1954	Newbery Medal: Joseph Krumgold's ...And Now Miguel
1959	Newbery Honor: Francis Kalnay's Chucaro: Wild Pony of the Pampa
1960	Caldecott Medal: Marie Hall Ets and Aurora Labastida for Nine Days to Christmas – A Story of Mexico
1961	Newbery Honor: Jack Schaefer's Old Ramon
1965	Newbery Medal: Maia Wojciechowska's Shadow of a Bull
1966	Newbery Medal: Elizabeth Borton de Trevino's I, Juan de Pareja
1967	Newbery Honor: Scott O'Dell's The King's Fifth
1968	Hans Christian Andersen International Medal: Jose Maria Sanchez-Silva (Spain)
1982	Hans Christian Andersen International Medal: Lygia Bojunga Nunes (Brazil)
1992	Nobel Prize to Mexican poet and essayist Octavio Paz, who becomes Mexico's first Nobel laureate for literature
1999	Americas Award given by the Consortium of Latin American Studies Programs to books published in 1998 that portray Latin America, the Caribbean, or Latinos in the United States, with winners including George Ancona's Barrio: Jose's Neighborhood, and Amelia Lau Carling's Mama and Papa Have a Store
2000	Mildred L. Batchelder Honor: Ineke Holtwijk's Asphalt Angels

Asian Timeline

800	Tuan Ch'eng Shish's Yu Yant Ts a Tsy, early Chinese "Cinderella"
1800s	Two thousand tales collected, translated, and published by Indian scholars, civil servants, and foreign missionaries
1926	Newbery: Arthur Bowie Chrisman's Shen of the Sea
1933	Newbery: Elizabeth Forman Lewis' Young Fu of the Upper Yangtze
1935	Newbery Honor: Elizabeth Seeger's Pageant of Chinese History
1939	Caldecott: Thomas Handforth's Mei Li
1951	Newbery Honor: Jeanette Easton's Ghandi, Fighter Without a Sword
1956	Caldecott Honor: Taro Yashima's Crow Boy
1973	Caldecott: Artist Blair Lent's The Funny Little Woman
1976	Newbery Honor and Children's Book Award: Laurence Yep's Dragonwings
1980	Hans Christian Andersen International Medal: Illustrator Suekichi Akaba (Japan)
1983	Mildred L. Batchelder Award: Toshi Maruki's Hiroshima No Pika
1984	Hans Christian Andersen International Medal: Illustrator Mitsumasa Anno (Japan)
1986	Newbery Honor: Rhoda Blumberg's Commodore Perry in the Land of the Shogun
1989	Caldecott Honor: Artist Allen Say's The Boy of the Three-Year Nap
1994	Caldecott: Allen Say's Grandfather's Journey
1994	Newbery Honor: Laurence Yep's Dragon's Gate
1994	Hans Christian Andersen International Medal: Illustrator Michio Mado (Japan)
1997	Mildred L. Batchelder Award: Peter Sís's Tibet: Through the Red Box
2000	National Book Award: Gloria Welan's Homeless Bird
2001	Newbery Award: Linda Sue Park's A Single Shard

Jewish Timeline

1887	Moses Gaster's collecting and publishing of Jewish Folklore in the Middle Ages
1938-9	Abraham Berger's early survey of Jewish folklore
1973	Newbery Honor: Johanna Reiss's The Upstairs Room
1977	Caldecott Honor: Artist Beverly Brodsky McDermott, The Golem, A Jewish Legend
1982	Newbery Honor: Aranka Siegal's Upon the Head of the Goat: A Childhood in Hungary, 1939-1944
1985	Mildred L. Batchelder Award: Uri Orlev's The Island on Bird Street
1986	Mildred L. Batchelder Award: Roberto Innocenti's Rose Blanche
1990	Newbery: Lois Lowry's Number the Stars
1990	Caldecott Honor: Illustrator Trina Schart Hyman for Hershel and the Hanukkah Goblins
1992	Mildred L. Batchelder Award: Uri Orlev's The Man from the Other Side
1993	Children's Book Award: Karen Hesse's Letters from Rifka
1994	Children's Book Award: Nancy S. Toll's Behind the Secret Window: A Memoir of a Hidden Childhood During World War Two
1995	Anne Frank: The Diary of a Young Girl: The Definitive Edition, including materials not found in the earlier diary
1996	Hans Christian Andersen International Medal: Uri Orlev
1996	Mildred L. Batchelder Award: Uri Orlev's The Lady with the Hat
1997	Caldecott: David Wisniewski's Golem

Middle Eastern Timeline

1704	Arabian Nights or The Thousand and One Nights, translated from Arabic to French by Antoine Galland
1885-88	Translation of The Thousand Nights and a Night from Arabic to English by Sir Richard Francis Burton
1910	Two hundred Arabian tales by Hans Schmidt published
1914	Edmund Dulac's illustrations for Sindbad the Sailor and Other Stories from the Arabian Nights, inspired by Persian miniatures of the fifteenth century
1971	Mildred L. Batchelder Award: Hans Baumann's In the Land of Ur: The Discovery of Ancient Mesopotamia
1974	Hans Christian Andersen International Medal: Illustrator Farshid Mesghali (Iran)
1980	Caldecott Honor: to artist Chris Van Allsburg's The Garden of Abdul Gasazi
1985	The Ancient Egyptian Book of the Dead translated by R. O. Faulkner
1990	Newbery Honor: Suzanne Fisher Staples's Shabanu, Daughter of the Wind
1991	Mildred L. Batchelder Honor Award: Rafik Schami's A Handful of Stars
1995	Mildred L. Batchelder Honor Award: Vedat Dalokay's Sister Shako and Kolo the Goat: Memories of My Childhood in Turkey
1998	The Space Between Our Footsteps: Poems and Paintings from the Middle East, a large anthology selected by Naomi Shihab Nye

Through the Eyes of a Child

AN INTRODUCTION TO CHILDREN'S LITERATURE

Sixth Edition

DONNA E. NORTON

Texas A & M University

SAUNDRA E. NORTON

with contributions by

AMY MCCLURE

Ohio Wesleyan University

Merrill
Prentice Hall

Upper Saddle River, New Jersey
Columbus, Ohio

Library of Congress Cataloging-in-Publication Data
Norton, Donna E.
  Through the eyes of a child : an introduction to children's literature / Donna E. Norton,
Saundra E. Norton ; with contributions by Amy McClure.
    7th ed. p. cm.
  ISBN 0-13-042207-X
    1. Children--Books and reading--United States. 2. Children's literature--History and
criticism. I. Norton, Saundra E. II. McClure, Amy A. III. Title.

Z1037.A1 N68 2003
[PN1009.A1]
028.1'62--dc21   2002023081

Vice President and Publisher: Jeffery W. Johnston
Editor: Linda Ashe Montgomery
Development Editor: Hope Madden
Production Editor: Mary M. Irvin
Design Coordinator: Diane C. Lorenzo
Text Design: Ceri Fitzgerald
Cover Designer: Ceri Fitzgerald
Cover Art: Yangsook Choi
Production Manager: Pamela D. Bennett
Director of Marketing: Ann Castel Davis
Marketing Manager: Krista Groshong
Marketing Services Manager: Tyra Cooper

This book was set in Gill Sans by Carlisle Communications, Ltd., and was printed and bound by Courier Kendallville, Inc.
The cover was printed by The LeHigh Press, Inc.

Photo Credits: p. 20, Courtesy of Macmillan; p. 59, Courtesy of Dial Books for Young Readers; p. 81, Courtesy of
HarperCollins Publishers; p. 136, © Suki Coughlin, courtesy of G. P. Putnam's; p. 184, Courtesy of Simon & Schuster;
p. 237, Henry Kruth, courtesy of HarperCollins Publishers; p. 298, Kenneth S. Lewis; p. 325, Courtesy of Random House
Children's Books; p. 394, Alan McEwen, courtesy of HarperCollins Publishers; p. 416, Courtesy of Houghton Mifflin
Company; p. 464, Matthew Wysocki, courtesy of Simon & Schuster; p. 532, Courtesy of G. P. Putnam's.

Pearson Education Ltd.
Pearson Education Australia Pty. Limited.
Pearson Education Singapore Pte. Ltd.
Pearson Education North Asia Ltd.
Pearson Education Canada, Ltd.
Pearson Educación de Mexico, S.A. de C.V.
Pearson Education—Japan
Pearson Education Malaysia Pte. Ltd.
Pearson Education, *Upper Saddle River, New Jersey*

Merrill
Prentice Hall

10 9 8 7 6 5 4 3 2 1
ISBN 0-13-042207-X

PREFACE

 you are an adult who wants to share books with children, *Through the Eyes of a Child* is written for you. Whether the children's literature course is offered in the department of Education, English, or Library Science, the text's unique two-part chapter organization and special features provide a meaningful guide to understanding children's literature.

What you will find in this new edition is a stronger focus on teaching, with voices from the field, new teaching ideas, and student artifacts. The same quality of literary criticism; the strongest, most researched treatment of multicultural literature; streamlined prose; integrated technology; innovative and meaningful special features; and a balance between new and classic titles are other strong components of this revision.

Organization

Unique Two-Part Chapter Organization

Beginning in Chapter 3 and extending through Chapter 12, each chapter is purposely divided into two parts. The first discusses in depth the characteristics, history, and the classic and best new titles of each genre suitable for courses emphasizing Education, English, or Library Science.

The second part of each genre chapter contains streamlined, classroom-tested strategies for teaching children with the best literature, providing readers with the best methods for using children's literature in their classrooms. These chapters are now connected to an online activities book, which contains many more such strategies, that can be found at www.prenhall.com/norton.

Strong Multicultural Theme

Always the leader in multicultural literature scholarship, this new edition continues the strong multicultural theme with a dedicated chapter, as well as complete integration of important multicultural titles in every chapter, reflecting the importance of the literature, and the necessity of understanding and studying its contributions to all genres.

New to This Edition

New Titles for the Sixth Edition

As in the past, there has been a careful selection of new books, which has resulted in the addition of hundreds of new titles representing the best children's books published since 1999. The books discussed in this edition were chosen for their quality of literature and to create a

balance between new books and those that have stood the test of time and are considered to be classics. In addition to the newest literature, the text includes numerous adult references that reflect the viewpoints, issues, and scholarly findings of professionals who write and work in the area of children's literature.

While hundreds of new titles were studied and included in this edition, hundreds of other titles were cut because the books are no longer in print. The exclusion of books that are out of print is meant to assist librarians, educators, and other professionals who may want to order the books that are discussed or mentioned in the text. However, a very limited number of out of print books are included, because they are still available in libraries, are the best examples for a specific discussion, or are just too good to be ignored.

Emphasis on the Artistry

Heartfelt thanks are extended to cover artist Yangsook Choi, whose distinctive illustrative style and writing have received acclaim from *The New York Times* (Outstanding Book of the Year), *Publisher's Weekly* (one of the most prominent new children's book artists of 1997), International Reading Association (Children's Book Award), American Library Association (Notable Book), and Oppenheim (Toy Portfolio Gold Award). Her beautiful original piece for our cover expresses the joy and celebration to be found, savored, and shared in quality literature, and we are grateful for and honored by her work for us.

The beauty and artistry of children's literature begin with our cover and are carried throughout this beautiful text. The full-color illustrations that appear as the frontispiece and at the beginning of each chapter represent carefully selected illustrations in a variety of media crafted by some of the most talented children's book illustrators. From cut paper to woodcuts, through watercolors and oil paintings, and through the camera's eye, the illustrators represented on the opening pages of each chapter give children special stimulation for their visual, interpretive skills.

Special Features

NEW! **Through the Eyes of a Teacher.** This new feature of voices from the field in every chapter clearly illustrates the ways teachers and media specialists use good children's literature to engage students. Master teachers model good instruction and provide ideas for teaching with good literature.

Through the Eyes of an Author. These interviews with top writers, illustrators, and storytellers in the field of children's literature bring readers into the world of creating books for kids, and open students up to the world behind children's literature. These features have been expanded for this edition.

NEW! **Video Profile.** Many of the authors interviewed in the *Through the Eyes of an Author* feature, as well as numerous other children's book authors and illustrators, are part of a video of extended conversations that are available with the text.

NEW! **Through the Eyes of a Student.** In this new feature, students respond to the work of each chapter's author or illustrator highlighted in the *Through the Eyes of an Author* feature. These student writing samples introduce readers to the kinds of responses they can expect from their own students being introduced to good literature.

NEW! **Technology Resources.** The technology features, found in every chapter, connect chapter content with both the *Companion Website* and the *CD database* that accompany the text, linking users to the technological resources that will provide them a wealth of children's literature and related teaching materials, all of which will be an excellent resource for users for years to come.

Evaluation Criteria. Professors tell us that the one thing their students *must* know is how to choose the best titles from among all the available children's literature. As in previous editions, this feature in every genre chapter gives users the information they need to choose the best titles for their students.

Issues. This important feature, great for class discussion and research projects, has been updated to include the constant and the new issues facing the field of children's literature, particularly as they affect teaching. The feature introduces readers to the issues they will face when choosing and teaching with children's literature, presents information, and asks readers to reflect upon different controversies facing the field, including issues of censorship and culturally sensitive literature.

In-Depth Look. Many professors have indicated that their students would benefit from models of deep discussion related to the literary elements in children's literature. This section in each chapter uses one title at a time to explore, contextualize, and fully illustrate important literary concepts for readers. For example, Chapter 3 focuses on Christopher Paul Curtis' *The Watsons Go to Birmingham—1963* to explore plot and conflict. These pieces have been expanded in this edition to include elements in every genre chapter.

Supplements

CD-ROM Database. Included in the back of this text is a free database of children's literature. It includes approximately 5000 titles and is intended to be an ongoing resource for teachers and media specialists who choose titles for students. An award winner field has been added to give users a feel for the best of the best titles. Every title discussed in the booklists can be brought up on the CD, which provides users with plot summaries, appropriate reading level, awards won, and publisher information. The CD has been further integrated in the text through the *Technology Resource* feature.

Companion Website. This completely text-integrated supplement contains self-assessments, activities, an online activity book with strategies for teaching with children's literature, and many, many links to award sites, author sites, research sites, classroom sites, and others.

Conversations with Children's Literature Authors and Illustrators Video. Integrated into the text, this free supplement includes interviews with many excellent children's book authors and illustrators, including Eve Bunting, Floyd Cooper, Paula Danziger, Brian Pinkney, Jack Gantos, and many more.

Instructor's Manual. This free supplement for professors includes test questions, chapter outlines, and syllabus samples.

Acknowledgements

Thank you, Dr. Amy McClure, for your thorough research, thoughtful compilation, and masterful organization of the *Through the Eyes of a Teacher* material. Readers will gain true insight for teaching because of the thought-provoking and meaningful coverage of classrooms learning with children's literature.

A special thanks to all the teachers and students who allowed us and our readers to learn through their involvement with children's literature.

Pam Wilson and her students at Western Row Elementary in Mason, OH.

Kevin Spink and his students at Chugiak Elementary School in Chugiak, American Samoa.

Monica Edinger and her students at Dalton School in New York, NY.

Patricia Taverna and Terry Hongell and their students at Pocantico Hills School in Sleepy Hollow, NY.

Steve Schack, Howard Anderson, and Melissa Wilson and their students at Beck Urban Academy in Columbus, OH.

Susan Anderson-McElveen and Connie Dierking and their students at Curtis School in Clearwater, FL.

Connie Rosenblatt and her students at Yarbrough Elementary School in Auburn, AL.

Barry Hoonan and his students at Bainbridge School in Bainbridge Island, WA.

Lisa Siemans and her students at Riverview School in Winnipeg, Manitoba, Canada.

Kathryn Mitchell-Pierce and her students at Glenridge Elementary School in Glenridge, MO.

Robin Groce and her students at Iola Junior High in Tyler, TX.

Sallie Barker and her students at Salisbury Elementary School in Salisbury, MD.

Ruth Nathan and her students at Rancho Romero Elementary in Alomo, CA.

As always, colleagues and professors from around the country are appreciated for their thoughtful responses and meaningful suggestions regarding this revision: Tina Cummings, Iowa State University; Sam Sebesta, University of Washington; Tonya Hameister, University of Wisconsin, Oshkosh; and Virginia Harris, Wayland Baptist University; Cyndi Giorgis, University of Nevada—Las Vegas; Shirley B. Ernst, Eastern Connecticut State University; Nancy J. Johnson, Western Washington University; Richard M. Kerper, Millersville University of Pennsylvania; and Sylvia Vardell, University of Texas at Arlington. I am also grateful to Dr. Sandy H. Smith and Dr. Ernest L. Bond for their contributions to the text's Companion Website.

Finally, I wish to dedicate this book to my husband, Verland, and my children, Saundra and Bradley, for their constant support, immense understanding, and insightful viewpoints.

COMPANION WEBSITE

Discover the Companion Website Accompanying This Book

Through the Eyes of a Child: A Virtual Learning Environment

Technology is a constantly growing and changing aspect of our field that is creating a need for content and resources. To address this emerging need, Prentice Hall has developed an online learning environment for students and professors alike—a Companion Website—to support this text.

In creating a Companion Website, our goal is to build on and enhance what *Through the Eyes of a Child* already offers. For this reason, the content for this user-friendly website is organized by chapter and provides the professor and student with a variety of meaningful resources.

For the Professor

Every Companion Website integrates **Syllabus Manager™**, an online syllabus creation and management utility.

- **Syllabus Manager™** provides you, the instructor, with an easy, step-by-step process to create and revise syllabi, with direct links into the Companion Website and other online content without having to learn HTML.
- Students may log on to your syllabus during any study session. All they need to know is the web address for the Companion Website and the password you've assigned to your syllabus.
- After you have created a syllabus using **Syllabus Manager™**, students may enter the syllabus for their course section from any point in the Companion Website.
- Clicking on a date, the student is shown the list of activities for the assignment. The activities for each assignment are linked directly to actual content, saving time for students.
- Adding assignments consists of clicking on the desired due date, then filling in the details of the assignment—name of the assignment, instructions, and whether or not it is a one-time or repeating assignment.
- In addition, links to other activities can be created easily. If the activity is online, a URL can be entered in the space provided, and it will be linked automatically in the final syllabus.
- Your completed syllabus is hosted on our servers, allowing convenient updates from any computer on the Internet. Changes you make to your syllabus are immediately available to your students at their next logon.

Common Companion Website features for students include:

For the Student

- **Chapter Objectives** – outline key concepts from the text
- **Interactive Self-quizzes** – complete with hints and automatic grading that provide immediate feedback for students

After students submit their answers for the interactive self-quizzes, the Companion Website **Results Reporter** computes a percentage grade, provides a graphic representation of how many questions were answered correctly and incorrectly, and gives a question-by-question analysis of the quiz. Students are given the option to send their quiz to up to four email addresses (professor, teaching assistant, study partner, etc.).

- **Activities**
  - *Web-based Activities* include Webquests, treasure hunts, subject samplers, thematic multimedia projects, and material on creating an educational website
  - *Communicating Activities* provide avenues and ideas for dialoguing with authors, students in other places, resource people, academic list serves, and online literature circles
  - *Writing and Publishing Activities* look at specific online opportunities with book reviews, character sketch booktalks, lessons, projects, creative and collaborative writing
  - *Reading Activities* provide links to online literature, author/illustrator biographies, book reviews, and supplemental information
  - *Research Activities* provide numerous links, ideas, and opportunities to do research online
- **Online Activity Book** – contains numerous lesson suggestions to build on those in the Teaching Children with Literature sections of the text.
- **Web Destinations** – links to www sites that relate to chapter content
- **Message Board** – serves as a virtual bulletin board to post—or respond to—questions or comments to/from a national audience
- **Chat** – real-time chat with anyone who is using the text anywhere in the country—ideal for discussion and study groups, class projects, etc.

To take advantage of the many available resources, please visit the *Through the Eyes of a Child* Companion Website at

www.prenhall.com/norton

Brief Contents

Contents

CHAPTER 1

The Child Responds to Literature 1

CHAPTER 2

The History of Children's Literature 41

Chapter 6

Tradition Literature 207

Chapter 7

Modern Fantasy 271

CHAPTER 10
Historical Fiction 411

CHAPTER 11
Multicultural Literature 455

Chapter 12

Nonfiction: Biographies and Informational Books 529

SPECIAL FEATURES

Through the Eyes of . . . .

Through the Eyes of a Child

Through the Eyes of a Teacher

Issues

In-Depth Analysis Features

iterature entices, motivates, and instructs. It opens doors to discovery and provides endless hours of adventure and enjoyment. Children need not be tied to the whims of television programming nor wait in line at the theater to follow a rabbit down a hole into Wonderland, save a wild herd of mustangs from slaughter, fight in the Revolutionary War, learn about a new hobby that will provide many enjoyable hours, or model themselves after real-life people of accomplishment. These experiences are available at any time on the nearest bookshelf.

Adults have a responsibility to help children become aware of the enchantment in books. The extent to which books, however, play a significant role in the life of young children depends upon adults. Adults provide the books and, through sharing literature, adults transmit the literary heritage contained in nursery rhymes, picture storybooks, and traditional tales. Eden Ross Lipson (2001) believes so strongly in the power of literature that he conducted a discussion about the power of summer reading. Participants concluded that they could see positive differences in children who read for fun in the summer. These differences enhanced both attitudes toward reading and skills associated with reading. Unfortunately, the panelists also concluded that many children will not read if their parents do not.

As you read this book, you will gain knowledge about literature so that you can share stimulating books and book-related experiences with children. This chapter introduces various values of literature for children to help you search for books that can play significant roles in children's lives. It also looks at the importance of considering children's stages of language and cognitive, personality, and social development when selecting literature for children and suggests books that reflect children's needs during different stages of the maturing process. All of these developmental areas influence children's understanding and appreciation of literature and their responses to literature.

Values of Literature for Children

Following a rabbit down a rabbit hole or walking through a wardrobe into a mythical kingdom sounds like fun. There is nothing wrong with admitting that one of the primary values of literature is pleasure, and there is nothing wrong with turning to a book to escape or to enjoy an adventure with new or old book friends. Time is enriched, not wasted, when children look at beautiful pictures and imagine themselves in new places. When children discover enjoyment in books, they develop favorable attitudes toward them that usually extend into a lifetime of appreciation.

Books are the major means of transmitting our literary heritage from one generation to the next. Each new generation can enjoy the words of Lewis Carroll, Louisa

May Alcott, Robert Louis Stevenson, and Mark Twain. Through the work of storytellers such as the Brothers Grimm, each generation can also experience the folktales originally transmitted through the oral tradition.

Literature plays a strong role in helping us understand and value our cultural heritage as well. Developing positive attitudes toward our own culture and the cultures of others is necessary for both social and personal development. Carefully selected literature can illustrate the contributions and values of the many cultures. It is especially critical to foster an appreciation of the heritage of the ethnic minorities in American society. A positive self-concept is not possible unless we respect others as well as ourselves; literature can contribute considerably toward our understanding and thus our respect.

The vicarious experiences of literature result in personal development as well as pleasure. Without literature, most children could not relive the European colonists' experiences of crossing the ocean and shaping a new country in North America; they could not experience the loneliness and fear of a fight for survival on an isolated island; they could not travel to distant places in the galaxy. Historical fiction provides children with opportunities to live in the past. Science fiction allows them to speculate about the future. Contemporary realistic fiction encourages them to experience relationships with the people and the environment of today. Because children can learn from literature how other people handle their problems, characters in books can help children deal with similar problems, as well as understand other people's feelings.

Another value of literature is that of developing emotional intelligence. Daniel Golman (1995) identifies five basic elements of emotional intelligence that are needed by children: self-awareness, managing emotions, handling anxiety in appropriate ways, motivating oneself, and sensitivity toward others. Marjorie N. Allen (1999) states that children's literature is an excellent source for helping adolescents deal with emotions because "Books are a way to face grief, deal with perceived differences, and gain self-confidence. When written well, they create empathy and understanding at a time when young people are trying to adjust to the unexpected complexities of growing up" (p. 87).

Informational books relay new knowledge about virtually every topic imaginable, and they are available at all levels of difficulty. Biographies and autobiographies tell about the people who gained knowledge or made discoveries. Photographs and illustrations show the wonders of nature or depict the processes required to master new hobbies. Realistic stories from a specific time bring history to life. The use of concept books that illustrate colors, numbers, shapes, and sizes may stimulate the cognitive development of even very young children. On the flyleaf of his *A History of Reading,* Alberto Manguel (1996) summarizes the values gained through literature. He states:

At one magical instant in your early childhood, the page of a book—that string of confused, alien ciphers—shivered into meaning. Words spoke to you, gave up their secrets; at that moment, whole universes opened. You became, irrevocably, a reader.

Any discussion about the values of literature must stress the role that literature plays in nurturing and expanding the imagination. Books take children into worlds that stimulate additional imaginative experiences when children tell or write their own stories and interact with each other during creative drama inspired by what they have read. Both well-written literature and illustrations, such as those found in picture books and picture storybooks, can stimulate aesthetic development. Children enjoy and evaluate illustrations and may explore artistic media by creating illustrations of their own.

The values gained from literature in childhood often have profound influences on adults. David L. Russell (1999) chronicles the importance of reading to historical fiction author Scott O'Dell. Russell states:

O'Dell's early formal education had little impact on him, but he always enjoyed reading. When he was 10, his parents gave him the works of his ancestor Sir Walter Scott, and he fell in love with them. Perhaps from that time forward he was destined to be a historical novelist himself. (p. 3)

Promoting Child Development Through Literature

Research in child development has identified stages in the language, cognitive, personality, and social development of children. Not all children progress through these stages at the same rate, but all children do pass through each stage as they mature. The general characteristics of children at each developmental stage provide clues for appropriate literature. Certain books can benefit children during a particular stage of development, helping the children progress to the next stage. Understanding the types and stages of child development is useful for anyone who works with children.

Language Development

Literature has profound influences on children's language development. Chart 1.1 lists characteristics, implications, and books that are appropriate for language development.

Preschool Children. During their first few years, children show dramatic changes in language ability. Most children learn language very rapidly. They speak their first words at about one year of age; at about eighteen months, they begin to put words together in two-word combinations. Speech during this stage of language development consists of nouns, verbs, and adjectives. It usually contains no prepositions, articles, auxiliary verbs, or pronouns. When children say "pretty flower" or "milk gone," they are using telegraphic speech. The number of different two-word combinations increases slowly. Then, it shows a sudden upsurge around age two.

CHART 1.1 (PP. 4–6)   Language development

Characteristics	Implications	Literature Suggestions
Preschool: Ages Two–Three		
1 Very rapid language growth occurs. By the end of this period, children have vocabularies of about nine hundred words.	1 Provide many activities to stimulate language growth, including picture books and Mother Goose rhymes.	Ho, Minfong. *Hush!: A Thai Lullaby.* Lobel, Arnold. *The Random House Book of Mother Goose.* Simmons, Jane. *Daisy Says "Coo!"* Wells, Rosemary. *Max's Birthday.*
2 Children learn to identify and name actions in pictures.	2 Read books that contain clear, familiar action pictures; encourage children to identify actions.	Fleming, Denise. *In the Tall, Tall Grass.* Opie, Iona. *Here Comes Mother Goose.* Steptoe, John. *Baby Says.* Wells, Rosemary. *Max's Breakfast.*
3 Children learn to identify large and small body parts.	3 Allow children to identify familiar body parts in picture books.	Oxenbury, Helen. *Dressing.*
Preschool: Ages Three–Four		
1 Vocabularies have increased to about fifteen hundred words. Children enjoy playing with sound and rhythm in language.	1 Include opportunities to listen to and say rhymes, poetry, and riddles.	Aylesworth, Jim. *Old Black Fly.* Barton, Byron. *The Wee Little Woman.* Griego, Margot C., et al. *Tortillitas Para Mama.* Priceman, Marjorie. *Froggie Went a-Courting.* Rosen, Michael. *We're Going on a Bear Hunt.* Wilson, Karma. *Bear Snores On.* Yolen, Jane. *The Three Bears Rhyme Book.* Cooper, Helen. *Pumpkin Soup.*
2 Children develop the ability to use past tense but may overgeneralize the *ed* and *s* markers.	2 Allow children to talk about what they did yesterday; discuss actions in books.	Hill, Eric. *Spot's First Walk.* _____. *Spot Goes to School.* Keats, Ezra Jack. *The Snowy Day.* Weiss, Nicki. *Where Does the Brown Bear Go?*
3 Children use language to help find out about the world.	3 Read picture storybooks to allow children to find out about and discuss pets, families, people, and the environment.	Brown, Ruth. *Toad.* Carle, Eric. *The Very Busy Spider.* Fleming, Denise. *In the Small, Small Pond.* Keller, Holly. *Geraldine's Big Snow.* Potter, Beatrix. *The Tale of Peter Rabbit.* Tafuri, Nancy. *Early Morning in the Barn.* Waddell, Martin. *Let's Go Home, Little Bear.*
4 Speech becomes more complex, with more adjectives, adverbs, pronouns, and prepositions.	4 Expand the use of descriptive words through detailed picture books and picture storybooks. Allow children to tell stories and describe characters and their actions.	Barton, Byron. *Machines at Work.* Frampton, David. *The Whole Night Through: A Lullaby.* Hill, Eric. *Spot Goes to the Beach.* Narahashi, Keiko. *I Have a Friend.*

CHART 1.1 *(Continued)*

Characteristics	Implications	Literature Suggestions
Preschool: Ages Four–Five		
1 Language is more abstract; children produce grammatically correct sentences. Their vocabularies contain approximately twenty-five hundred words.	1 Children enjoy books with slightly more complex plots. Ask them to tell longer and more detailed stories. They enjoy retelling folktales and can tell stories using wordless books.	Brett, Jan. *Goldilocks and the Three Bears.* Haas, Irene. *A Summertime Song.* Hamanaka, Sheila. *I Look Like a Girl.* McCully, Emily Arnold. *School.* McPhail, David. *Pigs Aplenty, Pigs Galore!* Wiesner, David. *Free Fall.* _____. *Tuesday.* Zimmerman, H. Werner. *Henny Penny.*
2 Children understand the prepositions *over, under, in, out, in front of,* and *behind.*	2 Use concept books or other picture books in which prepositions can be reinforced.	Hutchins, Pat. *Rosie's Walk.* _____. *What Game Shall We Play?* Noll, Sally. *Watch Where You Go.*
3 Children enjoy asking many questions, especially those related to *why* and *how.*	3 Take advantage of natural curiosity and find books to help answer children's questions. Allow them to answer each other's questions.	Barton, Byron. *Airport.* Gammell, Stephen. *Is That You, Winter?* Oppenheim, Joanne. *Have You Seen Birds?* Prelutsky, Jack. *The Frogs Wore Red Suspenders.* Showers, Paul. *Look at Your Eyes.*
Preschool—Kindergarten: Ages Five–Six		
1 Most children use complex sentences frequently and begin to use correct pronouns and verbs in present and past tense. They understand approximately six thousand words.	1 Give children many opportunities for oral language activities connected with literature.	Aardema, Verna. *Bringing the Rain to Kapiti Plain.* Appelt, Kathi. *Where, Where Is Swamp Bear?* Cronin, Doreen. *Click, Clack, Moo: Cows That Type.* Gág, Wanda. *Millions of Cats.* Hoberman, Mary Ann. *The Eensy-Weensy Spider.* Moss, Lloyd. *Zin! Zin! Zin! A Violin.* Opie, Iona. *My Very First Mother Goose.* Taback, Simms. *There Was an Old Lady Who Swallowed a Fly.*
2 Children enjoy taking part in dramatic play and producing dialogue about everyday activities such as those at home and the grocery store.	2 Read stories about the home and community. Allow children to act out their own stories.	Demarest, Chris. L. *Firefighters A to Z.* Hurd, Edith Thacher. *I Dance in My Red Pajamas.* Mathers, Petra. *A Cake for Herbie.* Martin, Rafe. *Will's Mammoth.* Seeber, Dorothea. *A Pup Just for Me: A Boy Just for Me.* Seuss, Dr. *And to Think That I Saw It on Mulberry Street.*
3 Children are curious about the written appearance of their own language.	3 Write chart stories using the children's own words. Have children dictate descriptions of pictures.	Baker, Jeannie. *Window.* Bloom, Suzanne. *The Bus for Us.* McCully, Emily Arnold. *Picnic.* Newman, Lesléa. *Cats, Cats, Cats!* Willard, Nancy. *Night Story.*

(continues)

CHART 1.1 *(Continued)*

Characteristics	Implications	Literature Suggestions
Early Elementary: Ages Six–Eight		
1 Language development continues. Children add many new words to their vocabularies.	1 Provide daily time for reading to children and allow for oral interaction.	Defelice, Cynthia. *Willy's Silly Grandma.* Drummond, Allan. *Casey Jones.* George, Kristine O'Connell. *Toasting Marshmallows: Camping Poems.* Hoberman, Mary Ann. *You Read to Me, I'll Read to You.* Johnston, Tony. *Desert Song.* Lewin, Hugh. *Jafta.* Prelutsky, Jack. *Awful Ogre's Awful Day.* Silverstein, Shel. *A Light in the Attic.*
2 Most children use complex sentences with adjectival clauses and conditional clauses beginning with *if.* The average oral sentence length is seven and one-half words.	2 Read stories that provide models for children's expanding language structure.	Burton, Virginia Lee. *The Little House.* Hodges, Margaret. *Saint George and the Dragon.* McCloskey, Robert. *Make Way for Ducklings.*
Middle Elementary: Ages Eight–Ten		
1 Children begin to relate concepts to general ideas. They use connectors such as *meanwhile* and *unless.*	1 Supply books as models. Let children use these terms during oral language activities.	Schotter, Roni. *Nothing Ever Happens on 90th Street.* Steptoe, John. *Mufaro's Beautiful Daughters: An African Tale.* Young, Ed. *Lon Po Po: A Red Riding Hood Story from China.*
2 The subordinating connector *although* is used correctly by 50 percent of children. Present participle active and perfect participle appear. The average sentence length is nine words.	2 Use written models and oral models to help children master their language skills. Literature discussions allow many opportunities for oral sentence expansion.	Kennedy, Caroline. *The Best-Loved Poems of Jacqueline Kennedy Onassis.* Levine, Arthur A. *The Boy Who Drew Cats: A Japanese Folktale.* Mayer, Marianna. *The Twelve Dancing Princesses.* Paolilli, Paul, and Dan Brewer. *Silver Seeds: A Book of Nature Poems.* Sandburg, Carl. *More Rootabagas.* Sierra, Judy. *Tasty Baby Belly Buttons.* Walter, Mildred Pitts. *Brother to the Wind.*
Upper Elementary: Ages Ten–Twelve		
1 Children use complex sentences with subordinate clauses of concession introduced by *nevertheless* and *in spite of.* Auxiliary verbs *might, could,* and *should* appear frequently.	1 Encourage oral language and written activities that permit children to use more complex sentence structures.	L'Engle, Madeleine. *A Swiftly Tilting Planet.* Lisle, Janet Taylor. *The Gold Dust Letters.* McKinley, Robin. *The Hero and the Crown.* Paulsen, Gary. *Hatchet.* _____. *The Winter Room.* Pullman, Philip. *The Golden Compass.* Whelan, Gloria. *Homeless Bird.*

Sources: Bartel (1995); Brown (1973); Gage and Berliner (1992); Hendrick (1996); and Loban (1976).

Speech usually becomes more complex by age three, when most children have added adverbs, pronouns, prepositions, and more adjectives to their vocabularies. Children also enjoy playing with the sounds of words at this stage of language development. By age four, they produce grammatically correct sentences. This stage is a questioning one, during which language is used to ask why and how.

Literature and literature-related experiences can encourage language development in preschool children. Joanne Hendrick (1996) recommends children's books and related activities to enhance language development. Steven Herb (1997) reviews research findings and concludes, "Children's early experiences with books directly relate to their success in learning to read in school" and "storybook reading is a more effective influence on literacy development when children have opportunities to engage in conversation about the story" (p. 23).

Book experiences in the home, at the library, and at nursery school can help children use language to discover the world, identify and name actions and objects, gain more complex speech, and enjoy the wonder of language. Many children first experience literature through picture books, which help children give meaning to their expanding vocabularies. For example, children who are just learning to identify their hands and other parts of their bodies may find these parts in drawings of children. Parents of very young children may share Helen Oxenbury's excellent baby board books. (Board books are toy books made of cardboard for young children.) *Dressing*, for example, includes a picture of a baby's clothing, followed by a picture of the child dressed in those items. The illustrations are sequentially developed to encourage talking about the steps in dressing.

Young children also learn to identify actions in pictures, and enjoy recognizing and naming familiar actions, such as those in Sheila Hamanaka's *I Look Like a Girl*. The text stimulates children to imagine themselves in many different shapes and experiences. The language also enhances the imagination as in this example: "And when I am sleeping, like a jaguar I'm creeping through the jungle of my dreams" (unnumbered). Even though she looks like a girl she sometimes is a tiger, a dolphin, a wild horse, a condor, or a wolf.

Many excellent books allow children to listen to the sounds of language and experiment with these sounds. For example, Woody Guthrie's *Woody's 20 Grow Big Songs* includes songs that contain both repetition and actions that are enjoyed by younger children.

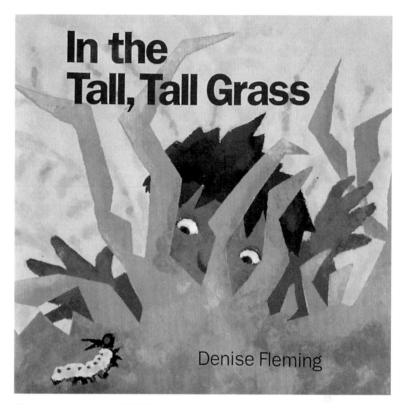

The language in In the Tall, Tall Grass *encourages both observation and play with words.* From In The Tall, Tall Grass *by Denise Fleming. Copyright © 1991 by Denise Fleming. Reprinted by permission of Henry Holt and Company, Inc.*

Books with repetitive language are excellent for enticing listeners to join in during oral reading. In *Off We Go!* Jane Yolen creates a rhythmic, rhyming text as various animals move off to find grandmother's house. For example, notice the appealing language as "Slither-slee, slithery slee, Down the branch and round the tree" (unnumbered) goes the little snake in search of grandmother. There are numerous rhyming sentences: Frogs slop, stop; moles sleep, creep; ducks scratch, hatch; and spiders crawl, fall. Another good source of a rhythmic text to read to young children is Lesléa Newman's *Cats, Cats, Cats!* in which cats are tucked in tight every night and *fiddle dee dee* is rhymed with *me*. Jim Aylesworth's *Old Black Fly* is another rhythmic chant that encourages listeners to join in the story as they say, "Shoo fly! Shoo fly! Shooo." Children may respond in both Spanish and English when they interact with the rhymes in *Tortillitas Para Mama* by Margot C. Griego et al. Mary Ann Hoberman's adaptation of *The Eensy-Weensy Spider* includes both music and hand and body movements that may be used to accompany the text.

Books that encourage children to play with and appreciate language are also excellent for language development. The vivid language in Lloyd Moss's *Zin! Zin! Zin! A Violin* is especially appealing. Children can join in as the trombone plays mournful tones by "gliding, sliding" or the oboe plays "gleeful, bleating, sobbing, pleading." This book provides an excellent source for acting out the sounds and movements related to the instruments of the orchestra.

Unusual words and stories in rhyme encourage children to play with language. In *Good Zap, Little Grog,* Sarah Wilson uses unusual language to create a story in rhyme. As the fantasy story progresses, ooglets are tuzzling, parobbies are churling, and glipneeps are jumping. Rob and Amy Spence's *Clickety Clack* includes both a story in rhyme and rhythm associated with a railroad. Children can easily join in with all the words that rhyme with *clack* such as *track, back, yak, quack, crack,* and *attack.* A similar rhyme and rhythm is developed in Kevin Lewis's *Chugga-Chugga Choo-Choo.* Considerable onomatopoeia provides humor in Libba Moore Gray's language for *When Uncle Took the Fiddle* as the strings on the violin go "zee zee, saw saw, and ziggle, ziggle, zang" and gourds shake "click and clatter, shu, sha, shu, and rick-a-rack-a MEW!" (unnumbered).

Repetitive language and a satisfying ending make Bryon Barton's *The Wee Little Woman* a good choice for reading aloud to preschool children who may join in by describing the wee little woman, the wee little stool, the wee little table, and even the wee little cat. Repetitive language in Suzanne Bloom's *The Bus for Us* encourages language development as readers join in the repetitive chorus and identification of vehicles that are not the bus.

The poems in Jane Dyer's collection *Animal Crackers: A Delectable Collection of Pictures, Poems, and Lullabies for the Very Young* include rhythm, rhyme, and sound patterns that appeal to young children. Iona Opie's *My Very First Mother Goose* is a collection of over 60 rhymes illustrated with Rosemary Wells's humorous illustrations.

Elementary-Age Children. Language development of course continues as children enter school and progress through the grades. Walter Loban (1976) conducted the most extensive longitudinal study of language development in school-age children. Loban's study is so important that Marilyn Hanf Buckley (1992) states that Loban's work established the firm relationship between oral language development and success at reading and writing and "provided the base upon which our present-day thinking about the integrated language arts curriculum rests" (p. 622). Loban examined the language development of the same group of over two hundred children from age five to age eighteen. He found that children's power over language increases through successive control over different forms of language, including pronouns, verb tenses, and connectors, such as *meanwhile* and *unless.*

Loban (1976) identified dramatic differences between children who ranked high in language proficiency and those who ranked low. The high group reached a level of oral proficiency in first grade that the low group did not attain until sixth grade and a level of written proficiency in fourth grade that the low group did not attain until tenth grade. Those who demonstrated high language proficiency excelled in the control of ideas expressed,

showing unity and planning in both their speech and writing. These students spoke freely, fluently, and easily, using a rich vocabulary and adjusting the pace of their words to their listeners. They were attentive and creative listeners themselves, far outranking the low group in listening ability. The oral communication of those with low language proficiency was characterized by rambling and unpurposeful dialogue that demonstrated a meager vocabulary.

Children who were superior in oral language in kindergarten and first grade also excelled in reading and writing in sixth grade. They were more fluent in written language than were the low-ranked children, used more words per sentence, showed a richer written vocabulary, and were superior in using connectors and subordination to combine thoughts into complex forms of expression. Given the demonstrated connection between oral and written language skills, Loban (1976) concluded that teachers, librarians, and parents should give greater attention to developing children's oral language. Discussion should be a vital part of elementary school and library programs because it helps children organize ideas and make complex generalizations. Unfortunately, however, Marie Clay (1991) concludes, "[W]hile teachers see oral language as central to writing and reading acquisition, they often do not recognize the need to foster its further development" (p. 41).

Books with repetitive language are excellent for enticing listeners to join in during oral reading. Mem Fox's *Hattie and the Fox* includes both a cumulative plot and repetitive refrains. The illustrations are excellent for predicting language because they show various features of the approaching fox. John Ivimey's *The Complete Story of the Three Blind Mice* includes repetitive lines, rhyming language, and descriptive terms. This extended story, illustrated by Paul Galdone, allows readers to discover what caused the loss of the tails. This version even has a happy ending. Repetitive lines and interesting words are found in Judy Sierra's *Tasty Baby Belly Buttons,* a folktale from Japan. Repetitive words such as *boro, boro* and *zushin, zushin* are part of the vocabulary of traditional Japanese storytellers.

Wordless picture books are excellent stimuli for oral and written language. Emily Arnold McCully's *School* follows the exploits of the littlest mouse child, who discovers what happens during a real school day. Peter Collington's *The Angel and the Soldier Boy* provides an exciting adventure, in which an angel and a soldier rescue a coin from pirates and return it to a sleeping child.

 Technology Resources

You can use the database to select books that will improve language development focusing on rhyme. If you are unfamiliar with using the database, please select the Help button for specific directions.

David Wiesner's *Free Fall* shows the adventures that are possible within dreams. Wiesner's *Tuesday* is a story filled with surprising and unexpected elements as frogs fly around the neighborhood. Readers enjoy extending the book into the next Tuesday. Wiesner's final illustration shows that now the pigs have their opportunity to fly, to explore the neighborhood, and to baffle the people. The book provides an interesting stimulus for oral stories, creative writing, and drawing illustrations and for children to create their own stories about "The Night the Pigs Could Fly."

Books with vivid language, similes, and metaphors stimulate language development and appreciation for literary style. The text for Jane Yolen's *Owl Moon* is filled with figurative language. It personifies trees, dogs, and shadows. For example, footprints in the snow "follow us," shadows "bumped after me," and cold places an "icy hand . . . palm-down on my back." Similes and metaphors produce vivid comparisons; voices in the night fade away "as quiet as a dream," snow is "whiter than milk in a cereal bowl," and an owl moves "like a shadow without a sound." The vivid language in Nancy Willard's *Pish, Posh, Said Hieronymus Bosch* presents a fantasy world in which the housekeeper wrestles with dragons "while the cats chase the cucumbers, slickity-slink." The language in Nancy Carlstrom's *Raven and River* sounds like the actions of various animals as they wake the sleeping river from its icy slumber.

Poetry collections are another good source for language development. *Silver Seeds: A Book of Nature Poems* by Paul Paolilli encourages readers to view nature in new ways as the poems use vivid metaphors to describe such common natural occurrences as the stars, the moon, and the clouds.

Literature is a crucial resource, providing both a model for language and a stimulus for oral and written activities. This text suggests a wealth of literature for use in the elementary grades: literature to be read aloud to children; literature to provide models for expanding language proficiency; and literature to stimulate oral discussion, creative dramatics, creative writing, and listening enjoyment.

Literature provides stimulus for the dramatic play and creative dramatics that inspire children in the primary grades to express themselves verbally with much enjoyment. For example, in Maurice Sendak's *Where the Wild Things Are*, Max gets into so much mischief when he is wearing his wolf suit that his mother sends him to his room without any supper. His vivid imagination turns the room into a forest inhabited by wild things. Max stays in the forest and becomes its king, but finally, he gets lonely and wants to return to the land where someone loves him. Children can relate to Max's experience and use it to stimulate their own

A boy turns a day in the snow into a very imaginative experience. Illustration by Stephen Gammell, reproduced with permission of G. P. Putnam's Sons from Will's Mammoth *by Rafe Martin, illustrations copyright © 1989 by Stephen Gammell.*

wild experiences. Children enjoy using their imaginations and turning common occurrences into creative experiences.

Books that encourage children to make up their own stories are also excellent for language development. Authors may develop their books on the premise of what would happen if a character from a book came to life. In Susan Cooper's *Matthew's Dragon*, the dragon from a boy's favorite book comes to life and the boy and the dragon share an adventure. By reading and viewing *The Flying Dragon Room*, text by Audrey Wood and illustrations by Mark Teague, children can use their imaginations to create their own fantasy worlds inhabited by strange animals and unusual experiences, or they can pretend that they are riding the flying dragon or sailing on the Jolly Mermaid. In *Edward and the Pirates*, David McPhail uses a young boy's love for reading and his powerful imagination to create adventures. Any of these books can encourage children to create their own stories. For example, children can choose a figure from a fictional book and pretend that it comes to life. What would happen? What might the figure do for good or for bad? How would they control the figure?

"What if" stories may encourage children to explore vicariously new worlds and to tell about experiences if they could accompany the literary characters. Paul Fleischman's *Time Train* provides a marvelous opportunity for children to enter the Rocky Mountain Unlimited and to go back in time chronologically until they finally enter a tropical world inhabited by dinosaurs. Jon Scieszka's *Your Mother Was a Neanderthal* allows children to accompany a time-warp trio back to the time of woolly mammoths and saber-toothed tigers. Alison Lester's *The Journey Home* encourages readers to accompany two children who dig a hole that takes them to the other side of the world. They have numerous adventures as they explore the earth in their endeavor to reach home. These books encourage children to create imaginative fantasies.

Older children will gain insights about the dramatic use of language by reading Susan Cooper's *King of Shadows*. This time-warp story takes a young actor back to the original Globe Theatre where he acts with Shakespeare. Cooper uses many lines from various Shakespearean plays in her writing.

Cognitive Development

Factors related to helping children remember, anticipate, integrate perceptions, and develop concepts fill numerous textbooks and have been the subject of both research and conjecture. Jean Piaget and B. Inhelder (1969) maintained that the order in which children's thinking matures is the same for all children, although the pace varies from child to child. Stimulation is also necessary for cognitive development. Children who grow up without a variety of experiences may be three to five years behind other children in developing the mental strategies that aid recall. Chart 1.2 lists books that can promote cognitive development in children.

According to child development authority David Shaffer (1989), cognitive development "refers to the changes that occur in children's mental skills and abilities over time" (p. 306). Shaffer states, "We are constantly attending to objects and events, interpreting them, comparing them with past experiences, placing them into categories, and encoding them into memory" (p. 306). Mussen, Conger, and Kagan (1989) define cognition as the process involved in

(1) perception—the detection, organization, and interpretation of information from both the outside world and the internal environment, (2) memory—the storage and retrieval of the perceived information, (3) reasoning—the use of knowledge to make inferences and draw conclusions, (4) reflection—the evaluation of the quality of ideas and solutions, and (5) insight—the recognition of new relationships between two or more segments of knowledge.

George Maxim (1993) emphasizes cognitive development that includes two major areas: physical knowledge and logicomathematical ability. Physical knowledge is gained through observing properties of objects within the child's experience. The child learns about the physical environment through observation and experimentation. Logicomathematical ability includes the ability to classify or group objects on some common criterion; to arrange objects according to size, quality, or quantity and then compare likenesses and differences among objects in the same category and order them according to relative differences; to understand spatial relations in terms of direc-

tion, distance, and perspective; to understand temporal relations that allow perception of time sequences; and to conceptualize properties of objects.

Scientist and author Chet Raymo (1992) highlights the role of children's books in developing a scientific imagination. He states, "Creative science depends crucially upon habits of mind that are most readily acquired by children: curiosity; voracious observation; sensitivity to rules and variations within the rules; and fantasy. Children's books that instill these habits of mind sustain science" (p. 561).

All of the preceding processes are essential for success in both school and adult life. Each is also closely related to understanding and enjoying literature. Without visual and auditory perception, literature could not be read or heard; without memory, there would be no way to see the relationships among literary works and to recognize new relationships as experiences are extended. Literature is also important in stimulating cognitive development by encouraging the oral exchange of ideas and the development of thought processes. Children's literature is especially effective for developing the basic operations associated with thinking: (1) observing, (2) comparing, (3) classifying, (4) hypothesizing, (5) organizing, (6) summarizing, (7) applying, and (8) criticizing.

Observing. Colorful picture books are excellent means of developing observational skills in both younger and older children. Young children discover how many animals they can locate in *Keep Looking!* by Millicent Selsam and Joyce Hunt. Suse MacDonald's *Alphabatics* encourages young children to observe how a letter changes within three or four drawings to a picture of an object that begins with that letter. Keith Baker's *Hide and Snake* encourages viewers to search through the illustrations to find the snake that is mixed in with colored yarns, curled around hats, wrapped among presents, and napping with cats. The colors of the snake blend with the colors in the illustrations. Consequently, this book becomes a game of hide and seek. Using Stephen T. Johnson's *Alphabet City*, students may search for the various letters of the alphabet captured through paintings of various scenes. For example, the letter A is a construction sawhorse, the letter M is a bridge structure, and the letter Z is formed with fire escapes. The illustrations in Lucy Micklethwait's *A Child's Book of Play in Art: Great Pictures, Great Fun* encourage children to find details, imitate sounds, adapt patterns, and interpret costumes.

The author's note in Scott Russell Sanders' *Crawdad Creek* states that he wrote the book "in hopes of inviting today's children to go outside, hunt for moving water, open their eyes and ears and hearts to the wilderness that wells up everywhere" (unnumbered). Robert Hynes's illustrations show readers some of the life they will observe including frogs, crayfish, turtles, and insects as well as fossils.

CHART 1.2 (PP. 11–14)   Cognitive development

Characteristics	Implications	Literature Suggestions
Preschool: Ages Two–Three		
1 Children learn new ways to organize and classify their worlds by putting together things that they perceive to be alike.	1 Provide opportunities for children to discuss and group things according to color, shape, size, or use. Use picture concept books with large, colorful pictures.	Cabrera, Jane. *Cat's Colors.* Hoban, Tana. *Look! Look! Look!* _____. *Of Colors and Things.* _____. *1, 2, 3.* _____. *What Is It?* Gunson, Christopher. *Over On the Farm: A Counting Picture Book Rhyme.*
2 Children begin to remember two or three items.	2 Exercise children's short-term memories by providing opportunities to recall information.	
Preschool: Ages Three–Four		
1 Children develop an understanding of how things relate to each other: how parts go together to make a whole, and how they are arranged in space in relation to each other.	1 Give children opportunities to find the correct part of a picture to match another picture. Use simple picture puzzles.	Hutchins, Pat. *Changes, Changes.* Oxenbury, Helen. *I See.*
2 Children begin to understand relationships and classify things according to certain perceptual attributes that they share, such as color, size, shape, and what they are used for.	2 Share concept books on color, size, shape, and use. Provide opportunities for children to group and classify objects and pictures.	Carle, Eric. *My Very First Book of Colors.* de Brunhoff, Laurent. *Babar's Book of Color.* Hoban, Tana. *Shapes, Shapes, Shapes.* _____. *So Many Circles, So Many Squares.*
3 Children begin to understand how objects relate to each other in terms of number and amount.	3 Give picture counting books to children. Allow them to count.	Bang, Molly. *Ten, Nine, Eight.* Carle, Eric. *My Very First Book of Numbers.* Christelow, Eileen. *Five Little Monkeys Jumping on the Bed.* Fleming, Denise. *Count!* Tafuri, Nancy. *Who's Counting?*
4 Children begin to compare two things and tell which is bigger and which is smaller.	4 Share and discuss books that allow comparisons in size, such as a giant and a boy, a big item and a small item, or a series of animals.	Campbell, Rod. *Dear Zoo.* Hutchins, Pat. *Shrinking Mouse.* Voake, Charlotte. *Mrs. Goose's Baby.*
Preschool: Ages Four–Five		
1 Children remember to do three things told to them or retell a short story if the material is presented in a meaningful sequence.	1 Tell short, meaningful stories and allow children to retell them. Use flannelboard and picture stories to help children organize the story. Give practice in following three-step directions.	Asbjørnsen, Peter Christen. *Three Billy Goats Gruff.* Galdone, Paul. *The Gingerbread Boy.* Gray, Libba Moore. *Is There Room on the Feather Bed?* Carle, Eric. *My Very First Book of Shapes.*
2 Children increase their ability to group objects according to important characteristics but still base their rules on how things look to them.	2 Provide many opportunities to share concept books and activities designed to develop ideas of shape, color, size, feel, and use.	Emberley, Ed. *Go Away, Big Green Monster!* Hoban, Tana. *Circles, Triangles, and Squares.* _____. *Is It Red? Is It Yellow? Is It Blue?* Sís, Peter. *Trucks Trucks Trucks.*

(continues)

CHART 1.2   *(Continued)*

Characteristics	Implications	Literature Suggestions
Preschool: Ages Four–Five		
3 Children pretend to tell time but do not understand the concept. Things happen "now" or "before now."	3 Share books to help children understand sequence of time and when things happen, such as the seasons of the year and different times of the day or different days of the week.	Johnson, Angela. *Tell Me a Story, Mama.* Peters, Lisa Westberg. *October Smiled Back.* Rockwell, Anne. *First Comes Spring.*
Preschool—Kindergarten: Ages Five–Six		
1 Children learn to follow one type of classification (such as color or shape) through to completion without changing the main characteristic partway through the task.	1 Continue to share concept books and encourage activities that allow children to group and classify.	Falwell, Cathryn. *Turtle Splash!: Countdown at the Pond.* Lobel, Arnold. *On Market Street.* Theodorou, Rod, and Carole Telford. *Big and Small.*
2 Children count to ten and discriminate ten objects.	2 Reinforce counting skills with counting books and other counting activities.	Carle, Eric. *My Very First Book of Numbers.* Parker, Vic. *Bearobics: A Hip-Hop Counting Story.* Sierra, Judy. *Counting Crocodiles.*
3 Children identify primary colors.	3 Reinforce identification through the use of color concept books and colors found in other picture books.	Ehlert, Lois. *Color Zoo.* Hutchins, Pat. *Changes, Changes.*
4 Children learn to distinguish between "a lot of" something and "a little of" something.	4 Provide opportunities for children to identify and discuss the differences between concepts.	Gág, Wanda. *Millions of Cats.* Zemach, Margot. *It Could Always Be Worse.*
5 Children require trial and error before they can arrange things in order from smallest to biggest.	5 Share books that progress from smallest to largest. Have children retell stories using flannelboard characters drawn in appropriate sizes.	Galdone, Paul. *The Three Billy Goats Gruff.* Jenkins, Steve. *Big & Little.*
6 Children still have vague concepts of time.	6 Share books to help children understand time sequence.	Braun, Trudi. *My Goose Betsy.* Moser, Barry. *The Three Little Pigs.*
Early Elementary: Ages Six–Eight		
1 Children are learning to read; they enjoy reading easy books and demonstrating their new abilities.	1 Provide easy-to-read books geared to children's developing reading skills.	Byars, Betsy. *My Brother, Ant.* Lobel, Arnold. *Frog and Toad All Year.* Rylant, Cynthia. *Henry and Mudge and the Long Weekend.* _____. *Mr. Putter and Tabby Pour the Tea.* Seuss, Dr. *The Cat in the Hat.* Van Leeuwen, Jean. *Oliver Pig at School.*
2 Children are learning to write and enjoy creating their own stories.	2 Allow children to write, illustrate, and share their own picture books. Use wordless books to suggest plot.	Van Allsburg, Chris. *The Mysteries of Harris Burdick.* Waber, Bernard. *The Snake: A Very Long Story.* Wiesner, David. *Free Fall.* _____. *Sector 7.* _____. *Tuesday.*

CHART 1.2   *(Continued)*

Characteristics	Implications	Literature Suggestions
Early Elementary: Ages Six–Eight		
3 Children enjoy longer stories than they did when they were five because their attention spans are increasing.	3 Read longer storybooks to children, such as books in which the chapters can be completed in a short time.	Alexander, Lloyd. *The Fortune Tellers.* Lester, Julius. *The Last Tales of Uncle Remus.* Milne, A. A. *The House at Pooh Corner.* San Souci, Robert. *The Talking Eggs: A Folktale from the American South.* Van Allsburg, Chris. *The Polar Express.*
4 Children under seven still base their rules on immediate perception and learn through real situations.	4 Provide experiences that allow children to see, discuss, and verify information and relationships.	Emberley. Ed. *The Wing on a Flea: A Book About Shapes.* Micklethwait, Lucy. *A Child's Book of Play in Art: Great Pictures Great Fun.* Peters, Lisa Westberg. *The Sun, the Wind and the Rain.* Priceman, Marjorie, *How to Make an Apple Pie and See the World.*
5 Sometime during this age, children pass into the stage that Piaget refers to as concrete operational. Children have developed a new set of rules, called groupings, so they don't have to see all objects to group; they can understand relationships among categories.	5 Provide opportunities for children to read and discuss concept books.	Anno, Mitsumasa. *Anno's Counting Book.* _____. *Anno's Math Games II.* Feelings, Muriel. *Moja Means One: Swahili Counting Book.* Grossman, Bill. *My Little Sister Ate One Hare.* Haskins, Jim. *Count Your Way Through Italy.* Hoban, Tana. *26 Letters and 99 Cents.* Inkpen, Mick. *Kipper's A to Z: An Alphabet Adventure.* Kalman, Maira. *What Pete Ate from A–Z (Really!).* McMillan, Bruce. *Eating Fractions.* Wells, Rosemary. *Emily's First 100 Days of School.*
Middle Elementary: Ages Eight–Ten		
1 Children's reading skills improve rapidly, although there are wide variations in reading ability among children within the same age group.	1 For independent reading, provide books at appropriate reading levels. Allow children opportunities to share their book experiences with peers, parents, teachers, and other adults.	Blume, Judy. *Tales of a Fourth Grade Nothing.* Cleary, Beverly. *Ramona and Her Father.* Lowry, Lois. *Attaboy, Sam!* Nichol, Barbara. *Beethoven Lives Upstairs.* Wilder, Laura Ingalls. *Little House in the Big Woods.*
2 Children's level of interest in literature may still be above their reading levels.	2 Provide a daily time during which children can listen to a variety of books being read aloud.	Burnett, Frances Hodgson. *The Secret Garden.* Gantos, Jack. *Joey Pigza Loses Control.* Grahame, Kenneth. *The Wind in the Willows.* Konigsburg, E. L. *The View From Saturday.* Lewis, C. S. *The Lion, the Witch, and the Wardrobe.* White, E. B. *Charlotte's Web.*

(continues)

CHART 1.2   *(Continued)*

Characteristics	Implications	Literature Suggestions
Middle Elementary: Ages Eight–Ten		
3 Memory improves as children learn to attend to certain stimuli and ignore others.	3 Help children set purposes for listening or reading before the actual literature experience.	Cole, Joanna. *Ms. Frizzle's Adventures: Ancient Egypt.* Freedman, Russell. *The Wright Brothers: How They Invented the Airplane.* Koscielniak, Bruce. *The Story of the Incredible Orchestra.*
Upper Elementary: Ages Ten–Twelve		
1 Children develop an understanding of the chronological ordering of past events.	1 Encourage children to read historical fiction and books showing historical changes to help them understand differing viewpoints and historical perspectives.	Arnold, Caroline. *Stone Age Farmers Beside the Sea: Scotland's Prehistoric Village of Skara Brae.* Forbes, Esther. *Johnny Tremain.* McCurdy, Michael. *Escape from Slavery: The Boyhood of Frederick Douglass in His Own Words.* Meyer, Carolyn, and Charles Gallenkamp. *The Mystery of the Ancient Maya.* Speare, Elizabeth George. *The Sign of the Beaver.* Stolley, Richard B. *Life: Our Century in Pictures for Young People.* Orlev, Uri. *The Man from the Other Side.*
2 Children apply logical rules, reasoning, and formal operations to abstract problems.	2 Use questioning and discussion strategies to develop higher level thought processes. Children enjoy more complex books.	Avi. *Nothing But the Truth: A Documentary Novel.* *Beowulf.* Blumberg, Rhoda. *The Incredible Journey of Lewis & Clark.* Freedman, Russell. *Lincoln: A Photobiography.* Goodall, Jane. *The Chimpanzees I Love: Saving Their World and Ours.* Levin, Betty. *Shadow Catcher.*

Sources: Maxim (1997); Mussen, Conger, and Kagan (1989); and Piaget and Inhelder (1969).

Suse MacDonald's *Look Whooo's Counting* encourages readers to observe and count as they locate animals in a moonlit landscape. The objects progress from one to ten as a young owl flies through the night.

Older children enjoy searching for art objects, literary and historical characters, and present-day personalities in Mitsumasa Anno's detailed wordless books, such as *Anno's U.S.A. Lentil,* by Robert McCloskey, contains excellent drawings of a Midwestern town in the early 1900s: the town square, the houses on the streets, the interior of the schoolhouse, the train depot, and a parade. Single lines of text accompany each picture, but the pictures show the lifestyles and the emotions of the characters in the story. Kathy Jakobsen's *My New York* encourages children to locate the narrator within each picture and to describe the detailed New York settings.

Anthony Browne's *Willy's Pictures* provides an observational task in which readers are asked to identify the artistic works that inspired Browne's illustrations. The book concludes with copies of the original paintings. For example, one of Browne's illustrations includes a shell that is similar to the shell in "The Birth of Venus," painted in about 1485 by Sandro Botticelli. Roxie Munro's *Mazescaples* challenge readers to follow a series of mazes through cityscapes and over country roads. The opening shows a hand carrying the book to a car, which implies that the book might be used to provide entertainment during a car trip.

The detailed illustrations in The Inside-Outside Book of Washington, D.C. *provide an excellent source for observing. (From* The Inside-Outside Book of Washington, D.C. *by Roxie Munro. Copyright © 1987 by Roxie Munro. Reproduced by permission of the publisher, Dutton Children's Books, a division of Penguin Books USA, Inc.)*

Comparing. Picture books and other literature selections provide opportunities for comparing. For example, comparisons between two points of view may be made using Dorothea P. Seeber's *A Pup Just for Me; A Boy Just for Me*. Two stories are told in the book. One is told from the point of view of a boy who wants a puppy and the other from that of a puppy who wants a kind, loving master. The illustrations in Sandy Nightingale's *A Giraffe on the Moon* encourage children to compare reality and visions stimulated by the imagination. In Patrick Benson's *Little Penguin*, viewers compare the size of Pip, an Adélie penguin, with that of Emperor penguins. The illustrations also compare big and little fish.

Comparisons between work activities and nature activities can be made as the characters in D. B. Johnson's *Henry Hikes to Fitchburg* wager who will travel the thirty miles first: the one who walks and enjoys nature along the way or the one who works for money for the train ticket. The illustrator has contrasted the activities of the two characters. For example, one paints a fence while the other walks on stone walls and looks at nature through a magnifying glass; one sits on a train in a crowd of people while the other picks and eats blackberries in a berry patch. Readers can also decide if Henry David Thoreau was correct when he decided that walking was the best way to enjoy nature.

Different artists' renditions of the same story provide opportunities for artistic comparisons. For example, there are several illustrated versions of Margery Williams's *The Velveteen Rabbit*, originally published in 1922, including those by Allen Atkinson, Michael Hague, and Ilse Plume. Versions of the popular folktale "Beauty and the Beast" include those illustrated in different styles by Warwick Hutton, Barry Moser, Jan Brett, and Michael Hague. Students can consider the impact of color, line, design, and media on the interpretation of the text, as well as evaluate the accuracy of the illustrations. In addition to comparing artists' renditions, children may compare traditional versions of the tales and those adapted by authors such as William J. Brooke in *Untold Tales*, Jon Scieszka in *The Stinky Cheese Man and Other Fairly Stupid Tales*, and Eugene Trivizas in *The Three Little Wolves and the Big Bad Pig*.

A poetry collection, *Jump Back Honey: The Poems of Paul Laurence Dunbar*, provides an interesting comparative activity. The poems are illustrated by different artists including Ashley Bryan, Carol Byard, Jan Spivey Gilchrist, Brian Pinkney, Jerry Pinkney, and Faith Ringgold. Viewers can compare the various artistic styles. Three editions of "Aesop's Fables," all published in 2000, provide interesting comparisons. Jerry Pinkney's *Aesop's Fables* is a large collection of sixty fables illustrated in watercolors. Each fable

Henry decides to walk 30 miles to historic Fitchburg while his friend plans to work all day to earn the fare for the train. (From Henry Hikes to Fitchburg by D. B. Johnson. Copyright © 2000 by D. B. Johnson. Reprinted by permission of Houghton Mifflin Company. All rights reserved.)

concludes with a moral. Doris Orgel's *The Lion & the Mouse and Other Aesop Fables* includes twelve fables, each of which includes sidebars with information about ancient Greece rather than the more typical moral. Tom Lynch's *Fables from Aesop* includes twelve fables illustrated with fabric collages. Each fable ends with a short moral. Children can compare the styles of the retellings and the impact of the illustrations.

Upper-elementary children can compare the main characters, their struggles for survival, and their growing up in books such as Maia Wojciechowska's *Shadow of a Bull* and Elizabeth George Speare's *The Bronze Bow*. They can compare one author's depiction of characters and survival in Gary Paulsen's *Hatchet* and *The Voyage of the Frog*. They can compare themes, characterizations, and person-against-self conflicts in Marion Dane Bauer's *On My Honor* and Paula Fox's *One-Eyed Cat*. They can compare Russell Freedman's depiction of Lincoln in *Lincoln: A Photobiography* with the depiction of Lincoln by other biographers.

Two other interesting comparisons may be accomplished using Lois Duncan's *The Magic of Spider Woman* and Shonto Begay's *Navajo: Visions and Voices Across the Mesa*. Students may compare the similarities in values, beliefs, and themes in Duncan's folklore with the values, beliefs, and themes expressed in three poems in Begay's text: "Echoes," "Creation," and "Mother's Lace."

Classifying. Concept books provide excellent stimuli for classifying. Children must be able to classify objects or ideas before seeing or understanding the relationships among them. Various concept books use different levels of abstractness to introduce children to such concepts as color, shape, size, and usefulness. Eric Carle allows children to match blocks of color with the color shown in an illustration in his *My Very First Book of Colors* and illustrates the colorful story of a chameleon who wants to change his appearance in *The Mixed-Up Chameleon*.

Shape concept books vary in level of difficulty. Carle's *My Very First Book of Shapes* encourages children to match black shapes with similar shapes in color. John Reiss's *Shapes* presents shapes, their names, and their three-dimensional forms. Photographs in Tana Hoban's *Shapes, Shapes, Shapes* encourage children to search for circles, rectangles, and ovals.

Many other types of books can be used to develop children's classification skills and responses to literature. For example, after listening to the folktale "The Three Bears," children may classify the bears, porridge bowls, chairs, and beds according to their size and then identify which bear could best use a particular bowl, bed, or chair. (Flannelgraph characters and objects make classification more concrete for young children.) Stories can be classified using a category for wild animals or pets; a boy or girl category for the main character; or a category for settings such as country or city. Characteristics of a story can also be used for classification: realistic or unrealistic; likable or unlikable; happy or sad; and funny or serious. For example, children can compare the realistic and unrealistic qualities found in Patricia Lauber's *The News About Dinosaurs*, Henry Schwartz's *How I Captured a Dinosaur*, and Rafe Martin's *Will's Mammoth*.

Hypothesizing. Several illustrated books encourage younger children to hypothesize about what they will find when they turn the page. In *Look! Look! Look!*, Tana Hoban uses cutout squares to reveal portions of pictures. The total picture appears on the page following the portions. At a more complex level, students must turn the page to determine the possible dialogue in Chris Van Allsburg's *The Z Was Zapped*.

Hypothesizing is stimulated as children search for clues in pictures and text to answer various questions. In *Joseph Had a Little Overcoat*, Simms Taback uses cutouts in illustrations to provide clues about the next, always smaller, item that he makes out of the material that was once his old and worn jacket. In Mary Serfozo's *What's*

What?: A Guessing Game, readers hypothesize about the answer to a question such as "What's light?" After they guess, they can turn the page to discover the artist's answer. Finding objects may encourage both hypothesizing about the potential for the object and expanding the imagination. When a young girl finds a red ribbon on the ground in Carole Lexa Schaefer's *The Squiggle,* she twists and twirls the ribbon as she imagines it to be objects such as a thunder cloud and a dragon. In Edith Baer's *This Is the Way We Go to School: A Book About Children Around the World,* readers must locate clues in the illustrations and then identify where in the world the children attend school. A map with the correct answers appears in the back of the book.

Books that encourage hypothesizing include texts or illustrations in which children are asked to speculate about what may happen next. Adults who read Janet Stevens's *Tops & Bottoms* could stop after the second time in which Hare tricks Bear by getting the best part of the vegetable crop. Adults can ask students to speculate about how Hare will trick Bear during the third year when Bear states that he wants both the tops and bottoms. In a humorous ending, Hare plants corn so that Bear gets the roots (bottoms) and the tassels (tops), while Hare gets the ears of corn (middles). Before reading Betty Levin's *Shadow Catcher* children can speculate about the content of this book set in the 1890s. The book is a mystery in which considerable insights and knowledge are gained as the protagonist sees life through the camera's lens.

Hypothesizing about the subject, plot, or characters in a story helps children develop their cognitive skills and interests. It also motivates them to read or listen to literature. For example, before reading Ian Strachan's *The Flawed Glass,* older children can speculate about the author's purposes for using a plot that parallels the struggles of a girl with a physical handicap that makes it difficult to walk and to speak and the struggles of a weak eagle that tries to survive on the island. Before reading Patricia Lauber's *The News About Dinosaurs,* children can speculate about the content of the text.

Descriptive chapter titles and titles to subsections of books are excellent stimuli for verbal or written speculations by older children. For example, before reading or listening to Kathryn Lasky's *Think Like an Eagle: At Work with a Wildlife Photographer,* children can discuss what information they believe will be in each of the following sections: "A Walk Through the Night," "A Key to the Forest," "Dreams of Birds," "Corkscrew Swamp," "Thinking Like a Beaver," "Another Wilderness," and "The Last Golden Days." After reading each section, they can review the accuracy of their predictions.

Organizing. Books that allow children to follow changes in seasons increase children's understandings about sequences of time. In *Sky Tree: Seeing Science Through Art,* Thomas Locker follows the seasonal cycle of a tree begin-

ning in summer and progressing through the seasons until the tree again experiences summer. Lisa Westberg Peters's *October Smiled Back* portrays each of the months in both text and illustrations. Longer sequences of time are also presented in many books. For example, the organizational structure in Donald Hall's *Old Home Day* follows the evolution of a pond in New Hampshire from the Ice Age to the late 1990s. Patricia Lauber's *What You Never Knew About Tubs, Toilets, and Showers* begins with the Stone Age and then traces the development of these "fictures" through time and different civilizations. For older children, Kathryn Lasky's *Sugaring Time* follows the sequential order in which maple syrup is collected and processed, and Russell Freedman's *The Wright Brothers: How They Invented the Airplane* traces the major events in the lives of these two inventors.

Anne Millard's *A Street Through Time: A 12,000-Year Walk Through History* includes detailed illustrations that depict the same street from the Stone Age to modern times. Considerable opportunities exist for observation as readers are asked to locate Henry Hyde who is hidden in the pictures from each historical period.

Plot development in literature encourages children to learn forms of logical organization. After listening to or reading a literature selection, children can improve their abilities to put ideas into order by retelling the story or developing a creative drama based on the story. With their strong sequential plots and repetition of sequence and detail, folktales are especially appropriate for developing organizational skills. "The Little Red Hen" uses chronological order. The story progresses from the seed, to the planting, to the tilling, to the harvesting, to the baking, and finally to the eating.

"Why" tales also frequently depict a series of events to explain something. For example, Verna Aardema's *Why Mosquitoes Buzz in People's Ears: A West African Tale* describes the sequence of events that prevented the owl from waking the sun and bringing in a new day. Such folktales make excellent selections for flannelboard stories. When children retell the stories using the flannelgraphs or use the stories as the basis for creative drama, they develop and reinforce their organizational skills.

Summarizing. Summarizing skills can be developed with literature of any genre or level of difficulty. Children may summarize stories orally or in writing. Oral summaries may motivate other children to read the same book or story. After a recreational reading period in the classroom, library, or home, members of the group can retell a story, retell the part of the story they liked best, discuss the most important information that they learned, describe the funniest part of the story, discuss the most exciting part, and describe the actions of the character they admired the most or the least.

Summaries can be related to specific content. For example, children can summarize the most important historical information in Rhoda Blumberg's *The Incredible*

The wheels on a train, the hole in a key.

The Wing on a Flea introduces the concept that geometric forms are all around us. From The Wing on a Flea *by Ed Emberley. Text and illustrations copyright © 2001 by Ed Emberley. Reprinted by permission of Little, Brown & Company.*

Journey of Lewis & Clark and *Commodore Perry in the Land of the Shogun,* or the most important scientific information in Patricia Lauber's *Volcano: The Eruption and Healing of Mount St. Helens.* They may summarize the major contributions of Theodore Roosevelt after reading Jean Fritz's *Bully for You, Teddy Roosevelt!* or of Eleanor Roosevelt after reading Russell Freedman's *Eleanor Roosevelt: A Life of Discovery.*

Applying and Responding. Young children need many opportunities to apply the skills, concepts, information, or ideas in books. When children read concept books, for example, they should see and manipulate concrete examples, not merely look at pictures. Children who read Tana Hoban's *26 Letters and 99 Cents* can count and group objects. Using Anita Lobel's *One Lighthouse, One Moon,* readers can respond to colors, days of the week, months, and numbers from one to ten.

Humorous situations may provide opportunities to discover unusual ways to apply knowledge. Paul Fleischman uses such a technique in *Weslandia* when his main character, Wesley, discovers that "He could actually use what he'd learned that week for a summer project that would top all others. He would grow his own staple food crop—and found his own civilization!" (unnumbered). This text could also stimulate interesting discussions in science and social studies.

How-to books provide numerous opportunities for applying directions found in the books. *Ed Emberley's Picture Pie 2: A Drawing Book and Stencil* includes a group of stencils and directions for turning the stencil drawings into various animal forms such as birds, lions, and mice. The step-by-step instructions show which shape to use, its color, its size, and where to place it. Denis Roche's *Loo-Loo, Boo, And Art You Can Do,* includes step-by-step instructions for making eleven art projects such as face masks, potato prints, and papier-mâché.

Books that not only enhance children's appreciation of nature but also provide directions for science projects are excellent sources. For example, in *Butterfly House,* Eve Bunting presents directions for "How to Raise a Butterfly." Vivian French's *Growing Frogs* provides directions for collecting frogs' eggs, watching tadpoles develop, and releasing frogs back into the environment. Kathryn Lasky's *Science Fair Bunnies* shows that even two first-grade bunny friends can solve a problem when it appears that their science fair project has failed. Lasky shows that if students apply their knowledge and imagination to problems they can succeed. Using Ed Emberley's *The Wing on a Flea: A Book About Shapes* students can search for examples of rectangles, triangles, and circles found in the world around them.

Criticizing. Neither adults nor children should be required or encouraged to accept everything that they hear or read without criticism. Children should be given many opportunities to evaluate critically what they read or hear. Children develop critical evaluation skills when they sense the appropriateness, reliability, value, and authenticity of literature selections. Historical fiction selections are excellent for investigating and discussing the authenticity of plots, characters, and settings. For older readers, evaluation might include assessing the authenticity of biographies, such as Gary Schwartz's *Rembrandt* or informational books such as Francine Jacobs's *The Tainos: The People Who Welcomed Columbus.* Research indicates that the levels and types of questioning strategies used with children affect their levels of thinking and their development of critical evaluative skills.

Books provide many opportunities for students to critically evaluate the effectiveness of the literature. For example, older students can summarize the development of themes in Sharon Creech's *Walk Two Moons* and critically evaluate the effectiveness of the messages in developing themes, conflict, and characterization. Using Lloyd

Alexander's *The Arkadians,* students can search for and critically evaluate the effectiveness of Alexander's use of Greek mythology in this modern fantasy. Using Carol Fenner's *Yolanda's Genius,* students can critically evaluate the effectiveness of Fenner's use of music to develop themes and characterizations.

Nonfiction information books provide many opportunities for readers to critically evaluate how the information is presented and the effectiveness of the information. For example, readers can evaluate the author's ability to show that the Nazi government tried to turn the 1936 Olympic games held in Berlin into a propaganda tool for their cause. In *The Nazi Olympics: Berlin 1936,* Susan D. Bachrach provides background information, a discussion titled "The Nazification of German Sport," a review of "The Boycott Debate," and a summary of "The Nazi Olympics." The text also provides many opportunities for debate as students consider the negative or positive aspects of incorporating politics into sports.

Personality Development

According to George Maxim (1993), personality characteristics are "the traits that give each person a unique style of reacting to other people, places, things, and events" (p. 81). To gain these traits, children go through many stages of personality development. Children gradually learn to express emotions acceptably, experience empathy toward others, and develop feelings of self-esteem.

Child development authority Joanne Hendrick (1992) states that children "pass through a series of stages of emotional development wherein basic attitudes are formed. Early childhood encompasses three of these: the stages of trust versus mistrust, autonomy versus shame and doubt, and initiative versus guilt" (p. 112). Hendrick maintains that people who work with children must foster mental health in young children by providing many opportunities to develop healthy emotional attitudes. Slowly, with guidance, children learn to handle their emotions productively rather than disruptively. Expanded experiences, adult and sibling models, and personal success show positive ways of dealing with emotions.

Overcoming fears, developing trust, relinquishing the desire to have only one's own way, and learning acceptable forms of interaction with both peers and adults inevitably involve traumatic experiences. Progressing through the stages of personality development is part of the maturing process, and books can play a very important role in that process.

 Technology Resources

Visit our Companion Website at www.prenhall.com/norton for more resources on promoting children's personality development with literature.

Bibliotherapy is interaction between readers and literature. In bibliotherapy, the ideas inherent in the reading materials have a therapeutic effect. Experts in child development frequently suggest bibliotherapy to help children through various times of stress, such as hospitalization, loss of a friend, and parents' divorce. Although most of the emotional problems that young children experience are not as severe as coping with loss and separation, all children must face numerous smaller crises that require personal adjustment. Literature can help children understand their feelings, identify with characters who experience similar feelings, and gain new insights into how others have coped with the same problems. According to Masha Rudman and Anna Pearce (1988), "Books can serve as mirrors for children, reflecting their appearance, their relationships, their feelings and thoughts in their immediate environment" (p. 159). In addition, books can act as windows on the world, inviting children to look beyond themselves and to form bonds with characters and circumstances.

Joan Glazer (1991) identifies four ways in which literature contributes to the emotional growth of children. First, literature shows children that many of their feelings are common to other children and that those feelings are normal and natural. Second, literature explores a feeling from several viewpoints, giving a fuller picture and providing a basis for naming the feeling. Third, actions of various characters show options for ways of dealing with particular emotions. Fourth, literature makes clear that one person experiences many emotions and that these emotions sometimes conflict.

Jan Ross (1993) emphasizes that because children are small and are constantly dwarfed by their environment, they frequently suffer from lack of self-esteem. She states:

Books can help children understand that size is relative. Mary Norton's "Borrowers" books, which concern tiny creatures who live in people's houses and survive by "borrowing" from "Human Beans," are wonderful examples. After all, if Arriety, who is small enough to stand in a child's hand, can be stalwart, then surely a child can be, too. (p. 53)

Animal characters in books for young children frequently act very much like people. The problems that the characters face, especially their fears, can assist the personality development of young children. Books with animal characters are very satisfying for readers because the authors allow the animal characters to face and overcome common fears and emotions. For example, Martin Waddell's *Can't You Sleep, Little Bear?* focuses on a young bear's fear of the dark. In *Let's Go Home, Little Bear,* Waddell's characters focus on overcoming fears of sounds. In both books, Big Bear's compassion and understanding help the young bear overcome his fears. The kitten in Mary Wormell's *Why Not?* learns a lesson about not bothering other animals and listening to her mother. The circus dog in Lisa Campbell Ernst's *Ginger Jumps* overcomes fear of jumping because of the companionship of

Through the Eyes of an AUTHOR

Eve Bunting

Visit the CD-ROM that accompanies this text to generate a complete list of Eve Bunting titles.

Selected Titles by Eve Bunting:

Butterfly House

Dandelions

Fly Away Home

The Wall

How Many Days to America? A Thanksgiving Story

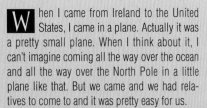

When I came from Ireland to the United States, I came in a plane. Actually it was a pretty small plane. When I think about it, I can't imagine coming all the way over the ocean and all the way over the North Pole in a little plane like that. But we came and we had relatives to come to and it was pretty easy for us.

But a friend of mine in Los Angeles who is a teacher had children in her class who spoke something like thirty different languages among them. A lot of them had come to the United States as immigrants, often in small boats, and it was hard for them coming here. I had asked my friend if she could tell me about her students, and she said, "No, I'll ask them to write their experiences for you."

So they all wrote their experiences for me, and many of them suffered severe hardships. But in the end they came here and ended up happy. I wanted to write a book about them, so I asked the children's permission. I said, "May I write a book about your experiences?" And they said, "Oh, sure." So then I wrote *How Many Days to America?*, which is based on their experiences.

Now, I don't scratch down ideas. I usually have a terrible memory, but when I'm thinking about a book I remember every little detail. I never really make outlines. I think it all out very carefully before I write anything. With a picture book, I would say I know every word before I write it down. So when people ask "How long did it take you to write a picture book?," I have to really give it some consideration, because sometimes I've been thinking about it off and on for a long, long time. I wrote a book called *The Wall*, which is about the Vietnam Veteran's Memorial in Washington, D.C. I really thought about that book for three years before I wrote it. When I actually began to write it, I had every word in my head, so I was able to write it very quickly. It seems silly to say it took three years, but it really did.

I got the idea for *Nasty Stinky Sneakers* because I saw an article in the paper about a competition in some school or town for who had the nastiest, stinkiest sneakers and I thought, "Boy, if my two sons were just the right age to go in for that competition, they would win." So I decided to write the *Nasty Stinky Sneakers* book. I had so much fun writing that book. I have fun writing all of my books, but that was a particularly fun one. Then after I had written it and published it, the publisher decided that they were going to have a nasty, stinky sneaker competition in different classrooms. And so they organized these competitions at different schools. It was really neat because what happened was that first the kids brought their nasty, stinky sneakers into the classroom and then they asked me if I would judge this competition nationwide. I said, "I don't think so." I love my book and I love my work, but I just didn't think I wanted to do that!

So they had the students create poems about their nasty, stinky sneakers or do drawings; some of them even made sculptures. They were really great. My whole house was covered with all of these things while I tried to decide. My husband helped choose the best one, which actually turned out to be a long poem a boy had written. As the prize, his whole class was given new, not nasty, not stinky, but brand new sneakers.

Video Profiles: The accompanying video contains more of this conversation with Eve Bunting, as well as conversations with Lynne Cherry and Mary E. Lyons concerning students' responses to literature.

---

an understanding girl. Searching for identity is a common theme in books with young animal characters. In Molly Bang's *Goose,* a goose egg falls out of the nest, and the baby is raised by a loving family of woodchucks. The baby goose, however, feels like an outsider until she discovers that she has her own special abilities: She can fly. Now she is able to be herself and return to her adoptive family. The main character in Bob Graham's *Benny: An Adventure Story* discovers pride in his abilities and a family who loves a dancing dog.

Many of these books are very satisfying for readers because the authors allow animal characters to face and overcome common emotions. For example, *In the Rain with Baby Duck,* by Amy Hest, allows Baby Duck to discover that when his mother was little she also disliked rain, puddles, mud, and getting her feet wet. Grampa Duck solves the problem by giving Baby Duck the umbrella and boots that his mother wore when she was young. This text shows that two generations had the same feelings about going out in the rain. Grampa Duck again helps Baby Duck to overcome fear in *Off to School, Baby Duck!* Grampa understands just how to help Baby Duck on that very first day of school. In Helen Lester's *Hooway for Wodney Wat,* a rodent with a speech impediment discovers that he can be a hero when his speech difficulty helps him overcome the class bully.

Jealousy is an emotion that is familiar to most children when they feel threatened by a new baby. Books about new babies can help children express their fears and realize that their parents still love them but that it is not unusual to feel fearful about a new relationship. Ezra Jack Keats's *Peter's Chair* shows how one child handles fear and jealousy when he not only gets an unwanted baby sister but also sees his own furniture painted pink for the new arrival. The older sister in Lenore Look's *Henry's First–Moon Birthday* discovers that her baby brother is not as bad as she thought when she becomes involved in the preparations for his one-month birthday.

In Jacqueline Martin's *Buzzy Bones and the Lost Quilt,* a mouse child experiences troubled dreams when he loses his security quilt. An understanding uncle and numerous friends help him search for the quilt. After the tattered quilt is found, the friends create a new quilt that includes pieces from the old one. Thus, books can help children anticipate and prepare themselves for situations that frighten them.

Many children fear going to school for the first time or moving into a new school or neighborhood. In *Miss Bindergarten Gets Ready for Kindergarten,* Joseph Slate creates two parallel stories as both the teacher, who is a black-and-white dog, and a group of animals prepare for the first day of school. All the animals except a reluctant iguana discover a very satisfying experience. In Kathryn Lasky's *Lunch Bunnies,* Clyde worries about all the terrible things that might happen during lunch on his first day of school. Fortunately, the experience is more pleasant than he imagined. Eric Carle's *Do You Want to Be My Friend?,* Miriam Cohen's *Will I Have a Friend?,* and Rosemary Wells's *Timothy Goes to School* present heroes who successfully cope with this problem. The conflict between individuality and conformity provides the plot in Peggy Rathmann's *Ruby the Copycat.* Many children who are unsure of their capabilities relate to this story of a girl who feels so unsure of herself that she copies a classmate's actions. By the end of the story, the girl discovers that she has her own creative resources. In fact, she is so good at hopping that the class now copies her. In Kevin Henkes's *Chrysanthemum,* a mouse child experiences problems adjusting to other children in school who make fun of her name. An understanding adult helps her learn to appreciate her name. Harlow Rockwell has written and illustrated *My Dentist* to help answer young children's questions about the procedures and equipment used during dental checkups.

The necessity of love is developed as an important theme in Martin Waddell's humorous book, *What Use Is a Moose?* The theme develops as Jack brings a moose home and tries to justify the animal's presence in his home. Jack fails miserably as he tries to show the usefulness of the animal only to have his mother banish the moose. When Jack becomes very unhappy, his mother realizes that being loved is a good use for a moose. The need to overcome loneliness is developed in Kay Chorao's *Pig and Cow* as Pig uses his nurturing experience to care for an egg that eventually hatches into a goose. He finally has a friend.

Literature provides children with many examples of how to cope with anger. Many children have days when absolutely nothing goes right. Books can act as stimuli for discussing how children handled or could have handled similar situations. Young children, for example, can certainly identify with Judith Viorst's Alexander in *Alexander and the Terrible, Horrible, No Good, Very Bad Day* or with Patricia Giff's Ronald in *Today Was a Terrible Day.* Betsy Everitt's *Mean Soup* shows that a child, with his mother's assistance, can release anger through proper channels rather than by locking it inside. Overcoming emotional problems associated with adjusting to a new school, a new community, and new friends is a common experience in today's society. In *Morgy Makes His Move* a third-grade boy has to face and eventually overcome prob-

In Can't You Sleep, Little Bear?, *a young bear experiences fears that are similar to those expressed by children. Illustration from* Can't You Sleep, Little Bear? *by Martin Waddell. Illustration © 1988 Barbara Firth. Used by permission of Candlewick Press, Cambridge, MA.*

lems related to moving. The author, Maggie Lewis, uses letters written to Morgy's old friend in California to highlight his problems. In a satisfying ending Morgy overcomes his problems and develops new friends. Readers understand that Morgy has really overcome his problems when he tells his new baby sister that it will be great for her because he will be there to help her with anything that she does not know.

Literature can play a dramatic role in helping children develop positive and realistic self-concepts. Infants do not think of themselves as individuals. Between the ages of two and three, children slowly begin to realize that they have identities separate from those of other members of the family. By age three, with the assistance of warm, loving environments, most children have developed a set of feelings about themselves; they consider themselves "I."

Egocentric feelings continue for several years, and children consider themselves the center of the universe. If the development of self-esteem is to progress positively, children need to know that their families, friends, and the larger society value them. Jane Yolen's *Owl Moon* and Karen Ackerman's *Song and Dance Man* are books in which children are valued by family members.

Books also show children that it is all right to be different from their families. Jan Mark's *Fun* shows that a boy who prefers quiet, contemplative activities can be happy living with an active, boisterous mother and father.

Books that stress creative problem solving are especially valuable for the personal development of young children. Denys Cazet's *A Fish in His Pocket* follows a young bear who accidentally causes the death of a fish, discovers a solution to the problem, and concludes a satisfactory ending to his dilemma. In Dayal Kaur Khalsa's *I Want a Dog,* a young girl finds a way to show her parents that she will be ready to take care of a dog when she is old enough to own a pet. Her solution, to practice taking care of a roller skate as if it were a dog, is both novel and humorous. In Amy Hest's *The Purple Coat,* a young girl finds a way to have the purple coat she wants and still have the navy blue coat preferred by her mother. The reversible coat results when Gabrielle and her grandfather work on the problem together.

Picture storybooks written for younger children may help children cope with the loss of a loved one. A young girl and her grandfather share many happy experiences in Rosemary Wells's *The Language of Doves.* Grandfather tells Julietta how he and his carrier pigeons (doves) sent messages during World War I. Now Grandfather continues to raise doves. After Grandfather dies, Julietta is heartbroken when the doves are sold. Her grief is lightened when a dove flies home with a final message from her grandfather.

In a book for slightly older readers, *When Dinosaurs Die: A Guide to Understanding Death,* Laurie Krasny Brown and Marc Brown provide a more detailed exploration of death by asking and answering questions such as "Why does someone die?" and "What does dead mean?" Various emotions and feelings about death are explored through the text. The book concludes with a positive section, "Ways to Remember Someone."

Divorce is another emotional and stressful experience faced by many children. Fred Rogers's *Let's Talk About It: Divorce* provides examples of ways that children can deal with their emotions. Through such statements as "Their divorce is not your fault," Rogers approaches one of the greatest concerns of young children and provides them with reassurance. Rogers recommends that adults use this book to discuss the topic with children. Photographs show three families whose members are experiencing divorce.

Adoption is another emotional experience. In *Tell Me Again About the Night I Was Born,* Jamie Lee Curtis tells a story that develops a loving relationship between the child and the adoptive parents. This book encourages children to overcome fear by celebrating adoption and suggesting that it is a very important decision for both parents and children.

Several excellent books for older children are based on the themes of overcoming problems. In Scott O'Dell's *Island of the Blue Dolphins,* a girl survives alone on an island off the coast of California. She is not rescued for eighteen years and must overcome loneliness, develop weapons that violate a taboo of her society, and create a life for herself. Gary Paulsen's *Hatchet* follows a boy as he learns about personal and physical survival in the Canadian wilderness. *Call It Courage,* by Armstrong Sperry, is another survival book. In this book, a boy must overcome his fear of the sea before he can return home. Survival during the Holocaust is developed in Livia Bitton-Jackson's *I Have Lived A Thousand Years: Growing Up in the Holocaust* as the heroine survives the ghetto, labor camps, and Auschwitz. Her bravery and determination help her realize that she is happy to be Jewish.

All children must feel pride in their accomplishments and cultural heritage and must develop positive sex-role identifications. Those who develop positive feelings of self-worth will be able to assume responsibility for their own successes and failures. Literature can help young children discover the capabilities they have and realize that acquiring some skills takes considerable time. For example, in Ezra Jack Keats's *Whistle for Willie,* Peter tries and tries to whistle. After considerable practice, he finally learns this skill. The importance of feeling pride in one's accomplishments is developed in Florence Parry Heide and Judith Heide Gilliland's *The Day of Ahmed's Secret.* This story, set in Cairo, follows a boy through his day of work and encourages readers to empathize with his excitement as he shares his secret with his family: He can write his own name.

The importance of being independent and developing your own interests is developed in Laurence Anholt's biography *Stone Girl, Bone Girl: The Story of Mary Anning.* The author focuses on the characteristics of a young girl who continues her hunt for fossils even though she is teased by children of the village. Her persistence pays off when she finds a large ichthyosaur skeleton. Her various finds increase her interest in paleontology and eventually make it possible for her to make a living in that field. You may compare Anholt's biography with Catherine Brighton's *The Fossil Girl: Mary Anning's Dinosaur Discovery.*

Using talent and wisely pursuing one's dreams are important themes in Oliver Dunrea's *The Painter Who Loved Chickens.* In this story the painter discovers that it is possible to both live where he wants to live—on a farm—and paint the subjects he wants to paint—chickens. Dunrea develops this important message when "The painter became famous. And he never again painted anything that he did not love to paint" (unnumbered). Helen Lester's *Author: A True Story* focuses on how the author overcame both learning disabilities as a child and rejection slips as an adult to become an author of children's books. Kathleen Krull's *Wilma Unlimited: How Wilma Rudolph Became the World's Fastest Woman* provides an excellent model for achievement through overcoming obstacles that would discourage many people. Wilma overcame polio, competed in a male-dominated sport, and as an African American grew up in the segregated South of the 1940s. Another book that emphasizes the accomplishments of female sports

Through the Eyes of a CHILD

Matt

Pam Wilson's Fourth Grade
Western Row Elementary
Mason, Ohio

TITLE: A Picnic in October

AUTHOR: Eve bunting

The book A Picnic in October is a very good book. I Like the part When tony's family comes in to the scene how you gave details about what they are wearing, and how They Look Like. I really like the Illustrations to they're really good. I noticed each page Tommy gets nicer, and happier. This a story about a boy who is Learnig to Like The Statue of Liberty. He also Learns that the Statue is important to him. I would recommed to Someone because it is a good book. I really Like this book because its a little bit of history.

Matt

---

stars is Sue Macy's *Winning Ways: A Photohistory of American Women in Sports.*

The importance of maintaining one's dreams is a common theme in books by Paolo Guarnieri and by Florence Parry Heide and Judith Heide Gilliland. In *A Boy Named Giotto* Guarnieri creates a fictional story about the early life of the painter (1266?–1334) who was a shepherd in Italy but dreamed of becoming an artist. He maintains his dream until he is invited to study with the painter Cimabue and eventually paints beautiful frescoes in Assisi and Padua. The dream for Heide and Gilliland's protagonist in *The House of Wisdom* is to follow in his father's footsteps and become a revered scholar in ancient Baghdad. When the caliph chooses Ishaq to lead a worldwide expedition to search for books, he knows that he can have two dreams: to see the world and to be a scholar who brings back the best manuscripts to the great library in Baghdad.

Personality development in children is extremely important. If children do not understand themselves and believe that they are important, how can they value anyone else? Many literary selections and literature-related experiences reinforce positive personality development. Such experiences include reading orally in a warm and secure environment, discussing and acting out various roles from literature, and simply enjoying a wide variety of literature.

A young girl discovers the first Ichthyosaur remains and surprises the scientific world of the early 19th century. From The Fossil Girl: Mary Anning's Dinosaur Discovery. *Text and illustrations © 1999 by Catherine Brighton. Published by The Millbrook Press. Reprinted by permission.*

ISSUE The Impact of Scary Content in Books: Is It Good or Bad for Children's Development?

A review of many series books suggests that terror is stalking children. This same conclusion may be reached by viewing current television programs and movies. Compilations of best-selling children's books such as those reported monthly in *Publishers Weekly*[1] suggest that children are buying and/or reading the books in record numbers. Two series by R. L. Stine, "Goosebumps" and "Fear Street," are bestsellers.

In an article in *The New York Times,* Doreen Carvajal[2] discusses this phenomenon as books, movies, and television become "grittier, scarier, edgier, and more violent than ever before" (p. E5) and seem to appeal to younger and younger audiences. Carvajal reports both positive and negative responses to this increase in frightening content.

On the positive side, publishers report that they are trying to make books as interesting and exciting as television. In addition, publishers argue that the scary content entices reluctant readers to read books.

In contrast, Carvajal cites responses of experts on child behavior who are concerned with the increase in nightmares and other responses by young children. Carvajal states, "Some librarians worry about the impact on girls who are often featured as victims of violence. There are also female characters who can dish out violence as well as take it—the high-school heroine of Buffy the Vampire Slayer, for example. Are TV portrayals of feminine aptitudes for violence a good thing? A bad thing? Both?" (p. E5).

Ask yourself these same three questions as you read a book with particularly scary content. Also, what is your response to Carvajal's concluding paragraph? "Ms. Pipher (a psychologist and author) advises parents to form small cooperatives to share information about books, films and television programs appropriate for their children. 'My grandmother used to tell me to choose your books like your own friends,' she said. Grandma never had friends like these" (p. E5).

---

[1]"Publishers Weekly: Children's Bestsellers." *Publishers Weekly* 244 (July 21, 1997): 177.
[2]Carvajal, Doreen. "In Kids' Pop Culture, Fear Rules." *The New York Times.* June 1, 1997, E5.

Social Development

According to David Shaffer (1989), socialization "is the process by which children acquire the beliefs, values, and behaviors deemed significant and appropriate by the older members of their society" (p. 560). Shaffer identifies three ways in which socialization serves society: (1) as a means of regulating children's behavior and controlling their undesirable or antisocial impulses, (2) as a way to promote the personal growth of the individual, and (3) as a means to perpetuate the social order. George Maxim (1993) emphasizes the role of literature in influencing positive racial and cultural attitudes. He believes that we must start to enhance self-concepts and cultural identity, develop social skills and responsibility, broaden the cultural base of the curriculum, and study particular groups by integrating multicultural education into the curriculum of the very young. To meet this multicultural component, Maxim recommends reading or telling stories that describe the lives of people in other cultures, inviting guest speakers from other cultures, visiting museums, and playing with games and toys from various cultures. Chart 1.3 lists books that can promote the social development of children.

Socialization. Socialization is said to occur when children learn the ways of their groups so that they can function acceptably within those groups. Children must learn to exert control over aggressive and hostile behavior if they are to have acceptable relationships with family members, friends, and the larger community. Acceptable relationships require an understanding of the feelings and viewpoints of others. Quite obviously, socialization is a very important part of child development. Understanding the processes that influence social development is essential for anyone who works with children. Researchers have identified three processes influential in the socialization of children.

First, reward or punishment by parents and other adults reinforces socially acceptable attitudes and behaviors and discourages socially unacceptable ones. For example, a child who refuses to share a toy with another child may be deprived of the toy, while appropriate sharing may be rewarded with a hug and a favorable comment.

Second, observation of others teaches children the responses, behaviors, and beliefs considered appropriate within their culture. Children learn how to act and what to believe by imitating adults and peers. For example, a girl may learn about gender distinctions in our culture by observing and trying to copy her mother's role in the family. Children also observe what other members of the family fear and how members of their group react to people who belong to different racial or cultural groups.

The third process, identification, may be the most important for socialization. It requires emotional ties with models. Children's thoughts, feelings, and actions become similar to those of people they believe are like them.

Children's first relationships usually occur within the immediate family, then extend to a few friends in the neighborhood, to school, and finally to the broader world. Literature and literature-related activities can aid in the development of these relationships by encouraging children to become sensitive to the feelings of others. For example, Ann Herbert Scott's *Sam* is very unhappy when the members of his family are too busy to play with him. When they realize what is wrong, they remember to include Sam in their activities. The four-year-old in Eve Rice's *Benny Bakes a Cake* helps his

CHART 1.3 (PP. 27–31) Social development

Characteristics	Implications	Literature Suggestions
Preschool: Ages Two–Three 1 Children learn to organize and represent their world; they imitate actions and behaviors they have observed. 2 Children transform things into make-believe: a yardstick may be a horse.	1 Encourage children to role-play so they can begin to take others' points of view and learn about other behavior. 2 Provide objects and books that suggest creative interpretations.	Carle, Eric. *The Mixed-Up Chameleon.* Oxenbury, Helen. *Family.* Steptoe, John. *Baby Says.* Hutchins, Pat. *Changes, Changes.*
Preschool: Ages Three–Four 1 Children begin to realize that other people have feelings, just as they do. 2 Children enjoy playing together and develop strong attachments to other children. 3 Children begin to enjoy participating in group activities and group games. 4 Children begin to identify others' feelings by observing facial expressions.	1 Encourage children to talk about how they felt when something similar happened to them; provide books that show feelings. 2 Encourage the growing social skills of sharing, taking turns, and playing cooperatively. 3 Let children be both leaders and followers during group activities after reading a book. 4 Encourage children to become sensitive to their own and others' feelings by talking about the feelings that accompany different facial expressions in books.	Keats, Ezra Jack. *Peter's Chair.* McBratney, Sam. *Guess How Much I Love You.* Winthrop, Elizabeth. *Bear and Mrs. Duck.* Cohen, Miriam. *Best Friends.* Hoban, Russell. *Best Friends for Frances.* Lindgren, Barbro. *Sam's Ball.* Bulla, Clyde. *Keep Running, Allen!* Scott, Ann Herbert. *Sam.* Henkes, Kevin. *Jessica.* Hutchins, Pat. *Where's the Baby?* Schaefer, Carol Lexa. *Snow Pumpkin.* Wells, Rosemary. *Bunny Cakes.*
Preschool: Ages Four–Five 1 Children start to avoid aggression when angry and instead look for compromises. They are, however, frequently bossy, assertive, and prone to using alibis. 2 Children begin to understand consequences of good and bad and may engage in unacceptable behavior to elicit reactions. 3 Children seldom play alone, but they begin to work by themselves. 4 Children increase their awareness of the different roles people play—nurse, police officer, grocery clerk, man, woman, etc. 5 Children exhibit unreasonable fears, such as fear of the dark, thunder, and animals.	1 Praise children for talking out anger, help them to calm down and talk about the situation, direct them toward finding solutions. Choose books in which aggression is avoided. 2 Explain actions in terms that children understand. Let children discuss alternative actions. 3 Encourage persistence; let children work at something until it is completed to their satisfaction. This is crucial for problem solving and self-directed learning. 4 Provide opportunities to meet different kinds of people through real life and books; encourage dramatic play around different roles. 5 Help children overcome fears by sharing experiences of others who had fears but overcame them.	Reiser, Lynn. *Best Friends Think Alike.* Shannon, David. *David Goes to School.* Viorst, Judith. *I'll Fix Anthony.* Zolotow, Charlotte. *The Quarreling Book.* Galdone, Paul. *The Little Red Hen.* Howe, James. *Horace and Morris But Mostly Dolores.* Burton, Virginia Lee. *Mike Mulligan and His Steam Shovel.* Carle, Eric. *The Very Busy Spider.* Morozumi, Atsuko. *My Friend Gorilla.* Barton, Byron. *I Want to Be an Astronaut.* Bunting, Eve. *Ghost's Hour, Spook's Hour.* Ernst, Lisa Campbell. *Ginger Jumps.*

(continues)

CHART 1.3   *(Continued)*

Characteristics	Implications	Literature Suggestions
Preschool—Kindergarten: Ages Five–Six		
1 Children like to help parents around the house; they are developing dependable behavior.	1 Allow children to be responsible for jobs that they can realistically complete. Read stories about children helping.	Rice, Eve. *Benny Bakes a Cake.* Rylant, Cynthia. *When I Was Young in the Mountains.* Spinelli, Eileen. *Night Shift Daddy.* Williams, Vera B. *A Chair for My Mother.*
2 Children protect younger brothers and sisters and other children.	2 Let children help and read to younger children, encourage them to become aware that they are growing into independent people. Share reasons why all people need security.	Howe, James. *There's a Monster Under My Bed.* Hughes, Shirley. *Dogger.* Schwartz, Amy. *Annabelle Swift, Kindergartner.*
3 Children are proud of their accomplishments; they take pride in going to school and in their possessions.	3 Encourage a feeling of self-worth: praise accomplishments, encourage children to share school and home experiences, and allow them to talk about their possessions.	Fassler, Joan. *Howie Helps Himself.* Miller, Margaret. *Now I'm Big.* Schwartz, Amy. *Annabelle Swift, Kindergartner.* Udry, Janice May. *What Mary Jo Shared.*
4 Children continue to show anxiety and unreasonable fear.	4 Help children overcome their fears and anxieties; stress that these are normal.	Waber, Bernard. *Ira Sleeps Over.* Wells, Rosemary. *Timothy Goes to School.*
5 Children enjoy playing outside on their favorite toys, such as tricycles and sleds.	5 Provide opportunities for play, discussions about play, reading and drawing about outside play, and dictating stories about outside play.	Keats, Ezra Jack. *The Snowy Day.* Martin, Rafe. *Will's Mammoth.* McLeod, Emilie Warren. *The Bear's Bicycle.* Smalls-Hector, Irene. *Jonathan and His Mommy.*
6 Children enjoy excursions to new places and familiar ones.	6 Plan trips to zoos, fire stations, historic sites, and such. Read about these places, encourage children to tell about family trips.	Asch, Frank. *Moonbear's Pet.* Coy, John. *Night Driving.* Griffith, Helen V. *Grandaddy's Place.*
7 Children enjoy dressing up, role playing, and creative play.	7 Provide opportunities for children to dress up and play different roles. Read stories that can be used for creative play.	Aardema, Verna. *Who's in Rabbit's House?* Ichikawa, Satomi. *Nora's Castle.* Wells, Rosemary. *Max and Ruby's First Greek Myth: Pandora's Box.*
Early Elementary: Ages Six–Eight		
1 Children may defy parents when they are under pressure; they have difficulty getting along with younger siblings.	1 Encourage children to become more sensitive to family needs and to talk and read stories about similar situations. Direct children toward finding solutions.	Blume, Judy. *The One in the Middle Is the Green Kangaroo.* Hartmann, Wendy, and Niki Daly. *The Dinosaurs Are Back and It's All Your Fault Edward!* Hoberman, Mary Ann. *Mr. and Mrs. Muddle.* Ness, Evaline. *Sam, Bangs, and Moonshine.* Nomura, Takaaki. *Grandpa's Town.* Sendak, Maurice. *Where the Wild Things Are.*
2 Children want to play with other children but frequently insist on being first.	2 Encourage children both to lead and follow, read books in which children overcome similar problems.	Kellogg, Steven. *Best Friends.* Udry, Janice May. *Let's Be Enemies.*

CHART I.3 *(Continued)*

Characteristics	Implications	Literature Suggestions
Early Elementary: Ages Six–Eight		
3 Children respond to teachers' help or praise. They try to conform and please teachers.	3 Allow children to share work and receive praise. Show and tell is especially enjoyable for six- and seven-year-olds. Praise their reading and sharing of books.	Henkes, Kevin. *Lilly's Purple Plastic Purse.* Lobel, Arnold. *Frog and Toad All Year.* Van Leeuwen, Jean. *More Tales of Oliver Pig.*
4 Children enjoy sitting still and listening to stories read at school, at home, or in the library.	4 Provide frequent storytelling and story-reading times.	Fleischman, Sid. *The Scarebird.* Godden, Rumer. *Premlata and the Festival of Lights.* Hopkins, Deborah. *Under the Quilt of Night.* Melmed, Laura Krauss. *Little Oh.* Polacco, Patricia. *The Butterfly.* Say, Allen. *Grandfather's Journey.*
5 Children have definite, inflexible ideas of right and wrong.	5 Discuss attitudes and standards of conduct in books.	Cline-Ransome, Lesa. *Satchel Paige.* Friedman, Ina R. *How My Parents Learned to Eat.* Hanson, Regina. *The Face at the Window.* Schotter, Roni. *Captain Snap and the Children of Vinegar Lane.* Wild, Margaret. *Mr. Nick's Knitting.*
6 Children are curious about differences between boys and girls.	6 Ask children questions about differences between boys and girls and where babies come from. Provide books that help answer such questions.	Andry, Andrew, and Steven Schepp. *How Babies Are Made.*
Middle Elementary: Ages Eight–Ten		
1 Concepts of right and wrong become more flexible; the situation in which the wrong action occurred is taken into consideration.	1 Provide experiences and books to help children relate to different points of view; they begin to realize there are attitudes, values, and standards different from those their parents stress.	Adler, David A. *America's Champion Swimmer: Gertrude Ederle.* Bradley, Kimberly. *Ruthie's Gift.* Callen, Larry. *Who Kidnapped the Sheriff? Tales from Tickfaw.* Goble, Paul. *The Girl Who Loved Wild Horses.*
2 Children begin to be influenced by their peer groups.	2 Read and discuss books in which peer groups become more important; these groups can influence attitudes, values, and interests.	Allard, Harry. *Miss Nelson Is Missing!* Rappaport, Doreen. *Martin's Big Words.* Soto, Gary. *Taking Sides.* Byars, Betsy. *The Animal, the Vegetable, and John D. Jones.*
3 Children's thinking is becoming socialized; children can understand other people's points of view. They feel that their reasoning and solutions to problems should agree with others.	3 Provide many opportunities for children to investigate differing points of view. Literature is an excellent source.	Lacapa, Kathleen, and Michael Lacapa. *Less Than Half, More Than Whole.* Monjo, F. N. *The Drinking Gourd.* Peet, Bill. *Bill Peet: An Autobiography.* Sandin, Joan. *The Long Way to a New Land.*

(continues)

CHART 1.3 *(Continued)*

Characteristics	Implications	Literature Suggestions
Upper Elementary: Ages Ten–Twelve		
1 Children have developed racial attitudes; low-prejudiced children increase in perception of non-racial characteristics; high-prejudiced children increase in perception of racial characteristics.	1 Provide literature and instructional activities to develop multiethnic values and stress contributions of ethnic minorities.	Adoff, Arnold. *All the Colors of the Race.* Bat-Ami, Miriam. *Two Suns in the Sky.* Curtis, Christopher Paul. *Bud, Not Buddy.* Freedman, Russell. *An Indian Winter.* Highwater, Jamake. *Anpao—An American Indian Odyssey.* McKissack, Patricia, and Fredrick McKissack. *The Civil Rights Movement in America from 1865 to the Present.* Paulsen, Gary. *Dogsong.* Soto, Gary. *Neighborhood Odes.*
2 Children want to do jobs well instead of starting and exploring them; feelings of inferiority and inadequacy may result if children feel that they cannot measure up to their own personal standards.	2 Encourage expansion of knowledge in high-interest areas; provide books in these areas; provide assistance and encouragement to allow children to finish jobs to meet their expectations.	Cobb, Vicki, and Kathy Darling. *Bet You Can't! Science Impossibilities to Fool You.* Giblin, Jame Cross. *The Century That Was: Reflections on the Last One Hundred Years.* Arnold, Caroline. *Saving the Peregrine Falcon.* Kuklin, Susan. *Irrepressible Spirit.*
3 Children have a sense of justice and resist imperfections in the world.	3 Read and discuss stories where people overcome injustice, improve some aspect of life, or raise questions about life.	Lasky, Kathryn. *The Night Journey.* Lowry, Lois. *Number the Stars.* Riskind, Mary. *Apple Is My Sign.* Sachar, Louis. *Holes.* Severance, John B. *Gandhi, Great Soul.* Yates, Elizabeth. *Amos Fortune, Free Man.*

mother in the kitchen but faces disappointment when his dog eats the cake.

Books for younger children frequently deal with such problems as developing satisfactory relationships with family, friends, and neighbors. In Martin Waddell's *You and Me, Little Bear,* the author develops the importance of loving parent and child relationships as Little Bear wants to play, but Big Bear has work to do. Both the text and Barbara Firth's illustrations reflect the warm relationships between the two animals and the possibilities of resolving these types of family conflicts. In *Guess How Much I Love You,* Sam McBratney creates a loving bond between two rabbits as the father and son try to explain the measure of their love for each other.

In Leah Komaiko's *Just My Dad & Me,* a young girl wishes she could spend the day alone with her father only to find many extended family members joining them on the water. After a fanciful dive alone in the ocean, she dis-

covers that she needs her family, especially her father. Aliki's *Those Summers* details the carefree times at the beach and the interactions with children and adults. This book could be used to motivate discussions about special times during the summer.

Close relationships with a grandmother are important in Lenore Look's *Love as Strong as Ginger.* This Chinese American story was inspired by the author's grandmother who worked in a cannery in Seattle in the 1960s and 1970s. The girl learns a very important lesson from her grandmother when she discovers that it is important to become whatever you dream. Relationships with a neighbor who becomes a mentor are very important in Nikki Grimes's *My Man Blue.* Through a series of poems, Grimes develops this strengthening relationship until the boy concludes that someday he wants to be just like his friend Blue: gentle, trustworthy, and wise.

CHART 1.3 (PP. 27–31) *(Continued)*

Characteristics	Implications	Literature Suggestions
Upper Elementary: Ages Ten–Twelve		
4 Peer groups exert strong influences on children; conformity to parents decreases and conformity to peers increases in social situations. Children may challenge their parents.	4 If differences between peer and family values are too great, children may experience conflicts. Provide literature selections and discussions to help.	Brooks, Bruce. *The Moves Make the Man.* Byars, Betsy. *The Cybil War.* Fine, Anne. *The Book of the Banshee.* Greenberg, Jan. *The Iceberg and Its Shadow.* Hahn, Mary Downing. *Stepping on the Cracks.* Lisle, Janet Taylor. *Afternoon of the Elves.*
5 Children have developed strong associations with gender-typed expectations: Girls may fail in "masculine" tasks, boys in "feminine" tasks.	5 Provide books and discussions that avoid sex-stereotyped roles; emphasize that both sexes can succeed in many roles.	Cleary, Beverly. *A Girl from Yamhill: A Memoir.* Crowe, Chris. *Presenting Mildred D. Taylor.* Cummings, Pat. *Talking with Artists.* Freedman, Russell. *Eleanor Roosevelt: A Life of Discovery.* Johnson, Rebecca L. *Braving the Frozen Frontier: Women Working in Antarctica.* Macy, Sue. *Winning Ways: A Photohistory of American Women in Sports.* Paige, David. *A Day in the Life of a Marine Biologist.* Russell, David L. *Scott O'Dell.*
6 Boys and girls accept the identity of the opposite sex. Girls more than boys begin to feel that marriage would be desirable.	6 Provide books that develop relationships with the opposite sex; such books interest girls especially.	Cole, Brock. *The Goats.* Cooper, Susan. *Seaward.* L'Engle, Madeleine. *A Ring of Endless Light.* Lunn, Janet. *The Root Cellar.* MacLachlan, Patricia. *The Facts and Fictions of Minna Pratt.*

Sources: Mussen et al. (1989); Piaget and Inhelder (1969); and Shaffer (1989).

Kathleen and Michael Lacapa in *Less Than Half, More Than Whole* explore the questions asked by a boy who is part Native American and part Anglo. The authors use the symbol of the Creator's gift of corn to show the boy that like the corn of many colors he is also special. Consequently, like the corn, he is more than whole.

Overcoming problems related to sibling rivalry is a frequent theme in children's books and is one that children can understand. In *Stevie,* by John Steptoe, Robert is upset when his mother takes care of a child from another family, but he discovers that he actually misses Stevie when Stevie leaves.

Many books for preschool and early-primary children deal with various emotions related to friendship. Best friends may have strong attachments with each other, as shown in Miriam Cohen's *Best Friends* and Russell Hoban's *Best Friends for Frances.* The importance of an interracial friendship is developed in Carole Lexa Schaefer's *Snow Pumpkin.*

What happens to people when they want to be different from those around them is the subject of Toni Morrison's *The Big Box.* The story, told as a poem, provides interesting discussions as children are placed in a box because they cannot handle their freedom and act differently than their teachers and parents desire.

Social development includes becoming aware of and understanding the different social roles that people play. One of the greatest contributions made by literature and literature-related discussions is the realization that both boys and girls can succeed in a wide range of roles. Books that emphasize nonstereotyped sex roles and achievement are excellent models that can stimulate discussion. Biographies about women leaders and women authors show that women have made many

Grandpa's Town

By Takaaki Nomura

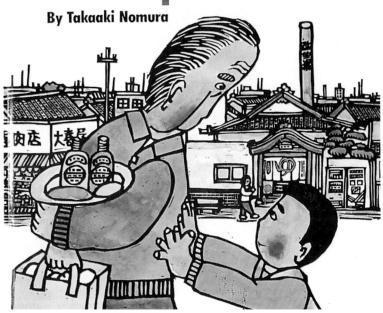

In Grandpa's Town, *a close and understanding relationship is shown between a boy and his grandfather. Illustration from* Grandpa's Town © *1989 Takaaki Nomura, translated by Amanda Mayer Stinchecum.* © *1991 Kane/Miller Book Publishers. Used by permission of Kane/Miller Book Publishers.*

important contributions, even during historical time periods when women did not usually have leadership roles. For example, Diane Stanley and Peter Vennema's *Good Queen Bess: The Story of Elizabeth I of England* presents a strong female who overcame many obstacles to rule her people. Biographies such as Norma Johnston's *Louisa May: The World and Works of Louisa May Alcott* and Angelica Shirley Carpenter and Jean Shirley's *Frances Hodgson Burnett: Beyond the Secret Garden* show that there were important female authors even during a time when writing was dominated by male authors.

Becoming aware of different views of the world is important in socialization, and literature can help accomplish this. Children may sympathize with the Native American girl who loves her family but longs for a free life among the wild horses in *The Girl Who Loved Wild Horses* by Paul Goble. They may view a cross-cultural Christmas as they read Allen Say's *Tree of Cranes* and become involved in a Christmas celebration that includes elements from both the Japa-nese and American cultures. They may understand the slave's viewpoint and the consequences of prejudice when they read F. N. Monjo's *The Drinking Gourd.* Older children discover the consequences of prejudice when they read Mildred Taylor's *Let the Circle Be Unbroken,* Belinda Hurmence's *A Girl Called Boy,* or Virginia Hamilton's *Many Thousand Gone: African Americans*

from Slavery to Freedom. When children read Ellen Levine's *Freedom's Children: Young Civil Rights Activists Tell Their Own Stories,* they may empathize with young people who worked for civil rights in the 1950s and 1960s.

Patricia Polacco's *The Butterfly* helps readers visualize the conflict and fear surrounding people during the German occupation of France during World War II. This story of friendship between a Jewish and a French family highlights the significance of strong social values during times of inhumanity.

Moral Development. Acquiring moral standards is an important part of each child's social development. Preschool children start to develop concepts of right and wrong when they identify with their parents and with parental values, attitudes, and standards of conduct. The two-year-old knows that certain acts are wrong. According to Piaget and Inhelder (1969), children younger than seven or eight have rigid and inflexible ideas of right and wrong, which they have learned from their parents. Piaget and Inhelder suggest that between the ages of eight and eleven, many changes occur in the moral development of children. At this time, children start to develop a sense of equality and to take into account the situation in which a wrong action occurs. Children become more flexible and realize that there are exceptions to their original strict rules of behavior; at this time, peer groups begin to influence conduct.

Lawrence Kohlberg (1981) defines the stages of moral judgment of adults and children according to the choices made when two or more values conflict. Kohlberg considers the moral decisions made, as well as the reasons for the decisions, when he identifies the stages in moral development. At Stages 1 and 2, Kohlberg's "preconventional" level, a child responds to external, concrete consequences. During Stage 1, a child chooses to be good, or to obey rules, in order to escape physical punishment. During Stage 2, a child obeys or conforms in order to obtain rewards. Kohlberg's stages and children's ages cannot be equated because some people progress more rapidly through the sequence. However, Stages 1 and 2 apparently dominate the behavior of most children during the primary years.

At Stages 3 and 4, Kohlberg's "conventional" level, a child is concerned with meeting the external social expectations of family, group, or nation. During Stage 3, a child desires social approval and consequently makes decisions according to the expectations of the people who are important to the child. Stage 4 has a law-and-order orientation; a child conforms because of a high regard for social order and for patriotic duty. Although one stage builds on another, the transition between stages is gradual. Stage 3 behaviors usually begin in the upper-elementary grades, and Stage 4 behaviors usually emerge in adolescence.

Stages 5 and 6 (which may be incorporated into a single stage) are at the "postconventional," autonomous, or principled level. At this level, a person establishes his or her own moral values. At Stage 5, a person responds to equal rights and consequently avoids violating the rights of others. At Stage 6, an individual conforms to his or her inner beliefs in order to avoid self-condemnation. Kohlberg estimates that only 25 percent of the population moves on in late adolescence or adulthood to a morality of equal rights, justice, and internal commitment to the principles of conscience.

Kohlberg suggested that a Stage 7 in moral development is the highest level of ethical and religious thinking. He refers to this stage as one of qualitatively new insight and perspective, in which a person experiences wholeness—a union with nature, a deity, and the cosmos. Although Kohlberg recognizes Stage 7 as an aspiration rather than as a complete possibility, he maintains that Stage 7 behaviors support individuals through experiences of suffering, injustice, and death.

Children's literature contains numerous moments of crisis, when characters make moral decisions and contemplate the reasons for their decisions. If adults expect children to understand the decision-making process of characters in a story, they should be aware of the level of the decisions that the characters are

The characters' actions in this book set during WWII demonstrate Kohlberg's stages of development.. From The Butterfly by Patricia Polacco. Copyright © 2000 by Patricia Polacco. Used by permission of Philomel Books, an imprint of Penguin Putnam Books for Young Readers, a division of Penguin Putnam, Inc.

making and consider whether or not the children are at a stage when they can appreciate those decisions. Teachers or other adults may need to help children understand decision making if the decisions are beyond their moral development.

For example, let us consider the decision making by the characters in Patricia Polacco's The Butterfly. At Stage 1, punishment and obedience, Monique obeys her mother and does not argue when she is told to go to school. At Stage 3, the maintaining of good relations, the children pretend they do not see the Nazi soldiers. "Don't look for too long. . . . If we do they'll come for us." At Stage 5, the morality of contract, Monique is upset when a Jewish shopkeeper is arrested. She worries that the Nazis will treat him like they treated the butterfly they killed. At Stage 6, the morality of individual principles of conscience, Monique understands the sadness in her mother's eyes and realizes that she must protect the Jewish family hiding in her basement. She understands the importance of being free as a butterfly and she gives away her cat as a symbol of friendship. Now consider which of these decisions might require adults to help children understand the moral development.

Technology Resources

Visit our Companion Website at www.prenhall.com/norton for more information on helping children understand decision making.

Children's Responses to Literature

Encouraging children to respond to the literature that they read is one of the most important tasks for adults who interact with children and literature. Thomas W. Bean and Nicole Rigoni (2001) state that "Intergenerational studies of reader responses to literature show the tremendous potential these exchanges have for increasing reader interest, engagement, and critical thinking" (p. 235). Lee Galda (1988) states, however:

Responding to literature is a complex process involving readers, texts, and contexts. Responding to literature has to do with what we make of a text as we read, how it becomes alive and personal for us, the pleasure and satisfaction we feel, and the way in which we display these feelings. Our responses to the books we read are influenced by many factors and come in many forms. (p. 92)

Cedric Cullingford (1998) emphasizes the complexities associated with children's responses when he states: "The more that the responses of readers are studied the more complicated they become. Readers bring all their idiosyncrasies to bear. They do not become the text, but connect the text to their own ways and to their own interpretations" (p. 1).

This section discusses each of the factors related to literature responses and relates the factors to specific literature.

Factors Within Readers

Readers bring past experiences, present interests, and expectations of stories with them when they read a selection. Consequently, different readers often read, interpret, and respond to the same piece of literature in different ways. The stories children hear lead the children to expectations about what a story should be and about what new stories will be like. Consequently, early and continual reading to children is extremely important.

In addition, children's responses to literature are influenced by the developmental factors discussed in this chapter. Children's language, cognitive, personality, social, and moral development affect the ways in which children interpret and respond to a story. In a review of response research, Miriam Martinez and Nancy Roser (1991) state that "Researchers have identified numerous reader characteristics that influence response, including reader beliefs and expectations, reading ability, socioeconomic status, cultural background, cognitive development, sex, and personal style" (p. 644). Robert Probst (1991) adds that insights gained from Piaget's work on cognitive development and Kohlberg's research on the development of moral reasoning are important for understanding and examining children's responses to literature.

As children bring their developmental, emotional, cultural, and scholastic backgrounds to their reading of literature, they approach the reading with their previous knowledge of the subject, their purposes for reading that literature, and their various strategies for gaining meaning from text. Rewarding interpretations of literature require personal responses that allow readers to connect experiences, emotions, and text; to understand and appreciate the unique requirements of different literary elements and genres; and to use various types of responses to expand their reactions to the literature. Consequently, the descriptions of various types of development and knowledge gained from the age and stage charts in this chapter will add to your knowledge of factors that influence readers and the examples of literature that you may use at different stages of development to enhance children's responses to literature.

Factors Within Texts

Literature texts vary from fairly simple narrative structures in folktales to elaborate novel-length plots with interwoven themes, detailed characterizations, and vivid, complex styles and language. In addition, each of the genres of literature has unique requirements: Poetry has a form different from that of biography; expository texts have reading requirements and purposes for reading different from those of realistic fiction; and mythology has a fundamental belief system different from that of fantasy. Even within expository writing, texts vary from simple, literal descriptions to structures that develop complex ideas such as cause and effect.

Galda (1988) states that factors in texts are important because "The text guides the response of the reader in that it presents content in a specific style and form which generate and modify expectations as a reader reads" (p. 98). Galda then identifies specific characteristics that influence response. The characteristics that influence readers' emotional involvement include aspects of style and characterization, the point of view of the story, the level of abstraction, and the complexity of the syntax. The age and maturation level of the main character frequently influence interest in the story and the type of response generated. The genre of the literature also influences types of responses. For example, fantasy frequently elicits a type of response different from that of realistic fiction. Likewise, readers may respond to poetry in different ways than they respond to biography.

FIGURE 1.1   So Why Might the World Wide Web Be Used with Literature?

 Technology Resources

1. So much information is available on the WWW—information about the books and the authors and ideas for use in the classroom.
2. Some works are extended or enhanced by narrative and graphics existing only on a website.
3. Connectivity: Teachers can share information about books, students can ask questions of their favorite authors, students in Maryland can discuss a book set in San Diego with students in San Diego (or Africa or China).
4. Quality literature for children is available on the WWW that is unavailable or hard to find anywhere else.
5. Numerous other claims (all of which depend on how the technology is utilized):
   - Enhances collaboration
   - Promotes student-centered and directed learning
   - Allows students to publish their own writing and reviews in a high-quality format for a large audience
   - Provides multimedia possibilities that might draw students into the literature
   - Prepares students for tomorrow's workplace

 Visit our Companion Website at www.prenhall.com/norton to find out about the wealth of resources available to you online.

Factors Within Contexts

The literature environment influences children's responses to literature. When adults support and encourage growth in children's responses and provide numerous experiences with many types of literature, they create an environment that stimulates children's responses. Martinez and Roser (1991) summarized some of the context factors that influence children's responses within home and school settings. They found that adults who positively influence children's responses make books accessible to children, select titles that emphasize quality and that allow children to make connections among literature selections, read to children daily, discuss books using critical terminology, suggest literature-related activities and share the results of those activities with peers, plan numerous experiences with literature, provide repeated opportunities for children to interact with the same books, and model personal responses to literature for the children.

A report published in *Reading Today* (2001) highlights the importance of this literary environment for reading achievement. Factors attributed to achievement included reading for fun; discussing studies at home; and having books, magazines, newspapers, and encyclopedias in the home.

Responses

When literary critics and authorities discuss responses related to literature, they frequently emphasize at least two major types of responses: efferent and aesthetic. Rosenblatt (1985) distinguishes between the two when she states that efferent reading focuses attention on "actions to be performed, information to be retained, conclusions to be drawn, solutions to be arrived at, analytic concepts to be applied, propositions to be tested"

(p. 70). Aesthetic reading, according to Rosenblatt, focuses on "what we are seeing and feeling and thinking, on what is aroused within us by the sound of the words, and by what they point to in the human and natural world" (p. 70). A worthy literature program should include both efferent and aesthetic responses to literature.

Robert Ruddell (1992) states:

A critical issue in this process is for the teacher to recognize the instructional stance taken toward literature in the classroom. One stance focuses attention on aesthetic-type reading, leading to identification with story characters, personal interpretation, and transaction with the text as the child steps through the "magic curtain" into the book with the character. A different stance, however, may focus attention on efferent-type reading, emphasizing content and information to be "taken away" from the book. Both aesthetic and efferent stances are needed in the instructional setting but serve very different purposes. Our overall literacy program must have balance across these two stances. (p. 615)

Alan C. Purves and Dianne L. Monson (1984) also emphasize the importance of encouraging both efferent and aesthetic responses within a literature program. They emphasize the relationships between texts and readers as the readers draw meaning. They describe two important functions in any literature program that prepares readers through a transactional approach. First, the program provides a broad background of literary genres and allows the students to talk about books using words like *plot, metaphor, characterization, theme, style,* and *tone.* This function encourages students to understand the reasons for deciding that one book is better than another book (efferent responses). The program also exposes students to a variety of approaches and critical questions that allow the students to consider "How does the literature or character affect me? What does it mean? How good is it?" Such responses allow aesthetic involvement and individual transactions.

Notice how Purves and Monson (1984) stress both the efferent and the aesthetic responses to literature when they state:

It would seem therefore that students should be exposed to a variety of critical questions, including those which are personal and affective, those which are analytical, those which are interpretive, and those which are evaluative. Each of these questions can be answered intelligently and answering each can help a student learn to read and think and feel. And you can teach your students how to answer them. (p. 189)

Cedric Cullingford (1998) states that teachers should be concerned with the "development of a reader who is aware and discriminating, who can analyze as well as react to what is read. Our first concern is to bring out the critical abilities of the reader, without which no demanding text can be enjoyed" (p. 193).

Analyzing Responses

Use of realistic fiction and other types of books for role playing and bibliotherapy is more effective when there is a general understanding of children's responses to literature. Louise Rosenblatt (1978) states that literature selection "should not be thought of as an object, an entity, but rather as an active process lived through during the relationship between a reader and a text" (p. 12). Readers bring past experiences, present interests, and expectations that influence their responses to texts.

Studies of children's oral and written responses to literature analyze the types of comments that children make when they retell a selection or talk about a story. In a review of children's responses to literature, Purves and Monson (1984) identify characteristic responses of children in different grades. For example, children up to the third grade tend to respond to and retell literal aspects of a story. In addition to literal responses, fourth- and fifth-grade students tend to elaborate on their responses by placing themselves in the roles of the characters, comparing themselves to the characters, and talking about their personal reactions. By sixth grade, students begin to emphasize and interpret characters. In seventh and eighth grades, students increase their interpretations and frequently emphasize meaning and understanding in their evaluations. Eighth-grade students begin to look for deeper or hidden meanings in stories.

Working with children and literature, you can learn a great deal about children's responses to literature by analyzing what children choose to say or write about when they discuss literature. Purves and Monson (1984) recommend a classification system to use when analyzing children's comments about literature (see Chart 1.4).

CHART 1.4 Classifying children's responses to books

Type of Response	Examples
Descriptive	Retelling the story, naming the characters, listing the media used in illustration.
Analytic	Pointing to the uses of language, structure, point-of-view in the work.
Classificatory	Placing the work in its literary historical context.
Personal	Describing the reader's reactions to the work and the emotions and memories that have been evoked.
Interpretive	Making inferences about the work and its parts, relating the work to some way of viewing phenomena (e.g., psychology).
Evaluative	Judging the work's merit on personal, formal, or moral criteria.

Source: From Alan C. Purves and Dianne L. Monson. Experiencing Children's Literature. *Glenview, Ill.: Scott, Foresman, 1984, p. 143.*

The Role of Motivation

Ruddell (1992) emphasizes the importance of the aesthetic stance in encouraging readers to "step into the story, experience, and live through the story" (p. 616). Ruddell identifies the following six internal motivators that foster aesthetic responses in readers and build personal connections with literature: problem resolution, prestige, aesthetic motivation, escape, intellectual curiosity, and understanding of self. Numerous examples of literature may be associated with each of these internal motivators and consequently may encourage aesthetic responses from children.

Problem resolution books encourage readers to see themselves as successful problem solvers. In this response, readers relate to characters who are able to solve or resolve problems and vicariously associate with successful characters. Young children can become successful problem solvers as they respond to the boy who uses his wits to encourage the king to leave the bathtub in Audrey Wood's *King Bidgood's in the Bathtub.*

Older children can see themselves as successful problem solvers by responding to Marty in Phyllis Reynolds Naylor's *Shiloh* when Marty resolves to save the dog from being mistreated by its owner and then uses much initiative to solve his problem by bargaining successfully for the dog. With Molly Cone's *Come Back, Salmon,* children can associate with the members of a fifth-grade class who cleaned up a salmon stream in Washington. With Susan Cooper's *The Boggart,* children can accompany three Canadian children as they figure out how to send a mischievous spirit back to his castle. With E. B. White's *Charlotte's Web,* children can respond to Charlotte, certainly one of the most successful problem solvers in children's fantasy.

The internal motivation of prestige enables a child to vicariously become a person of significance, who receives attention and exerts influence and control. Through picture *storybooks,* children can visualize themselves as heroines or heroes.

Highly illustrated biographies allow children to respond to characters who have had prestige in history, such as those in Diane Stanley and Peter Vennema's *Good Queen Bess: The Story of Elizabeth I of England, Bard of Avon: The Story of William Shakespeare,* and *Shaka: King of the Zulus.* The prestige of an artist may appeal to readers who can associate themselves with the successful career of an animator for Disney Studios and an illustrator of children's books in Bill Peet's *Bill Peet: An Autobiography.* Pat Cummings's *Talking with Artists* presents interviews with fourteen illustrators of children's books and shows examples of their works. Jeanette Winter's *My Name Is Georgia* follows the life of Georgia O'Keeffe and shows how she drew her inspiration from nature.

Aesthetic motivation involves the elevation of an aesthetic sense and ranges from appreciation of beauty in nature to the enjoyment of family harmony and interaction. Children are motivated to respond to both the aesthetic beauty in nature and to the beauty of language when they read Jane Yolen's *Owl Moon.* In Monro Leaf's *The Story of Ferdinand,* children can respond to a bull who favors the aesthetic response to nature to the glory of the bull ring. Aesthetic responses to beautiful language are heightened through poetry books such as Nancy Willard's *Pish, Posh, Said Hieronymus Bosch* and Stephen Dunning, Edward Lueders, and Hugh Smith's *Reflections on a Gift of Watermelon Pickle . . . and Other Modern Verse.* Enjoyment of family harmony and interactions are found in Pat Mora's *A Birthday Basket for Tia.* This book develops loving relationships between a Hispanic girl and her aunt. Laura Ingalls Wilder's *Little House in the Big Woods* develops strong family relationships in pioneer times.

Escape literature enables readers to vicariously accompany literary characters to unfamiliar or even fantasy places. Readers can escape to Africa with a carpenter who discovers how to tell fortunes in Lloyd Alexander's *The Fortune Tellers.* Africa is also the escape location for an African American girl who imagines what it would be like to live in East Africa in Virginia Kroll's *Masai and I.* The illustrations in David Wiesner's *Free Fall* allow readers to escape through a character's dreams. Anne Lindbergh's *Travel Far, Pay No Fare* follows children as they travel through the pages of several books. Books such as A. A. Milne's *Winnie-the-Pooh* allow readers to escape to the Hundred Acre Wood of personified toys. J. R. R. Tolkien's

I looked closely at the flowers.

Georgia O'Keeffe saw the world in her own way. From My Name is Georgia, A Portrait *by Jeannette Winter. Copyright © 1998 by Jeannette Winter. Reprinted by permission of Silver Whistle, an imprint of Harcourt Brace & Company.*

The Hobbit takes children into Middle Earth and allows them to become heroes as they accomplish their quest and regain the realm of the dwarfs. Lloyd Alexander's *The Remarkable Journey of Prince Jen* allows children to accompany a hero on a quest through a mythical land that has oriental characteristics.

Fiction and nonfiction set in other time periods encourage children to vicariously escape into those times. Avi's *Who Was That Masked Man, Anyway?* takes children back to World War II and allows them to interact with a boy who is infatuated with the radio shows of that time. Tracy Barrett's *Anna of Byzantium* takes readers back to the intrigue of the eleventh-century Byzantine Empire to discover a princess who wanted to write history. Rhoda Blumberg's *Commodore Perry in the Land of the Shogun* encourages readers to accompany Commodore Perry to Japan in 1853. Classics such as Robert Louis Stevenson's *Treasure Island* have encouraged generations to escape into the adventures that are possible with treasure maps, mysterious islands, and questionable characters.

The motivator of intellectual curiosity encourages curious minds to explore and learn about new words and new ideas. Some picture books, such as Arthur Geisert's *Pigs from 1–10,* challenge readers to find animals that are hiding within the illustrations. Numerous nonfiction books also encourage intellectual curiosity. Lois Ehlert's *Red Leaf, Yellow*

Leaf follows a child's curiosity as she plants a sugar maple tree and discovers how the seedling arrived at the nursery. Joanna Cole's *The Magic School Bus on the Ocean Floor* presents science facts through an amusing excursion through the ocean. Anne Baird's *Space Camp: The Great Adventure for NASA Hopefuls* includes numerous photographs and descriptions that will motivate and excite future astronauts. Kathryn Lasky's *Think Like an Eagle: At Work with a Wildlife Photographer* challenges readers to think like animals in order to acquire the best photographs.

Understanding of self is a powerful motivator. Books allow children to understand and respond to personal motivations and motivations that influence others. Many of the books listed under personal development may be used to elicit and increase personal responses to literature because they are closely related to emotions faced by children. In Cynthia Rylant's *Missing May*, a girl faces her aunt's death and makes discoveries about herself and those whom she loves. In Nina Bawden's *Humbug*, the heroine learns about deceit and honesty. Anne Fine's *The Book of the Banshee* allows readers to respond to the various emotional reactions in a family when one of the family members is a teenager. Avi's *Nothing But the Truth: A Documentary Novel* elicits very personal responses and insights into the motives of older students. Memos, letters, diary pages, phone and personal conversations, speeches, and telegrams encourage readers to develop and defend their own point of view about which character is telling the truth.

Throughout, this book contains many literature recommendations and literature-related activities that entice and enhance children's responses to literature. These recommendations encourage both efferent and aesthetic responses to literature. For example, through oral responses such as drama, discussions, role playing, and storytelling, children can respond to and critically evaluate development of the literary elements such as plot, conflict, characterization, and theme (efferent responses) and can provide personal reactions to those literary elements (aesthetic responses). Likewise, readers can evaluate the effectiveness of the setting and mood as created by the author or illustrator (efferent responses) and provide personal responses that emphasize emotional reactions through their own drawings (aesthetic responses).

Suggested Activities

For more suggested activities, visit our Companion Website at www.prenhall.com/norton

- Select several books, such as Eve Rice's *Oh, Lewis!*, to encourage young children to identify familiar actions in books. Share these books with a few preschool children and let the children interact orally with the text.
- With a group of your peers, compile a list of picture books that would be useful when developing one of the following cognitive skills: observing, comparing, hypothesizing, organizing, summarizing, applying, or criticizing. Share your findings with your class.
- Read several books in which young children must overcome such problems as jealousy, fear, or anger. Compare the ways in which the authors have allowed the children to handle their problems. Do the feelings seem normal and natural? Is more than one aspect of a feeling developed? Are options shown for handling each emotion?
- The cover of *School Library Journal* for September 2000 carries the headline "You Are What You Read." Conduct your own research on your reading habits. What literature influenced you at different times in your life? By looking at your list, how would you answer this question about yourself?

All literature discussed in Chapter 1 can be found in the appropriate genre chapters as well as the appropriate Children's Literature lists at the ends of Chapters 3 through 12.

For an extensive list of children's literature, visit the CD-ROM that accompanies this book.

Kevin Spink
Third/Fourth-Grade Teacher
Chugiak Elementary School
Chugiak, Alaska

Literature Strategy Plan: Children Using Trade Books Across the Curriculum

Chugiak Elementary is a foreign language immersion school. The children are taught in their native language—Spanish, Russian, or Japanese—for half a day, then work with a teacher in English for the second half. Kevin Spink teaches two groups of third and fourth graders English language arts and social studies, allowing him the opportunity to integrate these subjects. Kevin combines the use of *historical fiction* and *nonfiction* to help children make connections with the past. "The way that you present history has a definite impact on the way children understand it. I really try to show children how people in history are real, like ourselves, and that what happened in the past is still rippling through us and is a continuous thing."

Kevin's goal is to show how historical events interact with each other and how geography and climate influenced how people lived and why they acted as they did. He avoids relying on textbooks because he thinks that textbook writing is very artificial. "When my students read fiction, like MacLachlan's *Sarah, Plain and Tall,* they appreciate the story, but they also become interested in the prairie ecosystem, what the people wore, the foods they ate and so on. Then we read related nonfiction because the children become genuinely interested in wanting to know more. They don't read the nonfiction in an efficient way; just to do the report. Rather, they are truly curious about it. Fiction stimulates our wondering. Then we search more deliberately for answers to specific questions."

Building Students' Background Knowledge

Kevin's class studies eight ecosystems throughout the year. One of their favorites is the prairie. "We live at the base of mountains [so] the terrain of a broad, flat prairie is unfamiliar to my students. It is interesting for them to contrast the prairie with the tundra, which is very familiar to them. We begin by reading together *Sarah, Plain and Tall* by Patricia MacLachlan. The first time through we enjoy the book as good literature, responding to the feelings evoked, savoring the language, connecting to the characters. Then we return to it and more closely examine how the author integrated facts about prairie life with the story." The class then breaks into small book groups and reads other fictional works set on the prairie, such as those written by Laura Ingalls Wilder.

Purposeful Reading and Writing

Once the students have acquired a general sense of prairies and the lives of people who lived on them, they begin researching so they can create short historical fiction stories for their first-grade buddies. Kevin creates text sets of poetry, short stories, and nonfiction related to the prairie theme and the children use these as well as materials they find on their own to begin their studies. The research is used to provide authenticity to the stories they will eventually write, in the same way that authors research the background for their stories and then subtly incorporate the information into their writing. "We toy with the term *research* and we talk about how to do research. As we go through the text sets, we become curious and we return to books over and over to acquire background about prairie life. So we go back and search again to see, for example, how Patricia MacLachlan weaves what she knows about the plains into her story."

The class breaks into several smaller groups to study specific aspects of the topic. Some study prairie wildlife, plants, and climate. Others research the types of violent weather (tornadoes, thunderstorms, etc.) that occur in the Midwest but are rarely seen in Alaska. Still other groups examine facets of history that occurred one hundred and two hundred years ago, asking questions such as: "How did people live?" "How big were towns and cities?" "Did most people live in cities or on farms?"

Kevin helps his students find resources to answer their questions. "Some of the books are challenging for them. So I teach them how to use illustrations and captions and how to skim to find specific information. These became strategies for working through the denser texts." Once the children have completed their research, they present what they've learned to the class, using fact sheets, bar graphs, posters, and other means to organize the information. Kevin encourages them to compare what they've learned about prairies with what they know about where they live. "I think it's important to make the connection. I think it's natural that when we learn something new, we wrap it around our own memories and connect it to our lives as a way of making sense. So we always try to compare and contrast the information gathered from our nonfiction stories with our Alaskan environment."

Once the research is complete, the children begin writing their creative stories. Kevin supports the process by sharing examples of good historical fiction writing from award-winning writers like Karen Hesse, Pam Conrad, and Lois Lowry. He makes overheads of excerpts from different books so the group can discuss how the author developed authentic characters or a realistic setting or how historical facts are woven into the story. "I have them think about, for example, how Patricia MacLachlan described the setting so it seems real without just coming out and telling us? What language does Pam Conrad use in *Prairie Songs* so that the conversations sound authentic? How does Jerry Stanley take historical facts and weave them into a compelling narrative with the feel of poetry in *Children of the Dust Bowl*? I also tell them how just before *Number the Stars* (1989) was published, Lois Lowry stopped everything to visit Copenhagen so she was sure the descriptions of setting were true." What he discovers is that the children begin to read with eyes opened to the crafting of both fiction and nonfiction.

The children use all they've learned to create their own books, incorporating authentic detail, dialogue, and well-developed characters into an interesting story line. Most are several pages long and include illustrations. They then get into editing groups and help each other verify the historical details. Because the books will be read by first graders, they work hard to make sure the spelling and punctuation are perfect. The books are shared with the buddies, then left in the younger children's class library for rereading.

Assessment

Kevin believes that numerical ratings and grades don't adequately measure student progress in reading and writing. "I think the obsession with numbers to evaluate kids is a very distorting thing. It becomes a mask for things that are hard to pin down—and it actually leads to knowing less about children's progress." What he prefers to do is compare first and last drafts based on several factors that have been agreed on by the group. So issues like the following are considered: "When the readers are done with this story, will they have a good sense of how it was to live in prairie times?" "Is there enough detail to make the story come

alive?" "Is your story coherent, following a logical sequence?" "Have you used appropriate spelling, grammar, and punctuation?" Usually the class develops a rubric that describes specific criteria in each category that would make a story "outstanding," "satisfactory," or "unsatisfactory."

 For ideas on adapting Kevin Spink's lesson to meet the needs of older or younger readers, please visit Chapter 1 on our Companion Website at www.prenhall.com/norton

Sam H.

I was going to go outside one day but my mom stopped me so I went to wake up my seven brothers and seven sisters My brothers and I started by feeding the chickens. then we moved on to the pigs but before we did I checked what the girls were doing. Mom said they went to get water and my dad took the cows to the pasture next we fed the pigs.

A page from Sam's historical fiction book.

2 THE HISTORY OF CHILDREN'S LITERATURE

From The Pied Piper of Hamelin, *by Robert Browning. Illustrated by Kate Greenaway. Copyright © 1986 by F. Warne, London. Used by permission.*

any people are surprised to discover that childhood has not always been considered an important time of life. When students of children's literature look at the beautiful books published to meet children's needs, interests, and reading levels, many are amazed to learn that not long ago books were not written specifically for children. Changes in printing technology provided affordable books, but more important were changes in social attitudes toward children. When society looked upon children as little adults who must rapidly step into the roles of their parents, children had little time or need to read books. When childhood began to be viewed as a special part of the human life cycle, literature written specifically for children became very important.

Within the context of human history as a whole, the history of children's literature is very short. Neither early tales told through the oral tradition nor early books were created specifically for children. When eventually written, children's books usually mirrored the dominant cultural values of their place and time. Thus, a study of children's literature in Western Europe and North America from the fifteenth century through contemporary times reflects both changes in society as a whole and changes in social expectations of children and the family.

Literature researchers view children's literature as a vehicle for studying social values and changing attitudes. Karen J. Winkler (1981) maintains that the 1970s and 1980s have been characterized by an ever-increasing interest in the scholarly study of children's literature as an index to the social attitudes of a particular time. Robert Gordon Kelly's (1970) "Mother Was a Lady: Self and Society in Selected American Children's Periodicals, 1865–1890," Mary Lystad's (1980) *From Dr. Mather to Dr. Seuss: Two Hundred Years of American Books for Children,* Cedric Cullingford's (1998) *Children's Literature and Its Effects,* and Gwen Athene Tarbox's (2000) *The Club-women's Daughters: Collective Impulses in Progressive-Era Girl's Fiction, 1890–1940* are examples of such research.

Numerous edited texts are available in which writings of various researchers and critics are collected. For example, *Aspects and Issues in the History of Children's Literature,* edited by Maria Nikolajeva (1995), includes articles on theories and methods of conducting studies on the history of children's literature and aspects of national histories. *Literature and the Child: Romantic Continuations, Post-modern Contestations,* edited by James Holt McGavran (1999), provides articles on topics such as "Romanticism Continuing and Contested" and "Romantic Ironies, Post-modern Texts." *Children's Book Publishing in Britain Since 1945,* edited by Kimberley Reynolds and Nicholas Tucker (1998), includes critical articles on topics such as picture books and movable books.

CHART 2.1   Historic milestones in children's literature

—	The Oral Tradition
	    "Beowulf"
	    "Jack the Giant Killer"
			1800s	The Romantic Movement in Europe
				    The Brothers Grimm
				    Hans Christian Andersen

1400s	Early Books
	    Hornbooks
	    Caxton's Printing Press—1476
				The Impact of Illustrators on
				        Children's Books
				    Walter Crane
				    Randolph Caldecott
				    Kate Greenaway

1500s	The Introduction of Chapbooks
	    "Jack the Giant Killer"
			1860s	The Victorian Influence
				    Charlotte Yonge's *The Daisy Chain*
				        and *The Clever Woman of the*
				        Family

1600s	The Puritan Influence
	    Spiritual Milk for Boston Babes in
	        Either England, Drawn from the
	        Breasts of Both Testaments for
	        Their Souls' Nourishment
	    Pilgrim's Progress
			1840–1900	Childhood Seen as an Adventure, Not
				        a Training Ground for Adulthood
				Fantasy
				    Lewis Carroll's *Alice's Adventures*
				        in Wonderland
				    Edward Lear's *A Book*
				        of Nonsense

1693	A View of Childhood Changes
	    John Locke's *Some Thoughts*
	        Concerning Education
				Adventure
				    Robert Louis Stevenson's *Treasure*
				        Island

1697	First Fairy Tales Written for Children
	    Charles Perrault's *Tales of Mother*
	        Goose
				Howard Pyle's *The Merry*
				        Adventures of Robin Hood
				    Jules Verne's *Twenty Thousand*
				        Leagues Under the Sea

1719	Great Adventure Stories
	    Daniel Defoe's *Robinson Crusoe*
	    Jonathan Swift's *Gulliver's Travels*
				Real People
				    Margaret Sidney's *The Five Little*
				        Peppers and How They Grew

1744	Children's Literature: A True Beginning
	    John Newbery's *A Little Pretty Pocket*
	        Book and *History of Little Goody*
	        Two-Shoes (1745)
				Louisa May Alcott's *Little Women*
				    Johanna Spyri's *Heidi*

1762	Guidance of Children in Their Search for
	        Knowledge
	    Jean-Jacques Rousseau's *Emile*			

1789	Poetry About Children William Blake's *Songs of Innocence*			

The increasing number of doctoral dissertations that critically evaluate certain aspects of children's literature also suggest the current importance of children's literature as a research subject. For example, from the 1930s until 1970, approximately two hundred dissertations covered topics related to children's literature. In contrast, the 1970s alone produced nearly eight hundred such dissertations. Several of these studies suggest the interrelatedness of social, cultural, and economic factors and the story themes and values presented in children's literature of a certain period.

Milestones in the History of Children's Literature

This chapter first considers some milestones in the development of children's literature. Then, it looks at changing views of children and the family as reflected in early books for children and in more contemporary stories. Chart 2.1 provides a brief overview of the historical milestones.

The Oral Tradition

Long before recorded history, family units and tribes shared their group traditions and values through stories told around the campfire. On every continent around the globe, ancient peoples developed folktales and mythologies that speculated about human beginnings, attempted to explain the origins of the universe and other natural phenomena, emphasized ethical truths, and transmitted history from one generation to the next. When hunters returned from their adventures, they probably told about the perils of the hunt and hostile encounters with other tribes. Heroic deeds were certainly told and retold until they became a part of a group's heritage. This tradition has existed since the first oral communication among human beings and goes back to the very roots of every civilization on earth. These tales were not told specifically to children, but children were surely present—listening, watching, learning, and remembering.

The various native peoples of North America developed mythologies expressing their reverence for the rolling prairies, lush forests, ice floes, deserts, and blue lakes of their continent. In Latin and South America, storytellers of the Yucatán Peninsula and the Andes chronicled the rise of Mayan, Aztec, and Incan empires, wars of expansion, and, eventually, the Spanish conquest of their homelands. Across Africa, highly respected storytellers developed a style that encouraged audiences to interact with storytellers in relating tales of dramatic heroes, personified animals, and witty tricksters. In the extremely ancient cultures of Asia, from Mesopotamia to Japan, early myths and folktales were eventually incorporated into the complex mythologies and philosophical tenets of Taoism, Confucianism, Hinduism, and Buddhism. In Europe, the earliest oral traditions of the Celts, Franks, Saxons, Goths, Danes, and many other groups eventually influenced one another as a result of migration, trade, and warfare; and the mythologies of ancient Greece and Rome became widely influential as the Roman Empire expanded over much of the continent.

The European oral tradition, according to Robert Leeson (1977), reached its climax in the feudal era of the Middle Ages. What are often called *castle tales* and *cottage tales* provided people with literature long before those tales were widely accessible in writing or print. The ruling classes favored poetic epics about the reputed deeds of the lord of the manor or his ancestors. In the great halls of castles, minstrels or bards accompanied themselves on lyres or harps while singing tales about noble warriors, such as Beowulf and King Arthur, or ballads of chivalrous love in regal surroundings, such as those found in the French version of *Cinderella*.

Around cottage fires or at country fairs, humbler people had different heroes. Storytellers shared folktales about people much like the peasants themselves, people who daily confronted servitude, inscrutable natural phenomena, and unknown spiritual forces. In these tales, even the youngest or poorest person had the potential to use resourcefulness or kindness to go from rags to riches and to live "happily ever after." Often, such achievement required outwitting or slaying wolves, dragons, malevolent supernatural beings, or great lords.

By whatever name they were known—bards, minstrels, or devisers of tales—the storytellers of medieval Europe were entertainers: If they did not entertain, they lost their audiences or even their meals and lodging. Consequently, they learned to tell stories that had rapid plot development and easily identifiable characters. These storytellers also possessed considerable power. Sir Philip Sidney (1595), a sixteenth-century English poet, described storytellers as able to keep children away from their play and old people away from their chimney corners. Whether woven from imagination or retold from legends and stories of old, the tales of storytellers could influence the people who heard them. Thus, if a minstrel's story offended or discredited a lord, the minstrel could be punished. By the end of the fourteenth century, feudal authority sought to control the tales being told and often jailed storytellers who angered either a ruler or the church.

German scholar August Nitschke (1988) describes the role of fairy tales in earlier times. He states:

In the fifteenth and sixteenth centuries fairy tales were told to children, but grown men took fairy tales so seriously that they would interpret them symbolically. Geiler of Kaiserberg, for instance, and Martin Luther were able to interpret the Cinderella story in such a way. They foretold a good future for those persons working in the kitchen as humbly and shyly as Cinderella did. Others such as Cardinal Giovanni Dominici opposed fairy tales because he thought they could foster vanity such as toys might—like the wooden horses or the pretty trumpets or the artificial birds or the golden drums—or because they might frighten children. (p. 164)

Today, many early European folktales, myths, and legends are considered ideal for sharing with children, but this was not the attitude of feudal Europe. Storytellers addressed audiences of all ages. A child was considered a small adult who should enter into adult life as quickly as possible, and stories primarily for young people were considered unnecessary. Consequently, the stories about giants, heroes, and simpletons that relieved the strain of adult life also entertained children. These favorite tales, which had been told and retold for hundreds of years, were eventually chosen for some of the first printed books in Europe.

Early Printed Books

Prior to the mid-1400s, the literary heritage of Europe consisted of the oral tradition and parchment manuscripts laboriously handwritten by monks and scribes. Manuscript books were rare and costly, prized possessions of the nobles and priests, who were among the few Europeans able to read and write. To the extent that these books were meant for the young, they were usually designed to provide instruction in rhetoric, grammar, and music for the children privileged enough to attend monastery schools. Children were rarely trusted with the books themselves and usually wrote on slates as monks dictated their lessons.

A significant event occurred in the 1450s, when the German Johannes Gutenberg discovered a practical method for using movable metal type, which made possible the mass production of books. After learning the printing process in Germany, William Caxton established England's first printing press in 1476. The use of printing presses led to the creation of hornbooks, which were printed sheets of text mounted on wood and covered with translucent animal horn. Hornbooks were used to teach reading and numbers. The books were in the shape of a paddle. Gillian Avery (1995) states that "This convenient and relatively indestructible form of presenting the alphabet (followed by a syllabary, invocation to the Trinity, and the Lord's Prayer) was in common use from the sixteenth century until well on in the eighteenth" (p. 3).

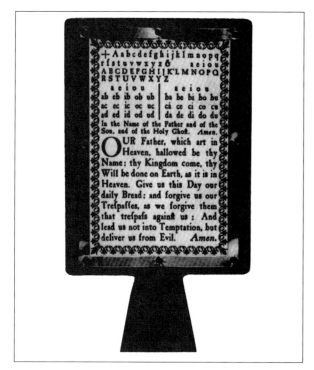

The hornbook, which was used for instruction, usually contained the alphabet, numerals, and the Lord's Prayer. (Photo courtesy of The Horn Book, Inc.)

This lesson book, or battledore, was made from folded paper or cardboard. (Courtesy of The Horn Book, Inc.)

Hornbooks remained popular into the 1700s, when the battledore, a lesson book made of folded paper or cardboard, became more prevalent. Like hornbooks, battledores usually contained an alphabet, numerals, and proverbs or prayers.

When William Caxton opened his printing business in 1476, most of the books used with children were not written for their interest. Instead, books for children adhered to the sentiment that young readers should read only what would improve their manners or instruct their minds. *Caxton's Book of Curtesye*, first printed in 1477 (Furnivall, 1868), contained directions for drawing readers away from vice and turning them toward virtue. Verses guided readers toward personal cleanliness (comb your hair, clean your ears, clean your nose but don't pick it), polite social interactions (look people straight in the face when speaking, don't quarrel with dogs), suitable reverence in church (kneel before the cross, don't chatter), and correct table manners (don't blow on your food or undo your girdle at the table).

The majority of books that Caxton published were not meant to be read by children, but three of his publications are now considered classics in children's literature. In 1481, Caxton published the beast fable *Reynart the Foxe* (*The History of Reynard the Fox*), a satire of oppression and tyranny. This tale of a clever fox who could outwit all his adversaries became popular with both adults and children.

Caxton's most important publication may be *The Book of the Subtyle Historyes and Fables of Esope* (*The Fables of Aesop*), which Caxton translated from a manuscript by the French monk Machault in 1484. These fables about the weaknesses of people and animals were popular with readers of various ages and are still enjoyed by children. F. J. Harvey Darton (1966) maintains that Caxton's version of Aesop, "with infinitely little modernization, is the best text for children today" (p. 10). Caxton's publication in 1485 of Sir Thomas Malory's *Le Morte d'Arthur* (*The Death of Arthur*) preserved the legendary story of King Arthur and his knights, which has been published since in many versions suitable for young readers.

Caxton's translations, standardization of English, and literary style had a major impact upon English literature, according to Jane Bingham and Grayce Scholt (1980). At least eight of Caxton's books are mentioned in the "Famous Prefaces" volume of *The Harvard Classics* (Lenaghan, 1967). Cornelia Meigs et al. (1969) also stress Caxton's importance in creating the first printed books in the English language. In outward form, these books were of a standard not easily equaled. The ample pages, the broad margins, and the black-letter type that suggested manuscript contributed to their beauty, dignity, and worthiness to be England's first widespread realization of her own literature.

Caxton's books were beautiful, but they were too expensive for the common people. Soon, however, peddlers (or chapmen) were selling crudely printed chapbooks for pennies at markets and fairs, along with ribbons, patent medicines, and other wares. Customers could also go directly to a printer and select from large uncut sheets of as many as sixteen pages of text, which then were bound into a hardcover book.

From the sixteenth to the nineteenth centuries, peddlers sold inexpensive chapbooks in Europe and North America. (From Chap-Books of the Eighteenth Century *by John Ashton. Published by Chatto and Windus, 1882. From the John G. White Collection, Cleveland Public Library.)*

Some of the first chapbooks were based on ballads, such as "The Two Children in the Wood," and traditional tales, such as "Jack the Giant Killer." According to Lou J. McCulloch (1979), the content of chapbooks fell into the following categories: religious instruction, interpretations of the supernatural, romantic legends, ballad tales, and historic narratives. John Ashton's (1882) *Chap-Books of the Eighteenth Century* includes religious titles, such as "The History of Joseph and His Brethren" and "The Unhappy Birth, Wicked Life, and Miserable Death of the Vile Traytor and Apostle Judas Iscariot"; traditional tales, such as "Tom Thumb" and "A True Tale of Robin Hood"; and supernatural tales, such as "The Portsmouth Ghost."

Chapbooks were extremely popular in both England and the United States during the 1700s, but their popularity rapidly declined during the early 1800s. Zohar Shavit (1995) states that "During the eighteenth century, chapbooks became the most important reading material for children. However, neither the religious nor the educational establishment were delighted about the reading of chapbooks by children. On the contrary, the more important the child's education (and consequently his reading matter) became, the less the educational establishment was ready to accept children's reading of chapbooks. When the religious establishment began to scrutinize the education of children as well as

their reading material, chapbooks had to retreat underground" (p. 31).

The Puritan Influence

According to Bingham and Scholt (1980), political upheaval, religious dissent, and censorship affected English literature in the 1600s. As printing increased and literacy spread, the British monarchy realized the power of the press. In 1637, it decreed that only London, Oxford, Cambridge, and York could have printing establishments.

According to Anne Scott MacLeod (1995), "The story of children's reading in America begins with the Puritans. . . . From the beginning, Puritans thought about the children and provided for their schooling, at home and in the tiny communities they called towns. By the 1640s, Massachusetts law required heads of families to teach their children and apprentices to read" (p. 102).

The beliefs of the Puritans, dissenters from the established Church of England who were growing in strength and numbers in England and North America, also influenced literature of the period. Puritans considered the traditional tales about giants, fairies, and witches found in chapbooks to be impious and corrupting. They urged that children not be allowed to read such materials and instead be provided with literature to instruct them and reinforce their moral development. Puritans expected their offspring to be children of God first and foremost. Bernard J. Lonsdale and Helen K. Macintosh (1973) describe:

Family worship, admonitions from elders, home instruction, strict attendance at school, and close attention to lessons all were aimed at perpetuating those ideals and values for which the parents themselves had sacrificed so much. To the elders, the important part of education was learning to read, write, and figure. Only literature that would instruct and warn was tolerated. (p. 161)

Awesome titles for books that stressed the importance of instructing children in moral concerns were common in Puritan times. In 1649, the grandfather of Cotton Mather (a Puritan who was influential during the Salem witch-hunts in New England) wrote a book called *Spiritual Milk for Boston Babes in Either England, Drawn from the Breasts of Both Testaments for Their Souls' Nourishment.* In 1671, the leading Puritan writer, James Janeway, published a series of stories about children who had led saintly lives until their deaths at an early age. His *A Token for Children, Being an Exact Account of the Conversion, Holy and Exemplary Lives, and Joyful Deaths of Several Young Children* was meant not for enjoyment, but to instruct Puritan children in moral development.

The most influential piece of literature written during this period was John Bunyan's *The Pilgrim's Progress from this world, to that which is to come. Delivered under the similitude of a Dream. Wherein is discovered, the manner of his*

A	In *Adam's* Fall We Sinned all.
B	Thy Life to Mend This *Book* Attend.
C	The *Cat* doth play And after flay.
D	A *Dog* will bite A Thief at night.
E	An *Eagles* flight Is out of fight.
F	The Idle *Fool* Is whipt at School.

The New England Primer *taught both Puritan ideals and the alphabet. (From* The New England Primer, Enlarged, *Boston, 1727 edition. From the Rare Books and Manuscript Division, The New York Public Library, Astor, Lenox, and Tilden Foundations.)*

setting out, his dangerous journey and safe arrival at the Desired Country, or *Pilgrim's Progress,* published in England in 1678. While moral improvement was the primary purpose of this book, *Pilgrim's Progress* also contained bold action that appealed to both children and older readers, some of whom adopted it for its entertainment, as well as religious, value. Bunyan's hero, Christian, experiences many perilous adventures as he journeys alone through the Slough of Despond and the Valley of Humiliation in his search for salvation. Characters such as Mr. Valiant-for-Truth and Ignorance appear in such settings as the Valley of the Shadow of Death, the Delectable Mountains, and the Celestial City. Christian acquires a companion, Faithful, who is executed in the town of Vanity Fair. Then another companion, Hopeful, helps him fight the giant Despair and finally reach his goal.

Pilgrim's Progress and the *Spiritual Milk for Boston Babes in Either England* were required reading for colonial children in North America. Another important book in colonial homes was *The New England Primer,* a combination alphabet and catechism designed to teach Puritan ideals. The primer was written in such a way that spiritual instruction was the main theme. The primer appeared around 1690 and was printed in hundreds of editions until 1830. According to Cornelia Meigs et al. (1969), the

influence of the primer lasted so long because in that era "the chance of life for young children was cruelly small" (p. 114), and spiritual preparation for an early death was thus imperative.

John Locke's Influence on Views of Childhood

In a social environment that viewed children as small adults and expected them to behave accordingly, few considered that children might have interests and educational needs of their own. The Puritans and other Calvinist Christians believed that everyone was born predestined to achieve either salvation or damnation. Thus, all must spend their lives attempting to prove predestined worthiness to be saved.

The English philosopher John Locke, however, envisioned the child's mind at birth as a *tabula rasa,* a blank page on which ideas were to be imprinted. In *Some Thoughts Concerning Education* (1910), published in 1693, Locke stressed the interrelatedness of healthy physical development and healthy mental development, and he advocated milder ways of teaching and bringing up children than had been recommended previously. According to John Rowe Townsend (1975), Locke believed that children who could read should be provided with easy, pleasant books suited to their capacities—books that encouraged them to read and rewarded them for their reading efforts but that did not fill their heads with useless "trumpery" or encourage vice.

Locke found a grave shortage of books that could provide children with pleasure or reward, but he did recommend *Aesop's Fables* and *Reynard the Fox* for the delight that they offered children and the useful reflections that they offered the adults in children's lives. Locke's attitude was quite enlightened for his time. It provided a glimmer of hope that children might be permitted to go through a period of childhood rather than immediately assume the same roles as their parents. While seventeenth-century European and North American culture contained few books appropriate for children, a realization dawned that children might benefit from books written to encourage their reading.

Charles Perrault's Tales of Mother Goose

An exciting development in children's literature occurred in seventeenth-century France. Charles Perrault, a gifted member of the Academie Française, published a book called *Contes de ma Mère l'Oye (Tales of Mother Goose).* The stories in this collection were not those normally referred to as Mother Goose rhymes today. Instead, they were well-known fairy tales, such as "Cinderella," "Sleeping Beauty," "Puss in Boots," "Little Red Riding Hood," and "Blue Beard." Perrault did not create these tales; he retold stories from the French oral tradition that had entranced children and provided entertainment in the elegant salons of the Parisian aristocracy for generations.

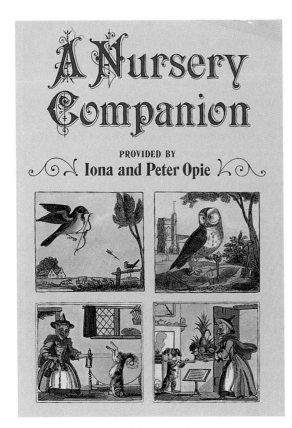

A Nursery Companion *is a collection of Mother Goose rhymes that were originally published in the early 1800s. (From* A Nursery Companion *by Iona and Peter Opie, Oxford University Press, 1980.)*

Perrault was one of the first writers to recognize that fairy tales have a special place in the world of children. Readers can thank Perrault or, as many scholars (Muir, 1954) now believe, his son Pierre Perrault d'Armancour, for collecting these tales, which have been translated and retold by many different contemporary writers and illustrators of children's books. At last, entertainment was written for children rather than adopted by them because nothing else was available.

The Adventure Stories of Defoe and Swift

Two adventure books that appeared in the early eighteenth century were, like virtually all literature of the time, written for adults, but these two were quickly embraced by children. A political climate that punished dissenters by placing them into prison molded the author of the first great adventure story, *Robinson Crusoe,* which was published in 1719. Daniel Defoe was condemned to Newgate Prison after he wrote a fiery pamphlet responding to the political and religious controversies of his time. However, Defoe wrote constantly, even while in jail.

Defoe was motivated to write *Robinson Crusoe* when he read the personal accounts of a Scottish sailor, Alexander Selkirk, who had been marooned on one of the Juan Fernandez Islands, located off the coast of Chile. This Scottish sailor had deserted ship after a disagreement

with the captain and had lived alone on the island for four years before he was discovered by another ship and brought back to England. Defoe was so captivated by Selkirk's experience that he wrote an adventure story to answer his questions about how a person might acquire food, clothing, and shelter if shipwrecked on an island.

The resulting tale appeared first in serial publication and then in a book. Children and adults enjoyed the exciting and suspenseful story. The book was so influential that thirty-one years after Defoe's death, French philosopher Jean-Jacques Rousseau, the founder of modern education, said that *Robinson Crusoe* would be the first book read by his son, Emile.

According to Brian W. Alderson (1959) *Robinson Crusoe* reflects an era in Western history when people had begun to believe in the natural goodness of human beings uninfluenced by corruption in the world around them. *Robinson Crusoe* became and remained so popular that it stimulated a whole group of books written about similar subjects, which came to be known as Robinsonades. The most popular Robinsonade was Johann Wyss's *The Swiss Family Robinson.* Susan Naramore Maher (1988) states:

Robinsonades commanded an eager juvenile readership ready to devour the latest fiction about castaways, no matter how didactic or improbable the tale. In the nineteenth century, *Robinson Crusoe* itself became a prized nursery book, favored by children for its detail and adventure, by parents for its religious sentiment and work ethic. (p. 169)

The second major adventure story written during the early eighteenth century also dealt with the subject of shipwreck. Jonathan Swift's *Gulliver's Travels,* published in 1726, described Gulliver's realistic adventures with strange beings encountered in mysterious lands: tiny Lilliputians, giant Brobdingnagians, talking horses, and flying islands. Swift wrote *Gulliver's Travels* as a satire for adults. Children, however, thought of the story as an enjoyable adventure and adopted Gulliver as a hero.

These adventure stories must have seemed truly remarkable to children otherwise surrounded by literature written only to instruct or to moralize. The impact of these eighteenth-century writers is still felt today, as twentieth-century children enjoy versions of the first adventure stories.

Newbery's Books for Children

The 1740s are commonly regarded as the time when the idea of children's books began in Europe and North America. New ways of thought emerged as the middle

 Technology Resources

Use the database to generate a list of Newbery award winners. Just search under Awards, type "New" in the field, then click on Retain to complete the list.

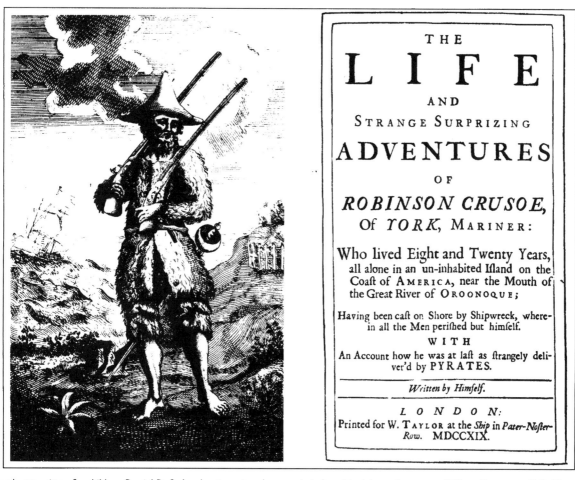

Although not written for children, Daniel Defoe's adventure story became popular with eighteenth-century children. (Courtesy of Lilly Library, Indiana University, Bloomington, Indiana.)

class became larger and strengthened its social position. Because more people had the time, money, and education necessary for reading, books became more important. Middle-class life also began to center on the home and family rather than on the marketplace or the great houses of nobility. With the growing emphasis on family life, a realization began that children should be children rather than small adults.

Into this social climate came John Newbery, an admirer of John Locke and an advocate of a milder way of educating children. Newbery was also a writer and publisher, who began publishing a line of books for children in 1744 with *A Little Pretty Pocket Book*. "Although his work reflected the didactic tone of the time," say Jane Bingham and Grayce Scholt (1980), "his books were not intended to be textbooks. Their gilt-paper covers, attractive pages, engaging stories and verses—and sometimes toys which were offered with the books—provided 'diversion' for children of the English-speaking world" (p. 86). *A Little Pretty Pocket Book* included a letter from Jack the Giant Killer written to both instruct and entertain children. Modern readers would not consider this early book for

children very entertaining compared with books written to amuse today's children, but it must have been revolutionary for its time. In 1765, Newbery published a more famous book, *History of Little Goody Two-Shoes,* a fictitious story by Oliver Goldsmith. Sylvia Patterson Iskander (1988) identifies several features that characterized this book: Like its predecessors, it had a lengthy title page, a dedication, an introduction, descriptive chapter headings, and stories and poems interrelated within the text.

Newbery's company, set up in London, became a success. His accomplishments are often attributed to his bustling energy, his interest in literature and writers, his love for children, and his taking note of children's tastes as measured by the popularity of their favorite chapbooks. Newbery's publications included *Nurse Truelove's New Year's Gift, Mother Goose, Tom Thumb's Folio,* and old favorites, such as *Aesop's Fables, Robinson Crusoe,* and *Gulliver's Travels.* Because of Newbery's success, publishers realized that there was indeed a market for books written specifically for children. It is fitting that the coveted award given annually to the outstanding author of a children's literature selection bears Newbery's name.

Rousseau's Philosophy of Natural Development

While John Locke had advocated a milder and more rational approach to educating children, Jean-Jacques Rousseau recommended a totally new approach. Locke believed that children should be led in their search for knowledge, but Rousseau believed that they should merely be accompanied. Rousseau maintained that children could and should develop naturally, with gentle guidance from wise adults who could supply necessary information. Margaret C. Gillespie (1970) maintains:

At a time when the major emphasis was on sharpening the muscles of the mind and filling it to the brim with all the knowledge in the world it could absorb, Jean Jacques Rousseau's exhortations to "retournez à la nature" had a strong impact on the complacency of educators. (p. 21)

In his *Emile,* published in 1762, Rousseau described stages of children's growth, stressing the importance of experiences in harmony with children's natural development physically and mentally. Rousseau's stages progressed from early sensory motor development, through a concrete learning period, into a period where intellectual conceptualization was possible. As mentioned, Rousseau believed that Daniel Defoe's *Robinson Crusoe* was the most important piece of literature because it emphasized the necessity of using one's own ideas to cope with one's environment. Rousseau's impact on parents' attitudes toward children was "forceful and unmistakable," says Gillespie. "Now children were looked upon as 'little angels' who could do no wrong. They were permitted to be children rather than 'little adults.' They became the center of the educational scene rather than satellites around the curriculum" (p. 23).

William Blake's Poetry About Children

The English poet William Blake, who is credited with writing verses as if a child had written them, published his *Songs of Innocence* in 1789 and his *Songs of Experience* in 1794. F. J. Harvey Darton (1932, 1966) characterizes Blake in the spiritual sense as "a child happy on a cloud, singing and desiring such songs as few but he could write" (p. 179). Blake's often quoted poem that introduces *Songs of Innocence* provides readers an opportunity to visualize this happy child (the punctuation and spelling are from the engraved first edition cited in Darton, 1932):

Introduction

Piping down the valleys wild
Piping songs of pleasant glee
On a cloud I saw a child.
And he laughing said to me.

Pipe a song about a Lamb:
So I piped with merry chear,
Piper pipe that song again—
So I piped, he wept to hear.

Drop thy pipe thy happy pipe
Sing thy songs of happy chear.
So I sung the same again
While he wept with joy to hear.

Piper sit thee down and write
In a book that all may read—
So he vanish'd from my sight.
And I pluck'd a hollow reed

And I made a rural pen,
And I stain'd the water clear,
And I wrote my happy songs,
Every child may joy to hear.

The Fairy Tales of Andersen and the Brothers Grimm

Sir Walter Scott's novels about the Middle Ages, enthusiasm for Gothic architecture, lyrical ballads, and Rousseau's philosophy of a return to nature typified the Romantic Movement in late-eighteenth-century Europe. This atmosphere encouraged an interest in folk literature.

In the early 1800s, two German scholars, Jacob and Wilhelm Grimm, became interested in collecting folktales that reflected the ancient German language and tradition. In researching their subject, the brothers listened to tales told by Dortchen and Gretchen Wild; the Wilds' maid, Marie; a farmer's wife called Frau Viehmännin; and other storytellers from throughout Germany. Although scholars disagree about how exactly the Brothers Grimm transcribed the tales they heard, Bettina Hürlimann (1980) maintains that the brothers

did not just write down what they heard. Even for the first edition they did a lot of revising, comparing with other sources, and trying to find a simple language which was at the same time full of character. With time and with later editions it became clear that Jacob, the more scholarly, tried to keep the tales in the most simple, original form, more or less as they had heard them, and that Wilhelm, more of a poet, was for retelling them in a new form with regard to the children. (p. 71)

The Grimms' first edition of tales, published in 1812, contained eighty-five stories, including "Cinderella," "Hansel and Gretel," "Little Red Riding Hood," and "The Frog Prince." According to Hürlimann, the second edition, published in 1815, was designed more specifically for children, with illustrations and a minimum of scholarly comment on the tales it contained.

In 1823, the tales collected by the Brothers Grimm were translated into English and published under the title *German Popular Stories.* Since that time, artists in many countries have illustrated such tales as "Snow White and the Seven Dwarfs," "Rumpelstiltskin," and "The Elves and the Shoemaker," which have become part of our literary heritage.

Most of the published folktales and fairy tales discussed thus far were written down by either Charles Perrault or the Brothers Grimm. The stories had been told in

German Popular Stories, *such as this 1826 edition, introduced the Grimms' folktales to English-speaking children. (Courtesy of Lilly Library, Indiana University, Bloomington, Indiana.)*

castles and cottages for many generations. Hans Christian Andersen, however, is generally credited with being the first to create and publish an original fairy tale. Andersen used his own experiences to stimulate his writing. "The Ugly Duckling," "The Little Mermaid," and "The Red Shoes" are among Andersen's famous stories.

Andersen was born to a poor but happy family in Odense, Denmark. His cobbler father shared stories with him and even built a puppet theater for Andersen. Even when his father died and it seemed that Andersen would have to learn a trade, Andersen retained his dream of becoming an actor. During these poverty-stricken years, he tried to forget his troubles by putting on puppet shows and telling stories to children.

Because Andersen wanted to write stories and plays, he returned to school to improve his writing skills. While there, he suffered from cruel jokes about his looks; he was thin and had large feet and a large nose. (Doesn't this sound like a theme for one of his fairy tales?)

In 1828, when Andersen was twenty-three, he began to write stories and poems. Five years later, he was recognized as a promising writer by the Danish government, whose financial support allowed him to travel and write about his experiences. When his *Life in Italy*, a rather scholarly work, was published, Andersen at last started to

make money. His next book was far different; it was the first of his famous fairy tale books, and it was written in the same colloquial language used to tell stories.

When *Fairy Tales Told for Children* was published, a friend told Andersen that his *Life in Italy* would make him famous but his fairy tales would make people remember him forever. Although Andersen did not believe his fairy tales were as good as his other books, he enjoyed writing them and produced a new fairy tale book each Christmas as a gift to children of all ages. When Andersen was sixty-two, he was invited back to Odense, the town in which he had known happiness, poverty, and sadness. This time, however, he was the honored guest at a celebration that lasted for an entire week.

Andersen's fairy stories are still popular; newly illustrated versions are published every year. These colorful picture-book versions, as well as tales in anthologies, are still enjoyed by children of many ages.

Early Illustrators of Children's Books

The identity of the first picture book for children is debated. Eric Quayle (1971) identifies *Kunst und Lehrbüchlein (Book of Art and Instruction for Young People)*, published in 1580 by the German publisher Sigmund Feyerabend, as the "first book aimed at the unexplored juvenile market"

A typical woodcut from Orbis Pictus, *the first picture book for children. (A reprint of the* Orbis Pictus *has been published by Singing Tree Press, Gale Research Company, Detroit, Michigan.)*

(p. 11). The detailed, full-page woodcuts showing European life were the work of Jost Amman. Of particular interest are the pictures of a young scholar reading a hornbook and of a child holding a doll.

Johann Amos Comenius, a Moravian teacher and former bishop of the Bohemian Brethren, is usually credited with writing the first nonalphabet picture book that strove to educate children. Bettina Hürlimann (1980) describes Comenius as a great humanist, who wanted children to observe God's creations—plants, stars, clouds, rain, sun, and geography—rather than to memorize abstract knowledge.

To achieve this goal, Comenius took children out of the conventional classrooms and into the natural world. He then wrote down their experiences in simple sentences, using both Latin and the children's own language. He published these simple sentences and accompanying woodcuts in 1658 as *Orbis Pictus* (*Painted World*). Educational historian Ayers Bagley (1985) identifies allegorical meanings in the illustrations and text. According to Bagley, Comenius saw true understanding, right action, and correct speech as important contributors to the attainment of wisdom.

Scholars disagree about whether Comenius drew the illustrations for *Orbis Pictus* himself or whether he instructed artists in their execution. Jane Bingham and Grayce Scholt (1980) credit the woodcuts in the 1658 edition to Paul Kreutzberger and the wood engravings in the 1810 American edition to Alexander Anderson. Whoever the artist was, Hürlimann emphasizes that "the pictures are in wonderful harmony with the text, and the book was to become for more than a century the most popular book with children of all classes" (p. 67).

Most book illustrations before the 1800s, especially those in the inexpensive chapbooks, were crude woodcuts. If color was used, it was usually hand applied by amateurs who filled in the colors according to a guide. Thomas Bewick is credited with being one of the earliest artists to illustrate books for children. His skillfully executed woodcuts graced *The New Lottery Book of Birds and Beasts,* published in 1771, and *A Pretty Book of Pictures for Little Masters and Misses; or Tommy Trip's History of Beasts and Birds,* published in 1779.

Three nineteenth-century English artists had enormous impact on illustrations for children's books. According to Ruth Hill Viguers in the introduction to Edward Ernest's (1967) *The Kate Greenaway Treasury,* the work of these artists "represents the best to be found in picture books for children in any era: the strength of design and richness of color and detail of Walter Crane's pictures; the eloquence, humor, vitality, and movement of Randolph Caldecott's art; and the tenderness, dignity, and grace of the very personal interpretation of Kate Greenaway's enchanted land of childhood" (p. 13).

Walter Crane's illustrated texts, characterized by subdued colors, strong design, and rich detail, are credited with marking the beginning of the modern era in color illustrations. (From The Baby's Own Aesop. *Reproduced by permission of the Department of Special Collections, Research Library, University of California, Los Angeles.)*

Randolph Caldecott's illustrations suggest action and vitality. (From The Hey Diddle Diddle Picture Book *by Randolph Caldecott. Reproduced by permission of Frederick Warne & Co., Inc., Publishers.)*

Walter Crane's *The House That Jack Built,* published in 1865, was the first of his series of toy books, the name used for picture books published for young children. These books, engraved by Edmund Evans, are credited with marking the beginning of the modern era in color illustrations. From 1865 through 1898, Crane illustrated over forty books, including folktales, such as *The Three Bears* and *Cinderella,* and alphabet books, such as *The Farmyard Alphabet* and *The Absurd ABC.*

Many of Crane's illustrations reflect his appreciation of Japanese color prints. Crane (1984) specified this appreciation in lectures that he gave before the Society of Arts in 1889, when he stated that Japanese art was "a living art, an art of the people, in which traditions and craftsmanship were unbroken, and the results full of attractive variety, quickness, and naturalistic force" (p. 133).

Randolph Caldecott's talent was discovered by Edmund Evans, the printer. Caldecott's illustrations for *The Diverting History of John Gilpin,* printed by Evans in 1878, demonstrated his ability to depict robust characters, action, and humor. (The Caldecott Medal for children's book illustration, named for the artist, is embossed with the picture of Gilpin galloping through an English village.) Caldecott's lively and humorous figures jump fences, dance to the fiddler, and flirt with milkmaids in such picture books as *The Fox Jumps over the Parson's Gate, Come Lasses and Lads,* and *The Milkmaid.*

Caldecott's picture books are now reissued by Frederick Warne. Brian Alderson's (1986) *Sing a Song of Six-*

pence provides a pictorial history of English picture books and Randolph Caldecott's art.

Printer and engraver Edmund Evans also encouraged and supported the work of Kate Greenaway. Delighted by Greenaway's drawings and verses, Evans printed her first book, *Under the Window,* in 1878. It was so successful that 70,000 English editions and over 30,000 French and German editions were sold.

Greenaway continued illustrating books that reflected happy days of childhood and the blossoming apple trees and primroses that dotted the English countryside of her youth. In a letter to her friend John Ruskin, Greenaway described her view of the world:

> I go on liking things more and more, seeing them more and more beautiful. Don't you think it is a great possession to be able to get so much joy out of things that are always there to give it, and do not change? What a great pity my hands are not clever enough to do what my mind and eyes see, but there it is! (Ernest, 1967, p. 19)

Other picture books illustrated by Greenaway include *Kate Greenaway's Birthday Book* (1880), *Mother Goose* (1881), *The Language of Flowers* (1884), and Robert Browning's *Pied Piper of Hamelin* (1880). Greenaway's name, like Caldecott's, has been given to an award honoring distinguished artistic accomplishment in the field of children's books. The Kate Greenaway Medal is given annually to the most distinguished British illustrator of children's books.

By the late 1800s, when Crane, Caldecott, and Greenaway began drawing for children, European and North American attitudes toward children were also changing. According to Frederick Laws (1980), these three artists

> were under no public compulsion to be morally edifying or factually informative. Children were no longer supposed to be "young persons" whose taste would be much the same whether they were five or fifteen. So long as they pleased children, artists were free; indeed, Crane wrote that "in a sober and matter-of-fact age Toybooks afford perhaps the only outlet for unrestricted flights of fancy open to the modern illustrator who likes to revolt against the despotism of facts." (p. 318)

This brief discussion of illustrators does not mention all of the artists who made contributions in the nineteenth century, but it does outline the relatively short history of children's book illustration. Chart 2.2 summarizes some milestones in the illustration of children's books from the fifteenth century into the early twentieth century.

Kate Greenaway was one of the early influential illustrators. Her name is now attached to the Kate Greenaway Medal for outstanding illustrators in Great Britain. (From Almanack for 1884 by Kate Greenaway.)

Students of children's literature who are interested in investigating the history of illustrations will enjoy *Landmarks in Print Collecting,* edited by Antony Griffiths (1996). This highly illustrated book published by the British Museum provides a history of print collecting beginning with Sir Hans Sloane in the 1600s and extending to collections in the twentieth century.

The Victorian Influence

English-speaking people identify the reign of Great Britain's Queen Victoria, from 1837 to 1901, with a distinct social epoch, the Victorian Age, although so-called Victorian social influences certainly preceded and followed the queen's life. The rise of a highly competitive industrial technology, the growth of large cities and the decline of rural traditions, an emphasis on strictly controlled social behavior and Christian piety, and a romantic focus on home and family are factors usually associated with the Victorian Age in Europe, North America, and elsewhere. Alan Rauch (1989) describes this period as one of "scientific didacticism," a time when authors used scientific subjects for moral and religious instruction of children. In addition, the increasingly prosperous middle and upper classes began to view childhood sentimentally, as an even more special stage in the human life cycle, while children of the working poor labored many hours a day in mines and factories.

Juliana Horatia Ewing was one of the most prolific authors of the Victorian period. Many of her popular tales for children first appeared in such English periodicals as *The Monthly Packet* and *Aunt Judy's Magazine for Young People.* Her first book, *Melchior's Dream and Other Stories,* was published by the Society for the Promotion of Christian

CHART 2.2 Milestones in the history of children's illustration

1484	William Caxton, *Aesop's Fables,* contained over one hundred woodcuts.
1658	Johann Amos Comenius, *Orbis Pictus* (Painted World), considered by many to be the first picture book for children.
1771	Thomas Bewick, *The New Lottery Book of Birds and Beasts.*
1784	Thomas and John Bewick, *The Select Fables of Aesop and Others.*
1789	William Blake, *Songs of Innocence.*
1823	George Cruikshank, translation of Grimms' *Fairy Tales.*
1853	George Cruikshank, *Fairy Library.*
1865	John Tenniel, illustrations for Lewis Carroll's *Alice's Adventures in Wonderland.*
1865	Walter Crane, *The House That Jack Built,* the first of the toy books engraved by Evans.

1878	Randolph Caldecott, *The Diverting History of John Gilpin,* the first of sixteen picture books.
1878	Kate Greenaway, *Under the Window.*
1883	Howard Pyle, *The Merry Adventures of Robin Hood.*
1900	Arthur Rackham, illustrations for Grimms' *Fairy Tales.*
1901	Beatrix Potter, *The Tale of Peter Rabbit.*
1924	E. H. Shepard, illustrations for A. A. Milne's *When We Were Very Young.*
1933	Kurt Wiese, illustrations for Marjorie Flack's *The Story of Ping.*
1933	E. H. Shepard, illustrations for Kenneth Grahame's *The Wind in the Willows.*
1937	Dr. Seuss, *And to Think That I Saw It on Mulberry Street.*

MRS. EWING'S STORIES.

"What's your name, boy?" — PAGE 247.

JAN OF THE WINDMILL.
A STORY OF THE PLAINS.
By Mrs. EWING. Price, $1.00.
ROBERTS BROTHERS, Publishers,
BOSTON

From Mrs. Ewing's Stories *by Mrs. Ewing, Roberts Brothers, Publishers, Boston.*

Knowledge in 1862. Among her other books were *Mrs. Overtheway's Remembrances* (1869), *Jan of the Windmill* (1876), *Brothers of Pity, and Other Tales* (1882), *Jackanapes* (1884), and *Daddy Darwin's Dovecot* (1884). The last two books were illustrated by Randolph Caldecott.

Literary critics considered Mrs. Ewing's writing to be among the best of the time. Their comments also reflected typically Victorian concerns and values. For example, a critic for the *Worcester Spy* described Mrs. Ewing as a genius whose writing touched the heart, excited tender and noble emotion, encouraged religious feeling, and deepened the scorn for the mean and the cowardly. This same critic recommended that children read Mrs. Ewing's stories because they nourished everything that was lovely in children's characters. Mrs. Ewing's "refining" and "ennobling" stories were popular for many years, remaining in print until the 1930s.

Fred Raymond Erisman (1966) has concluded that American children's literature of the late nineteenth and early twentieth centuries chiefly reflected upper-middle-class values, although it fell into two main categories: fiction and nonfiction. Nonfiction was realistic, dealing with the social, technological, and biographical concerns of an urban society. Fiction presented the ideal values of the well-to-do, implying that these were the typical American values.

Robert Gordon Kelly's (1978) research also reveals that American children's literature in the nineteenth century presented children with an ideal concept of selfhood for emulation. As well, it indicated unresolved tensions about America's growing cities, a beginning emphasis on the responsibilities of a cultural elite, and changing ideas about childhood. According to Kelly, the "gentleman and lady" in children's literature "offered models for negotiating the difficult and precarious passage from childhood to adulthood as well as for moderating the economic competition . . . that was the most important social fact of American life" (p. 42). Children's literature encouraged the young to confront a dog-eat-dog world with courage, temperance, prudence, courtesy, self-reliance, and presence of mind. "So great was the emphasis on self-control," says Kelly, "that one author warned that carelessness is worse than stealing" (p. 41).

Kelly identifies two typical story patterns in children's literature of the period. In the *ordeal,* a child loses the protection and influence of parents or other adults for a short time. Circumstances force the child to act decisively; the situations described often seem contrived to emphasize sound character rather than sound reasoning. The child demonstrates the expected behaviors and then returns to the safety of the family and is justly rewarded.

The heroine of "Nellie in the Light House," published in an 1877 edition of *St. Nicholas* magazine, is the seven-year-old daughter of a lighthouse keeper. When her father goes to the mainland for supplies, the housekeeper is called away to nurse a neighbor, the housekeeper's husband collapses from a stroke, a storm causes high winds, and the beacon light is extinguished. Alone, Nellie must overcome her fear and find a way to rekindle the beacon. She remembers a hymn her mother sang to her and rekindles the light, which then saves her father, who is caught in the storm.

In the second type of story, *change of heart,* a child who has not yet reached the ideal of self-discipline and sound moral character realizes the need for improvement. In "Charlie Balch's Metamorphosis," which appeared in an 1867 edition of the *Riverside Magazine for Young People,* the hero is a sullen and lazy boy who has withdrawn into himself after his mother's death. His father sends him to a boarding school, where he joins a rough crowd of boys. Charlie realizes the errors of his ways during a sermon, and the rest of the story places him in situations that test his resolution for a change of heart. By the end of the story, Charlie has a cheerful disposition and better manners.

Charlotte Yonge was a prolific author of children's literature. She wrote about the large families so common in Victorian times; her own childhood involved close ties with her brother and many cousins. Conversations among the people in her extended family later provided her with realistic settings and dialogue for her fiction. Yonge's stories also reflect the pronounced Christian ethic of the Victorian period.

In Yonge's *The Daisy Chain,* for example, a husband and wife become missionaries in the Loyalty Islands. In typical Victorian fashion, Yonge's fiction portrays females as inferior to males. In *The Daisy Chain,* the hero's sister is advised not to compete with her brother at the university because a woman cannot equal a man scholastically. In *The Clever Woman of the Family,* published in 1865, the heroine thinks for herself, but whenever there is a disagreement between her ideas and those of a man, she must adhere to the superior wisdom of a brother, father, or husband.

Myra Stark (1979) maintains that the Victorian Age was in the grip of an ideology that viewed women as either wives and mothers or failed wives or mothers. Stark declares:

Woman was the center of the age's cult of the family, "the angel in the house," tending to the domestic altar. She was viewed as man's inferior—less rational, weaker, needing his protection; but at the same time, she was exalted for her spirituality, her moral influence. Man was the active one, the doer; woman was the inspirer and the nurturer. The spheres of work in the world and in the home were rigidly divided between the sexes. (p. 4)

Consequently, most Victorian literature for children directed middle- and upper-class girls and boys into the rigidly distinct roles expected of them as adults.

Robert MacDonald's analysis of illustrations in the boys' magazine *Chums* defines the masculine role model found in Victorian illustrations. MacDonald (1988) states that by

repetition and emphasis, a vocabulary of patriotic images was developed and exploited, which for a generation of British males dramatized the myth of Empire. The primary motifs of these illustrations defined manhood, race, and individual action: manhood shown in the heroics of courageous soldiers or brave frontiersmen; lessons of race demonstrated by the examples of barbarous natives or uncivilized Dutchmen; and the complicated relationship between choice and duty set forth as an insistent expectation that the wars of school led to the games of war. A close relationship was established between the world of boys and the world of men. (p. 33)

Some Victorian authors were sensitive to the realities of life for poor children. In 1862, the English poet Elizabeth Barrett Browning wrote of the woes of these children in her poem, "The Cry of the Children," describing the weeping of children in mines and factories while other children played. Another famous English author of the period, Charles Dickens, aroused the Victorian conscience to the plight of unfortunate children, such as the fictional orphan in *Oliver Twist.*

The "Ragged Dick" series, published in 1868, told of the sad plight of children who tried to survive in a city without family or friends. They often worked long hours in factories or on farms. Many died. Horatio Alger, Jr., wrote the series in the hope that readers would be sympathetic to the cause of poor children and the Children's Aid Soci-

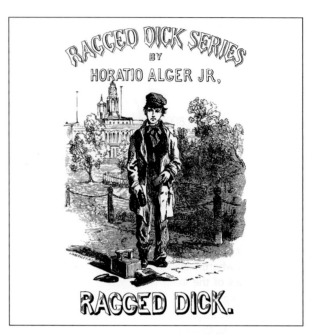

The Ragged Dick *series, published in 1868, told of the sad plight of children who tried to survive in a city without family or friends.*

ety. Since 1854, the society has been finding homes for abandoned children.

Horatio Alger's *Frank's Campaign* (1864) was the first of a series of books in which poor American youths went from rags to riches. Other books by Alger that have a similar theme include *Fame and Fortune* (1868), *Sink or Swim* (1870), *Strong and Steady* (1871), *Brave and Bold* (1874), *Risen from the Ranks* (1874), and *From Farm Boy to Senator: Being the History of the Boyhood and Manhood of Daniel Webster* (1882).

Reissues of lesser known books and stories published during the Victorian period provide opportunities for further study. For example, *What I Cannot Tell My Mother Is Not Fit for Me to Know* is a collection of stories, poems, and songs selected by Gwladys and Brian Rees-Williams (1981) from texts published in the nineteenth century. Andrew Tuer's *Stories from Forgotten Children's Books* (1986) is a facsimile edition of a book published in 1898.

Fantasy, Adventure, and Real People

As the world was changing, views of childhood were changing, too. Emphases in children's literature mirrored the new attitudes and world developments. Childhood was becoming, at least for middle- and upper-class children, a more carefree and enjoyable period of life, and this change was reflected in the increase in fantasy stories for children. As adventurers explored unknown areas of the world, their experiences inspired new adventure stories. Also, the characters of specific families and localities were captured in the growing popularity of literature about ordinary people, places, and events in sometimes extraordinary circumstances.

Technology Resources

Visit our Companion Website at www.prenhall.com/norton to link to a nice collection of Lewis Carroll–related materials.

Fantasy. By the mid-1800s, the puritanical resistance to fantasy in children's literature was on its way toward extinction in most segments of European and North American society. Children had been reading and enjoying the folktales of Perrault and the Brothers Grimm, and Andersen's stories had been translated into English. More and more educators and parents believed that literature should entertain children rather than merely instruct them.

According to Raymond Chapman (1968), fantasy created a world where fears could be projected onto impossible creatures of the imagination while a child remained safe. Although growing to maturity seemed dangerous, the happiest people acquired new knowledge while retaining childlike qualities. Brian W. Alderson (1959) describes the creation of one of the landmarks in fantasy and nonsense:

One summer's day on the river at Oxford [England] a thirty-year-old lecturer in mathematics at Christ Church was taking the three daughters of his Dean, Edith, Lorina, and Alice, out for a row. His name was Charles Lutwidge Dodgson. The day was hot and the children wanted to have a story told them, a thing they had come to expect from Mr. Dodgson. So the young lecturer complied, his mind relaxing in the drowsy heat and his thoughts, which did not tire so easily, following paths of their own making. (p. 64)

The paths led directly down the rabbit hole and into adventures in Wonderland with the Cheshire Cat, the Queen of Hearts, and the Mad Hatter. The story told that afternoon in 1862 made such an impression on Alice that she pestered Dodgson to write it down. He wrote it for her, gave it to her as a gift, and, after it had been thoroughly enjoyed by many people, published it for others under the pseudonym Lewis Carroll.

According to Cornelia Meigs et al. (1969), the revolutionary nature of Lewis Carroll's *Alice's Adventures in Wonderland* and *Through the Looking Glass* when compared with earlier books written for children is due to "the fact that they were written purely to give pleasure to children. . . . Here . . . for the first time we find a story designed for children without a trace of a lesson or moral" (p. 194).

Edward Lear, the other great writer of fantasy for children in the nineteenth century, created absurd and delightful characters in nonsense verses. Lear's *A Book of Nonsense* appeared in 1846, his *More Nonsense* in 1872. *Nonsense Songs, Botany and Alphabets,* published in 1871, contained Lear's "Nonsense Stories," "Nonsense Geography," "Natural History," and "Nonsense Alphabets." *Laughable Lyrics* (1877) included the nonsense verses "The

The illustrations and text for Alice's Adventures in Wonderland *were designed to give pleasure, not to teach a lesson. (Illustrated by John Tenniel. From* Alice's Adventures in Wonderland *by Lewis Carroll. Published by Macmillan and Co., 1865. Courtesy of Lilly Library, Indiana University, Bloomington, Indiana.)*

There was an Old Person of Pinner,
As thin as a lath, if not thinner;
They dressed him in white,
And roll'd him up tight,
That elastic Old Person of Pinner.

Edward Lear's illustrations heightened the humor of his limericks. (From A Book of Nonsense *by Edward Lear. Published by Heinrich Hoffman, 1846. Courtesy of Lilly Library, Indiana University, Bloomington, Indiana.)*

Quangle-Wangle's Hat," "The Dong with the Luminous Nose," and "The Youghy-Bonghy-Bo."

Lear's work, like Carroll's, was popular with both young and adult readers. Today, both writers are often quoted and enjoyed as much as they were when their works were created.

Adventure. Europeans and North Americans were having many real-life adventures in the nineteenth century. Explorers were seeking the North Pole, Florence Nightingale was pioneering for female independence as a director of nursing in the Crimean War, and a railroad was being constructed across the United States. If a person could not go to a remote region and overcome the perils lurking there, the next best adventure was the vicarious one offered through books.

Robert Louis Stevenson was the master of the adventure stories written during this time. When *Treasure Island* was published, it was considered the greatest adventure story for children since *Robinson Crusoe*. Brian W. Alderson (1959) agrees that Stevenson had the greatest influence on children's literature after Daniel Defoe.

Stevenson was born in Edinburgh, Scotland, the son of a lighthouse engineer. When he was a young boy, his father told him bedtime tales filled with "blood and thunder," and his nurse told him stories of body snatchers, ghosts, and martyrs. As an adult, Stevenson traveled to many lands, but he still loved the lochs, islands, and misty forests of his home. Stevenson's early experiences are evident in his two most famous adventure stories, *Treasure Island* and *Kidnapped*.

Treasure Island had an interesting beginning. While trying to entertain his stepson, Stevenson drew a watercolor map of an island, then followed his drawing with the now famous story of pirates, buried treasure, and a young boy's adventures.

Both *Treasure Island* and *Kidnapped* have the ingredients of outstanding adventure literature: action, mystery, and pursuit and evasion in authentic historical settings. Stevenson believed that an adventure story should have a specific effect on its readers: It should absorb and delight them, fill their minds with a kaleidoscope of images, and satisfy their nameless longings. According to Bernard J. Lonsdale and Helen K. Macintosh (1973), Stevenson believed that Robinson Crusoe discovering a footprint on his lonely beach, Achilles shouting against the Trojans, and Ulysses bending over his great bow were culminating moments that have been printed in the mind's eye forever. In addition, according to Brian W. Alderson (1959), Stevenson believed that children and adults should demand such moments in their literature, and Stevenson achieved that quality in tales of "treasure and treachery . . . the comings and goings of . . . pirates, the ominous hints of the fearful events which are to come" (p. 257).

The historical novel became popular in the 1800s with the publication of stories by Sir Walter Scott and Charlotte Yonge.

While Robert Louis Stevenson wrote of pirates and buried treasure in the not-so-distant past, Howard Pyle took readers back to the Middle Ages to fight evil, overcome Prince John's injustice, and have a rollicking good time in the green depths of Sherwood Forest. Pyle's *The Merry Adventures of Robin Hood,* published in 1883, retold the old English ballad about Robin Hood, Little John, Friar Tuck, and the other merry men who robbed the rich to give to the poor and constantly thwarted the evil plans of the Sheriff of Nottingham. Here was swashbuckling entertainment that also provided children with a glimpse of an early period in European history.

The historical novel became popular in the 1800s with the publication of stories by Sir Walter Scott. Scott's story of medieval English life, *Ivanhoe: A Romance* (1820), was often used as a school assignment for older children. Other popular books by Scott included *The Lady of the Lake* (1810), *Waverly: Or, 'Tis Sixty Years Since* (1814), *Rob Roy* (1818), and *Tales of the Crusaders* (1825).

The Industrial Revolution, the invention of the steam engine, and the prevalent feeling of new possibilities always just around the corner laid the groundwork for a new kind of adventure story in the last half of the nineteenth century. Jules Verne's science fiction adventure stories can certainly be classified as another benchmark in children's literature. Verne envisioned submarines, guided missiles, and dirigibles long before such things were possible. His first science fiction book, *Five Weeks in a Balloon,* was published in France in 1863. His two most famous books, *Twenty Thousand Leagues Under the Sea,* published in 1869, and *Around the World in Eighty Days,* published in

Through the Eyes of an AUTHOR/ILLUSTRATOR

Steven Kellogg

Visit the CD-ROM that accompanies this text to generate a complete list of Steven Kellogg titles.

Selected Titles by Steven Kellogg:

Yankee Doodle

Jack and the Beanstalk

Paul Bunyan

Mystery of the Missing Red Mitten

A Rose for Pinkerton

I think one of the functions of literature is to keep legends, tales, myths, and old ballads alive and re-create them in new forms for succeeding generations. I think one of the roles of the author, the storyteller, or the artist is to keep our heritage alive and pass it on, and encourage the people to whom you pass it on to do the same thing for the generation that comes after them. Our American tall tale literature really is our mythology, our folklore. Actually it was an editor who mentioned to me quite a number of years ago that it had been somewhat overlooked in the picture-book form, and he was anxious that I undertake a picture book retelling the adventures of Paul Bunyan. That was the beginning of the tall tale series that I've been working on, on and off ever since, for almost twenty-five years now.

These tales were oral to begin with. Then they were printed in some anthologies earlier on, but they tended to be underillustrated, illustrated with small black-and-white line drawings. One of the exciting things that has been happening to picture books in the last thirty years is that there have been great advances in full-color printing, so there have been a lot of opportunities open to artists that were not there before. Full-color printing is a lot less expensive now, and it became possible to obtain really high-quality results without the enormous financial investment that had been commanded earlier. So there was a real renaissance in picture books in terms of the quality of their illustrations, and a lot more artists were drawn to express themselves in that format.

Also, there's been a growing awareness of the importance of literature to children and that they are shaped by the stories they're exposed to. So there was a real desire to make available to them the highest quality writing and artwork so their aesthetic judgment would respond to that and they would enjoy literature and the arts on that level, we hope, for the rest of their lives.

When I write, I think a lot about the audience, which is, of course, primarily the kids, and I really want them to have as many positive experiences as possible during these years of crucial development. This is really important, especially because they are still learning the nuts and bolts of reading and mastering all the nuances of language and the complexities of verbal communication. We want to present that in as appealing a way as possible. So I think I lean in the direction of making the books really welcoming, positive, enjoyable, and fun so that the kids will find them compelling and really be drawn to them.

The *Jack and the Beanstalk* that I did, though, like a lot of fairy tales, has a lot of very dark overtones to it. I tried to really honor that and not shy away from it—to capture the moments of Jack's distress when he is trapped in the ogre's house and feeling very vulnerable and very frightened. I tried to really capture that feeling because I know that's important. You want to deal with real feelings, not just the lighthearted, positive ones, by giving readers a chance to explore the darker corridors as well.

Yankee Doodle has so much vitality and so much energy that I tried to infuse the illustrations with the same kind of really exuberant activity, the explosive energy and frenetic cadence of the song and the whole upbeat quality of it. I tried to capture that in the illustrations and have that harmonize with the text.

My own illustrations come from a lot of background work, and thought, and sketching, and trial and error, by trying out different pictorial compositions and then altering them in a way that seems to make them more effective and harmonize more completely with the text, and also to give nuances and meaning to the text that are only hinted at or not even there. A picture book is really a duet between the two voices, the verbal and the visual. They both make a very important contribution, but don't necessarily rehash the same material. The pictures bring different meaning to the story. Sometimes it's the way the two combine that is really the essence of the picture book as a storytelling form.

Video Profiles: The accompanying video contains conversations from such authors and illustrators as Jack Gantos, Roland Smith, Molly Bang, and Floyd Cooper.

1872, have also been immortalized on film. Consequently, the heroes of these books, Captain Nemo and Phileas Fogg, are well known to both readers and movie fans.

Verne admired the work of an earlier author, Daniel Defoe, and Verne's *The Mysterious Island*, published in 1875, was written because of Verne's interest in *Robinson Crusoe*. Verne's genius can be seen in the popularity of his works even today, after his glorious inventions have become reality. Verne's detailed descriptions are so believable they seem as modern now as they did when they were published in the 1800s. The popularity of Verne's literature also caused other authors to write science fiction and to expand the new genre.

Real People. During the later nineteenth and early twentieth centuries, the local-color story came into its own.

Realistic situations and people are the settings and subjects of such stories, in which place, plot, and characters are tightly integrated. According to James H. Fraser (1978), "This integration, which reveals the complex involvement of human, cultural, and geographical influences, produces a rich literature—peculiarly rich for the student of American culture, and extraordinarily rich for the young persons fortunate enough to read it" (p. 55). The diversity of American geography and people are found in books like Edward Eggleston's *The Hoosier School Boy* (rural Indiana), Thomas Bailey Aldrich's *The Story of a Bad Boy* (a New England seafaring town), Kate Douglas Wiggins's *Rebecca of Sunnybrook Farm* (rural Maine), Mark Twain's *The Adventures of Huckleberry Finn* (Mississippi River towns), and Frances Courtenay Baylor's *Juan and Juanita*

Mark Twain wrote adventures about life in the Mississippi River environment in which he himself had grown up. (From The Adventures of Huckleberry Finn *by Mark Twain. Published by Charles L. Webster and Co., 1885. Courtesy of Lilly Library, Indiana University, Bloomington, Indiana.)*

(the Southwest). Fraser maintains that these local-color stories also transmit a conservative, traditional view of American life to the next generation. Their characters are "carryovers from an earlier age, an agrarian, preindustrial age, which the stories sentimentalize for their modern readers" (p. 59).

The greatest American writer of realistic adventure in this period was Mark Twain (Samuel Clemens). While Robert Louis Stevenson was writing about adventures on far-off islands, Twain was immortalizing life on the Mississippi River before the Civil War. Twain captured the human, cultural, and geographical influences that affected a boy's life in this era of American history. Twain grew up in the river town of Hannibal, Missouri, where he lived many of the adventures about which he later wrote. He explored the river, raided melon patches, and used a cave as a rendezvous to plan further adventures and mischief with his friends. These adventures made Tom Sawyer and Huckleberry Finn come alive for many

adventure-loving children. Twain's heroes did not leave the continent, but they did have exciting adventures on a nearby island, return in time to hear plans for their own funerals, and then attend those momentous occasions. Characters such as Injun Joe, Aunt Polly, Tom Sawyer, Becky Thatcher, and Huckleberry Finn still provide reading pleasure for children and adults. Donald A. Barclay (1992) concludes that Mark Twain's *The Adventures of Huckleberry Finn* is also one of the most frequently illustrated novels in history. Barclay estimates that there are approximately eight hundred editions of the novel, most of which are illustrated.

Many American books in the Victorian era took the family as their subject, and series stories dealing with the everyday lives of large families became popular. Margaret Sidney, for example, wrote a series of books about the five little Peppers. The first book, *The Five Little Peppers and How They Grew,* published in 1881, was followed by *The Five Little Peppers Midway* and *The Five Little Peppers Grown Up.*

Louisa May Alcott's account of family life in *Little Women,* published in 1868, is so real that readers feel they know each member of the March family intimately. This book showing the warm relationships and everyday struggles in a family of meager means is actually about Alcott's own family.

In many ways, Alcott's life was quite different from the usual Victorian model, which accounts for the ways in which *Little Women* was ahead of its time. Alcott's father believed in educating his daughters. Consequently, Alcott was first educated at home by her father and then sent to the district school.

In 1867, a publisher asked Alcott to write a book for girls, and she decided to write about her own family. The resulting book, *Little Women,* was an overwhelming success. Readers enjoyed the intimate details of a warm, loving, and very human family. The most popular character, Jo, shares many characteristics with Alcott herself. Jo is courageous, warm, and honest, but she has a quick temper that often gets her into difficulty. She also leaves home to earn a living as a writer and to help support her family. *Little Women* was so popular that in 1869 Alcott wrote a sequel, *Little Women, Part II.* She also wrote other favorites, such as *An Old-Fashioned Girl, Little Men,* and *Eight Cousins.*

One very popular realistic story published in the nineteenth century had a setting foreign to most readers of its English translation. Mountains that climb into the sky, sheepherders, tinkling bells, rushing streams, flower-strewn

Through the Eyes of a CHILD

Brendan

Pam Wilson's Fourth Grade
Western Row Elementary
Mason, Ohio

TITLE: Ralph's Secret Weapon

AUTHOR: Steven Kellogg

I really liked the book. It had such good details I almost didn't need the pictures. I thought the pictures were good too. The book is about Ralf and his bassoon. His Aunt has three great danes and he gets to play with them. Another thing I liked is how Ralf won the contest and the trophy was bigger than him. I think you should read this book to find out what happens to Ralf and his bassoon.

Brendan

---

meadows, a hut with a bed of fresh hay, and the freedom to wander in delightful Swiss surroundings were found in Johanna Spyri's *Heidi,* published in Switzerland in 1880 and translated into English in 1884. Spyri based her book on her own childhood experiences in the Swiss Alps, which may help explain its realistic appeal.

Actual experience in a foreign land was not the only basis that an author had for providing a believable setting. Mary Mapes Dodge used research and imagination to provide credible background and characters in *Hans Brinker, or the Silver Skates, a Story of Life in Holland.* Readers in the Netherlands accepted this story as authentic in 1865, even though Dodge had never visited their country.

Space does not allow a complete discussion of all the books written for children or written for adults and read by children in earlier eras of our history. Chart 2.3 lists some previously discussed literature that brings the world of children's books into the twentieth century. As you read this chart, however, remember that book publishing for children is a fairly recent activity. As Betsy Hearne (1988) points out, the first children's book department to be established in a publishing house in the United States was Macmillan's children's book department, established in 1918. Although children's books were published prior to this date, this is certainly a milestone in the publication of children's literature.

CHART 2.3 Notable authors of children's literature

1477	William Caxton, *Caxton's Book of Curtesye*
1484	William Caxton, *The Fables of Aesop*
1485	William Caxton, *Le Morte d'Arthur*
1678	John Bunyan, *Pilgrim's Progress*
1698	Charles Perrault or Pierre Perrault d'Armancour, *Tales of Mother Goose*
1719	Daniel Defoe, *Robinson Crusoe*
1726	Jonathan Swift, *Gulliver's Travels*
1744	John Newbery, *A Little Pretty Pocket Book*
1789	William Blake, *Songs of Innocence*
1812	First volume of Grimm Brothers' fairy tales, *Kinder-und Hausmärchen*
	Johann Wyss, *Swiss Family Robinson*
1820	Sir Walter Scott, *Ivanhoe: A Romance*
1823	Clement G. Moore, *A Visit from St. Nicholas*
1826	James Fenimore Cooper, *The Last of the Mohicans*
1843	Charles Dickens, *A Christmas Carol*
1846	Edward Lear, *A Book of Nonsense*
	Hans Christian Andersen's fairy tales in English translations
1851	John Ruskin, *King of the Golden River*
1856	Charlotte Yonge, *The Daisy Chain*
1862	Christina Georgina Rossetti, *Goblin Market*
1863	Charles Kingsley, *The Water Babies*
1865	Lewis Carroll, *Alice's Adventures in Wonderland*
	Mary Elizabeth Mapes Dodge, *Hans Brinker, or the Silver Skates, a Story of Life in Holland*
1868	Louisa May Alcott, *Little Women*
1870	Thomas Bailey Aldrich, *The Story of a Bad Boy*
1871	George MacDonald, *At the Back of the North Wind*
1872	Jules Verne, *Around the World in Eighty Days*
1873	*St. Nicholas: Scribner's Illustrated Magazine for Girls and Boys,* edited by Mary Mapes Dodge
1876	Mark Twain, *The Adventures of Tom Sawyer*
1877	Anna Sewell, *Black Beauty*
1881	Margaret Sidney, *The Five Little Peppers and How They Grew*
	Joel Chandler Harris, *Uncle Remus; His Songs and Sayings: The Folklore of the Old Plantation*
1883	Howard Pyle, *Merry Adventures of Robin Hood of Great Renown, in Nottinghamshire*
	Robert Louis Stevenson, *Treasure Island*
1884	Johanna Spyri, *Heidi; Her Years of Wandering and Learning*
1885	Robert Louis Stevenson, *A Child's Garden of Verses*
1886	Frances Hodgson Burnett, *Little Lord Fauntleroy*
1889	Andrew Lang, *The Blue Fairy Book*
1892	Carlo Collodi, *The Adventures of Pinocchio*
	Arthur Conan Doyle, *The Adventures of Sherlock Holmes*
1894	Rudyard Kipling, *The Jungle Book*
1901	Beatrix Potter, *The Tale of Peter Rabbit*
1903	L. Leslie Brooke, *Johnny Crow's Garden*
	Kate Douglas Wiggins, *Rebecca of Sunnybrook Farm*
	J. M. Barrie, *Peter Pan; or The Boy Who Would Not Grow Up*
1904	Howard Garis, *The Bobbsey Twins; or Merry Days Indoors and Out* (There are over seventy books in the series.)
1908	Kenneth Grahame, *The Wind in the Willows*
1911	Frances Hodgson Burnett, *The Secret Garden*
1913	Eleanor H. Porter, *Pollyanna*
1918	O. Henry, *The Ransom of Red Chief*
1921	Hendrik Willem Van Loon, *The Story of Mankind* (One of the first informational books attempting to make learning exciting; first Newbery Medal, 1922)
1922	Margery Williams Bianco, *The Velveteen Rabbit*
1924	A. A. Milne, *When We Were Very Young*
1926	A. A. Milne, *Winnie-the-Pooh*
1928	Wanda Gág, *Millions of Cats*
	Carl Sandburg, *Abe Lincoln Grows Up*
1929	Rachel Field, *Hitty, Her First Hundred Years*
1932	Laura Ingalls Wilder, *Little House in the Big Woods*
	Laura E. Richards, *Tirra Lirra: Rhymes Old and New*
1933	Jean de Brunhoff, *The Story of Babar*
1937	Dr. Seuss, *And to Think That I Saw It on Mulberry Street*
	John Ronald Reuel Tolkien, *The Hobbit*
1939	James Daugherty, *Daniel Boone*
1940	Armstrong Sperry, *Call It Courage*
	Doris Gates, *Blue Willow*
1941	Lois Lenski, *Indian Captive, The Story of Mary Jemison*
	Robert McCloskey, *Make Way for Ducklings*
1942	Virginia Lee Burton, *The Little House*

CHART 2.3   *(Continued)*

1944	Robert Lawson, *Rabbit Hill*
1946	Esther Forbes, *Johnny Tremain*
1947	Marcia Brown, *Stone Soup*
1950	Beverly Cleary, *Henry Huggins*
1951	Olivia Coolidge, *Legends of the North*
1952	Lynd Ward, *The Biggest Bear*
	E. B. White, *Charlotte's Web*
	David McCord, *Far and Few*
1953	Mary Norton, *The Borrowers*
1954	Rosemary Sutcliff, *The Eagle of the Ninth*
1955	L. M. Boston, *The Children of Green Knowe*
1957	Else Holmelund Minarik, *Little Bear*
1958	Jean Fritz, *The Cabin Faced West*
	Elizabeth George Speare, *The Witch of Blackbird Pond*
1959	Leo Lionni, *Little Blue and Little Yellow*
	Jean George, *My Side of the Mountain*
1960	Michael Bond, *A Bear Called Paddington*
	Scott O'Dell, *Island of the Blue Dolphins*
1961	C. S. Lewis, *The Lion, the Witch, and the Wardrobe*
1962	Ronald Syme, *African Traveler, The Story of Mary Kingsley*
	Madeleine L'Engle, *A Wrinkle in Time*
	Ezra Jack Keats, *The Snowy Day*
1964	Louise Fitzhugh, *Harriet the Spy*
	Irene Hunt, *Across Five Aprils*
	Lloyd Alexander, *The Book of Three*
1967	John Christopher, *The White Mountains*
	E. L. Konigsburg, *Jennifer, Hecate, MacBeth, William McKinley and Me, Elizabeth*
	Virginia Hamilton, *Zeely*
1969	John Steptoe, *Stevie*
	William H. Armstrong, *Sounder*
	Theodore Taylor, *The Cay*
	Vera and Bill Cleaver, *Where the Lilies Bloom*
	William Steig, *Sylvester and the Magic Pebble*
1970	Betsy Byars, *Summer of the Swans*
	Judy Blume, *Are You There God? It's Me, Margaret*
1971	Arnold Lobel, *Frog and Toad Are Friends*
	Muriel Feelings, *Moja Means One: Swahili Counting Book*
	Robert Kraus, *Leo, the Late Bloomer*

1972	Judith Viorst, *Alexander and the Terrible, Horrible, No Good, Very Bad Day*
1973	Doris Smith, *A Taste of Blackberries*
1974	Janet Hickman, *The Valley of the Shadow*
1975	Laurence Yep, *Dragonwings*
1976	Mildred Taylor, *Roll of Thunder, Hear My Cry*
1977	Jamake Highwater, *Anpao: An Indian Odyssey*
	Patricia Clapp, *I'm Deborah Sampson: A Soldier in the War of the Revolution*
	Katherine Paterson, *Bridge to Terabithia*
	Margaret Musgrove, *Ashanti to Zulu: African Traditions*
1978	Tomie de Paola, *The Clown of God*
1979	José Aruego and Ariane Dewey, *We Hide, You Seek*
1981	Nancy Willard, *Visit to William Blake's Inn*
1982	Nina Bawden, *Kept in the Dark*
	Laurence Pringle, *Water: The Next Great Resource Battle*
	Cynthia Rylant, *When I Was Young in the Mountains*
1984	Paula Fox, *One-Eyed Cat*
1985	Rhoda Blumberg, *Commodore Perry in the Land of the Shogun*
1986	Jean Fritz, *Make Way for Sam Houston*
1987	Russell Freedman, *Lincoln: A Photobiography*
1988	Paul Fleishman, *Joyful Noise: Poems for Two Voices*
1989	Janet Taylor Lisle, *Afternoon of the Elves*
1990	Dr. Seuss, *Oh, the Places You'll Go!*
1991	Avi, *Nothing But the Truth: A Documentary Novel*
1993	Lois Lowry, *The Giver*
1997	E. L. Konigsburg receives her Second Newbery Medal for *The View from Saturday*
1999	Louis Sachar's *Holes* receives both the Newbery Medal and the National Book Award
2001	Richard Peck, *A Year Down Yonder*

The History of Censorship

According to *Webster's Dictionary: The New Lexicon of the English Language,* 1988 edition, a censor is "a person empowered to suppress publications or excise any matter in them thought to be immoral, seditious, or otherwise undesirable" (p. 158). What is considered immoral, sedi-tious, or undesirable changes, however, with various time periods and with political and social attitudes.

According to Kirk Polking (1990), although "censorship has always existed to some degree, the criteria for propos-ing that books be banned seem to shift with social trends. In the late 1960s and early 1970s, racism, sexism, and other forms of discrimination were considered objectionable; in

CHART 2.4 Milestones in the history of censorship

411 B.C.	Works of Protagoras were burned in Athens.
387 B.C.	Plato suggested expurgating Homer's *The Odyssey* for immature readers.
213 B.C.	Chinese Emperor Shih Huang-ti tried to burn all the books in his realm because he disapproved of the traditional Chinese culture.
168 B.C.	Jewish library in Jerusalem was destroyed during the Maccabean uprising.
1st century	Augustus exiled poets and banned their works. Emperor Caligula ordered books by Homer and Virgil burned.
A.D. 303	Diocletian condemned and burned all Christian books.
1497	Works of Ovid and Dante were burned in Florence.
1559	The Sacred Congregation of the Roman Inquisition published the first *Index of Forbidden Books*—books considered dangerous to the faith and morals of Roman Catholics (abandoned in 1996).
1624	The Bible, translated by Martin Luther in 1534, was burned in Germany.
1660	Charles II of England decreed that the Council for Foreign Plantations instruct natives, servants, and slaves of the British colonies in the precepts of Christianity by teaching them to read. But British slave owners feared literate blacks might find dangerous revolutionary ideas in books.
1683	John Locke escaped from England to Holland because his theory of civil, religious, and philosophical liberty was considered too radical.
1713	Daniel Defoe was prosecuted and imprisoned by the Whigs for writing treasonable anti-Jacobite pamphlets. In 1720, his *Robinson Crusoe* was placed on the *Index of Forbidden Books.*
1726	*Gulliver's Travels* by Jonathan Swift was denounced as wicked and obscene because of its satire on courts, political parties, and statesmen.
1760	South Carolina passed strict laws forbidding all blacks from being taught to read.
1762	Jean-Jacques Rousseau's *Emile* was condemned and burned by Parliament of Paris.
1872	Anthony Comstock founded in New York the Society for the Suppression of Vice. This was the first effective censorship board in the United States.
1884	Mark Twain's *Huckleberry Finn* was banned in Massachusetts. The sales of the book increased.
1925	John Scopes was found guilty of teaching evolution based on *The Origin of Species.*
1933	In Berlin, propaganda minister Paul Goebbels spoke during the burning of over 20,000 books while a crowd of more than 100,000 cheered.
	Rudolf Frank was arrested in Germany for writing *No Hero for the Kaiser,* a juvenile literature book with an antiwar theme.
1942	In Athens, performances of classic Greek plays were banned by Nazi occupation authorities.
1955	In Connecticut, African Americans protested against a dramatized version of Harriet Beecher Stowe's *Uncle Tom's Cabin, or Life Among the Lowly.*
1957	New York City dropped works of Mark Twain from lists of approved books for junior and senior high schools because of racial language.
1980	Parents took Hawkins County Tennessee Public Schools to court because an elementary school series was believed to violate their fundamentalist religious beliefs.
1984	*The Adventures of Huckleberry Finn* was removed from the high school reading list in Waukegan, Illinois.
1989	A survey of schools showed that Mark Twain's *The Adventures of Huckleberry Finn* was one of the most read books in high schools.
1994–95	List compiled by People for the American Way of the ten leading books that various groups tried to ban during the year and the reasons for the banning:
	Alvin Schwartz. *More Scary Stories to Tell in the Dark* (supernatural tales).
	Alvin Schwartz. *Scary Stories to Tell in the Dark* (supernatural tales).
	Maya Angelou. *I Know Why the Caged Bird Sings* (sexual content).
	Lois Lowry. *The Giver* (profanity, violence, depressing story).
	Eve Merriam. *Halloween ABC* (supernatural theme).
	Alvin Schwartz. *Scary Stories 3: More Tales to Chill Your Bones* (supernatural tales).
	Katherine Paterson. *Bridge to Terabithia* (sexual content, profanity, "satanic" material).
	Robert Cormier. *The Chocolate War* (profanity, violence, sexual content).
	John Steinbeck. *Of Mice and Men* (profanity, sexual content).
	Christopher and James Lincoln Collier. *My Brother Sam Is Dead* (profanity, violence, challenge to patriotism, challenge to parental authority).
1997	February 17 issue of *Publishers Weekly* lists *The Giver* as number four in "Children's Bestsellers" (one of the books groups sought to ban in 1995).

the 1980s, it was material alleged to be anti-American, anti-family, or obscene that was challenged. While educators traditionally have chosen books for use by school children for their literary value and for their handling of controversial topics in what they consider to be a tasteful manner, some conservative lobbying groups emerged in the early 1980s as opponents of certain works of literature" (p. 67). Peter Hunt (1997) identifies two limitations on the freedom to read that he considers to be serious invisible censorship that influences the availability of books in both Great Britain and the United States: "What is available for British children to read is severely circumscribed by a combination of two silent forces: government policies, which have in recent years severely cut school library budgets and school library services, and (as in the U.S.) the selection procedures of those powerful bookselling companies that dominate the market" (p. 96).

In his book, *A History of Reading,* Alberto Manguel (1996) identifies some of the milestones in the history of censorship beginning in 411 B.C. and relates censorship with power. He states, "Censorship, therefore, in some form or another, is the corollary of all power, and the history of reading is lit by a seemingly endless line of censors' bonfires, from the earliest papyrus scrolls to the books of our time" (p. 283). Another source for milestones in the history of censorship is Gail Blasser Riley's (1998) *Censorship.* Riley includes legal issues in a chapter, "The Law of Censorship," and a section on "How to Research Censorship."

In Chart 2.4, the milestones in the history of censorship include some of the landmarks identified by Manguel in his chapter "Forbidden Reading" and listings in Anne Lyon Haight's *Banned Books: 387 B.C. to 1978 A.D.* (1978) and in William Noble's *Bookbanning in America: Who Bans Books?—and Why* (1990). Additional milestones in censorship that specifically influenced children's literature have also been added to the list. As you read the list of books in the chart, try to identify the social, religious, or political attitudes that might have been behind these actions.

Children and the Family in Children's Literature

Attitudes toward the place for children in the family have changed considerably over time. Before the Middle Ages, children were not greatly valued, and infanticide was a regular practice. During the Middle Ages, poor children shared the poverty and hard work of their parents, while children from the upper class and nobility spent most of their childhood separated from their families, receiving instruction and training in the roles that they would assume as adults. Not until relatively recently has childhood become the time for the close family interaction that we are familiar with today.

Books written for children or adopted by children during the last few centuries have usually reflected views

of childhood and the family typical of their time. Researchers are increasingly viewing children's literature as an important source of information about these changing attitudes. In *Fifteen Centuries of Children's Literature: An Annotated Chronology of British and American Works in Historical Context,* Jane Bingham and Grayce Scholt (1980) consider the historical background of children's books, including attitudes toward and treatment of children, discuss the development of children's books, and provide an annotated chronology of children's books.

Other researchers have analyzed children's literature over time: Mary Cadogan and Patricia Craig (1976) have looked at the changing role of females in *You're a Brick, Angela! A New Look at Girls' Fiction from 1839 to 1975;* Alma Cross Homze (1963) has analyzed the changing interpersonal relationships depicted in realistic fiction published between 1920 and 1960; and Jean Duncan Shaw (1966) has studied themes in children's books published between 1850 and 1964. Lynne Vallone (1988) analyzed the role of females in eighteenth-century adolescent fiction. Studies of more recent historical periods include Carolyn Wilson Carmichael's (1971) analysis of social values reflected in contemporary realistic fiction; John Rowe Townsend's (1975) analysis of the relationships between generations depicted in the literature of the 1950s and the 1960s; Beverly Young's (1985) analysis of female protagonists in literature of the 1930s, the 1950s, and the 1970s; and Anita P. Davis and Thoma R. McDaniel's (1999) analysis of gender portrayal in recent Caldecott-winning books.

Unsurprisingly, a prominent theme in children's literature has been the relationships of children within the family. Changing views about children and the family over time necessarily reflect other social attitudes as well. The following time periods reflect the publication dates of a few popular American children's books in eras otherwise not easily demarcated by precise years. All of these books are available today. The older books have been published in reproductions by Garland Publishing Company of New York and London.

The Child and the Family, 1856–1903

An emphatic sense of duty to God and parents, the rise of the public school and Sunday School movements, and the beginning of a belief that children are individuals in their own right are among the characteristics of the Victorian era identifiable in children's literature of the time. According to Karen I. Adams (1989), "In the latter half of the nineteenth century and early decades of the twentieth century, religion was most often represented by the moralizing of Louisa May Alcott in *Little Women*" (p. 5). Much Victorian children's literature stresses the development of conscience, the merit of striving for perfection, and the male and female roles exemplified by family members. Illuminating examples of the social attitudes of this period may be drawn from Charlotte Yonge's *The Daisy Chain* (1856), Louisa May Alcott's *Little Women*

May Alcott's illustrations for her sister Louisa May Alcott's Little Women *reinforce the vision of a warm, loving Victorian family. (Illustration by May Alcott. From* Little Women or, Meg, Jo, Beth and Amy *by Louisa M. Alcott. Published by Roberts Brothers, 1868. Courtesy of Lilly Library, Indiana University, Bloomington, Indiana.)*

(1868), Thomas Bailey Aldrich's *The Story of a Bad Boy* (1870), Margaret Sidney's *The Five Little Peppers and How They Grew* (1880), and Kate Douglas Wiggins's *Rebecca of Sunnybrook Farm* (1903).

While these books have their differences, all of them stress the importance of accepting responsibility, whether for one's family, the poor and unfortunate, or self-improvement. For example, the older children in *The Daisy Chain* assume the task of raising the younger children when their mother dies; their greatest concerns are instilling Christian goodness in their siblings and living up to their father's wishes. Likewise, the children in *Little Women* and *The Five Little Peppers and How They Grew* feel responsible for their siblings and their mothers. Rebecca, in *Rebecca of Sunnybrook Farm,* feels this responsibility to such an extent that she completes four years of work at the academy in three years so that she can earn a living and help educate her siblings.

The characters in these books respect adult authority. Children strive to live up to their parents' ideals or want the acceptance and respect of their parents. The protagonist in *The Story of a Bad Boy* may not always ask or follow his grandfather's advice, but he admits that he deserves the terrible things that usually happen to him when he disobeys.

Respect for authority is underscored by the characteristic religious emphasis in these books. In *The Daisy Chain,* family members read the Bible together, discuss the meaning of the minister's sermons, debate the relative importance of the temptations in their lives, and organize a church and school for the poor. In *Little Women,* the family members receive strength from prayer and Bible reading. In *The Story of a Bad Boy,* Sundays are solemn days in which the family attends church, reads the scriptures, and eats food prepared the day before. The five little Peppers voice admiration for the clergy and want to become "good." Rebecca of Sunnybrook Farm's aunt, like her father before her, is an influential member of her church.

Family life in these books reiterates the definite social roles assigned to males and females in the Victorian era. Females usually run the household and make decisions related to everyday life, but the husband and father is usually the undisputed head of the family. The author may even state this fact point-blank, so there is no misunderstanding on the part of readers—as Louisa May Alcott does in *Little Women:*

To outsiders, the five energetic women seemed to rule the house, and so they did in many things; but the quiet scholar, sitting among his books, was still the head of the family, the household conscience, anchor, and comforter: to him the busy, anxious women always turned in troublous times, finding him, in the truest sense of those sacred words, husband and father. (p. 294)

Males and females attend separate schools in *The Story of a Bad Boy,* and only male characters attend the university in *The Daisy Chain* and *Little Women.* Education may also stress different objectives for males and females. Yonge's heroine in *The Daisy Chain* completes her brother's school assignments but is not expected to understand mathematical concepts. Aldrich's hero wants training in manly arts, such as boxing, riding, and rowing. In contrast, drawing, writing, and music are desired accomplishments for the females in *Little Women,* piano lessons are sought by the oldest female Pepper, and writing is Rebecca's desire.

Insights about the children and families in these books are gained by viewing the problems that the heroes and heroines experience. Many of these problems involve attempts to abide by the period's standards of moral rectitude. Yonge's heroine strives to raise her family and help the poor. She works to keep the youngest baby an "unstained jewel" until the baby returns to her mother. She and her brother also face the problems associated with providing spiritual guidance to the poor. Many of Jo's problems in *Little Women* are related to controlling her "unfeminine" high energy and self-assertiveness. Jo looks to her pious mother for guidance in how to be "good":

Jo's only answer was to hold her mother close, and, in the silence which followed, the sincerest prayer she had ever prayed left her heart without words; for in that sad, yet happy hour, she had learned not only the bitterness of remorse and despair, but the sweetness of self-denial and self-control; and, led by her mother's hand, she had drawn nearer to the Friend who welcomes every child with a love stronger than that of any father, tenderer than that of any mother. (p. 103)

Rebecca of Sunnybrook Farm also confronts problems caused by the conflicts between her own high-spirited nature and adults' strict expectations about a young girl's behavior. She, too, experiences personal misgivings when her actions do not live up to her desire to be good. The advantages of these conflicts, however, are stated by Rebecca's English teacher at the academy: "Luckily she attends to her own development. . . . In a sense she is independent of everything and everybody; she follows her saint without being conscious of it."

The problems that Thomas Bailey Aldrich creates for his protagonist allow the "bad" boy to consider and strengthen his own moral code. Although he has several unhappy and even disastrous experiences, the boy does not dwell upon them, believing that they have caused him to become more manly and self-reliant.

Overcoming problems related to poverty and growing up without a father are major concerns of the Pepper children, but Margaret Sidney has their mother encourage them in this way: "You keep on a-tryin', and the Lord'll send some way; don't you go to botherin' your head about it now . . . it'll come when it's time." The family's financial problems are finally solved when a wealthy old gentleman invites them to share his home.

The Child and the Family, 1938–1960

The 1900s brought much change to the lives of American children. Many states passed child labor laws, John Dewey's influential theories encouraged a more child-centered educational philosophy, the quality and extent of public education improved, and religious training placed less emphasis on sinfulness and more emphasis on moral development and responsibility toward others. Children's literature reflected these changes, and children's book publishing expanded to meet the needs of an increasingly literate youthful population. Optimism was a keynote in the twentieth-century "Age of Progress," and, especially after World War II, "children's book editors saw a bright future for the children of this country and the world" (McElderry, 1974, p. 89).

This optimism is reflected in the views of the children and families depicted in American children's books of the late 1930s through the beginning of the 1960s. John Rowe Townsend's (1975) conclusions about depictions of family life in children's literature of the 1950s apply to earlier literature as well: Children live in stable communities, where most children are happy and secure, the older generations are wise and respected, and the generations follow one another into traditional social roles in an orderly way.

The following books, written by award-winning authors, characterize the social values, the stability of family life, and the types of personal relationships depicted in children's literature of this period: Elizabeth Enright's *Thimble Summer* (1938), Eleanor Estes's *The Moffats* (1941), Sydney Taylor's *All-of-a-Kind Family* (1951), and Madeleine L'Engle's *Meet the Austins* (1960). The families in these books live in different locations around the United States and range from lower-middle class to upper-middle class, but the values that they support are similar. The characters admire and emulate the traditional family model of bread-winning father, housewife mother, and their children, living together in one place for a number of years.

Family members have happy and secure relationships with one another, complemented by mutual respect, warmth, and humor. The actions of the Moffats express confidence and trust in the family unit. The children in *All-of-a-Kind Family* cannot imagine what it would be like not to have a family. In *Meet the Austins,* Vicky is pleased because her mother looks just the way that she believes a mother should look.

Religious values are suggested in these stories by Sunday School attendance, preparation for the sabbath, or prayers before meals. Dignity is stressed. The family in *Thimble Summer* brings an orphaned boy into its home on trust without checking his background. The parents in *All-of-a-Kind Family* tell their children to accept people and to not ask them about their personal lives. The Austin family feels empathy for others' problems, and the parents include their children in serious discussions.

Patriotism is strong in all of the books, and the law is respected. Education is considered important; children enjoy reading, go to school with the expectation that it will increase their understanding, and finish their homework before playing. Families prize even small collections of books. The work ethic is a powerful force in the lives of these families. Children talk about saving their money to buy a farm, a mother takes in sewing to keep the family together, and a father works long hours, saving for the day when he can make life better for his family. Children respect adult wisdom and authority; they obey rules, minding their teachers and complying with parental desires. Children also enjoy listening to their elders tell about their own experiences.

Unsurprisingly, given their secure lives and confident adherence to established social standards, the children in these books have few emotional problems. They usually feel good about themselves and other family members. Their actions suggest dependence upon the family for emotional stability, but independence in their daily experiences, as they move without fear around the neighborhood, city, or countryside.

The Child and the Family, 1969–2000

Researchers who have analyzed children's literature over time have identified the 1960s, 1970s, and 1980s as decades in which traditional social, family, and personal values appeared to be changing. Alma Cross Homze (1963) found that in the late 1950s, adult characters in children's books were becoming less authoritarian and critical in their relationships with children, while children were becoming more outspoken, independent, and critical of adults. John Rowe Townsend (1975) later concluded that children's literature of the 1960s suggested an erosion of adult authority and a widening of the generation gap. When Beverly Young (1985) compared female protagonists of the 1930s, the 1950s, and the 1970s, she concluded that the characters became increasingly protest oriented. Craig Werner and Frank Riga (1989) used religious questions developed by authors in the late 1900s to analyze changes in questions pertaining to religious matters in literature written in the 1800s. They found that nineteenth-century authors such as George MacDonald addressed questions such as "What must I do to enter the kingdom of God?" or "How should I pray?" In contrast, contemporary authors such as Cynthia Rylant and M. E. Kerr address questions such as "Is there a Kingdom of God?" or "Does it do any good to pray?" Werner and Riga conclude that the questions have shifted radically from the searchable to the searching because modern authors present partial answers, "not the full-blown declarations of faith that characterized earlier religious writings for children" (p. 2).

Binnie Tate Wilkin (1978) connects these trends in the children's literature of the 1960s and 1970s with changing "educational, social and political, and economic concerns" (p. 21), citing as examples the civil rights movements, protest marches, and assassinations of the period. Wilkin says:

Almost all levels of society were challenged to respond to the activism. Book publishers responded with new materials reflecting dominant concerns. Distress about children's reading problems, federal responses to urban unrest, the youth movements, new openness about sexuality, religious protest, etc. were reflected in children's books. (p. 21)

In 1981, polls quoted by John F. Stacks (1981) showed that about 20 percent of Americans still expressed belief in most of the traditional values of hard work, family loyalty, and sacrifice, while the majority of respondents embraced only some of those values, doubted that self-denial and moral rectitude were their own rewards, and held tolerant views about abortion, premarital sex, remaining single, and not having children. Still, Stacks concluded that people who believed in tradi-

tional values were becoming an increasingly vocal group that "could set to a significant degree the moral tone for the 1980s" (p. 18).

Statistics cited by Nancy Lee Cecil and Patricia L. Roberts (1998) to support their view of the changing American family show the rapid decline of the former typical family of two parents—a father who works outside the home and a mother who is a homemaker. They cite Census Bureau reports that indicate that 26 percent of the U.S. population consists of married couples with at least one child living at home. Single-parent households now make up 29 percent of the households. Of these households, 90 percent have women as the head of the family.

A William A. Galston article published in *The Family* (Mary E. Williams, 1998) discusses the changing influences of divorce on families. He states, "Since the 1960s, the number of children directly touched by divorce has jumped from 485,000 to one million a year. The percentage of children living in mother-only households has more than doubled, and about 40 percent of children have not seen their fathers during the past year" (p. 81).

Comparison of children's literature written between the 1930s and the early 1960s with children's literature written in the 1970s through the 1990s reveals both similarities and differences between the American families in the two periods. Many books still portray strong family ties and stress the importance of personal responsibility and human dignity, but the happy, stable unit of the earlier literature is often replaced by a family in turmoil as it adjusts to a new culture, faces the prospects of surviving without one or both parents, handles the disruption resulting from divorce, or deals with an extended family, exemplified by grandparents or a foster home. Later literature also suggests that many acceptable family units do not conform to the traditional American model.

While many children's books could be selected for this discussion, the following books contain some of the diverse attitudes toward family and children in the period from 1969 into the 1990s: Vera and Bill Cleaver's *Where the Lilies Bloom* (1969), Norma Klein's *Mom, the Wolf Man, and Me* (1972), Paula Fox's *The Moonlight Man* (1986), Ruth White's *Belle Prater's Boy* (1996), and Jack Gantos's *Joey Pigza Loses Control* (2000). While children in the literature of the 1940s and 1950s had few personal and emotional problems, children between 1969 and the 1990s may have much responsibility and may experience emotional problems as they try to survive. The strongest character in *Where the Lilies Bloom* attempts to hold the family together, but she discovers that she needs people outside her immediate family. The heroine of *Mom, the Wolf Man, and Me* fears that her life will change if her mother marries. The main character in *The Moonlight Man* must

ISSUE   What Is the Future of Children's Book Publishing and Literacy?

In an article edited by Diane Roback and Shannon Maughan,[1] several publishers and editors speculate about the future of children's book publishing. Many of these speculations provide issues that can be analyzed, researched, and discussed in children's literature courses. For example, the following quotes and concerns provide interesting discussion topics:

Stephen Roxburgh, president and publisher, Front Street Books, provides two issues that are of interest. First, he maintains that we are currently dealing with an industry that has changed from privately held businesses to publicly held businesses whose investors demand return on their money. He states, "The potential for profit and growth is enormous, hence, the headlong rush and ruthless tactics" (p. 152). Second, he believes that the old publishing model based on serving libraries has been replaced by the media industry model that sells entertainment to the masses. He states, "Those who publish books supported primarily by the institutions (hardcover fiction, nonfiction, poetry, 'high-end' picture books) will find themselves under siege to justify their existence" (p. 152).

Tracy Tang, vice president and publisher, Puffin Books, discusses the results of the market-driven type of publishing that may cause publishers to lose sight of more traditional, book-based publishing. She states, "I'm speaking optimistically when I say I hope that there will be a return to publishing books for the strength of their story and their illustrations" (p. 153). Tang's second issue focuses on the quality of the huge numbers of paperbacks for middle-grade and young adult series. She states, "A lot of people are trying to clone Goosebumps and the Baby-sitters Club. I think it's safe to say that most of these series aren't working as well as publishers hoped. I'm not sure that there will ever be fewer new series being published, but hopefully we'll see more high-quality, author-based series" (p. 153).

Jasan Higgins, vice president and director of marketing of children's books, William Morrow, discusses the impact on purchasing power for both public and school libraries. She emphasizes the controversy between book and technology purchases as the libraries try to stretch dollars to meet both demands.

David Ahlender, vice president and editorial director, Children's Book-of-the-Month Club, argues for the future of books and literacy. He believes that "It really does come down to a book and a child. Parents today cannot take literacy for granted the way they used to; they need to provide books in the home if they want their children to be literate. Our industry has a tremendous cultural relevance and a bright future. I hope that publishers will take that as a cause and a mission, because that's what really matters" (p. 153).

There are differences of opinion provided among these comments by publishers. Their comments, however, provide interesting topics for discussion and debate. You may consider questions such as the following: What is the impact on children's literature of each of these positions? How does the newer impact of a market-driven economy influence the types of books that will be published? How can the public ensure that there will be high-quality books for children? What will happen to children's literacy if there is a reduction in higher quality books? What do you believe will be the future outcome of the debate between book purchases and technology?

The authors of *Media and Literacy*[2] speculate about the future of technology and literacy: "As new interlocking technologies shape our future, it is important to explore the possibilities and the problems. The power of today's information, communications, and networking media requires special attention. But it would be foolish to provide too warm a welcome without more serious thought. Will developing multimedia technology provide a transforming vision and a new awareness? Possibly. But developments have been moving so fast that few have taken the time to consider where we are going or where we might end up" (pp. 3–4).

---

[1]Roback, Diane, and Shannon Maughan, eds. "Fall 1996 Children's Books: The Road Ahead." *Publishers Weekly* 243 (July 22, 1996): 151–153.

[2]Adams, Dennis, and Mary Hamm. *Media and Literacy,* Second edition. Springfield, Ill.: Charles C. Thomas, 2000.

accept her father and his behavior as well as her parents' divorce. The main characters in *Belle Prater's Boy* learn how to overcome the inner hurt caused by the suicide of a parent and the disappearance of another parent. The main character in *Joey Pigza Loses Control* has a hyperactive disorder, divorced parents, and an alcoholic father.

Characters in the literature of this period may express concern about equal opportunities and question respect for the law, education, and adult authority. In *Mom, the Wolf Man, and Me,* the mother is a successful photographer and allows the daughter to accompany her on women's rights and peace marches.

The strongest story related to the dignity of human beings and acceptance of responsibility is Vera and Bill Cleaver's *Where the Lilies Bloom,* which is about the proud, independent mountain people who earn their livings through wildcrafting (the gathering of wild plants for human use). Before the father dies, he asks his daughter to keep the family together without accepting charity and to instill in the children pride in having the name Luther. *Belle Prater's Boy* is also a strong story about the dignity of human beings as the children discover the truth in Grandpa's belief that it is what is in the heart that counts.

An opposite condition is found in *The Moonlight Man.* The father is an alcoholic, and when his daughter says, "See you," as she leaves him, he whispers, "Not if I see you first" (p. 179). The father in *Joey Pigza Loses Control* is an alcoholic who needs help but refuses to accept assistance. The happy ending occurs when Joey returns home with his mother and realizes that he is not like his father. Clearly, children's literature now presents a greater range and more realistic representations of family diversity.

Through the Eyes of a TEACHER

Monica Edinger
Fourth-Grade Teacher
Dalton School
New York, New York

Literature Strategy Plan—
Teaching Classic Children's Books:
The Many Faces of Alice in Wonderland

Should children read classic literature like Robert Louis Stevenson's *Treasure Island* or Frank Baum's *Wizard of Oz*? Or are those books, with their sophisticated, sometimes archaic language and references to cultural practices and mores that have disappeared, irrelevant to today's children?

Fourth-grade teacher Monica Edinger believes children should be exposed to classic stories. "We need to perpetuate our literary heritage. There's a reason why these books have endured for generations." But more important than perpetuating our literary heritage is Monica's belief that books, like *Alice in Wonderland,* should be read for enjoyment. Monica loves Alice's story. "*Alice in Wonderland* was my favorite book as a child. My father first read it aloud to me, then I read it again and again on my own. I loved the funny, meandering stories, the eccentric collection of characters, and the sophisticated word play. This fascination with the book stayed with me as an adult.

"A summer NEH Fellowship at Princeton University provided the opportunity to study the different illustrated versions of the book. It's like *Hamlet* for actors—many of the great illustrators have attempted it. Studying the different ways illustrators have interpreted the book seemed like an engaging, thought-provoking literature unit. The book really lends itself to supporting children's responses through many different modalities: talk, art, writing, drama, and technology."

Building Students' Background Knowledge

Before beginning the unit, Monica usually sets up an "Alice" center in her classroom. This consists of many different illustrated versions of the book as well as photographs, artifacts, and printed materials on Lewis Carroll and the Victorian period. "I collect everything I can find about Lewis Carroll and his books. People often make references to Alice in puns, newspaper headlines, advertisements, and cartoons. Or they make comparisons to characters. I have copies of letters Carroll wrote to Alice and other children as well as articles written about the books. Caldecott award-winning author Faith Ringgold created an Alice story quilt and I have a picture of that. All this is available to students during our reading time." Monica also shows them videos of the BBC series *1900 House,* in which a modern-day family reenacts what daily life was like in Victorian England. "Although *Alice* was published in the mid-nineteenth century, the series does give the children a feel for the cultural context of the book," she says.

She then begins by sharing her own experiences with the story, asking for students to share what they know about the book. Some have seen the Disney film or an adapted stage version but few have actually read it. Thus, she knows she will need to carefully frame the unit so children understand the language, story structure, and cultural context. The first entry in their reading journal is usually a short description of what they know about the book and their past experiences with it.

Focused Reading and Writing

Monica feels that *Alice in Wonderland* should be read aloud by an adult. "The vocabulary is difficult and there are many cultural references that need to be explained as the reading progresses," she states. "Also, much of the book is dialogue. It's more enjoyable for students if an experienced reader with knowledge of phrasing and the ability to project different voices reads it. Students can then concentrate on enjoying and comprehending the story rather than worrying about the mechanics of decoding." She reads from Martin Gardner's annotated *Alice* (Meridian, 1960), which includes background on things like the poems from Carroll's era that he parodies, the mathematical puzzles he uses, word plays, and other aspects of the book.

During the read-aloud time children listen to or follow along in one of the illustrated versions they have selected. As Monica reads, she stops to examine the illustrations, considering why different artists made the choices they made in terms of style or media as well as why they chose to illustrate particular parts of the book. She also interrupts the reading to discuss the jokes, puzzles, unusual vocabulary, or cultural references the children might not understand. How often they stop depends on the group's choice. Some classes like waiting until the end of the chapter to discuss; others prefer stopping when the references occur in the story. "It's tricky to balance the talk with the reading," says Monica. "You don't want to interrupt the flow of the story but you also want them to understand it. So I'm constantly monitoring this."

Once the day's chapter has been read, the group studies the different ways illustrators decided to portray that chapter's characters and events by looking at each other's books. They also discuss the story itself, including issues like how it is like a fairy tale, how it is like "Cinderella" (their previous literature unit), their response to particular characters, and what they think might happen next. Monica creates class charts of what they discuss so that she has a permanent record of the group's ideas about the book.

At the end of each week the children are asked to comment on the book in their reading journal. "Sometimes I have them pick an illustration or character they like and write an explanation of why they like it. At other times the children or I will generate questions we want to consider. Typical questions might be 'How is Alice like Dorothy in *The Wizard of Oz*?' or 'Why do some illustrators show Alice looking like a little girl while others portray her as much more adult looking?'"

After Monica finishes reading the book aloud, she invites her students to create their own illustrations for the story, encouraging them to think carefully about the scenes they wish to portray and how they can portray them creatively. Some do a series of illustrations while others create one large poster that incorporates many elements from the book. Those who don't feel comfortable drawing might use collage or computer drawing programs. Some children create stories placing Alice in modern contexts like a New York street (she falls down a manhole to reach Wonderland).

In 2001, the class decided to create a Victorian toy theater production of the story. Teams of children each wrote adaptations of the book's chapters; created characters, props, and scenery; practiced their plays; and performed them for each other. They then videotaped their plays and posted them on student-made web pages, which included a Quicktime movie of the theater production, essays by the students, and a sampling of their scenery and characters.

Technology Resources

Visit Ms. Edinger's classroom's Alice site at www.dalton.org/ms/alice/content.html or link to it from our Companion Website at www.prenhall.com/norton

The last day of the study features a Mad Hatter tea party. "We transform the classroom into the Mad Hatter's garden by moving all the desks into a long line. The children dress up in fancy hats or as Wonderland characters and bring scones, biscuits, and other food suitable for tea. We share all the projects we've created," says Monica. "That's also when I show them the Disney movie. It's fun to see what they notice in the movie after they've spent so much time in Lewis's version of Wonderland."

Evaluation

All Monica's students achieve beyond minimum expectations in this unit. Whether or not they're comprehending is never an issue. The various activities demonstrate that the children not only enjoy the book but also are able to interpret it in quite sophisticated ways. She uses their journal responses in particular as evidence that they understand the story and can construct a response to it that shows evidence of critical thinking. "Some students are rather literal in their interpretations, while others write very detailed responses that show evidence of critical thinking." She also evaluates their ability to write more formal responses later in the year after her *Wizard of Oz* unit. At that point each child writes a structured

Alice in Wonderland by Lewis Carroll, is a great story. I've read it many times and don't even think of getting bored of it! After Ms. Edinger read the book to us, we studied the illustrators. Some of them like: John Tenniel, Peter Newell, Disney, and many more. I liked Abelardo Morrel a lot. He makes really nice illustrations with his photos.

I loved making the Alice toy theatre. We were all assigned a chapter from Alice in Wonderland in pairs. We had to adapt the dialog from the book and make the scenes and characters.

I love Alice and the things we did with it. It's a great story!

A short multimedia essay on Alice by Lily and Rachel.

essay comparing the characters of Alice and Dorothy. Monica evaluates their ability to synthesize their understandings of each character along with assessing traditional writing competencies like sentence structure and complexity, organization, ability to develop a thesis, and the like.

"I am continually amazed by my students' responses to the Alice unit. While I anticipated positive responses from my higher level readers, it was my weaker readers who surprised me. These literal thinkers who might have been expected to find the story difficult to follow are often the most enthusiastic of all. My reading it aloud and providing context as well as the many illustrated versions makes it pleasurable—and accessible—for all."

 For more ideas on adapting Monica Edinger's lesson to meet the needs of older or younger readers, please visit Chapter 2 on our Companion Website at www.prenhall.com/norton

Suggested Activities

 For more suggested activities for understanding the history of children's literature, visit our Companion Website at www.prenhall.com/norton

- Investigate the life and contributions of William Caxton. What circumstances led to his opening a printing business in 1476? Why were *Reynart the Foxe*, *The Book of the Subtyle Historyes and Fables of Aesop*, and *Le Morte d'Arthur* considered such important contributions to children's literature?

- Choose a tale published by Charles Perrault in his *Tales of Mother Goose*, such as "Cinderella," "Sleeping Beauty," "Puss in Boots," "Little Red Riding Hood," "Blue Beard," or "Little Thumb." Compare the language and style of Perrault's early edition with the language and style in a twentieth-century version of the same tale. What differences did you find? Why do you believe that the changes were made?

- Choose one of the following great nineteenth-century English artists who had an impact on children's illustrations: Kate Greenaway, Walter Crane, or Randolph Caldecott. Read biographical information and look at examples of their illustrations. Share your information and reactions with your literature class.

- Read Mark Twain's *The Adventures of Tom Sawyer* or *The Adventures of Huckleberry Finn*. Consider the controversy about racism in Twain's work. Compare Mark Twain's writing for the nineteenth century with writing for the twentieth century.

3 EVALUATING AND SELECTING LITERATURE FOR CHILDREN

Illustration from Golem by David Wisniewski. Copyright © 1996 by David Wisniewski. Reprinted by permission of Clarion books/Houghton Mifflin Company. All rights reserved.

ecause thousands of books have been published for children, selecting books appropriate to the needs of children can be difficult. Teachers and librarians, who share books with groups of children as well as with individual children, should select books that provide balance in a school or public library. The objectives of literature programs also affect educators' selections of children's books.

A literature program should have five objectives. First, a literature program should help students realize that literature is for entertainment and can be enjoyed throughout their lives. Literature should cater to children's interests as well as create interests in new topics. Consequently, educators must know these interests and understand ways to stimulate new ones.

Second, a literature program should acquaint children with their literary heritage. To accomplish this, literature should foster the preservation of knowledge and allow its transmission to future generations. Therefore, educators must be familiar with fine literature from the past and must share it with children.

Third, a literature program should help students understand the formal elements of literature and lead them to prefer the best that our literature has to offer. Children need to hear and read fine literature and to appreciate authors who not only have something to say but also say it extremely well. Educators must be able to identify the best books in literature and share these books with children.

Fourth, a literature program should help children grow up understanding themselves and the rest of humanity. Children who identify with literary characters confronting and overcoming problems like their own learn ways to cope with their own problems. Educators should provide literature that introduces children to people from other times and nations and that encourages children to see both themselves and their world in a new perspective.

Fifth, a literature program should help children evaluate what they read. Literature programs should extend children's appreciation of literature and their imaginations. Therefore, educators should help students learn how to compare, question, and evaluate the books that they read.

Rosenblatt (1991) adds an important sixth objective, encouraging "readers to pay attention to their own literary experiences as the basis for self-understanding or for comparison with others' evocations. This implies a new, collaborative relationship between teacher and student. Emphasis on the reader need not exclude application of various approaches, literary and social, to the process of critical interpretation and evaluation" (p. 61). Children need many opportunities to respond to literature.

If children are to gain enjoyment, knowledge of their heritage, recognition and appreciation of good literature, and understanding of themselves and others, they must explore balanced selections of literature. A literature program should include classics and contemporary stories, fanciful stories as well as realistic ones, prose as well as poetry, biographies, and books containing factual information. To provide this balance, educators must know about many kinds of literature. Alan Purves (1991) identifies basic groups of items usually found in literature programs: literary works, background information, literary terminology and theory, and cultural information. He states that some curricula also include the responses of the readers themselves.

This text provides information about numerous types of books written for children. This chapter looks at standards for evaluating books written for children. It presents and discusses the literary elements of plot, characterization, setting, theme, style, and point of view. It also discusses children's literature interests, characteristics of literature found in books chosen by children, and procedures to help children evaluate literature.

Standards for Evaluating Books and Literary Criticism

According to Jean Karl (1987), in true literature, "there are ideas that go beyond the plot of a novel or picture-book story or the basic theme of a nonfiction book, but they are presented subtly and gently; good books do not preach; their ideas are wound into the substance of the book and are clearly a part of the life of the book itself" (p. 507). Karl maintains that in contrast, mediocre books overemphasize their messages or they oversimplify or distort life; mediocre books contain visions that are too obvious and can be put aside too easily. If literature is to help develop children's potential, merit rather than mediocrity must be part of children's experiences with literature. Both children and adults need opportunities to evaluate literature. They also need supporting context to help them make accurate judgments about quality.

Literary critic Anita Silvey (1993) provides both a useful list for the qualities of a reviewer and questions for the reviewer to consider. She first identifies the characteristics of fine reviewers and fine reviews. These include a sense of children and how they will respond to the book as well as an evaluation that, if the book is good, will make readers want to read the book. The review should also evaluate the literary capabilities of the author and also be written in an enjoyable style. The reviewer needs a sense of the history of the genre and must be able to make comparisons with past books of the author or illustrator. This sense of genre also requires knowledge of contemporary adult literature, art, and film so that the reviewer is able to place the book in the wider context of adult literature and art. The review should also include a balance between a discussion of plot and critical commentary. A sense of audience for the review also requires that the

reviewer understand what the audience knows about books. Finally, Silvey recommends that a reviewer have a sense of humor, especially when evaluating books that are themselves humorous.

Silvey's (1993) list of questions that the reviewer should consider is divided according to literary questions (How effective is the development of the various literary elements?), artistic questions (How effective are the illustrations and the illustrator's techniques?), pragmatic questions (How accurate and logical is the material?), philosophical questions (Will the book enrich a reader's life?), and personal questions (Does the book appeal to me?).

Northrop Frye, Sheridan Baker, and George Perkins (1985) identify five focuses of all literary criticism, two or more of which are usually emphasized in an evaluation of a literary text:

(1) The work in isolation, with primary focus on its form, as opposed to its content; (2) its relationship to its own time and place, including the writer; the social, economic, and intellectual milieu surrounding it; the method of its printing or other dissemination; and the assumptions of the audience that first received it; (3) its relationship to literary and social history before its time, as it repeats, extends, or departs from the traditions that preceded it; (4) its relationship to the future, as represented by those works and events that come after it, as it forms a part of the large body of literature, influencing the reading, writing, and thinking of later generations; (5) its relationship to some eternal concept of being, absolute standards of art, or immutable truths of existence. (p. 130)

The relative importance of each of the preceding areas to a particular critic depends on the critic's degree of concern with the work itself, the author, the subject matter, and the audience.

Book reviews and longer critical analyses of books in the major literature journals are valuable sources for librarians, teachers, parents, and other students of children's literature. As might be expected from the five focuses of Frye, Baker, and Perkins, reviews emphasize different aspects of evaluation and criticism. Phyllis K. Kennemer (1984) identified three categories of book reviews and longer book analyses: (1) descriptive, (2) analytical, and (3) sociological. Descriptive reviews report factual information about the story and illustrations of a book. Analytical reviews discuss, compare, and evaluate literary elements (plot, characterization, setting, theme, style, and point of view), the illustrations, and relationships with other books. Sociological reviews emphasize the social context of a book, concerning themselves with characterizations of particular social groups, distinguishable ethnic characteristics, moral values, possible controversy, and potential popularity.

Although a review may contain all three types of information, Kennemer concludes that the major sources of information on children's literature emphasize one type of evaluation. For example, reviews in the *Bulletin of the Center for Children's Books* tend to be descriptive, but they also mention literary elements. Reviews in *Booklist, The Horn Book, Kirkus Reviews,* and *The School Library Journal* chiefly analyze literary elements. *The School Library Journal* also places great emphasis on sociological analysis.

Selection criteria and reviews in specific journals also emphasize the particular content and viewpoints of the group that publishes the journal. For example, each year the Book Review Subcommittee of the National Council for the Social Studies—Children's Book Council Joint Committee publishes in *Social Education* their recommended list of Notable Children's Trade Books in the Field of Social Studies (1992). The criteria for books selected in this bibliography, for children in grades K–8, "emphasize human relations; represent a diversity of groups and are sensitive to a broad range of cultural experiences; present an original theme or a fresh slant on a traditional topic; are easily readable and of high literary quality; and have a pleasing format and, when appropriate, illustrations that enrich the text" (p. 253).

The reviews accompanying the books in *Social Education* (1992) emphasize human relationships and social studies issues. For example, the review for Milton Meltzer's *Thomas Jefferson: The Revolutionary Aristocrat* states:

This biography details the complex and productive life of the third U.S. president and considers the contradictions between his words and actions on issues such as slavery, freedom of the press, and the limits of presidential power. The author explains his own efforts to weigh evidence, shape information, and interpret Jefferson's life. (p. 254)

Likewise, standards for evaluating science trade books have specific evaluation criteria as recommended by science professionals. Kathleen S. Johnston (1991) states that accuracy in facts presented and in depictions of scientific methods is of primary consideration. In addition, the criteria include clarity of purpose, organization, and accuracy in presenting the process of science; scope and completeness of the subject; quality of the illustrations and graphic design; and instructional value.

Reading and discussing excellent books as well as analyzing book reviews and literary criticism can increase one's ability to recognize and recommend excellent literature for children. Those of us who work with students of children's literature are rewarded when for the first time people see literature with a new awareness, discover the techniques that an author uses to create a believable plot or memorable characters, and discover that they can provide rationales for why a book is excellent, mediocre, or poor. Ideally, reading and discussing excellent literature can help each student of children's literature become a worthy critic, what Mary Kingsbury (1984) defines as one "who offers us new perspectives on a text, who sees more in it than we saw, who motivates us to return to it for another reading" (p. 17).

 Technology Resources

You can use the database to print a list of Carnegie award winners. Simply search under Awards, type in "Crn" (award name abbreviations are listed in the Field information), click "Retain" and print your completed list.

New perspectives may be of special concern when evaluating books written by authors from other countries. Jeffrey Garrett (1992/1993), a member of the Hans Christian Andersen Award Committee, makes a strong case for including the works of the best international authors and illustrators. Garrett states, "We have much to gain by reading and sharing the works of international authors and illustrators. Let's begin by learning who other cultures regard as their great writers, and then approach them with the respect they deserve. The experience may be eye-opening" (p. 314).

In addition to books that are chosen for various literary awards such as the Newbery, the Carnegie, and the Hans Christian Andersen Award, students of children's literature may consider and discuss the merits of books identified by Karen Breen, Ellen Fader, Kathleen Odean, and Zena Sutherland (2000) on their list of the one hundred books that they believe were the most significant books for children and young adults in terms of shaping the twentieth century. When citing their criteria for these books, they state: "We decided that our list should include books with literary and artistic merit, as well as books that are perennially popular with young readers, books that have blazed new trails, and books that have exerted a lasting influence on the world of children's book publishing" (p. 50).

Of the one hundred books on the list, twenty-three were selected unanimously by the six experts on the first round of balloting. These twenty-three are listed in Chart 3.1. As you may have noticed when you read this list, the books range from picture storybooks for young children to novels for older readers. The books also include all of the various genres of literature that are discussed in this textbook. The list provides an interesting discussion for literary elements. Why are these particular books included on such a distinguished list?

Alleen Pace Nilsen and Kenneth L. Donelson (2001) warn that adults add another element when evaluating literature: "We should caution, however, that books are selected as 'the best' on the basis of many different criteria, and one person's best is not necessarily yours or that of the young people with whom you work. We hope that you will read many books, so that you can recommend them not because you saw them on a list, but because you enjoyed them and believe they will appeal to a particular student" (p. 11).

CHART 3.1   Twenty-three significant children's books that shaped the twentieth century

Author	Book Title
Natalie Babbitt	*Tuck Everlasting*
Ludwig Bemelmans	*Madeline*
Judy Blume	*Are You There God? It's Me, Margaret*
Margaret Wise Brown	*Goodnight Moon*
Robert Cormier	*The Chocolate War*
Louise Fitzhugh	*Harriet the Spy*
Anne Frank	*Anne Frank: The Diary of a Young Girl*
Russell Freedman	*Lincoln: A Photobiography*
Jean Craighead George	*Julie of the Wolves*
Ezra Jack Keats	*The Snowy Day*
E. L. Konigsburg	*From the Mixed-Up Files of Mrs. Basil E. Frankweiler*
Madeleine L'Engle	*A Wrinkle in Time*
C. S. Lewis	*The Lion, the Witch and the Wardrobe*
Arnold Lobel	*Frog and Toad Are Friends*
Patricia MacLachlan	*Sarah, Plain and Tall*
A. A. Milne	*Winnie-the-Pooh*
Scott O'Dell	*Island of the Blue Dolphins*
Katherine Paterson	*Bridge to Terabithia*
Beatrix Potter	*The Tale of Peter Rabbit*
Maurice Sendak	*Where the Wild Things Are*
Dr. Seuss	*The Cat in the Hat*
E. B. White	*Charlotte's Web*
Laura Ingalls Wilder	*Little House in the Big Woods*

Literary Elements

The focus of this chapter is literary elements. This section looks at the ways in which authors of children's books use plot, characterization, setting, theme, style, and point of view to create memorable stories.

Plot

Plot is important in stories, whether the stories reflect the oral storytelling style of Chaucer's *The Canterbury Tales* or the complex interactions in a mystery. When asked to tell about a favorite story, children usually recount the plot, or plan of action. Children want a book to have a good plot: enough action, excitement, suspense, and conflict to develop interest. A good plot also allows children to become involved in the action, feel the conflict developing, recognize the climax when it occurs, and respond to a satisfactory ending. Children's expectations and enjoyment of conflict vary according to their ages. Young children are satisfied with simple plots that deal with everyday happenings, but as children mature, they expect and enjoy more complex plots.

Following the plot of a story is like following a path winding through it; the action develops naturally. If the plot is well developed, a book will be difficult to put down unfinished; if the plot is not well developed, the book will not sustain interest or will be so prematurely predictable that the story ends long before it should. The author's development of action should help children enjoy the story.

Developing the Order of Events. Readers expect a story to have a good beginning, one that introduces the action and characters in an enticing way; a good middle section, one that develops the conflict; a recognizable climax; and an appropriate ending. If any element is missing, children consider a book unsatisfactory and a waste of time. Authors can choose from any of several approaches for presenting the events in a credible plot. In children's literature, events usually happen in chronological order. The author reveals the plot by presenting the first happening, followed by the second happening, and so forth, until the story is completed. Illustrations reinforce the chronological order in picture storybooks for younger children.

Very strong and obvious chronological order is found in cumulative folktales. Actions and characters are related to each other in sequential order, and each is mentioned again when new action or a new character is introduced. Children who enjoy the cumulative style of the nursery rhyme "The House That Jack Built" also enjoy a similar cumulative rhythm in Verna Aardema's *Bringing the Rain to Kapiti Plain: A Nandi Tale.* Cumulative, sequential action may also be developed in reverse, from last event to first, as in Verna Aardema's *Why Mosquitoes Buzz in People's Ears.*

Authors of biographies frequently use chronological life events to develop plot. Jean Fritz, for example, traces the life of a famous president and constitutional leader in *The Great Little Madison.* In *Lincoln: A Photobiography,* Russell Freedman begins with Lincoln's childhood and continues through his life as president. In *The Wright Brothers: How They Invented the Airplane,* Freedman follows the lives of the Wright brothers and emphasizes major changes in aeronautics, and in *Eleanor Roosevelt: A Life of Discovery,* Freedman follows the life of one of the great women in American history. Dates in these texts help readers follow the chronological order.

The events in a story also may follow the maturing process of the main character. In *The Borning Room,* Paul Fleischman begins with the birth of the heroine in a borning room on a farm in Ohio in 1851. The plot then develops according to major events that occurred in the borning room as the family uses the special room at times of births and deaths. The book concludes as the heroine, after years of a rewarding life, is herself waiting in the borning room for her probable death.

Books written for older readers sometimes use flashbacks in addition to chronological order. At the point when readers have many questions about a character's background or wonder why a character is acting in a certain

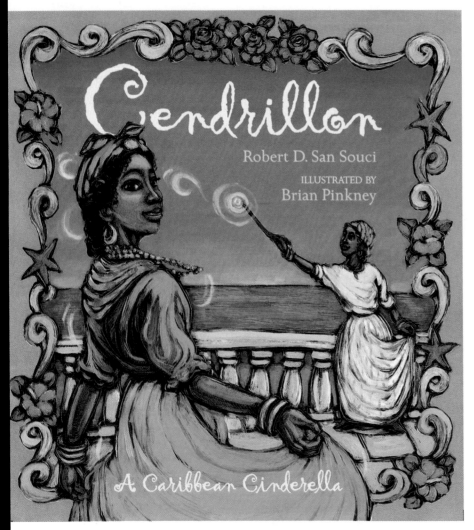

The story of Cinderella and its many variations present a person-against-person conflict. From Cendrillon: A Caribbean Cinderella by Robert D. San Souci. Text copyright © 1998 by Robert D. San Souci. Illustrations copyright © 1998 by Brian Pinkney. Reprinted by permission of Simon & Schuster Books for Young Readers.

dren usually develop only one kind of conflict, but many of the stories for older children use several conflicting situations.

Person Against Person. One person-against-person conflict that young children enjoy is the tale of that famous bunny, Peter Rabbit, by Beatrix Potter. In this story, Peter's disobedience and greed quickly bring him into conflict with the owner of the garden, Mr. McGregor, who has sworn to put Peter into a pie. Excitement and suspense develop as Peter and Mr. McGregor proceed through a series of life-and-death encounters. Mr. McGregor chases Peter with a rake, Peter becomes tangled in a gooseberry net, and Mr. McGregor tries to trap Peter inside a sieve. Knowledge of Peter's possible fate increases the suspense of these adventures. The excitement intensifies each time Peter narrowly misses being caught, and young readers' relief is great when Peter escapes for good. Children also sympathize with Peter when his disobedience results in a stomachache and a dose of chamomile tea.

Conflicts between animals and humans, or animals and animals, or humans and humans are common in children's literature, including many popular folktales. Both Little Red Riding Hood and the three little pigs confront a wicked wolf. Cinderella and Sleeping Beauty are among the fairytale heroines mistreated by stepmothers, and Hansel and Gretel are imprisoned by a witch.

A humorous person-against-person conflict provides the story line in Beverly Cleary's *Ramona and Her Father.* Seven-year-old Ramona's life changes drastically when her father loses his job and her mother must work full time. Ramona's new time with her father is not so enjoyable as she had hoped that it would be, however. Her father becomes tense and irritable as his period of unemployment lengthens. Ramona and her father survive their experience, and by the end of the story, they have returned to their normal, warm relationship.

Katherine Paterson develops a more complex person-against-person conflict for older children in *Jacob Have I Loved.* In this story, one twin believes that she is like the despised Esau in the Old Testament, while her sister is the adored favorite of the family. The unhappy heroine's descriptions of her early experiences with her sister, her growing independence as she works with her father, and her final discovery that she, not her

way, the author interrupts the order of the story and reveals information about a previous time or experience. For example, memories of a beloved aunt allow readers to understand the character and the conflict in Cynthia Rylant's *Missing May.* The memories of twelve-year-old Summer allow readers to understand the grief following the aunt's death and to follow Summer and her uncle as they try to overcome the grief and begin a new life for themselves. Without the memories, readers would not understand May's character.

Developing Conflict. Excitement in a story occurs when the main characters experience a struggle or overcome conflict. Conflict is the usual source of plots in literature. According to Rebecca J. Lukens (1999), children's literature contains four kinds of conflict: (1) person against person, (2) person against society, (3) person against nature, and (4) person against self. Plots written for younger chil-

The 1998 Newbery winner, Karen Hesse's Out of the Dust, is the story of 14-year-old Billie Jo's pain, forgiveness, and growth after the accidental death of her mother in Depression-era Oklahoma. (Out of the Dust, by Karen Hesse. Copyright © 1997. New York, Scholastic Press. Reprinted by permission of Scholastic, Inc.)

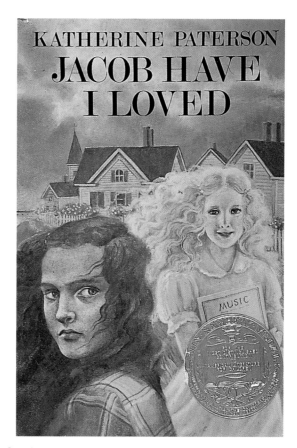

Complex person-against-person conflict develops between twin sisters in Jacob Have I Loved by Katherine Paterson. (Jacket by Kinoko Craft, Thomas Y. Crowell Co. Copyright © 1980 by Katherine Paterson.)

sister, is the strong twin create an engrossing plot and memorable characters.

Person Against Society. Conflicts also develop when the main character's actions, desires, or values differ from those of the surrounding society. This society may consist of groups of children who cannot tolerate children who are different from themselves. In Brock Cole's *The Goats,* a boy and a girl who are considered social outcasts by their peers at camp are stripped of their clothing and marooned on a deserted island. The author reveals the social attitudes of this camp when girls are classified as queens, princesses, dogs, and real dogs. The girl on the island is considered a real dog. Cole reveals the feelings of the children through their ordeal when he uses terms such as *they* and *them* to identify the society. When the girl wants the boy to leave her, his actions, thoughts, and dialogue reveal the strength of his dislike for the society that placed him in this isolation: " 'I'm afraid. Maybe you'd better go without me.' 'No,' he said. He didn't try to explain. He knew he was afraid to leave her alone, but even more

important, it wouldn't be good enough. He wanted them both to disappear. To disappear completely'' (p. 16).

Children's books often portray person-against-society conflicts that result from being different from the majority in terms of race, religion, or physical characteristics. Gary Paulsen's *Nightjohn* develops the brutality of a society that mistreats slaves. Life for twelve-year-old Sarney becomes even more miserable when Nightjohn secretly teaches her how to read and both of them are punished for this action. Judy Blume's *Blubber* shows the cruelty to which a fat child is subjected by her peers. For the conflict between person and society in such books to be believable, the social setting and its values must be presented in accurate detail.

Numerous survival stories set in wartime develop person-against-society conflicts. In Uri Orlev's *The Island on Bird Street,* the conflict is between a Jewish boy and the society that forces him to live in loneliness and starvation rather than surrender. Throughout the story, Orlev describes the boy's fear and the society that causes him to feel and respond in this way. For example, in the following quote, notice how Orlev describes the actions of the society and the boy's responses to that society when a group of Jewish people are found living in a hidden bunker:

> Its inhabitants began to come out. It took a long while for the last of them to emerge. The Germans and the policemen kept shouting and footsteps kept crossing the ruins from the cellar to the front gate. Now and then someone stumbled. . . . Somebody fell once or maybe twice. A shot rang out. Nobody screamed, though. Even the children had stopped crying. The last footsteps left the building. I heard voices in the street and an order to line up in threes. The same as had been given us. Then they were marched away. A few more shots. Finally, the car started up and drove away. . . . It was strange to think that all those people had been hiding with me in one house without us even knowing about each other. . . . They'd never take me away like that. (p. 81)

Jewish characters also experience person-against-society conflicts in refugee situations. In Miriam Bat-Ami's *Two Suns in the Sky,* the author develops the anti-Semitic attitudes of various people in the town. A teenage girl defies her father, visits the camp, and develops a friendship with Adam, a Yugoslavian Jew who is living in the camp after he escapes the Nazis.

Person Against Nature. Nature—not society or another person—is the antagonist in many memorable books for older children. When the author thoroughly describes the natural environment, readers vicariously travel into a world ruled by nature's harsh laws of survival. This is the case in Jean Craighead George's *Julie of the Wolves.* Miyax, a thirteen-year-old Eskimo girl also called by the English name Julie, is lost and without food on the North Slope of Alaska. She is introduced lying on her stomach, peering at a pack of wolves. The wolves are not her enemy, however. Her adversary is the vast cold tundra that stretches for hundreds of miles without human presence, a land so harsh that no berry bushes point to the south, no birds fly overhead so that she can follow, and continuous summer daylight blots out the North Star that might guide her home:

> No roads cross it; ponds and lakes freckle its immensity. Winds scream across it, and the view in every direction is exactly the same. Somewhere in this cosmos was Miyax; and the very life in her body, its spark and warmth, depended upon these wolves for survival. And she was not so sure they would help. (p. 6)

The constant wind; the empty sky; and the cold, deserted earth are ever present as Miyax crosses the Arctic searching for food, protecting herself from the elements, and making friends with the wolves, who bring her food. The author encourages readers to visualize the power and beauty of this harsh landscape and to share the girl's sorrow over human destruction of this land, its animals, and the Eskimo way of life.

Another book that pits a young person against the elements of nature is Armstrong Sperry's *Call It Courage.*

The hero's conflict with nature begins when the crashing, stormy sea—"a monster livid and hungry"—capsizes Mafatu's canoe during a hurricane:

> Higher and higher it rose, until it seemed that it must scrape at the low-hanging clouds. Its crest heaved over with a vast sigh. The boy saw it coming. He tried to cry out. No sound issued from his throat. Suddenly the wave was upon him. Down it crashed. Chaos! Mafatu felt the paddle torn from his hands. Thunder in his ears. Water strangled him. Terror in his soul. (p. 24)

The preceding quote makes clear that there are two adversaries in the story: The hero is in conflict with nature and also in conflict with himself. The two adversaries are interwoven in the plot as Mafatu sails away from his island in order to prove that he is not a coward. Each time that the boy wins a victory over nature, he also comes closer to his main goal, victory over his own fear. Without victory over fear, the boy cannot be called by his rightful name Mafatu, "Stout Heart," nor can he have the respect of his father, his Polynesian people, and himself. In *A Girl Named Disaster,* Nancy Farmer develops a survival story set in Mozambique and Zimbabwe. As the heroine struggles to escape starvation on her lonely journey, she discovers that the spirits of her ancestors help both her physical and emotional survival.

You may compare Farmer's story of survival with Anton Quintana's *The Baboon King* set in the African land of the Kikuyu and the Masai. Quintana also develops the need for both physical and emotional survival after a young man is banished by his people. The author describes not only the physical geography of the landscape but also the predators that might attack a lone hunter. The need for emotional survival is developed as the young man joins a baboon troop in order to regain the companionship that he lost.

Authors who write strong person-against-nature conflicts use many of the techniques shown in the quotes by George and Sperry. Personification gives human actions to nature, vivid descriptions show that characters are in a life-and-death struggle, sentences become shorter to show increasing danger, and actions reveal that characters know that they are in serious conflict with nature.

Person Against Self. In *Hatchet,* Gary Paulsen creates person-against-self and person-against-nature conflicts for his major character, thirteen-year-old Brian. These two major conflicts are intertwined throughout the book. For example, Paulsen creates an excellent transition between unconsciousness at the end of Chapter 3 and consciousness at the beginning of Chapter 4. In the following quote, notice how Paulsen ties together the two most destructive experiences in Brian's life: the plane crash that could have killed him and the secret about his mother that caused his parents' divorce.

> Without knowing anything. Pulling until his hands caught at weeds and muck, pulling and screaming until his hands caught at

Through the Eyes of an AUTHOR

David Wisniewski

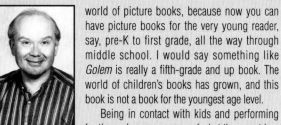

Visit the CD-ROM that accompanies this text to generate a complete list of David Wisniewski titles.

Selected Titles by David Wisniewski:

Golem

Sundiata, Lion King of Mali

Rain Player

Tough Cookie

The Secret Knowledge of Grown-Ups: The Second File

It pays to be in contact with the audience you work for, and I find that by being in the schools providing a good service at a reasonable price (I might even say an excellent service at a reasonable price!), you excite children about the processes of writing, illustrating, and reading, but you also stay in contact. I think sometimes you can be in this profession and get to a point where if you don't stay in contact with your audience, you end up writing things that are out of whack with them.

The world of children's books has outgrown the public perception of children's books. The general public still agrees in a very diffuse fashion that picture books are for the very young. And yet the world of children's books has grown to the point where you have to subdivide the world of picture books, because now you can have picture books for the very young reader, say, pre-K to first grade, all the way through middle school. I would say something like *Golem* is really a fifth-grade and up book. The world of children's books has grown, and this book is not a book for the youngest age level.

Being in contact with kids and performing for them give you a sense of what they want in a story. *The Warrior and The Wise Man,* which was my first book, came out of my background in puppetry doing folktales. It seemed only natural to use a folktale or a folkloric tale to capitalize on that familiarity. And I also did not want to do anything trivial. I wanted to do something that had a point, but I also knew enough from puppetry that if you are going to make a point, it has to be demonstrated by the story plot and character. It cannot be laid on top.

I learned from the puppetry that if you are going to have a point, it has to be organically built into the tale and demonstrated by the tale, not preached at you. So with *The Warrior and The Wise Man,* I started off with the point that it's better to think your way through a problem than fight your way through a problem. Knowing that, I knew I could set the story in Japan, because they had two classes: They had the Samurai and they had the Shinto monks coming into Japanese history at the same time. So I could have a dichotomy already set up there. By making my characters twins, I start them off evenly. By making them sons of the emperor vying for the throne, then I've got what Alfred Hitchcock called "the maguffin." I had the point of the story set up.

Because it is a nature-oriented religion, the Shinto religion provided my wind/water/fire—all those elements required by the twins in order to gain the throne. And then the final inspiration was the kids' game of "Scissors/Paper/Rock," which was one element canceling out another element. And then the twist at the end was really not something I had planned. That was a bright idea that came to me. What I like about this story is that the warrior is not evil. He simply has what has proved to be an inferior way of doing things. And that's brought up at the very end—being strong is nice, but unless that strength is directed intelligently, it's worthless.

So that is what got me started on the culturally entrenched tales with a sensible way of working. I came up with the idea that I needed to know what point I wanted the story to make. Where is the culture that supports the point of my story? What culture could this story have happened in? And then I do research from there to make sure that I'm not breaking any cultural norms that would preclude the use of my original tale in it.

Video Profiles: The accompanying video contains conversations from such authors and illustrators as Roland Smith, Paula Danziger, and E. B. Lewis.

---

last in grass and brush and he felt his chest on land, felt his face in the coarse blades of grass and he stopped; everything stopped. A color came that he had never seen before, a color that exploded in his mind with the pain and he was gone, gone from it all, spiraling out into the world, spiraling out into nothing. Nothing. (p. 30, end of chapter 3)

The Memory was like a knife cutting into him. Slicing deep into him with hate. The Secret. (p. 31, beginning of chapter 4)

Symbolically, the secret is the first thing that Brian remembers after waking from unconsciousness. Paulsen reveals the destructive nature of the secret through flashbacks, as Brian's memory returns, and through comparisons between the hate that cut him like a knife and the sharp pain caused by the crash. As Brian gains confidence and ability to survive in the Canadian wilderness, he gains understanding about his parents' conflict and ability to face his own person-against-self conflict.

While few children face the extreme personal challenges described in *Hatchet, Call It Courage,* and *Julie of the Wolves,* all children must overcome fears and personal problems while growing up. Person-against-self conflict is a popular plot device in children's literature. Authors of contemporary realistic fiction often develop plots around children who face and overcome problems related to family disturbances. For example, the cause of the person-against-self conflict in Jerry Spinelli's *Wringer* is a boy's realization that if he does not accept the violence associated with killing pigeons, he must find the courage to oppose the actions and attitudes expressed by both his friends and the town. In Ruth White's *Belle Prater's Boy,* the characters struggle to understand the suicide of the girl's father and desertion by the boy's mother.

Good plots do not rely on contrivance or coincidence. They are credible to young readers because many of the same conflicts occur in the children's own lives. Credibility is an important consideration in evaluating plot in children's books. Although authors of adult books often rely on sensational conflict to create interest, writers of children's books like to focus on the characters and the ways in which they overcome problems.

An In-Depth Analysis of the Plot and Conflict in One Book

Christopher Paul Curtis's *The Watsons Go to Birmingham— 1963*, a 1996 Newbery Honor book, provides an excellent source for both literary analysis and historical authenticity. It is a book that changes mood at about the halfway point in the story. At the beginning of the book, the author develops a typical African American family who lives and works in Flint, Michigan. The problems of the various characters are typical for many families. The main character, ten-year-old Kenny, is a bright boy who reads very well. Kenny's scholastic achievements frequently place him in conflict with his older brother, Bryon, whose escapades vary from the humorous to the more serious. At the point in which the parents decide that Bryon is heading for a life of delinquency, they decide that he should spend time with his strict grandmother in Birmingham.

When they decide to travel to Alabama, the tone of the book changes. In this time of racial tension, person-against-society conflict is the most prominent. The racial conflict is developed early in the story when the mother wants to go from Flint to Birmingham because life is slower in Alabama and the people are friendlier. Dad responds, " 'Oh yeah, they're a laugh a minute down there. Let's see, where was that 'Coloreds Only' bathroom downtown?' " (p. 5). The culmination of this person-against-society conflict results toward the end of the book when a church is bombed and several African American children are killed.

Curtis develops parallels between the person-against-society and person-against-self conflicts. As Kenny tries to understand the hatred that could cause such deaths he also, with the help of his older brother, reaches a point where he releases his personal feelings and begins to cry. The author shows the impact of this release in the following quote: "he knew that was some real embarrassing stuff so he closed the bathroom door and sat on the tub and waited for me to stop, but I couldn't. I felt like someone had pulled a plug on me and every tear inside was rushing out" (p. 199).

At the moment of complete self-understanding Kenny admits to his brother that he was no longer afraid of the bombing incident; instead, he was ashamed of himself because he ran from the church rather than try to find his sister, who he believed was inside the church. His older brother helps him clarify the situation and makes him realize that he has no reason for embarrassment.

The themes and language in the book also relate to the person-against-society and person-against-self conflicts. Through the actions of various characters we learn that prejudice and hatred are harmful and destructive forces. To increase understanding of these conflicts, Curtis effectively uses comparative language and symbolism. For example, he compares the steering of a big car to being grown up when the father tells Kenny that both are scary at first, but with a lot of practice the car and life are under control. The symbolism of the Wool Pooh (Winnie-the-Pooh's evil twin brother) is of particular interest. When Kenny swims in dangerous waters he almost drowns. He believes it is the Wool Pooh who is trying to kill him. Later in the bombed church he believes he sees this same faceless monster. Students of literature may find interesting comparisons for discussion as they analyze the possible significance of this evil symbolism as it relates to both the conflicts and themes developed in the book.

When using this book with older students, adults may ask them to trace the parallels between person-against-society and person-against-self conflicts, conduct historical studies to analyze the 1963 setting and conflicts for authenticity and to relate them to the church bombings in 1996, and trace the emergence of the themes. Curtis's text provides an interesting discussion to show the relationships among conflict, theme, and author's style.

Characterization

A believable, enjoyable story needs main characters who seem lifelike and who develop throughout the story. Characterization is one of the most powerful of the literary elements, whether the story is a contemporary tale in which characters face realistic problems or an adaptation of classic literature.

The characters whom we remember fondly from our childhood reading usually have several sides; like real people, they are not all good or all bad, and they change as they confront and overcome their problems. Laura, from the various "Little House" books by Laura Ingalls Wilder, typifies a rounded character in literature. She is honest, trustworthy, and courageous, but she can also be jealous, frightened, or angry. Her character not only is fully developed in the story but also changes during its course.

One child who enjoyed Wilder's books described Laura this way: "I would like Laura for my best friend. She would be fun to play with but she would also understand when I was hurt or angry. I could tell Laura my secrets without being afraid she would laugh at me or tell them to someone else." Any writer who can create such a friend for children is very skilled at characterization.

Rosemary Chance (1999) reported on a study that analyzed the characteristics of novels that were on the list of young adult choices. She found that characterization was the most important criterion. Protagonists in these books are dynamic and well developed. The majority of the novels included conflicts that center on people including person-against-self and person-against-person conflicts. It would appear from such studies and comments from readers that memorable characterization is one of the most important literary elements.

How does an author develop a memorable character? How can an author show the many sides of a character as well as demonstrate believable change as this character matures? The credibility of a character depends

WHAT·ANGEL·WAKES·ME·FROM·MY·FLOWERY·BED

Strong characterization from Shakespeare's plays are available in a version for children. (From Tales from Shakespeare *by Charles and Mary Lamb with sundry pictures and illuminations both in color and in line by Elizabeth Shippen Green Elliott. Reproduced by permission of Children's Classics. Crown Publishers.)*

Yolonda's positive attitudes create strong characterization in a story about sister and brother relationships. The author uses the symbolism of music to show characterization. (From Yolonda's Genius *by Carol Fenner. Jacket illustration copyright © 1995 by Stephen Marchesi, Margaret K. McElderry Books. Reprinted by permission of Simon & Schuster, Inc.)*

upon the writer's ability to reveal the full nature of the character, including strengths and weaknesses. An author can achieve such a three-dimensional character by describing the character's physical appearance, recording the conversations of the character, revealing the character's thoughts, revealing the perceptions of other characters, and showing the character in action.

In *Call It Courage*, Armstrong Sperry uses all of these methods to reveal Mafatu's character and the changes that occur in him as he overcomes his fears. Sperry first tells readers that Mafatu fears the sea. Then, through narration, Sperry shows the young child clinging to his mother's back as a stormy sea and sharks almost end their lives. Mafatu's memories of this experience, revealed in his thoughts and actions, make him useless in the eyes of his Polynesian tribe, as Sperry reveals through the dialogue of other characters: "That is woman's work. Mafatu is afraid of the sea. He will never be a warrior" (p. 12).

The laughter of the tribe follows, and Sperry then describes Mafatu's inner feelings:

Suddenly a fierce resentment stormed through him. He knew in that instant what he must do: he must prove his courage to himself, and to the others, or he could no longer live in their

midst. He must face Moana, the Sea God—face him and conquer him. (p. 13)

Sperry portrays Mafatu's battle for courage through a combination of actions and thoughts: Terror and elation follow each other repeatedly as Mafatu lands on a forbidden island used for human sacrifice, dares to take a ceremonial spear even though doing so may mean death, confronts a hammerhead shark that circles his raft, and then overcomes his fear and attacks the shark to save his dog. Mafatu celebrates a final victory when he kills a wild boar, whose teeth symbolize courage. Mafatu's tremendous victory over fear is signified by his father's statement of pride: "Here is my son come home from the sea. Mafatu, Stout Heart. A brave name for a brave boy" (p. 115).

In *The Moves Make the Man*, Bruce Brooks develops character through basketball terminology. Brooks uses the words of Jerome Foxworthy, a talented black student, to express these thoughts about his own character:

Moves were all I cared about last summer. I got them down, and I liked not just the fun of doing them, but having them too,

Through the Eyes of a CHILD

John

Pam Wilson's Fourth Grade
Western Row Elementary
Mason, Ohio

TITLE: The secret Knowledge of Grown ups
AUTHOR: David Wisniewski

I like The Secret Knowlege of grown-ups because its funny and I like the pictures. I'll tell you some of the things I think are funny. Millions of years ago veggies ruled the earth. Big Bunches of Broccoli stomed through the jungles, followed by ferocious carrots and savage packs of peas. Huge heads of lettuce roamed the grass lands and giant celery stalked the planins. So you probably think thats funny. I think its true and maybe you will too. You should get this book Its really good! Get the book, read it. Don't show your parents. let me give you some advice. At dinner eat your veggies, don't play with your food, and drink your milk. Don't blow bubbles in it! At Bed time comb your hair, don't jump on your bed. When your light are off don't bite your finger nails or pick your noes.

John

---

like a little definition of Jerome. Reverse spin, triple jump, reverse dribble. . . . These are me. The moves make the man, the moves make me, I thought, until Mama noticed they were making me something else. (p. 44)

Brooks uses contrasting attitudes toward fake moves in basketball to reveal important differences between Jerome and Bix Rivers, a talented but disturbed white athlete.

In *The Wanderer* Sharon Creech introduces the main character by emphasizing her father's description as a person who has many sides. Notice in the following quote how Creech describes both the father's and the girl's interpretation of her character:

I am not always such a dreamy girl, listening to the sea calling me. My father calls me Three-Sided Sophie: One side is dreamy and romantic; one is logical and down-to-earth; and the third side is hardheaded and impulsive. He says I am either in dreamland or earthland or mule-land, and if I ever get the three together, I'll be

set, though I wonder where I will be then. If I'm not in dreamland or earthland or mule-land, where will I be? (p. 3).

By the end of the book the author shows the main character's progression through these same three characteristics. She now answers her own question when she realizes: "I'm not in dreamland or earthland or mule-land. I'm just right here, right now. When I close my eyes, I can still smell the sea, but I feel as if I've been dunked in the clear cool water and I've come out all clean and new." (p. 305).

This textbook discusses many memorable characters in children's literature. Some of these characters—such as the faithful spider Charlotte and a terrific pig named Wilbur, in E. B. White's *Charlotte's Web*—are old favorites who have been capturing children's imaginations for decades. Others—such as Max in Maurice Sendak's *Where the Wild Things Are* and Karana in Scott O'Dell's *Island of the Blue Dolphins*—are more recent arrivals in

An In-Depth Analysis of Characterization in One Book

Carol Fenner, the author of one of the 1996 Newbery Honor books, *Yolonda's Genius,* uses several techniques to develop the characteristics of two African American children, bright, fifth-grade Yolonda and her slower younger brother Andrew. For example, the author reveals both Yolonda's intelligence and her retaliation ability after she is teased about her size through an incident in which Yolonda responds to being called a whale: Yolonda tells her fellow bus rider that he knows nothing about whales because "Whales are the most remarkable mammals in the ocean—all five oceans" (p. 16). She then provides information about whales, such as "The whales sank, lifting their tails high above the water like a signal. Deep in the ocean, their voices sent out a high swelling cry, sharing their message of victory for a hundred miles" (p. 17). We learn later that Yolonda goes to the library each week to learn new facts.

Yolonda's positive attitudes and Andrew's possible musical genius are developed as Yolonda shares Andrew's abilities. She reviews what Andrew can do and not what he cannot do when she thinks, "If there was music on the TV or the blaster, he could keep it company by beating out a rhythm on anything—his knees, a table, a wall. Or he could play a sweet line of sound on his harmonica just underneath the music, like water under a bridge. He played people's voices—an argument, cries of surprise, hushed conversa-

tion. The harmonica lived in his pocket. He fell asleep with it in his hand" (p. 38).

Later, Yolonda's actions show both her respect for Andrew's talents and her dislike for those who torment her younger brother because he is a slower learner in school and gains his enjoyment from playing his harmonica. Yolonda takes vengeance on the three boys who destroy Andrew's harmonica. She does this while Andrew is watching because she wants it to be Andrew's vengeance as well as her own.

The author continues to show characterization through the symbolism of music. Andrew makes discoveries about people through sounds, he learns the alphabet after a teacher relates the alphabet to the instruments, and Andrew eventually plays his harmonica to reveal the character of Yolonda. As you read the following quote, analyze how the author describes Yolonda through Andrew's music: "Yolonda walking, a steady, strong beat—great big moves, slow, making waves of air pass by. Yolonda eating a chocolate eclair—full mouth—soft and happy. Yolonda reading to him, voice purring around the big words, Yolonda dancing. This is the sound of Yolonda's body—large, gobbling, space, powerful and protecting—great like a queen, frightening everyone with a scowl and a swelling of her shoulders" (p. 203).

Notice in this example how the author uses several different techniques to develop the characterizations of Yolonda and her brother. After reading the book, readers understand that both characters have well-rounded personalities.

---

the world of children's books. Authors of picture storybooks, historical fiction, science fiction, fantasy, and contemporary realistic fiction have created characters who are likely to be remembered long after the details of their stories have been forgotten.

Setting

The setting of a story—its location in time and place—helps readers share what the characters see, smell, hear, and touch, and also makes the characters' values, actions, and conflicts more understandable. Whether a story takes place in the past, present, or future, its overall credibility may depend on how well the plot, characterizations, and setting support one another. Different types of literature—picture storybooks, fantasy, historical fiction, and contemporary realistic fiction—have their own requirements as far as setting is concerned. When a story is set in an identifiable historical period or geographical location, details should be accurate. Plot and characters also should be consistent with what actually occurred or could have occurred at that time and place.

Jean Craighead George (1991), author of numerous survival stories, emphasizes the setting for the book. To do this, George walks through the setting, smells the environment, looks at the world to see careful details, and

searches for protagonists. During her final writing, she closes her eyes and re-creates in her imagination the land, the people, and the animals. George states:

I strive to put the reader on the scene. I want to make each child feel that he is under a hemlock tree with Sam Gribley in *My Side of the Mountain* or on his hands and knees talking to the tundra wolves in *Julie of the Wolves.* I want my reader to hear and see the ice on the Arctic Ocean in *Water Sky.* (p. 70)

In some books, setting is such an important part of the story that the characters and plot cannot be developed without understanding the time and place. In other stories, however, the setting provides only a background. In fact, some settings are so well known that just a few words place readers immediately into the expected location. "Once upon a time," for example, is a mythical time in days of yore when it was possible for magical spells to transform princes into beasts or to change pumpkins into glittering carriages. Thirty of the thirty-seven traditional fairy tales in Andrew Lang's *The Red Fairy Book* begin with "Once upon a time." Magical spells cannot happen everywhere; they usually occur in "a certain kingdom," "deep in the forest," in "the humble hut of a wise and good peasant," or "far, far away, in a warm and pleasant land." Children become so familiar with such phrases—and the visualizations of setting that such phrases trigger—that additional details and descriptions are not necessary.

Even a setting that is described briefly may serve several different purposes. It may create a mood, provide an antagonist, establish historical background, or supply symbolic meanings.

Setting as Mood. Authors of children's literature and adult literature alike use settings to create moods that add credibility to characters and plot. Readers would probably be a bit skeptical if a vampire appeared in a sunny American kitchen on a weekday morning while a family was preparing to leave for school and work. The same vampire would seem more believable in a moldy castle in Transylvania at midnight. The illustrations and text can create the mood of a location. Readers can infer the author's and illustrator's feelings about the setting. For example, Cynthia Rylant's text and Barry Moser's illustrations for *Appalachia: The Voices of Sleeping Birds* provide a setting that radiates warm feelings about the varied people, their strengths, and their way of life.

The epic story of Attila the Hun, a famous invader of Eastern Europe in the fifth century A.D., can be told as historical fiction, with a setting that emphasizes accuracy of geographical and biographical detail. In *The White Stag,* Kate Seredy takes a mythical approach to telling how a migratory Asiatic people reached their new homeland in what became Hungary. Gods, moonmaidens, and a supernatural animal are among the characters in this story, and Seredy uses setting to create a mood in which such beings seem natural. The leader of the tribe stands before a sacrificial altar in a cold, rocky, and barren territory, waiting to hear the voice of the god Hadur, who will lead his starving people to the promised land.

At this time, the white stag miraculously appears to guide the Huns in their travels—through "ghost hours" onto grassy hills covered with white birch trees, where they hear a brook tinkling like silver bells and a breeze that sounds like the flutes of minstrels. Readers expect magic in such a place, and they are not disappointed to see:

Moonmaidens, those strange changeling fairies who lived in white birch trees and were never seen in the daylight; Moonmaidens who, if caught by the gray-hour of dawn, could never go back to fairyland again; Moonmaidens who brought good luck. . . . (p. 34)

The setting becomes less magically gentle when Attila is born. Attila's father has just challenged his god, and the result is terrifying:

Suddenly, without warning it [the storm] was upon them with lightning and thunder that roared and howled like an army of furious demons. Trees groaned and crashed to the ground to be picked up again and sucked into the spinning dark funnel of the whirlwind. (p. 64)

This setting introduces Attila, the "Scourge of God," who in the future will lead his people home, with the help of the white stag.

The illustrations create a nostalgic look at childhood in In Coal Country. *(From* In Coal Country *by Judith Hendershot, illustrated by Thomas B. Allen. Illustration copyright © 1987 by Thomas B. Allen. Reprinted by permission of Alfred A. Knopf.)*

In the preceding quotes, notice how Seredy uses descriptive words that create the mood. Through word choice and ability to paint pictures with words, authors of excellent literature create moods that range from happy and nostalgic to frightening and forbidding.

In *The Thief,* Megan Whalen Turner also goes back to a time of the old legends in a country that resembles Greece. As the thief searches for an ancient treasure, readers are introduced to a setting complete with ancient temples, gods and goddesses, and objects of power that set the mythical mood.

Setting as Antagonist. Setting can be an antagonist in plots based on person-against-society or person-against-nature conflict. The descriptions of the Arctic in Jean Craighead George's *Julie of the Wolves* are essential. Without them, readers would have difficulty understanding the life-and-death peril facing Miyax. These descriptions make it possible to comprehend Miyax's love for the Arctic, her admiration of and dependence on the wolves, and her preference for the old Eskimo ways.

Sharon Creech's descriptions of the ocean during a storm in *The Wanderer* provide a vivid antagonist. For example, notice how Creech uses descriptive language and frightening similes in the following quotes: "Now the waves are more fierce, cresting and toppling over, like leering drooling monsters spewing heavy streaks of foam through the air" (p. 185) and "But this wave was unlike any other. It had a curl, a distinct high curl. I watched it growing up behind us, higher and higher, and then curled over *The Wanderer,* thousands of gallons of water, white and lashing" (p. 208).

The paintings depict the terrible destruction associated with a tornado in Irene Trivas's illustrations for George Ella Lyon's One Lucky Girl. *(From* One Lucky Girl *by George Ella Lyon. Copyright © 2000 by Dorling Kindersley Limited, London. Reprinted by permission of Dorling Kindersley.)*

Illustrated picture books also may develop the setting as antagonist. For example, Irene Travas's illustrations for George Ella Lyon's *One Lucky Girl* depict the destruction associated with a tornado.

In *The Witch of Blackbird Pond,* by Elizabeth George Speare, a Puritan colony in New England is the setting as well as the antagonist of newcomer Kit Tyler, whose colorful clothing and carefree ways immediately conflict with the standards of an austere society. Careful depiction of the colony's strict standards of dress and behavior helps readers understand why the Puritans accuse Kit of being a witch.

The setting in Ida Vos's *Hide and Seek* provides the antagonist, the Netherlands during German occupation. In the foreword to the text, Vos introduces the setting for the story and helps readers understand that the setting is the antagonist. For example, she states:

Come with me to a small country in Western Europe. To the Netherlands, a land also known as Holland. Come with me, back to the year 1940. I am eight years old. German soldiers are parading through the Dutch streets. They have helmets on their heads and they are wearing black boots. They are marching and singing songs that have words I don't understand. "They're going to kill all the Jews!" shouts my mother. I am afraid, I have a stomachache. I am Jewish. (p. vii)

The reactions of the characters and the descriptions of the occupation in the remainder of the book leave no doubt that this setting is an antagonist. Vos based *Hide and Seek* on her family's life during World War II.

Setting as Historical Background. Accuracy in setting is extremely important in historical fiction and in biography. Conflict in the story and the actions of the characters may

Lois Lowry develops a setting that is historically accurate for World War II Denmark. (From Number the Stars *by Lois Lowry, copyright © 1989. Reproduced with permission of Houghton Mifflin Co.)*

be influenced by the time period and the geographical location. Unless authors describe settings carefully, children cannot comprehend unfamiliar historical periods or the stories that unfold in them. *A Gathering of Days,* by Joan W. Blos, is an example of historical fiction that carefully depicts setting—in this case, a small New Hampshire farm in the 1830s. Blos brings rural nineteenth-century America to life through descriptions of little things, such as home remedies, country pleasures, and country hardships.

Blos describes in detail the preparation of a cold remedy. The character goes to the pump for water, blows up the fire, heats a kettle of water over the flames, wrings out a flannel in hot water, sprinkles the flannel with turpentine, and places it on the patient's chest. Blos describes discipline and school life in the 1830s. Disobedience can result in a thrashing. Because of their sex, girls are excused from all but the simplest arithmetic. Readers vicariously join the characters in breaking out of the snow with a team of oxen, tapping the maple sugar trees, and collecting nuts. Of this last experience, the narrator says, "O, I do think, as has been said, that if getting in the corn and potatoes are the prose of a farm child's life, then nutting's the poetry" (p. 131).

In *Number the Stars,* set in Copenhagen during the 1940s, Lois Lowry develops a fictional story around the actions of the Danish Resistance. Actions of King Christian add to the historical accuracy of the time period. In addition to developing historically accurate backgrounds, Lowry develops the attitudes of the Danish people. Consequently, readers understand why many Danes risked their lives to relocate the Jewish residents of Denmark.

Both the illustrations and the text develop the World War II background in Michael Foreman's *War Boy: A Country Childhood.* Detailed illustrations show life in England as characters build shelters, put on gas masks, watch bombs falling, work, and relax. The illustrations add much information and help readers understand the time period.

Detailed illustrations by Steve Noon for Anne Millard's *A Street Through Time: A 12,000-Year Walk Through History* allow viewers to identify many aspects of life as it would appear in the same setting beginning with 10,000 B.C. and progressing into a modern town. Times associated with early periods such as "Roman Times," "Viking Raiders," and "Medieval Village" provide numerous details that could be used with nonillustrated books of historical fiction.

The settings in Graham Salisbury's *Under the Blood-Red Sun* develop the historical time period associated with the bombing of Pearl Harbor on December 7, 1941. The author describes the sights and sounds of the bombing.

The authors of historical fiction and biography must not only depict the time and location but also be aware of values, vocabulary, and other speech patterns consistent with the time and location. To do this, the authors must be immersed in the past and do extensive research. Joan Blos researched her subject at the New York Public Library, libraries on the University of Michigan campus, and the town library of Holderness, New Hampshire. She also consulted town and county records in New Hampshire and discussed the story with professional historians. Lois Lowry visited Copenhagen and researched documents about the leaders of the Danish Resistance.

Setting as Symbolism. Settings often have symbolic meanings that underscore what is happening in the story. Symbolism is common in traditional folktales, where frightening adventures and magical transformations occur in the deep, dark woods, and splendid castles are the sites of "happily ever after." Modern authors of fantasy and science fiction for children often borrow symbolic settings from old folktales in order to establish moods of strangeness and enchantment, such as the parallel universes created in the high fantasies by authors such as J. K. Rowling in *Harry Potter and the Goblet of Fire* and Philip Pullman in *The Golden Compass,* but authors of realistic fiction also use subtly symbolic settings to accentuate plot or help develop characters.

In one children's classic, *The Secret Garden,* by Frances Hodgson Burnett, a garden that has been locked behind a wall for ten years symbolizes a father's grief after the death of his wife, his son's illness, and the emotional estrangement of the father and son from each other. The

A boy and girl create a secret kingdom in which they can escape the problems of the real world. (Illustration by Donna Diamond from Bridge to Terabithia *by Katherine Paterson. Copyright © 1977 by Katherine Paterson. A Newbery Medal winner. By permission of Thomas Y. Crowell, Publishers.)*

first positive change in the life of a lonely, unhappy girl occurs when she discovers the buried key to the garden and opens the vine-covered door: "It was the sweetest, most mysterious-looking place anyone could imagine. The high walls which shut it in were covered with the leafless stems of climbing roses which were so thick that they were matted together" (p. 76).

Finding the garden, working in it, and watching its beauty return bring happiness to the girl, restore health to the sick boy, and reunite the father and son. The good magic that causes emotional and physical healing in this secret kingdom is symbolized by tiny new shoots emerging from the soil and the rosy color that the garden's fresh air brings to the cheeks of two pale children.

In a more recent book, Katherine Paterson's *Bridge to Terabithia,* a secret kingdom in the woods is the "other world" shared by two young people who do not conform to the values of rural Virginia. The boy, Jess, would rather

An In-Depth Analysis of Setting in One Book

The settings in Philip Pullman's award-winning fantasy from England, *The Golden Compass,* reveal several purposes for setting that may be found in the same book. For example, in the beginning of the book notice how the author creates a suspenseful setting through the following quote showing the characters' actions: " 'Behind the chair—quick!' whispered Pantalaimon, and in a flash Lyra was out of the armchair and crouching behind it. It wasn't the best one for hiding behind: she'd chose one in the very center of the room, and unless she kept very quiet . . ." (p. 4).

On the following pages readers discover how dangerous this setting might be for Lyra: "What she saw next, however, changed things completely. The Master took from his pocket a folded paper and laid it on the table beside the wine. He took the stopper out of the mouth of a decanter containing a rich golden wine, unfolded the paper, and poured a thin stream of white powder into the decanter before crumpling the paper and throwing it into the fire. Then he took a pencil from his pocket, stirred the wine until the powder had dissolved, and replaced the stopper" (p. 6).

As the story moves from England to the far north, the setting frequently becomes an antagonist as Lyra faces both the cold and the fear found in the wilderness. Pullman creates both of these moods in quotes such as the following: "The other girls went on talking, but Lyra and Pantalaimon nestled down deep in the bed and tried to get warm, knowing that for hundreds of miles all around her little bed there was nothing but fear" (p. 246).

Pullman's settings both create a realistic background and suggest the fantasy settings of other worlds. For example, the following quote provides realistic background for a small town in the far north. It also allows readers to visualize, hear, and even smell the setting: "Directly ahead of the ship a mountain rose, green flanked and snowcapped, and a little town and harbor lay below it: wooden houses with steep roofs, an oratory spire, cranes in the harbor, and clouds of gulls wheeling and crying. The smell was of fish, but mixed with it came land smells too: pine resin and earth and something animal and musky, and something else that was cold and blank and wild: it might have been snow. It was the smell of the North" (p. 168).

Many of Pullman's settings also reflect a universe inhabited by witches, supernatural beings, and parallel worlds. Pullman describes this parallel world in this way: "The city hanging there so empty and silent looked new-made, waiting to be occupied; or asleep, waiting to be woken. The sun of that world was shining into this, making Lyra's hands golden, melting the ice on Roger's wolfskin hood, making his pale cheeks transparent, glistening in his open sightless eyes" (p. 397).

Pullman concludes his fantasy in a way that prepares readers for the next book in the series by summarizing some of the moods found in the previous settings and foreshadowing the fantasy to come: "She turned away. Behind them lay pain and death and fear; ahead of them lay doubt, and danger, and fathomless mysteries. But they weren't alone. So Lyra and her deamon turned away from the world they were born in, and looked toward the sun, and walked into the sky" (p. 399). To continue analyzing Pullman's fantasy setting, read *The Subtle Knife* and *The Amber Spyglass,* sequels to *The Golden Compass.*

---

be an artist than follow the more masculine aspirations of his father, who accuses him of being a sissy. Schoolmates taunt the girl, Leslie, because she loves books and has no television. Jess and Leslie find that they have much in common, so they create a domain of their own, in which a beautiful setting symbolizes their growing sense of comradeship, belongingness, and self-love.

Even the entrance to their secret country is symbolic: "It could be a magic country like Narnia, and the only way you can get in is by swinging across on this enchanted rope" (p. 39). They grab the old rope, swing across the creek, and enter their stronghold, where streams of light dance through the leaves of dogwood, oak, and evergreen, fears and enemies do not exist, and anything they want is possible. Paterson develops credible settings as Jess and Leslie go from the world of school and home to the world that they make for themselves in Terabithia.

A dilapidated house, with its uncared-for backyard, becomes a symbolic setting in Janet Taylor Lisle's *Afternoon of the Elves.* In this setting, two girls, Hillary and Sara-Kate, make discoveries about each other and the importance of accepting people who are different. The girls work together in a miniature village that Sara-Kate maintains was built by elves. Like Paterson, Lisle creates two credible settings: (1) Hillary's normal world of school and home and (2) the almost otherworld existence of a yard that is entered through a thick hedge. Like many other authors of books that have symbolic settings, Lisle relates the settings to the theme.

Theme

The theme of a story is the underlying idea that ties the plot, characters, and setting together into a meaningful whole. When evaluating themes in children's books, consider what the author wanted to convey about life or society and whether that theme is worthwhile for children. A memorable book has a theme—or several themes—that children can understand because of their own needs. Laurence Perrine (1983) states:

There is no prescribed method for discovering theme. Sometimes we can best get at it by asking in what way the main character has changed in the course of a story and what, if anything, the character has learned before its end. Sometimes the best approach is to explore the nature of the central conflict and its outcome. Sometimes the title will provide an important clue. (p. 110)

Authors of children's books often directly state the theme of a book, rather than imply it, as authors commonly do in books for adults. For example, Wendy Anderson Halperin's *Love Is . . .* develops various definitions of love such as "Love is kind." On one side of the double page the artist depicts the consequences when that type of love is not present. The facing page depicts the consequences when that love is added. Theme may be stated by characters or through the author's narrative. The characters' actions and the outcome of the story usually develop and support the theme in children's literature. Picture storybooks, with their shorter texts and fewer themes, allow readers to analyze, trace, and discuss evidence of theme in a briefer, whole story. For example, many readers identify the theme in Patricia Polacco's *Appelemando's Dreams* as "It is important to dream." The following evidence from the book supports this theme:

1. The boy who does not have anything to do in a drab village makes his life interesting by dreaming about magic chariots pulled by galloping hues of color.

2. Appelemando shares his beautiful colored dreams with his friends and makes them happy.

3. The friends try to capture Appelemando's dreams on paper so that they can keep the dreams forever.

4. The children fear that they will lose Appelemando's dreams after the villagers angrily make them wash the dreams off the village walls.

5. The dreams allow the children to be found after they lose their way in the forest.

6. The villagers weep for joy after they follow Appelemando's vision and find the children.

7. The villagers conclude, "Never again would they question the importance of dreams" (p. 28, unnumbered).

8. The village becomes a colorful and dreamy place that people enjoy visiting.

Themes in books written for younger children frequently develop around experiences and emotions that are important to the younger readers. For example, James Howe's *Horace and Morris But Mostly Dolores* develops the very understandable theme that friendship is important. The theme in Douglas Wood's *What Dads Can't Do* develops the importance of a father's love by showing numerous father and child relationships.

In contrast, themes developed in books written for older readers frequently focus on human development and the consequences that may result from choices. For example, Suzanne Fisher Staples's heroine in *Shiva's Fire* discovers " 'That is a basic human frailty—we always want to know what will happen if we do one thing rather than another. Not knowing is the mystery of destiny. If you are still for a moment, no doubt you will hear your heart tell you what you must do.' " (p. 264). Human frailty is also revealed in the concluding volume to Philip Pullman's trilogy, *The Amber Spyglass.*

Theme Revealed by Changes in Characters. In *The Whipping Boy,* Sid Fleischman develops the theme that friendship is important. Fleischman shows how the main characters change in their attitudes toward each other. For example, the names that the main characters call each other progress from hostility to comradeship. At the beginning of the story, Jemmy thinks of the prince as "Your Royal Awfulness." Likewise, the prince refers to Jemmy as "Jemmy-from-the-Street" and "contrary rascal." As the story develops and the two characters learn to respect and admire each other, Jemmy refers to the prince as "friend" and the prince calls himself "Friend-o-Jemmy's."

Theme and the Nature of Conflict. Stories set in other time periods frequently develop themes by revealing how the main characters respond to conflicts caused by society. For example, Rudolf Frank's *No Hero for the Kaiser,* set in World War I, develops several antiwar themes. Frank develops the harsh nature of war by exploring the actions and responses of a boy who is unwittingly drawn into battle. Through the viewpoint of the boy, Frank reveals that it takes more courage not to fight than to fight, that it is important to respect oneself, and that "guns never go off by themselves" (p. 13). Frank reinforces these themes through symbolism, similes, and contrasts. The contrasts are especially effective as Frank compares the same soldiers at home and on the battlefield and contrasts peacetime and wartime meanings for terms such as *bull's-eye, shot,* and *field.*

Janet Lunn's main character in *Shadow in Hawthorn Bay,* a historical novel set in 1800s Canada, discovers that prejudice is a harmful force and that respecting one's own beliefs is important. The impact of prejudice is explored when the main character, a girl with second sight, leaves Scotland and arrives in a community where her abilities are feared, not honored. Prejudice is a harmful force in other historical fiction, such as Elizabeth George Speare's *The Witch of Blackbird Pond,* Paula Fox's *The Slave Dancer,* Mary Stolz's *Cezanne Pinto: A Memoir,* Uri Orlev's *The Island on Bird Street,* and Mildred D. Taylor's *Roll of Thunder, Hear My Cry.*

The Theme of Personal Development. Literature offers children opportunities to identify with other people's experiences and thus better understand their own growing up. Consequently, the themes of many children's books deal with developing self-understanding. In an early study, Gretchen Purtell Hayden (1969) concluded that the following themes related to personal development are predominant in children's books that have received the Newbery Medal: difficulties in establishing good relationships between adults and children, the need for morality to guide one's actions, the importance of support from other people, an acceptance of oneself and others, a respect for authority, the ability to handle problems, and

Superior rats consider the morality of their actions in a complex plot. (Illustration by Zena Bernstein from Mrs. Frisby and the Rats of NIMH *by Robert C. O'Brien. Copyright © 1971 by Robert C. O'Brien. [New York: Charles Scribner's Sons, 1971]. Reprinted with the permission of Atheneum Publishers.)*

the necessity of cooperation. As you read more current books, search to see if these themes are still found in the literature.

In Robert O'Brien's *Mrs. Frisby and the Rats of NIMH,* intellectually superior rats search for a moral code to guide their actions. They have studied the human race and do not wish to make the same mistakes, but they soon realize how easy it is to slip into dishonest behavior. Some equipment that they find allows them to steal electricity, food, and water from human society, which then makes their lives seem too easy and pointless. Eventually, the rats choose a more difficult course of action, moving into an isolated valley and working to develop their own civilization. In Lois Lowry's *The Giver,* a boy discovers that his ideal world has dark secrets and that the people may be better off if they have memories of their history and are responsible for their actions.

One book that develops the importance of support from another human being is Theodore Taylor's *The Cay.* When Phillip and his mother leave Curaçao in order to find safety in the United States, their boat is torpedoed by a German submarine. Phillip, a white boy, and Timothy, a black West Indian, become isolated first on a life raft and then on a tiny Caribbean island. Their need for each other is increased when Phillip becomes blind after a blow to the head and must, in spite of his racial prejudice, rely on Timothy for his

Technology Resources

The *Bulletin of the Centre for Children's Books* is a review journal, providing starred reviews, editorials, and author/illustrator profiles. You can link to this valuable site from our Companion Website at **www.prenhall.com/norton**

survival. Phillip's superior attitudes gradually vanish, as he becomes totally dependent on another person. When Phillip is finally rescued, Phillip treasures the way in which a wonderful friend has helped change his life for the better.

The Cay also stresses the theme of accepting oneself and others, as does Joan W. Blos's *A Gathering of Days,* in which Catherine experiences injustice for the first time when she and her friends secretly help a runaway slave. Catherine learns to respect authority as well when after

An In-Depth Analysis of Theme in One Book

Sharon Creech's 1995 Newbery Medal winner, *Walk Two Moons,* allows readers to analyze the effectiveness of the author's use of theme and to consider how it relates to thirteen-year-old Sal, her grandparents, her friend, her father, and her mother, who has left home. The themes in Creech's book tie the plot, characters, and setting together into a meaningful whole. For example, Creech uses mysterious messages left by a stranger to tie together the plot, characters' actions, and motivation. The messages are also written in the form of themes.

The first message is "Don't judge a man until you have walked two moons in his moccasins" (p. 51). Father then interprets the meaning of the message on page 61. The second message is "Everyone has his own agenda" (p. 60). This message is tied to Gramps's interpretation of the message (p. 60), Prudence's and Sal's actions (p. 104), and Phoebe's thoughts about her agenda (p. 140). The third message is "In the course of a lifetime what does it matter" (p. 105). This message is related to Sal's thoughts about the meaning of the message (p. 106). The fourth message is "You can't keep the birds of sadness from flying over your head, but you can keep them from nesting in your hair" (p. 154). This message is related to Phoebe's story (p. 155), Phoebe's father's response (p. 162), Phoebe's crying and Sal's response (p. 169), hope related to the story of Pandora's box (pp. 174–175), the birds of sadness around Phoebe's family (p. 189), and the birds of sadness around Mrs. Cadaver (p. 220). The fifth message is "We never know the worth of water until the well runs dry" (p. 198). This message is related to the discussion about Mrs. Cadaver's and Sal's realization that the messages have changed the way they look at life.

The final and sixth message is the same as the first: "Don't judge a man until you have walked two moons in his moccasins" (p. 252). The importance of this message is developed when Gramps and Sal play the moccasin game in which they take turns pretending they are walking in someone else's moccasins (p. 275) and when Gramps's gift to Sal is to let her walk in her mother's moccasins. This book provides an interesting source for tracing the emergence of themes and the relation of those themes to various characters and conflicts developed in the text.

years of responsibility for her widowed father and little sister, she must trust and obey her new stepmother.

Many children's books deal in some way with the necessity of overcoming problems. Characters may overcome problems within themselves or in their relationships with others, or problems caused by society or nature. Memorable characters face their adversaries, and through a maturing process, they learn to handle their difficulties. Handling problems may be as dramatic and planned as Mafatu's search for courage in Armstrong Sperry's *Call It Courage* or may result from accident, as in Theodore Taylor's *The Cay*. In Phyllis Reynolds Naylor's *Shiloh*, Marty solves the problem of animal abuse and finds a way to keep a dog.

Cooperation, the importance of personal growth, and the need for kindness and sharing are all themes in E. L. Konigsburg's *The View from Saturday*. These themes are developed as a group of sixth graders form a winning team for the Academic Bowl.

Style

Authors have a wide choice of words to select from and numerous ways to arrange words in order to create plots, characters, and settings and to express themes. Many authors use words and sentences in creative ways. To evaluate style, read a piece of literature aloud. The sound of a story should appeal to your senses and be appropriate to the content of the story. The language should help develop the plot, bring the characters to life, and create a mood.

The Girl Who Loved Wild Horses, by Paul Goble, was a Children's Choice selection. The most frequent reason that children give for choosing this book is the author's use of language. Goble uses precise similes to evoke a landscape of cliffs and canyons, beautiful wild horses, and the high-spirited Indian girl who loves them. One stallion's eyes are "cold stars," while his floating mane and tail are "wispy clouds." During a storm, the horses gallop "faster and faster, pursued by thunder and lightning . . . like a brown flood across hills and through valleys" (p. 12, unnumbered).

Sid Fleischman uses many metaphors and similes to create the setting in *The Midnight Horse*, such as "It was raining bullfrogs. The coach lurched and swayed along the river road like a ship in rough seas. Inside clung three passengers like unlashed cargo. One was a blacksmith, another was a thief, and the third was an orphan boy named Touch" (p. 1).

Fleischman also uses similes to develop characters. For example, Touch, the orphan, is described as "skinny and bareheaded, with hair as curly as wood shavings" (p. 1), and "he chose to bring himself up, free as a sail to catch any chance wind that came along" (p. 29). Compare these similes with those for Otis Cratt, the thief, who is described as a long-armed man who looked "like a loosely wrapped mummy" (p. 3), was drawn to the blacksmith's billfold "like a compass needle to true north"

(p. 4), and ran "like a wolf returning to its den" (p. 29). Fleischman uses similes that relate to the actions of each character within the story.

Figurative language also helps develop characters, plot, and setting in Jan Hudson's *Sweetgrass*, a historical novel about the Blackfoot, set on the Canadian prairies. Early in the story, for example, sweet berries symbolize a young girl's happiness and hopes: "Promises hung shimmering in the future like glowing berries above sandy soil as we gathered our bags for the walk home" (p. 12). Later, the same girl's acceptance of a disillusioning reality is symbolized again by berries, which are then bitter.

Rudolf Frank's figurative language in *No Hero for the Kaiser* reinforces the antiwar themes developed within the story. In the following quote, Frank first uses contrasts to show the changing nature of terms previously understood and to reveal the destructiveness of cannons:

Jan could not help remembering that among those invisible men called enemies there was his own father. His own father was in the field and his father's son was in the field. Why could they not tend the field together as before? Because this field that the soldiers were taking was not a field at all. A real field does not kill, a field lies at peace under God's sun, rain, and wind, a field is where things grow. He had caught the military in a lie. The soldiers were sent into a field of deceit. Like huge wolves the four cannon of the Seventh Battery went "into the field," across Polish fields, deeper and deeper into Russia, and behind them walked the gunners. (p. 46)

Authors also may select words and sentence structures with rhythms evoking different moods. Armstrong Sperry creates two different moods for Mafatu in *Call It Courage*. As Mafatu goes through the jungle, he is preoccupied and moves leisurely. Sperry uses long sentences to set this mood: "His mind was not in this business at all: he was thinking about the rigging of his canoe, planning how he could strengthen it here, tighten it there" (p. 77). This dreamy preoccupation changes rapidly as Mafatu senses danger. Sperry's verbs become harsh and his sentences short and choppy as Mafatu's tension builds: "The boar charged. Over the ground it tore. Foam flew back from its tusks. The boy braced himself" (p. 78).

The language and style in Lloyd Alexander's *The Arkadians* seems appropriate for a fantasy formulated on Greek mythology. There are numerous words reflecting Greek terminology and poetry such as "rosy-fingered dawn," "your life-threads are spun," and "wine-dark seas."

Many of the enjoyable stories contain repetition of words, phrases, or sentences. Repetition is appealing because it encourages children to join in. It provides a pleasing rhythm in *When I Was Young in the Mountains*, by Cynthia Rylant. The author introduces her memories of Grandfather's kisses, Grandmother's cooking, and listening to frogs singing at dusk with "When I was young in the mountains," a phrase that adds an appropriate aura of loving nostalgia to the experiences that she describes.

An In-Depth Analysis of Author's Use of Style in One Book

Gloria Whelan, the author of a National Book Award winner, *Homeless Bird,* develops a strong heroine who must overcome the traditional life dictated for her by India's tradition of arranged marriages and lower esteem for women. One of the strengths of Whelan's book is her use of figurative language through similes, metaphors, and symbolism. This is especially important in the references to birds and the title of the book. Notice in the following quote how Koly uses positive comparisons to describe her father's writing: "I watched as the spoken words were written down to become like caged birds, caught forever by my clever baap" (p. 2). In another place the author uses a comparison with caged animals to reveal Koly's feelings of being trapped: "As I lay there in the strange house, I felt like a newly caged animal that rushes about looking for the open door that isn't there" (p. 24). The theme of the lonely and trapped feelings associated with a homeless bird is developed throughout the book to describe Koly's emotions until at the end of the book she finally finds happiness and the homeless bird is allowed to fly to its home.

The author also uses very descriptive similes and metaphors to describe Koly's feelings as the time of her arranged marriage approaches. When she realizes that the family of her prospective bridegroom is more interested in her dowry than in her, the author uses a simile that foreshadows Koly's future. Now she thinks, "Was my marriage to be like the buying of a sack of yams in the marketplace?" (p. 13). After her marriage, the author again uses a reference to the marketplace as her mother-in-law holds her arm "as I have seen women in the marketplace holding a chicken's neck before they killed it" (p. 22).

When Koly realizes fully the disastrous consequences of her marriage, the author compares her feelings to those of a small fly caught in the web of a cunning spider. After Koly discovers that her husband has tuberculosis and will probably die, the author again describes her feelings through a vivid simile: "My hope slipped away like a frightened mouse into a dark hole" (p. 42). After Koly's husband dies, the author uses numerous comparisons to develop characterizations: Koly's mother-in-law

is suspicious of books and she treats them like scorpions that might sting. Later her mother-in-law is compared to little red ants that swarm all over you and continually bite. When her mother-in-law deserts her in a town filled with begging widows, Koly feels like a kitten who has been dropped down a well.

The mood, developed through figurative language, changes after Koly discovers hope in a home for widows that is founded to help people like herself gain respect and an ability to earn a living. Notice how the mood of the comparisons changes as Koly also discovers hope. When with relief she takes off her widow's sari she feels like the snake that rids itself of its confining skin. Later, the author uses Koly's considerable ability with embroidery to show that if we use our talents, life can be like a beautiful tapestry.

The idea for a tapestry also becomes symbolic for the changes in Koly's life. Notice in the following quote how the author uses the symbolism of quilting as a way to show the changes in Koly's life as she proceeds from sadness to happiness: "Once again I began to quilt for my dowry. My first quilt was stitched as I worried about my marriage to Hari, the second in sorrow at Hari's death. Chandra's quilt was stitched to celebrate her happiness. This time as I embroidered, I thought only of my own joy. 'When it's finished,' I wrote Raji, 'we'll be married.' In the middle of the quilt, spreading its branches in all directions, I put a tamarind tree to remind me of the tree in my maa and baap's courtyard and the tree in the home I was going to. . . . I stitched a rickshaw and Raji in the fields and me embroidering in the room Raji had made for me. Around the quilt for a border I put the Yamuna Rier, the reeds and herons beside it" (pp. 207–208).

In addition to the symbolism found in embroidery, the author uses references to Indian poetry and mythology to develop the story's style. As students of children's literature, you might consider the importance of the author's references to this poetry. In the author's note, the poet is identified as Rabindranath Tagor, who lived between 1861 and 1941 and was considered one of India's greatest poets who also wrote plays and stories, composed music, and was an advocate for India's independence from Great Britain. In 1913 he received the Nobel Prize for literature.

Point of View

Several people may describe an incident in different terms. The feelings they experience, the details they choose to describe, and their judgments about what occurred may vary because of their backgrounds, values, and perspectives. Consequently, the same story may change drastically when told from another point of view. How would Peter Rabbit's story be different if Beatrix Potter had told it from the viewpoint of the mother rabbit? How would Armstrong Sperry's *Call It Courage* differ if told from the viewpoint of a Polynesian tribesman who loves the sea rather than from the viewpoint of a boy

who fears it? Author Patricia Lauber (1991) emphasizes the importance of point of view when she states, "The best stories have a point of view. They involve readers by making them care—care about the characters, whether people or animals, care about a town, care about an idea, and most of all, care about how it all comes out" (p. 46).

Avi's *Nothing but the Truth: A Documentary Novel* stimulates interesting discussions about point of view and fosters responses to literature. The book, a fictional novel written in documentary format, allows readers to interpret each incident, draw their own conclusions about the truthfulness of the documents, and decide which characters are changed

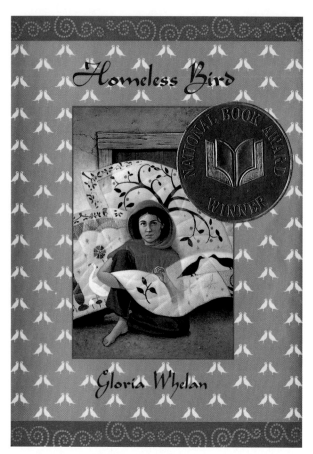

The author's style develops a strong heroine and reflects a vivid setting. (From **Homeless Bird** *by Gloria Whelan. Copyright © 2000 by Gloria Whelan. Published by HarperCollins. Reprinted by permission of the publisher.*

An In-Depth Analysis of Point of View in One Book

The point of view developed in Richard Peck's 2001 Newbery Medal winner, *A Year Down Yonder,* provides an opportunity for readers to analyze the effectiveness of several of the purposes for establishing a point of view. Readers may also develop an understanding of the techniques used by the author to make them care about the characters and what will happen in the story.

First, the author builds on his previous book, *A Long Way from Chicago,* which was a 1999 Newbery Honor book and a National Book Award finalist. In the first book the author develops the characters of two children who during each summer of the Depression travel from Chicago to a small town in southern Illinois to visit their grandmother. In the first book Peck develops characters who involve readers by making them care about the boy and the girl. Through the details he chooses to describe, we have a strong feeling about the backgrounds, values, and perspectives of the main characters, especially the feisty grandmother.

In *A Year Down Yonder,* Peck focuses on fifteen-year-old Mary Alice and her grandmother who spend a year together during the recession of 1937. The book begins as Mary Alice is asked to live with her grandmother after her father loses his job. Let us begin our discussion of point of view with Lauber's (1991) concern that a major purpose of point of view is to make readers care about the characters and how the story will develop. A considerable portion of Peck's novel is told through Mary Alice's point of view. Most readers will immediately sympathize with her and understand her feelings when she thinks: "Oh, didn't I feel sorry for myself when the Wabash Railroad's Blue Bird train steamed into Grandma's town. . . . My trunk thumped out onto the platform from the baggage car ahead. There I stood at the end of the world with all I had left. Bootsie [her cat] and my radio" (p. 4). In the first chapter Peck develops Mary Alice's point of view about the town as a place where everyone knows everything about you, about going to a school where she knows nobody and where the students do not want to make friends with a new girl who they consider a rich city girl, about missing her brother who always stuck up for her, and about her view of her grandmother who has definite opinions of her own and is considered not only feisty but also difficult to get along with.

the most. As a consequence, readers gain insights into how emotions can define and distort the truth.

As children read this novel, they can analyze how Avi documents various reactions to and points of view on the same incident through the use of memos, letters, diary pages, discussions, phone and personal conversations, speeches, and telegrams. Avi also develops characters, conflicts, and various emotional responses through these same documents. Consequently, the book may be used to stimulate personal responses among readers.

Two different points of view are developed in Dorothea P. Seeber's *A Pup Just for Me; A Boy Just for Me.* In this book written for younger children, readers discover how authors may use the same desire to create overlapping stories. The book could also be used to stimulate creative writing.

Paul Fleischman's *Bull Run* is a story of the first battle of the Civil War. It is unique because Fleischman develops the story around the points of view of sixteen different people involved in the battle. Eight characters tell their story from

the perspective of the Union and eight characters reflect the perspective of the Confederacy. Fleischman's characters range from generals to foot soldiers. Some of the characters tell their stories while waiting for men to return from battle, while others are artists, photographers, and doctors who observe or play important parts in the battle. By the end of the book, all of the characters reflect the disillusionment and horror associated with this first battle.

Tracing how Peck uses Mary Alice's changing point of view about her grandmother is an interesting way to show the importance of point of view. Through Mary Alice's point of view we understand how Mary Alice goes from someone who fears her grandmother and does not want to be with her, to someone who understands and respects her grandmother's actions, beliefs, and values. Early in the novel Peck describes Grandma's actions toward Halloween tricksters, her interpretation of being able to gather all the nuts on the ground in a neighbor's yard, and her attitude toward borrowing pumpkins from a neighbor's garden and then baking them into pies to donate to a school function. We discover through Mary Alice's point of view that "To Grandma, Halloween wasn't so much trick-or-treat as it was vittles and vengeance. Though she'd have called it justice" (p. 38).

Peck continues to develop a plot that focuses on Mary Alice's growing understanding of and respect for her feisty grandmother's actions, beliefs, and values. By the end of the book, we as readers care about both Mary Alice and her grandmother and what will happen to them. The closeness of the two characters is revealed when Mary Alice leaves school during a tornado alert because she wants to "come home" and make sure that her grandmother is all right. This closeness is again reinforced when Mary Alice realizes: "Sometimes I thought I was turning into her. I had to watch out not to talk like her. And I was to cook like her for all the years to come" (p. 123). This closeness is again highlighted through Mary Alice's first-person point of view when she declares " 'Grandma, I don't want to go back to Chicago. I want to stay here with you' " (p. 126).

By developing this relationship through Mary Alice's point of view, Peck helps us understand the changes that allow Mary Alice to progress from someone who thought she was at the end of the world with no one to care about her to a character who shows considerable love, respect, and admiration for her grandmother. Peck's last two pages are placed in the future when years later Mary Alice returns to her grandmother's house to be married.

As students of children's literature, you may wish to consider how Peck uses point of view to develop characterizations and plot in *A Long Way from Chicago*. Could you predict any of the happenings in *A Year Down Yonder*? Does Peck use any of the same techniques to develop point of view in *A Long Way from Chicago*?

An author has several options when selecting point of view. A first-person point of view speaks through the "I" of one of the characters. An author who wishes to use a first-person narrative must decide which character's actions and feelings should influence the story. An objective point of view lets actions speak for themselves. The author describes only the characters' actions, and readers must infer the characters' thoughts and feelings.

An omniscient point of view tells the story in the third person ("they," "he," or "she"). The author is not restricted to the knowledge, experiences, and feelings of one person. The feelings and thoughts of all characters can be revealed. A limited omniscient point of view, however, concentrates on the experiences of one character but has the option to be all-knowing about other characters. A limited omniscient point of view may clarify conflicts and actions that would be less understandable in a first-person narrative.

Although no point of view is preferred for all children's literature, an author's choice can affect how much children of certain ages believe and enjoy a story. Contemporary realistic fiction for children age eight and older often uses a first-person point of view or a limited omniscient point of view that focuses on one child's experiences. Older children often empathize with one character if they have had similar experiences.

Consistency of point of view encourages readers to believe in a story. Such belief is especially crucial in modern fantasy, where readers are introduced to imaginary worlds, unusual characters, and magical incidents. A writer may describe a setting as if it were being viewed by a character only a few inches tall. To be believable, however, the story cannot stray from the viewpoint of the tiny character. The character's actions, the responses of others toward the character, and the setting must be consistent.

Stereotypes

Consider stereotypes when evaluating literature for young children. Educators and other concerned adults strongly criticize stereotypical views of both race and sex. Of particular concern are literary selections that inadequately represent minority groups and females or that represent them in insensitive or demeaning ways.

Teachers, librarians, and parents may confront a shortage of high-quality stories about members of racial and ethnic minority groups, of works by authors who write from a minority perspective, and of materials that depict the literary, cultural, and historical influences of minorities. However, children's literature should present honest, authentic pictures of different people and their cultural and historical contributions.

When evaluating literature about minorities, for example, keep the following questions in mind: Are African American, Native American, Latino, and other minority characters portrayed as distinct individuals, or are they grouped in one category under depersonalizing clichés? Does the author recognize and accurately portray the internal diversity of minority cultures? Are minority cultures respected or treated as inferior? Does the author accurately describe the values, behavior, and environment of characters who are members of minority groups? Are illustrations realistic and authentic? Research indicates that if stereotypical attitudes are to change, reading of positive multicultural literature must be followed by discussions or other activities that allow interactions between children and adults.

In this book, set in the recession of 1937, the author develops several strong points of view. (Cover Art by Steve Cieslawski, copyright © 2000 by Steve Cieslawski, cover art, from A Year Down Yonder, by Richard Peck. Used by permission of Dial Books for Young Readers, a division of Penguin Putnam, Inc.

Sexism in children's literature also requires adults to evaluate children's books with care. Masha Kabakow Rudman (1984) states:

Books for children have reflected societal attitudes in limiting choices and maintaining discrimination. Most traditional books show females dressed in skirts or dresses even when they are engaged in activities inappropriate for this sort of costume. Illustrations also have conventionally placed females in passive observer roles, while males have been pictured as active. Studies have demonstrated time and time again that illustrations confirm the subordinate, less valued role for the female, while stressing the active, adventuresome, admirable role of the male. . . . When a female is permitted to retain her active qualities, it is usually made clear to the reader that she is the notable exception and that all the other girls in the story are "normal." (p. 105)

Some children's books also stereotype males in ways that limit the options of boys to express a wide range of feelings and interests. Books should treat all characters as

individuals. A book that groups all males or all females together and makes insulting remarks about either sex as a whole is sexist. However, you must read an entire book before you reach this decision, because you should not judge isolated quotes out of context.

The Right Book for Each Child

Because of developmental stages, children have different personal and literary needs at different ages. Children in the same age group or at the same stage of development also have diverse interests and reading abilities that you must consider. Understanding why and what children read is necessary in order to help them select materials that stimulate their interests and enjoyment. Studies show that the most powerful determinants of adult reading are accessibility, readability, and interest. These factors also influence children's reading. If developing enjoyment through literature is a major objective of your reading program for children, you must make available many excellent books, consider children's reading levels, and know how to gain and use information about children's reading interests.

Accessibility

Literature must be readily accessible if children are to read at all. To determine which books interest them, gain knowledge of their heritage, recognize and appreciate good literature, and understand themselves and others through literature, children must have opportunities to read and listen to many books. As suggested, a literature program for children should include a wide variety of high-quality literature, both old and new. Unfortunately, studies show that children do not have enough opportunities to read literature in school. Roger Poole (1986) surveyed schools in England and reported, "Findings of the research show that teachers do not make much use of quality narrative" (p. 179). Rebecca Barr and Marilyn Sadow (1989) analyzed American schools and found "little reading of literary selections other than those available in the basal program" (p. 69).

Accessibility in the home is also important for developing interest in books. In a review of studies of children who read early and who do voluntary reading, Lesley Mandel Morrow (1991) discusses environments that foster children's early interest in books. She concludes that the environments must have a large supply of accessible books, plus parents who read to children regularly and who are responsive to their children's questions about books. In addition, these parents must serve as models by reading a great deal themselves.

In a panel discussion on the importance of reading during the summer, educators interviewed by Eden Ross Lipson (2001) stressed the importance of reading for pleasure during this time because children gain a love for reading and also return to school as better readers.

Technology Resources

The Children's Literature Web Guide is an excellent site that includes award lists, conference information, and links to sources for parents, teachers, storytellers, writers, and illustrators. If you visit only one site concerning children's literature, this should be it. Link to it from our Companion Website at www.prenhall.com/norton

A survey by Susan Swanton (1984) showed that gifted students owned more books and used public libraries more than did other students. Fifty-five percent of the gifted students whom Swanton surveyed identified the public library as their major source of reading materials, as opposed to only 33 percent of the other students, most of whom identified the school library as their major source for books. Thirty-five percent of the gifted children owned more than one hundred books. Only 19 percent of other students owned an equal number of books. Swanton made the following recommendations for cooperation between public libraries and schools:

1. Promote students' participation in summer reading programs that are sponsored by public libraries.
2. Inform parents about the value of reading aloud to children, of giving children their own books, and of parents as role models for developing readers.
3. Encourage school librarians to do book talks designed to entice children into reading.
4. Provide field trips to public libraries.
5. Advertise public library programs and services.
6. Make obtaining the first library card a special event.

These recommendations have not changed. Nilsen and Donelson (2001) stress many of the same activities to promote reading by young adults, especially the need to match books with readers, provide book talks, make displays to promote books, and develop programs to interest readers.

Readability

Readability is another major consideration in choosing literature for children. A book must conform to a child's reading level in order for the child to read independently. Children become frustrated when books contain too many words that they don't know. A child is able to read independently when able to pronounce about 98–100 percent of the words in a book and to answer 90–100 percent of the comprehension questions asked about it. Reading abilities in any one age group or grade level range widely, so adults working with children must provide and be familiar with an equally wide range of literature. Many children have reading levels lower than their interest levels. Thus, they need many opportunities to listen to, and otherwise interact with, fine literature.

Books listed in the bibliographies at the end of chapters in this book are identified by grade level and readability, although a book will not be applicable to every child in the grade indicated.

Interest and Reader Response

Interests are also extremely important when developing literature programs. Margaret Early (1992/1993) states, "Decades of experience have shown that children are more likely to develop as thoughtful readers when they are pursuing content that interests them" (p. 307). You can learn about children's interests from studies of children's interests and from interest inventories. You should consider information gained from each source.

Dianne Monson and Sam Sebesta (1991) reviewed the research on children's interests and reading preferences. They conclude, "The results of a good number of studies reveal agreement of types of subject matter that appeal to students of a particular age level and support the notion that interests change with age" (p. 667). Monson and Sebesta found that children in the first and second grades prefer stories about animals, nature, fantasy, and child characters. Children in the third and fourth grades continue to be interested in nature and animals and begin to develop interest in adventure and familiar experiences. Boys in the fifth and sixth grades are interested in war, travel, and mystery, while girls are interested in animal stories, westerns, and fairy tales. Children in the intermediate grades show an increasing interest in history and science as well as continuing interest in mystery and adventure. By the seventh and eighth grades, girls prefer mysteries; romances; stories about animals, religion, and careers; humorous stories; and biographies. Boys prefer science fiction, mysteries, adventure stories, biographies, histories, and stories about animals and sports. Both boys and girls have an increased interest in nonfiction, romantic fiction, historical fiction, and books dealing with adolescence. All children like books that contain humor and adventure.

While this information can provide some general ideas about what subjects and authors that children of certain ages, sexes, and reading abilities prefer, do not develop stereotyped views about children's preferences. Without asking questions about interests, there is no way to learn, for example, that a fourth-grade boy is a Shakespeare buff, since research into children's interests does not indicate that a fourth grader should like Shakespeare's plays. A first-grade girl's favorite subject was dinosaurs, which she could identify by name. Discovering this would have been impossible without an interview; research does not indicate that first-grade girls are interested in factual, scientific subjects. These two cases point to the need to discover children's interests before helping children select books. Informal conversation is one of the simplest ways to uncover children's interests. Ask a child to describe what he or she likes to do and read about. Usually, you should record the information when working with a number of children.

ISSUE The Content of Children's Books: Pleasure Versus the Message

"Read This, It's Good for You" is the title of a critical evaluation of books. Children's author Natalie Babbitt[1] discusses books that have messages about instructing children in the values of reading. She asks, "What's the use of writing a story for children about the value of reading when it will be read only by those children who are already readers?" (p. 23). She argues that in many books there is no story. Instead, there is a message about the way life is supposed to be. In place of books whose main purpose is delivering a message, Babbitt wants children to learn to love reading by reading books such as *Millions of Cats, Make Way for Ducklings,* and *Where the Wild Things Are.*

Babbitt concludes, "Good stories are always a pleasure to read, and we like pleasure, regardless of our ages. The risk with message books, and

message attitudes, is that children's books will get classed with broccoli and end up shoved under the mashed potatoes of television" (p. 24).

Author John Neufeld[2] provides a contrasting view for evaluating books in an article titled "Preaching to the Unconverted." He states, "I have often been criticized for being didactic. Sometimes that criticism has been warranted. At other times, I have felt that reviewers were unable to distinguish between information offered—valuable information for young people—and what they perceive as a Message. . . . I may direct a reader's attention to, or help focus it on, an idea or problem, but I can only induce readers to decide whether that story applies to their lives" (p. 36).

Neufeld believes that the stories that last are the ones that encourage readers to think about

what they would do in similar circumstances. Neufeld concludes, "Stories about young people, for young people, are feasts authors serve their youthful readers. I like to think that some of what we offer sticks to their bones" (p. 36).

As you read and evaluate children's literature, consider the impact of the content to bring pleasure and increase joy in reading versus the importance of the message. Which is more important, pleasure or message? Which type of book do you remember from your own childhood? What was the impact of the book on you?

[1]Babbitt, Natalie. "Read This, It's Good for You." *The New York Times Book Review,* May 18, 1997, 23–24.
[2]Neufeld, John. "Preaching to the Unconverted." *School Library Journal* 42 (July 1996): 36.

The Child As Critic

Children are the ultimate critics of what they read, and you should consider their preferences when evaluating and selecting books to share with them. For the last few years, a joint project of the International Reading Association and the Children's Book Council has allowed approximately 10,000 children from around the United States to evaluate children's books published during a given year. Each year, their reactions are recorded, and a research team uses this information to compile a list called "Children's Choices" in the following categories: beginning independent reading, younger children, middle grades, older readers, informational books, and poetry. This very useful annotated bibliography is published each year in the October issue of *The Reading Teacher,* and it may be obtained from the Children's Book Council, 67 Irving Place, New York, NY 10003.

A summary of children's reading choices by Christine Hall and Martin Coles (1999) provides an interesting list for discussion. They conclude:

1. Children read fewer books as they grow older.

2. In the Children's Reading Choices Survey, the average number of books read in the month prior to the survey was 2.52.

3. Children at ages ten, twelve, and fourteen are eclectic in their reading habits.

4. Strongly plotted adventure stories are popular at all ages.

5. Ten-year-olds choose to read poetry, but interest in poetry declines with age.

6. Most children respond positively when asked their views about reading.

7. Younger children spend more of their leisure time reading than do older children.

Children choose books from a wide variety of genres. Some are on lists of highly recommended children's books; others are not. Many educators and authorities on children's literature are concerned about the quality of books that children read. To improve their ability to make valid judgments about literature, children must experience good books and investigate and discuss the elements that make books memorable. Young children usually just enjoy and talk about books, but older ones can start to evaluate what they do and do not like about literature.

Ted Hipple and Amy B. Maupin (2001) discuss the importance of encouraging students to find the artistry in the details of a novel. They state, "It is a good teaching tactic to ask students to find selections—passages, individual sentences, even single words—they like. When enough students have responded positively to something, that something, even a required novel, may suddenly take on a new significance: peers like it, too" (p. 41). In addition, they recommend that students read Lois Lowry's *The Giver,* Karen Hesse's *Out of the Dust,* and Louis Sachar's *Holes* and compare and contrast the measures of quality in the books using plots, characters, themes, artistry in details,

EVALUATION CRITERIA

Literary Criticism: Questions to Ask Myself When I Judge a Book

1. Is this a good story?

2. Is the story about something I think could really happen? Is the plot believable?

3. Did the main character overcome the problem, but not too easily?

4. Did the climax seem natural?

5. Did the characters seem real? Did I understand the characters' personalities and the reasons for their actions?

6. Did the characters in the story grow?

7. Did I find out about more than one side of the characters? Did the characters have both strengths and weaknesses?

8. Did the setting present what is actually known about that time or place?

9. Did the characters fit into the setting?

10. Did I feel that I was really in that time or place?

11. What did the author want to tell me in the story?

12. Was the theme worthwhile?

13. When I read the book aloud, did the characters second like real people actually talking?

14. Did the rest of the language sound natural? (Norton, 1993)

and emotional impact. These books are excellent choices because they have been identified as popular with readers as well as winners of the Newbery award.

One sixth-grade teacher encouraged her students to make literary judgments and to develop a list of criteria for selecting good literature (Norton, 1993). The motivation for this literature study began when the students wondered what favorite books their parents might have read when they were in the same grade. To answer this question, the children interviewed their parents and other adults, asking them which books and characters were their favorites. The children listed the books, characters, and number of people who recommended each book on a large chart.

Each student then read a book that a parent or another respected adult had enjoyed. (Many adults also reread these books.) Following their reading, the children discussed the book with the adult, considering what made or did not make the book memorable for them. At this time, the teacher introduced the concepts of plot, characterization, setting, theme, and style. The children searched the books that they had read for examples of each element. Finally, they listed questions to ask themselves when evaluating a book (see the accompanying Evaluation Criteria).

A review of the fourteen evaluative questions shows how closely they correspond to the criteria that should be used in evaluating plot, characterization, setting, theme, and style.

When children are encouraged to share, discuss, and evaluate books and are given opportunities to do so, they are able to expand their reading enjoyment and to select worthwhile stories and characters. Sharing and discussion can take place in the library, in the classroom, or at home.

Suggested Activities

 For more suggested activities for evaluating and selecting children's literature, visit our **Companion Website** at www.prenhall.com/norton

- Find examples of person-against-person, person-against-society, person-against-nature, and person-against-self conflicts in children's literature. Do some books develop more than one type of conflict? What makes the conflict believable? Share these examples with your class.

- Read one of Laura Ingalls Wilder's "Little House" books. Do you agree with the child who said that she would like the character Laura for her best friend? How has the author developed Laura into a believable character? Give examples of techniques that Wilder uses to reveal Laura's nature.

- The following five authors or illustrators from the United States have won the Hans Christian Andersen Award: Virginia Hamilton, Paula Fox, Meindert DeJong, Maurice Sendak, and Scott O'Dell. Pretend that you are a member of the worldwide committee. What qualities encourage you to select books of these authors and illustrators?

- Compare the top teachers' choices and the top children's choices ("Going Places," *Reading Today*, 2001). The top adult choices: E. B. White's *Charlotte's Web*, Chris Van Allsburg's *The Polar Express*, Dr. Seuss's *Green Eggs and Ham*, Maurice Sendak's *Where the Wild Things Are*, Robert N. Munsch's *Love You Forever*, Shel Silverstein's *The Giving Tree*, Eric Carle's *The Very Hungry Caterpillar*, Wilson Rawls's *Where the Red Fern Grows*, and Jan Brett's *The Mitten*. The top children's choices include J. K. Rowling's "Harry Potter" series, R. L. Stine's "Goosebumps" series, Dr. Seuss's *Green Eggs and Ham*, Dr. Seuss's *The Cat in the Hat*, Marc Brown's "Arthur" series, E. B. White's *Charlotte's Web*, Phyllis Reynold Naylor's "Shiloh" trilogy, Gary Paulsen's *Hatchet*, Louis Sachar's *Holes*, and Lois Lowry's *The Giver*.

Teaching with Literary Elements

Whether developing a literature program, developing literature-based reading instruction, or sharing literature on a one-to-one basis, remember the dual roles of literature: providing enjoyment and developing understanding. If you want children to respond to, love, and appreciate literature, provide them with a varied selection of fine literature and give them many opportunities to read, listen to, share, discuss, and respond to literature.

Involving Children in Plot

Creative drama interpretations based on story texts help children expand their imaginations, stimulate their feelings, enhance their language, and clarify their concepts. Through the playmaking process, children discover that plot provides a framework, that there is a beginning in which the conflict is introduced, that there is a middle that moves the action toward a climax, and that there is an end with a resolution to the conflict.

Nursery rhymes are excellent for introducing both younger and older children to the concept that a story has several parts—a beginning, a middle, and an end. The simple plots in many nursery rhymes make them ideal for this purpose. "Humpty Dumpty" contains three definite actions that cannot be interchanged and still retain a logical sequence: (1) a beginning—"Humpty Dumpty sat on a wall," (2) a middle—"Humpty Dumpty had a great fall," and (3) an end—"All the king's horses and all the king's men couldn't put Humpty Dumpty together again." Children can listen to the rhyme, identify the actions, discuss the reasons for the order, and finally act out each part. Encourage them to extend their parts by adding dialogue or characters to beginning, middle, or ending incidents. Other nursery rhymes illustrating sequential plots include "Jack and Jill," "Pat-a-Cake, Pat-a-Cake, Baker's Man," and "Rock-a-Bye Baby."

After children understand the importance of plot structure in nursery rhymes, proceed to folktales, such as "Three Billy Goats Gruff," in which there is also a definite and logical sequence of events. Divide the children according to the beginning incidents, middle incidents, and ending incidents. After each group practices its part, put the groups together into a logical whole. To help children learn the importance of order, have them rearrange the incidents. They will discover that if the ending incidents are enacted first, the story is over and there is no rising action or increasing conflict.

Diagramming plot structures is another activity that helps children appreciate and understand that many stories follow a structure in which the characters and the problems are introduced at the beginning of the story, the conflict increases until a climax or turning point is reached, and the conflict ends. Have children listen to or read stories and then discuss and identify the important incidents. For example, the important incidents in Dianne Snyder's *The Boy of the Three-Year Nap* are placed on the plot diagram in Figure 3.1.

Stories in which the conflict results because characters must overcome problems within themselves may also be placed on plot diagrams. Caron Lee Cohen (1985) identifies four major components in

The rhyme "Humpty Dumpty" contains three definite actions that cannot be interchanged and still retain a logical sequence. (From Humpty Dumpty.*)*

the development of person-against-self conflicts: (1) problem, (2) struggle, (3) self-realization, and (4) achievement of peace or truth. Literature selections such as Marion Dane Bauer's *On My Honor,* in which the author develops struggles within the main characters, are good for this type of discussion and plot diagramming. In this plot structure, identify (1) the problem and the characters, (2) the incidents that reflect increasing struggle with self, (3) the point of self-realization, and (4) the point at which the main character attains peace or truth. Because person-against-self conflicts are frequently complex, lead students in the identification of significant incidents and ask them to provide support for these major struggles.

For example, in *On My Honor,* the problem results for Bauer's character, Joel, because he betrays his parents' trust and swims with his friend in a treacherous river. The struggle continues as Joel feels increasing guilt, tries not to accept his friend's disappearance and probable death, and blames his father for allowing the two boys to go on a bike ride in the first place. Self-realization begins when Joel admits that Tony drowned and realizes that his father is not the cause of his problem: "But even as he slammed through the door and ran up the stairs to his room, he knew. It wasn't his father he hated. It wasn't his father at all. He was the one....Tony died because of him" (p. 81).

Peace and truth begin, although the seriousness of the problem does not allow complete resolution. After Joel sobbingly tells his father the whole truth, he feels "tired, exhausted, but tinglingly aware" (p. 89). Even though there cannot be a total resolution of the conflict, because Joel's father cannot give him the reassurance that he desires or take away his pain, Joel forgives his father and asks him to stay in the room until he (Joel) falls asleep.

Students may compare Bauer's person-against-self conflict with that in Paula Fox's *One-Eyed Cat* (see Chapter 9). Additional person-against-self conflicts for older students include Cynthia Rylant's *A Fine White Dust,* a traumatic conflict in which a thirteen-year-old boy becomes involved with an unscrupulous traveling evangelist and struggles to understand his own beliefs, Karen Hesse's *Out of the Dust,* a story in which the protagonist blames herself and her father for her mother's accidental death, and Audrey Couloumbis's *Getting Near to Baby* in which the protagonist must overcome her grief and gain insights into the healing process following the death of the baby in the family.

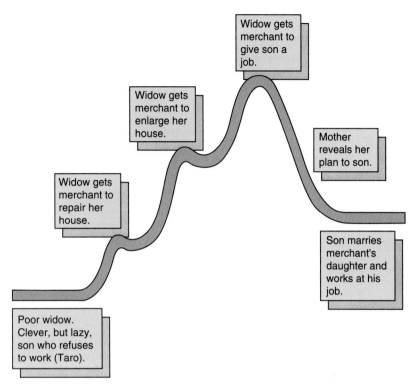

FIGURE 3.1   Plot diagram for Dianne Snyder's *The Boy of the Three-Year Nap*

Although many of the books with person-against-self conflicts are written for older students, several books may be used with younger students. For example, Arthur Yorinks's *Hey, Al* is a picture storybook in which Al and his dog Eddie overcome dissatisfaction and decide that "Paradise lost is sometimes Heaven found" (p. 27, unnumbered). Evaline Ness's *Sam, Bangs & Moonshine* is a picture storybook in which the main character faces the consequences of her lies.

Involving Children in Characterization

Authors of books with notable characters develop three-dimensional personalities that allow readers to gain insights into the strengths, weaknesses, pasts, hopes, and fears of the characters. You can help students understand how authors develop characters by discussing books in which the authors use several techniques for developing characters. You may also help students understand the often complex nature of inferencing about characters by modeling activities in which you show the students how to analyze evidence from the text and to speculate about the characters.

Characterization Techniques

Have students search for examples in which an author reveals a character through such techniques as narration, thoughts, actions, and dialogue. Have the students list examples in which each of these techniques is used and

CHART 3.2   Revealing characterization

Author's Technique	Characterization	Evidence
Narration	Plain and tall	"She was plain and tall." (p. 19)
	Loved by animals	"The dogs loved Sarah first." (p. 22)
	Loved animals	"The sheep made Sarah smile. . . . She talked to them." (p. 28)
	Intelligent	"Sarah was quick to learn." (p. 52)
Thoughts about the character	Loved the sea	Anna thought: "Sarah loved the sea, I could tell." (p. 12)
	Homesick	Anna thought: "Sarah was not smiling. Sarah was already lonely." (p. 20)
The character's actions	Adventurous	Sarah answers an advertisement asking for a wife. (p. 9)
	Sense of humor	When Sarah finished describing seals, she barked like one. (p. 27)
	Hardworking	Sarah learned how to plow the fields. (p. 33)
Dialogue	Strong	"I am strong and I work hard." (p. 9)
	Independent	Papa tells Sarah that the cat will be good in the barn. Sarah tells Papa that the cat will be good in the house. (p. 19)
	Confident	"I am fast and I am good." (p. 46)

identify what each example reveals. Have the students summarize what they know about a specific character and discuss whether the characterization is flat or rounded.

A group of students led by Diana Vrooman (1989) used this approach to identify and discuss the characterization of Sarah in Patricia MacLachlan's *Sarah, Plain and Tall.* First, Vrooman introduced the story and reviewed the techniques that authors may use to develop characters. Second, she listed on the board the techniques that MacLachlan uses to reveal Sarah's character in *Sarah, Plain and Tall.* Third, she read the first chapter to the students and asked them to identify the examples in the chapter and to stipulate what they learned about Sarah from those examples. Fourth, she asked the students to complete the search for other examples of Sarah's characterization in the remaining chapters. Finally, she asked the students to summarize Sarah's characterization and to defend whether or not they believed that Sarah was a rounded character.

Chart 3.2 shows a few of the characterizations and proofs for Sarah.

The students concluded that Sarah was a fully developed, three-dimensional character. In addition, they discovered the techniques that authors use to develop such well-rounded characters. The same book may be used to analyze the characterization of the young boy, Caleb, or the young girl, Anna.

Modeling Inferencing

Some of MacLachlan's characterizations in *Sarah, Plain and Tall* are stated, while others are implied. Students frequently need much assistance in analyzing implied characterizations. Researchers such as Laura Roehler and Gerald

Duffy (1984) and Christine Gordon (1985) have developed modeling approaches that place an adult in an active role with students and that show the adult's thought processing to the students. Modeling is one of the most effective ways to improve comprehension (Dole, Duffy, Roehler, and Pearson, 1991) and is an effective way to help students understand characterization (Norton, 1992). The following activity shows the modeling process with Patricia MacLachlan's *Sarah, Plain and Tall.*

Requirements for Effective Reasoning. Effective inferencing requires readers to go beyond the information that an author provides in a text. Readers must use clues from the text to hypothesize about a character's emotions, beliefs, actions, hopes, and fears. Readers must also be aware that authors develop characters by narration, a character's thoughts or the thoughts of others about the character, the character's actions, and the dialogue between the characters.

An Introduction to Inferencing. Review characterization by asking students to identify how authors develop three-dimensional, believable characters. Share examples of each technique of characterization as part of this review. Also explain that students will listen to you ask a question, answer the question, provide evidence from the story that supports the answer, and share the reasoning process used to reach the answer. Tell the students that after they have listened to you proceed through the sequence, they will use the same process to answer questions, identify evidence, and explore their own reasoning processes. As part of this introduction, discuss the meanings of *evidence* and *reasoning.* Encourage the students to identify evidence about a character in the literature and to share how to use this evidence.

The Importance of Inferencing. Ask students to explain why it is important to be able to make inferences about characters. Encourage the students to discuss how inferencing characterizations makes a story more exciting, enjoyable, and believable.

An Introduction to the Story. There are two important settings in *Sarah, Plain and Tall:* (1) the pioneer setting in one of the prairie states and (2) the pioneer setting in Maine. To identify students' understandings of these locations and time periods, ask the students to pretend that they are sitting on the front porch of a cabin in one of the prairie states in the 1800s, to look away from the cabin, and to describe what they see. Make sure that they describe prairie grass, wheat fields, few trees, a dirt road, and flat or gently rolling land. Ask them to tell which colors they see. Then, ask them to turn around and describe what they see through the open door of the cabin. Make sure that they describe a small space, a fireplace, and characteristic furnishings, such as wooden chairs and a wooden table.

The Maine setting is also important to this story because Sarah's conflict results from love of a very different setting. Ask the students to pretend that they are sitting on the coast of Maine, to look out at the ocean, and to describe what they see. Ask them to turn toward the land and describe the setting. Ask them to discuss the differences between the prairie and the Maine coast and to consider whether the differences in these settings could cause conflicts for a character.

The First Modeling Example. Read orally from the beginning of the book through the line, "That was the worst thing about Caleb," on page 5. Ask, "What was Anna's attitude toward her brother Caleb when he was a baby?" Answer, "Anna disliked her brother a great deal. We might even say she hated him." Provide the evidence. Say, "Anna thinks that Caleb is homely, plain, and horrid smelling. Anna associates Caleb with her mother's death." Provide the reasoning that you used to reach the answer. For example, "The words Anna uses, especially *horrid,* are often associated with things that we do not like. I know from the reference to the happy home that Anna loved her mother. When she says that her mother's death was the worst thing about Caleb, I believe that she blamed him for the death."

The Second Modeling Example. At this point, verify that the students understand the procedure. If they do not, continue by completely modeling another example. If the students understand the process, let them join the discussion by providing an answer, the evidence, and the reasoning. It is advisable to have the students jot down brief answers to the questions, evidence, and reasoning; these notes will increase the quality of the discussion that follows each question.

The next logical discussion point occurs at the bottom of page 5. Read through the line, "And Papa didn't sing." Ask the question, "What is Anna really telling us about her inner feelings?" Ask the students to answer the question. They should provide answers similar to this one: "She believes

that nothing can replace her lost mother and that the home will not be happy again." Ask the students to provide evidence, such as, "The author tells us that the relatives could not fill the house. The days are compared to long, dark winter days. The author states that Papa did not sing." Ask the students to provide reasoning, such as, "The author created a very sad mood. We see a house filled with relatives that do not matter to Anna. I know what long, dark, winter days are like. I can visualize a house without singing. I think Anna is very unhappy and it may take her a long time to get over her loss."

Continue this process, having the students discuss the many instances of implied characterization in the book. The letters written by Sarah to Mr. Wheaton (p. 9), to Anna (pp. 9–10), and to Caleb (p. 11) are especially good for inferencing about the characters because students need to infer what was in the letters written by Anna and Caleb. To help the students infer the contents of the letters, ask the students to write the letters themselves.

Longer stories, such as *Sarah, Plain and Tall,* lend themselves to discussions according to chapters. Students may read and discuss several chapters each day. After each session, however, ask the students to summarize what they know about Sarah, Anna, Caleb, and Papa. Ask them, "What do you want to know about these characters?"

Involving Children in Setting

Believable settings place readers in geographic locations and time periods that they can see, hear, and even feel. In literature, authors use settings for four purposes: (1) creating appropriate moods, (2) developing antagonists, (3) developing historical and geographical backgrounds, and (4) suggesting symbolic interpretations.

Settings That Create Moods

Authors use settings to create moods. Through word choices and the visual pictures created by words, authors create moods that range from humorous and happy to frightening and foreboding. Asking students to tell their reactions to words and illustrations and comparing words and illustrations in a text help students understand and evaluate the appropriateness of a mood. For example, students can respond to the frightening, eerie mood created by Marcia Brown's illustrations for Blaise Cendrars's *Shadow* and examine the influence of words, such as *prowler,* and descriptions, such as "teeming like snakes," in Cendrars's poem. When a house sits precariously under a wave, as in Shelley Jackson's *The Old Woman and the Wave,* readers can respond to the frightening mood or the more symbolic fear of the unknown.

Teachers may use illustrated texts, such as *Song and Dance Man,* to show students very different moods. Stephen Gammell's illustrations create a warm, happy mood as children watch their beloved grandfather recreate the joyful days of his youth. The transition from a common, dreary, crowded attic to an uncommon experience is enhanced by the artist's drawing of a brightly colored, shadowy shape.

Additional literature selections that develop warm, happy moods through both illustrations and text are Cynthia Rylant's *When I Was Young in the Mountains*, Kate Banks's *And if the Moon Could Talk*, Margaret Wild's *Our Granny*, and Alexandra Day's *Frank and Ernest Play Ball*. Funny, even absurd, moods are created in both the text and illustrations of Doreen Cronin's *Click, Clack, Moo: Cows That Type*, Simms Taback's *There Was an Old Lady Who Swallowed a Fly*, Mary Ann Hoberman's *Mr. and Mrs. Muddle*, Patricia Polacco's *Meteor!*, Jacqueline Briggs Martin's *Good Times on Grandfather Mountain*, Susan Meddaugh's *Martha Speaks*, Kevin Henkes's *Owen*, and Angela Johnson's *Julius*.

Authors of fantasy frequently prepare their readers for the fantastical experiences to come by creating settings and moods in which fantasy seems possible. Sharing and discussing introductions to fantasies allow students to appreciate and understand the techniques that authors use to prepare them for both fantasy and conflict. For example, read and discuss the following introduction to Natalie Babbitt's *Tuck Everlasting*:

The road that led to Treegap had been trod out long before by a herd of cows who were, to say the least, relaxed. It wandered along in curves and easy angles, swayed off and up in a pleasant tangent to the top of a small hill, ambled down again between fringes of bee-hung clover, and then cut sidewise across a meadow. Here its edges blurred. It widened and seemed to pause, suggesting tranquil bovine picnics: slow chewing and thoughtful contemplation of the infinite. And then it went on again and came at last to the wood. But on reaching the shadows of the first trees, it veered sharply, swung out in a wide arc as if, for the first time, it had reason to think where it was going, and passed around.

On the other side of the wood, the sense of easiness dissolved. The road no longer belonged to the cows. It became, instead, and rather abruptly, the property of people. And all at once the sun was uncomfortably hot, the dust oppressive, and the meager grass along its edges somewhat ragged and forlorn. On the left stood the first house, a square and solid cottage with a touch-me-not appearance, surrounded by grass cut painfully to the quick and enclosed by a capable iron fence some four feet high which clearly said, "Move on—we don't want you here." So the road went humbly by and made its way, past cottages more and more frequent but less and less forbidding, into the village. But the village doesn't matter, except for the jailhouse and the gallows. The first house only is important; the first house, the road, and the wood. (pp. 5–6)

After you read this introduction, to enhance personal response have the students consider the effect of the contrasts used by Babbitt, the influence of personification, and the impact of such wordings as "tranquil bovine picnics," "veered sharply," "touch-me-not," and "grass cut painfully to the quick." Have the students speculate about the changing mood in the introduction and the type of story that might follow. Of course, have them read the story to verify their predictions.

Settings That Develop Antagonists

Authors of both historical fiction and contemporary adventure stories frequently develop plots in which nature or society is the antagonist. Vivid descriptions of either nature or society are essential if readers are to understand why and how the setting has created conflicts or even life-and-death perils.

Sharing and discussing quotations will help students respond to, identify, and appreciate vivid descriptions. Kevin Crossley-Holland's *Storm* is written for young readers. The author, however, vividly describes a fearful storm and a girl who fears the storm and faces her fears of a ghostly creature who supposedly roams the English marshlands. Crossley-Holland uses personification and metaphor to develop believable settings. For example, Crossley-Holland says that the storm "whistled between its salty lips and gnashed its sharp teeth" (p. 14) and "gave a shriek" (p. 27). Other elements in nature respond. The moon "seemed to be speeding behind grey lumpy clouds, running away from something that was chasing it" (p. 23). The young girl responds in ways that suggest fear: "Annie felt a cold finger slowly moving from the base of her spine up to her neck, and then spread out across her shoulders" (p. 12) and she swayed in the saddle as she "thought she could bear it no longer—the furious gallop, the gallop of the storm, the storm of her own fears" (p. 35). By the end of the story, Annie has faced her fears of both the storm and the ghost.

In *Call It Courage*, Armstrong Sperry uses personification to give human actions to the sea and decreasing sentence lengths to show increasing danger. Have your students search for vivid descriptions throughout the book. After students discuss such examples, encourage them to find additional quotations in which nature is depicted through vivid descriptions, to share the quotations, and to tell why they believe that nature is the antagonist. Vivid descriptions of nature as an antagonist also are found in Gary Paulsen's *Hatchet*, Farley Mowat's *Lost in the Barrens*, Scott O'Dell's *Island of the Blue Dolphins*, Jean Craighead George's *Julie of the Wolves*, Michael Morpurgo's *Kensuke's Kingdom*, and Sharon Creech's *The Wanderer*.

It is more difficult for students to understand the setting if society, and not nature, causes the conflict because the students must understand both the larger societal attitudes and the reasons that the characters are in conflict with those attitudes. Thematic studies that allow students to read from several genres are usually best for developing understanding about complex subjects, such as anti-Semitism or slavery. In thematic studies, have students use nonfictional sources to authenticate the settings in historical fiction. For example, a series of books about the Holocaust might include nonfiction, biography, historical fiction, and even time-warp fantasy. Beginning with Barbara Rogasky's nonfictional *Smoke and Ashes: The Story of the Holocaust*, students can discover the historical background of the time period, the roots of anti-Semitism, the development of ghettos and concentration camps, and the tragic consequences. Have the students read Milton Meltzer's nonfictional *Rescue: The Story of How Gentiles Saved Jews in the Holocaust* to provide historical background about heroic people who risked their own lives to save the lives of other people and Michael Leapman's *Witnesses to War: Eight True-Life Stories of Nazi Persecution.* Next, have the students read Albert Marrin's biographical text, *Hitler.* Pages 17–20 are especially revealing. Within these pages, Marrin discusses the roots of Hitler's anti-Semitism and his developing hatred. For example:

Once Adolph began to hate, it became harder and harder to stop hating. From the age of nineteen, his hatred deepened, grew stronger, until it passed the bounds of sanity. He had only to hear Jews mentioned, to see them or think he saw them, to lose self-control. . . . One day, he vowed, he'd get even with them. They'd pay, every last one of them, for the humiliation they'd caused him. (p. 20)

Have the students read Uri Orlev's historical fiction, *The Island on Bird Street* and *The Man from the Other Side,* Lois Lowry's historical fiction about the Danish resistance, *Number the Stars,* and Jane Yolen's time-warp story, *The Devil's Arithmetic.* Then, have the students use the background information from the first three books to evaluate the authenticity of the settings that cause so much conflict in the fictional books.

Settings That Develop Historical and Geographical Backgrounds

Settings in historical fiction and biography should be so integral to the story and so carefully developed that readers are encouraged to imagine the sights, sounds, and even smells of the environment. For example, have groups of students choose one of the settings developed in Elizabeth George Speare's *The Sign of the Beaver,* such as the log cabin, the wilderness, or the Penobscot village. Lead them to discover as much information as possible about the sights, sounds, and even tastes associated with that environment. Have them identify and analyze quotations that describe the setting.

Students enjoy creating maps and illustrations depicting well-defined settings. Have students use details from historical fiction or fantasy to draw maps, homes, or other settings. Carefully crafted fantasy worlds provide evidence for map locations and show the importance of settings in creating believable worlds. For example, after students read J. R. R. Tolkien's *The Hobbit,* ask them to draw maps of Middle Earth. C. S. Lewis's *The Lion, the Witch and the Wardrobe* includes detailed information about Narnia. Likewise, Lewis Carroll's *Alice's Adventures in Wonderland* provides descriptions of Wonderland.

After students have read literature with well-developed settings, divide the class into groups and ask each group to draw a map so that visitors to the land would be able to travel through it. Ask the students to defend their map loca-

tions by providing evidence from the literature. After the maps are completed, ask each group to share its map with the larger group and to defend why it placed landmarks in specific places.

Two sources provide interesting stimulation for these drawing tasks. Alberto Manguel and Gianni Guadalupi's *The Dictionary of Imaginary Places* (1980) includes maps and descriptions of numerous fantasy worlds. Rosalind Ashe and Lisa Tuttle's *Children's Literary Houses: Famous Dwellings in Children's Fiction* (1984) includes interpretations of the homes found in Frances Hodgson Burnett's *The Secret Garden,* T. H. White's *The Sword in the Stone,* Esther Forbes's *Johnny Tremain,* and Louisa May Alcott's *Little Women.*

Settings That Are Symbolic

The easiest symbolic setting for students to understand is probably the once-upon-a-time setting found in folktales. Readers know that "once upon a time" means much more than long ago. When readers close their eyes, they often visualize deep woods or majestic castles, where enchantment, magic, and heroic adventures are expected. Folktale settings are excellent introductions to symbolic settings.

Authors of other types of literature also use symbolic settings to develop understandings of plots, characters, and themes. Frances Hodgson Burnett's *The Secret Garden* is one of the best literature selections for showing symbolic settings. Students can trace parallel changes that take place in the garden and in the people living in Misselthwaite Manor. For example, the story begins in a cold, dreary mansion surrounded by gardens that are dormant from winter. The characters are equally unresponsive. Mary is "the most disagreeable-looking child ever seen. . . . She had a little thin face and a little thin body, thin light hair and a sour expression" (p. 1). Colin is a disagreeable invalid, Mr. Craven is still in mourning for his dead wife, and Colin and his father are estranged. The setting and the people begin to change after Mary finds the door to the secret garden. Finding the key to the garden is the symbolic turning point, after which the characters and the garden are slowly nurtured back to both physical and emotional health.

As students trace the parallel changes in the garden and the people, they may ask themselves the following questions: Why does the author focus attention on a garden that has been locked and mostly uncared for for ten years? What is the significance of a key that opens a door? How do the people change and what happens to the garden? Why does the author draw parallels between nurturing a garden and healing people both physically and emotionally? Does the garden meet Perrine's requirements for symbolism in literature? Is the garden a good symbolic setting for both characterization and plot development? Why or why not?

Students may explore the symbolism of gardens in Philippa Pearce's *Tom's Midnight Garden* and other books.

Involving Children in Theme

Students need many opportunities to read and discuss literature in order to identify controlling ideas or central concepts in stories. Themes are difficult because they are frequently implied rather than directly stated. Students learn about themes, however, by studying the actions of characters, analyzing the central conflict, and considering the outcome of a story. When looking for theme, it is important to consider how the main character changes in the story, what conflicts are found in the story, what actions are rewarded or punished, and what the main character has learned as a result. Even the title may provide clues to the theme.

The following sequence of events develops an understanding of theme in Ann Grifalconi's *Darkness and the Butterfly*. First, explain to the students that theme is the controlling idea or central concept in a story. Themes often reveal important beliefs about life, and a story may contain more than one theme. When searching for theme, ask, "What is the author trying to tell us that would make a difference in our lives?" Review some of the ways in which authors reveal themes, such as through conflict, the characters' actions, the characters' thoughts, the outcome of the story, the actions that are rewarded or punished, and narrative. In addition, the title and illustrations may provide clues.

Next, read orally *Darkness and the Butterfly*. Ask the students, "What is the author trying to tell us that would make a difference in our lives?" They will probably identify two important themes: (1) It is all right to have fears—we all may have fears that cause us problems—and (2) we can and must overcome our fears.

After the students have identified the themes, ask them to listen to the story a second time. This time, ask them to search for proof that the author is developing these themes. Their discussion and evidence probably will include some of the following examples:

1. It is all right to have fears; we all may have fears that cause us problems.
   a. The illustrations show contrasts between the beauty of the world in the day, which is without fear, and the monsters that surface in Osa's mind at night.
   b. The actions of the mother show that she is understanding. She even gives beads to help Osa feel less fearful.
   c. The actions of Osa show that she is a normal child during the day but a fearful child at night.
   d. The wise woman tells Osa that she was once afraid, " 'specially at night!"
2. We can and must overcome our fears.
   a. The author tells the story of the yellow butterfly, the smallest of the small, as it flies into the darkness.
   b. The butterfly story is based on an important African proverb, "Darkness pursues the butterfly."
   c. The wise woman tells Osa, "You will find your own way."

d. The wise woman compares finding your way to the wings of the butterfly.
e. The dream sequence reveals the beauties of the night.
f. The actions of the butterfly show that it is not afraid.
g. Osa reveals her self-realization: "I can go by myself. I'm not afraid anymore."
h. The author states that Osa, the smallest of the small, "found the way to carry her own light through the darkness."
i. The butterfly symbolizes that the smallest, most fragile being in nature can light up the darkness, trust the night, and not be afraid.
j. The title of the book is *Darkness and the Butterfly*.

Folktales, with their easily identifiable conflicts and characterizations, are excellent for developing understanding of theme. For example, when searching for themes in John Steptoe's *Mufaro's Beautiful Daughters*, students discover that greed and selfishness are harmful and that kindness and generosity are beneficial.

Involving Children in Style

Many of the discussions and activities related to plot, characterization, setting, and theme emphasize an author's style. By selecting words that create visual images and arranging the words to create moods or to increase tension, authors show the power of carefully chosen words and sentence structures. When reading carefully crafted stories, you may not even notice the techniques that authors use. When you read aloud a carefully crafted story and one that is not so well developed, however, the differences become obvious. This section looks at developing students' appreciation for personification through narrative stories and for pleasing style.

Personification

Many of the most enjoyable books read to and by younger children develop characterizations through personification. This is probably so believable because children tend to give human characteristics to their pets and toys. Personification is an excellent introduction to style for younger children because the texts that include personification of objects and animals often are reinforced through illustrations that also personify the subjects.

Virginia Lee Burton's *The Little House* provides an enjoyable introduction to personification. As you read appropriate pages to the students, ask them: What pronoun is used when the author talks about the house? What actions can the house do that are similar to your actions? What feelings does the house express that are similar to your feelings? What causes the house to have each of these feelings? When have you had similar feelings? How do the illustrations help you understand the house's feelings and character? After the students have discussed the answers to these questions, share with them that the author is giving the house human feelings and behaviors through both the text and the illustrations.

Extend this understanding of personification in *The Little House* by asking the students to use pantomime or creative drama to enact the feelings expressed in the book. For example, have them listen to the text being read and pantomime the feelings expressed by the house. Have them create conversations that might occur between the house and her country or city neighbors. Have them tell the story from the point of view of one of the other objects found in the story.

Use similar discussions with books in which toys are personified, such as Anthony Browne's *Gorilla* and Margery Williams's *The Velveteen Rabbit.* Books in which animals are personified include Alexandra Day's *Frank and Ernest on the Road,* Diana Engel's *Josephina Hates Her Name,* and Lillian Hoban's *Arthur's Great Big Valentine.*

Pleasing Style

Jette Morache (1987) recommends having older students collect and share quotations from literature that they find pleasing or that support other literary elements, such as characterization, setting, and theme. Morache recommends having students work in groups to find quotes that illustrate a certain technique, to compare and discuss the quotes chosen by their group and other groups, to compile a page of quotes that they find particularly appealing, and to develop a list of qualities that make a "quotable quote." This type of activity is appropriate for developing appreciation for any of the literary elements discussed in this chapter. Have students find quotes to support characterization, setting, and theme.

Quotes also can emphasize specific literary techniques, such as personification, symbolism, simile, or metaphor. Older students might read Henry Wadsworth Longfellow's "Hiawatha" and Jamake Highwater's *Anpao: An American Indian Odyssey* to find examples of personification in nature. Jan Hudson's *Sweetgrass* is filled with symbolism, similes, and metaphors. Cynthia Voigt's *Dicey's Song* has many references to music, a sailboat, and a tree as symbols.

Students can also search books to find introductory paragraphs in which the author's style heightens their interest and makes them want to know more about the character and the story. For example, Tomie dePaola provides a vivid setting through words and references to known literature in *26 Fairmount Avenue.*

Webbing the Literary Elements

Webbing is an excellent way to help children understand important characteristics of a story (Norton, 1992). Webbing also helps students increase their appreciation of literature and improve their reading and writing competencies. In addition, webbing helps students understand the interrelationships among the literary elements. Prior to the webbing experience, introduce the literary elements of setting, characterization, conflicts (plot), and themes by including many of the activities previously discussed in this chapter. To introduce

the idea of webbing literary elements, read and discuss folktales with the children. Then, draw simple webs with the title of the book in the center and the elements of setting, characterization, conflicts, and themes on spokes that extend from the center. Lead discussions that help students identify the important characteristics being placed on the web.

The complex web presented in Figure 3.2 was completed with Karen Cushman's *Catherine, Called Birdy.* This historical fiction novel is set in medieval England. Notice on the web that the story takes place in an English manor. It also has strong characterizations, conflicts, and themes. An interesting comparison may be made by webbing Cushman's *The Midwife's Apprentice,* a tale set in the same time period but with a heroine from the lowest level of society.

Questioning to Encourage Aesthetic Responses

Many literature authorities stress that students' first responses to any literary work should be personal ones. For example, Patricia Cianciolo (1990) recommends that adults encourage personal responses during the sharing of a picture storybook before introducing any other activities related to the literature. These responses can take many forms. Children may discuss their reactions, write their responses, create responses through art, or even create or select music that depicts their responses to the moods or content of the literature.

Robert Probst (1989) states that adults who direct students' reading must encourage students "to attend not only to the text, but to their own experience with it as well—the emotions, associations, memories, and thoughts that are evoked during the reading of the work" (p. 180). Probst recommends the following types of questions to encourage students to provide aesthetic responses to literature:

1. Questions that encourage students' immediate emotional and intellectual responses to literature:
   a. What is your first response or reaction to the literature?
   b. What emotions did you feel as you read the literature?
   c. What ideas or thoughts were suggested by the literature?
   d. How did you respond emotionally or intellectually to the literature? Did you feel involved with the literature or did you feel distance from the text?
2. Questions that encourage students to pay attention to the text, without ignoring their roles while reading the literature:
   a. What did you focus on within the text? What word, phrase, image, or idea caused this focus?
   b. If you were to write about your reading, upon what would you focus? Would you choose an association or memory, an aspect of the text, something about the author, or something else about the literature?

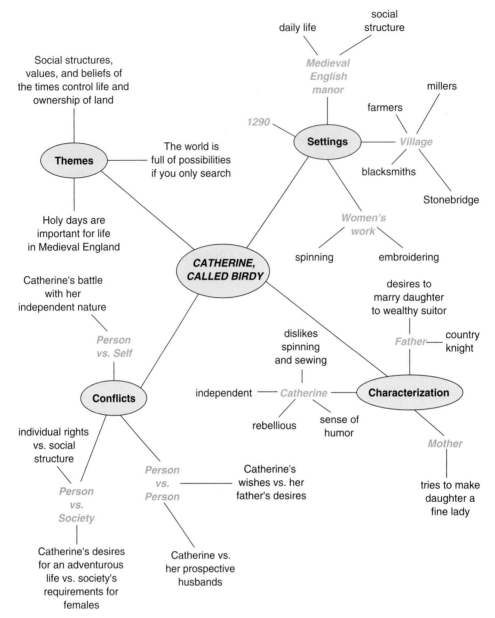

FIGURE 3.2 Semantic web of *Catherine, Called Birdy*. Source: Donna E. Norton's *The Effective Teaching of Language Arts*, 5th edition. Merrill, 1997.

c. Describe an image that was called to your mind by the text.

d. What in the text or in your reading of the literature caused you the most trouble?

e. Do you think that this is a good piece of literature? Why or why not?

3. Questions that direct attention to the context in which students encounter the literature, a context of other readers, other texts, and personal history:

a. What memories do you have after reading the literature: memories of people, places, sights, events, smells, feelings, or attitudes?

b. What sort of person do you think the author is?

c. How did your reading of the literature differ from that of your classmates? How was your reading similar?

d. What did you observe about others as they read or discussed the literature?

e. Does this text remind you of any other literary work, such as a poem, a play, a film, a story, or another genre? If it does, what is the literature and what connection do you see between the two works?

Throughout this text are many examples of literature that develops understanding of the various literary elements and that encourages various types of responses to that literature. Notice how the following Through the Eyes of a Teacher feature includes many of the strategies discussed in this section.

Patricia Taverna
Second-Grade Teacher

Terry Hongell
Computer Teacher
Pocantico Hills School
Sleepy Hollow, New York

Literature Strategy Plan— In-Depth Study of a Classic: Charlotte's Web by E. B. White

Sometimes teachers question the necessity of studying literary elements with children. "Shouldn't we just let them enjoy a story without asking them to do anything with it?" they ask. It *is* important to let children savor and "just enjoy" books. However, helping children appreciate how a character is revealed to a reader or the deliberate use of carefully selected words to evoke a mood, for example, can open up new possibilities for enjoyment that go far beyond passive or superficial response.

Building Students' Background Knowledge

Patricia Taverna believes in the power of a classic to transform children's lives. "*Charlotte's Web* is a wonderful book for introducing children to fantasy and to good literature. It's just one of the richest pieces of children's literature I've come across. It has everything to capture children's interest: talking animals, humor, a farm, a friendship—all the right elements to appeal to seven- and eight-year-olds. We all laugh when Wilbur tries to spin a web, then we are shocked along with Wilbur when the old sheep tells him that he is meant to be eaten, and we all cry when Charlotte dies. There are so many life situations we can talk about that children are drawn into the book."

Prior to her Charlotte's Web lesson, Patty gets her students used to some analysis and discussion of literature. "When we read Cynthia Rylant's 'Henry and Mudge' books at the beginning of the year, for example, we look at how Rylant uses descriptive phrases. Or we'll look at how we come to know characters. My class gets used to spending time as a group, discussing the techniques writers use to make their stories interesting."

Patty conducts these discussions with her entire class. Usually, they first brainstorm their own thoughts about a story in their small groups. They then go to a central meeting spot where they share their ideas with the whole group. Often Patty records these ideas on an easel. "We don't do formal literature circles yet, but I think it's important that they learn how to talk and share with each other and listen to other people's ideas," she says.

Purposeful Reading and Writing

Patty reads the book aloud to her students while they follow along in their own large print copies. "This allows us to go back if someone notices something, or we want to check a name or event we encountered earlier in the book, or we want to reexperience our favorite parts.

"Often we act out parts. We sort of become the farm for a month or two and live the parts of the characters. We read and reread favorite scenes. Sometimes we create a play of the book or rework a part to look at it from another character's perspective." The class also charts various literary elements such as characters, favorite quotes, fantastic versus realistic events, interesting descriptions, and favorite words. "I never know what they're going to notice—each year it's different. One year the quotes just seemed to jump out at the children so we charted those, discussing what about E. B. White's writing style makes these quotes so appealing. Another year they became intrigued with the cars that were pulled up to the Zuckerman's barn when the first miracle occurs. This led to a discussion of how life was different back when this story took place, and the influence of setting on story events."

As the reading progresses, Patty and her class begin writing chapter summaries. "This is really a stretch for them because summarizing is new to them," she says. "So we first do these as a group. Once the children are more comfortable with the concept, I put each with a partner and they banter back and forth about the chapter's main idea. By the end of the book they become quite skilled at summarizing. It helps that the book is so engaging and well structured."

They also create quizzes and games based on the book. "Charlotte's Web Mystery Quotes Quiz" and "Trivia Crossword Puzzles" are popular choices for this activity. "They really have to go back into the story and find the exact location of the quote not only so they can create the game, but also so they can provide a clue for someone who is having difficulty answering the question," says Patty. "This is an excellent skimming activity."

All this writing and sharing culminates in the creation of a *Charlotte's Web* website. Assisted by Terry Hongell, the school's computer teacher, the children put the games, summaries, and other materials they've produced on a website using Kid Pix, Microsoft Word, Puzzlemaker, and other programs. To help students create activities that are worthwhile learning experiences for potential site visitors, Patty and Terry continually urge them to ask themselves, "What can other children learn from this activity? What will they find interesting about it?" Students are also encouraged to revisit the book again and again to ensure accuracy. "The children are so proud of their work when they see it up on the site," says Patty. "They learn that everything must be high quality, accurate, detailed and understandable to an audience beyond their classroom. It really stretches them."

Charlotte's Web Chapter VI - Summer Days

It is summer and school is out for Fern and Avery. The goslings are hatching.
By Stacey

Next Chapter

A Charlotte's Web puzzle by a small group.

Charlotte's Web Trivia Crossword Puzzle #4
By Carolyn, David Y., Matthew, Silena & Stacey

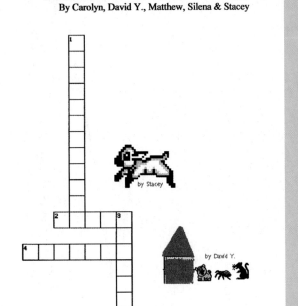

Across
2. What was Mrs. Zuckerman's first name? (See p. 12 in Charlotte's Web)
4. What did Avery have on his ear when he went back to the truck for lunch at the Fair? (See p. 136 in Charlotte's Web)
5. How much did Uncle Homer pay Fern to buy Wilbur?

Assessment

"Much of my assessment is in response to our oral discussions. I listen to their comments and contributions to our charting activities. When they do the summaries and games, I watch to see if they can go back into the story and find the location of the correct quote or the answer to their crossword puzzle question. I really don't worry about meeting the state language arts standards because what we do easily encompasses all the standards. When they analyze the story, write their understandings of it, and make and modify their predictions, they are going far beyond what's considered 'competency' in our state. When we set high expectations and engage them in high-quality literature, they succeed."

 For ideas on adapting Patricia Taverna and Terry Hongell's lesson to meet the needs of older or younger readers, please visit Chapter 3 on our Companion Website at www.prenhall.com/norton

Suggested Activities

For suggested activities to enhance children's understanding of literary elements, please visit our Companion Website at
www.prenhall.com/norton

Children's Literature

For full descriptions, including plot summaries and award winner notations, of these and other titles for enhancing children's understanding of literary elements, please visit the CD-ROM that accompanies this book.

Aardema, Verna. *Bringing the Rain to Kapiti Plain: A Nandi Tale.* Illustrated by Beatriz Vidal. Dial, 1981 (I:5–8 R:6).

_____. *Why Mosquitoes Buzz in People's Ears.* Illustrated by Leo and Diane Dillon. Dial, 1975 (I:5–9 R:6).

Ackerman, Karen. *Song and Dance Man.* Illustrated by Stephen Gammell. Knopf, 1988 (I:3–8 R:4).

Alcott, Louisa May. *Little Women.* Little, Brown, 1868 (I:10+ R:7).

Alexander, Lloyd. *The Arkadians.* Dutton, 1995 (I:10+ R:6).

Avi. *Nothing but the Truth: A Documentary Novel.* Orchard, 1991 (I:12+).

_____. *The True Confessions of Charlotte Doyle.* Orchard, 1990 (I:10+ R:6).

Babbitt, Natalie. *Tuck Everlasting.* Farrar, Straus & Giroux, 1975 (I:8–12 R:6).

Banks, Kate. *And If the Moon Could Talk.* Illustrated by Georg Hallensleben. Farrar, Straus & Giroux, 1998 (I:3–6 R:4).

Barber, Antonia. *The Enchanter's Daughter.* Illustrated by Errol Le Cain. Farrar, Straus & Giroux, 1987 (I:6–9 R:5).

Barrett, Tracy. *Anna of Byzantium.* Delacorte, 1999 (I:10+ R:5).

Barton, Byron. *I Want to Be an Astronaut.* Crowell, 1988 (I:2–6).

Bat-Ami, Miriam. *Two Suns in the Sky.* Front Street, 1999 (I:12+ R:6).

Bauer, Joan. *Hope Was Here.* Putnam, 2000 (I:10+ R:5).

Bauer, Marion Dane. *On My Honor.* Clarion, 1986 (I:10+ R:4).

Bemelmans, Ludwig. *Madeline.* Viking, 1939, 1977 (I:4–9 R:5).

Ben-Ezer, Ehud. *Hosni the Dreamer.* Illustrated by Uri Shulevitz. Farrar, Straus & Giroux, 1997 (I:5–9 R:5).

Benjamin, Carol Lea. *The Wicked Stepdog.* Crowell, 1982 (I:9–12 R:4).

Berenzy, Alix. *A Frog Prince.* H. Holt, 1989 (I:6–10 R:6).

Blos, Joan W. *A Gathering of Days.* Scribner, 1979 (I:8–14 R:6).

Blume, Judy. *Are You There God? It's Me, Margaret.* Bradbury, 1970 (I:10+ R:6).

_____. *Blubber.* Bradbury, 1974 (I:10+ R:4).

Bober, Natalie. *Countdown to Independence: A Revolution of Ideas in England and Her American Colonies: 1760–1776.* Simon & Schuster, 2001 (I:12+ R:6).

_____

I = Interest by age range.
R = Readability by grade level.

Brooks, Bruce. *The Moves Make the Man.* Harper & Row, 1984 (I:10+ R:7).

_____. *What Hearts.* HarperCollins, 1992 (I:101 R:6).

Brown, Margaret Wise. *Goodnight Moon.* Illustrated by Clement Hurd. Harper, 1947 (I:2–7).

Browne, Anthony. *Gorilla.* Watts, 1983 (I:3–8 R:4).

Bunting, Eve. *The Wednesday Surprise.* Illustrated by Donald Carrick. Clarion, 1989 (I:3–9 R:5).

Burnett, Frances Hodgson. *The Secret Garden.* Illustrated by Tasha Tudor. Lippincott, 1911, 1938, 1962 (I:8–12 R:7).

Burton, Virginia Lee. *The Little House.* Houghton Mifflin, 1942 (I:3–7 R:3).

Cadnum, Michael. *In a Dark Wood.* Orchard, 1998 (I:10+ R:6).

Carrick, Carol. *Stay Away from Simon!* Illustrated by Donald Carrick. Clarion, 1985 (I:7–10 R:3).

Carroll, Lewis. *Alice's Adventures in Wonderland.* Illustrated by John Tenniel. Macmillan, 1866; Knopf, 1984 (I:8+ R:6).

Cendrars, Blaise. *Shadow.* Illustrated by Marcia Brown. Scribner, 1982 (I:all).

Chaucer, Geoffrey. *The Canterbury Tales.* Retold by Barbara Cohen. Illustrated by Trina Schart Hyman. Lothrop, Lee & Shepard, 1988 (I:8+ R:5).

Cleary, Beverly. *The Mouse and the Motorcycle.* Illustrated by Louis Darling. Morrow, 1965 (I:7–11 R:3).

_____. *Ramona and Her Father.* Illustrated by Alan Tiegreen. Morrow, 1977 (I:7–12 R:6).

_____. *Ramona Quimby, Age 8.* Illustrated by Alan Tiegreen. Morrow, 1981 (I:7–12 R:6).

Cole, Brock. *The Goats.* Farrar, Straus & Giroux, 1987 (I:8+ R:5).

Cooper, Helen. *Pumpkin Soup.* Doubleday, 1999 (I:3–8).

Cormier, Robert. *The Chocolate War.* Laureleaf, 1999.

Couloumbis, Audrey. *Getting Near to Baby.* Putnam, 1999 (I:10+ R:4).

Creech, Sharon. *Walk Two Moons.* HarperCollins, 1994 (I:12+ R:6).

_____. *The Wanderer.* HarperCollins, 2000 (I:10+ R:6).

Cronin, Doreen. *Click, Clack, Moo: Cows That Type.* Illustrated by Betsy Lewin. Simon & Schuster, 2000 (I:4–7).

Crossley-Holland, Kevin. *Storm.* Illustrated by Alan Marks. Heinemann, 1985 (I:6–12 R:5).

Curtis, Christopher Paul. *The Watsons Go to Birmingham—1963.* Delacorte, 1995 (I:10+ R:6).

Cushman, Karen. *Catherine, Called Birdy.* Clarion, 1994 (I:12+ R:9).

_____. *The Midwife's Apprentice.* Clarion, 1995.

Dabcovich, Lydia. *Sleepy Bear.* Dutton, 1982 (I:3–6 R:1).

Day, Alexandra. *Frank and Ernest Play Ball.* Scholastic, 1990 (I:5–8 R:5).

_____. *Frank and Ernest on the Road.* Scholastic, 1994 (I:5–8 R:5).

DePaola, Tomie. *26 Fairmont Avenue.* Putnam, 1999 (I:6+).

Dorris, Michael. *Morning Girl.* Hyperion, 1992 (I:8 + R:4).

Edmonds, Walter D. *The Matchlock Gun.* Dodd, Mead, 1941 (I:8+ R:5).

Engel, Diana. *Josephina Hates Her Name.* Morrow, 1989 (I:5–8 R:4).

Farmer, Nancy. *A Girl Named Disaster.* Orchard, 1996 (I:10+ R:6).

Fenner, Carol. *Yolonda's Genius.* McElderry, 1995 (I:10+ R:3).

Fitzhugh, Louise. *Harriet the Spy.* Harper & Row, 1964 (I:8–12 R:3).

Fleischman, Paul. *The Borning Room.* HarperCollins, 1991 (I:10+ R:5).

———. *Bull Run.* Illustrated by David Frampton. HarperCollins, 1993 (I:10+ R:5).

———. *Dateline: Troy.* Illustrated by Gwen Frankfeldt and Glenn Morrow. Candlewick, 1996 (I:12+ R:7).

Fleischman, Sid. *The Midnight Horse.* Illustrated by Peter Sís. Greenwillow, 1990 (I:8–12 R:5).

———. *The Whipping Boy.* Illustrated by Peter Sís. Greenwillow, 1986 (I:8+ R:5).

Forbes, Esther. *Johnny Tremain.* Illustrated by Lynd Ward. Houghton Mifflin, 1943 (I:10I R:6).

Foreman, Michael. *War Boy: A Country Childhood.* Little, Brown, 1990 (I:all R:6).

Fox, Paula. *Monkey Island.* Orchard, 1991 (I:10+ R:6).

———. *One-Eyed Cat.* Bradbury, 1984 (I:10+ R:5).

———. *The Slave Dancer.* Illustrated by Eros Keith. Bradbury, 1973 (I:12+ R:7).

Frank, Anne. *Anne Frank: The Diary of a Young Girl.* Edited by Otto H. Frank and Mirjam Pressler. Translated by Susan Massotty. Doubleday, 1995 (I:12+ R:5).

Frank, Rudolf. *No Hero for the Kaiser.* Translated from German by Patricia Crampton. Illustrated by Klaus Steffens. Lothrop, Lee & Shepard, 1986 (I:10+ R:7).

Freedman, Russell. *Eleanor Roosevelt: A Life of Discovery.* Clarion, 1993 (I:10+ R:6).

———. *Lincoln: A Photobiography.* Clarion, 1987 (I:8I R:6).

———. *The Wright Brothers: How They Invented the Airplane.* Holiday, 1991 (I:8+ R:5).

Fritz, Jean. *Bully for You, Teddy Roosevelt!* Illustrated by Mike Wimmer. Putnam, 1991 (I:8+ R:5).

———. *The Cabin Faced West.* Illustrated by Feodor Rojankousky. Coward, McCann, 1958 (I:7–10 R:5).

———. *The Great Little Madison.* Putnam, 1989 (I:10+ R:6).

———. *Make Way for Sam Houston.* Illustrated by Elise Primavera. Putnam, 1986 (I:9+ R:6).

———. *Traitor: The Case of Benedict Arnold.* Putnam, 1981 (I:8+ R:5).

George, Jean Craighead. *Julie of the Wolves.* Illustrated by John Schoenherr. Harper & Row, 1972 (I:10–13 R:7).

———. *My Side of the Mountain.* Dutton, 1959 (I:10+ R:6).

———. *Water Sky.* Harper & Row, 1987 (I:10+ R:6).

Gipson, Fred. *Old Yeller.* Illustrated by Carl Burger. Harper & Row, 1956 (I:10+ R:6).

Goble, Paul. *The Girl Who Loved Wild Horses.* Bradbury, 1978 (I:6–10 R:5).

Grahame, Kenneth. *Wind in the Willows.* Illustrated by E. H. Shepard. Scribner, 1908 (I:7–12 R:7).

Grifalconi, Ann. *Darkness and the Butterfly.* Little, Brown, 1987 (I:4–8 R:4).

Grimm, Brothers. *Rumpelstiltskin.* Retold and illustrated by Paul O. Zelinsky. Dutton, 1986 (I:all R:5).

Halperin, Wendy Anderson. *Love Is . . .* Simon & Schuster, 2001 (I: all).

Hamilton, Virginia. *Anthony Burns: The Defeat and Triumph of a Fugitive Slave.* Knopf, 1988 (I:9+ R:6).

———. *Many Thousand Gone: African Americans from Slavery to Freedom.* Illustrated by Leo and Diane Dillon. Knopf, 1993 (I:8+ R:5).

Hansen, Joyce. *I Thought My Soul Would Rise and Fly: The Diary of Patsy, A Freed Girl.* Scholastic, 1997 (I:10+ R:4).

Hastings, Selina, retold by. *Sir Gawain and the Loathly Lady.* Illustrated by Juan Wijngaard. Lothrop, Lee & Shepard, 1985 (I:9–12 R:6).

Hendershot, Judith. *In Coal Country.* Illustrated by Thomas B. Allen. Knopf, 1987 (I:5–9 R:3).

Henkes, Kevin. *Owen.* Greenwillow, 1993 (I:3–7 R:4).

Hesse, Karen. *Out of the Dust.* Scholastic, 1997 (I:10+ R:6).

———. *Stowaway.* Simon & Schuster, 2000 (I:10+ R:6).

Highwater, Jamake. *Anpao: An American Indian Odyssey.* Illustrated by Fritz Scholder. Lippincott, 1977 (I:12+ R:5).

Hoban, Lillian. *Arthur's Great Big Valentine.* Harper & Row, 1989 (I:5–7 R:2).

Hoberman, Mary Ann. *Mr. and Mrs. Muddle.* Illustrated by Catharine O'Neill. Little, Brown, 1988 (I:3–8 R:4).

Howe, James. *Horace and Morris But Mostly Delores.* Illustrated by Amy Waldo. Atheneum, 1999 (I:4–8).

Hudson, Jan. *Sweetgrass.* Tree Frog, Philomel, 1984, 1989 (I:10+ R:4).

Hurmence, Belinda. *A Girl Called Boy.* Houghton Mifflin, 1982 (I:10+ R:6).

Ibbotson, Eve. *Journey to the River Sea.* Dutton, 2002 (I:10+ R:5).

Jackson, Shelley. *The Old Woman and the Wave.* DK, 1998 (I:4–7 R:4).

Johnson, Angela. *Julius.* Illustrated by Dav Pilkey. Orchard, 1993 (I:3–7 R:4).

———. *Tell Me a Story, Mama.* Illustrated by David Soman. Watts, 1989 (I:3–7 R:4).

Keats, Ezra Jack. *The Snowy Day.* Viking, 1962 (I:2–6 R:2).

Konigsburg, E. L. *From the Mixed-Up Files of Mrs. Basil E. Frankweiler.* Atheneum, 1967 (I:9–12 R:7).

———. *Journey to an 800 Number.* Atheneum, 1982 (I:10+ R:6).

———. *The View from Saturday.* Atheneum, 1996 (I:10+ R:6).

Lamb, Charles, and Mary Lamb, retold by. *Tales from Shakespeare.* Illustrated by Elizabeth Shippen Green Elliott. Crown, 1988 (I:8+).

Lang, Andrew. *The Red Fairy Book.* Illustrated by H. J. Ford and Lancelot Speed. McGraw-Hill, 1967 (I:all R:6).

Leapman, Michael. *Witnesses to War: Eight True-Life Stories of Nazi Persecution.* Puffin, 2000.

L'Engle, Madeleine. *A Wrinkle in Time.* Farrar, Straus & Giroux, 1962 (I:10+ R:5).

Levine, Ellen. *Freedom's Children: Young Civil Rights Activists Tell Their Own Stories.* Putnam, 1993 (I:all).

Levine, Gail Carson. *Ella Enchanted.* HarperCollins, 1997 (I:10+ R:6).

Lewis, C. S. *The Lion, the Witch and the Wardrobe.* Illustrated by Pauline Baynes. Macmillan, 1950 (I:9+ R:7).

Lisle, Janet Taylor. *Afternoon of the Elves.* Watts, 1989 (I:10+ R:5).

Lobel, Arnold. *Frog and Toad Are Friends.* Harper & Row, 1970 (I:5–8 R:1).

Lowry, Lois. *The Giver.* Houghton Mifflin, 1993 (I:10+ R:5).

———. *Number the Stars.* Houghton Mifflin, 1989 (I:8–12 R:5).

Lunn, Janet. *Shadow in Hawthorn Bay.* Scribner, 1986 (I:10+ R:5).

Lyon, George Ella. *One Lucky Girl.* Illustrated by Irene Trivas. Dorling Kindersley, 2000 (I:6+ R:4).

McCully, Emily Arnold. *The Ballot Box Battle.* Knopf, 1996 (I:7–9 R:4).

McCurdy, Michael, ed. *Escape from Slavery: The Boyhood of Frederick Douglass in His Own Words.* Knopf, 1994 (I:9+ R:6).

McKinley, Robin. *The Hero and the Crown.* Greenwillow, 1984 (I:10+ R:7).

McKissack, Patricia C. *The Dark-Thirty: Southern Tales of the Supernatural.* Illustrated by Brian Pinkney. Knopf, 1992 (I:all R:5).

MacLachlan, Patricia. *The Facts and Fictions of Minna Pratt.* Harper & Row, 1988 (I:7–12 R:4).

_____. *Mama One, Mama Two.* Illustrated by Ruth Lercher Bornstein. Harper & Row, 1982 (I:5–7 R:2).

_____. *Sarah, Plain and Tall.* Harper & Row, 1985 (I:7–10 R:3).

Marrin, Albert. *Hitler.* Viking Kestrel, 1987 (I:10+ R:7).

Martin, Jacqueline Briggs. *Good Times on Grandfather Mountain.* Illustrated by Susan Gaber. Orchard, 1992 (I:4–8 R:5).

Maruki, Toshi. *Hiroshima No Pika.* Lothrop, Lee & Shepard, 1982 (I:8–12 R:4).

Meddaugh, Susan. *Martha Speaks.* Houghton Mifflin, 1992 (I:4–8 R:4).

Meltzer, Milton. *Rescue: The Story of How Gentiles Saved Jews in the Holocaust.* Harper & Row, 1988 (I:10+ R:6).

_____. *Thomas Jefferson: The Revolutionary Aristocrat.* Watts, 1991 (I:10+ R:6).

_____, ed. *The Black Americans: A History in Their Own Words 1619–1983.* Crowell, 1984 (I:10+).

Merriam, Eve. *Halloween ABC.* Illustrated by Lane Smith. Macmillan, 1987 (I:all).

Millard, Anne. *A Street Through Time: A 12,000-Year Walk Through History.* Illustrated by Steve Noon. DK, 1998 (I: all).

Milne, A. A. *Winnie-the-Pooh.* Illustrated by Ernest H. Shepard. Dutton, 1926, 1954 (I:6–10 R:5).

Morpurgo, Michael. *Kensuke's Kingdom.* Illustrated by Michael Foreman. Mammoth, 2000 (I:8+ R:5).

Mowat, Farley. *Lost in the Barrens.* Illustrated by Charles Geer. McClelland & Stewart, 1956, 1984 (I:9+ R:6).

Myers, Walter Dean. *Now Is Your Time!: The African-American Struggle for Freedom.* HarperCollins, 1991 (I:10+ R:6).

Naylor, Phyllis Reynolds. *Shiloh.* Atheneum, 1991 (I:8+ R:5).

Ness, Evaline. *Sam, Bangs & Moonshine.* Holt, Rinehart & Winston, 1966 (I:5–9 R:3).

North, Sterling. *Rascal.* Dutton, 1963 (I:10+ R:6).

Noyes, Alfred. *The Highwayman.* Illustrated by Charles Keeping. Oxford, 1981 (I:10+).

O'Brien, Robert C. *Mrs. Frisby and the Rats of NIMH.* Illustrated by Zena Bernstein. Atheneum, 1971 (I:8–12 R:4).

O'Dell, Scott. *Island of the Blue Dolphins.* Houghton Mifflin, 1960 (I:10+ R:6).

Orlev, Uri. *The Island on Bird Street.* Translated by Hillel Halkin. Houghton Mifflin, 1984 (I:10+ R:6).

_____. *The Man from the Other Side.* Translated by Hillel Halkin. Houghton Mifflin, 1991 (I:10+ R:6).

Paterson, Katherine. *Bridge to Terabithia.* Illustrated by Donna Diamond. Crowell, 1977 (I:10–14 R:6).

_____. *Jacob Have I Loved.* Crowell, 1980. (I:10 R:6).

Paulsen, Gary. *Hatchet.* Bradbury, 1987 (I:10+ R:6).

_____. *Nightjohn.* Delacorte, 1993 (I:12+ R:6).

Pearce, Philippa. *Tom's Midnight Garden.* Illustrated by Susan Einzig. Lippincott, 1958 (I:8+ R:6).

Peck, Richard. *A Long Way from Chicago.* Dial, 1998 (I:10+ R:5).

_____. *A Year Down Yonder.* Dial, 2000 (I:10+ R:5).

Pieńkowski, Jan. *Haunted House.* Dutton, 1979 (I:all).

Polacco, Patricia. *Appelemando's Dreams.* Philomel, 1991 (I:6–9 R:5).

_____. *Meteor!* Dodd, Mead, 1987 (I:6–10 R:7).

Potter, Beatrix. *The Tale of Peter Rabbit.* Warner, 1902. (I:2–7 R:5).

Pullman, Philip. *The Amber Spyglass.* Knopf, 2000 (I:10+ R:7).

_____. *The Golden Compass.* Knopf, 1996 (I:10+ R:7).

_____. *The Subtle Knife.* Knopf, 1997 (I:10+ R:7).

Quintana, Anton. *The Baboon King.* Translated by John Nieuwenhuizen. Walker, 1999 (I:10+ R:5).

Raskin, Ellen. *The Westing Game.* Dutton, 1978 (I:10–14 R:5).

Rathmann, Peggy. *Ruby the Copycat.* Scholastic, 1991 (I:5–8 R:3).

Rodowsky, Colby. *Sydney Herself.* Farrar, Straus & Giroux, 1989 (I:11+ R:6).

Rogasky, Barbara. *Smoke and Ashes: The Story of the Holocaust.* Holiday House, 1988 (I:10+ R:6).

Rowling, J. K. *Harry Potter and the Goblet of Fire.* Scholastic, 2000 (I:all).

Rylant, Cynthia. *Appalachia: The Voices of Sleeping Birds.* Illustrated by Barry Moser. Harcourt Brace Jovanovich, 1991 (I:all R:5).

_____. *A Fine White Dust.* Bradbury, 1986 (I:10+ R:6).

_____. *The Islander.* DK, 1998 (I:10+ R:6).

_____. *Missing May.* Orchard, 1992 (I:10+ R:6).

_____. *When I Was Young in the Mountains.* Illustrated by Diane Goode. Dutton, 1982 (I:4–7 R:3).

Salisbury, Graham. *Under the Blood-Red Sun.* Doubleday, 1995 (I:10+ R:5).

San Souci, Robert D. *Cendrillon . . . A Caribbean Cinderella.* Illustrated by Brian Pinkney. Simon & Schuster, 1998 (I:All).

Scieszka, Jon. *The Stinky Cheese Man and Other Fairly Stupid Tales.* Illustrated by Lane Smith. Viking, 1992 (I: all R:4).

Seeber, Dorothea P. *A Pup Just for Me; A Boy Just for Me.* Illustrated by Ed Young. Philomel, 2000 (I:6+).

Sendak, Maurice. *Where the Wild Things Are.* Harper & Row, 1963 (I:4–8 R:6).

Seredy, Kate. *The White Stag.* Viking, 1937; Puffin, 1979 (I:10–14 R:7).

Seuss, Dr. *The Cat in the Hat.* Random House, 1957 (I:4–7 R:1).

Snyder, Dianne. *The Boy of the Three-Year Nap.* Illustrated by Allen Say. Houghton Mifflin, 1988 (I:4–9 R:4).

Speare, Elizabeth George. *The Sign of the Beaver.* Houghton Mifflin, 1983 (I:8–12 R:5).

_____. *The Witch of Blackbird Pond.* Houghton Mifflin, 1958 (I:9–14 R:4).

Sperry, Armstrong. *Call It Courage.* Macmillan, 1940 (I:9–13 R:6).

Spinelli, Jerry. *Wringer.* HarperCollins, 1997 (I:9+ R:4).

Staples, Suzanne Fisher. *Shiva's Fire.* Farrar, Straus & Giroux, 2000 (I:10+).

Steptoe, John. *Mufaro's Beautiful Daughters: An African Tale.* Lothrop, Lee & Shepard, 1987 (I:all R:4).

Stolz, Mary. *Cezanne Pinto: A Memoir.* Knopf, 1994 (I:10+ R:6).

Strachan, Ian. *Flawed Glass.* Little, Brown, 1990 (I:10+ R:6).

Taback, Simms. *There Was an Old Lady Who Swallowed a Fly.* Viking, 1997 (I:all).

Taylor, Mildred D. *Roll of Thunder, Hear My Cry.* Dial, 1976 (I:10+ R:6).

Taylor, Theodore. *The Cay.* Doubleday, 1969 (I:8–12 R:6).

Tolkien, J. R. R. *The Hobbit.* Houghton Mifflin, 1938 (I:9–12 R:6).

Treece, Henry. *The Magic Wood.* Illustrated by Barry Moser. HarperCollins, 1992 (I:8+).

Trivizas, Eugene. *The Three Little Wolves and the Big Bad Pig.* Illustrated by Helen Oxenbury. Macmillan, 1993 (I:4–8 R:5).

Turner, Megan Whalen. *The Thief.* Greenwillow, 1996 (I:11+ R:6).

Voigt, Cynthia. *Bad Girls.* Scholastic, 1996 (I:9+ R:7).

_____. *Dicey's Song.* Atheneum, 1982 (I:10+ R:5).

Vos, Ida. *Hide and Seek.* Translated by Terese Edelstein and Inez Smidt. Houghton Mifflin, 1991 (I:8–12 R:5).

Wells, Rosemary. *Max's Chocolate Chicken.* Dial, 1989 (I:2–6).

Whelan, Gloria. *Homeless Bird.* HarperCollins, 2000 (I:10+ R:5).

White, E. B. *Charlotte's Web.* Illustrated by Garth Williams. Harper & Row, 1952 (I:7–11 R:3).

_____. *Trumpet of the Swan.* Puffin, 1970 (I:7–11 R:5).

White, Ruth. *Belle Prater's Boy.* Farrar, Straus & Giroux, 1996 (I:10+ R:6).

White, T. H. *The Sword in the Stone.* Collins, 1938 (I:10+ R:7).

Wild, Margaret. *Our Granny.* Illustrated by Julie Vivas. Ticknor & Fields, 1994 (I:3–6 R:5).

Wilder, Laura Ingalls. *Little House in the Big Woods.* Harper & Row, 1932 (I:8–12 R:6).

Williams, Margery. *The Velveteen Rabbit.* Illustrated by William Nicholson. Doubleday, 1958 (I:6–9 R:5).

Williams, Vera B. *Stringbean's Trip to the Shining Sea.* Illustrated by Vera B. Williams and Jennifer Williams. Greenwillow, 1988 (I:5–10).

Wood, Douglas. *What Dads Can't Do.* Illustrated by Doug Cushman. Simon & Schuster, 2000 (I:3–8).

Yolen, Jane. *The Devil's Arithmetic.* Viking Kestrel, 1988 (I:8+ R:5).

Yorinks, Arthur. *Hey, Al.* Illustrated by Richard Egielski. Farrar, Straus & Giroux, 1986 (I:all).

4 ARTISTS AND THEIR ILLUSTRATIONS

Understanding Artists and Their Illustrations

Many young children mention the illustrations when asked what attracted them to a book. The bright colors of an East African setting may entice children into searching for camouflaged animals. Jagged lines and dark colors may excite children with the prospect of dangerous adventures, while delicate lines and pastel colors may set children to dreaming about fairyland. The textures in illustrations may invite children to "feel" a bear's fur or an eagle's feathers. In these and many other ways, illustrations are integral to picture books for young children. Outstanding artists illustrate books for older children—such as Laura Ingalls Wilder's "Little House" series—but in such books, the text can stand on its own. In picture books, however, the illustrations join the text in telling the stories.

This chapter discusses the visual elements, media, and styles used by illustrators of all books for children, but it focuses on the special requirements of picture books. It suggests criteria for evaluating illustrations in picture books, provides examples of high-quality books, and looks at some outstanding illustrators to see how they create memorable picture books.

Visual Elements: The Grammar of Artists

Writers create compelling stories by arranging words; artists arrange visual elements to create pictures that complement stories. A visual grammar consists of the elements of line, color, shape, and texture. Artists who organize these elements into unified wholes create visual designs that convey meaning.

Line

Artists use line to suggest direction, motion, energy, and mood. Artist William A. Herring (1997) defines the importance of line when he states: "I regard line as essential to beauty in any work of art" (p. 40). Lines can be thin or wide, light or heavy, feathery or jagged, straight or curved. H. W. Janson and Anthony F. Janson (1999) maintain that line is the most basic visual element. They state, "A majority of art is initially conceived in terms of contour line. Its presence is often implied even when it is not actually used to describe form" (p. 17). According to these authorities in art and art history, drawings represent line in its purest form and artists commonly treat drawing as a form of note taking. Artists such as Michelangelo based their finished art on carefully developed drawings, but line is also extremely important in children's book illustration. According to Edmund Burke Feldman (1992), line is the most crucial visual element for several reasons:

1. Line is familiar to virtually everyone because of experience with drawing and writing.

2. Line is definite, assertive, intelligible (although its windings and patternings may be infinitely complex); it is precise and unambiguous; it commits artists to specific statements.

3. Line conveys meaning through its identification with natural phenomena.

4. Line leads the eye and involves viewers in the line's "destiny."

5. Line permits eyes to do as children do when getting to know the world: handle objects and feel their contours. The outlines of things eventually become more important than their color, size, or texture as means of identifying them.

Feldman's discussion of the relationship between line and natural phenomena is especially interesting to people involved with children and the illustrations found in literature for them. Experiences with common natural phenomena may help children relate meaningfully to works of art. Vertical lines, for example, look like trees in a windless landscape or like people who stand rather than move. Consequently, they suggest lack of movement.

Horizontal lines, such as the surface of a placid lake or a flat horizon, suggest calm, sleep, stability, and an absence of strife. Most young children use a horizontal baseline in their drawings to convey the idea of the firm ground upon which they walk.

Vertical lines and horizontal lines joined at right angles depict artificial elements that differ considerably from the natural world of irregular and approximate shapes. Two vertical lines connected by a horizontal line at the top give the feeling of a solid, safe place: a doorway, house, or building.

In contrast, diagonal lines suggest loss of balance and uncontrolled motion—unless they form a triangle that rests on a horizontal base, which suggests safety. In both human design and nature, jagged lines have connotations of breakdown and destruction. Consequently, jagged lines suggest danger.

People see curved lines as fluid because of their resemblance to the eddies, whirlpools, and concentric ripples in water. Because of this, circles and curved lines seem less definite and predictable than do straight lines.

In *The Girl Who Loved Wild Horses,* Paul Goble uses line effectively to depict the natural setting of a Native American folktale. Goble introduces readers to the main character as she goes down to the river at sunrise to watch the wild horses. The illustration shows a calm, nonthreatening scene. The lines of the horses' legs are vertical,

since the horses are quietly drinking from the river. The calm mood is supplemented by the reflections in the water; not even a ripple breaks the tranquillity.

On the next page, the girl rests in a meadow close to home. Goble illustrates the triangular shapes of teepees sitting securely on the ground. The text relates, however, a rumble while the girl sleeps. The outlines of the clouds suggest this break in a peaceful afternoon: they are still rounded, but they are also heavy, with protrusions jutting into the sky.

Movement in the story and the illustrations becomes more pronounced as lightning flashes and as the horses rear and snort in terror. Sharp lines of lightning extend from black, rolling clouds to the ground. Even the lines of the plants are diagonal, suggesting dangerous wind as the horses gallop away in front of the storm. When night falls and the storm is over, the tired girl and horses stop to rest. Goble illustrates the hills with vertical lines connected by horizontal lines, suggesting the new feeling of safety and shelter under the moon and the stars.

In contrast to Paul Goble's depiction of familiar natural phenomena, the soft, delicate lines of Marcia Brown's illustrations for Charles Perrault's *Cinderella* create a mythical kingdom that could exist only "once upon a time." The drawing of Cinderella's fairy godmother transforming her into a beautiful princess has an ethereal quality, as if the scene were floating on air. Because these illustrations seem to be almost as diaphanous and changeable as clouds, viewers are not surprised when a pumpkin turns into a coach and a rat becomes the driver of the coach. Even the architecture has a magical quality. Delicately curved windows, softly flowing draperies, and graceful pillars provide fitting backgrounds for a favorite fairy tale.

Marjorie Priceman's illustrations for Lloyd Moss's *Zin! Zin! Zin! A Violin* create a flowing movement and a feeling that matches the text. For example, on the page in which the text reads, "And soaring high and moving in, With Zin! Zin! Zin! A Violin" (unnumbered), the violinist seems to float across the pages. Even the cats illustrated in the top of the illustration create a similar flowing movement as they chase a mouse across the page.

Mary Barrett Brown uses contrasting lighter and heavier lines in illustrations. In *Tiger with Wings: The Great Horned Owl* by Barbara Juster Esbensen, Brown supports Esbensen's text, which compares the horned owl and a tiger as fierce hunters. The accompanying illustration shows a tiger, drawn in almost transparent lines, following the horned owl, drawn with heavier dark lines.

In *The Highwayman,* Charles Keeping's illustrations for Alfred Noyes's ghost poem create quite a different mood. Stark black lines create ghostly, terrifying subjects and suggest sinister and disastrous consequences. Several of Roberto Innocenti's illustrations for Charles Dickens's *Christmas Carol* use thin white lines against a darker background to depict the ghostly apparitions that visit Mr. Scrooge.

In *Michael Foreman's Mother Goose*, Michael Foreman uses line to suggest movement and to take viewers into the next picture. Soldiers or animals move from one page to the next, lines continue on the next illustration, and hills or houses introduced on one page become the source for the action on the next page.

Even invisible lines, or suggestions of lines, have impact in illustrations. Lyn Ellen Lacy (1986) emphasizes the role of invisible vertical and horizontal lines as directional influences. For example, when analyzing pages 43 and 44 in Robert McCloskey's *Make Way for Ducklings*, Lacy states:

Tethered to a top coat button, the whistle manages to fly behind Michael like a free pixie spirit. It points in the direction opposite Michael's intended hasty path. Literally, it points toward the townscape; figuratively, it points our way back into the picture in case we missed something. We do not then turn the page too soon, but instead we follow the whistle's path of gesture along an invisible line, back into the maze of buildings whose vertical lines have a downward thrust to the sidewalk. This underlying structure in the picture is a gentle reminder that there are minute spots on the sidewalk. McCloskey did not want us to miss them. (p. 47)

The minute spots prove to be mother duck and her ducklings.

Color

Color plays an extremely important role in illustration. Janson and Janson (1999) contrast the role of line and color when they state, "The role of color in art rests primarily on its sensuous and emotive appeal, in contrast to the more cerebral quality generally associated with line" (p. 19).

Combining line and color is perhaps the most common way in which artists convey mood and emotion in picture books. Describing picture books of the 1990s, Dilys Evans (1992) emphasizes the roles of line and color in the illustrations of David Wiesner, Lane Smith, and David Wisniewski. Evans states, "Now the world of children's book illustration is witnessing bold new visual voices as they surface upon the page with bright vibrating color, strong black containing lines, and a new reverence for black as color" (p. 760).

Anthony Browne (Evans, 1998) describes the importance of line and color in developing the four parts for *Voices in the Park*. For example, the second voice of a man in winter uses dark and oppressive colors to reflect a bleak and cold park as a man looks through the paper for a job. When his daughter begins to talk happily to the man, Browne uses brighter colors to show the changing mood.

Many colors are associated with natural phenomena. Reds, yellows, and oranges are most associated with fire, sun, and blood, and they usually have warm or hot connotations: friendliness, high energy, or anger. Blues, greens, and

some violets are most associated with air, water, and plant life, and their coolness or coldness can suggest moods and emotions ranging from tranquillity to melancholy.

To evaluate an illustrator's use of color, consider how well the color language of the artist conveys or complements the mood, characters, setting, and theme that the writer develops in words. Marcia Brown complements the delicate lines in her illustrations for Charles Perrault's *Cinderella* by using soft pastels, bringing a shimmering radiance to the pictures. In contrast, Paul Goble uses bright colors and black, in addition to strong line, to illustrate a desert setting and the tension and movement of animals and forces of nature in *The Girl Who Loved Wild Horses*.

Color can reflect the mood of a story. In *Ox-Cart Man*, Barbara Cooney uses pastels and muted hues of darker colors to translate Donald Hall's gentle story about a quieter time in American history. Cooney portrays the hills of rural New England in the early 1800s as gentle curves of green, gray, and blue. The deep rusts, blues, and greens of the clothing look authentic for the time period.

Cooney's color choices also show the passing of time. When the farmer begins his journey over hills and past villages, the countryside is aflame with the rusts and oranges of fall. When he reaches Portsmouth, the trees have only a few brown leaves. As he returns home, a soft,

Color can be used to great effect to set the mood of the story. From The Blizzard's Robe, *written and illustrated by Robert Sabuda. Reprinted with the permission of Atheneum Books for Young Readers, an imprint of Simon & Schuster Children's Publishing Division. Copyright 1999 by Robert Sabuda.*

brown land awaits the first snowfall. The scene turns white in winter. Then, soft greens cover the hills before the trees explode with white and pink apple blossoms. One child said that the pictures made her feel homesick because she had lived in an area that had hills, valleys, quiet farms, and distinct seasons. You may compare Cooney's illustrations for Mary Lyn Ray's *Basket Moon* with those for *Ox-Cart Man.* In Michael Bedard's *Emily* and Jane Yolen's *Letting Swift River Go,* Cooney also uses colors that reflect the settings and times. Many readers of *Ox-Cart Man* mention its feeling of tranquillity. Cooney creates tranquillity in her illustrations for *Island Boy,* which she also wrote.

Blues and greens emphasize the cold setting in Michael Rothman's illustrations for Joanne Ryder's *White Bear, Ice Bear* and in Jon Van Zyle's illustrations for Debbie S. Miller's *A Polar Bear Journey.* Frosty whites and shades of blue and green reinforce the cold winds, ice, and blizzards.

Bright primary colors highlight the illustrations in Jessica Souhami's *The Leopard's Drum: An Asante Tale from West Africa.* In this retelling of an African folktale, Souhami uses bright primary colors and shapes that are very similar to paper puppets placed on sticks. According to the artist, the illustrations are adapted from the shadow puppets she uses in her oral performances of folktales. To bring a unity to the text, the various geometric designs in primary colors also illustrate the endpapers.

Rich, vivid colors attract attention and reinforce the happy mood of exploration in Denise Fleming's *In the Small, Small Pond.* Printed in deep black, the text stands out against the colorful illustrations.

Artists may use changes in color to contrast moods within a book. For example, Donald Carrick's illustrations for Eve Bunting's *Ghost's Hour, Spook's Hour* use color to create moods. The dark shades used in the early illustrations develop and reinforce the scary environment and the young boy's fear of the dark. When the father rescues his frightened son, the father is shown in an open doorway that has a warm yellow background. The warm yellows are retained as the boy is comforted by his parents and joins them in the big couch bed.

The colors in Thomas Allen's illustrations for Judith Hendershot's *In Coal Country* are appropriate for a story about growing up in a 1930s Ohio coal mining town. The impressionistic pastel and charcoal illustrations create a landscape observed through a combination of coal dust and nostalgia.

Artists may also use contrasts in illustrations to create drama and complement plot. Helen Oxenbury's illustrations for Michael Rosen's *We're Going on a Bear Hunt* alternate between black and white and color. On the pages with black-and-white illustrations, the characters chant the portion of the bear hunt that they are about to experience. The color illustrations show the family swishing through long grass, splashing across a river, squishing in mud, and stumbling through a dark forest.

A totally different mood may be created by black-and-white paintings. For example, the illustrations in Jonathan Frost's *Gowanus Dogs* develop the inner-city world of homeless people and homeless dogs. The illustrations show the moods of exuberant puppies and the harsh environment of the homeless. In a happy ending, the homeless man's life changes when he adopts one of the puppies. Now the black-and-white illustrations show the puppy and the no longer homeless man living snug and warm above a diner.

Black-and-white photographs may also reflect differences in mood. Interesting comparisons may be made between the effects of painterly photographs and photographs that are in sharp focus by viewing the photographs in Susan Goldman Rubin's photobiography *Margaret Bourke-White: Her Pictures Were Her Life.* For example, Rubin contrasts two photographs of the Terminal Tower, Cleveland, 1929. The photograph reproduced on page 28 shows a "painterly photograph" in soft focus. The photograph on page 29 is labeled "This image of the Terminal Tower, as viewed through the arches of a railroad viaduct, is in sharp focus."

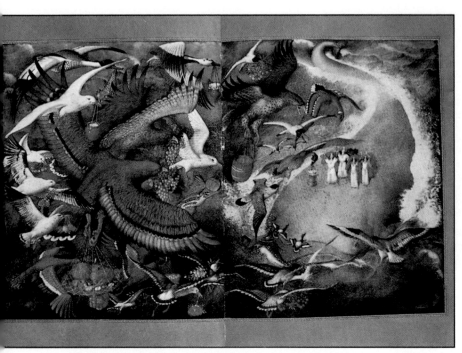

The Children of Lir *presents motifs from Irish folklore completed in watercolors.*
(From The Children of Lir, *by Sheila MacGill-Callahan, illustrated by Gennady Spirin.*
Copyright © 1993 by Gennady Spirin, pictures. Used by permission of Dial Books for
Young Readers, a division of Penguin Books USA Inc.)

Shape

Lines join and intersect to suggest shapes, and areas of color meet to produce shapes. Organic shapes, irregular and curving, are common in nature and in handmade objects. Geometric shapes—exact, rigid, and often rectangular—usually have mechanical origins. As discussed in relation to line, different shapes have different connotations. Illustrators may use organic, freeform shapes to convey anything from receptivity and imagination to frightening unpredictability. They may use geometric shapes to connote complexity, stability, assertion, or severity.

Gerald McDermott, illustrator and author of *Arrow to the Sun,* uses traditional Native American patterns of line and color to create shapes that draw readers into a desert world where humans, nature, and spiritual forces intertwine. Rich yellow, orange, and brown rectangles depict the pueblo home of the people. This building constructed by humans from natural materials is separated by a black void from the circular orange and yellow sun, which is the people's god. The people worship this god in the kiva, a circular ceremonial chamber. A rectangular ray from the sun to the pueblo represents the spark of life that becomes the sun god's earthly son. He is illustrated as a black and yellow rectangle, while his mother's form is more circular. Black and yellow rectangles predominate in the illustrations until the son

decides to search for his father and takes on the sun's power as well as the rainbow of colors available to the sun. He returns to earth as an arrow, and his people, now illustrated in all of the colors that he has brought with him, celebrate with the dance of life.

Shape and color are also important in the illustrations for Paul Owen Lewis's *Storm Boy.* The bold paintings and shapes reflect the cultures and the graphic art of the Haida, Tlingit, and other native peoples from the Pacific Northwest.

A person's shape says much about self-image. In *Crow Boy,* Taro Yashima uses line and color to create shapes that emphasize a small boy's growth from fright and alienation to self-confidence. Yashima first draws the boy as a small, huddled shape isolated from his classmates in white space. As an understanding teacher helps Crow Boy become more self-assured, his shape on the page becomes larger, more outreaching, and closer to the shapes of other characters. Yashima also stresses Crow Boy's transformation by outlining his new form with shades of white that suggest shimmering light.

Shape provides the most important element in alphabet books such as David Pelletier's *The Graphic Alphabet* and Stephen T. Johnson's *Alphabet City.* In *The Graphic Alphabet,* Pelletier relates the shape of the letters to meaning. For example, the letter *f* reflects the meaning of *fire* by showing red flames emerging from the top of the letter. There is no text in *Alphabet City.* Consequently, all of the paintings reflect the shapes of various letters of the alphabet.

Shape is another way to emphasize the mood of a picture and story. According to illustrator Uri Shulevitz (1985), two areas are related to shape and mood: (1) the overall form of an illustration if viewed as a silhouette (with no interior details) and (2) the edges of the picture, which can be hard, soft, jagged, or straight. Shulevitz states that symmetrical picture shapes, such as rectangles, squares, circles, and ovals, are calm and solid, while asymmetrical picture shapes are unbalanced, irregular, and dynamic.

To evaluate the impact of shape on mood in illustrated books, analyze several recent award-winning books and books on the Children's Literature Association's touchstone list. Consider David Wisniewski's illustrations for *Golem,* David Diaz's illustrations for Eve Bunting's

Geometric shapes and sunny colors give a powerful feeling to a Native American tale from the southwestern United States. (From Arrow to the Sun *by Gerald McDermott. Copyright © 1974 by Gerald McDermott. Used by permission of Viking Penguin, an imprint of Penguin Putnam Books for Young Readers, a division of Penguin Putnam Inc.)*

Smoky Night, Stephen Gammell's illustrations for Karen Ackerman's *Song and Dance Man,* John Schoenherr's illustrations for Jane Yolen's *Owl Moon,* Richard Egielski's illustrations for Arthur Yorinks's *Hey, Al,* Emily Arnold McCully's illustrations for *Mirette on the High Wire,* Paul O. Zelinsky's illustrations for Grimm's *Rapunzel,* David Small's illustrations for Sarah Stewart's *The Gardener,* and Simms Taback's illustrations for *There Was an Old Lady Who Swallowed a Fly.* Earlier illustrated books on the touchstone list include Robert McCloskey's *Make Way for Ducklings,* Dr. Seuss's *The 500 Hats of Bartholomew Cubbins,* L. Leslie Brooke's *Johnny Crow's Garden,* Kate Greenaway's *A: Apple Pie,* Walter Crane's *The Baby's Opera,* and Wanda Gág's *Millions of Cats.* Do the shapes reinforce the moods of these texts?

Texture

Looking at an object for the first time, a child usually wants to touch it to know how it feels. Experience in touching rough bark, smooth skin, sharp thorns, and soft fur enables children later to imagine how something feels without actually touching it. Illustrators use such visual elements as line, color, and shape to create textural imagery.

Frequently, illustrators who depict the wonders of nature use line to show texture in their illustrations. In Jane Yolen's *Owl Moon,* John Schoenherr (1988) re-creates the texture of the woods outside his studio windows. Viewers can almost feel the tree trunks, the snow-covered landscapes, the small animals peeking from behind trees, and the ultimate owl. The thick textures of animals are almost felt in Jon Van Zyle's illustrations for Debbie S. Millers *A Woolly Mammoth Journey.* The many textures of nature are felt through the watercolors used by Jerry Pinkney in his illustrations for Hans Christian Andersen's *The Ugly Duckling.* The textures range from the feathers of the mother duck to the almost transparent wings of a dragonfly.

The textures associated with the geography and the animals found in the Australian bush are found in Christian Birmingham's illustrations for Michael Morpurgo's *Wombat Goes Walkabout.* The textures range from the wombat's soft fur and whiskers to the spiky texture of the undergrowth. Textures allow readers to vicariously experience the wilderness environment of the Healesville Sanctuary in Australia.

In *Bear,* Schoenherr reproduces the hide of an angry moose and the fur on the hungry bear. In contrast, his stream imparts the impression of cool, smooth water. Animal fur, corn husks, and corn silks are important textures that bring to life Janet Stevens's *Tops & Bottoms.* Viewers can describe the feel of the lazy bear's fur, the corn husks, and the silk protruding from each ear of corn. Raven's feathers, bear's fur, and tree bark are all vicariously felt in Jon Van Zyle's illustrations for Nancy White Carlstrom's *Raven and River.*

In *The Story of Jumping Mouse,* Steptoe uses line and shades of black and white to create textures ranging from sharp spikes on cacti to delicate petals on flowers. John Sanford's oil paintings emphasize the textures found in nature in Judit Z. Bodnár's *Tale of a Tail.* The fur of bear and fox, the hatched roof of fox's cottage, and the roughness of tree bark all seem very appropriate for this Hungarian folktale.

A child's response to Kenneth Lilly's illustrations in Joyce Pope's *Kenneth Lilly's Animals: A Portfolio of Paintings* shows how effective texture can be in an informational book. The child did not want to put the book away because "I was there with the animals. I kept touching the Koala bears to see if they were real."

For one minute,
three minutes,
maybe even a hundred minutes,
we stared at one another.

Lines and color re-create the texture of an owl. (From Owl Moon *by Jane Yolen. Illustrated by John Schoenherr, text copyright 1987, by Jane Yolen, illustrations © 1987 by John Schoenherr. Reprinted by permission of Philomel books.)*

Design: Organizing the Visual Elements

Design, or composition, is the way in which artists combine the visual elements of line, color, shape, and texture into a unified whole. When an illustration has an overall unity, balance, and sense of rhythm, viewers experience aesthetic pleasure; when the design is weak, viewers often feel that they are looking at an incomplete, incoherent, or boring picture.

Illustrators of children's books emphasize certain characters, develop main ideas, and provide background information. They also organize their illustrations so that viewers can identify the most important element in a picture and follow a visual sequence within the picture. Artists show dominance in their work by emphasizing size (the largest form is seen first), contrasting intense colors (an intense area of warm color dominates an intense area of cool color of the same size), placing the most important item in the center, using strong lines to provide visual pathways, and emphasizing nonconformity (viewers' eyes travel to an item that is different). When evaluating illustrations in children's books, consider whether or not the dominant images are consistent with those of the story.

Tomie dePaola achieves balance through symmetry in his illustrations for Clement Moore's *The Night Before Christmas.* The strong vertical lines of the central fireplace are reinforced by stockings hanging beneath the mantle, candles on the mantle, rows of trees in a picture over the mantle, and the legs of a chair and a table in the room. To the left and the right of the fireplace, portraits face the center of the illustration, where Santa stands on the hearth. For further emphasis, Santa's beard and the fur on his jacket are strikingly white against the rich reds and greens of the room.

Both authors and illustrators of children's books use repetition for emphasis. In illustrations, repetition can create rhythms and provide visual pathways. Virginia Lee Burton's illustrations are excellent examples of this technique. Burton's background in ballet and interest in the spatial concepts of dance may help account for her success in capturing rhythm and movement on paper. In *The Little House,* for example, Burton shows the house sitting on a hill and trees on either side. A row of trees follows the curve of several hills behind the house. On each hill are progressively smaller trees, houses, people, and animals. Beyond the last curving line of trees, the text tells us, lies the city that will soon spread out and surround the little house with traffic and skyscrapers.

Page design can provide a unifying quality. Jeanne McLain Harms and Lucille J. Lettow (1998) emphasize the importance of borders in book and page design when they conclude: "These designs decorate, depict folk designs of a culture, focus on story elements, predict emerging plots, extend the messages of a text, bind the text and illustrations, and break the frame. Cameos in borders and margins of illustrations can play a supporting role by portraying minor elements of the story" (p. 23).

Several artists develop visual continuity by framing text pages or illustrations. Trina Schart Hyman frames each text page in Margaret Hodges's *Saint George and the Dragon* with drawings of plants that are indigenous to the British Isles. In Barbara Cohen's adaptation of Chaucer's *Canterbury Tales,* Hyman borders the illustrations with rich gold designs. In *Exodus* Brian Wildsmith uses gold to border the illustrations for a biblical story about Moses. In Paolo Guarnieri's *A Boy Named Giotto,* Bimba Landmann also uses gold to border illustrations that depict an early Italian setting and the boy who learns to paint frescoes at Assisi. In the illustrations for *Sindbad: From the Tales of the Thousand and One Nights,* Ludmila Zeman uses rich borders that reflect the Persian influence of the setting. Laszlo Gal borders each illustration in Eva Martin's *Canadian Fairy Tales* with lightly penciled sketches of objects chosen from the appropriate story. In *Hiawatha's Childhood,* derived from Henry Wadsworth Longfellow's famous poems, artist Errol LeCain borders each page with the tall birch trees shown in the cover illustration. Helen Davie uses Native American designs to add authenticity to the borders in Barbara Esbensen's *The Star Maiden.*

Page and book design are especially effective when the design matches and adds to the content of the book. For example, the page design in Janet Stevens's *Tops & Bottoms* provides an interesting topic for discussion as readers consider the impact of the book's design, which is illustrated and printed from top to bottom, with the book bound at the top instead of the normal side-to-side page turning. Notice how Helen Cooper in *Pumpkin Soup* places the text in different formats and changes the size and density of the text to match the story's actions. James J. Alison's text for *The Drums of Noto Hanto* uses a similar approach as the words representing the sounds of the drums become larger and darker as the drums boom.

DePaola achieves balance through symmetry. Notice the lines of the trees in the painting over the fireplace, the pictures on each side of the fireplace, and the fireplace decorations. (Copyright © 1980 by Tomie dePaola. Reprinted from The Night Before Christmas *by permission of Holiday House, Inc.)*

Repetition and line provide a visual pathway and suggest movement. (Illustration by Virginia Lee Burton from The Little House. *Copyright 1942 by Virginia Lee Demetrios. Copyright renewed 1969 by George Demetrios. Reprinted by permission of Houghton Mifflin Co.)*

The different formats of the text emphasize the informality of the story. (From Pumpkin Soup *by Helen Cooper. Copyright © 1998 by Helen Cooper. Reprinted by permission of Farrar, Straus and Giroux, LLC.)*

In addition to providing unifying qualities, page design should reflect the level of formality of the text. Lyn Ellen Lacy (1986) emphasizes choosing levels of formality or informality that are in harmony with the text. Lacy identifies five levels of formality in book and page design. As you look at total book design, analyze the impact and the appropriateness of each of the levels of formality. First, text placed opposite illustrations on adjacent pages is considered the most formal arrangement. *Saint George and the Dragon,* by Margaret Hodges, has such an arrangement. Each text page is blocked in black type and surrounded by a formal border. To add to this formal feeling, each illustrated page is also bounded by a consistent border. The resulting text provides the formal feeling of a traditional legend. Likewise, in *Fables,* Arnold Lobel carefully balances the text and illustrations on facing pages and places them within a border.

Second, text positioned above or beneath illustrations is considered formal. The text for Sid Fleischman's *The Scarebird* is consistently placed under Peter Sís's illustrations. Notice how texts such as *The Scarebird* and Donald Hall's *Ox-Cart Man* still appear formal but not as formal as *Saint George and the Dragon* and *Fables.*

Third, text shaped with irregular boundaries to fit inside, between, around, or to the side of illustrations is considered informal. For example, notice how the text is shaped in Virginia Lee Burton's *The Little House* or in Wanda Gág's *Millions of Cats.*

Fourth, text combined with two or more arrangements is very informal. Julian Scheer's *Rain Makes Applesauce* is a good example of a very informal arrangement. The text is printed in different forms, colors, and sizes, and it appears to be part of Marvin Bileck's illustrations. This level of informality seems appropriate for a nonsense poem.

Finally, lack of text, such as in wordless books and almost-wordless books, is considered the most informal. *Will's Mammoth,* with Rafe Martin's text and Stephen Gammell's illustrations, has such a level of informality. The words that introduce an imaginary experience are printed in different sizes and colors. The illustrations then continue the story wordlessly. Words again written in different sizes and colors conclude the story. This combination is appropriate for a text that encourages imaginative play. As you look at page design, consider the different responses that are possible.

Artistic Media

The elements of line, color, shape, and texture are expressed through the materials and techniques that artists use in illustrating. Ink, wood, paper, paint, and other media can create a wide variety of visual effects. Artist Harry Borgman (1979) indicates a few of the possibilities in stating his own preferences:

If I want a bright, translucent wash tone, I would either use watercolor or dyes. For an opaque paint that is water resistant, I would use acrylics. If I want to draw a line that will dissolve a bit when water is washed over it, I would use a Pentel Sign pen. (p. 113)

Borgman's remarks suggest the importance of choosing the media and artistic techniques most appropriate for conveying characterization, setting, and mood in a particular story.

Lines and Washes

Many illustrations discussed in this chapter rely on lines drawn in ink to convey meaning and develop the mood. For example, the crisp lines and repetition in Wanda Gág's pen-and-ink drawings help readers visualize and believe in a world inhabited by *Millions of Cats*, each of which has special qualities appealing to an old man.

Ink is a versatile medium. It may be applied with brush, sponge, cloth, or even fingers, as well as with pen. In the artist's note for Betsy Lewin's illustrations for Doreen Cronin's *Click, Clack, Moo: Cows That Type*, the artist states that she applied watercolor washes to the black drawings.

Artists also use varying qualities of pen-and-ink line to convey emotions corresponding to characterizations in books. Ray Cruz's drawings for Judith Viorst's *Alexander and the Terrible, Horrible, No Good, Very Bad Day* communicate the essence of a boy who experiences unhappy and frustrating emotions. The scowling expressions and hair on end convey the spirit of a boy who has lost his best friend and doesn't have any dessert in his lunch box.

Shades of water-thinned ink, sparely drawn figures, and textured paper suggest a traditional Japanese setting in Sumiko Yagawa's *The Crane Wife*. Illustrator Suekichi Akaba's traditional Japanese painting techniques complement the story of a transformed crane who rewards a poor farmer

The transparent quality of watercolors suggests a close relationship with nature in this spider's web in Laurel Molk's illustrations for Jane Yolen's Off We Go! *(From* Off We Go! *by Jane Yolen. Text copyright © 2000 by Jane Yolen. Illustrations © 2000 by Laurel Molk. Published by Little, Brown & Company. Reprinted by permission of the publisher.)*

for his care but returns to animal form when the young man becomes greedy and breaks his promise.

Watercolors, Acrylics, Pastels, and Oils

Watercolor is one of the most common artistic media chosen by illustrators of children's books. According to art director Lucy Bitzer (1992), "The opportunities offered by the luminous and transparent hues of the watercolor medium make this form a pliant choice to evoke mood, mystery, and timelessness. Specifically, it allows the structure of descriptive drawing to hold its own against a color style" (p. 227). Bitzer identifies Arthur Rackham, who illustrated books in the late 1800s and early 1900s, as one of the first illustrators to recognize the transparent qualities obtainable with watercolors. Edmund Dulac was another early artist who used watercolors, especially when illustrating folktales.

Laurel Molk's watercolors for Jane Yolen's *Off We Go!* suggest a close relationship with nature. The transparent qualities are especially noticeable in an illustration

The illustrations for Jennifer Armstrong's Pierre's Dream *provide a good source for viewing the effectiveness of acrylics. (From* Pierre's Dream *by Jennifer Armstrong, pictures by Susan Gaber. Copyright © 1999 by Susan Gaber, pictures. Used by permission of Dial Books for Young Readers, an imprint of Penguin Putnam Books for Young Readers, a division of Penguin Putnam Inc.)*

Greg Couch's watercolors used to illustrate Jane Cutler's *The Cello of Mr. O.* exemplify the range of moods that can be created by this medium. There is the desolation of a war-torn city, but also the glowing feelings associated with music. When Mr. O begins playing, the paintings take on an almost transparent appearance as birds and flowers rise out of the instrument. The illustrations match the moods that go from fear to happiness.

Humor can also be created through the use of watercolors, as shown in the watercolors of James Marshall in his illustrations for Edward Lear's *The Owl and the Pussycat.* Read the comments written by Maurice Sendak in the Afterword of the book and see if you agree with Sendak's conclusion: "There never was such an Owl and Pussycat, certainly not since Edward Lear, and for my money James surpasses Lear's original pictures in sheer giddy humor and heartfeltness" (unnumbered). Another artist who develops humor in a retelling of a tale is Barry Moser in his adaptation of *The Three Little Pigs.* Watercolors effectively give personalities to both the pigs and the wolf.

The effects of three color media—watercolors, pastels, and acrylics—are seen in Leo and Diane Dillon's illustrations for Margaret Musgrove's *Ashanti to Zulu: African Traditions.* Vibrantly colored jewelry and designs on artifacts contrast with the soft shades of the flowing garments. The river in the illustration that depicts the Lozi people is so transparent that the bottom of the boat shimmers through the water. In other pictures, the sky vibrates with heat from the sun and jewel-like tones express the breathtaking beauty of exotic birds and plants.

Jerry Pinkney's illustrations for Barbara Diamond Goldin's *Journey with Elijah: Eight Tales of the Prophet* are a combination of graphite, colored pencil, pastel, and watercolor. Wendy Anderson Halperin's illustrations for Jim Aylesworth's *The Full Belly Bowl* provide a source for analyzing an artist's ability using colored pencil.

depicting a fragile spider's web with blues and greens in the background.

David Wiesner's *Tuesday* is an excellent example of watercolors in illustration. The paintings go from the transparency of a curtain to the heavy leaves and trees of the outdoors setting. Likewise, the lighting changes from dark shadows to brilliant moonlight. A similar feeling is developed in Spirin's illustrations for Aaron Shepard's *The Sea King's Daughter: A Russian Legend.* In Frances Ward Weller's *I Wonder If I'll See a Whale,* Ted Lewin's illustrations contrast the colors of life above the sea and the blues and greens of life below the sea. Several pictures create a feeling of looking through the water with its levels of color and changes in current. A very different setting is created by Uri Shulevitz's use of watercolors in Ehud Ben-Ezer's *Hosni the Dreamer: An Arabian Tale.* Now watercolors create the hues of the desert. Watercolors seem appropriate for creating these settings.

Strong line and repetition in pencil-and-ink drawings complement a story. (Illustration by Wanda Gág from Millions of Cats. *Copyright 1928; renewed 1956, by Wanda Gág. Reprinted by permission of Coward McCann & Geoghegan, Inc.)*

Oil paints on board create the desired textures. (From The Stinky Cheese Man and Other Fairly Stupid Tales *by Jon Scieszka and Lane Smith. Copyright © 1992 by Jon Scieszka. Reprinted by permission of Viking Penguin, a division of Penguin Books USA Inc.)*

Dark, somber tones in full-page oil paintings create an appropriately menacing setting for a dramatic folktale. (From Hansel and Gretel. *Illustrated by Paul O. Zelinsky and retold by Rika Lesser. Illustrations copyright © 1984 by Paul O. Zelinsky, Dodd Mead. Reprinted by permission.)*

According to an interview with Marisa Bulzone (1993), illustrator Gary Kelley is inspired by oil paintings, but he creates his works in pastels. Kelley used pastels in the illustrations for Washington Irving's *The Legend of Sleepy Hollow* because he was influenced by the paintings of John Singleton Copley, Charles Wilson Peale, and the Hudson River and Naive schools of painting. He states, "I wanted my illustrations to reflect their color palettes and the way these painters handled similar subject matter" (p. 96). As you look at illustrations by Gary Kelley, try to analyze how he was influenced by oil paintings.

Paul O. Zelinsky's full-page oil paintings create a somber mood for *Hansel and Gretel*, as told by the Brothers Grimm. Zelinsky's woods are menacing, where evil is likely to exist. The rich highlights that are possible with oil are shown in Zelinsky's illustrations for Brothers Grimm's *Rumpelstiltskin* and *Rapunzel.* Likewise, Thomas Locker's full-page oil paintings for Jean Craighead George's *The First Thanksgiving* show the shadings, highlights, colors, and textures possible with oils. Jill Kastner's oil paintings found in Cynthia Rylant's *In November* develop the warm autumn colors that correspond with Rylant's seasonal fall activities such as a Thanksgiving feast, November trees prepared for winter, and birds leaving for their southern migration. Lane Smith (1993), the illustrator of Jon Scieszka's *The True Story of the 3 Little Pigs!* and *The Stinky Cheese Man and Other*

Fairly Stupid Tales, describes how he uses oil paint on illustration board to acquire the desired effects:

Everything I do is oil paint on board. I get texture from a variety of means. Usually it involves some sort of acrylic paints or sprays to cause a reaction. . . . Sometimes, if the painting gets really thick, I'll sand down areas to another layer. I've always been attracted to texture. (p. 70)

Woodcuts

Woodcuts are among the oldest and most influential artistic media in both Western and Eastern cultures. In the fifteenth century, the black-and-white woodcuts of the German artist Albrecht Dürer brought this medium to a new level of sophistication in Europe. These early woodcuts, which were often drawings of animals, influenced the ways in which people saw nature and thought about it (Quammen, 1993). The first printed books, including the earliest books for children, were illustrated with black-and-white woodcuts. Later, Japanese artists pioneered in the creation of full-color woodcuts, inspiring other artists in Europe and North America, such as the famous French artist Paul Gauguin.

To create a woodcut, an artist draws an image on a block of wood and cuts away the areas around the

The collage illustrations reflect the changing moods of the Mississippi River. (From Steamboat! The Story of Captain Blanche Leathers *by Judith Heide Gilliland, illustrated by Holly Meade. Copyright © 2000 by DK Publishing. Reprinted by permission of the publisher.)*

design. After rolling ink onto this raised surface, the artist presses the woodblock against paper, transferring the image from the block to the paper. Color prints require a different woodblock for each color in the picture. Woodcuts can be printed in colors with varying degrees of transparency, and the grain and texture of the wood can add to the effect of the composition. Carol Finley's *Art of Japan* focuses on the woodblock prints made in Japan between 1600 and 1868. The paintings reproduced in the book show landscapes that celebrate the beauty and meditative quality of nature, birds, and flowers, and the dramatic style of Kabuki acting. The author also describes the creation of the woodblock prints as well as how this period in Japanese art influenced European artists.

The strong lines and bold colors of woodcuts create a simplicity often desired by illustrators of folktales. Gail Haley used woodcuts to illustrate her version of an African folktale *A Story, a Story.* The grain of the wood replicates the texture of native huts and communicates the earthy nature of a traditional setting. The strong lines possible with woodcuts are found in David Frampton's illustrations for Miriam Chaikin's *Clouds of Glory,* a collection of Jewish tales from the Midrash.

The effects of Betsy Bowen's woodcuts may be analyzed in her illustrations for Lise Lunge-Larsen's *The Troll* with *No Heart in His Body and Other Tales of Trolls from Norway.* The rough texture seems very appropriate for illustrating hags, shaggy goats, and all types of trolls.

Kevin Crossley-Holland illustrates his story set in the Middle Ages, *Arthur: The Seeing Stone,* with woodcuts from the publication "Medieval Life Illustrations." The use of these reproductions of early woodcuts adds a sense of authenticity to a book set in England and Wales in 1199.

In *Bayberry Bluff,* Blair Lent uses cardboard cuts. Cardboard cuts are similar to woodcuts or linoleum cuts, except that the designs are cut into thick cardboard with single-edged razor blades.

Collage

Collage—a word derived from the French word *coller,* meaning "to paste" or "to stick"—is a recent addition to the world of book illustration. Pasting and sticking are exactly what artists do when using this technique. Any object or substance that can be attached to a surface can be used to develop a design. Artists may use cardboard, paper, cloth, glass, leather, metal, wood, leaves, flowers, or even butterflies. They may cut up and rearrange their own paintings or use paint and other media to add background. When photographically reproduced, collages still communicate texture. In an analysis of current illustration in picture storybooks, Dilys Evans (1992) emphasizes the increased use of cut paper and collage, fabrics, plasticine, and embroidery in illustrations.

Eric Carle, a popular artist of picture books for children, is known for his striking, colorful storybooks. *The Very Hungry Caterpillar* won the American Institute of Graphic Art's award for 1970. Carle develops his collages through a three-step process. He begins by applying acrylic paints to tissue paper. Then, he uses rubber cement to paste the paper into the desired designs. Finally, he applies colored crayon to provide accents. In *Eric Carle's Animals Animals,* tissue-paper collage creates a dazzling array of animals. In Laura Whipple's *Eric Carle's Dragons Dragons & Other Creatures That Never Were,* Carle painted onto thin tissue papers and then cut or tore the tissue papers into shapes and glued them onto the illustration boards. The painted tissue papers create smooth and silky illustrations. Carle's collages for *From Head to Toe* compare movements among animals and children. Carle adds a sensory feature to his large, colorful collages in *The Very Clumsy Click Beetle.* Readers can hear a loud click as the beetle overcomes his clumsiness and learns how to accomplish somersaults.

Another artist who illustrates with collage is Ezra Jack Keats. In *Peter's Chair,* lace looks realistic as it cascades from

Outstanding Illustrators of Children's Books

A close look at several artists reveals the wide range of excellence in children's book illustration and the ways in which individuals fluent in artistic grammar create visual narratives that appeal to young children. The artists discussed in this chapter use the elements of line, color, shape, and texture to create memorable illustrations that highlight the moods of the texts. These illustrations provide numerous opportunities for both children and adults to interact with visual elements and to improve their appreciation of art.

Barbara Cooney

Barbara Cooney's illustrations for Donald Hall's *Ox-Cart Man* use gentle colors and rounded shapes to evoke the peaceful countryside of early nineteenth-century New England. Cooney creates the same mood in *Island Boy*. Soft colors and curved landscapes add to the feeling of an unhurried way of life in which a young boy can explore the joys of his New England home. In Cooney's illustrations for *Chanticleer and the Fox*, however, bold, black lines create a strutting, vain rooster in the earlier portion of the book and a frightened, humble one as the story reaches its climax in the life-and-death struggle between Chanticleer and his enemy, the fox.

Cooney is skilled in using artistic techniques that best complement a particular text. Her illustrations for Margot Griego et al.'s *Tortillitas Para Mama and Other Spanish Nursery Rhymes* re-create the varied settings associated with Spanish nursery rhymes. Warm browns depict the interior of a Mexican home, cool blues warmed by the shining moon suggest a village by the water, and warm fuchsia pinks reflect the warmth of a mother and father sharing a quiet time with their baby.

Cooney's illustrations for Jane Yolen's *Letting Swift River Go* take viewers back to the rural life in western Massachusetts and to the memories of a town that was submerged when the Quabbin Reservoir was formed. Before illustrating Michael Bedard's *Emily*, Cooney con-

Barbara Cooney uses gentle colors and rounded shapes to recreate the feeling of an earlier rural setting in Mary Lynn Ray's Basket Moon. *(From* Basket Moon *by Mary Lynn Ray. Text copyright © 1999 by Mary Lynn Ray, illustrations copyright © 1999 by Barbara Cooney. Published by Little, Brown & Company. Reprinted by permission of the publisher.)*

ducted research at Emily Dickinson's home in Amherst, Massachusetts. Cooney painted the illustrations for *Emily* on China silk mounted on illustration board, using liquitex acrylic paints, prismacolor, and Derwent colored pencils and pastels. Cooney also illustrates the earlier rural setting of Columbia County, New York, for Mary Lyn Ray's *Basket Moon*. Oils, pastels, and acrylics, gentle colors, and rounded shapes are similar to those used by Cooney in Hall's *Ox-Cart Man*. You may compare the illustrations for the two texts and consider the moods suggested by the artist's choice of colors and shapes.

Tomie dePaola

Tomie dePaola has illustrated, or written and illustrated, over one hundred books, including traditional folktales from Italy, Scandinavia, and Mexico; informational books; realistic fiction; and Bible stories. DePaola's illustrations for *The Clown of God* reveal the influence of two pre-Renaissance artists, Giotto and Fra Angelico, whose simplicity and strength of line dePaola admires: "I almost reduce features to a symbol. And yet I think of my faces as good and warm. I try to show expression in very few lines" (Hepler, 1979, p. 299). For *The Clown of God,* dePaola first penciled in the lines and then went over the sketches with raw sienna waterproof ink, a second brown pencil line, and brown ink. He completed the artwork with watercolors.

DePaola emphasizes that his great love of folk art is a strong element in his work. Consequently, according to Masha Rudman (1993b), he was inspired by the early works of Alice and Martin Provensen. Strong feelings for Americana are found in dePaola's *An Early American Christmas.* Many of dePaola's illustrations and texts such as *Christopher: The Holy Giant* reflect his belief that children and adults should be exposed to the rich heritage of ethnic folklore. In his illustrations for *The Legend of the Bluebonnet, The Legend of the Indian Paintbrush,* and numerous folktales from various European countries, dePaola combines folk art and folktale.

DePaola also values his theater experience and makes use of it in his illustrations: "There are so many ways picture books are like theater-scenes, settings, characterization. A double page spread can be like a stage" (Hepler, 1979, p. 300). DePaola's illustrations often have the symmetry of stage settings, with actions that appear to take place in front of a backdrop. *Giorgio's Village,* for example, a pop-up book that re-creates an Italian Renaissance village, is itself a stagelike setting in which windows open and tabs allow movement. Some of the illustrations in *Tomie dePaola's Mother Goose* also have the appearance of stage settings.

Other books show the influence of films. In *Watch Out for the Chicken Feet in Your Soup,* the action in the story and illustrations starts before the title page, which becomes part of both the narrative and the action. In these and other ways, dePaola's large body of work demonstrates his belief that children should be exposed to many types of visual imagery.

Leo and Diane Dillon

Leo and Diane Dillon's strong interest in the folklore of traditional peoples is evident in their award-winning books. Their work reflects careful research into the decorative motifs of many cultures and helps re-create and preserve traditional ways of life.

The text for Mildred Pitts Walter's *Brother to the Wind* is rich in folklore, symbols, and dreams. The Dillons use light

Acrylics are used to illustrate this book based on Inuit tales. (From The Girl Who Dreamed Only Geese by Howard Norman. Text © 1997 by Howard Norman. Illustrations © 1997 by Leo and Diane Dillon. Published by Harcourt Brace & Company. Reprinted by permission.)

and dark, pastels and deep colors, to contrast a boy's mythical quest to fly and the earthbound unbelievers who are sure that he will fail. In one illustration, the wind, which makes it possible for the boy to fly, is a transparent woman whose color and shape blend into the pale, cloudy sky. Viewers are given the impression that only they and the boy, not the doubting villagers, can see the wind.

The Dillons also use shades of black and white to contrast myth and reality in the illustrations for Virginia Hamilton's *The People Could Fly: American Black Folktales.* Their illustrations for Verna Aardema's *Why Mosquitoes Buzz in People's Ears* re-create the setting of a traditional African folktale. In Virginia Hamilton's *Her Stories: African American Folktales, Fairy Tales, and True Tales* the artists painted with acrylics on illustration board. Acrylics are also used to illustrate Howard Norman's *The Girl Who Dreamed Only Geese and Other Tales of the Far North.* In every case, careful research preceded the Dillons' illustrations.

Technology Resources

Visit our Companion Website at www.prenhall.com/norton to link to a Leo and Diane Dillon website containing biographies and an assortment of related sites.

Susan Jeffers

Susan Jeffers uses texture and line to convey differences between reality and fantasy in her realistic but magical illustrations. Her skilled use of line is especially apparent in her illustrations for Hans Christian Andersen's *The Wild Swans*. Strong lines depict forest, hillside, and stormy sea. More delicate, cross-hatched lines depict the sunshine and plants within the fragrant cedar grove. When a beautiful fairy enters the girl's dreams to guide her in freeing her brothers, Jeffers contrasts the reality of the characters sleeping on the ground and the fairyland of the palace in the clouds. The girl herself is in warm greens and browns, while the fairy and the fairy castle are almost transparent blues and grays.

Jeffers uses variety of line to depict similar distinctions of nature and the mythical spirit world in her illustrations for Henry Wadsworth Longfellow's *Hiawatha*. Other books in which Jeffers develops mood and setting through detailed line drawings include the Grimms's *Hansel and Gretel*, Eugene Field's *Wynken, Blynken and Nod*, Charles Perrault's *Cinderella*, adapted by Amy Ehrlich, and Jeffers's own *Brother Eagle, Sister Sky*.

Ezra Jack Keats

Ezra Jack Keats combines collage, paint, and empathy for children's needs and emotions in compositions that portray inner-city life. Sometimes, the environment is peaceful, as in *The Snowy Day*, where Keats uses brilliantly white torn paper to convey the snow covering chimneys and rooftops as Peter looks out on a fresh, white world. Later, shadowy blue footprints bring the text and the illustrations together, asking readers to look at Peter's footprints in the snow. Snowbanks are rounded shapes, and buildings are rectangles of color in the background. Peter's simple, red-clad figure stands out against the snowy background.

Keats evokes quite a different mood with collage and paint in *Goggles!* Here, two children confront harsher realities, as they try to escape from bigger boys who want their possessions. The colors are dark, and the collages include thrown-away items that one might find in back alleys. Keats shows the frightening big boys as almost featureless. In one picture, a hole in a piece of wood frames the scene as the two small boys look through it and plan how to get home. In other books—such as *Louie*, *The Trip*, and *Peter's Chair*—illustrations by Keats complement the loneliness, daydreams, or jealousy described in the text.

Joseph Schwarcz (1982) believes that children respond to books by Keats, such as *Apt. 3*, because

the illustrations dramatize the lyrical mood, probably also making it more easily accessible for the younger reader. The gestures and postures of the people in the story are down to earth, outspoken. The important visual motifs are the ones we know well.

The apartment building is muddy and ugly. The large shapes of the boys, painted from a close angle, evoke intimacy. From the beginning there is visual metaphor. (p. 188)

W. Nikola-Lisa (1991) analyzes the art of Ezra Jack Keats and discusses Keats's use of lines to direct the viewers' attention to a portion of his illustrations.

Robert McCloskey

Robert McCloskey's illustrations present the real world of boys, girls, families, and animals. Detailed black-and-white drawings depict the settings in most of his books, although McCloskey also uses color to evoke the essence of an island susceptible to forces of nature in *Time of Wonder*. In that book, McCloskey's watercolors first depict a serene world. When gentle rain approaches, the painting is so transparent that the first thing seen is a thin mist descending. Later, diagonal lines of raindrops break the surface of the peaceful water, and light fog surrounds two children, who experience the whispering sound of growing ferns. The island is not always serene, however. A hurricane bends the lines of the trees, as the illustrations themselves almost move on the page. McCloskey's use of line is so compelling that Lyn Ellen Lacy (1986) uses page-by-page discussion of *Make Way for Ducklings* and *Time of Wonder* to analyze line in McCloskey's Caldecott award-winning books.

Black-and-white drawings illustrate McCloskey's delightful *Blueberries for Sal*. The child, whether stealing berries from a pail or mistakenly following a mother bear instead of her own mother, looks as if she could walk right off the page.

Alice and Martin Provensen

Color, symmetry, and effective use of space are noteworthy elements in the work of Alice and Martin Provensen. Many illustrations by the Provensens, whose collaborative efforts include more than fifty books, reflect the world in earlier times or worlds of fantasy. The Provensens create a feeling of flying through space in their book about the first flight across the English Channel, *The Glorious Flight Across the Channel with Louis Bleriot, July 25, 1909*. Consecutive illustrations proceed from a close-up of the plane before it soars to a wide-angle view of the small plane surrounded by clouds and sky. The corresponding text reveals that Louis Bleriot is alone, lost in a world of swirling fog. The illustrators' use of space and color reinforces this mood of danger and exhilaration.

The impact of symmetry in design is felt in several of the Provensens' illustrations for Nancy Willard's *A Visit to William Blake's Inn: Poems for Innocent and Experienced Travelers*. In one illustration, for example, the Wonderful Car hovers over buildings that provide a visual center for the car; the steps of the flying vehicle lead viewers toward the passengers; and the two smaller sets of propeller blades balance the larger center blade.

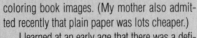

Through the Eyes of an ILLUSTRATOR

Tomie dePaola

Visit the CD-ROM that accompanies this text to generate a complete list of Tomie dePaola titles.

Selected Titles by Tomie dePaola:

Strega Nona

Clown of God: An Old Story

The Mysterious Giant of Barletta

The Art Lessons

Nana Upstairs & Nana Downstairs

Illustrating and Books

I am a doodler. In fact, I *love* to doodle. I always have. I keep pads of scratch paper and black and red fine-line markers by the telephones, at my drawing table, on my desk, in my carry-on bag when I fly; and when I was teaching, I never went to a meeting (faculty, committee, etc.) without my handy pad and markers.

Growing up, coloring books were absent from our house . . . at least, in my room. My tools were plain paper, pencils, and my trusty Crayolas. After all, I was going to be an artist when I grew up. And besides, my own drawings and doodles seemed to be far more interesting to me, and those around me, than the simple coloring book images. (My mother also admitted recently that plain paper was lots cheaper.)

I learned at an early age that there was a definite difference between out-and-out drawing and serious doodling. A drawing had more structure, more direction. A definite idea was usually the beginning of a drawing. For example, I might say, "I think I will do a drawing of a girl ice skating, wearing a fancy Ice Follies-type costume." (Yes, the Ice Follies were around way back then.) Then the problem would be to try to do a drawing that coincided with my original idea or vision.

Doodles were (and are) totally different. I would just put pencil to paper and see what happened. All sorts of interesting images would result. I might start out not really concentrating on my doodle but on what else I was doing at the time. Talking on the phone was a very good activity for doodling. Late at night under the covers with a flashlight and listening to the radio was another activity that produced more terrific doodles—some actually on sheets rather than on paper. The "state of the art" doodles of this early period, though, appeared as if by magic on my arithmetic papers. There would be columns of figures copied from the blackboard and before I knew it, the paper would be covered with pictures with no room for the answers. My teachers—well, at least, a few of them—were *not* amused. They warned me. I'd never learn to add, subtract, multiply, etc. They were right, but for me as an artist, the doodling proved to be a far more important activity. I was able to buy a calculator with a royalty check, and now, I have an accountant.

"Meeting doodles," especially faculty meeting doodles, proved to be among the most valuable for me. It was during a college faculty meeting that was about the same issues the previous dozen meetings had been about that "Strega Nona" appeared on my pad. I didn't know who she was at that moment, but a few months on my studio wall, and she soon let me know all about herself.

I've just opened a drawer and found some doodles that were done several years ago. (I stash doodles in different drawers so they can show up later and surprise me. My assistant saves all the phone-call doodles for me. My mother and an old friend both have doodles of mine in special drawers, waiting for the day they can cash in on them.)

The newfound doodles are on the wall of my studio. There is a rather fetching sheep and two classy cats, dressed to kill. Who knows . . . someday. . . . But remember! You read about them here first!

Video Profiles: The accompanying video contains conversations from such children's book artists as E. B. Lewis, Molly Bang, Floyd Cooper, and Lynne Cherry.

Copyright © by Tomie dePaola.

 ### Technology Resources

Use the database to generate a list of works by your favorite illustrator. You can add your own comments concerning individual titles by clicking on the hotlink in the third column, viewing the complete record, and typing in the comment field.

Other books demonstrating the Provensens' skill in re-creating historical periods include *Leonardo da Vinci.*

Maurice Sendak

Time magazine has called Maurice Sendak "the Picasso of children's books." Sendak's artistic versatility in using color, line, and balance is evident in the many books that Sendak has illustrated or written and illustrated, including Janice Udry's *The Moon Jumpers.* One of Sendak's primary aims in illustrating a text is to make "the pictures so organically akin to the text, so reflective of its atmosphere, that they look as if they could have been done in no other way. They should help create the special world of the story . . . creating the air for a writer" (Moritz, 1968, p. 352).

Sendak's special relationship between text and illustrations may be most apparent in *Outside over There* and *Where the Wild Things Are.* Sendak (Davis, 1981) described the steps that he took in creating the illustrations for *Outside over There,* which he considers his best and most significant children's book. One of his first concerns was drawing ten-year-old Ida holding a baby. To reproduce realistic body postures, Sendak made photographs of a child holding a baby. The baby kept slipping out of the child's arms, so that the clothes on both children drooped and became disheveled. Sendak referred to watercolors by the British poet and artist William Blake for inspiration in choosing colors that communicate the setting, characterization, and mood:

The colors belong to Ida. She is rural, of the time in the country when winter sunsets have that certain yellow you never see in other seasons. There's a description of women's clothing, watered silk, and that's what those skies are like—moist, sensuous, silken, almost transparent—the color I copied in the cape Ida wears and in other things showing up against soft mauve, blue, green, tan—all part of the story's feeling. (p. 46)

The illustrations for *Where the Wild Things Are* are totally integrated with the text and play a crucial role in the plot

Maurice Sendak was inspired by the watercolors in William Blake's paintings in creating his illustrations for this book. (Illustrations from Outside over There *by Maurice Sendak. Copyright © 1981 by Maurice Sendak. By permission of Harper & Row, Publishers, Inc.)*

Symmetry of design directs viewers toward the distant garden. (Illustration by Chris Van Allsburg from The Garden of Abdul Gasazi. *Copyright 1979 by Chris Van Allsburg. Reprinted by permission of Houghton Mifflin Company.)*

grass. As the story progresses, the illustrations cover more and more of the page; when Max becomes king of the wild things, six pages of illustrations are uninterrupted by text. Sendak creates a believably mischievous boy and humorous but forceful wild things with terrible rolling eyes and horrible gnashing teeth.

Brian Alderson (1993b) maintains that with the illustration of *Where the Wild Things Are,* Sendak shifted the load-bearing responsibility in his books from words to pictures. As you look at books illustrated by Maurice Sendak, notice how much of the story is extended, or even totally told, through the illustrations. The illustrations are especially important in Sendak's *We Are All in the Dumps with Jack and Guy,* where Sendak uses two nursery rhymes to provide minimal text. The illustrations, however, develop a contemporary story about the harsh reality of homelessness and poverty. Even the newspapers used as protection emphasize the contemporary social conflict between wealth and poverty.

Selma Lanes's *The Art of Maurice Sendak* (1980) provides biographical information as well as examples from Sendak's numerous books. Sendak's *Posters by Maurice Sendak* (1986) provides examples from many occasions. The posters also show how important wild things are in Sendak's art.

Chris Van Allsburg

Chris Van Allsburg's *The Garden of Abdul Gasazi, Jumanji, The Mysteries of Harris Burdick,* and *The Widow's Broom* demonstrate the effectiveness of black-and-white illustrations. Both line and subtle shading focus attention along a visual pathway in the illustrations for *The Garden of Abdul Gasazi.* In one picture, the main character is framed by a central doorway. On either side of the doorway, a bright statue against dark leaves points down a black tunnel toward a circle of white. This circle represents the garden in which the story line develops. (Symmetry is one way that artists create balance in their designs.)

In *The Wreck of the Zephyr,* Van Allsburg uses line to create movement and color to convey mood. As the story begins, rolling waves and billowing dark clouds suggest movement and the ominous forces of angry sea and sky. Later, the mood changes to fantasy, and Van Allsburg uses color to create a calm sea

and characterization, as well as the setting. When Max is banished to his room for bad behavior, the room gradually becomes the kingdom of the wild things, with trees growing naturally out of the bedposts and the shag rug turning into

Through the Eyes of a CHILD

Kayla

Pam Wilson's Fourth Grade
Western Row Elementary
Mason, Ohio

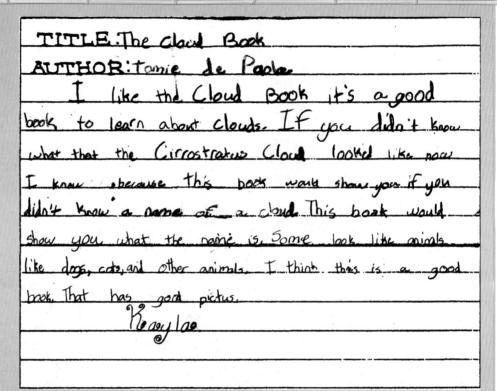

TITLE: The Cloud Book

AUTHOR: tomie de Paola

I like the Cloud Book it's a good book to learn about clouds. IF you didn't know what that the Cirrostratus Cloud looked like now I know because this book would show you if you didn't know a name of a cloud. This book would show you what the name is. Some look like animals like dogs, cats, and other animals. I think this is a good book. That has good pictus.

Kayla

The glowing colors and contrasts between light and dark are appropriate for a children's fantasy. (Illustrations from The Polar Express *by Chris Van Allsburg, copyright © 1985 by Chris Van Allsburg. Reproduced with permission from Houghton Mifflin Co.)*

sparkling with light, a fantasy harbor town seen through shadows, soft clouds tinged with sunset, and a star-studded sky.

Compare Van Allsburg's use of line and shading in his black-and-white illustrations with his use of line and color in *The Wreck of the Zephyr, The Polar Express, Swan Lake* (retold by Mark Helprin), *The Wretched Stone,* and *The Sweetest Fig.* In *The Polar Express,* Van Allsburg uses line to create the furry textures of lean wolves roaming the dark forests and the feathery texture of newly fallen snow. Even Santa Claus's beard and mittens seem to have texture. Van Allsburg also uses contrasting light and dark colors and shadings effectively. Moonlight focuses attention on the boy in his darkened bedroom, train windows glow with warmth as the train winds through cold forests and up snow-covered mountains, and city lights stream from windows to pierce the darkness.

David Wiesner

David Wiesner is best known for his wordless books, Caldecott Medal winner *Tuesday* and Caldecott Honor

Watercolors allow the artist to create illustrations that appear to vary from transparent to heavy. (From Tuesday *by David Wiesner. Copyright © 1991 by David Wiesner. Reprinted by permission of Clarion Books/Houghton Mifflin Co. All rights reserved.)*

book *Free Fall.* In an interview conducted by Susan Caroff and Elizabeth Moje (1992/1993), Wiesner states:

Wordless books have been my passion for a long time. It's something that goes way back. I've always liked telling stories with pictures, more than just painting a single painting. If I came up with an image that I liked—I would always be interested in seeing what had happened before or after the particular image I had painted. (p. 284)

Wiesner is pleased when his wordless books are used to stimulate creativity. He maintains that his books need readers because the author's voice is not there in the form of text. Words do not anchor the stories to reality. Instead, readers must interpret the illustrations themselves and create their own interpretations.

In *Free Fall,* Wiesner's illustrations seem to move into the next page. As you look at these illustrations, notice how the squares in the boy's blanket become the fields in a countryside divided into geometric shapes and then become a lifelike chess board. When the boy returns from his fantasy experience, the squares return to the bed covering. Flying shapes are important in creating the fantasy in both Wiesner's *Tuesday* and *June 29, 1999.*

Wiesner uses color to create moods appropriate for the settings. In *Tuesday,* blues and greens create the coolness of the night and provide an appropriate background for a story in which frogs explore their environment at night.

Suggested Activities

For more suggested activities for understanding artists and their illustrations, visit our Companion Website at **www.prenhall.com/norton**

▥ With some of your peers, select one of the following criteria for evaluating the illustrations and narrative portions of a picture book, find books that clearly exemplify the criteria, and share them with the class:
  a. The illustrations help readers anticipate both the action of the story and the climax (for example, Richard Egielski's illustrations for Arthur Yorinks's *Hey, Al* or Maurice Sendak's illustrations for *Where the Wild Things Are*).
  b. The pictures help create the basic mood of the story (for example, Paul Goble's *The Girl Who Loved Wild Horses* or Marcia Brown's illustrations for *Cinderella,* by Charles Perrault).
  c. The illustrations portray convincing characters (for example, Taro Yashima's *Crow Boy*).
  d. All pictures are accurate and consistent with text (for example, Barbara Cooney's illustrations for Donald Hall's *Ox-Cart Man*).
▥ Consider the ways in which lines are related to natural phenomena. Look carefully at the illustrations in several books. Are there examples in which vertical lines suggest lack of movement, horizontal lines suggest calmness or an absence of strife, vertical and horizontal lines connected at the top suggest stability and safety, diagonal lines suggest motion, and jagged lines symbolize danger?
▥ Ian Falconer (Brown, 2000) discusses the power of red in his illustrations for *Olivia.* He cites the influence of traditional Russian political posters, which use black and white and red. Research the traditional political posters and compare the posters with Falconer's illustrations.
▥ Choose an outstanding illustrator of children's books. Find as many of the illustrator's works as you can. Analyze the artist's use of the elements of art—line, color, shape, and texture— and the various media and styles used by the artist. Compare the books. Does the artist use a similar style in all works, or does the style change with the subject matter of the text? Compare earlier works with later ones. Are there any changes in the use of artistic elements, style, or media?

Teaching with Artists and Their Illustrations

A growing trend is helping children appreciate, respond to, and understand art. Children's librarian and author Sylvia S. Marantz (1992) argues that to awaken their visual perceptions, children need experiences designed to help them learn. She states:

Unfortunately most of their experience comes to them through a barrage of photographed images from a television screen. The children have no opportunity to examine what they see, to question its form or validity, to compare or contrast it critically with other pictures their eyes are receiving or with those their imaginations might provide if given the chance. (p. v)

Marantz uses her experience with children and books to recommend a program in which children, with the aid of adults, examine, discuss, question, and compare the illustrations in books and accomplish art activities that relate to the specific illustrations. Marantz progresses through a series of activities that focus on the book jacket, the front end papers, the title page, and each illustration, leading children to understand and appreciate such elements as color, movement, page design, and format. She recommends viewing and discussing additional books by the same illustrator and books to use for comparisons.

Susan Boulanger (1996) emphasizes using art education books that provide "opportunities for sharing the experience of looking at, thinking about, and discussing art" (p. 298). Such books allow children living in all locations to develop an appreciation for and an understanding of art, even if museum collections are not available.

Carol Finley in her author's note to *Art of the Far North: Inuit Sculpture, Drawing, and Printmaking* provides another reason for studying art: "One way to learn about the traditions of another people is to study their art. It could be said that art is a universal language and a window into cultures different from our own" (unnumbered).

This section of the chapter presents a few of the ways that you can help children experience "breathtaking, ingenious aspects of pictures" (Nodelman, 1984a, p. 40). The techniques include aesthetic scanning, visual literacy, studying inspirations for art, and investigating the works of great artists.

Aesthetic Scanning

Art educators who are involved with developing programs that encourage informed aesthetic responses in children recommend a technique called aesthetic scanning. Hallowell Judson (1989) states:

Aesthetic scanning consists of locating and identifying the aesthetic properties of an artwork while looking at it. It is a pedagogical version of what artists do when they are making art and what connoisseurs do when contemplating it. The aesthetic properties involved in aesthetic scanning include the sensory, the formal, the expressive, and the technical. (p. 62)

The sensory properties include the visual elements of art, such as line, color, shape, and texture. The formal properties include the principles of art used to organize or compose art, such as balance, repetition, variety, and contrast. Expressive qualities are visual characteristics used to express feelings or ideas, such as mood, conflict, energy, and meaning. The technical properties are the media, such as watercolor and chalk, and techniques used by artists.

Judson recommends using the aesthetic scanning approach developed by H. S. Broudy (1981) and described by Gloria J. Hewett and Jean C. Rush (1987) when encouraging students to respond to the illustrations in children's literature. Hewett and Rush also identify two rules for this type of treasure hunt: (1) the aesthetic property must be in the artwork and observable by others and (2) the viewer must be able to identify and describe the property. Chart 4.1 presents examples of questions that adults may ask to encourage children to examine a work of art carefully and to volunteer information based on their own perceptions. Hewett and Rush recommend that adults build confidence by beginning with easier questions. Notice that the questions are presented in order of difficulty. The questions toward the end of the chart require higher levels of artistic knowledge and lead to better informed aesthetic responses. As children become experienced at looking at art and talking about aesthetic properties, expect longer, more detailed descriptions of the properties and ask more open-ended questions.

Hewett and Rush (1987) also recommend encouraging students to expand their responses by asking questions that clarify and elaborate the responses. Hewett and Rush warn, however, that the questions in the table are merely examples to be modified, amended, changed, or rearranged to meet the goals of instruction. They state that if the questions are followed mechanically or methodically and are used with every lesson, discussions may be limited rather than enhanced. Remember that questions should expand children's responses to art.

You may use Jan Greenberg and Sandra Jordan's text *The Sculptor's Eye: Looking at Contemporary American Art* to provide guidance for developing discussions about art. The text begins with a discussion of contemporary American art, including steps in which viewers describe what they see by using sensory words that remind them of things that they touch, taste, see, hear, or smell. Next, it considers how artists use the elements of painting, including line, shape, texture, and color, and different styles, media, and methods. Other sections emphasize the meaning of various paintings; putting all of the elements together; and visual effects, including balance, visual

CHART 4.1   Aesthetic scanning: Initiating questions

Kind of Question*	Properties	Sample Questions
Leading (Agreement, disagreement)	Sensory	This painting has a lot of red, doesn't it?
	Formal	The balance in this fabric pattern is symmetrical, isn't it?
	Expressive	Don't you agree that the smooth shapes in this sculpture convey a feeling of peace?
	Technical	You can feel how rough the surface texture of this pot is, can't you?
Selective (Choice)	Sensory	Do you see more red or blue in this painting?
	Formal	Is this balance symmetrical or asymmetrical?
	Expressive	Do the shapes make you feel peaceful or upset?
	Technical	Is the surface texture rough or smooth?
Parallel (Additional information)	Sensory	What other colors are there in this painting besides red?
	Formal	Is there any kind of balance here other than symmetrical?
	Expressive	What else might these smooth shapes suggest?
	Technical	Are there more surfaces on this clay piece than rough ones?
Constructive (Specific new information)	Sensory	What colors can you find in this painting?
	Formal	What kinds of balance do you see here?
	Expressive	What kinds of shapes can you find in this sculpture, and what mood do they evoke?
	Technical	How has the artist treated the surface of this clay pot?
Productive (General new information)	Sensory	How would you describe one of the painting's sensory properties?
	Formal	Can you describe one of the formal properties in this fabric pattern?
	Expressive	What does this sculpture express?
	Technical	What medium and techniques did the artist use in constructing this pot?

*Initiating questions are presented in order of how difficult they are to answer.
Reprinted from Gloria J. Hewett and Jean C. Rush, "Finding Buried Treasures: Aesthetic Scanning with Children," Art Education 40 (January 1987).

rhythms that form patterns, emphasis, and space. The text is written to encourage interactions among readers and text. Thus, you may use it to develop aesthetic discussions with your students.

Use the discussion of various artistic elements, design, artistic media, artistic styles, and outstanding illustrators of children's books presented earlier in this chapter to help you select interesting artwork from children's illustrators and to develop your own treasure hunt. Lyn Ellen Lacy's *Art and Design in Children's Picture Books* (1986) provides in-depth suggestions for analyzing the visual elements in several Caldecott Medal-winning illustrations. Use Chart 4.1 to help you include questions related to sensory, formal, expressive, and technical aspects of the artistic work. Many children enjoy develop-

ing their own observations and formulating questions that allow them to interact with art.

Visual Literacy

You may use many books for finding insights into visual art. According to museum curator Daniel Rice (1988):

It is only when these elements are considered in the context of the subject matter and the emotional effect that they communicate that they are truly related to visual literacy. If diagonal lines communicate motion in a painting, it is important to know why, and also how that dynamism relates to the particular subject that is being depicted, the personal style of the artist as well as the style of the period or location. It is not enough to merely identify and notice them. (p. 16)

Readers are asked to respond to Diego Rivera's painting, Piñata. *(From* Come Look with Me: World of Play *by Gladys S. Blizzard. Published by Thomasson-Grant, 1993. Diego Rivera Piñata 1953. Tempera on canvas 97" 3 171½" Hospital Infantil de Mexico "Federico Gomez," Mexico City. Reproduced by permission of the hospital.)*

An In-Depth Analysis of Aesthetic Scanning in One Book

Many books provide opportunities for developing aesthetic scanning and cultural understanding. Paul Goble's *The Girl Who Loved Wild Horses* includes excellent examples of visual elements and illustrations that develop understanding of the Native American culture, specifically that of the Plains Indians. (Although the pages in the book are unnumbered, page numbers here refer to pages as if the title page were page 1.)

Information about the artist. Paul Goble grew up in England, where he listened to his mother read him stories that interested him in the culture of the Plains Indians. Later, he visited Montana and South Dakota, where he studied the Native American culture. He lives in the Black Hills of South Dakota, writing and illustrating many stories about Native American peoples. His special area of interest is traditional literature of the Plains Indians. He has been adopted into the Yakima and Sioux tribes. Additional books that you may use for aesthetic scanning and comparisons include *Beyond the Ridge, Buffalo Woman, Death of the Iron Horse, The Gift of the Sacred Dog, Iktomi and the Berries, Iktomi and the Boulder: A Plains Indian Story,* and *Star Boy.* Many of Goble's books include helpful notes about the stories and the illustrations.

Endpapers, both front and back. The color red develops a feeling of warmth and provides a harmonious introduction

to the title page, in which red also dominates. Consider the possible mood for a book that is introduced by red.

Page 1, the title page. The title here is written in the same form as it is on the cover of the book. The color red develops a feeling of warmth and high energy. The sun in this illustration shines on a Native American girl on her Appaloosa stallion. According to Goble (1978), the geometric sun design comes from the Plains Indians. Women painted this geometric sun design on buffalo robes that men wore. The circle surrounded by white space creates a sense of balance. The plants in the foreground increase this sense of balance.

Pages 2 and 3. The horizontal lines suggest calm, sleep, and stability. The vertical lines in the plants and horses' necks suggest lack of movement and reinforce the feeling of calm. The sleeping girl adds to this total, nonthreatening scene.

Pages 6 and 7. The running buffalo herd creates the sense of movement and direction. According to Goble, the buffalo hunters approach the sacred buffalo on the right side so that they can use the bow and arrow to the best effect. Several hunters are trying to help the hunter who has had a mishap.

Pages 8 and 9. This two-page spread uses horizontal and vertical lines to create a peaceful, nonthreatening scene. Notice that the horizontal lines of the horses are reflected in the surface of the lake. Not a ripple mars the tranquillity. Also notice that the vertical lines of the cattails and the horses' manes mirror the peaceful setting described in the text. Because the horses are not frightened by the girl, we can infer a close relationship. The gold colors in the aspens show that it is autumn. According to Goble, reflection, as seen through the water, is a theme found in Indian painting. The quill and beadwork designs frequently have reflections (or up and down motifs), which symbolize sky and earth.

Pages 10 and 11. The teepees sitting securely on the ground suggest a safe place. Changes in color and movement are found, however, in the far left. The black, circular clouds suggest changes. The jagged lines protruding from the clouds even indicate the direction that the storm is moving. These changes of color and line foreshadow danger.

Pages 12 and 13. Diagonal lines suggest loss of balance and uncontrolled motion. Notice the jagged diagonal line of the lightning. Feelings of fear explode in this picture because lightning is one of nature's most fearsome elements. The danger is imminent because the black clouds cover almost half of the two-page spread. Notice that the lines of the birds, the horses' legs, and the horses' manes suggest movement and danger.

Pages 14 and 15. Notice that Goble develops movement and direction through the horses, other animals, and even the plants leaning away from the wind. The jagged yellow lines and the black clouds approach and cover portions of the sun that earlier provided warmth.

Pages 16 and 17. Horizontal lines on the mountain tops and the horses' backs show that the danger is over and that peace and tranquillity exist once again. The high canyon walls have a special awe and quietness at night. The stars and the sky are important in this illustration. According to Goble, much Native American mythology concerns the Sky World. When a person dies, his spirit walks along the Milky Way to the world above. A sense of peace in the dark is provided by knowing that one has relatives in the sky and by remembering that the moon is the sun's wife.

Pages 20 and 21. According to Goble, pairs of scouts were sent out to find the buffalo herds so that when returning to camp each scout could vouch for the truth of the other's report. The stallion takes a position of defense at the rear of his mares, whom he drives in front of him.

Pages 24, 25, 26, and 27. According to Goble, this is a Blackfoot camp. Looking at all four pages at the same time, one sees half of the camp circle. Each teepee design is divinely revealed. The top portion represents the sky, and the cross at the very top symbolizes the morning star and a wish for wisdom and good dreams, while the discs represent stars. The middle portion of the teepee contains the animals, who have their feet on earth and their heads in heaven. These designs display vital tracts, kidneys, and leg joints because they are sources of the animals' power. The bottom border of the teepee represents the earth, and the projecting triangles or rounded shapes represent mountains or hills. Such lodges are still held sacred by the Blackfoot Indians.

Pages 30 and 31. According to Goble, these pages parallel page 1. The girl, however, may have become a horse. The figures share the warmth of each other and the sun. The crocuses and the bluebirds show that winter is over and springtime is here.

After discussing the illustrations in this book, ask students to respond to and compare the illustrations in other books by Paul Goble.

Studying Inspirations for Art

After children have had many opportunities to look at and to discuss the art in picture books, make connections between artists' illustrations and the artists' inspirations. Lynn Hoffman (2000) emphasizes that "Picture book illustration is not separate from other art forms; rather, it copies and imitates and pays homage to the body of work that has come before it, just as in other art forms" (p. 16). Hoffman describes the effectiveness of displays that pair illustrations from children's books with examples from traditional fine art. It is interesting to discover what artists, artistic time periods, artistic styles, or works have inspired contemporary artists and to compare the picture-book illustrations.

For example, for *Outside over There,* Maurice Sendak was inspired, as we have discussed, by the watercolors of British poet and artist William Blake in his choice of colors. H. W. Janson and Anthony F. Janson (1995) describe Blake, who lived from 1757 to 1827, as a painter of the Romantic movement who was inspired by literature to develop new ranges of subjects, emotions, and attitudes. Encourage children to discuss Sendak's illustrations in *Outside over There* and to compare them with illustrations by William Blake in art texts.

Help children make connections between the art of Maurice Sendak and the art of Randolph Caldecott, who lived from 1846 to 1886. In a review of Sendak's *We Are All in the Dumps with Jack and Guy,* Brian Alderson (1993a), the children's book editor of *The Times of London,* states: "Put it all down to Randolph Caldecott. As you may know, Maurice Sendak is a devotee of that Victorian picture-book artist, and indeed he designated an early book, *Hector Protector,* 'an intentionally contrived homage to this beloved teacher'" (p. 17). Like Caldecott, Sendak transforms rhymes into epics by introducing a pictorial narrative inspired by the slender texts of the rhymes. Alderson compares Sendak and Caldecott because "Caldecott loved to play with such visual counterpointing (the tragic demise of the dish eloping with the spoon; the decrepit beggar man fiddling while bonny lasses and lads dance around the maypole). The exercise probably helped to keep up his interest in his rudimentary copy" (p. 17). Many reissues of Caldecott's books, as discussed earlier, are available.

There are interesting connections between Clement Hurd's illustrations for Margaret Wise Brown's *Goodnight Moon* and a painting by Goya. Leonard S. Marcus (1991) describes how Hurd created the illustrations:

All March and for the rest of the spring, the artist worked on the illustrations for *Goodnight Moon.* Margaret had not given him many

ISSUE   Messages in Picture Books: Moralizing Versus Art

Is moralizing an appropriate role for picture books, or should the main role be the development of art and storytelling? In "The New Didacticism," Anita Silvey[1] states that creating messages in books for children is "an issue which has long been a cause for concern for those of us connected with children's books" (p. 5). Silvey points out:

"Children's books have always alternated between periods when art for art's sake prevailed and times when using books to impart values prevailed. And until recently I believed that we were fortunate to be working with books in a period when the art of the book for children was of prime importance—what it taught, less so. But there seems to be a growing trend toward a new didacticism by the best of our authors and creators. The picture book these days seems particularly prone to moralizing. . . . But once we accept that moralizing is the appropriate role of a picture book, we begin to throw art and storytelling aside and invite the preachers and teachers into our books for children." (p. 5)

Silvey identifies books such as Chris Van Allsburg's *The Wretched Stone* and Susan Jeffers's *Brother Eagle, Sister Sky* as recent books that exemplify the new didacticism.

In the same issue of *The Horn Book*, Robert Hale[2] discusses the role of messages in books such as *Brother Eagle, Sister Sky* and Roald Dahl's *The Minpins*. He states:

"Regardless of author's intent—whether there was meant to be a message or merely a very good story—what comes across to the child can depend upon the slant given by whoever is doing the reading. However, I can remember times when my children were little when they seemed to understand better than I the meaning of a book I was reading to them. Perhaps they would have seen through the truth of the story no matter how I slanted it. That's hopeful, isn't it? It confirms my faith in the young. They will get the message if we just make sure they get the books." (p. 113)

Authors of articles in the popular press are also questioning the role of didacticism in children's literature. Writing in *Newsweek*, Malcolm Jones[3] states:

"In the current crop of children's literature, linguistic anarchy—any kind of anarchy—is largely passé. The emphasis is all on being good—respecting others, respecting yourself, allowing for cultural differences. It's tough stuff to knock, but you have to wonder whatever happened to old-fashioned fun like gluing your sister's hair to the bedpost. You wonder even harder if the people who create these 'good' books ever had childhoods themselves." (p. 54)

After reading these three brief articles, debate the following issues:

1 What is the major role of a picture storybook written and illustrated for children?
2 If moralizing is appropriate in picture storybooks, what type of moralizing should be found in books for young children?
3 What should be the role of adults when sharing books with children?

Analyze recent illustrated picture books to decide if you believe that there is a new didacticism in the illustrations and stories. Find examples of books in which you believe that what is taught is of prime importance in the illustrations and in the text and find examples of books in which you think that the art and the storytelling are of prime importance.

[1]Silvey, Anita. "The New Didacticism." *The Horn Book* 68 (January/February 1992): 5.
[2]Hale, Robert. "Musings." *The Horn Book* 68 (January/February 1992): 112–113.
[3]Jones, Malcolm, Jr. "Kid Lit's Growing Pains: Books: Multiculturalists and Postmodern Ironists Invade the Nursery." *Newsweek*, November 22, 1993, 54–57.

suggestions for the art, as she sometimes did. She simply scribbled a few brief notes and, along with them, offered inspiration in the form of a small color reproduction of Goya's dashing *Boy in Red*, which she pasted onto the notebook's front cover. (p. 20)

Ask students to look carefully at Hurd's illustrations for *Goodnight Moon* and respond to the mood created by colors, lines, shapes, and light. Ask the students to aesthetically scan Goya's painting and discuss the sensory and expressive qualities found in that art (see Ann Waldron's *Francisco Goya*). Are there any similarities between Goya's and Hurd's works? Was Hurd motivated by the *Boy in Red*? Why do you believe that Margaret Wise Brown sent Hurd the photo?

Leo Lionni identified the inspirational connections for his illustrations in an interview with Amanda Smith (1991). When Smith asked him about the artists whom he admired and who were his role models, Lionni said, "I think it's impossible today not to have Picasso as a hero, a role model. . . . I love Bonnard because of his way of handling his brush and color. For each [aspect] you have a different role model. My heroes are here" (p. 118). Hanging in his studio, Lionni has works of Giacometti, Calder, Klee, and Moore. Encourage children to view a number of Lionni's picture books and to compare his works with those of his heroes and role models.

In an interview with David Wiesner, Susan Caroff and Elizabeth Moje (1992/1993) report that the greatest impact on Wiesner's work and the ways in which he tells stories is a book illustrated by Lynd Ward, *Mad Man's Drum*. Ward developed this novel for adults completely in woodcuts, without words. Wiesner states that he was very impressed with Ward's ability to develop a complex story dealing with complicated themes and imagery in a 250-page book with no words.

Encourage students to either compare Ward's and Wiesner's illustrations or to analyze Wiesner's ability to convey themes and imagery through wordless books.

Jennifer M. Brown's interview with Ian Falconer (2000) identifies the children's books that most influenced the author/illustrator of *Olivia*. Encourage students to analyze the following books and discuss how they might have influenced Falconer: Ludwig Bemelman's *Madeline*, Robert McCloskey's *One Morning in Maine* and *Blueberries for Sal*, Dr. Seuss's *The 500 Hats of Bartholomew Cubbins*, Jean de Brunhoff's *Babar*, and John Tenniel's drawings for *Alice in Wonderland*.

Quite different art works influenced artist Lane Smith (1993). Smith states that he was influenced by Monty Python, *Mad* magazine, and comic books. Smith says:

I think my palette, my sensibilities, and my composition were greatly influenced by films I saw as a child, especially the old Disney films like *Snow White* and *The Jungle Book*. Some of my work in *The Stinky Cheese Man*—the ugly duckling sequence in particular—is directly influenced by Tex Avery. He was an animation director from the forties—the one who always had his cartoon characters' eyeballs popping right out of their heads. All his work was very exaggerated. (p. 68)

Encourage students to compare Lane Smith's illustrations with those that inspired his art.

You may use many additional illustrators for similar activities. For example, Peter Sís (1992) states that he has always admired medieval artists like Bosch and Breughel and artists from the German Gothic school. Henrik Drescher's illustrations have been compared to those of Paul Klee and the German expressionists. John Steptoe, who illustrated *Stevie*, has been compared to the French painter Georges Rouault. According to Herbert R. Lottman (1993), illustrator Satomi Ichikawa was motivated to illustrate books after she discovered the art of Maurice Boutet de Monvel. In an interview with Masha Kabakow Rudman (1993b), Ashley Bryan says that he was inspired by early religious books printed by hand using woodcuts when he illustrated texts based on African American spirituals, such as *I'm Going to Sing: Black American Spirituals*.

Investigating the Works of Great Artists

Many books currently published for children encourage the children to make discoveries about the history of art, to learn about elements and style in art, and to explore the art of renowned artists. Art history is introduced in a unique way in books by Bob Knox and by Laurene Krasny Brown and Marc Brown. In Knox's *The Great Art Adventure,* two children tour an art gallery, the Museum of World Art, beginning in the Hall of Ancient Egypt and continuing historically through such areas as Ancient Greece, Scandinavia, China, Oceania, North American Indian, and Mexico. You may use this book in several ways. Have students follow the trail through the museum and discuss the art. In addition to great art of the areas and periods, Knox illustrates Dave and Jane, the two picture-book characters, within the paintings. Consequently, you may use this book as a model for students to create their own tour of a museum in art. Have them place themselves in the settings. Have them focus on the details of an artistic period in order to draw themselves into appropriate settings.

The illustrations in Anthony Browne's *Willy's Pictures,* winner of the Hans Christian Andersen Medal for excellence in illustrations, feature items from original paintings by

Two contemporary children are included in the artworks of specific periods. (Illustration by Bob Knox from **The Great Art Adventure**. Copyright © 1993 by Bob Knox and Rizzoli International Publications. Reprinted by permission of Rizzoli International Publications.)

artists such as Henri Rousseau, Vincent van Gogh, and Edouard Manet. Readers are asked to look carefully at each of Browne's illustrations and then search the copies of the original paintings reprinted at the conclusion of the book.

Two books for older readers introduce students to the history of art. H. W. Janson and Anthony F. Janson's *History of Art for Young People,* fifth edition, is a comprehensive text that proceeds from prehistoric art through twentieth-century art. It includes both color and black-and-white photographs of great paintings. A chronological chart lists milestones in political history, religion and literature, science, architecture, sculpture, painting, and photography from 1750 through 1980. Use this source to stimulate various research projects into time periods, artists, or connections among great contributions and events in history.

You may use Jill Bossert's (1998) *Children's Book Illustration: Step By Step Techniques* to explore the artistic styles and techniques developed by nine artists including Charles Santore, Emily Arnold McCully, and Jerry Pinkney. Younger children can follow the techniques described by Debra Cooper-Solomon (1999) as she uses the illustrations of Eric Carle to introduce collage. Cooper-Solomon presents detailed guidelines for developing an art project following the reading of Carle's *The Mixed-Up Chameleon.*

Use Kathleen Westray's *A Color Sampler* to encourage students to experiment with color. In addition to discussing and illustrating primary, secondary, intermediate,

Through the Eyes of a TEACHER

Steve Schack

Third-Grade Teacher

Howard Anderson

Fifth-Grade Teacher

Melissa Wilson

Reading Specialist
Beck Urban Academy
Columbus, Ohio

Literature Strategy Plan: Studying the Work of Jerry Pinkney

Picture books are an excellent resource for developing children's awareness of how artists use elements such as media, style, and color deliberately to complement and extend the meaning of a story. Most adapt their work to fit a particular story. However, many also develop a personal style that children can come to know through repeated encounters with their work. Studying how a particular artist adapts his or her own personal style while also adapting that style to fit individual stories helps children learn how the visual and narrative elements of a picture book work together.

Third-grade teacher Steve Schack, fifth-grade teacher Howard Anderson, and reading specialist Melissa Wilson decided to collaborate on a unit to support children's exploration of artist Jerry Pinkney's work. They selected Pinkney because of the children they teach: a blend of African American, Latino, White, Ethiopian, and Somalian students. "We are really trying to create an atmosphere in our school that affirms the urban child and is culturally relevant," says Steve. "I think Pinkney is a marvelous model because he is an African American man and is very outspoken about what he does and he has lived through a lot of changes. I also find that if I link my activities to a theme, it makes me think through how things are coming together for me. In turn, I'm much better able to help the kids figure out how things are related."

Building Students' Background Knowledge

Steve, Howie, and Melissa began by sharing the video "A Visit with Jerry Pinkney" (Penguin Author Video Series, 1995) with students to give them an idea of Pinkney's composing process, which includes making a thumbnail sketch, posing people for photographs, and then creating a painting based on the photos. The children were fascinated by the process, particularly the photography step. Many compared his process to the writing process. As one student said, "A thumbnail sketch is just like a sloppy copy." Following the viewing, they wrote video summaries and created time lines of Pinkney's life. Melissa also dis-

> A Visit with Jerry Pinkney, a video summary by Tyler Brad
> The main point about the video was his art work. 1st he gets friends or family. 2nd he gets them to pose like the Charicter. 3rd he takes his camra and takes theire picture. 4th he draws the picture. 5th he paints the picture. And finily he puts it in a Book. He also can do thumb nail scetches. The video also said he was still a good artist when he was a boy.

cussed the illustrator's role in creating pictures that not only tell a story, but expand the story. She also helped them explore how to draw human figures.

Steve and Melissa then placed a collection of books illustrated by Pinkney on the carpet and asked the children to sort them by genre. "Jerry Pinkney illustrates books from a wide variety of genres, which makes his work perfect for an activity like this," said Steve. As children sorted, Steve asked them questions such as "How do you know that's fiction?" "How do you categorize a book like Minty (about Harriet Tubman) that is about a real person but is essentially a fictionalized account?" "Do you notice that some books link to one another [sequels]?" "Was John Henry real? Some say yes; others disagree and would put his story in the category of a legend." Steve also asked them to examine the art, noticing differences and speculating as to why these differences occurred. "We hoped they might be drawn to certain books or genres to encourage their self-selection of literature. We also wanted them to become familiar with Pinkney's distinctive artistic style."

Steve also thought his transitional third-grade readers could be helped to engage in self-selected reading of chapter books if he provided modeling of how to read longer texts through small-group guided reading sessions. "The Adventures of Spider, illustrated by Jerry Pinkney, was a good place to start. This book has seven chapters, each with its own distinct story. Reading and discussing a chapter or two together—showing them how you look at the table of contents, predict what the stories will be about, skim and evaluate—help children realize, 'Hey, I can handle a long book like this,'" says Melissa. "Third grade is a very transitional year because some kids feel confident they can read a chapter book while others haven't yet begun to get over that hurdle. It can be scary. Books of short stories, folktales, or poetry can help them." This book was also useful because Pinkney used a spare, graphic style for the illustrations rather than the lush watercolors he is now known for. "The children couldn't believe the book was illustrated by Pinkney," says Steve. "They were just taken aback that this was one of his books because it was so different from the others they'd seen. It helped them better understand how an author's style can change over time."

Steve also read aloud several books illustrated by Pinkney. *Minty* and *Sam and the Tigers* were two favorites. The children were intrigued by the fact that Minty was about a real person but was considered historical fiction because the text wasn't based strictly on historical fact. They marveled at the soft watercolor illustrations and how they brought this historical figure to life along with the era in which she lived.

Purposeful Reading, Writing, and Illustrating

Soon the children were reading Jerry Pinkney's books on their own. After completing a book, they wrote summaries, created Venn diagrams or wrote letters to classmates. For example, Christen and Tyler wrote letters to the class pretending they were Brer Rabbit and Tar Baby. Sierra compared *The Patchwork Quilt* and *Tanya's Reunion* in a Venn diagram. As they became increasingly familiar with his work, they could readily identify Pinkney's style and the kinds of books he usually selected to illustrate.

Fifth-grade teacher Howard Anderson took a different direction, focusing specifically on Pinkney's illustration technique. "My class first viewed the videotape and took notes, which is part of what I try to teach them about doing research. We then wrote our own stories and used his artistic technique as models for illustrating ours." Pinkney often poses people in scenes, photographs them, then paints from the photographs. Howie decided that using this technique with his students would help them become more familiar with Pinkney's work, while also giving them a focus for their own writing. Thus, they first created thumbnail sketches related to their own creative stories, arranged their classmates in tableaux that mirrored the sketches, and then snapped the pictures. One print stayed in their writing portfolio to provide continued visual support for the writing and the other was used for a model in the illustration process. "What I discovered

Alicia's Pinkney-inspired watercolor.

was that the kids loved seeing each other in photographs," laughs Howie. "Even more importantly, however, it helped them keep the idea of their story in their head more. So instead of a story wandering all over the place, you've got a story that's more focused. They seemed to have a sense of writing in general but also of some of the specific literary and artistic techniques used in the Jerry Pinkney books."

Assessment

These teachers believe that effective assessment is informal and very individualized. They look at issues such as "What kinds of things are they saying to each other and to us about an illustrator's work as they share books?" and "Are they tuning in to the kinds of things we hope they will notice about an illustrator's work?" "It's very individual," says Steve. "You take what they're doing and respond individually back to them; acknowledging what they're doing right and pushing them to go a little further." Evaluation is also a process of comparing work throughout the year, examining writing at different points in time to see if they've incorporated some more sophisticated techniques or if they've incorporated what they've learned about an artist in their literature discussions or illustrations.

One of the most interesting things the teachers learned from this experience was the link between creating art and creating story. The children began to see that in both processes an image is created. A thumbnail sketch in art is like a rough draft in writing. The artist completes a painting in stages, revising and polishing, just like the writer revises. Jerry Pinkney makes this connection himself: "I'm not one who sits right down and does a lot of sketches at first. I work best by thinking about an assignment for a while, jotting down notes as ideas come to me. Then I do rough sketches...." The children learn to respect this connection.

 For ideas on adapting Steve Schack's lesson to meet the needs of older or younger readers, please visit Chapter 4 on our Companion Website at www.prenhall.com/norton

LOTS AND LOTS AND LOTS OF DOTS
We gradually started to notice some
very strange things in the park.

Viewers may search for aspects of original paintings found in the illustrations such as this one based on Sunday Afternoon on the Island of LaGrande Jatte by George Seurat. (From Willie's Pictures by Anthony Brown. Copyright © 2000 by Anthony Brown. Reproduced by permission of the publisher, Candlewick Press, Inc., Cambridge, MA.

and complementary colors, Westray develops color concepts, such as the influences of darker and lighter backgrounds, placement of colors, and optical illusions created by colors. Creating optical illusions is of special interest to many students.

Have students investigate specific artistic styles, using books by Jude Welton and by Jan Greenberg and Sandra Jordan. Welton's *Impressionism* interweaves biographical information about the artists with color reproductions of their paintings. Use this book as introductory research for artistic style or to stimulate students to conduct further research into the lives and works of specific artists.

Older students may be fascinated by the processes associated with the paper engineering required to construct pop-up books. Directions for creating three-dimensional books are presented in *The Elements of Pop-Up* by David A. Carter and James Diaz.

You may use numerous highly illustrated books for research projects in which students investigate the works of one artist. One of the most interesting books for all children is Christina Bjork's *Linnea in Monet's Garden.* Along with Linnea, readers can learn about Monet and discover the excitement of visualizing nature and paintings in new ways. After children read *Linnea in Monet's Garden,* have them conduct their own research into the work and life of Monet. Jude Welton's *Monet* is a source for numerous reproductions of paintings, discussions about the paintings, and

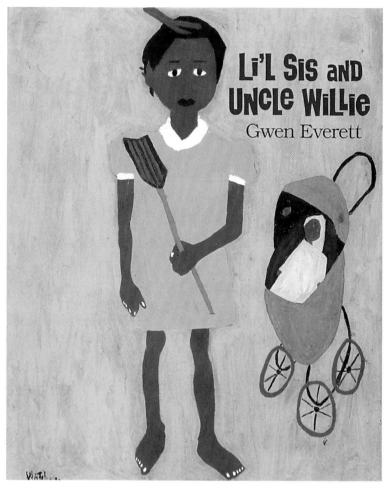

The author used William Johnson's paintings to illustrate a fictional story. (From Li'l Sis and Uncle Willie: A Story Based on the Life and Paintings of William H. Johnson *by Gwen Everett, illustrations by William H. Johnson. Published by Rizzoli International Publications, Inc., 1991. Illustration reprinted by permission of the National Museum of American Art, the Smithsonian Institution, Washington, D.C.)*

tional creative stories as told through the possible viewpoints of the horses.

Use the paintings of one artist to stimulate students to write a story to accompany existing art. For this task, use Gwen Everett's *Li'l Sis and Uncle Willie: A Story Based on the Life and Paintings of William H. Johnson* as a model. Everett uses paintings and events in the life of African American painter William Johnson to create a fictional story. The artist's paintings appear to be the illustrations for the story. In addition, you may use many of the previously discussed art texts as sources for such activities.

The Treasury of Saints and Martyrs provides a source for a study of early artwork associated with the history of art. Margaret Mulvihill's text, written for older readers, includes numerous labeled reproductions of artworks proceeding from the early centuries through modern times. The picture acknowledgments include the locations of the original art.

For a focus on illustrators of children's books, have students begin their study with Pat Cummings's *Talking with Artists.* This book provides information on fourteen artists, including Leo and Diane Dillon, Steven Kellogg, Jerry Pinkney, Lane Smith, Chris Van Allsburg, and David Wiesner. Throughout this text are suggestions for motivating children to respond to literature through artistic interpretations of books or to create their own illustrations using specific art media.

biographical information about Monet. Patricia Wright's *Manet* is another source for researching French artists and impressionism.

Use *Linnea in Monet's Garden* as a model to stimulate students to create stories in which they make discoveries about great artists. Leonardo da Vinci is an excellent subject for such a visual journey. For this task, have students use Richard McLanathan's *Leonardo da Vinci,* Diane Stanley's *Leonardo da Vinci,* or Rosabianca Skira-Venturi's *A Weekend with Leonardo da Vinci.*

Christina Björk's *Vendela in Venice* may be used to motivate children to research and write stories in which they explore architecture, painting, statues, and sculptures associated with a location. The four golden horses and the numerous statues of lions are of special interest. There is also enough mystery associated with the creation of the horses (Greece, 300 B.C., or Rome, 300 A.D.) to stimulate speculation and creative writing. The dates at the end of the book could motivate addi-

Suggested Activities

 For suggested activities for teaching children about artists and their illustrations, visit our Companion Website at www.prenhall.com/norton

Children's Literature

 For full descriptions, including plot summaries and award winner notations, of these and other titles for teaching children about artists and their illustrations, visit the CD-ROM that accompanies this book.

Aardema, Verna. *How the Ostrich Got Its Long Neck: A Tale from the Akamba of Kenya.* Illustrated by Marcia Brown. Scholastic, 1995 (I:4–7 R:5).

_____. *Why Mosquitoes Buzz in People's Ears.* Illustrated by Leo and Diane Dillon. Dial, 1975 (I:5–9 R:6).

Ackerman, Karen. *Song and Dance Man.* Illustrated by Stephen Gammell. Knopf, 1988 (I:3–8 R:4).

Andersen, Hans Christian. *The Nightingale.* Retold by Eva LeGalliene. Illustrated by Nancy Ekholm Burkert. Harper & Row, 1968 (I:6–12 R:8).

_____. *The Ugly Duckling.* Adapted and illustrated by Jerry Pinkney. Morrow, 1999 (I:6–9 R:7).

_____. *The Wild Swans.* Retold by Amy Ehrlich. Illustrated by Susan Jeffers. Dial, 1981 (I:7–12 R:7).

Arkhurst, Joyce Cooper. (reteller) *The Adventures of Spider: West African Folktales.* Illustrated by Jerry Pinkney, Little, Brown, 1992 (I:8–11 R:4+).

Armstrong, Jennifer. *Pierre's Dream.* Illustrated by Susan Gaber. Dial, 1999 (I:6+ R:5).

Aylesworth, Jim. *Country Crossing.* Illustrated by Ted Rand. Atheneum, 1991 (I:3–7).

_____. *The Full Belly Bowl.* Illustrated by Wendy Anderson Halperin. Atheneum, 1999 (I:5–8 R:4).

Baker, Jeannie. *Where the Forest Meets the Sea.* Greenwillow, 1988 (I:4–10).

_____. *Window.* Greenwillow, 1991 (I:all).

Baker, Olaf. *Where the Buffaloes Begin.* Illustrated by Stephen Gammell. Warne, 1981 (I:8+ R:7).

Banks, Kate. *And If the Moon Could Talk.* Illustrated by Georg Hallensleben. Farrar, Straus & Giroux, 1998 (I:3–6 R:4).

Beckett, Sister Wendy. *A Child's Book of Prayer in Art.* Dorling Kindersley, 1995 (I:all).

Bedard, Michael. *Emily.* Illustrated by Barbara Cooney. Doubleday, 1992 (I:all).

Bemelmans, Ludwig. *Madeline.* Viking, 1939, 1977 (I:4–9 R:5).

_____. *Madeline in London.* Viking, 1961, 1977 (I:4–9 R:3).

Ben-Ezer, Ehud. *Hosni the Dreamer: An Arabian Tale.* Illustrated by Uri Shulevitz. Farrar, Straus & Giroux, 1997 (I:4–8 R:4).

Björk, Christina. *Linnea in Monet's Garden.* Illustrated by Lena Anderson. Farrar, Straus & Giroux, 1987 (I:all R:6).

_____. *Vendela in Venice.* Translated by Patricia Crampton. Illustrated by Inga-Karin Eriksson. R&S, 1999 (I:8+ R:5).

Blizzard, Gladys S. *Come Look with Me: World of Play.* Thomasson-Grant, 1993 (I:all).

Bodnár, Judit Z. *Tale of a Tail.* Illustrated by John Sandford. Lothrop, Lee & Shepard, 1998 (I:4–8 R:4).

Bowen, Betsy. *Antler, Bear, Canoe: A Northwoods Alphabet Year.* Little, Brown, 1991 (I:all).

Brett, Jan. *Berlioz the Bear.* Putnam, 1991 (I:5–8 R:6).

Brooke, L. Leslie. *Johnny Crow's Garden.* Warne, 1903, 1986 (I:all).

Brown, Laurene Krasny, and Marc Brown. *Visiting the Art Museum.* Dutton, 1986 (I:6+).

Brown, Marcia. *Once a Mouse.* Scribner, 1961 (I:3–7 R:6).

Brown, Margaret Wise. *Goodnight Moon.* Illustrated by Clement Hurd. Harper, 1947 (I:2–7).

Browne, Anthony. *Willy's Pictures.* Candlewick, 2000 (I:all).

Bryan, Ashley. *I'm Going to Sing: Black American Spirituals,* Vol. 2. Atheneum, 1982 (I:all).

Bunting, Eve. *Ghost's Hour, Spook's Hour.* Illustrated by Donald Carrick. Clarion, 1987 (I:2–7 R:2).

_____. *Smoky Night.* Illustrated by David Diaz. Harcourt Brace, 1994 (I:all).

Burkert, Nancy Ekholm. *Valentine & Orson.* Farrar, Straus & Giroux, 1989 (I:10+).

Burton, Virginia Lee. *The Little House.* Houghton Mifflin, 1942 (I:3–7 R:3).

_____. *Mike Mulligan and His Steam Shovel.* Houghton Mifflin, 1939 (I:3–7 R:3).

Caldecott, Randolph. *Come Lasses and Lads.* New Orchard, 1988.

_____. *The Fox Jumps over the Parson's Gate.* New Orchard, 1988.

_____. *A Frog He Would A-Wooing Go.* New Orchard, 1988.

_____. *Hey Diddle Diddle and Baby Bunting.* New Orchard, 1988.

_____. *Ride a Cock Horse to Banbury X & a Farmer Went Trotting upon His Grey Mare.* New Orchard, 1988.

Carle, Eric. *Catch the Ball.* Philomel, 1982 (I:3–6).

_____. *Eric Carle's Animals Animals.* Philomel, 1989 (I:3–9).

_____. *From Head to Toe.* HarperCollins, 1997 (I:3–7).

_____. *The Honeybee and the Robber: A Moving/Picture Book.* Philomel, 1981 (I:3–6).

_____. *Let's Paint a Rainbow.* Philomel, 1982 (I:3–6).

_____. *The Mixed-Up Chameleon.* Crowell, 1975, 1984 (I:3–6).

_____. *The Very Clumsy Click Beetle.* Philomel, 1999 (I:1–5).

_____. *The Very Hungry Caterpillar.* Crowell, 1971 (I:2–7).

Carlstrom, Nancy White. *Raven and River.* Illustrated by Jon Van Zyle. Little, Brown, 1997 (I:4–8).

Carroll, Colleen. *How Artists See Animals: Mammal Fish Bird Reptile.* Abbeville, 1996 (I:8–12).

_____. *How Artists See the Elements: Earth Air Fire Water.* Abbeville, 1996 (I:8–12).

_____. *How Artists See People: Boy Girl Man Woman.* Abbeville, 1996 (I:8–12).

_____. *How Artists See the Weather: Sun Rain Wind Snow.* Abbeville, 1996 (I:8–12).

Carroll, Lewis. *Alice in Wonderland.* Illustrated by John Tenniel. Grossett & Dunlap, 1946 (I:5–8 R:8+).

Carter, David A., and James Diaz. *The Elements of Pop-Up.* Simon & Schuster, 1999 (I:10+).

Catalanotto, Peter. *Emily's Art.* Simon & Schuster, 2001 (I:4–8).

Cendrars, Blaise. *Shadow.* Illustrated by Marcia Brown. Scribner, 1982 (I:all).

Chaikin, Miriam. *Clouds of Glory.* Illustrated by David Frampton. Clarion, 1998 (I:8+ R:5).

Chaucer, Geoffrey. *Canterbury Tales.* Adapted by Barbara Cohen. Illustrated by Trina Schart Hyman. Lothrop, Lee & Shepard, 1988 (I:8+).

Cooney, Barbara. *Chanticleer and the Fox.* Adapted from Geoffrey Chaucer. Crowell, 1958 (I:5–10 R:4).

_____. *Eleanor.* Viking, 1996 (I:6–8 R:4).

_____. *Island Boy.* Viking Kestrel, 1988 (I:3–8 R:3).

Cooper, Helen. *Pumpkin Soup.* Doubleday, 1999 (I:3–7).

Crane, Walter. *The Baby's Opera.* Simon & Schuster, 1981 (I:all).

Cronin, Doreen. *Click, Clack, Moo: Cows That Type.* Illustrated by Betsy Lewin. Simon & Schuster, 2000 (I:4–7).

Crossley-Holland, Kevin. *Arthur: The Seeing Stone.* Orion, 2000 (I:8+ R:6).

_____. *Beowulf.* Illustrated by Charles Keeping. Oxford, 1982 (I:10+ R:6).

Cummings, Pat, ed. *Talking with Artists.* Bradbury, 1992 (I:8+).

Cutler, Jane. *The Cello of Mr. O.* Illustrated by Greg Couch. Dutton, 1999 (I:7+ R:5).

Day, Nancy Raine. *The Lion's Whiskers: An Ethiopian Folktale.* Illustrated by Ann Grifalconi. Scholastic, 1995 (I:5–8 R:5).

dePaola, Tomie. *Big Anthony and the Magic Ring.* Harcourt Brace Jovanovich, 1979 (I:5–9 R:3).

_____. *Charlie Needs a Cloak.* Prentice-Hall, 1973 (I:3–6 R:4).

_____. *Christopher: The Holy Giant.* Holiday, 1994 (I:4–8 R:4).

_____. *The Clown of God.* Harcourt Brace Jovanovich, 1978 (I:all R:4).

_____. *An Early American Christmas.* Holiday House, 1987 (I:4–7 R:6).

_____. *Giorgio's Village.* Putnam, 1982 (I:all).

_____. *Helga's Dowry: A Troll Love Story.* Harcourt Brace Jovanovich, 1977 (I:5–9 R:4).

_____. *The Legend of the Bluebonnet.* Putnam, 1983 (I:all R:6).

_____. *The Legend of the Indian Paintbrush.* Putnam, 1987 (I:all R:6).

_____. *Tomie dePaola's Mother Goose.* Putnam, 1985 (I:2–6).

_____. *Watch Out for the Chicken Feet in Your Soup.* Prentice-Hall, 1974 (I:3–7 R:2).

Dickens, Charles. *Christmas Carol.* Illustrated by Roberto Innocenti. Stewart, Tabori & Chang, 1990 (I:10+ R:6).

Duggleby, John. *Artist In Overalls: The Life of Grant Wood.* Chronicle, 1995 (I:8+ R:8).

Dunbar, Paul Laurence. *Jump Back, Honey: The Poems of Paul Laurence Dunbar.* Hyperion, 1999 (I:all).

Dunrea, Olivier. *The Trow-Wife's Treasure.* Farrar, Straus & Giroux, 1998 (I:4–8).

Ehlert, Lois. *Cuckoo/Cucu.* Harcourt Brace, 1997 (I:4–7).

_____. *Red Leaf, Yellow Leaf.* Harcourt Brace Jovanovich, 1991 (I:3–7).

Emberley, Barbara. *Drummer Hoff.* Illustrated by Ed Emberley. Prentice-Hall, 1967 (I:3–7 R:6).

Emberley, Ed. *Ed Emberley's Picture Pie 2: A Drawing Book and Stencil.* Little, Brown, 1996 (I:all).

Esbensen, Barbara. *The Star Maiden.* Illustrated by Helen Davie. Little, Brown, 1988 (I:all).

_____. *Tiger with Wings: The Great Horned Owl.* Illustrated by Mary Barrett Brown. Orchard, 1991 (I:6–10).

Everett, Gwen. *Li'l Sis and Uncle Willie: A Story Based on the Life and Paintings of William H. Johnson.* Illustrated by William H. Johnson. Rizzoli, 1992 (I:5–8 R:5).

Fain, Moira. *Snow Day.* Walker, 1996 (I:6–10 R:4).

Falconer, Ian. *Olivia.* Simon & Schuster, 2000 (I:3–8 R:4).

Field, Eugene. *Wynken, Blynken and Nod.* Illustrated by Susan Jeffers. Dutton, 1982.

Finley, Carol. *Art of Japan.* Lerner, 1998 (I:10+ R:6).

_____. *Art of the Far North: Inuit Sculpture, Drawing, and Printmaking.* Lerner, 1998 (I:8+ R:6).

Fleischman, Sid. *The Scarebird.* Illustrated by Peter Sís. Greenwillow, 1988 (I:7+ R:4).

Fleming, Denise. *In the Small, Small Pond.* Holt, 1993 (I:3–6).

Flournoy, Valerie. *The Patchwork Quilt.* Illustrated by Jerry Pinkney. Dial, 1985 (I:7–10 R:5).

_____. *Tanya's Reunion.* Illustrated by Jerry Pinkney. Dial, 1995 (I:7–10 R:4).

Foreman, Michael. *Michael Foreman's Mother Goose.* Harcourt Brace Jovanovich, 1991 (I:6+).

_____. *Seal Surfer.* Harcourt Brace, 1997 (I:5–9).

Frampton, David. *The Whole Night Through.* HarperCollins, 2001 (I:3–7).

Frost, Jonathan. *Gowanus Dogs.* Farrar, Straus & Giroux, 1999 (I:5–8).

Gág, Wanda. *Millions of Cats.* Coward, McCann, 1928 (I:3–7 R:3).

Gauch, Patricia Lee. *Presenting Tanya the Ugly Duckling.* Illustrated by Satomi Ichikawa. Philomel, 1999 (I:6+).

George, Jean Craighead. *The First Thanksgiving.* Illustrated by Thomas Locker. Philomel, 1993 (I:all).

Gilliland, Judith Heide. *Steamboat! The Story of Captain Blanche Leathers.* Illustrated by Holly Meade. DK, 2000 (I:7+).

Goble, Paul. *Beyond the Ridge.* Bradbury, 1989 (I:all R:5).

_____. *Buffalo Woman.* Bradbury, 1984 (I:all R:6).

_____. *Death of the Iron Horse.* Bradbury, 1987 (I:8+ R:5).

_____. *The Gift of the Sacred Dog.* Bradbury, 1980 (I:all R:6).

_____. *The Girl Who Loved Wild Horses.* Bradbury, 1978 (I:6–10 R:5).

_____. *Iktomi and the Berries.* Watts, 1989 (I:4–10 R:4).

_____. *Iktomi and the Boulder: A Plains Indian Story.* Orchard, 1988 (I:4–10 R:4).

_____. *Star Boy.* Bradbury, 1983 (I:6–10 R:5).

Goldin, Barbara Diamond. *Journeys with Elijah: Eight Tales of the Prophet.* Illustrated by Jerry Pinkney. Harcourt Brace, 1998 (I:all).

Greenaway, Kate. *A: Apple Pie.* Castle, 1979 (I:all).

_____. *Kate Greenaway.* Rizzoli, 1977 (I:all).

Greenberg, Jan, and Sandra Jordan. *The American Eye: Eleven Artists of the Twentieth Century.* Delacorte, 1995 (I:10+ R:7).

_____. *The Sculptor's Eye: Looking at Contemporary American Art.* Delacorte, 1993 (I:10+ R:6).

Griego, Margot C., Betsy L. Bucks, Sharon S. Gilbert, and Laurel H. Kimball. *Tortillitas Para Mama and Other Spanish Nursery Rhymes.* Illustrated by Barbara Cooney. Holt, Rinehart & Winston, 1981 (I:3–7).

Grimes, Nikki. *My Man Blue.* Illustrated by Jerome Lagarrigue. Dial, 1999 (I:all).

_____. *A Pocketful of Poems.* Illustrated by Javaka Steptoe. Clarion, 2001 (I:6–10).

Grimm, Brothers. *The Golden Bird,* retold by Neil Philip. Illustrated by Isabelle Brent. Little, Brown, 1995 (I:all).

_____. *Hansel and Gretel.* Illustrated by Susan Jeffers. Dial, 1980 (I:5–9 R:6).

_____. *Hansel and Gretel.* Retold by Rika Lesser. Illustrated by Paul O. Zelinsky. Dodd, Mead, 1984 (I:all R:6).

_____. *Little Red Riding Hood.* Illustrated by Trina Schart Hyman. Holiday House, 1983 (I:6–9 R:7).

_____. *Rapunzel.* Retold and illustrated by Paul O. Zelinsky. Dutton, 1997 (I:all).

_____. *Rumpelstiltskin.* Retold and illustrated by Paul O. Zelinsky. Dutton, 1986 (I:all).

_____. *Snow White and the Seven Dwarfs.* Illustrated by Nancy Ekholm Burkert. Farrar, Straus & Giroux, 1972 (I:7–12 R:6).

Grimm, Wilhelm. *Dear Mili.* Translated by Ralph Manheim. Illustrated by Maurice Sendak. Farrar, Straus & Giroux, 1988 (I:all R:6).

Guarnieri, Paolo. *A Boy Named Giotto.* Illustrated by Bimba Landman. Farrar, Straus & Giroux, 1999 (I:5–8 R:4).

Haley, Gail E. *A Story, a Story.* Atheneum, 1970 (I:6–10 R:6).

Hall, Donald. *Ox-Cart Man.* Illustrations by Barbara Cooney. Viking, 1979 (I:3–8 R:5).

Halperin, Wendy Anderson. *Love Is . . . .* Simon & Schuster, 2001 (I:all).

Hamilton, Virginia. *Her Stories: African American Folktales, Fairy Tales, and True Tales.* Scholastic, 1995 (I:all).

_____. *The People Could Fly: American Black Folktales.* Illustrated by Leo and Diane Dillon. Knopf, 1985 (I:9+ R:6).

Helprin, Mark. *Swan Lake.* Illustrated by Chris Van Allsburg. Houghton Mifflin, 1989 (I:all R:8).

Hendershot, Judith. *In Coal Country.* Illustrated by Thomas Allen. Knopf, 1987 (I:5–9 R:3).

Ho, Minfong. *Hush! A Thai Lullaby.* Illustrated by Holly Meade. Orchard, 1996 (I:3–8).

Hoban, Tana. *Shadows and Reflections.* Greenwillow, 1990 (I:all).

Hodges, Margaret. *Saint George and the Dragon.* Illustrated by Trina Schart Hyman. Little, Brown, 1984 (I:9+ R:7).

Holling, Holling Clancy. *Paddle-to-the-Sea.* Houghton Mifflin, 1941 (I:7–12 R:4).

_____. *Seabird.* Houghton Mifflin, 1948 (I:7–12 R:4).

Hughes, Langston. *The Sweet and Sour Animal Book.* Illustrated by students from the Harlem School of Arts. Oxford University Press, 1994 (I:all).

Innocenti, Roberto. *Rose Blanche.* Stewart, Tabori & Chang, 1990 (I:8+ R:4).

Irving, Washington. *The Legend of Sleepy Hollow.* Illustrated by Gary Kelley. Creative Education, 1990 (I:9+).

_____. *The Legend of Sleepy Hollow.* Illustrated by Will Moses. Philomel, 1995 (I:all).

Isaacs, Anne. *Swamp Angel.* Illustrated by Paul O. Zelinsky. Dutton, 1994 (I:all).

Jackson, Shelley. *The Old Woman and the Wave.* DK, 1998 (I: 4–7 R:4).

Janson, H. W., and Anthony F. Janson. *History of Art for Young People,* 5th Ed. Abrams, 1997 (I:10+).

Jeffers, Susan. *Brother Eagle, Sister Sky.* Dial, 1991 (I:all).

_____. *Three Jovial Huntsmen.* Bradbury, 1973 (I:4–8).

Jenkins, Steve. *The Top of the World: Climbing Mount Everest.* Houghton Mifflin, 1999 (I:7+).

Johnson, James Weldon. *The Creation.* Illustrated by Carla Golembe. Little, Brown, 1993 (I:all).

Johnson, Stephen T. *Alphabet City.* Viking, 1995 (I:all).

Johnston, Tony. *Desert Song.* Illustrated by Ed Young. Sierra Club, 2000 (I:all).

Keats, Ezra Jack. *Apt. 3.* Macmillan, 1974 (I:3–8 R:3).

_____. *Goggles!* Macmillan, 1969 (I:5–9 R:3).

_____. *Louie.* Greenwillow, 1975 (I:3–8 R:2).

_____. *Peter's Chair.* Harper & Row, 1967 (I:3–8 R:2).

_____. *Regards to the Man in the Moon.* Four Winds, 1981 (I:4–8 R:3).

_____. *The Snowy Day.* Viking, 1962 (I:2–6 R:2).

_____. *The Trip.* Greenwillow, 1978 (I:3–8 R:2).

Kleven, Elisa. *Hooray, A Pinata!* Dutton, 1996 (I:4–7).

Knox, Bob. *The Great Art Adventure.* Rizzoli, 1992 (I:all).

Kolar, Bob. *Do You Want to Play? A Book About Being Friends.* Dutton, 1999 (I:all).

Krauss, Ruth. *A Hole Is to Dig.* Illustrated by Maurice Sendak. Harper & Row, 1952 (I:2–6 R:2).

Krensky, Stephen. *Breaking Into Print: Before and After the Invention of the Printing Press.* Illustrated by Bonnie Christensen. Little, Brown, 1996 (I:7–10 R:4).

Lawson, Robert. *Ben and Me.* Little, Brown, 1939 (I:7–11 R:6).

_____. *Rabbit Hill.* Viking, 1944 (I:7–11 R:7).

Leaf, Munro. *The Story of Ferdinand.* Illustrated by Robert Lawson. Viking, 1936 (I:4–10 R:6).

Lear, Edward. *The Owl and The Pussycat.* Illustrated by James Marshall. HarperCollins, 1998 (I:all).

Lenski, Lois. *Sing a Song of People.* Illustrated by Giles Laroche. Little, Brown, 1987. (I:all).

Lent, Blair. *Bayberry Bluff.* Houghton Mifflin, 1987 (I:3–8 R:6).

Lester, Julius. *The Tales of Uncle Remus: The Adventures of Brer Rabbit as Told by Julius Lester.* Illustrated by Jerry Pinkney. Dial, 1987 (I:6–9 R:4).

_____. *Further Tales of Uncle Remus: The Misadventures of Brer Rabbit, Brer Fox, the Doodang and All the Other Creatures.* Illustrated by Jerry Pinkney. Dial, 1990 (I:6–11 R:5).

_____. *Sam and the Tigers: A New Telling of Little Black Sambo.* Illustrated by Jerry Pinkney. Dial, 1996 (I:6–9 R:4).

Lewis, Paul Owen. *Storm Boy.* Beyond Words, 1995 (I:7+ R:6).

Lindbergh, Reeve. *Johnny Appleseed.* Illustrated by Kathy Jakobsen. Little, Brown, 1990 (I:all).

Lionni, Leo. *Alexander and the Wind-up Mouse.* Pantheon, 1969 (I:3–6 R:3).

_____. *A Color of His Own.* Random House, 1975 (I:2–7 R:5).

_____. *Swimmy.* Pantheon, 1963 (I:2–6 R:3).

Livingston, Myra Cohn. *A Circle of Seasons.* Illustrated by Leonard Everett Fisher. Holiday House, 1982 (I:all).

Lobel, Arnold. *Fables.* Jonathon Cape, 1980 (I:all).

Locker, Thomas. *Sailing with the Wind.* Dial, 1986. (I:all).

_____. *Where the River Begins.* Dial, 1984 (I:all).

London, Jonathan. *Baby Whale's Journey.* Illustrated by Jon Van Zyle. Chronicle, 1999 (I:all).

Longfellow, Henry Wadsworth. *Hiawatha.* Illustrated by Susan Jeffers. Dial, 1983 (I:all).

_____. *Hiawatha's Childhood.* Illustrated by Errol LeCain. Farrar, Straus & Giroux, 1984 (I:all).

Lunge-Larsen, Lise, retold by. *The Troll with No Heart in His Body and Other Tales of Trolls from Norway.* Illustrated by Betsy Bowen. Houghton Mifflin, 1999 (I:7+).

McCloskey, Robert. *Blueberries for Sal.* Viking, 1948 (I:4–8 R:6).

_____. *Lentil.* Viking, 1940 (I:4–9 R:7).

_____. *Make Way for Ducklings.* Viking, 1941 (I:4–8 R:4).

_____. *One Morning in Maine.* Viking, 1952 (I:4–8 R:3).

_____. *Time of Wonder.* Viking, 1957 (I:5–8 R:4).

McCully, Emily Arnold. *The Ballot Box Battle.* Knopf, 1996 (I:4–8 R:5).

_____. *The Bobbin Girl.* Dial, 1996 (I:6–9 R:5).

_____. *Mirette on the High Wire.* Putnam, 1992 (I:all).

McDermott, Beverly Brodsky. *The Golem.* Lippincott, 1976 (I:9–14 R:5).

McDermott, Gerald. *Arrow to the Sun.* Viking, 1974 (I:3–9 R:2).

MacDonald, Suse. *Look Whooo's Counting.* Scholastic, 2000 (I:3–6).

MacGill-Callahan, Sheila. *The Children of Lir.* Illustrated by Gennady Spirin. Dial, 1993 (I:6+ R:5).

MacLachlan, Patricia. *What You Know First.* Illustrated by Barry Moser. HarperCollins, 1995 (I:all).

McLanathan, Richard. *Leonardo da Vinci.* Abrams, 1990 (I:10+).

Mallat, Kathy, and Bruce McMillan. *The Picture That Mom Drew.* Walker, 1997 (I:8+).

Marcus, Leonard S. *A Caldecott Celebration: Six Artists and Their Paths to the Caldecott Medal.* Walker, 1998 (I:8+ R:5).

Martin, Eva. *Canadian Fairy Tales.* Illustrated by Laszlo Gal. Douglas & McIntyre, 1984 (I:7–16 R:4).

Martin, Rafe. *Will's Mammoth.* Illustrated by Stephen Gammell. Putnam, 1989 (I:2–7).

Maruki, Toshi. *Hiroshima No Pika.* Lothrop, Lee & Shepard, 1982 (I:8–12 R:4).

Meggendorfer, Lothar. *The City Park.* Collins, 1982.

Meryman, Richard. *Andrew Wyeth.* Abrams, 1991 (I:10+).

Miller, Debbie S. *A Polar Bear Journey.* Illustrated by Jon Van Zyle. Little, Brown, 1997 (I:6–9 R:5).

_____. *A Woolly Mammoth Journey.* Illustrated by Jon Van Zyle. Little, Brown, 2001 (I:6–9 R:5).

Mitchell, B. *Edmund Dulac's Fairy Book: Fairy Tales of the World.* Omega, 1984.

Moore, Clement. *The Night Before Christmas.* Illustrated by Tomie dePaola. Holiday House, 1980 (I:all).

Morpurgo, Michael. *Wombat Goes Walkabout.* Illustrated by Christian Birmingham. Candlewick, 2000 (I:4–8).

Mosel, Arlene. *Tikki Tikki Tembo.* Illustrated by Blair Lent. Holt, Rinehart & Winston, 1968 (I:5–9 R:7).

Moser, Barry, retold by. *The Three Little Pigs.* Little, Brown, 2001 (I:4–8).

Moss, Lloyd. *Zin! Zin! Zin! A Violin.* Illustrated by Marjorie Priceman. Simon & Schuster, 1995 (I:all).

Mulherin, Jennifer, ed. *Favourite Fairy Tales.* Granada, 1982. (I:8+).

Mulvihill, Margaret. *The Treasury of Saints and Martyrs.* Consultant David Hugh Farmer. Viking, 1999 (I:10+ R:7).

Musgrove, Margaret. *Ashanti to Zulu: African Traditions.* Illustrated by Leo and Diane Dillon. Dial, 1976 (I:7–12).

Myers, Christopher. *Wings.* Scholastic, 2000 (I:all).

Myers, Walter Dean. *Toussaint L'Ouverture: The Fight for Haiti's Freedom.* Illustrated by Jacob Lawrence. Simon & Schuster, 1996 (I:8+ R:5).

Newberry, Clare Turlay. *Marshmallow.* Harper & Row, 1942 (I:2–7 R:7).

Nister, Ernest. *Animal Tales.* London: Benn, 1981.

_____. *Revolving Pictures.* Putnam, 1979.

Norman, Howard, retold by. *The Girl Who Dreamed Only Geese and Other Tales of the Far North.* Illustrated by Leo and Diane Dillon. Harcourt Brace, 1997 (I:9+ R:6).

Noyes, Alfred. *The Highwayman.* Illustrated by Charles Keeping. Oxford, 1981 (I:10+).

Oppenheim, Joanne. *Have You Seen Trees?* Illustrated by Jean and Mou-sien Tseng. Scholastic, 1995 (I:all).

Peet, Bill. *Bill Peet's Autobiography.* Houghton Mifflin, 1989 (I:all R:5).

Pelletier, David. *The Graphic Alphabet.* Orchard, 1996 (I:all).

Perrault, Charles. *Cinderella.* Adapted by Amy Ehrlich. Illustrated by Susan Jeffers. Dial, 1985 (I:5–8 R:4).

_____. *Cinderella.* Illustrated by Marcia Brown. Harper & Row, 1954 (I:5–8 R:5).

Pope, Joyce. *Kenneth Lilly's Animals: A Portfolio of Paintings.* Illustrated by Kenneth Lilly. Lothrop, Lee & Shepard, 1988 (I:all).

Potter, Beatrix. *The Tale of Peter Rabbit.* Warne, 1902, 1986 (I:all).

Priceman, Marjorie. *Froggie Went A-Courting.* Little, Brown, 2000 (I:3–5).

Provensen, Alice, and Martin Provensen. *The Glorious Flight Across the Channel with Louis Bleriot, July 25, 1909.* Viking, 1983 (I:all R:4).

_____. *Leonardo da Vinci.* Viking, 1984 (I:all R:8).

Pyle, Howard. *Bearskin.* Illustrated by Trina Schart Hyman. Morrow, 1997 (I:6–9 R:5).

Quiller-Couch, Sir Arthur, retold by. *The Sleeping Beauty and Other Fairy Tales.* Illustrated by Edmund Dulac. London: Hodder and Stoughton, 1981.

Ransome, Arthur. *The Fool of the World and the Flying Ship.* Illustrated by Uri Shulevitz. Farrar, Straus & Giroux, 1968 (I:6–10 R:6).

Ray, Mary Lyn. *Basket Moon.* Illustrated by Barbara Cooney. Little, Brown, 1999 (I:all).

Richardson, Judith Benét. *Come to My Party.* Illustrated by Salley Mavor. Macmillan, 1993 (I:3–7).

_____. *The Way Home.* Illustrated by Salley Mavor. Macmillan, 1991 (I:3–7).

Rogasky, Barbara. *The Golem.* Illustrated by Trina Schart Hyman. Holiday, 1996 (I:9+ R:5).

Rosen, Michael, retold by. *Crow and Hawk: A Traditional Pueblo Indian Story.* Illustrated by John Clementson. Harcourt Brace, 1995 (I:4–8 R:6).

_____. *We're Going on a Bear Hunt.* Illustrated by Helen Oxenbury. Macmillan, 1989 (I:2–6).

Rubin, Susan Goldman. *Margaret Bourke-White: Her Pictures Were Her Life.* Photographs by Margaret Bourke-White. Abrams, 1999 (I:10+).

Ryder, Joanne. *White Bear, Ice Bear.* Illustrated by Michael Rothman. Morrow, 1989 (I:3–8 R:4).

Rylant, Cynthia. *In November.* Illustrated by Jill Kastner. Harcourt, 2000 (I:4–7).

Sabuda, Robert. *The Blizzard's Robe.* Atheneum, 1999 (I:all).

Sanderson, Ruth. *The Nativity: From the Gospels of Matthew and Luke.* Little, Brown, 1993 (I:all).

Say, Allen. *Allison.* Houghton Mifflin, 1997 (I:4–8 R:4).

Scheer, Julian. *Rain Makes Applesauce.* Illustrated by Marvin Bileck. Holiday House, 1964 (I:3–8).

Schoenherr, John. *Bear.* Philomel, 1991 (I:5–8 R:4).

Schreiber, J. F. *The Great Menagerie.* Viking, 1979. (I:all).

Schroeder, Alan. *Minty: A Story of Young Harriet Tubman.* Illustrated by Jerry Pinkney. Puffin, 1996 (I:8–11 R4+).

Schwartz, Delmore. *"I Am Cherry Alive," The Little Girl Sang.* Illustrated by Barbara Cooney. Harper & Row, 1979.

Schwartz, Gary. *Rembrandt.* Abrams, 1992 (I:10+ R:7).

Scieszka, Jon. *The Stinky Cheese Man and Other Fairly Stupid Tales.* Illustrated by Lane Smith. Viking, 1992 (I:all).

_____. *The True Story of the 3 Little Pigs!* Illustrated by Lane Smith. Viking, 1989 (I:all).

Sendak, Maurice. *In the Night Kitchen.* Harper & Row, 1970 (I:5–7).

_____. *Outside over There.* Harper & Row, 1981 (I:5–8 R:5).

_____. *We Are All in the Dumps with Jack and Guy.* HarperCollins, 1993 (I:all).

_____. *Where the Wild Things Are.* Harper & Row, 1963 (I:4–8 R:6).

Seuss, Dr. *The 500 Hats of Bartholomew Cubbins.* Vanguard, 1938 (I:4–9 R:4).

Shannon, George. *Dance Away.* Illustrated by Jose Aruego and Ariane Dewey. Greenwillow, 1982 (I:2–6).

Shepard, Aaron, retold by. *Master Man: A Tall Tale of Nigeria.* Illustrated by David Wisniewski. HarperCollins, 2001 (I:all).

_____, retold by. *The Sea King's Daughter: A Russian Legend.* Illustrated by Gennady Spirin. Atheneum, 1997 (I:7+ R:5).

Simon, Seymour. *Jupiter.* Morrow, 1985 (I:all R:7).

Simont, Marc. *The Goose That Almost Got Cooked.* Scholastic, 1997 (I:3–7 R:4).

Singer, Isaac Bashevis. *The Golem.* Illustrated by Uri Shulevitz. Farrar, Straus & Giroux, 1982 (I:81 R:5).

_____. *Zlateh the Goat.* Illustrated by Maurice Sendak. Harper & Row, 1966 (I:6–10 R:6).

Sís, Peter. *Starry Messenger: Galileo Galilei.* Farrar, Straus & Giroux, 1996 (I:all).

Skira-Venturi, Rosabianca. *A Weekend with Leonardo da Vinci.* Translated by Ann Keay Beneduce. Rizzoli, 1992 (I:10+).

Souhami, Jessica. *The Leopard's Drum: An Asante Tale from West Africa.* Little, Brown, 1995 (I:4–8 R:6).

Spier, Peter. *The Fox Went Out on a Chilly Night.* Doubleday, 1961 (I:all).

_____. *Noah's Ark.* Doubleday, 1977 (I:3–9).

_____. *The Star-Spangled Banner.* Doubleday, 1973. (I:8+).

Stanley, Diane. *Leonardo da Vinci.* Morrow, 1996 (I:8+ R:6).

_____. *Saving Sweetness.* Illustrated by G. Brian Karas. Putnam, 1996 (I:5–8 R:5).

Steig, William. *The Amazing Bone.* Farrar, Straus & Giroux, 1976 (I:6–9 R:5).

Steptoe, Javaka. *In Daddy's Arms I Am Tall: African Americans Celebrating Fathers.* Lee & Low, 1997 (I:all).

Steptoe, John. *The Story of Jumping Mouse.* Lothrop, Lee & Shepard, 1984 (I:all R:4).

Stevens, Janet. *Tops & Bottoms.* Harcourt Brace, 1995 (I:4–7).

Stevenson, Robert Louis. *My Shadow.* Illustrated by Ted Rand. Putnam, 1990 (I:all).

Stewart, Sarah. *The Gardener.* Illustrated by David Small. Farrar, Straus & Giroux, 1997 (I:5–8 R:4).

Strickland, Carol. *The Annotated Mona Lisa: A Crash Course in Art History from Prehistoric to Post-Modern.* Andrews and McMeel, 1992 (I:10+).

Sykes, Julie. *This and That.* Illustrated by Tanya Linch. Farrar, Straus & Giroux, 1996 (I:4–7).

Taback, Simms. *Joseph Had a Little Overcoat.* Viking, 1999 (I:all).

_____. *There Was an Old Lady Who Swallowed a Fly.* Viking, 1997 (I:all).

Tseng, Grace, retold by. *White Tiger, Blue Serpent.* Illustrated by Jean and Mou-sien Tseng. Lothrop, Lee & Shepard, 1999 (I:all).

Turner, Robyn Montana. *Faith Ringgold.* Little, Brown, 1993 (I:9+ R:5).

_____. *Frida Kahlo.* Little, Brown, 1993 (I:9+ R:5).

_____. *Georgia O'Keeffe.* Little, Brown, 1991 (I:9+ R:5).

_____. *Mary Cassatt.* Little, Brown, 1992 (I:9+ R:5).

_____. *Rosa Bonheur.* Little, Brown, 1991 (I:9+ R:5).

Udry, Janice May. *The Moon Jumpers.* Illustrated by Maurice Sendak. Harper & Row, 1959 (I:3–9 R:2).

Van Allsburg, Chris. *The Garden of Abdul Gasazi.* Houghton Mifflin, 1979 (I:5–8 R:5).

_____. *Jumanji.* Houghton Mifflin, 1981 (I:5–8 R:6).

_____. *The Mysteries of Harris Burdick.* Houghton Mifflin, 1984. (I:all).

_____. *The Polar Express.* Houghton Mifflin, 1985 (I:5–8 R:6).

_____. *The Sweetest Fig.* Houghton Mifflin, 1993 (I:all R:6).

_____. *The Widow's Broom.* Houghton Mifflin, 1992 (I:5–8 R:6).

_____. *The Wreck of the Zephyr.* Houghton Mifflin, 1983 (I:5–8 R:6).

_____. *The Wretched Stone.* Houghton Mifflin, 1991 (I:5–8 R:6).

Viorst, Judith. *Alexander and the Terrible, Horrible, No Good, Very Bad Day.* Illustrated by Ray Cruz. Atheneum, 1972 (I:3–8 R:6).

Waber, Bernard. *The Lion Named Shirley Williamson.* Houghton Mifflin, 1996 (I:5–8 R:5).

Waddell, Martin. *Farmer Duck.* Illustrated by Helen Oxenbury. Candlewick, 1992 (I:4–7).

Waldron, Ann. *Francisco Goya.* Abrams, 1992 (I:10+).

Walker, Barbara K., retold by. *The Dancing Palm Tree: And Other Nigerian Folktales.* Illustrated by Helen Siegl. Texas Tech University Press, 1990 (I:all R:4).

Walter, Mildred Pitts. *Brother to the Wind.* Illustrated by Diane and Leo Dillon. Lothrop, Lee & Shepard, 1985 (I:all R:3).

Ward, Lynd. *The Biggest Bear.* Houghton Mifflin, 1952 (I:5–8 R:4).

Waring, Richard. *Hungry Hen.* Illustrated by Caroline Jayne Church. HarperCollins, 2002 (I:4–8).

Weller, Frances Ward. *I Wonder If I'll See a Whale.* Illustrated by Ted Lewin. Philomel, 1991 (I:6–10 R:4).

Welton, Jude. *Impressionism.* Kindersley/The Art Institute of Chicago, 1993 (I:10+).

_____. *Monet.* Kindersley/The Musee Marmottan, Paris, 1992 (I:10+).

Westervelt, Linda. *Roger Tory Peterson's ABC of Birds: A Book for Little Birdwatchers.* Illustrated by Roger Tory Peterson. Photographs by Seymour Levin. Rizzoli, 1995 (I:all).

Westray, Kathleen. *A Color Sampler.* Ticknor & Fields, 1993 (I:all).

Whipple, Laura, compiled by. *Eric Carle's Dragons Dragons & Other Creatures That Never Were.* Illustrated by Eric Carle. Philomel, 1991 (I:all).

Wiesner, David. *Free Fall.* Lothrop, Lee & Shepard, 1988. (I:all).

_____. *June 29, 1999.* Clarion, 1992 (I:all).

_____. *Tuesday.* Clarion, 1991 (I:all).

Wild, Margaret. *Let the Celebrations BEGIN!* Illustrated by Julie Vivas. Orchard, 1991 (I:all).

Wildsmith, Brian. *Exodus.* Eerdmans, 1998 (I:all).

Willard, Nancy. *Pish, Posh, Said Hieronymus Bosch.* Illustrated by Leo and Diane Dillon. Harcourt Brace Jovanovich, 1991 (I:all).

_____. *A Visit to William Blake's Inn: Poems for Innocent and Experienced Travelers.* Illustrated by Alice and Martin Provensen. Harcourt Brace Jovanovich, 1981 (I:all).

Winter, Jonah. *Diego.* Translated by Amy Prince. Illustrated by Jeanette Winter. Knopf, 1991 (I:6–10 R:5).

Wisniewski, David. *Golem.* Clarion,1996 (I:all).

_____. *Rain Player.* Clarion, 1991 (I:5–8 R:5).

Wood, Audrey. *King Bidgood's in the Bathtub.* Illustrated by Don Wood. Harcourt Brace Jovanovich, 1985 (I:6–9 R:1).

Wood, Douglas. *Old Turtle.* Illustrated by Cheng-Khee Chee. Pfeifer-Hamilton, 1992 (I:all).

Wright, Patricia. *Manet.* Kindersley/National Gallery, London, 1993 (I:10+).

Yagawa, Sumiko. *The Crane Wife.* Translated by Katherine Paterson. Illustrated by Suekichi Akaba. Morrow, 1981 (I:all R:6).

Yashima, Taro. *Crow Boy.* Viking, 1955 (I:4–8 R:4).

_____. *Umbrella.* Viking, 1958 (I:3–7 R:7).

Yolen, Jane. *Letting Swift River Go.* Illustrated by Barbara Cooney. Little, Brown, 1992 (I:all).

_____. *Off We Go!* Illustrated by Laurel Molk. Little, Brown, 2000 (I:3–5).

_____. *Owl Moon.* Illustrated by John Schoenherr. Philomel, 1987 (I:all).

Yorinks, Arthur. *Hey, Al.* Illustrated by Richard Egielski. Farrar, Straus & Giroux, 1986 (I:all).

_____. *The Miami Giant.* Illustrated by Maurice Sendak. HarperCollins, 1995 (I:all).

Young, Ed, translated by. *Lon Po Po: A Red-Riding Hood Story from China.* Philomel, 1989 (I:all R:5).

_____. *Seven Blind Mice.* Philomel, 1992 (I:all).

Zeman, Ludmila, retold and illustrated by. *Sindbad: From the Tales of the Thousand and One Nights.* Tundra, 1999 (I:all).

Zheng, Zhensun, and Alice Low. *Young Painter: The Life and Paintings of Wang Yani—China's Extraordinary Young Artist.* Scholastic, 1991 (I:all R:5).

Zolotow, Charlotte. *Mr. Rabbit and the Lovely Present.* Illustrated by Maurice Sendak. Harper & Row, 1962 (I:3–8 R:2).

_____. *When the Wind Stops.* Illustrated by Stefano Vitale. HarperCollins, 1995 (I:4–8).

Illustration from Storm Boy, written and illustrated by Paul Owen Lewis, copyright © 1995 by Paul Owen Lewis. Beyond Words Publishing, Inc., 1-800-284-9673.

The thought of a child, a lap, and a picture book arouses warm feelings and recollections in many adults. When a loving adult provides opportunities for a child to experience the enchantment found in picture books, both the child and the adult benefit.

The books included in the genre of picture books have many values in addition to pleasure. The rhythm, rhyme, and repetition in nursery rhymes stimulate language development as well as auditory discrimination and attentive listening skills in young children. Alphabet books reinforce ability to identify letter/sound relationships and help expand vocabularies. Concept books enhance intellectual development by fostering understanding of abstract ideas. Wordless books encourage children to develop their observational skills, descriptive vocabularies, and abilities to create stories characterized by logical sequence. Illustrations found in picture books stimulate sensitivity to art and beauty. Well-written picture storybooks encourage children to appreciate literary style. Thus, picture books have important roles in children's development.

What a Picture Book Is

Most children's books are illustrated, but not all illustrated children's books are picture books. As Perry Nodelman (1990) points out, picture books "communicate information or tell stories through a series of many pictures combined with relatively slight texts or no texts at all" (p. VII, preface).

In picture books, the illustrations are as important as the text or even more important than the text. Because children respond to stories told visually as well as verbally, some picture books are quite effective with no words at all. Many picture books, however, maintain a balance between the illustrations and the text, so that neither is completely effective without the other.

Thus the term *picture books* covers a wide variety of children's books, ranging from Mother Goose books and toy books for very young children to picture storybooks with plots that satisfy more experienced, older children. Many of the picture books discussed in this chapter rely heavily upon illustrations to present content. In some, each scene or rhyme is illustrated. Other books, with more complex verbal story lines, are not so dependent upon pictures to develop their plots.

Many picture books have a characteristic not often shared by other children's books: The writer and the illustrator may be the same person. Well-known artists often create picture books. This chapter emphasizes authors, author-illustrators, and their literature.

Literary Criticism: Evaluating Picture Books

Because the text and the illustrations in picture books should complement each other, consider the relationships between the words and pictures when evaluating a picture book. Zena Sutherland (1997) makes recommendations for evaluating picture books if the books are written for young children. She states:

A story should be brief and straightforward if it is for young children; it should contain few concepts and none that are beyond comprehension if they are not familiar concepts; it should be written in a direct and simple style; and it should have illustrations that complement the text and are not in conflict with it. (p. 64)

The questions in the Evaluation Criteria box on this page can help you select high-quality picture books for children.

Educators, researchers, and authorities in children's literature are increasingly interested in children's responses to picture books and in the characteristics of picture books that appeal to children. You should consider children's own evaluations when selecting picture books to share with children.

The first interactions of a very young child with a picture book are largely physical, as the child investigates the size, shape, texture, and moving parts of the unfamiliar object. The child may stick the book into his or her mouth to become acquainted with it or turn the pages even if the book is upside down. With adult guidance, the child soon learns the specific purposes and pleasures associated with books and responds to the symbolic nature of books, focusing on the content of the pictures and connecting illustrated objects and concepts with the sounds and names given to them. The child quickly begins to assume that books will contain stories.

As a sense of time develops, a child begins to see connections among past, present, and future in pictures and text and to expect that a story will have a beginning, a middle, and an end. Finally, after time and experience with both books and everyday living, a child evaluates book text and illustrations in terms of his or her own view of reality and his or her own feelings and desires. Thus, different types of books and book-related experiences are appropriate for children at different ages and stages of development.

Patricia Cianciolo (1997) identified four major factors that influence how a child perceives and evaluates the illustrations in picture books: (1) the child's age and stage of cognitive and social development, (2) the way in which an adult has (or has not) prepared the child for the experience with a picture book, (3) the child's emotional state of readiness, and (4) the number of times the child looks

EVALUATION CRITERIA

Selecting High-Quality Picture Books

1. Are the illustrations accurate, and do they correspond to the content of the story?

2. Do the illustrations complement the setting, plot, and mood of the story?

3. Do the illustrations enhance the characterizations?

4. Do both the text and illustrations avoid stereotypes of race and sex?

5. Will the plot appeal to children?

6. Is the theme worthwhile?

7. What is the purpose for sharing this book with children or recommending that they read it?

8. Are the author's style and language appropriate for the children's interests and age levels?

9. Are the text, the illustrations, the format, and the typography in harmony?

at the illustrations. Cianciolo's (1983) analysis of picture books listed in the Children's Choices also reveals that children prefer illustrations that depict here-and-now situations, fantasies of all kinds, and humorous exaggerations and slapstick; illustrations that are colorful and add more detail to the descriptions of characters, action, and setting in the text; and illustrations that are drawn in either a realistic or a cartoon-like style. Such preferences may help adults select picture books for children, but Cianciolo stresses that adults can and should also use books and book-related activities to teach children "how to be more evaluative and discriminating in their selections" (p. 28).

Additional insights into evaluating picture books are gained by analyzing picture books that are highly rated in journals that review books written for children. Journals such as *The Horn Book, School Library Journal, Publishers Weekly,* and *Booklist* provide extensive reviews. Each of these journals includes starred reviews of books that the reviewers consider to have exceptional merit.

Most of the reviews for outstanding picture books emphasize a close integration between the illustrations and text as well as author style that excites readers. As you read picture books, decide if you do or do not agree with reviewers.

Mother Goose

Mother Goose rhymes are the earliest literature enjoyed by many young children; the rhymes, rhythms, and pleasing sounds of these jingles appeal to young children, who are

Mother GOOSE's Melody.   **37**

*J*ACK and *Gill*
 Went up the Hill,
 To fetch a Pail of **Water**;
Jack fell down
And broke his Crown,
 And *Gill* came tumbling after.

Maxim.

The more you think of dying, the better
you will live.

ARISTOTLE'S

38 Mother GOOSE's Melody.

ARISTOTLE's STORY.
THERE were two Birds fat on
 a Stone,
 Fa, la, la, la, lal, de;   [one,
One flew away, and then there was
 Fa, la, la, la, lal, de;
The other flew after,
And then there was none,
 Fa, la, la, la, lal, de;
And fo the poor Stone
 Was left all alone,
 Fa, la, la, la, lal, de.
This may ferve as a Chapter of Confequence
in the next new Book of Logick.

Mother Goose rhymes, which contained maxims or morals, were popular in both Great Britain and North America. (The Original Mother Goose's Melody printed in London by John Newbery, 1760.)

Children also respond to the repetition of sounds in a phrase or line of a nursery rhyme. Alliteration, the repetition of an initial consonant in consecutive words, creates phrases that children enjoy repeating just to experience the marvelous feelings that result from the repetition of beginning sounds: "One misty, moisty, morning"; "Sing a song of sixpence"; and "Diddle, diddle, dumpling." Sentences that contain a great deal of alliteration become tongue twisters. Children love the challenge of this jingle:

Peter Piper picked a peck of pickled peppers.
A peck of pickled peppers Peter Piper picked.
If Peter Piper picked a peck of pickled peppers,
Where's the peck of pickled peppers Peter Piper picked?

experimenting with their own language patterns, and aid children's language development. Betsy Hearne (1992) emphasizes the appeal of Mother Goose when she states, "Nursery rhymes are only a step away from song in their changing cadence and compressed story elements" (p. 22). A brief review of the basic characteristics of nursery rhymes indicates why children enjoy them, as well as why nursery rhymes encourage language development in children.

Appealing Characteristics

The rhythm in many nursery rhymes almost forces children to react. For example, children may clap their hands or jump up and down to the rhythm of this jingle:

Handy dandy, Jack-a-Dandy
Loves plum cake and sugar candy;
He bought some at a grocer's shop
And out he came, hop, hop, hop.

Rhyme is another aspect of many nursery verses that children enjoy. Rhyming words, such as *dandy* and *candy,* and *shop* and *hop,* invite children to join in and add the rhyming word or to make up their own rhymes. Rhymes enhance the adventures of many favorite characters: "Little Miss Muffet sat on a tuffet"; "Jack and Jill went up the hill"; "Bobby Shafto's gone to sea, Silver buckles on his knee." Many verses rhyme at the end of each line, but some verses also use internal rhyming elements: "Hickory, dickory, dock, the mouse ran up the clock" and "Rub, a dub, dub, three men in a tub." To test the influence of these rhyming verses, ask older children to share one of their favorite Mother Goose rhymes. They can probably say several although they may not have heard or recited them for years.

Humor is another great appeal of Mother Goose verses for children:

Hey, diddle, diddle!
The cat and the fiddle,
The cow jumped over the moon;
The little dog laughed
To see such sport,
And the dish ran away with the spoon.

This verse is also an example of hyperbole, the use of exaggeration for effect, which is common in Mother Goose rhymes. Children appreciate exaggerated, ridiculous situations, such as an old woman's living in a shoe with so many children she doesn't know what to do, a barber's trying to shave a pig, or Simple Simon's going for water with a sieve:

He went for water with a sieve,
But soon it ran all through;
And now poor Simple Simon
Bids you all adieu.

Rhyme, repetition of sounds, humor, and exaggeration combine to create appealing subjects for young children.

Collections

The many different collections of Mother Goose rhymes contain more or less the same verses, but their formats, sizes, and illustrations are quite different. Some editions contain several hundred verses in large-book format, while others have fewer verses and are small enough for a young child to hold. Some editions have illustrations reminiscent of eighteenth-century England, while others have modern illustrations. Many adult students in Ameri-

TOMMY was a silly boy.
" I can fly," he said ;
He started off, but very soon
He tumbled on his head.

His little sister Prue was there,
To see how he would do it ;
She knew that, after all his boast,
Full dearly Tom would rue it !

K.G

Kate Greenaway was an influential illustrator of children's books in the nineteenth century. (From Kate Greenaway's Mother Goose, *copyright © 1988. Reprinted by permission of Dial Books for Young Readers.)*

can university classes prefer the Mother Goose editions with settings in the England of the 1600s and 1700s— either reissues of the original early editions or editions first published in the twentieth century.

Two popular early editions, John Newbery's *The Original Mother Goose's Melody* and *Kate Greenaway's Mother Goose: Or, the Old Nursery Rhymes,* continue to be reissued. Newbery's edition may be of greater interest to adults than to children (the text contains a history of Mother Goose), although many older children enjoy looking at the early orthography in Newbery's edition and comparing the verses and illustrations with twentieth-century editions, which do not share Newbery's tendency to add a moral to the close of each nursery rhyme. In Newbery's edition, for example, "Ding, dong, bell, the cat is in the well," is followed by this maxim: "He that injures one threatens a Hundred" (p. 25).

The edition illustrated by the well-known author-illustrator Kate Greenaway was first published in 1881. Greenaway's book is a small text suitable for sharing with one child. She illustrates the nursery rhymes with pictures of delicate children that appeal to the sentiments of most readers.

Collections assembled by Iona and Peter Opie provide older children and adults with an opportunity to examine early illustrated versions of Mother Goose. A

Nursery Companion is a large, highly illustrated collection of nursery rhymes originally published in the early 1800s. The *Oxford Nursery Rhyme Book* contains eight hundred rhymes categorized according to contents. Black-and-white woodcuts, from both earlier editions and newly created works, illustrate this large volume. An informative preface and a list of sources for the illustrations increase the usefulness for those who wish to study early editions of nursery rhymes. *Tail Feathers from Mother Goose: The Opie Rhyme Book* is a collection of lesser known rhymes, many of which are previously unpublished. The rhymes are illustrated by contemporary artists.

In *I Saw Esau: The Schoolchild's Pocket Book,* the Opies assemble a collection of rhymes, chants, and riddles that are appropriate for various ages. The illustrations by Maurice Sendak and the rhymes appeal to younger children. Older children and adults benefit from the notes section, which explains the origins of the rhymes.

Another large-format book that appeals to younger children is *Here Comes Mother Goose,* also edited by Iona Opie. Illustrations by Rosemary Wells add humor to a book that is appropriate for sharing with a group of children.

Arnold Lobel's *Gregory Griggs and Other Nursery Rhyme People* contains rhymes about lesser known characters, such as Theophilus Thistle, the successful thistle sifter; Gregory Griggs, who had twenty-seven different wigs; Charley, Charley, who stole the barley; Michael Finnegan, who grew a long beard right on his chinnigan; and Terence McDiddler, the three-stringed fiddler. The language and strong rhyming patterns in these verses make the book appropriate for reading aloud. The humorous, nonsensical rhymes are enriched by Lobel's pastel illustrations. Each rhyme is illustrated with a large picture, making it especially good for sharing with a group of children. Lobel's *The Random House Book of Mother Goose* is a collection of 306 rhymes. The illustrations emphasize Lobel's ability to create humorous situations in pictures.

The placement of illustrations next to the matching nursery rhyme, the large-page format, and the humorous folk-art illustrations make *Tomie dePaola's Mother Goose* especially appealing to younger children. The pictures that accompany multiple verses illustrate the sequential development in longer rhymes, such as "Simple Simon." The plots of some of the rhymes are extended through the illustrations. For example, the illustrations accompanying "Jack and Jill" show the actions on a marionette stage.

Michael Foreman's Mother Goose, selected and illustrated by Michael Foreman, is another large collection of nursery rhymes. Because of the visual links, the illustrations provide interesting opportunities to increase observational abilities and interactions. For example, the illustration on page 23 shows someone falling off the wall in front of the Pretty Maid, who is gathering roses in her garden. When readers turn the page, they find that the legs belong to Humpty Dumpty, who now cannot be put back together again.

Humorous illustrations and large-book format provide an appealing volume for young children. (Illustration by Tomie dePaola reprinted by permission of G. P. Putnam's Sons from Tomie dePaola's Mother Goose. *Copyright © 1985 by Tomie dePaola.)*

In *We Are All in the Dumps with Jack and Guy,* a potentially controversial Mother Goose, Maurice Sendak provides social commentary in illustrations showing newspaper headlines on papers worn by homeless children. Sendak's images, which reflect poverty, crime, AIDS, and unemployment, should encourage much discussion.

Books That Illustrate One Rhyme or Tale

Children often want to know more about their favorite nursery rhyme characters. The humor and simple plots found in nursery rhymes lend themselves to expansion into picture storybook format. Each verse of Sarah Josepha Hale's *Mary Had a Little Lamb* has several full-page color illustrations of nineteenth-century farm and school settings by Tomie dePaola.

Picture storybook versions of Mother Goose rhymes may stimulate creative interpretations if children think about what might happen, expanding and illustrating the plots in other nursery rhymes. John Ivimey's text and Paul Galdone's illustrations for *The Complete Story of the Three Blind Mice* reveal how the mice lost their sight as well as tails. This version has a happy ending, as the mice regain their sight and tails and become "three wise mice." Texts that extend the story line beyond that found in the Mother Goose rhyme provide motivation for children to

create their own expanded story lines of other favorite Mother Goose rhymes.

Susan Ramsay Hoguet's *Solomon Grundy* extends the nursery rhyme through historical illustrations. The illustrations allow readers and viewers to visualize what life was like in the United States at an earlier time. This Solomon Grundy is born in 1836 and is buried in 1910 near the church in which he was christened.

"Old MacDonald Had a Farm" provides the foundations for Jan Ormerod's *Ms. MacDonald Has a Class.* In this variant of the rhyme, Ms. MacDonald's class takes a field trip to a farm and then prepares a show that depicts their adventures. Young children enjoy joining in with a "Here a hop, there a waddle, everywhere a quack quack" (unnumbered). This variant may also be compared with the original rhyme.

Nursery Rhymes in Other Lands

Traditional nursery rhymes and jingles for children are found in many different lands. The language and style may differ from the English Mother Goose, but the content is amazingly alike. Nursery rhymes everywhere tell about good and bad children, wise and foolish people, animals, and nature. The multicultural nature of nursery rhymes is emphasized with a collection of Chinese nursery rhymes that were adapted and illustrated by Demi. The rhymes in *Dragon Kites and Dragonflies* are illustrated with drawings that depict an ancient culture. Illustrations show kites, emperors, dragons, boats, dancers, weavers, acrobats, and pagodas.

Robert Wyndham has translated Chinese nursery rhymes into English versions that are designed to appeal to English-speaking readers and listeners. *Chinese Mother Goose Rhymes* are about dragons, Buddhas, carriage chairs, the Milky Way, and ladybugs, which seem to fascinate children of many nationalities. Each of the sprightly rhymes is shown in both English and Chinese, with a simple, colorful drawing to illustrate it. Turning games and nonsense words are well represented, as they are in English nursery rhymes.

> Gee lee, gu lu, turn the cake,
> Add some oil, the better to bake.
> Gee lee, gu lu, now it's done;
> Give a piece to everyone. (p. 40, unnumbered)

N. M. Bodecker has translated and illustrated Danish nursery rhymes in *It's Raining, Said John Twaining.* Wooden shoes and royalty are common characters in the Danish verses. Like English verses, Danish nursery rhymes use rhyming elements, tongue-twisting nonsense words, and riddles. The names of some characters in the rhymes, such as Skat Skratterat Skrat Skrirumskrat, appeal to young children, who love nonsense and alliterative sounds. Each rhyme in this book is illustrated with a colorful, full-page picture.

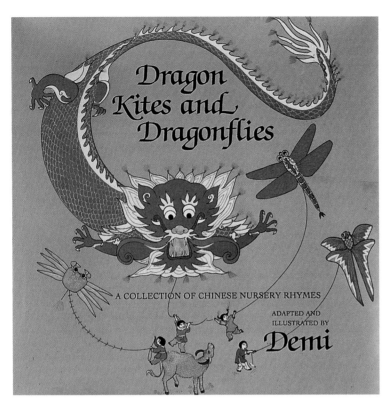

The illustrations reinforce the Chinese settings for the nursery rhymes. (Jacket cover from Dragon Kites and Dragonflies *copyright © 1986 by Demi. Reprinted by permission of Harcourt Brace & Company.)*

Margot C. Griego et al. have collected nursery rhymes and lullabies from Mexico and Spanish-speaking communities in the United States. *Tortillitas Para Mama and Other Spanish Nursery Rhymes* contains finger plays, counting rhymes, and clapping rhymes written in both Spanish and English.

Nursery rhymes from many nations are important contributions to our cultural heritage. They foster the self-esteem and language skills of the children who are members of ethnic minorities in the United States and help all American children appreciate the values and contributions of cultures other than their own.

Toy Books

An increasing number of toy books, including board books, pop-up books, flap books, cloth books, and plastic books, entice children into interacting with stories, developing their vocabularies, counting, identifying colors, and discussing book content with adults. These books are valuable additions to children's literature because they stimulate the language, cognitive, personal, and social development of preschool children. They also provide happy experiences with books that, ideally, extend into later childhood and adulthood. Board books range from identifying a baby's clothing to describing experiences at school or in a doctor's office.

Some of Helen Oxenbury's board books are especially appropriate for younger children. In *Dressing, Family,* and *Working,* each page contains an easily identifiable picture of a baby's actions as he or she gets dressed, interacts with family members, or accomplishes a new skill. Another book by Oxenbury, *I Hear,* identifies sounds within the environment.

Board books help children understand their expanding experiences and environments. Lucy Cousins's *Maisy's Colors* and *Count with Maisy* encourage counting and identifying familiar objects. Todd Parr's *Black & White* and *Big & Little* encourage understanding of basic concepts related to color and size.

Jane Simmons's board books about a duck, *Daisy Says Coo!, Daisy's Day Out,* and *Daisy's Hide-and-Seek,* encourage young children to join in the language of the story. They can repeat sounds and in the third book play with Daisy by looking under flaps.

Two "Sam" board books, *Sam's Ball* and *Sam's Bath,* written by Barbro Lindgren and illustrated by Eva Eriksson, encourage language development through identification of objects and discussion of actions. A humanized rabbit provides similar subjects for discussion and enjoyment in *Max's Bath, Max's Bedtime,* and *Max's Breakfast,* by Rosemary Wells.

Five board books written and illustrated by Cynthia Rylant introduce everyday experiences. Colorful collages in *Everyday Children, Everyday Garden, Everyday House, Everyday Pets,* and *Everyday Town* encourage children to describe what they find in each illustration.

Four board books by Sophie Fatus develop concepts in *Spots, Stripes, Holes,* and *Squares.* Concepts are also developed in Patrick Yee's *Rosie Rabbit's Colors, Rosie Rabbit's Numbers, Rosie Rabbit's Opposites,* and *Rosie Rabbit's Shapes.*

Pop-up books, flap books, and other mechanical books encourage children to interact with text. Pop-up books also may introduce children to beloved storybook characters, tell simple stories, or create fascinating three-dimensional settings such as those in Margaret Wise Brown's *The Goodnight Moon Room: A Pop-Up Book.*

Lucy Cousins's *Maisy Goes to the Playground* and *Maisy Goes to School* use flaps and pull tabs to tell the simple story of a mouse's adventures. Eric Carle's *The Very Clumsy Click Beetle* includes sound effects that add a sensory feature.

Eric Hill has written and illustrated an excellent series of flap books for preschool children. *Where's Spot?,* for

FIGURE 5.1   Children respond to Maurice Sendak's *We Are All in the Dumps with Jack and Guy*

Responses to Maurice Sendak's *We Are All in the Dumps with Jack and Guy*

Maurice Sendak's book *We Are All in the Dumps with Jack and Guy* has received considerable attention. It has been featured in *The New York Times Book Review* and *The New Yorker* magazine, as well as in journals that review children's literature. Reviewers usually comment on the relevancy of the subject, but some question whether or not older elementary children will appreciate and understand the message, which is a plea for social responsibility. This plea is developed through the details in the illustrations, which include newspaper headlines, pictures of homeless children, and references to landmarks, art, and even the Holocaust. The images provide numerous topics to study and discuss.

In an effort to discover how children respond to this book, we shared the book with a group of gifted fifth-grade children in a suburb of Dallas, Texas. In order to receive responses that were not influenced by the other children, we first asked each child to respond individually to the book. Then, the children shared their responses orally with the group. Each child responded to the pictures and told why he or she liked or did not like the book. It is interesting to note that all of these fifth-grade children liked the book.

First, consider their impression of the total book and then identify what images influenced them as they looked at the illustrations and read the text. As you read the following reasons, notice why the children liked the story and what made it popular:

"I liked the book because I like books that need a sharp reader and have hidden messages in the pictures."
"I liked it because you had to piece the story together."
"I loved the significance and the pictures. But, the story about being poor is very sad."
"I liked the way he put the story together and how things in the book fit together."

Next, consider some of the characteristics of the book that encouraged responses: The first characteristic of the book noted by several students was the quality of the endpapers. One girl commented that the endpapers were like recycled paper bags. She thought that the endpapers were appropriate because the story also used a recycling rhyme. She said, "Recycled paper, recycled rhymes, give a modern story that tells about hunger and homelessness. I think it is important."

On the dedication page, the children discussed the possible significance of the stars in the sky and the rope that several thought looked like the Star of Bethlehem. They speculated about why the star was either broken or being used to hang clothes for the homeless.

example, revolves around a dog's full dinner bowl and discovering where the dog could be. Children join Spot's mother as they open a door or lift a covering in search of Spot. Each opening reveals a different animal. The lettering of Hill's books is large and clear against a white background, and the illustrations are both colorful and humorous. Young children return many times to rediscover what is behind each flap.

Tana Hoban's *Look! Look! Look!* uses square openings on black pages to reveal small portions of the colored photograph on the next page. A child can guess what the object is and then turn the page to see if he or she is correct. Harriet Ziefert's *Night Knight* and *Baby Buggy* use flaps to help readers explore homonyms. Lionel's *Peekaboo Babies: A Counting Book* uses tabs and flaps to encourage counting.

Toy books may be created for older readers. For example, pulling the tabs in Robert Crowther's *Pop-Up Olympics: Amazing Facts and Record Breakers* allows readers to both move the athletes in their respective sports and to discover information about records or the people who have been active in the sport. Some of the paper-engineered movements allow readers to visualize the actions of the athletes participating in the sport.

Dorothea P. Seeber's *A Pup Just for Me; A Boy Just For Me* includes two stories. It is an upside-down book that when turned over tells the story from a different point of view.

The numerous toy books discussed here and listed in the children's literature at the end of the chapter indicate a trend toward publishing more books for very young children. A visit to a bookstore or a search through publishers' catalogues will show even more texts. *Booklist,* the journal for the American Library Association, regularly reviews toy books as part of its coverage of children's books.

Alphabet Books

Alphabet books have long been used to help young children identify familiar objects, as well as letters and sounds. The objects pictured in alphabet books should be easy for children to identify and should not have more than one commonly used name. For example, since young children often call a rabbit a bunny, *rabbit* might not be the best choice for illustrating the letter *r* in an alphabet book for very young children. If letter/sound identification is a major concern, the letters and corresponding illustrations

FIGURE 5.1 *Continued*

All of the children responded to the child calling for help and the other children in the dump. They thought that it was important that the child calling for help was black because "there is a great deal of hunger in Africa." They noticed the boy identifying his own private property while living in the crowded conditions of the dump. The children thought that it is important for everyone to identify what is "mine," even if it is only a box or a sack.

The children all commented on the moon's changing expressions: It seemed to show sadness, anger, and tears. They thought that the moon was sad because "he sees these kids, their hunger, and their homelessness and no one seems to be doing anything to help them." They also noted that as life became more difficult for the children, the moon became angrier, until he finally changed into a cat and came to earth to rescue the children.

The rats caused much speculation. Several children thought that the rats were probably in disguise because they had hands. They worried about what the rats would do to the kittens and to the boy. The fact that they seemed to be gambling over the fate of their captives caused concern.

These fifth graders were interested in every detail in the book. They found "Trumped Tower" and discussed the significance of placing the homeless children below this setting. They were particularly interested in reading the newspaper headlines that formed both the clothes of and shelter for many of the children. They discussed the importance of the changing headlines that went from the availability of expensive housing to chaos in shelters, job layoffs, and AIDS. Several of the children concluded that one cannot create a strong shelter with newspapers. They discussed the possible connections between a bakery and an orphanage and noticed how the black smoke from the building partially covered the face of the moon. At the end of the story, they were pleased that the boy and the kittens were saved (one child referred to the moon, the kittens, and the boy "as the moon's family"), but they were not pleased that the final setting in the book was again the dump.

When asked if there is a message in this book, the children provided several important messages. One child stated, "We must remember to give money to the poor and to try to change their lives." Another child said, "The moon is watching over all of us." Still another felt that rats should not be able to take kids away. When asked what age children they thought should read the book, most of them responded with age ten. They thought that children much younger than ten would not understand the message in the book or recognize the symbolism. As you read *We Are All in the Dumps with Jack and Guy,* compare your responses with those of these fifth-grade children.

should be easily identifiable. If young children use the book independently, the pages should not be cluttered with numerous objects that can confuse letter/sound identification.

When adults share alphabet books with older children, however, pages rich with detail and numerous objects may help children develop their observational and discussion skills. A child's age and the educational objectives are basic considerations when evaluating any alphabet book. Some alphabet books are most appropriate for young children, while others contain enough detail or historical insight to interest even older children.

Steven Engelfried (2001) maintains that the best creators of alphabet books "come up with ways to surprise, engage, and instruct, with new twists that expand the original concept to enhance youngsters' love of language and sharpen their powers of deduction and observation" (p. 32). Alphabet books that meet Engelfried's criteria for being innovative include Henry Horenstein's *A Is For. . . ?: A Photographer's Alphabet of Animals* in which viewers are challenged to identify the animals after viewing photographs that show parts of animals, Suse MacDonald's *Alphabatics,* in which the letters are transformed into objects that begin with that letter, and Richard Wilbur's *The Disappearing Alphabet,* in which poetry is used to show what would happen if the various letters were missing.

Early Alphabet Books

Like Mother Goose rhymes, alphabet books were among the first books published for children. Some early alphabet books have been reissued, and some new books are reminiscent of earlier texts. One very early ABC rhyme, "History of an Apple Pie," tells how "B bit it," "C cut it," and so forth, until the end of the alphabet and the pie. In 1886, Kate Greenaway illustrated the pie's alphabetical history in *A—Apple Pie,* and her original woodblock designs have been used in a reissue of this charming text.

Ruth Baldwin's *One Hundred Nineteenth-Century Rhyming Alphabets in English* contains a version of "History of an Apple Pie," as well as other early alphabets. The 296 pages of this large book are filled with colorful reproductions of nineteenth-century pictures and verses. Each rhyme is identified according to title, illustrator, publisher, and date of publication.

Alice and Martin Provensen have illustrated another early ABC, *A Peaceable Kingdom: The Shaker Abecedarius.* The Shaker alphabet book was first published in the Shaker Manifesto of July 1882 under the title "Animal

The illustrations and the text reveal what would be missing if that letter was not in the alphabet, such as this reference to werewolf and watermelon (From The Disappearing Alphabet *by Richard Wilbur. Text copyright © 1998. Illustrations copyright © 1998 by David Diaz. Reprinted by permission of Harcourt.*

The letters of the alphabet are shown in animals. (From Animal Alphabet *by Bert Kitchen. Copyright © 1984 by Bert Kitchen. Reprinted by permission of Dial Books.)*

Rhymes." According to Richard Barsam (1978), it was written to teach reading. While Shaker teachers were strict disciplinarians, singing and dancing were part of children's school life. The rhyme and rhythm of these verses must have appealed to Shaker children, as they appeal to children today. The Provensens' charming illustrations show people engaged in typical Shaker occupations, wearing the dress of an earlier time in American history. Such historical alphabet books give contemporary children a sense of what life was like in the past because they share a reading and learning experience that children in earlier eras also enjoyed.

Animal Themes

The animal theme in the Shaker alphabet book is still very popular. Contemporary animal alphabet books range in complexity. Some show one letter and a single animal for each entry; some have a single letter, a single animal, and a rhyming phrase; some have very descriptive phrases with each letter; and some develop an integrated story in alphabetical order.

Mick Inkpen uses an alphabetical format as a dog, a pig, and a zebra take readers on an adventure in *Kipper's A to Z: An Alphabet Adventure.* Cartoonlike illustrations help develop the humor in the tale.

Roger Tory Peterson's ABC of Birds: A Book for Little Birdwatchers includes text by Linda Westervelt, paintings by Roger Tory Peterson, and photographs by Seymour Levin. The text for each bird includes a large uppercase letter, a short description, and either a painting or a photograph.

For example, the text on the *O* page states: "O is for Owl. In the night, sharp eyes and ears watch and listen. 'Whoo, whoo, whoo' " (unnumbered).

Interaction with text is also encouraged in Arthur Geisert's *Pigs from A to Z.* In this detailed text, each letter is introduced by one or two sentences. Full-page illustrations depict pigs performing the accompanying actions. Within each illustration are hidden several examples of the specific letter as well as the letter that precedes the applicable letter and the letter that follows it. The book concludes with a key so that readers may verify the locations of the letters within the picture puzzle.

Mary Beth Owens's *A Caribou Alphabet* is unusual because the illustrations and alphabetical order reveal information about one of the large wild animals. The text begins "A caribou's antlers can grow mighty large/Bulls spar in the autumn to see who's in charge" (unnumbered). Each page continues with a letter, an illustration, and a rhyming text that highlights a word beginning with that letter.

Ann Jonas's *Aardvarks, Disembark!* focuses on endangered and now-extinct animals as they leave the ark. Jonas pictures the animals in reverse alphabetical order, proceeding from zebus to aoudads. A glossary in the back of the book defines the animals and indicates whether the animals are endangered or are extinct.

Cathi Hepworth's *Antics!* is another unusual animal ABC for older children. Each of the words illustrated from A to Z has the word *ant* somewhere within the word. For example, a wizard ant illustrates an ench*ant*er for the let-

F l a m b o y a n t

The alphabetical order is based on words containing ant.
("Flamboyant" from Antics! *by Cathi Hepworth, copyright © 1992 by Catherine Hepworth. Reprinted by permission of G. P. Putnam's Sons.)*

ter *E.* Adults who work with older children indicate that this book provides an interesting motivation for writing ABC books that use a similar approach.

Other Alphabet Books

In *Firefighters A to Z,* Chris L. Demarest uses a rhyming format to convey concepts related to firefighting. For example, the text on the *H* page reads: "H is for Hoses and Hydrants we need." The illustrations drawn in pastels depict the action associated with each letter.

Food and ogres provide the subjects in Nicholas Heller's *Ogres! Ogres! Ogres!: A Feasting Frenzy from A to Z,* illustrated by Jos A. Smith. Each illustration and text include the major letter plus the next letter in the alphabet, as found in "Dermot dispatches deviled eggs" and "Fergusen flips frogs' legs on the griddle" (unnumbered).

Two award-winning alphabet books provide opportunities for careful observation and comparisons. For example, Stephen T. Johnson's *Alphabet City* presents the letters through paintings of city scenes. Viewers look carefully to discover letters such as *p* as part of a handrail or *v* as part of the structure on an electric transmission pole. David Pelletier's *The Graphic Alphabet* presents each of the letters through the interpretations of a graphic designer. In the illustrator's note, Pelletier states that the book grew

out of his interest in letterforms: "Expanding on a traditional form for children, the alphabet book, he decided that the illustration of the letterform had to retain the natural shape of the letter as well as represent the meaning of the word" (unnumbered). Viewers will observe this relationship through examples such as a *y* that is yawning and an *f* that is burning with a fire.

A buying excursion in an old-fashioned market provides an enjoyable trip through the alphabet in Arnold Lobel's *On Market Street,* illustrated by Anita Lobel. The child buys gifts from the shopkeepers: apples, books, clocks, doughnuts, . . . and finally zippers. The colorful illustrations help children develop concepts as they see and discuss the goods offered for sale. Lois Ehlert's *Eating the Alphabet: Fruits and Vegetables from A to Z* is another theme approach to introducing the alphabet to young children.

Suse MacDonald's *Alphabatics* is an extremely creative alphabet book. The illustrator uses a series of pictures that proceed from the original letter to an object that represents the letter. For example, the *A* proceeds from a drawing of a capital *A,* to an *A* tilted on blue waves, to an *A* upside down on the waves, to an *A* turned into an ark, and finally to an ark filled with animals. This book can be used to motivate children's drawings of similar examples.

Alphabet books by Betsy Bowen, Jim Aylesworth, Oscar de Mejo, and Cynthia Chin-Lee are organized around specific locations. Bowen's *Antler, Bear, Canoe: A Northwoods Alphabet Year* follows the seasons in the Northwoods of Minnesota, beginning in January and proceeding into the following winter. The woodblock prints depict activities such as kayaking in spring, watching northern lights in summer, and taking part in potluck dinners of grouse and wild rice in the autumn. Aylesworth's *The Folks in the Valley: A Pennsylvania Dutch ABC* is illustrated with pictures depicting the Pennsylvania Dutch heritage. De Mejo's *Oscar de Mejo's ABC* depicts an earlier time in United States history. Chin-Lee's *A Is for Asia* presents information about Asia.

The Z Was Zapped by Chris Van Allsburg also encourages interaction between the text and readers. Van Allsburg presents the alphabet in the form of a twenty-six-act play. Each act is a letter being treated to some action that begins with that sound. For example, the play is introduced with the letter *A* as it is bombarded with falling rocks. Readers become involved because they must turn the page to discover that Act 1 is "The A was in an Avalanche." Teachers may encourage writing by asking students to create their own descriptions of each act.

 Technology Resources

Use the database to generate a list of alphabet books by searching under the topic *alphabet.* **You can limit your search to a specific age range by adding the appropriate grade to the Grade Level field.**

Eve Merriam's *Halloween ABC,* an alphabet poetry book for older students, uses the ABC format to introduce poems about Halloween topics. For example, the *K* page has an illustration of the letter *K* and a key. The accompanying poem is about a key that opens a mysterious gate that in turn leads to adventure. This poem is another selection that may stimulate writing. Students may write a second verse to the key poem to reveal what happens when they find the key that spells "Follow me." Rhythmic verse also provides the focus for Bill Martin, Jr., and John Archambault's ABC, *Chicka Chicka Boom Boom.*

Several alphabet books are designed to provide information to older students rather than to teach letter/sound relationships to younger ones. Two award-winning books present information about African life. Margaret Musgrove's *Ashanti to Zulu: African Traditions,* vividly illustrated by Leo and Diane Dillon, depicts the customs of twenty-six African peoples. *Jambo Means Hello: Swahili Alphabet Book,* by Muriel Feelings, introduces Swahili words and customs. These beautiful books can encourage children of all cultural backgrounds to learn more about African people. Jonathan Hunt's *Illuminations* focuses on the people and events of the Middle Ages, alphabetically presenting terms such as *Excalibur, falconry,* and *Grail.* The book makes an interesting accompaniment for English legends such as those about King Arthur.

Bruce Whatley and Rosie Smith's *Whatley's Quest* includes illustrations of numerous objects that begin with the sound. A secret scroll on the inside of the dust jacket provides a guide through this colorful alphabet. For example, the guide for the *Q* page: "Sitting on the quay is a Queen. The Queen wants to join the treasure hunt, and she is using a quill to chart her course. She is in a quandary about where to look for the treasure, though, so one of the Quintuplets is telling the other four to be quiet so the Queen can think" (inside dust jacket).

Counting Books

Counting books, like alphabet books, are often used for specific educational purposes. To develop one-to-one correspondence and ability to count sequentially from one through ten, a counting book should contain easily identifiable numbers and corresponding objects. Effective number books for young children usually show one large number, the word for the number, and the appropriate number of objects—all on one page or on facing pages. The actual number represented should be clear. For example, one star showing five points may be a poor choice for depicting the number five, since children may not understand that five, not one, is being depicted.

Books that stimulate the manipulation of concrete objects are especially useful. For example, a counting book showing the number two and two blocks might encourage a young child to count two real blocks. One very sim-

Anta Lobel presents concepts related to counting, the months of the year, the days of the week, and colors. (From One Lighthouse, One Moon. *Copyright © 2000 by Greenwillow Books. Reprinted by permission of the publisher.)*

ple counting book for young children, Eric Carle's wordless *My Very First Book of Numbers,* is designed so that children can easily match numbered squares with their corresponding illustrations.

Counting books for children may stimulate language development and interaction with the text. In *Roll Over!* Mordicai Gerstein uses a nursery rhyme, fold-out flaps, and humorous illustrations to involve children in counting the number of people in a bed. In Molly Bang's *Ten, Nine, Eight,* an African American father and child observe objects and then say a rhythmic counting lullaby that proceeds backward from ten to one until the drowsy child is ready for bed.

Bénédicte Guettier's *The Father Who Had 10 Children* focuses on counting the ten children and activities associated with them. Suse MacDonald's *Look Whooo's Counting* combines careful observation as an owl flies through a moonlit landscape. Each turn of the page reveals a group of animals whose numbers match the numbers from one to ten.

Readers find many opportunities to apply their counting skills as found in this illustration from Emily's First 100 Days of School. *(From* Emily's First 100 Days of School *by Rosemary Wells. Copyright © 2000 by Rosemary Wells. Reprinted by permission of Hyperion Books for Children.)*

Christopher Gunson's *Over On the Farm: A Counting Picture Book Rhyme,* another book for young children, uses farm animals and rhyming text to develop numbers from one through ten. Language is also a strength in Vic Parker's *Bearobics: A Hip-Hop Counting Story.* The text uses a hip-hop beat, alliteration, and onomatopoeia.

One Hole in the Road, by W. Nikola-Lisa and illustrated by Dan Yaccarino, uses the idea of a tremendous hole that requires such counting concepts as four flashing stoplights, five sirens, and six engineers to try to control the situation. Young children enjoy the action in this setting with its vivid colors.

Some books develop both observational skills and counting abilities. Arthur Geisert's *Pigs from 1 to 10* encourages children to find the numbers and count the pigs that are hidden within the illustrations. This counting book includes a story line in which the ten pigs go on a quest to find a lost land. There is a key to the location of the numbers in the back of the book.

Counting books for older children may develop the concept of numbers, addition, or subtraction, or they may encourage children to search for many groups of the same number on a single page. You should consider children's abilities so that you select books of appropriate difficulty.

Count and See and *26 Letters and 99 Cents*, by Tana Hoban, are simple counting books with easy-to-identify number concepts that also extend to sets and higher numbers. In *Count and See*, each number, its corresponding written word, and a circle or circles illustrating the number appear in white on a black background. On the opposite page, a photograph illustrates the number with things found in the environments of many children: one fire hydrant, two children, . . . twenty watermelon seeds, . . . forty peanuts shown in groups of ten, . . . and one hundred peas shown in pods of ten each. The book may also be used for counting and grouping concrete items. (Counting and grouping aid cognitive development.) This book may be used as either a counting book or an alphabet book. In one direction, the illustrations and text emphasize counting, and in the other direction it is an alphabet book.

Emily's First 100 Days of School by Rosemary Wells introduces the numbers from one to one hundred through various activities associated with a young bunny as she experiences her days at school. The numbers are introduced as the teacher tells the class that each morning they will learn a new number and create their own number notebook. Some of the activities are associated with school ("There are nine planets in our solar system"), while others relate to home ["I collect twenty-five Japanese beetles from the garden"]. (unnumbered).

Handtalk Birthday: A Number & Story Book in Sign Language, by Remy Charlip, Mary Beth Miller, and George Ancona, presents an unusual story. It is about a surprise party for a deaf woman. Photographs show the characters using sign language as the woman guesses the contents of her presents and the guests question her about her age.

Muriel Feelings's *Moja Means One: Swahili Counting Book* is the counting-book partner to her Swahili alphabet book. Each two-page spread provides a numeral from one to ten, the Swahili word for the number, a detailed illustration (by Tom Feelings) that depicts animal or village life in Africa, and a sentence describing the contents of the illustration. This book may be more appropriate for stimulating interest in an African culture or providing information for older children than for presenting number concepts to younger children.

Counting concepts in English and Spanish are reinforced in Ginger Foglesong Guy's *¡Fiesta!* The text develops counting and vocabulary concepts as children go through a village gathering items for a fiesta. The items eventually become the objects in a piñata, which is broken during the party.

Jim Haskins's *Count Your Way Through Italy* is part of the "Count Your Way Through" series of counting books. Haskins develops counting concepts from one through ten in Italian. He then provides background information about Italian culture and geography. Beth Wright's illustrations depict the numbers and the text for such things as Mount Etna

Ashley Bryan uses poetry to develop a unique alphabet book. *(From* Ashley Bryan's ABC of African American Poetry. *Illustrations copyright © 1997 by Ashley Bryan. Published by Atheneum Books for Young Readers. Reprinted by permission.)*

(one), the products for which Italy is known (nine), and the horses that are chosen to race in the Corsa del Palio (ten). Additional books in this series provide counting opportunities through Africa, the Arab world, Canada, China, Germany, Japan, Korea, Mexico, and Russia.

Counting books may also be written for older students. *The History of Counting* by Denise Schmandt-Besserat is a fascinating book that describes the evolution of counting, including examples of body counting, concrete counting, and abstract counting.

Concept Books

Many of the books recommended for use in stimulating the cognitive development of children are concept books. These books rely on well-chosen illustrations to help children grasp both relatively easy concepts, such as *red* and *circle,* and more abstract concepts (which may be difficult for children to comprehend), such as prepositions (*through,* for example) and antonyms (*fast* and *slow,* for example). Like counting books, concept books come in various degrees of difficulty, so teachers should consider a child's level of understanding when selecting concept books.

Numerous books have been designed to help young children learn basic concepts, such as colors and shapes.

ISSUE Picture Books and Controversy

Several books discussed in this chapter have stirred controversy and subsequently have been removed from library shelves. Other books have had illustrations altered to meet specific standards.

In the 1960s, Garth Williams's *The Rabbit's Wedding* was criticized because the illustrations showed the marriage of a black rabbit and a white rabbit. In 1969, William Steig's *Sylvester and the Magic Pebble* was criticized because some parents objected to his portrayal of police officers as pigs and others objected to his having the mother do housework while Sylvester and his father relaxed.

When Maurice Sendak's *In the Night Kitchen* was published in 1970, some parents, teachers, and librarians deplored the child's nudity. In several incidents, the nudity was covered with a drawn-on washcloth or the book was removed from the shelf. In the 1970s, too, some people criticized *Changes, Changes,* by Pat Hutchins, because the man has a more active role than does the woman. He drives and decides what to make from the blocks, while the woman pulls the train whistle and hands him the blocks.

One book not discussed in this chapter illustrates the changing sensitivities of Americans toward certain social issues. Helen Ban-nerman's *Little Black Sambo* (1899) was popular for many years. Eventually, however, many people considered the crudely drawn features of the characters and the story line to be offensive, and the book was taken off many library shelves.

As you evaluate picture books, consider which books might be controversial and the reasons for the controversy. Does controversy change with the times? What subjects might have caused controversy in picture books published in the 1950s, 1960s, 1970s, 1980s, or 1990s? Are those subjects still controversial? Are any new areas of controversy developing today?

Eric Carle's *My Very First Book of Colors* is a simple, wordless book that asks a child to match a block of color with the picture of an object illustrated in that color. In *Of Colors and Things,* Tana Hoban uses both colors and photographs of objects to invite children to search for matching colors. In *Circles, Triangles, and Squares,* Hoban uses large black-and-white photographs to show common shapes in everyday objects. In *Shapes, Shapes, Shapes,* she uses photographs to depict such shapes as circles, rectangles, and ovals. Photographs also depict shapes in Hoban's *So Many Circles, So Many Squares.* These books also encourage readers to look for similar shapes in their own environments. In *Over, Under and Through and Other Spatial Concepts,* Tana Hoban uses photographs that show children jumping *over* fire hydrants, walking *under* outstretched arms, and crawling *through* large pipes.

Pat Hutchins's *What Game Shall We Play?* presents concepts in a game format. Readers follow the various animals across the fields, among the grasses, over the wall, and into the hole. Sally Noll's *Watch Where You Go* follows a gray mouse through the grass, up a tree, along branches, down vines, between rocks, into marsh grass, and into a hole that is home. This trip is not as easy as it might appear, however. The journey includes going through, along, and down many areas that are dangerous for the mouse.

Donald Crews familiarizes children with various concepts in *Freight Train.* The cars of the train are different colors, and the movement of the train *across* trestles, *through* cities, and *into* tunnels encourages understanding of spatial concepts and of opposites, such as *darkness* and *daylight.* Trains fascinate many young children, and children eagerly learn concepts while enjoying the colors, movements, and sounds developed in this book. Brian Floca uses trucks at an airport in *Five Trucks* to introduce concepts associated with trucks such as *large* and *heavy, small* and *quick,* and *long* and *straight.* The activities of trucks are shown as airplanes are prepared for takeoff.

Anne Rockwell helps children understand seasonal changes and appropriate activities for each season in *First Comes Spring,* while Lisa Westberg Peters in *October Smiled Back* uses the twelve months of the year to help readers understand concepts related to changes in nature. Nancy Tafuri encourages concept and language development with large illustrations of animals in her almost wordless book *Early Morning in the Barn.* These concept books and others offer children pleasure as well as important learning experiences.

Wordless Books

In a newer type of picture book, the illustrations tell the whole story, without words. Children enjoy the opportunity to provide the missing text for wordless books—an excellent way of developing their oral and written language skills. Wordless books stimulate creative thinking and enhance visual literacy abilities, because children must watch the pages for clues to the action. Wordless books are especially valuable because they allow children of different backgrounds and reading levels to enjoy the same book.

Wordless books have various degrees of detail and plot complexity. Some contain much detail, while others do not. Some develop easily identifiable plots, while others can be interpreted in many different ways. Some are large, making them appropriate for sharing with a group, while others are small, easily held by one child or one adult with a child in the lap. You should consider all of these characteristics when choosing wordless books for children of different ages, reading levels, and interests.

Pat Hutchins's *Changes, Changes* is a simple wordless book that appeals to children in preschool and kindergarten who enjoy building with blocks. The illustrations show two wooden dolls building a house of blocks, coping with a fire by turning the house into a fire truck, solving the problem of too much water by building a boat, reaching land by constructing a truck, and eventually rebuilding their home. The large and colorful pictures make actions easily identifiable. The book stimulates oral language, as well as problem solving and manipulation of children's own blocks.

Realistic humor is a popular theme of wordless books for young children. A series of wordless books by Mercer Mayer shows the humorous adventures of a boy, a dog, and a frog. *Frog Goes to Dinner*—the most detailed book in the series and, to many children, the funniest— illustrates the humorous disruptions that can occur if a frog hides in a boy's pocket and accompanies a family to a fancy restaurant. Each of Mayer's books is small, just the right size for individual enjoyment or for sharing with an adult. The illustrations are expressive and contain sufficient detail to stimulate language development and enjoyment.

Several wordless books develop plots involving the antics of animals from the world of fantasy. John S. Goodall's *Paddy Under Water* follows Paddy Pork as he dives underwater and discovers a sunken ship. Emily Arnold McCully's *Picnic* follows a family of mice as they jubilantly go on a picnic, unhappily discover that a small mouse is missing, and joyfully reunite the whole family. McCully's *School* follows the same family as they experience common occurrences. The illustrations depict enough plot to stimulate the creation of narrative even by older children.

Peter Collington's *The Angel and the Soldier Boy* is a large-format book that can be viewed and discussed by groups of students. The wordless plot follows the actions in a young girl's dream. Her toy soldier and angel come to life and challenge the pirates who rob the girl's piggy bank, capture the soldier, and return to their ship on top of the piano. The illustrations include enough detail to stimulate storytelling.

Another dream sequence forms the plot in David Wiesner's *Free Fall*. This beautifully illustrated, wordless book takes the dreamer on a fantasy in which he explores uncharted lands. Interestingly, many of the objects that seem so real in his dream are by his bed when he awakes. Plots in wordless books frequently take characters on magical excursions. Wiesner's *Sector 7* encourages viewers to accompany a boy in a fantasy during which he discovers how clouds are shaped and sent throughout the country. In Lisa Maizlish's *The Ring,* a boy finds a magical object in a New York City park, puts it on, and flies through the air. Photographs follow the boy and reveal his adventures. Ask students to compare the influence of the illustrator's use of black-and-white and color photographs. In *Tuesday,* Wiesner uses the wordless format and glowing watercolors to create a book filled with surprising and unexpected elements. Readers enjoy not only creating their own story to accompany the illustrations but also extending the book into the next Tuesday. Wiesner's final illustration shows the following Tuesday, when the pigs have their opportunity to fly, to explore the neighborhood, and to baffle the people.

The sequential organization and detail of the illustrations provide a story line that stimulates language development. (Illustration on unnumbered page 11 from Picnic *by Emily Arnold McCully. Copyright © 1984 by Emily Arnold McCully. Reprinted by permission of Harper & Row Publishers, Inc.)*

The book provides interesting stimuli for creative writing and illustrating, allowing students to create their own stories about "The Night the Pigs Could Fly."

Peter Spier's *Noah's Ark* is another excellent picture book. The only words occur at the beginning of the book. The pictures show the building of the ark, the boarding of the animals, the long wait, and the starting of life again on the land, which is plowed and cultivated. The pictures contain so much detail that children can discover something new each time they read the book.

Jeannie Baker's *Window* is an exceptional example of collage illustrations that explore textures found in various settings. The illustrations use a window to show the changes that occur in an Australian neighborhood. These changes, which are shown through the growth of a child and the changing view from the window, also develop a strong environmental theme: People affect the environment. By tracing the changes, the artist shows how rapidly a community can change from rural to urban and investigates the possible consequences of moving to a rural area again. The artist reinforces the theme through her endnotes when she states, "By understanding and changing the way we personally affect the environment, we can make a difference."

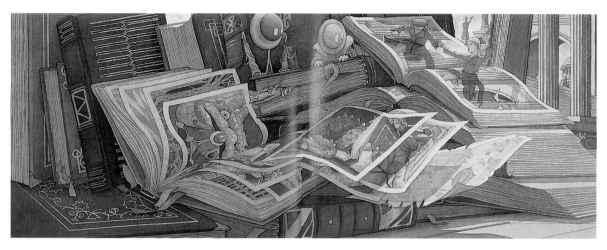

The illustrations show the dream world of the boy in **Free Fall** *by David Wiesner. (Illustration by David Wiesner from* **Free Fall** *by David Wiesner. Copyright © 1988 by David Wiesner. Reprinted by permission of Lothrop, Lee and Shepard Books, a division of William Morrow & Co., Inc.)*

Several beautifully illustrated wordless books by Mitsumasa Anno also encourage oral discussion and storytelling by older children. The detailed drawings in *Anno's Journey,* for example, are the result of the artist's travels through the countryside, villages, and larger towns of Europe. Anno adds to the enjoyment by suggesting that readers look for certain details in the pictures, such as paintings and characters from children's literature. The pictures are detailed enough to keep even adults occupied. The illustrations in Peter Sís's *Dinosaur!* provide opportunities for children to identify specific types of dinosaurs as a young boy takes his toy dinosaur into the tub only to be joined by many other dinosaurs. The dinosaurs are identified inside the front and back covers.

One enticing, almost wordless book is Chris Van Allsburg's *The Mysteries of Harris Burdick.* A title and a one-line caption precede each picture. In the introduction to the book, Van Allsburg asks readers to provide the missing stories. Teachers and librarians report that the illustrations contain enough elements of mystery and fantasy to motivate excellent oral and written stories.

Many wordless books are ideal for promoting oral language development. Others, however, are so obscure in story line that children may be frustrated when asked to tell the story. When choosing wordless books, consider the questions posed in the Evaluation Criteria box on this page.

The varied levels of complexity found in wordless books indicate that wordless books are appropriate for young children as well as older ones. This same complexity, however, means that adults must select the materials carefully. As an example of the differences in wordless books and relationships with age, compare wordless books for young readers such as those by Mercer Mayer with Tom Feelings's *The Middle Passage: White Ships/Black Cargo,* a wordless book about the slave trade.

EVALUATION CRITERIA

Selecting High-Quality Wordless Books

1. Is there a sequentially organized plot that provides a framework for children who are just developing their own organizational skills?

2. Is the depth of detail appropriate for the age level of the children? (Too much detail will overwhelm younger children, while not enough detail may bore older ones.)

3. Do the children have enough experiential background to understand and interpret the illustrations? Can they interpret the book during individual reading, or is adult interaction necessary?

4. Is the size of the book appropriate for the purpose? (Larger books are necessary for group sharing.)

5. Will the subject appeal to the children?

Easy-to-Read Books

Easy-to-read books are designed to be read by children with beginning reading skills. These beginner books serve as transitions between basal readers and library trade books. Like picture storybooks, these books contain many pictures designed to suggest the story line. Unlike picture storybooks, however, the vocabulary is controlled so that young readers can manage independently. Controlling the vocabulary to fit the needs of beginning readers may result in contrived language, however, because it is difficult to write stories that sound natural if all of the words must be selected from the easiest level of readability.

Authors, teachers, and librarians use several different readability formulas to determine the approximate level of reading skill required to read a book. The Fry Readability Formula (Fry, 1977), for example, measures the reading level by finding the average number of sentences and syllables per hundred words. These averages are plotted on a graph that identifies the corresponding grade level for the book. Readability experts assume that easier books have shorter sentences and more monosyllabic words. As the reading level becomes higher, the sentences become longer and multisyllabic words become more numerous.

Compare the readability of an easy-to-read book and another picture storybook. A one hundred-word selection from one popular easy-to-read book, Dr. Seuss's *The Cat in the Hat,* shows sixteen sentences and one hundred syllables for those one hundred words. The sentences are very short and all words are of one syllable. Plotting these two findings on the Fry graph indicates a first-grade reading level. In contrast, a picture storybook also written for first-grade interests by Dr. Seuss, *And to Think That I Saw It on Mulberry Street,* has seven and one-half sentences and 126 syllables in a one hundred-word selection. The reading level for this book is fifth grade. While both books appeal to children of about the same age, children themselves usually read the first book, and adults usually read the second to children.

Even though easy-to-read books may not meet all standards for literary quality, they may meet the needs of beginning readers. Because children need experiences with books that allow them to reinforce their reading skills independently and to develop pride in their accomplishments, you should include easy-to-read books in every book collection for primary-age children. Easy-to-read books are also helpful to students who need successful experiences in remedial reading classes. Because of controlled use of language and sentence structure, easy-to-read books are less appropriate for adults to read aloud to children, although children may enjoy reading them aloud to appreciative adults.

Animal antics appeal to young children, and many favorite easy-to-read books have animals as the main characters. In Dr. Seuss's *The Cat in the Hat,* a cat amazes and entertains two children when he balances a fish bowl, a bottle of milk, and a cake simultaneously. Dr. Seuss's humorous illustrations and rhyming dialogue appeal to children. The cat emphasizes this enjoyment:

> Look at me!
> Look at me!
> Look at me Now!
> It is fun to have fun
> But you have to know how. (p. 8)

Arnold Lobel has written and illustrated several enchanting easy-to-read books. The soft brown and green illustrations in Lobel's stories about Frog and Toad recreate the atmosphere of a woodland setting and show

Humorous illustrations enhance an unexpected experience in a favorite easy-to-read book. (*From* The Cat in the Hat, *by Dr. Seuss. TM and copyright © 1957 and renewed 1989 by Dr. Seuss Enterprises, L.P. Reprinted by permission of Random House, Inc.*)

the friendship felt by these two characters. In *Frog and Toad Are Friends,* Frog tries to entice Toad out of his home in order to enjoy the new spring season. Children enjoy Toad's reactions when Frog knocks on the door:

> "Toad, Toad," shouted Frog,
> "wake up. It is spring!"
> "Blah," said a voice
> from inside the house.

In Lobel's *Grasshopper on the Road,* a curious insect decides to follow a winding country lane just to discover where it leads. Lobel's characterization is fuller than that found in many other easy-to-read books. Lobel has the grasshopper encounter the rural inhabitants and then try to change their behaviors.

Easy-to-read books may be series books, such as those written by Cynthia Rylant. Rylant includes several books in her Henry and Mudge series. *Henry and Mudge and the Happy Cat* develops the new relationship between the dog Mudge and a stray cat. *Henry and Mudge and the Bedtime Thumps* is set in Grandmother's house in the country. A strange noise shows Henry and Mudge that it is better to be together during scary times. In *Henry and Mudge and the Long Weekend,* Rylant tells a warm story in which boredom and "February cranks" are overcome by creating a castle out of large boxes. An elderly man and an old yellow-and-white cat develop a strong companionship in *Mr. Putter and Tabby Pour the Tea* and *Mr. Putter and Tabby Walk the Dog. Poppleton* includes stories about a pig. Rylant's easy-to-read books are unique because of their interesting stories and their descriptive language.

Charlotte Pomerantz's "I Can Read Book" *Outside Dog* takes place in a Puerto Rican neighborhood. Pomerantz has incorporated Spanish words and phrases into the text. Short, scary stories are found in both Edward Marshall's *Four on the Shore* and Alvin Schwartz's *In a Dark, Dark Room.*

Ready ... Set ... Read! is an anthology of easy-to-read stories, poems, and games compiled by Joanna Cole and Stephanie Calmenson. The stories are written by such well-known authors as Dr. Seuss, Else Minarik, Arnold Lobel, Joanna Cole, and Bernard Wiseman. This anthology lets students of children's literature analyze and compare several sources of this type of literature.

Picture Storybooks

A characteristic common to many picture books discussed thus far is the use of illustrations to present all or most of the content of a book. Reliance on pictures is especially crucial in concept books, counting books, a majority of the alphabet books, and all wordless picture books. Many of these books do not have continuous story lines; instead, the illustrations are grouped according to common themes or are presented in numerical or alphabetical sequence.

Although picture storybooks contain many illustrations, they also develop strong story lines in text. In a well-written picture storybook, the text and narrative complement each other, so children cannot deduce the whole story merely by viewing the pictures. The illustrations are integral to the story line, enhancing the actions, settings, and characterizations (Norton, 1993).

Elements in Picture Storybooks

When adults think about enjoyable book experiences shared by adults and children during story hour or at bedtime, they usually remember picture storybooks. Childhood would be less exciting without friends like Mike Mulligan, Frances the badger, and Ferdinand the bull. What makes some books so memorable for both children and adults? Originality and imagination are crucial in outstanding picture books, but so are strong plot, characterization, setting, theme, style, and humor.

Originality and Imagination. A man and his dog discover that "Paradise lost is sometimes Heaven found"; a young man goes to a fortune teller and discovers that the predictions about his future can come true; and a child's bedroom becomes the kingdom of wild things. Some adults

never lose touch with the dreams, fears, and fantasies of childhood and, as authors of picture storybooks for children, they create imaginative new worlds in which the impossible becomes both real and believable.

In *Hey, Al,* Arthur Yorinks's plot helps a janitor and his dog find a more satisfying way of life. Through experience in a beautiful location, where they do not need to work, they discover that beautiful places can have dangerous secrets.

In *The Fortune-Tellers,* Lloyd Alexander develops the story of a young carpenter who is unhappy with his life. When he seeks a fortune teller to reveal what will happen in his life, he discovers that his life will change in unexpected ways. In humorous dialogue, the fortune teller gives the carpenter his wishes. For example, when the carpenter asks, "Do you see me rich, then?" the fortune teller answers, "Rich you will surely be. . . . On one condition: that you earn large sums of money" (p. 5, unnumbered). After the seer mysteriously disappears, the carpenter discovers an unexpected way for the prophesies to come true. Older readers will also enjoy the irony in the conclusion.

A child's imagination structures the delightful story in Maurice Sendak's *Where the Wild Things Are.* Only in such fantasy can young children who have been disciplined turn their rooms into kingdoms inhabited by other wild things like themselves and then return home in safety before their suppers get cold.

The moral in *Joseph Had a Little Overcoat* by Simms Taback states: "You can always make something out of nothing . . . over and over again!" (unnumbered). In this humorous and imaginative story, the main character keeps recycling his old overcoat into smaller and smaller objects until he loses the final object. But all is not lost because he makes a book about it which proves "You can always make something out of nothing."

Picture storybooks and their accompanying illustrations are filled with many imaginative episodes. They provide hours of enjoyment and are excellent for stimulating children's imaginations during creative play, storytelling, and creative writing.

Plot. The short attention spans of children who read or hear picture storybooks place special demands on plot development. The plots of picture storybooks are usually simple, clearly developed, and brief. They involve few subplots or secondary characters. Such plots usually allow young children to become involved with the action, identify the problem, and solve it rapidly.

For example, in the first three pages of Maurice Sendak's *Where the Wild Things Are,* children know that Max is in so much trouble that he has been sent to bed without supper. Even though the thirty-seven words used thus far do not reveal what Max has done, the pictures explain his problems. Children see him standing on books, hammering nails into the wall, and chasing the dog with a fork. The plot is swiftly paced, and children rapidly join

The original plot suggests that beautiful places may be dangerous. (Illustrations from Hey, Al *by Arthur Yorinks. Illustrated by Richard Egielski. Illustrations copyright © 1986 by Richard Egielski. Reprinted by permission of Farrar, Straus & Giroux, Inc.)*

Max in his imaginary world, as the room becomes wilder and wilder.

Sendak introduces additional conflict and excitement when Max encounters the wild things and overcomes them with a magic trick. Children empathize with Max when he has played long enough, sends his new subjects off to bed, and returns home to his mother's love and his supper. The author uses only thirty-eight words to tell what happens between the time Max leaves the wild things and returns home. This book is an excellent example of the important relationship between illustrations and plot development; the illustrations become larger and larger as the drama increases and then become smaller again as Max returns to his everyday life.

It is interesting to compare Sendak's illustrations and Richard Egielski's illustrations for *Hey, Al.* Both illustrators increase the sizes of their illustrations as conflict develops, use two-page spreads at the height of interest, and include much information about characters and settings within the illustrations.

Some picture books have plots that are very similar to those found in folktales. For example, in Brock Cole's humorous *Buttons,* three daughters are asked to go on a quest in search of buttons to replace those destroyed when their father pops the buttons on his britches. The eldest seeks a husband who will give her buttons in exchange for her hand in marriage. The second decides to join the army to find buttons on a soldier's uniform. The youngest runs through a meadow with her apron held before her, expecting buttons to drop from the sky. As in many humorous folktales it is the least likely plan that brings buttons to the father and happiness to the family.

Other picture books deal with children's problems in more realistic plots. In *Like Jake and Me,* Mavis Jukes por-trays the strained relationship between Alex and his big, powerful stepfather, Jake, who refuses to allow Alex to help with various chores. When a large, hairy spider crawls into Jake's clothes, Alex discovers that even a powerful, ex-rodeo cowboy can be afraid, and Jake discovers that even a small boy can provide assistance. In Ana Zamorano's *Let's Eat!* a boy experiences grown-up responsibilities when Mama is expecting a baby.

Whether a plot is based on fantasy or realism, it usually involves a rapid introduction to the action, a fast pace, and a strong, emotionally satisfying climax. In Patricia Polacco's *Thunder Cake,* a grandmother and her grand-daughter assemble a special cake as a thunderstorm grows nearer. These actions help the girl realize that she is brave enough to face the storm. In *Yo! Yes?,* Chris Raschka uses only thirty-four words to show the beginning of friendship when an African American boy and a white boy meet on the street. Their brief exchanges, accompanied by cartoonlike illustrations, show many universal feelings and emotions as the two boys become acquainted.

Characterization. The characters in picture storybooks must have specific traits that make them appealing to young children and that meet the demands of the short format. Since a short story does not allow for the fully developed characters that older children and adults prefer, the characters in picture storybooks must experience situations and emotions immediately familiar and credible to the children.

Maurice Sendak, for example, did not need to describe Max, the wild things, or the rumpus that takes place between them. His illustrations show these effectively. Likewise, Stephen Gammell's illustrations for Karen Ackerman's *Song and Dance Man* re-create the magic of vaudeville and express the love between grandchildren and their grandfather.

Any child can understand the feelings of Judith Viorst's hero in *Alexander and the Terrible, Horrible, No Good, Very Bad Day.* Alexander wakes up with gum in his hair, does not get a prize in his cereal when everyone else does, receives reprimands from his teacher, loses his best friend, has a cavity filled by the dentist, gets into trouble for making a mess in his dad's office, has to eat lima beans for dinner, and is ignored by the cat, who goes to sleep with his brother. In this book, as in most picture storybooks, the illustrations supplement the characterizations in the text by showing the characters' actions and reactions.

Children can understand stories about loneliness and friendship. In *The Scarebird,* Sid Fleischman develops a story of friendship between a lonely older farmer and his creation of a lifelike scarecrow and then between the farmer and an equally lonely and homeless young farm worker. As the human friendship increases, the farmer takes needed objects from the scarecrow and gives them to the boy. In *Captain Snap and the Children of Vinegar Lane,* Roni Schotter's characters use friendship and thoughtfulness to change the life of a lonely older man. In *The Gardener,* both Sarah Stewart's text and David Small's illustrations show changes that may be brought to a city landscape and a scowling man through flowers.

Children frequently have close attachments with older people and want to hear more about their lives. Such a character is developed in Gloria Houston's *My Great-Aunt Arizona.* The tone of Houston's text and Susan Condie Lamb's illustrations develop the loving character of a woman who gave her life to teaching. Houston tells readers that although she never traveled from the Blue Ridge Mountains, she educated generations of children and touched their lives wherever they traveled. This book stimulates a strong response in adults. When using this book for the first time with adults (college students), the adults decided it would be a good book to give as a present to their favorite teacher.

Many storybooks contain animal characters that act and speak like humans. Margaret Wise Brown's *The Runaway Bunny* uses a credible little bunny to demonstrate a child's need for independence and love. The dialogue between the mother rabbit and the bunny stresses the bunny's desire to experience freedom by running away. Each time that he suggests ways to run away, however, the mother rabbit counters with actions that she would take to get him back. The love between the two animals is visible in the dialogue and pictures, and the bunny decides to stay with the mother who loves him.

Setting. In picture storybooks, as in all literature, setting is used to establish the location of a story in time and place, create a mood, clarify historical background if necessary, provide an antagonist, and emphasize symbolic meaning. Picture storybooks, however, strongly rely on illustrations

Children and an old man develop a warm relationship. (From Captain Snap and the Children of Vinegar Lane *by Roni Schotter, illustrated by Marcia Sewall. Copyright © 1989 by Roni Schotter, illustrations copyright © 1989 by Marcia Sewall. Reprinted by permission of Orchard Books.)*

to serve these functions. Many books, such as Judith Viorst's *Alexander and the Terrible, Horrible, No Good, Very Bad Day* and Vera Williams's *Something Special for Me,* take place in the familiar contemporary world of television sets, blue jeans, and shopping centers. Other books take place in locations or times unfamiliar to the readers.

Carole Byard's illustrations for Sherley Anne Williams's *Working Cotton* create the world of an African American child as she labors in the migrant farming fields of central California. Holly Meade's illustrations for Minfong Ho's *Hush! A Thai Lullaby* create the environment of rural Thailand.

Ronald Himler's illustrations for Byrd Baylor's *The Best Town in the World* show how important illustrations are for illuminating time in picture storybooks. The brief poetic text alone cannot describe the details of a turn-of-the-century general store, the warmth created by a kerosene lamp, and the many activities associated with a picnic celebration in the days when a picnic was a major social event. Rachel Isadora's illustrations for *Young Mozart* take readers back to the historical setting of the composer's youth.

Toshi Maruki's dramatically expressive illustrations for *Hiroshima No Pika (The Flash of Hiroshima)* clarify the horrifying nature of the story's antagonist and the mood as seven-year-old Mii confronts the consequences of atomic warfare on August 6, 1945. The colors are especially dramatic. Swirling red flames pass over fleeing people and animals. Black clouds cover huddling masses and destroyed buildings. The illustrations suggest both the setting as antagonist and a destructive, frightening mood.

In *The Wreck of the Zephyr,* Chris Van Allsburg's illustrations create a light mood, subtly mixing reality and make-believe. A boy who dreams of becoming the best sailor in the world experiences a calm sea sparkling with light and a star-studded night disturbed only by a magical ship flying through the sky. The illustrations in all such worthy picture storybooks enhance the times, places, conflicts, and moods of the stories.

Theme. The themes in picture storybooks for young children are closely related to children's needs and understandings. The importance of adjusting to new siblings and the need for security are popular themes in books. In *Darcy and Gran Don't Like Babies,* Jane Cutler uses a unique approach to help Darcy accept the new baby. When Gran arrives for a visit, Gran agrees with Darcy as they discuss what they do not like about babies. After they have a fun-filled day together, however, Gran gently helps Darcy understand that she will eventually like the baby.

In *Owen,* Kevin Henkes explores the need for security. The mouse child outmaneuvers his parents in their efforts to take away his security blanket, but in a very satisfying ending, the mother mouse cuts the blanket into handkerchiefs so that Owen can take his security with him wherever he goes. The need for love is a related theme developed in books such as Natalie Babbitt's *BUB: Or the Very Best Thing.* A young child lets his parents know that love is the best. A similar theme is developed in Mary Murphy's *I Like It When . . .* as a young penguin tells about happy shared experiences such as holding hands.

The importance of happy and secure moments between father and child provides the theme in Eileen Spinelli's *Night Shift Daddy.* Warm, loving relationships are shown as the father tucks the little girl in at night and then she tucks her father in bed when he comes home from work.

An understanding grandparent figure plays a key role in Patricia Polacco's *Babushka Baba Yaga.* Instead of the fearsome Russian witch, Polacco develops a kinder, gentler Baba Yaga, who learns to love Victor, a small boy in her care. Victor's devotion to her and Baba Yaga's actions when she saves Victor develop the themes that loving relationships between generations and tolerance when judging others are important.

Authors who develop conflicts usually develop the theme that overcoming fear is important. In *Lester's Dog,* Karen Hesse develops the theme as she introduces the fearful boy who was bitten by a neighbor's dog. With the help of a deaf friend, the boy bravely overcomes his fear and saves a homeless kitten. In *Mirette on the High Wire,* Emily Arnold McCully shows how debilitating fear can be. The heroine helps the Great Bellini, a former master wire walker, face and overcome his fear.

Themes related to friendship are also very important in picture storybooks. In *Santa Calls,* William Joyce develops a unique story set in Abilene, Texas, in 1908. Art Atchinson Aimesworth, his sister Esther, and his friend Spaulding discover a mysterious box left by Santa Claus. The directions accompanying the flying machine invite the children to join Santa at the North Pole. While at the North Pole, they not only meet Santa but also combat dark elves and an evil queen. Readers do not know why the children are asked by Santa to come to the North Pole until they read two letters that are folded and attached to the final two pages. The first letter, from Esther, is addressed to Santa: "You can send me toys if you like, but what I *really* wish for is for my brother Art to be my friend." The final letter, from Santa, states, "Such a rare and wonderful request could not be refused. I am glad our little adventure did the trick."

The importance of friendships during times of great stress is a theme found in storybooks set during World War II. In *The Butterfly* Patricia Polacco develops a close friendship between a Jewish girl and the daughter of a French family who protects and hides the Jewish family. The author's note stresses the importance of the French underground and resistance in helping Jewish families during the Nazi occupation.

The importance of friendships, the need to respect others, and the necessity for conducting wise negotiations are all important themes found in picture books. Peggy Rathmann's *Officer Buckle and Gloria* develops a theme about the importance of friendship as the story concludes with the safety tip, "Always Stick With Your Buddy!" (unnumbered). Both Lynn Reiser's *Best Friends Think Alike* and A. M. Monson's *Wanted: Best Friend* stress friendship, the obligations of friendship, and the often difficult task of sharing. The importance of getting along with one's neighbors and developing respect for and understanding of others is an important theme in Eve Bunting's *Smoky Night.* Conducting wise negotiations, using one's wits, and doing one's share of the work are developed in Janet Stevens's *Tops & Bottoms.*

Style. Because a picture storybook contains so few words, its author must select those words very carefully. In an interview with Carolyn Phelan (1993), author Mem Fox emphasizes the need for rhythm when writing for children. She states, "I think rhythm is important in all writing, but I think it's of particular importance in a picture book because of the deep-seated, collective unconscious need for rhythm" (p. 29). The presence of rhythm in many of the Mother Goose rhymes, discussed earlier, indicates just how important this rhythm is in books for young children. A storybook also must be designed to catch children's attention and to stimulate their interest when adults read the story aloud. Adults can evaluate the effectiveness of style by reading a storybook orally to themselves or to a child.

Authors of picture storybooks frequently use repetition of single words or phrases to create stronger impressions when the books are read aloud. African folktales, for example, sometimes repeat words several times. In Gail E. Haley's *A Story, a Story,* the Sky God describes Ananse, the tiny spider man, as "so small, so small, so small." Similar use of repetition conveys the impression of a dancing fairy and rain on a hornet's nest. Verna Aardema uses this form of repetition to make a strong statement stronger in *Why Mosquitoes Buzz in People's Ears.* When a mother owl finds her dead baby, she is "so sad, so sad, so sad." The night that doesn't end is described as "long, long, long."

Young children enjoy listening to words that create vivid images. In the preface to *A Story, a Story,* Gail Haley says that many African words are found in the book and asks readers to listen carefully to the sounds so they can tell what the words mean. Haley uses many unknown words to describe the movements of animals. A python slithers "wasawusu, wasawusu, wasawusu" down a rabbit hole; a rabbit bounds "krik, krik, krik" across an open space; and sticks go "purup, purup" as they are pulled out of the iguana's ears. Minfong Ho uses a similar style in *Hush! A Thai Lullaby* as the various animals are introduced with the sounds they might create. For example, a monkey goes "Jiak-jiak! Jiak-jiak!" and a water buffalo goes "MAAAU, MAAAU."

Careful word choice also creates evocative moods in well-written picture storybooks. In *The Seeing Stick,* Jane Yolen creates a mood of wonder as Hwei Ming, the unhappy, blind daughter of a Chinese emperor, "sees" her father for the first time:

She reached out and her fingers ran eagerly through his hair and down his nose and cheek and rested curiously on a tear they found there. And that was strange, indeed, for had not the emperor given up crying over such things when he ascended the throne? (p. 19, unnumbered)

Carefully chosen words allow readers or listeners to place themselves in the setting and to feel the mood, as in Michael Bedard's *Emily,* in which a young girl sits in Emily Dickinson's parlor and listens to her mother play the piano: "I sat upon the parlor chair. Still the music played—but now I felt it breathe. My hand felt in my pocket. I thought of sunlight dancing on the sun-room floor, of Father plucking petals, and of poetry" (p. 25, unnumbered).

Humor. Selecting and sharing books that contribute to merriment are major goals of any literature program. Research shows that humorous literature is particularly effective in attracting children to the pleasures of reading and writing. In a study of children's reading preferences, Dianne Monson and Sam Sebesta (1991) identified humor as a very important element in books preferred by children. They state:

Some forms of humor seem to have greatest appeal and perhaps are better understood by children in elementary and junior

high school than others. The totally ridiculous situation and humorous characters are well liked, as is the humor associated with exaggeration, a surprising event, and play on words. (p. 668)

Many elements in picture storybooks can cause children to laugh out loud. An investigation by Sue Anne Martin (1969) concluded that humor in books awarded the Caldecott Medal had five general sources: (1) word play and nonsense, (2) surprise and the unexpected, (3) exaggeration, (4) the ridiculous and caricatures, and (5) superiority.

Word Play and Nonsense. Theodor Geisel, better known as Dr. Seuss, is one of the most popular authors of books for children and was an undisputed authority on word play and nonsense. Dr. Seuss often made up totally new words and names to describe the animals found in his imagination. In *Good Zap, Little Grog* Sarah Wilson uses a style similar to that of Dr. Seuss. Wilson creates new words for her story in rhyme. Here little Grog must "zoodle opp," the "ooglets are tuzzling," and "smibblets are giggling." A "Grog Guide" at the end of the book reveals the identity of the various animals in this fantasy world.

In Seuss's *If I Ran the Zoo,* Gerald McGrew's imaginary zoological garden contains an elephant-cat, a bird known as a Bustard, a beast called Flustard, and bugs identified as thwerlls and chugs. Of course, no one could find such animals in the usual jungles, so Gerald must search for them in Motta-fa-Potta-fa-Pell, in the wilds of Nantasket, and on the Desert of Zind. Children enjoy not only the nonsense found in the rhyming text but also the nonsensical illustrations of these strange animals.

Bill Peet's nonsense rhymes and nonsensical illustrations in *No Such Things* appeal to children. Peet uses both internal and end-of-line rhyming to create text such as the following:

The blue-snouted Twumps feed entirely on weeds,
And along with the weeds they swallow the seeds.
Eating seeds causes weeds to sprout on their backs,
Till they look very much like walking haystacks. (p. 5)

Surprise and the Unexpected. Both Audrey Wood's text and Mark Teague's illustrations in *The Flying Dragon Room* create surprise and the unexpected. In this fantasy world created by a bored child are rooms in which people slide down a snake, fly through the air in the jumping room, sail into a world inhabited by friendly alligators, and give carrots to Tyrannosaurus Rex. The illustrations in Peggy Rathmann's *Officer Buckle and Gloria* add considerable humor and unexpected situations when the police dog performs behind Officer Buckle's back as he gives safety tips to school children. The dog's actions, unknown by Officer Buckle, change a presentation from dull to exciting.

What difficulties might arise if cows could type and hens decided to go on strike unless the farmer meets their demands? This is the unexpected plot developed by Doreen Cronin in *Click, Clack, Moo: Cows That Type.* The story ends with a what-could-happen-next experience. After the cows and hens receive their demands, the ducks

Click, clack, **moo.**
Click, clack, **moo.**
Clickety, clack, **moo.**

Cows demanding better working conditions and other funny surprises fill out the unexpected plot. (From Click, Clack, Moo: Cows That Type, *by Doreen Cronin. Copyright © 2000 by Doreen Cronin, illustrations copyright © 2000 by Betsy Lewin. Reprinted with the permission of Simon & Schuster Books for Young Readers, an imprint of Simon & Schuster Children's Publishing Division.)*

now go "Click, clack, quack./Click, clack, quack./Clickety, clack, quack" (unnumbered) and demand a diving board because the pond is too boring.

Irony creates surprise and the unexpected in Amy Hest's *In the Rain with Baby Duck.* Hest tells the story of a duck who dislikes to get wet feet, hop in puddles, or waddle through the water. Instead of loving rainy weather, he dawdles, dallies, pouts, and drags behind his parents who are thoroughly enjoying the setting. In a satisfying conclusion, Grampa gives Baby Duck a red umbrella and matching boots that once belonged to Baby Duck's mother, who also did not like the rain. Now Grampa and Baby Duck enjoy the weather together.

Surprise occurs in Jon Agee's *The Incredible Painting of Felix Clousseau* when the paintings come to life. Chaos takes place and imprisonment of the artist results until a dog in one of the paintings captures a jewel thief. The unexpected also occurs in Mem Fox's *Night Noises*—the frightening night noises are caused by family members who are coming to give a surprise birthday party for the grandmother.

The humor in *The Chanukkah Guest* by Eric A. Kimmel emerges through the unexpected when an old

woman mistakes a bear for the rabbi and serves the bear the delicious latkes that she has prepared for her special guest. A surprise ending and repetitive language provide humor in Candace Fleming's *Muncha! Muncha! Muncha!*

Exaggeration. Children's imaginations are often filled with exaggerated tales about what they can do or would like to do. In James Stevenson's *Could Be Worse!,* however, the grandfather is the one who exaggerates. Grandpa does and says the same things day after day. Whenever anyone complains, Grandpa responds, "Could be worse." When he overhears his grandchildren commenting on his dull existence, he tells them what happened to him the previous evening: He was captured by a large bird and dropped in the mountains, where he encountered an abominable snowman. Then, he crossed a burning desert, escaped from a giant animal, landed in the ocean, and finally returned home on a paper airplane. After the grandchildren hear his story, they respond with his favorite expression, "Could be worse!"

Patricia Polacco uses exaggeration to develop her humorous *Meteor!* After a meteor lands on a farm, the whole town exaggerates the power of the meteor. Individuals claim that it gives the ability to play a trumpet, create a marvelous recipe, and even see extraordinary distances. The book is humorous because readers know that such an incident might really happen.

Exaggeration is the source of humor in both Anne Isaacs's text and Paul O. Zelinsky's illustrations for *Swamp Angel.* This tall-tale story set in the American frontier develops a female character with unusual powers such as the ability to wrestle a bear. The exaggeration begins on the day of her birth, when "The newborn was scarcely taller than her mother and couldn't climb a tree without help" (unnumbered). The story concludes when Swamp Angel turns Thundering Tarnations (the bear) into a rug. Unfortunately, the bear skin is too big for Tennessee so she moves to Montana where she can spread the rug on the ground in front of her cabin. "Nowadays, folks call it the Shortgrass Prairie" (unnumbered).

In *I Was Born About 10,000 Years Ago,* Steven Kellogg also uses the exaggeration of a tall tale as the narrator romps through history and reports being part of momentous occasions such as eating the core of the apple (Adam and Eve) and building the pyramids. The exaggeration of a tall tale is important in Debbie Dadey's *Shooting Star: Annie Oakley, the Legend* as Dadey creates a heroine whose skills include being able to shoot the points off a star and hit the moon.

A humorous exaggerated experience accompanies a young boy when he has a sleepover at his grandmother's in Kate Lum's *What! Cried Granny: An Almost Bedtime Story.* The story takes on tall-tale characteristics when Grandmother answers each of the child's protests about going to bed by completing an almost impossible task. For example, because he has no bed, she cuts down a tree and makes him a bed. She also shears sheep and knits a blanket. The final humor results when she tells him to go to bed but he cannot because it is now morning.

The Ridiculous and Caricatures. The consequences of having antlers suddenly appear on a young girl's head provide the humor in *Imogene's Antlers,* in which author David Small caricatures the ridiculousness of the fears of some people. To extend the humor, the story concludes with another what-if: The antlers disappear, but an even more beautiful appendage replaces the antlers.

Foolishness and ridiculous situations may change to wisdom, as shown in Eric Kimmel's *The Chanukkah Tree.* In this Jewish tale, the people of Chelm believe a peddler when he sells them a Christmas tree as "a Chanukkah tree. From America. Over there Chanukkah trees are the latest thing" (unnumbered). The townspeople decorate the tree with potato latkes and candles. The only star that they can find for the top is on a door, so they place the whole door on top of the tree. When they discover that they have been duped by the peddler, they are unhappy at first. Later, birds take sanctuary on the tree during a snowstorm, and the people discover that their tree is not so ridiculous: The potato latkes feed the birds, the candles warm them, and the door protects them.

The humor in Janet Stevens's *Tops & Bottoms* results from the ridiculous situation and foolish actions of rich, lazy Bear when he is tricked out of the garden produce by Hare, who uses his wits to secure the best portions of the crop. The illustrations of Bear are particularly interesting as they epitomize this humorous and ridiculous situation.

Superiority. Some humorous picture storybooks gratify the desire of young children to be superior to everyone else for a change or to easily overcome their problems. When a town simpleton surpasses not only his clever brothers but also the czar of the land, the result is an unusual tale of humorous superiority. Arthur Ransome's *The Fool of the World and the Flying Ship* is a Russian tale. In it, the good deeds performed by a simple lad allow him to obtain a flying ship, discover companions who have marvelous powers, overcome obstacles placed in his path by the czar, win the hand of the czar's daughter, and live happily ever after.

A singing cow solves her problems by using superiority against a greedy human in Lisa Campbell Ernst's *When Bluebell Sang.* When the cow and the farmer become tired of being taken advantage of by a talent agent, the cow hides herself among a herd of cows, where the agent cannot identify her without her dress, hat, and shoes.

Typical Characters and Situations

Children's picture storybooks include stories about people disguised as animals, talking animals with human emotions, personified objects, humans in realistic situations, and humorous and inventive fantasies. This section dis-

On rainy days, Olivia likes to go to the museum.

She heads straight for her favorite picture.

Readers find many opportunities to hypothesize about what the main character will do following an experience in Ian Falconer's Olivia *(From* Olivia *by Ian Falconer. Copyright © 2000 by Ian Falconer. Published by Atheneum Books for Young Readers. All rights reserved. Used by permission.)*

cusses stories by some outstanding writers of books on these subjects.

People Disguised as Animals. Many children's stories with animal characters are so closely associated with human lifestyles, behavior patterns, and emotions that it is difficult to separate them from stories with human characters. If these stories were read without reference to the illustrations or to a specific type of animal, children might assume that the stories are about children and adults like themselves. These stories may be popular with children because the children can easily identify with the characters' emotions and the actions.

Russell Hoban's Frances the badger, for example, lives in a nice house with her two parents, loves bread and jam, and feels jealous when she gets a new baby sister. Children identify with Frances when, in *Bread and Jam for Frances,* she refuses to eat anything but her two favorite foods. Hoban has her parents, like good human parents, carefully guide Frances into her decision that eating only bread and jam is boring and that trying different foods is pleasant.

In *A Baby Sister for Frances,* the young badger decides to run away from home when her mother becomes busy with the new baby. She packs a lunch to take with her on her journey, but she goes only as far as the next room, from which she looks longingly at her parents and her sister. In this warm story, Hoban shows how Frances's need for her family helps her overcome her jealousy and decide to accept the new arrival. The warmth is expressed in Hoban's choice of language:

> Big sisters really have to stay
> At home, not travel far away,
> Because everybody misses them
> And wants to hug-and-kisses them. (p. 26, unnumbered)

In *Leo the Late Bloomer*, Robert Kraus develops a credible character through experiences shared by many children: Leo, a young tiger, cannot read, write, draw, talk, or even eat neatly. One of Leo's parents worries, while the other suggests that Leo is merely a late bloomer. Kraus uses repetition to emphasize Leo's problem as the seasons go by: "But Leo still wasn't blooming." A satisfactory ending results in both the text and illustrations when Leo finally discovers that he can do everything that he couldn't do before, and a happy father and mother hear their happy child declare, "I made it!" Ian Falconer's heroine, *Olivia,* is a precocious pig who believes that she can do anything that she desires to accomplish. The feisty heroine sees herself as a prima ballerina, a builder of great buildings, and even an artist. When she paints a wall at home, she earns very childlike punishment: a time-out. The pig continues her exploits in *Olivia Saves the Circus.*

Fears and experiences that result in temporary unhappiness are popular causes of conflict in stories about animals disguised as people. In *Rockin' Reptiles* by Stephanie Calmenson and Joanna Cole, two alligator friends must work out a fair solution to a conflict that at first threatens their friendship. David McPhail uses a temporarily unhappy experience to create a happy ending in *Fix-It.* A bear, Emma, who could easily be a young child, cries when the television does not work. After successive disappointments, her mother reads a book to try to calm the unhappy Emma. Emma discovers that reading is so much fun that she stays with the book rather than returning to the television. In *Owen,* Kevin Henkes uses a mouse child's fear of losing his security blanket to create a story that could be about any young child. In *Off to School, Baby Duck!* Amy Hest develops a story that could easily be about a human child as Baby Duck has jitters in her stomach and shows reluctance to go to school on the first day. It is Grampa who introduces Miss Posy, the teacher, to Baby Duck and talks with her about all the fun Baby Duck will have in school.

D. B. Johnson uses the human nature of and the characteristics associated with Henry David Thoreau to create the story *Henry Hikes to Fitchburg.* Two animal friends complete a wager in which they determine who will be the first to arrive in Fitchburg, thirty miles away. Henry decides to walk so he can see and enjoy the country. His friend decides to work to buy a train ticket. The illustra-

Grampa Duck helps Baby Duck overcome his fear of going to school in Off to School, Baby Duck! *(From* Off to School, Baby Duck! *by Amy Hest. Text copyright © 1999 by Amy Hest, illustrations copyright © 1999 by Jill Barton. Reproduced by permission of the publisher Candlewick Press, Inc., Cambridge, MA.)*

tions show the contrasting activities. For example, while the friend fills a woodbox, Henry is hopping from rock to rock across a river, and while the friend is pulling weeds in a garden, Henry is picking flowers and pressing them into a book to keep. At the conclusion, his friend states that the train was faster while Henry concludes, "I know. I stopped for blackberries" (unnumbered). The author provides information "About Henry" that includes an excerpt from *Walden* in which Henry David Thoreau discusses the pleasures of walking and enjoying nature.

In Marc Brown's *Arthur's Family Vacation,* the aardvark family plans and goes on a vacation to the seashore. Like many human vacations, their vacation at first looks like a disaster because it rains every day, the motel room is too small, the pool is not as large as a bathtub, and the children complain that their friends are not with them. The disaster is averted when Arthur decides to plan field trips for the family. Trips to a cow festival, Gatorville, Flo's Fudge Factory, and Jimmy's Jungle Cruise provide entertainment until the last day, when the sun shines and the family spends a glorious day at the beach. Children respond to the experiences and the problem solving by the oldest aardvark child. If the book were read without pictures, however, the story could be about any family.

Talking Animals with Human Emotions. In other animal stories, the animals live in traditional animal settings, such as meadows, barnyards, jungles, and zoos. The animals in these stories display some animal traits, but they still talk like humans and have many human feelings and problems.

Although the main characters in Martin Waddell's *Can't You Sleep, Little Bear?* live in a cave in the woods, the cave has furnishings, the bears talk, and they express emotions that are very human. The universal fear of darkness and the need to be comforted by a caring adult provide the story line in this warm, loving story. The father, who continually leaves his book to soothe the child and provide security, develops a good response among children. In a totally satisfying ending, "Big Bear carried Little Bear back into the Bear Cave, fast asleep, and he settled down with Little Bear on one arm and the Bear Book on the other, cozy in the Bear Chair by the fire" (p. 25, unnumbered). In *Let's Go Home, Little Bear,* Waddell continues the loving relationship between the two bears, and Little Bear is helped to overcome his fears of the sounds that he hears in the woods. In *You and Me, Little Bear,* the bear tries to get mother bear's attention.

The main character in Munro Leaf's *The Story of Ferdinand* lives in a meadow with his mother and other cattle. Leaf develops contrasts between Ferdinand, who sits under his favorite cork tree smelling the flowers, and the bulls who run, jump, and butt their heads together practicing for the bullring. The theme of the story is relevant to any human child: All individuals should be themselves, and being different is not wrong. Leaf allows Ferdinand to remain true to his individual nature. When Ferdinand is taken to the bullring, he merely sits and smells the flowers.

Jean de Brunhoff uses a variety of emotional experiences in the various Babar books. Emotionally, Babar grows up; grieves when his mother dies; runs away to the city; returns to the jungle, where he is crowned king; and raises a family.

In Roger Duvoisin's *Petunia,* a goose becomes conceited when she finds a book and believes that merely carrying it around gives her wisdom. Petunia's advice creates an uproar in the barnyard when she maintains that firecrackers discovered in the meadow are candy and thus good to eat. Her true wisdom begins when she discovers that books have words and that she will need to learn to read if she really wants to be wise.

A farm setting is also the location for Martin Waddell's *Farmer Duck.* In the beginning, the duck does all the work while the lazy human farmer lies in bed, eats chocolates, and reads the paper. In a satisfying ending, the animals

Technology Resources

Visit a great site dedicated to the work of Eric Carle by linking to our Companion Website at www.prenhall.com/norton

work together, chase the farmer away, and retrieve the farm for the duck and the other animals.

Many young children like a combination of fast, slapstick adventure and an animal with easily identifiable human characteristics, such as Hans Rey's *Curious George.* Readers are introduced to this comedic monkey as he observes a large yellow hat lying on the jungle floor. His curiosity gets the better of him, he is captured by the man with the yellow hat, and his adventures begin. The text and illustrations develop one mishap after another. George tries to fly but falls into the ocean, grabs a bunch of balloons and is whisked away by the wind, and is finally rescued again by the man with the yellow hat. The rapid verbal and visual adventures bring delight to young children, who are curious about the world around them and would like to try some of the same activities.

Other picture storybooks with animal characters satisfy children's desires for absurd situations, flights of fancy, and magical transformations. In William Steig's *Sylvester and the Magic Pebble,* for example, a young donkey accidentally changes himself into a rock and must figure out how to communicate with his grieving parents and return to his donkey form.

Personified Objects. The technique of giving human characteristics to inanimate objects is called *personification.* Children usually see nothing wrong with a house that thinks, a doll that feels, or a steam shovel that responds to emotions. Virginia Lee Burton, a favorite writer for small children, is the highly skilled creator of things that have appealing personalities and believable emotions. In Burton's *Katy*

There once was a duck who had the bad luck to live with a lazy old farmer. The duck did the work. The farmer stayed all day in bed.

The animals in Farmer Duck *display human emotions and traits. (Reproduced from* Farmer Duck *by Martin Waddell with permission from Candlewick Press, Cambridge, MA. Illustration copyright © by Helen Oxenbury.)*

Through the Eyes of an ILLUSTRATOR

E. B. Lewis

Visit the CD-ROM that accompanies this text to generate a complete list of titles illustrated by E. B. Lewis.

Selected Titles by E. B. Lewis:

Fire on the Mountain

Big Boy

Little Cliff and the Porch People

The Other Side

Virgie Goes to School with Us Boys

Since I am the illustrator, I'm going to basically tell you how an illustrator works. Basically we start from an idea; sometimes we start with a manuscript. A manuscript is something that's sent to an illustrator and has only words; no pictures. I have to create pictures to go with these words. This is how I start as an illustrator—by coming up with an idea for a page.

I get the manuscript and read the story, for example, *Fire on the Mountain.* This is a story about a little boy who loses his parents in Ethiopia and goes out to find his sister to tell her the news. He encounters his sister, who works for a rich man, and together they end up working for this rich man. The rich man tries to outwit the little boy, to take advantage of him. Together, the boy and his sister conspire to get him back. It's a great little Ethiopian folktale—it tells the reader that if you're truthful and honest, your hopes and dreams will come true.

I go to the library in Philadelphia—I'm from Philadelphia—where there is a department called the Print and Picture Department, and in that department I do my research. Since this is an Ethiopian folktale, that means I have to do all kinds of research on Ethiopia, the country—what the terrain is like, what the people are like, and what have you. The people who work in the department bring me a photograph or samples of artwork from which I can choose.

The next part of the process is to find a model. Since this is an Ethiopian folktale and I wanted my book to be authentic to Ethiopia, I had to go find a model. I went to a community here in Philadelphia, an Ethiopian community, and I found a little boy.

And since I did the research, I knew what the terrain was like in Ethiopia and found that a forest in back of the Philadelphia Museum of Art closely resembled the terrain in Ethiopia. So I took my model and placed him in that terrain and took photographs. I work from photographs as an artist.

Video Profile: The accompanying video contains more of this conversation with E. B. Lewis, as well as conversations with Molly Bang, Leonard Everett Fisher, Keith Baker, and Brian Pinkney on illustrating children's books.

---

and the Big Snow, an extraordinary red tractor named Katy responds to calls for help from the chief of police, the postmaster, the telephone company, the water department, the hospital, the fire chief, and the airport. "Sure," she says, and digs the town of Geoppolis out from a big snow that is two stories deep. When city departments believe in Katy, it is easy for the readers to believe in her also.

In *Mike Mulligan and His Steam Shovel,* also by Burton, Mike's best friend is a large piece of machinery named Mary Anne. A suspenseful story unfolds as the two friends try to dig the basement of Popperville's town hall in only one day. *The Little House* is a heroine who is strong and also needs love. In this story, a growing city encroaches upon the house and she becomes dilapidated and lonely. The house proceeds, like a real person, through a series of emotions until she is moved away from the city and settles down happily on a new foundation, where "once again she was lived in and taken care of" (p. 39).

Humans in Realistic Situations. Young children enjoy stories about other children who share their concerns, problems, and pleasures. The heroine in Cari Best's *Shrinking Violet* shows that a shy child can win against a bothersome bully and save the class play. The numerous books written and illustrated by Ezra Jack Keats, for example, easily draw young children into the private worlds of other children. Louie, one of Keats's realistic heroes, is very lonely when his family moves to a new neighborhood. He solves his problems in *The Trip* by building a model of his old neighborhood and going on an imaginative adventure with his old friends. In *Regards to the Man in the Moon,* other children tease Louie because his father is a junk dealer. His father's advice—that Louie build a spacecraft from junk—and his own imagination allow Louie and a friend to experience flight into outer space. When the other children hear of these adventures, they want to take part in them also.

While Keats's books usually have inner-city settings, the settings created by another well-known children's author are usually the country or the coast of Maine. Robert McCloskey stresses warm family relationships in books such as *Blueberries for Sal.* This delightful story allows readers to share the berry-picking expeditions of a human mother and daughter and an adult bear and her cub. McCloskey develops drama when the youngsters get mixed up and start following the wrong parents. He provides a satisfying ending as both children are reunited with their mothers.

Stories about relationships between grandparents and grandchildren are also popular in current picture storybooks. In *The Day Gogo Went to Vote: South Africa, April 1994,* Elinor Batezat Sisulu tells the story of how Thembi's great-grandmother, who has not left the house in years, casts her vote for the first time. This story told through Thembi's viewpoint shows the importance of this milestone in South African history.

Vera Williams's *A Chair for My Mother* shows that even a young child can help her mother fulfill a dream. After a fire destroys the family's furniture, Williams's heroine earns money to help fill the large coin jar that represents her mother's and grandmother's desire: a new, soft, comfortable chair. This goal is not easily reached, however; mother and daughter must work together.

Through the Eyes of a CHILD

Kelly

Pam Wilson's Fourth Grade
Western Row Elementary
Mason, Ohio

TITLE: The Other side
AUTHOR: Jacqueline Woodson   illustrated by E.B. Lewis

I liked this book because it was about how two girls from different backgrounds could get along. They didn't care what other people thought. They just acted liked everything was fine. I also liked the book because the author told how things really were back then. I really liked how the illustrater made the pictures look like photographs. Everything looked so realistic, it looked like the people were real. I also liked how all the colors blended in so well, it looked like one big picture instead of little seperate pictures on one page.

Kelly

Emily Arnold McCully's heroine in *Mirette on the High Wire* is an independent female protagonist. When Mirette meets a retired high-wire walker, the Great Bellini, she wants to learn the art. Despite his refusal, Mirette practices and teaches herself. Later, Mirette rescues her friend from the high wire by helping him overcome his fear. In the sequel, *Starring Mirette & Bellini,* McCully develops the theme about the importance of freedom.

In Sharon Bell Mathis's *The Hundred Penny Box* a young boy develops an important relationship with his Great-great-aunt Dew, who moves into his home with an old box containing a penny for every year of her long life. This is one of many picture storybooks, such as those of Ezra Jack Keats, that share with children of all backgrounds the warm relationships in nonwhite families. Close relationships between a young Chinese girl and her grandfather are developed in Margaret Holloway Tsubakiyama's

Mei-Mei Loves the Morning. The text and illustrations show activities such as preparing breakfast, riding to the park on a bicycle, and doing tai-chi with friends.

Of course, young children also confront problems in their families, including sex-role biases. In Charlotte Zolotow's *William's Doll,* a young boy wants a doll to hug, cradle, and play with. His brother calls him a creep, and his neighbor calls him a sissy. His father tries to interest him in "masculine" toys and brings him a basketball and an electric train. William enjoys both toys but still wants a doll. When his grandmother visits, he explains his wish to her, shows her that he can shoot baskets, and tells her that his father does not want him to play with a doll. Grandmother understands William's need, buys him a baby doll, and then explains to William's upset father that William wants and needs a doll so that he can practice being a father just like his own father. Tomie dePaola deals with a similar situation in *Oliver Button Is a Sissy*. Such books can reassure children that there is nothing wrong with non-stereotypical behavior.

Some picture storybooks that deal with realistic situations show protagonists trying to solve their problems. In *Letting Swift River Go*, Jane Yolen creates a happy childhood for Sally in rural Massachusetts. It is a life filled with walking through the countryside, sleeping under the stars, catching and releasing fireflies, and gathering sap from maple trees. This life changes when the river is dammed and the people are moved. The author develops the theme that "You have to let go" as Sally and her father row across the new lake and she hears her mother reminding her years ago that you have to let the fireflies go. Then, Sally realizes that she must let the past go, too.

Two picture storybooks about the Holocaust show that the realistic situations in picture books may sometimes be about very serious subjects. These books also make interesting comparisons for both content and illustrations. In *Rose Blanche*, Roberto Innocenti develops a strong protagonist who discovers the concentration camp near her home in Germany during World War II. As a consequence, she hides food and takes it to the Jewish prisoners. Unfortunately, Rose Blanche is killed by stray bullets as she stands in the woods. The somber colors in the illustrations reflect the sadness of both the concentration camps and Rose Blanche's death. In *Let the Celebrations Begin!*, Margaret Wild focuses on the same time in history. In Wild's book, however, the Jewish prisoners are preparing for soldiers to liberate the camp. Compared with Innocenti's somber shades, Julie Vivas's illustrations for *Let the Celebrations Begin!* are colorful pastels. As you read these two books, compare the illustrations and the contents. Both books have received some criticisms. Is *Rose Blanche* too depressing for children? Do the pastel illustrations and the party preparations found in *Let the Celebrations Begin!* trivialize a very serious subject? You decide as you read the two books.

The fiftieth anniversary of the end of World War II saw numerous books produced about the time period. Topics in current picture storybooks include war experiences in both Europe and Japan. For example, Jo Hoestlandt's *Star of Fear, Star of Hope* is set in Nazi-occupied France on the eve of Helen's ninth birthday. Her best friend, Lydia, is Jewish and leaves Helen's celebration to go home to warn her family that the Nazis are forcibly collecting the Jewish residents of the city. Helen feels abandoned by her friend and lets her know that she is no longer her friend. Unfortunately, Helen never sees Lydia again. Now, years later, Helen hopes that her best friend will see the message in the book and call her. The story ends with an important message that is also one of the themes of the book: "I'll always have hope . . ." (unnumbered). In Tatsuharu Kodama's *Shin's Tricycle*, a young atomic bomb victim in Hiroshima is remembered through his tricycle, which is now on display at the Peace Museum.

Both of these books about different World War II experiences are reminders about the tragedy of war.

Another picture storybook with a wartime setting is Jane Cutler's *The Cello of Mr. O*. In this modern war-torn setting, an older man brings comfort to the neighborhood by first playing on his cello and later, after his cello is destroyed by exploding shells, he plays on his harmonica. The book ends on a hopeful note because "The music makes us feel happy. And the courage of the harmonica player makes us less afraid" (unnumbered).

Humorous and Inventive Fantasies. Dr. Seuss is one of the most popular authors of books for children. In his many outlandish stories, he develops characters who are original and humorous and who talk in a style that children enjoy. In *The 500 Hats of Bartholomew Cubbins*, both conflict and humor result when the king orders a peasant to remove his magical hat. Every time that Bartholomew tries to remove one hat, another hat appears. When the number reaches 157 hats, the magicians cast a spell:

> Dig a hole five furlongs deep,
> Down to where the night snakes creep,
> Mix and mold the mystic mud,
> Malber, Balber, Tidder, Tudd. (p. 31, unnumbered)

As the hats begin to number in the hundreds, the king threatens Bartholomew with execution. Then, hat number five hundred is so beautiful that the king offers to buy it for five hundred gold pieces. With that offer, the spell is broken and a rich Bartholomew returns home.

Several of Dr. Seuss's characters face moral issues. In *Horton Hatches the Egg*, Horton the elephant remains 100 percent faithful to his promise to hatch a lazy bird's egg in spite of jeering bystanders and other unpleasant experiences. He gains his reward when the egg hatches and is an elephant-bird.

Chris Van Allsburg's *Jumanji* begins with a realistic scene involving two children who are asked to keep the house neat until their parents return with guests. Bored, the children make a mess with their toys and then go to the park, where they find instructions for a jungle adventure game that cannot be ended until one player reaches the golden city. When the children take the game home, they realize the consequences of the rules. A lion appears on the piano and chases one of them around the house. Other jungle animals and jungle-related actions enter the scene each time that the children frantically throw the dice. Van Allsburg ends the story on a note of suspense and speculation. The children return the game, but two other children, who are notorious for never reading directions, pick up the game and run through the park.

The plot in Van Allsburg's fantasy *The Widow's Broom* develops after a witch leaves her broom with a widow, Minna Shaw. As in all fantasies with witches, the broom has special powers and does Minna's work for her. Complications arise when suspicious neighbors express fear of the broom and then burn it. In a happy ending, the broom arises, rejoins the widow, and plays music for their pleasure. The positive power of books versus the negative hypnotic power of a strange glowing stone provides the conflict in Van Allsburg's fantasy *The Wretched Stone*. Children understand the message when they discover that the people who know how to read books recover more rapidly than do others from the debilitating power of the glowing stone.

Suggested Activities

 For more suggested activities for understanding picture books, visit our Companion Website at www.prenhall.com/norton

- Read a journal that evaluates children's literature such as *The Horn Book Guide to Children's and Young Adult Books.* Select two picture books that are highly rated and two books that are not. Compare the literary elements and the illustrations in the books. Do you agree with the evaluation of the journal? Why or why not?

- Choose several different editions of Mother Goose that contain the same nursery rhymes. Compare the artists' interpretations of these characters.

- Select a common animal or object that often appears in books for children. Find several picture books that develop a story about that animal or object. Compare the ways in which the different artists depict the animal or object through the illustrations and the ways in which the writers describe the animal or object and develop the plots.

- This text includes various responses to Maurice Sendak's *We Are All in the Dumps with Jack and Guy.* Respond to the illustrations and text in *The Miami Giant,* written by Arthur Yorinks and illustrated by Maurice Sendak. This book has also received mixed reviews. As you read the book, analyze the effectiveness of the satire.

Teaching with Picture Books

To truly share picture books, you must care enough to select books and prepare book-related activities that children find stimulating and enjoyable. Picture-book experiences involve sharing nursery rhymes to stimulate oral language development and dramatization; wordless books that encourage children to find objects in pictures, tell their own stories, or write creatively; picture storybooks ideal for reading aloud; illustrations that encourage aesthetic sensitivity; and picture books of all sorts that encourage children to join in with songs and movement. Picture books are important for developing experiences with song and story because, according to Betsy Hearne (1992): "Meaning emerges from experience patterned by artistry, an artistry in association with the senses. Song and story are sensuous. . . . Children's books are the continuation of speech, song, and story" (p. 31).

Patricia Cianciolo (1990) develops a strong argument for using picture books with students at all grade levels, from three-year-old children who cannot yet read to sophisticated young adults who can analyze the illustrations and grasp new meaning and significance. Cianciolo states:

In these picture books the illustrations are superbly accomplished works of visual and graphic art, and the texts are written in beautifully expressive language. . . . In addition to bringing out and emphasizing the text, they convey other meanings and impressions that readers would not have envisioned from the verbal information on its own. They encourage higher-level thinking and imaginative thinking. Readers can and do grasp their meaning and significance and can go well beyond what the illustrator and author suggested. (p. 2)

Whatever the book, if it is worth sharing, the sharing experience is worth thoughtful preparation. This section discusses a few of the many ways in which you can use picture books to enhance personal development in children and to increase children's responses to literature.

Sharing Mother Goose

Mother Goose rhymes are natural means of stimulating language development and listening appreciation in very young children because the rhymes include a simple story line that encourages finger play, a story or song with a repeated chorus, a verse with nonsense words, a description of daily actions, and a choral reading in which children join in with the rhyming words.

Even two- and three-year-olds thoroughly enjoy and respond to the rhyme, rhythm, and nonsense found in nursery rhymes. Because passive listening may not encourage language development, adults must create experiences that motivate children to interact with the verses in enjoyable ways. Once children have heard the simpler Mother Goose rhymes several times, they usually can help you finish the verses by filling in missing words or rhyming elements: "Jack and Jill, went up the _____ to fetch a pail of water. Jack fell down, and broke his _____, and Jill came tumbling after." In addition to providing enjoyment during shared experience, this activity encourages auditory discrimination and attentive listening, skills necessary for later successes in reading and language arts.

You may also insert an incorrect word into a rhyme familiar to children and have the children correct the error. Children especially enjoy this exercise when the nursery rhyme book has large, colorful illustrations in which the children can point out what is wrong with your version. For example, say, "Jack be nimble, Jack be quick, Jack jump over a pumpkin," or "Little Boy Blue come blow your horn. The pig's in the meadow, the chick's in the corn." Many children also enjoy making up their own incorrect versions.

Books such as Joanna Cole and Stephanie Calmenson's *Miss Mary Mac: And Other Children's Street Rhymes* help children become involved in the rhythmic elements of rhyme. This collection includes hand-clapping, ball-bouncing, and counting rhymes.

Young children enjoy creative play and spontaneously dramatize many of their favorite rhymes. Dramatization allows children to explore body movements, develop their senses, expand their imaginations and language, and experiment with characterization. Read or tell various nursery rhymes while children pretend to be each character in the rhyme and perform the actions expressed in the verses. Following each line, allow enough time for the children to act out each part. Children especially enjoy acting out such action rhymes as "Little Miss Muffet," "Jack Be Nimble," and "Hey Diddle Diddle."

You can encourage children to expand upon one of their favorite nursery rhymes, as do several delightful picture books devoted to one rhyme—such as John Ivimey's *The Complete Story of the Three Blind Mice*. You may use Susan Ramsay Hoguet's *Solomon Grundy* to encourage children to extend the nursery rhyme through historical illustrations. Children may select a time period for any Mother Goose rhyme, conduct research to make discoveries about the time period, and illustrate the rhyme accordingly. Other Mother Goose rhymes that lend themselves to extended oral, written, or artistic versions are "Old Mother Hubbard," "Old King Cole," and "Simple Simon." After sharing one of these books or rhymes with children, ask the children if they would like to know more about any other Mother Goose characters.

A discussion with first graders, for example, revealed that several children wanted to know what it would be like to live in a pumpkin. They talked about how they might decorate its interior, what they could do inside a pumpkin, and how neighbors might react to a pumpkin in the neighborhood. They dictated their story to the teacher and then divided it into separate sentences, each written and illustrated on tagboard by one child and then placed in the classroom library. This book was read by many children and became one of the most popular picture storybooks in the classroom. When more children created their own books, the children's librarian developed a library display of both commercially published Mother Goose books and books printed and illustrated by the children. Some illustrated stories are take-offs on earlier nursery rhymes. After reading Jan Ormerod's *Ms. MacDonald Has a Class,* have students compare the story to "Old MacDonald Had a Farm." Then have them write interpretations of other nursery rhymes.

University students in children's literature classes have developed other stimulating ways of using Mother Goose with older children. For example, they have had children compare the illustrations in different editions of Mother Goose, discuss their personal responses to the illustrations, discover more information about art media used by illustrators, demonstrate certain techniques to a group, and illustrate their own picture books to be shared with younger children.

Sharing Wordless Books

Wordless books are ideal for encouraging language growth, stimulating intellectual development, motivating creative writing, developing text for reading, and evaluating language skills. Consider children's ages and the complexity of plot or details when choosing wordless books. Some wordless books have much detail, which stimulates observational skills and descriptive vocabularies. Other wordless books are more appropriate for encouraging understanding and interpretation of sequential plot.

Stimulating Cognitive and Language Development

Literature is valuable in promoting cognitive development in children. Several skills associated with the thinking process—observing, comparing, and organizing—can be developed through the use of wordless books. Children can describe what is happening in each picture and the details that they observe, compare pictures or changes that occur, and organize their thoughts into sequentially well-organized stories. Describing, comparing, and storytelling also help children expand their vocabularies.

Children can describe the action in each detailed picture in Peter Spier's *Noah's Ark,* for example, as they follow the building of the ark; the loading of food, utensils, and animals; the problems that develop inside the ark; and the final landing and starting of life anew. One group of seven-year-olds did the following:

1. Identified the animals they recognized in a two-page spread showing animals boarding the ark.

2. Described the color, size, mode of travel, and natural habitat of the animals.

3. Identified humorous details in the illustrations.

4. Identified Noah's problems and suggested possible causes and solutions.

5. Speculated about Noah's feelings as he tried to rid the roof of too many birds, dealt with a reluctant donkey, and finally closed the doors of the ark.

6. Thought of descriptive words for the animals, such as *slithering* for snakes, *leaping* for frogs, and *lazy, brown* for monkeys.

7. Compared the positions of the snails in the illustrations at the beginning of the book and at the end.

8. Chose one picture each and told or wrote a detailed description of the picture.

Spier's wordless book can be compared with Lisbeth Zwerger's illustrations in Heinz Janisch's *Noah's Ark.* Mercer Mayer's funny wordless book *Frog Goes to Dinner* encourages before-and-after comparisons. People enjoy a leisurely meal in one picture, for example, and in the next experience the disruptions caused by Frog. A first grader made this comparison when he discussed two pictures of the band:

The band was playing beautifully. They had their eyes closed and were enjoying the music. All of a sudden the frog jumped in the saxophone. Now the saxophone player tried to play but couldn't. His face puffed out and he looked funny. The other players jumped. The frog made the drum player fall into his drum. The horn player thought it was funny.

The detailed illustrations in Jeannie Baker's *Window* are excellent for encouraging comparisons of the same setting across time. Children can observe, describe, and compare the illustrations that show changes in the Australian environment and ecology over a period of twenty-four years.

Motivating Writing and Reading

Educators in reading and language arts frequently recommend the use of language experiences that stimulate children's oral language and writing by exploring ideas and expressing feelings. These experiences in turn provide the content for group and individual stories composed by children and recorded by adults, who then use these stories for reading instruction.

Many teachers introduce students to the language experience approach to literature through group chart stories. These activities are appropriate for all age groups, but they are used most as reading-readiness or early reading activities in kindergarten or first grade. Usually, an entire group (guided by the teacher) writes a chart story after a shared motivational experience, such as a field trip, an art project, a film, music, or a story. Many of the wordless books discussed in this text are excellent sources for motivational activities.

If you use a wordless book to motivate the writing of a chart story, first share the book with the group. Following oral discussion, have the children dictate the story, as you record it on posterboard, the chalkboard, or large sheets of newsprint, repeating each word aloud. (Some teachers identify each child's contribution to the chart story by placing the child's name after the contribution.) It is essential that children be able to see each word as it is written. As you write the chart story, children will see that sentences flow from the top to the bottom on a page, follow a left-to-right sequence, begin with capital letters, and end with periods. Following completion of the chart story, read the whole story. Then, ask the children to reread the story with you. Following this experience, some individual children may choose to read the whole story aloud while others may choose to read only their own contributions.

Place wordless books and their accompanying chart stories in areas easily accessible to children, so that the children can enjoy reading the stories by themselves. Some teachers tape-record the children's reading of the chart stories and then place the recordings, the chart stories, and the wordless books in a listening center. The stories may also be read to children in other classes or added to the library.

Picnic and *School* by Emily Arnold McCully provide opportunities for children to write dialogue, describe settings, develop conflicts and characterizations, and discuss themes. David Wiesner's *Free Fall* encourages children to write interpretations of a fanciful dream. University students report that Chris Van Allsburg's *The Mysteries of Harris Burdick* is one of the most enticing nearly wordless books for older elementary students. Children can speculate about each fantasy in Van Allsburg's book, write their own stories, and share the stories with other children who have different interpretations. Because there is no correct answer, children may choose to write more than one story about a picture.

Reading to Children

An adult who reads to children accepts an opportunity and a responsibility for sharing a marvelous experience.

Author and illustrator Leo Lionni (quoted by Smith, 1991) states this very well when he describes the role of children's books in children's lives:

When a child is four or five, he has lived four or five years in a totally chaotic verbal environment. The picture book is the first thing that gets into his head where he is confronted with a verbal structure. If it's a good book, it has a beginning, a middle and an end. It's the first time that he will say "more, again" after the reading is over. Now he knows what the end and the beginning is—just think of what a complicated notion that is. Which means that he also has a notion of what's in between, so that he has a sense of whole. He's not conscious of it, but for the first time, he's faced with structure. That I think is an enormously convincing consideration on the importance of the picture book. (p. 119)

There is probably no better way to interest children in the world of books than to read to them. Listening to books read aloud is a way for children to learn that literature is a form of pleasure. June Brown (1999) emphasizes that because younger children's listening level is greater than their reading level "reading aloud can build background knowledge, teach new words, and provide a positive role model. It also hooks children on quality literature, demonstrates the pleasure involved in the process, and motivates them to read alone" (p. 520). Without parents, librarians, or other adults, a very young child would not experience nursery rhymes or such stories as Beatrix Potter's *Peter Rabbit,* and younger elementary children would not experience the marvelous verses and stories of A. A. Milne or enter the joyous world of Dr. Seuss. For children just struggling to learn to read, a book may not be a source of happiness. In fact, books actually arouse negative feelings in many children. Being read to helps beginning readers develop an appreciation for literature that they could not manage with their own reading abilities.

The pleasure of the listening experience usually motivates children to ask for a book again or to read it themselves. Very young children may ask for a book to be reread so many times that they memorize it and then feel proud of being able to "read" it. When a teacher reads a particularly enjoyable selection to children in an elementary classroom, the children tend to check out all copies of that book in the class or school library.

Choosing the Books

An appropriate book for reading aloud depends, of course, upon the ages of the children, their interests, the need to balance the types of literature presented, the number of children who will share the listening experience, and the quality of the literature. A book selected for reading aloud should be worthy of the time spent by the readers and the listeners. It should not be something picked up hurriedly to fill in time.

The style and the illustrations are both considerations when choosing books to read aloud. Mary Ann Hoberman's *You Read to Me, I'll Read to You: Very Short Stories to Read Together* is designed especially for pairing beginning readers with older children or adults. Humorous selections encourage children to share the experience. Michael Emberley's humorous cartoon illustrations add to the fun. The language in A. A. Milne's *Winnie-the-Pooh* and Dr. Seuss's *The 500 Hats of Bartholomew Cubbins* appeals to young listeners. The rhyming text in Linnea Riley's *Mouse Mess* is fun to listen to and read aloud. Likewise, young children enjoy illustrations that are integral to the story. For example, illustrations in Robert McCloskey's *Lentil* help children visualize a midwestern town in the early 1900s, and the illustrations in Maurice Sendak's *Where the Wild Things Are* bring Max's exceptional adventure to life. Other books, such as Arthur Yorinks's *Hey, Al* and Jane Yolen's *Owl Moon*, have such beautiful illustrations that they should be chosen to encourage aesthetic appreciation. Books such as Martin Waddell's *Can't You Sleep, Little Bear?*, Minfong Ho's *Hush! A Thai Lullaby*, and Kathi Appelt's *Where, Where Is Swamp Bear?* provide warm, satisfying moments to be shared with children.

Children's ages, attention spans, and reading ability are also important when selecting stories to be read aloud. The books chosen should challenge children to improve their reading skills and to increase their appreciation of outstanding literature. The numerous easy-to-read books should usually be left for children to read independently. Young children respond to short stories; in fact, four- or five-year-olds may benefit from several short story times a day rather than a twenty- or thirty-minute period. Books such as Michael Rosen's *We're Going on a Bear Hunt*, Lloyd Moss's *Zin! Zin! Zin! A Violin*, Robert Kraus's *Leo the Late Bloomer*, and Doreen Cronin's *Click, Clack, Moo: Cows That Type* are short and have colorful pictures. *We're Going on a Bear Hunt* uses repetitive language to encourage children to join in during reading. *Zin! Zin! Zin! A Violin* uses rhyming words and sounds of instruments. *Leo the Late Bloomer* relates the problems of a young tiger who cannot talk, eat, or read correctly until all at once, when he finally blooms.

As children enter kindergarten and advance into first grade, they begin to enjoy longer picture storybooks with more elaborate plots. Robert McCloskey's *Make Way for Ducklings* and the various Dr. Seuss books are favorites with beginning elementary school children. Books such as William Steig's *Caleb & Kate*, Eugene Trivizas's *The Three Little Wolves and the Big Bad Pig*, Peggy Rathmann's *Officer Buckle and Gloria*, and Robert San Souci's *The Hobyahs* have enough plot to appeal to second-grade children. Steven Kellogg's humorous exploits of a Great Dane in *A Penguin Pup for Pinkerton* encourages listeners to enjoy Pinkerton's antics as he decides that a football is really a penguin egg and it is his responsibility to care for the egg.

By the time children reach the third grade, they are ready for stories read a chapter at a time. (A reading period should not end in the middle of a chapter.) Third graders usually enjoy E. B. White's *The Trumpet of the Swan*, *Charlotte's Web*, and *Stuart Little*. Fourth and fifth graders often respond to books like Madeleine L'Engle's *A Wrinkle in Time* and C. S. Lewis's *The Lion, the Witch and the Wardrobe*. Armstrong Sperry's *Call It Courage*, Esther Forbes's *Johnny Tremain*, the various "Harry Potter" books by J. K. Rowling, Louis Sachar's *Holes*, and Gloria Whelan's *Homeless Bird* discussed in other chapters in this text often appeal to sixth- and seventh-grade students.

Reading to children should not end in the elementary grades. Unfortunately, June Brown (1999) reports that many upper-grade teachers have abandoned the practice of reading aloud. Without enjoyable oral listening experiences, many older children are not exposed to good literature because they cannot read it independently. Alleen Pace Nilsen and Kenneth L. Donelson (2001) make a strong case for reading aloud to older students when they state: "English teachers ought to know enough about dramatic techniques and oral interpretation to be comfortable reading aloud to students. We need teachers eager and able to read material to students that just might interest, intrigue, amuse, or excite them, material that might make young people aware of new or old books or writers or techniques or ideas. . . . Poetry must be read aloud. So must drama. Reading fiction aloud is half the fun of teaching short stories. If students are to learn how to read poetry or drama, it will come from English teachers comfortable with their own oral reading" (p. 358).

Preparing to Read Aloud

Many adults mistakenly believe that children's stories are so simple that there is no need for an adult to read a selection before reading it to children. Many embarrassing situations, such as being unable to pronounce a word or selecting an inappropriate book, can be avoided if you first read the story silently—in order to understand it, identify the sequence of events, recognize the mood, and identify any problems with vocabulary or concepts—and then read it aloud in order to practice pronunciation, pacing, and voice characterization. Adults with little or no experience in reading to children can listen to themselves on tape recorders. You should also decide how to introduce the story and what type of discussion or other activity, if any, to use following the reading.

The Reading Itself

What makes the story hour a time of magic or an insignificant part of the day? An effective reading experience begins with adult knowledge of the story and is enhanced through child involvement, eye contact, expressive reading, pointing to meaningful words or pictures, and highlighting words and pictures. You should consider all of these factors when preparing for an oral presentation and when actually reading a story to an audience of children. Properly prepared, you can take children on a much-appreciated literary journey.

Let us consider an example of a reading aloud experience that accompanies a book for early elementary students developed by Donna Norton (1992):

While reading Michael Rosen's *We're Going on a Bear Hunt* to kindergarten or first-grade students, emphasize the repetitive language and the descriptive words. Show the students that the illustrator, Helen Oxenbury, places the repetitive verses on black-and-white backgrounds and the descriptive action words on colored backgrounds. Ask the students: "Why would an illustrator choose both black-and-white and colored backgrounds in the same book? How should we read this story to show the differences between black-and-white and colored backgrounds?" After orally reading the first series of repetitive text, encourage the students to join in the reading. On the colored action pages ask them to predict the sounds that the family will make as they go through each obstacle. Ask them to notice that each action is repeated three times and that each line increases in size. Ask the students: "Why would an author increase the size of the letters? How could we use our voices and actions to show this increasing size?" Then have the students read and act out the lines such as:

Splash splosh!
Splash splosh!
Splash splosh!

Students enjoy acting out this whole rhyme as they start the bear hunt, swishy swashy through the grass, splash splosh through the river, squelch squerch through the mud, stumble trip through the forest, hoooo wooooo through the snowstorm, tiptoe through the cave, discover the bear and then go back through each obstacle until they reach the safety of home and bed. This book encourages students to become involved in the text and their own vocabulary development as they join in the repetitive language, act out the action words, and discover how an author and an illustrator might show how words should be spoken by changing the size of the text or by alternating the backgrounds. (p. 63)

Developing Aesthetic Sensitivity

If the word *aesthetic* denotes sensitivity to art and beauty, then looking at the beautiful illustrations in children's books must be aesthetic. Children learn to appreciate the artistic media used in book illustrations when they are given the stimulation and time to become actively involved in making their own illustra-

tions. Some artistic media are too complex for very young children, of course, but Debra Cooper-Solomon (1999) believes that collage is an ideal medium for stimulating creative interpretations of literature and for developing fine-motor skills. In the process of making their own collages and reacting to the collages in book illustrations, children can also improve their vocabularies and oral discussion skills. Ezra Jack Keats, Leo Lionni, Jeannie Baker, and David Wisniewski are among the well-known illustrators of children's books who use collage. Adults can use works of such artists first to enlighten themselves and then as sources of material for children to discuss and compare. (Jeannie Baker's collage illustrations for *Where the Forest Meets the Sea* and *Window* are fine sources of inspiration for both adults and children because Baker uses many different textures to create large, colorful pictures.)

You might use the following sequence when introducing children to collage:

1. Encourage children to experiment with the collage technique by having them tear and cut shapes and pictures from plain paper or magazines and then to paste the shapes onto another piece of paper.

2. Provide opportunities for children to experience different textures in the world around them and then to use those textures in collages. Have the children take a texture exploration walk, for example, during which they feel and describe the textures of tree bark, leaves, grass, flowers, sidewalks, building materials, fabrics, paper, foods, and so forth. After they have experienced and discussed various textures, have them collect items with different textural qualities and then use the items in charts and texture collages. Encourage the children to touch their collage experiments, look at the textures carefully, and discuss their reactions to different texture combinations.

3. Have the children create their own collages or series of collages using as many different textures as they wish. Then, ask the children to share these illustrations with one another, along with accompanying stories or descriptions.

4. Share with the children a picture book illustrated with collage. While reading the story and showing the children the pictures, ask the children to recognize the collage technique, discuss the feelings produced by each collage object, tell why they think the illustrator chose a certain material to represent it, and describe the texture they would feel if they could touch the original collage. Let them decide whether or not the collage illustrations make the story better.

Hopkins, Lee Bennett (ed.). *Surprises.* Illustrated by Megan Lloyd. Harper & Row, 1984 (I:5–9).

Kessler, Leonard. *Kick, Pass, and Run.* Harper & Row, 1966 (I:5–8 R:1).

Levinson, Nancy Smiler. *Snowshoe Thompson.* Illustrated by Joan Sandin. HarperCollins, 1992 (I:5–8).

Lobel, Arnold. *Frog and Toad All Year.* Harper & Row, 1976 (I:5–8 R:1).

_____. *Frog and Toad Are Friends.* Harper & Row, 1970 (I:5–8 R:1).

_____. *Frog and Toad Together.* Harper & Row, 1972 (I:5–8 R:1).

_____. *Grasshopper on the Road.* Harper & Row, 1978 (I:5–8 R:2).

_____. *Owl at Home.* Harper & Row, 1975 (I:5–8 R:2).

_____. *Uncle Elephant.* Harper & Row, 1981 (I:5–8 R:2).

Marshall, Edward. *Four on the Shore.* Illustrated by James Marshall. Dial, 1985 (I:5–9 R:1).

Pomerantz, Charlotte. *Outside Dog.* Illustrated by Jennifer Plecas. HarperCollins, 1993 (I:5–8 R:2).

Rylant, Cynthia. *Henry and Mudge and the Bedtime Thumps.* Illustrated by Sucie Stevenson. Bradbury, 1991 (I:5–8).

_____. *Henry and Mudge and the Happy Cat.* Illustrated by Sucie Stevenson. Bradbury, 1990 (I:5–8).

_____. *Henry and Mudge and the Long Weekend.* Illustrated by Sucie Stevenson. Bradbury, 1992 (I:5–8).

_____. *Mr. Putter and Tabby Pour the Tea.* Illustrated by Arthur Howard. Harcourt Brace Jovanovich, 1994 (I:6–9).

_____. *Mr. Putter and Tabby Walk the Dog.* Illustrated by Arthur Howard. Harcourt Brace Jovanovich, 1994 (I:6–9).

_____. *Poppleton.* Illustrated by Mark Teague. Scholastic, 1997 (I:4–7).

Schwartz, Alvin. *In a Dark, Dark Room.* Illustrated by Dirk Zimmer. Harper & Row, 1984 (I:6–9 R:2).

Seuss, Dr. *The Cat in the Hat.* Random House, 1957 (I:4–7 R:1).

_____. *The Cat in the Hat Comes Back.* Random House, 1958 (I:4–7 R:1).

Van Leeuwen, Jean. *More Tales of Oliver Pig.* Dial, 1981 (I:5–7 R:2).

_____. *Oliver and Amanda's Halloween.* Illustrated by Ann Schweninger. Dial, 1992 (I:5–8).

_____. *Oliver Pig at School.* Illustrated by Ann Schweninger. Dial, 1990 (I:5–8).

_____. *Tales of Oliver Pig.* Illustrated by Arnold Lobel. Dial, 1979 (I:5–7 R:2).

Wiseman, Bernard. *Morris Goes to School.* Harper & Row, 1970 (I:5–8 R:1).

PICTURE STORYBOOKS

Aardema, Verna. *Why Mosquitoes Buzz in People's Ears.* Illustrated by Leo and Diane Dillon. Dial, 1975 (I:5–9 R:6).

Ackerman, Karen. *Song and Dance Man.* Illustrated by Stephen Gammell. Knopf, 1988 (I:3–8 R:4).

Ada, Alma Flor. *Jordi's Star.* Putnam, 1996 (I:4–8 R:4).

Adoff, Arnold. *Black Is Brown Is Tan.* Illustrated by Emily Arnold McCully. Harper & Row, 1973 (I:3–7).

Agee, Jon. *The Incredible Painting of Felix Clousseau.* Farrar, Straus & Giroux, 1988 (I:5–8 R:4).

_____. *The Return of Freddy LeGrand.* Farrar, Straus & Giroux, 1992 (I:5–8 R:4).

Ahlberg, Janet, and Allan Ahlberg. *Each Peach Pear Plum: An I-Spy Story.* Viking, 1978 (I:3–7).

_____. *The Jolly Postman.* Little, Brown, 1986 (I:3–8).

Alexander, Lloyd. *The Fortune-Tellers.* Illustrated by Trina Schart Hyman. Dutton, 1992 (I:all).

Appelt, Kathi. *Where, Where Is Swamp Bear?.* Illustrated by Megan Halsey. HarperCollins, 2002 (I:4–7).

Asch, Frank. *Moonbear's Pet.* Simon & Schuster, 1997 (I:4–6).

Ashforth, Camilla. *Monkey Tricks.* Candlewick, 1992 (I:3–6 R:4).

Auch, Mary Jane. *The Easter Egg Farm.* Holiday, 1992 (I:3–7 R:4).

_____. *Peeping Beauty.* Holiday, 1993 (I:4–8 R:4).

Babbitt, Natalie. *BUB: Or the Very Best Thing.* HarperCollins, 1994 (I:all).

Baker, Jeannie. *Where the Forest Meets the Sea.* Greenwillow, 1988 (I:4–10 R:5).

Baker, Keith. *Little Green.* Harcourt, 2001 (I:2–5).

Bang, Molly. *Goose.* Scholastic, 1996 (I:4–7).

Bannerman, Helen. *The Story of Little Babaji.* Illustrated by Fred Marcellino. HarperCollins, 1996 (I:all).

Baylor, Byrd. *The Best Town in the World.* Illustrated by Ronald Himler. Scribner, 1983 (I:all).

Bedard, Michael. *Emily.* Illustrated by Barbara Cooney. Doubleday, 1992 (I:all).

Best, Cari. *Shrinking Violet.* Illustrated by Giselle Potter. Farrar, Straus & Giroux, 2001.

Bogacki, Tomek. *Cat and Mouse.* Farrar, Straus & Giroux, 1996 (I:3–5).

Brown, Marc. *Arthur's Baby.* Little, Brown, 1987 (I:3–6 R:3).

_____. *Arthur Goes to Camp.* Little, Brown, 1982 (I:3–6 R:3).

_____. *Arthur's Family Vacation.* Little, Brown, 1993 (I:3–6 R:3).

Brown, Margaret Wise. *On Christmas Eve.* Illustrated by Nancy Edwards. Calder, 1996 (I:5–8).

_____. *The Runaway Bunny.* Rev. ed. Illustrated by Clement Hurd. Harper & Row, 1972 (I:2–7 R:6).

_____. *The Important Book.* Illustrated by Leonard Weisgard. Harper, 1949 (I:3–8 R:4).

Buchholz, Quint. *The Collector of Moments.* Translated by Peter F. Neumeyer. Farrar, Straus & Giroux, 1999 (I:all).

Bunting, Eve. *Flower Garden.* Illustrated by Kathryn Hewitt. Harcourt Brace Jovanovich, 1994 (I:3–6).

_____. *Ghost's Hour, Spook's Hour.* Illustrated by Donald Carrick. Clarion, 1987 (I:2–7 R:2).

_____. *The Mother's Day Mice.* Illustrated by Jan Brett. Clarion, 1986 (I:3–6).

_____. *My Backpack.* Illustrated by Maryann Cocca-Leffler. Boyds Mills, 1997 (I:4–8).

_____. *Smoky Night.* Illustrated by David Diaz. Harcourt Brace Jovanovich, 1994 (I:all).

_____. *The Wednesday Surprise.* Illustrated by Donald Carrick. Clarion, 1989 (I:3–9 R:5).

Burton, Virginia Lee. *Katy and the Big Snow.* Houghton Mifflin, 1943, 1971 (I:2–6 R:4).

_____. *The Little House.* Houghton Mifflin, 1942 (I:3–7 R:3).

_____. *Mike Mulligan and His Steam Shovel.* Houghton Mifflin, 1939 (I:2–6 R:4).

Calmenson, Stephanie, and Joanna Cole. *Rockin' Reptiles*. Illustrated by Lynn Munsinger. Morrow, 1997 (I:7–9 R:4).

Cannon, Janell. *Verdi*. Harcourt Brace, 1997 (I:4–10 R:5).

Carlstrom, Nancy White. *Jesse Bear, What Will You Wear?* Illustrated by Bruce Degen. Macmillan, 1986 (I:3–6).

Cazet, Denys. *A Fish in His Pocket*. Watts, 1987 (I:3–6 R:4).

Cendrars, Blaise. *Shadow*. Illustrated by Marcia Brown. Scribner, 1982 (I:all).

Cole, Brock. *Buttons*. Farrar, Straus & Giroux, 2000 (I:6+ R:4).

Condra, Estelle. *See the Ocean*. Illustrated by Linda Crockett-Blassingame. Ideals, 1994. (I:6–10 R:4).

Conrad, Pam. *Call Me Ahnighito*. Illustrated by Richard Egielski. HarperCollins, 1995 (I:7+ R:5).

Cooney, Barbara. *Miss Rumphius*. Viking, 1982. (I:5–8).

Cooper, Helen. *The Boy Who Would Not Go to Bed*. Dial, 1997 (I:3–6).

Crews, Donald. *Night At the Fair*. Greenwillow, 1998. (I:4–7).

_____. *Shortcut*. Greenwillow, 1992 (I:4–8 R:4).

Cronin, Doreen. *Click, Clack, Moo: Cows That Type*. Illustrated by Betsy Lewin, Simon & Schuster, 2000 (I:4–7).

Crunk, Tony. *Big Mama*. Illustrated by Margot Apple. Farrar, Straus & Giroux, 2000 (I:5–8 R:4).

Curtis, Jamie Lee. *Tell Me Again About the Night I Was Born*. Illustrated by Laura Cornell. HarperCollins, 1996 (I:4–7 R:4).

Cutler, Jane. *The Cello of Mr. O*. Illustrated by Greg Couch. Dutton, 1999 (I:7+ R:5).

_____. *Darcy and Gran Don't Like Babies*. Illustrated by Susannah Ryan. Scholastic, 1993 (I:3–7 R:3).

Dadey, Debbie. *Shooting Star: Annie Oakley, the Legend*. Illustrated by Scott Goto. Walker, 1997 (I:5–9 R:5).

Darling, Benjamin. *Valerie and the Silver Pear*. Illustrated by Dan Lane. Four Winds, 1992 (I:5–8).

de Brunhoff, Jean. *The Story of Babar*. Random House, 1933, 1961 (I:3–9 R:4).

_____, and Laurent de Brunhoff. *Babar's Anniversary Album: 6 Favorite Stories*. Random House, 1981 (I:3–9 R:4).

Defelice, Cynthia. *Willy's Silly Grandma*. Illustrated by Shelley Jackson. Orchard, 1997 (I:5–8 R:4).

dePaola, Tomie. *The Clown of God*. Harcourt Brace Jovanovich, 1978 (I:all R:4).

_____. *An Early American Christmas*. Holiday House, 1987 (I:4–7 R:6).

_____. *Nana Upstairs & Nana Downstairs*. Putnam, 1973 (I:3–7 R:6).

_____. *Oliver Button Is a Sissy*. Harcourt Brace Jovanovich, 1979 (I:5–8 R:2).

Duvoisin, Roger. *Petunia*. Knopf, 1950 (I:3–6 R:6).

Ehlert, Lois. *Mole's Hill*. Harcourt Brace Jovanovich, 1994 (I:3–8).

Emberley, Barbara. *Drummer Hoff*. Illustrated by Ed Emberley. Prentice-Hall, 1967 (I:3–7 R:6).

Engel, Diana. *Josephina Hates Her Name*. Morrow, 1989 (I:5–8 R:4).

Ericsson, Jennifer A. *No Milk!* Illustrated by Ora Eitan. Tambourine, 1993 (I:3–8).

Ernst, Lisa Campbell. *Miss Penny and Mr. Grubbs*. Bradbury, 1991 (I:5–8 R:4).

_____. *Walter's Tail*. Bradbury, 1992 (I:4–8 R:4).

_____. *When Bluebell Sang*. Bradbury, 1989 (I:4–8 R:5).

Falconer, Ian. *Olivia*. Simon & Schuster, 2000 (I:3–8 R:4).

_____. *Olivia Saves the Circus*. Simon & Schuster, 2001 (I:3–8 R:4)

Fleischman, Paul. *Time Train*. Illustrated by Claire Ewart. HarperCollins, 1991 (I:4–8 R:4).

_____. *Weslandia*. Illustrated by Kevin Hawkes. Candlewick, 1999 (I:8+ R:5).

Fleischman, Sid. *The Scarebird*. Illustrated by Peter Sís. Greenwillow, 1988 (I:5–9 R:5).

Fleming, Candace. *The Hatmaker's Sign: A Story by Benjamin Franklin*. Illustrated by Robert Andrew Parker. Orchard, 1998 (I:5–9 R:5).

_____. *When Agnes Caws*. Illustrated by Giselle Potter. Atheneum, 1999 (I:4–9 R:4).

_____. *Muncha! Muncha! Muncha!* Illustrated by G. Brian Karas. Atheneum, 2002 (I:5–8).

Fleming, Denise. *Lunch*. Holt, 1992 (I:2–7).

Fletcher, Ralph. *Twilight Comes Twice*. Illustrated by Kate Kiesler. Clarion, 1997. (I:6–10 R:3).

Forward, Toby. *Ben's Christmas Carol*. Illustrated by Ruth Brown. Dutton, 1996 (I:5–8).

Fox, Mem. *Hattie and the Fox*. Illustrated by Patricia Mullins. Bradbury, 1987 (I:3–7).

_____. *Night Noises*. Illustrated by Terry Denton. Harcourt Brace Jovanovich, 1989 (I:3–8 R:5).

_____. *Wombat Divine*. Illustrated by Kerry Argent. Harcourt Brace, 1996 (I:4–7).

Gág, Wanda. *Millions of Cats*. Coward, McCann, 1929 (I:3–7 R:3).

Galbraith, Kathryn O. *Laura Charlotte*. Illustrated by Floyd Cooper. Putnam, 1990 (I:4–6 R:4).

Gammell, Stephen. *Wake Up Bear . . . It's Christmas!* Lothrop, Lee & Shepard, 1981 (I:5–8 R:4).

Gantos, Jack. *Rotten Ralph's Rotten Romance*. Houghton Mifflin, 1997 (I:4–8 R:4).

Gauch, Patricia Lee. *Christina Katerina and the Time She Quit the Family*. Illustrated by Elise Primavera. Putnam, 1987 (I:4–8 R:6).

Gliori, Debi. *Flora's Blanket*. Scholastic, 2001 (I:1–3).

_____. *The Snow Lambs*. Scholastic, 1996 (I:4–8 R:4).

Graff, Nancy Price. *In the Hush of the Evening*. Illustrated by Brian G. Karas. HarperCollins, 1998 (I:7–11 R:4).

Graham, Bob. *Benny: An Adventure Story*. Candlewick, 1999 (I:3–7 R:4).

Gray, Libba Moore. *My Mama Had a Dancing Heart*. Illustrated by Raúl Colón. Orchard, 1995. (I:7–11 R:5).

Griffith, Helen V. *Grandaddy and Janetta*. Illustrated by James Stevenson. Greenwillow, 1993 (I:6–10 R:5).

_____. *Grandaddy's Place*. Illustrated by James Stevenson. Greenwillow, 1987 (I:4–8 R:4).

Haas, Irene. *A Summer Song*. Simon & Schuster, 1997 (I:4–8 R:4).

Haley, Gail E. *A Story, a Story*. Atheneum, 1970 (I:6–10 R:6).

Hanson, Regina. *The Face at the Window*. Illustrated by Linda Saport. Clarion, 1997 (I:5–8 R:4).

Hartmann, Wendy, and Niki Daly. *The Dinosaurs Are Back and It's All Your Fault Edward!* McElderry, 1997 (I:5–8 R:4).

Henkes, Kevin. *Jessica*. Greenwillow, 1989 (I:3–6 R:5).

_____. *Lilly's Purple Plastic Purse*. Greenwillow, 1996 (I:4–8 R:4).

_____. *Owen*. Greenwillow, 1993 (I:2–5 R:4).

Herriot, James. *Moses the Kitten.* Illustrated by Peter Barrett. St. Martin's, 1984 (I:all R:5).

Hesse, Karen. *Lester's Dog.* Illustrated by Nancy Carpenter. Crown, 1993 (I:6–9 R:5).

Hest, Amy. *Baby Duck and the Bad Eyeglasses.* Illustrated by Jill Barton. Candlewick, 1996 (I:3–8 R:5).

_____. *The Crack-of-Dawn Walkers.* Illustrated by Amy Schwartz. Macmillan, 1984 (I:5–8 R:3).

_____. *In the Rain with Baby Duck.* Illustrated by Jill Barton. Candlewick, 1995 (I:3–8 R:5).

_____. *Off to School, Baby Duck!* Illustrated by Jill Barton. Candlewick, 1999 (I:3–6 R:4).

Ho, Minfong. *Hush! A Thai Lullaby.* Illustrated by Holly Meade. Orchard, 1996 (I:3–8).

Hoban, Russell. *A Baby Sister for Frances.* Illustrated by Lillian Hoban. Harper & Row, 1964 (I:5–8 R:4).

_____. *A Bargain for Frances.* Illustrated by Lillian Hoban. Harper & Row, 1970 (I:4–8 R:2).

_____. *Best Friends for Frances.* Illustrated by Lillian Hoban. Harper & Row, 1969 (I:4–8 R:4).

_____. *Bread and Jam for Frances.* Illustrated by Lillian Hoban. Harper & Row, 1964 (I:4–8 R:4).

Hoberman, Mary Ann. *Mr. and Mrs. Muddle.* Illustrated by Catharine O'Neill. Little, Brown, 1988 (I:3–8 R:4).

_____. *You Read to Me, I'll Read to You: Very Short Stories to Read Together.* Illustrated by Michael Emberley. Little, Brown, 2001 (I:4–8).

Hoestlandt, Jo. *Star of Fear, Star of Hope.* Illustrated by Johanna Kang. Walker, 1995 (I:all).

Houston, Gloria. *My Great-Aunt Arizona.* Illustrated by Susan Condie Lamb. HarperCollins, 1992 (I:5–9 R:5).

Hughes, Shirley. *Alfie Gives a Hand.* Lothrop, Lee & Shepard, 1983 (I:3–6 R:4).

Hunter, Anne. *Possum's Harvest Moon.* Houghton, Mifflin, 1996 (I:3–6).

Hurd, Edith Thacher. *I Dance in My Red Pajamas.* Illustrated by Emily Arnold McCully. Harper & Row, 1982 (I:3–7 R:3).

Hutchins, Pat. *Happy Birthday, Sam.* Greenwillow, 1978 (I:3–6 R:4).

_____. *Where's the Baby?* Greenwillow, 1988 (I:3–6 R:4).

_____. *The Wind Blew.* Macmillan, 1974 (I:3–6 R:4).

Innocenti, Roberto. *Rose Blanche.* Stewart, Tabori & Chang, 1985 (I:all).

Isaacs, Anne. *Swamp Angel.* Illustrated by Paul O. Zelinsky. Dutton, 1994 (I:all).

Isadora, Rachel. *Young Mozart.* Viking, 1997 (I:4–8 R:5).

James, Simon. *Dear Mr. Blueberry.* Macmillan, 1991 (I:4–7 R:4).

Jennings, Dana Andrew. *Me, Dad & Number 6.* Illustrated by Goro Sasaki. Harcourt Brace, 1997 (I:4–8 R:5).

Johnson, Angela. *Julius.* Illustrated by Dav Pilkey. Orchard, 1993 (I:3–8 R:4).

_____. *The Rolling Store.* Illustrated by Peter Catalanotto. Orchard, 1997 (I:4–8 R:4).

Johnson, D. B. *Henry Hikes to Fitchburg.* Houghton Mifflin, 2000 (I:4–8 R:5).

Johnson, Paul Brett. *The Cow Who Wouldn't Come Down.* Orchard, 1993 (I:5–8 R:5).

Jorgensen, Gail. *Gotcha!* Illustrated by Kerry Argent. Scholastic, 1997 (I:3–7).

Joyce, William. *Dinosaur Bob and His Adventures with the Family Lazardo.* Harper & Row, 1988 (I:5–9 R:5).

_____. *Santa Calls.* HarperCollins, 1993 (I:4–9 R:6).

Jukes, Mavis. *Like Jake and Me.* Illustrated by Lloyd Bloom. Knopf, 1984 (I:6–9 R:4).

Keats, Ezra Jack. *Dreams.* Macmillan, 1974 (I:3–8 R:3).

_____. *Goggles!* Macmillan, 1969 (I:5–9 R:3).

_____. *A Letter to Amy.* Harper & Row, 1968 (I:3–8 R:3).

_____. *Maggie and the Pirate.* Four Winds, 1979 (I:4–8 R:3).

_____. *Peter's Chair.* Harper & Row, 1967 (I:3–8 R:2).

_____. *Regards to the Man in the Moon.* Four Winds, 1981 (I:4–8 R:3).

_____. *The Trip.* Greenwillow, 1978 (I:3–8 R:2).

Keller, Holly. *Island Baby.* Greenwillow, 1992 (I:4–8 R:4).

Kellogg, Steven. *I Was Born About 10,000 Years Ago.* Morrow, 1996 (I:all).

_____. *A Penguin for Pinkerton.* Dial, 2001 (I:4–8 R:3).

_____. *A Rose for Pinkerton.* Dial, 1981 (I:4–8 R:3).

Kessler, Christina. *Jubela.* Illustrated by JoEllen McAllister Stammen. Simon & Schuster, 2001 (I:4–8).

Khalsa, Dayal Kaur. *I Want a Dog.* Clarkson, 1987 (I:4–7 R:5).

Kimmel, Eric A. *The Chanukkah Guest.* Illustrated by Giora Carmi. Holiday House, 1990 (I:5–9 R:5).

_____. *The Chanukkah Tree.* Illustrated by Giora Carmi. Holiday House, 1988 (I:5–9 R:5).

Kleven, Elisa. *The Puddle Pail.* Dutton, 1997 (I:4–8).

Kodama, Tatsuharu. *Shin's Tricycle.* Illustrated by Noriyuki Ando. Walker, 1995 (I:all).

Kraus, Robert. *Leo the Late Bloomer.* Illustrated by Jose and Ariane Aruego. Windmill, 1971 (I:2–6 R:4).

Kurtz, Jane. *Faraway Home.* Illustrated by E. B. Lewis. Harcourt, 2000 (I:5–8 R:5).

Leaf, Munro. *The Story of Ferdinand.* Illustrated by Robert Lawson. Viking, 1936 (I:4–10 R:6).

L'Engle, Madeleine. *The Other Dog.* Illustrated by Christine Davenier. North-South, 2001 (I:5–8).

Lent, Blair. *Bayberry Bluff.* Houghton Mifflin, 1987 (I:3–8 R:6).

Lester, Helen. *Hooway for Wodney Wat.* Illustrated by Lynn Munsinger. Houghton Mifflin, 1999 (I:6+).

Lester, Julius. *Sam and the Tigers: A New Tale of Little Black Sambo.* Illustrated by Jerry Pinkney. Dial, 1996 (I:all).

Lindbergh, Reeve. *The Day the Goose Got Loose.* Illustrated by Steven Kellogg. Dial, 1990 (I:5–8 R:4).

Lindenbaum, Pija. *Boodil My Dog.* Henry Holt, 1992 (I:5–9 R:5).

Lionni, Leo. *Alexander and the Wind-up Mouse.* Pantheon, 1969 (I:3–6 R:3).

_____. *Tillie and the Wall.* Knopf, 1989 (I:2–7 R:4).

Littlesugar, Amy. *Marie in Fourth Position: The Story of Degas' "The Little Dancer."* Illustrated by Ian Schoenherr. Philomel, 1996 (I:6–8).

London, Jonathan. *The Owl Who Became the Moon.* Illustrated by Ted Rand. Dutton, 1993 (I:4–8).

Loomis, Christine. *Astro Bunnies.* Illustrated by Ora Eitan. Putnam, 2001 (I:4–7).

Lum, Kate. *What! Cried Granny: An Almost Bedtime Story.* Illustrated by Adrian Johnson. Dial, 1999 (I:2–6 R:4).

Lyon, George Ella. *Come a Tide*. Illustrated by Stephen Gammell. Orchard, 1990 (I:5–8 R:5).

_____. *Dreamplace*. Illustrated by Peter Catalanotto. Orchard, 1993 (I:all).

Macaulay, David. *Why the Chicken Crossed the Road*. Houghton Mifflin, 1987 (I:5–9 R:6).

McCloskey, Robert. *Blueberries for Sal*. Viking, 1948 (I:4–8 R:6).

_____. *Lentil*. Viking, 1940 (I:4–9 R:7).

_____. *Make Way for Ducklings*. Viking, 1941 (I:4–8 R:4).

_____. *One Morning in Maine*. Viking, 1952 (I:4–8 R:3).

_____. *Time of Wonder*. Viking, 1957 (I:5–8 R:4).

McCully, Emily Arnold. *Mirette on the High Wire*. Putnam, 1992 (I:5–9 R:5).

_____. *Starring Mirette & Bellini*. Putnam, 1997 (I:all).

McDonald, Megan. *The Great Pumpkin Switch*. Illustrated by Ted Lewin. Orchard, 1992 (I:5–8 R:4).

McKissack, Patricia. *The Honest-to-Goodness Truth*. Illustrated by Giselle Potter. Atheneum, 2000 (I:5–9 R:4).

_____. *Nettie Jo's Friends*. Illustrated by Scott Cook. Knopf, 1989 (I:5–9 R:5).

McPhail, David. *Edward and the Pirates*. Little, Brown, 1997 (I:5–8 R:4).

_____. *Fix-It*. Dutton, 1984 (I:3–R:2).

Marshall, James. *George and Martha One Fine Day*. Houghton Mifflin, 1978 (I:3–8).

Martin, Bill, and John Archambault. *Up and Down on the Merry-Go-Round*. Illustrated by Ted Rand. Holt, Rinehart & Winston, 1988 (I:3–8).

Martin, Jacqueline Briggs. *Buzzy Bones and the Lost Quilt*. Illustrated by Stella Ormai. Lothrop, Lee & Shepard, 1988 (I:4–8 R:6).

_____. *Good Times on Grandfather Mountain*. Illustrated by Susan Gaber. Orchard, 1992 (I:4–8 R:4).

Martin, Rafe. *Will's Mammoth*. Illustrated by Stephen Gammell. Putnam, 1989 (I:2–8).

Maruki, Toshi. *Hiroshima No Pika*. Lothrop, Lee & Shepard, 1982 (I:10+ R:4).

Mathis, Sharon Bell. *The Hundred Penny Box*. Illustrated by Leo and Diane Dillon. Viking, 1975 (I:6–9 R:3).

Mayer, Mercer. *There's a Nightmare in My Closet*. Dial, 1969 (I:3–7 R:3).

Meddaugh, Susan. *The Best Place*. Houghton Mifflin, 1999 (I:4–8 R:4).

_____. *Martha Speaks*. Houghton Mifflin, 1992 (I:4–8 R:4).

Melmed, Laura Krauss. *The First Song Ever Sung*. Illustrated by Ed Young. Lothrop, 1993 (I:3–6).

Milne, A. A. *Winnie-the-Pooh*. Illustrated by Ernest H. Shepard. Dutton, 1926, 1954 (I:6–10 R:5).

Modarressi, Mitra. *Yard Sale*. DK, 2000 (I:3–7 R:4).

Monson, A. M. *Wanted: Best Friend*. Illustrated by Lynn Munsinger. Dial, 1997 (I:4–8 R:4).

Moss, Lloyd. *Zin! Zin! Zin! A Violin*. Illustrated by Marjorie Priceman. Simon & Schuster, 1995 (I:all).

Murphy, Mary. *I Like It When . . .* Harcourt Brace, 1997 (I:3–5).

Myers, Walter Dean. *Harlem*. Illustrated by Christopher Myers. Scholastic, 1997 (I: all).

Narahashi, Keiko. *I Have a Friend*. Macmillan, 1987 (I:2–6+ R:3).

Naylor, Phyllis Reynolds. *Keeping a Christmas Secret*. Illustrated by Lena Shiffman. Atheneum, 1989 (I:3–7 R:3).

Ness, Evaline. *Sam, Bangs & Moonshine*. Holt, Rinehart & Winston, 1966 (I:5–9 R:3).

Newman, Lesléa. *Cats, Cats, Cats!* Illustrated by Erika Oller. Simon & Schuster, 2001 (I:4–8).

Nivola, Claire. *Elisabeth*. Farrar, Straus & Giroux, 1997 (I:4–8 R:4).

Numeroff, Laura. *The Chicken Sisters*. Illustrated by Sharleen Collicott. HarperCollins, 1997 (I:4–7).

Oakley, Graham. *Hetty and Harriet*. Atheneum, 1982 (I:5–10 R:6).

Opkinson, Deborah. *Birdie's Lighthouse*. Illustrated by Kimberly Bulcken Root. Simon & Schuster, 1997 (I:5–9 R:5).

Paz, Octavio. Translated by Catherine Cowan. *My Life with the Wave*. Illustrated by Mark Buehner. Lothrop, Lee & Shepard, 1997 (I:4–8).

Peet, Bill. *Cyrus the Unsinkable Sea Serpent*. Houghton Mifflin, 1975 (I:5–9 R:7).

_____. *The Gnats of Knotty Pine*. Houghton Mifflin, 1975 (I:5–9 R:6).

_____. *No Such Things*. Houghton Mifflin, 1983 (I:4–8 R:6).

Plourde, Lynn. *Pigs in the Mud in the Middle of the Rud*. Illustrated by John Schoenherr. Scholastic, 1997 (I:3–7).

Polacco, Patricia. *Appelemando's Dreams*. Philomel, 1991 (I:6–9 R:5).

_____. *Babushka Baba Yaga*. Philomel, 1993 (I:5–8 R:5).

_____. *The Bee Tree*. Philomel, 1993 (I:5–8 R:5).

_____. *The Butterfly*. Philomel, 2000 (I:6–9 R:5).

_____. *Meteor!* Dodd, Mead, 1987 (I:6–10 R:7).

_____. *Thunder Cake*. Philomel, 1990 (I:5–8 R:5).

Porte, Barbara Ann. *Harry in Trouble*. Illustrated by Yossi Abolafia. Greenwillow, 1989 (I:3–7 R:2).

Purdy, Carol. *Least of All*. Illustrated by Tim Arnold. Macmillan, 1987 (I:5–8 R:5).

Ransome, Arthur. *The Fool of the World and the Flying Ship*. Illustrated by Uri Shulevitz. Farrar, Straus & Giroux, 1968 (I:6–10 R:6).

Raschka, Chris. *Yo! Yes?* Orchard, 1993 (I:3–7).

Rathmann, Peggy. *Officer Buckle and Gloria*. Putnam, 1995 (I:all).

Reiser, Lynn. *Best Friends Think Alike*. Greenwillow, 1997 (I:3–6).

Rey, Hans. *Curious George*. Houghton Mifflin, 1941, 1969 (I:2–7 R:2).

Riley, Linnea. *Mouse Mess*. Scholastic, 1997 (I:4–7).

Root, Phyllis. *Mrs. Potter's Pig*. Illustrated by Russell Ayto. Candlewick, 1996 (I:4–8).

Rosen, Michael. *We're Going on a Bear Hunt*. Illustrated by Helen Oxenbury. Macmillan, 1989 (I:2–7).

Rosenberg, Liz. *Eli and Uncle Dawn*. Illustrated by Susan Gaber. Harcourt Brace, 1997 (I:3–8).

_____. *Moonbathing*. Illustrated by Stephen Lambert. Harcourt, Brace, 1996 (I:3–8).

Rylant, Cynthia. *Mr. Griggs' Work*. Illustrated by Julie Downing. Watts, 1989 (I:4–8 R:5).

_____. *The Old Woman Who Named Things*. Illustrated by Kathryn Brown. Harcourt Brace, 1996 (I:4–8).

_____. *When I Was Young in the Mountains*. Dutton, 1985 (I:4–7 R:3).

Sanfield, Steve. *The Great Turtle Drive.* Illustrated by Dirk Zimmer. Knopf, 1996 (I:7–10).

San Souci, Robert. *The Hobyahs.* Illustrated by Alexi Natchev. Doubleday, 1994 (I:4–7 R:5).

Schotter, Roni. *Captain Snap and the Children of Vinegar Lane.* Illustrated by Marcia Sewall. Orchard, 1989 (I:5–9 R:5).

_____. *Nothing Ever Happens on 90th Street.* Illustrated by Kyrsten Brooker. Orchard, 1997 (I:6–9 R:4).

Schwartz, Amy. *Annabelle Swift, Kindergartner.* Orchard, 1988 (I:4–7 R:4).

Sendak, Maurice. *In the Night Kitchen.* Harper & Row, 1970 (I:5–7).

_____. *Seven Little Monsters.* Harper & Row, 1977 (I:5–8).

_____. *The Sign on Rosie's Door.* Harper & Row, 1960 (I:5–9 R:2).

_____. *Where the Wild Things Are.* Harper & Row, 1963 (I:4–8 R:6).

Seuss, Dr. *And to Think That I Saw It on Mulberry Street.* Vanguard, 1937 (I:3–9 R:5).

_____. *The 500 Hats of Bartholomew Cubbins.* Vanguard, 1938 (I:4–9 R:4).

_____. *Horton Hatches the Egg.* Random House, 1940, 1968 (I:3–9 R:4).

_____. *Hunches in Bunches.* Random House, 1982 (I:6–10 R:4).

_____. *If I Ran the Zoo.* Random House, 1950 (I:4–10 R:3).

Sharmat, Marjorie Weinman. *The Best Valentine in the World.* Illustrated by Lilian Obligado. Holiday House, 1982 (I:3–7 R:4).

Simont, Marc, retold by. *The Stray Dog: From a True Story by Reiko Sassa.* HarperCollins, 2001 (I:4–8 R:4).

Sís, Peter. *Starry Messenger.* Farrar, Straus & Giroux, 1996 (I:all).

Sisulu, Elinor Batezalt. *The Day Gogo Went to Vote: South Africa, April 1994.* Illustrated by Sharon Wilson. Little, Brown, 1996 (I:4–8 R:5).

Small, David. *Imogene's Antlers.* Crown, 1985 (I:5–8 R:6).

Spier, Peter. *The Star-Spangled Banner.* Doubleday, 1973 (I:8+).

Spinelli, Eileen. *Night Shift Daddy.* Illustrated by Melissa Iwa. Hyperion, 2000 (I:3–6).

Standiford, Natalie. *Astronauts Are Sleeping.* Illustrated by Allen Garns. Knopf, 1997 (I:4–8).

Steig, William. *The Amazing Bone.* Farrar, Straus & Giroux, 1976 (I:6–9 R:3).

_____. *Caleb & Kate.* Farrar, Straus & Giroux, 1977 (I:6–9 R:3).

_____. *Spinky Sulks.* Farrar, Straus & Giroux, 1988 (I:3–7 R:5).

_____. *Sylvester and the Magic Pebble.* Simon & Schuster, 1969 (I:6–9 R:5).

_____. *Toby Where Are You?* Illustrated by Teryl Euvremer. Harcourt Brace, 1997 (I:3–6).

Stevens, Janet. *Tops & Bottoms.* Harcourt Brace, 1995 (I:4–7).

Stevenson, James. *Could Be Worse!* Greenwillow, 1977 (I:5–9 R:3).

_____. *Don't You Know There's a War On?* Greenwillow, 1992 (I:all).

_____. *July.* Greenwillow, 1990 (I:5–8 R:4).

Stock, Catherine. *Armien's Fishing Trip.* Morrow, 1990 (I:5–8 R:4).

Stewart, Sarah. *The Gardener.* Illustrated by David Small. Farrar, Straus & Giroux, 1997 (I:5–8 R: 4).

Sutcliff, Rosemary. *The Minstrel and the Dragon Pup.* Illustrated by Emma Chichester Clark. Candlewick, 1993 (I:6–10 R:5).

Sykes, Julie. *Dora's Eggs.* Illustrated by Jane Chapman. Little Tiger, 1997 (I:3–7 R:4).

Taback, Simms. *Joseph Had a Little Overcoat.* Viking, 1999 (I:all).

Trivizas, Eugene. *The Three Little Wolves and the Big Bad Pig.* Illustrated by Helen Oxenbury. Macmillan, 1993 (I:4–9 R:4).

Tsubakiyama, Margaret Holloway. *Mei-Mei Loves the Morning.* Illustrated by Cornelius Van Wright and Ying-Hwa Hu. Albert Whitman & Co., 1999.

Turner, Ann. *Shaker Hearts.* Illustrated by Wendell Minor. HarperCollins, 1997 (I:all).

Ungerer, Tomi. *The Beast of Monsieur Racine.* Farrar, Straus & Giroux, 1971 (I:5–9 R:5).

Van Allsburg, Chris. *Jumanji.* Houghton Mifflin, 1981 (I:5–8 R:6).

_____. *The Polar Express.* Houghton Mifflin, 1985 (I:5–8 R:6).

_____. *The Sweetest Fig.* Houghton Mifflin, 1993 (I:all R:6).

_____. *The Widow's Broom.* Houghton Mifflin, 1992 (I:5–8 R:5).

_____. *The Wreck of the Zephyr.* Houghton Mifflin, 1983 (I:5–8 R:6).

_____. *The Wretched Stone.* Houghton Mifflin, 1991 (I:5–8 R:5).

Vincent, Gabrielle. *Ernest and Celestine's Picnic.* Greenwillow, 1982 (I:3–5 R:4).

Viorst, Judith. *Alexander and the Terrible, Horrible, No Good, Very Bad Day.* Illustrated by Ray Cruz. Atheneum, 1972 (I:3–8 R:6).

Voake, Charlotte. *Mrs. Goose's Baby.* Little, Brown, 1989 (I:2–6).

Waber, Bernard. *A Lion Named Shirley Williamson.* Houghton Mifflin, 1996 (I:4–7 R:4).

Waddell, Martin. *Can't You Sleep, Little Bear?* Illustrated by Barbara Firth. Candlewick, 1992 (I:2–4 R:4).

_____. *Farmer Duck.* Illustrated by Helen Oxenbury. Candlewick, 1992 (I:4–7 R:3).

_____. *Let's Go Home, Little Bear.* Illustrated by Barbara Firth. Candlewick, 1993 (I:2–4 R:4).

_____. *What Use Is A Moose?* Illustrated by Arthur Robins. Candlewick, 1996 (I:5–8 R:4).

_____. *You and Me, Little Bear.* Illustrated by Barbara Firth. Candlewick, 1996 (I:3–6 R:4).

Ward, Lynd. *The Biggest Bear.* Houghton Mifflin, 1952 (I:5–8 R:4).

Waring, Richard. *Hungry Hen.* Illustrated by Caroline Jayne Church. HarperCollins, 2002 (I:5–7).

Wayland, April Halprin. *To Rabbittown.* Illustrated by Robin Spowart. Scholastic, 1989 (I:3–8 R:5).

Wegman, William. *William Wegman's Farm.* Hyperion, 1997 (I:all).

Wells, Rosemary. *Bunny Cakes.* Dial, 1997 (I:2–6).

_____. *The Language of Doves.* Illustrated by Greg Shed. Dial, 1996 (I:5–8 R:4).

_____. *A Lion for Lewis.* Dial, 1982 (I:3–7 R:4).

_____. *Max and Ruby's First Greek Myth: Pandora's Box.* Dial, 1993 (I:3–8 R:3).

_____. *McDuff Moves In.* Illustrated by Susan Jeffers. Hyperion, 1997 (I:2–5).

_____. *Timothy Goes to School.* Dial, 1981 (I:4–7 R:4).

Wiesner, David. *June 29, 1999.* Clarion, 1992 (I:all).

Wild, Margaret. *Let the Celebrations Begin!* Illustrated by Julie Vivas. Orchard, 1991 (I:all).

_____. *Mr. Nick's Knitting.* Illustrated by Dee Huxley. Harcourt Brace Jovanovich, 1989 (I:4–8 R:4).

Williams, Jay. *Everyone Knows What a Dragon Looks Like.* Illustrated by Mercer Mayer. Four Winds, 1976 (I:5–10).

Williams, Sherley Anne. *Working Cotton.* Illustrated by Carole Byard. Harcourt Brace Jovanovich, 1992 (I:all).

Williams, Vera. *A Chair for My Mother.* Greenwillow, 1982 (I:3–7 R:6).

_____. *Something Special for Me.* Greenwillow, 1983 (I:3–7 R:6).

_____. *Stringbean's Trip to the Shining Sea.* Greenwillow, 1988 (I:all).

Wilson, Sarah. *Good Zap, Little Grog.* Illustrated by Susan Meddaugh. Candlewick, 1995 (I:3–8).

Winthrop, Elizabeth. *Bear and Mrs. Duck.* Illustrated by Patience Brewster. Holiday House, 1988 (I:3–6 R:2).

Wood, Audrey. *The Flying Dragon Room.* Illustrated by Mark Teague. Scholastic, 1996 (I:4–8 R:6).

_____. *The Red Racer.* Simon & Schuster, 1996 (I:4–8 R:5).

Wood, Don. *Piggies.* Harcourt Brace Jovanovich, 1991 (I:2–7).

Woodson, Jacqueline. *The Other Side.* Illustrated by E. B. Lewis. Putnam, 2001 (I:6–8 R:4).

Yolen, Jane. *Letting Swift River Go.* Illustrated by Barbara Cooney. Little, Brown, 1992 (I:5–8 R:5).

_____. *Owl Moon.* Illustrated by John Schoenherr. Philomel, 1987 (I:all).

_____. *Welcome to the Sea of Sand.* Illustrated by Laura Regan. Putnam, 1996. (I:5–8 R:4).

Yorinks, Arthur. *Hey, Al.* Illustrated by Richard Egielski. Farrar, Straus & Giroux, 1986 (I:all R:5).

_____. *The Miami Giant.* Illustrated by Maurice Sendak. HarperCollins, 1995 (I:all).

Zamorano, Ana. *Let's Eat!* Illustrated by Julie Vivas. Scholastic, 1997 (I:4–7 R:4).

Zemach, Margot. *It Could Always Be Worse: A Yiddish Folktale.* Farrar, Straus & Giroux, 1976 (I:5–9 R:2).

Zimmerman, Andrea, and David Clemesha. *My Dog Toby.* Illustrated by True Kelley. Harcourt, 2000 (I:4–8).

Zolotow, Charlotte. *William's Doll.* Illustrated by William Pène du Bois. Harper & Row, 1972 (I:4–8 R:4).

TRADITIONAL LITERATURE

Illustration from Pappa Gatto, An Italian Fairy Tale, retold by Ruth Sanderson, copyright © 1995 by Ruth Sanderson. Used by permission of Little, Brown & Company.

Of Castle and Cottage

nchanted swans who regain human form because of a sister's devotion, a brave boy who climbs into the unknown world at the top of a beanstalk, witches, warriors, supernatural animals, royal personages, and humans are brought to life in traditional literature. Such literature contains something that appeals to all interests: humorous stories, magical stories, and adventure stories. The settings of the stories are as varied as the enchanted places in the human imagination and as the geography of our world, from scorching deserts to polar icecaps. Regardless of location or subject, such tales include some of the most beloved and memorable stories of everyone's childhood. This chapter discusses the nature of our traditional literary heritage—its basic forms and themes and what it has to offer children.

Our Traditional Literary Heritage

The quest for traditional literary heritage takes students of children's literature to times before recorded history and to all parts of the world. Tales of religious significance allowed ancient people to speculate about their beginnings. Mythical heroes and heroines from all cultures overcame supernatural adversaries to gain their rewards. Stories of real people who performed brave deeds probably gratified the rulers of ancient tribes. According to folklorist Stith Thompson (1977), similarities in the types of tales and in the narrative motifs and content of traditional stories from peoples throughout the world constitute tangible evidence that traditional tales are both universal and ancient.

Traditionally, young and old alike heard the same tales, but each social class cultivated the art of storytelling, reflecting the culture, natural environment, and social contacts of the storyteller and the audience. For example, storytellers who earned their livings in medieval European castles related great deeds of nobility. The English court heard about King Arthur, Queen Guinevere, and the Knights of the Round Table, and the French court heard stories of princely valor, such as "The Song of Roland." In ancient China, stories for the ruling classes often portrayed benevolent dragons, symbols of imperial authority.

Commoners in medieval Europe lived lives quite different from those of the nobility, and the traditional stories of the commoners differed accordingly. The stories that peasants told one another reflected the harsh, unjust, and often cruel circumstances of their existence as virtual slaves to the nobles. A common theme in their folktales is overcoming social inequality to attain a better way of life. In many tales, a poor lad outwits a nobleman, wins his daughter in marriage, and gains lifelong wealth. This theme is found in "The Flying Ship," a Russian tale; "The Golden Goose," a German tale; and "The Princess and the Glass Hill," a Norwegian tale.

Other traditional stories, such as the English "Jack the Giant Killer," tell of overcoming horrible adversaries with cunning and bravery. The peasants in these stories are not always clever. The consequences of stupidity are emphasized, for example, in the Norwegian tale "The Husband Who Has to Mind the House" and in the Russian tale "The Falcon Under the Hat." In place of the benevolent imperial dragon, the tales of early China's common people often involved cruel and evil dragons, whose power the heroines or heros overcame.

In the seventeenth century, the Puritans of England and its colonies considered folktales about giants, witches, and enchantment to be immoral for everyone. They maintained that children in particular should hear and read only what instructed them and reinforced their moral development. Other social groups in Europe and North America felt differently, however. In 1697, the Frenchman Charles Perrault published a collection of folktales called *Tales of Mother Goose,* which included "Cinderella" and "Sleeping Beauty."

Over one hundred years later, the Romantic movement in Europe generated enthusiasm for exploring folklore to discover more about the roots of European languages and traditional cultures. In Germany, the Brothers Grimm carefully collected and transcribed oral tales from the storytellers themselves. These tales have been retold or adapted by many contemporary writers. Perrault and the Brothers Grimm thus brought new respect to traditional tales and ensured their availability for all time. Their work influenced collectors in other countries, as well as writers of literature.

By the end of the nineteenth century, European and North American societies generally considered childhood a distinct, necessary, and valuable stage in the human life cycle. Improved technology created more leisure hours for the middle and upper classes and a need for literature to entertain children. Traditional literature became a valuable part of the childhood experience.

According to Betsy Hearne (1988), a significant happening in children's book publishing in the early 1900s also influenced the availability of traditional literature: Numerous children's book departments were established. The editors were drawn from librarians who had knowledge of storytelling and the tales from the oral tradition. At the same time, illustrators with close cultural ties to their folklore and art immigrated from Europe. Consequently, newly illustrated folktales became an important part of the children's literature market.

Today, folk literature is considered an important part of every child's cultural heritage. It is difficult to imagine the early childhood and elementary school years of American children without "The Little Red Hen," "The Three Bears," and "Snow White and the Seven Dwarfs."

The literary experiences of older children would not be complete without tales of Greek and Norse mythology.

Types of Traditional Literature

Traditional tales have been handed down from generation to generation by word of mouth. In contrast to a modern story, a traditional tale has no identifiable author. Instead, storytellers tell what they have received from previous tellers of tales. Folklorists and others interested in collecting and analyzing traditional literature do not always agree about how to categorize and define different types of traditional tales. This text discusses four types of traditional tales—folktales, fables, myths, and legends—drawing on definitions recommended by folklorist William Bascom (1965). Chart 6.1 summarizes and clarifies the differences among folktales, fables, myths, and legends, providing examples of each type of traditional literature.

Folktales

According to Bascom, folktales are "prose narratives which are regarded as fiction. They are not considered as dogma or history, they may or may not have happened, and they are not taken seriously" (p. 4). Because the tales are set in any time or place, they seem almost timeless and placeless. Folktales usually tell the adventures of animal or human characters. They contain common narrative motifs—such as supernatural adversaries (ogres, witches, and giants), supernatural helpers, magic and marvels, tasks and quests—and common themes—such as reward of good and punishment of evil. (Not all themes and motifs are found within one tale.) Subcategories of folktales include cumulative tales, humorous tales, beast tales, magic and wonder tales, *pourquoi* tales, and realistic tales.

Cumulative Tales. Tales that sequentially repeat actions, characters, or speeches until a climax is reached are found among all cultures. Most cumulative tales give their main characters—whether animal, vegetable, human, or inanimate object—intelligence and reasoning ability. Adults often share these stories with very young children because the structure of cumulative tales allows children to join in as each new happening occurs. A runaway baked food is a popular, culturally diverse subject for cumulative tales. It is found in not only the German "Gingerbread Boy" but also a Norwegian version, "The Pancake"; an English version, "Johnny Cake"; and a Russian version, "The Bun." In each of these tales, the repetition builds until the climax. Other familiar cumulative tales include the English "Henny Penny"; "The Fat Cat," a Danish tale; and "Why Mosquitoes Buzz in People's Ears," an African tale.

Humorous Tales. Folktales allow people to laugh at themselves as well as at others, an apparently universal pleasure. In tales such as the Russian "The Peasant's Pea Patch," the humor results from absurd situations or the

CHART 6.1 Characteristics of folktales, fables, myths, and legends

Form and Examples	Belief	Time	Place	Attitude	Principal Characters
Folktale	*Fiction*	*Anytime*	*Anyplace*	*Secular*	*Human or Nonhuman*
1. "Snow White and Seven Dwarfs" (European)	Fiction	"Once upon a time"	"In the great forest"	Secular	Human girl and dwarfs
2. "The Crane Wife" (Asian)	Fiction	Long ago	"In a faraway mountain village"	Secular	Human man, supernatural wife
3. "Why Mosquitoes Buzz in People's Ears" (African)	Fiction	"One morning"	In a forest	Secular	Animals
Fable	*Fiction*	*Anytime*	*Anyplace*	*Secular/Allegorical*	*Animal or Human*
1. "The Hare and the Frog" (Aesop)	Fiction	"Once upon a time"	On the shore of a lake	Allegorical	Animals
2. "The Tyrant Who Became a Just Ruler" (Panchatantra—India)	Fiction	"In olden times"	In a kingdom	Allegorical	Human king
Myth	*Considered Fact*	*Remote Past*	*Other World or Earlier World*	*Sacred*	*Nonhuman*
1. "The Warrior Goddess: Athena" (European)	Considered fact	Remote past	Olympus	Deities	Greek goddess
2. "Zuñi Creation Myth" (Native American)	Considered fact	Before and during creation	Sky, earth, and lower world	Deities	Creator Awonawilona, Sun Father, Earth Mother
Legend	*Considered Fact*	*Recent Past*	*World of Today*	*Secular or Sacred*	*Human*
1. "King Arthur Tales" (European)	Considered fact	Recent past	Britain	Secular	King
2. "The White Archer" (Native American)	Considered fact	Recent past	Land of Eskimos	Secular	Indian who wanted to avenge parents' death

stupidity of the characters. Human foolishness resulting from unwise decisions provides the humor and a moral in the English folktale "Mr. and Mrs. Vinegar" and in the Norwegian tale "The Husband Who Has to Mind the House."

Beast Tales. Beast tales are among the most universal folktales, being found in all cultures. For example, the coyote is a popular animal in Native American tales, while the fox and wolf are found in many European tales. The rabbit and the bear are popular characters in the folktales of African American culture in the United States. Beasts in folktales often talk and act quite like people. In some stories, such as "The Bremen Town Musicians," animal characters use their wits to frighten away robbers and claim wealth. In other tales, such as "The Three Billy Goats Gruff," animals use first their wits and then their strength to overcome an enemy. Still other animals win through industrious actions, such as those in "The Little Red Hen." Tales about talking animals may show the cleverness of one animal and the stupidity of another.

Magic and Wonder Tales. The majority of magic and wonder tales contain some element of magic. The fairy godmother transforms the kind, lovely, mistreated girl into a beautiful princess ("Cinderella"), the good peasant boy earns a cloth that provides food ("The Lad Who Went to the North Wind"), a kindhearted simpleton attains a magical ship ("The Fool of the World and the Flying Ship"), or the evil witch transforms the handsome prince into a beast ("Beauty and the Beast"). Transformations from humans to animals and animals to humans are also common in folktales. Mingshui Cai (1993) describes the relationships between humans and animals in both Eastern and Western folktales. He describes several tales in which magical animals become brides for humans. Cai categorizes these bride stories as brides from the sky, as in the Japanese story "The Crane Wife"; brides from the earth, as in the Native American folktale "The Serpent of the Sea"; and brides from the water, as in the Japanese story "Urashima Taro." Magic in wonder tales can be good or bad. When it is good, the person who benefits has usually had misfortune or is considered inferior by a parent or society. When it is bad, love and diligence usually overcome the magic—as in the German tale "The Six Swans" and the Norwegian tale "East of the Sun and West of the Moon."

Pourquoi Tales. *Pourquoi* tales—or "why" tales, in an English translation of the French word—answer a question or explain how animals, plants, or humans were created and why they have certain characteristics. For example, why does an animal or a human act in a certain way? Children enjoy *pourquoi* tales and like to make up their own stories about why animals or humans have certain characteristics.

Realistic Tales. The majority of folktales include supernatural characters, magic, or other exaggerated incidents. A few tales, however, have realistic plots and involve people who could have existed. One such tale, "Dick Whittington," tells about a boy who comes to London looking for streets paved with gold. He doesn't find golden streets, but he does find work with an honest merchant, and eventually, he wins his fortune. Some versions of this story suggest that at least parts of it are true—a Dick Whittington was lord mayor of London.

Fables

Fables are brief tales in which animal characters that talk and act like humans indicate a moral lesson or satirize human conduct. For example, in the familiar "The Hare and the Tortoise," the hare taunts the tortoise about her slow movements and boasts about his own speed. The tortoise then challenges the hare to a race. The hare starts rapidly and is soon far ahead, but he becomes tired and, in his confidence, decides to nap. Meanwhile, the tortoise, keeping at her slow and steady pace, plods across the finish line. When the hare awakens, he discovers that the tortoise has reached the goal. The moral of this fable is that perseverance and determination may compensate for lack of other attributes.

Myths

According to Bascom, myths are

prose narratives which, in the society in which they are told, are considered to be truthful accounts of what happened in the remote past. They are accepted on faith; they are taught to be believed; and they can be cited as authority in answer to ignorance, doubt, or disbelief. Myths are the embodiment of dogma; they are usually sacred; and they are often associated with theology and ritual. (p. 4)

Myths account for the origin of the world and humans; for everyday natural phenomena, such as thunder and lightning; and for human emotions and experiences, such as love and death. The main characters in myths may be animals, deities, or humans. The actions take place in an earlier world or another world, such as the underworld or the sky. Many ancient Greek myths, for example, explain the creation of the world, the creation of the gods and goddesses who ruled from Mount Olympus, and the reasons for natural phenomena. The myth about Demeter and Persephone, for example, explains seasonal changes.

Legends

Legends, Bascom says, are

prose narratives which, like myths, are regarded as true by the narrator and his audience, but they are set in a period considered less remote, when the world was much as it is today. Legends are more often secular than sacred, and their principal characters are human. (p. 4)

Many legends embroider the historical facts of human wars and migrations, brave deeds, and royalty. Legends from the British Isles tell about Robin Hood, the protector of the poor in the Middle Ages, who may have been an actual person. Legends from France tell about the miraculous visions of Joan of Arc, who led French armies into battle against the English. Legends from Africa describe how the prophet Amakosa saved the Juba people from extinction.

Values of Traditional Literature for Children

Traditional literature helps children understand the world and identify with universal human struggles. It also provides pleasure.

Understanding the World

Traditional tales help children improve their understanding of the world. Storyteller Diane Wolkstein (1992) declares, "Every story is rooted in a culture, and the world of culture is limitless" (p. 704). (See the Evaluation Criteria on this page.) In her introduction to *The Troll with No Heart in His Body and Other Tales of Trolls from Norway,* Lise Lunge-Larsen emphasizes that "Telling or reading folktales is one way to cultivate a child's soul and humanity. With their ancient symbolic images, such stories reach deep inside children to connect them with their essential nature" (p. 9).

World understanding is increased as children gain understanding of early cultural traditions, learn about cultural diffusion as they read variants of tales, develop

appreciation of culture and art from different countries, and become familiarized with many languages and dialects of cultures around the world.

Betsy Hearne (1993a) considers the identification of cultural sources in folktales so important that she makes the following proposals: "that the producers of picture-book folktales provide source notes that set these stories in their cultural context; that those of us who select these materials for children judge them, at least in part, on how well their authors and publishers meet this responsibility" (p. 22). Without cultural knowledge, readers cannot speculate about cultural diffusion. The similarities among tales indicate movement of people through migration and conquests. They also emphasize that humans throughout the world have had similar needs and problems. Some folktales from different countries are almost identical. For example, the German tale "The Table, the Donkey, and the Stick" is very similar to both the Norwegian tale "The Lad Who Went to the North Wind" and the English folktale "The Donkey, the Table, and the Stick." Also, almost every country has its traditional trickster, such as the fox in Palestine and the mousedeer in Malaysia; its stupid, easily fooled creature, such as the bear in Lapland and the giraffe in West Africa; and its benevolent, good-natured animal, such as the kangaroo in Australia. The tales are very similar, although the animals and the settings are characteristic of the countries in which they are told.

Traditional tales encourage children to realize that people from all over the world have inherent goodness, mercy, courage, and industry. In a Chinese tale, a loving brother rescues his sister from a dragon; in a German tale, a sister suffers six years of ordeals in order to bring her brothers back to human form. A Jewish folk character works hard to cultivate fig trees that may benefit his descendants but not himself, while the Norse Beowulf's strength of character defeats evil monsters.

Identifying with Universal Human Struggles

In *The Uses of Enchantment: The Meaning and Importance of Fairy Tales,* Bruno Bettelheim (1976) provides strong rationales for using traditional tales with children. In his psychoanalytic approach to traditional tales, Bettelheim claims that nothing is so enriching as traditional literature. To reinforce this claim, he argues that traditional tales allow children to learn about human progress and possible solutions to problems. Because tales state problems briefly, children can understand them. In addition, traditional tales subtly convey the advantages of moral behavior. Children learn that struggling against difficulties is unavoidable, but they can emerge victorious if they directly confront hardships.

Traditional tales present characters who are both good and bad. According to Bettelheim, children gain the conviction that crime does not pay. The simple, straightforward characters in traditional tales allow children to

---

EVALUATION CRITERIA

Literary Criticism: Increasing World Understanding Through Traditional Tales

1. Does the literature help children better understand the nonscientific cultural traditions of early humanity?

2. Does the literature show the interrelatedness of various types of stories and narrative motifs?

3. Does the literature help explain how different versions of a tale are dispersed?

4. Does the literature help children learn to appreciate the culture and art of a different country?

5. Does the literature provide factual information about a different country?

6. Does the literature familiarize children with another language or dialect of the world?

7. Can the literature be used to stimulate creative drama, writing, and other forms of artistic expression?

8. Does the literature encourage children to realize that people from another part of the world have inherent goodness, mercy, courage, and industry?

ISSUE Whose Cultural Values and Belief Systems Should Be Reflected in Folklore?

One of the issues we face as we read and evaluate folklore from around the world is whose cultural values and belief systems the tales should reflect. Should the stories be rewritten to reflect current American beliefs? Or should the tales reflect their original cultures in both text and illustrations? Comments in articles by Nina Jaffe[1] and David Sacks[2] provide interesting points for discussion.

Jaffe evaluates the work of Harold Courlander as he collected and retold tales that preserved the values of the cultures. Jaffe highlights Courlander's difficulties in his desire to retain authenticity. She quotes his difficulties with editors who frequently wanted him to change style or content. Courlander states, "In one collection, there was a Hottentot tale. It was about how people die and don't live again. That was the theme of it—how that came about. It was a kind of how it began story. An editor I

was dealing with said, 'A lot of people don't believe that, they believe you do live again.' And I have to be adamant about it and say, 'This is the story!' They didn't think it was suitable for children. Well too bad, they have to learn other people don't think the same way as we do— that's what it's all about' " (p. 133). Jaffe believes that retellers can have creative integrity "as long as values of respect, sensitivity, and self-knowledge are present in the interpretation, research, and retelling" (p. 133).

Sacks provides an equally strong argument for using myths and other literature reflecting ancient Greece and Rome. He believes in retaining the authenticity even in highly illustrated books. He states, "In a collection of myths for elementary-aged audiences, it could mean using illustrations that convey immortal grandeur, not a trivializing goofiness" (p. 38). He then presents an anno-

tated list of myths, history, and historical fiction that he recommends.

As you consider Jaffe and Courlander's concerns for cultural authenticity in the tales and Sacks's concern for cultural authenticity in the illustrations, ask yourself: What do you believe is the value in reading tales from another culture? Should the tales reflect the values and beliefs of the original culture or should they be rewritten to reflect the values and beliefs of contemporary American audiences? What happens to our understandings of earlier and frequently different cultures if the stories are changed? How does authenticity in illustrations add to or detract from folktales?

[1]Jaffe, Nina. "Reflections on the Work of Harold Courlander." *School Library Journal* 42 (September 1996): 132–133.
[2]Sacks, David. "Breathing New Life into Ancient Greece and Rome." *School Library Journal* 42 (November 1996): 38–39.

---

identify with the good and to reject the bad. Children empathize with honorable characters and their struggles, learning that while they may experience difficulty or rejection, they, too, will be given help and guidance when needed. Author and folklorist Gail E. Haley (1986) emphasizes the importance of reading about heroes in folklore because

heroes of the past teach us solutions for coping with today and tomorrow. They were synthesized out of the dreams and wishes of the people who created and consumed them. Those that survive are those whose faces, forms, and stature have fulfilled the nature and needs of succeeding generations. We still need heroes. (p. 118)

Joyce Thomas (1987) also emphatically supports the use of traditional tales with children. She states, "To deny fairy tales to children or to allow only those with 'acceptable' morals and innocuous fantasy is to retard their psychological and imaginative growth and expression" (p. 111).

Pleasure

Traditional literature is extremely popular with children. In particular, folktales—with their fast-paced, dramatic plots and easily identifiable good and bad characters—are among the types of literature most appealing to young audiences. Although folktales may appeal primarily to young children, children of various ages and interests find them enjoyable. Animal tales, such as "The Three Little Pigs," "The Little Red Hen," and "The Three Bears," have been illustrated in picture-book format for young children,

while fairy tales, such as "Beauty and the Beast," are of interest to upper-elementary school children.

F. André Favat (1977) reviewed the relevant research and reached the following conclusions about interest in folktales among children of different ages:

1. Children between the ages of five and ten—or roughly from kindergarten through the fifth grade—are highly interested in folktales, whether they select books or are presented with books and asked for their opinions.

2. This interest follows a curve of reading preference— that is, children's interest in folktales emerges at a prereading age and gradually rises to a peak between the approximate ages of six and eight. It then gradually declines.

3. Concurrent with the decline in interest in folktales emerges an interest in realistic stories.

Favat maintains that the characteristics of folktales correspond with the characteristics that Jean Piaget ascribed to children. First, children believe that objects, actions, thoughts, and words can exercise magical influence over events in their own lives. Folktales are filled with such occurrences, as spells turn humans into animals, or vice versa, and humble pumpkins become gilded coaches.

Second, children believe that inanimate objects and animals have consciousness much like that of humans. In folktales, the objects and animals that speak or act like people are consistent with children's beliefs.

Third, young children believe in punishment for wrongdoing and reward for good behavior. Folktales satisfy children's sense of justice. The good Goose Girl, for example, is rewarded by marrying the prince, and her deceitful maid is punished harshly.

Fourth, the relationship between heroes and heroines and their environments is much the same as the relationship between children and their own environments. Children are the center of their universes, while heroes and heroines are the centers of their folktale worlds. For example, when Sleeping Beauty sleeps for a hundred years, so does the whole castle.

Authenticating the Folklore

If students are to gain the values associated with folklore, especially the values associated with understanding a culture that is different from their own, they require literature that depicts the values, beliefs, and cultural backgrounds of various groups. The need for accuracy and authenticity is emphasized in numerous articles. For example, two articles by Betsy Hearne emphasize the importance of authenticity in picture books. In "Cite the Source: Reducing Cultural Chaos in Picture Books, Part One" (1993a), Hearne states: "How do you tell if a folktale in picture-book format is authentic, or true to its cultural background? What picture books have met the challenge of presenting authentic folklore for children? These two questions . . . are especially pressing in light of our growing national concern about multicultural awareness. And they generate even broader questions: How can an oral tradition survive in print? How do children's books pass on—and play on—folklore?" (p. 22).

In her second article, "Respect the Source: Reducing Cultural Chaos in Picture Books, Part Two" (1993b), Hearne discusses the importance of establishing cultural authority, citing the sources for folklore, and training adults who select and interact with the literature. She concludes her article with the following statements: "We can ask for source citations and more critical reviews; we can compare adaptations of their printed sources (interlibrary loan works for librarians as well as their patrons) and see what's been changed in tone and content; we can consider what context graphic art provides for a story; we can make more informed selections, not by hard and fast rules, but by judging the balance of each book. . . . We can, in short, educate ourselves on the use and abuse of folklore at an intersection of traditions" (p. 37).

Retellers of folklore are beginning to include more information that readers and critics can use to evaluate the authenticity of the folktales. For example, Paul Robert Walker includes considerable information in his retelling of *Little Folk: Stories from Around the World.* He includes an author's note, a discussion about the tale following each story, and a bibliography of sources for each of the tales. Consider in the excerpts from the following discussion of the retelling of "Rumpelstiltskin" how you might use this information when checking the authenticity of the tale:

"Rumpelstiltskin" was included in the first volume of the first edition of folktales by Jacob and Wilhelm Grimm, published in 1812 as *Kinderund Hausmarchen* (The Children's and Household Tales). . . . In this telling, I have generally followed the Grimms' tales, but I've added ideas from a version of "Tom Tit Tot" collected in Suffolk County, England, and first published in 1878. . . . The most significant addition is that the king—rather than a messenger—happens upon the strange little man singing his song, to my mind at least, makes for a better story. (p. 13)

The sources cited in the bibliography provide enough original editions that evaluators can make their own decisions about the cultural authenticity of this retelling.

For an in-depth look at how you might conduct an authenticity project, Norton's *Multicultural Literature: Through the Eyes of Many Children* (2001) includes examples of authenticating an African folktale (pp. 28–29), authenticating a Mayan folktale (pp. 143–144), and authenticating a Jewish folktale (pp. 244–245).

Folktales

Many folktales have similar characteristics and motifs. The folktales discussed in this section have many similar characteristics. They also reflect cultural differences. Chart 6.2 summarizes some of these similarities and differences by comparing tales from several cultures. This section looks at British, French, German, Norwegian, Russian, Jewish, Asian, Middle Eastern, African, and Native American tales. You may analyze other tales from each culture to identify common characteristics.

Characteristics

Because folktales differ from other types of literature, they have characteristics related to plot, characterization, setting, theme, and style that may differ from other types of children's stories.

Plot. Conflict and action abound in folktales. The nature of the oral tradition made it imperative that listeners be brought quickly into the action. Consequently, even in written versions, folktales immerse readers into the major conflict within the first few sentences. For example, the conflict in Paul Galdone's *The Little Red Hen* is between laziness and industriousness. The first sentence introduces the animals who live together in a little house. The second sentence introduces the lazy cat, dog, and mouse. The third sentence introduces the industrious hen and the conflict. The remainder of the story develops the conflict between the lazy animals and the industrious fowl. The conflict is resolved when the hen eats her own baking and doesn't share it with her lazy friends.

Conflict between characters representing good and characters representing evil is typical of folktales. Even though the odds are uneven, the hero overcomes the giant in "Jack the Giant Killer," the girl and boy outsmart the witch in "Hansel and Gretel," the intelligent animal

CHART 6.2 Comparisons of folktales from different cultures

Culture and Examples	Protagonist—Main Character	Portrayal of Hero or Heroine	Portrayal of Other Characters	Setting
British "Jack the Giant Killer"	Simple peasant lad	The lad is brave and is clever enough to outwit the villain.	The giants are evil. The king is weak.	Mountain cave
French "Sleeping Beauty"	Adolescent princess (about fifteen)	The prince is "pursued by love and honor" and is valiant.	The fairy is wicked. The father cannot protect his daughter.	Castle with a series of rooms similar to Versailles
German "Hansel and Gretel"	Boy and girl (a wood-cutter's children)	Hansel is caring, but Gretel is clever enough to outwit the witch.	The stepmother is uncaring. The father is weak. The witch is wicked.	Forest
Norwegian "The Lad Who Went to the North Wind"	Simple peasant lad	The lad is simple but honest.	The north wind is powerful. The mother is scolding. The innkeeper is dishonest and greedy.	Rural Far North
Russian "The Fool of the World and the Flying Ship"	Simple, young peasant	The young peasant is foolish but kindhearted.	The czar is dishonorable. The four companions have great powers.	Rural countryside and the czar's palace
Jewish "Mazel and Schlimazel"	Poor peasant	The bungler does poorly until good luck intercedes.	The spirit of good luck is happy and attractive. The spirit of bad luck is slumped and angry.	King's court and the countryside
Chinese "The Golden Sheng"	Poor adolescent girl	The boy grows up very rapidly.	The girl is helpless. The dragon is evil and cruel.	Rural
African "How Spider Got a Thin Waist"	Tricky and greedy spider	The greedy spider does not work; instead, he plays in the sun.	The villagers are hard-working.	Forest and village
Native American "The Fire Bringer"	Young Paiute Indian boy	The boy is concerned about his people.	The coyote is intelligent. The runners are swift.	Mesa and mountain
British "Jack the Giant Killer"	Common people	The hero is sent to rid the kingdom of giants.	Intelligence and bravery	Happy ending. The hero is rewarded with knighthood when the villains are slain.

(continues)

CHART 6.2 Continued

Culture and Examples	Protagonist—Main Character	Portrayal of Hero or Heroine	Portrayal of Other Characters	Setting
French "Sleeping Beauty"	Nobility	A threatened girl is rescued by a prince.	Beauty, wit, grace, dancing, and singing	Happy ending. The prince and princess are married.
German "Hansel and Gretel"	Common people	Abandoned children outwit a wicked witch.	Caring and cleverness	Happy ending. The children are rewarded with jewels after the witch is burned to death.
Norwegian "The Lad Who Went to the North Wind"	Common people	The hero sets out to retrieve a lost object.	Honesty and kindness	Happy ending. The boy beats the innkeeper and is rewarded with magical objects.
Russian "The Fool of the World and the Flying Ship"	Common people	A simple boy sets out on a quest. He is aided by a magical ship and companions.	Kindness and honesty	Happy ending. The peasant marries royalty.
Jewish "Mazel and Schlimazel"	Common people	A simple boy is accompanied by good luck and then bad luck on a series of quests.	Diligence, honesty, sincerity, and helpfulness	Happy ending. The hero marries the princess and eventually becomes the wisest of prince consorts.
Chinese "The Golden Sheng"	Common people	A young boy goes on a quest to save his sister from a dragon.	Helpfulness, diligence, and loyalty	Happy ending. After the dragon whirls himself to death, the brother and sister return to their mother.
African "How Spider Got a Thin Waist"	Common people	The spider tries to get food without working.	Industriousness	Unhappy ending. The greedy spider gets a thin waist.
Native American "The Fire Bringer"	Common people	A boy and a coyote set out to get fire for the Paiutes.	Intelligence, swiftness, and bravery	Happy ending. The boy and the coyote are honored.

outwits the ogre in "Puss in Boots," and a brother saves his sister from a dragon in "The Golden Sheng."

Actions that recur in folktales have been the focus of several researchers. Vladimir Propp (1968) analyzed one hundred Russian folktales and identified thirty-one recurring actions that account for the uniformity and repetitiveness of folktales. While not all tales included all actions, actions occurred in the same sequence in most tales. More importantly, Propp discovered that similar patterns were apparent in non-Russian tales. Propp concluded that consistency of action in folktales does not result from the country of origin. Instead, consistency results from the fact that tales remain true to the folk tradition.

F. André Favat (1977) summarized Propp's findings and analyzed French and German tales according to their actions. The following list of recurring sequential actions that may be found in various combinations is adapted from Favat. In some tales, females are the primary actors, but most folktales, reflecting the values and social realities of their times and places of origin, assign actions primarily to male characters.

1. One family member leaves home.
2. The hero or heroine is forbidden to do some action.
3. The hero or heroine violates an order by doing something forbidden.
4. The villain surveys the situation.
5. The villain receives information about the victim.
6. The villain attempts to trick or deceive the victim in order to possess the victim or the victim's belongings.
7. The victim submits to deception and unwittingly helps the enemy.
8. The villain causes harm or injury to a member of a family.
9. One family member either lacks something or desires to have something.
10. A misfortune or lack is made known; the hero or heroine is approached with a request or command; and he or she is allowed to go or is sent on a mission.
11. The seeker agrees to, or decides upon, a counteraction.
12. The hero or heroine leaves home.
13. The hero or heroine is tested, interrogated, or attacked, which prepares the way for him or her to receive a magical agent or a helper.
14. The hero or heroine reacts to the actions of the future donor.
15. The hero or heroine acquires a magical agent.
16. The hero or heroine is transferred, delivered, or led to the whereabouts of an object.
17. The hero or heroine and the villain join in direct combat.

18. The hero or heroine is marked.
19. The villain is defeated.
20. The initial misfortune or lack is eliminated.
21. The hero or heroine returns.
22. The hero or heroine is pursued.
23. The hero or heroine is rescued from pursuit.
24. The hero or heroine, unrecognized, arrives home or in another country.
25. A false hero or heroine presents unfounded claims.
26. A difficult task is proposed to the hero or heroine.
27. The task is resolved.
28. The hero or heroine is recognized.
29. The false hero/heroine or the villain is exposed.
30. The hero or heroine is given a new appearance.
31. The villain is punished.
32. The hero or heroine is married and ascends to the throne.

Many of the folktales discussed in this chapter contain various combinations of these actions. All folktales have similar endings, just as they have similar beginnings and plot development, and most tales end with some version of "and they lived happily ever after."

Characterization. Folktale characters are less completely developed than are characters in other types of stories. Oral storytellers lacked the time to develop fully rounded characters. Thus, characters in folktales are essentially symbolic and flat—that is, they have a limited range of personal characteristics and do not change in the course of the story. A witch is always wicked, whether she is the builder of gingerbread houses in the German tale "Hansel and Gretel" or the fearsome Baba Yaga in the Russian "Maria Morevna." Other unchangeably evil characters include giants, ogres, trolls, and stepmothers.

Characters easily typed as bad are accompanied by those who are always good. The young heroine is fair, kind, and loving. The youngest son is honorable, kind, and unselfish even if he is considered foolish. Isaac Bashevis Singer's *Mazel and Shlimazel, or the Milk of the Lioness* demonstrates characteristic differences between good and bad characters: Mazel, the spirit of good luck, is young, tall, and slim, with pink cheeks and a jaunty stride; Shlimazel, the spirit of bad luck, is old, pale-faced, and angryeyed, with a crooked red nose, a beard as gray as a spider's web, and a slumping stride.

Folktales usually establish the main characters' natures early on, as Charles Perrault does in the first paragraph of "Cinderella: or The Little Glass Slipper":

There was once upon a time, a gentleman who married for his second wife the proudest and most haughty woman that ever was known. She had been a widow, and had by her former husband two daughters of her own humor, who were exactly like her in all things. He had also by a former wife a young daughter, but of an unparalleled goodness and sweetness of temper, which she took from her mother, who was the best creature in the world. (*Histories or Tales of Past Times,* p. 73)

The characteristics of two female characters in an Italian folktale reveal honored and disrespected human characteristics in folktales. The actions of Sophia, who is beautiful, greedy, and lazy, and Beatrice, who is plainer but generous, loving, and hardworking, provide the plot and develop the theme in Ruth Sanderson's *Papa Gatto: An Italian Fairy Tale.* The two girls either prove their worthlessness or their worth when they each take care of Papa Gatto's family of kittens. Even though Sophia tries to trick both her stepsister and a handsome prince, it is Beatrice's kind and generous nature that wins the prince, because "he knew he would do all in his power to win the one whose beauty shone from within" (unnumbered). Both Beatrice's lazy stepsister and stepmother earn their just rewards: "As for Sophia and the widow, they were left behind in the cottage, with no one to cook and clean and tend the garden but themselves" (unnumbered).

Children easily identify the good and bad characters in folktales. This easy identification of heroes and heroines, as well as lively action, may account for the popularity of folktales with young children.

Setting. Setting in literature includes both time and place. The time in folktales is always the far-distant past, usually introduced by some version of "once upon a time." The first line of a folktale usually places listeners into a time when anything might happen. A Russian tale, "The Firebird," begins "Long ago, in a distant kingdom, in a distant land, lived Tsar Vyslar Andronovich." Native American folktales may begin with some version of "When all was new, and the gods dwelt in the ancient places, long, long before the time of our ancients." A French tale is placed "on a day of days in the time of our fathers," while a German tale begins "In the olden days when wishing still helped one." These introductions inform listeners that enchantment and overcoming obstacles are possible in the tales about to unfold.

The symbolic settings found in many folktales are not carefully described because there is no need for description. One knows immediately that magic can happen in the great forest of the Grimms' "Snow White and the Seven Dwarfs" or in the great castle of Madame de Beaumont's version of "Beauty and the Beast." The title of a Romanian tale, "The Land Where Time Stood Still," establishes a setting where the imagination will accept and expect unusual occurrences.

The introduction that places the folktale in the far-distant past may also briefly sketch the location. A Chinese tale, "The Cinnamon Tree in the Moon," suggests a nature setting, "where not even a soft breeze stirs the heavens and one can see the shadows in the moon." After introducing such settings, folktales immediately identify the characters and develop the conflict.

Theme. Folktales contain universal truths and reflect the values of the times and societies in which they originated, many of which are still honored today. The characters, their actions, and their rewards develop themes related to moral and material achievement. Good overcomes evil; justice triumphs; unselfish love conquers; intelligence wins out over physical strength; kindness, diligence, and hard work bring rewards. The tales also show what happens to those who do not meet the traditional standards. The jealous queen is punished, the wicked stepsisters are blinded by birds, the foolish king loses part of his fortune or his daughter, and the greedy man loses the source of his success or his well-being.

The universality of these themes suggests that people everywhere have responded to similar ideals and beliefs. Consider, for example, the universality of the theme that intelligence is superior to physical strength. The hero in the English "Jack the Giant Killer" outwits the much larger and less intelligent giant. In the African tale "A Story, a Story," Spider outwits a series of animals and wins his wager with the being who controls stories. The hero in the Jewish "The Fable of the Fig Tree" is rewarded because he considers the long-range consequences of his actions. The heroine in the Chinese "The Clever Wife" uses her wits to bring the family power.

In contrast, another universal theme is that foolishness causes the loss of possessions. In an English tale, "Mr. and Mrs. Vinegar," the characters lose their possessions because of foolish actions. In a German tale, "The Fisherman and His Wife," the couple returns to a humble position because of foolish choices and greed. The Russian characters in "The Falcon Under the Hat" lose their possessions because of foolish actions. These themes are found in traditional literature around the world.

Style. Charles Perrault, the famed collector of French fairy tales in the seventeenth century, believed "that the best stories are those that imitate best the style and the simplicity of children's verses" (Hearn, 1977, p. viii). Such style permits few distracting details or unnecessary descriptions. Simplicity is especially apparent in the thoughts and dialogues of characters in folktales: They think and talk like people. For example, the dialogue in the Grimms' "The Golden Goose" sounds as if the listener were overhearing a conversation. The little old gray man welcomes the first son with "Good morning. Do give me a piece of that cake you have got in your pocket, and let me have a draught of your wine—I am so hungry and thirsty."

The clever, selfish son immediately answers, "If I give you my cake and wine I shall have none left for myself; you just go your own way." Disaster rapidly follows this exchange.

When Dullhead, the youngest, simplest son, begs to go into the woods, his father's response reflects his opinion of his son's ability: "Both your brothers have injured themselves. You had better leave it alone; you know nothing about it." Dullhead begs hard, and his father replies, "Very well, then—go. Perhaps when you have hurt yourself, you may learn to know better." This German folktale is filled with rapid exchanges as Dullhead is rewarded with the golden goose and moves humorously on toward his destiny with the king and the beautiful princess.

The language of folktales is often enriched with simple rhymes and verses. In "Jack and the Beanstalk," the giant chants:

Fee, fi-fo-fum,
I smell the blood of an Englishman,
Be he alive, or be he dead,
I'll have his bones to grind my bread.

The enchanted frog from the Grimms' "The Frog King" approaches the door of the princess with these words:

Princess! Youngest princess!
Open the door for me!
Dost thou not know what thou saidst to me
Yesterday by the cool waters of the fountain?
Princess, youngest princess!
Open the door for me!

Likewise, the witch asks Hansel and Gretel:

Nibble, nibble, gnaw,
Who is nibbling at my little house?

As the story nears its end, another rhyme asks the duck for help:

Little duck, little duck, dost thou see
Hansel and Gretel are waiting for thee?
There's never a plank or bridge in sight,
Take us across on thy back so white.

The simple style, easily identifiable characters, and rapid plot development make folktales appropriate for sharing orally with children.

Motifs

Kind or cruel supernatural beings, magical transformations of reality, and enchanted young people who must wait for true love to break spells that confine them are elements that take folktales out of the ordinary and encourage people to remember and repeat the tales. Folklorists have identified hundreds of such elements, or motifs, found in folktales.

Although a folktale may be remembered for one dramatic story element, most tales have multiple elements. Consider the following motifs in "Jack and the Beanstalk": (1) The hero makes a foolish bargain, (2) the hero acquires a magical object, (3) a plant has extraordinary powers, (4) the ogre repeats "fee-fi-fo-fum," (5) the ogre's wife hides the hero, (6) the hero steals a magical object from the ogre, (7) the magical object possesses the power of speech, and (8) the hero summons the ogre.

Researchers use motifs to analyze and identify the similarities in tales from various cultures. Some motifs are practically universal, suggesting similar thought processes in people living in different parts of the world. Other motifs help trace diffusion from one culture to another or identify a common source. Chart 6.3 summarizes the discussion of motifs and demonstrates that folktales from many parts of the world contain the same motifs. The search for common motifs is enlightening and rewarding for children as well as adults. Some of the most common of the many motifs in folktales are supernatural beings; extraordinary animals; and magical objects, powers, and transformations.

Supernatural Adversaries and Helpers. Supernatural beings in folktales are usually either adversaries or helpers. The wicked supernatural beings, such as ogres and witches, may find heroines or heroes, entice them into their cottages or castles, and make preparations to feast upon them. The main character may deliberately seek out the adversary, as in the Chinese tale "Li Chi Slays the Serpent," or the encounter with the evil being may be the result of an unlucky chance meeting, as in "Hansel and Gretel." Luckily, the intended victims usually outwit the adversaries. In addition to being evil, supernatural adversaries are usually stupid; consequently, they are overcome by characters who use wit and trickery.

Supernatural helpers support many folklore heroes and heroines in their quests. Seven dwarfs help Snow White in her battle against her evil stepmother. A supernatural old man causes hardships to the selfish older brothers and rewards the generous younger brother in the Russian tale "The Fool of the World and the Flying Ship." The same motif is found in tales from western Asia, eastern Europe, and India.

Extraordinary Animals. Whether cunning or stupid, deceitful or upstanding, extraordinary animals are popular characters in the folktales of all cultures. In the English and German versions of "Little Red Riding Hood," the wolf plays the role of ogre, deceives a child, and is eliminated. In Japanese folklore, the fox has a malicious nature. It can assume human shape, and it has the power to bewitch humans. Tricky foxes and coyotes are important characters in African American and Native American folktales as well.

Some extraordinary animals are loyal companions and helpers to deserving human characters. The cat in the French "Puss in Boots" outwits an ogre and provides riches for his human master. The German version of "Cinderella" collected by the Brothers Grimm contains no fairy godmother; instead, white doves and other birds help Cinderella complete the impossible tasks that her wicked stepmother requires. The variety of extraordinary animals is apparent in texts such as Margaret Mayo's *Mythical Birds & Beasts from Many Lands*. Mayo includes folktales and mythology as well as notes on the stories.

Magical Objects, Powers, and Transformations. The possession of a magical object or power is crucial in many folktales. When all seems lost, the hero may don the cloak

CHART 6.3 Common motifs in folktales from different cultures

Common Motif	Culture	Folktale
Supernatural Adversaries		
Ogre	England	"Jack the Giant Killer"
Ogress	Italy	"Petrosinella"
Troll	Norway	"Three Billy Goats Gruff"
Giant	Germany	"The Valiant Little Tailor"
Dragon	China	"The Golden Sheng"
Witch	Africa	"Marandenboni"
Supernatural Helpers		
Fairies	France and Germany	"The Sleeping Beauty"
Fairy godmother	Vietnam	"The Land of Small Dragon"
Jinni	Arabia	"The Woman of the Well"
Cat (fairy in disguise)	Italy	"The Cunning Cat"
Deceitful or Ferocious Beasts		
Wolf	Germany	"The Wolf and the Seven Little Kids"
Wolf	France	"Little Red Riding Hood"
Wolf	England	"The Three Little Pigs"
Wild hog, unicorn, and lion	United States	"Jack and the Varmints"
Magical Objects		
Cloak of invisibility	Germany	"The Twelve Dancing Princesses"
Magical cloth	Norway	"The Lad Who Went to the North Wind"
Magical lamp	Arabia	"Aladdin and the Magic Lamp"
Magical mill	Norway	"Why the Sea Is Salt"
Magical Powers		
Granted wishes	Germany	"The Fisherman and His Wife"
Wish for a child	Russia	"The Snow Maiden"
Humans with extraordinary powers	Mexico	"The Riddle of the Drum"
Humans with extraordinary powers	Russia	"The Fool of the World and the Flying Ship"
Magical Transformations		
Prince to bear	Norway	"East of the Sun and West of the Moon"
Prince to beast	France	"Beauty and the Beast"
Bird to human	Japan	"The Crane Wife"
Human to animal	United States (Native American)	"The Ring in the Prairie"

of invisibility and follow "The Twelve Dancing Princesses" to solve a mystery and win his fortune, or the heroine's loving tears may fall into her true love's eyes and save him from blindness, as in "Rapunzel."

Folktale characters often obtain magical objects in extraordinary manners, lose them or have them stolen, and eventually recover them. This sequence occurs in the Norwegian "The Lad Who Went to the North Wind," in which a boy goes to the North Wind demanding the return of his meal, is given a magical object, loses it to a dishonest innkeeper, and must retrieve it. The dishonest innkeeper is eventually punished. In folktales, stealing a magical object often results in problems for the thief.

Magical spells and transformations are also common in folktales around the world. The spell of a fairy godmother turns a pumpkin into a golden coach, and the spell of a witch puts a princess to sleep for a hundred

years. One of the most common transformation motifs is the transformation of a prince into an animal ("The Frog Prince") or a beastlike monster ("Beauty and the Beast"). A gentle, unselfish youngest daughter usually breaks the enchantment when she falls in love with the animal or beast. In a Basque tale, the beast is a huge serpent; a Magyar Hungarian tale has the prince transformed into a pig; and a Lithuanian tale tells of a prince who becomes a white wolf. "The Crane Wife," a Japanese folktale, contains another example of the transformation from animal to human, as a poor farmer gains a wife when a wounded crane he cares for transforms herself into a lovely woman.

Many Native American tales include humans who are transformed into animals. "The Ring in the Prairie," a Shawnee Indian tale, includes transformations of humans and sky dwellers: A human hunter transforms himself into a mouse to capture a girl who descends from the sky, and the sky dwellers secure part of an animal and are transformed into that specific animal. Many of the Native American transformation stories suggest close relationships between humans and animals.

Folktales from the British Isles

British folktales about ogres, giants, and clever humans were among the first stories published as inexpensive chapbooks in the 1500s. Joseph Jacobs collected the tales, and in 1890, he published over eighty of them as *English Fairy Tales*. In 1892, Jacobs published a collection of Celtic fairy tales. These books, in reissue or modern editions, are still available today. The number of possible folktales from the British Isles is further emphasized when we read Katharine Briggs's *Dictionary of British Folk-Tales* (1970–1971), which was originally published in four volumes and 2,558 pages. The fast plots and unpromising heroes of British tales are popular with children. For example, the various "Jack tales"—including "Jack the Giant Killer" and "Jack and the Beanstalk"—develop plots around villainous ogres or giants who terrorize a kingdom and the heroes who overcome their adversaries with trickery and cleverness rather than magical powers.

Steven Kellogg retells "Jack and the Beanstalk," which was first collected by Jacobs. Kellogg's *Jack and the Beanstalk* retains the familiar language: "Fee-fi-fo-fum! I smell the blood of an Englishman. Be he alive or be he dead, I'll grind his bones to make my bread" (p. 14, unnumbered). Kellogg's illustrations reinforce the gentle mood of the cow, Milky-White, and the contrasting villainous mood of the ogre, whose food preferences include young boys. The story clearly defines good and bad characters and shows that a person with physical strength does not always succeed.

Other villains in British folktales play adversarial roles similar to those of giants and ogres. For example, "Three Little Pigs" must outwit a wolf, and a young girl is frightened by "The Three Bears." Glen Rounds's *Three Little Pigs and the Big Bad Wolf* includes a huffing, puffing wolf who tries unsuccessfully to lure the wittier third pig out of his home. Steven Kellogg's *The Three Little Pigs* includes a strong and industrious mother and a wolf that is not as bad as that portrayed in usual versions. In *What's in Fox's Sack? An Old English Tale*, retold and illustrated by Paul Galdone, the villain is a sly fox who manages to get a boy into his sack. A clever woman outsmarts the fox by placing a large bulldog inside the sack. The mother goat in "Grey Goat," retold in Alan Garner's *A Bag of Moonshine*, saves her three kids by killing the fox. In *Whuppity Stoorie: A Scottish Folktale*, retold by Carolyn White, the heroine must outwit a fairy.

In addition to clearly defined good and bad characters, repetitive language in many British folktales appeals to storytellers and listeners. In "The Three Little Pigs," the wolf threatens, "I'll huff and I'll puff and I'll blow your house in," and the pig replies, "Not by the hair on my

RETOLD AND ILLUSTRATED BY
Barry Moser

Moser's version of the Three Little Pigs includes all of the characters found in the classic folktale. (From The Three Little Pigs. *Copyright © 2001 by Barry Moser. Published by Little, Brown and Company. Reprinted by permission of Little, Brown and Company.)*

chinny chin chin." "Goldilocks and the Three Bears" repeats chairs, bowls of porridge, and beds, and the three bears' questions: Who has been sitting in my chair? Who has been eating my porridge? Who has been sleeping in my bed? Several versions of this folktale appeal to young children. Lorinda Bryan Cauley's *Goldilocks and the Three Bears* has compelling illustrations. Paul Galdone's *The Three Bears*, which may be used to develop size concepts, has pictures that differentiate the sizes of bears, bowls, beds, and chairs. James Marshall's *Goldilocks and the Three Bears* frolic in humorous illustrations. Jan Brett's *Goldilocks and the Three Bears* includes large, detailed illustrations on pages bordered with objects and characters from the story.

British folk literature is filled with tales that stress foolishness, making a point about human foibles. Vivian French's retelling of *Lazy Jack* provides a humorous version of this tale about a boy who is so lazy that "He got out of bed in the afternoon and he yawned and he stretched and he ate and he burped. Then he went back to bed without ever doing anything for anybody" (unnumbered). After his mother insists that he go to work, a series of misunderstandings cause him to take his mother's previous advice. Consequently, he puts milk in his pocket, places cheese on his head, and drags fish home with a rope. The activities related to each of these actions is developed in a sequence of humorous illustrations.

The consequences of greed, a universal motif in folktales from many countries, are found in Susan Cooper's *The Silver Cow: A Welsh Tale*. In this tale, the magic people, the Tylwyth Teg, send a marvelous cow out of Bearded Lake as a reward for a young boy's music. The greed of the boy's father causes the cow and her offspring to return to the lake, where they are turned into water lilies.

An impossible task created by foolish boasting is a motif in Harve Zemach's *Duffy and the Devil*, a Cornish tale resembling "Rumpelstiltskin." An inefficient maid named Duffy misleads her employer about her spinning ability and makes an agreement with the devil, who promises to do the knitting for three years. At the end of that time, she must produce his name or go with him. When the time arrives, the squire goes hunting and overhears the festivities of the witches and the devil as the little man with the long tail sings this song:

Tomorrow! Tomorrow! Tomorrow's the day!
I'll take her! I'll take her! I'll take her away!
Let her weep, let her cry, let her beg, let her
  pray—
She'll never guess my name is . . . Tarraway!
  (p. 30, unnumbered)

Thus, Duffy learns the magic name and cheats the devil from claiming her soul. The importance of a secret name is reflected in folktales from many cultures. In the English version of "Rumpelstiltskin," the name is Tim Tit Tot; a Scottish secret name is Whuppity Stoories; a tale from Nigeria is "The Hippopotamus Called Isantim."

A Cinderella-type story is found in several British folktales. In "Tattercoats," recorded by Joseph Jacobs in *More English Fairy Tales*, the heroine is mistreated by her grandfather, who mourns his daughter's death in childbirth and rejects the child who survived, and by the grandfather's cruel servants. In this British version, the prince invites her to attend the ball even though she is dressed in her rags. Only after she is at the ball does the gooseherd transform her into a beautifully dressed lady. Kevin Crossley-Holland's "Mossycoat," found in his *British Folk Tales*, is also mistreated by servants before she marries the young master.

In *Princess Furball*, retold by Charlotte Huck, the Cinderella-type heroine is at first ignored by her father, the king, and then promised in marriage to an ogre. Unlike many of the Cinderella tales, this heroine does not rely on magic to overcome obstacles. Instead, she relies on her own ingenuity. She demands and receives three gowns and a coat made from one thousand kinds of fur as a bridal gift from her father, but in order to escape the marriage, she runs away. Later, she is captured by a young king from a neighboring kingdom. At the castle, she becomes a servant to the servants. In this role she sweeps ashes, washes dishes, and fetches wood. When the king gives a ball, Furball wears one of her gowns, attends the ball, and dazzles the king. These actions continue through three balls, until a ring she is wearing shows the king that she is the girl that he loves.

A Cinderella variant, "Fair, Brown, and Trembling," is included in *Celtic Fairy Tales* retold by Neil Philip. In this variant from Ireland, a hen wife provides beautiful clothes for Trembling so that she can go to church with the admonition that she must not go inside the church and must rush home when people rise at the end of the service. During the third visit to the church the son of a king takes her shoe and then searches for the owner. Trembling's two sisters hide her until she is finally discovered by the nobleman. In this variant, after the wedding Trembling is pushed into the sea by her wicked sister, swallowed by a whale, and must be rescued by her husband.

Folktales from Ireland are filled with fairies, leprechauns, and other little people. Jacob's "Guleesh," found in *Celtic Fairy Tales*, shows that the fairies do not always outwit people. A young man races with the "sheehogues," tricks those fairy hosts out of a captured princess, and breaks a spell so that the princess can speak. This tale has an ending characteristic of Irish folk literature: "But I heard it from a birdeen that there was neither cark nor care, sickness nor sorrow, mishap nor misfortune on them till the hour of their death, and may the same be with me, and with us all!" (p. 25).

Colorful language is a style of many Irish folktales. For example, Brendan Behan introduces *The King of Ireland's Son* in this way: "Once upon a time houses were whitewashed with buttermilk and the pigs ran around with knives and forks in their snouts shouting, 'Eat me, eat me!'" (unnumbered).

The Children of Lir, by Sheila MacGill-Callahan, is based on Irish folklore. In this tale, an evil stepmother transforms four children into swans; however, with the help of animals, the children finally break the evil spell. Some folklorists believe the Irish folktale to be the basis for Shakespeare's *King Lear*.

Peasants rather than royalty are usually the heroes and heroines in folktales of the British Isles. Consequently, readers or listeners can learn much about the problems, beliefs, values, and humor of common people in early British history. Themes in British folktales suggest that intelligence wins over physical strength, that hard work and diligence are rewarded, and that love and loyalty are basic values for everyone.

French Folktales

The majority of French folktales portray splendid royal castles rather than humble peasant cottages. Charles Perrault, a member of the Académie Française, collected and transcribed many of these tales. In 1697, he published a collection of folktales called *Tales of Mother Goose*, which included "Cinderilla" (original spelling), "Sleeping Beauty,"

"Puss in Boots," "Little Red Riding Hood," "Blue Beard," "Little Thumb," and "Diamond and the Toads." These stories had entertained children and adults of the Parisian aristocracy and, consequently, are quite different from tales that stress wicked, dishonest kings being outwitted by simple peasants. These folktales collected by Perrault provide the foundation for most of the French folktales published today.

Many illustrators and translators of French fairy tales depict royal settings. For example, Marcia Brown's *Cinderella* (based on Charles Perrault's version) is quite different from the German version. Cinderella has a fairy godmother who grants her wishes. A pumpkin is transformed into a gilded carriage, six mice become beautiful horses, a rat becomes a coachman with an elegant mustache, and lizards turn into footmen who are complete with fancy livery and lace. Cinderella is dressed in a beautiful gown, which is embroidered with rubies, pearls, and diamonds. This version also has the magical hour of midnight, when everything returns to normal. Perrault's *Cinderella* contains stepsisters who are rude and haughty, but they are not as cruel as they are in the German version. Cinderella even finds it possible to forgive them:

Now her stepsisters recognized her. Cinderella was the beautiful personage they had seen at the ball! They threw themselves at her feet and begged forgiveness for all their bad treatment of her. Cinderella asked them to rise, embraced them and told them she forgave them with all her heart. She begged them to love her always. (p. 27)

Cinderella not only forgives them but also provides them with a home at the palace and marries them to the lords of the court. Brown's illustrations, drawn with fine lines and colored with pastels, depict a kingdom where life in the royal court is marvelous. Compare the influence of illustrations in William Wegman's *Cinderella,* in which Wegman photographs dogs in costumes.

The French version of "Sleeping Beauty" suggests traditional French values. Seven good fairies bestow the virtues of intelligence, beauty, kindness, generosity, gaiety, and grace on the infant princess. David Walker's version, *The Sleeping Beauty,* shows his background in theatrical set and costume design. His illustrations create the feeling of a stage setting, especially as his fairies dance lightly across the great hall of the castle. The collaboration between Lincoln Kirstein's retelling and Alain Vais's illustrations for *Puss in Boots* also shows the influence of backgrounds that come from the New York City Ballet. The text includes fast-paced storytelling, and the illustrations develop a world of baroque splendor that could provide stage settings for ballet. In addition, the common French motifs of enchantment and animals who help their masters attain high goals are developed through both the text and the illustrations. Readers will also enjoy searching the illustrations to find examples of seventeenth-century architecture and figures from art history.

The illustrations in this version of Puss in Boots *feature seventeenth-century architecture. (From* Puss in Boots *by Lincoln Kirstein. Text copyright © 1992 by Lincoln Kirstein. Illustrations copyright © 1992 by Alain Vais. Reprinted by permission of Little, Brown and Company.)*

Diane Goode has translated and illustrated an edition of Madame de Beaumont's *Beauty and the Beast.* Meant originally for the wealthy classes in French society, de Beaumont's tale begins with the traditional "Once upon a time," but it provides descriptions tailored for an aristocratic audience. For example, Beauty enjoys reading, playing the harpsichord, and singing while she spins. When she enters the beast's castle, he provides her with a library, a harpsichord, and music books. Goode's illustrations create the magical settings in which Beauty eventually loves the beast for his virtue, although he lacks good looks and wit. Beauty's moral discrimination permits the beast's transformation back into a handsome prince.

Jan Brett's *Beauty and the Beast* includes illustrations that Brett modeled after the work of Walter Crane. The tapestries in the illustrations include messages and show the people in the castle before they were enchanted.

Nancy Willard's *Beauty and the Beast* has an American setting, but the locations are just as grand and magical as those in France. In this retelling, the wealthy merchant leaves his home, a splendid townhouse in New York overlooking Central Park, and eventually seeks shelter from the storm in a rural mansion that is magically untouched by the storm. Willard's descriptions allow readers to visualize and sense the grandeur of the occasion:

As he passed through room after room, his amazement grew. Each room seemed charged with the invisible presence of some loving soul who had lit candles in the sconces and fires in the fireplaces and moved on, leaving behind a fragrance of cloves and roses. In all his travels, the merchant had never seen rarities to compare with what the rooms contained. In one he found a cabinet of ivory centaurs that danced in a circle when he bent to admire them. Another held a chair carved like a merman from a single chunk of apricot jade. In a third he discovered a chess set with diamond and ruby pieces facing each other invitingly, ready for a game. On the walls were portraits of handsome men and women, elegantly dressed in the cloaks and ruffles of a hundred years ago. (p. 24)

Barry Moser's wood engravings add to the dramatic feeling of the tale.

Warwick Hutton's shorter *Beauty and the Beast* is not aimed at the wealthy classes. His Beauty is the youngest daughter of a merchant who has had bad luck. Unlike her ill-tempered and resentful older sisters, she looks on the bright side of their situation and tries to keep her family happy.

French folktales contain more enchantment than do tales from other countries. The motifs in these tales include fairy godmothers, other fairies, remarkable beasts who help their young masters, unselfish girls who break enchantments, and deceitful beasts.

German Folktales

The following words bring to mind one of the most popular childhood tales:

> Mirror, mirror on the wall.
> Who is the fairest of them all?

German folktales—whether they are about enchanted princesses and friendly dwarfs, clever animals, or poor but honest peasants—are among the most enjoyed folktales in the world. German scholar August Nitschke (1988) emphasizes the role of the German folktales historically. He states that by telling folktales, German "mothers allowed their children to come to an understanding of the world in which familiar and discomforting aspects were clearly separated, thus reaffirming that these two states of community existed" (p. 173). According to Nitschke, the storytelling and the stories allowed both mother and child to gain courage.

The accessibility of German folktales to modern audiences is owed to the work of Wilhelm and Jacob Grimm, German professors who researched the roots of the German language through the traditional tales, which had been told orally for generations. The Grimms asked village storytellers throughout Germany to tell them tales. Then, they wrote down the stories and published them as *Kinder-und Hausmärchen*. The stories ultimately were translated into many languages and became popular in Europe, North America, and elsewhere.

A wolf is the villain in several German folktales that young children enjoy. Wolves in these tales are cunning and dangerous, and they receive just punishments. Trina

Schart Hyman's version of *Little Red Riding Hood* is involved and more appropriate for older children. In addition to the story, Hyman stresses the importance of a moral in the Grimms' folktales. The incident with the dangerous wolf teaches Red Riding Hood a lesson: "I will never wander off the forest path again, as long as I live. I should have kept my promise to my mother."

Quite a different mood is created by James Marshall's humorous text and cartoon-type illustrations in his *Red Riding Hood*. The last page even includes a crocodile. Little Red Riding Hood has learned her lesson, however, and refuses to speak to him. For another mood, see William Wegman's *Little Red Riding Hood,* which contains photographs of dogs in the various roles.

Not all animals in German folklore are as fearsome as the wolf. For example, in "The Bremen Town Musicians," old animals about to be destroyed by their owners have humorously appealing human qualities. P. K. Page gives *The Traveling Musicians of Bremen* a contemporary feeling through modern language, conversations, and situations. Kady MacDonald Denton's illustrations show the robbers as teenagers with punk hair styles whose loot includes television sets. Ilse Plume's softly colored illustrations for another version of this tale suggest the gentle nature of the animals and the setting, a sunlit forest.

Poor peasants and penniless soldiers are common heroes in German folklore. The peasant may not be cunning, but he is usually good. In "The Golden Goose," for example, the youngest son is even called Simpleton. When his selfish brothers leave home, their parents give each one a fine, rich cake and a bottle of wine, which they refuse to share with anyone. The despised Simpleton, however, is generous with the cinder cake and sour beer that his parents give him. His kind heart is rewarded when he acquires a golden goose with magical powers that allow him to marry a princess. In Neil Philip's retelling of *The Golden Bird,* the youngest son accomplishes his quest for three objects through honesty and dedication.

"Hansel and Gretel" is the classic tale of an evil witch, a discontented and selfish mother, an ineffectual father, and two resourceful children. Rika Lesser's *Hansel and Gretel* with Paul O. Zelinsky's illustrations provides a rich retelling of this favorite tale. James Marshall adds humorous text and cartoon-type illustrations to his *Hansel and Gretel.* In comparing these two books, consider the impact of illustrations on the mood of the tales.

Many of the best-loved German folktales are stories of princesses who sleep for a hundred years, have wicked stepmothers, and are enchanted by witches. One lovely version of the Grimms' "Snow White" is translated by Randall Jarrell and illustrated by Nancy Ekholm Burkert. Burkert undertook research in German museums and visited the Black Forest before creating her drawings for *Snow White and the Seven Dwarfs,* which portrays every

Technology Resources

Visit our Companion Website at www.prenhall.com/norton to link to Brothers Grimm fairy tales, with beautifully presented versions of a dozen fairy tales collected by the Brothers Grimm.

aspect of the mystical forest, the dwarfs' cottage, and the wicked stepmother's secret tower room. Samuel Denis Fohr (1991) argues that "Snow White" is filled with spiritual symbolism. He states: "The changed mother in 'Snow White' not only represents the world but also worldliness. Similarly, Snow White not only symbolizes human beings but also the innocence or non-worldliness of youth" (p. 85). He argues that the story is consequently of value for adults as well as for children. The text and illustrations in the Jarrell and Burkert editions may be compared with *Snow White* translated by Paul Heins and illustrated by Trina Schart Hyman. Another folktale featuring a sleeping female is Trina Schart Hyman's retelling of Grimms' *The Sleeping Beauty.*

The German version of "Cinderella" in *The Complete Brothers Grimm Fairy Tales* differs from the French rendering of this tale in both detail and mood. A bird in the hazel tree growing by her mother's grave, not a fairy godmother, gives Cinderella a dress made of gold and silver and satin slippers for the ball. When Cinderella is united with the prince, no softness of heart leads her to forgive her cruel stepsisters. On her wedding day, the sisters join the bridal procession, but doves perched on Cinderella's shoulders peck out the sisters' eyes.

The elegance of the Italian renaissance is reflected in Paul O. Zelinsky's illustrations for *Rapunzel.* The elegance of courtly life is also reflected in tales such as *The Twelve Dancing Princesses.* Kinuko Craft's paintings re-create beautiful costumes, gardens, and magical settings in Marianna Mayer's retelling of this magical tale. Ruth Sanderson's *The Twelve Dancing Princesses* includes both enchantment and a supernatural helper who assists the poor but honest peasant break the spell, marry the princess, and inherit the kingdom.

Breaking enchantments through unselfish love is another common theme in German folklore. In the Grimms' "The Six Swans," the heroine can restore her brothers to human form only by sewing six shirts out of starwort. She cannot speak during the six years required for her task and suffers many ordeals before she is successful.

Jan Ormerod and David Lloyd's *The Frog Prince* is the classic tale of enchantment complete with rhythmical language, such as

> Let me eat from your plate,
>   my honey, my heart.

> Let me eat from your plate,
>   my own darling.
> Remember the promise
>   you made in the woods.
> Remember your promise
>   to love me. (p. 12, unnumbered)

Nonny Hogrogian's version of the Grimms' *The Devil with the Three Golden Hairs* contains many of the characteristics of German folktales. A poor, brave boy is rewarded; a wicked, greedy king is punished; a kind miller cares for the boy; a beautiful princess is rewarded; the devil's grandmother uses enchantment to help the boy; and the devil is outwitted. Common folktale motifs in this tale include a physical sign of luck, a quest, the importance of threes (three hairs, three questions), and magical transformations. The text concludes with a characteristic moral: "The youth, together with his bride, lived well and reigned well, for he who is not afraid can even take the hairs from the devil's head and conquer the kingdom" (unnumbered).

After reading a number of German folktales first recorded by Jacob and Wilhelm Grimm, you may approach the challenge of Wilhelm Grimm's *Dear Mili,* illustrated by Maurice Sendak. What is the origin of the tale recently found in a letter written to a young girl in 1816? Is it part of the oral tradition collected by this famous recorder of German folktales, or did Grimm use characteristics of traditional tales to write his own literary folktale?

German folktales are ideal candidates for storytelling. Their speedy openings, fast-paced plots, and drama keep listeners entertained for story after story. In these tales, adversaries include devils, witches, and wolves. The good-hearted youngest child is often rewarded, but selfishness, greed, and discontent are punished. The noble character frequently wins as a result of intervention by supernatural helpers, and magical objects and spells are recurring motifs.

Norwegian Folktales

Norwegian scholars Peter Christian Asbjörnsen and Jörgen Moe's interest in collecting the traditional tales of the Norwegian people was stimulated by reading the Grimms' *Kinder-und Hausmärchen.* They were also inspired by the renaissance that was then sweeping Europe. Asbjörnsen and Moe's collection of traditional tales was published under the title *Norwegian Folk Tales* in 1845.

 Technology Resources

Generate a list of Red Riding Hood variants by searching the database for "Red Riding Hood" in the fields Title, Topics, and Description simultaneously.

Four illustrations of a familiar tale show the impact of the pictures on the moods of the story. A, The formal border and illustration style create a traditional mood in the illustrations from Little Red Riding Hood. (Illustrations from Little Red Riding Hood by Trina Schart Hyman, copyright © 1983 by Trina Schart Hyman. Reprinted by permission of Holiday House.) B, The black-and-white photographs suggest a frightening mood in Rita Marshall's illustrations for Little Red Riding Hood. (From Little Red Riding Hood by Charles Perrault, edited by Ann Redpath and Etienne Delessert, illustrations by Rita Marshall. Copyright © 1983. Reprinted by permission of Creative Education, Inc.) C, James Marshall's cartoon illustrations add a humorous context to Little Red Riding Hood. (From Little Red Riding Hood by James Marshall. Illustrated by James Marshall, Dial Books for Young Readers. Copyright © 1987.) D (p. 227), Dark colors and frightened girls suggest the dangerous nature of the tale. (From Lon Po Po: A Red-Riding Hood Story from China, translated and illustrated by Ed Young, copyright © 1989 by Ed Young. Reprinted by permission of Philomel Books.)

A

B

C

Shang listened through the door. "Po Po," she said, "why is your voice so low?"

"Your grandmother has caught a cold, good children, and it is dark and windy out here. Quickly open up, and let your Po Po come in," the cunning wolf said.

Tao and Paotze could not wait. One unlatched the door and the other opened it. They shouted, "Po Po, Po Po, come in!"

At the moment he entered the door, the wolf blew out the candle.

"Po Po," Shang asked, "why did you blow out the candle? The room is now dark."

The wolf did not answer.

D

The first translation of the tales into English was by Sir George Webbe Dasent in 1859. According to Naomi Lewis (1991),

It was not surprising that Dasent was so captivated by Scandinavia. The plots of fairy tales everywhere have many likenesses; what changes them is the place where they are told—the country and the people. Wherever the landscape is wild, the winters long and bitter, and the villages small and isolated, magic and mystery thrive. Why should the folk there doubt that trolls live in the forest, as well as wolves and bears; or that animals, who share the same scene and hardships, can speak if they will, and even change into humans and back again? (Introduction)

It is interesting to compare Norwegian story elements with those of other European cultures. Consider, for example, Mercer Mayer's *East of the Sun and West of the Moon*. The story in this tale is similar to those in the French "Beauty and the Beast" and other tales of human enchantment and lost loves: An enchanted human demands a promise in return for a favor; the promise is at first honored; the maiden disenchants the human; he must leave because she does not honor her promise; she searches for him; and she saves him finally. The adversaries and helpers in this tale reflect a northern climate and culture. The human is enchanted by a troll princess who lives in a distant, icy kingdom. The loving maiden receives help from, among others, Father Forest, who understands the body of earth and stone; Great Fish, who knows the blood of salt and water; and North Wind, who understands the mind of the earth, the moon, and the sun. The gifts that each helper gives to the maiden allow her to overcome the trolls and free the prince. A tinderbox makes it possible to melt the ice encasing the youth, a shot from the bow and arrow causes the troll princess to turn to wood, and reflections in the fish scale cause the remaining trolls to turn to stone. Mayer's illustrations of snowy winters, creatures frozen in ice, icy mountains, and tree-covered landscapes also evoke northern settings.

Claire Booss's version of the tale in *Scandinavian Folk & Fairy Tales* differs from Mayer's version. In *East O' the Sun and West O' the Moon*, translated by George Webbe Dasent and illustrated by P. J. Lynch, a white bear offers a family riches if its youngest daughter is allowed to live in his castle. In *East of the Sun & West of the Moon: A Play*, Nancy Willard develops a style that is appropriate for oral presentations, as shown in the song that the woodcutter's daughter sings as she goes to the bear's palace:

When you go through the forest at midnight,
and your friends and relations are few,
just remember the crow and the cricket
are twice as nervous as you. (p. 17)

The tale of enchanted princesses emphasizes a regal setting. (From **Twelve Dancing Princesses** *retold by Marianna Mayer. Illustrated by K.Y. Craft. Text © 1989 by Marianna Mayer. Illustrations © 1989 by K.Y. Craft. Reprinted by permission of Morrow Junior Books, a division of William Morrow & Co.)*

touches her, Tom forms a parade of unwilling followers: an old woman, an angry man who kicks at the woman, a smithy who waves a pair of tongs, and a cook who runs after them waving a ladle of porridge. At the sight of this ridiculous situation, the sad princess bursts into laughter. Tom wins the princess and half of the kingdom. Compare this tale with the Grimms' "The Golden Goose."

The humor in Asbjørnsen and Moe's *The Man Who Kept House,* illustrated by Otto S. Svend, results from another ridiculous situation. A man who claims that keeping house is easy exchanges his field work for his wife's housework. Hilarious situations result when the man faces such common household chores as washing clothes.

Norwegian folktales help children appreciate Norwegian traditions as well as provide children with pleasure and excitement. Themes suggest the rewarding of unselfish love and the punishment of greed. The sharp humor, the trolls, and the poor boys who overcome adversity are excellent elements for storytelling.

Norwegian folktale collections provide many excellent stories for retelling. Several favorites are found in Virginia Haviland's *Favorite Fairy Tales Told in Norway.* Young children love to listen to and dramatize "Three Billy Goats Gruff." Glen Rounds's *Three Billy Goats Gruff* is an excellent source for creative drama. Children can re-create the world of the hairy troll and the goats who finally are victorious.

Lise Lunge-Larsen's collection of Norwegian folktales found in *The Troll with No Heart in His Body and Other Tales of Trolls from Norway* focuses on nine tales that feature hags, trolls, and enchantments in rugged, mountainous settings. There are well-known stories in the collection such as "The Three Billy Goats Gruff" and "The Boy and the North Wind." There are also less known tales such as "The Boy Who Became a Lion, a Falcon, and an Ant." All of the stories, however, have certain characteristics in common: It is possible to overcome even the worst evil by using intelligence, courage, persistence, and kindness.

Another favorite for storytelling and creative drama is "Taper Tom," found in Asbjørnsen and Moe's *Norwegian Folk Tales,* whose hero is the characteristic youngest son. Tom sits in a chimney corner amusing himself by grubbing in the ashes and splitting tapers for lights. His family laughs at his belief that he can win the hand of the princess in marriage and half of the kingdom by making the princess laugh. With the assistance of a magical golden goose who does not relinquish anyone who

Russian Folktales

Heroes and heroines who may be royalty or peasants, settings that reflect deep snows in winter, dark forests, the wooden huts of peasants, the gilded towers of palaces, and villains such as the witch Baba Yaga and dishonest nobility or commoners are found in Russian folktales. Talent, beauty, and kindness are usually appreciated and rewarded. In contrast, foolish actions, greed, broken promises, and jealousy are usually condemned. Peasants sometimes outwit tsars (or *czars*), and females are often strong and resourceful. Lenny Hort's retelling of Alexander Nikolayevich Afanasyév's *The Fool and the Fish: A Tale from Russia* shows that even a peasant can be accepted by the tsar and marry his daughter. The humor of the fool's actions expresses the universal need to laugh at oneself and others. The illustrations by Russian artist Gennady Spirin depict a prerevolutionary Russia. Compare Spirin's illustrations in this book with his illustrations in Aaron Shepard's retelling of *The Sea King's Daughter.*

Many Russian folktales are complex stories of quests, longing, and greed. Ruth Sanderson's *The Golden Mare, the Firebird, and the Magic Ring* includes a greedy tsar, a young horseman, and a magical horse whose talents allow the young man to succeed. The mare comes to the rescue even when the tsar demands such impossible tasks as capturing the firebird.

J. Patrick Lewis's adaptation of *At the Wish of the Fish: A Russian Folktale* shows that even a simpleton can be

The northern climate is found throughout the illustrations for this Norwegian tale. (Illustration from East O' the Sun and West O' the Moon *with an introduction by Naomi Lewis. Illustration © 1991 P. J. Lynch. Used by permission of Candlewick Press, Cambridge, MA.)*

rewarded for his kindness. At the conclusion of the tale, after he has won the tsar's daughter, he asks the pike to make him less a fool. The tale ends, "The once-upon-a-time simpleton never forgot the great good fortune bestowed upon him by the pike. And often he was heard to say, as he strolled through the gardens in his princely caftan, 'By the will of a fish, I have done all I wish' " (unnumbered).

Universal folktale themes found in Russian folktales include a desire for children, developed in a story about a childless couple who create "The Snow Maiden," and hatred of a beautiful child by her stepmother and stepsisters, developed in "Vassilissa the Fair," a Russian version of the Cinderella story. The latter tale and six others are collected in Alexander Nikolayevich Afanasyév's *Russian Folk Tales,* with illustrations by Ivan Bilibin, the late-nineteenth-century Russian illustrator, who depicts traditional costumes and early Russian settings. John Cech's retelling of *First Snow, Magic Snow* also presents the story of parents who wish for a child and find themselves parents of a snow child.

Alexander Pushkin was one of the first Russian writers to transcribe the orally transmitted folktales of his country. Four of Pushkin's tales are found in *The Golden Cockerel and Other Fairy Tales,* originally published in French in 1925. This translation includes "The Dead Princess and the Seven Heroes," a tale similar to the German "Snow White."

Patricia Tracy Lowe has translated and retold *The Tale of Czar Saltan, or the Prince and the Swan Princess.* This tale reflects the importance of keeping promises and the consequences of jealously and greed. The consequences of greed are also developed in Elizabeth Winthrop's adaptation, *The Little Humpbacked Horse: A Russian Tale.* In this tale wisdom and friendship overcome greed.

The familiar theme of kindness rewarded and the motifs of magical powers and foolish but kindhearted peasants are found in Arthur Ransome's *The Fool of the World and the Flying Ship.* The tsar has offered his daughter's hand in marriage to anyone who can build a flying ship. Kindness to an old man provides an aspiring peasant with a magical ship. Companions with extraordinary powers also aid the peasant in his quest. This tale implies that the tsar does not want a peasant to marry his daughter.

Russian protagonists may be strong and resourceful females. Josepha Sherman's *Vassilisa the Wise: A Tale of Medieval Russia* shows that a clever and courageous female is able to outwit the prince and save her unwise husband from the prince's dark dungeon.

These and many other Russian folktales reflect a vast country containing numerous cultures. Talent, beauty, and kindness are appreciated and rewarded. People must pay the consequences for foolish actions, greed, broken promises, and jealousy. Humor suggests the universal need to laugh at oneself and others.

Jewish Folktales

Folktales, according to Rahel Musleah (1992), may be identified as Jewish if they contain any one of the following elements:

The components are a Jewish place (under a wedding canopy; in a synagogue); a Jewish character (King Solomon instead of a nameless judge); Jewish time (a holiday or life-cycle event); and most importantly, a Jewish message (faith, learning, remembrance, hospitality, family). (p. 42)

Jewish folktales are filled with stories in which sincerity, unselfishness, and true wisdom are rewarded. The stories also contain bunglers, ironic humor, and human foibles. According to Charlotte Huck, Susan Hepler, and Janet Hickman (1997), Jewish folktales "have a poignancy, wit, and ironic humor that is not matched by any other folklore" (p. 289). Wit and humor are found in Margot Zemach's *It Could Always Be Worse.* This Yiddish folktale relates the story of nine unhappy people who share a small, one-room hut. The father desperately seeks the advice of the rabbi, who suggests that he bring a barnyard animal inside. A pattern of complaint and advice continues until most of the family's livestock is in the house. When the rabbi tells the father to clear the animals out of the hut, the whole family appreciates its large, peaceful home.

Advice from a rabbi is a frequent story plot technique that develops both the ridiculous situation and the moral of the story in Jewish folktales. Joan Rothenberg's

This Russian folktale depicts magic and brave deeds. (From The Golden Mare, the Firebird, and the Magic Ring *by Ruth Sanderson. Copyright © 2001 by Ruth Sanderson. Reprinted by permission of Little, Brown and Company.)*

Yettele's Feathers is a cautionary tale against spreading rumors and gossip. When the situation becomes extreme and no one will speak to Yettele Babbelonski, she asks the rabbi for advice. When Yettele declares that words are like feathers and not like rocks because words and feathers cannot hurt anyone, the rabbi tells her to cut off the top of her largest goose feather pillow and bring it to him. When the wind snatches the pillow from her arms, she is lost in a blizzard of feathers. Now the rabbi tells her he will help her after she retrieves all of the feathers. After Yettele becomes extremely fatigued trying to gather the feathers she concludes that in a lifetime she could never put all the feathers back into the pillow. Now the rabbi uses her own words to teach the moral of the story: "And so it is with those stories of yours, my dear Yettele. Once the words leave your lips, they are as impossible to put back as those feathers" (p. 31).

Isaac Bashevis Singer's *Mazel and Shlimazel, or the Milk of the Lioness* is longer and more complex. It pits Mazel, the spirit of good luck, against Shlimazel, the spirit of bad luck. To test the strength of good luck versus bad, the two spirits decide that each of them will spend a year manipulating the life of Tam, a bungler who lives in the poorest

hut in the village. As soon as Mazel stands behind Tam, he succeeds at everything he tries. He fixes the king's carriage wheel and is invited to court, where he accomplishes impossible tasks. Even Princess Nesika is in love with him.

Just as Tam is about to complete his greatest challenge successfully, Mazel's year is over, and an old, bent man with spiders in his beard stands beside Tam. With one horrible slip of the tongue encouraged by Shlimazel, Tam is in disfavor and condemned to death. Shlimazel has won. But wait! Mazel presents Shlimazel with the wine of forgetfulness, which causes Shlimazel to forget poor Tam. Mazel rescues Tam from hanging and helps Tam redeem himself with the king and marry the princess. Tam's success is more than good luck, however: "Tam had learned that good luck follows those who are diligent, honest, sincere and helpful to others. The man who has these qualities is indeed lucky forever" (p. 42).

Singer's *When Shlemiel Went to Warsaw & Other Stories* contains several folktales that reflect both human foibles and folklore themes. For example, "Shrewd Todie & Lyzer the Miser" pits foolish, greedy actions against cunning and trickery. To his discomfort, the miser learns, "If you accept nonsense when it brings you profit, you must also accept nonsense when it brings you loss" (p. 12).

The Feather Merchants & Other Tales of the Fools of Chelm, retold by Steve Sanfield, is made up of thirteen traditional Eastern European Jewish tales about the good and decent people of Chelm, who can also be silly and foolish. Sanfield states that no one knows how Chelm came to be known as the town of fools. He declares:

Our Chelm is the Chelm of the spirit and imagination that has existed, generation after generation, in the minds and hearts of those who've told and listened to these tales. Our Chelm is a magical place filled with honest and righteous men and women for whom the idea of defeat passes as quickly as a gaggle of geese flying south. Our Chelm has a soul which yearns for beauty, which is full of mercy, which possesses faith, which seeks justice. Chelm is where hopes and dreams and laughter go on living—and will go on living as long as you and I go on telling these stories. (p. 97)

As you read Jewish folktales, notice how this spirit of Chelm emerges from the tales. Additional stories of Chelm are found in Francine Prose's *The Angel's Mistake: Stories of Chelm.*

The fools of Chelm as well as stories about witches, goblins, and King Solomon are found in Howard Schwartz and Barbara Rush's collection of stories, *The Diamond Tree: Jewish Tales from Around the World*. These fifteen tales originated in many countries, including Palestine, Iraq, Turkey, Babylon, and Poland. The text concludes with sources and commentary that are extremely useful to scholars and others who are interested in evaluating the sources of the stories. In addition, each tale is classified according to the Aarne-Thompson (AT) system. (Aarne-Thompson is a folklorist who identified tales according to specific characteristics.) For example, notice the useful information found in the notations for "The Bear and the Children" (Eastern Europe):

From *Yiddisher Folklor* (Yiddish), edited by Yehuda L. Cahan (Vilna: 1931). AT 123.

This is probably the best-known Jewish nursery tale of Eastern Europe—with the exception of the song "Had Gadya" ("One Kid"), sung at the end of the Passover seder. The story offers young children the assurance that if there is danger, their parents will do everything possible to save them. It is a variant of "The Wolf and the Seven Kids" from *Grimms' Fairy Tales*. (p. 119)

Asian Folktales

Asian folktales, like other folktales, portray the feelings, struggles, and aspirations of common people; depict the lives of the well-to-do; and reflect the moral values, superstitions, social customs, and humor of the times and societies in which they originated. Like medieval Europe, ancient Asia contained societies in which royalty and nobles led lives quite different from those of peasants. Females had less freedom and social influence than did males. Asian tales tell about the rich and the poor, the wise and the foolish, mythical quests, lovers, animals, and supernatural beings and powers, motifs common to all folklore, but they also reflect the customs and beliefs of specific cultures.

Chinese Folktales. Traditional Chinese sayings (Wyndham, 1971) suggest Chinese values and philosophical viewpoints expressed in Chinese folktales over the centuries, for example: "A teacher can open the door, but the pupil must go through it alone," and "The home that includes an old grandparent contains a precious jewel."

According to Louise and Yuan-hsi Kuo (1976), Chinese tales often develop universal themes and contain roguish humor. Respect for ancestors, ethical standards, and conflict between nobility and commoners are popular topics in Chinese tales.

A dislike for imperial authority is evident in several Chinese equivalents to the cottage tales of medieval European peasants. The defeat of an evil ruler is the main conflict in Rosalind C. Wang's *The Treasure Chest: A Chinese Tale*. The hero in this tale is a poor widow's son who rescues a fish and earns the gratitude of the Ocean King. The gift from the King of three bamboo sticks helps the young man save the woman he loves from Funtong, the evil ruler who desires the young woman.

These Jewish tales collected from many countries reflect many of the values of the Jewish people. (From The Diamond Tree: Jewish Tales from Around the World *selected and retold by Howard Schwartz and Barbara Rush. Copyright © 1991 by Uri Shulevitz. Used by permission of HarperCollins Publishers.)*

The hero in Grace Tseng's *White Tiger, Blue Serpent* is a Chinese boy who faces perils when he tries to rescue a beautiful brocade woven by his mother from the greedy goddess. The boy's efforts free the animals and beautiful vegetation captured within the brocade. In addition to defeating the goddess, the boy's bravery makes it possible for "Kai and his mother to live happily in the beauty of the magnificent brocade" (unnumbered).

A benevolent dragon is found in "Green Dragon Pond" in Neil Philip's *The Spring of Butterflies and Other Folktales of China's Minority Peoples*. According to the tale, "From the very beginning to the end, this dragon did no harm, but only good deeds. For this reason, the villagers around Malong peak lived a happy life" (p. 119). In this tale of transformation, the dragon changes himself into a man and plays chess with an old monk who lives in the temple by the pond. The story has an unhappy ending because of the carelessness of the dragon and the monk, not because the dragon is cruel.

Marilee Heyer's *The Weaving of a Dream: A Chinese Folktale* reveals rewarded behavior: bravery, unselfish love, understanding, respect for one's mother, faithfulness, and kindness. In contrast, disrespect for one's mother and selfishness are punished. This tale also shows the power of a dream and the perseverance that may be required to gain the dream. Ed Young's *Lon Po Po: A Red-Riding Hood Story from China* shows that the cleverness of the eldest daughter and the cooperation of the three sisters are powerful enough to outwit the intentions of the evil wolf.

In *Tiger Woman,* Laurence Yep uses a rhyming format to retell a Shantung folktale in which selfishness is punished and sharing is rewarded. When a beggar approaches a selfish woman and asks for some of her bean curd, she replies that she will not give up any of her food because she is a tiger when she is famished. The beggar then casts a spell so that whatever the selfish woman says she becomes. Consequently, she becomes an ox, a bird, an elephant, and a sow. At that point when she almost becomes a pork roast, she repents and turns back into a human. Now she realizes the importance of sharing her food.

In *Two of Everything,* Lily Toy Hong develops the importance of both humor and wisdom. A poor farmer and his wife discover the unusual characteristics of a brass pot that the farmer unearths in his garden. If one item is placed in the pot, two identical items appear. This happy situation continues until the wife falls head first into the pot, but the woman uses her wits and solves the problem.

Numerous tales in *The Spring of Butterflies and Other Chinese Folktales* reveal the consequences of kindness, humor, and greed. Moss Roberts's large collection, *Chinese Fairy Tales and Fantasies,* is divided into tales about enchantment and magic, folly and greed, animals, women and wives, ghosts and souls, and judges and diplomats. Laurence Yep's *The Rainbow People* is a collection of twenty Chinese folktales from Chinese Americans in the United States. The text is divided according to tales about tricksters, fools, virtues and vices, Chinese America, and love. Yep has included introductory comments for each of the sections.

Japanese Folktales. Ellen S. Shapiro in her introduction to Grace James's *Green Willow and Other Japanese Fairy Tales* (1987) summarizes some of the characteristics of Japanese folktales. According to Shapiro, the stories include appreciation for the beauty and mystery of life, belief in the power of the spirit to accomplish its will, and ridicule for pretensions. Shapiro states that within Japanese folktales, "Anything is possible; magic abounds, as long as it is faithful to the truths of the heart. Some stories are lighthearted, others disturbing, but all reveal the deep human values underlying the apparent transience of the physical world" (p. viii). In her discussion of style associated with Japanese folktales, Shapiro emphasizes that short phrases and repetitive sentences have great emotional impact, as in this quote from "The Wind in the Pine Tree": "the heavenly deity descended. Lightly, lightly he came by way of the Floating Bridge, bearing the tree in his right hand. Lightly, lightly his feet touched the earth" (p. x).

Chinese culture influenced Japanese culture, and many Japanese tales are similar to Chinese tales. Dragons, for example, are common in tales from both countries.

The tiger, usually considered a symbol of power, is a creature often found in Japanese tales. The cat is important in *The Boy Who Drew Cats: A Japanese Folktale,* retold by Arthur Levine. When a boy paints cats on screens after he is trapped in an abandoned temple, the cats come alive to save him from a giant rat. "The Boy Who Drew Cats" is also included in Rafe Martin's *Mysterious Tales of Japan.* This is a collection of ten traditional tales such as "Urashima Taro," "Green Willow," and "The Crane Maiden." The book includes story notes that either provide additional information about the context of the story or about the source. For example, the source note for "The Snow Woman" includes: "My version is based on Lafcadio Hearn's 'Yuki-Onna,' a retelling of a story a Japanese farmer told him, which can be found in Hearn's *Kwaidan, Stories and Studies of Strange Things* (Kwaidan means 'weird tales')" (p. 71).

Japanese folktales reflecting respected values and disliked human qualities include Katherine Paterson's *The Tale of the Mandarin Ducks.* Paterson develops strong messages, such as kindness will be rewarded, creatures cannot survive when held captive, honor is important, and sharing helps people through trouble. These respected values are developed when two servants help a coveted mandarin duck, who has been captured by a greedy lord. When the kitchen maid releases the duck against the lord's command, she and another servant are sentenced to death. The grateful drake and his mate, however, outwit the lord and reward the kindness of the servants.

Cranes, like sparrows, are frequently important in Japanese folktales. Molly Bang's *The Paper Crane* suggests the desirability of friendship between humans and supernatural creatures. A hungry man rewards a restaurant owner with a paper crane that can be brought to life by clapping hands, and this attraction creates many customers for the business. Odds Bodkin's *The Crane Wife* develops the tragic consequences that result from greed.

Dianne Snyder's *The Boy of the Three-Year Nap* has a strong female protagonist who outwits her lazy son. The tale is a humorous match of wits. The lazy son tries to trick a wealthy merchant into letting him marry the merchant's daughter. The mother, however, shows that she is the equal of the son. She not only convinces the merchant to repair and enlarge her house but also tricks her son into getting a job. Another strong female protagonist is found in Judy Sierra's *Tasty Baby Belly Buttons,* in which a girl battles the terrible oni, whose favorite food is human navels. The author uses words such as *boro, boro* and *zushin, zushin,* which are part of the oral vocabulary of traditional Japanese storytellers. Another strong female protagonist is found in Robert D. San Souci's *The Samurai's Daughter: A Japanese Legend.* In this tale, the beautiful daughter slays a sea monster and restores the sanity of the ruler who had banished her father into exile.

"Ah!" came a voice from within. At the same time Yohei cried out in horror and fell back from the doorway.

What Yohei saw was not human. It was a crane, smeared with blood, for with its beak it had plucked out its own feathers to place them in the loom.

At the sight Yohei collapsed into a deep faint.

You may compare the text illustrations in these two versions of "The Crane Wife." (Top: from The Crane Wife, *retold by Odds Bodkin, illustrated by Gennady Spirin. Copyright © 1998 by Odds Bodkin. Published by Gulliver Books, Harcourt Brace & Company. Reprinted by permission. Bottom: from* The Crane Wife, *retold by Sumiko Yagawa, illustrated by Suekichi Akaba, © 1979. English translation copyright © 1981 by Katherine Peterson. Published by William Morrow and Company, Inc. Reprinted by permission.)*

Strong associations with nature and ecology are developed in Sheila Hamanaka's *Screen of Frogs*. A landowner responds favorably when a large frog appears in a dream and begs the man not to sell his home. Through the dream, the frog stresses the disasters that will occur if the frogs do not retain their land. As a reward for not selling the land, a tattered white screen belonging to the man is transformed into a beautifully painted screen of frogs.

Other Asian Folktales. The Asian Cultural Centre for UNESCO has published a series of five books called *Folk Tales from Asia for Children Everywhere*. The series contains stories from many Asian countries. For example, a story from Burma, "The Four Puppets," stresses the harm that wealth and power can bring if they are not tempered with wisdom and love. "The Carpenter's Son," a tale from Afghanistan, is similar to the Arabian story of Aladdin and his magic lamp.

Many folktales from India are included in a series of animal stories traditionally known as the *Panchatantra*. The original tales were moralistic and included reincarnations of the Buddha. English translations, however, usually delete the morals and the references to Buddha. Consequently, the stories have characteristics of folktales. In Judith Ernst's retelling of *The Golden Goose King: A Tale Told by the Buddha,* the storyteller uses a tale told by the Buddha to reveal how a golden goose instructs the king and queen how to rule wisely. In *The Golden Carp and Other Tales from Vietnam,* a collection of six folktales, Lynette Dyer Vuong includes sources for the tales, interpretive notes, and pronunciation guides.

Mirra Ginsburg's *The Chinese Mirror* is a Korean folktale about humorous consequences when a group of people see themselves in a mirror for the first time. They cannot convince each other that each one sees something else in the mirror until the mirror is broken into a hundred shiny splinters. Then, "that was the end of the stranger who looked at the traveler, the young beauty from China, the wrinkled old crone, the neighbor's grandpa, the nasty brat who stole pebbles, and the big fat bully who hurt little boys" (unnumbered).

Nami Rhee's *Magic Spring: A Korean Folktale* develops both humorous irony and the consequences of greed. When a poor, older couple discover a magic spring in the forest, they learn that a drink returns them to their youth. When their rich, greedy neighbor learns about their secret, he goes in search of the spring. Unfortunately, his greed causes him to drink too much water and he becomes an infant. The renewed couple find him in the forest and raise him as their own child.

The theme in Nina Jaffe's *Older Brother, Younger Brother: A Korean Folktale* shows that greed will be punished and kindness will be rewarded. An author's note places this story in the mid-eighteenth century "when it was sung as part of the classic repertoire called pahn-

SOH-ree. These epic poems were performed in the courtyards of rural aristocrats and are still preserved by Korean musicians and singers today. The story reflects the strong influence of Confucianism, the ancient Chinese philosophy of life and code of ethics, which was brought to Korea as early as the first century. Different versions of the tale also exist in the folklore of China and Japan, but the core story probably originated in Northeast Asia from Mongol sources" (author's note).

Laurence Yep's *The Khan's Daughter: A Mongolian Folktale* develops both a quest motif and a change in character as Mongke, a shepherd boy, accomplishes three trials in order to win the Khan's daughter. Two of the trials are imposed by the girl's mother: He must demonstrate proof of strength and proof of bravery. The third trial is formulated by the Khan's daughter. It is this third trial that shows both the character of the girl in determining her own destiny and the changes in Mongke as he goes from a rather foolish and boastful character to one who is both contrite and filled with considerable wisdom.

Eastern folktales contain such universal motifs as reward for unselfishness, assistance from magical objects, cruel adversaries, and punishment for dishonesty. The tales also emphasize the traditional values of the specific people: Homage is paid to ancestors, knowledge and cleverness are rewarded, and greed and miserly behavior are punished.

Middle Eastern Folktales

According to Inea Bushnaq in *Arab Folktales,* the collection of Arab tales began as early as the eighth century when scholars centered in Baghdad began collecting the tales. In 1704 *The Arabian Nights or The Thousand and One Nights* was translated from Arabic into French. This translation introduced Persian tales into Europe. Between 1885 and 1888, Sir Richard Francis Burton, the British consul in Trieste, translated the text from Arabic to English. Burton's translation is a primary source for many retellings in English.

In *Arab Folktales,* Bushnaq identifies the following categories for Arabic tales: Bedouin tales told by desert nomads; tales of magic and supernatural or household tales that include djinn, ghouls, and afreets; animal tales, which include fables and anecdotes; famous fools and rascals; religious tales and moral instruction; and tales of wit and wisdom that tell about clever men and wily women. We will use Bushnaq's categories because much of the folklore published for children falls under these categories.

The Bedouin tales collected from the nomadic peoples of the desert include characteristics such as generosity in which a person's worth is counted not by what he owns but by what he gives to others; hospitality to those who enter the home and encampment (traditionally the period of Bedouin hospitality is three and one-third days); the importance of ancestry and birth in a culture in which the family is the most important social unit; and pride, independence, and self-sufficiency of the nomadic characters. Many Bedouin tales reflect these values when the storyteller concludes with a sentence such as "So it is when men are noble."

Generosity and hospitality are the major values depicted in Bushnaq's "The Last Camel of Emir Hamid." In this tale from Saudi Arabia, a reward is given for generosity. Hospitality is important in "The Boy in Girl's Dress," a story from Syria that shows the value of hospitality in a treeless, waterless region in which to deny food and shelter could mean denying life.

Many of the highly illustrated single-volume tales are tales of magic and supernatural. Eric A. Kimmel's *The Three Princes: A Tale from the Middle East* has a characteristically vague, contradictory opening: "Once there was and once there was not a princess who was as wise as she was beautiful" (p. 1). The princess challenges her three suitors to bring back the rarest things that they find in their year-long travels and promises to marry the prince who returns with the greatest wonder. In a dramatic ending, the prince who returns with the orange that cures any illness uses the fruit to heal the princess and thus wins her for his wife. The importance of generosity, sacrifice, and wisdom is revealed as the princess chooses the prince who sacrificed the most.

Neil Philip's *The Arabian Nights* presents several magical tales, including a variant of the Cinderella story. This variant includes both motifs related to Cinderella and motifs that are characteristic of Arabic folklore. Notice how the following motifs suggest that this is an Arabic story: A plot with a jinni provides the heroine with whatever she fancies, including anklets studded with diamonds. The heroine enters the King's harem where the women's part of the entertainment is held. In her haste to leave the feast, she drops the diamond anklets. The queen organizes a search party for the person who can wear the anklet. After the girl is found, she is taken back to the palace where the celebration lasts for forty days and forty nights while the wedding is prepared. The evil sisters learn the secret of the jinni and turn their younger sister into a white dove by jabbing her with diamond pins. The prince sends out search parties. Without the heroine, he begins to sicken and waste away. Every day the white dove comes to the prince's window and the prince grows to love the bird. The prince finds the diamond pins, pulls them out, and the bride reappears. You may compare this "Cinderella" variant with another tale from the Middle East: Rebecca Hickox's *The Golden Sandal: A Middle Eastern Cinderella Story.*

The stories told by Shahrazad to King Shahriyar are popular for retelling and illustrating. *Sindbad: From the Tales of the Thousand and One Nights,* retold and illustrated by Ludmila Zeman, includes a tale of adventure, magic, and wonder. The author's note relates the Sindbad tales to actual historical routes and stresses that they may contain a mixture of fact and fiction. Zeman states: "Their route resembled that of Sindbad. They sailed on the Arabian Sea

The illustrations in Sindbad *reflect the jewel-like carpets. (From* Sindbad: From the Tales of the Thousand and One Nights, *retold and illustrated by Ludmila Zeman. Copyright © 1999 by Ludmila Zeman. Reprinted by permission of Tundra Books. All rights reserved.)*

around India and Sri Lanka. In Sindbad's adventures, we visit the Valley of Diamonds, possibly the island of Sri Lanka, known for precious stones, such as rubies, blue sapphires, and topazes. Later, Sindbad is captured by manlike creatures—could they be the orangutans that Arabian sailors first encountered in Sumatra?" (author's note). The illustrations in the text reflect the Persian influence.

According to Bushnaq, the favorite type of animal story in Arabic is a trickster tale in which two animals, or a human and an animal, try to outwit each other. These tales usually end with a punch line that is wise and witty. For example, "The Cat Who Went to Mecca," an animal tale from Syria, concludes: "The king of the mice jumped back into his hole and rejoined his subjects. 'How is the king of the cats after his pilgrimage?' they asked. 'Let's hope he has changed for the better.' 'Never mind the pilgrimage,' said the king of the mice. 'He may pray like a Hajji but he still pounces like a cat'" (p. 216).

Many of the religious tales are discussed under mythology.

Tales reflecting wit and wisdom are numerous in folklore from the Middle East. Several of the tales in Sharon Creeden's *Fair Is Fair: World Folktales of Justice* include wise people whose actions change the course of events. "Ali

Cogia, Merchant of Baghdad" concludes with a motif of wisdom: "The caliph scolded the cadi for his incompetence. 'Learn from the wisdom of this child,' he said. Last of all, he sent the boy home with one hundred pieces of silver as a mark of his favor" (p. 51). In "The Quality of Mercy," a tale from Morocco, it is the Princess and her wisdom that encourage the King to rule with kindness and justice. In "The Stoning," another tale from Morocco, it is a woman's wisdom that changes a judge's actions and allows for forgiveness and healing.

As you notice from these stories, tales from the Middle East include the importance of generosity and hospitality, using wit and wisdom, and may include moral instruction.

African Folktales

African folktales are characterized by a highly developed oral tradition. Repetitive language and styles that encourage interaction with the storyteller make them excellent choices for sharing with children. Many of the stories are "why" tales. Such tales explain animal and human characteristics. Verna Aardema's *Why Mosquitoes Buzz in People's Ears* uses cumulative language to explain the buzz. Personified animals, often tricksters, are popular subjects. The hare, the tortoise, and Ananse the spider use wit and trickery to gain their objectives. Chapter 11, "Multicultural Literature," discusses other tales that reflect traditional values of African peoples.

North American Folktales

Many North American folktales have roots in the cultures of other parts of the world or have been influenced by written literature and characters created by professional writers. Consequently, identifying tales that began in a specifically North American oral tradition is often difficult or impossible.

Folklorists identify four types of folktales found in North America: (1) Native American (and Native Canadian) tales that were handed down over centuries of tribal storytelling; (2) folktales of African Americans that reflect African and European themes but that were changed as slaves faced difficulties in a new land; (3) variants of European folktales containing traditional themes, motifs, and characters that were changed to meet the needs of a robust, rural North America; and (4) boisterous, boastful tall tales that originated on this continent. Some collections of folktales, such as Amy L. Cohn's *From Sea to Shining Sea: A Treasury of American Folklore and Folk Songs,* include all of these types of tales. Other sources contain only one type of tale.

Native American Folktales. Native American tales are usually considered the only traditional tales truly indigenous to the United States. Any study of the traditional literature of native peoples in North America reveals not one group of folktales, but tales different from region to

region and tribe to tribe, although most Native American folklore has motifs in common.

Animal trickster tales are popular in Native American culture, as elsewhere. The tricksters are often ravens, rabbits, or coyotes that have powers of magical transformation. In Gerald McDermott's *Raven: A Trickster Tale from the Pacific Northwest,* the trickster character brings light to the people. Heroes and heroines may also use transformation in undertaking their quests. In McDermott's *Arrow to the Sun: A Pueblo Indian Tale,* for example, a boy becomes an arrow as he searches for his father, the sun-god.

The importance of folklore for passing on tribal beliefs is revealed in Olaf Baker's *Where the Buffaloes Begin.* A young Native American of the Great Plains learns from a tribal storyteller about a sacred spot where the buffaloes rise out of a lake. After he finds the lake, he waits quietly in the night. As he waits, he hears the words of the storyteller singing in his mind:

> Do you hear the noise that never ceases?
> It is the Buffaloes fighting far below.
> They are fighting to get out upon the prairie.
> They are born below the Water but are fighting
>   for the Air.
> In the great lake in the Southland where the
>   Buffaloes begin! (p. 20)

The diversity of Native American cultures, customs, and folklore is illustrated in Jamake Highwater's *Anpao: An Indian Odyssey.* Highwater's book emphasizes the importance of traditional tales in transmitting Native American culture. Chapter 11, "Multicultural Literature," discusses these tales and others.

African American Folktales. Many African American folktales reflect both an African origin and an adaptation to a new environment and the harsh reality of slavery. For example, a rabbit trickster who triumphs over more powerful animals is popular in African folklore. He is also one of the most popular characters in tales collected from black people on southern plantations. This character's popularity with African Americans was probably related to the experience of slavery. Cunning, wit, and deception were often the only weapons available against oppression. (The tortoise and Ananse the spider play similar trickster roles.) The trickster Brer Rabbit is famous in the African American folktales collected by Joel Chandler Harris in nineteenth-century Georgia and published as *Uncle Remus and His Friends* (1892) and *Told by Uncle Remus* (1905).

Other African American tales about a trickster rabbit are found in West Virginia. Though not as powerful as his adversaries, the rabbit is more intelligent, and he manages to outwit them. Some of these stories contain a serious moral: "Don't go looking for trouble, else you might find it." Such morals are often found in African American folklore.

William H. Hooks's *The Ballad of Belle Dorcas* is a tale set in the tidewater section of the Carolinas during the time of slavery. The protagonists are a free issue woman

Through the Eyes of an AUTHOR

Jamake Highwater

Selected Titles by Jamake Highwater:

Anpao: An American Indian Odyssey

Legend Days

Many Smokes, Many Moons: A Chronology of American Indian History Through Indian Art

Moonsong Lullaby

Rama: A Legend

I Wear the Morning Star

Traditional Native American Tales

In a very real sense, I am the brother of the fox. My whole life revolves around my kinship with four-legged things. I am rooted in the natural world. I'm two people joined into one body. The contradiction doesn't bother me. But people always assume the one they're talking to is the only one there is. That bothers me. There is a little of the legendary Anpao in me, but also a little of John Gardner. I stand in both those worlds, not between them. I'm very much a twentieth-century person, and yet I'm traditional Northern Plains Indian.

I've always had an enormous regard for the intellect. Still, I like to go home to my people, who are in touch with the beginning of things. At home, people are carpenters; some are poets, painters, and teachers; some work on construction jobs. They are people who perceive the importance of small things that are easily missed by those of us who move much too quickly.

I came to terms with the solemn aspects of life very early. I was always among Indians, for we traveled the powwow circuit. I was always listening to some older person telling stories. They are nameless to me now, and countless, because there were so many. I was introduced to the Indian world as children in my tribe were in the 1870s, when we were a nomadic people. I was rootless yet connected to a vital tradition. The elders talked to me and gave me a sense of the meaning of my existence.

I talk and think as a poet, but I don't want to perpetuate the romantic notion of the Indian as watching chipmunks his entire life [and] waiting to see which side of the tree the moss grows on.

For the Indian, art is not reserved for a leisure class, as it is in Anglo society. It is part of our fundamental way of thinking. We are an aesthetic people. Most primal people are. We represent a constant chord that's been resounding ever since man began. While those Cro-Magnon people in the caves of southern France (at least according to Western mentality) should have been out worrying about the great likelihood that they wouldn't survive, they were building scaffolds fifty or sixty feet high and with tiny oil lamps were painting the ceilings of their caves with marvelous magical images. These images were an implicit and important part of their lives. For us, this aesthetic reality is a continuous process. The kiva murals of the Hopi and the Mimbres pottery rival the finest accomplishments of Western art. This idea of life as art is part of being Indian. It's not quaint or curious or charming. It's fundamental, like plowing a field. There's great beauty in plowing a field.

I think Indians have become a metaphor for a larger idea. We are building bridges toward cultures. Some people in white society are also building bridges toward us, and they sometimes join together. That means that it's possible for everyone to find the Indian in himself. It's a kind of sensibility that I'm talking about.

Video Profiles: The accompanying video contains conversations with Joseph Bruchac, Jack Gantos, Roland Smith, and other writers of children's literature.

Drawn from an interview with Jane B. Katz, 1980. The world of literature recently lost Jamake Highwater, who died in June, 2001.

---

and a slave who fall in love, but they are threatened with separation when the master wishes to sell the slave. In addition to revealing the consequences of social injustice, the tale reveals the power of love and the belief in the magical ability of the spells created by conjurers. These tales and other tales are discussed in Chapter 11, "Multicultural Literature."

Variants of European Tales. The traditional literatures of the United States and Canada contain many variants of traditional European folktales. European settlers from England, France, and elsewhere brought their oral traditions with them. Then, they adapted the stories to reflect a new environment. Consequently, many North American folktales involve familiar European themes, motifs, and characters in settings that portray the unknown wilderness and harsh winters confronted by the early colonizers of North America. The only indigenous Canadian traditional literature comes from the Native Canadian and Inuit peoples.

Eva Martin's *Canadian Fairy Tales* contains twelve French-Canadian and English-Canadian variations of traditional European tales. Ti-Jean tales contain several familiar story elements. The lazy fellow kills one thousand flies with one blow, uses his wits to capture a unicorn and steal a giant's seven-league boots, and eventually marries the princess. In the Canadian variant of "Beauty and the Beast," the enchanted beast is female and the prince stays in her castle. William H. Hooks's *Moss Gown* is an adaptation of the English Cinderella tale. It also contains elements of King Lear and the plantation South.

The best-known North American variants of European tales belong to the Jack cycle. In these tales, a seemingly nonheroic person overcomes severe obstacles and outwits adversaries. The American "Jack and the Varmits," for example, is similar to the English "The Brave Little Tailor." In keeping with the European tradition, the American Jack is rewarded by a king. Instead of a giant, Jack must overcome a wild hog, a unicorn, and a lion. The influences of rural America are found in both the setting and language. The lion, who was killing cattle, horses, and humans, came over the mountains from Tennessee. Both the king and Jack speak in frontier dialect. Gail E. Haley's *Jack and the Bean Tree* is an Appalachian variant of "Jack and the Beanstalk." Haley's *Mountain Jack Tales,* a collection of stories from the

Through the Eyes of a CHILD

Riley

Pam Wilson's Fourth Grade
Western Row Elementary
Mason, Ohio

TITLE: Jamake Highwater
AUTHOR: Moonsong Lullaby

Moonsong Lullaby sounds very poetic. I like that you can't get the exact meaning, but Jamake Highwater gets across the basic point. Jamake Highwater's writing will give you clues for what he's writing about until the very end of the sentence, when he just brings it right out to you. I would recommend this book to anyone.

Riley

Jack cycle, has foundations in the mountain regions of America. A resourceful female becomes the heroine in Mary Pope Osborne's variant of "Jack and the Beanstalk," *Kate and the Beanstalk.* There is also considerable humor in this story.

Tall Tales. Boastful frontier humor is found in North American tall tales. These tales reflect the hardships of settlers, who faced severe climatic changes, unknown lands, and people whose lives reflected strange cultures. Exaggerated claims in tall tales—such as those found in Walter Blair's *Tall Tale America: A Legendary History of Our Humorous Heroes*—declare that the American soil is so rich that fast-growing vines damage pumpkins by dragging them on the ground; that frontier people are so powerful that they can lasso and subdue cyclones; and that the leader of the river boaters can outshoot, outfight, outrun, and outbrag everyone in the world.

The North American heroes and heroines who faced extremes in weather, conquered humans and beasts, and subdued the wilderness are not the godlike heroes and heroines of European mythology. Instead, their lives reflect the primitive virtues of brute force, animal cunning, and courage. The characters and situations in tall tales reflect frontier idealism. People are free to travel. They live self-sufficient lives and are extremely resourceful.

American tall tales contain fictional heroes and heroes based on real people. Hardworking, persevering characters—such as Johnny Appleseed, who considered it his mission to plant apple trees across the country—

demonstrate duty and endurance. Boisterous, bragging roughnecks—such as Davy Crockett, Calamity Jane, and Paul Bunyan—perform otherwise impossible feats, out-shooting a thousand enemies or conquering mighty rivers and immense forests. Other characters—such as the steel-driving man, John Henry—reflect a country that was changing from a rural and agricultural way of life to an urban and mechanized one. *John Tabor's Ride,* by Edward C. Day, reflects the whaling industry and the yarns told by whalers in New England. *Mike Fink: A Tall Tale,* retold by Stephen Kellogg, is another story that emphasizes numerous fantastic feats.

You may find additional information about the folklore associated with Davy Crockett by reading *The Tall Tales of Davy Crockett: The Second Nashville Series of Crockett Almanacs 1839–1841,* which is published by the University of Tennessee Press. In the introduction to the text, Michael Lofaro (1987) states that Crockett's heroic death increased his image as a boasting, brawling backwoodsman. Lofaro continues:

The "wretched caricatures" soon became fantastic tall tales in the popular comic almanacs that bore Crockett's name. In these works Davy once again "assumed the character drawn for him by others"; it was, however, a character no longer bounded by the achievements of a mortal man, but only by the imagination. (p. x)

Robert D. San Souci's *Cut from the Same Cloth: American Women of Myth, Legend, and Tall Tale* is an excellent tall-tale collection about women in heroic conflicts. San

Souci presents tales from different regions and ethnic groups. He also includes source notes and a bibliography. Nancy Van Laan's *With a Whoop and a Holler: A Bushel of Lore from Way Down South* is an anthology of tales from the Bayou region, the deep South, and Appalachia. Scott Cook's illustrations add humor to many of the tall tales. The author includes a list of source notes. These stories would be especially good for oral storytelling.

Fables

Legend credits the origin of the fable in Western culture to a Greek slave named Aesop, who lived in the sixth century B.C. Aesop's nimble wit supposedly got Aesop's master out of numerous difficulties. Aesop may not have been one person, however. Several experts attribute the early European fables to various sources. Fables are found worldwide; the traditional literatures of China and India, for example, contain fables similar to Aesop's. Whatever their origins, fables are excellent examples of stories handed down over centuries of oral and written literary tradition.

The Book of the subtyl historyes and Fables of Esope, *published in the fifteenth century, is considered one of William Caxton's most important contributions to European literature.* (The Book of the Subtyl Historyes and Fables of Esope *by William Caxton, published in the fifteenth century.)*

Characteristics

According to R. T. Lenaghan (1967) in his introduction to *Caxton's Aesop,* fables have the following characteristics: (1) They are fiction in the sense that they did not really happen, (2) they are meant to entertain, (3) they are poetic, with double or allegorical significance, and (4) they are moral tales, usually with animal characters. In fables, animals usually talk and behave like humans and possess other human traits. Fables are short, and they usually have not more than two or three characters. These characters perform simple, straightforward actions that result in a single climax. Fables also contain human lessons expressed through the foibles of personified animals.

The characteristics of fables apparently appealed to traditional storytellers around the world. In fifteenth-century England, fables were among the first texts that William Caxton printed on his newly created printing press. Lenaghan (1967) credits the popularity of fables to their generic ambiguity. They could be used as entertaining stories, teaching devices, or sermons. They could also reach people of various degrees of intelligence, be bluntly assertive or cleverly ironic, and be didactic or skeptical. Storytellers could emphasize whatever functions they chose.

The continuing popularity of fables led Randolph Caldecott to create his own edition of Aesop in the

nineteenth century. *The Caldecott Aesop,* first published in 1883 and reissued in 1978, provides modern readers with an opportunity to enjoy fables accompanied by hand-colored drawings of a great illustrator of children's books. Caldecott's illustrations show first the animals in a fable, then the people replacing the animals. Sir Roger L'Estrange's seventeenth-century translation of *Aesop's Fables* is also available in a reissued text.

Contemporary Editions

Fables are popular subjects for modern storytellers and illustrators. In his introduction to *Feathers and Tails: Animal Fables from Around the World,* David Kherdian (1992) states his reasons for believing that fables are popular:

These stories speak to our limitations as well as our possibilities, since one without the other is meaningless. We are confused by our potential, our possibilities. Each of us is born knowing there is more—but more of what? As we grow and begin to define what the more is for ourselves, we see that it is nothing more or less than our own wholeness. We need guidance, but we are uncertain how to seek it, or how to apply it once it has been found. In all of this the ancient teaching story can be our guide, for it speaks to us with humor, laughter, and enjoyment, from a source that we can all recognize because it is as old as mankind, as universal as the sun and stars. (p. 8)

Young children like the talking animals and the often humorous climaxes. Authors and illustrators of fables for young children sometimes expand fables into longer, more detailed narrative stories. In *The Tortoise and the Hare,* Janet Stevens expands the story line of the fable by including the exercises Tortoise undertakes to prepare for

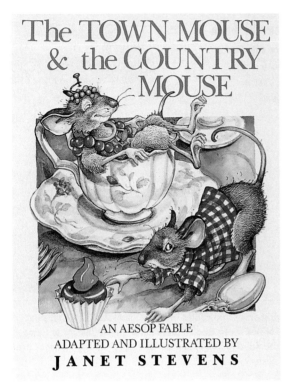

The author has expanded on a fable to create a picture storybook in The Town Mouse & the Country Mouse. *(From* The Town Mouse & the Country Mouse, *adapted and illustrated by Janet Stevens. Copyright © 1987 by Janet Stevens. Reprinted by permission of Holiday House. All rights reserved.)*

the race and the actions of Tortoise's friends as they try to deter Hare. Stevens uses a similar approach in her picture storybook version of Aesop's *The Town Mouse & the Country Mouse.* Another heavily illustrated version of this fable is Helen Craig's *The Town Mouse and the Country Mouse.* Compare the impact of the illustrations and the retellings by each author.

Numerous collections of Aesop's fables have been compiled and illustrated for slightly older children, too. It is interesting to compare the various editions to see how the fables have been interpreted and illustrated. For example, a version of Aesop first published in 1919, *The Aesop for Children,* is in simple narrative form and dialogue. The capture of the mouse in "The Lion and the Mouse" is described in this way:

A Lion lay asleep in the forest, his great head resting on his paws. A timid little Mouse came upon him unexpectedly, and in her fright and haste to get away, ran across the Lion's nose. Roused from his nap, the Lion laid his huge paw angrily on the tiny creature to kill her.

"Spare me!" begged the poor Mouse. "Please let me go and some day I will surely repay you."

The Lion was much amused to think that a Mouse could ever help him. But he was generous and finally let the Mouse go. (p. 19)

The moral is simply stated in this version: "A kindness is never wasted."

Tom Paxton retells fables in verse in his *Aesop's Fables.* Paxton describes the incident in which the mouse is captured in "The Lion and the Mouse":

He ran over the lion, who awoke with a roar:
"Who's treating my back like the jungle floor?"
He grabbed the poor mouse by his poor little tail.
"Oh, please, Mister Lion, I swear without fail,
    If you'll please just release me, I promise someday
The debt will be one that I'll gladly repay."
The proud lion laughed and let the mouse go.
(unnumbered)

The moral of this fable is presented in verse form in the last two lines:

Yes, sometimes the weak and sometimes the
    strong
Must help each other to save right from wrong.
(unnumbered)

Jerry Pinkney's *Aesop's Fables* is a large collection of sixty fables all ending with a short moral such as "Don't count your chickens before they're hatched."

Jane Yolen's *A Sip of Aesop* provides an interesting version for comparison with more traditional versions of the fables. Yolen retells the fables in poetic form, including the moral at the end of the fable. For example, "The Dog and the Bone" ends with the moral:

You may not have time
For a final correction.
Don't open your mouth
Without proper reflection. (unnumbered)

Contemporary versions of fables differ in the illustrator's style as well as the author's style. Heidi Holder's *Aesop's Fables* contains detailed, elegant paintings surrounded by equally detailed borders. Michael Hague's *Aesop's Fables* is illustrated with full-page paintings in somber, earthy tones. Fulvio Testa's *Aesop's Fables* also follows each fable with a full-page illustration. Each illustration is framed with a colorful design. Pinkney's *Aesop's Fables* is illustrated with large watercolor paintings. Tom Lynch's *Fables from Aesop* is illustrated with fabric collages.

An interesting cross-cultural comparison of both texts and illustrations may be made with John Bierhorst's *Doctor Coyote: A Native American Aesop's Fables.* Bierhorst identifies both Spanish-Aztec and ancient Latin connections. Bierhorst states:

The Aztec Aesop's was adapted in the 1500s by one or more Indian retellers, using a now-lost Spanish collection of the standard fables. All of these, however, can be traced to Latin and Greek manuscripts of late classical and medieval times. Compared with the originals, the Aztec variants differ mainly in the cast of characters, which includes Coyote and Puma, two of the best-known animal tricksters in Native American folklore. (author's note, unnumbered)

enced by an old Norse tale when he wrote *Hamlet;* J. R. R. Tolkien, a professor of Anglo-Saxon literature at Oxford University, relied on his knowledge of the northern sagas when he wrote *The Hobbit* and *The Lord of the Rings.*

The tales of the northern gods and goddesses were collected during the twelfth and thirteenth centuries from the earlier oral tradition. These original tales formed two volumes, the *Elder Edda* and the *Younger Edda.* These texts are now the sources for most of our knowledge about Norse mythology. According to Olivia Coolidge (1951), Norse mythology maintains that the earth began when a frost giant, Ymir, came out of swirling mists. The shifting particles formed a great cow, whose milk nourished Ymir. As time went by, sons and daughters were also created out of the mists. Gods took form when the cow began to lick the great ice blocks that filled the mists. As she licked, a huge god appeared. When he stood up, his descendants were formed from his warm breath.

The frost giants were evil, so the gods vowed to destroy them. A mighty battle resulted between the gods and the frost giants, with the gods finally overpowering the giants. Ymir was destroyed, and the remaining giants fled into the outer regions and created a land of mists and mountains. The mightiest of the gods, Odin, looked at the dead frost giant, Ymir, and suggested that the gods use his body to make a land where they could live. They formed Ymir's body into the round, flat earth, and on its center, they built mountains to contain their home, Asgard. Ymir's skull was used to form the great arch of heaven; his blood was the ocean, a barrier between the earth and giantland. The gods stole sparks from the fiery regions to light the stars, and they built chariots in which they placed sun and moon spirits to ride over the earth.

The Norse world of tales filled with heroism, humor, and wisdom and peopled with gods, goddesses, giants, and dwarfs comes alive in Mary Pope Osborne's *Favorite Norse Myths.* These tales retold from the *Elder Edda* and the *Younger Edda* are introduced with quotes from the *Poetic Edda,* written down in the tenth century. For example, the first myth, "Creation: The Nine Worlds," begins with the following quote:

> Twas the earliest of times
> When Ymir lived:
> There was no sand nor sea
> Nor cooling wave.
> Earth had not been,
> Nor heaven on high,
> There was a yawning void
> And grass no where. (p. 1)

Osborne then begins the tale in a similar manner that places readers into this far distant time: "In the morning of time there was no sand, no sea, and no clouds. There was no heaven, no earth, and no grass. There was only a region of icy mist called Niflheim, a region of fire called Muspell, and a great yawning empty void between them

"The Hammer of Thor" is an excellent choice for storytelling. (From Legends of the North, *by Olivia Coolidge. Copyright © 1951 and renewed 1979 by Olivia E. Coolidge. Reprinted by permission of Houghton Mifflin Co.)*

called Ginnugagap" (p. 1). The author provides an introduction that places the Norse myths into their historic time and setting. In addition, sections contain pronunciation guides and identifications of the gods, goddesses, giants, and other creatures; meanings of symbols and runes; a bibliography; and an index.

Padraic Colum portrays the strong moral code of Odin in his version of "The Building of the Wall," found in *The Children of Odin: The Book of Northern Myths.* Even though a protective wall is built around Asgard, Odin grieves:

> But Odin, the Father of the Gods, as he sat upon his throne was sad in his heart, sad that the Gods had got their wall built by a trick, that oaths had been broken, and that a blow had been struck in injustice in Asgard. (p. 12)

Olivia E. Coolidge's *Legends of the North* is an excellent source of stories about the Norse gods and goddesses who lived on earth in the mighty citadel of Asgard and the heroes and heroines who lived under their power. In "The Apples of Idun," the divine beings often walked on earth because the mighty Odin believed they should know their realm intimately, in stone, flower, and leaf.

In Coolidge's text, Thor, the god of war, strides around with red hair bristling and fierce eyes ablaze. Sometimes, he rides in his chariot drawn by red-eyed goats, which are as shaggy and fierce as their master.

One humorous selection from this book is "The Hammer of Thor." In this story, Thor searches loudly for his missing hammer. Children probably feel close to Thor as he responds in exasperation when Freyja, the goddess of beauty, asks him where he put it. He shouts, "If I knew where I put it, I should not be looking for it now" (p. 35).

Thor discovers that the giant Thyrm has stolen the hammer and wants Freyja as ransom. When the goddess vehemently refuses to become the giant's bride, the suggestion is made that Thor dress up as a bride and go to giantland to retrieve his own hammer. After considerable argument, the huge god dresses in gown and veil to cover his fierce eyes and bristling beard, and accompanied by the impish Loki, he leaves for giantland.

Mighty Thor remains quiet as the wedding feast progresses, and fast-witted Loki answers the giant's questions and calms his suspicions. Finally, Thor is able to touch his hammer as the wedding ceremony begins. This is what he has been waiting for; he regains his hammer, overpowers the giant, removes his skirts, and leaves for home.

Thor's courage, loyalty, and willingness to take vengeance are recurring strains found in this mythology. The humor and action in this tale make it excellent for storytelling. Other enjoyable Norse tales suitable for sharing with children include Ingri and Edgar Parin D'Aulaire's *Norse Gods and Giants* and Kevin Crossley-Holland's *The Faber Book of Northern Legends*.

Myths from Other Cultures

All cultures include mythology that allows their peoples to experience and to explain the awe of the universe. As do the Greek and Norse myths, these myths reflect the cultures and the settings from which they originated. For example, Kiri Te Kanawa's *Land of the Long White Cloud: Maori Myths, Tales, and Legends* is a collection of ancient folklore told by the Polynesian sailors who discovered New Zealand—The Land of the Long White Cloud. Here are creation stories, trickster tales, and legends of various Maori tribes. The first tale, "The Birth of Maui," describes the birth of this trickster character and explains why he grew up to be a maker of mischief. The setting is appropriate for a culture that is so influenced by the ocean:

Out in the middle of the wide, wide ocean, where the sky rests on the edges and there is no land to be seen, a little bundle of seaweed rose and fell in the swell. Seabirds wheeled around overhead, their lonely cries echoing across the water. The sun beat down and a breeze stirred the surface, pushing the seaweed for miles and miles. (p. 12)

Michael Foreman's predominantly blue and green illustrations create a mood of a land surrounded by water.

Virginia Hamilton's *In the Beginning: Creation Stories from Around the World* includes twenty-five myths from various cultures. Each myth includes a comment in which Hamilton provides information about the source of the myth and some interpretive information. For example,

the myth "Apsu and Tiamat the Creators" includes the following comment:

This myth is taken from the stunning Babylonian creation verse narrative, *Enuma elish,* perhaps the most famous of the Near Eastern texts. It symbolizes unity from which all life begins, and it also represents a World-Parent myth type. Apsu and Tiamat are not only ancestors of the gods, they also symbolize the living, unformed matter of the world.

One of the purposes of the *Enuma elish* was to praise Marduk, who was the main god of Babylon—to establish him as supreme, and to honor Babylon as the highest city.

The *Enuma elish* was discovered in the ruins of King Ashurbanipal's library at Nineveh dating back to 668–626 B.C., but it has been traced back to the First Babylonian Dynasty, 2050–1750 B.C., and the age of King Hammurabi, 1900 B.C., and even further back to the Sumerians who lived in the region before the Babylonians. The narrative takes its name from the first line: "Enuma elish la nabu shamanu . . . ," meaning "When on high the heaven had not been named. . . ." (p. 85)

Barry Moser's illustrations add to the feelings of wonder that are reflected in these myths.

Some of the folklore from the Middle East reflects the common ground between Islam and Christianity. Shulamith Levy Oppenheim's *Ibis,* thought to date back to the ninth century B.C., is both a creation story explaining the beginnings of humankind and our troubles and a cautionary tale showing the dangers of disobeying God's orders. The author tells us that this version of the Adam and Eve story "can be found in the work of Jarir at-Tabari, a famous Islamic scholar who was a religious authority and historian. Born about 839 A.D. in Amul, a city near the southern shore of the Caspian Sea, he traveled throughout the Islamic world as a young man and finally settled in Baghdad, in what is now Iraq. He acquired material for his history of the world from oral storytelling and literary sources, as well as from the Koran" (author's note, unnumbered). You may compare this variant of the Adam and Eve story with the Christian version.

Legends

According to Richard Cavendish in his introduction to *Legends of the World* (1982):

Legends stand the test of time, better than genuine history does. . . . The territory of legend has history on one of its borders, myth on another and folk-tale on a third. The frontier zones are vague and shifting, and perhaps no two people will ever agree about precisely where the boundary lines fall. . . . Everywhere in the world, legendary stories of what happened in the past have been handed down from generation to generation. They are part of the inherited conglomerate of accepted beliefs, values and attitudes which give a people its identity. These stories consequently provide invaluable evidence about the societies that give birth to them, and insights into human nature in general. (p. 9)

The great legends in traditional literature are closely related to mythology. Many of these legends have been transmitted over the centuries in the form of epics. Epics are long narrative poems about the deeds of traditional or historical human heroes and heroines of high station. Two of the better-known Greek epics are *The Iliad* and *The Odyssey*. *The Iliad* is an account of the Trojan War. *The Odyssey* reports the journey of Odysseus (Ulysses in Latin) as he defeats the Cyclops, overcomes the song of the sirens, and manages to survive ten long years of hazardous adventures. Gods, goddesses, and other supernatural beings play important roles in such epics, but the focus is human characters.

"Beowulf," the story of a human warrior, is usually considered the outstanding example of Norse epic poetry. Beowulf's struggle against evil has three main episodes. First, Beowulf fights and kills the monster Grendel. Second, Beowulf dives to the depths of a pool and attacks Grendel's mother, She. Third, Beowulf fights the dragon Firedrake and is mortally wounded.

Versions of this epic are available in both narrative and poetic form. One version, which the author Robert Nye calls a new telling, is written in narrative form for young readers. In this version, Beowulf is strong, but he is also good—loyal, courageous, and willing to take vengeance. His character epitomizes the heroic code found in Norse myths. A combination of heroic deeds and honorable characteristics makes it possible for his good name to live after him. For example, Nye describes the hero as having real strength. It "lay in the balance of his person—which is perhaps another way of saying that he was strong because he was good, and good because he had the strength to accept things in him which were bad" (p. 25). His good is so powerful that it is felt by the evil monsters and is instrumental in their defeat.

Fate, a strong code of honor, and a willingness to avenge wrong are emphasized in Kevin Crossley-Holland's *Beowulf*. Crossley-Holland develops the importance of fate as Beowulf ponders the outcome of his forthcoming struggle with the monster Grendel: "Who knows? Fate goes always as it must" (p. 11) and "If a man is brave enough and not doomed to die, fate often spares him to fight another day" (p. 13). The importance of fate is reemphasized after Beowulf's victory, as King Hrothgar declares: "Beowulf, bravest of men, fate's darling! Your friends are fortunate, your enemies not to be envied" (p. 34).

Crossley-Holland develops a strong code of honor when Beowulf refuses to use a sword or a shield because the monster fights without weapons. Crossley-Holland combines honor and vengeance as Beowulf cries that he will avenge the Danes, the people who gave refuge to his father. Honor and vengeance are also part of the monster's code, and Beowulf is pleased when he discovers: "There is honor amongst monsters as there is honor amongst men. Grendel's mother came to the hall to avenge the death of her son" (p. 25). The conclusion emphasizes Beowulf's heroic characteristics: "They said

that of all kings on earth, he was the kindest, the most gentle, the most just to his people, the most eager for fame" (p. 46).

The newest retelling of the Beowulf epic poem is Seamus Heaney's translation titled *Beowulf*. The text written in both Old English and modern English was the 2000 winner of the Whitbread Award.

Many of the heroes and heroines in epic legends reflect a strong sense of goodness as they overcome various worldly evils. The line between legend and myth is often vague, however. The early legends usually enlarged upon the lives of religious figures, such as martyrs and saints. In more recent times, legends developed around royal figures and folk heroes and heroines. Chart 6.6 shows similarities and differences between myth and legend.

We consider the tales of King Arthur to be legends rather than myths because they are stories primarily about humans rather than supernatural beings and because historical tradition maintains that King Arthur actually existed in fairly recent times. Tales of this legendary British king were so popular in early England that Sir Thomas Malory's *Le Morte d'Arthur* was one of the first books published in England.

Another early version of the tale is Howard Pyle's *The Story of King Arthur and His Knights*. The first section of Pyle's version, "The Book of King Arthur," reveals how Arthur removed the sacred sword Excalibur from a stone and signified that he was the rightful king of England, claimed his birthright, wed Guinevere, and established the Round Table. The second section, "The Book of Three Worthies," tells about Merlin the magician, Sir Pellias, and Sir Gawaine. The original version of this book, with Pyle's illustrations, has been reissued. Other editions of Arthurian legends include Rosemary Sutcliff's *The Sword and the Circle: King Arthur and the Knights of the Round Table, The Light Beyond the Forest*, and *The Road to Camlann: The Death of King Arthur*. In *Parzival: The Quest of the Grail Knight*, Katherine Paterson retells a legendary tale about another knight from Arthur's court.

Selina Hastings's *Sir Gawain and the Loathly Lady* retells one of the Arthurian legends in a picture-book format. Characteristically, the tale includes a challenge, a quest, enchantment, and a promise demanded by the code of chivalry. Juan Wijngaard's illustrations capture both the evil menace of the black knight and the ancient splendor of Arthur's court.

The importance of the Arthurian legends as subjects for more contemporary authors is easily seen by reading Cindy Mediavilla's *Arthurian Fiction: An Annotated Bibliography* (1999). Mediavilla includes more than two hundred book-length Arthurian novels that she categorizes under areas such as "Romance of Camelot" and "Merlin, Kingmaker and Mage." To make the bibliography more useful to all readers, she identifies a reading level for each book from middle school to high school.

CHART 6.6 Similarities and differences between myth and legend

Myth: "The Birth of Athena"	Legend: "Tales of King Arthur"
Belief Told as factual—the birth of a goddess	Told as factual—the life of a British chieftain of the fifth and sixth centuries
Setting Mount Olympus, Greece	British Isles
Time In a remote past, when gods and goddesses dwelt on the earth	In the time of kings and knights, within a recognizable world
Attitude Sacred—Athena (a goddess) sprang from the head of Zeus (father of the gods)	Sacred—a quest for the Holy Grail Secular—King Arthur established the Round Table and was the leader of the knights
Principal Characters Nonhuman—the goddess assists heroes and heroines in quests	Human—the king does not have supernatural powers

Another legendary figure in English culture is Robin Hood, the hero of Sherwood Forest. Stories about Robin Hood were told orally for centuries and were mentioned in manuscripts as early as 1360. Legend suggests that he was born Robert Fitzooth, Earl of Huntingdon, in Nottinghamshire, England, in 1160. According to the tales, he was a great archer. He and his band of outlaws poached the king's deer, robbed the rich, and gave to the poor.

Stories of Robin Hood are popular with children. Movies and television plays have been produced about his adventures. Howard Pyle's *The Merry Adventures of Robin Hood* provides visions of what it would be like to live "in merry England in the time of old" and to interact with Little John, Maid Marian, Friar Tuck, the Sheriff of Nottingham, and King Richard of the Lion's Heart. Margaret Early's *Robin Hood* is a highly illustrated version of the legend. Children enjoy comparing the various editions and describing the strengths and weaknesses of each. For this purpose, even the Walt Disney movie that presents Robin Hood as a fox, Little John as a bear, and Prince John as a lion adds to a lively discussion, especially about characterization.

The Outlaws of Sherwood is Robin McKinley's interpretation of the Robin Hood legend. McKinley has created a vivid and readable story that includes both a castle-versus-cottage conflict and romanticism of the original time. For example, through the words of Alan-a-Dale, she shows the conflict between the outlaws and their wealthier antagonists:

Indeed, perhaps I have heard of this band for enough of time that I have written a ballad or two about them; a ballad or two received well enough at market day among the yeoman farmers

Page design is enhanced by plain-colored borders on illustrated pages and drawings of plants and scenes bordering text pages. (From Saint George and the Dragon. *Retold by Margaret Hodges and illustrated by Trina Schart Hyman. Illustration copyright © 1984 by Trina Schart Hyman. Used by permission of Holiday House.)*

and goodwives, but not so well among those who live in great castles and feel the need to have an eye to their own wealth. (p. 71)

This text is good for reading and for making comparisons among Robin Hood legends. You may also compare Michael Cadnum's *In a Dark Wood*, which is told from the point of view of the sheriff.

The hero in Margaret Hodges's adaptation of the English legend *Saint George and the Dragon* exemplifies the characteristics found in legendary heroes. He is noble, courageous, and willing to avenge a wrong. A legendary fight for freedom and independence is retold by Margaret Early in *William Tell*. This beautifully illustrated text captures the mood of the historic period as well as the life of the Swiss hero, William Tell.

The Hawaiian Islands provide the setting for Marcia Brown's *Backbone of the King: The Story of Pakáa and His Son Ku*. The characters display the qualities of other legendary heroes. Bravery, honor, and willingness to avenge a wrong characterize the chief, a trusted adviser to the king, who is unjustly wronged and then brought back to honor through the brave actions of his son.

Jewish legends with Biblical sidelights are important for understanding the Jewish culture. Sandy Eisenberg Sasso's *But God Remembered: Stories of Women from Creation to the Promised Land* includes legends about Lilith, who tradition tells us was Adam's first wife, and other little-known female figures such as Serach, the Granddaughter of Jacob, and the five daughters of Zelophehad, who come to Moses after their father dies and ask to inherit their father's land. The characteristics of these women reflect many of the important values found in Jewish folklore. For example, in "The Psalm of Serach," Serach has the characteristics of grace and wisdom. She feels honored because her father taught her the wisdom of the ancestors. Through her beautiful singing voice and the Psalm she writes, the storyteller shows the importance of music and of Psalms to impact knowledge and understanding. Through the Psalm, readers discover the importance of hope, forgiveness, and God's role in Jewish history.

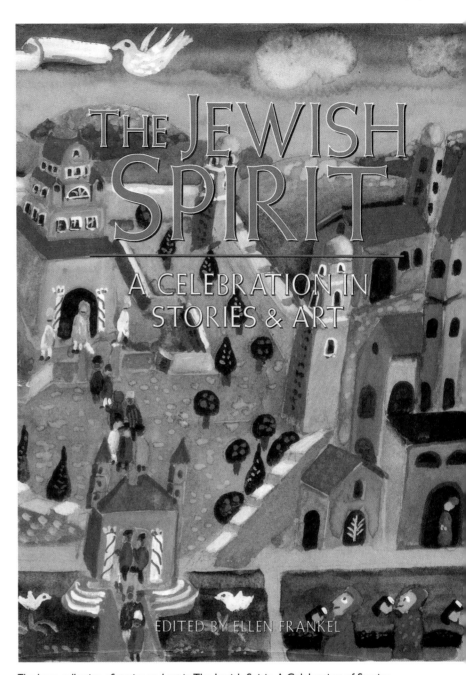

The large collection of stories and art in The Jewish Spirit: A Celebration of Stories & Art *provides an excellent source of Jewish materials. (From* The Jewish Spirit: A Celebration of Stories & Art *edited by Ellen Frankel. Copyright © 1998. A Fair Street/ Welcome Book, published by Stewart, Tabori & Chang. Reprinted by permission.)*

Barbara Diamond Goldin places *Journeys with Elijah: Eight Tales of the Prophet* in different times and in different places "to emphasize the age-old idea that Elijah can appear anywhere, anytime, if people will but welcome him and what he stands for—hope and peace" (p. x). Each of the eight stories includes an introduction that identifies the time, place, and circumstances used in telling the tale. Miriam Chaikin's *Clouds of Glory* includes twenty-one myths and legends retold from Midrash. The author's "Notes and References" section includes a combination of sources for each tale. "From the Bible" includes quotes and Bible commentary; "From Legend" includes elements of Midrash, commentary, and legends on which the stories are based. You may compare Chaikin's text and interpretations with Julius Lester's *When the Beginning Began: Stories About God, the Creatures, and Us,* which is also based on Midrash tales.

Three versions of the legend about the Golem provide opportunities for comparisons of both illustrations and text. For example, David Wisniewski's *Golem* is a highly illustrated tale about a rabbi who brings to life a clay giant to help the people during a very dangerous time in sixteenth-century Prague. The cut-paper illustrations give a three-dimensional appearance to both the architecture and the characters. They also stress the power that is found in the form of the Golem. Within the illustrations are numerous examples of Jewish culture such as Hebrew letters, the rabbi, the holy texts, the yellow circles worn on the left shoulders or sleeves of many of the characters, and the synagogue.

Wisniewski's version may be compared with Barbara Rogasky's *The Golem,* illustrated by Trina Schart Hyman, and Isaac Bashevis Singer's *The Golem,* illustrated by Uri Shulevitz. Both of these books present longer versions of the Golem story and include fewer illustrations. As you read these three texts, compare the power of the writing, consider the information provided in the author's or illustrator's notes, and view the impact of the illustrations.

Legends help children understand the conditions of times that created a need for brave and honorable men and women. These tales of adventure stress the noblest actions of humans. In legends, justice reigns over injustice. Children can feel the magnitude of the oral tradition as they listen to these tales, so reading legends aloud is the best way to introduce them to children.

Suggested Activities

For more suggested activities for understanding traditional literature, visit our Companion Website at www.prenhall.com/norton

- Read the stories included in Charles Perrault's *Tales of Mother Goose* and some tales collected by the Brothers Grimm. Note similarities and differences in the characterizations, settings, and actions. Describe the people for whom you believe the stories were originally told.
- Choose a common theme found in folktales, such as that in Cinderella or in trickster stories. Find examples of similar stories in folktales from several countries. What are the similarities and differences? How do the stories reflect cultural characteristics?
- Read a fable in *Caxton's Aesop* and in *The Caldecott Aesop.* Compare these versions of the fables with a modern version. Are there differences in writing style, language, spelling, and illustrations between the earlier and later versions? If there are, what do you believe are the reasons for the differences? Share the versions with a child. How does the child respond to each version?
- To gain an understanding of the numerous subjects that are studied within the area of folklore, search editor Thomas A. Green's *Folklore: An Encyclopedia of Beliefs, Customs, Tales, Music, and Art,* Volumes I and II (1997). Share your findings with the class.

Teaching with Traditional Literature

Traditional tales are among the most memorable that children experience in literature. With their well-defined plots, easily identifiable characters, rapid action, and satisfactory endings, the tales lend themselves to enjoyable experiences. This section explores ways to recapture the oral tradition through telling stories, comparing folktales from different countries, investigating folktales from a single country, and motivating writing.

Telling Stories

Learning the ancient art of storytelling is worth the effort in the pleasure it affords both the teller and the audience. This is true whether the storyteller is an adult or a child. The current emphasis on storytelling is seen not only in the increase of university and public school programs that focus on storytelling, but also in the development of community programs such as "Spellbinders Programs" that connect storytellers, community volunteers, libraries, and children. For example, the values of storytelling as identified by *Spellbinders Volunteer Storytelling* (1999) include the following:

1. Provide children with positive, character-building role models.

2. Provide natural and nourishing communication between generations.

3. Enhance children's language development, listening skills, and aural comprehension.

4. Stimulate children's creative imagination.

5. Acquaint children with the folktales, legends, and true stories of many cultures and many lives, told in traditional oral form.

6. Give older adult volunteers an opportunity to be of traditional significance and purpose to their communities (p. 3).

It was my pleasure to be an observer of and a participant in a Spellbinders Program sponsored by the Pitkin Library in Aspen, Colorado, during the summer of 2001. Each of the weekly sessions began with stories told by a professional storyteller. The audience consisted of more than one hundred children. Following an interactive storytelling session that involved children with both stories and songs, adult volunteers helped children who had joined a children's storytelling club prepare their own stories for

telling. Children first told their stories to small groups and then to larger groups. It was an exciting experience to witness the power of storytelling.

Choosing a Story

The most important factor in choosing a story is selecting one that is really enjoyable. Narrators should enjoy spending time preparing stories and should retell them with conviction and enthusiasm.

Storytelling demands an appreciative audience. Storytellers must be aware of the interests, ages, and experience of the listeners involved. Young children have short attention spans, so story length must be considered when selecting a tale. Children's ages also should influence the subject matter of a tale. Young children like stories about familiar subjects, such as animals, children, or home life. They respond to the repetitive language in cumulative tales and enjoy joining in when stories such as "Henny Penny" reach their climax. Simple folktales, such as "The Three Bears," "The Three Little Pigs," and "The Three Billy Goats Gruff," are excellent to share with young children. Children from roughly ages seven through ten enjoy folktales with longer plots, such as those collected by the Brothers Grimm. "Rapunzel" and "Rumpelstiltskin" are favorites. Other favorites include such Jewish folktales as "It Could Always Be Worse." Older children enjoy adventure tales, myths, and legends. Anne Pellowski's *Hidden Stories in Plants* (1990) and *The Family Story-Telling Handbook* (1987), Sue McCord's *The Storybook Journey: Pathways to Literacy Through Story and Play* (1995), Robin Moore's *Creating a Family Storytelling Tradition: Awakening the Hidden Storyteller* (1999), and Doug Lipman's *Improving Your Storytelling: Beyond the Basics for All Who Tell Stories in Work or Play* (1999) include recommended stories and suggestions for how to use them.

Folktales have several characteristics that make them appropriate for storytelling: strong beginnings that bring listeners rapidly into the fast-paced action; several characters with whom listeners easily identify; climaxes that are familiar to children; and satisfying endings. These characteristics suggest worthwhile criteria for selecting tales.

Storytellers should also consider the mood that they wish to create, whether it be humorous and lighthearted or serious and scary. If, for example, you want to choose a story appropriate for Halloween, then mood is important. Even the site for storytelling may affect the mood and story selection. Assume, for example, that a group of people is sitting on high rocks overlooking Lake Superior. The wind is causing the waves to crash with a mighty roar onto the rocks below. When the people look out over the lake, they can see only a wide stretch of water. No one else is in sight. The view to the north is one of thick forests, ferns, and distant waterfalls. The Norse myth "The Hammer of Thor," from Olivia E. Coolidge's *Legends of the North,* seems ideal for this setting.

Preparing the Story for Telling

Storytelling does not require memorization, but it does require preparation. Certain steps will help you prepare for an enjoyable experience. An experienced storyteller, Patti Hubert (Norton, 1997), recommends the following sequence of steps:

1. Read the story completely through about three times.

2. List mentally the sequence of events. You are giving yourself a mental outline of the important happenings.

3. Reread the story, noting the events you did not remember.

4. Go over the main events again and add the details that you remember. Think about the meaning of the events and ways to express that meaning, rather than memorize the words in the story.

5. When you believe that you know the story, tell the story to a mirror. (You will be surprised at how horrible the story sounds the first time.)

6. After you have practiced two or three more times, the wording will improve, and you can change vocal pitch to differentiate characters.

7. Change your posture or hand gestures to represent different characters.

8. Do not be afraid to use pauses to separate scenes.

9. Identify background information, share information about hearing the story for the first time, or share an object related to the story.

Sharing the Story with an Audience

Because you have spent considerable time in preparation, you should present the story effectively. However, you can enhance your presentation by creating an interest in the story, setting a mood, creating an environment where children can see and hear you, and presenting the story with effective eye contact and voice control. You may use book jackets, giant books, miniature books, travel posters, art objects and everyday objects, puppets, or music to stimulate children's interest in the story. A librarian or teacher who regularly tells stories to large groups of children can use any of these methods so that children will look forward to the story hour.

Colorful book jackets from folktales or myths not only entice children but also help set a mood for storytelling. For example, you might develop a display around the book jacket for Steven Kellogg's *Jack and the Beanstalk*. In addition to the book jacket, you could display a picture of a beanstalk (or even a real beanstalk), a toy chicken, an egg, and a picture of a castle. To show comparative sizes, you might include a picture of a giant and a picture of a boy. Your accompanying questions might include the following: How could a beanstalk make it possible for a boy to reach a castle that is up in the sky? How could a chicken and eggs cause a boy and his mother to obtain great wealth?

Stories about giants also lend themselves to displays of large books. One librarian drew huge figures of giants and beanstalks on large sheets of tagboard and then placed the sheets together to form a gigantic book that stimulated interest in "Jack and the Beanstalk." The giant book worked well in this case: The children speculated about the size or strength of anyone who could read such a large book. Drawings of a huge hammer stimulated interest about Thor when another librarian prepared the Norse myth for telling. Miniature books stimulated children's interest before another story hour when "Tom Thumb" was the story. The storyteller used other tiny objects, many formed out of clay, that would be appropriate for a little person.

Identifying sources for folklore is important according to George Shannon (1986). He stresses that we must acknowledge the sources for the folktales because "sources are a part of the folk process—the chain of human sharing—both oral and written" (p. 117). Consequently, information about the sources for the folklore should be included in the introduction.

Travel posters can stimulate interest and provide background information. They are especially appealing when used with folktales from other countries. Travel posters showing ancient English sites might introduce an oral telling of Barbara Cohen's adaptation of Geoffrey Chaucer's *Canterbury Tales*. You may use travel posters about Greece and Italy with Greek and Roman mythology. Travel posters showing Norwegian fjords and mountains can accompany Norse myths, while posters showing the Black Forest and old European castles are appropriate for "Snow White and the Seven Dwarfs" and "Sleeping Beauty."

Objects from the story or from the country that is the setting of the story can also increase children's interest. Dolls, plates, figurines, stuffed animals, and numerous other everyday objects and curios can add to the story hour.

After interest is high, concentrate on setting the mood for story time. Many storytellers use story-hour symbols. For example, if a small lamp is the symbol for story hour, children know that when the lamp is lit, it is time to listen. Music can also be a symbol; a certain recording, music box tune, piano introduction, or guitar selection can introduce story hour. These techniques are usually effective, since children learn to associate them with enjoyable listening experiences. Donna E. Norton (1997, p. 84) has the following suggestions for telling the story:

1. Find a place in the room where all of the children can see and hear the presentation.

2. Either stand in front of the children or sit with them.

3. Select an appropriate introduction. Use a prop, tell something about the author, discuss a related event, or ask a question.

4. Maintain eye contact with the children. This engages them more fully in the story.

5. Use an appropriate voice rate and appropriate volume for effect.

6. While telling the story, use a short step or shift in footing to indicate a change in scene or character or to heighten the suspense. If seated, lean forward or away from the children.

7. After telling the story, pause to give the audience a chance to soak in everything you said.

Observing Children's Responses to Storytelling

Children may have emotional responses to the story, to the interpretation of the story, or to various literary elements within the story. The responses may be as subtle as facial expressions or as expressive as vocal interactions with the story and the storyteller. Zena Sutherland (1997) recommends that you ask yourself the following questions after telling a story to a group of children:

1. Which children showed response during the story period?

2. What parts of the story evoked the most response?

3. How did the children show their reactions?

4. Did the reactions influence, in any way, your telling of the story?

5. Did any child comment about the story at some time after the story hour? If so, did the comment indicate emotional response? interpretation of the story? attention to literary characteristics such as style?

6. Do their reactions give you ideas for future story choices for this group? (p. 552)

Encouraging Children to Be Storytellers

Storytelling by children is frequently a natural continuation of storytelling by adults because children learn to tell and appreciate oral storytelling by imitating adults. Storytellers Martha Hamilton and Mitch Weiss (1993) believe that when children tell stories, they gain confidence, improve verbal skills, learn how to think inventively, and develop a love of language and stories.

Hamilton and Weiss (1993) provide valuable guidelines for helping children choose their stories, learn their stories, and tell their stories. These storytellers stress that when helping children choose their stories, adults should select a pool of appropriate stories from which the children can select so that the children choose stories appropriate to the age and interests of their audience. A sign-up

sheet will help children avoid duplicating stories that they are preparing for telling.

The techniques for helping students learn the story are similar to those identified for adults. You should ask children to read their stories a number of times. Use pictorial outlines to help children understand and visualize the sequence of the story rather than memorize the story. It is also helpful to have the children practice their stories by tape recording them, telling the stories in front of a mirror, telling the stories to only one person, and then telling the stories to a larger audience.

Encourage children to use their voices to bring expression and life to the story. Have them practice varying their speed of speaking to convey various moods. Facial expressions, gestures, and movements should be natural and be appropriate for the story. Additional guidelines for helping children learn to tell stories are found in Hamilton and Weiss's *Children Tell Stories: A Teaching Guide* (1990).

Using Feltboards to Share Folktales

Storytelling does not require any props. In fact, some of the best storytellers use nothing except their voices and gestures to recapture the plots and characters found in traditional tales. Most storytellers, however, enjoy adding variety to their repertoire. Children also enjoy experimenting with different approaches to storytelling; the flannelboard or feltboard lends itself to storytelling by both adults and children.

A feltboard is a rectangular, lightweight board covered with felt, flannel cloth, or lightweight indoor-outdoor carpeting. This board acts as the backdrop for figures cut from felt, pellon, or another material. Felt or pellon figures will cling directly to a feltboard, while any object, even leather, wood, or foam rubber, will adhere to the felt if backed with a small square or strip of Velcro. Other materials, such as yarn or cotton balls, will also cling to a feltboard and may be used to add interest and texture to a story.

Stories that lend themselves to feltboard interpretations have only a few major characters, plots that depend upon oral telling rather than physical action, and settings that do not demand exceptional detail. These characteristics are similar to those already stipulated for the simple folktales that young children enjoy. Pleasing stories to retell on the feltboard include the folktales "Three Billy Goats Gruff," "The Three Bears," "The Gingerbread Boy," and "Henny Penny." Stories should include actions that can be shown on the board. In addition, the number of figures should not overwhelm the board (see Figure 6.1).

Consider the Norwegian folktale "The Three Billy Goats Gruff." First, use simple cutouts or objects to represent the characters. The three goats range in size from a small goat to a great big goat with curved horns. The ugly old troll has big eyes and a long, long nose. You can

FIGURE 6.1 Stories that lend themselves to feltboard interpretations have only a few major characters, plots that depend on oral telling rather than physical action, and settings that do not demand exceptional detail.

show the setting easily: a bridge crossing a stream and green grass on the other side of the bridge. You can illustrate the action effectively: each goat can go "Trip, trap! Trip, trap!" over the bridge. The troll can challenge each goat with "Who's that tripping over my bridge?" You can also illustrate the climax easily: The big billy goat knocks the troll off the bridge and continues to cross to the other side. The plot develops sequentially from a small billy goat, to a medium-sized billy goat, and finally to a great big billy goat.

Cumulative tales are excellent for feltboard presentations. As you introduce each new character, place it on the feltboard. Have the children join the dialogue as "The Fat Cat," for example, encounters first the gruel, then the pot, the old woman, Skahottentot, Skilinkenlot, five birds, seven dancing girls, the lady with the pink parasol, the parson, and the woodsman.

Through such presentations, children learn about sequential order and improve their language skills. Using feltboard stories with children, you will often find that the children either ask if they can retell the stories or make up their own feltboard stories to share. If you provide feltboards and materials, children naturally enjoy telling stories in this manner. Whether you tell a story to one child or to a group, storytelling is well worth the effort of preparation and presentation. Watching children as they respond to a magical environment and then make their own efforts as storytellers will prove to you that storytelling should be included in every child's experience.

Comparing Folktales from Different Countries

Understanding how various types of traditional stories are related, becoming aware of cultural diffusion, and learning about different countries are benefits of traditional literature. One way to help children gain these benefits is to compare folktales from different countries.

Comparing Different Versions of the Same Tale

Many older children are fascinated to discover that some tales appear in almost every culture. The names vary, magical objects differ, and settings change, but the basic elements of the story remain the same. Folklorist Alan Dundes (1988) claims that over one thousand versions of the Cinderella story have been found throughout the world. Compile questions such as the following with the children's assistance to guide their search and discovery:

1. What caused Cinderella to have a lowly position in the family?
2. What shows that Cinderella has a lowly position in the household?
3. How is Cinderella related to other household members?
4. What happens to keep Cinderella away from the ball?
5. How does Cinderella receive her wishes or transformation?
6. Where does Cinderella meet the prince?
7. What is the test signifying the rightful Cinderella?
8. What happens to the stepsisters?

Sources for comparisons include Mary Ann Nelson's (1972) anthology, Bingham and Scholt's (1974) synopses of twelve variants of the Cinderella story, Sutherland and Livingston's anthology (1984), and folklore collections from around the world. Jerry D. Flack's *From the Land of Enchantment: Creative Teaching with Fairy Tales* (1997) includes " 'Cinderella' Resources" such as Tradition Sources (twenty-nine summaries), Variations and Other Treatments (twelve summaries), Stepmothers and Stepsisters (four summaries), and Videocassettes (five summaries). There are also numerous "Cinderella" tales published in single editions such as Rebecca Hickox's *The Golden Sandal: A Middle Eastern Cinderella Story* (Iraq). Chart 6.7 represents some key variants found in Cinderella tales from different countries.

Hundreds of versions of the Cinderella story from around the world have been found. The illustrations are just as variant. Top left, from a Chinese variant. (Illustration by Ed Young reprinted by permission of Philomel Books from Yeh Shin: A Cinderella Story from China *retold by Ai-Ling Louie, illustrations © 1982 by Ed Young.) Top right, Native American. (Illustration by David Shannon reprinted by permission of G.P. Putnam's Sons from* The Rough Face Girl *by Rafe Martin, illustrations © 1992 by David Shannon.) Bottom, Cinderella as a dog. (From* Cinderella *by William Wegman. Text and photos © 1993 by William Wegman. Reprinted by permission of Hyperion Books for Children, a Walt Disney Company. All rights reserved.)*

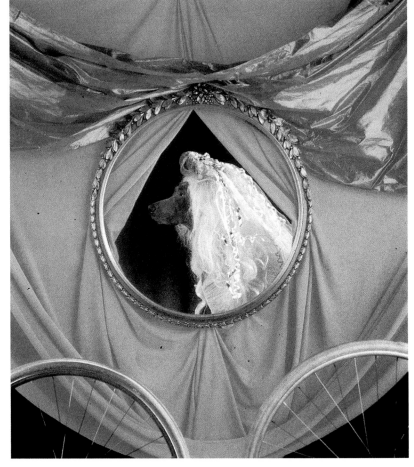

CHART 6.7 Variations found in Cinderella stories from different countries

Origin	Cause of Lowly Position	Outward Signs of Lowly Position	Cinderella's Relationship to Household	How She Receives Wishes	What Keeps Her from Social Occasion	Where She Meets the Prince	Test of Rightful Cinderella	What Happens to Stepsisters
French Perrault's "Cinderella"	Mother died. Father remarried.	Sitting in ashes. Vilest household tasks.	Stepdaughter to cruel woman. Unkind stepsisters.	Wishes to fairy godmother.	(Ball) No gown. Family won't let her go.	Castle ball. Beautifully dressed.	Glass slipper.	Forgiven. Live in palace. Marry lords.
German Grimm's "Cinderella"	Mother died. Father remarried.	Wears clogs, old dress. Sleeps in cinders. Heavy work.	Stepdaughter to cruel woman. Cruel stepsisters.	Wishes to bird on tree on mother's grave.	(Ball) Must separate lentils.	Castle ball. Beautifully dressed.	Glass slipper.	Blinded by birds.
English "Tattercoats"	Mother died at her birth. Grandfather blames her.	Ragbag clothes. Scraps for food.	Despised granddaughter. Hated by servants.	Gooseherd plays pipe.	(Ball) Grandfather refuses.	In forest. Dressed in rags.	None.	Grandfather weeps. Hair grows into stones.
Vietnamese "In the Land of Small Dragon"	Mother died. Father's number two wife hates her.	Collects wood. Cares for rice paddies.	Stepdaughter to hateful woman. Hated by half-sisters.	Fairy. Bones of fish.	(Festival) Must separate rice from husks.	Festival. Beautifully dressed.	Jeweled slipper (hai).	Not told.
Chinese "Beauty and Pock Face"	Mother turned into cow.	Straightens hemp. Hard work.	Stepdaughter to cruel woman. Cruel stepsister.	From bones of mother in earthenware pot.	(Theater) Straighten hemp. Separate sesame seeds.	Theater. Scholar picks up shoe from road.	Walks on eggs. Climbs ladder of knives. Jumps into oil.	Roasted in oil.
Micmac— Native American "Little Burnt Face"	Mother died.	Burned face. Ragged garments.	Despised by two jealous sisters.	The Great Chief's sister changes her.	She must make her own dress.	Wigwam by the lake.	Describe the Great Chief.	Sent back to wigwam in disgrace.

This chapter suggests criteria for evaluating modern fantasy. It stresses the ways in which modern authors of fantasy literature follow in the footsteps of the anonymous storytellers who created and transmitted the traditional fantasies of oral literature. It also discusses various types of modern fantasy and recommends numerous outstanding fantasy stories.

Evaluating Modern Fantasy

Like all authors of fiction, authors of high-quality modern fantasy use basic literary elements to create stories that are interesting, engrossing, and believable. In evaluating modern fantasy for children, you should use the criteria recommended in Chapter 3, while considering the special uses of literary elements that the fantasy genre requires. Consider the questions in the Evaluation Criteria box on this page when selecting modern fantasy to share with children.

Many books of modern fantasy admirably satisfy these criteria and provide great enjoyment to children and adults alike.

Suspending Disbelief: Plot

The author's ability to make readers suspend disbelief and to accept the possibility that the story could have happened is one of the greatest requirements for modern fantasy. Fantasy writer Patricia Wrightson (1990) states this very well:

Fantasy is story, and no story has any business to begin by asking you weakly to suspend disbelief. It is the business of story to require and work for your belief. It may be more difficult in fantasy, but that is the writer's affair; no one is forcing him to try. If he invites you to go flying with him, the very least he can do is to build a strong pair of wings. The freedom of fantasy is not license: if it abandons the laws and logic of reality, it must provide other laws and logic to govern itself. It may invent circumstances to suit its purpose, but the purpose must be the story's obligation to explore life and humanity. It has great strengths: the power of the extraordinary, the broad definition of symbol, the evocative voice of poetry; having them, it mustn't also ask for your weak and complaisant credulity. If fantasy is not strong, it is nothing. (p. 75)

A story may seem believable if it begins in a realistic context and then moves into the realm of fantasy. In "The Chronicles of Narnia," C. S. Lewis develops normal human characters who visit a realistic English home and enter into childhood games familiar to most children. When these realistic characters confront the fantastic and believe it, readers believe it too. Likewise, Margaret Anderson's characters in *In the Keep of Time* have a strong foundation in reality before they enter their time-warp fantasies, encouraging readers' belief.

When an author develops a logical framework and develops characters' actions consistently within this framework, there is an internal consistency in the story. This consistency is important. If, for example, animals supposedly live and behave like animals, they should do so *consistently* unless the author carefully develops when they change, why they change, and how they change.

EVALUATION CRITERIA

Selecting Modern Fantasy

1. Is every action consistent with the framework developed by the author?

2. How does the author's characterization allow children to suspend disbelief? Do characters begin in a real world before they travel to the world of fantasy? Does a believable character accept a fanciful world, characters, or happenings? Does the author use an appropriate language or create a believable language consistent with the story?

3. Does the author pay careful attention to the details in the setting? If the author develops several time periods, are the settings authentic and integral to the story?

4. Is the theme worthwhile for children?

5. Does the author encourage readers to suspend disbelief by developing a point of view that is consistent in every detail, including sights, feelings, and physical reactions?

Suspending Disbelief: Characterization

Of course, the character from whose point of view a story is told must be believable for readers to suspend disbelief. Whether an author humanizes animals and inanimate objects, gives supernatural beings human traits, or places realistic human characters into fantastic situations, the characters in a fantasy story must be internally coherent as well as accessible to the readers.

Language is one way that authors of fantasy can make characters believable. In *The Hobbit* and *The Lord of the Rings*, for example, J. R. R. Tolkien creates distinct languages for different groups of characters. Ruth Noel (1977), in her evaluation of Tolkien's use of language, concludes that the musical flow of Elfish words and names implies that the Elves are noble people and that they love beauty and music. In contrast, the guttural Dwarfish, which sounds less familiar to English-speaking readers, indicates that the Dwarfs themselves are different from humans and Elves. Likewise, the croaked curses of the Orcs establish them as coarse, cruel, and unimaginative, and the prolonged chants of the Ents demonstrate their peaceful life in the forest. David Rees (1988) states that Joan Aiken has a similar talent for characterization through language because in such fantasies as *The Wolves of Willoughby Chase,* she is able to create "the dialects, vocabulary, and speech rhythms of various periods in history" (p. 42).

Creating a World: Setting

The magical settings of traditional tales let children know that anything is possible in those environments. Writers of modern fantasy may also create worlds in which unusual circumstances are believable, or they may combine reality and fantasy as characters or stories go back and forth between two worlds. In either case, if the story is to be credible, the author must develop the setting so completely that readers can see, hear, and feel it.

The settings for Mary Norton's "Borrowers" books, described through the eyes of little people, are integral to each story. The inside of a cottage drain becomes both an escape route and an antagonist in *The Borrowers Afloat.* Readers experience a new world as they vicariously join the Borrowers inside the drain:

There were other openings as they went along, drains that branched into darkness and ran away uphill. Where these joined the main drain, a curious collection of flotsam and jetsam piled up over which they had to drag the soap lid . . . the air from that point onwards, smelled far less strongly of tea leaves. (p. 105)

The setting in the drain changes from a fairly calm escape route to one filled with drumming noises and fright as a bath drain opens. Norton describes an antagonistic setting:

A millrace of hot scented water swilled through her clothes, piling against her at one moment, falling away the next. Sometimes it bounced above her shoulders, drenching her face and hair; at others it swirled steadily about her waist and tugged at her legs and feet. (p. 110)

Norton provides so much detail in her description of this setting that readers can see the contents of the inside of the drain as if they too were only six inches tall, can smell the soap and tea leaves deposited in the drain, and can hear the changing sounds of water echoing through the drainage system or gushing down in thundering torrents.

Other authors create convincing new worlds as characters go from realistic to fantasy settings. In *Alice's Adventures in Wonderland,* by Lewis Carroll, Alice begins her adventures on a realistically peaceful river bank in nineteenth-century England and then travels down a rabbit hole into a unique world quite different from her normal one, which Carroll describes in great detail from her viewpoint.

In Janet Lunn's *The Root Cellar,* twelve-year-old Rose goes down into a root cellar on an old dilapidated farm in twentieth-century Canada. When she leaves the root cellar, she enters a nineteenth-century world in which the farm is prosperous. The people in that earlier time are engrossed

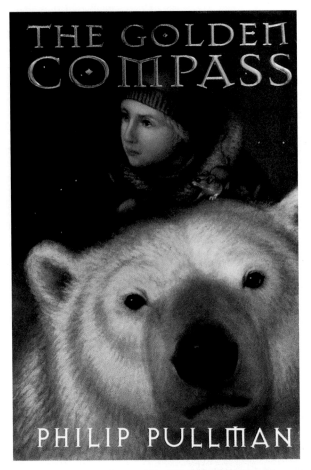

Detailed descriptions of a parallel universe create a believable setting. (Cover illustration by Eric Rohmann, copyright © 1996 by Eric Rohmann, from The Golden Compass by Philip Pullman. Used by permission of Alfred A. Knopf Children's Books, a division of Random House, Inc.)

by the approaching American Civil War. Believable descriptions of the same setting in two different centuries are important to the story. Lunn develops an authentic Civil War setting by describing the sights, sounds, feelings, and concerns that the main character experiences as she travels throughout the northeastern United States to find a boy who has not returned from the war. Authors whose characters travel in time warps must create believable, authentic settings for two time periods.

Jane Yolen uses a similar approach in *The Devil's Arithmetic.* After a contemporary girl steps through a door and finds herself in a Jewish village in the 1940s, the sights, sounds, conflicts, and concerns become those of people living in a death camp during the Holocaust.

Universality: Themes

Memorable modern fantasies develop themes related to universal struggles, values, and emotions. The constant battle between good and evil, faith and perseverance in the face of obstacles, personal and social responsibility, love, and friendship are important themes in works of modern fantasy ranging from George MacDonald's Victorian story *At the Back of the North Wind* to Madeleine L'Engle's contemporary books of science fiction. Children easily identify with such themes, especially when an author develops them within the framework of consistently believable plots, characterizations, settings, and points of view.

As found in David Almond's *Skellig*, modern fantasy exemplifies some of the strongest, most powerful themes in literature. Through the characters and plot, Almond develops the themes that love has a redemptive power, that humans have power to change their environments, and that life is fragile. Philip Pullman's humorous, lighter fantasy *I Was a Rat!* also develops the power of love as an older couple befriends a boy who has magically been transformed from a rat to a human. After a series of adventures and humorous, sometimes dangerous experiences as the boy tries to overcome his rat behaviors, the boy is reunited with the couple and together they conclude: "The world outside was a difficult place, but toasted cheese and love and craftsmanship would do to keep them safe" (p. 165).

Suspending Disbelief: Point of View

Rebecca J. Lukens (1990) says:

If fantasy is to be successful, we must willingly suspend disbelief. If the story's characters, conflict, and theme seem believable to us, we find it plausible and even natural to know the thoughts and feelings of animal characters or tiny people. In fact, the story may be so good that we wish it were true. . . . This persuasion that the writer wishes to bring about—persuasion that "what if" is really "it's true"—is most successful when the writer is consistent about point of view. (p. 108)

The point of view of a story is determined by the author's choice of the person telling it. A story could be told quite differently from the perspective of a child, a mother, a wicked witch, an animal or a supernatural beast, or an objective observer. Authors of fantasy must decide which point of view best facilitates a believable telling of a story and then sustain that point of view in order to persuade readers to keep suspending disbelief in the fantastic elements of the story.

The Borrowers, by Mary Norton, seems believable because most of this story about "little people" is told from the viewpoint of Arrietty, who is only six inches tall. The little people's family sitting room seems authentic because readers see, through Arrietty's eyes, the postage-stamp-sized portraits on the walls, a work of art created by a pillbox that is supporting a chess piece, and a couch made from a human's padded trinket box. Even the reaction to a miniature book that is Arrietty's diary is dealt with through the physical capabilities of a miniature person: "Arrietty braced her muscles and heaved the book off her knees, and stood upright on the floor" (p. 20). Readers

are ready to believe the story because Norton describes sights, feelings, and physical reactions as if a six-inch-tall person were actually living through the experience.

In *The Tale of Peter Rabbit*, Beatrix Potter creates believable situations by telling the story from both Peter Rabbit's point of view and the first-person point of view of the storyteller, who occasionally interjects comments such as "I am sorry to say that Peter was not very well during the evening." In this case, the authoritative, realistic voice of the storyteller reassures readers that the fantastic events being described are normal and understandable.

Perry Nodelman (1984b) emphasizes the need for an author to consider both the storyteller and the audience when creating a credible fantasy. Nodelman says:

Only by ignoring the fact that it is fantastic, by pretending to be a true story about a real world shared by characters in the story, the storyteller, and the people who hear the story, can a fantasy establish its credibility and work its magic on those who actually hear it. (p. 16)

Jane Yolen (1986) emphasizes the importance of these elements in making a real world for children. She states that the fantasy world seems real to children because

the world of fantasy has three very persuasive parts to it. First, it has identifiable laws that always work. Second, it has a hero or heroine who is often lost, unlikely, powerless at first glance, or unrecognized, which makes him or her easy for the child reader (who feels lost, unlikely, unrecognized or powerless) to identify with. And third, in a fantasy world things end justly though not always happily. (p. 89)

Bridges Between Traditional and Modern Fantasy

In many ways, modern fantasy stories are direct descendants of the folktales, fables, myths, and legends of the oral tradition. Tales about talking animals, wise and foolish humans, supernatural beings, heroic adventurers, and magical realms are as popular with children and adults today as they were hundreds of years ago. Many authors of modern fantasy have drawn upon themes, motifs, settings, and characterizations common in traditional literature. Of course, in the distant past, people believed that the content of some fairy tales, myths, and legends had basis in fact, while most readers of modern fantasy suspend their disbelief only in extraordinary beings and events. Still, to entice their readers into out-of-the-ordinary experiences, authors of modern fantasy play roles similar to those of storytellers of old, who enchanted live audiences with tales that had been orally transmitted over generations. The bridges between traditional fantasy and modern fantasy are evident in many contemporary tales of wonder, but they are especially strong in literary folktales, allegories, and tales about mythical quests and conflicts.

Literary Folktales

In the past hundred years or so, some authors of fantasy have deliberately attempted to replicate the "Once upon a time" of traditional folktales, with their dark forests, castles, princesses and princes, humble people of noble worth, and "happily ever afters." The traditional theme that goodness is rewarded and evil is punished is common in literary folktales, as are motifs involving magic. Betsy Hearne (1992) states that many folklore elements are found in William Steig's *The Amazing Bone,* and archetypal characters from folktales abound in the fantasies of James Marshall.

Ursula K. LeGuin's *A Ride on the Red Mare's Back* is a literary folktale that contains many elements from folklore. First, the setting is similar to that in a folktale: "A long time ago, when the world was wild, a family lived in the forests of the North, far from any other house" (p. 11). Second, the heroine is a young girl who bravely sets out to rescue her brother, who has been stolen by trolls. The plot is advanced by a magical object, a small toy horse that turns into a real horse during a time of need. This magical object then gives aid and advice to the heroine. The importance of threes is revealed when the girl takes three objects with her and these objects allow her to successfully rescue her brother: (1) Bread baked by her mother is given to the troll under the bridge, (2) knitting needles made by her father and a

ball of yarn are given to the old troll who guards the children, and (3) a scarf she knitted for her little brother makes him aware that he wants to come home.

Likewise, Walter Dean Myers's literary folktale, *The Story of Three Kingdoms,* begins in a folkloric style: "Long ago, when the earth had not settled in its turning and the stars had not found their places in the night sky, there were three kingdoms" (unnumbered). In addition, the fantasy has elements that are similar to those found in folktales including types of conflict, characteristics of characters, and theme. Notice in the following ending how Myers has used a folkloric style: "From that day on the People held their heads high, never forgetting to sit by the fire and tell their stories. Never forgetting that in the stories could be found wisdom and in wisdom, strength" (unnumbered). The battle between good and evil is found in folklore and many literary folktales as revealed in Eric A. Kimmel's *Hershel and the Hanukkah Goblins.*

Fantasies by Jennifer Armstrong, Shulamith Levy Oppenheim, and Jim Aylesworth also have folkloric elements. Armstrong's *Wan Hu Is in the Stars* ends in a folkloric tradition as a new star formation appears in the sky: "And some believe Wan Hu achieved his hope and one desire. The gardener is sure that he did" (unnumbered). The setting for Oppenheim's *The Hundredth Name* is similar to a folktale because it is set "far back in time" in Muslim Egypt. This literary folktale has an emphasis on Allah as the young hero tries to discover through his camel the hundredth name for Allah. Aylesworth's *The Full Belly Bowl* is set "In a tiny house at the edge of a forest, there once lived a very old man and a cat" (unnumbered). The story has a folktale quality as the old man rescues a wee small man from a fox, is rewarded for his kindness with a magic bowl, and then discovers that he must be careful to follow the directions or he will lose his treasure.

Hans Christian Andersen. Charles Perrault is usually credited with publishing the first children's book of fairy tales, but Hans Christian Andersen is credited with writing, a century later, the first fairy tale for children. While Perrault wrote down stories from the oral tradition, Andersen created new stories for theater audiences and readers.

Zena Sutherland (1997) points out that although Andersen's first stories for children were

elaborations of familiar folk and fairy tales, . . . he soon began to allow his imagination full rein in the invention of plot, the shaping of character, and the illumination of human condition. These later creations, solely from Andersen's fertile imagination, are called literary fairy tales, to distinguish them from the fairy tales of unknown origin, those created by common folk. Andersen's work served as inspiration for other writers. (p. 230)

Andersen's "The Wild Swans" is a literary fairy tale quite similar to the Grimms' traditional tale "The Six Swans." Both stories involve enchantment by an evil stepmother and the courage and endurance of a young girl who is willing to suffer in order to free her brothers.

The battle between good and evil is found in literature that bridges traditional and modern fantasy. (From Hershel and the Hanukkah Goblins *by Eric A. Kimmel, illustrated by Trina Schart Hyman. Reprinted by permission of Holiday House. Text copyright 1989 by Eric A. Kimmel. Illustrations copyright 1989 by Trina Schart Hyman. All rights reserved.)*

Experts in children's literature believe that some of Andersen's other literary fairy tales are based on his own life. For example, Andersen's unpleasant experiences in school, where the teacher poked fun at the poor boy's lack of knowledge, large size, and looks, may have inspired his story "The Ugly Duckling." Jerry Pinkney's illustrations for a book-length version of this story show the transformation of the ugly duckling into the most beautiful swan in the pond. When the children exclaim that he is the best one of all, "The swan knew that it was worth having undergone all the suffering and loneliness that he had. Otherwise, he would never have known what it was to be really happy" (unnumbered).

Andersen's *The Tinderbox*, adapted and illustrated by Barry Moser, includes many of the motifs found in folklore: a poor tattered soldier who eventually wins riches and the beautiful girl; challenges in the form of three doors, each guarded by a huge dog; a magical object; and a leader who tries to prevent the soldier from marrying his daughter. This book can also be used to analyze the change in setting from the original story. Moser places his adaptation in the Tennessee mountains at the end of the Civil War. His characters include a Confederate soldier and the people who live in a mountain village.

Nancy Ekholm Burkert has beautifully illustrated one of Andersen's stories that reflects the beauty of natural life versus the heartbreak associated with longing for mechanical perfection or metallic glitter. *The Nightingale* tells of a Chinese emperor who turned from the voice of a faithful nightingale to a jeweled, mechanical bird. He learns, however, that only the real, unjeweled bird's song can bring comfort and truth. Compare Alison Claire Darke's illustrations for *The Nightingale* with Burkert's illustrations. Both illustrators emphasize the beauty of the Chinese setting.

Illustrator Susan Jeffers and author Amy Ehrlich have combined their talents to create three beautiful versions of Andersen's tales. Jeffers's finely detailed drawings suggest fantasy settings in *Thumbelina* and *The Wild Swans*. Contrast her illustrations for and Amy Ehrlich's retelling in *The Snow Queen* with two other versions of the same tale, one retold by Naomi Lewis and illustrated by Errol LeCain and the other retold by Naomi Lewis and illustrated by Angela Barrett.

Three adapters and illustrators have chosen to retell Andersen's *The Steadfast Tin Soldier*. The version translated by Naomi Lewis and illustrated by P. J. Lynch includes illustrations drawn as if they were from a toy's-eye view. The version retold by Tor Seidler and illustrated by Fred Marcellino is illustrated with a Christmas setting, because according to the illustrator, the story was first published during the Christmas of 1838. Rachel Isadora's illustrations for her version reflect her background in theater and dance.

Michael Hague, Kay Nielson, and Edward Ardizzone are among those who have illustrated collections of

Finely detailed lines enhance the dreamlike quality of the fairy tale setting. (From The Wild Swans, *retold by Amy Ehrlich, illustrated by Susan Jeffers. Illustrations copyright ©1981 by Susan Jeffers. Used by permission of the publisher Dial Books for Young Readers.)*

Andersen's tales for adults to read aloud to children or for children to read independently. *Michael Hague's Favorite Hans Christian Andersen Fairy Tales* includes nine stories in large print. More extensive collections include *Hans Andersen: His Classic Fairy Tales*, illustrated by Michael Foreman.

Religious and Ethical Allegory

Religious themes provide strong links between traditional and modern fantasy. According to Bruno Bettelheim (1976), "Most fairy tales originated in periods when religion was a most important part of life; thus, they deal, directly or by inference, with religious themes" (p. 13). Traditional tales from around the world reflect the religions prominent in their times and places of origins, including Islam, Buddhism, and Judaism, to name but a few.

Some European folktales, such as the German "Our Lady's Child," directly refer to the Roman Catholic beliefs of the Middle Ages. In this tale recorded by the Brothers Grimm, a young girl becomes mute when she disobeys the Virgin Mary and then lies about what she has done. After suffering severe ordeals, she desires only to confess her sin, and the Virgin Mary rewards her confession by renewing her power of speech and granting her happiness. Other European folktales and legends develop less explicit religious themes by using allegory, or prolonged metaphors. Characters representing goodness or wisdom must confront and overcome characters representing evil or foolishness.

Many authors writing in the 1800s created strong stories with ethical and religious themes. John C. Hawley (1989) contends that Charles Kingsley's *The Water-Babies* is a classic example of children's literature employed to disarm and to teach. He states:

> As unusual and even quirky as the water world of Kingsley's novel may be, however, this priest/novelist somehow succeeds in showing readers young and old something very familiar and even comforting in the strange and mysterious, sugaring a pill he considers necessary medicine for his generation. (p. 19)

In our more secular age, as Bettelheim (1976) points out, "these religious themes no longer arouse universal and personally meaningful associations" in the majority of people, as they once did. However, modern authors of fantasy still create religious and ethical allegories. Some authors actually replicate the heroic humans, witches, personified animals, and magical settings of traditional literature. Others use characters and settings consistent with their own times. Readers may respond to these stories on different levels, since they are both allegories and tales of enchantment and high adventure.

George MacDonald. The strongly moralistic atmosphere of Victorian England and training as a Congregational minister influenced a writer who used allegorical fantasy to portray and condemn the flaws in his society. Cynthia Marshall (1988) states that George MacDonald's concern for distinguishing good from evil leads to "moralizing interventions" (p. 61) in books such as *At the Back of the North Wind*. First published in 1871 and reissued in 1966, is the story of Diamond, the son of a poor coach driver. Diamond lives two lives: the harsh existence of impoverished working-class Londoners, and a dreamlike existence in which he travels with the North Wind, who takes him to a land of perpetual flowers and gentle breezes, where no one is cold or sick or hungry.

MacDonald uses the North Wind, a beautiful woman with long flowing hair, to express much of his own philosophy. "Good people see good things; bad people, bad things" (p. 37), she tells Diamond, whom Mac-Donald describes as a good boy, "God's baby." When Diamond questions her reality, she says, "I think ... that if I were only a dream, you would not have been able to love me so. You love me when you are not with me, don't you?" (p. 363). Diamond clings to the back of the North Wind. With her streaming hair enfolding him, they fly to a land where it is always May. Diamond returns home from that visit, but the end of the story has further allegorical implications:

> I walked up the winding stair, and entered his room. A lovely figure, as white and almost as clear as alabaster, was lying on the bed. I saw at once how it was. They thought he was dead. I knew that he had gone to the back of the North Wind. (p. 378)

The flowing lines of the North Wind seem to enfold little Diamond. (Illustration by E. H. Shepard from At the Back of the North Wind, *by George MacDonald. Copyright © 1956, 1994. J. M. Dent, Children's Classics Series. Reprinted with permission of J. M. Dent & Sons, Ltd.)*

C. S. Lewis. A professor of medieval and Renaissance literature at Cambridge University, C. S. Lewis used his interest in theology and his knowledge about medieval allegory, classical legend, and Norse mythology to create a highly acclaimed and popular fantasy saga. "The Chronicles of Narnia" (winner of the Carnegie Medal for best children's books), beginning with *The Lion, the Witch and the Wardrobe* and ending seven books later with *The Last Battle*, develop marvelous adventure stories interwoven with Christian allegory. Children can enjoy the series for its high drama alone, or they can read it for its allegorical significance.

While *The Lion, the Witch and the Wardrobe* is the first book in the series, *The Magician's Nephew* explains how the saga began and how the passage between the magical world of Narnia and earth was made possible. The tree grown from the magical Narnia apple has blown over, and its wood is used to build a large wardrobe. This is the same wardrobe through which the daughters of Eve and

 Technology Resources

Visit our Companion Website to link to Narnia, an incredible site dedicated to the world created by C. S. Lewis.

the sons of Adam enter into the kingdom, meet the wicked White Witch, and help the great lord-lion Aslan defeat the powers of evil.

In *The Lion, the Witch and the Wardrobe,* Aslan gives his life to save Edmund, who has betrayed them all. Aslan, however, rises from the dead and tells the startled, bereaved children that the deeper magic before the dawn of time has won:

It means that though the witch knew the Deep Magic, there is a magic deeper still which she did not know. Her knowledge goes back only to the dawn of Time. But if she could have looked a little further back, into the stillness and the darkness before Time dawned, she would have read there a different incantation. She would have known that when a willing victim who has committed no treachery was killed in a traitor's stead, the Table would crack and Death itself would start working backward. (pp. 132–133)

From Aslan, the children learn that after they have once been crowned, they will remain kings and queens of Narnia forever.

The remaining books in the chronicle tell other fantastic tales of adventure in which the characters overcome evil. The final Christian allegory is contained in the last book of the series, *The Last Battle.* Here, the children are reunited with Aslan after their death on earth and discover:

for them it was only the beginning of the real story. All their life in this world and all their adventures in Narnia had only been the cover and the title page: now at last they were beginning Chapter One of the Great Story which no one on earth has read: in which every chapter is better than the one before. (p. 184)

The stories in the chronicles of Narnia are filled with adventures and characters that appeal to children. There are magical spells, centaurs, dwarfs, unicorns, ogres, witches, and minotaurs. Throughout the stories, characters strive to meet high ideals and recognize the importance of faith.

Brian Sibley's *The Land of Narnia* (1989) provides additional information about C. S. Lewis and Narnia. The book includes photographs of Lewis and his environment as well as an overview of the various Narnia books. The book includes "C. S. Lewis's Outline of Narnian History."

Mythical Quests and Conflicts

Quests for lost or stolen objects of power, descents into darkness to overcome evil, and settings where lightning splinters the world and sets the stage for battles between two opposing forces are found in traditional myths, legends, and modern fantasy. Some authors of modern fantasy borrow magical settings and characters from traditional tales of heroism, while others create new worlds of enchantment. Modern stories may contain some threads of the allegory that characterizes many traditional tales—such as the English legends about King Arthur, his knights

of the Round Table, and the quest for the Holy Grail. Most modern fantasies about mythical quests and conflicts, however, emphasize adventure. Their characters acquire new knowledge and learn honorable uses of personal power.

Mythical elements are found in Megan Whalen Turner's *The Thief,* set in the time of a belief in gods and legends. Turner develops the mythical setting by describing the statues of the gods and goddesses and then encouraging the hero to hear them speak. Turner's themes are closely related to those found in mythology and legend: Fate rules our lives, dreams are important as a way to predict what will happen, and the old stories about gods are very important for people's lives.

Several authors develop fantasies built on various Arthurian legends and characters. For example, Gerald Morris states in his author's note to *The Squire, His Knight, and His Lady:* "I took the battle with the Emperor of Rome from *Le Morte D'Arthur,* by Sir Thomas Malory, and I've borrowed minor characters from *Parzival* by Wolfram von Eschenbach." In *Arthur: The Seeing Stone,* Kevin Crossley-Holland develops stories across two time periods: the borders of England and Wales in 1199 and the earlier time of the boy's namesake, King Arthur. Nancy Springer in *I Am Morgan LeFay: A Tale from Camelot* interprets the legend through the viewpoint of the villainous sorceress.

Philip Pullman's *The Golden Compass* is a high fantasy that has numerous fantasy elements that may be identified and analyzed. Characters with supernatural powers include humans with their daemons (spirits, souls in animal form), witches who fly, and talking bears wearing armor. Objects of power include an ancient gold and crystal disk or alethiometer that always tells the truth. The symbols on this alethiometer also reveal both themes and possible conflict. For example, the various meanings for the anchor symbol are revealed to be hope, because hope holds you fast like an anchor; steadfastness; snag or prevention; and the sea. The importance of this object of power is revealed through quotes such as the following: "She knew one thing: she was not pleased or proud to be able to read the alethiometer—she was afraid. Whatever power was making that needle swing and stop, it knew things like an intelligent being" (p. 147). Pullman's sequels to *The Golden Compass, The Subtle Knife,* and *The Amber Spyglass* provide other sources for identifying and analyzing fantasy elements.

Students of children's literature will discover a challenge as they read the final book in the trilogy, *The Amber Spyglass.* Several reviews of the book suggest contradictory responses. For example, Kathleen Odean (2000) states, "Philip Pullman has penned a 1,000-plus-page fantasy that's near impossible to put down" (p. 50). Although Brian Alderson's (2000) review stresses Pullman's literary ability, Alderson also states, "Needless to say, Philip Pullman's parallel purposes are hard to reconcile. The author as God must lean from his heaven and direct affairs in the way he requires them to go, and we mortal readers must erect small gantries from which to suspend our varieties of disbelief" (p. 22). As you read this book decide for yourself if the book is an exciting adventure or is too didactic.

J. R. R. Tolkien. Destiny, supernatural immortals, evil dragons, and rings of power are found in J. R. R. Tolkien's popular stories. According to Ruth S. Noel (1977), Tolkien's writings "form a continuation of the mythic tradition into modern literature. . . . In no other literary work has such careful balance of mythic tradition and individual imagination been maintained" (pp. 6–7). This balance between myth and imagination is not accidental in Tolkien's writing. Tolkien studied mythology for most of his life; he was a linguistic scholar and professor of Anglo-Saxon literature at Oxford University. His chief interest was the literary and linguistic tradition of the English West Midlands, especially as revealed in *Beowulf* and *Sir Gawain and the Green Knight.* Tolkien respected the quality in myths that allows evil to be unexpectedly averted and good to succeed. He masterfully develops this battle between good and evil in *The Hobbit* and in *The Lord of the Rings,* its more complex sequel. According to Tolkien (1965), these stories were at first a philological game in which he invented languages: "The stories were made rather to provide a world for the languages than the reverse. I should have preferred to write in 'Elvish' " (p. 242). These languages with their own alphabets and rules help make Tolkien's characters believable.

Careful attention to detail and vivid descriptions of setting in Middle Earth also add credibility to Tolkien's stories. For example, he introduces the reluctant hobbit, Bilbo Baggins, to the challenge of a quest to regain the dwarfs' treasures by using a dwarfs' chant:

> Far over the misty mountains cold
> To dungeons deep and caverns old
> We must away ere break of day
> To find our long-forgotten gold. (*The Hobbit,* p. 37)

As Bilbo, the wizard Gandalf, and the thirteen dwarfs proceed over the mountains toward the lair of the evil dragon Smaug, Tolkien describes a lightning that splinters the peaks and rocks that shiver. When Bilbo descends into the mountain dungeons to confront Smaug, Tolkien's setting befits the climax of a heroic quest: Red light, wisps of vapor, and rumbling noises gradually replace the subterranean darkness and quiet. Ahead, in the bottom-most cellar, lies a huge red-golden dragon surrounded by precious gold and jewels. As in traditional tales, the quest is successful, the dragon is slain, and the goblins are overthrown. The hero retains his decency, his honor, and his pledge always to help his friends.

The ring found during the hobbit's quest becomes the basis of the plot in the ring trilogy: *The Fellowship of the Ring, The Two Towers,* and *The Return of the King.* In his foreword to *The Fellowship of the Ring,* Tolkien says that he

The mythological text and illustrations are strongly interrelated in this edition of J. R. R. Tolkien's books, illustrated by Michael Hague. (From **The Hobbit** *by J. R. R. Tolkien, illustrated by Michael Hague. Illustrations copyright © 1984 by Oak, Ash & Thorn, Ltd. Reprinted by permission of Houghton Mifflin Company.)*

had no intention of writing a story with an inner meaning or message. The story is not meant to be allegorical:

> As the story grew it put down roots (into the past) and threw out unexpected branches; but its main theme was settled from the outset by the inevitable choice of the Ring as the link between it and *The Hobbit.* (*The Fellowship of the Ring,* p. 6)

Many junior-high and high-school students, college students, and other adults have been brought back into the world of mythology through Tolkien's books.

Lloyd Alexander. The stories that unfold in Lloyd Alexander's mythical land of Prydain reflect Alexander's vivid recollections of Wales, favorite childhood stories, and knowledge of Welsh legends. When Alexander researched the Mabinogion, a collection of traditional Welsh legends, he discovered the characters of Gwydion Son of Don, Arawn Death-Lord of Annuvin, Dallben the enchanter, and Hen Wen the oracular pig (Tunnell and Jacobs, 1989). In Alexander's outstanding Prydain chronicles, these characters become involved in exciting adventures of good versus evil.

Alexander's books take place in a time when fairy folk lived with humans, a time of enchanters and enchantments, a time before the passages between the world of enchantment and the world of humans were closed. In the first Prydain chronicle, *The Book of Three,* Alexander

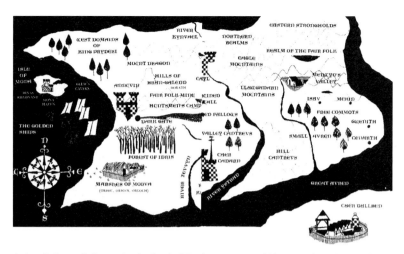

A detailed map helps make the land of Prydain more credible to readers. (From The High King, *by Lloyd Alexander. Map by Evaline Ness. Copyright © 1968 by Lloyd Alexander. Copyright © 1968 by Holt, Rinehart and Winston. Reproduced by permission of Holt, Rinehart and Winston.)*

introduces the forces of good and evil and an assistant pig-keeper, Taran, who dreams of discovering his parentage and becoming a hero. (Alexander tells readers that all people are assistant pig-keepers at heart because their capabilities seldom match their aspirations and they are often unprepared for what is to happen.)

The forces of good include the enchanter Dallben, who reads the prophecy written in *The Book of Three;* the sons of Don and their leader Prince Gwydion, who in ancient times voyaged from the Summer Country to stand as guardians against the evil Annuvin; and the Princess Eilonwy, descendant of enchanters. They are aided by Hen Wen, a pig who can foretell the future by pointing out ancient symbols carved on letter sticks. The forces of evil are led by a warlord who wants to capture Hen Wen because she knows his secret name. This name is powerful because "once you have the courage to look upon evil, seeing it for what it is and naming it by its true nature, it is powerless against you, and you can destroy it" (p. 209).

Throughout his Prydain series—*The Black Cauldron, The Castle of Llyr, Taran Wanderer,* and *The High King*— Alexander develops strong, believable characters with whom upper-elementary and older children can identify. The world of fantasy becomes relevant to the world of reality. The characters gain credibility through Alexander's history of the people and their long struggle against the forces of evil. Alexander encourages readers to believe in the tangible objects of power because the characters place so much faith in the legend of the sword, the prophecies written in *The Book of Three,* and the fearsome black cauldron.

Alexander's literary style also strengthens the credibility of the fantasy, the plot, and the characterization in his other fantasy adventure stories, such as *Westmark, The*

Iron Ring, and *The Beggar Queen.* In *The Beggar Queen,* Alexander carefully builds a foundation for the action that follows. He develops strong person-against-person, person-against-self, and person-against-society conflicts. He uses ghosts from the past to introduce the various conflicts and factions; he uses animal symbolism to describe characters; and he concludes each chapter at a point of tension and excitement, foreshadowing the conflict to come.

In *The Arkadians,* Alexander develops a high fantasy with foundations in Greek mythology. Alexander encourages readers to suspend disbelief in the mystical setting by introducing the setting through a map showing Arkadia. Mystical places and magical substances include the Water of Forgetting and the Water of Remembering; groves of trees, rings of stones, and fountains; and amulets that protect heroes. Alexander's fantasy includes many similarities with Greek mythology such as a wooden animal with a hollow stomach, men with special abilities, winged horses, prophecies that come true, and voyages that include fantastic adventures. In *The Iron Ring* Alexander develops a high fantasy with foundations in mythology from India.

Ursula K. LeGuin. Somewhere in the land of fantasy lies Earthsea, an archipelago of imaginary islands where wizards cast their spells and people live in fear of fire-blowing winged dragons. Responsible wizards attempt to retain a balance between the forces of good and the forces of evil that seek dominance. LeGuin helps her readers suspend disbelief through detailed descriptions of Earthsea, its inhabitants, and a culture permeated with magic. LeGuin's series of Earthsea books develops the theme that responsibility is attached to great power by tracing the life of Sparrowhawk from when he is an apprentice wizard until he is finally the most powerful wizard in the land.

In the first book of the series, *A Wizard of Earthsea,* the young boy has powers strong enough to save his village, but pride and impatience place him in grave danger. A master wizard cautions Sparrowhawk about wanting to learn and use powers of enchantment that he is not yet mature enough to understand:

Have you never thought how danger must surround power as shadow does light? This sorcery is not a game we play for pleasure or for praise. Think of this: that every act of our Art is said and is done either for good, or for evil. Before you speak or do you must know the price that is to pay! (p. 35)

Sparrowhawk, renamed Ged, does not understand the warning. Conflict with another apprentice leads to a duel of sorcery skills, in which Ged calls up a dead spirit and accidentally unleashes an evil being onto the world.

LeGuin's descriptions of the rent in the darkness, the blazing brightness, the hideous black shadow, and Ged's reaction to the beast convince readers that evil really is released, important because the remainder of the book follows Ged as he hunts the shadow-beast across the islands to the farthest waters of Earthsea and develops an understanding that he is responsible for his own actions. The series ends with *Tehanu: The Last Book of Earthsea.*

Alan Garner. According to John Rowe Townsend (1975), Alan Garner was the most influential writer of fantasy in Great Britain of the 1960s. Garner's books are full of magic: the old magic of sun, moon, and blood that survives from crueler times, as well as the high magic of thoughts and spells that checks the old magic and serves as a potent but uncertain weapon against the old evil. Garner's stories transcend time barriers by allowing children from the present to discover objects that contain ancient spells influential in old legends. The ancient masters of good and evil then emerge either to pursue or to safeguard the children.

Garner creates a believable fantasy in *The Weirdstone of Brisingamen* by first placing two realistic characters into a realistic English country setting. He achieves credibility through the reactions of these children as they discover the powers in a tangible object, a tear-shaped piece of crystal that has been handed down over many generations. The plot then revolves around this "weirdstone." It is sought by both the forces of good and the forces of evil. The children, aided by two dwarfs, set out to return the stone to the good wizard who is its guardian. Along the way, however, they encounter evil characters—a shape-changing witch, giant troll women, and a wolf who chases them through underground tunnels and across the countryside. The final confrontation reveals the power of the weirdstone.

Robin McKinley. Magical objects are the focus of quests in Robin McKinley's *The Blue Sword* and *The Hero and the Crown.* McKinley makes *The Blue Sword* believable by depicting a realistic colony called Daria and realistic characters—colonial officials of Her Majesty's government, career army officers—who are unlikely to be influenced by the extraordinary. Fantasy elements enter the story when Harry is kidnapped by the leader of the Hillfolk and taken to the kingdom of Damar. From Harry's point of view, McKinley reveals a people who have the ability to speak in the old tongue, the language of the gods.

In *The Hero and the Crown,* which McKinley describes as a "prequel" to *The Blue Sword,* the power of a magical object is revealed through the sword that brings power from its original owner, Lady Aerin, who was the savior of her people. There is a strong feeling of destiny as the heroine sets forth to regain the objects of power and restore the power to her kingdom. As in many traditional epics, Aerin's quest results in increasingly difficult tests. She proceeds from slaying small dragons to finally overcoming an evil magician. McKinley strongly emphasizes responsibility, as Aerin discovers that even though the price is high, her destiny and her responsibility to her people require this quest.

Susan Cooper. Students of children's literature may identify the influence of English, Celtic, and Welsh legends and myths in Susan Cooper's series of modern fantasies. Her books about the guardians of light combating the forces of darkness contain references to the legend in which King Arthur does not die but lies resting in a place from which he will arise when the need is greatest. According to Celtic tradition, the words on Arthur's tomb mean "Here lies Arthur, King once and King to be."

Richard Cavendish (1982) reports that the Welsh version of the legend places Arthur's resting place in a cave in Snowdonia. A similar cave is important in Cooper's *The Grey King,* and Arthur and his knights rise again in *Silver on the Tree* to assist in the final battle against evil. The wizard Merlin, Arthur's legendary confidant, plays a crucial role throughout Cooper's series. Introduced as Merriman Lyon, Merlin has the ability to suspend the laws of nature and to travel into the past as well as the future. Throughout the series, Merriman retains Merlin's profound wisdom from an ancient past that leads the powers of good against the powers of evil.

Legendary objects, places, and occurrences are found throughout the series. For example, the power of a seventh son of a seventh son dominates the characters on heroic quests. Arthur's sword, his ship, and even his dog's name are important in Cooper's books. Quests for the objects of power form a thread of continuity in Cooper's stories. In *Over Sea, Under Stone,* three children visit Cornwall and find an old map that discloses a hidden treasure. This treasure, the grail, could hinder the forces of darkness. With the help of the good Old Ones, the children find the grail, but they lose the manuscript that is the key to its inscriptions.

In *The Dark Is Rising,* the responsibility for continuing the quest falls upon eleven-year-old Will Stanton. While born in twentieth-century England, Will has a special responsibility as the seventh son of a seventh son and the last born of the Old Ones, whose powers can be used against the powers of darkness. Early in Will's quest, his impatience and ignorance cause him to help the forces of darkness. He swears that he will never again use his powers unless he knows the consequences. His knowledge increases until he finally understands the magnitude of his powers and is able to use them successfully:

Will realized once more, helplessly, that to be an Old One was to be old before the proper time, for the fear he began to feel now was worse than the blind terror he had known in

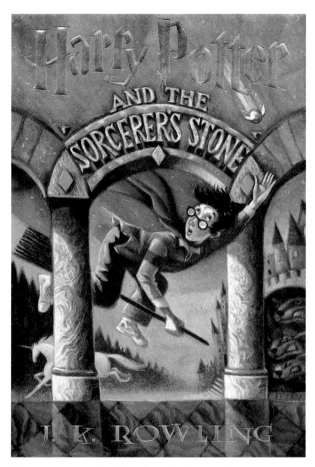

The high fantasy in the Harry Potter books appeals to many readers. (From Harry Potter and the Sorcerer's Stone, *by J. K. Rowling. Harry Potter, characters, names, and all related indicia are trademarks of Warner Bros. © 2001.)*

An In-Depth Analysis of Fantasy in the Writings of One Author

What is it about J. K. Rowling's "Harry Potter" books that places them all on the best-seller lists, shows worldwide sales of more than 100 million copies, and encourages the *New York Times* film critic, A. O. Scott (2000), to state, "Harry Potter is the biggest mass-culture phenomenon to come out of Britain since the Beatles" (p. 11)? Or, why does the adult fantasy novelist Stephen King (2000) declare, "Although they bear the trappings of fantasy, and the mingling of the real world and the world of wizards and flying broomsticks is delightful, the Harry Potter books are, at heart, satisfyingly shrewd mystery tales" (p. 13)? King continues, "The fantasy writer's job is to conduct the willing reader from mundanity to magic. This is a feat of which only a superior imagination is capable, and Rowling possesses such equipment" (p. 14).

The Harry Potter series begins with *Harry Potter and the Sorcerer's Stone,* in which a very unhappy orphan boy is described as living with the Dursleys, his horrible aunt and uncle and their even more despicable son, Dudley. Readers are encouraged to suspend disbelief as they are introduced into this real world of middle-class Britain. Readers along with Harry discover the possibilities that Harry has magical powers. This discovery is reinforced when Harry is accepted into Hogwarts School of Witchcraft and Wizardry and he begins his journey into a parallel world that allows his dismal life to change and his magical powers to develop. Rowling uses a jagged scar to foreshadow the possibilities that Harry is different from those around him.

Rowling suspends disbelief in the fantasy setting by introducing a fantasy environment through detailed descriptions of Diagon Alley with its wizard's bank and stores selling course books in wizardry, magical wands, cauldrons, and flying broomsticks. There is the journey to the school that begins as the students proceed through Platform Nine and Three-Quarters at King's Cross Station. There are detailed descriptions of Hogwarts School with its long history of training witches and a sorting hat that uses a student's capabilities and personality to place each student in one of the four divisions of the school; its special faculty of witches and wizards who teach courses such as spells, magical animals, and defense against the dark arts; and even Quidditch, which is a school sport played on flying broomsticks.

Rowling suspends disbelief by developing universal themes that are important to readers. There is the importance of friendship and trust as Harry develops close friendships with Ron Weasley and Hermione Granger and the three friends join forces to overcome evil. The author develops the need to use your own special abilities to solve problems and complete a quest: Hermione, the brightest witch in the school, uses her intelligence to solve a riddle; Ron uses his chess-playing ability to cross an enchanted area; and Harry uses his ability to ride a broomstick to capture a flying key.

Each of the books helps readers to suspend their disbelief and to increase their enjoyment of the series by developing

his attic bed, worse than the fear the Dark had put into him in the great hall. This time, his fear was adult, made of experience and imagination and care for others, and it was the worst of all. (p. 127)

Greenwitch, the third book of the series, continues the quest for the grail and the missing manuscript. *The Grey King* and *Silver on the Tree* complete the series.

Cooper encourages readers to suspend disbelief in her fantasies by developing a strong foundation in the reality of the twentieth century. When her realistic contemporary characters travel into earlier centuries and mythical worlds, her readers follow them willingly and share their quests for greater knowledge. There is a tie, however, between the past and present. For example, in *The Dark Is Rising,* Will goes back into the past to recover the Sign of Fire. When he has fulfilled his quest, a great crashing roar and rumbling and growling ensue. Back in the present, thunder is creating earsplitting sounds. The action is believable, and readers feel that the old ways are actually awakening and that the powers live again.

believable conflicts. These conflicts exemplify the characteristics of high fantasy: There is a constant battle between good versus evil, the characters have a high purpose, the tone is mythically charged, there are objects of power that help the hero, and the conflicts consider high social and moral issues.

In *Harry Potter and the Sorcerer's Stone,* Harry and his friends capture the stone that could be used by the evil Lord Voldemort to gain everlasting life. Through considerable danger, the friends cause the stone to be destroyed so it cannot be used for evil purposes. In *Harry Potter and the Chamber of Secrets,* Harry is in danger from a dark power that has the ability to petrify or to kill. Now Harry and his friends overcome the deadly Basilisk, the gigantic King of Serpents. In *Harry Potter and the Prisoner of Azkaban,* Harry discovers the secret of his newly found godfather and the relationship among his dead father and Moony, Wormtail, Padfoot, and Prongs. In *Harry Potter and the Goblet of Fire,* Harry discovers the truth about Lord Voldemort and faces him in a deadly combat that could have easily killed Harry. In this fourth book the author concludes with a chapter titled "The Beginning," which foreshadows the coming dangers and battles caused by Voldemort's return. Elizabeth D. Schafer, in *Exploring Harry Potter* (2000), identifies some the mythology, legends, and folktale connections that she found in the various Harry Potter books.

Technology Resources

You can link to two excellent Harry Potter websites by visiting our Companion Website at www.prenhall.com/norton

Categories of Modern Fantasy

Modern fantasies cover a wide range of topics. These topics include articulate animals, toys that come alive, preposterous characters and situations, strange and curious worlds, little people, friendly and frightening spirits, time warps, and science fiction.

Articulate Animals

Concerned rabbit parents worry about what will happen to their family when new folks move into the house on the hill, a mongoose saves his young owner from a deadly cobra, and a mole and a water rat spend an idyllic season floating down an enchanting river. Animals who talk like people but still retain some animal qualities are among the most popular modern fantasy characters. Authors such as Beatrix Potter and Kenneth Grahame have been able to create animal characters who display a balance between animal and human characteristics. This balance is

ISSUE   Harry Potter and Censorship

The "Harry Potter" books are both among the most popular books of all time and the most censored or criticized. In 2001, the first four books were all concurrently on various best-seller lists. The books have been highly praised and have won numerous awards. They are also listed on various best books lists such as "Top 10 Fantasy Books for Youth" (*Booklist,* April 15, 2000) and "Best Children's Books, 2000" (*Publishers Weekly,* November 6, 2000). Various letters to the editors also attest to children's positive responses to the books. For example, a letter in *The Horn Book* (March/April 2000) states that fifth through eighth graders in Old Greenwich, Connecticut, voted *Harry Potter and the Sorcerer's Stone* "the best book of 1998, tied for first place with the Newbery winner, *Holes*" (p. 133) and "Children's Voices: A Response to Harry Potter" in *The New Advocate* (Winter, 2001) stresses the importance of being lost in a book and letting your imagination soar. In addition, the author J. K. Rowling has been awarded an honorary doctorate from St. Andrews University in Scotland and is an Officer of the Order of British Empire.

In contrast, the "Harry Potter" series is listed among the top one hundred titles identified as banned books by the American Library Association's Office for Intellectual Freedom. The Potter books have been attacked because of the witchcraft and wizardry that are found in them.

Kimbra Wilder Gish (2000) voices the concerns of conservative Christian parents to books such as the "Harry Potter" series and other books that feature magic, witchcraft, and wizardry. For example, Gish cites Deuteronomy 18:9–12 as the reason that some people are concerned about the potential influences on children. "The above-referenced section of Deuteronomy specifically states that witches and wizards are an abomination unto the Lord that will be driven out, [so] one can see why someone who firmly believes this scripture might not want his or her child reading 'Harry Potter.' In these books, witchcraft and wizardry are generally portrayed as having many positive aspects" (p. 267).

In addition to issues related to witchcraft and wizardry, Gish cites problems with divination, Hermione's approval of the Egyptian magicians' work, possession of another person, and

trances. Gish's final issue relates to the portrayal of Muggles, the nonmagical people in the books. Gish states, "there remains a tone suggesting more or less overtly that Muggles do not understand magic and that their fear of witches/wizards stems from ignorance or spite rather than sincere and positive faith in a belief system . . . it isn't that we feel other views should be stifled; we are simply concerned about the negative portrayal of non-witches/ wizards painted in such sharp contrast to the more positive view of these supernaturally endowed" (pp. 268–299).

Gish concludes her article with ways that she believes conservative, Christian parents should discuss their family's beliefs with their children, talk about what they find of concern in the books, and use interest in the books to spark an in-depth discussion of faith.

As students of children's literature, you should explore different responses to the Harry Potter books. Find as many supportive and dissenting views as possible. Share these views with your children's literature class. This would be an interesting topic for debate as you share the pros and cons of these books.

not accidental; many successful authors write from close observations of animal life.

Young children are drawn to the strong feelings of loyalty that the animals in modern fantasies express as they help each other out of dangerous predicaments, stay with friends when they might choose other actions, or protect their human owners while risking their own lives. The memorable animal characters, like all memorable characters in literature, show a wide range of recognizable traits. Children often see themselves in the actions of their animal friends.

Retaining a consistent point of view is very important in believable modern fantasy. This may be particularly important in articulate animal stories. In Mary James's *Shoebag*, a cockroach changes into a boy. In this humorous story, James's protagonist retains his cockroach point of view.

Robert O'Brien's *Mrs. Frisby and the Rats of NIMH* is an excellent example of an author's use of believable plot, characters, and setting; interesting theme; and consistent point of view in modern fantasy. This consistency continues in Jane Leslie Conly's sequel, *Racso and the Rats of NIMH*, in which the author, who is the daughter of O'Brien, extends the story. In this sequel, the intelligent rat colony must save their Thorn Valley home from the threat of a dam and the accompanying tourism.

Beverly Cleary develops humorous animal stories for young children through imaginative and unusual plots. *The Mouse and the Motorcycle* and Cleary's other books about a mouse named Ralph are good introductions to modern fantasy.

Ursula K. LeGuin's *Catwings* and *Catwings Return* are also good introductions to fantasy for young children. LeGuin's *Catwings* introduces a family of kittens whose mother wishes a better life for them than her own city slums. As a result of her dreams, the kittens are born with wings and are able to fly to a safe home in the country. In *Catwings Return*, two of the cats return to the city because they miss their mother. In a satisfying conclusion, they discover and save their sister, who also has wings. In addition, children lovingly protect and care for the cat family in the end.

The characterization in Brian Jacques's *Redwall* is effective. For example, Jacques introduces Matthias, an unlikely and frequently clumsy mouse protagonist, with a description that reveals a great deal about the character's physical and emotional characteristics:

Matthias cut a comical little figure as he wobbled his way along the cloisters, with his large sandals flip-flopping and his tail peeping from beneath the baggy folds of an oversized novice's habit. He paused to gaze upwards at the cloudless blue sky and tripped over the enormous sandals. Hazelnuts scattered out upon the grass from the rush basket he was carrying. Unable to stop, he went tumbling cowl over tail. (p. 13)

After Matthias lands at the feet of Abbot Mortimer, the language reinforces the bumbling nature of the apologetic

These articulate animals talk like humans but have the additional power of flight. (From Catwings Return by Ursula K. LeGuin, illustrated by S. D. Schindler. Copyright © 1989 by Ursula K. LeGuin, illustrations copyright © 1989 by S. D. Schindler. Reprinted by permission of Orchard Books, a division of Franklin Watts, Inc.)

mouse: "Er, sorry, Father Abbot, I tripped, y'see. Trod on my Abbot, Father Habit. Oh dear, I mean . . ." (p. 13).

Compare the description of Matthias and the description of Cluny, the vicious antagonist:

Cluny was a bilge rat; the biggest, most savage rodent that ever jumped from ship to shore. He was black, with grey and pink scars all over his heavy vermin-ridden back to the enormous whiplike tail which had earned him his title: Cluny the Scourge! (p. 17)

Thus, Jacques sets the tone for a contest between two opposite characters.

Readers who enjoy Jacques's *Redwall* will enjoy additional books in the series. In *Mossflower*, a prequel to *Redwall*, Jacques goes back in time to reveal the story of Martin the Warrior, the original hero of Redwall Abbey and the savior of the land of Mossflower. *Mattimeo*, a sequel to *Redwall*, is about the exploits of Matthias's son, Mattimeo. In *Mariel of Redwall*, a mousemaid leads a battle at sea and saves Redwall animals from a savage pirate rat. As in his other books, Jacques stresses prophecies and provides readers with clues in a poem and a dream. All of Jacques's books have strong characters who reveal the best or the worst of animalkind.

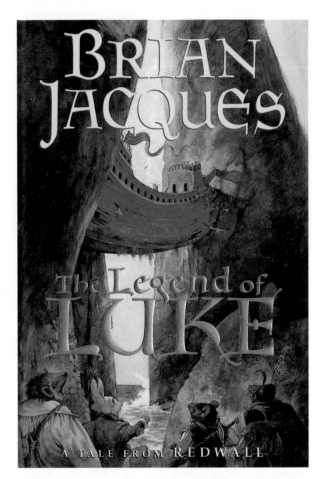

The Legend of Luke *is one of the* Redwall *stories. (Jacket art by Troy Howell, copyright © 2000 by Troy Howell, jacket art, from* The Legend of Luke: A Tale from Redwall *by Brian Jacques. Used by permission of Philomel Books, a division of Penguin Putnam, Inc.)*

Beatrix Potter. Children of all ages can identify the following sentence as the beginning of an enjoyable story, *The Tale of Peter Rabbit:* "Once upon a time there were four little Rabbits, and their names were—Flopsy, Mopsy, Cotton-tail, and Peter" (p. 3). Beatrix Potter, who wrote so knowledgeably about small animals, spent many holidays in the country observing nature, collecting natural objects, and making detailed drawings. Potter had small pets, including a rabbit, a hedgehog, and mice, who later became very real in her illustrated books for children. As an adult, Potter purchased a farm that offered further stimulation for her stories about articulate animals.

Potter's first book, *The Tale of Peter Rabbit,* began as a letter sent to a sick child. When she later submitted the story to a publisher, it was rejected. She did not let this rejection dissuade her; she had the book printed independently. When young readers accepted Peter Rabbit with great enthusiasm, the publisher asked if he might print the book.

Potter's characters may seem real to children because they show many characteristics that children themselves demonstrate. Peter Rabbit, for example, wants to go to the garden so badly that he disobeys his mother. In a vast store of vegetables, happiness changes rapidly to fright when Peter encounters the enemy, Mr. McGregor. Children can sympathize with Peter's fright as he tries unsuccessfully to flee. They also can respond to a satisfying ending, as Peter narrowly escapes and reaches the security of his mother. Children know that such behavior cannot go unpunished. Peter must take a dose of chamomile tea for a stomachache, while his sisters feast on milk and blackberries.

Potter's illustrations, drawn in careful detail, complement the story and suggest the many moods of the main character. Peter stealthily approaches and squeezes under the garden gate. He appears ecstatic as he munches carrots. When Peter discovers that he is too fat to squeeze under the gate, his ears hang dejectedly, a tear trickles down his cheek, one front paw is clenched in fright against his mouth, and his back paws are huddled together. The illustrated moods are so realistic that children feel a close relationship with Peter. *The Tale of Peter Rabbit* is found in a reissue of the 1902 Warne publication, as well as collections such as *A Treasury of Peter Rabbit and Other Stories* and *Tales of Peter Rabbit and His Friends.*

Michael Bond. Paddington Bear is another animal character whose warmth and appeal are related to the author's ability to encourage children to see themselves in the actions of an animal. Unlike Beatrix Potter's Peter Rabbit, who lives in an animal world, Michael Bond's Paddington lives with an English family after the family discovers the homeless bear in Paddington Station. Acceptance of the bear by the family and neighborhood creates a credible and humorous series of stories beginning with *A Bear Called Paddington.*

Bond's Paddington may seem real to children because Paddington displays many childlike characteristics. He gets himself into trouble, and he tries to hide his errors from people who would be disappointed in or disapprove of his actions. Paddington is hard to communicate with when he is in one of his difficult moods, and like a human child, he often is torn between excitement and perplexity. The excitement of preparing the itinerary for a trip in *Paddington Abroad* is balanced by Paddington's trouble in spelling hard words, his difficulty understanding why the bank does not return the same money that he put into his savings account, and his inability to read his prepared map. Children in the early elementary grades greatly enjoy these humorous episodes.

Rudyard Kipling. While the majority of articulate animal stories familiar to Americans occur in the woods and farmlands of the United States and Europe, one series uses the jungles of India. Rudyard Kipling spent his early years in Bombay, India, and this time had a great influence on his later writing. He spent much time in the company of Indian *ayahs* (nurses) who told him native

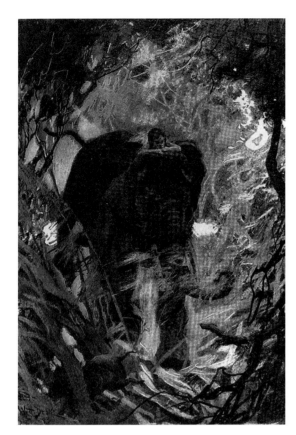

Kipling's young children were the first to hear his stories of articulate animals and a boy raised by the jungle animals. Illustration by W. H. Drake. (From The Jungle Book *by Rudyard Kipling. Illustrated by W. H. Drake, copyright © 1894. Macmillan and Co.)*

tales about the jungle animals. His own young children were the first to hear his most famous stories about the man-cub Mowgli and his brothers, Akela the wolf, Baloo the bear, and Bagheera the panther, published in *The Jungle Book* in 1894.

The story "Mowgli's Brothers" is one of Kipling's most popular. Kipling develops animal characters as diverse as the man-eating tiger Shere Khan, who claims the young Mowgli as his own, and Mother Wolf, who demonstrates her maternal instincts as she protects the man-cub and encourages him to join her own cubs. The law of the jungle is a strong element in the story, as the animals sit in council to decide Mowgli's fate. This story has the flavor of a traditional tale. The suspense rises until old Baloo the bear finally speaks for the man-cub. As in traditional tales about articulate animals, powerful feelings of loyalty grow as Mowgli saves the life of his old friend Akela, the wolf.

The characters, plot, and language of "Rikki-Tikki-Tavi" make it an excellent choice for oral storytelling. The wicked cobras Nag and Nagaina live in the garden of a small boy and his parents. They plan a battle against the humans and the heroic mongoose, Rikki-Tikki-Tavi, a hunter with eyeballs of flame and the sworn enemy of all

snakes. In keeping with the oral tradition, the action develops rapidly. The boy's loyal mongoose kills Nag. Then, he faces his most deadly peril, a female cobra avenging her mate and protecting her unborn babies. Kipling's language is excellent for oral recitation. As the tension mounts, Rikki-Tikki-Tavi asks:

What price for a snake's egg? For a young cobra? For a young king-cobra? For the last—the very last of the brood? The ants are eating all the others down by the melon-bed. (p. 117)

A happy-ever-after ending has Rikki-Tikki-Tavi defeating his enemy and remaining on guard so there will not be another threat in the garden.

Humorous incidents and language that is most effective when shared orally are characteristics of Kipling's *Just So Stories*. Young children enjoy the language in such favorite tales as "The Elephant's Child," the story of an adventurous young animal who lives near the banks of the "great, gray-green, greasy Limpopo River."

Kenneth Grahame. Kenneth Grahame first told his stories to his young children; however, scholarly analysis reveals that *The Wind in the Willows* may be read at several levels. For example, Michael Mendelson (1988) analyzed the contrast between the values of the dusty road and the riverbank. Peter Hunt (1988) analyzed the language and class structure. Richard Gillin (1988) searched for evidence of romanticism.

The animals in *The Wind in the Willows* are much more human than are Mowgli's friends in Kipling's jungle (Townsend, 1975). Grahame creates characters who prefer the idyllic life and consider work a bore, who long for wild adventures, who demonstrate human frailties through their actions, and who are loyal to friends. The idyllic life is exemplified in the experiences of Mole and Water-Rat as they explore their river world. Grahame introduces his readers to Mole as the scent of spring is penetrating Mole's dark home with a spirit of longing and discontent. Lured out of his hole, Mole observes the busy animals around him and muses that the best part of a holiday is not resting. Instead, it is seeing other animals busy at work. Through detailed description, Grahame communicates this perpetual vacationer's delight and carefree joy to readers:

He thought his happiness was complete when, as he meandered aimlessly along, suddenly he stood by the edge of a full-fed river. Never in his life had he seen a river before—this sleek, sinuous, full-bodied animal, chasing and chuckling, gripping things with a gurgle and leaving them with a laugh, to fling itself on fresh playmates that shook themselves free, and were caught and held again. All was a-shake and a-shiver—glints and gleams and sparks, rustle and swirl, chatter and bubble. The Mole was bewitched, entranced, fascinated. (p. 6)

Grahame creates credibility for the adventures of his most eccentric character, Toad of Toad Hall, by taking him away from the peaceful surroundings of his ancestral home. In the Wide World, where presumably such adventures could happen, he wrecks cars, is imprisoned, and escapes in a washerwoman's clothing basket. While he is gone, the less desirable animals who live in the Wild Wood, the stoats and the weasels, take over his home. When he returns, Toad's friends—brave Badger, gallant Water-Rat, and loyal Mole—help Toad recapture Toad Hall and tame the Wild Wood. Grahame suggests that a subdued and altered Toad, accompanied by his friends, recaptures his life of contentment along the river, at the edge of the Wild Wood, far away from the Wide World beyond.

Grahame's writing creates strong characters and visual images of the settings. Many children find the text difficult to read, however, so it may be preferable for adults to read this story to children. Many adults find Grahame's writing to be very enjoyable. As illustrator Fritz Eichenberg (1990) states in his Arbuthnot Lecture address, "At my age I can still read with pleasure and profit The Wind in the Willows. That should prove a pleasant platform on which we all can meet, peacefully, or better still let's meet at Toad Hall!" (p. 53).

Robert Lawson. This winner of the Newbery Award, the Caldecott Medal, and the Lewis Carroll Shelf Award has created a believable world in which animals retain their individualized characters. Unlike the river world of Mole in The Wind in the Willows, Robert Lawson's animal kingdom is influenced by humans. Like other distinguished authors of articulate animal stories, Lawson spent time closely observing animals (Weston, 1970). In 1936, Lawson built a house called Rabbit Hill in Connecticut. He says that he had wanted to write a story about the animals who ate everything he planted, the deer who trampled his garden, the skunks who upset his garbage pail, and the foxes who killed his chickens. Instead, when he started to write, he found himself growing fond of Little Georgie, a young rabbit, and the other animals on the hill.

The resulting book, Rabbit Hill, presents the impact of humans on the animals from the point of view of the animals. Lawson maintains this point of view to create believable characters. The animals on the hill wait expectantly after they learn that new folks are coming. They wonder if this change will bring about a renewal of older and pleasanter days when the fields were planted, a garden cultivated, and the lawns manicured. However, Mother Rabbit fears that the folks will be lovers of shotguns, traps, and poison gases, or worst of all, boys.

Lawson centers his book on the exploits of the exuberant Little Georgie, a rabbit who retains his curiosity and love for a good chase even when his father warns him that misbehavior and parental indulgence can have swift and fatal consequences. The animals believe that all will be well when the new owners put up a sign saying "Please drive carefully on account of small animals." Then, Little Georgie has a dreadful experience with a car on the black road, and the folks from the hill take the limp rabbit into the house. Gloom settles over the animals. Is Georgie alive, and, if so, why does he not appear? What terrible experiences are the folks planning for Little Georgie? The animals learn that the new folks are considerate and caring. The story has a satisfying ending, and the animals pay tribute to their new folks on the hill.

George Selden. Like Robert Lawson, George Selden loves the Connecticut countryside and creates animals with strong and believable personalities. His The Cricket in Times Square, however, has an urban setting, the subway station at Times Square. Two animal characters, Tucker Mouse and Harry Cat, are city dwellers. The other animal, Chester Cricket, arrives accidentally, having jumped into a picnic basket in Connecticut and been trapped until he arrived in New York.

Selden tells their story from the point of view of the animals and develops additional credibility by retaining some of each animal's natural characteristics: The city-wise Tucker Mouse lives in a cluttered drainpipe because he enjoys scrounging and does not consider neatness important. Chester Cricket is a natural musician and prefers to play when the spirit moves him rather than when people want to hear him. The plot develops around Chester's remarkable ability to play any music he hears and his need for returning kindness to the poor owner of the newsstand in the subway. Selden concludes his story with a longing that might be felt by anyone taken from his native environment. Chester becomes homesick for autumn in Connecticut and leaves the city to return home. When Tucker asks him how he'll know that he has reached home, Chester reassures him, "Oh, I'll . . . I'll smell the trees and I'll feel the air and I'll know" (p. 154).

This is a touching story of friendship, of longing for one's home, and of the love and understanding that can be felt between even a child and a tiny insect. Additional stories about these animals are found in Selden's Tucker's Countryside, Harry Cat's Pet Puppy, and Chester Cricket's Pigeon Ride. Chester Cricket's Pigeon Ride has a large format and illustrations designed to appeal to young children.

E. B. White. E. B. White introduces his characters within the reality of an authentically described working farm. His human characters have no unusual powers. They do not treat animals like people, and White does not give his animals human characteristics. The harsh reality is that the farmer must keep only animals that can produce a profit. In this setting, Mr. Arable moves toward the hoghouse with an ax in his hand to kill the runt in a newly born litter of six pigs. His daughter, Fern, pleads with him to let her raise the pig. As Wilbur grows, the profitability of the farm again influences Wilbur's fate. Mr. Arable is not willing to provide for Wilbur's growing appetite. Fern again saves Wilbur, but without a hint of fantasy: She sells him to Uncle Homer Zuckerman, who lives within easy visiting distance.

Wilbur's new home also begins on a firm foundation of reality. White describes the barn in which Wilbur will live and the afternoons when Fern visits Wilbur. On an afternoon when Fern does not arrive, White changes the story from reality to fantasy. Wilbur discovers that he can talk. As he realizes this, his barnyard neighbors begin to talk to him. From this point on, White develops the animal characters into distinct individuals, consistent in speech, actions, and appearance.

Wilbur feels lonely, friendless, and dejected. He often complains. He is a character who must be helped by others. When he discovers that he is being fattened to become smoked bacon and ham, he acts nonheroically: He bursts into tears, screams that he wants to live, and cries for someone to save him. Fern does not rescue him this time. Instead, White answers Wilbur's needs by giving him a barnyard friend, Charlotte A. Cavatica, a beautiful gray spider. Charlotte has quiet manners, and she is intelligent and loyal. She reassures Wilbur during their quiet talks, spins the webs that save Wilbur's life, and accompanies him on his trip to the fair.

The character of Templeton, the barnyard rat, is revealed through his convincing actions. He creeps furtively in his search for garbage, talks sneeringly to the barnyard animals, and eats until he gorges himself. White underscores this characterization by describing Templeton as having no morals or decency.

Through the reactions of the farm families, White allows readers to suspend disbelief about the possibility of a spider's spinning a web containing words. When the local residents react in "joyful admiration" and notify their local newspaper (the *Weekly Chronicle*), White's readers tend to believe this could really have happened. Readers can accept even the final, natural death of Charlotte, because life and friendship continue through Charlotte's offspring. Wilbur understands this as he welcomes three of Charlotte's daughters to his home:

Welcome to the barn cellar. You have chosen a hallowed doorway from which to string your webs. I think it is only fair to tell you that I was devoted to your mother. I owe my very life to her. She was brilliant, beautiful, and loyal to the end. I shall always treasure her memory. To you, her daughters, I pledge my friendship, forever and ever. (p. 182)

You may wish to compare E. B. White's *Charlotte's Web* with Dick King-Smith's believable characters and plot in *Pigs Might Fly*. Like Wilbur, Daggie Dogfoot is the runt of the litter. Unlike Wilbur, Daggie Dogfoot has a physical disability.

Toys

When children play with dolls or have conversations with their stuffed animals and other toys, they demonstrate belief in the human characteristics that they give their playthings. An author who tells a story from the point of view of a toy encourages young readers to draw upon their imaginative experiences with toys and to suspend disbelief.

Rumer Godden. Telling *The Dolls' House* from the viewpoint of a doll, Godden creates a believable story about a group of small dolls who long to leave a shoebox and live in their own house. Godden tells her readers:

It is an anxious, sometimes a dangerous thing to be a doll. Dolls cannot choose; they can only be chosen; they cannot "do"; they can only be done by; children who do not understand this often do wrong things, and then the dolls are hurt and abused and lost; and when this happens, dolls cannot speak, nor do anything except be hurt and abused and lost. If you have any dolls, you should remember that. (p. 13)

Godden creates dolls who have a range of human characteristics. For example, Mr. and Mrs. Plantagenet are quite ordinary dolls with extraordinary hearts; Tottie is an antique Dutch doll with a warm, friendly character; and Marchpane is an elegant nineteenth-century china doll with a vile disposition. These characteristics play important roles as the dolls express the desire for a new home. When an elegant dollhouse arrives, Marchpane declares that the house is rightfully hers and that the rest of the dolls are her servants. Godden describes the dolls' increasing unhappiness until a tragedy opens the eyes of the two children and the story ends on a note suggesting that justice is related to one's conduct.

Margery Williams. *The Velveteen Rabbit* is told from the viewpoint of a stuffed toy that lives in a nursery and learns to know his owner. Conversations between the stuffed rabbit and an old toy horse are especially effective. They allow Margery Williams to share her feelings about the reality of toys. When the rabbit asks the wise, old Skin Horse what it means to be real, the Skin Horse informs him, "Real isn't how you are made. . . . It's a thing that happens to you. When a child loves you for a long, long time, not just to play with, but REALLY loves you, then you become Real" (p. 17). The horse tells the rabbit that becoming real usually happens after a toy's hair has been loved off, its eyes have dropped out, and its joints have loosened. Then, even if the toy is shabby, it does not mind because it has become real to the child who loves it.

The story develops around the growing companionship between a boy and the boy rabbit. Children's reactions to this story suggest how meaningful the toy–child relationship is. Teachers and librarians describe the concern of young children when the rabbit is placed on the rubbish pile because the rabbit spent many hours in bed with the boy when he had scarlet fever. When the nursery fairy appears and turns the toy into a real rabbit, however, children often say that this is the right reward for a toy who has given so much love. These reactions suggest the credibility of a story written from the point of view of a toy. You may wish to compare the versions of this book illustrated by William Nicholson (the original edition), Michael Green, Ilse Plume, Allen Atkinson, and Michael Hague.

Companionship and love between a boy and a toy seem believable in this fantasy. (From The Velveteen Rabbit, *by Margery Williams. Illustrated by Michael Hague. Illustrations copyright © 1983 by Michael Hague. Reprinted by permission of Henry Holt and Company, Inc.)*

A. A. Milne.   According to his creator, A. A. Milne (1966), Winnie-the-Pooh does not like to be called a teddy bear because a teddy bear is just a toy, whereas Pooh is alive. The original Pooh was a present to Milne's son, Christopher Robin, on his first birthday. The boy and Pooh became inseparable, playing together on the nursery floor, hunting wild animals among the chairs that became African jungles, and having lengthy conversations over tea. Christopher Robin's nursery contained other "real" animals, including Piglet, Eeyore, Kanga, and Roo. When Milne wrote his stories about Christopher Robin's adventures with these animals, he was not only thinking about his own son but also remembering himself as a boy.

Winnie-the-Pooh and *The House at Pooh Corner* are filled with stories about Pooh because Pooh likes to hear stories about himself. Milne develops credibility for the actions in his stories by taking Pooh and the others out of the nursery and into the hundred-acre wood, where an inquisitive bear can have many adventures. Several stories suggest Pooh's reality: He climbs trees looking for honey and eats Rabbit's honey when he pays a visit. The text and illustrations leave no doubt that Pooh is a toy, however. No real bear would be so clumsy as to fall from branch to branch or to become stuck in Rabbit's doorway. Children may feel a close relationship with Christopher Robin

because every time that Pooh gets into difficulty, the human child must rescue the "silly old bear."

Carlo Collodi.   The adventures of a wooden marionette who is disobedient, prefers the joys of playtime to the rigors of school, and finally learns his lesson and wins an opportunity to become a real boy are similar to the experiences of Carlo Collodi, his creator. The Italian author of *The Adventures of Pinocchio* described himself as "the most irresponsible, the most disobedient and impudent boy in the whole school" (De Wit, 1979, p. 74). His story reflects a lesson that Collodi learned in school:

I persuaded myself that if one is impudent and disobedient in school he loses the good will of the teachers and the friendship of the scholars. I too became a good boy. I began to respect the others and they in turn respected me. (p. 76)

Pinocchio's insistence on doing only what he wants leads to a series of adventures: He sells his spelling book instead of attending school, he becomes involved with a devious fox and cat, he goes to a land of perpetual playtime, and he is transformed into a donkey. After Pinocchio learns some bitter lessons, he searches for his creator, Geppetto, who works to restore his health. Pinocchio begins to practice his reading and writing, and eventually becomes a real person. Through the words of the blue fairy, Collodi explains why Pinocchio is rewarded:

Because of your kind heart I forgive you for all your misdeeds. Boys who help other people so willingly and lovingly deserve praise, even if they are not models in other ways. Always listen to good counsel and you will be happy. (p. 193)

The influence of traditional folktales and fables is evident in Collodi's use of animals with human traits to teach lessons. Magical transformations punish and reward Pinocchio on his path to self-improvement (Heins, 1982).

Preposterous Characters and Situations

Children love exaggeration, ridiculous situations, and tongue-twisting language. Stories that appeal to a sense of humor usually include repetition, plays on words, and clever and original figures of speech. The characters in this section are developed through vivid descriptions of dress, features, or actions.

Floating through the air inside a huge peach propelled by five hundred and two seagulls provides a getaway for an unhappy child in Roald Dahl's *James and the Giant Peach*. Children thoroughly enjoy the freshness and originality of this story. Other enjoyably preposterous journeys occur when a housepainter is granted an unusual wish in *Mr. Popper's Penguins*, by Richard and Florence Atwater; when an eccentric inventor restores an old car in Ian Fleming's *Chitty Chitty Bang Bang*; and when a bed takes flight in Mary Norton's *Bed-Knob and Broomstick*. Pamela L. Travers's preposterous nanny, Mary Poppins, goes on many adventures.

After they harvested the crop one year, they had the barns, the cribs, the sheds, the shacks, and all the cracks and corners of the farm, all filled with popcorn.

"We came out to Nebraska to raise popcorn," said Jonas Jonas, "and I guess we got nearly enough popcorn this year for the popcorn poppers and all the friends and relations of all the popcorn poppers in these United States."

The Huckabuck family displays more of Carl Sandburg's humor. (Illustration from The Huckabuck Family and How They Raised Popcorn in Nebraska and Quit and Came Back *by Carl Sandburg, pictures by David Small. Pictures copyright © 1999 by David Small. Printed by permission of Farrar, Straus & Giroux, LLC.)*

Carl Sandburg. Readers might expect some unusual characters to be the residents of Rootabaga Country, where the largest city is a village called Liver and Onions. They are usually not disappointed when they hear Carl Sandburg's *Rootabaga Stories.* Told originally to the author's own children, these stories lose part of their humor if they are read rather than heard. The alliteration and nonsensical names are hard for children to read themselves, but they are fun to listen to.

Sandburg begins his ridiculous situation by describing how to get to Rootabaga Country by train: Riders must sell everything that they own, put "spot-cash money" into a ragbag, and then go to the railroad station and ask for a ticket to the place where the railroad tracks run into the sky and never come back. They will know that they have arrived when the train begins running on zigzag tracks; when they have traveled through the country of Over and Under, where no one gets out of the way of anyone else; and when they look out the train windows and see pigs wearing bibs.

The residents of Rootabaga Country have tongue-twisting names, such as Ax Me No Questions, Rags Habakuk, Miney Mo, and Henry Hagglyhoagly, and they become involved in tongue-twisting situations. For exam-

ple, when Blixie Bimber puts a charm around her neck, she falls in love with the first man that she meets with one *x* in his name (Silas Baxby), then with a man with two *x*'s (Fritz Axanbax), and finally with a man with three *x*'s (James Sixbixdix).

Sandburg's characters often talk in alliteration, repeating an initial sound in consecutive words. When the neighbors see a family selling their possessions, for example, they speculate that the family might be going "to Kansas, to Kokomo, to Canada, to Kankakee, to Kamchatka, to the Chattahoochee" (p. 6). The stories are brief enough to share with children during a short story time, but the uncommon names and the language require preparation by a storyteller or an oral reader. *More Rootabagas* is a new collection of previously unpublished stories. *The Huckabuck Family and How They Raised Popcorn in Nebraska and Quit and Came Back* is one of Sandburg's stories illustrated with humorous drawings by David Small.

Astrid Lindgren. In *Pippi Longstocking,* Swedish author Astrid Lindgren creates an unusual and vivacious character, who wears pigtails and stockings of different colors. Lindgren relies on exaggeration to develop a character who is supposedly the strongest girl in the world. Pippi demonstrates her ability when she lifts her horse onto the porch of her house.

Pippi's unconventional behavior and carefree existence appeal to many children. Pippi is a child who lives in a home all by herself. She sleeps on a bed with her feet where her head should be and decides to attend school because she doesn't want to miss Christmas and Easter vacation. Pippi's adventures continue in *Pippi in the South Seas,* in which Pippi saves her friend Tommy from a shark attack.

Strange and Curious Worlds

While on their way to Carl Sandburg's Rootabaga Country, young readers may find themselves falling down rabbit holes or flying off into even stranger and more curious worlds of modern fantasy.

Lewis Carroll. A remarkable realm unfolds when one falls down a rabbit hole, follows an underground passage, and enters a tiny door into a land of cool fountains, bright flowers, and unusual inhabitants. The guide into this world is also unusual: an articulate white rabbit who wears a waistcoat complete with a pocket watch.

Perhaps even more remarkable is the fact that this world of fantasy was created by a man who was dreadfully shy with adults, had a tendency to stammer, and displayed prim and precise habits. Charles Lutwidge Dodgson, better known as Lewis Carroll, was a mathematics lecturer at Oxford University during the sedate Victorian period of English history. Warren Weaver (1964) describes the life of this Victorian don:

Dodgson's adult life symbolized—indeed, really caricatured—the restraints of Victorian society. But he was essentially a wild and free spirit, and he had to burst out of these bonds. The chief outlet was fantasy—the fantasy which children accept with such simplicity, with such intelligence and charm. (p. 16)

Dodgson may have been shy with adults, but he showed a very different personality with children. He kept himself supplied with games to amuse them, made friends with them easily, and enjoyed telling them stories. A story told on a warm July afternoon to three young daughters of the dean of Dodgson's college at Oxford made Lewis Carroll almost immortal. As the children—Alice, Edith, and Lorina Liddell—rested on the riverbank, they asked Dodgson for a story. The result was the remarkable tale that later became *Alice's Adventures in Wonderland.* Even the first line of the story is reminiscent of a warm, leisurely afternoon:

Alice was beginning to get very tired of sitting by her sister on the bank and having nothing to do: Once or twice she had peeped into the book her sister was reading, but it had no pictures or conversations in it, "And what is the use of a book" thought Alice, "without pictures or conversations?" (p. 9)

From that point on, however, the day enters another realm of experience. Alice sees a strange white rabbit

A tea party with unusual guests adds to Alice-in-Wonderland's confusion. (From The Nursery "Alice," *by Lewis Carroll. Illustrated by John Tenniel. Published by Macmillan Publishing Co., 1890, 1979.)*

muttering to himself and follows him down, down, down into Wonderland, where the unusual is the ordinary way of life. Drinking mysterious substances changes one's size; strange animals conduct a race with no beginning and no finish that everyone wins; a hookah-smoking caterpillar gives advice; Dormouse, March Hare, and Mad Hatter have a very odd tea party; Cheshire Cat fades in and out of sight; and the King and Queen of Hearts conduct a ridiculous trial. According to Weaver (1964), the strange adventures have a broad appeal to children everywhere because:

Something of the essence of childhood is contained in this remarkable book—the innocent fun, the natural acceptance of marvels, combined with a healthy and at times slightly saucy curiosity about them, the element of confusion concerning the strange way in which the adult world behaves, the complete and natural companionship with animals, and an intertwined mixture of the rational and the irrational. For all of these, whatever the accidents of geography, are part and parcel of childhood. (p. 6)

Throughout the book, Alice expresses a natural acceptance of the unusual. When she finds a bottle labeled "Drink Me," she does so without hesitation. When the White Rabbit sends her to look for his missing gloves, she thinks to herself that it is queer to be a messenger for a rabbit, but she goes without question. During her adventures in this strange land she does, however, question her own identity. When the caterpillar opens their conversation by asking, "Who are you?" Alice replies:

I—I hardly know, Sir, just at present—at least I know who I was when I got up this morning, but I think I must have been changed several times since then. . . . I can't explain myself. I'm afraid, Sir, because I'm not myself, you see. (p. 23)

Lewis Carroll's language is appealing to children, especially if an adult reads the story to them, but children have difficulty reading the story for themselves, and some of the word plays are difficult for them to understand.

Carroll's version of the story for young children, *The Nursery "Alice,"* is written as though the author were telling the tale directly to children:

This is a little bit of the beautiful garden I told you about. You see Alice had managed at last to get quite small, so that she could go through the little door. I suppose she was about as tall as a mouse, if it stood on its hind legs; so of course this was a very tiny rose-tree: and these are very tiny gardeners. (p. 41)

Carroll is noted for his nonsense words as well as for his nonsensical situations. He claimed that even he could not explain the meanings of some words. Myra Cohn Livingston (1973) quotes a letter in which Carroll explains at least some words in his popular poem "Jabberwocky":

I am afraid I can't explain "vorpal blade" for you—nor yet "tulgey wood:" but I did make an explanation once for "uffish thought"—It seems to suggest a state of mind when the voice is gruffish, the manner roughish, and the temper huffish. Then again, as to "burble"; if you take the three verbs, "<u>b</u>leat," "<u>mur</u>mur" and "<u>war</u>ble," and select the bits I have underlined, it certainly makes "burble": though I am afraid I can't distinctly remember having made it that way.

The appeal of Carroll's nonsensical characters and fantasy, both to himself and to children, may be explained in a quote from a letter that he wrote in 1891:

In some ways, you know, people that don't exist are much nicer than people that do. For instance, people that don't exist are never cross: and they never contradict you: and they never tread on your toes! Oh, they're ever so much nicer than people that do exist!

You may find it interesting to compare the original version of *Alice's Adventures in Wonderland* with two more recent editions. You can compare John Tenniel's illustrations for the text published in 1890 with Helen Oxenbury's illustrations for *Alice's Adventures in Wonderland* and Lisbeth Zwerger's illustrations for *Alice in Wonderland.* Both of these editions were published in 1999.

James Barrie. *Peter Pan,* the classic flight of James Barrie's imagination into Never Land, was first presented as a play in 1904. Barrie begins his fantasy in the realm of reality, describing the children of Mr. and Mrs. Darling in their nursery as their parents prepare to leave for a party. When the parents leave the house, the world of fantasy immediately enters it in the form of Peter Pan and Tinker Bell, who are looking for Peter's lost shadow. Thus begins an adventure in which the Darling children fly, with the help of fairy dust, to Never Land, the kingdom that is "second to the right and then straight on till morning" (p. 31).

In Never Land, they meet the lost boys, children who have fallen out of their baby carriages when adults were not looking, and discover that there are no girls in Never Land because girls are too clever to fall out of their baby carriages. Along with Peter Pan, who ran away from home because he didn't want to grow up, the children have a series of adventures in Mermaids' Lagoon with the fairy Tinker Bell and against their archenemy, Captain Hook, and his pirates. The children finally decide to return home and to accept the responsibility of growing up.

Barrie's description of Mermaids' Lagoon encourages readers to visualize this fantasy land:

If you shut your eyes and are a lucky one, you may see at times a shapeless pool of lovely pale colours suspended in the darkness; then if you squeeze your eyes tighter, the pool begins to take shape, and the colours become so vivid that with another squeeze they must go on fire. But just before they go on fire you see the lagoon. This is the nearest you ever get to it on the mainland, just one heavenly moment; if there could be two moments you might see the surf and hear the mermaids singing. (p. 111)

Barrie's settings and characters seem real. They may seem especially real to children who do not wish to grow up. Readers who do not want to take on the responsibility of adulthood may sympathize with the adult Wendy, who longs to accompany Peter Pan but cannot. The book closes on a touch of nostalgia, as Peter Pan returns to claim each new generation of children who are happy and innocent.

Little People

Traditional folktales and fairy tales describe the kingdoms of small trolls, gnomes, and fairies; Hans Christian Andersen wrote about tiny Thumbelina, who sleeps in a walnut shell; and J. R. R. Tolkien created a believable world for the hobbit. Eloise McGraw in *The Moorchild* creates a world in which the Folk, or fairy people, live in their own world near that of the human occupants of the moor. Saaski, the heroine of the story, cannot survive with the Folk because she does not have their ability to make herself invisible to humans. McGraw creates her fantasy plot when the Folk exchange Saaski for a human child. The author creates tension between the villagers and Saaski's parents when the villagers blame Saaski for various misfortunes and threaten the child. Now Saaski must discover who she is and try to save the human child and the foster parents she has grown to admire. Contemporary authors of fantasy satisfy children's fascination with people who are a lot like them, only much smaller.

Carol Kendall. In *The Gammage Cup,* Carol Kendall creates a new world, the Land between the Mountains, in which little people in the valley of the Watercress River live in twelve serene towns with names like Little Dripping, Great Dripping, and Slipper-on-the-Water. Kendall gives credibility to this setting by tracing its history, carefully describing its buildings, and creating inhabitants who have lived in the valley for centuries.

The valley has two types of residents. The Periods display smug conformity in their clothing, their insistence on neat houses, and their similar attitudes and values. In contrast, the five Minnipins—whom the Periods refer to as "Oh Them"—insist upon being different. Gummy roams the hills rather than working at a suitable job; Curley Green paints pictures and wears a scarlet cloak; Walter the Earl digs for ancient treasure; Muggles refuses to keep her house organized; and Mingy questions the rulers' authority.

The conflict between the two sides reaches a climax when the five Minnipins refuse to conform to one standard and decide that they would rather outlaw themselves, leave their homes, and become exiles in the mountains than conform to the Periods' wishes. However, Kendall allows nonconformity to save the valley; the Minnipins discover the ancient enemy, the Mushrooms, or Hairless Ones, who have tunneled a way into the valley through an old gold mine. The five exiles rally the villagers and lead the Periods in a glorious victory over the enemy. At this point, the exiles return to their homes as heroes.

Mary Norton. The little people in Mary Norton's stories do not live in an isolated kingdom of their own. Instead, they are found in "houses which are old and quiet and deep in the country—and where the human beings live to a routine. Routine is their safeguard. They must know which rooms are to be used and when. They do not stay long where there are careless people, or unruly children, or certain household pets" (p. 9). In *The Borrowers*, Norton persuades readers to suspend disbelief by developing a foundation in reality. She describes an old country house in detail, including a clock that has not been moved for over eighty years. Realistic humans living in the house see and believe in the little people.

Norton describes normal-sized people through the eyes of the Clock family, who are only six inches tall. The Clocks' size forces them to lead precarious lives. They borrow their furnishings from the human occupants of the house.

Norton further encourages readers to suspend disbelief through the effort made to catch the little people. *The Borrowers* reaches an exciting climax when the housekeeper vows to have the borrowers exterminated by all available means: The rat-catcher arrives, complete with dogs, rabbit snares, sacks, spade, gun, and pickax. When a human boy takes an ax and desperately tries to dislodge the grating from the brick wall so that the little people can escape, readers have no doubt that those extraordinary beings are waiting in the shadows for his aid.

The Borrowers Afloat, The Borrowers Afield, The Borrowers Aloft, and *The Borrowers Avenged* continue the Clocks' adventures in fields and hedgerows. Sights, sounds, smells, and experiences seem original and authentic as readers look at the world from this unusual perspective.

Spirits Friendly and Frightening

Most children love good ghost stories or tales about beings from the spirit realm, whether frightening or friendly. Authors who write about these subjects may develop elements from folklore and the historic past.

Never Trust a Dead Man is a fast-paced tale that has elements of intrigue and mystery. (From Never Trust a Dead Man *by Vivian Vande Velde, copyright © 1999 by Vivian Vande Velde. Cover art copyright © 1999 by Tristan Elwell. Published by Harcourt Brace & Co. Reprinted by permission of Harcourt.*

Older children who enjoy stories about ghosts and goblins like the suspense and humor of Mollie Hunter's *The Wicked One*. They also like Paul Fleischman's three short tales of the supernatural in *Graven Images*. Fleischman's tales are successful because they build upon suspenseful turns of events, human folly, and comic mishaps. In *Seven Strange & Ghostly Tales*, Brian Jacques develops strange and unexpected stories featuring ghosts, demons, and vampires. To entice readers, Jacques introduces each of his stories with a poem.

Vivian Vande Velde's *Never Trust a Dead Man* (which won the Edgar Allan Poe Award for Young People) has the elements of a mystery when Farold is found with a knife in his back. Unfortunately, the protagonist, Selwyn, is convicted of the murder, sealed alive in the village burial cave along with the corpse, and has to bargain with a witch to raise Farold from the dead in order to discover the identity of the murderer. In a fast-paced, often humorous tale, Farold rises from the dead but is in the form of a talking

Technology Resources

One way to motivate a child to read is to recommend books on a favorite topic. Use the database to generate a list of titles concerning "ghosts" by searching the Title, Description and Topics fields with the term *ghost*. Add a grade specification to the Grade Level field to streamline your search.

bat. With the help of the witch's spell Selwyn's appearance is changed. The two characters go through a series of adventures, gather clues, and finally solve the mystery of who really stabbed Farold.

In a ghost story, Mary Downing Hahn helps present-day characters deal with their problems. In *Wait till Helen Comes,* Hahn's characters overcome their resentment against their stepfather and stepsister when they help the stepsister overcome her fascination with a ghost who is trying to lure the girl to her death. In *Ghost Abbey,* by Robert Westall, an abbey plays two different roles: (1) it protects those who care for it and (2) it threatens those who harm it. In *Whispers from the Dead,* by Joan Lowery Nixon, the ghost of a murdered character helps solve a mystery and prevent a second murder. In *The Ghost of Fossil Glen* by Cynthia DeFelice, the ghost of a murdered child convinces the protagonist that she should investigate the mysterious disappearance of the younger girl. In a climactic ending the ghost saves the protagonist from being killed by the murderer.

In *The Boggart,* Susan Cooper develops a conflict of wills between the Boggart, an ancient spirit, and the children who visit a castle in the western highlands of Scotland. The conflict increases when the spirit accidentally accompanies the children to their home in Toronto, Canada. There, the children must use modern technology to return the spirit to his castle home. In Cooper's sequel, *The Boggart and the Monster,* the spirit interacts with the Loch Ness Monster.

For older readers, *Silver Kiss* by Annette Curtis Klause has a mysterious teenage boy help a girl face her own problems and acquire self-realization. In this book, Zoe, a contemporary girl, and Simon, a three-hundred-year-old vampire, help each other accept what has happened in their lives. In Francesca Lisa Block's *Missing Angel Juan,* the ghost of Witch Baby's grandfather helps her find her missing boyfriend. Authors of fantasy frequently help characters face issues and overcome problems that could be self-destructive. In Peter Dickinson's *The Lion Tamer's Daughter: And Other Stories* teenagers are helped by supernatural friends, while Patricia Windsor's *The Blooding* is a story of good versus evil.

Lucy Boston. The winner of the Lewis Carroll Shelf Award for *The Children of Green Knowe,* Lucy Boston uses her own historic manor house at Hemingford Grey near Cambridge, England, as the setting for her stories. The

house and the way of life that past generations experienced in it provided Boston with ideas for a series of stories written about an old manor house and the friendly presences who return there from generations past.

The first book of a series, *The Children of Green Knowe* introduces the house, its owner Mrs. Oldknowe, her great-grandson Tolly, and the children who have previously lived in the house. Boston describes the house through the eyes of Tolly, a lonely, shy boy who comes to live in this old house with furnishings similar to those found in a castle. The past comes alive for Tolly as children who have lived there in previous generations come back to play with each other and bring vitality to the house and gardens. Readers are not surprised by these actions because Great-grandmother Oldknowe expects the children to return and enjoys having them visit. Boston allows readers to learn more about the people in the past through the stories that Mrs. Oldknowe tells Tolly.

Other books in this series are *The Treasure of Green Knowe, The River at Green Knowe, A Stranger at Green Knowe,* and *An Enemy at Green Knowe.* In all of the stories, ancestors return because someone wanted to keep their memories alive.

Time Warps

Children who read time-warp stories discover that there are more things in this world than progress and theories about the future. Time-warp stories encourage children to consider what might have happened in their own towns or geographic locations hundreds of years ago, as well as what the future might hold in centuries to come. Symbols and tangible objects unite past, present, and future. Believable characters travel to a distant past or see a future yet to materialize. Unlike many of the modern fantasies that bridge the world between old and new fantasy, time-warp stories focus on human development rather than on the forces of good and evil. The problems are solved by the characters, not by supernatural powers.

Authors frequently use the time-warp technique to allow their characters to make discoveries about themselves, their families, or the past. These discoveries usually allow the characters to gain new understandings. In *A Dig in Time,* Peni R. Griffin uses artifacts found in the backyard to allow a boy and a girl to go back to a time when their grandparents and parents were much younger. During this process, the protagonists make discoveries that help them in their contemporary world.

Detailed descriptions of a farm and countryside in the twentieth century and during the American Civil War create a believable story in Janet Lunn's time-warp fantasy *The Root Cellar.* In this book, the problems that an unhappy orphan confronts in both the present and the past encourage her personal development. Time-warp experiences help children overcome problems related to growing up and to family in Cynthia Voigt's *Building Blocks.* In *Stonewords: A Ghost Story* and the sequel, *Zoe Rising,*

Pam Conrad develops a theme of friendship. A contemporary girl interacts with a girl who lived in the same house during a different time. In *Zoe Rising,* fourteen-year-old Zoe goes back in time to solve a mystery in her estranged mother's past.

Belinda Hurmence uses a historical time and person-against-society conflict to help her protagonist understand a conflict that influenced her family. In *A Girl Called Boy,* Hurmence has a contemporary girl go back in time and experience slavery in 1853. In *Trapped Between the Lash and the Gun,* Arvella Whitmore uses a time-warp experience to help a contemporary African American boy make decisions about his life. When he contemplates running away from home and joining a street gang, he steals his grandfather's watch, which had been owned by an early ancestor. This is the tangible object that unites the present with the past as the boy finds himself transported to the plantation on which his ancestors were slaves. A contemporary actor is helped to overcome his grief and sorrow when he goes back to the late 1500s in Susan Cooper's *King of Shadows.* In the earlier time, he finds himself in the Globe Theatre acting with Shakespeare. Cooper develops a historically believable earlier setting by describing the theatre, using quotes from Shakespeare, and adding political intrigue associated with the time period. The need for healing from grief is a thread that runs through both time periods and allows the author to develop themes associated with the need to overcome grief and the power of great poetry to transcend time. Jane Yolen uses a similar approach in *The Devil's Arithmetic.* In this book, a contemporary Jewish girl faces the Holocaust.

These books are believable because the authors develop historical backgrounds that are authentic and characters who are changed by their experiences. These books may seem real because the authors allow their contemporary protagonists to experience the problems of another time.

Science Fiction

Writers of science fiction rely on hypothesized scientific advancements and imagined technology to create their plots. To achieve credibility, they provide detailed descriptions of this technology, portray characters who believe in the technology or the results of the technology, and create a world where science interacts with every area of society. Like other modern fantasies, science fiction relies on an internal consistency among plot, characters, and setting to encourage readers' suspension of disbelief. Science fiction written for young children often emphasizes the adventure associated with traveling to distant galaxies or with encountering unusual aliens. Stories for older readers often hypothesize about the future of humanity and stress problem solving in future societies.

Critics do not agree on the identity of the first science fiction novel. Margaret P. Esmonde (1984) identifies

Mary Godwin Shelley's *Frankenstein,* published in 1817, as the earliest science fiction story because the protagonist is a scientist, not a wizard, and the central theme is the proper use of knowledge and the moral responsibility of a scientist for his discovery.

Jules Verne published one of the first popular science fiction novels, *Five Weeks in a Balloon,* in 1863. Verne focused that book and later famous books enjoyed by older children and adults, such as *Twenty-Thousand Leagues Under the Sea,* on technology and invention but did not develop a society around them. Later in the nineteenth century, H. G. Wells began writing science fiction novels, such as *War of the Worlds,* that had a strong influence on the genre. According to Green, the writings of Wells differed from those of Jules Verne in that they included the systematic "extrapolation of social trends to create a detailed picture of a future society, revolutionary inventions, interplanetary warfare, and time travel" (p. 46).

After World War I, as technology advanced at an even faster pace, science fiction writing was influenced by the growth of magazines, such as *Amazing Stories.* John W. Campbell, Jr.'s, editorship of *Astounding Science Fiction,* beginning in 1938, was highly influential. Campbell insisted that the authors of stories he published develop strong characters, plausible science and technology, and logical speculation about future societies. He encouraged such talented science fiction writers as Robert A. Heinlein and Isaac Asimov.

In the 1960s, an increasing number of authors began to write science fiction stories. These stories were more suited to older children and young adults than to young children because the plots often relied on a developed sense of time, place, and space. Science fiction became a topic of interest for university and high-school courses. The media were extremely influential during this period. The movie *2001: A Space Odyssey* and the television program "Star Trek" created a devoted science fiction audience and suggested the imaginative potential of science fiction subjects. In the 1970s and 1980s, audiences flocked to such pictures as *Star Wars* and *E.T.* In the 1990s, the possible cloning of dinosaurs became a debated issue in *Jurassic Park.* Young people today read and reread the paperback versions of these movies.

Many writers are creating high-quality science fiction for young people and are considering responses to future catastrophes or scientific possibilities in their plots. The years following the destruction of modern civilization due to the Flash provide the setting for Caroline Stevermer's *River Rats.* In this story, a group of teenagers crew an old salvaged paddle-wheel steamer on the toxic Mississippi River. Their fight for physical survival is increased after they rescue a man who is being chased because he knows the location of a hoard of weapons. Stevermer presents a setting filled with ruined cities and the consequences of toxic pollution. The protagonists work together and survive in this desolate environment.

Authors who place their characters in science fiction environments tend to develop strong survival stories in addition to cautionary tales. The future aboard a space freighter is the setting for Annette Curtis Klause's *Alien Secrets*. While en route to the planet where her parents are based, the heroine makes friends with an alien and becomes involved in a mystery that allows her to make discoveries about the alien beings and their culture. Vivid descriptions of the characters and space travel create believable situations and settings. Interactions with aliens also provides the conflict in Neal Shusterman's *The Dark Side of Nowhere* as the protagonist must decide where to place his loyalties.

In *The Giver*, Lois Lowry develops a future in which poverty, inequality, and unemployment have been eliminated. This society, however, is devoid of conscience, emotion, and even color. Accompanying twelve-year-old Jonas as he discovers the truth about his society, readers must ponder and reexamine many of their own beliefs.

Gains in time research form the scientific probability and provide the plot in Robert Silverberg's *Letters from Atlantis*. Possible breakthroughs in time research in the twenty-first century allow a scientist to go back in time to the island of Atlantis by transferring the scientist's mind into the mind of a royal prince who lived in Atlantis. The scientist writes letters to another scientist, who also went back in time, and these letters detail what Atlantis might have been like 180 centuries ago.

The transcendent time between the technologically advanced, but polluted, twenty-first century and the sixteenth-century world of warriors who plunder the borders of England and Scotland forms the setting for scientists in Susan Price's *The Sterkarm Handshake*. This winner of the *Guardian*'s Children's Fiction Award presents a plot and characters that depict the clashes between two cultures. Readers can consider the responsibilities of and the possibilities for a future culture that might try to solve their problems by taking over a culture, a people, and a land.

In *Invitation to the Game*, Monica Hughes speculates about what might happen in the year 2154 if there is high unemployment, if workers have been replaced by robots, and if teenagers, after graduating from high school, are given permanent unemployed status rather than jobs. This is the predicament of eight teenagers who are relegated to a Designated Area. As they investigate their area, they discover not only the harsh realities of perpetual unemployment but also the mysterious something referred to as "The Game." When they receive an invitation to participate in the game, they experience lifelike computer simulations that place them in unfamiliar settings and give them challenges in which they must work together. The group discovers that each has unique capabilities.

Hughes provides the ultimate answer to unemployment and overcrowding when the members of the group find themselves on a distant planet and realize that they

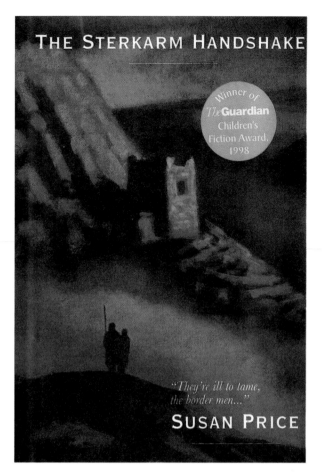

Transcending time forms the plot structure in Susan Price's The Sterkarm Handshake. *(Cover from the* Sterkarm Handshake *by Susan Price, cover illustration by Mark Edwards, first published in the UK by Scholastic Children's Books 1998, reproduced by permission of Scholastic Ltd.)*

will not be going back to Earth. In a survival story, the members of the group must use the training that they gained during the simulation sessions and their unique skills to work together and to survive. As in her other science fiction books, Hughes considers the consequences of projected contemporary issues and provides at least a glimmer of hope for the future.

Madeleine L'Engle. Do we all need each other? Is every atom in the universe dependent on every other? Questions like these confront Madeleine L'Engle's characters as they travel the cosmos, face the problem of being different, fight to overcome evil, understand the need for all things to mature, and discover the power of love.

It is interesting to note L'Engle's thoughts about herself as she wrote *A Wrinkle in Time*:

I was trying to discover a theology by which I could live, because I had learned that I cannot live in a universe where there's no hope of anything, no hope of there being somebody to whom I could say, "Help!" (p. 254)

Through the Eyes of an AUTHOR

Madeleine L'Engle

Visit the CD-ROM that accompanies this text to generate a complete list of titles by Madeleine L'Engle.

Selected Titles by Madeleine L'Engle:

A Wrinkle in Time

A Swiftly Tilting Planet

An Acceptable Time

Meet the Austins

Ring of Endless Light

The Search for Truth

Long ago when I was just learning to read, and the world was (as usual) tottering on the brink of war, I discovered that if I wanted to look for the truth of what was happening around me, and if I wanted to know what made the people tick who made the events I couldn't control, the place to look for that truth was in story. Facts simply told me what things were. Story told me what they were about, and sometimes even what they meant. It never occurred to me then, when I was little, nor does it now, that story is more appropriate for children than for adults. It is still, for me, the vehicle of truth.

As for writing stories for children, whether it's fantasy or "slice-of-life" stories, most people are adults by the time they get published.

And most of us adults who are professional writers are writing for ourselves, out of our own needs, our own search for truth. If we aren't, we're writing down to children, and that is serving neither children, nor truth.

I'm sometimes asked, by both children and their elders, why I've written approximately half of my books for children, and I reply honestly that I've never written a book for children in my life, nor would I ever insult a child by doing so. The world is even more confused now than it was when I first discovered story as medium for meaning, and story is still, for me, the best way to make sense out of what is happening, to see "cosmos in chaos" (as Leonard Bernstein said). It is still the best way to keep hope alive, rather than giving in to suicidal pessimism.

Books of fantasy and science fiction, in particular, are books in which the writer can express a vision, in most cases vision of hope. A writer of fantasy usually looks at the seeming meaninglessness in what is happening on this planet, and says, "No, I won't accept that. There has got to be some meaning, some shape and pattern in all of this," and then looks to story for the discovery of that shape and pattern.

In my own fantasies I am very excited by some of the new sciences; in *A Wrinkle in Time* it is Einstein's theories of relativity, and Planck's Quantum theory; tesseract is a real word, and the theory of tessering is not as far fetched as at first it might seem. If anyone had asked my grandfather if we'd ever break the sound barrier,

he'd have said, "Of course not." People are now saying "Of course not" about the light barrier, but, just as we've broken the sound barrier, so, one day, we'll break the light barrier, and then we'll be freed from the restrictions of time. We will be able to tesser.

In *A Wind in the Door*, I turn from the macrocosm to the microcosm, the world of the cellular biologist. Yes, indeed, there are mitochondria, and they live within us; they have their own DNA, and we are their host planet. And they are as much smaller than we are as galaxies are larger than we are. How can we—child or adult—understand this except in story?

Concepts which are too difficult for adults are open to children, who are not yet afraid of new ideas, who don't mind having the boat rocked, or new doors opened, or mixing metaphors! That is one very solid reason my science fiction/fantasy books are marketed for children; only children are open enough to understand them. Let's never underestimate the capacity of the child for a wide and glorious imagination, an ability to accept what is going on in our troubled world, and the courage to endure it with courage, and respond to it with a realistic hope.

Video Profiles: The accompanying video contains conversations with Gary Soto, Paula Danziger, Robert Kimmel Smith, and other writers of children's literature.

In *A Wrinkle in Time*, L'Engle creates characters who are different from the people around them but have high intelligence and strong bonds of love and loyalty to one another. Meg Murry and Charles Wallace are the children of eminent scientists. Meg worries about the way the people in their town make fun of her brother as backward and strange. Her father consoles her by telling her that her brother is doing things in his own way and time. In fact, Charles Wallace has very special powers: He can probe the minds of his mother and sister, and he is also extremely bright.

L'Engle's development of the characters provides a realistic foundation for the science fiction fantasy that follows. The children discover that their scientist father is fighting the "dark thing"—a thing so evil that it could overshadow a planet, block out the stars, and create fear beyond the possibility of comfort. The children travel in the fifth dimension to a far-distant planet, where their father has been imprisoned by the evil power of "It."

L'Engle states that this villain is a naked brain because "the brain tends to be vicious when it's not informed by the heart" (Wintle and Fisher, 1974, p. 254). The heart proves more powerful than the evil It in this story: Meg's ability to love deeply saves her father and Charles.

The battle against evil continues in *A Wind in the Door*, in which Charles appears to be dying. In *A Swiftly Tilting Planet*, readers discover the climactic purpose of Charles's special abilities. L'Engle creates a realistic foundation for the science fiction when fifteen-year-old Charles and his father construct a model of a tesseract, a square squared and then squared again, which is considered the dimension of time. Because Charles and his father can construct the tesseract, readers feel that the story must be true.

Another credible character adds realism to the story: The president of the United States asks for help. Elements of traditional fantasy enter this science fiction story in the form of an ancient rune designed to call the elements of

Through the Eyes of a CHILD

Tommy

Pam Wilson's Fourth Grade
Western Row Elementary
Mason, Ohio

TITLE: A Wrinkle in Time
AUTHOR: Madeleine L'Engle

A Wrinkle in time is a very good chapter book. It gives fictional answers to to questions that we can't find the answer to, such as: Is there other life in the universe? etc. There is so much detail that pictures are not needed. The book sort of tells you at the end: this the beginning of a series. The genre is some where between science fiction and fanasty. This is a perfect book for a sixth grader, but not a fourth grader. There are still many words that I don't understand. Still, I'd like to read the rest of the series called the Time Quartet, but there are only 4 books in the series. I hope the author writes more!

Tommy

---

light and hold back evil and a unicorn that aids Charles in a perilous journey. In all of her books, L'Engle emphasizes the mystery and beauty of the cosmos and the necessity of maintaining a natural balance in the order of the universe.

Anne McCaffrey. In Anne McCaffrey's *Dragonsong,* Pern is the third planet of Rukbat, a golden G-type star in the Sagittarian sector. When a wildly erratic bright red star approaches Pern, spore life, which proliferates at an incredible rate on the red star's surface, spins into space and falls in thin threads toward Pern's hospitable earth. The spore life is not hospitable to life on Pern, however. In order to counteract this menace, the colonists enlist a life form indigenous to the planet. These creatures, called

dragons, have two remarkable characteristics: (1) They can travel instantly from place to place by teleportation and (2) they can emit flaming gas when they chew phosphine-bearing rock. When guided by dragonriders, they can destroy the spore before it reaches the planet.

In this setting, a young girl fights for her dream to become a harpist. Because her father believes that such a desire is disgraceful for a female and forbids her to play her music, Menolly runs away and makes friends with the dragons. After a series of adventures in both *Dragonsong* and *Dragonsinger,* Menolly learns that she need no longer hide her skill or fear her ambitions:

The last vestige of anxiety lifted from Menolly's mind. As a journeyman in blue, she had rank and status enough to fear no one and nothing. No need to run or hide. She'd a place to fill and a craft that was unique to her. She'd come a long, long way in a sevenday. (*Dragonsinger*, p. 264)

Nancy Farmer. The year is 2194; the location is Harare, Zimbabwe. By analyzing the 1995 Newbery Honor book, Nancy Farmer's *The Ear, the Eye and the Arm,* you will discover several of the themes frequently developed in science fiction: Toxic contamination can change lives, the world of the future may be influenced by technology, and some members of the society search for their traditional heritage. The three main characters have unique characteristics that make them ideal detectives. Arm has a long snaky arm that can outreach all other arms. Ear has extremely sensitive hearing, and Eye has excellent vision. These detectives use their unique abilities to search for the three kidnapped children of the general.

In addition to unusual characters, the text includes both technology and mythology. For example, an automatic doberman guards the mansion, robot gardeners clip the grass, and a programmed pantry prepares the food. The author also uses ancient customs and references to mythology to create a credible history for the country. The author develops two quite different settings. One is the toxic dump where outcasts live. This setting is developed in the first half of the book when the children are kidnapped and forced to work in the mines by digging out refuse that can be sold. Resthaven, a compound in which people live by the ancient rules and customs, is developed in the second half of the book when the children are brought into the compound. In the compound they learn not only about the history of their country but also what it is like to live under separate roles and rules for males and females, to believe in superstitions such as witchcraft, and to live without modern medical knowledge. As in all good science fiction, the author provides detailed descriptions for her futuristic environment.

John Christopher. The future world that John Christopher envisions in *The White Mountains* is quite different from the world hoped for by people today. In Christopher's future, people have lost free will, and machines called Tripods have taken over. These machines maintain control through a capping ceremony that places a steel plate on the skull, making the wearer docile and obedient. Fourteen-year-old Will

Parker, who is angered by the prospect of an inescapable voice inside his head, discovers that a colony of free people lives in the White Mountains, which are far to the south. Will escapes with two other young people, but the Tripods follow them. Will discovers that freedom and hope are the most important luxuries in life.

In *The City of Gold and Lead* and *The Pool of Fire,* the free humans plan battle against the Tripods and then defeat them. Yet, quarreling factions defeat Will's attempts to plan for new unity among the victorious humans. Christopher's stories are exciting, but they are also sober reminders of what can happen if humanity allows itself to lose free will.

Suggested Activities

 For more suggested activities for understanding modern fantasy, visit our Companion Website at www.prenhall.com/norton

■ Discuss C. S. Lewis's "The Chronicles of Narnia" with another adult who has read the books and with a child who has read them. What are the differences, if any, in the interpretations of the two people?

■ After reading J. R. R. Tolkien's *The Hobbit* or *The Lord of the Rings,* identify common elements and symbols in Tolkien's work and mythology. Consider the use of fate, subterranean descents, denial of death, mortals and immortals, supernatural beings, and power granted to objects.

■ Authors who write believably about articulate animals balance reality and fantasy by allowing the animals to talk but still retain some animal characteristics. Choose an animal character such as Beatrix Potter's Peter Rabbit, Little Georgie from Robert Lawson's *Rabbit Hill,* or Mole from Kenneth Grahame's *The Wind in the Willows.* What human characteristics can you identify? What animal characteristics can you identify? Has the author developed a credible character? Why or why not?

■ Read an article that analyzes a modern fantasy selection such as Lisa Paul's "A Second Look: The Return of the Iron Man" (2000), Betsy Hearne's "Circling Tuck: An Interview with Natalie Babbitt" (2000), or Brian Alderson's "Harry Potter, Dido Twite, and Mr. Beowulf" (2000). Summarize the article and share it with your class. Stress points of agreement or disagreement.

Teaching with Modern Fantasy

Y ou can extend the magic that children gain from modern fantasy by providing varied opportunities to interact with the plots, characters, and settings of such stories. In a presentation to the National Council of Teachers of English, Marcia Bagham (2000) provides a strong reason for sharing fantasy with children. She states, "In fantasy, readers are empowered and assured that they can succeed and overcome obstacles. Fantasy-based stories give readers hope—hope to keep on living and hope to keep on reading."

Helping Children Recognize, Understand, and Enjoy Elements in Fantasy

Fantasy is a worthy genre of literature for all children. It challenges the intellect, reveals insights, stimulates the imagination, and nurtures the affective domain. However, many children have difficulty comprehending modern fantasy. Unlike realistic fiction, which mirrors a more or less real world, modern fantasy presents an altered picture. One of the first ways to help children understand and appreciate modern fantasy is to read several fantasy selections and encourage the students to identify and discuss what makes each story modern fantasy. The following questions address the altered literary elements in the stories (Norton, 1992):

1. How has the author manipulated or altered the literary elements so that the story takes place in a world other than the real world of today?

2. What is the evidence that the setting has been altered? How was the setting altered? How does this setting differ from the real world? (The author does not need to alter all of these elements.)

3. What is the evidence that the characters are different from characters living in the real world? How are the characters altered? How do these characters differ from characters that you know in the real world?

4. What is the evidence that time has been altered? How was time altered? How is this experience with time different from experiences with time in the real world?

5. How did the author suspend disbelief and encourage readers to believe in the fanciful experience?

Again, be sure to remind students that they will not find all of these altered elements in every piece of modern fantasy.

Books that vividly describe settings encourage children to visualize the settings, respond to the language, and understand why authors must select words carefully to set the stage for their books. One of the ways to help students recognize the importance of setting in fantasy is to ask them to close their eyes and to listen to a passage (Norton, 1992). As they listen to the passage, have them try to visualize the setting and then describe what they see.

Numerous books have vivid paragraphs that can be used for visualization and discussion. In *The Wish Giver*, Bill Brittain uses rich and colorful imagery to create a memorable story. Fantasies in picture-book format written for younger children are also excellent selections for this type of activity. For example, have children visualize and describe the settings and the personified characters in Virginia Lee Burton's *The Little House*, Munro Leaf's *The Story of Ferdinand*, and Leo Lionni's *Swimmy*. Pointing out the author's use of similes and metaphors helps students understand the story.

Authors often enrich their fantasies with allegory, irony, figurative language, and traditional elements. Such elements may increase the appreciation of the stories for gifted children but cause confusion for less able readers. Susan Swanton's (1984) survey of the literary choices of gifted students supports this contention. Gifted students indicated that they liked science fiction and fantasy because of the challenges presented. While almost half of the books preferred by gifted students were classified as modern fantasy (29 percent science fiction, 18 percent other fantasy), none of the top choices of other students were similarly classified. Because modern fantasy can be pleasurable for all readers, the difference in the reading preferences is unfortunate.

With detailed illustrations and simple plots, picture books can help children understand the more complex elements found in modern fantasy. Picture books can stimulate discussion, illuminate meanings, and form bridges between illusion and understanding. Chart 7.1 identifies elements in modern fantasy and selections that develop and illustrate the elements. The picture books include both modern fantasy and traditional tales. (See the Children's Literature for Chapter 6 for the traditional tales.) Have the children read and discuss the picture books in each category before they read and discuss the fantasy. After children can recognize the literary elements in picture books, they find it easier to identify similar elements in fantasy selections.

Each of the picture books in Chart 7.1 illustrates an important element in fantasy. For example, Hugh Lewin's highly illustrated *Jafta* and *Jafta's Mother* are excellent sources for figurative language. Lewin

CHART 7.1   Books for helping children understand modern fantasy

Elements	Picture Books	Modern Fantasy
Allegory	Holder's *Aesop's Fables* Lobel's *Fables*	Lewis's "Chronicles of Narnia"
Irony	Gage's *Cully, Cully and the Bear*	Brittain's *The Wish Giver*
Figurative language	Lewin's *Jafta* and *Jafta's Mother*	Brittain's *The Wish Giver* and *Dr. Dredd's Wagon of Wonders*

Folklore elements
   Power in tangible objects
   A quest
 	
   Magical powers
 	
   Transformations
 	
   Punishment for misused ability
	Aylesworth's *The Full Belly Bowl*
	
	 Marshak's *The Month Brothers*
	 Severo's *The Good-Hearted Youngest Brother*
	 Hodges's *Saint George and the Dragon*
	 Grimms's *The Devil with the Three Golden Hairs*
	 Andersen's *The Wild Swans*
	 Williams's *The Velveteen Rabbit*
	 Van Allsburg's *The Wreck of the Zephyr*
		Crossley-Holland's *Arthur: The Seeing Stone*
		 Lunn's *The Root Cellar*
		 Cooper's *Seaward*
		
		 McKinley's *The Hero and the Crown*
		 McKinley's *The Blue Sword*
		 Pullman's *I Was a Rat!*
		
		 Cooper's *Seaward*
		 Brittain's *The Wish Giver*

describes and illustrates Jafta's feelings by comparing them to the feelings and actions of animals in Jafta's African environment. The double-spread illustrations show both the boy and the particular animal demonstrating such actions as skipping (like a spider), stamping (like an elephant), and grumbling (like a warthog). In the modern fantasy *The Wish Giver*, Bill Brittain also uses figurative language to suggest character traits and to enhance the rural setting.

Older students may discover the mythological and legendary foundations of Tolkien's modern fantasy by tracing the important motifs in J. R. R. Tolkien's *The Hobbit* back to Norse myths and legends. Have older students identify the elements and motifs in Padraic Colum's *The Children of Odin*, Kevin Crossley-Holland's *The Faber Book of Northern Legends* and *The Norse Myths*, and Michael Harrison's *The Curse of the Ring*. Children who identify the important motifs in Colum's *The Children of Odin* will discover a constant battle between forces of good and evil for the control of humanity. Children also will discover that the remote past is considered a golden age, that there is a magical significance for runes, that the ring is a symbol of power, that a dragon must be slain, that promises are contracts to be kept, that fate governs the lives of all beings, that tricksters may help or hinder, and that heroes frequently make personal sacrifices for common good. (See also Chapter 6.)

In addition to identifying the important motifs in *The Children of Odin,* ask older students to identify quotes that show these elements. For example, following are a few of the quotes showing that Norse mythology includes a constant battle between good and evil: "Always there had been war between the Giants and the Gods—between the Giants who would have destroyed the world and the Gods who would have protected the race of men and would have made the world more beautiful" (p. 6), the dwarf Brock's bargain with Loki was an evil bargain and "all its evil consequences you must bear" (p. 42), and "East of Midgard there was a place more evil than any region in Jotunheim. It was Jarnid, the Iron Wood. There dwelt witches who were the most foul of all witches. The son of the most evil witch would be the wolf who would swallow up the Moon and stain the heavens and earth with blood" (p. 168).

After Norse mythology, have the students identify similar elements in *The Hobbit* and provide evidence for those elements. The following examples show the battle between good and evil in *The Hobbit:* The evil goblins battle against the good dwarfs, Bilbo verbally battles against the Gollum, the evil forces lie to the east, evil wolves threaten the dwarfs, Bilbo battles against the dragon Smaug, evil Smaug battles the Lake Men, and the battle of the Five Armies has good and evil forces.

Through the Eyes of a TEACHER

Barry Hoonan

Fifth/Sixth-Grade Teacher
Bainbridge School
Bainbridge Island, Washington

Literature Strategy Plan: Helping Children Appreciate Fantasy Literature

Fantasy is a worthy genre for children. It challenges the intellect, stimulates the imagination, and helps us understand the basic struggles we all face as human beings. Some people, however, think children should not read fantasy; it's not contemporary enough, these critics argue, or it will lead children to practice magic or believe in the occult. Others say fantasy is too difficult because of qualities often characteristic of books in this genre: more complex language, sophisticated themes, and settings far removed from children's direct experience.

Yet, the enduring popularity of books like E. B. White's *Charlotte's Web* and C. S. Lewis's *The Lion, the Witch and the Wardrobe,* along with the phenomenal success of J. K. Rowling's "Harry Potter" series, suggests that children are hungry for these books. Middle-school teacher Barry Hoonan agrees: "I think fantasy works well because it lets kids explore worlds that stimulate their imaginations; it gives images to the ethereal." Barry also believes his job is to model a passion for reading and to support his students' understanding of how to respond deeply to books. Fantasy is an excellent genre for advancing those goals.

Building Students' Background Knowledge

Barry always has a few students who are fans of Brian Jacques's "Redwall" series. He builds on this natural base by reading aloud a challenging fantasy and showing his class the strategies readers use to appreciate more complex literature. T. A. Barron's *Heartlight* is an excellent book for these purposes. "In *Heartlight,* Kate, the heroine, goes into an alternative universe. We have to really work together to make sense of this and understand Barron's imagery. Barron also has characters that are excellent role models for my students—a spunky, intuitive, intelligent thirteen-year-old girl and a strong, wise, sensitive male in the grandfather figure."

Barry uses this book to teach reading strategies, particularly how readers sometimes must wrestle with a text in order to fully appreciate it. "There's a complacency in my students when it comes to reading. Fantasy pushes them. I want them to understand that we're always growing as readers and we continue to grow—even as adults," says Barry. So when they encounter a difficult or unsettling part of the book, he stops and leads a discussion. Sometimes they act out the scene several times, considering character motivations, themes, or what might be causing tension in the story. "When I stop the story for these discussion, I try to get two dialogues going: talking about things through the perspective of the characters as well as the reader."

Barry also uses this time to show his students the many ways in which they can respond to literature. "Students generally don't like to prepare written responses. Because of this reluctance, I like to demonstrate my own written responses, using the overhead. As I project what I wrote, I highlight why I wrote what I did and what I was doing as a reader." Barry also demonstrates how to use Post-It notes to mark favorite passages, puzzling parts, particularly compelling descriptions. "Post-Its are a great strategy for response because you can stick a Post-It in a book and keep on reading. You don't interrupt the flow."

Barry also encourages children to respond to books through art. Sometimes his students do an activity called "Save the Last Word for the Artist" in which a sketch representing key concepts from a chapter or section of the book is created. The other members of the class or small

Kirsten's artistic response to Tamora Pierce's *Magic Steps:* "The book swirls with color, magic, and danger."

group "read" the illustration, offering their response to the picture in light of their own knowledge about the book. Then the artist shares his or her intended meaning. Sometimes children select quotes to accompany their sketches. "It's like going to a museum and interpreting the paintings," says Barry. "It's just glorious for them to see that there are multiple ways of thinking about a text. There is a great flowering that brings our reading and writing to a whole new level."

Children also create symbolic representations after reading an entire book, particularly following *Heartlight*. First they fold a paper into four quadrants. Barry then asks them to consider the following questions: What colors come to mind when you think of *Heartlight*? What images? If there was a symbol for this book, what would it look like? How did you enjoy the book? Their responses are quickly recorded in each box. They then create a collage, three-dimensional model, or drawing of colors, words, and images that represents their response to the book.

Purposeful Reading and Writing

Soon students take off on their own, finding books of fantasy to read independently during silent reading time. They also participate in small-group literature studios in which they discuss a book read in common. One year, for example, some of the girls became interested in studying Tamora Pierce's "Circle of Magic" books. Many of the boys that year decided to explore T. A. Barron's "Merlin" books. Children are encouraged to participate in several groups. Many do.

All group members are expected to read their selected book, then write responses in their literature journals. Barry doesn't provide specific questions for them to answer. Rather, they are asked to record thoughts about the evolving plot, aspects of the book that intrigue or puzzle them, interesting words, speculations about what they think will happen next, and other open-ended responses. Favorite passages are marked with Post-Its, following the model Barry demonstrated with *Heartlight*. They then come to the literature circles and discuss what they've read. "The discussion is so much richer if they've thought about things before they come to the group," says Barry. "It really makes a difference in their level of reading to not only talk about books but to think about what they will do next. However, literature groups are not there to serve my purposes. Rather, I hope they serve the purpose of encouraging kids to read more and enjoy their reading."

Barry uses several other strategies to help children deepen their responses. One is "Fishbowl." In this activity the class forms two circles, one inside the other. The inside group discusses their literature circle book for ten to fifteen minutes while the outside group listens. The observers later make observations about what they noticed about the discussion and how to conduct their own discussions. Both groups gain from demonstrating and listening to how circle discussions evolve. "At first the discussions have almost a performance or 'TV show' effect," says Barry. "But gradually the children get into it and they forget they're being observed. Then they really show the others how to help each other work through a text."

Assessment

"I believe the best reading assessment is a good conversation," says Barry. So he regularly conducts small-group "book chats" to discover how effectively his students are using various reading strategies. Five or six children at a time bring their reading notebooks and book lists to a round table. "I take out my notebook and tell them their job is to tell me what they're reading and what they're thinking about as they read. And I write down their responses as if I'm noting a recommendation." Sometimes he asks questions to stimulate their thinking, for instance, "I notice Margaret Haddix's books are becoming popular. Why do you think this is the case?" or "What's your favorite fantasy book so far? Why is it your favorite?" After talking for a while, Barry tries to summarize what they've said, asks more questions to help them expand their book choices, or helps them expand their use of strategies. "I think assessment should lead to action," he says. "So if a child isn't finding a fantasy book she likes, I'll help her reflect on what has appealed in the past to support her selection process. Or if someone is not recalling important parts of the book, we'll talk about how Post-Its might help."

Barry also conducts an informal reading interview with each new student at the beginning of the year in which he tries to discern their interests, attitudes, and skills as readers and writers. In addition to having them read and respond to text selections, he also explores issues with them like "How do you choose a book?" "How do you write a response to a book?" "How do you draw responses?" "What do you do when you read a book?" This helps him support their progress.

"It's a really great time to be a middle-school teacher. We've grown tremendously in our notions of how to help kids in the middle grades who have a great deal of knowledge and experience stay motivated about learning. Fantasy books are excellent for helping them become dreamers and creators."

 For ideas on adapting Barry Hoonan's lesson to meet the needs of older or younger readers, please visit Chapter 7 on our Companion Website at
www.prenhall.com/norton

Interpreting Modern Fantasy by Identifying Plot Structures

Writings by Joseph Campbell such as *The Power of Myth* (1988) and *The Hero with a Thousand Faces* (1949, 1968) and research by Christopher Vogler in *The Writer's Journey: Mythic Structure for Storytellers and Screenwriters* (1992) suggest that successful authors map the journey or plot of the story by identifying and describing specific stages as the hero or heroine progresses in his or her journey and reaches the ultimate reward. We find these stages of the hero's journey in traditional literature classics such as "The Iliad of Homer," the "Myths of Greece and Rome," and Howard Pyle's *The Story of King Arthur and His Knights.*

Author Katherine Paterson (1995), winner of two Newbery Medals and two National Book Awards, also emphasizes that excellent literature follows the stages in a hero's journey. When writing about the process she uses in writing her own novels, she states, "The hero must leave home, confront fabulous dangers, and return the victor to grant boons to his fellows. Or, a wandering nobody must go out from bondage through the wilderness and by the grace of God become truly someone who can give back something of what she was given. That—incredible as it may seem—is the story of my lives" (p. 154). These stages in a writer's journey may also be used to help students either analyze structure in literature or to write their own stories. (I also use the stages when I teach a writing institute.)

As we proceed through this technique we will first model the approach using Philip Pullman's *The Golden Compass* (the 1996 Carnegie Medal winner) and then identify the stages in two additional fantasies that are appropriate for students in the upper elementary of middle school: Lois Lowry's *The Giver* (1994 Newbery Award) and Megan Whalen Turner's *The Thief* (1997 Newbery Honor).

Students should first read Pullman's *The Golden Compass* and then become part of the discussion as the plot structures and stages in the hero's journey are identified and discussed. Consequently, let us first identify the stage in plot development and then discuss how Pullman develops that stage in his writing. The following information may be used as you model and discuss the identification of the stages with your students.

The first stage in the hero's journey begins by placing the protagonists in the ordinary world before placing them into a new or alien experience. Authors use this technique to create a vivid contrast with the strange new world that the heroes are about to enter.

Pullman begins his story at Oxford University where the heroine, Lyra, has lived most of her life. The author describes the Hall with pictures of scholars, the library, and the scholars' common room. We see and hear normal people such as the Master of the college. Pullman's use of dialogue such as "You have been safe here in Jor-

dan, my dear. I think you have been happy" helps readers understand this ordinary world. (You may discuss with students how the author has been successful in creating an ordinary world.)

Vogler's second stage in plot development is the call to adventure in which the hero is presented with a problem, challenge, or adventure to undertake. Once presented with a call to adventure, the hero can no longer remain indefinitely in the comfort of the ordinary world. Pullman's call to adventure occurs rapidly when the heroine hides in the Oxford Professor's Meeting Room and learns about a problem that could change the nature of the world, especially the easy life that she has led at Oxford. The author uses a technique in which Lyra summarizes her discoveries over the previous few weeks and she realizes that she must try to rescue her friends.

The third stage is the refusal of the call during which experience the protagonist shows fear or expresses reluctance, especially toward facing the unknown. Pullman uses techniques such as avoidance and excuses as his heroine tries to convince herself that she does not want to leave the safety of Oxford University and proceed to the far North and into the unknown.

The fourth stage in plot structure occurs when the protagonist meets the mentor, the wise old man or woman, the Merlin-like character, who assists the hero or heroine. Pullman uses a plot technique in which the Master of Jordan College presents Lyra with an object of power: an alethiometer that tells the truth and gives advice. Pullman also develops a spirit soul in animal form that helps the heroine find her way and gives her advice.

Crossing the first threshold is the fifth stage in which the hero or heroine commits to the adventure, decides to face the challenge, and fully enters the special world. This plotting occurs when Pullman allows Lyra to discover that Lord Asriel is being held by Armored Beasts and the Oblation Board. Now she knows that she must run away to try to rescue him. The author presents this crossing of the threshold when he states, "Now that Lyra had a task in mind, she felt much better" (p. 110).

Tests, allies, and enemies occur throughout the sixth stage in which the protagonist encounters new challenges, faces new tests, and makes allies and enemies. These tests allow the author to develop both the character of the protagonist and to explore the depth of the antagonists that are working against the character. Pullman contrasts the roles of good spirits and bad spirits as the heroine faces various tests along the way.

During the seventh stage the protagonist approaches the innermost cave in which he or she comes to the edge of a dangerous place where the object of the quest is hidden. Pullman uses foreshadowing and prophesying to reveal the possible dangers that will come through dialogue such as this: "The witches have spoken of a child such as this, who has a great destiny that can only be fulfilled elsewhere—not in this world, but far beyond. Without this child, we shall all die. . . . But she must fulfill her destiny in ignorance of what she is doing, because only in her ignorance can we be saved" (p. 176).

The supreme ordeal, or eighth stage, occurs when the protagonist faces the greatest fear, the most harrowing moments. This may be a life-or-death moment in which the character or the character's goals are in mortal jeopardy. Pullman uses the encounter between Mrs. Coulter, the ultimate evil, and Lyra to develop the supreme ordeal in which she plans to save the children who are under Mrs. Coulter's power.

The reward occurs during the ninth stage in which the protagonist takes possession of the treasure or the object of the quest that he or she has come to seek. Pullman uses a device in which Lyra and the children escape as Lyra tries to rescue her father and give him the powerful alethiometer. When she rescues her father she discovers the meaning of the dust that makes the alethiometer work and also discovers why her enemies are trying to control the dust.

The road back, or tenth stage, deals with the consequences of confronting the dark forces of the supreme ordeal. The character is frequently pursued by the vengeful forces disturbed by seizing the reward. Pullman uses a technique in which the heroine deals with the forces of evil, and the author is now able to reveal the magnitude of this evil. Because this is the first book in a three-volume series, the author allows the heroine to confront the dark forces and her own inability to accomplish the total quest through inner thoughts of the character such as "Oh, the bitter anguish! She had thought she was saving Robert, and all the time she'd been diligently working to betray him. Lyra shook and sobbed in a frenzy of emotion. It couldn't be true" (p. 380).

The eleventh stage is the resurrection in which the hero or heroine is purified, cleansed, or reborn before returning to the ordinary world. It usually occurs when the protagonist is transformed by the experience and returns to the real world with new insights. Pullman allows his heroine to realize that she is not alone in her quest to rid the world of the terrible evils. Her main realization is that she is not alone. The author uses this resurrection and purification to allow her to continue with added strength on her journey for the ultimate quest. Lyra's actions reveal this new strength: "She turned away. Behind them lay pain and death and fear; ahead of them lay doubt, and danger, and fathomless mysteries. But they were not alone. So Lyra and her daemon turned away from the world they were born in, and looked toward the sun, and walked into the sky" (p. 399).

The final stage is the return in which the protagonist journeys back to the ordinary world with some elixir, treasure, or lesson learned from the special world. Pullman develops the continuation of the plot as Lyra realizes that she has strength and can search for answers. It is interesting that the plot structures found in Pullman's high fantasy parallel those identified by both Campbell and Vogler.

Many high fantasy books can be used for a similar activity. Both Lois Lowry's *The Giver* and Megan Whalen Turner's *The Thief* follow similar plot structures. *The Giver,* a science fiction novel set in a futuristic world in which society has tried to rid itself of contemporary problems, is considered a controversial book by some because it has been identified as one of the most censored of recently published books. *The Thief,* a legendary fantasy, has foundations in Greek mythology.

The following examples include points that you might use when discussing the stages in the hero's journey with students. In *The Giver* the author presents the characters in an ordinary world that revolves around life in the community. The community is a highly controlled atmosphere where few, or no, choices are found because choices lead to pain and ultimately confusion. Lowry reveals this setting by having various characters describe the many rules of the society that influence their lives. The ordinary world in *The Thief* begins in the King's prison as the protagonist is bound in chains. Turner reveals this ordinary world through descriptions of setting and also through the pleasant memories in which the protagonist contrasts the cell with memories of a previous time in which he lived within the marble floors and painted walls of the King's palace.

The call to adventure occurs in *The Giver* when the protagonist, Jonas, is selected to be the next Receiver of Memory. The importance of this selection is revealed as the author describes Jonas's excitement and apprehension as he meets the demands placed on him on his crucial birthday. The call to adventure occurs in *The Thief* when the King's adviser offers to release the protagonist from prison if he will steal one of the most valuable objects in their world.

The refusal of the call in *The Giver* is developed as Jonas reveals his feelings of fear, of being alone, and of losing his friendships if he is to take on this very important task. In *The Thief* the refusal of the call is in the form of reluctance to live under the requirements of the quest.

The mentors in both books take on fantasy characteristics. The Elder who is the previous Receiver of Memory becomes the Giver when he begins to transmit the memories of the past, including both pain and joy, to the new Receiver of Memory. During a series of experiences the mentor reveals the memories of history to the protagonist. The mentors in *The Thief* are both the human magus, the king's honored helper, and the woman in a dream who gives the thief valuable advice that saves his life.

In *The Giver* Jonas crosses the first threshold when he accepts the new responsibility and believes that he can accomplish the task after he has had an especially pleasant memory with snow and sliding down a hill. The protagonist in *The Thief* crosses the first threshold when he realizes the power of his own ambition and decides to join in the quest for the powerful stone.

The tests, allies, and enemies in *The Giver* take the form of memories that bring pain as well as pleasure. Now the protagonist discovers the consequences of choices: Should society be ordinary and predictable so life is free of pain? Or, should people experience everything so that they can make their own decisions? The tests in *The Thief* result as the protagonist must transcend a maze. Allies include the characters from ancient mythology that are revealed during storytelling.

The innermost cave or the most dangerous place is reached in *The Giver* when Jonas becomes "weighted with new knowledge" (p. 99) and realizes that the people know nothing because "without the memories it is all meaningless" (p. 105). The most dangerous place in *The Thief* is found as the protagonist faces the disappearing river that allows the temple to be dry for a brief time. He knows that the river will reappear and that if he has not found the stone by then he will drown.

The supreme ordeal occurs in *The Giver* when Jonas faces the worst of the memories such as those related to war and discovers that memories are essential for the development of wisdom. The supreme ordeal in *The Thief* occurs during the protagonist's third and last try to locate the secret door and obtain the powerful stone.

The rewards in the two books are quite different. In *The Giver* Jonas realizes that he has the power to give memories to others and that he can take much of the pain and responsibility away from the previous Giver. In *The Thief* the protagonist discovers the secret door and the throne with the statues of the Goddess surrounded by her court. Within this court is the powerful stone, the object of his quest.

The road back is not an easy trip for either of the protagonists. In *The Giver* Jonas does not want to return to the honor, pain, or wisdom associated with the memories. But, he realizes that life could change for his world, that love is important. The protagonist's road back in *The Thief* includes being swept away by the river, being attacked by thieves, and being betrayed by a member of the quest.

The third threshold is crossed in *The Giver* when Jonas develops deeper feelings, especially when he discovers that in his world people are trained to kill without feelings. The author describes Jonas's vivid reactions to this killing: "Jonas felt a ripping sensation inside himself, the feeling of terrible pain clawing its way forward to emerge in a cry" (p. 151). Crossing the threshold that results in transformation in *The Thief* occurs when the protagonist gives up a supposedly rich reward and helps the members of the quest team escape.

In *The Giver* the final return to the ordinary world depends on the reader's interpretation. Jonas escapes from his community and releases all of the memories back to the community members. To what world does he return? Is he able to return to the world of beyond, the world he sees in his memories? Does he return to the world of his own community, one that now has all of the past memories? Or, does he die and the warm colors that he sees ahead of him represent heaven? This book, like many of the excellent high fantasies, has strong themes and several different interpretations. In *The Thief* the protagonist is revealed as a highly honored member of the royal family and that his original desire was to obtain the powerful stone for his Queen. At the conclusion of the book, the Queen destroys the powerful stone so that it can no longer control people's lives.

Although each of these high fantasy selections has very different content, they each include stages in plot structures that are similar to those described by Campbell and Vogler. You may ask students to compare the various books and to consider why they believe that *The Golden Compass*, *The Giver*, and *The Thief* conclude with strong themes that reveal the importance of being responsible for one's own decisions and the negative situations that are possible when society tries to control the lives of the people.

Involving Children with Science Fiction

Science fiction stories have inspired children to become scientists and writers. Scientist Carl Sagan (1980) credited the science fiction stories of H. G. Wells with stimulating his boyhood dreams of flying to the moon and Mars and with eventually leading him to become an astronomer. Robert Goddard, the inventor of modern rocketry, read *War of the Worlds* by Wells. Stories about the space traveler Buck Rogers influenced George Lucas, the creator of the movies *Star Wars* and *The Empire Strikes Back*. Science fiction provides enjoyment but it can also stimulate interaction between science fiction and science or social studies.

Interdisciplinary Studies: Interaction Between Social Studies and Science Fiction

Science fiction relates to not only scientific principles and technology but also the possible impacts of technological changes, such as mechanization, space travel, and life on other planets, upon people and societies. Using science fiction in social studies classrooms allows students to understand and discuss broad themes like the nature of government, the merits of different types of social organization, and cultural differences. Science fiction can stimulate debate that is unhindered by children's stereotypes. Science fiction also encourages children to acquire a sense of the relationship between cause and effect, and in so doing, children can begin to grasp the sweep of history that is important to any study of social studies.

CHART 7.2 Issues and books to motivate children to consider different viewpoints

Issue: *People who differ from those around them are often misunderstood, feared, and even hated. This treatment is inconsistent with the prevalent belief that fellowship and love are essential if society is to survive. How should people deal with those who are different? What could happen if fellowship and love are not emphasized by society?*	**Issue:** *Should society allow its members to have free will? What could happen if people do not strive to retain freedom of choice?*
Science Fiction to Share with Children 1 Lowry, Lois. *The Giver.* This world of the future has solved many problems but the inhabitants appear to be devoid of conscience. 2 L'Engle, Madeleine. *A Wrinkle in Time.* People fear and whisper about Charles Wallace because he is different from the other children in the town: He can communicate without speaking.	**Science Fiction to Share with Children** 1 Christopher, John. *The White Mountains.* People in the twenty-first century are controlled by machines called Tripods. When human members of the society reach the age of fourteen, steel plates are inserted into their skulls so that they can be controlled by the state. 2 Christopher, John. *The City of Gold and Lead.* Will tries to discover the secrets of the Tripod culture by spying inside the major Tripod city. 3 Christopher, John. *The Pool of Fire.* People try to set up a new government after defeating the Tripods; dissident groups, however, cannot agree on a unified approach.

Many science fiction books lend themselves to debates on issues related to society and social studies. Classroom teachers have successfully used the issues and books in Chart 7.2 to motivate children to consider different viewpoints during social studies classes.

Because science fiction stories often describe futuristic cities on earth or other inhabited planets, they can inspire children to create their own model cities. Have children consider what a city of the future would look like and how it would function if they could build it any way that they wished. One sixth-grade class designed such a city. The children researched known design possibilities and used their imaginations.

For the project, the children investigated energy-efficient buildings, transportation systems, sanitation systems, and suburban/urban growth before they began to build. They chose high-rise office and apartment buildings for their efficient use of urban space. For energy efficiency and beauty, their suburban homes were partially or totally below ground and had solar collectors. Shopping centers used below- and above-ground space, and they utilized light shafts to bring in light for plants and people. The children's transportation included clean, electric mass transit; computerized road systems for private cars to ensure safe, steady traffic; and moving sidewalks. Their sanitation system used a three-phase treatment process that produced drinkable water; and their power plant incinerated garbage to provide recycled power. The children planned museums and recreational facilities, including parks, trees, and an arboretum. They considered the issues of control-ling growth, providing an ideal number of people for their city, and satisfying their city's future energy needs.

Have children think about the impact on their own lives and society if an alien people landed on earth or if space exploration discovered life forms on other planets. Through role playing, have them imagine a first meeting, ways in which they might communicate, and ways in which humans and aliens could function together without destroying either culture. Television programs such as "Star Trek" can lead to the issue of interfering with another culture. Have children consider the possibility of earth's being invaded or colonized by aliens who are far superior intellectually to people on earth or a space exploration's discovering human life forms who have not progressed as far as those on earth.

Have children discuss the impact of various environments on space travelers who are trying to colonize them. Have the children construct whole new environments in their classrooms. Have them design settings that include atmosphere, plants, animals, and land characteristics; create new languages; develop communication systems; and suggest fine arts possibilities.

Unit Plan: Using One Book of Modern Fantasy

Teachers and librarians can develop numerous enjoyable activities around one book of modern fantasy. Madeleine L'Engle's *A Wrinkle in Time,* for example, is a popular science fiction book. It has a plot, characters, settings, and themes that stimulate discussion, artwork, and creative dramatization. Many outstanding books can serve as bases for such activities. Therefore, you may wish to use the suggestions related to L'Engle's book as guidelines for activities in connection with other books.

Oral Discussion

Some of the suggestions for discussion of L'Engle's text involve questions that require children to consider information presented at different points in the text and then to integrate this information. Leading a discussion, interject appropriate text passages as the children consider their answers. Listen to the children's responses and, if appropriate, ask divergent questions. Divergent questions encourage more than one "correct" answer. Let the children verbalize different interpretations to the story. Encourage the children to consider their own experiences and reactions and thus to interact with the text.

Your discussion of L'Engle's text can focus on plot, characterization, setting, theme, and style, too. The following questions and suggestions are listed in the order of the material in the book (which is indicated by page or chapter). If you wish to focus on plot, characterization, setting, theme, or style at one time, group the following suggestions accordingly:

1. *Characterization.* What did Meg's father mean when he told Meg not to worry about Charles Wallace because "he does things in his own way and in his own time"? Was her father right? What exceptional behavior does Charles Wallace display? Why is Charles Wallace considered strange by the villagers? Why doesn't he want the people in the village to know his real capabilities? (Chapter 2)

2. *Plot.* A tesseract is mentioned in several places in the book. Present ideas about what students think is meant by a tesseract. For example, Mrs. Whatsit informs Mrs. Murry that there is such a thing as a tesseract (p. 21). Mrs. Murry tells the children that she and their father used to have a joke about a thing called a tesseract (p. 23). The term *tessering* is described as traveling in the fifth dimension—going beyond the fourth dimension. The five dimensions are described as first, a line; second, a flat square; third, a cube; fourth, time; and fifth, the square of time, a tesseract in which people can travel through space without going the long way around (p. 76).

3. *Style: emotional response to language.* Throughout the book, L'Engle makes associations between smells and emotions. Discuss some of these associations: Mrs. Whatsit's statement that she found Charles Wallace's house by the smell; and then her reaction in which she describes how lovely and warm the house is inside (p. 17); or the delicate fragrance that Meg smells when the gentle beast with tentacles relieves her of her pain (p. 175). Express your associations between smells and emotions.

4. *Theme.* Mrs. Who tells Meg that if she wants to help her father, she will need to stake her life on the truth. Mrs. Whatsit agrees and tells the children that their father is staking his life on the truth. What do Mrs. Who and Mrs. Whatsit mean by their remarks (p. 92)? How does Mrs. Whatsit stake her life in the battle against evil (p. 92)?

5. *Characterization, theme.* Throughout the book, L'Engle develops descriptions and associations around "It." Discuss these associations and meanings:

   p. 72   It is described as a dark thing that blotted out the stars, brought a chill of fear, and is the evil that their father is fighting.

   p. 88   It is described as evil; It is the powers of darkness. It is being fought against throughout the universe. The great people of the earth who have fought against It include Jesus, Leonardo da Vinci, Michelangelo, Madame Curie, Albert Einstein, and Albert Schweitzer. Discuss how these people fought against darkness, and identify other people who fought or are fighting against darkness.

   p. 108   It makes its home in Camazotz, the most oriented city on the planet, the location of the Central Intelligence Center.

   p. 118   The man is frightened about the prospect of being sent to It for reprocessing.

   p. 141   It sometimes calls itself "The Happiest Sadist."

   p. 158   It is a huge brain.

   p. 170   Meg feels iciness because she has gone through the dark thing.

6. *Characterization, plot.* Mrs. Whatsit gives each child a talisman to strengthen the child's greatest ability: For Calvin, it is the ability to communicate with all kinds of people; for Meg, it is her faults; and for Charles Wallace, it is the resilience of his childhood (p. 100). How do the children use these abilities throughout the story in their fight against It and in their endeavors to free Mr. Murry? Which ability is most important? Why?

7. *Characterization, theme, setting.* Why did L'Engle introduce Camazotz by showing the children skipping and bouncing in rhythm, identical houses, and women who opened their doors simultaneously (p. 103)? Why is the woman so frightened about an Aberration? What eventually happened to the Aberration? What is the significance of these actions?

8. *Characterization, theme.* Compare the people living in Camazotz with Meg, Charles Wallace, and Calvin. How do you account for these differences (p. 118)? Could the people living in a city on earth become like the people in Camazotz? Why or why not? Why

does the man at Central Intelligence Center tell the children that life will be easier for them if they don't fight It? What would happen if everyone took the man's suggestion (p. 121)? What are the consequences of allowing someone to accept all the pain, the responsibility, and the burdens of thought and decision? Would this be good or bad? Give a reason for your answer.

9. *Plot.* What is Meg's reason for saying the periodic table of elements when she is standing before It (p. 161)?

10. *Characterization, plot, theme.* What characteristics does Meg have that make her the only one who is able to go back to Camazotz and try to save Charles Wallace from the power of It (p. 195)? What is the only weapon that Meg has that It does not possess (p. 203)? How does Meg use this weapon to free Charles Wallace? Do any people ever use this weapon? Has anyone here ever used this weapon? Is it a weapon for good or for bad?

Artwork

Art activities accompanying *A Wrinkle in Time* can stimulate children's interpretations of setting and characters. Ideally, children can demonstrate their divergent thinking as they interpret the author's descriptions. Following are several suggestions for art interpretations:

1. *Characterization.* Mrs. Whatsit goes through several different transformations in the course of the book. Encourage your students to illustrate these transformations. Suggestions include Mrs. Whatsit's appearance as a plump, tramplike character in her blue and green paisley scarf, red and yellow flowered print, red and black bandanna, sparse grayish hair, rough overcoat, shocking pink stole, and black rubber boots (pp. 16–17). Readers then see her transformed from this comical character into a beautiful winged creature with "wings made of rainbows, of light upon water, of poetry" (p. 64). Readers also discover that Mrs. Whatsit had been a star who gave her life in the battle against It (p. 92).

2. *Setting.* The medium is able to show the children visions through her globe. Ask your students to pretend to be sitting before a magical globe and to draw either the series of visions that the children see or the visions that people would like to see if they could ask the globe to show them anything.

3. *Setting.* Meg, Mr. Murry, and Calvin travel to a planet inhabited by creatures with four arms and five tentacles attached to each hand. The planet also has a different appearance from earth or Uriel. Ask your students to create a shadowbox showing the inhabitants and their planet.

Creative Dramatization

Creative drama allows children to interact with the characters in a story, interpret aspects of plot, and express their reactions to the author's style. Following are several suggestions for creative dramatizations:

1. *Characterization.* Have your students role-play Mrs. Whatsit's first visit to Charles Wallace's home and Meg's and Mrs. Murry's reactions to her.

2. *Setting, style.* Use chapter 4 to create a Reader's Theater presentation for upper-elementary classes. Have your students accompany their oral readings with music that depicts the mood as Meg describes the light disappearing (p. 56); the sensations of moving with the earth (p. 58); leaving the silver glint of autumn behind and arriving in a golden field filled with light, multicolored flowers, singing birds, and an air of peace and joy (pp. 59–61); the transformation of Mrs. Whatsit into a beautiful winged creature with a voice as warm as a woodwind, with the clarity of a trumpet, and the mystery of an English horn; and ascending into the atmosphere to observe the moon and then seeing the dark, ominous shadow that brought a chill of fear—the dark thing that their father was fighting.

3. *Style.* Have your students pantomime the passages on pages 56 and 57, when Meg experiences the black thing, complete with darkness, the feeling of her body's being gone, legs and arms tingling, traveling through space, and reuniting with Charles and Calvin on Uriel.

4. *Theme.* Have your students debate the argument between Meg and It, talking through Charles Wallace, found on page 160. Have them consider the question, and encourage one group to take It's view—like and equal are the same thing; people will be happy if they are alike—while another group argues Meg's point—like and equal are two different things; people cannot be happy if they are the same.

5. *Characterization, plot extension.* Have your students pretend that the story continues and role-play the scene in the kitchen after Mr. Murry, Charles Wallace, Meg, and Calvin return home. What would they say to Mrs. Murry and the two boys? What would Mrs. Murry and the boys say to them?

Many science fiction books encourage creative thinking and imagination. If science fiction can inspire children as it did Carl Sagan, then it can open new universes for other children.

Suggested Activities

 For suggested activities for teaching children with modern fantasy, visit our Companion Website at www.prenhall.com/norton

Children's Literature

 For full descriptions, including plot summaries and award winner notations, of these and other titles for teaching children with modern fantasy, please visit the CD-ROM that accompanies this book.

Aiken, Joan. *The Wolves of Willoughby Chase.* Illustrated by Pat Marriott. Doubleday, 1963 (I:7–10 R:5).

Alexander, Lloyd. *The Arkadians.* Dutton, 1995 (I:10+ R:6).

_____ . *The Beggar Queen.* Dutton, 1984 (I:10+ R:7).

_____ . *The Black Cauldron.* Holt, Rinehart & Winston, 1965 (I:10+ R:7).

_____ . *The Book of Three.* Holt, Rinehart & Winston, 1964 (I:10+ R:5).

_____ . *The Castle of Llyr.* Holt, Rinehart & Winston, 1966 (I:10+ R:5).

_____ . *Gypsy Rizka.* Dutton, 1999 (I:10+ R:5).

_____ . *The High King.* Holt, Rinehart & Winston, 1968 (I:10+ R:5).

_____ . *The Iron Ring.* Dutton, 1997 (I:10+ R:6).

_____ . *The Remarkable Journey of Prince Jen.* Dutton, 1991 (I:10+ R:6).

_____ . *Taran Wanderer.* Holt, Rinehart & Winston, 1967 (I:10+ R:5).

_____ . *Westmark.* Dutton, 1981 (I:10+ R:7).

Almond, David. *Skelling.* Delacorte, 1999 (I:10+ R:6).

Andersen, Hans Christian. *The Emperor's New Clothes.* Retold by Anne Rockwell. Translated by H. W. Dulcken. Illustrated by Anne Rockwell. Harper & Row, 1982 (I:6–9 R:6).

_____ . *The Emperor's New Clothes.* Retold by Riki Levison. Illustrated by Robert Byrd. Dutton, 1991 (I:6–9 R:6).

_____ . *The Emperor's New Clothes.* Illustrated by Dorothee Duntz. North-South Books, 1986 (I:6–9 R:6).

_____ . *The Emperor's New Clothes.* Illustrated by S. T. Mendelson. Stewart, Tabori & Chang, 1992 (I:6–9 R:6).

_____ . *The Emperor's New Clothes.* Illustrated by Janet Stevens. Holiday, 1985 (I:6–9 R:6).

_____ . *Hans Andersen: His Classic Fairy Tales.* Translated by Erik Haugaard. Illustrated by Michael Foreman. Doubleday, 1974 (I:7–10 R:7).

_____ . *The Little Match Girl.* Adapted and illustrated by Jerry Pinkney. Penguin, 1999 (I:6–8).

_____ . *Michael Hague's Favorite Hans Christian Andersen Fairy Tales.* Illustrated by Michael Hague. Holt, Rinehart & Winston, 1981 (I:5–8 R:7).

_____ . *The Nightingale.* Illustrated by Alison Claire Darke. Doubleday, 1989 (I:6–12 R:5).

_____ . *The Nightingale.* Translated by Eva Le Gallienne. Illustrated by Nancy Ekholm Burkert. Harper & Row, 1965 (I:all R:7).

_____ . *The Snow Queen.* Retold by Amy Ehrlich. Illustrated by Susan Jeffers. Dial, 1982 (I:6–9 R:6).

_____ . *The Snow Queen.* Adapted by Naomi Lewis. Illustrated by Errol LeCain. Viking, 1979 (I:6–9 R:6).

_____ . *The Snow Queen.* Adapted by Naomi Lewis. Illustrated by Angela Barrett. Holt, Rinehart & Winston, 1988 (I:6–9 R:6).

_____ . *The Steadfast Tin Soldier.* Illustrated by Thomas DiGrazia. Prentice-Hall, 1981 (I:6–8 R:6).

_____ . *The Steadfast Tin Soldier.* Retold and illustrated by Rachel Isadora. Putnam, 1996 (I:6–10 R:5).

_____ . *The Steadfast Tin Soldier.* Translated by Naomi Lewis. Illustrated by P. J. Lynch. Gulliver, 1992 (I:6–9 R:6).

_____ . *The Steadfast Tin Soldier.* Retold by Tor Seidler. Illustrated by Fred Marcellino. HarperCollins, 1992 (I:6–9 R:6).

_____ . *Thumbelina.* Retold by Amy Ehrlich. Illustrated by Susan Jeffers. Dial, 1979 (I:6–8 R:6).

_____ . *Thumbelina.* Retold by Jane Falloon. Illustrated by Emma Chichester Clark. Simon & Schuster, 1997 (I:6–8 R:6).

_____ . *The Tinderbox.* Adapted and illustrated by Barry Moser. Little, Brown, 1990 (I: 4–9 R:5).

_____ . *The Ugly Duckling.* Retold and illustrated by Lorinda Bryan Cauley. Harcourt Brace Jovanovich, 1979 (I:6–8 R:2).

_____ . *The Ugly Duckling.* Adapted and illustrated by Jerry Pinkney. Morrow, 1999 (I:6–8).

_____ . *The Wild Swans.* Retold by Amy Ehrlich. Illustrated by Susan Jeffers. Dial, 1981 (I:7–12 R:7).

Anderson, Margaret J. *In the Keep of Time.* Knopf, 1977 (I:9+ R:6).

Armstrong, Jennifer. *Wan Hu Is in the Stars.* William Morrow, 1995.

Atwater, Richard, and Florence Atwater. *Mr. Popper's Penguins.* Illustrated by Robert Lawson. Little, Brown, 1938 (I:7–11 R:7).

Aylesworth, Jim. *The Full Belly Bowl.* Illustrated by Wendy Anderson Halperin. Atheneum, 1999 (I:5–8).

Babbit, Natalie. *Tuck Everlasting.* Farrar, Straus & Giroux, 1975 (I:8–12 R:6).

Baker, Keith. *The Magic Fan.* Harcourt Brace Jovanovich, 1989 (I:5–8 R:4).

Barber, Antonia. *The Enchanter's Daughter.* Illustrated by Errol LeCain. Farrar, Straus & Giroux, 1987 (I:6–9 R:5).

Barrie, James. *Peter Pan.* Illustrated by Nora S. Unwin. Scribner, 1911, 1929, 1950 (I:8–10 R:6).

Barron, T. A. *The Fires of Merlin.* Putnam, 1998 (I:10+ R:6).

_____ . *Heartlight.* Philomel, 1990 (I:10+ R:6).

_____ . *The Lost Years of Merlin.* Putnam, 1996 (I:10+ R:6).

_____ . *The Mirror of Merlin.* Putnam, 1999 (I:10+ R:6).

_____ . *The Seven Songs of Merlin.* Putnam, 1997 (I:10+ R:6).

_____ . *The Wings of Merlin.* Philomel, 2000 (I:10+ R:6).

Baum, L. Frank. *The Wizard of Oz.* Illustrated by W. W. Denslow. Reilly, 1956 (I:8–11 R:6).

_____ . *The Wizard of Oz.* Illustrated by Michael Hague. Holt, Rinehart & Winston, 1982 (I:8–11 R:6).

Bellairs, John. *The Spell of the Sorcerer's Skull.* Dial, 1984 (I:8–12 R:4).

Billingsley, Fanny. *The Folkkeeper.* Atheneum, 1999 (I:10+ R:5).

_____ . *Well Wished.* Simon & Schuster, 1997 (I:10+ R:5).

Block, Francesca Lisa. *Missing Angel Juan.* HarperCollins, 1993 (I:12+ R:6).

Bond, Michael. *A Bear Called Paddington.* Illustrated by Peggy Fortnum. Houghton Mifflin, 1960 (I:6–9 R:4).

_____ . *Paddington Abroad.* Illustrated by Peggy Fortnum. Houghton Mifflin, 1972 (I:6–9 R:4).

_____ . *Paddington Helps Out.* Illustrated by Peggy Fortnum. Houghton Mifflin, 1961 (I:6–9 R:4).

_____ . *Paddington Marches On.* Illustrated by Peggy Fortnum. Houghton Mifflin, 1965 (I:6–9 R:4).

Boston, Lucy M. *The Children of Green Knowe.* Illustrated by Peter Boston. Harcourt Brace Jovanovich, 1955 (I:8–12 R:6).

_____ . *An Enemy at Green Knowe.* Illustrated by Peter Boston. Harcourt Brace Jovanovich, 1964 (I:8–12 R:6).

_____ . *The River at Green Knowe.* Illustrated by Peter Boston. Harcourt Brace Jovanovich, 1959 (I:8–12 R:6).

_____ . *A Stranger at Green Knowe.* Illustrated by Peter Boston. Harcourt Brace Jovanovich, 1961 (I:8–12 R:6).

_____ . *The Treasure of Green Knowe.* Illustrated by Peter Boston. Harcourt Brace Jovanovich, 1958 (I:8–12 R:6).

Brittain, Bill. *The Devil's Donkey.* Illustrated by Andrew Glass. Harper & Row, 1981 (I:9–12 R:5).

_____ . *Dr. Dredd's Wagon of Wonders.* Illustrated by Andrew Glass. Harper & Row, 1987 (I:9–12 R:6).

_____ . *The Wish Giver.* Illustrated by Andrew Glass. Harper & Row, 1983 (I:8–12 R:5).

Burton, Virginia Lee. *The Little House.* Houghton Mifflin, 1942 (I:3–7 R:3).

Calmenson, Stephanie. *The Principal's New Clothes.* Illustrated by Denise Brunkus. Scholastic, 1989 (I:6–12 R:6).

Cameron, Eleanor. *The Wonderful Flight to the Mushroom Planet.* Illustrated by Robert Henneberger. Little, Brown, 1954 (I:8–10 R:4).

Carris, Joan. *Aunt Morbelia and the Screaming Skulls.* Illustrated by Doug Cushman. Little, Brown, 1990 (I:8+ R:5).

Carroll, Lewis. *Alice in Wonderland.* Illustrated by Lisbeth Zwerger. North-South, 1999 (I:9+ R:6).

_____ . *Alice's Adventures in Wonderland.* Illustrated by Helen Oxenbury. Candlewick, 1999 (I:8+ R:6).

_____ . *Alice's Adventures in Wonderland.* Illustrated by S. Michelle Wiggins. Ariel/Knopf, 1983 (I:8+ R:6).

_____ . *Alice's Adventures in Wonderland.* Illustrated by Justin Todd. Crown, 1984 (I:8+ R:6).

_____ . *Alice's Adventures in Wonderland.* Illustrated by John Tenniel. Macmillan, 1866; Knopf, 1984 (I:8+ R:6).

_____ . *Alice's Adventures in Wonderland.* Illustrated by John Tenniel. Macmillan, 1865, 1963 (I:all R:6).

_____ . *Alice's Adventures in Wonderland, Through the Looking Glass, and the Hunting of the Snark.* Illustrated by Sir John Tenniel. Chatto, Bodley Head & Jonathan Cape, 1982 (I:all R:6).

_____ . *The Nursery "Alice."* Illustrated by John Tenniel. Macmillan, 1890, 1979 (I:6–10 R:5).

_____ . *Through the Looking-Glass, and What Alice Found There.* Illustrated by John Tenniel. Macmillan, 1872; Knopf, 1984 (I:8+ R:6).

Christopher, John. *The City of Gold and Lead.* Macmillan, 1967 (I:10+ R:6).

_____ . *The Pool of Fire.* Macmillan, 1968 (I:10+ R:6).

_____ . *The White Mountains.* Macmillan, 1967 (I:10+ R:6).

Clark, Margaret. *A Treasury of Dragon Stories.* Kingfisher, 1997. (I:8+).

Cleary, Beverly. *The Mouse and the Motorcycle.* Illustrated by Louis Darling. Morrow, 1965 (I:7–11 R:3).

_____ . *Ralph S. Mouse.* Illustrated by Paul O. Zelinsky. Morrow, 1982 (I:7–11 R:3).

_____ . *Runaway Ralph.* Illustrated by Louis Darling. Morrow, 1970 (I:7–11 R:3).

Collodi, Carlo. *The Adventures of Pinocchio.* Illustrated by Naiad Einsel. Macmillan, 1892, 1963 (I:7–12 R:7).

_____ . *The Adventures of Pinocchio.* Retold by Neil Morris. Illustrated by Frank Baber. Rand McNally, 1982 (I:7–12 R:7).

_____ . *The Adventures of Pinocchio.* Illustrated by Roberto Innocenti. Knopf, 1988 (I:4–12 R:7).

_____ . *The Adventures of Pinocchio: Tale of a Puppet.* Translated by M. L. Rosenthal. Illustrated by Troy Howell. Lothrop, Lee & Shepard, 1983 (I:9+ R:7).

Conly, Jane Leslie. *Racso and the Rats of NIMH.* Harper & Row, 1986 (I:8–12 R:5).

Conrad, Pam. *Stonewords: A Ghost Story.* HarperCollins, 1990 (I:10+ R:6).

_____ . *Zoe Rising.* HarperCollins, 1996 (I:10+ R:6).

Cooper, Susan. *The Boggart.* Macmillan, 1993 (I:10+ R:5).

_____ . *The Boggart and the Monster.* Simon & Schuster, 1997 (I:10+ R:5).

_____ . *The Dark Is Rising.* Illustrated by Alan E. Cober. Atheneum, 1973 (I:10+ R:8).

_____ . *Greenwitch.* Atheneum, 1974 (I:10+ R:8).

_____ . *The Grey King.* Atheneum, 1975 (I:10+ R:8).

_____ . *King of Shadows.* Simon & Schuster, 1999 (I:10+ R:6).

_____ . *Over Sea, Under Stone.* Illustrated by Margery Gill. Harcourt Brace Jovanovich, 1965 (I:10+ R:8).

_____ . *Seaward.* Atheneum, 1983 (I:10+ R:5).

_____ . *Silver on the Tree.* Atheneum, 1977, 1980 (I:10+ R:8).

Crossley-Holland, Kevin. *Arthur: The Seeing Stone.* Orion, 2000 (I:8+ R:5).

Dahl, Roald. *James and the Giant Peach.* Illustrated by Nancy Ekholm Burkert. Knopf, 1961 (I:7–11 R:7).

Darling, Christina. *Mirror.* Illustrated by Alexandra Day. Farrar, Straus & Giroux, 1997 (I:5–9 R:4).

DeFelice, Cynthia. *The Ghost of Fossil Glen.* Farrar, Straus & Giroux, 1998 (I:10+ R:5).

Dengler, Marianna. *The Worry Stone.* Illustrated by Sibyl Graber Gerig. Northland, 1996 (I:8+ R:5).

Dickinson, Peter. *Eva.* Delacorte, 1989 (I:10+ R:6).

_____ . *The Lion Tamer's Daughter: And Other Stories.* Delacorte, 1997 (I:10+ R:5).

Doyle, Arthur Conan. *The Lost World.* Random House, 1959 (I:10+ R:7).

Farmer, Nancy. *The Ear, the Eye and the Arm.* Orchard, 1994 (I:12+ R:6).

Fleischman, Paul. *Graven Images.* Illustrated by Andrew Glass. Harper & Row, 1982 (I:10+ R:6).

Fleischman, Sid. *The Midnight Horse.* Illustrated by Peter Sís. Greenwillow, 1990 (I:8–12 R:5).

Fleming, Ian. *Chitty Chitty Bang Bang.* Illustrated by John Burningham. Random House, 1964 (I:7–11 R:6).

Garner, Alan. *Elidor.* Walck, 1967 (I:10+ R:7).

_____ . *The Owl Service.* Walck, 1968 (I:10+ R:5).

_____ . *The Weirdstone of Brisingamen.* Walck, 1969 (I:10+ R:5).

Gerstein, Mordicai. *The Mountains of Tibet.* Harper & Row, 1987 (I:6–8 R:4).

Godden, Rumer. *The Dolls' House.* Illustrated by Tasha Tudor. Viking, 1947, 1962 (I:6–10 R:2).

Grahame, Kenneth. *The Wind in the Willows.* Illustrated by E. H. Shepard. Scribner, 1908, 1940 (I:7–12 R:7).

Griffin, Peni R. *A Dig in Time.* Macmillan, 1991 (I:8+ R:5).

_____ . *Switching Well.* Macmillan, 1993 (I:10+ R:6).

Hahn, Mary Downing. *Wait till Helen Comes.* Clarion, 1986 (I:8–12 R:5).

Hamilton, Virginia. *Dustland.* Greenwillow, 1980 (I:10+ R:7).

_____ . *The Gathering.* Greenwillow, 1981 (I:10+ R:7).

_____ . *Justice and Her Brothers.* Greenwillow, 1978 (I:10+ R:7).

_____ . *The Magical Adventures of Pretty Pearl.* Harper & Row, 1983 (I:10+ R:5).

Howe, James. *The Celery Stalks at Midnight.* Illustrated by Leslie Morrill. Atheneum, 1983 (I:8–10 R:5).

Hughes, Carol. *Toots and the Upside-Down House.* Illustrated by Garrett Sheldrewnson and Anthony Stacchi. Random, 1997 (I:8+ R:5).

Hughes, Monica. *Invitation to the Game.* Simon & Schuster, 1991 (I:10+ R:7).

Hunter, Mollie. *The Mermaid Summer.* Harper, 1988 (I:10+ R:6).

_____ . *The Wicked One.* Harper & Row, 1977 (I:10+ R:7).

Hurmence, Belinda. *A Girl Called Boy.* Houghton Mifflin. 1982 (I:10+ R:6).

Jacques, Brian. *Mariel of Redwall.* Philomel, 1991 (I:10+ R:7).

_____ . *Martin the Warrior.* Illustrated by Gary Chalk. Philomel, 1994 (I:10+ R:7).

_____ . *Mattimeo.* Putnam, 1990 (I:10+ R:7).

_____ . *Mossflower.* Putnam, 1988 (I:10+ R:7).

_____ . *Pearls of Leitra.* Philomel, 1997 (I:10+ R:7).

_____ . *Redwall.* Philomel, 1986 (I:10+ R:7).

_____ . *Seven Strange & Ghostly Tales.* Putnam, 1991 (I:8+ R:6).

_____ . *The Legend of Luke: A Tale from Redwall.* Philomel, 2000 (I:10+ R:7).

James, Mary. *Shoebag.* Scholastic, 1990 (I:8+ R:4).

Jennings, Patrick. *Faith and the Electric Dogs.* Scholastic, 1996 (I:8–12 R:5).

Juster, Norton. *The Phantom Tollbooth.* Illustrated by Jules Feiffer. Random House, 1961 (I:9+ R:8).

Kendall, Carol. *The Gammage Cup.* Illustrated by Erik Blegvad. Harcourt Brace Jovanovich, 1959 (I:8–12 R:4).

Key, Alexander. *The Forgotten Door.* Westminster, 1965 (I:8–12 R:6).

Kimmel, Eric A. *Hershel and the Hanukkah Goblins.* Illustrated by Trina Schart Hyman. Holiday, 1989 (I:all).

King-Smith, Dick. *Martin's Mice.* Illustrated by Jez Alborough. Crown, 1989 (I:8–12 R:6).

_____ . *Pigs Might Fly.* Illustrated by Mary Rayner. Viking, 1982 (I:9–12 R:6).

Kipling, Rudyard. *The Elephant's Child.* Illustrated by Lorinda Bryan Cauley. Harcourt Brace Jovanovich, 1983 (I:5–7 R:7).

_____ . *The Jungle Book.* Doubleday, 1894, 1964 (I:8–12 R:7).

_____ . *Just So Stories.* Doubleday, 1902, 1907, 1952 (I:5–7 R:5).

_____ . *Just So Stories.* Illustrated by Victor G. Ambrus. Rand McNally, 1982 (I:5–7 R:5).

Klause, Annette Curtis. *Alien Secrets.* Delacorte, 1993 (I:12+ R:6).

_____ . *Silver Kiss.* Delacorte, 1990 (I:12+ R:6).

Lawrence, Louise. *Dream-Weaver.* Clarion, 1996 (I:12+ R:7).

Lawson, Robert. *Ben and Me.* Little, Brown, 1939 (I:7–11 R:6).

_____ . *Rabbit Hill.* Viking, 1944 (I:7–11 R:7).

Leaf, Munro. *The Story of Ferdinand.* Illustrated by Robert Lawson. Viking, 1936 (I:4–10 R:6).

LeGuin, Ursula K. *Catwings.* Illustrated by S. D. Schindler. Watts, 1988 (I:3–8 R:4).

_____ . *Catwings Return.* Illustrated by S. D. Schindler. Watts, 1989 (I:3–8 R:4).

_____ . *The Farthest Shore.* Illustrated by Gail Garraty. Atheneum, 1972 (I:10+ R:6).

_____ . *A Ride on the Red Mare's Back.* Illustrated by Julie Downing. Orchard, 1992 (I:6–10 R:5).

_____ . *Tehanu: The Last Book of Earthsea.* Atheneum, 1990 (I:10+ R:6).

_____ . *A Wizard of Earthsea.* Illustrated by Ruth Robbins. Parnassus, 1968 (I:10+ R:6).

L'Engle, Madeleine. *A Swiftly Tilting Planet.* Farrar, Straus & Giroux, 1978 (I:10+ R:7).

_____ . *A Wind in the Door.* Farrar, Straus & Giroux, 1973 (I:10+ R:7).

_____ . *A Wrinkle in Time.* Farrar, Straus & Giroux, 1962 (I:10+ R:5).

Levine, Gail Carson. *Ella Enchanted.* HarperCollins, 1997 (I:8+ R:5).

Lewis, C. S. *The Last Battle.* Illustrated by Pauline Baynes. Macmillan, 1956. (I:9+ R:7).

_____ . *The Lion, the Witch and the Wardrobe.* Illustrated by Pauline Baynes. Macmillan, 1950 (I:9+ R:7).

_____ . *The Magician's Nephew.* Illustrated by Pauline Baynes. Macmillan, 1955 (I:9+ R:7).

_____ . *Prince Caspian, the Return to Narnia.* Illustrated by Pauline Baynes. Macmillan, 1951 (I:9+ R:7).

_____ . *The Silver Chair.* Illustrated by Pauline Baynes. Macmillan, 1953 (I:9+ R:7).

_____ . *The Voyage of the Dawn Treader.* Illustrated by Pauline Baynes. Macmillan, 1952 (I:9+ R:7).

Lewis, Naomi, trans. *Proud Knight, Fair Lady: The Twelve Lais of Marie de France.* Viking/Kestrel, 1989 (I:10+ R:6).

Lindgren, Astrid. *Pippi Longstocking.* Illustrated by Louis S. Glanzman. Viking, 1950 (I:7–11 R:5).

_____ . *Pippi in the South Seas.* Illustrated by Louis S. Glanzman. Viking, 1959 (I:7–11 R:5).

Lionni, Leo. *Swimmy.* Pantheon, 1963 (I:2–6 R:3).

Lowry, Lois. *The Giver.* Houghton Mifflin, 1993 (I:10+ R:5).

Lunn, Janet. *The Root Cellar.* Scribner, 1983 (I:10+ R:4).

McCaffrey, Anne. *Dragonquest.* Ballantine, 1981 (I:10+ R:6).

_____ . *Dragonsinger.* Atheneum, 1977 (I:10+ R:6).

_____ . *Dragonsong.* Atheneum, 1976 (I:10+ R:6).

MacDonald, George. *At the Back of the North Wind.* Illustrated by Arthur Hughes. Dutton, 1871, 1966 (I:10+ R:6).

_____ . *The Princess and the Goblin.* Illustrated by Nora S. Unwin. Macmillan, 1872, 1951 (I:10+ R:9).

McGraw, Eloise. *The Moorchild.* Simon & Schuster, 1996 (I:10+ R:5).

McKinley, Robin. *The Blue Sword.* Greenwillow, 1982 (I:10+ R:7).

_____ . *The Hero and the Crown.* Greenwillow, 1984 (I:10+ R:7).

_____ . *Spindle's End*. Putnam, 2000 (I:10+ R:6).

Mahy, Margaret. *The Changeover*. Atheneum, 1984 (I:10+ R:7).

_____ . *The Five Sisters*. Illustrated by Patricia MacCarthy. Viking, 1997 (I:7–9 R:5).

McCaffrey, Ann. *Dragonriders of Pern*. Ballentine, 1988 (I:10+ R:6).

Mills, Lauren. *Fairy Wings*. Illustrated by Dennis Nolan. Little, Brown, 1995 (I:7–9 R:4).

Milne, A. A. *The House at Pooh Corner*. Illustrated by Ernest H. Shepard. Dutton, 1928, 1956 (I:6–10 R:3).

_____ . *Winnie-the-Pooh*. Illustrated by Ernest H. Shepard. Dutton, 1926, 1954 (I:6–10 R:5).

Morris, Gerald. *The Savage Damsel and the Dwarf*. Houghton Mifflin, 2000 (I:10+ R:6).

_____ . *The Squire, His Knight, and His Lady*. Houghton Mifflin, 1999 (I:10+ R:6).

_____ . *The Squire's Tale*. Houghton Mifflin, 1998 (I:10+ R:6).

Myers, Walter Dean. *The Story of Three Kingdoms*. Illustrated by Ashley Bryan. HarperCollins, 1995 (I:7+ R:5).

Nix, Garth. *Sabriel*. HarperCollins, 1996 (I:12+ R:7).

Nixon, Joan Lowery. *Whispers from the Dead*. Delacorte, 1989 (I:10+ R:6).

Norton, Mary. *Bed-Knob and Broomstick*. Illustrated by Erik Blegvad. Harcourt Brace Jovanovich, 1943, 1971 (I:7–11 R:6).

_____ . *The Borrowers*. Illustrated by Beth and Joe Krush. Harcourt Brace Jovanovich, 1952, 1953 (I:7–11 R:3).

_____ . *The Borrowers Afield*. Illustrated by Beth and Joe Krush. Harcourt Brace Jovanovich, 1955 (I:7–11 R:4).

_____ . *The Borrowers Afloat*. Harcourt Brace Jovanovich, 1959 (I:7–11 R:4).

_____ . *The Borrowers Aloft*. Harcourt Brace Jovanovich, 1961 (I:7–11 R:4).

_____ . *The Borrowers Avenged*. Illustrated by Beth and Joe Krush. Harcourt Brace Jovanovich, 1982 (I:7–11 R:4).

O'Brien, Robert C. *Mrs. Frisby and the Rats of NIMH*. Illustrated by Zena Berstein. Atheneum, 1971 (I:8–12 R:4).

Oppenheim, Shulamith Levy. *The Hundredth Name*. Illustrated by Michael Hays. Boyd Mills, 1995 (I:4–8 R:5).

O'Shea, Pat. *The Hounds of the Morrigan*. Holiday House, 1986 (I:10+ R:6).

Park, Ruth. *Playing Beatie Bow*. Atheneum, 1982 (I:10+ R:6).

Pearson, Kit. *Awake and Dreaming*. Viking, 1997 (I:8+ R:5).

Philbrick, Rodman. *The Last Book in the Universe*. Scholastic, 2000 (I:9–12 R:6).

Pierce, Mamora. *Circle of Magic*. Brior's, 1999 (I:10+ R:6).

Potter, Beatrix. *The Tailor of Gloucester, from the Original Manuscript*. Warne, 1969, 1978 (I:5–9 R:8).

_____ . *The Tale of Peter Rabbit*. Warne, 1902.

_____ . *The Tale of Squirrel Nutkin*. Warne, 1903 (I:3–9 R:6).

_____ . *Tales of Peter Rabbit and His Friends*. Chatham, 1964 (I:3–9 R:6).

_____ . *A Treasury of Peter Rabbit and Other Stories*. Avenel, 1979 (I:3–7 R:6).

Price, Susan. *The Sterkarm Handshake*. Scholastic, 1998 (I:12+ R:7).

Pullman, Philip. *The Amber Spyglass*. Knopf, 2000 (I:10+ R:7).

_____ . *The Golden Compass*. Knopf, 1995 (I:10+ R:7).

_____ . *I Was a Rat!* Illustrated by Kevin Hawkes. Knopf, 2000 (I:8+ R:4).

_____ . *The Subtle Knife*. Knopf, 1997 (I:10+ R:6).

Rodgers, Mary. *Summer Switch*. Harper & Row, 1982 (I:8–12 R:6).

Rodowsky, Colby F. *The Gathering Room*. Farrar, Straus & Giroux, 1981 (I:10+ R:7).

Rowling, J. K. *Harry Potter and the Chamber of Secrets*. Scholastic, 1999 (I:all).

_____ . *Harry Potter and the Goblet of Fire*. Scholastic, 2000 (I:all).

_____ . *Harry Potter and the Prisoner of Azkaban*. Scholastic, 1999 (I:all).

_____ . *Harry Potter and the Sorcerer's Stone*. Scholastic, 1998 (I:all).

Sandburg, Carl. *The Huckabuck Family and How They Raised Popcorn in Nebraska and Quit and Came Back*. Illustrated by David Small. Farrar, Straus & Giroux, 1999 (I:6–8).

_____ . *More Rootabagas*. Illustrated by Paul O. Zelinsky. Knopf, 1993 (I:8–11 R:7).

_____ . *Rootabaga Stories*. Illustrated by Maud and Miska Petersham. Harcourt Brace Jovanovich, 1922, 1950 (I:8–11 R:7).

_____ . *Rootabaga Stories*. Illustrated by Michael Hague. Harcourt Brace Jovanovich, 1922, 1988 (I:8–11 R:7).

Seabrooke, Brenda. *The Care and Feeding of Dragons*. Illustrated by Mark Robertson. Dutton, 1998 (I:9+).

Selden, George. *Chester Cricket's Pigeon Ride*. Illustrated by Garth Williams. Farrar, Straus & Giroux, 1981 (I:6–9 R:4).

_____ . *The Cricket in Times Square*. Illustrated by Garth Williams. Farrar, Straus & Giroux, 1960 (I:7–11 R:3).

_____ . *Harry Cat's Pet Puppy*. Farrar, Straus & Giroux, 1975 (I:7–11 R:3).

_____ . *Tucker's Countryside*. Farrar, Straus & Giroux, 1969 (I:7–11 R:3).

Sherman, Josepha. *Child of Faerie, Child of Earth*. Illustrated by Rick Farley. Walter, 1992 (I:10+ R:5).

Shusterman, Neal. *The Dark Side of Nowhere*. Little, Brown, 1997 (I:12+ R:6).

Silverberg, Robert. *Letters from Atlantis*. Illustrated by Robert Gould. Atheneum, 1990 (I:10+ R:6).

Sleator, William. *Interstellar Pig*. Dutton, 1984 (I:10 R:8).

Smith, Sherwood. *Wren's Quest*. Harcourt Brace Jovanovich, 1993 (I:10+ R:6).

Springer, Nancy. *I Am Morgan LeFay: A Tale from Camelot*. Philomel, 2001 (I:12+ R:6).

Steig, William. *The Amazing Bone*. Farrar, Straus & Giroux, 1976 (I:6–9 R:3).

Stevermer, Caroline. *River Rats*. Harcourt Brace Jovanovich, 1992 (I:10+ R:6).

Sutcliff, Rosemary. *The Light Beyond the Forest: The Quest for the Holy Grail*. Penguin, 1980 (I:10+ R:7).

_____ . *The Road to Camlann: The Death of King Arthur*. Penguin, 1982 (I:10+ R:7).

_____ . *The Sword and the Circle: King Arthur and the Knights of the Round Table*. Penguin, 1981 (I:10+ R:7).

Thurber, James. *Many Moons*. Illustrated by Marc Simont. Harcourt Brace Jovanovich, 1990. Thurber's original copyright, 1943 (I:6–9 R:4).

Tolkien, J. R. R. *Farmer Giles of Ham.* Illustrated by Pauline Baynes. Houghton Mifflin, 1978 (I:7–10 R:6).

———. *The Fellowship of the Ring.* Houghton Mifflin, 1967 (I:12+ R:8).

———. *The Hobbit.* Houghton Mifflin, 1938 (I:9–12 R:6).

———. *The Lord of the Rings.* Houghton Mifflin, 1974 (I:12+ R:8).

———. *The Return of the King.* Houghton Mifflin, 1967 (I:12+ R:8).

———. *The Two Towers.* Houghton Mifflin 1965 (I:12+ R:8).

Travers, Pamela L. *Mary Poppins.* Illustrated by Mary Shepard. Harcourt Brace Jovanovich, 1934, 1962 (I:7–11 R:7).

Turner, Megan Whalen. *The Thief.* Greenwillow, 1996 (I:10+ R:6).

Van Allsburg, Chris. *The Wreck of the Zephyr.* Houghton Mifflin, 1983 (I:5–8 R:6).

Vande Velde, Vivian. *Curses, Inc.: And Other Stories.* Harcourt Brace, 1997 (I:10+ R:6).

———. *Never Trust a Dead Man.* Harcourt Brace, 1999 (I:10+ R:6).

Voigt, Cynthia. *Building Blocks.* Atheneum, 1984 (I:9 R:7).

Westall, Robert. *Ghost Abbey.* Scholastic, 1989 (I:10+ R:6).

White, E. B. *Charlotte's Web.* Illustrated by Garth Williams. Harper & Row, 1952 (I:7–11 R:3).

———. *Stuart Little.* Illustrated by Garth Williams. Harper & Row, 1945 (I:7–11 R:6).

Whitmore, Arvella. *Trapped Between the Lash and the Gun.* Dial, 1999 (I:10+ R:6).

Wiesner, David. *Free Fall.* Lothrop, Lee & Shepard, 1988 (I:all).

Williams, Margery. *The Velveteen Rabbit.* Illustrated by Allen Atkinson. Knopf, 1984 (I:6–9 R:5).

———. *The Velveteen Rabbit.* Illustrated by Michael Hague. Holt, Rinehart & Winston, 1983 (I:6–9 R:5).

———. *The Velveteen Rabbit.* Illustrated by Ilse Plume. Godine, 1982 (I:6–9 R:5).

———. *The Velveteen Rabbit: Or, How Toys Become Real.* Illustrated by Michael Green. Running Press, 1982 (I:6–9 R:5).

———. *The Velveteen Rabbit: Or How Toys Become Real.* Illustrated by William Nicholson. Doubleday, 1958 (I:6–9 R:5).

Windsor, Patricia. *The Blooding.* Scholastic, 1996 (I:12+ R:7).

Wolff, Ferida. *Seven Loaves of Bread.* Illustrated by Katie Keller. Tambourine, 1993 (I:4–8 R:4).

Wright, Betty Ren. *The Ghosts of Mercy Manor.* Scholastic, 1993 (I:10+ R:6).

Wrightson, Patricia. *A Little Fear.* Hutchinson, 1983 (I:9 R:6).

———. *Balyet.* McElderry, 1989 (I:10+ R:6).

Yolen, Jane. *The Devil's Arithmetic.* Viking/Kestrel, 1988 (I:8+ R:5).

———. *Dragon's Blood.* Delacorte, 1982 (I:10+ R:5).

———. *The Girl Who Loved the Wind.* Illustrated by Ed Young. Crowell, 1972 (I:7–10 R:6).

———. *Here There Be Witches.* Illustrated by David Wilgus. Harcourt Brace, 1995 (I:8+).

———. *Hobby.* Harcourt Brace, 1996 (I:10+ R:5).

———. *Merlin.* Harcourt Brace, 1997 (I:10+ R:5).

———. *Passager.* Harcourt Brace, 1995 (I:10+ R:5).

The Best-Loved Poems of

JACQUELINE KENNEDY ONASSIS

SELECTED AND INTRODUCED BY

CAROLINE KENNEDY

According to Eve Merriam (1976), poetry is "Rainbow Writing" because it colors the human mind with the vast spectrum of human experience:

> *Rainbow Writing*
>
> Nasturtiums with
> their orange cries
> flare like trumpets;
> their music dies.
> Golden harps
> of butterflies;
> the strings are mute
> in autumn skies.
> Vermillion chords,
> then silent gray;
> the last notes of
> the song of day.
> Rainbow colors
> fade from sight,
> come back to me
> when I write.
>
> Eve Merriam
> *Rainbow Writing,* p. 3

As a rainbow inspires an awe of nature, so may a poem inspire an awe for words and the expression of feelings. Poetry often has a musical quality that attracts children and appeals to their emotions. The poet's choice of words can suggest new images and create delightful word plays.

Many poems allow children to see or feel with fresh insights. The first section of this chapter discusses the values of poetry, the characteristics of poems that children prefer, criteria for selecting poetry, elements of poetry, and forms of poetry. It concludes with a discussion of children's poem classifications and poets.

The Values of Poetry for Children

Children can share feelings, experiences, and visions with poets. Poetry also brings new understandings of the world. It encourages children to play with words and to realize some of the images possible when words are chosen carefully. Through poetry, children may discover the power of words, a power that poets can release. Kathy A. Perfect (1999) states this value:

Poetry appeals to the near universal fondness children have for rhyme and rhythm. It nurtures a love and appreciation for the sound and power of language. Poetry can help us see differently, understand ourselves and others, and validate our human experience. It is a genre especially suited to the struggling or unmotivated reader. Poetry easily finds a home in all areas of the curriculum, enhances thinking skills, and promotes personal connections to content area subjects. Such attributes deserve a closer look. (p. 728)

When we read why authors are attracted to poetry we discover many of the values of poetry. For example, poet Brian Moses (1999) states:

Because I'm attracted so much to music and the rhythms of music, I'm attracted to the rhythms of poetry and language. I love words and how poetry allows you to string words together in a variety of ways. For me, a poem is a snapshot giving you a brief glimpse, but a glimpse that is often so powerful that it can stay with you forever. It enables you to look at the world in a different way. Writing poetry is something I'll always do. (p. 6)

In *Crosscurrents,* the program for the Aspen Music Festival and School, Jane Vial Jaffe (2001) highlights the connections between music and literature, "especially when it comes to poetry; literally thousands of songs bear the shape of verse" (p. 3). She then discusses the impact of literature on various composers such as Leonard Bernstein and Claude Debussy. Debussy was attracted to the poetry of Pierre Louÿs written in 1895. In 1900 and 1901, Debussy staged a reading of the poetry that was accompanied by his newly written compositions. Music may be used today to provide backgrounds for poetry readings.

The connections between poetry and art are shown in Jan Greenberg's *Heart to Heart: New Poems Inspired by Twentieth-Century American Art.* Each of the poems in the collection is paired with the painting that inspired it.

Poet Lilian Moore (1988) describes the power of words when she relates her reactions to the poetry of Valerie Worth. She states that she "felt a delicious shock, a pleasure at the clarity with which real things were seen" (p. 470). She continues to compare reading poetry to taking a field trip with binoculars that allow readers to look in new ways at the details of the world, at the bugs, the earthworms, and the dandelions. Moore (1993) also reveals, "The response to what is genuine in a poem is a kind of happiness" (p. 303). Poet Valerie Worth (1992) describes the impact of poetry for her when she states that poetry has such power that it can "reveal, extol, and even preserve the many beauties of the world" (p. 568).

Rumer Godden (1988) equates giving a child a love of poetry to giving a child the ability to enjoy life. She states:

To give a child a love of poetry is like instilling a spring or fountain of perpetual private refreshment—and not only refreshment; a love and understanding of poetry brings a perception, a sort of sixth sense that makes its possessor quick to life—quick in the sense of being very much alive—quick to the world around him; it rescues him from dullness, gives him a sense of form, a mental discipline, and because it is limitless it will grow as he grows. (p. 306)

Poet Charles Causley (Merrick, 1988) emphasizes the illuminating quality of poetry. He believes that one of the values of poetry is that a poem may suggest something different each time it is read. The ultimate value of poetry is cited by David McCullough in his biography of *John Adams* (2001). McCullough describes Adams's love of literature and that he was likely to carry a volume of English poetry with him on journeys because Adams felt that " 'You will never be alone with a poet in your pocket' " (p. 19).

As we can see, there are numerous values for sharing poetry. A brief summary of these values includes these: First, poetry provides enjoyment. Young children begin to discover the enjoyment in poetry by hearing and sharing nonsense poems, Mother Goose rhymes, and tongue twisters. They grow into poetry through story poems, such as those written by A. A. Milne, and they gradually discover the many exciting forms available to poets. Second, poetry provides children with knowledge about concepts in the world around them: size, numbers, colors, and time. Third, because precise and varied words play such important roles in poetic expression, poetry encourages children to appreciate language and to expand their vocabularies. Horses not only run, they clop; kittens jump, but they also pounce; and the moon may be not only bright but also a silver sickle. Fourth, poetry helps children identify with people and situations. With Robert Louis Stevenson, they go up in a swing; with Robert Frost, they share a snowy evening in the woods; and with Mike Makley, they are "The New Kid" on the baseball team who plays just as well as Dutch, PeeWee, or Earl, even though she is a girl. Fifth, poetry expresses moods familiar to children and helps children understand and accept their feelings. Other children empathize with the child in Charlotte Zolotow's "Nobody Loves Me." Sometimes, it seems as if nobody loves the speaker, and sometimes it seems as if everybody loves him—feelings common to all children. Finally, poetry grants children insights into themselves and others, developing their sensitivity to universal needs and feelings. Through poems written by other children, as well as by adults, children discover that others have feelings similar to their own.

What Poetry Is

What is this literary form that increases enjoyment, develops appreciation for language, and helps children gain insights about themselves? Poetry is not easily defined nor is it easily measured or classified. There is no single accepted definition of poetry. Some definitions specify the characteristics of poetry, including the poetic elements and the functions of words, while other definitions emphasize the emotional impact of poetry. Try to develop your own definition of poetry as you read the following definitions by poets, critics, and children. Author Rumer Godden (1988) states, "True poetry, even in its smallest shape, should have form, meter, rhythm bound into a whole with words that so match and express its subject they seem inevitable" (p. 310).

Critic Patrick Groff (1969) maintains that poetry for children is writing that, in addition to using the mechanics of poetry, transcends literal meaning. He explains:

The use of original combinations of words is probably the easiest, the best, and the most obvious way to write poetry that transcends the literal and goes beyond a complete or obvious meaning. Consequently, in poetry a word has much more meaning than a word in prose. In the former the emphasis is connotative rather than denotative. Words possess suggested significance apart from their explicit and recognized meanings. It is the guessing element that requires the reader to go below the surface of words, to plumb their literal meanings. Figurative language most often provides the guessing element. (p. 185)

Emotional and physical reactions defined poetry for poet Emily Dickinson, who related poetry to a feeling: If she read a book that made "her body so cold no fire could warm" her, she knew it was poetry; if she felt physically as if the top of her head were taken off, she also knew it was poetry. Michael Bedard's *Emily* (1992) is a picture storybook in which a father gives his daughter a similar definition for poetry:

Listen to Mother play. She practices and practices a piece, and sometimes a magic happens and it seems the music starts to breathe. It sends a shiver through you. You can't explain it, really; it's a mystery. Well, when words do that, we call it poetry. (p. 12, unnumbered)

Poet Valerie Worth (1992) also talks about the power and magic of poetry and the need to select the right words, "the right verbs, the right adjectives, or the precious image would fade away and be gone—and the magic as well" (p. 569). Judson Jerome (1968) contends that poetry is words performed. He stresses that meaning cannot be separated from the sounds of words. Just as visual shape is important to sculptors or painters, tonal shape is important to poets. Jerome compares the work of poets to the composition of musicians; in both forms, tonal quality is essential.

Lee Bennett Hopkins's (1987) interviews with poets in *Pass the Poetry, Please!* include numerous and varied definitions of poetry. Poets express such phrases as "music of words," "celebration of life," and "revelation of feelings." Poet David McCord (1977) provides definitions such as the shiver down the spine, the translation of words that do not exist, the dripping of hot coffee from an icicle, and a calculus of the imagination.

Teacher Anne Clark (1992) identifies poetry as one of the purest literary art forms, in which "Capturing a moment, a glimpse, a sensation in a handful of words was magic to me" (p. 624).

Author Margaret Mahy presents a definition of poetry in her short story "The Cat Who Became a Poet," found in *Nonstop Nonsense.* After the cat cannot stop himself from speaking in poetic form, he thinks, "I became a poet through eating the mouse. Perhaps the mouse became a poet through eating seeds. Perhaps all this poetry stuff is just the world's way of talking about itself" (p. 19). Following the cat's rendition of a poem that tricks a dog, the cat concludes, "If only he knew. I wasn't meaning to praise him. Poetry is very tricky stuff and can be taken two ways" (p. 19).

John Drury (1995) emphasizes that "the writers of children's poems will usually simplify the language and ideas and highlight the rhythms and sound effects . . . . William Blake's *Songs of Innocence and Experience,* while symbolic and profound, are at the same time simple and musical and full of what might be called primary images" (p. 58).

Overall, the various definitions of poetry highlight the importance of an original combination of words, distinctive sound, and emotional impact. Visual elements are also significant in poetry. Some poems are like paintings; they must be seen to be appreciated. Poets may use shape and space to increase the impact of their words. They may group lines into stanzas, use open spaces to emphasize words, capitalize important words, or arrange a whole poem to suggest the subject matter.

The essential elements of poetry must be savored to be enjoyed. Like painting or sculpture, poetry cannot be experienced rapidly. It must be read slowly, even reread several times to immerse its readers or listeners in its sounds and imagery. In other words, children must have time to see, hear, and feel the world of poets.

Characteristics of Poems That Children Prefer

Consider children's individual interests when choosing poetry for them. When children honestly judge what speaks to their imaginations, their judgments must be respected. Even though children's interests and experiences vary widely, research into children's poetry choices contains valuable information. Several researchers have identified poems that children generally enjoy and have analyzed the subjects and elements in these poems. As you read the results of these studies that were conducted over different time periods, try to decide if the results would be similar or different if conducted today.

Carol Fisher and Margaret Natarella (1982) examined poetry preferences in the first through the third grades. They found that the children preferred narrative poems and limericks, poems about strange and fantastic events, traditional poems, and poems that rhymed or used alliteration and onomatopoeia to create sound patterns.

Karen Sue Kutiper (1985) surveyed preferences of students in the seventh, eighth, and ninth grades. She concluded that these students prefer rhyme, humorous narrative, and content based on familiar experiences.

Ann Terry (1974) investigated the poetry preferences of children in the fourth, fifth, and sixth grades. She also analyzed poetic elements in the poems that the children preferred. She concluded the following:

1. Children's enthusiasm for poetry declines as children advance in the elementary grades.

2. Children respond more favorably to contemporary poems than to traditional ones.

3. Children prefer poems dealing with familiar and enjoyable experiences.

4. Children enjoy poems that tell a story or have a strong element of humor.

5. Children prefer poems that feature rhythm and rhyme.

6. Among the least popular poems are those that rely too heavily on complex imagery or subtly implied emotion.

7. The majority of teachers in the fourth, fifth, and sixth grades pay little attention to poetry, seldom read it to children, and do not encourage them to write their own poems.

When Terry analyzed the forms of poetry that the children preferred or disliked, she found that narrative poems and limericks were among the most preferred, while haiku and free verse were among the least popular. The most popular poems were humorous, even nonsensical, about familiar experiences or animals. As stated, in a study based on Terry's earlier research, Carol Fisher and Margaret Natarella (1982) reported that children prefer rhythm, rhyme, alliteration, and onomatopoeia.

Terry stresses that adults should provide children with many experiences with poetry and should include a wide range of poetry. Terry also recommends that books of poetry be made accessible to children, that listening centers include tapes and records of poetry, and that a rich poetry environment be used to stimulate children to write their own poetry.

One reason for the narrow range of poems that children enjoy may be that adults infrequently share poetry with children. The enjoyment of poetry, like the enjoyment of other types of literature, can be increased by an enthusiastic adult who reads poetry to children. Because Terry's research indicates that teachers of older children seldom use poetry with them, enthusiasm for poetry first must be stimulated among teachers themselves. The lack of interest in poetry when children choose literature is reinforced in a *Reading Today* article, "An Adventure with Books" (2001). This article reports the results of a study in which elementary students identified the books they read during the summer. The only poetry book chosen was Matthew Gollub's *Cool Melons—Turn to Frogs! The Life and Poems of Issa.* This combination of biography and haiku poetry about the Japanese poet was selected by third graders.

The need for and the advantages of longer interactions with poetry are indicated by an analysis of poetry included in the International Reading Association's Chil-

dren's Choices. Sam Sebesta (1983) reports, "serious poetry, blank and free verse, and extended imagery—all qualities that children disapproved of in other preference studies—are present on the lists of Children's Choices" (p. 67). For example, children liked serious traditional poems, such as Robert Frost's "Stopping by Woods on a Snowy Evening" and the poems of Arnold Adoff's *My Black Me: A Beginning Book of Black Poetry.* They liked the personified desert in Byrd Baylor's *The Desert Is Theirs.* They chose the imagistic poems about everyday things in Valerie Worth's *More Small Poems.* In addition, Sebesta found that the number of poetry books included in children's literary preferences implied a greater affection for poetry than was found in many previous studies.

Sebesta's conclusions about the reasons for the discrepancies between the previous studies and the Children's Choices provide valuable insights for anyone responsible for selecting and sharing poetry. First, unlike many of the research studies that present poetry in a brief fashion, the poetry on the Children's Choices list is available in the classroom and is shared with children over a two- to six-week period. Second, unlike most of the studies that present poetry orally, the poetry on the Children's Choices list includes books that emphasize the visual aspects of poetry. The selections frequently develop unique arrangements on the page, and the illustrations arouse interests and feelings. Third, recent developments in teaching poetry emphasize both the study of the structure of poetry and readers' responses to poetry. A merger of the two approaches may expand the range of poetry that children enjoy.

As you begin the study of poetry, you should also heed a warning given by William and Betty Greenway (1990). They state, "We may be teaching students the poetry they like as children, but not the poetry they'll like as adults" (p. 138). Poetry, however, is receiving national recognition among adults. Lee Gomes (2001) reports: "Poets laureate are sprouting like Wordsworth's daffodils all over the country. Even suburbs whose only previous literary culture had been the chain bookstore at the shopping mall can have bards of their own" (p. 1). The United States has had a poet laureate consultant to the Library of Congress since the 1930s. These poets include Robert Frost and James Dickey. It is just recently, however, that the idea of poets laureate has emerged throughout the country.

In a review of the editors' selections of the fifty-three books that were chosen by the *School Library Journal* for 2001, the editors state: "This was a banner year for poetry. Whether light and funny or serious and thoughtful, the poems and in many cases, their accompanying artwork, made a strong showing in a variety of formats" (p. 44). The following poetry books are included in this list: Kristine O'Connell George's *Toasting Marshmallows: Camping Poems,* Jan Greenberg's *Heart to Heart: New Poems Inspired by Twentieth-Century American Art,* Paul B.

Janeczko's *A Poke in the I: A Collection of Concrete Poems,* Henry Wadsworth Longfellow's *The Midnight Ride of Paul Revere,* and Jack Prelutsky's *Awful Ogre's Awful Day.*

Criteria for Selecting Poetry for Children

Both Rumer Godden (1988) and Charles Causley (Merrick, 1988) emphasize that a good poem need not be understood all at once. Godden states that a good poem "has a mysterious capacity for growing, unfolding more and more of itself in the mind, and very soon a child whose ear is tuned, mind made alert, is ready to go beyond children's poets and the lively, quickly assimilable poems—far, far beyond" (p. 310). Liz Rosenberg (1991) stresses that the best children's poems accompany you through life, growing with you. Consequently, poetry "must be vibrant, skillful, mysterious, thrilling" (p. 55).

Elements of Poetry

How important to you is a knowledge of the literary elements found in poetry? Avi (1993) states that of the various criteria, "only knowing the elements of good prose and poetry contributes meaningfully to an understanding of what is children's literature" (p. 42).

Poets use everyday language in different ways to encourage readers to see familiar things in new lights, to draw on their senses, and to fantasize. Poets also use certain devices to create medleys of sounds, suggest visual interpretations, and communicate messages. The criteria for selecting poetry for children suggest the importance of such poetic elements as rhythm, rhyme and other sound patterns, repetition, imagery, and shape in the creation of poetry. In their poetry anthology, *Knock at a Star: A Child's Introduction to Poetry,* X. J. Kennedy and Dorothy M. Kennedy highlight the elements of poetry through a section titled "What's Inside a Poem?" In this section they include poems that develop "Images," "Word Music," "Beats that Repeat," "Likenesses," and "Word Play." When you read these poems you will notice that the poems develop the elements of poetry.

Rhythm

The word *rhythm* is derived from the Greek *rhythmos,* meaning to flow. In poetry, this flowing quality refers to the movement of words in the poem. Stress, the number of syllables, and the pattern of syllables direct the feelings expressed in a poem. Many poems have a definite, repetitive cadence, or meter, with certain lines containing a certain number of pronounced beats. For example, limericks have a strict rhythmic structure easily recognizable even when one is hearing them in a foreign language. Free verse, however, usually has a casual, irregular rhythm similar to that of everyday speech.

The poems in Knock at a Star: A Child's Introduction to Poetry *are excellent for developing understanding of poetic elements. (Cover from* Knock at a Star: A Child's Introduction to Poetry, *illustrated by Karen Lee Baker. Cover copyright © 1999 by Karen Lee Baker. Published by Little, Brown and Company. Reprinted by permission of Little, Brown and Company.)*

Poets use rhythm for four specific purposes. First, they use rhythm to increase enjoyment in hearing language. Young children usually enjoy the repetitive cadences of nursery rhymes, chants, and nonsensical verses. Rhythm encourages children to join in orally, experiment with language, and move with it. Second, poets use rhythm to highlight and emphasize specific words. Poets often use stress to suggest the importance of words. Third, poets use rhythm to create dramatic effects. Irregular meter or repeatedly stressed words may immediately attract attention. Fourth, poets use rhythm to suggest mood. For example, a rapid rhythm can suggest excitement and involvement, while a slow, leisurely rhythm can suggest laziness and contemplation. David McCord uses rhythm to suggest the sounds that a stick might make if a child dragged it along a fence. Rhythm in the following poem emphasizes specific words, attracts and holds attention, and suggests a certain mood.

The Pickety Fence

The pickety fence
The pickety fence

Give it a lick it's
The pickety fence
Give it a lick it's
A clickety fence
Give it a lick it's
A lickety fence
Give it a lick
Give it a lick
Give it a lick
With a rickety stick
Pickety
Pickety
Pickety
Pick

From Poem "The Pickety Fence" from *Far and Few: Rhymes of the Never Was and Always Is*, p. 7 by David McCord. Copyright © 1974, Little, Brown & Company.

As you share poetry with children you will notice that the rhythm of a poem works particularly well when it reinforces the content of the poem. Consider, for example, Robert Louis Stevenson's "From a Railway Carriage." The rhythm suggests the dash and rattle of a train as it crosses the country. You can easily imagine yourself peering out the window as the scenery rushes by.

From a Railway Carriage

Faster than fairies, faster than witches,
Bridges and houses, hedges and ditches;
And charging along like troops in a battle,
All through the meadows the horses and cattle:
All of the sights of the hill and the plain
Fly as thick as driving rain;
And ever again, in the wink of an eye,
Painted stations whistle by.
Here is a child who clambers and scrambles,
All by himself and gathering brambles;
Here is a tramp who stands and gazes;
And here is the green for stringing the daisies!
Here is a cart run away in the road
Lumping along with man and load;
And here is a mill and there is a river:
Each a glimpse and gone forever!

Robert Louis Stevenson
A Child's Garden of Verses, 1883

Rhythm and the sounds of language are important elements in *Talking Like the Rain: A First Book of Poems* selected by X. J. and Dorothy M. Kennedy. The book is introduced with a quote from Isak Dinesen's *Out of Africa,* in which the workers ask Dinesen to "Speak again. Speak like rain." The poems in the anthology are meant to be read aloud to children and to bring them rhythm and pleasure.

Rhythm and repetition are important poetic elements in Lee Bennett Hopkins's *Good Rhymes, Good Times.* There is the rhythm and sound of the city as "Quiet rumbling/traffic/roars" (p. 8); the rhythm and feel of valentine feelings that go "flippy/fizzy, whoopy, whizzy" (p. 12); and

EVALUATION CRITERIA

Literary Criticism: Selecting Poetry for Children

1. Poems that are lively, with exciting meters and rhythms, are most likely to appeal to young children.

2. Poems for young children should emphasize the sounds of language and encourage play with words.

3. Sharply cut visual images and words used in fresh, novel manners allow children to expand their imaginations and see or hear the world in a new way.

4. Poems for young children should tell simple stories and introduce stirring scenes of action.

5. The poems selected should not have been written down to children's supposed level.

6. The most effective poems allow children to interpret, to feel, and to put themselves into the poems. They encourage children to extend comparisons, images, and findings.

7. The subject matter should delight children, say something to them, enhance their egos, strike happy recollections, tickle their funny bones, or encourage them to explore.

8. Poems should be good enough to stand up under repeated readings.

the motion and rhythm of a kite that "flitters/twirls/tumbles/twitters" (p. 14). The repeated line "Sing a song of cities" (p. 5) emphasizes the sound of the city. The repetition of the word "good" in the poem "Good Books, Good Times!" (p. 28) emphasizes the importance of the things that are good in children's lives. The poems and songs in Alvin Schwartz's *And the Green Grass Grew All Around: Folk Poetry from Everyone* include the rhythms that children chant in games and sing in songs.

Rhyme and Other Sound Patterns

Sound is an important part of the pleasure of poetry. One of the ways in which poets can emphasize sound is rhyming. Many beloved traditional poems for children—such as Edward Lear's "The Owl and the Pussy-Cat"—use careful rhyme schemes.

Rhyming words may occur at the ends of lines and within lines. Poets of nonsense verse even create their own words to achieve humorous, rhyming effects. Consider, for example, Zilpha Keatley Snyder's use of rhyme in "Poem to Mud." The end rhymes—*ooze–slooze,*

Technology Resources

crud–flood, and *thickier–stickier*—suggest visual and auditory characteristics of mud. The internal rhymes—*fed–spread, slickier–stickier–thickier*—create a tongue-twisting quality.

Poem to Mud

Poem to mud—
Poem to ooze—
Patted in pies, or coating the shoes.
Poem to slooze—
Poem to crud—
Fed by a leak, or spread by a flood.
Wherever, whenever, whyever it goes,
Stirred by your finger, or strained by your toes,
There's nothing sloopier, slipperier, floppier,
There's nothing slickier, stickier, thickier,
There's nothing quickier to make grown-ups sickier,
Trulier coolier,
Than wonderful mud.

Zilpha Keatley Snyder
Today Is Saturday, pp. 18–19

Numerous internal rhymes are found in Robert Southey's classical poem, "The Cataract of Lodore." In the following excerpt from the poem, notice how internal rhymes create the sound and feel of the water as it flows toward a waterfall in the Lake District of England.

Retreating and beating and meeting and sheeting,
Delaying and straying and playing and spraying,
Advancing and prancing and glancing and dancing,
Recoiling, turmoiling and toiling and boiling,
And gleaming and streaming and steaming and beaming,
And rushing and flushing and brushing and gushing,
And flapping and rapping and clapping and slapping,
And curling and whirling and purling and twirling,
And thumping and plumping and bumping and jumping,
And dashing and flashing and splashing and clashing, ...

Robert Southey, 1774–1843.

A humorous picture-book version of the total poem is illustrated by David Catrow. Catrow's illustrations for *The Cataract of Lodore* present the English countryside as a Georgian gentleman and his family descend the river toward the mighty waterfall.

Poets also use alliteration, the repetition of initial consonants or groups of consonants, to create sound patterns. In "The Tutor," Carolyn Wells uses repetition of the beginning consonant *t* to create a humorous poem about a teacher trying to teach "two young tooters to toot." "The Tutor" is one of the poems selected by Isabel Wilner

for *The Poetry Troupe,* a collection of over two hundred poems that children have selected for reading aloud. Mary Ann Hoberman's four-line poem "Gazelle," also in Wilner's collection, contains fifteen words beginning with *g*. If a poem contains a great deal of alliteration, a tongue twister results. "Sing Me a Song of Teapots and Trumpets" by N. M. Bodecker is one of the poems selected for X. J. Kennedy and Dorothy M. Kennedy's *Knock at a Star: A Child's Introduction to Poetry.* Each verse uses a different alliteration. In the first verse are *teapots* and *trumpets, tippets* and *taps,* and *trippers* and *trappers.* The second verse includes *sneakers* and *snoopers, snappers* and *snacks,* and *snorkels* and *snarkles.* By the third verse the alliteration includes *parsnips* and *pickles, picsnips* and *parkles,* and *pumpkins* and *pears.*

Assonance, the repetition of vowel sounds, is another means of creating interesting and unusual sound patterns. Another poem selected by Kennedy and Kennedy, "Did You Eever, Iver, Over?" by Anonymous uses repetitions of vowel sounds in words such as *leef, life, loaf,* and *neever, niver, nover.* This poem becomes a tongue twister if read aloud at a rapid pace. Jack Prelutsky uses the frequent repetition of the long *e* sound in the following poem.

Don't Ever Seize a Weasel by the Tail

You should never squeeze a weasel
for you might displease the weasel,
and don't ever seize the weasel by the tail.
Let his tail blow in the breeze;
if you pull it, he will sneeze,
for the weasel's constitution tends to be a little
    frail.
Yes the weasel wheezes easily;
the weasel freezes easily;
the weasel's tan complexion rather suddenly
    turns pale.
So don't displease or tease a weasel,
squeeze or freeze or wheeze a weasel
and don't ever seize a weasel by the tail.

Jack Prelutsky
A Gopher in the Garden and Other Animal Poems, p. 19

The sounds of some words suggest the meanings that they are intended to convey. The term *onomatopoeia* refers to words that imitate the actions or sounds with which they are associated. Words such as *plop, jounce,* and *beat* suggest the loud sound of rain hitting the concrete in Aileen Fisher's "Rain."

Eve Merriam effectively uses onomatopoeia in her poem "Owl," found in *Halloween ABC.* Merriam's repeated use of "who" sounds like the subject of her poem. One of her other poems, "Weather," found in Beatrice Schenk de Regniers's *Sing a Song of Popcorn,* begins with "Dot a dot dot" and continues with words like "spack a spack speck" to sound like rain. In *Earth Verses and Water Rhymes,* poet J. Patrick Lewis suggests in "Sounds of Winter" that October Ogres lumber in with a "tum-tum-titum."

Through the Eyes of a POET

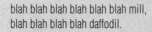

Jack Prelutsky

Visit the CD-ROM that accompanies this text to generate a complete list of Jack Prelutsky titles.

Selected Titles by Jack Prelutsky:

The Headless Horseman Rides Tonight

The New Kid on the Block

It's Raining Pigs and Noodles: Poems

Monday's Troll

Nightmares: Poems to Trouble Your Sleep

Poetry Doesn't Have to Be Boring!

Once there was a teacher who had charge of thirty-three open and eager young minds. One Monday morning, the teacher opened her curriculum book, which indicated that she should recite a poem to her students. She did, and it came out something like this:

Blah blah the flower,
blah blah the tree,
blah blah the shower,
blah blah the bee.

When she had finished her recitation she said, "Please open your geography books to page one-hundred-thirty-seven."

On Tuesday morning, the teacher (a wonderful person who happened to be rather fond of poetry) decided, on her own initiative, to read another poem to her class. This poem, which was somewhat longer than the first, came out something like this:

blah blah blah blah blah blah hill,
blah blah blah blah blah blah still,

blah blah blah blah blah blah mill,
blah blah blah blah daffodil.

Then she said, "Please open your history books to page sixty-two."

She went on like this for the entire week, and by Friday, the children (who knew what was coming when she opened her book of verse) began making peculiar faces and shifting restlessly in their seats. The staunchest aesthetes in the group had begun to lose interest in flowers, bees, hills, etc. Many of the children were harboring strange feelings about poetry. They began saying things about poetry to themselves and to each other. Here are some of the things they said:

"Poetry is boring."

"Poetry is dumb."

"Poetry doesn't make any sense."

"Poetry is about things that don't interest me."

"I hate poetry."

Once there was another teacher with a class of thirty-three young students. She was also a wonderful person with a fondness for poetry. One Sunday evening, she opened her curriculum book and saw that a unit of poetry was scheduled for the next day's lesson. "Hmmmmmm," she mused. "Now what poem shall I share with them tomorrow?" After giving it some careful thought, she settled on a poem about a silly monster, which the poet had apparently created out of whole cloth, and which she thought might stimulate her pupils' imaginations. "Hmmmmmm," she mused again. "Now how can I make this poem even more interesting?" She deliberated a bit more and, in the course of memorizing the poem, came up with several ideas. The next morning, this is what happened:

"Children," she said. "Today is a special day. It is the first day of silly monster week, and to honor the occasion, I am going to share a silly monster poem with you." She held up a small tin can, and continued. "The monster lives in this can, but I am not going to show it to you yet, because I would like you to imagine what it looks like while I'm reciting the poem."

She then recited the poem, and upon reaching the last word in the last line, suddenly unleashed an expanding snake from the can. The children reacted with squeals of mock terror and real delight. Then they asked her to recite the poem again, which she did. Afterward, she had them draw pictures of the silly monster. No two interpretations were alike.

The drawings were photographed and later presented in an assembly as a slide show, with the children reciting the poem in chorus. She shared a number of other poems during "silly monster week," always showing her honest enthusiasm and finding imaginative methods of presentation. She used masks, musical instruments, dance, sound-effects recordings, and clay sculpture. The children grew so involved that she soon was able to recite poems with no props at all. At the end of the week, these are some of the things her students said about poetry:

"Poetry is exciting."

"Poetry is fun."

"Poetry is interesting."

"Poetry makes you think."

"I love poetry."

Video Profiles: The accompanying video contains conversations with Lynne Cherry, Mary E. Lyons, Keith Baker, and other writers of children's literature.

Repetition

Poets frequently use repetition to enrich or emphasize words, phrases, lines, or even whole verses in poems. David McCord uses repetition of whole lines in "The Pickety Fence," and Lewis Carroll uses repetition to accent his feelings about soup.

Beautiful Soup

Beautiful Soup, so rich and green,
Waiting in a hot tureen!
Who for such dainties would not stoop?
Soup of the evening, beautiful Soup!
Soup of the evening, beautiful Soup!
Beau—ootiful Soo—oop!
Beau—ootiful Soo—oop!
Soo—oop of the e—e—evening,

Beautiful, beautiful Soup!
Beautiful Soup! Who cares for fish,
Game, or any other dish?
Who would not give all else for two
Pennyworth only of beautiful Soup?
Beau—ootiful Soo—oop!
Beau—ootiful Soo—oop!
Soo—op of the e—e—evening,
Beautiful, beauti—FUL SOUP!

Lewis Carroll
Alice's Adventures in Wonderland, 1865

"Beautiful Soup" is another favorite for oral reading because children find that they can re-create that marvelous sound of rich, hot soup being taken from the spoon and placed into their mouths.

The illustrations provide an appropriate setting for a poem about the Lake District in England. (From The Cataract of Lodore by Robert Southey. Illustrated by David Catrow. Illustrations copyright © 1992 by David Catrow. Reprinted by permission of Henry Holt and Company, Inc.)

Lullabies shared with young children are often enhanced by repetition. Christina G. Rossetti's "Lullaby" uses repetition to suggest a musical quality.

Lullaby

Lullaby, oh, lullaby!
Flowers are closed and lambs are sleeping;
Lullaby, oh, lullaby!
Stars are up, the moon is peeping;
Lullaby, oh, lullaby!
While the birds are silence keeping,
(Lullaby, oh, lullaby!)
Sleep, my baby, fall a-sleeping,
Lullaby, oh, lullaby!

Christina Rossetti
Sing-Song, 1872

Young children enjoy the numerous poems that contain repetition in Jane Yolen's *The Three Bears Rhyme Book*. Poems that are especially strong in repetition include "Three Bears Walking," "Photographs," "Bears' Chairs," and "Poppa Bear's Hum."

Imagery

Imagery is a primary element in poetry. It encourages children to see, hear, feel, taste, smell, and touch the worlds created by poets. You have already seen how rhythm, sound patterns, and repetition cause readers to experience what poets describe. Poets also use figurative language (language with nonliteral meanings) to clarify, add vividness, and encourage readers to experience things in new ways. Several types of figurative language are used in poetry. This discussion looks at metaphor, simile, personification, and hyperbole.

Metaphors are implied comparisons between things that have something in common but are essentially different. Metaphors highlight certain qualities in things to make readers see them in new ways. In the introduction to *Flashlight and Other Poems*, Judith Thurman (1976) uses metaphor when she asserts that a "poem is a flashlight, too: the flashlight of surprise. Pointed at a skinned knee or at an oil slick, at pretending to sleep or at kisses, at balloons, or snow, or at the soft, scary nuzzle of a mare, a poem lets us feel and know each in a fresh, sudden and strong light" (introduction). Thurman demonstrates her command of metaphor when she compares the Milky Way to thick white breath in cold air, or clay to a clown without bones. In "Spill," Thurman compares a flock of flying sparrows to loose change spilling out of a pocket.

Spill

the wind scatters
a flock of sparrows—
a handful of small change
spilled suddenly
from the cloud's pocket

Judith Thurman
Flashlight and Other Poems, p. 16

Paul Paolilli and Dan Brewer use metaphors effectively in *Silver Seeds: A Book of Nature Poems*. For example, they compare stars to silver seeds that have been planted in the sky, while the moon is a marvelous melon that offers flavor to the night.

Through the Eyes of a CHILD

Katie

Pam Wilson's Fourth Grade
Western Row Elementary
Mason, Ohio

TITLE: The New Kid on the Block

AUTHOR: Jack Prelutsky

Mr. Jack Prelutsky likes to make people laugh by poetry. How James did his illustrations was he drew one picture that represented the poem. He drew black and white pictures. Jack doesn't rhyme that much in his poetry. The title is The New Kid on the Block. He does 18 poems in this book. Jack writes funny and fiction poems. James sometimes did funny illustrations. On the front cover it looks like it was painted. But on the inside it looks like it was done in marker. James draws his pictures in detail. Jack doesn't just write about the new kid he also writes about other poems too. I like this book because I like the funny poems. Some poems in this book made me laugh aloud. I dedicate this book to my 10 year old cousin Jennifer Smith because I think this would make her laugh aloud too.

Katie

While metaphors are implied comparisons, similes are direct comparisons between things that have something in common but are essentially different. The comparisons made by similes are considered direct because the word *like* or *as* is included in the comparison. In "The Path on the Sea," a thirteen-year-old Russian child uses simile to capture the mystery and allure of moonlight on the ocean. Notice the use of the word *like* in the first line. What are the commonalities between a silver sickle and a new moon?

The Path on the Sea

The moon this night is like a silver sickle
Mowing a field of stars.
It has spread a golden runner
Over the rippling waves.
With its winking shimmer
This magic carpet lures me
To fly to the moon on it.

From the poem "The Path on the Sea" by Inna Miller,
from *The Moon Is Like a Silver Sickle* by
Miriam Morton. Reprinted by permission.

Insightful comparisons can develop meaning that transcends words. Poetic imagery can open the minds of children to new worlds and can allow children to ascend to different levels of consciousness.

Personification allows poets to give human emotions and characteristics to inanimate objects, abstract ideas, and nonhuman living things. For example, personification is an important element in Byrd Baylor's poetry about Native Americans and Native American legends. In *Moon Song*, Baylor personifies the moon as a mother who gives birth to Coyote Child, wraps him in her magic, caresses him with pale white mist, and shines on him with love.

Kaye Starbird uses personification in the following poem to encourage readers to visualize a wind with human characteristics.

The Wind

In spring, the wind's a sneaky wind,
A tricky wind,
A freaky wind,
A wind that hides around the bends
And doesn't die, but just pretends;
So if you stroll into a street
Out of a quiet lane,
All of a sudden you can meet
A smallish hurricane.
And as the grown-ups gasp and cough
Or grumble when their hats blow off,
And housewives clutch their grocery sacks
While all their hairdos come unpinned . . .
We kids—each time the wind attacks—
Just stretch our arms and turn our backs,
And then we giggle and relax
And lean against the wind.

Kaye Starbird
The Covered Bridge House and Other Poems,
p. 11

Hyperbole is exaggeration that creates specific effects. John Ciardi's humorous "Mummy Slept Late and Daddy Fixed Breakfast" says that a waffle is so tough that it cannot be dented by a hacksaw.

Mummy Slept Late and Daddy Fixed Breakfast

Daddy fixed the breakfast.
He made us each a waffle.
It looked like gravel pudding.
It tasted something awful.

"Ha, ha," he said, "I'll try again.
This time I'll get it right." But what I got was in
between
Bituminous and anthracite.

"A little too well done? Oh well,
I'll have to start all over."
That time what landed on my plate
Looked like a manhole cover.

I tried to cut it with a fork:
The fork gave off a spark.
I tried a knife and twisted it
into a question mark.
I tried it with a hack-saw.
I tried it with a torch.
It didn't even make a dent.
It didn't even scorch.

The next time Dad gets breakfast
When Mummy's sleeping late,
I think I'll skip the waffles.
I'd sooner eat the plate!

John Ciardi
You Read to Me, I'll Read to You, p. 18

Many of the poems in Shel Silverstein's *Where the Sidewalk Ends* also include exaggeration.

Shape

Poets may place their words on pages in ways designed to supplement meaning and to create greater visual impact. Word division, line division, punctuation, and capitalization can emphasize content, as when Lewis Carroll writes about "Beau—ootiful Soo—oop!"

The shape of a poem may represent the thing or the physical experience that the poem describes. In Regina Sauro's "I Like to Swing," the poem becomes wider and wider toward the bottom, as the sweep of the swing becomes wider and wider. In "Seals," by William Jay Smith (anthologized in Stephen Dunning, Edward Lueders, and Hugh Smith's excellent *Reflections on a Gift of Watermelon Pickle . . . and Other Modern Verse*), the poem forms the shape of a supple seal and is reinforced by an accompanying photograph of a seal. Several of the poems in Myra Cohn Livingston's *Space Songs* are shaped like objects in space. For example, "Moon" looks like a crescent, "Meteorites" has a tail, and "Satellites" looks like a mechanical object. Children enjoy discovering that shape may be related to the meaning of a poem and experimenting with shape in their own poetry writing.

Forms of Poetry

Some children do not believe that they are reading a poem unless the lines rhyme. While adults should not spend time with young children analyzing the form of a poem, children should realize that poetry has many different forms.

Children should be encouraged to write their own poetry. When they write poetry, they enjoy experimenting with different forms. For such experiments, however, they must be immersed in poetry and led through many enjoyable experiences with poems. This section takes a brief look at various forms of poetry, including lyric, narrative, ballad, limerick, concrete, and haiku.

Lyric Poetry

According to Northrop Frye, Sheridan Baker, and George Perkins (1985), a lyric poem is "a poem, brief and discontinuous, emphasizing sound and picture imagery rather than narrative or dramatic movement. Lyrical poetry began in ancient Greece in connection with music, as poetry sung, for the most part, to the accompaniment of a lyre" (p. 268). The epic poems of the Greeks were narratives emphasizing heroic deeds. Now, as in the past, lyric poems emphasize musical, pictorial, and emotional qualities. The musical roots of lyric poetry are indicated by the fact that the words of songs are now termed *lyrics*.

John Drury (1995) states "Originally lyric poetry was sung, chanted, or recited to a musical accompaniment. The word lyric refers to the poet's lyre, the harp-like instrument the poet or musician would play. . . . Lyric poetry now tends to be quiet, inward, meditative" (p. 156). Many of the poems discussed in this chapter have lyrical quality.

Children's early experiences with poetry may be through Mother Goose rhymes sung to music and traditional lullabies sung at bedtime. Consider the melody associated with the words in the following traditional lullaby.

Hush, Little Baby

Hush, little baby, don't say a word,
Mama's going to buy you a mocking bird.
And if that mocking bird don't sing,
Mama's going to buy you a diamond ring.
And if that diamond ring turns to brass,
Mama's going to buy you a looking glass.
And if that looking glass gets broke,
Mama's going to buy you a billy goat.
And if that billy goat won't pull,
Mama's going to buy you a cart and bull.
And if that cart and bull turn over,
Mama's going to buy you a dog named Rover.
And if that dog named Rover won't bark,
Mama's going to buy you a horse and cart.

And if that horse and cart fall down,
You'll still be the sweetest little baby in town.

Traditional poem

Dan Fox's *Go In and Out the Window: An Illustrated Songbook for Young People* contains numerous traditional lyrics. John Langstaff's *What a Morning! The Christmas Story in Black Spirituals* shows the emotional power associated with some lyrics. *On Christmas Day in the Morning,* with a foreword by Langstaff, is a traditional English folksong. Langstaff's "Foreword" provides directions for acting out the words that accompany the lyrics. Langstaff states: "Hundreds of years ago, farmers celebrated planting time with songs and dances. They believed that dancing and singing would help push the plants out of the earth, so they danced and sang as energetically as they could" (foreword). Mary Ann Hoberman's adaptation of a traditional folksong, *There Once Was a Man Named Michael Finnegan,* includes considerable repetition as well as humorous illustrations that appeal to young children. The text includes the musical score.

Children's favorite storybook characters make up verses and sing their poems—as does A. A. Milne's Winnie-the-Pooh, for example. Many poets write poems that have singing qualities. Jack Prelutsky's anthology *The Random House Book of Poetry for Children* contains, for example, Lois Lenski's "Sing a Song of People," which re-creates the tempo of people traveling through a city. John Ciardi's "The Myra Song" captures the personality of a little girl who enjoys singing, skipping, chattering, and playing. William Blake's "Introduction to 'Songs of Innocence' " has its piper of "happy songs/Every child may joy to hear."

The songs of two well-known singers and songwriters are the sources for illustrated texts. *Island in the Sun* by Harry Belafonte and Lord Burgess pays tribute to Belafonte's island childhood. The lines of the song are divided and illustrated to form a picture book. The text begins and concludes with the music. *This Land Is Your Land* by Woody Guthrie is a highly illustrated version of the popular song with paintings by Kathy Jakobsen. The text includes "A Tribute to Woody Guthrie" and the words and music by Guthrie. The illustrations provide a panorama of the United States.

The universality of songs and chants are shown through Nikki Siegen-Smith's *Songs for Survival: Songs and Chants from Tribal Peoples Around the World.* The anthology includes selections from six continents. The anthology is divided according to songs about beginnings, songs about the living world, songs that discuss the elements, and songs about survival. An introduction and an appendix present information about the importance of songs and customs of tribal groups.

Narrative Poetry

Poets may be expert storytellers. A poem that tells a story is narrative poetry. With rapid action and typically chronological order, story poems have long been favorites of children. They are excellent for increasing children's

The poems and illustrations take readers across America. (From This Land Is Your Land. *Words and music by Woodie Guthrie, paintings by Kathy Jackson. Illustrations © 1998 by Kathy Jakobsen. Published by Little, Brown and Company. Reprinted by permission.)*

interest in, and appreciation of, poetry. Robert Browning's "The Pied Piper of Hamelin," first published in 1882, contains many of the characteristics that make narrative poems appealing to children. The actions of the villainous rats, for example, are easy to visualize.

> Rats!
> They fought the dogs, and filled the cats,
> And bit the babies in the cradles,
> And ate the cheeses out of the vats,
> And licked the soup from the cook's own ladles,
> Split open the kegs of salted sprats,
> Made nests inside men's Sunday hats,
> And even spoiled the women's chats
> By drowning their speaking
> With shrieking and squeaking
> In fifty different sharps and flats.

The plot develops rapidly, as the townspeople approach the mayor and the town council demanding action. Into this setting comes the hero.

> And in did come the strangest figure!
> His queer long coat from heel to head
> Was half of yellow and half of red;
> And he himself was tall and thin,
> With sharp blue eyes, each like a pin,
> And light, loose hair, yet swarthy skin,

> No tuft on cheek nor beard on chin,
> But lips where smiles went out and in—
> There was no guessing his kith and kin!
> And nobody could enough admire
> The tall man and his quaint attire:

With rapidity, the council offers the stranger a thousand gilders to rid the town of its rats, and the piper places the pipe to his lips. At this point, the tempo of the poem resembles the scurrying of rats.

> And out of the house the rats came
>   tumbling.
> Great rats, small rats, lean rats, brawny rats,
> Brown rats, black rats, gray rats, tawny rats,
> Grave old plodders, gay young friskers,
> Fathers, mothers, uncles, cousins,
> Cocking tails and pricking whiskers,
> Families by tens and dozens,
> Brothers, sisters, husbands, wives—
> Followed the piper for their lives.
> From street to street he piped advancing,
> And step for step they followed dancing,

> Robert Browning
> *The Pied Piper of Hamelin*, 1882

After the efficient disposal of the rats comes the confrontation, when the mayor refuses to pay the thousand gilders. In retribution, the piper puts the pipe to his lips and blows three notes. At this point, the tempo of the poem resembles the clapping of hands and the skipping of feet. Every child in the town merrily follows the piper through a wondrous portal into the mountain.

Highly illustrated picture books for young children frequently develop a story in rhyme. For example, Kathi Appelt shows the love between a very personified Mama Bird and her child in *Oh My Baby, Little One*. The narrative poem describes Mama's love as her little one goes to school. Similes help develop this love that is always with the young bird just as the leaves are with the trees, the sand is with the sandbox, or the kite is with the breeze.

Other narrative poems long popular with children include Clement Moore's "A Visit from St. Nicholas" (now better known as "The Night Before Christmas"), which has been produced as books illustrated by Tomie dePaola and by Tasha Tudor; Lewis Carroll's delightful "The Walrus and the Carpenter," in which some young oysters go for a walk on the beach with one hungry animal and one hungry human; and Henry Wadsworth Longfellow's romantic dramas from early American history, "The Song of Hiawatha" and "Paul Revere's Ride."

Many contemporary poets—including John Ciardi, Jack Prelutsky, and Beatrice Curtis Brown—write narrative poems. Their topics are both nonsensical and realistic. Several contemporary poets have written highly illustrated narrative poems. For example, Nancy Willard's *The Tale I Told Sasha* follows a yellow ball as it rolls over the Bridge of Butterflies and encounters all types of beasts and even the King of Keys. The girl who follows the ball has an imaginative adventure that ends with the girl trying to recapture her strange adventures as she returns home.

Roy Gerrard's *Sir Francis Drake: His Daring Deeds* tells a lively story about the explorer. Gerrard's *Sir Cedric* is a heroic tale of Cedric the Good and Matilda the Pure. Gerrard's *Wagons West!* tells the story of a group of pioneers as they live their adventures on a wagon train heading westward to Oregon. The adventures along the way are developed through both the narrative poem and the illustrations. Along the way, the pioneers experience inclement weather, cattle thieves, and frontier entertainment.

Julia Fields's *The Green Lion of Zion Street* follows the exploits of a group of urban children as they wait for a bus on a foggy morning. In epic fashion, the children decide to challenge their fears and approach the dangerous lion that crouches "Fierce/Smirking/Vain" on Zion Street. Thankfully, they are able to walk through the frightening mists, face the lion, and laugh at their fears. After all, the scowling lion is made of stone.

Ballads

The ballad is a form of narrative folk song developed in Europe during the Middle Ages. Minstrels and bards (*bard* is the Welsh word for poet) sang the tales of legend or history, often accompanying themselves on stringed instruments. Marla Frazee's *Hush, Little Baby* is an English folk song that includes a musical accompaniment. Modern poets have used the ballad form for poems to be read rather than sung. However, traditional ballads are part of the oral literary heritage of European culture, passed on by word of mouth.

Action, usually heroic or tragic, is the focus of such traditional ballads. Samuel Taylor Coleridge's "The Rime of the Ancient Mariner," a sea ballad published in 1798, was based on the legend that it is fatal to shoot an albatross. The text is dramatic, including memorable lines that are frequently quoted. Notice the drama in the following excerpt from the longer poem.

> The fair breeze blew, the white foam flew,
> The furrow follow'd free;
> We were the first that ever burst
> Into that silent sea.
>
> Down dropt the breeze, the sails dropt down,
> 'Twas sad as sad could be;
> And we did speak only to break
> The silence of the sea!
>
> All in a hot and copper sky,
> The bloody Sun, at noon,
> Right up above the mast did stand,
> No bigger than the Moon.
>
> Day after day, day after day,
> We stuck, nor breath nor motion;
> As idle as a painted ship
> Upon a painted ocean.
>
> Water, water, everywhere,
> And all the boards did shrink;
> Water, water, everywhere
> Nor any drop to drink.

Samuel Taylor Coleridge
From "The Rime of the Ancient Mariner," 1798

Salt-Sea Verse, compiled by Charles Causley, contains a number of sea ballads, including portions of Coleridge's "The Rime of the Ancient Mariner." Gene Kemp's anthology *Ducks and Dragons: Poems for Children* contains a variety of English, Scottish, and American ballads that children enjoy reading or hearing read aloud. Jane Yolen's *The Ballad of the Pirate Queens* is the story of Anne Bonney and Mary Reade, two women aboard the *Vanity.* This ballad is full of adventure. Yolen provides notes about the history. Steven Kellogg's *I Was Born About 10,000 Years Ago* is an illustrated version of a ballad that includes considerable exaggeration.

Limericks

The short, witty poems called limericks are popular with children. All limericks have the same basic structure and rhythm: They are five-line poems in which the first, second, and fifth lines rhyme and have three pronounced beats each, and the third and fourth lines rhyme and have two pronounced beats each. The limerick form was

Climb Mount Fuji,

Snail, but slowly,

slowly!

The illustration reinforce the images of the haiku. (From Cool Melons—Turn to Frogs!: The Life and Poems of Issa. *Story and haiku translations by Matthew Golub. Illustration by Kazuko G. Stone. Illustrations copyright © 1998 by Kazuko G. Stone. Published by Lee & Low Books, Inc. Reprinted by permission of Lee & Low Books, Inc.)*

popularized by Edward Lear in the nineteenth century. Following is an example of humorous verse from Lear's *A Book of Nonsense.*

> There was an Old Man with a beard,
> Who said, "It is just as I feared!—
> Two Owls and a Hen,
> Four Larks and a Wren
> Have all built their nests in my beard."
>
> Edward Lear
> *A Book of Nonsense,* 1846

Children enjoy the visual imagery that this poem creates. They can see and laugh at the predicament of having those fowl nesting in a beard. They also enjoy reciting the definite rhythm and rhyme found in the limerick.

David McCord (1977), who has written numerous contemporary limericks himself, says that for a limerick to be successful, it must have perfect rhyming and flawless rhythm. McCord's amusing limericks in his *One at a Time: Collected Poems for the Young* illustrate the author's ability to play with words and the sounds of language. These limericks may also stimulate children to experiment with language by writing their own limericks.

Concrete Poems

Concrete is something that can be seen or touched, something that is physically real. When a poet emphasizes the meaning of a poem by shaping it into the form of a picture, concrete poetry results. Robert Froman's poem "Dead Tree," from *Seeing Things: A Book of Poems,* is lettered in the shape of a dead tree trunk. Mary Ellen Solt was inspired to create both a poem and a picture about the promise of spring in a forsythia bush. Children should turn this poem on its side to read the thoughts of the author.

The poems in Joan Bransfield Graham's *Flicker Flash* are all written as concrete poetry. Some of these shapes include "Candle," "Firefly," and "Full Moon." Jack Prelutsky's *"A Triangular Tale,"* found in his *A Pizza the Size of the Sun,* is another enjoyable poem that is written in the shape of the content of the poem.

Children find concrete poetry exciting to look at. Observing concrete objects and writing picture poems about them also stretches children's imaginations.

Haiku

Haiku is a very old form of Japanese poetry. A traditional haiku has three lines. The first line has five syllables, the second line has seven, and the final line has five. According to John Drury (1995), "The essential elements of haiku are brevity, immediacy, spontaneity, imagery, the natural world, a season, and sudden illumination" (p. 125).

Poets of haiku link themselves with nature and the cycle of the seasons. A photograph of a beach scene, in which a stream of water is placing its mark upon the land, accompanies the following example of Ann Atwood's (1971) haiku.

> A blank page of sand—
> at the water's cutting edge
> the pattern shaping.
>
> From poem *Haiku: The Mood of Earth,*
> by Ann Atwood,
> Scribner's Sons, copyright 1971.
> p. 4, unnumbered

Nikki Grimes structures her haiku poems around the seasons in *A Pocketful of Poems.* Words associated with each season are introduced with a brief poem followed by a haiku that highlights the same word.

Haiku by the great Japanese poet Issa, among other geniuses of this art, illustrate how this ancient form of verse has been used to express feelings, experiences, and visions in just the right words. Poems by Issa and important information about his life are included in Richard Lewis's *Of This World: A Poet's Life in Poetry.* Ann Atwood's haiku are col-

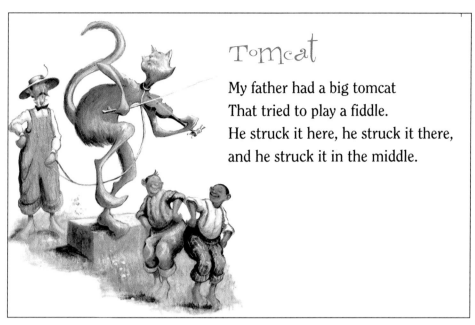

Tomcat

My father had a big tomcat
That tried to play a fiddle.
He struck it here, he struck it there,
and he struck it in the middle.

The poems in With a Whoop and a Holler: A Bushel of Love from Way Down South *are filled with nonsense and ridiculous situations. (Reprinted with the permission of Atheneum Books for Young Readers, an imprint of Simon & Schuster Children's Publishing Division from* With a Whoop and a Holler: A Bushel of Love from Way Down South *by Nancy Van Laan, illustrated by Scott Cook. Illustrations copyright © 1998 by Scott Cook.)*

lected in her *Haiku: The Mood of the Earth* and other books. Demi's collection of poems in *In the Eyes of the Cat: Japanese Poetry for All Seasons* includes a selection of Japanese poetry that has been translated by Tze-si Huang. Demi's illustrations combine with the poetry to provide a feeling for nature. Myra Cohn Livingston's *Cricket Never Does: A Collection of Haiku and Tanka* provides an introduction to the traditional Japanese forms of poetry.

One of the most interesting introductions both to the eighteenth-century Japanese poet and to his haiku is Matthew Gollub's *Cool Melons—Turn to Frogs! The Life and Poems of Issa.* The text includes both a brief biography of the poet and haiku translations that highlight Issa's life. Kazuko G. Stone's illustrations add to the impact of the poetry. In addition, Japanese calligraphy adds a visual appeal and conveys the feeling of the delicate brush strokes that were part of Issa's skill. As you read these poems notice how they support Drury's essential elements of haiku. Also notice how the illustrations add to the meaning of both the biography and the haiku. For example, what is the impact of an illustration of a snail on the tree branch overlooking Mount Fuji, the haiku telling readers to climb the mountain slowly like the snail, and the biographical portion on the same page that describes Issa's struggles as he trains under a master poet?

Poems and Poets

To share poetry with children, you may select from many classic and contemporary poems. Poets who write for chil-

dren use subject matters interesting to children. Children's poets write humorous poems; nature poems; poems that encourage children to identify with characters, situations, and locations; poems that suggest moods and feelings; animal poems; and poems about witches and ghosts. Although these categories sometimes overlap and some poets write about many different topics, many children's poets focus on certain subjects and types of poetry.

Nonsense and Humor: Poems for Starting Out Right

Nonsense rhymes are logical successors to Mother Goose rhymes for enjoyably introducing children to poetry. The nonsense poems of such great poets as Edward Lear and Lewis Carroll are ideal: They suggest spontaneous fun through emphatic, regular rhythms that are heightened by alliteration. Nonsense verses convey absurd meanings or even no meaning at all. Collections of rhymes, superstitions, and riddles such as those found in Nancy Van Laan's *With a Whoop and a Holler: A Bushel of Lore from Way Down South* suggest that nonsense and humor are universal characteristics that have appealed to people across time and geographical locations.

Humorous poetry, while closely related to nonsense poetry, deals with amusing happenings that might actually befall a person or an animal. Numerous contemporary poets also write nonsensical or humorous verse to entice children into the fun and life-enriching world of poetry.

The poems in *Animals That Ought to Be: Poems About Imaginary Pets*, written by Richard Michelson, provide humorous viewpoints about animals that "ought to be" because they could be of great service. For example, there is a poem about a "Roombroom" that cleans up messes. Other poems such as the "Nightmare Scarer" suggest that some of these pets might be difficult to control.

Samuel Marshak's *The Pup Grew Up* presents the comical dilemma of a lady's placing a Pekingese on a train and collecting a Great Dane when she gets off the train. The poem, written by a famous Russian poet, is a dig at bureaucracy.

An early love of William Blake's *Songs of Innocence* and *Songs of Experience* inspired Nancy Willard's *A Visit to William Blake's Inn: Poems for Innocent and Experienced Travelers*. The nonsense and lyric poems in the book, evocatively illustrated by Alice and Martin Provensen, present an odd assortment of guests and workers at the inn, including a rabbit that makes the bed and two dragons that bake the bread. "The Man in the Marmalade Hat Arrives" shows another of the guests.

> The man in the marmalade hat
> arrived in the middle of March,
> equipped with a bottle of starch
> to straighten the bends in the road, he said.
> He carried a bucket and mop.
> A most incommodious load, he said,
> and he asked for a room at the top.
>
> Now beat the gong and the drum!
> Call out the keepers
> and waken the sleepers.
> The man in the marmalade hat has come!
>
> The man in the marmalade hat
> bustled through all the rooms,
> and calling for dusters and brooms
> he trundled the guests from their beds,
> badgers and hedgehogs and moles.
> Winter is over, my loves, he said.
> Come away from your hollows and holes.
>
> Now beat the gong and the drum!
> Call out the keepers
> And waken the sleepers.
> The man in the marmalade hat has come!
>
> Nancy Willard
> *A Visit to William Blake's Inn*, p. 22

Humor is also found in the imagery, situations, and descriptive language in Willard's *Pish, Posh, Said Hieronymus Bosch*, inspired by the odd creatures found in artist Hieronymus Bosch's paintings. The artist, who painted in the late 1400s and early 1500s, was known for his bizarre creatures. When writing this poetry, Willard speculated about what it would be like to live and work in a household filled with Bosch's creatures. Consequently, the poetry is filled with three-legged thistles, pickle-winged fish, pigeon-toed rats, and a troop of jackdraws.

William Cole's *Poem Stew* includes humorous poems. Two larger anthologies contain sections of nonsense poetry. Jack Prelutsky's *The Random House Book of Poetry for Children* contains a section titled "Nonsense! Nonsense!" *Sing a Song of Popcorn: Every Child's Book of Poems*, by Beatrice Schenk de Regniers et al., includes poems categorized "Mostly Nonsense."

Edward Lear. Edward Lear, introduced earlier as the popularizer of the limerick form, had many loyal friends among the leaders and creative artists of Great Britain in the nineteenth century. He was welcomed into their homes and became an "Adopty Duncle" to their children, for whom he wrote and illustrated the nonsense verses collected in *A Book of Nonsense* and *Nonsense Songs and Stories*: limericks, narrative poems, tongue twisters, and alphabet rhymes.

Lear's nonsense poems can be found in many anthologies. They have also been illustrated in single editions by several well-known illustrators. *Hilary Knight's The Owl and the Pussy-Cat* is an excellent choice for young children. The highly illustrated text begins with a fantasy situation and presents the poem as a story told by Professor Comfort. A careful search of the illustrations reveals numerous references to Lear's works and interests. Compare Knight's illustrated version with Jan Brett's illustrations for Lear's *The Owl and the Pussycat*. Brett places her characters in a Caribbean setting. Fred Marcellino's illustrated version of *The Pelican Chorus and Other Nonsense* written by Edward Lear includes "The New Vestments," "The Owl and the Pussycat," and "The Pelican Chorus." The delightfully humorous illustrations make interesting comparisons with other illustrated versions of Lear's poetry.

Lewis Carroll. Lewis Carroll was the pen name for Charles Lutwidge Dodgson, a mathematician. Carroll's works are historical milestones of children's literature. His nonsense verses are found in *Alice's Adventures in Wonderland* and *Through the Looking Glass*. One of Carroll's most famous poems is "Jabberwocky," from *Through the Looking Glass*, which introduces the marvelous nonsense words *brillig*, *slithy toves*, and *borogoves*. This poem has been published as a lovely book illustrated by Jane Breskin Zalben.

Laura E. Richards. Contemporary children may be surprised to discover that a well-known author of nonsense poetry is the daughter of Julia Ward Howe, who wrote a beautiful but somber poem, "The Battle Hymn of the Republic." Like Lear and Carroll, Richards has shared marvelous words and sounds with children. There are *wizzy wizzy woggums*, *ditty dotty doggums*, and *diddy doddy dorglums*. There are *Rummy-jums*, *Viddipocks*, and *Orang-Outang-Tangs*. Richards's collection *Tirra Lirra, Rhymes Old and New* contains many rhymes that emphasize the sound of language and encourage children to play with words. One of her best-loved nonsense poems follows.

Eletelephony

Once there was an elephant,
Who tried to use the telephant—
No! No! I mean an elephone
Who tried to use the telephone—
(Dear me! I am not certain quite
That even now I've got it right.)

Howe'er it was, he got his trunk
Entangled in the telephunk;
The more he tried to get it free,
The louder buzzed the telephee—
(I fear I'd better drop the song
Of elephop and telephong!)

From poem "Eletelephony" from *Tirra Lirra,
Rhymes Old and New,* p. 31, by Laura E. Richards.
Copyright © 1955, Little, Brown & Company.

Shel Silverstein. One of the most popular children's poets, Shel Silverstein writes much nonsense and humorous poetry. Librarians report that Silverstein's *Where the Sidewalk Ends* and *A Light in the Attic* are in much demand by young readers. Improbable characters and situations in *A Light in the Attic* include a Quick-Digesting Gink, Sour Ann, and a polar bear in the Frigidaire. Silverstein covers slightly more realistic topics in poems like "The Boa Constrictor," from *Where the Sidewalk Ends.* In this poem, the narrator describes the experience of being swallowed by a boa constrictor. Children enjoy dramatizing this popular action poem. Silverstein's *Fall Up* includes poems about additional humorous situations.

Consider Silverstein's use of rhythm, rhyme, sound patterns, and repetition in "Ickle Me, Pickle Me, Tickle Me Too."

Ickle Me, Pickle Me, Tickle Me Too

Ickle Me, Pickle Me, Tickle Me too
Went for a ride in a flying shoe.
"Hooray!"
"What fun!"
"It's time we flew!"
Said Ickle Me, Pickle Me, Tickle Me too.

Ickle was captain, and Pickle was crew
And Tickle served coffee and mulligan stew
As higher
And higher
And higher they flew,
Ickle Me, Pickle Me, Tickle Me too.

Ickle Me, Pickle Me, Tickle Me too,
Over the sun and beyond the blue.
"Hold on!"
"Stay in!"
"I hope we do!"
Cried Ickle Me, Pickle Me, Tickle Me too.

Ickle Me, Pickle Me, Tickle Me too
Never returned to the world they knew,
And nobody
Knows what's

Happened to
Dear Ickle Me, Pickle Me, Tickle Me too.

From poem "Ickle Me, Pickle Me" by Shel Silverstein.
Copyright 1974. Reprinted by permission of
HarperCollins.

Jack Prelutsky. The world created by Prelutsky's nonsense and humorous poetry for children could be described as the kingdom of immortal zanies and improbable situations such as those already shown in his poem "Don't Ever Seize a Weasel by the Tail." Within the pages of *The Queen of Eene* are preposterous characters, such as peculiar Mister Gaffe, Poor Old Penelope, Herbert Glerbertt, and the Four Foolish Ladies (Hattie, Harriet, Hope, and Hortense).

Rolling Harvey Down the Hill describes the humorous experiences of a boy and his four friends. In *The Sheriff of Rottenshot,* eccentric characters include Philbert Phlurk, Eddie the spaghetti nut, and a saucy little ocelot. *The Baby Uggs Are Hatching* contains poems about oddly named creatures, such as Sneepies and Slitchs. Prelutsky's *The Dragons Are Singing Tonight* contains poems about all types of dragons, and Peter Sís's illustrations add to the believability. *The Gargoyle on the Roof,* also illustrated by Peter Sís, includes humorous poems about all types of monsters including werewolves, vampires, and, of course, gargoyles. *Awful Ogre's Awful Day* illustrated by Paul O. Zelinsky is another collection of humorous poems. Prelutsky's *Monday's Troll* features poems about enchanted characters such as witches and ogres. Other improbable creatures are found in his *A Pizza the Size of the Sun.* Many of the poems in *The Frog Wore Red Suspenders* use place names such as Tucumcari and Tuscaloosa.

William Jay Smith. Smith's *Laughing Time* contains many funny and entrancing poems, including limericks similar to those of Edward Lear. Smith's poem about escape to a strange land illustrates the spirit of fun that makes his poetry appealing to children.

The Land of Ho-Ho-Hum

When you want to do wherever you please,
Just sit down in an old valise,
And fasten the strap
Around your lap,
And fly off over the apple trees.

And fly for days and days and days
Over rivers, brooks, and bays
Until you come
To Ho-Ho-Hum
Where the Lion roars, and the Donkey brays.

Where the unicorn's tied to a golden chain,
And Umbrella Flowers drink the rain.
After that,
Put on your hat,
Then sit down and fly home again.

William Jay Smith
Laughing Time, p. 8

John Ciardi. A poet who has been both a professor of English and a columnist for *Saturday Review World,* Ciardi

Technology Resources

The database can be used to generate a list of appropriate titles to get a class on course to writing their own nature poetry. Begin by searching for "nature" in the Title, Description, and Topics fields. You might consider using both poetry (P) and nonfiction (INF) in the Genre field.

has written two books with a simple vocabulary to appeal to children with beginning reading skills: *I Met a Man* and *You Read to Me, I'll Read to You*. In the second book, Ciardi tells readers, "All the poems printed in black, you read to me, and all the poems printed in blue, I'll read to you." This collection contains "Mummy Slept Late and Daddy Fixed Breakfast." Other popular poems in this book tell about such characters as Change McTang McQuarter Cat and Arvin Marvin Lillisbee Fitch.

Ciardi's *The Hopeful Trout and Other Limericks* contains numerous poems about funny situations supplemented by tongue-twisting sounds. However, some of Ciardi's poems are better understood by older children. Poems by Ciardi often contain satirical observations about human behavior or problems of society, and the humorous poems in *Doodle Soup* tend to be caustic.

N. M. Bodecker. Poems suggesting that children should wash their hands with number-one dirt, shampoo their hair with molasses, and rinse off in cider are welcomed by young readers. Bodecker uses word play in "Bickering" to create humorous verse enjoyed by older children.

Bickering

The folks in Little Bickering
they argue quite a lot.
Is tutoring in bickering
required for a tot?
Are figs the best for figuring?
Is pepper ice cream hot?
Are wicks the best for wickering
a wicker chair or cot?
They find this endless dickering
and nonsense and nit pickering
uncommonly invigor'ing
I find it downright sickering!
You do agree!

From poem "Bickering" from *Hurry, Hurry Mary Dear!*, by N. M. Bodecker, copyright 1976. Reprinted by permission of Atheneum/Macmillan/Simon & Schuster, Inc.

In *Hurry, Hurry Mary Dear!*, the title poem has a harassed woman who is told to pick apples, dill pickles, chop trees, dig turnips, split peas, churn butter, smoke hams, stack wood, take down screens and put up storm windows, close shutters, stoke fires, mend mittens, knit sweaters, and brew tea. This might not be so bad, but the man who is giving the orders sits in a rocking chair all of the time. Finally, Mary has enough: She places the teapot carefully on the demanding gentleman's head.

Nature Poems

Like children, poets have marveled at the opening of the first crocus, seen new visions in a snowflake, or stopped to watch a stream of crystal-clear water tumbling from a mountaintop. They have understood that people should feel reverence and respect for nature. Such reverence and respect require special ways of hearing as well as special ways of looking. In *The Great Frog Race and Other Poems*, Kristine O'Connell George captures not only frogs but also Canada geese and other pleasures associated with a rural setting. In *Toasting Marshmallows: Camping Poems* George again captures the feelings of nature. In *Earth Verses and Water Rhymes*, J. Patrick Lewis encourages readers to try to catch the first snowflake on the tongue, feel the wind, and see the rays of a lighthouse. In *I'm Going to Pet a Worm Today and Other Poems*, Constance Levy encourages readers to explore many things in nature, including bees, old leaves, and water. One of the thematic sections in Siyu Liu and Orel Protopopescu's *A Thousand Peaks: Poems from China* explains and presents poetry that explores the love of nature.

The poetry of Emily Dickinson reflects a reverence for nature. *Poems for Youth* and *Poetry for Young People: Emily Dickinson* include a collection of Dickinson's poetry. Poems such as "The Moon Was But a Chin of Gold" personify nature by describing the moon's forehead, her cheeks, and her lips. See also Dickinson's more self-contemplative poems such as "Have You Got a Brook in Your Little Heart" and "I Took My Power in My Hand."

Photographs form the accompaniment for the nature poems in Peggy Christian's *If You Find a Rock*. Instead of identifying the rock, the poet identifies activities that could accompany the rock such as skipping in water, climbing a large rock, or kicking it all the way home. The photographs show children's curiosity associated with nature.

Charlotte Zolotow's poetry is about childhood experiences and nature. Two different editions of Zolotow's *River Winding* make possible interesting comparisons of the effects of illustrations. Children may enjoy evaluating the illustrations by Regina Shekerjian (1970 edition) and by Kazue Mizumura (1978 edition). The poem "Change" demonstrates how Zolotow is able to bring nature and children's experiences together in poetry.

Change

The summer
still hangs
heavy and sweet
with sunlight
as it did last year.

The autumn
still comes
showering gold and crimson
as it did last year.

The winter
still stings
clean and cold and white
as it did last year.

The spring
still comes
like a whisper in the dark night.

It is only I
who have changed.

From poem "Change" from *River Winding,*
by Charlotte Zolotow. Copyright 1978. Reprinted
by permission of Crowell/HarperCollins.

Creation and the ancient world are also subjects for poets. James Weldon Johnson's *The Creation,* newly illustrated by Carla Golembe, develops feelings of mystery and majesty. Douglas Wood's *Old Turtle* develops an understanding of the earth and our relationship with the beings who inhabit it. Cheng-Khee Chee's watercolors reinforce this fragility.

Nature also provides the focus for many of the selections included in John Bierhorst's *The Sacred Path: Spells, Prayers & Power Songs of the American Indians.* Seymour Simon's *Star Walk* is a collection of poetry about astronomy. The collection includes poems by poets such as Archibald MacLeish, Sara Teasdale, and May Swenson. Several Native American poems are included. The anthology is illustrated with photographs. *The Mermaid: And Other Sea Poems,* selected by Sophie Windham, is a collection of poems about both real and mythical sea creatures. Examples of poems include Rudyard Kipling's "Seal Lullaby," E. V. Rieu's "The Flattered Flying Fish," and Ted Hughes's "My Other Granny."

Nature poems frequently stimulate artists to create the settings described by poets. Ed Young illustrated Robert Frost's poem "Birches." Marcia Brown illustrated a series of "Mostly Weather" poems in de Regniers's *Sing a Song of Popcorn: Every Child's Book of Poems.* Wendell Minor's illustrations for Diane Siebert's *Mojave* illuminate the desert landscape, his illustrations in *Heartland* illuminate the land and people of the Midwest, and his illustrations for *Sierra* show the grandeur of the mountains. In Kenneth Koch and Kate Farrell's *Talking to the Sun,* an anthology containing artwork from the Metropolitan Museum of Art, many of the poems are nature poems.

Robert Frost. The nature poems of Robert Frost are frequently included in anthologies of children's literature or are heavily illustrated in versions containing only one poem. As you read one of Frost's most famous poems, "Stopping by Woods on a Snowy Evening," try to visualize nature through the viewpoint of the poet. What emotions do you believe that the poet is experiencing?

Stopping by Woods on a Snowy Evening

Whose woods these are I think I know.
His house is in the village though;
He will not see me stopping here
To watch his woods fill up with snow.

My little horse must think it queer
To stop without a farmhouse near
Between the woods and frozen lake
The darkest evening of the year.

He gives his harness bells a shake
To ask if there is some mistake.
The only other sound's the sweep
Of easy wind and downy flake.

The woods are lovely, dark and deep,
But I have promises to keep,
And miles to go before I sleep,
And miles to go before I sleep.

Robert Frost, 1923

Aileen Fisher. Fisher's poetry communicates the excitement and wonder of discovering nature. Her vision is fresh and full of the magic possible when a person really looks at the natural world. Fisher creates images that are real to children and that children may extend to other observations. In her poems about insects, found in *When It Comes to Bugs,* and her poems about seasons and rabbits, found in *Listen, Rabbit* and *Rabbits, Rabbits,* Fisher encourages readers to closely observe nature.

In Fisher's poems about winter, evergreens after a snowfall wear woolly wraps and snow fills the garden chairs with teddy bears. Fisher's "Frosted-Window World" allows children to visit Winter's house by going inside a frosted windowpane.

Frosted-Window World

The strangest thing,
the strangest thing
came true for me today:
I left myself beneath the quilt
and softly slipped away.

And do you know
the place I went
as shyly as a mouse,
as curious as a cottontail,
as watchful as a grouse?
Inside the frosted windowpane
(it's rather puzzling to explain)
to visit Winter's house!

How bright it was.
How light it was.
How white it was all over,
with twists and turns
through frosted ferns
and crusted weeds and clover,
through frost-grass
reaching up to my knees,
and frost-flowers
thick on all the trees.

The brightest sights,
the whitest sights
kept opening all around,
for everything

was flaked with frost,
the plants, the rocks,
the ground,
and everything was breathless-still
beneath the crusty rime—
there wasn't any clock to tick
or any bell to chime.
Inside the frosted windowpane
(it's rather puzzling to explain)
there wasn't any Time.

How clear it was.
How queer it was.
How near it was to heaven!
Till someone came
and called my name
and said, "It's after seven!"
And heaven vanished like an elf
and I whisked back, inside myself.

From poem "Frosted-Window World" from
In One Door and Out the Other:
A Book of Poems, by Aileen Fisher, copyright 1969.
Reprinted by permission of Crowell.

Byrd Baylor. The closeness between the land and the creatures who live upon it is strikingly presented in Baylor's poetry. Baylor tells readers that they must learn *The Other Way to Listen* if they are to be fortunate enough to hear corn singing, wildflower seeds bursting open, or a rock murmuring to a lizard. The old man in the poem teaches the child that nature will not talk to people who feel superior. A person must respect every aspect of nature, humble as well as grand, and must begin with the small things: one ant, one horned toad, one tree. In several of Baylor's books, Peter Parnall's sensitive illustrations are attuned to both nature and Baylor's words.

The poems in *Desert Voices* are written from the viewpoints of various inhabitants of the desert, animal and human. In *The Desert Is Theirs,* a poem about Native Americans, the poetry and accompanying illustrations develop the theme that the land is meant to be shared; it belongs to not only people but also spiders, scorpions, birds, coyotes, and lizards. This beautifully illustrated poem tells how Earthmaker created the desert, Spider People sewed the sky and earth together, and Elder Brother taught the people to live in the sun and to touch the power of the earth. Readers discover that the Papagos know how to share the earth. Baylor develops the close relationship between people and nature through terms such as *brother* and actions that emphasize respect:

Papagos try
not to anger
their animal brothers.

They don't
step on
a snake's track
in the sand.

They don't disturb
a fox's bones.
They don't shove
a horned toad
out of the path.

They know
the land belongs
to spider and ant
the same as it does
to people.

They never say,
"This is my land
to do with as I please."
They say,
"We share . . .
we only share."

From poem *The Desert Is Theirs,*
by Byrd Baylor. Reprinted by permission
of Simon & Schuster, Inc.

Paul Fleischman. Sound and motions in nature are strongly depicted in Paul Fleischman's *Joyful Noise: Poems for Two Voices* and *I Am Phoenix: Poems for Two Voices.* The texts are designed to be read aloud by two readers, one taking the left side, the other taking the right side. The poems are read from top to bottom, with some parts solo and some parts duet. For example, read aloud the poem "Cicadas" in Figure 8.1 with another reader. Notice the effect created by the solo parts and the two voices.

Characters, Situations, and Locations

Poems about experiences that are familiar to children make up a very large category of poetry for children. Familiar experiences may be related to friends or family, may tell about everyday occurrences, or may provide insights into children's environments.

Eloise Greenfield's *Honey, I Love* emphasizes the things a young girl loves, such as the way her cousin talks, the hose on a hot day, riding in a crowded car, and mama's soft and warm arm. The poems selected by Javaka Steptoe in *In Daddy's Arms I Am Tall: African Americans Celebrating Fathers* explore the bond between fathers and their children. Jo Carson's *Stories I Ain't Told Nobody Yet* is a collection of poetry written by people from the Appalachian region of the United States. Walter Dean Myers's *Harlem* celebrates the people, their dreams, and their environment. *When the Rain Sings: Poems by Young Native Americans,* published by the National Museum of the American Indian, includes poems that reflect traditional cultural values as well as poems embedded with historical conflict and dreams for the future.

Developing an understanding of poetry is the motivation for the poems in X. J. Kennedy's anthology *Knock at a Star: A Child's Introduction to Poetry.* The poems in the text are organized to help readers understand types and elements of poetry.

FIGURE 8.1 "Cicadas" (From Paul Fleischman. "Cicadas." *Joyful Noise: Poems for Two Voices.* Text © 1998 by Paul Fleischman. Illustrations © by Eric Beddows. Harper & Row Publishers, Inc. Reprinted by permission of HarperCollins.)

Cicadas	
Afternoon, mid-August Two cicadas singing	
	Two cicadas singing Air kiln-hot, lead-heavy
Five cicadas humming Thunderheads northwestward Twelve cicadas buzzing	Five cicadas humming
	Twelve cicadas buzzing Up and down the street
the mighty choir's assembling Shrill cica- das droning	the mighty choir's assembling
	Ci- cadas droning in the elms
Three years spent underground	*Three years*
	among the roots
in darkness Now they're breaking ground	in darkness
	and climbing up the tree trunks
splitting skins and singing	
	and singing Jubilant
rejoicing	cicadas pouring out their
fervent praise	fervent praise for heat and light
their hymn sung to the sun Cicadas whin- ing	their hymn
	Cicadas whining ci- cadas whirring
whir- ring	
	ci- cadas pulsing
pulsing chanting from the treetops sending forth their booming boisterous joyful noise!	chanting from the treetops sending forth their booming joyful noise!

R. R. Knudson and May Swenson's *American Sports Poems* is a large anthology that includes poems about both specific sports and well-known athletes. *At the Crack of the Bat* is a collection of baseball poems compiled by Lillian Morrison. The poems in Barbara Esbensen's *Who Shrank My Grandmother's House: Poems of Discovery* explore childhood discoveries about everyday objects, such as pencils, clouds, and doors.

Myra Cohn Livingston. Whether about whispers tickling children's ears or celebration of such holidays as Thanksgiving, Christmas, and Martin Luther King Day, Livingston's verses create images and suggest experiences to which children can relate. One child felt his mouth puckering as he read Livingston's poem about learning to whistle.

> *I Haven't Learned to Whistle*
>
> I haven't learned to whistle.
> I've tried—
> But if there's anything like a whistle in me,
> It stops
> Inside.
>
> Dad whistles.
> My brother whistles
> And almost everyone I know.
>
> I've tried to put my lips together with wrinkles,
> To push my tongue against my teeth
> And make a whistle
> Come
> Out
> Slow—
>
> But what happens is nothing but a feeble gasping
> Sound
> Like a sort of sickly bird.
>
> (Everybody says they never heard
> A whistle like *that*
> And to tell the truth
> Neither did I.)
>
> But Dad says, tonight, when he comes home,
> He'll show me again how
> To put my lips together with wrinkles,
> To push my tongue against my teeth,
> To blow my breath out and really make a whistle.
>
> And I'll *try!*
>
> Myra Cohn Livingston
> *O Sliver of Liver*, p. 12

In additional poems, Livingston deals with characters, situations, and locations. Livingston's books of poems include *Celebrations* and *A Circle of Seasons*.

Valerie Worth. In *More Small Poems*, Valerie Worth poetically describes looking at a moth's wing through a magnifying glass, observing a kitten with a stiffly arched back, and seeing fireworks in the night sky. Something as simple as taking off one's shoes becomes a sensual experience for Worth, as in the following poem:

> *Barefoot*
>
> After that tight
> Choke of sock
> And blunt
> Weight of shoe,
>
> The foot can feel
> Clover's green
> Skin
> Growing,
>
> And the fine
> Invisible
> Teeth
> Of gentle grass,
>
> And the cool
> Breath
> Of the earth
> Beneath.
>
> Valerie Worth
> *Still More Small Poems*, p. 13

In the poems of Valerie Worth, common things in the worlds of children contain magical qualities. In *Still More Small Poems*, Worth sees common objects with uncommon insights: Grandmother's door with the fancy glass pattern, a kite riding in the air, and rags that are no longer faithful pajamas but crumpled cloths used to wash windows. The poems from all four of Valerie Worth's series of small poems appear in *All the Small Poems*.

David McCord. The poetic genius of McCord has won him numerous honors, including the Sarah Josepha Hale Medal, a Guggenheim Fellowship, and, in 1977, the first national award for excellence in children's poetry awarded by the National Council of Teachers of English. Clifton Fadiman (McCord, 1977) said, "David McCord stands among the finest of living writers of children's verse. He is both an acrobat of language and an authentic explorer of the child's inner world" (coverleaf).

One at a Time: Collected Poems for the Young contains over two hundred of McCord's poems: favorite chants, such as "Song of the Train," alphabet verses, riddles, poetic conversations, and numerous poems about animals, children's experiences, nature, and nonsense. The last section of the book, "Write Me Another Verse," attempts to show readers how to write different poetry forms, including the ballad, the tercet, the villanelle, the clerihew, the cinquain, and the haiku. Earlier in the book, McCord gives directions for writing the couplet (two-line verse), the quatrain (four-line verse), the limerick (five-line verse), and the triolet (eight-line verse).

McCord's skill in using shape to supplement meaning is illustrated in the following poem.

> *The Grasshopper*
>
> Down
> a
> deep
> well

a
grasshopper
fell.

By kicking about
He thought to get out.
He might have known better,
For that got him wetter.

To kick round and round
Is the way to get drowned,
And drowning is what
I should tell you he got.

But
the
well
had
a
rope
that
dangled
some
hope.
And sure as molasses
On one of his passes
He found the rope handy
And up he went, *and he*

it
up
and
it
up
and
it
up
and
it
up
went
And hopped away proper
As any grasshopper.

From poem "The Grasshopper" from
*One at a Time: Collected Poems
for the Young,* pp. 28–30 by David McCord.
Copyright © 1980, Little, Brown & Company.

Moods and Feelings

The many moods and feelings associated with love are reflected in the poems compiled by William Jay Smith in *Here Is My Heart: Love Poems.* These poems range from "My Valentine" by Robert Louis Stevenson, in which love is reflected in bird song at morning and palaces fit for the loved one, to the humor of Jack Prelutsky in "I Love You More Than Applesauce," in which love is equated with feelings for lollipops and candy drops.

The many moods related to friendship are also understood by children. The poems selected by Paul B. Janeczko in his anthology *Very Best (Almost) Friend: Poems of Friendship* range from the wishful thinking in Janeczko's "If I Could Put a Curse on You," in which the unhappy friend visualizes a

locker full of killer bees and busted spokes on a new bike, to the happiness expressed in Barbara Esbensen's "Friends," in which even drawings of the friends' houses lean toward each other as the friend runs up the walk.

A bedtime fantasy forms the setting for the poems in Janet S. Wong's *Night Garden: Poems from the World of Dreams.* Poems such as "Night Garden" are enhanced through the poet's use of visualization, similes, and metaphors. Imagine a setting in which dreams grow wild and are compared with dandelion weeds with feathery heads that are alive with seeds. Or, imagine a world in which the dream person is able to answer a stranger in French that flies out of the mouth as fast as a goose flies south in winter. Or, imagine being able to swim free like a fish following a moonlit path down a stream. These are the fantasy possibilities found in the world of dreams.

Other moods and feelings related to nighttime, bedtime, and happy dreams are the focus of Thomas Hood's *Before I Go to Sleep* and Kay Chorao's anthology *The Baby's Bedtime Book,* in which a full-page painting accompanies each selection. Fantastic events in a dream world create a happy, imaginative setting in Nancy Willard's *Night Story.*

Moods and feelings about loss are found in Naomi Shihab Nye's anthology *What Have You Lost?* Many of the poems in this collection for older readers probe deeper feelings such as the lost promises we never return to, as found in Jane Hirshfield's "Autumn Quince" or Nicanor Parra's "Fame," which laments the eluded fame that eventually comes after years of desire. The poems selected by Lydia Omolola Okutoro in the anthology *Quiet Storm: Voices of Young Black Poets* are divided into sections that reflect such areas as "Black Pride," "Keeper of the Oral Tradition," and "Poems That Reflect on Self and Spirit." Moods and feelings also provide the focus in Carol Ann Duffy's *I Wouldn't Thank You for a Valentine: Poems for Young Feminists.* These poems express a variety of feelings such as humor, anger, and conflict.

In a book of poetry for older readers, *Pierced by a Ray of Sun: Poems About the Times We Feel Alone,* Ruth Gordon selects poems that emphasize various moods and feelings from alienation through hope. The note to the reader provides an introduction to the various moods reflected in the poems as the poet asks, "Am I the only such person on Earth? . . . This collection was put together with the thought that throughout time and history many have felt as we feel. If we realize that we are not the only such people on Earth, perhaps poets' words of the distant past and recent present will help us face not only our differences, but also our sameness" (p. xvii). As you read the poems in Janet S. Wong's *Behind the Wheel: Poems About Driving,* written for older readers, try to decide what the poet is saying about life. According to the introduction, "Janet S. Wong looks at driving as a metaphor for life" (unnumbered).

In *My Man Blue* Nikki Grimes uses a series of poems to develop the relationship between a young African American boy and his older friend, Blue. Simile and imagery develop Blue's characterization and appearance as Grimes describes his skin as looking like indigo ink and his harmless "gentle-giant" side. In the final poem the boy wants to grow up like Blue who both says and shows that he cares. You may compare the moods and feelings in Grimes's poetry with those expressed in the various poems found *In Daddy's Arms I Am Tall: African Americans Celebrating Fathers,* edited and illustrated by Javaka Steptoe, and in Walter Dean Myers's *Harlem.*

Some of the poems written by children may reveal very emotional experiences or times of great unhappiness or fear in their lives. For example, the poems that are included in *... I Never Saw Another Butterfly ...,* edited by Hana Volavkova were written in the Terezin Concentration Camp from 1942 through 1944. As you read the following poem, try to imagine the experiences of and the mood felt by the author, who was also a child.

The Butterfly

The last, the very last,
So richly, brightly, dazzlingly yellow.
Perhaps if the sun's tears would sing
   against a white stone....

Such, such a yellow
Is carried lightly 'way up high.
It went away I'm sure because it wished to
   kiss the world good-bye.

For seven weeks I've lived in here,
Penned up inside this ghetto.
But I have found what I love here.
The dandelions call to me
And the white chestnut branches in the court.
Only I never saw another butterfly.

That butterfly was the last one.
Butterflies don't live in here, in the ghetto.

Pavel Friedman, 1942

Langston Hughes. Although Hughes is not considered primarily a children's poet, his poetry explores feelings, asks difficult questions, and expresses hopes and desires that are meaningful to readers of any age. Some of his poems—such as "Merry-Go-Round"—can be used to help children understand and identify with the feelings and experiences of African Americans in earlier eras of American history. In another poem, Hughes vividly describes what life would be like without dreams.

Dreams

Hold fast to dreams
For if dreams die
Life is a broken-winged bird
That cannot fly.
Hold fast to dreams
For when dreams go
Life is a barren field
Frozen with snow.

Langston Hughes
The Dream Keeper, 1932, 1960

The photograph that accompanies "Dreams" in the anthology *Reflections on a Gift of Watermelon Pickle ... and Other Modern Verse,* edited by Dunning, Lueders, and Smith, shows a solitary dried weed surrounded by ice crystals. When this poem was shared with a group of fifth graders, one of the students reminded the class that dreams do not need to die: Like the weed, they can be reborn in the spring.

Cynthia Rylant. Moods and feelings related to growing up form the unifying theme in Rylant's *Waiting to Waltz: A Childhood.* Rylant's poems paint word pictures of a young girl feeling pride in her small town, pondering the relationships within the town, and revealing the experiences that influence her own maturation. In "Teenagers," for example, Rylant explores the longings of a child who is too big for some things and not big enough for others.

Teenagers

Watching the teenagers
in Beaver
using hairspray and
lipstick.
Kissing at ballgames.
Going steady.
And wanting it fast,
wanting it now.
Because all my pretend
had to be hidden.
All my games
secret.
Wanting to be a wide-open child
but too big,
too big.
No more.
Waiting to shave
and wear nylons
and waltz.
Forgetting when
I was last time
a child.
Never knowing
when it
ended.

Cynthia Rylant
Waiting to Waltz: A Childhood, p. 44

A combination of sadness and nostalgia is created in Patricia MacLachlan's *What You Know First.* The poem has a historical setting of a prairie farm during the Depression. As readers follow the girl's last tour of the farm they realize how important are these early experiences and keeping the memories even as you are forced to move to a new location. The mood of this poem could be compared with the mood created by the rhythmic language and the choice of experiences in Cynthia Rylant's *When I Was Young in the Mountains.*

Animals

When reporting a summary of the studies that investigated children's poetry preferences, Dianne Monson and Sam

Eric Carle's collage illustrations add to the beauty in a poetry collection about animals. *(From* Eric Carle's Animals, Animals. *Illustrations copyright © 1989 by Eric Carle. Philomel Books.* Snail *by John Drinkwater, © 1929. Reprinted by permission of Samuel French, Inc.)*

Sebesta (1991) concluded, "The popularity of humorous poems and poems about animals is evident from responses by English as well as U.S. children" (p. 668). Animals, whether teddy bears, cuddly puppies, purring kittens, or preposterous beasts of imagination, hold special places in the hearts of both children and adults. Therefore, it is not surprising that many poets write about animals. In *Feathered Ones and Furry*, Aileen Fisher shares with children her love for all types of animals, including the furry.

> *The Furry Ones*
>
> I like
> the furry ones—
> the waggy ones
> the purry ones
> the hoppy ones
> that hurry,
>
> The glossy ones
> the saucy ones
> the sleepy ones
> the leapy ones
> the mousy ones
> that scurry,
>
> The snuggly ones
> the huggly ones
> the never, never
> ugly ones . . .
> all soft
> and warm
> and furry.
>
> Aileen Fisher
> *Feathered Ones and Furry*, p. viii

The illustrations reinforce the spooky mood of the poems. (From Poems of Halloween Night: Ragged Shadows *by Lee Bennett Hopkins. Illustrated by Giles Laroche. Copyright © 1993 by Giles Laroche. Reprinted by permission of Little, Brown and Company.)*

The best-known collection of cat poems by a single author is probably T. S. Eliot's *Old Possum's Book of Practical Cats*. These poems, which were composed for Eliot's godchildren, are full of vivid language, interesting characterizations, and lyrical quality, as revealed when the poems were set to music in the Broadway show, *Cats*. Errol Le Cain has illustrated two poems from *Old Possum's Book of Practical Cats* in *Mr. Mistoffelees with Mungojerrie and Rumpelteazer*. It is interesting to compare the original illustrations by Edward Gorey with the new illustrations by Le Cain.

William Blake's "The Tyger," written in the eighteenth century, begins with the memorable lines "Tyger, Tyger, burning bright/In the forests of the night." In *The Tyger*, newly illustrated in a single volume, the paintings by Neil Waldman add to the energy, mood, and animals depicted in the poem. In *Mammalabilia* Douglas Florian creates poems about twenty-one animals in which he depicts often humorous characteristics. He uses considerable rhyming elements such as when he describes "The Otter" as aquatic, fanatic, acrobatic, and charismatic.

Several anthologies about animals offer works by various poets. Laura Whipple's *Eric Carle's Animals, Animals,* an anthology, includes poems about a variety of animals. Carle's collage illustrations are vivid. *The Beauty of the Beast: Poems from the Animal Kingdom,* selected by Jack Prelutsky, provides an interesting comparison.

Laura Whipple selected poems about mythical creatures for *Eric Carle's Dragons Dragons & Other Creatures That Never Were*. Eric Carle's large, colorful collages created from painted tissue paper introduce the right mood for poems about dragons, minotaurs, griffins, unicorns, krackens, and manticores. A detailed glossary contains information about these fabulous beasts and their origins. In addition, there are an index of poets and an index of creatures. Compare Whipple's collection with *The Dragons Are Singing Tonight*, written by Jack Prelutsky and illustrated by Peter Sís.

Three poetry collections are about dinosaurs. Compare the mood of the poems and the influence of Arnold Lobel's watercolor illustrations that accompany Jack Prelutsky's poems in *Tyrannosaurus Was a Beast: Dinosaur Poems* with the influence of Murray Tinkelman's black-and-white illustrations in Lee Bennett Hopkins's *Dinosaurs*. You may also compare the mood of these poems with that developed by William Wise in *Dinosaurs Forever*. Wise includes a "Pronunciation Guide" to assist the oral reader.

Witches and Ghosts

Haunted houses, ghostly appearances, mysterious happenings, and diabolic demons are found in Eve Merriam's *Hal-*loween ABC*. The spooky nature of the poems is intensified by Lane Smith's dark, dramatic illustrations. Merriam uses repetition, alliteration, and vivid imagery to capture the essence of witches and other ghostly creatures.

Alfred Noyes's classic poem *The Highwayman* has a ghostly conclusion to a tale of love, horror, and unselfish motives. Charles Keeping's black-and-white illustrations in *The Highwayman* reinforce the drama in this poem for older readers. Prior to death, the characters are sketched in black. Following death, the horseman becomes a predominantly white figure, who rides through ghostly trees, approaches the old inn door, and finds the landlord's daughter, who is now a ghostly figure herself.

Other vivid poems about ghoulies, ghosties, and graveyards are found in Daisy Wallace's collection, *Ghost Poems,* illustrated by Tomie dePaola. The world of spirits and eerie images is also evoked by Blaise Cendrars's words and Marcia Brown's illustrations in *Shadow*. Cendrars's carefully chosen words suggest a shadow that prowls, mingles, watches, spies, and sprawls in silence. Brown's collages reinforce this ghostly world. Several more ghostly poems are found in the section of poems titled "Spooky Poems" in *Sing a Song of Popcorn: Every Child's Book of Poems* by de Regniers, Moore, White, and Carr.

Suggested Activities

 For more suggested activities for understanding poetry, visit our Companion Website at www.prenhall.com/norton

- Compare the poetry selections chosen in the Children's Choices, a list published each year in the October issue of *The Reading Teacher*. What types of poetry are children selecting? Has the poetry changed throughout the years?
- Look through an anthology of poetry and find some poems that rely on sound patterns to create excitement. Prepare for oral presentation a poem that relies on alliteration (the repetition of initial consonant sounds) or assonance (the repetition of vowel sounds). Share the poem orally with a peer group.
- Compile a list of similes and metaphors found in a poem. What images does the poet suggest? Are similes or metaphors more effective or more easily visualized in word pictures than are realistic words?
- Compare the content and style of a poet who wrote humorous verse in the nineteenth century (such as Lewis Carroll or Edward Lear) with those of a contemporary author (such as Jack Prelutsky or N. M. Bodecker). What are the similarities and differences between the writers in the two time periods?

Teaching with Poetry

Appreciation for language, knowledge about concepts, empathy with characters and situations, insights about oneself and others, self-expression, and enjoyment are values of poetry for children. According to John Gough (1988), "Poetry is an acquired taste, and the taste can only be acquired by using poetry, rolling it around the tongue, spitting out words, chewing ideas, putting oneself into the action, taking risks, allowing oneself to be disturbed" (p. 194). Gough maintains that the disturbing aspect of poetry is especially important because "good poetry is disturbing. That is, it challenges our sense of reality, and breaks down our complacency with strange ideas, new feelings and alternative pictures of the world" (p. 194).

Gough (1984) also argues that the anthology format of many poetry collections discourages enjoyment. Individual poems are presented in isolation, rather than in a continuity that sustains interest. Gough believes that appreciation of poetry should be carefully developed and nurtured through a logical sequence: nursery rhymes and songs; rhymed stories, such as Dr. Seuss's *The Cat in the Hat;* narrative poems that are highly but carefully illustrated; stories, such as A. A. Milne's *Winnie-the-Pooh,* in which characters, adventures, and poems are strongly interrelated; narrative poems that give contextual support to the poetry; and then a coherent, related sequence of poems by one poet to encourage understanding of the personality of the poet and appreciation of the poems.

Rumer Godden (1988) stresses that children can be enticed with good poetry. She believes that children should proceed from singing and saying nursery rhymes to exploring lively poems that emphasize movement and rhythm, such as Stevenson's "Windy Nights," to hearing and reading small anthologies of poems to sharing poetry in which poets tell stories, such as Browning's "The Pied Piper of Hamelin," Rossetti's "Goblin Market," Noyes's "The Highwayman," and Scott's "Lochinvar."

University students often say that their aversion to poetry stems from the way in which it was presented in their elementary, middle-school, and high-school classrooms. They fondly remember the rhymes and jingles shared in kindergarten and first grade, but the pleasant associations are undercut by later forced memorization of poems and exercises in which everyone had to agree with the teacher's analysis of a poem. One student recalled her feelings of terror every Friday when she had to recite a memorized poem in front of the class and then had points deducted from her presentation for each error that she made.

Other university students, however, describe more positive memories of poetry in their elementary classrooms. The students remembered teachers who spontaneously shared a wide variety of poetry with their classes; who encouraged students to write poems and share them with an appreciative audience; and who had their students experiment with choral readings of poetry, sometimes accompanied by rhythm instruments. One student remembered a teacher who always had a poem to reflect the mood of a gentle rain, a smiling jack-o-lantern, or a mischievous child. Another remembered going outside on a warm spring day, looking at the butterflies and wildflowers in a meadow, listening to the world around her, sharing her feelings with the class, and then writing a poem to express the promise of that beautiful day. Yet another remembered a librarian who always included poetry in story-hour presentations.

After university students explore the various ways of sharing poetry with children, many of them sadly conclude that something was left out of their own educations.

Poetry Workshop

This portion of the chapter includes a series of activities developed and taught by Donna and Saundra Norton as part of several poetry workshops. The participants were teachers and graduate students. The workshops were introduced by discussing the values of poetry and asking participants to define poetry and identify their favorite poems and poets. Eve Merriam's "How to Eat a Poem" and Naoshi Koriyama's "Unfolding Bud" in Stephen Dunning, Edward Lueders, and Hugh Smith's *Reflections on a Gift of Watermelon Pickle . . . and Other Modern Verse* were then read and discussed.

A possible progression of poetry was then analyzed and discussed. Examples of this poetry began with poetry for very young children such as nursery rhymes. Anthologies of poetry for young children included Jack Prelutsky's *Read-Aloud Rhymes for the Very Young* and Jane Dyer's *Animal Crackers: A Delectable Collection of Pictures, Poems, and Lullabies for the Very Young.* Narrative poems were then discussed in which the illustrations help children interpret the poetry. Easier narrative poems included Kathi Appelt's *Oh My Baby, Little One* and Nancy Willard's *The Tale I Told Sasha.* This progression expanded to more difficult illustrated narrative poems such as Roy Gerrard's *Sir Francis Drake: His Daring Deeds* and *Sir Cedric.* Participants discussed how the illustrations helped students understand and appreciate the plot, characters, and time period in narrative poetry. These illustrated poems were then compared with narrative poems that were not illustrated, such as Henry Wadsworth Longfellow's "The Song of Hiawatha" and "Paul Revere's Ride." The nonillustrated poems were compared with illustrated versions of the same poem such as Susan Jeffers's *Hiawatha,* Errol LeCain's *Hiawatha's Childhood,* and Ted Rand's *Paul*

Revere's Ride. The groups discovered how much the illustrations added to understanding and appreciation, especially of setting and time period.

Workshop participants then progressed to reading, listening, and discussing poems by one poet along with biographical information about the poet. The poets for younger children included Lucille Clifton, Eve Merriam, David McCord, Jack Prelutsky, and Shel Silverstein. The poets for older students included Gwendolyn Brooks, Emily Dickinson, Robert Frost, Langston Hughes, Edgar Allan Poe, and Robert Louis Stevenson.

The workshop then introduced and discussed poetic elements and forms of poetry. Examples of rhythm, rhyme, alliteration, assonance, onomatopoeia, repetition, metaphors, similes, and personification were introduced. The participants had opportunities to locate, share, and discuss examples found in many anthologies that were provided for them. This same type of activity accompanied various forms of poetry including lyric, narrative, ballad, limerick, concrete, and haiku. The participants found that *Knock at a Star: A Child's Introduction to Poetry* selected by X. J. and Dorothy M. Kennedy was especially useful. The poems in sections titled "What's Inside a Poem?" and "Special Kinds of Poetry" provided numerous examples. You may use the identification of poetic elements and forms discussed earlier in this chapter to help you learn about the different forms of poetry.

The participants in these workshops were very interested in identifying poetry that could accompany various areas of the curriculum and ideas for developing strategies to be used with the poetry. The workshop then focused on identifying poetry that could accompany a study of a culture such as Native American, African American, Latino, Asian, or Jewish. The participants chose a culture, searched for appropriate poetry, and shared the poetry with the group. [They used Donna Norton's *Through the Eyes of Many Children: An Introduction to Multicultural Literature* (2001) to help them identify poetry.] Next, they identified various content areas that they taught in the curriculum. They then searched for, identified, and shared poetry that they found appropriate for the content areas of language arts, science, social studies, and math. (An excerpt from a curriculum poetry unit developed by a participant is included in a later section, Choosing Poetry to Accompany Content.)

The workshop progressed to the identification of and participation in various activities to accompany poetry. The following activities are discussed next: Reading poetry aloud, dramatizing poetry, developing choral speaking arrangements, choosing poetry to accompany content, and writing poetry with and for students.

Listening to Poetry

Poetry is meant to be read, reread, and shared. The sounds, the rhythms, the vivid words, and the unexpected phrases lend themselves to oral reading. Research shows that poetry is rarely shared with children, and even when poetry is shared, it is often isolated from other experiences. Poet Lee Bennett Hopkins (1987) argues that poetry may be disliked by children because it is frequently taught as an isolated unit instead of shared at appropriate times throughout the day. Hopkins maintains that poetry deserves to be added to the total curriculum, not limited to the language arts. Hopkins provides the following guidelines for reading poetry orally to children, whether you are a parent, teacher, or librarian:

1. Before reading a poem to an audience, read it aloud several times to get the feel of the words and rhythm. Mark the words and phrases that you would like to emphasize.

2. Read the poem naturally, following the rhythm of the poem. Allow the physical appearance of the poem to dictate the rhythm and mood of the words. Some poems are meant to be read softly and slowly; others must be read at a more rapid pace.

3. Make pauses that make sense and that please you.

4. When reading a poem aloud, speak in a natural voice. Read a poem as though you were interested in the subject.

Reading poetry aloud is also an excellent activity for children. Teacher Lisa Lenz (1992) describes the benefits of immersing her elementary students in reading poetry aloud when she states:

Listening to poetry and reading it aloud has helped my first and second graders develop a feel for the texture and power of language. The poetry they've read has stepped off the printed page and become part of their lives. The poetry they've written continues to spill out of their own hearts and into those of their listeners. (p. 597)

Lenz describes the process that she used with her students to help them prepare for reading aloud their poems. They chose poems they loved and then progressed through a series of rehearsals with peer coaches. These coaches helped them listen to themselves and consider how they wanted each poem to sound. After they could read the poems smoothly, they listened for words or phrases that had interested them and marked up a photocopy of the poem by circling special words and making notes in the margins. When they felt prepared, they videotaped their presentations. In *Let's Do a Poem* (1991), Nancy Larrick emphasizes introducing poetry through such activities as listening, singing, and body movement.

Moving to Poetry

The rhythms, sounds, characters, and images in many poems encourage physical responses from children. An observer of children on a playground is likely to see two children swinging a rope while a third child jumps to the rhythm and the actions described in a chant such as the following:

> Teddy bear, teddy bear, turn around.
> Teddy bear, teddy bear, touch the ground.
> Teddy bear, teddy bear, close your eyes.
> Teddy bear, teddy bear, be surprised.
> Teddy bear, teddy bear, climb up the stairs.
> Teddy bear, teddy bear, say your prayers.
> Teddy bear, teddy bear, turn out the light.
> Teddy bear, teddy bear, say good night.

In a similar way, children may be inspired to move when you slowly read a poem aloud. Valerie Worth's *More Small Poems* provides children with an opportunity to become a "Kitten," arching their backs, dancing sideways, tearing across the floor, crouching against imagined threats, and pouncing with claws ready, or to become "Fireworks," exploding in the air, billowing into bright color, and spilling back down toward earth in waterfalls. They can be spectacular in a much quieter way as a "Soap Bubble" that bends into different shapes, rises shimmering into the air, then pops and disappears. Worth's *Still More Small Poems* encourages children to experience the free flight of a "Kite" as the wind tears it from a hand and sends it soaring; to become a "Mushroom" pushing up through the soil; or to go "Barefoot," as their feet emerge from choking socks and they feel cool clover and gentle blades of grass between their toes.

Dramatizing Poetry

One of the values of poetry for children is encouragement to identify with characters and situations. Narrative poetry is especially good for helping children identify with characters and situations. In addition, narrative poetry is a favorite among children. Creative dramatization is one of the ways that you can enhance children's enjoyment of the situations found in poetry.

Clement C. Moore's narrative poem "A Visit from St. Nicholas" (now familiarly known as "The Night Before Christmas") suggests several scenes to dramatize. Children can prepare for the Christmas celebration by trimming the tree and decorating the room. They can imagine the sugarplum dreams and act them out. They can reenact the father's response to hearing the clatter of hoofs. They can be reindeer pulling the loaded sleigh or St. Nicholas as he comes down the chimney, fills the stockings, and then bounds up the chimney and drives out of sight.

The poem has many other dramatic possibilities. Children have created the dialogue for an imaginary meeting between the father and St. Nicholas or the children and St. Nicholas. What would they say to each other? How would they act? If the children could ask St. Nicholas questions, what would they ask? If St. Nicholas could ask questions, what would he want to know? Children have imagined themselves as St. Nicholas going into many homes on Christmas Eve. What was the most unusual experience they had? They also have imagined themselves going back to St. Nick's workshop at the North Pole. What kind of a welcome did they receive?

Adults have used the nonsensical situations found in Jack Prelutsky's poems in *The Queen of Eene* to stimulate humorous dramatizations. One group, for example, dramatized the conversation and actions of the four foolish ladies (Hattie, Harriet, Hope, and Hortense) as they roped a rhinoceros and took him to tea. Then, the group imagined and acted out other predicaments that could have been created by the actions of the foolish ladies. "Gretchen in the Kitchen" can stimulate spooky dramatizations at Halloween. The quarts of curdled mud, salted spiders, ogre's backbone, and dragon's blood provide a setting appealing to children who are preparing to be spooks, witches, and black cats.

Other poems can be used to stimulate creative dramatizations, including the following:

1. "The Pied Piper of Hamelin," by Robert Browning, located in numerous sources, including Iona and Peter Opie's *The Oxford Book of Children's Verse*. The piper lures rats to their deaths. Then, after the mayor refuses to pay for his services, the piper entices the children of the town to follow him.

2. "The Adventures of Chris," by David McCord, found in *One at a Time: Collected Poems for the Young*. A toad and a boy discuss arithmetic, spelling, and what not to miss on earth.

3. *Sir Cedric*, by Roy Gerrard. Cedric the Good, Black Ned, and Matilda the Pure have knightly adventures.

4. *Sir Francis Drake: His Daring Deeds*, by Roy Gerrard. This explorer has numerous adventures that can stimulate dramatizations.

5. *Night Story*, by Nancy Willard. A small boy has a series of adventures in dreamland.

6. *The Midnight Ride of Paul Revere*, by Henry Wadsworth Longfellow. A classic poem related to history.

7. *A Visit to William Blake's Inn: Poems for Innocent and Experienced Travelers*, by Nancy Willard. Many unusual characters, such as the man in the marmalade hat, visit the inn. The characters and incidents can stimulate many dramatizations.

Developing Choral Speaking

Choral speaking, the interpretation of poetry or other literature by two or more voices speaking as one, is a group activity that allows children to experience, enjoy, and increase their interest in rhymes, jingles, and other types of poetry. During a choral-speaking or choral-reading experience, children discover that speaking voices can be combined as effectively as singing voices. Young children who cannot read can join in during repeated lines or can take part in rhymes and verses that they know from memory; older children can select anything suitable within their reading ability. Choral speaking is useful in a variety of situations: library programs, classrooms, and extracurricular organizations.

Increasing children's enjoyment of poetry and other literature, not developing a perfect performance, is the main purpose for using choral speaking with elementary children. Allow children to enjoy the experience and experiment with various ways of interpreting poetry. Donna Norton (1997) suggests the following guidelines for encouraging children to interact in choral arrangements:

1. When selecting materials for children who cannot read, choose poems or rhymes that are simple enough to memorize.

2. Choose material of interest to children. Young children like nonsense and active words; consequently, humorous poems are enjoyable first experiences and encourage children to have fun with poetry.

3. Select poems or nursery rhymes that use refrains, especially for young children. Refrains are easy for nonreaders to memorize and result in rapid participation from each group member.

4. Let children help select and interpret the poetry. Have them experiment with the rhythm and tempo of a poem, improvise the scenes of the selection, and try different voice combinations and various choral arrangements before they decide on the best structure.

5. Let children listen to each other as they try different interpretations within groups.

Adults should also understand the different phases through which children should be guided in their choral interpretations of poetry. First, because young children delight in the rhythm of nursery rhymes, encourage them to explore the rhythm in poetry. They can skip to the rhythm of "Jack and Jill," clap to the rhythm of "Hickory Dickory Dock," and sway to the rhythm of "Little Boy Blue." They can sense fast or slow, happy or sad rhythms through their bodies. They can explore rhythm and tempo as they "hoppity, hoppity, hop" to A. A. Milne's poem "Hoppity" (found in *When We Were Very Young*).

Second, encourage children to experiment with the color and quality of voices available in the choral-speaking choir. McIntyre says that children do not need to know the meaning of *inflection* (rise and fall within a phrase), *pitch levels* (change between one phrase and another), *emphasis* (pointing out of the most important word), and *intensity* (loudness and softness of voices), but adults must understand these terms so that they can recommend materials that excite children and allow them to try different interpretations. Third, encourage children to understand and experiment with different choral arrangements, such as refrain, line, antiphonal, cumulative, and unison arrangements.

Refrain Arrangement

In refrain arrangement, an adult or a child reads or recites the body of a poem, and the other children respond in unison, repeating a refrain or chorus. Poems such as Maurice Sendak's *Pierre: A Cautionary Tale,* Lewis Carroll's "Beautiful Soup," and Jack Prelutsky's "The Yak" have lines that seem to invite group participation.

A nursery rhyme that encourages young children to participate is "A Jolly Old Pig."

Leader:	A jolly old pig once lived in a sty, And three little piggies she had, And she waddled about saying,
Group:	"Grumph! grumph! grumph!"
Leader:	While the little ones said,
Group:	"Wee! Wee!"
Leader:	And she waddled about saying,
Group:	"Grumph! grumph! grumph!"
Leader:	While the little ones said,
Group:	"Wee! Wee!"

The poetic retelling of "The Fox and the Grapes" in Tom Paxton's version of *Aesop's Fables* contains lines in parentheses such as "(A very high tree, Yes, a very high tree.)" that encourage group responses.

Line Arrangement

To develop a line arrangement, have one child or a group of children read the first line, another child or group read the next line, a third child or group read the next line, and so forth. Continue this arrangement with a different child or different group reading each line until the poem is finished. Use a familiar nursery rhyme to introduce this arrangement, such as:

Child 1 or Group 1:	One, two, buckle my shoe;
Child 2 or Group 2:	Three, four, shut the door;
Child 3 or Group 3:	Five, six, pick up sticks;
Child 4 or Group 4:	Seven, eight, lay them straight;
Child 5 or Group 5:	Nine, ten, a good fat hen.

Enjoyable poems for line-a-child arrangements include Zilpha Keatley Snyder's "Poem to Mud," Laura E. Richards's "Eletelephony," and Jack Prelutsky's "Pumberly Pott's Unpredictable Niece."

Antiphonal, or Dialogue, Arrangement

This arrangement highlights alternate speaking voices. Boys' voices may be balanced against girls' voices, or high voices may be balanced against low voices. Poems such as "Eskimo Chant," found in *The New Wind Has Wings: Poems from Canada,* compiled by Mary Alice Downie and Barbara Robertson, encourage children to respond in either joyful or fearful voices. Poems with question-

and-answer formats or other dialogue between two people are obvious choices for antiphonal arrangements. Poems such as Kaye Starbird's "The Spelling Test" and the nursery rhyme "Pussy-Cat, Pussy-Cat" are enjoyable in dialogue arrangements. Paul Fleischman's *I Am Phoenix: Poems for Two Voices* includes poems about birds. Fleischman's *Joyful Noise: Poems for Two Voices* allows children to experiment with sounds and movements of insects. The poems are written to be read by more than one person. Children also enjoy chorally reading the lyrics from folk songs. The words of "Yankee Doodle," for example, can be used with one group of children reading each verse and another group responding with the chorus. Many traditional songs are found in Dan Fox's *Go In and Out the Window: An Illustrated Songbook for Young People*. The folk song "A Hole in the Bucket" presents an enjoyable dialogue between Liza and Henry for choral speaking activity.

Try the following Mother Goose rhyme as a dialogue arrangement:

Boys: The man in the wilderness asked me
How many strawberries grew in the sea.
Girls: I answered him as I thought good,
As many red herrings as grew in the wood.

Cumulative Arrangement

A crescendo arrangement may be used effectively to interpret a poem that builds to a climax. Have the first group read the first line or verse; the first and second groups read the second line or verse; the first, second, and third groups read the third line or verse; and so forth, until the climax. Then, have all of the groups read together.

Edward Lear's "The Owl and the Pussy-Cat" may be read in a cumulative arrangement by six groups; John Ciardi's "Mummy Slept Late and Daddy Fixed Breakfast" is also fun for six groups to develop into a climax, as Daddy's waffles become impossible to eat. Other poems appropriate for cumulative reading include Arnold Lobel's *The Rose in My Garden*. The nursery rhymes "There Was a Crooked Man" and "This Is the House That Jack Built" are also enjoyable.

Try the following traditional folk song, "Skin and Bones," as a cumulative arrangement:

Group 1:	There was an old woman all skin and bones, Oo—oo—oo!
Groups 1 and 2:	She lived down by the graveyard, Oo—oo—oo!
Groups 1, 2, and 3:	One night she thought she'd take a walk, Oo—oo—oo!
Groups 1, 2, 3, and 4:	She went to the closet to get a broom, Oo—oo—oo!

Groups 1, 2, 3, 4, and 5:	She opened the door and BOO!

As a variation, develop a reverse arrangement. Have all groups begin together; then, with each subsequent line or verse, have a group drop out until only one group remains. This arrangement works well with such poems as Barbara Kunz Loots's "Mountain Wind" and James Reeves's "The Wind." Both poems begin with louder expressions and end in silence or quiet. These poems are found in Jack Prelutsky's *The Random House Book of Poetry for Children*.

Unison Arrangement

In unison arrangement, the entire group or class reads or speaks a poem together. This arrangement is often the most difficult to perform, because it tends to create a singsong effect. For this reason, shorter poems, such as Myra Cohn Livingston's "O Sliver of Liver," Lillian Morrison's "The Sidewalk Racer" or "On the Skateboard," and Judith Thurman's "Campfire," are appropriate.

Choosing Poetry to Accompany Content

An example of a poetry unit developed by a student in a workshop exemplifies how teachers develop understanding of poetry with their students. Jana Wright Prewitt (2001), a fourth-grade teacher, developed "Poetry for the Fourth-Grade Classroom: A Collection of Poems and Activities" as a unit in which she incorporates poems and activities that will allow her also to teach the various content areas of the elementary curriculum including language arts, science, social studies, and mathematics. Jana's introduction to the unit clarifies her purposes:

I decided to do a poetry collection for fourth grade students and teachers because, in my experience, I have not seen enough teachers integrating poetry into their instruction. I have not used poetry extensively with my students. I have conducted some research and discovered the importance of incorporating poetry on a daily basis in the classroom. The imagery, style, abstract nature, humor, and organization of poetry are all characteristics that attract children. What better way to encourage children to become strong readers and writers than exposing them to poetry that is humorous, descriptive, and thought provoking. I look forward to using this unit in my classroom and adding to this collection in years to come. (introduction)

The following poems are used in the unit. Each poem is followed by discussions that reinforce the following areas:

Language Arts:

Making predictions: Jack Prelutsky's "Chocolate Cake" in Prelutsky's *My Parents Think I'm Sleeping*, Greenwillow, 1985.

Comparing and contrasting things or ideas: Mary Austin's "Rathers" in Helen Ferris's *Favorite Poems Old and New,* Doubleday, 1957.

Persuasive writing or speech: Jack Prelutsky's "The Multilingual Mynah Bird" in Prelutsky's *Zoo Doings,* Greenwillow, 1983.

Acrostic poetry and description: Emily Dickinson's "I'm Nobody! Who Are You?" in Dickinson's *The Complete Poems of Emily Dickinson,* Little, Brown, 1924.

Antonyms, description, and elaboration: Jana wrote her own examples of diamante poetry.

Spelling: Robert Pottle's "Bak Too Skool" in "Giggle, Giggle, Snicker, Laugh!" and in the "Gigglepict," <http://www.robertpottle.com/>, posted July 2, 2001.

Mathematics:

Studying money: Shel Silverstein's "Smart" in *Where the Sidewalk Ends,* HarperCollins, 1974.

Geometry and shapes: Jack Prelutsky's "A Triangular Tale" in *A Pizza the Size of the Sun,* Greenwillow, 1996.

Science:

Living things: Douglas Florian's "The Daddy Longlegs" in *Insectiopedia,* Harcourt Brace, 1998.

X. J. Kennedy's "Electric Eel" in *Eric Carle's Animals Animals,* edited by Laura Whipple, Philomel, 1989.

Douglas Florian's "The Gorilla" and "The Bear" in *Mammalabilia,* Harcourt, 2000.

Importance of research and experiments: Jack Prelutsky's "Miss Misinformation" in *A Pizza the Size of the Sun,* Greenwillow, 1996.

Social Studies:

State history: Lillian Davis Terrill's "Texas, Our Texas" in Peggy Zuleika Lynch and Edmund C. Lynch's *From Hide and Horn: A Sesquicentennial Anthology of Texas Poets,* Eakin, 1985.

Jana included regional poems on culture, geography, and climate. As you identify social studies poems, expand their use to other regions of the United States and the world. Many excellent poems emphasize U.S. history such as Henry Wadsworth Longfellow's *Paul Revere's Ride* in Ted Rand's illustrated version. Poetry such as Woody Guthrie's *This Land Is Your Land* illustrated by Kathy Jakobsen, Little, Brown, 1998, provides many opportunities to incorporate content areas and poetry.

Writing Poetry

Research into the development of the writing process of children, conducted by Donald Graves (1988) and George Hillocks (1986), suggests that adults should work with children during the writing process rather than after the materials are completed. Research

emphasizes using phases in the writing process to encourage students to explore, plan, draft, and revise. For example, Jackie Proett and Kent Gill (1986) report a sequence of events and recommend activities from experiences at the Bay Area Writing Project and the University of California. These educators sequence the process according to activities that should be done (1) before the students write (content and idea building through observing, remembering, imagining, experiencing, logging, reading, brainstorming, listing, dramatizing, developing details, and structuring), (2) while the students write (developing rhetorical stance and linguistic choices by deciding voice, audience, purpose, form, word choice, figurative language, structure, and syntax), and (3) after the students write (encouraging revision and highlighting by sharing with editing groups, raising questions, expanding, clarifying, proofreading, sharing, reading, and publishing).

The various phases are certainly crucial to poetry writing. By reading or listening to poetry, children obtain motivational and observational opportunities to develop their awareness and to stimulate their imaginations. Children require opportunities to incubate and clarify ideas, to compose and revise their poetry, and to share their poetry with an appreciative audience. To share poetry writing experiences with children, use the sequence in Chart 8.1, adapted from research by Donna Norton (1997).

Motivations

The three categories of motivational activities outlined in Chart 8.1 suggest that numerous topics can stimulate the writing of poetry. Many activities already occurring in classrooms, libraries, or extracurricular organizations are natural sources of topics for self-expression through poetry. For example, while teaching a social studies unit, a second-grade teacher showed a film about farm life. The teacher encouraged the children to observe the characteristics and actions of the farm animals and then to write about them in poetic form. A Girl Scout leader encouraged children to describe and write about their feelings following a soccer game. A librarian asked children to write their own color poems after they heard Mary O'Neill's poems about colors in *Hailstones and Halibut Bones.*

University students have used both poetry written by adult authors and poetry written by children as ways of stimulating children to write their own poems. For example, they have used Kenneth Koch's *Wishes, Lies, and Dreams* (1970), reading the poems under a certain topic to children and then using the suggestions developed by Koch to encourage the children to write their own poems. Several of the categories include experiences that are common to children but allow the children to think of these experiences in new ways. A third-grade teacher encouraged his students to consider the wishes that they

CHART 8.1 An instructional sequence for poetry writing

I. Motivation
   A. Ongoing activities
   B. Everyday experiences
   C. New, adult-introduced experiences
II. Oral exchange of ideas
   A. Questions and answers to extend stimulation activities
   B. Brainstorming of subjects, vocabulary, images, and such
   C. Idea clarifications
III. Transcription
   A. Individual dictation of poems to adults
   B. Individual writing
   C. Teacher interaction to help development
   D. Adult assistance when required
   E. Revision and editing through small-group interaction and teacher interaction during individual writing
IV. Sharing
   A. Reading of the poetry to a group
   B. Audience development
   C. Permanent collections
   D. Poetry extensions, if desired, to poetry dramatizations, choral reading, art interpretations, and so forth
V. Post-transcription
   A. Permanent writing folders
   B. Writing conferences
   C. Modeling of the writing process

might make if they had the opportunity and then asked them to write a poem expressing those wishes. The following is an example of a third grader's wishes.

> I wish I had a puppy,
>   not a dog, a puppy
>   not a cat, a puppy
>   not a kitten, a puppy.
> I wish I was rich
>   not poor, but rich
>   not a little bit of money, a lot
>   so I'm really rich.
> I wish I had a Genie
>   not a pony, a Genie
>   not a pig, a Genie
>   not a pig or a pony
>   a Genie.
> I wish I could
>   have anything
>   know anything
>   be anything
>   see anything
>   and do anything
>   I wish.

Eight-year-old

Many adults encourage children to write poetry by introducing them to experiences that allow the children to nurture their awareness and their observational powers. The children may go for a walk in a flowering park or meadow, listen to the noises around them, smell the air in spring, touch trees and flowers, describe their sensations with new feelings, and then write poems about their experiences. The following poem resulted from a sixth grader's visual experiences out-of-doors.

> *Woodland*
>
> Cool crisp air calls me
> Late September afternoon
> Crimson, gold, green, rust
> Falling leaves whisper softly
> Come look, what's new in the woods?

Eleven-year-old

Oral Exchanges of Ideas

During an oral exchange of ideas, encourage children to think aloud about a subject. For example, through brainstorming, children may gain many ideas from each other and look at old ideas in new ways.

During an outside observational session, have children look at clouds and share their impressions, describe the ways the light filters through the leaves, or close their eyes and describe the sounds they hear. The librarian who encouraged children to write color poems after listening to Mary O'Neill's poems in *Hailstones and Halibut Bones* asked the children to observe the colors around them. They searched for objects that reminded them of the colors in the poems and talked about their moods as reflected by colors. For example, brainstorming the color white produced the following associations, and more: snowflakes, winter silence, puffy clouds, a wedding veil, the flash of winning, a frost-covered window, quivering vanilla pudding, heaps of popcorn, a plastered wall, apple blossoms, pale lilac blossoms, sails skimming across a lake, a forgotten memory, fog rising from a marsh, a polar bear, and a gift wrapped in tissue paper. After this experience, the children began to look at common objects and feelings with new awareness.

Transcriptions

You can help young children compose by taking dictation. Encourage the children to tell you their thoughts while you write them down. Parents indicate that even very young children enjoy seeing their creative jingles, rhymes, and poems in print. Children enjoy playing with language and feeling the tickle of new ways of expression falling off their tongues.

One university student found it meaningful that her mother had kept a notebook of her early experiences writing poetry. Another university student, who had several poems published, felt that his early spontaneous

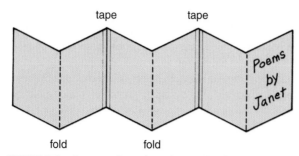

FIGURE 8.2   An accordion-pleated poem book

FIGURE 8.3   Shapes of various poetry books

poetry, written down by his mother, had stimulated his desire to become a professional writer. Parents who have been successful in this type of dictation have been careful not to force dictation upon a child or to criticize any thoughts or feelings expressed. The experiences have been warm, trusting relationships, in which children discover that their thoughts can be written down and saved for themselves and for sharing with others.

When children have mastered the mechanics of writing, they usually write their own poems. However, when working with children, continue to interact with them as they progress with their writing. Encourage them to reread their poems aloud, ask questions to help clarify a problem or an idea, or answer questions pertaining to spelling and punctuation.

Sharing

The ideal way to share poetry is to read it to an appreciative audience. Consequently, many adults encourage children to share their creations with others. Attractive bulletin boards of children's poems may also stimulate children to read one another's poems and write more poems.

Children enjoy making permanent collections of their poems. One teacher had each child develop an accordion-pleated poem book (see Figure 8.2). To construct their books, the children folded large sheets of heavy drawing paper in half, connected several sheets with tape, and printed an original poem and an accompanying illustration on each page.

Other classes have made their own books by constructing covers in various appropriate shapes, cutting paper to match the shapes, and binding the covers and pages together. A group of second graders placed Halloween poems inside a jack-o-lantern book, fourth graders wrote city poems inside a book resembling a skyscraper, and third graders placed humorous mythical animal poems inside a book resembling a beast from Dr. Seuss (see Figure 8.3). Although it is not necessary to extend writing of poetry to other activities, children often enjoy using their own poetry for choral reading, art interpretations, or dramatizations.

Various Forms of Poetry

Many children enjoy experimenting with writing different types of poems, such as limericks, cinquains, and diamantes. Limericks, for example, are among the poetry most enjoyed by children. David McCord's *One at a Time: Collected Poems for the Young* describes the content and form of limericks and provides examples that you can share with children. Use the nonsense limericks of Edward Lear, N. M. Bodecker, and William Jay Smith to stimulate these five-line poems. Follow this form: Lines 1, 2, and 5 rhyme and have a three-beat rhythm; lines 3 and 4 rhyme and have a two-beat rhythm. Brainstorming words that rhyme helps children complete their rhyming lines. After reading and listening to a number of limericks, a sixth grader wrote about and illustrated the following predicament.

> There once was a girl named Mandy
> Whose hair was dreadfully sandy
> She never did wash it
> Instead she did frost it
> The icing made Mandy smell dandy
>
> Eleven-year-old

Cinquains are another form of poetry having specific structural requirements. These poems help children realize that descriptive words are important when expressing feelings in poetry and that rhyming words are not necessary. A cinquain uses the following structure.

Line 1:	One word for the title.
Line 2:	Two words that describe the title.
Line 3:	Three words that express action related to the title.
Line 4:	Four words that express a feeling about the title.
Line 5:	One word that either repeats the title or expresses a word closely related to the title.

Brainstorming descriptive words and action words adds to children's enjoyment in writing and sharing their cinquains. The following cinquains were written by middle-school children.

Tree

Huge,   woody
Expanding,   reproducing,   entertaining
Leaves   are   colorfully   crisp
Oak

Eleven-year-old

Lasagna

Hot,   delectable
Steaming,   bubbling,   oozing
Always   great   on   Fridays
Paisans

Eleven-year-old

A diamante is a diamond-shaped poem. Poems written in the diamante format progress from one noun to a final noun that contrasts with the first noun. Because this form is more complex than the cinquain is, you should describe each line and draw a diagram of the diamante to help children see the relationships among the lines. Diamantes have the following structure.

Line 1:	One noun.
Line 2:	Two adjectives that describe the noun.
Line 3:	Three words that express action related to the noun.
Line 4:	Four nouns or a phrase that expresses a transition in thought between the first noun and the final contrasting noun.
Line 5:	Three words that express action related to the contrasting noun.
Line 6:	Two adjectives that describe the contrasting noun.
Line 7:	One contrasting noun.

Diagramming this type of poem as follows is also helpful:

noun
describing describing
action   action   action
transition nouns or phrase
action   action   action
describing describing
noun

Children find it helpful to brainstorm suggestions for contrasting nouns to form the framework for the ideas developed in a diamante. One teacher brainstormed with upper-elementary students and developed the following contrasts.

sun—moon	tears—smiles
day—night	young—old
life—death	happy—sad
friends—enemies	man—woman
summer—winter	war—peace
sky—ground	love—hate
angel—devil	darkness—light
boredom—excitement	dreams—reality

Next, each group wrote a poem. The following poems were created by this experience.

Light

Beautiful, bright
Seeing, glistening, refreshing
Light is sometimes blinding
Groping, cautioning, frightening
Evil, insecure
Dark

Ten-year-old

Friends

Happiness, security
Understanding, caring, laughing
Reaching out your hand
Hating, hurting, fighting
Silence, tension
Enemies

Ten-year-old

Through the Eyes of a TEACHER

Lisa Siemans
Multiage Primary Teacher
Riverview School
Winnipeg, Manitoba, Canada

Literature Strategy Plan: Helping Children Write Poetry

Lisa Siemans delights in helping her children express their thoughts and dreams through poetry. She believes that writing is more than picking up a pencil and setting words on paper. It is about "seeing and hearing and receiving the world in an open way." Lisa encourages children to find those little seeds of images that can be nurtured into a poem.

Building Students' Background Knowledge

Lisa reads poems aloud several times a day throughout the year. "It is important that the children be surrounded by voices—each other's as well as the voices of the finest authors and poets we can find," she says. "Our bookshelves are filled with hundreds of books: Our days are filled with listening to writers, both the ones we find between the pages of books and the ones who live inside our classroom." Published poems written by children, such as *The Palm of My Heart: Poetry by African American Children,* can help the students see themselves as poets, while selections from *Soul Looks Back in Wonder,* for example, exposes children to the poetic language of the greatest American poets. Sometimes the reading is done as part of the morning circle time at which everyone is given regular opportunities to share their favorite pieces, or Lisa reads the same poem aloud for several days during their daily meditation time, letting children savor the words and meanings. She also often reads aloud poetry children have written either that day or in previous classes.

This continual exposure to poetic language is vitally important. Reading many examples of fine poetry not only develops an appreciation for poetic language but also models poetry for children. They are then more willing to attempt writing poetry of their own. This experimentation with poetic form through writing makes children more appreciative of the crafting involved in the poetry they read.

Purposeful Reading and Writing

Lisa often begins the year with a class sharing of personal stories or special treasures they've brought into the classroom. Children sign up to share by writing a title on a sign-up sheet. "The entire month of September is about more than stories: It is about voices, about listening to each other, about widening our horizons," says Lisa. In this way she develops a community where children feel that their true voices will be heard and valued.

Gradually, through all this exposure to language, particularly poetic language, the children begin writing their own pieces. Sometimes Lisa gives a specific assignment after reading poetry aloud or following a significant event like the first snow. Most of the time, however, they are on their own, pursuing their own topics. Most of the poetry they create is not revised. "Somehow it loses its freshness when they start revising it. With the younger ones, I think it's that

> ## Sandpiper
>
> Gone Sandpiper
> Gone like the north wind
> Tracked memories in the sand
> Feathers flying in the air
> Waves slapping against the sandy beach
> Other footprints
> Kids' footprints
> Beside sandpipers
> padding against the sand
> Making a warm blanket for every sandy step she takes
> Then heading home to her nest
> Thinking of the beauty she planted in the sand
>
> Gone   Sandpiper
>
> by Thomas

Thomas was inspired to write "Gone Sandpiper."

initial impulse of what they want to say that makes their poem strong. As they get a bit older, they might work on line breaks or achieving a consistent rhythm."

With the youngest children, the writing process often begins with pictures. "I think that a lot of their wonderful pieces come through their art. Somehow when you sit down and paint or draw, it seems to take you to a different place in your head that allows you to access words, images, language that you otherwise might not have been able to reach." Thomas was one child who showed Lisa the importance of drawing in relation to writing. He had spent one whole art workshop coloring the shore by an ocean and the ocean itself. While sharing it with Lisa, he used his fingernail to sketch little footprints in the sand. "Those are sandpiper prints," he told her. Then suddenly he erased the prints, returned to his seat and wrote "Gone Sandpiper." "His mom came to me after that and said he couldn't go to sleep last night; he kept writing poems and would hold them out the door and she would go type them. She had all these scribbled pieces of paper she brought to me. He was on fire! So, maybe what art does is get you into a flow or a mind-set."

Often the children borrow ideas from each other. Because Lisa has the children for three years, they bring a history of writing to the classroom, particularly what was shared in previous years. "A lot of their voices and a lot of their words come from each other," says Lisa. "For example, one of my girls was working on this poem and the

last line was 'Don't worry my heart is always open.'" I told her that sounds so much like a poem we did last year and she looked at me quietly and said, 'I know.'"

Assessing Student Learning

"I do a lot of my assessment through observation: Are they engaged; are they moving forward with using language in more sophisticated ways; how willing are they to try new things? I really can't measure one poem against another. Our students keep portfolios which they share with their parents. During this time they have an hour to do whatever they want with their parents—often they share poetry or have parents try to write some. They don't really judge themselves or compare themselves with other children. There is just a lot of valuing of what they do."

Lisa also publishes the children's work in the weekly class newsletter. She believes that when parents see how the children's work is honored, they honor it too.

Lisa does have to give some sort of numerical rating to mark each child's progress in language arts. However, it is done on the basis of 4/3/2/1 with "1" being the highest rating. These ratings are very broadly defined.

 For ideas on adapting Lisa Siemans's lesson to meet the needs of older or younger readers, please visit Chapter 8 on our Companion Website at www.prenhall.com/norton

Poetry Writing Exercises

Robin Behn and Chase Twichell, the editors of *The Practice of Poetry: Writing Exercises from Poets Who Teach* (1992), provide strong reasons for using poetry writing exercises with anyone who wants to improve his or her writing. They state:

Poetry, like any art, requires practice. It's easy for us to accept the idea of practice when we think of a painter's figure studies or the sounds coming from the hives of practice rooms in a conservatory. But, since we consider ourselves already fluent in language, we may imagine that talent is the only requirement for writing poetry. . . . The aspiring poet must master the elements of language, the complexities of form and its relation to subject, the feel of the line, the image, the play of sound that make it possible to respond in a voice with subtlety and range when he hears that music in his inner ear, or she sees in the world that image that's the spark of a poem. (p. xi)

Several of the exercises described by various poets in Behn and Twichell's collection of writing exercises are appropriate for students in the elementary and middle

grades. For example, to improve an understanding of language and abstract thoughts, have students list their associations with words such as *love* and then ask them to translate the ideas into abstractions and mental pictures, metaphors, or images. These images then become the foundations for poetry. To enhance the visualization of images in a poem, ask them to listen to a poem and then write down all of the evocative words triggered by the poem. To help students structure or organize a poem, ask them to choose an ordinary object such as a door and then make a list of the functions for that object. Hopefully, the object has a symbolic meaning such as a door opens, closes, separates, or blocks the view. Now begin the poem with a title that identifies the object and follow it with a list of functions. Finally, conclude the poem with a summary statement that also suggests the more symbolic meaning.

I have used several of the poetry writing exercises associated with photography described by poet Maggie Anderson (Behn and Twichell, 1992, pp. 231–235). Now a photograph provides the details, the images, the setting, and the characters that provide the details for the content of the poem. Anderson recommends that students write at least three different poems using the same photograph but writing from different viewpoints or perspectives. For example, a poem could be written from the point of view of the photographer or from someone or something that is shown in the photograph. The poem might be written from the perspective of what happened just before, during, or after the photograph was taken. The poem might be written from the perspective of someone finding the photograph years after it was taken. Photographs of experiences that are close to children or people who are important in their lives are especially meaningful. In one classroom we created photo albums that included pictures of students and poems that described each of the students. Activities such as a school field trip, sports, music, or drama provide excellent photographic subjects.

Another excellent source of ideas and suggestions for exercises in poetry writing is Stephen Dunning and William Stafford's *Getting the Knack: 20 Poetry Writing Exercises* (1992). Each of the exercises includes an introduction, steps to follow, and examples of poems that were written using the writing exercise.

Adults Writing Poetry for Juvenile Audiences

The poetry writing workshop mentioned earlier in this chapter concluded with several sessions on recommendations for adults who want to write poetry for children. The participants in the workshops were either interested in publishing poetry or in creating poetry that they could use as models when teaching their own students.

For this activity, Jean E. Karl's chapter "Writing Poetry and Verse for Children" in *How to Write and Sell Children's Books* (1994) was very useful. Karl provides ten steps that should be followed by prospective authors. As you read through these steps, notice how the steps include many of the activities already discussed in this chapter. You will also discover that you can use the following steps when teaching children to be poetry writers:

Step 1: Discover the nature of verse and poetry. You should choose verse and poetry as a form for writing when you are convinced that no other form of writing is as good for your purpose.

Step 2: Search for the experiences, emotions, and imagination associated with childhood. This search will enable you to understand and speak to a child when writing your poetry.

Step 3: Understand the traditional structure of verse and poetry. Study the writing of poetry and verse to discover how to create patterns of meter and rhyme.

Step 4: Explore more modern forms of verse and poetry. Experiment with ways of putting ideas into form where rhythm does not constrict your expression.

Step 5: Decide what you will write. Will it be a collection of poems, a single poem for a magazine, or a longer narrative poem that will be illustrated?

Step 6: Begin with an idea and a vision. Write with language that is colorful, evocative, and fresh.

Step 7: Revise even as you write. Keep the vision in mind as you write and revise. Keep revising until the final version matches the initial idea and the inspiration that caused you to write the poem.

Step 8: Put the poem away for a few days. Let someone whose judgment you respect read and respond to the poem.

Step 9: Decide what you want to do with the poem. Will you send it to a magazine? Will you try to have a longer poem illustrated?

Step 10: Final rewrite. Prepare your manuscript for submission.

This part of the workshop always concludes with poetry readings in which participants share their own poems with an audience. Some of the participants may prepare their works for manuscript submission. Whatever happens to the poetry, the participants discover a great deal about poetry and how they might motivate their own students to appreciate and understand it. Ralph Fletcher's *Poetry Matters: Writing a Poem from the Inside Out* is written for students in the upper grades.

Children's Literature

Adedjourna, Davida (editor). *The Palm of My Heart: Poetry by African American Children.* Illustrated by Gregory Christie. Lee, 1996 (I:7+ R:1).

Adoff, Arnold. *All the Colors of the Race.* Illustrated by John Steptoe. Lothrop, Lee & Shepard, 1982.

_____ . *Love Letters.* Illustrated by Lisa Desimini. Scholastic, 1997.

_____ . *My Black Me: A Beginning Book of Black Poetry.* Dutton, 1974.

_____ . ed. *The Poetry of Black America: Anthology of the 20th Century.* Harper & Row, 1973.

_____ . *Sports Pages.* Illustrated by Steve Kuzma. Lipplncott, 1986.

Aesop. *Aesop's Fables.* Retold by Tom Paxton. Illustrated by Robert Rayevsky. Morrow, 1988.

Alarcón, Francisco X. *Laughing Tomatoes.* Illustrated by Maya Christina Gonzalez. Children's, 1997.

Angelou, Maya (editor). *Soul Looks Back in Wonder.* Illustrated by Tom Feelings. Dial, 1993 (I:7+ R:2).

Appelt, Kathi. *Oh My Baby, Little One.* Illustrated by Jane Dyer. Harcourt, 2000.

Attenborough, Liz (compiled by). *Poetry by Heart.* Scholastic, 2001.

Atwood, Ann. *Haiku: The Mood of Earth.* Scribner's Sons, 1971.

Baylor, Byrd. *The Desert Is Theirs.* Illustrated by Peter Parnall. Scribner's Sons, 1975.

_____ . _Moon Song._ Illustrated by Ronald Himler. Scribner's Sons, 1982.

_____ . _The Other Way to Listen._ Illustrated by Peter Parnall. Scribner's Sons, 1978.

Baylor, Byrd, and Peter Parnall. _Desert Voices._ Scribner's Sons, 1981.

Belafonte, Harry, and Lord Burgess. _Island in the Sun._ Illustrated by Alex Ayliffe. Dial, 1999.

Bierhorst, John, ed. _The Sacred Path: Spells, Prayers & Power Songs of the American Indians._ Morrow, 1983.

Blake, William. _The Tyger._ Illustrated by Neil Waldman. Harcourt Brace Jovanovich, 1993.

Bodecker, N. M. _Hurry, Hurry Mary Dear!_ Atheneum, 1976.

Brenner, Barbara, selected by. _Voices: Poetry and Art from Around the World._ National Geographic, 2000.

Brooks, Gwendolyn. _Bronzeville Boys and Girls._ Illustrated by Ronni Solbert. Harper & Row, 1956.

Browning, Robert. _The Pied Piper of Hamelin._ Illustrated by Kate Greenaway. Warne Classic, 1888.

Bryan, Ashley. _I'm Going to Sing: Black American Spirituals._ Vol. 2. Atheneum, 1982.

_____ . _Sing to the Sun._ HarperCollins, 1992.

Burkert, Nancy Ekholm. _Valentine and Orson._ Farrar, Straus & Giroux, 1989.

Carroll, Lewis. _Jabberwocky._ Illustrated by Jane Breskin Zalben. Warne, 1977.

_____ . _Poems of Lewis Carroll._ Selected by Myra Cohn Livingston. Crowell, 1973.

Carson, Jo, ed. _Stories I Ain't Told Nobody Yet._ Watts, 1989.

Causley, Charles, ed. _Salt-Sea Verse._ Illustrated by Antony Maitland. Kestrel, Puffin, 1981.

Cendrars, Blaise. _Shadow._ Translated and illustrated by Marcia Brown. Scribner's Sons, 1982.

Chorao, Kay. _The Baby's Bedtime Book._ Dutton, 1984.

Christian, Peggy. _If You Find A Rock._ Photographs by Barbara Hirsch Lember. Harcourt, 2000.

Ciardi, John. _Doodle Soup._ Illustrated by Merle Nacht. Houghton Mifflin, 1985.

_____ . _The Hopeful Trout and Other Limericks._ Illustrated by Susan Meddaugh. Houghton Mifflin, 1989.

_____ . _You Read to Me, I'll Read to You._ Illustrated by Edward Gorey. Lippincott, 1962.

Cole, William, ed. _Poem Stew._ Illustrated by Karen Ann Weinhaus. Lippincott, 1981.

Demi, ed. _In the Eyes of the Cat: Japanese Poetry for All Seasons._ Illustrated by Demi, translated by Tze-si Huang. Holt, 1992.

de Regniers, Beatrice Schenk, Eva Moore, Mary Michaels White, and Jean Carr. _Sing a Song of Popcorn: Every Child's Book of Poems._ Scholastic, 1988.

Dickinson, Emily. _The Complete Poems of Emily Dickinson._ Little, Brown, 1924.

_____ . _Poetry for Young People: Emily Dickinson,_ edited by Frances Schoonmaker Bolin. Illustrated by Chi Chung. Sterling, 1994.

_____ . _Poems for Youth,_ edited by Alfred Leete Hampson. Illustrated by Thomas B. Allen. Little, Brown, 1996.

Downie, Mary Alice, and Barbara Robertson, eds. _The New Wind Has Wings: Poems from Canada._ Illustrated by Elizabeth Cleaver. Oxford University Press, 1984.

Duffy, Carol Ann, ed. _I Wouldn't Thank You for a Valentine: Poems for Young Feminists._ Illustrated by Trisha Rafferty. Holt, 1994.

Dunning, Stephen, Edward Lueders, and Hugh Smith, eds. _Reflections on a Gift of Watermelon Pickle . . . and Other Modern Verse._ Lothrop, Lee & Shepard, 1967.

Dyer, Jane. _Animal Crackers: A Delectable Collection of Pictures, Poems, and Lullabies for the Very Young._ Little, Brown, 1996.

Eliot, T. S. _Mr. Mistoffelees with Mungojerrie and Rumpelteazer._ Illustrated by Errol Le Cain. Harcourt Brace Jovanovich, 1991.

_____ . _Old Possum's Book of Practical Cats._ Illustrated by Edward Gorey. Harcourt Brace Jovanovich, 1939, 1967, 1982.

Esbensen, Barbara. _Who Shrank My Grandmother's House? Poems of Discovery._ Illustrated by Eric Beddows. HarperCollins, 1992.

Ferris, Helen, ed. _Favorite Poems Old and New._ Doubleday, 1957.

Field, Eugene. _Wynken, Blynken and Nod._ Illustrated by Susan Jeffers. Dutton, 1982.

Fields, Julia. _The Green Lion of Zion Street._ Illustrated by Jerry Pinkney. Macmillan, 1988.

Fisher, Aileen. _Feathered Ones and Furry._ Illustrated by Eric Carle. Crowell, 1971.

_____ . _In One Door and Out the Other: A Book of Poems._ Illustrated by Lillian Hoban. Crowell, 1969.

_____ . _Listen, Rabbit._ Illustrated by Simeon Shimin. Crowell, 1964.

_____ . _Rabbits, Rabbits._ Illustrated by Gail Nieman. Harper & Row, 1983.

_____ . _When it Comes to Bugs._ Illustrated by Chris and Bruce Degen. Harper & Row, 1986.

Fleischman, Paul. _I Am Phoenix: Poems for Two Voices._ Illustrated by Ken Nutt. Harper & Row, 1985.

_____ . _Joyful Noise: Poems for Two Voices._ Illustrated by Eric Beddows. Harper & Row, 1988.

Fletcher, Ralph. _Poetry Matters: Writing a Poem from the Inside Out._ HarperCollins, 2002.

Florian, Douglas. _Insectiopedia._ Harcourt Brace, 1998.

_____ . _Mammalabilia._ Harcourt, 2000.

Fox, Dan, ed. _Go In and Out the Window: An Illustrated Songbook for Young People._ Metropolitan Museum of Art and Holt, Rinehart & Winston, 1987.

Frazee, Marla. _Hush, Little Baby._ Harcourt, 1999.

Froman, Robert. _Seeing Things: A Book of Poems._ Crowell, 1974.

Frost, Robert. _Birches._ Illustrated by Ed Young. Holt, Rinehart & Winston, 1988.

_____ . _Stopping by Woods on a Snowy Evening._ Illustrated by Susan Jeffers. Dutton, 1978.

George, Kristine O'Connell. _The Great Frog Race and Other Poems._ Illustrated by Kate Kiesler. Clarion, 1997.

_____ . _Toasting Marshmallows: Camping Poems._ Illustrated by Kate Kiesler. Clarion, 2001.

Gerrard, Roy. _Sir Cedric._ Farrar, Straus & Giroux, 1984.

_____ . _Sir Francis Drake: His Daring Deeds._ Farrar, Straus & Giroux, 1988.

_____ . _Wagons West!_ Farrar, Straus & Giroux, 1996.

Gollub, Matthew. _Cool Melons—Turn to Frogs! The Life and Poems of Issa._ Illustrated by Kazuko G. Stone. Lee & Low, 1998.

Gordon, Ruth, selected by. _Pierced by a Ray of Sun: Poems About the Times We Feel Alone._ HarperCollins, 1995.

Graham, Joan Bransfield. _Flicker Flash._ Illustrated by Nancy Davis. Houghton Mifflin, 1999.

Greenberg, Jan, ed. *Heart to Heart: New Poems Inspired by Twentieth-Century American Art.* Abrams, 2001.

Greenfield, Eloise, *Honey, I Love.* Illustrated by Jan Spivey Gilchrist. HarperCollins, 1995.

_____. *Nathaniel Talking.* Illustrated by Jan Gilchrist. Black Butterfly Children's Books, 1989.

Grimes, Nikki. *Come Sunday.* Illustrated by Michael Bryant. Eerdmans, 1996.

_____. *My Man Blue.* Illustrated by Jerome Lagarrigue. Dial, 2001.

_____. *A Pocketful of Poems.* Illustrated by Javaka Steptoe. Clarion, 2001.

Guthrie, Woody. *This Land Is Your Land.* Illustrated by Kathy Jakobsen. Little, Brown, 1998.

Hall, Donald, ed. *The Oxford Illustrated Book of American Children's Poems.* Oxford, 1999.

Hoberman, Mary Ann, adapted by. *There Once Was a Man Named Michael Finnegan.* Illustrated by Nadine Bernard Westcott. Little, Brown, 2001.

Hood, Thomas. *Before I Go to Sleep.* Illustrated by Mary Jane Begin-Callanan. Putnam, 1990.

Hopkins, Lee Bennett. ed. *Dinosaurs.* Illustrated by Murray Tinkelman. Harcourt Brace Jovanovich, 1987.

_____. *Good Rhymes, Good Times.* Illustrated by Frané Lessac. HarperCollins, 1995.

_____, ed. *Surprises.* Illustrated by Megan Lloyd. Harper & Row, 1984.

Hughes, Langston. *The Dream Keeper.* Knopf, 1932, 1960.

_____. *Selected Poems of Langston Hughes.* Knopf, 1942, 1959.

Janeczko, Paul B. *A Poke in the I: A Collection of Concrete Poems.* Illustrated by Chris Raschka. Candlewick, 2001.

_____, collected by. *Very Best (Almost) Friends: Poems of Friendship.* Illustrated by Christine Davenier. Candlewick, 1999.

Johnson, James Weldon. *The Creation.* Illustrated by Carla Golembe. Little, Brown, 1993.

Katz, Bobbi. *Truck Talk: Rhymes on Wheels.* Scholastic, 1997.

Kellogg, Steven. *I Was Born About 10,000 Years Ago.* Morrow, 1996.

Kemp, Gene, ed. *Ducks and Dragons: Poems for Children.* Illustrated by Carolyn Dinan. Faber & Faber, 1980; Puffin, 1983.

Kennedy, X. J. *The Beasts of Bethlehem.* Illustrated by Michael McCurdy. Macmillan, 1992.

_____, and Dorothy M. Kennedy, eds. *Knock at a Star: A Child's Introduction to Poetry.* Illustrated by Karen Lee Baker. Little, Brown, 1999.

_____, and Dorothy M. Kennedy, eds. *Talking Like the Rain: A First Book of Poems.* Illustrated by Jane Dyer. Little, Brown, 1992.

Kipling, Rudyard. *Gunga Din.* Illustrated by Robert Andrew Parker. Harcourt Brace Jovanovich, 1987.

Knudson, R. R., and May Swenson, eds. *American Sports Poems.* Watts, 1988.

Koch, Kenneth, and Kate Farrell, eds. *Talking to the Sun.* Metropolitan Museum of Art/Holt, Rinehart & Winston, 1985.

Langstaff, John, foreword by. *On Christmas Day in the Morning.* Illustrated by Melissa Sweet. Candlewick, 1999.

_____, ed. *What a Morning! The Christmas Story in Black Spirituals.* Illustrated by Ashley Bryan. Macmillan, 1987.

Larrick, Nancy, ed. *Songs from Mother Goose.* Illustrated by Robin Spowart. Harper & Row, 1989.

_____, ed. *When the Dark Comes Dancing: A Bedtime Poetry Book.* Illustrated by John Wallner. Philomel, 1982.

Lear, Edward. *A Book of Bosh.* Compiled by Brian Alderson. Penguin, 1982.

_____. *The Complete Nonsense Book.* Dodd, Mead, 1946.

_____. *Hilary Knight's The Owl and the Pussy-Cat.* Illustrated by Hilary Knight. Macmillan, 1983.

_____. *The Nonsense Books of Edward Lear.* New American Library, 1964.

_____. *Nonsense Omnibus.* Warne, 1943.

_____. *Nonsense Songs.* Illustrated by Bee Willey. Simon & Schuster, 1997.

_____. *The Owl and the Pussycat.* Illustrated by Jan Brett. Putnam, 1991.

_____. *The Pelican Chorus and Other Nonsense.* Illustrated by Fred Marcellino. HarperCollins, 1995.

Lee, Dennis. *The Ice Cream Store.* Illustrated by David McPhail. HarperCollins, 1991.

Levy, Constance. *I'm Going to Pet a Worm Today and Other Poems.* Illustrated by Ronald Himler. Macmillan, 1991.

Lewis, J. Patrick. *Earth Verses and Water Rhymes.* Illustrated by Robert Sabuda. Atheneum, 1991.

Lewis, Richard. *Of This World: A Poet's Life in Poetry.* Photographs by Helen Buttfield. Dial, 1968.

Little, Jean. *Hey World, Here I Am!* Illustrated by Sue Truesdell. Harper & Row, 1989.

Liu, Siyu, and Orel Protopopescu. *A Thousand Peaks: Poems from China.* Illustrated by Siyu Liu. Pacific View, 2002.

Livingston, Myra Cohn. *Celebrations.* Illustrated by Leonard Everett Fisher. Holiday House, 1985.

_____. *A Circle of Seasons.* Illustrated by Leonard Everett Fisher. Holiday House, 1982.

_____. *Cricket Never Does: A Collection of Haiku and Tanka.* Illustrated by Kees de Kiefte. McElderry, 1997.

_____. *O Sliver of Liver.* Illustrated by Iris Van Rynbach. Atheneum, 1979.

Lobel, Arnold. *The Rose in My Garden.* Illustrated by Anita Lobel. Greenwillow, 1984.

_____. *Whiskers and Rhymes.* Greenwillow, 1985.

Longfellow, Henry Wadsworth. *Hiawatha.* Illustrated by Susan Jeffers. Dutton, 1983.

_____. *Hiawatha.* Illustrated by Keith Mosely. Putnam, 1988.

_____. *Hiawatha's Childhood.* Illustrated by Errol LeCain. Farrar, Straus & Giroux, 1984.

_____. *The Midnight Ride of Paul Revere.* Illustrated by Christopher Bing. Handprint, 2001.

_____. *Paul Revere's Ride.* Illustrated by Paul Galdone. Crowell, 1963.

_____. *Paul Revere's Ride.* Illustrated by Ted Rand. Dutton, 1990.

Loveday, John, ed. *Over the Bridge: An Anthology of New Poems.* Illustrated by Michael Foreman. Kestrel, Penguin, 1981.

Lynch, Peggy Zuleika, and Edmund C. Lynch. *From Hide and Horn: A Sesquicentennial Anthology of Texas Poets.* Eakin, 1985.

MacLachlan, Patricia. *What You Know First.* Illustrated by Barry Moser. HarperCollins, 1995.

McCord, David. *Far and Few: Rhymes of the Never Was and Always Is.* Illustrated by Henry B. Kane. Little, Brown, 1952.

———. *One at a Time: Collected Poems for the Young.* Illustrated by Henry B. Kane. Little, Brown, 1977.

Mahy, Margaret. *Nonstop Nonsense.* Illustrated by Quentin Blake. Macmillan, 1989.

Marshak, Samuel. *The Pup Grew Up.* Translated by Richard Pevear. Illustrated by Vladimir Radunsky. H. Holt, 1989.

Merriam, Eve. *Halloween ABC.* Illustrated by Lane Smith. Macmillan, 1987.

———. *Rainbow Writing.* Atheneum, 1976.

———. *The Singing Green: New and Selected Poems for All Seasons.* Illustrated by Kathleen Collins Howell. Morrow, 1992.

Michelson, Richard. *Animals that Ought to Be: Poems About Imaginary Pets.* Illustrated by Leonard Baskin. Simon & Schuster, 1996.

Milne, A. A. *When We Were Very Young.* Illustrated by Ernest H. Shepard. Dutton, 1961.

———. *Winnie-the-Pooh.* Illustrated by Ernest H. Shepard. Dutton, 1954.

———. *The World of Christopher Robin.* Illustrated by E. H. Shepard. Dutton, 1958.

Moore, Clement. *The Night Before Christmas.* Illustrated by Tomie dePaola. Holiday House, 1980.

———. *The Night Before Christmas.* Illustrated by Tasha Tudor. Little, Brown, 1999.

Moore, Lilian. *Adam Mouse's Book of Poems.* Illustrated by Kathleen Garry McCord. Atheneum, 1992.

Morrison, Lillian, ed. *At the Crack of the Bat.* Illustrated by Steve Cieslawski. Hyperion, 1992.

Morton, Miriam, ed. *The Moon Is Like a Silver Sickle: A Celebration of Poetry by Russian Children.* Illustrated by Eros Keith. Simon & Schuster, 1972.

Myers, Walter Dean. *Harlem.* Illustrated by Christopher Myers. Scholastic, 1997.

Noyes, Alfred. *The Highwayman.* Illustrated by Charles Keeping. Oxford University Press, 1981.

Nye, Naomi Shihab, ed. *This Same Sky: A Collection of Poems from Around the World.*

———, ed. *What Have You Lost?* Photographs by Michael Nye. Greenwillow, 1999.

Okutoro, Lydia Omolola, selected by. *Quiet Storm: Voices of Young Black Poets.* Hyperion, 1999.

O'Neill, Mary. *Hailstones and Halibut Bones.* Illustrated by Leonard Weisgard. Doubleday, 1961.

Opie, Iona, and Peter Opie, eds. *The Oxford Book of Children's Verse.* Oxford University Press, 1984.

———. *Tail Feathers from Mother Goose: The Opie Rhyme Book.* Little, Brown, 1988.

Paolilli, Paul, and Dan Brewer. *Silver Seeds: A Book of Nature Poems.* Illustrated by Steve Johnson and Lou Fancher. Viking, 2001.

Prelutsky, Jack. *Awful Ogre's Awful Day.* Illustrated by Paul O. Zelinsky. Greenwillow, 2001.

———. *The Baby Uggs Are Hatching.* Illustrated by James Stevenson. Greenwillow, 1982.

———. ed. *The Beauty of the Beast: Poems from the Animal Kingdom.* Illustrated by Meilo So. Knopf, 1997.

———. *The Dragons Are Singing Tonight.* Illustrated by Peter Sís. Greenwillow, 1993.

———. *The Frog Wore Red Suspenders.* Illustrated by Petra Mathers. Greenwillow, 2002.

———. *The Gargoyle on the Roof.* Illustrated by Peter Sís. Greenwillow, 1999.

———. *A Gopher in the Garden and Other Animal Poems.* Illustrated by Robert Leydenfrost. Macmillan, 1966, 1967.

———. *The Headless Horseman Rides Tonight.* Illustrated by Arnold Lobel. Greenwillow, 1980.

———. *Monday's Troll.* Illustrated by Peter Sís. Greenwillow, 1996.

———. *My Parents Think I'm Sleeping.* Greenwillow, 1985.

———. *A Pizza the Size of the Sun.* Illustrated by James Stevenson. Greenwillow, 1996.

———. *The Queen of Eene.* Illustrated by Victoria Chess. Greenwillow, 1978.

———, ed. *The Random House Book of Poetry for Children.* Illustrated by Arnold Lobel. Random House, 1983.

———, ed. *Read-Aloud Rhymes for the Very Young.* Illustrated by Marc Brown. Knopf, 1986.

———. *Rolling Harvey down the Hill.* Illustrated by Victoria Chess. Greenwillow, 1980.

———. *The Sheriff of Rottenshot.* Illustrated by Victoria Chess. Greenwillow, 1982.

———. *Tyrannosaurus Was a Beast: Dinosaur Poems.* Illustrated by Arnold Lobel. Greenwillow, 1988.

———. *Zoo Doings.* Greenwillow, 1983.

Richards, Laura E. *Tirra Lirra, Rhymes Old and New.* Illustrated by Marguerite Davis. Little, Brown, 1955.

Rosen, Michael, ed. *Poems for the Very Young.* Illustrated by Bob Graham, Kingfisher, 1993.

Rossetti, Christina. *Goblin Market.* Illustrated and adapted by Ellen Raskin. Dutton, 1970.

———. *Sing-Song.* Illustrated by Arthur Hughes. Routledge, 1872.

Rylant, Cynthia. *Waiting to Waltz: A Childhood.* Illustrated by Stephen Gammell. Bradbury, 1984.

Schwartz, Alvin. *And the Green Grass Grew All Around: Folk Poetry from Everyone.* Illustrated by Sue Truesdell. HarperCollins, 1992.

Seeger, Ruth Crawford. *American Folksongs for Children—In Home, School, and Nursery School.* Illustrated by Barbara Cooney. Doubleday, 1948.

Sendak, Maurice. *Pierre: A Cautionary Tale.* Harper & Row, 1962.

Seuss, Dr. *The Cat in the Hat.* Random House, 1957.

Siebert, Diane. *Heartland.* Illustrated by Wendell Minor. Crowell, 1989.

———. *Mojave.* Illustrated by Wendell Minor. Crowell, 1988.

———. *Sierra.* Illustrated by Wendell Minor. HarperCollins, 1991.

Siegen-Smith, Nikki. *Songs for Survival: Songs and Chants from Tribal Peoples Around the World.* Illustrated by Bernard Lodge. Dutton, 1996.

Silverstein, Shel. *Fall Up.* HarperCollins, 1996.

———. *A Light in the Attic.* Harper & Row, 1981.

———. *Where the Sidewalk Ends.* Harper & Row, 1974.

Simon, Seymour, ed. *Star Walk.* Morrow, 1995.

Smith, William J., compiled by. *Here Is My Heart: Love Poems.* Illustrated by Jane Dyer. Little, Brown, 1999.

_____. *Laughing Time.* Illustrated by Juliet Kepes. Little, Brown, 1955.

Snyder, Zilpha Keatley. *Today Is Saturday.* Illustrated by John Arms. Atheneum, 1969.

Southey, Robert. *The Cataract of Lodore.* Illustrated by David Catrow. Holt, 1992.

Starbird, Kaye. *The Covered Bridge House and Other Poems.* Illustrated by Jim Arnosky. Four Winds, 1979.

Steptoe, Javaka, edited and Illustrated by. *In Daddy's Arms I Am Tall: African Americans Celebrating Fathers.* Lee & Low, 1997.

Stevenson, Robert Louis. *A Child's Garden of Verses.* Longmans, Green, 1885.

Thurman, Judith. *Flashlight and Other Poems.* Illustrated by Reina Rubel. Atheneum, 1976.

Tiller, Ruth. *Cats Vanish Slowly.* Illustrated by Laura Seeley. Peachtree, 1995.

Turner, Ann. *Mississippi Mud: Three Prairie Journals.* Illustrated by Robert J. Blake. HarperCollins, 1997.

Van Laan, Nancy. *With a Whoop and a Holler: A Bushel of Lore from Way Down South.* Illustrated by Scott Cook. Atheneum, 1998.

Viorst, Judith. *If I Were in Charge of the World and Other Worries: Poems for Children and Their Parents.* Illustrated by Lynne Cherry. Atheneum, 1981.

Volavkova, Hana, ed. *. . . I Never Saw Another Butterfly. . . .* Schocken, 1993.

Wallace, Daisy. *Ghost Poems.* Illustrated by Tomie dePaola. Holiday House, 1979.

Westcott, Nadine Bernard. *Peanut Butter and Jelly: A Play Rhyme.* Dutton, 1987.

When the Rain Sings: Poems by Young Native Americans. National Museum of the American Indian and Simon & Schuster, 1999.

Whipple, Laura, ed. *Eric Carle's Animals, Animals.* Illustrated by Eric Carle. Philomel, 1989.

_____. *Eric Carle's Dragons Dragons & Other Creatures That Never Were.* Philomel, 1991.

Willard, Nancy. *Night Story.* Illustrated by Ilse Plume. Harcourt Brace Jovanovich, 1986.

_____. *Pish, Posh, Said Hieronymus Bosch.* Illustrated by Leo and Diane Dillon. Harcourt Brace Jovanovich, 1991.

_____. *The Tale I Told Sasha.* Illustrated by David Christiana. Little, Brown, 1999.

_____. *A Visit to William Blake's Inn: Poems for Innocent and Experienced Travelers.* Illustrated by Alice and Martin Provensen. Harcourt Brace Jovanovich, 1981.

Wilner, Isabel, ed. *The Poetry Troup: An Anthology to Read Aloud.* Scribner's Sons, 1977.

Windham, Sophie. Selected by. *The Mermaid: And Other Sea Poems.* Scholastic, 1996.

Wise, William. *Dinosaurs Forever.* Illustrated by Lynn Munsinger. Dial, 2000.

Wong, Janet S. *Behind the Wheel: Poems About Driving.* Simon & Schuster, 1999.

_____. *Night Garden: Poems from the World of Dreams.* Illustrated by Julie Paschkis. Simon & Schuster, 2000.

Wood, Douglas. *Old Turtle.* Illustrated by Cheng-Khee Chee. Pfeifer-Hamilton, 1992.

Worth, Valerie. *All the Small Poems.* Illustrated by Natalie Babbitt. Farrar, Straus & Giroux, 1987.

_____. *More Small Poems.* Illustrated by Natalie Babbitt. Farrar, Straus & Giroux, 1976.

_____. *Still More Small Poems.* Illustrated by Natalie Babbitt. Farrar, Straus & Giroux, 1978.

Yolen, Jane. *The Ballad of the Pirate Queens.* Illustrated by David Shannon. Harcourt Brace, 1995.

_____. *The Three Bears Rhyme Book.* Illustrated by Jane Dyer. Harcourt Brace Jovanovich, 1987.

Zemach, Margot. *Some from the Moon, Some from the Sun: Poems and Songs for Everyone.* Farrar, Straus & Giroux, 2001.

Zolotow, Charlotte. *River Winding.* Illustrated by Kazue Mizumura. Crowell, 1978.

_____. *River Winding.* Illustrated by Regina Shekerjian. Abelard-Schuman, 1970.

9 CONTEMPORARY REALISTIC FICTION

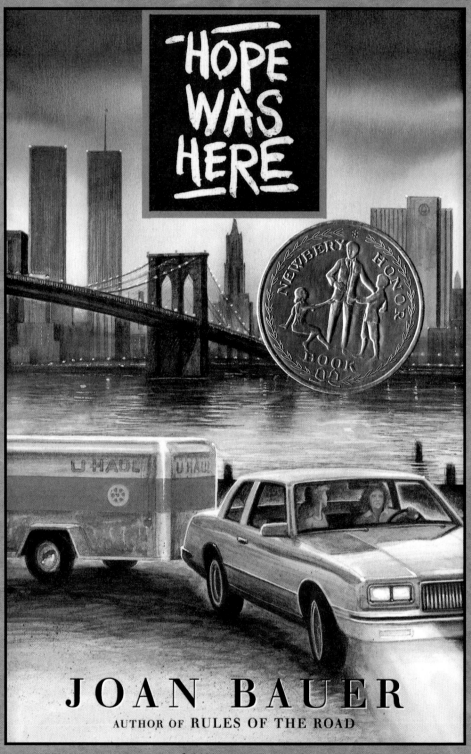

"Jacket Art" by Wendell Minor, copyright © 2000 by Wendell Minor, from Hope Was Here by Joan Bauer. Used by permission of G. P. Putnam's Sons, an imprint of Penguin Putnam Books for Young Readers, a division of Penguin Putnam Inc.

New terminology enters the discussion of children's books as you leave the realm of Mother Goose, most picture storybooks, traditional literature, and modern fantasy. Such terms as *relevant books, extreme realism, problem novel,* and *everyday occurrences* are found in critiques and discussions of contemporary realistic fiction.

While some of the books in this genre are among the most popular with older children, they are also among the most controversial. Interest groups, educators, and parents criticize and debate the value of some realistic stories for children. Many adults are concerned about such issues as censorship, sexism, promiscuity, violence, profanity, alienation from society, and racism. This chapter discusses what contemporary realistic fiction is, why it should be shared with children, how realistic fiction has changed, issues related to realistic fiction, and criteria for evaluating realistic fiction.

What Contemporary Realistic Fiction Is

The term *contemporary realistic fiction* implies that everything in a realistic story—including plot, characters, and setting—is consistent with the lives of real people in our contemporary world. The word *realistic* does not mean that the story is true, however; it means only that the story could have happened.

Use of the words *realistic* and *fiction* together is confusing to some children, who have trouble distinguishing contemporary realistic fiction from modern fantasy or from stories that really happened. Certainly, authors of modern fantasy attempt to make their stories realistic in the sense that they try to create believable plots, characters, and settings; to make their stories as internally consistent as possible; and to ground their stories in familiar reality before introducing elements of fantasy. Contemporary realistic fiction, however, requires that plots deal with familiar, everyday problems, pleasures, and personal relationships and that characters and settings seem as real as the contemporary world we know. The supernatural has no part in such stories, except occasionally in the beliefs of realistic human characters.

The differences between modern fantasy and contemporary realistic fiction are summarized in Chart 9.1. Two popular animal stories demonstrate the differences. In Beatrix Potter's fantasy *The Tale of Peter Rabbit,* Peter talks, thinks, acts, and dresses like an inquisitive, sometimes greedy, sometimes frightened human child who needs his mother's love and care. While the story's garden setting is realistic, Peter's home is furnished with human furniture. In this fantasy, conflict develops because Peter demonstrates believable childlike desires.

CHART 9.1 Differences between modern fantasy and contemporary realistic fiction

	Modern Fantasy	Contemporary Realistic Fiction
Believable stories	Authors must encourage readers to suspend disbelief	Authors may rely on "relevant subjects," everyday occurrences, or extreme realism
Plot	Conflict may be against supernatural powers Problems may be solved through magical powers	Conflict develops as characters cope with such problems as growing up, survival, family discord, and inner-city tensions Antagonists may be self, other family members, society, or nature
Characters	Personified toys, little people, supernatural beings, real people who have imaginary experiences, animals who behave like people	Characters act like real people Animals always behave like animals
Setting	Past, present, or future Imaginary world May travel through time and space	The contemporary world is as we know it

In contrast, the three animals in Sheila Burnford's *The Incredible Journey* retain their animal characteristics as they struggle for survival in a realistically depicted Canadian wilderness. A trained hunting dog leads his companions across the wilderness; an English bull terrier, who is a cherished family pet, seeks people to give him food; and a Siamese cat retains her feline independence. Conflict in this realistic story develops as the animals become lost and face problems while trying to return to their home. Burnford does not give the animals human thoughts, values, or other human characteristics. The characters and settings are not only believable but also completely realistic in our everyday world.

Values of Realistic Fiction

One of the greatest values of realistic fiction for children is that many realistic stories allow children to identify with characters of their own age who have similar interests and problems. Children like to read about people whom they can understand. Thus, their favorite authors express a clear understanding of children. For example, one girl said about Judy Blume's *Are You There God? It's Me, Margaret,* "I've read this book five times; I could be Margaret."

Realistic fiction can help children discover that their problems and desires are not unique and that they are not alone in experiencing certain feelings and situations. Children who are unhappy about the death of a loved one may identify with Howard Kaplan's *Waiting to Sing* or Audrey Couloumbis's *Getting Near to Baby,* for example, or children who are having preadolescent anxieties, especially about boy–girl relationships, may find a comrade in Phyllis Naylor's *Alice in Rapture, Sort Of.* The young characters in these books face and overcome their problems while remaining true to themselves.

Realistic fiction also extends children's horizons by broadening their interests, allowing them to experience new adventures, and showing them different ways to view and deal with conflicts in their own lives. Children can vicariously live a survival adventure and mature in the process as they read Scott O'Dell's *Island of the Blue Dolphins,* for example, or experience the death of a father in Vera and Bill Cleaver's *Where the Lilies Bloom.*

According to Joanne Bernstein (1989), reading about children who are facing emotional problems can help other children discharge repressed emotions and cope with fear, anger, or grief. For example, books about divorce or abuse may help children cope with a traumatic period in their lives. In Beverly Cleary's *Dear Mr. Henshaw* or Kate DiCamillo's *Because of Winn-Dixie,* readers discover that parents as well as children are hurt by divorce or separation. Children may realize the consequences of wife and child abuse by reading Betsy Byars's *Cracker Jackson.* (A word of caution: Realistic fiction should *not* be used to replace professional help in situations that warrant such intervention. Children experiencing severe depression, anger, or grief may require professional help.) Many of the books discussed in this chapter can stimulate discussion and help children share their feelings and solve their problems. Of course, realistic fiction also provides children with pleasure and escape. Realistic animal stories, mysteries, sports stories, and humorous stories are enjoyable getaways for young people.

How Realistic Fiction Has Changed

Synonyms for *realistic* include other adjectives, such as *lifelike, genuine,* and *authentic.* Of course, what people consider lifelike depends upon the social context. What seems realistic to us might seem fantastic to people in different societies or other eras.

In the Victorian era of the late nineteenth and early twentieth centuries, realistic fiction emphasized traditional family roles and ties in warm, close, and stable family units that lived in one place for generations; strict roles for males and females, stressing higher education and careers for males and wifehood and motherhood for females; respect for law and adult authority; strong religious commitment; duty to educate, Christianize, or care for the poor; and problems related to overcoming sinfulness and becoming good.

Realistic fiction continued to emphasize many of these values well into the second half of the twentieth century, although the literature began to depict both female and male children gaining more independence. The characters in realistic children's fiction were usually white, middle-class, and members of stable families consisting of a father, a mother, and their children. Nontraditional families and family disturbances were virtually unrepresented in this literature.

Beginning roughly in the 1960s, however, the content of contemporary realistic fiction became more diverse—no doubt reflecting the increasingly diverse and complex social life in the United States and elsewhere. Maria Nikolajeva (1995) states: "Many taboos that existed in children's literature during its early periods are today being withdrawn" (p. 40). Contemporary realistic stories for children depict some unhappy and unstable families, single-parent families, and families in which both parents work outside the home. Career ambitions are not as confined to traditional gender roles as they were in the past. Children often have much responsibility and independence. Fear of or disrespect for law and authority is more common. Education and religion receive less stress. Ethnic and racial minorities are more in evidence, and in general, people's economic, emotional, and social problems receive more emphasis.

John Rowe Townsend (1975) is among the researchers who have pointed out the striking contrasts between children's realistic fiction of the 1950s and the late 1960s. The 1950s was one of the quietest decades in children's literature: In keeping with traditional values, children were pictured as part of a stable community—grandparents were wise, parents were staunch and respected, and childhood was happy and secure. In contrast, children's literature of the late 1960s implied an erosion of adult authority and an apparent widening of the generation gap. It was no longer self-evident that parents knew best and that children could be guided into accepting the established codes and behavior.

Author Betsy Byars (1993), who has been writing for more than thirty years, states that children's publishing has changed a great deal. She says,

I think there's been a great evolution. When I first started writing, children's books had to be nice. I can remember some editor writing in the margin, "Don't have him lie" or something like that. And now you're very free. You don't feel any pressure, you don't find yourself thinking things like, "I can't say this" or "This will be too tough a subject for kids." (p. 906)

In a study of themes found in contemporary realistic fiction published in the late 1970s, Jane M. Madsen and Elaine B. Wickersham (1980) found that popular themes for young children were overcoming fear and meeting responsibility and that stories about problems related to adoption, divorce, disabilities, and minority social status were more common than in the past. In the 1980s, contemporary realistic fiction for older children often depicted children overcoming family and personal problems. Children confronted quarreling or divorcing parents, deserting or noncaring parents, cruel foster families, conflicts between personal ambitions and parental desires, and death of loved ones. Discovery of self and development of maturity as children face and overcome their fears were other popular themes in stories written for older children. Such stories often stressed the importance of self-esteem and being true to oneself.

Contemporary realistic fiction in the 1990s and 2000s reflects both the mirror of society's problems and changes that have occurred in books because of past criticisms. An introduction to recommended books titled "Curriculum Connectors: Family Secrets" in *School Library Journal* (1997) highlights many of the characteristics of current realistic fiction: "All of the families in the books listed below harbor secrets. Some are dark and grim; others are quirky and quite funny. Abuse, desertion, hidden pasts, feuds, and even a grandmother's elopement play a part. Some of the young protagonists draw on inner strengths they didn't know they had; others turn to siblings and friends for help. What these young people have in common is resilience, resourcefulness, and a feeling of hope for the future" (p. 112).

Literary Criticism: New Realism and the Problem Novel

Alleen Pace Nilsen and Kenneth L. Donelson (2001) characterize books that are identified under the area of new realism as books that include serious coming-of-age stories:

In addition to their candor and the selection of subject matter, they differ from earlier books in four basic ways. The first difference lies in the choice of characters. These protagonists come mostly from lower-class families, which ties in with the second major difference, setting. Instead of living in idyllic, pleasant suburban homes, the characters in these books come from settings that are harsh, difficult places to live. To get the point across about the characters and where they live, authors used colloquial language, which is the third major difference. Authors began to write the way people really talk (e.g., in dialogue using profanity and ungrammatical constructs). (pp. 113–114)

Nilsen and Donelson identify the fourth difference as a change in attitude, a change in mode in which stories no longer had to have upbeat, happy endings.

Some literary critics question the merit of at least portions of this new realism. Sheila Egoff (1980), for example, applauds realistic novels that have strong literary qualities, including logical flow of narrative, delicate complexity of characterization, insights that convey the conduct of life as characters move from childhood to adolescence and to adulthood, and a quality that touches both the imagination and the emotions. In an outstanding realistic novel, says Egoff, conflict is integral to the plot and characters, and resolution of conflict has wide implications growing out of the personal vision or experience of the writer. In contrast, Egoff maintains, conflict in a problem novel stems from the writer's social standards more than from personal feelings and emotions. The author's intentions may be good, but in an effort to make a point or argue a social position, the author creates a cardboard story instead of one that really comes alive. The conflict is specific rather than universal and narrow rather than far-reaching in its implications. Egoff identifies other typical characteristics of the problem novel:

1. Concern is with externals, with how things look rather than how things are. The author begins with a problem rather than with a plot or characters.

2. The protagonist is burdened with anxieties and grievances that grow out of alienation from the adult world.

3. The protagonist often achieves temporary relief through association with an unconventional adult from outside the family.

4. The narrative is usually in the first person, and its confessional tone is self-centered.

5. The vocabulary is limited, and observation is restricted by the pretense that an ordinary child is the narrator.

6. Sentences and paragraphs are short, the language is flat, without nuance, and the language may be emotionally numb.

7. Inclusion of expletives seems obligatory.

8. Sex is discussed openly.

9. The setting is usually urban.

Jack Forman (1985) adds that in contrast to the fully developed characters in books of literary quality, many topical novels "are peopled with characters who are more mouthpieces of a particular point of view than fully developed protagonists" (p. 470). Beverly Cleary (Connell, 1984) further articulates the difference between stories that focus on problems and stories that focus on people:

I'm more interested in writing about people than problems. *Dear Mr. Henshaw* [the winner of the 1984 Newbery Medal] is about a boy that had a problem, not a problem that had a boy. I don't search for a new problem. (p. 1F)

Educators and critics of children's literature in the mid-1980s disagreed, however, about how prominent new realism and problem novels actually are in contemporary realistic fiction for children. Critics such as Bertha M. Cheatham (1985) maintained that novels "mirroring real-life situations and tackling controversial subjects (drugs, sex, suicide) are increasing in numbers" (p. 25), while critics such as Marilyn F. Apseloff (1985) saw "a definite swing away from the serious 'new realism' which dominated the lists half a decade ago" (p. 32) in the United States, Europe, and Japan. Apseloff noted an apparently increasing demand for adventure stories, humorous stories, and realistic fiction of high literary quality.

Today's students of children's literature are living in an interesting era of book publishing for children. They may analyze new books of contemporary realistic fiction and contemplate the different directions that authors can choose to pursue.

Controversial Issues

Barbara Feldstein (1993) identifies the major controversies in children's books as political views that differ from those of censors, treatment of minorities, stereotyped roles of women, problems of contemporary society, and profane language. When any of these subjects are in books, you may expect varied reactions. The degree to which realistic fiction should reflect the reality of the times leads to controversy when writers create characters who face problems relating to sexism, sexuality, violence, and drugs. There is no simple solution: What one group considers controversial, another does not. Realistic fiction has resulted in more controversy and calls for censorship than has any other genre. Therefore, educators must be aware of some concerns in this area of literature, including sexism, sexuality, violence, profanity, and family problems.

Sexism

Sexism has been a major concern for the past few decades. The following position statement by the Association of Women Psychologists (1970), written more than thirty years ago, stresses the dangers of the traditional roles created by society and reflected in literature:

Psychological oppression in the form of sex role socialization clearly conveys to girls from the earliest ages that their nature is to be submissive, servile, and repressed, and their role is to be servant, admirer, sex object and martyr. . . . The psychological consequences of goal depression in young women . . . are all too common. In addition, both men and women have come to realize the effect on men of this type of sex role stereotyping, the crippling pressure to compete, to achieve, to produce, to stifle emotion, sensitivity and gentleness, all taking their toll in psychic and physical traumas.

Marsha M. Sprague and Kara K. Keeling (2000) quote research that concludes: "In the U.S., girls are at risk of academic failure, substance abuse, pregnancy, sexual disease, and suicide to a degree unimaginable to most parents and teachers" (p. 640). These authors recommend that schools use literature as a means for dialogues and real-world learning and especially for creating opportunities that help girls and boys explore and discuss gender issues. Sprague and Keeling recommend using nonstereotypical books in which a central female character searches for her true voice. Three of the recommended contemporary realistic fiction books discussed include Katherine Paterson's *Jacob Have I Loved,* Suzanne Staples's *Shabanu: Daughter of the Wind,* and Cynthia Voigt's *Dicey's Song.*

Colleen A. Ruggieri (2001) also recommends reading and discussing the characteristics of strong female protagonists such as those found in *Shabanu: Daughter of the Wind.* Ruggieri states that "Perhaps one of the most important points that *Shabanu* makes for young readers is that no one deserves to be the victim of physical violence" (p. 49).

People concerned with sexism have evaluated the roles of males and females in children's literature and in elementary classrooms. The evaluations are usually harshly critical of the negative forces of sex-role stereotyping. Ramona Frasher (1982), for example, reviewed research on sexism and sex-role stereotyping in children's literature and identified some trends. In Newbery Award-winning books published prior to the 1970s, male main characters outnumbered female main characters by about three to one. In addition, negative comments about females and stereotyping were common. Frasher's analysis of Newbery Award winners published between 1971 and 1980 showed the ratio of male characters to female characters was about equal. In addition, female characters tended to be portrayed with more positive and varied personality characteristics and to exhibit a greater variety of behaviors.

Even though these changes reflect a heightened sensitivity to feminist concerns, Frasher's article identifies three areas still of major concern: (1) changes are found predominantly in books written for children in middle- and late-childhood years, (2) the rush to respond to criticism resulted in too many examples of poor or marginal literature, and (3) until more authors are able to write with ease about both sexes engaged in a broad scope of activities and exhibiting a range of characteristics, children's literature will remain stereotyped. Frasher's conclusion emphasizes the need for critical evaluation in this area: "The number of books accessible to children is immense; it will take many years of publishing quality nonsexist literature to insure that a random selection is as likely to be nonstereotyped as it is to be stereotyped" (p. 77).

Educators, psychologists, and other concerned adults also criticize the sexism and sex-role stereotyping in realistic picture books. In an earlier study, Alleen Pace Nilsen (1971) analyzed the role of females in eighty Caldecott Medal winners and honor books. She chose picture books because illustrated books are "the ones influencing children at the time they are in the process of developing their own sexual identity. Children decide very early in life what roles are appropriate to male and female" (p. 919). Of the books that were realistic (as compared with fantasy), she found fewer stories having girls as the leading characters. She also compared the number of girl- and boy-centered stories over a twenty-year period; the percentage of girl-centered stories had decreased from a high of 46 percent in 1951–1955 to a low of 26 percent in 1966–1970.

Anita P. Davis and Thomas R. McDaniel (1999) analyzed the percentages of male and female characters in more recent Caldecott Medal winners. They found that 39 percent of the characters in books published in the 1990s were female.

Many female protagonists in books for older children behave in ways quite different from those of the heroines of traditional literature. They reflect the fairly recent realization that females are also *heroes,* with intellectual, emotional, and physical potential in their actions. Some of the most memorable girl characters—including Karana in Scott O'Dell's *Island of the Blue Dolphins,* Queenie in Robert Burch's *Queenie Peavy* (who insisted that she would grow up to be a doctor, not a nurse), Harriet in Louise Fitzhugh's *Harriet the Spy,* and even Jo in Louisa May Alcott's Victorian novel, *Little Women*—are believable and exciting because they do not follow stereotypical behavior patterns.

Nontraditional behaviors can, of course, also result in controversy. Women's roles and women's rights are political issues. Advocates express strong opinions on both sides. One of the areas that illustrates women's changing roles is the portrayal of the minor characters in stories. Mothers may be photographers who travel on assignments and join peace marches accompanied by their daughters, as in Norma Klein's *Mom, the Wolf Man and Me;* book illustrators who travel on consulting contracts, as in Lois Lowry's *Anastasia on Her Own;* and authors whose children consider them eccentric, as in Patricia MacLachlan's *The Facts and Fictions of Minna Pratt.* Recent books suggest that the roles of males and females may be changing, as increasingly varied occupations and behavior patterns are found in the books. Teachers, librarians, and parents should be aware, however, that not all people look on these changes favorably.

Sexuality

Today is a time of increasing sophistication and frankness about sexuality. Television programs and movies portray sexual relationships that would not have been shown to earlier generations of adults, let alone children. Premarital and extramarital sex, sexual development, homosexual experiences, and sex education are controversial topics in children's literature. The subjects of books written for older readers may be particularly controversial. For example, M. E. Kerr's *"Hello," I Lied* deals with problems associated with being gay; Suzanne Fisher Staples's *Dangerous Skies* deals with sexual abuse; and Francesca Lisa Block's *Girl Goddess #9: Nine Stories* describes a peer world that includes casual sex, drugs, and alcohol. Laurie Halse Anderson's *Speak* deals with a high school freshman's trauma after being raped. The author voices the girl's resolution about her conflict when she thinks: "It happened. There is no avoiding it, no forgetting. No running away, or flying, or burying, or hiding. Andy Evans raped me in August when I was drunk and too young to know what was happening. It wasn't my fault. He hurt me. It wasn't my fault. And I'm not going to let it kill me. I can grow" (p. 197).

Several books written for older children describe nontraditional living situations in which a child's mother lives with a male friend. In Norma Klein's controversial *Mom, the Wolf Man and Me,* Theodore spends weekends with Brett's mother, which leads eleven-year-old Brett to ask her mother if she is having sexual relations with him. This results in a frank discussion about sexual intercourse. As might be expected, this book has met with varying reactions.

In a book for older audiences, *Dear Nobody,* Berlie Doherty explores feelings and issues associated with the pregnancy of an unmarried high school girl. The author explores the unhappiness and confusion that surround the decision to keep the baby as well as the responses of the mother, the baby's father, and their families.

A study of books that focus on teen pregnancy and parenting by Joy B. Davis and Laurie MacGillivray (2001) found the following eight common messages: Do not have unprotected sex; most mothers keep their babies; having a baby may cause changes in educational plans, but you can still achieve your goals; when pregnant you are on your own; young men are often portrayed as sexual predators; young women have to live with the consequences, while young men do not; teen pregnancies do not mandate marriage; and teens from troubled homes are more likely to become pregnant.

Books describing children's concerns about their developing sexuality may also be controversial. For example, Judy Blume's popular *Are You There God? It's Me, Margaret* has been reviewed favorably as a book that realistically conveys preadolescent girls' worries over menstruation and body changes. Yet in 1981, this book

Books for older readers, such as Speak, *may deal with controversial issues related to sexuality. (Jacket design from* Speak, *by Laura Halse Anderson. Copyright © 1999 by Laurie Halse Anderson. Reprinted by permission of Farrar, Straus & Girroux, LLC.)*

was one of several taken from library shelves and burned because some adults viewed it as a negative influence on children. In that same year, the national television news showed angry adults criticizing the morality of this book, as well as the morality of many other books, and the resulting flames of protest.

Violence

Television, movies, and books have been accused of portraying too much violence. Children's cartoons are often criticized for their excessive violence. Children's books become the object of controversy when they portray what some people define as inappropriate behavior or excessive violence. Many realistic books containing violence have inner-city settings in which both violence and drugs play a role. For example, drugs figure prominently in Walter Dean Myers's *Scorpions.* Some people believe that children should read about the reality of drugs in the world around them, while others believe that the minds of children should not be contaminated by the mention of drugs.

Shannon Maughan (1992) discusses the controversy around Clark Taylor's picture book, *The House That Crack Built.* Maughan states that much of the controversy centers around the appropriate age for this book, which is based on the nursery rhyme "The House That Jack Built." People living in suburban neighborhoods believe that the book is appropriate for students in high school and maybe junior high. In contrast, those living in urban environments see the book as appropriate for children as young as first grade and extending through high school.

Profanity

Profanity and other language objectionable to some people are also controversial. What is considered objectionable has changed over the years, however. Mary Q. Steele (1971) describes her own experiences with writing. In the 1950s, editors deleted "hecks" and "darns" from manuscripts written for children, but now, authors can write relevant dialogue. Ken Donelson's (1985) survey on censorship reports that a committee unsuccessfully challenged the placement of Katherine Paterson's *The Great Gilly Hopkins* in an elementary library because the author used language that the committee members considered objectionable.

In 1990, a teacher in Donna Norton's children's literature class successfully met a challenge to Paterson's *Bridge to Terabithia.* One parent wanted the book removed from the class reading list because of mild profanity. The teacher successfully defended the book for literary merit, especially the importance of its themes.

Family Problems and Other Controversial Issues

Strong young protagonists in contemporary novels frequently overcome obstacles related to family problems caused by adult family members. The antagonists are frequently adults who have less than desirable qualities. The lack of strong adult role models in many contemporary books is also controversial. For example, Robert Unsworth (1988) praises the fully developed fathers in several published books, but he also states, "The bad news is the portrayal of that Dad at home. A grander group of adulterers, philanderers, child abusers, wife-beaters, drunks, and all-around ne'er-do-wells hasn't been seen since the fall of Rome" (p. 48).

Abandonment of children is another family problem that is depicted in many contemporary stories. According to Marilyn Fain Apseloff (1992), there are three types of abandonment:

Newer books portray mothers so intent upon finding themselves and doing their own thing that they are willing to leave their families in the process. . . . In other novels the abandonment is temporary. . . . Still another kind of abandonment occurs in books for older readers: the desertion of the mother when the child is still an infant. (pp. 102–103)

Apseloff concludes:

Here is unsoftened realism, an indictment of contemporary society, where adults no longer want to assume the traditional roles of protectors and nurturers of children. Such people have always existed, of course, but their numbers seem to be increasing, more adults being concerned with their own welfare and well-being first, before those of the rest of the family. (p. 105)

The role of the absent parent is highlighted in a review of *The Goats.* In a review of Brock Cole's *The Goats,* Anita Silvey (1988) states:

Like all powerful books, *The Goats* will repel some readers and attract others. Critics of the book are concerned with the absence of positive adult characters—as was the case with *Harriet the Spy*—and the change in the young protagonists from innocents to thieves. (p. 23)

Silvey goes on to praise the book, saying that the publication of the novel "signifies that we are still creating children's books that affirm the human spirit and the ability of the individual to rise above adversity" (p. 23). In another review of *The Goats,* Wendy J. Glenn (1999) focuses on the contrasts between the independent nature of the young protagonists and the immaturity of the adults. She states, "When faced with difficult problems, the grown-ups back down or act irresponsibly" (p. 26).

Current award-winning books such as Jack Gantos's *Joey Pigza Loses Control,* Kate DiCamillo's *Because of Winn-Dixie,* and Joan Bauer's *Hope Was Here* include some form of parental abandonment. In *Joey Pigza Loses Control,* Joey spends the summer with an alcoholic father who he has never known. In *Because of Winn-Dixie,* the mother has deserted her daughter and husband. In *Hope Was Here,* the heroine longs for the father she has never known.

The controversy surrounding the award given to a book in England illustrates issues in contemporary realistic fiction. According to Julie Eccleshare (1997), "The prestigious Carnegie Medal was awarded last month to Melvin Burgess for *Junk* (Andersen Press). A novel about a group of teenage drug addicts who think that they can handle heroin, *Junk* has attracted enormous media coverage, ranging from adults who find it frightening and even morally wrong that a children's book should deal with these issues, to those who see it as 'a book waiting to be written.' Holt will publish the book in the U.S. in spring '98" (p. 25). As you read *Junk* and books with similar content, ask yourself, "What is my own response to this content? Is it beneficial? Is it harmful?"

According to Michelle Mittelstadt (1993), "Increasingly, the schools are the battle ground for struggles mirroring broader societal debates collectively known as the 'cultural war'" (p. A9). Other issues that can be controversial in children's books are viewpoints on war and peace, religion, death, and racial matters. (Chapter 11 discusses critics' concerns about books related to African Americans, Hispanic Americans, Native Americans, and Asian Americans.)

Literary Criticism: Guidelines for Selecting Controversial Fiction

The question of how "realistic" realistic fiction should be is answered differently by various groups. Historically, schools have often been under the pressures of censorship because different groups have tried to impose their values. While modern censors might laugh at the literary concerns of the Puritans, there is still concern over appropriate subjects for children's literature. Children's books that explore sexuality, violence, moral problems, racism, and religious beliefs are likely to be thought objectionable by individuals and groups who believe that children should not be exposed to such ideas. Arbuthnot Lectures recipient Dorothy Butler (1990) warns that

we must confront those who would cut wild swaths through the body of children's books, rejecting some because they believe them to advance ideas which are in conflict with ones they wish children to espouse, embracing others because they appear to recommend currently approved attitudes—and all with little or no regard to literary merit, or reference to the opinions of those who might advise. We are in danger, in the hands of these well-meaning but misguided evangelists, of banishing at least half the classics of the English language; in vain to protest that the real liberators of the world have always been the informed, the readers; that the burning of books has always been in the cause of human oppression. The dictates of such critics, whether in the cause of antiracism, antisexism, or any other philosophy, denote an arrogance which may be excused as ignorance, but must not be tolerated. Good and true books engender true thought and feeling, and so allow children to think clearly and to feel deeply. (p. 37)

Teachers and librarians need to be knowledgeable about their communities, subjects that may prove controversial, and the merits of controversial books that they would like to share with children. Wholesale avoidance of books containing controversial topics, in addition to encouraging overt censorship, is inappropriate because (1) books about relevant sociological or psychological problems can give young people opportunities to grow in their thinking processes and to extend their experiences; (2) problems in books can provide some children with opportunities for identification and allow other children opportunities to empathize with their peers; and (3) problems in books invite decisions, elicit opinions, and afford opportunities to take positions on issues.

Given the controversial issues and the need for books that are relevant to the interests, concerns, and

EVALUATION CRITERIA

Literary Criticism: Controversial Books

1. Know what might be considered controversial.
2. Determine the author's viewpoint and weigh the positive influences against perceived negative influences.
3. Be sure that the book meets normal literary criteria and is not chosen merely for its high interest and possibly controversial topic.
4. Know and be able to explain your purpose for using a particular book.
5. Review and be able to discuss both sides of the censorship question.

problems of today's children, you should consider some guidelines when choosing realistic fiction for children. Day Ann K. McClenathan (1979) provides teachers a useful guide for selecting books that might be considered controversial. (See the Evaluation Criteria box on this page for a summary of her guidelines.)

Dianne McAfee Hopkins (1993) provides useful recommendations for librarians who face challenges to literature. She recommends that you examine your district's materials selection policy carefully, ensure that principals and teachers are aware that the policy is intended for all who challenge the appropriateness of materials, take every challenge seriously, follow the reconsideration section of the policy fully, seek support when an oral or written challenge occurs, communicate at all levels to ensure that challenges are handled in an effective and objective manner, and recognize that you can be the key person in shaping the outcome of challenges to library materials.

Author Richard Peck (1992) provides an excellent observation for all of those who are developing defenses for books. Peck states, "Only the nonreader fears books" (p. 816).

In addition to the basic literary criteria, high-quality contemporary realistic fiction should satisfy the following requirements.

Know exactly what might be considered controversial. This means that you have to really read the book. You can't rely on the opinion of someone else or even on a good review. As a member of a school and a community, you must be able to appraise specific content. What offends in one community might go unnoticed or unchallenged in another.

Ascertain the author's point of view and weigh the power of the positive influence against exposure to a theme that some people perceive negatively. For example, if an author writes about the drug culture but events in

---

ISSUE Positive Versus Negative Role of Censorship:
Could There Be a Positive Role for Censorship?

The title of an article by Leigh Ann Jones,[1] "Better Libraries Through Censorship," seems at first to be an oxymoron. How could there be a positive side for censorship? Jones, a school librarian, argues that in her school district a censorship controversy changed the district for the better because "it prompted us to examine current practices and policies, and provided impetus for us to" (p. 54) make the following changes: (1) Strengthen selection policy by adding parents to the committee, creating a district-level review committee for appeals, and adding a time frame with deadlines for responses; (2) broaden library support by mobilizing parents into "Friends" groups and other supportive organizations for the library; (3) affirm intellectual freedom by articulating the importance of the right to read; (4) empower librarians by reaffirming the role of professional personnel in the careful selection of materials; and (5) enhance the library role by stressing access to all library books through a policy of intellectual freedom.

As you read about the experiences of this school district, consider both the positive and potentially negative impacts of censorship.

Why do you believe that this challenge to books was handled successfully? Why does Jones claim that censorship created a climate for positive change? Interview librarians and other personnel associated with selecting books. How have they approached issues related to censorship?

---

[1]Jones, Leigh Ann. "Better Libraries Through Censorship." *School Library Journal* 42 (October 1996): 54.

---

the story clearly point to harmful effects of drug use, then you may miss an opportunity for shaping healthy attitudes if you pass up the book.

Apply literary criteria to the selection of library books so that vulnerability to the arguments of would-be censors is at least partially reduced by the obvious overall quality of the book choices. Occasionally, teachers and librarians select books of inferior quality because they deal with topics having high interest for middle-grade or older children (for example, books involving experimentations with sex). The information in such books may be harmless (or even useful), but the books may fall short of accepted literary criteria. Then, if a book is targeted because it offends community groups, you will have difficulty defending it, and having it in your school collection will suggest that considerations other than literary quality determine choices. In addition, examine books that attempt to counter stereotypes for what can be thought of as overcorrection. Sometimes, in a passion to change images, authors work too hard on issues and neglect plot and characterizations.

Know and be able to explain your purpose for using a particular book. Have answers ready to the following questions:

1. Will the topic be understood by the students with whom I intend to use the book?

2. What merits of this particular book have influenced me to use it rather than another book of comparable literary, sociological, or psychological importance?

3. Is the book an acceptable model in terms of writing style and use of language?

4. Are my objectives in using this book educationally defensible (for example, refinement of attitudes, promotion of reading habits)?

To clarify and maintain your objectivity, review and be prepared to discuss both sides of the censorship question.

Literary Elements

Contemporary realistic fiction should meet the basic literary criteria discussed in Chapter 3. Conflicts that could really occur in our contemporary world should be integral to the plot, characterization, setting, and theme. In realistic contemporary settings, authors should thoroughly develop internal and external conflicts, developing credible stories through credible plots, good characterizations, meaningful themes, and effective styles. (See the Evaluation Criteria box page 371.)

Plot

Conflicts at the center of plots in contemporary realistic fiction may arise from external forces, with characters trying to overcome problems related to families, peers, or the society around them, or conflicts may arise with characters trying to overcome problems related to inner conflicts. However, internal conflicts often result from conflict with external forces. Consequently, person-against-self conflicts are common in contemporary realistic fiction.

As in traditional literature, conflict in contemporary realistic fiction may involve protagonists in quests. Caron Lee Cohen (1985) identifies four major components in person-against-self conflicts: (1) problem, (2) struggle, (3) realization, and (4) achievement of peace or truth. She says:

The point at which the struggle wanes and the inner strength emerges seems to be the point of self-realization. That point leads immediately to the final sense of peace or truth that is the resolution of the quest. The best books are those which move readers and cause them to identify with the character's struggle. (p. 28)

Of course, if readers are to understand conflicts and empathize with characters' responses, the characters themselves must be convincingly developed. The pres-

EVALUATION CRITERIA

Literary Criticism: Realistic Fiction

1. The content should be presented honestly. Sensationalizing and capitalizing on the novelty of a subject should be avoided.

2. A story should expose personal and social values central to our culture, at the same time revealing how overt expression of those values may have changed.

3. The story should allow readers to draw personal conclusions from the evidence. The author should respect the readers' intelligence.

4. The author should recognize that today's young readers are in the process of growing toward adult sophistication.

5. The language and syntax should reveal the background and the nature of characters and situations.

6. The author should write in a hopeful tone. A story should communicate in an honest way that there is hope in this world.

7. Children's literature should reflect sensitivity to the needs and rights of girls and boys without preference, bias, or negative stereotypes.

8. If violence is included in a story, the author should treat the subject appropriately. Does the author give the necessary facts? Are both sides of the conflict portrayed fully, fairly, and honestly? Is the writing developed with feeling and emotion? Does the author help children develop a perspective about the subject?

9. A story should satisfy children's basic needs and provide them with insights into their own problems and relationships.

10. A story should provide children with enjoyment.

sures that characters experience and the motives that characters act upon must be very clear.

As an example of credible conflict, consider the person-against-self conflict that Paula Fox develops in *One-Eyed Cat.* Fox sets the stage for the forthcoming conflict by describing an incident in which Uncle Hilary gives Ned a loaded Daisy air rifle for his eleventh birthday. Ned's father, the Reverend Wallace, forbids Ned to use the gun until he is at least fourteen. Instead of hiding the gun, Ned's father takes it to the attic, where Ned can easily find it. A conflict is developed as Ned considers, "The painful thing was that, though Ned didn't always trust his father, his father trusted him, and that seemed to him unfair, although he couldn't explain why it was so" (p. 40).

Ned cannot resist the temptation of the gun, and fires it, shooting a wild stray cat. Then the person-against-self conflict deepens. Fox vividly describes Ned's fear and accompanying guilt when he sees the "gap, the dried blood, the little worm of mucus in the corner next to the cat's nose where the eye had been" (p. 70). Metaphor explains Ned's emotional response as "the gun was like a splinter in his mind" (p. 90). Ned's quest becomes to save the wild cat from sickness and starvation during the approaching winter. It also becomes a quest to overcome his sense of guilt and remorse and to tell the truth about what has happened.

Fox's novel follows Cohen's four major components. The problem results because Ned betrays his parent's trust; the struggle continues when Ned feels increasingly guilty because of his lies as he tries to save the wounded animal; the point of self-realization begins when Ned feels relief by confessing his guilt to a critically ill older neighbor; and peace and truth finally result on a moonlit night when Ned confesses his actions to his mother after they see a one-eyed cat and kittens emerging from the woods. In a satisfying conclusion, Ned and his mother exchange revealing confessions.

This book may be successful because the conflict appeals to more than one age or ability group. Most readers can empathize with the desire to commit a forbidden action and the terror of the consequences. More mature readers can appreciate the portrayal of a boy who successfully overcomes a hurdle in the maturation process.

Marion Dane Bauer's *On My Honor* develops a person-against-self conflict that is similar to the conflict in *One-Eyed Cat.* Consequently, the two books are excellent for comparisons. For example, the problem results for Bauer's character, Joel, because Joel betrays his parents' trust and swims with his friend in a treacherous river. The struggle continues when Joel feels increasing guilt, tries not to accept his friend's disappearance and probable death, and blames his father for allowing the two boys to go on a bike ride in the first place. Self-realization begins when Joel admits that Tony drowned and realizes that his father is not the cause of his problem. Although the seriousness of the problem does not allow complete resolution, peace begins after Joel sobbingly tells his father the whole truth. One of Bauer's themes, we have to live with our choices, is revealed when Joel's father says, "But, we all made choices today, Joel. You, me, Tony. Tony's the only one who doesn't have to live with his choice" (p. 88).

Characterization

The characterization of Ned in Fox's *One-Eyed Cat* is an integral part of the conflict. For example, Fox describes Ned's actions, clarifies his response to his parents and to the wounded cat, and reveals his thoughts during his traumatic experiences. Readers know Ned intimately. They understand his hopes, his fears, his past, his present, and his relationships with his parents.

Complex characterizations that lead to self-discovery and personal relationships are also important in Cynthia Voigt's books about the Tillerman family. In *Homecoming*, Voigt focuses on the children's experiences after their emotionally ill mother deserts them. In the sequel, *Dicey's Song*, Voigt focuses on the four children and their grandmother: a young girl who is trying to hold her family together, a girl with a learning disability who has a gift for music, a gifted boy who tries to hide his giftedness because he does not want to be different, a younger brother who strikes out in anger, and a grandmother whom the townspeople consider eccentric. In all of Voigt's books, as in Fox's *One-Eyed Cat*, readers discover that the protagonists have many-sided personalities, like their own. Readers come to know these characters intimately, sharing their hopes, fears, pasts, and presents.

Throughout her books, Voigt effectively uses symbolism in her characterizations. Her use of symbolism associated with the blue heron is especially meaningful in *A Solitary Blue*. Consider the implications for Jeff's character in the following examples: When Jeff has low self-esteem, he views the heron as a creature that occupies "its own insignificant corner of the landscape in a timeless, long-legged solitude" (p. 45). Later, when Jeff feels angry, broken, and bruised due to his mother's behavior, he again views the heron; " 'Just leave me alone,' the heron seemed to be saying. Jeff rowed away, down the quiet creek. The bird did not watch him go" (p. 91). Finally, when Jeff discovers that he is a worthwhile person, he realizes that the solitary heron reminds him of his best friend, Dicey Tillerman. When Dicey laughingly states that she was thinking that the bird reminded her of Jeff, Jeff is flattered by the comparison. Jeff knows that he, like the heron, is a "rare bird," with staying power and a gentle spirit.

The synthesis of symbolism and character traits is equally important in *Dicey's Song*. For example, a careful tracing of musical selections, including the title, shows that Voigt uses music to develop character and to illustrate changes in personal development. Likewise, a dilapidated boat and a tree have important symbolic meanings.

Norma Fox Mazer also synthesizes symbols and characters in *After the Rain*. Mazer uses the symbolism of rain at the end of the book both to reveal and to review Rachel's changing feelings for her grandfather, Izzy. For example, after Izzy's death, Mazer states:

Then, behind her closed eyes, she sees a road, a narrow sandy road with tall trees on both sides, and she sees herself walking down this road in the rain . . . dark, blue-green of the trees . . . hard, dark lines of water sleeting down . . . nothing else exists but the wet road, the trees lashed by wind, and herself, a solitary figure walking in the rain. (p. 267)

Later, Rachel uses these words when talking about Izzy to her brother Jeremy:

"Anyway, I'm glad that I finally _____ ," she begins, and then she can't say it, can't say she's finally glad she got to know him. The sky is clear and cloudless, the trees are blazing purely with autumn color, but she is all at once in a storm. Hard rain again, this time with thunder and lightning. This time, not grief but anger. Anger at Izzy, hard strikes of anger splitting the blue sky she's created out of their feeling for each other. Anger for all those years he let slip by when they could have been knowing each other, when she could have loved him so much. (p. 278)

After Rachel has spent days searching for and finally finding Izzy's handprint and initials on the bridge he helped construct, "They are here now she thinks, and they will still be here years from now, when she, herself, is old. And then, though today the whole sky is covered by gray clouds, for a moment she feels the sun on her head, as warm as a loving hand" (p. 288). Mature readers enjoy the development of and the interactions with such characters as Dicey, Jeff, and Rachel. The symbolism makes the reading experience even more vivid and meaningful.

Cynthia Rylant develops both credible characters and the need to overcome personal sorrow after death in *Missing May*. By allowing Summer and Uncle Ob to remember May, Rylant allows readers to understand this remarkable woman. For example, notice how Rylant encourages readers to visualize May by contrasting her with other people:

May was gardening when she died. That's the word she always used: gardening. Everybody else in Fayette County would say they were going out to work in the garden, and that's the picture you'd get in your mind—people out there laboring and sweating and grunting in the dirt. But Aunt May gardened, and when she said it your mind would see some lovely person in a yellow-flowered hat snipping soft pink roses, little robins landing on her shoulders. (p. 9)

Throughout the book, Rylant develops May's character through such memories. By sharing their memories, both Summer and Uncle Ob can bury their sorrow and finally go on with the life that May would have wanted.

Theme

The underlying ideas that tie the plot, characters, and settings together in contemporary realistic fiction are closely related to the needs of modern children. For example, authors frequently show that children become stronger as they make discoveries about themselves. In *What Hearts*, Bruce Brooks's protagonist, Asa, learns that he needs to receive and give love if he is to be a total person. In *Western Wind*, Paula Fox's heroine, Elizabeth, makes discoveries about herself and develops important understandings as she interacts with her eccentric artist grandmother, with whom she spends the summer on an island off the coast of Maine.

When four sixth-grade students became the Academic Bowl team for their school in E. L. Konigsburg's *The*

View from Saturday, they discover several important meanings in their own lives. For example, they discover the importance of expressing courtesy to one another, the importance of kindness, the importance of sharing, and the need to take careful notice of their actions and surroundings. By tracing the changes in the students as they interact with the team, Konigsburg develops the importance of these themes for each of the students and for their teacher, who needs to regain her confidence after an automobile accident.

In Joan Bauer's *Hope Was Here,* the author develops the theme that hope is something that everyone needs. Obtaining and retaining hope is, however, difficult for the heroine as she moves with her aunt to many different locations. It is during their final move, when she discovers the strength and honesty of a man who has cancer, that the heroine makes discoveries about herself and realizes that "hope was here."

The books in this chapter develop many additional themes, such as children have common hopes and fears, life is filled with important choices that must be carefully considered, and friends should support rather than hurt each other.

Style

An effective literary style greatly enhances plot, characterization, and theme in realistic fiction. Vivid descriptions, believable dialogue, symbolism, figures of speech, and other stylistic techniques subtly provide readers with in-depth understanding of characters and situations. In *Dicey's Song,* for example, Cynthia Voigt develops a synthesis of symbols and character traits. Allusions to familiar music are among Voigt's symbolic means of emphasizing changes in the character.

In *Walk Two Moons,* Sharon Creech develops two parallel stories. As the heroine tells the story of her best friend Phoebe and her experiences when her mother left, Sal makes discoveries about her own life and learns to accept her own mother's actions. The author uses considerable symbolism to develop the feelings and characterizations in the story. For example, smoke symbolizes her feelings after her mother leaves: "There goes my mother" and "I watched the trail of smoke disappearing in the air" (p. 74). There is the symbolism of a dream about mother climbing a ladder and never coming down (p. 169). There is also the story of the mother dog as she weans and trains her children to be independent (pp. 257–258) and the symbolism of the singing trees that ends on page 268 at Sal's mother's grave.

Anne Fine's *Step by Wicked Step* provides an interesting book for analyzing an author's style that not only grabs the reader's attention, but also changes the plot in an unpredictable way. For example, the introductory chapters lead readers to believe that they may be approaching a mystery. Fine's first paragraph states: "Even before they reached the haunted house, the night had turned wild.

The face of the minivan driver flicked from blue to white under the lightning. Each peal of thunder made the map in Mr. Plumley's hand shiver. The five leftover pupils from Stagfire School peered anxiously through the rain-spattered windows into the storm and the black night" (p. 3). As the minivan approaches Old Harwick Hall in England, the children comment on the forlorn appearance of the towering mansion with its turrets standing black against storm clouds. When they enter and go to their rooms they see a mark on the wall and find a hidden door with stretched and broken cobwebs. As they cautiously go through the door they find a hidden room with a book on the table titled: *Richard Clayton Harwick—My Story, Read and Weep.*

Now the children who are on a school field trip read the mysterious journal and discover the story of a boy who runs away from home after his father dies and he finds himself under the sinister influence of a stepfather. Fine changes the plot from an obvious mystery to one of self-discovery as each of the students realize that if Richard Clayton Harwick can tell his story, so can they. The remainder of the chapters focus on each child's telling his own story about divorce. The stories include sad, happy, and even humorous experiences. By the end of their stories, they discover that they are not alone and that someone has to make the effort because "as we all know, the ones who mess everything up in the first place aren't quite so good at fixing things again after" (p. 136).

In *Missing May,* Cynthia Rylant uses contrasts to encourage readers to understand the treatment of Summer in two locations, to emphasize how Summer felt about this treatment, and to introduce the special bond that develops between May and Summer. Notice the impact of the following contrasting situations:

I stood there before those shelves, watching these wonders begin to spin as May turned on the fan overhead, and I felt like a magical little girl, a chosen little girl, like Alice who had fallen into Wonderland. This feeling has yet to leave me.

And as if the whirligigs weren't enough. May turned me to the kitchen, where she pulled open all the cabinet doors, plus the refrigerator, and she said, "Summer, whatever you like you can have and whatever you like that isn't here Uncle Ob will go down to Ellet's Grocery and get you. We want you to eat, honey."

Back in Ohio, where I'd been treated like a homework assignment somebody was always having to do, eating was never a joy of any kind. Every house I had ever lived in was so particular about its food, and especially when the food involved me. There's no good way to explain this. But I felt like one of those little mice who has to figure out the right button to push before its food will drop down into the cup. Caged and begging. That's how I felt sometimes. (p. 7)

As you read this quote, notice the emotional impact of the comparison between the magical girl in Alice in Wonderland and the caged mouse who must beg for every morsel.

An In-Depth Analysis of a Contemporary Realistic Fiction Novel

How does an author combine a contemporary story about a juvenile detention camp, the irony of a one-hundred-year-old curse that still influences a contemporary plot and the characters, a parallel plot that sounds like a tall tale, and a mysterious search for a buried treasure that is also one hundred years old? This is the challenge that Louis Sachar took on in *Holes,* the winner of both the 1999 Newbery Medal and a National Book Award. In addition, the book has been listed as a best-seller in the area of children's literature.

Let us first consider the importance of the parallel plots, both of which are built around a treasure that is more than one hundred years old. The contemporary story, which is at times extremely humorous and also deadly serious, begins with a boy, Stanley Yelnats, who believes that all of his bad luck is due to the curse that was placed on his great-great-grandfather who had stolen a pig from a one-legged gypsy. Stanley's problem increases when he is sent to Camp Green Lake because he is accused of stealing a pair of shoes valued at more than five thousand dollars because they belong to a famous athlete. While at this juvenile detention center he experiences person-versus-person conflicts between himself and the warden, the various guards, and a few of his fellow inmates. As the plot progresses we find Stanley and the other inmates digging large holes in the hot, dry desert. The author identifies the reasons for digging the holes toward the climax of the story when Stanley uncovers evidence pointing toward a treasure that may have been buried in the desert. The story nears a climax when Stanley runs away in order to locate a friend who has run from the guards and may be dying of thirst in the desert. After Stanley finds his friend he helps him reach and climb a mountain in the distance. We later discover that carrying the friend up the mountain is very important as a way to resolve the conflict and the curse. Stanley and his friend eventually go back to camp, dig for the treasure at night, and are finally rewarded with the treasure and a verdict that Stanley was wrongly accused of stealing the shoes.

Without the parallel plots, readers would not understand the humor and irony associated with Stanley's situation and his belief that all of his bad luck is caused by the curse placed on his great-great-grandfather by the one-legged gypsy when he refuses to carry her up the mountain after stealing her pig. This parallel plot resembles a tall tale as the author reveals that the first Stanley Yelnats had made a fortune in the stock market but lost his entire fortune when he moved from New York to California and the stagecoach was robbed by the outlaw Kissin' Kate Barlow. Periodically, the author interrupts the first story to tell various tales about the family history that add both humor and background. For example, Sachar explains the curse in which Madame Zeroni dooms the descendants because the great-great-grandfather fails to carry the gypsy up the mountain, sing a song to her, and allow her to drink from the stream. Sachar provides stories about the early ancestors, the schoolteacher who later becomes the outlaw Kissin' Kate Barlow, the African American healer who picks and sells onions, and the belief in and the search for Kissin' Kate's treasures—the stolen loot.

The two plots converge when Stanley carries his friend Zero up the mountain, sings him a song that they both recognize, and together they dig up a suitcase that belonged to Stanley's great-great-grandfather. The author reveals that Zero is the great-great-grandson of the gypsy who created the curse. We know that the curse is broken when the sky turns dark and rain falls for the first time in more than one hundred years onto the empty lake. The contents of the great-great-grandfather's suitcase contain stock certificates, deeds of trust, and promissory notes that are worth several million.

Sachar also develops strong characters who support the plot. The main protagonists are Stanley and his friend Zero and the antagonists are the warden and the guards. A considerable amount of the characterization is developed through actions. For example, Stanley's letters to his mother show his feelings toward her and his desire not to worry her. He is also willing to risk his life to help a friend who is lost in the desert. His friend Zero helps Stanley dig his holes each day so that Stanley will have enough strength left to teach Zero to read. The warden and the guards play the roles of antagonists as they give harsh punishments for disobedience or inability to dig fast enough. The warden's character is revealed as she opens a bottle of fingernail polish that contains rattlesnake venom that she claims is harmless when dry but toxic when wet. Later she reveals that she has been searching for the treasure for years. In an ironic ending the suitcase that she claims is hers is taken away from her by the attorney general because it is engraved with the name Stanley Yelnats, Stanley's great-great-grandfather.

This is an example of a book that at first glance appears to have a fairly simple plot and characters. Many students, however, indicate that they needed to reread the book when they discovered the importance of the parallel plots.

Subjects in Realistic Fiction

To help you recommend or choose specific books for children, this section emphasizes personality and social development in children. The various subject matters within the genre of contemporary realistic fiction encompass a wide range of themes.

Family Life

The family stories of the late 1930s through the early 1960s depict some of the strongest, warmest family relationships in contemporary realistic fiction for children. Today's children still enjoy the warmth and humor represented by the families in Elizabeth Enright's *Thimble Summer,* Eleanor Estes's *The Moffats,* Sydney Taylor's *All of a*

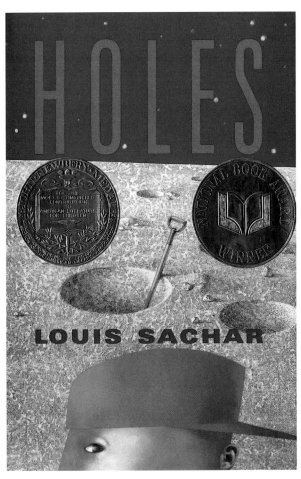

Parallel plots provide both mystery and adventure in this novel. (Jacket design from Holes *by Louis Sachar. Copyright © 1998 by Louis Sachar. Reprinted by permission of Farrar, Straus & Giroux, LLC.)*

Sydney Taylor creates family stories that show warmth, humor, and strong family relationships. (From Ella of All of a Kind Family, *by Sydney Taylor. Copyright © 1978 by Sydney Taylor. Illustrations copyright © 1978 by Gail Owens. Reprinted by permission of E. P. Dutton.)*

Kind Family, and Madeleine L'Engle's *Meet the Austins.* The actions of the characters suggest that security is gained when family members work together, that each member has responsibility to other members, that consideration for others is desirable, and that family unity and loyalty can overcome hard times and peer conflicts.

Since the early 1960s, many changes have taken place in the characterizations of the American family in realistic fiction. Authors writing in the 1970s, 1980s, and 1990s often have focused on the need to overcome family disturbances, as children and adults adjust to new social realities. Death of one or both parents, foster families, single-parent families, children of unmarried females, the disruptions caused by divorce and remarriage, and child abuse are some of the issues related to children and their families that now appear in contemporary realistic fiction for children.

Such literature may help children realize that many family units other than the traditional one are common and legitimate in society today. Children may also see that problems often can be solved if family members work

together. Even when depicting the most disturbing of relationships, authors of realistic fiction may show a strong need for family unity and a desire to keep at least some of the members together.

Authors of realistic stories about family disturbances use several literary techniques to create credible plots and characters. Often, they look at painful and potentially destructive situations and feelings that are common in society today. These situations are usually familiar to readers, who may have experienced similar situations, who may have known someone who had such experiences, or who may fear that they will have similar experiences. Authors often tell such stories from the perspective of a child or children involved. First-person or limited omniscient point of view from a child's perspective can successfully depict the emotional and behavioral reactions as the children first discover a problem, experience a wide range of personal difficulties and emotions when they try to change or understand the situation, and finally arrive at acceptance of the situation.

The characterizations may portray the vulnerability of the characters, create sympathy for them, and describe how they handle jolting disruptions and personal discoveries that affect their lives. Symbolism and allusion may emphasize conflicts and characters. Authors often use characters' reactions to change, trouble, and new discoveries to trace the development of better relationships with others or positive personal growth.

Some authors, however—such as those trying to make a point about child abuse—use specific situations or discoveries to allow children to escape from all reality. In realistic stories about family life, the antagonist may be a family member or an outside force, such as death of a parent, divorce, or moving to a new location. To relieve the impact of painful situations, authors may add humor. Humor can make situations bearable, create sympathy for characters, or clarify the nature of confrontations.

Elizabeth Strehle (1999) emphasizes the importance of using literature to help shape children's understandings by providing opportunities to observe characters and experience social issues. She states, "Class discussions provide opportunities for students to understand their own beliefs and reconstruct an existing understanding of a concept such as homelessness. Students form their understandings of the world through knowledge of themselves and personal experiences, as well as from the radio news and the books they read" (p. 219).

Desertion, Divorce, and Remarriage. In *Dear Mr. Henshaw*, Beverly Cleary effectively uses letters and diary entries written by her sixth-grade hero, Leigh Botts, to develop believable characters and plot and to show changes in Leigh as he begins to accept the actuality of his parents' divorce. As a classroom assignment, Leigh sends his favorite author a list of ten questions. Mr. Henshaw answers Leigh's questions and sends Leigh a list of ten questions that he wants Leigh to answer about himself.

At first, Leigh refuses to answer the questions. Then, his mother insists that because Mr. Henshaw answered Leigh's questions, Leigh must answer Mr. Henshaw's questions. The answers to the questions allow Cleary to provide important background information and to reveal Leigh's feelings about himself, his family, and his parents' divorce. Eventually, Leigh begins to write a diary—both because Mr. Henshaw suggests it and because Leigh's mother refuses to fix the television.

By midpoint in the book, the diary entries begin to change and Leigh realizes changes in his own character:

I don't have to pretend to write to Mr. Henshaw anymore. I have learned to say what I think on a piece of paper. And I don't hate my father either. I can't hate him. Maybe things would be easier if I could. (p. 73)

The entries seem believable because Cleary includes both humorous and painful experiences that are important in Leigh's life.

In *Strider*, the sequel to *Dear Mr. Henshaw*, Cleary again uses a series of diary entries to reveal changes in character. By caring for an abandoned dog, fourteen-year-old Leigh Botts finally learns to accept his parents' divorce and gains self-confidence. Cleary develops parallels to

The companionship of a dog helps a girl make new friends in Because of Winn-Dixie *by Kate DiCamillo. (Cover illustration by Chris Sheban,* © *2001 Candlewick Press, Inc. Reproduced by permission of the publisher Candlewick Press, Inc., Cambridge, MA.)*

Leigh's divorced parents as Leigh and his best friend argue over the custody of the dog.

A dog is also the means used by Kate DiCamillo in *Because of Winn-Dixie* to help a ten-year-old heroine, Opal, make new friends, understand herself, and accept the desertion of her mother. The dog allows her to make discoveries through the wisdom and advice of these new friends. For example, one older friend reminds her that "you got to remember, you can't judge people by the things they done. You got to judge them by what they are doing now" (p. 96). The librarian teaches Opal that most people have their share of sorrow and sadness. When the dog, Winn-Dixie, is lost the author compares the mother's leaving with Opal's feelings when the dog is lost. A happy ending results when the dog is found and all of the new friends have a party. Opal now understands that her mother will probably not return, but she and her father have made a happy life for themselves.

Mother–child relationships and the consequences that occur when mothers are no longer with their children are common plots in current realistic fiction. The plot in Creech's *Walk Two Moons* develops as Sal tries to discover why her mother left. In *Belle Prater's Boy*, Ruth

ticular are forced to suffer the effects of poverty and how poverty destroys the very fabric of society. Her novel was inspired by a true incident reported in the Turkish press" (endnotes).

The Batchelder Honor Award for 2000 was presented to Ineke Holtwijk's *Asphalt Angels*. This book was also inspired by a real homeless character living with a street gang in Rio de Janeiro. The author depicts the dangerous world of drugs, suicide, dishonest authorities, sex, and gang violence. The content of the book makes it more appropriate for older, mature audiences.

Surviving in a Dangerous World. A new type of survival literature is emerging in both American and British children's literature: realistic fiction that mirrors international headlines about new dangers in our modern age. In the person-against-society conflicts of this survival literature, the protagonists are usually innocent children and the antagonists are terrorist groups, oppressive military governments, and mass violence.

Terrorists create the person-against-society conflicts in Gillian Cross's *On the Edge*. In this book, the hostage is the kidnapped son of a journalist. Cross explores important choices. For the mother, it is complying with the terrorists' demands for the release of her son versus revealing information that could save the life of a world leader and destroy the assassination plot of the terrorists. For the son, it is what to do with the last few moments of his life.

In *AK*, Peter Dickinson develops the conflicts faced by Paul Kagomi, an orphan and a child guerrilla, who tries to survive in a war-torn African setting. Dickinson develops strong themes related to peace and war. Notice the impact of the following quote:

Now, you can't just say, "Let there be peace and happiness." It has to be built, by men and women working together. And even when it is built you can't leave it alone. It has to be tended, it has to be fed and repaired and altered to fit with changing times. It's like a railway, an engine on the railway. That doesn't run by itself. It has to be stoked and driven, its track must be kept sound and the signals working and the bridges inspected—all that. (p. 15)

Dickinson's conclusions are interesting for discussion and responses. Dickinson develops two contrasting scenarios for twenty years after the conclusion of the book. One is a very positive prediction in which the forces for freedom and peace have won. The other scenario is that guerrilla warfare and hatred are still the major way of life.

Other authors place their characters in the political turmoil of South America or Syria. James Watson's *Talking in Whispers*, a 1983 British Carnegie Honor book for older children, is a survival story in which the main character is hunted by the security forces of a South American government that denies basic human rights. Rafik Schami's *A Hand Full of Stars* places the hero in the political turmoil of modern Damascus. Showing how dangerous society can be, the story follows a teenager who

wants to become a journalist within this suppressed society. His wishes come true when he and his friends begin an underground newspaper. After reading this book, you may speculate about the symbolism in the title. The author states at the end of the book what *A Hand Full of Stars* means: "The Hand is the hand of Uncle Salim, always there to guide the narrator; in the saddest moments, it points the way out of despair. Like the stars that illuminate the dark night sky, the Stars in the hand stand for hope" (endnote).

The political turmoil of Romania provides the setting and conflict in Bel Mooney's *The Voices of Silence*. The major conflict results when a girl betrays her parents to her friend.

In Lois Duncan's *Don't Look Behind You,* a family is threatened by hired assassins. Duncan develops the frightening adjustments that the family must make when it is placed under the federal witness security program. Older readers will understand the conflicts of the teenage girl who tries to salvage parts of her former life.

Death

Part of growing up is realizing and gradually accepting the fact of death. An increasing number of realistic fiction stories develop themes related to the acceptance of death and the overcoming of emotional problems following the death of a loved one. Louis Rauch Gibson and Laura M. Zaidman (1992) identify the importance of literature that deals with death:

Since children, like adults, are so deeply affected by the loss of a relative or friend, contemporary realistic fiction and biography help resolve some of the conflicts death presents. Literature about real and fictional people satisfies a desperate need to comfort children who are justifiably bewildered and fearful about death. (p. 233)

As might be expected, different authors treat the subject differently. Treatments also depend on the developmental levels of their intended readers.

Differences in cause of conflict, resolution of conflict, and depth of emotional involvement are apparent in books of realistic fiction about death. Consider how several authors develop these areas in books written for younger readers, preadolescents, and teenagers. For comparative purposes, consider Howard Kaplan's *Waiting to Sing,* written for five- to eight-year-olds; Constance C. Greene's *Beat the Turtle Drum,* written for ten- to twelve-year-olds; Richard Peck's *Remembering the Good Times* and Judy Blume's *Tiger Eyes,* written for readers in their early teens; and Robert Cormier's *The Bumblebee Flies Anyway,* written for teenagers and young adults.

In Howard Kaplan's *Waiting to Sing,* the author first develops a strong family that is nurtured by love for and playing of the piano. This closeness ends with the death of the mother. It is the piano, however, that finally allows father and son to begin their healing. This begins when, "I walked from my bedroom to the piano bench, as if holding on to the music for balance, and sat by my father's side.... We let the piano speak for us. It is our way of crying, the way it had once been our way of laughing.... I felt as though we could quench our thirst on one bright drop. Sometimes I think the greatest distance to be traveled is that between two beating hearts" (unnumbered).

Stories written for ten- through twelve-year-olds have more fully developed characters and deal with more difficult emotions than those written for younger readers. Constance C. Greene's *Beat the Turtle Drum* develops the basis for a girl's reactions to her sister's accidental death by describing the warm relationship between ten-year-old Joss and her twelve-year-old sister, Kate. Kate believes that her parents prefer her younger sister. After Joss dies as a result of a fall from a tree, Kate faces both the sorrow of losing a sister and the inner conflict resulting from her belief that her sister was the favorite. Readers glimpse Kate's inner turmoil when she finally admits her feelings to an understanding relative, who responds:

I bet Joss would've felt the same way. If it'd been you, she might've said the same thing. And both of you would've been wrong. I think when a child dies, it's the saddest thing that could ever happen. And the next saddest is the way the brothers and sisters feel. They feel guilty, because they fought or were jealous or lots of things. And here they are, alive, and the other one is dead. And there's nothing they can do. It'll take time, Kate. (p. 105)

Kate gradually understands that overcoming her grief and conflicting emotions will take more than a moment but that she will receive pleasure from her memories of Joss.

The believable characters in Richard Peck's *Remembering the Good Times* help readers in their teens identify with this story about the suicide of a best friend. Peck first carefully develops the distinct personalities of two boys and a girl in their junior-high years. Kate is involved with people and believes in herself; Buck does not know which group he belongs with; and Trav is angry, unsure of himself, and afraid of the future. Peck develops the main person-against-self conflict by describing Trav's increasing fears as he discusses current events and as he reacts to evidence that he is expected to grow up to be like his successful parents. Trav becomes angry when he feels that he is not being prepared for the realities of life.

Peck develops a strong relationship among the three friends. After Trav's suicide, Kate admonishes herself because she did not notice the little things that should have warned them about Trav's approaching suicide. Peck explores various responses to Trav's death, as high-school administrators blame the parents, the parents blame the school, a knowledgeable older friend states the community's responsibility, and Kate and Buck discover that they can remember the good times of their friendship.

The causes of the conflict in Blume's story for older readers, *Tiger Eyes,* are the sudden, violent death of a par-

ent and a society that creates such violence. Blume develops a person-against-self conflict as a teenage girl, Davey, tries to adjust emotionally and physically to the death of her father, who was a robbery victim. Blume also develops a person-against-society conflict as the characters respond to and reflect about a society in which there is violent death, vandalism, excessive teenage tension, and powerful weapons. Blume's characterization encourages readers to understand Davey's turmoil. Blume shows Davey's emotional ties with her father, Davey's physical reactions when she faces her peers (she faints at school but cannot tell the nurse her problem), Davey's need for a quiet place to reflect, Davey's interactions with a man who is dying from cancer and an uncle who will not allow her to take chances but designs weapons at Los Alamos, and Davey's interactions with two friends who are also facing inner conflicts. The resolutions of the conflicts require much time, but Davey can finally face what happened, tell new friends how her father died, and consider her own future.

The setting in *The Bumblebee Flies Anyway,* Robert Cormier's psychological novel for teenagers and young adults, is a terminal care facility in which a sixteen-year-old boy, Barney, realizes that his treatment is only experimental and that he is actually dying. Cormier uses symbolism to convey Barney's feelings about being a terminally ill guinea pig: The complex is a facility for experimental medicine; "the Handyman" is a doctor who treats the patients and creates illusions; "the merchandise" is special medicines, chemicals, and drugs that are calculated to produce expected responses; and "the bumblebee" is a sportscar in a junkyard that at first appears to be shining and new but is actually only a cardboard mockup of reality.

Several responses by fourteen-year-olds to *Tiger Eyes* demonstrate how personal the reactions to realistic fiction can be. One reader said, "This is not a good book to read in class. You need to be by yourself so you can cry if you want to." Another child said, "It's great. You get into the story and forget everything. I was afraid Davey was going to kill herself, but I thought, Judy Blume wouldn't kill her main character." A third reader said that the story was sad but its moral was happy: "Take a chance on your talents; planning someone's life for them doesn't make them happy; it's always better to face the truth rather than run from it; life is a great adventure; you can't go back in time. So pick up the pieces and move ahead; and some changes happen down inside of you and only you know about them." These responses indicate that a fourteen-year-old grasped many of the complex themes that Blume wove into her novel. It is also interesting to note that the themes identified are positive rather than negative.

As seen from the previous discussion, books on death focus on various aspects of death. Books such as Sharon Creech's *Chasing Redbird* deal with a child's struggle to accept her aunt's death. Audrey Couloumbis's *Getting Near to Baby* explores how two sisters, a thirteen-year-old and a seven-year-old, learn about grief and healing after the tragic death of a sibling. Two recent books deal with responses to death through violence. In Colby Rodowsky's *Remembering Mog,* the author proceeds through a series of family reactions to Mog's murder. The contemporary nightmare of dealing with a missing relative is also developed in Michael Cadnum's *Zero to the Bone,* a book for older readers.

People as Individuals, Not Stereotypes

Stereotypical views of males and females, people with disabilities, and the elderly are becoming less prevalent than they once were in children's literature. Chapter 11, "Multicultural Literature," also discusses contemporary realistic fiction that portrays racial and ethnic minorities in unstereotyped ways.

Male and Females. Publishers are becoming sensitive to the need for literature that does not portray either sex in stereotypical roles. For example, since 1981, the Houghton Mifflin Publishing Company has had guidelines for eliminating sex stereotypes in materials that it publishes. Following are several guidelines:

1. Published materials should balance female and male protagonists and female and male contributors to society, and should present females and males in a variety of jobs. Stories should suggest that both females and males can prepare for and succeed in a variety of occupations.

2. Literature should recognize that males and females share the same basic emotions, personality traits, and capabilities. Both sexes should be portrayed in active pastimes and in solitary pursuits.

3. Sensitivity, taste, and nonstereotypic images should be employed in humor used to characterize the sexes.

4. Literature should present a broad range of historical references to women, including women whose contributions are well known and less well known.

5. Where appropriate, literature should include reference to legal, economic, and social issues related to women.

6. Historical books should include coverage of the roles and activities of women in past centuries.

As the roles of females in our society shift away from the stereotypes of the past, female characters in children's literature reflect these changes. Contemporary realistic fiction contains more girls who are distinct individuals. Girls may be brave, they may be tomboys, and they may be unorthodox. Mothers in realistic fiction are also taking on different roles. Often, they work outside the home; they may even have jobs more demanding than those of their husbands. Whatever roles females in recent realistic fiction play, the female characters are quite different from the female characters in earlier children's literature, even literature of the fairly recent past.

Consider, for example, the popular contemporary character Ramona, created by Beverly Cleary. Stories of her exploits span the years from the early 1950s into the 1980s. In *Henry and Beezus,* published in 1952, readers discover that the girls, Beezus and Ramona, are considered worthy playmates *even* by an active boy, such as Henry Huggins. These thoughts at least imply that active pastimes are not usually considered appropriate for girls; girls may not be considered creative playmates.

In later books, however, Ramona comes into her own. In *Ramona the Pest* (1968), she is not the stereotypical quiet girl; instead, she is the "worst rester" in kindergarten. By the time *Ramona and Her Father* was published in the late 1970s, the roles in her family have changed: Her father loses his job and stays home, while her mother returns to work on a full-time basis. Ramona humorously tries to help her father through this change in his life. *Ramona and Her Mother* explores a working mother's life as viewed by her seven-year-old daughter. By 1981, *Ramona Quimby, Age 8* is helping her family while her father returns to college. The Ramona books are popular with children who enjoy reading about the exploits of a spunky, humorous girl.

Louise Fitzhugh's hero in *Harriet the Spy* is an eleven-year-old girl whom other characters describe as exceptional, intelligent, and curious. Harriet's actions support these descriptions. Harriet hides in her secret places, observes her neighbors and classmates, and writes down her observations. The extent of this popular character's resourcefulness and self-confidence is revealed when her classmates find her notebook and organize "The Spy Catcher Club." Harriet uses all of her creativity to devise a plan that will convince her friends to forgive her. She is far from the fainting female of most traditional literature and Victorian fiction, who must be rescued from her failures by the males in the story. She is even able to return to her real loves, spying and writing. More tales about Harriet are found in *The Long Secret.*

E. L. Konigsburg's *From the Mixed-up Files of Mrs. Basil E. Frankweiler* is another book of realistic fiction in which a female protagonist belies the traditional stereotypes about passive femininity. Claudia Kincaid leads her brother in running away from home and hiding out in the Metropolitan Museum of Art. When the two children are given one hour to search the files and discover the answer to a mystery involving a statue of an angel, Claudia tells her impatient brother that five minutes of planning are worth fifteen minutes of haphazard looking. Her techniques prove successful, and they discover the answer.

Stereotyped views of males are also changing in our society and children's literature. In Katherine Paterson's *Bridge to Terabithia,* for example, a boy hates football, aspires to be an artist, and feels pressured by his father's traditionally masculine expectations of him. Although the father is afraid that Jess is becoming a "sissy," Jess finds support for being himself in a strong friendship with the story's other protagonist, a girl named Leslie, who is also a nonconformist in their rural community.

One outstanding book of realistic fiction from the mid-1960s reveals that wider options for males are becoming more prevalent in children's literature today. In Maia Wojciechowska's *Shadow of a Bull,* the son of a famous and supposedly fearless bullfighter learns that a male doesn't have to prove his manliness through acts of physical daring or violence. Manolo's village expects him to follow in his dead father's footsteps. As the men of the village begin training him in the art of bullfighting, Manolo believes that he is a coward because he has no interest in being a bullfighter. Manolo eventually learns that in order to be truly brave, he must be true to himself and not attempt to satisfy others' expectations. Wojciechowska effectively resolves Manolo's person-against-self conflict when Manolo tells the waiting crowd in the bullring that he prefers medicine to bullfighting.

Individuals Who Are Physically Different or Have a Disability.

Most children and adults dislike standing out in a crowd because of their appearance or physical capabilities. They also may feel discomfort when they see someone who does not conform to the customary standards of appearance or who is physically disabled. Children's realistic fiction is becoming increasingly sensitive to the importance of overcoming cruel or condescending stereotypes.

In *Blubber,* Judy Blume shows how peer cruelty to someone who is physically different can have negative consequences for all concerned. Classmates torment a girl whom they consider grossly overweight. A strong peer leader manipulates her friends into composing a list entitled "How to Have Fun with Blubber" and forces the girl herself to make self-demeaning statements, such as "I am Blubber, the smelly whale of class 206" (p. 72). The main character realizes the crushing impact of what she has done when she tries to stop the cruelty and her classmates then turn on her.

Authors who develop realistic plots around credible characters who have physical disabilities often describe details related to a disability, the feelings and experiences of the person who has the disability, and the feelings and experiences of family members and others who interact with the character. Well-written books help other children empathize with and understand children with disabilities. While adults should evaluate such books by literary standards, they also should evaluate them by their sensitivity.

The resolution of conflict can be a special concern in realistic fiction dealing with physical disabilities. Does the author concoct a happy ending because he or she believes that all children's stories should have happy endings, or does the resolution of conflict evolve naturally and honestly? Through fiction that honestly deals with disabilities, readers can empathize with children who are courageously overcoming their problems and who, with their families, are facing new challenges. Writers of such literature often express the hope that their stories will encourage positive attitudes toward individuals with physical disabilities. As mainstreaming brings more children with disabilities into regular classrooms, this goal becomes more important.

Stories set in different historical periods often reflect changing attitudes about physical disabilities and provide bases for discussion with children. Julia Cunningham's story of a mute boy in *Burnish Me Bright* takes place in a French village of the past. The boy encounters prejudice, misunderstanding, fear, and even hostility. Monsieur Hilaire, a retired performer who befriends the boy and brings him into his world of pantomime, clarifies the reasons behind society's prejudice:

These people you have known are no worse than the others that walk the world but they share with the others a common enemy, and the enemy is anyone who is different. They fear the boy who can't speak, the woman who lives by herself and believes in the curative power of herbs, the man who reads books instead of going to the café at night, the person like me who has lived in the distant differences of the theater. They are not willing to try to understand, so they react against them and occasionally do them injury. (p. 18)

Ellen Howard sets *Edith Herself* in the pioneer America of the 1890s. The girl, Edith, faces her own fears and the ignorance of others who do not understand her epileptic seizures. The story may seem realistic because the experience happened to a relative of the author. Carol Carrick's *Stay Away from Simon* shows the damage inflicted on a boy with mental disabilities in the early 1800s. Both texts develop strong themes about the consequences of prejudice caused by ignorance.

In *From Anna,* Jean Little develops a credible perspective on visual impairment by describing a girl's frightening experiences as a result of blurred letters, letters that look the same, or even appear to jiggle across the page. In *The Gift of the Girl Who Couldn't Hear,* Susan Shreve develops the interactions between Eliza and her best friend, Lucy, who has been deaf since birth. In this book, Lucy helps Eliza understand her own self-worth. The theme of the book may be used as a basis for students to ponder the role of real and self-imposed limitations and the courage to distinguish between the two.

Disabilities include mental capacities that are not up to the social norm. Authors who write plausible books about the relationships between children with mental disabilities and their normal siblings often portray the conflicting emotions of normal characters who experience both protective feelings and feelings of anger toward children with disabilities. In Betsy Byars's *The Summer of the Swans,* Sara is a normal teenager who is discontented with her looks, sometimes miserable for no apparent reason, and often frustrated with her mentally retarded brother as she cares for him.

Byars encourages readers to understand and empathize with Charlie's gentle nature. He is fascinated by the swans who glide silently across the lake, but he becomes confused and terrified when he follows the swans and becomes lost. During a frantic search for Charlie, Sara forgets her personal miseries. When the siblings are reunited, Sara discovers that she feels better about herself and life in general than she had before.

Virginia Euwer Wolff's *Probably Still Nick Swansen* develops a many-sided character, Nick, who faces the realities of his learning disability. The author explores the similarities between sixteen-year-old Nick and other teens as well as individual differences among the students in Nick's special education class. In a strong ending, Nick learns to accept himself. In *Reaching Dustin,* Vicki Grove uses an assignment in which a fifth-grade girl makes discoveries about a classmate's emotional problems when she interviews him.

The Elderly. When children's literature students evaluate the characterizations of elderly people in children's books, they often discover stereotypes. Some authors of contemporary realistic fiction are exploring the problems related to old age with greater sensitivity than authors expressed in books of the past. When evaluating books dealing with the elderly, you should select books that show elderly people in a wide variety of roles. Close experiences between grandparents and grandchildren are common in books for young children, such as Sharon Bell Mathis's *The Hundred Penny Box* and Benjamin Darling's *Valerie and the Silver Pear.* Books for older children, such as Susan Campbell Bartoletti's *Dancing with Dziadziu,* often stress the worthwhile contributions that are still being made by the elderly, the warm relationships that can develop between grandparents and grandchildren, and the desire of elderly people to stay out of nursing homes. Some books are very serious; others develop serious themes through humorous stories.

In *Old John,* Peter Hartling explores the need for independence and strong relationships between generations. When a seventy-five-year-old father and grandfather comes to live with his family, Hartling describes a strong elderly man who has not only idiosyncrasies but also needs for love and independence. In *Everywhere,* Bruce Brooks develops the strong bond between grandfather and grandson. This bond increases after the grandfather suffers a heart attack. The healing power of love is the theme.

The growing relationships and understandings between a girl and her grandfather form the basis for Norma Fox Mazer's *After the Rain.* At first, Rachel resents the time that she is asked to spend with her ailing grandfather, but she mourns the loss of their precious moments together after his death. Well-developed characters help readers understand the needs of the two different generations and the changes that can result because people learn to understand each other.

Other outstanding books about the elderly and young people who love and respect them include Gary and Gail Provost's *David and Max* and Patricia MacLachlan's *Journey.* With their diverse, nonstereotyped depictions of elderly people, such books provide discussion materials that encourage older children to explore the roles of elderly people in literature and their own feelings about the elderly. Additional books about the elderly are found in Sandra McGuire's bibliography, "Promoting Positive Attitudes Toward Aging" (1993).

Animal Stories, Mysteries, Sports Stories, and Humor

Animal stories include stories about dogs, horses, and birds. Mysteries use clues and suspense to help readers develop their powers of observation. Sports stories may be about baseball, football, or flying. Humorous stories use ridiculous situations, exaggeration, and the unexpected to create humor.

Animals

The animals in contemporary realistic fiction are quite different from the animals in traditional literature and modern fantasy. In traditional literature and modern fantasy, animals talk and act like people or have other magical powers. The animals in realistic fiction have a strong sense of reality and sometimes tragedy. Realistic animal stories place specific demands upon authors. When evaluating realistic animal stories for children, you should consider the following questions:

1. Does the author portray animals objectively, without giving them human thoughts or motives?
2. Does the behavior of the animal characters agree with information provided by knowledgeable observers of animals and authorities on animal behavior?
3. Does the story encourage children to respond to the needs of animals or the need of people to love animals without being too sentimental or melodramatic?

Authors who write credible animal stories often depict warm relationships between children and pets. The conflict in such stories usually occurs when something happens to disrupt the security of a pet's life. The antagonist may be a physical change in the animal, an environment different from the pet's secure home, or a human character whose treatment of the animal is cruel or even life threatening. Detailed descriptions of physical changes, settings that become antagonists, or cruel human characters may encourage children to understand the vulnerability of animals to such forces.

Credible stories about wild animals usually reflect research about animal behavior and natural habitats. Conflict may arise when animals face natural enemies, when humans take them from natural surroundings and place them in domestic environments, or when humans hunt or trap them.

Some authors use animal-against-society or animal-against-person conflicts to advocate protection of animals. Other authors stress the human development made possible by interaction with animals. Many authors also stress the positive effects of loyalty and devotion between humans and animals.

Consider, for example, the various techniques used by Theodore Taylor in *The Trouble with Tuck*. Taylor first develops a believably close relationship between Helen and her golden Labrador. Helen's love for Tuck and her family's devotion to the dog are strengthened by two incidents in which Tuck saves Helen from harm or possible death. The reactions of the family members when the veterinarian declares that Tuck is going blind and cannot be helped reflect their devotion to the dog and make plausible their acceptance of Helen's resolution of the problem. She calls a trainer for Seeing Eye dogs and makes an appointment for her parents without telling the trainer that the blind individual is a dog.

Although the trainer's initial reaction is negative, the family is finally offered an older Seeing Eye dog whose master has died. Taylor describes Helen's trials and frustrations as she tries to train Tuck to follow the Seeing Eye dog. After weeks of disappointment, she is rewarded when Tuck accepts and follows the older dog. This story, based on a true incident, emphasizes determination, loyalty, and self-confidence that may develop because of animal and human interaction.

In *Shiloh*, Phyllis Reynolds Naylor uses several techniques to develop the theme that cruelty to animals is wrong. For example, Marty thinks that something really hurts inside when a dog cringes like that. The theme is emphasized when the author compares a jar of lightning bugs to a chained dog: Both are prisoners. The thoughts of others reveal the theme when Marty's father tells Marty to open his eyes and understand that there are many hard-hearted people. In the end, Marty is able to bargain for Shiloh because Judd, Shiloh's cruel owner, illegally killed a deer and Marty saw him. *Shiloh Season* is a sequel to the book and extends the conflict between Marty and Judd.

A classic book with a notable dog as the main character is Jack London's *Call of the Wild*, first published in 1903. This story depicts life in the Klondike during the Alaskan gold rush. London develops a credible story of transformation. Buck progresses from a docile pet to a rugged work dog and finally to an animal who is inescapably drawn by the wild cries of the wolf pack. London develops these remarkable changes in Buck by providing details of his life before and after he is stolen from his home in California and brought, raging and roaring, to face the primitive law of the Klondike. Buck changes as he reacts to a beating and the fierce fangs of fighting dogs, but he retains his

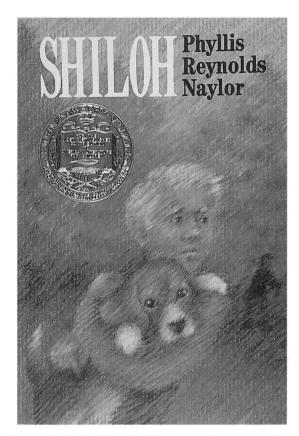

A strong relationship is developed between an abused dog and a boy. (From Shiloh by Phyllis Reynolds Naylor. Copyright © 1991 by Phyllis Reynolds Naylor. Published by Atheneum, an imprint of Macmillan Publishing Company. Reprinted by permission of Dilys Evans Fine Illustrations.)

spirit. While crossing the countryside in a dogsled harness, his long-suppressed instincts come alive.

This is also the story of strong bonds between dog and human. After a succession of sometimes cruel owners, Buck is purchased by kind John Thornton. Buck apparently feels an adoration for John that causes him continually to return from his wilderness treks until the terrible day when he returns to camp to find that John has been killed. Only then are the bonds between man and dog broken, allowing Buck to roam with the wolf pack:

His cunning was wolf cunning, and wild cunning; his intelligence shepherd intelligence and St. Bernard intelligence; and all this, plus an experience gained in the fiercest of schools, made him as formidable a creature as any that roamed the wild. (p. 114)

Horse stories also have qualities that make them marvelous for children. The horses and their owners, or would-be owners, usually have devoted relationships. Often, the little horse, which may have been laughed at or scorned, becomes the winner of a race and begins a famous line of horses. Sadness in many of these stories results when both horse and owner must overcome severe obstacles and even mistreatment.

Two outstanding authors of horse stories are Marguerite Henry and Walter Farley. Henry's stories reflect research and knowledge about horses and their trainers, and several of them report the history of a breed of horses. One memorable story narrates the ancestry of Man o' War, the greatest racehorse of his time. In *King of the Wind,* readers travel back two hundred years to the royal stables of a sultan of Morocco, where Agba, a young horse tender, has a dream of glory for a golden Arabian stallion with a white chest.

The boy and horse travel from Morocco to France when the Sultan sends six of his best horses to King Louis XV, who rejects the horses, which have become thin from their voyage. Agba and the once-beautiful Sham are handed over to several degrading and even cruel masters before the English Earl of Godolphin discovers their plight and takes them home with him. In England, Agba's dream comes true. Three of the golden Arabian's offspring win various important races. When the great Arabian horse, renamed the Godolphin Arabian, stands before royalty, Agba's thoughts flash back to a promise that he made in Morocco:

"My name is Agba. Ba means father. I will be a father to you, Sham, and when I am grown I will ride you before the multitudes. And they will bow before you, and you will be the king of the Wind. I promise it." He had kept his word! (p. 169)

A beautiful black stallion and his descendants are the chief characters in a series of books written by Walter Farley. The first, *The Black Stallion,* introduces a beautiful wild horse that is being loaded, unwillingly, onto a large ship. On this same ship is Alec Ramsay, who understands and loves horses. The two are brought together as the ship sinks, and the black horse pulls Alec through the waves to a small deserted island. Friendship develops as the two help each other survive, and Alec discovers the joy of racing on the back of the amazing horse.

Mysteries

Mysteries provide escape and enjoyable reading because of their suspense. They allow children to become involved in the solutions through clues. They also suggest that children themselves—if they are observant, creative, and imaginative—can solve mysteries.

Footsteps on a foggy night, disappearing people, mysterious strangers, and unusual occurrences woven together into exciting, fast-paced plots create mystery stories that appeal to older children. One eleven-year-old girl, an avid reader of mysteries, listed the following four characteristics that make a mystery exciting for her: (1) It should have an exciting plot that holds the interest of readers, (2) it should contain suspense, (3) it should have enough clues to allow readers to follow the action, and (4) the clues should be written in such a way that readers can try to discover "who done it." In answer to the question "What has caused your interest in mysteries?" she

 Technology Resources

Visit our Companion Website at www.prenhall.com/norton to link to a site on which Joan Lowery Nixon guides you through the process of writing a mystery.

replied that she had read Donald J. Sobol's *Encyclopedia Brown* in third grade and enjoyed trying to follow the clues. She said that her favorite suspense story was Virginia Hamilton's *The House of Dies Drear,* a tale about the Underground Railroad.

The best-known mysteries for young readers are probably contained in Donald J. Sobol's "Encyclopedia Brown" series. In each of the books, ten-year-old Leroy Brown helps his father, the police chief of Idvalle, solve crimes by figuring out the clues. For example, in *Encyclopedia Brown Tracks Them Down,* Leroy solves the case of a missing ambassador by reviewing the gifts presented to him at a birthday party. In another case in that book, Leroy solves the riddle of a flower can and discovers the identity of the boy who stole an 1861 Confederate coin worth $5,000. *Encyclopedia Brown Sets the Pace* contains ten more cases in which young readers can try to identify a thief or solve the problem of a bully who picks on smaller children. Sobol provides readers with the solutions and the reasoning behind them.

In *A Kind of Thief,* Vivien Alcock's introduction draws readers into the suspense. As you read the following quotes, notice how Alcock creates the mood and draws you into the conflict:

They came early, ringing at the bell, knocking at the door, and shouting. Elinor's room was at the back of the house. The noise disturbed her dreams, and she pulled her quilt over her head. Unlike her sister Judy, she was bad at waking up. It took her a long time to clear her mind of sleep. (p. 1)

There were two strange men in the hall, standing stiffly by the door. The older one was regarding her gloomily, as if he thought she only added to his troubles. The younger one was watching her father. Somehow they frightened her, coming here before the sun was properly up. She knew at once they meant her family no good. (p. 2)

The mystery deepens as Elinor's father is arrested. Before he is taken away, however, he slips a baggage claim receipt into her pocket and whispers words that she does not hear. When Elinor redeems the receipt and acquires her father's locked briefcase, she suspects the worst. The rest of the story accompanies Elinor through suspected family betrayal. Not until an accident occurs does Elinor learn the truth about her father and his interactions with his family.

Observation plays an important role in Robert Newman's mysteries, two of which are set in the London of Sherlock Holmes's time. *The Case of the Baker Street Irregular* and *The Case of the Vanishing Corpse* include suspense, sinister characters who must be outwitted, and several mysteries that seem not to be related but actually are.

In *The Original Freddie Ackerman*, Hadley Irwin introduces readers to the two personalities of Trevor Frederick Ackerman, who is going reluctantly to spend the summer with his great-aunts on an island off the coast of Maine. As you read the following quote, notice how Irwin separates the real experience from the imaginary one:

As they waited for the traffic light to turn green, he wondered what would happen if he opened the car door and disappeared. Great-Aunt Calla would probably be relieved, and Great-Aunt Louisa, sitting beside him, might not even notice, since she hadn't looked over at him yet and, besides that, seemed to have used up her quota of words for the day.

Freddie Ackerman, World War II ace, his B-24 Liberator bomber shot down in flames and his parachute buried deep in the Black Forest, would never allow himself to be captured alive with all the secret invasion plans he was carrying. Freddie Ackerman would fling open the car door, slide down into the river that bordered the autobahn, and fade like a ghost into the rain and mist of the German countryside. (p. 6)

Trevor's eccentric aunts provide mysterious quests for information to entice Trevor's interest. On the island, Trevor searches for physical evidence that will identify whether or not a book is a first edition. Strong relationships between the aunts and Trevor help him overcome feelings of alienation in his life.

Ellen Raskin's several books challenge readers to join often preposterous characters in working out puzzle clues. These clues include word puzzles, a series of obscurely written messages, and even observations gained through reading. *The Mysterious Disappearance of Leon (I Mean Noel)* is a humorous word puzzle, a game about names, liberally sprinkled with clues. As the story of Leon and Little Dumpling, the heirs to Mrs. Carillon's Pomato Soup fortune, proceeds, Raskin informs readers that there is a very important clue in a particular section or that they should mark the locations of Leon's fourteen messages because they contain important clues. Noel's final words, for example, as he bobs up and down in the water cause Little Dumpling years of searching. What is meant by "Noel glub C blub all . . . I glub new . . ."?

In *Figgs & Phantoms,* the clue that Raskin provides is "the bald spot." This clue eventually helps Mona Figg discover whether she has or has not actually visited Capri, the Figg family's idea of a perfect heaven. Raskin's *The Westing Game* includes many clues that must be worked through before the teams of players solve the mystery.

Zilpha Keatley Snyder's mysteries involve kidnapping, complex games, and mysterious secret environments. In *The Famous Stanley Kidnapping Case,* masked strangers kidnap five unusual children who accompany their parents to Italy. In *The Egypt Game,* six children create an ancient Egyptian world in an abandoned storage yard and solve a murder mystery.

Suspense, revenge, and mysterious happenings are all part of Robert Cormier's mystery for older readers, *In the Middle of the Night.* The novel begins with a foreshadowing of the suspense to follow: "Ten minutes later, Lulu was dead. And the nightmare began" (p. 9). Cormier uses several techniques to encourage readers to understand the conflict and its influence on the characters. For example, he described the son's reactions to his father as he burns letters, responds to reporters, and sees his face flashing on television. Tension builds as Cormier reviews old newspaper articles and relates telephone messages that change from calling the father in the middle of the night to calling the son in the afternoon. Now the tension increases as Cormier goes back and forth between Lulu, the child victim, and her brother and Denny, the son. In a dramatic ending, Denny's life is saved and he learns lessons about himself. Cormier's *Tenderness* is another taut mystery for older readers. This novel presents the portrait of a serial killer.

Sports

Sports stories rate highly with children who are sports enthusiasts. Some quite reluctant readers will finish a book about their favorite sport or sports hero. The majority of the sports stories are about boys, however, and few authors yet write about girls who enjoy participating in sports. Many stories deal with the ideal of fair play, the values of sports, the overcoming of conflicts between fathers and sons, and the overcoming of fears connected with sports. Unfortunately, many of the stories are didactic and have familiar plot lines and stock characters.

Sports stories for children are also apparently important to sport franchises. Karen Raugust (1997) reports a merger between major league sports teams and the publishing of sports-related books. According to a quote by the director of marketing for the National Hockey League, "The sport depends on the long-term development of fans. Publishing helps to support all of the other fan development programs" (p. 35). As these books become available, you may compare them with other books about sports and sports heroes.

Authors who write about baseball often imply that the sport has therapeutic value. Often, the emphasis in these books is on the role that baseball can play in helping children overcome problems at home, develop new friendships, face physical disabilities, or feel accomplishment. Matt Christopher's *The Fox Steals Home,* for example, tells the story of troubled Bobby Canfield, who is facing his parents' divorce and the prospect of his father's taking a job far from home. His father and his grandfather have coached him and nicknamed him "Fox." His proudest moment comes when he steals home and demonstrates to his father what a good player he has become.

Overcoming a severe accident in which a baseball player loses an eye provides the plot and conflict in Scott

Johnson's *Safe at Second.* This is also a strong story of friendship in which a best friend helps a boy who had been destined for the major leagues.

In *Hang Tough, Paul Mather,* Alfred Slote writes about a leukemia victim whose greatest interest is baseball. The boy must face the knowledge that he has a short time to live and that his parents are trying to prevent him from playing to protect him. However, an understanding doctor helps him play his last season with dignity and courage. In *The Trading Game,* Slote's story is about a ten-year-old boy who matures during his interactions with his grandfather. The grandfather is a former baseball player.

In *Herbie Jones and the Monster Ball,* Suzy Kline humorously develops a story about a young boy who hates baseball until his uncle coaches a baseball team for eight- and nine-year-olds. The book does not stereotype girls, who play on the team. The boy's older sister also gives him baseball lessons.

Written for older readers, Chris Crutcher's *Athletic Shorts* is a collection of six short stories about various types of athletes. The characters in many of these stories are taken from Crutcher's previous books.

The sport of flying provides the adventure in Betsy Byars's *Coast to Coast.* Developing a strong grandfather and granddaughter relationship, Byars takes readers on an adventurous trip in a Piper Cub when the grandfather and his granddaughter fly from South Carolina to California. This book shows that girls can be just as adventurous as boys.

Matt Christopher's collection of sports stories includes stories about almost every sport. Several of his more recent titles include *Skateboard Renegade,* in which a boy faces a challenge when he tries to fit in with his friends; *Soccer Duel,* in which team rivalry and friendship are in conflict; *Wheel Wizards,* in which a boy learns to play basketball from a wheelchair; and *Tennis Ace,* in which a girl is unhappy when her father ignores her talent and focuses on her brother.

Humor

Humorous stories, whether involving figures of fantasy or realistic people living in the contemporary world, are among children's favorites. Authors who write about humorous situations that could happen to real people (these situations and characters may stretch probability) allow children to understand that life can be highly entertaining and that it is not always serious. Writers may encourage readers to laugh at themselves and at numerous human foibles. Humorous situations and characters may highlight real problems and make reading about them palatable.

Authors of humorous realistic fiction use many of the sources of humor discussed in Chapter 5—word play, surprise and the unexpected, exaggeration, and ridiculous sit-

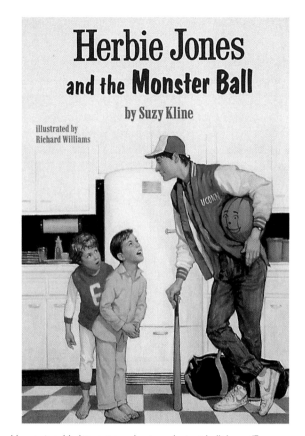

Humor is added to a story about a reluctant ballplayer. (From Herbie Jones and the Monster Ball *by Suzy Kline, illustrations by Richard Williams, copyright © 1988 by Richard Williams. Reprinted by permission of G. P. Putnam's Sons.)*

uations. For example, authors may use a play on words or ideas to create humorous situations or clarify characters' feelings. Consider Betsy Byars's *The Cybil War,* an entertaining story about a fifth-grade boy who has a crush on a girl. The war develops as Cybil Ackerman responds in various ways to Simon's advances, which are intentionally misinterpreted by his best friend.

Beverly Cleary uses a twist on the words of a familiar television commercial to create a funny incident in *Ramona Quimby, Age 8.* When Ramona gives her book report, she presents it in the style of a television commercial. Her statement, "I can't believe I read the whole thing," causes a hilarious reaction among her classmates. In *The One in the Middle Is the Green Kangaroo,* Judy Blume uses a humorous analogy to clarify a middle child's feelings: "He felt like the peanut butter part of a sandwich squeezed between Mike and Ellen" (p. 7).

Judy Blume uses a surprising and unexpected situation in *Tales of a Fourth Grade Nothing.* In this story, a humorous conflict between two brothers is brought to a climax when the younger boy swallows the older brother's pet turtle. An unexpected situation provides humor in Lois Lowry's *Anastasia on Her Own* when a

Through the Eyes of an AUTHOR

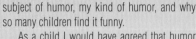

Beverly Cleary

Visit the CD-ROM that accompanies this text to generate a complete list of Beverly Cleary titles.

Selected Titles by Beverly Cleary:

Dear Mr. Henshaw

The Mouse and the Motorcycle

Ramona and Her Father

Runaway Ralph

Ramona Quimby, Age 8

The Laughter of Children

Although for over thirty years I have been absorbed in stories that spring from the humor of everyday life, I try not to think about humor while writing, because of the sound advice given me by my first editor, Elisabeth Hamilton, whom I met after writing *Henry Huggins & Ellen Tebbits*. In discussing writing for children, I happened to mention humor. Elisabeth, a forceful woman, interrupted. "Darlin'," she said, "don't *ever* analyze it. Just do it." I have followed her advice. While I am writing, if I find myself thinking about humor and what makes a story humorous, I am through for the day; and that chapter usually goes into the wastebasket, for spontaneity has drained out of my work. Although introspection is valuable to every writer, I find that analyzing my own work is harmful because it makes writing self-conscious rather than intuitive. When I am not writing, however, I find myself mulling over the subject of humor, my kind of humor, and why so many children find it funny.

As a child I would have agreed that humor is "what makes you laugh." I could not find enough laughter in life or in books, so the stories I write are the stories I wanted to read as a child in Portland, Oregon—humorous stories about the problems which are small to adults but which loom so large in the lives of children, the sort of problems children can solve themselves. I agree with James Thurber's statement: "Humor is the best that lies closest to the familiar, to that part of the familiar which is humiliating, distressing, even tragic. . . . There is always a laugh in the utterly familiar."

My first book, *Henry Huggins*, a group of short stories about the sort of children I had known as a child, was written with a light heart from memories of Portland. As I wrote I discovered I had a collaborator, the child within myself—a rather odd, serious little girl, prone to colds, who sat in a child's rocking chair with her feet over the hot air outlet of the furnace, reading for hours, seeking laughter in the pages of books while her mother warned her she would ruin her eyes. That little girl, who has remained with me, prevents me from writing down to children, from poking fun at my characters, and from writing an adult reminiscence about childhood instead of a book to be enjoyed by children. And yet I do not write solely for that child; I am also writing for my adult self. We are collaborators who must agree. The feeling of being two ages at one time is delightful, one that surely must be a source of great pleasure to all writers of books enjoyed by children.

By the time I had published five books, several things had happened which forced me to think about children and humor: I had children of my own, twins—a boy and a girl; reviews said my books were hilarious or genuinely funny; a textbook of children's literature said my books were to be read "purely for amusement"; and enough children had written to me to give me some insight into their thoughts about my books.

One phrase began to stand out in these letters from children. Letter after letter told me my books were "funny and sad." Until these letters arrived, I had not thought of *Henry Huggins* as sad. The words, at that time never used by adults in reference to my books, began to haunt me. Funny and sad, or even funny and tragic, describes my view of life. To borrow another phrase from James Thurber, I had chosen "reality twisted to the right into humor rather than to the left into tragedy"—for that is my nature. I feel that comedy is as illuminating as tragedy—more so for younger readers who may be frightened or discouraged by tragedy in realistic fiction.

Video Profiles: The accompanying video contains conversations with Paula Danziger, Eve Bunting, Gary Soto, and other authors of contemporary realistic fiction.

Abridged from "The Laughter of Children," *The Horn Book* (October 1982): 555–564. Copyright © 1982 by Beverly Cleary.

---

naive cook, trying to prepare a gourmet dinner, asks for and receives cooking advice from a stranger who is calling to sell tap dancing lessons. In *Anastasia's Chosen Career*, Lowry uses excerpts from Anastasia's writings from a school assignment about careers.

An unexpected situation in Anne Fine's *Alias Madame Doubtfire* occurs when an ex-husband disguises himself as a cleaning woman and babysitter in his ex-wife's house. The humorous and surprising situations in Joan Bauer's *Squashed* occur when a girl tries to grow the largest pumpkin for the Rock River Pumpkin Weigh-In. She tries everything including playing motivational tapes to make the pumpkin grow.

Comic twists, flamboyant characters, and humorous situations are part of the pleasure in reading Polly Horvath's *When the Circus Came to Town*. Although most of the incidents are humorous, the actions of the characters reflect and highlight human foibles, and the main characters learn something about themselves when they experience situations that are more humorous to readers than to them.

Through the Eyes of a CHILD

Amy

Pam Wilson's Fourth Grade
Western Row Elementary
Mason, Ohio

> TITLE: Dear Mr. Henshaw
>
> AUTHOR: Beverly Cleary
>
> Dear Mr. Henshaw is a really good book. I like the book because, it's all letters. I have never read a book that was just someone writing to a person, like pen pals. I like chapter books, like this one. I don't like pictures because, I would rather read the book and imagine my own pictures. That's why I like that the book only has six pictures out of the whole book. I would really recommend this book to someone because, All you have to read is letters taking place by months. The book is about a boy who wants to be a author when he grows up. Leigh is writing to his favorite author, named Mr. Henshaw. he only reads his books. Leigh's parents got divorced. Leigh just moved to a new school, he does not have friends. Someone keeps stealing good stuff from his lunch. Leigh wished that his dad would come to see Leigh someday. Amy

Suggested Activities

 For more suggested activities for understanding contemporary realistic fiction, visit our Companion Website at www.prenhall.com/norton

▓ Sexism in literature, including the harmful sex-role socialization resulting from female- and male-role stereotyping, is a major concern of many educators and psychologists. In a school, public, or university library, choose a random sampling of children's literature selections. If these books were the only sources of information available about male and female roles, what information would be acquired from the books and their illustrations? Is this information accurate?

▓ Analyze the list of books identified by Marsha M. Sprague and Kara K. Keeling in the April 2000 issue of *Journal of Adolescent & Adult Literacy*. Why do you believe that these twenty books have been identified as books that encourage gender dialogue?

▓ Interview children's librarians in public or school libraries. Ask these librarians to state the guidelines used by the library when selecting books considered controversial for children. What issues, if any, do the librarians feel are relevant in the community? Can they identify any books that have caused controversy in the libraries? If there are such books, how did they handle the controversy?

▓ Many realistic fiction stories deal with the problems that children must face and overcome when they experience separation from a friend, a neighborhood, or a parent, or they face the ultimate separation caused by death. Choose one area, read several books that explore the problem, and recommend books to share with younger children and books more appropriate for older children. Explain your decisions. Annotated bibliographies such as those found in Joanne E. Bernstein's "Bibliotherapy: How Books Can Help Young Children Cope" (1989) may be helpful in the search.

Teaching with Realistic Fiction

1 f realistic fiction is to help children identify with others, extend their horizons, and gain personal insights, then adults who work with children must be aware of a wide range of realistic fiction and activities. It is not necessary, or even advisable, to attach literature-related activities to all realistic fiction that children read, but some activities are appropriate.

This section considers how you may use realistic fiction to stimulate role playing that strengthens understanding of the world and offers suggestions for handling real problems. This section also takes an in-depth look at a children's literature unit that stresses the theme of island survival. In addition to activities and discussions stressing the influence of settings upon the conflicts in stories, a unit may relate literature to the science curriculum through activities that increase understanding of geography and botany. This section also tells you how to use literature to develop an appreciation for the contributions of females and an understanding of the various roles that both males and females can play in life. The section concludes with questioning strategies that can accompany realistic fiction or any other genre of literature.

Using Role Playing

Role playing is a creative dramatics activity in which children consider a problem, contemplate possible actions of people in reaction to the problem, and then act out the situation as they believe it might unfold in real life. According to child-development authorities, role playing fosters social development, increases problem-solving capabilities, and enhances creativity. Role playing helps children develop an understanding of the world around them and enhances children's understanding of various ways to handle common problems. Even young children can benefit from role-playing activities. Three- and four-year-olds can role-play experiences about family life while four- and five-year-olds can role-play situations that increase and extend their interests beyond family and school and into the world around them.

Shaffer (1989) provides guidelines that can help you select meaningful role-playing activities. He adapts Selman's stages of social perspective and describes characteristic student responses to others' perspectives. Understanding these typical responses can help you plan activities and observe or interact with students during role playing. For example, three- to six-year-olds are unaware of any perspective other than their own; six- to eight-year-olds recognize that people have perspectives different from theirs; eight- to ten-year-olds know that their points of view can conflict with others'; ten- to twelve-year-olds can consider their own and another person's point of view simultaneously; and twelve- to fifteen-year-olds attempt to understand another person's perspective by comparing it with that of the social system in which they operate.

Literature can be the stimulus for activities that satisfy the purposes of role playing. Use realistic picture books about doctors, dentists, and other neighborhood helpers to encourage young children to act out the roles of adults with whom they come in contact. Such role playing can decrease the fears of children by allowing them to experience a role before facing a real situation. Use books about families to encourage children to role-play interactions between different members of a family, nuclear or extended.

The plots in realistic fiction provide many opportunities for children to role-play problems. Zena Sutherland (1997) recommends that literature selected for stimulating, thought-provoking problem situations should (1) contain characters who are well developed and have clearly defined problems, (2) have plots that contain logical stopping places so that children can role-play the endings, (3) include problems, such as universal fears and concerns, that allow children to identify with the situations, and (4) present problems that help children develop their personal value systems. In role playing, you may either choose stories in which problems are developed to certain points and then have children role-play the unfinished situations or have children role-play various solutions to problems after they have read or listened to the whole stories.

Sutherland recommends the following procedures for role playing: First, encourage students to think about what will happen next in the story, to consider how the story might end, and to identify with the characters. Second, ask the students to describe the characters and then to play those roles. Third, ask the audience to observe and to decide if the solution is a realistic one. Fourth, ask the students who are role playing to decide what they will do to practice dialogue. Encourage them to describe the staging that they will use. Fifth, have the students role-play the situation, with each student playing the character that he or she represents. The focus should be solving a problem, not acting. Sixth, engage the players and the audience in a discussion of the role playing, the consequences of the actions, and alternative behaviors. Next, have the role players try new interpretations based on the ideas generated from the discussion. Finally, encourage students to assess the outcomes and determine the best ways to deal with the problems.

The books of realistic fiction discussed in this chapter offer many stimuli for role-playing situations. Because the books are categorized according to their content, you may refer to this chapter when searching for specific situations connected with family life, peer relationships, individuality, and so forth. The following books also contain problem situations that adults have used to stimulate children's role playing in connection with family life (Norton, 1992):

Family Life

1. *Responsibility toward family members (picture books).* Patricia Gauch's *Christina Katerina and the Time She Quit the Family. Problem:* What should happen in a family when a child wants to do only what pleases her and not what would make her part of the family? Mavis Jukes's *Like Jake and Me. Problem:* How should a stepfather and his new son adjust to each other? Phyllis Naylor's *Keeping a Christmas Secret. Problem:* How can a child redeem himself when he reveals an important family secret? How should the rest of the family respond? William Steig's *Spinky Sulks. Problem:* What should happen when a sulky boy discovers that his family really is trying to help him? Mildred Pitts Walter's *Two and Too Much. Problem:* What type of interaction should take place when a seven-year-old is asked to take care of his two-year-old sister?

2. *Interpersonal relationships.* Sharon Bell Mathis's *The Hundred Penny Box. Problem:* How should a boy respond when he makes friends with his great-great-aunt and tries to explain her feelings about an old box of pennies to his mother? How should the aunt and the mother interact with each other? Roni Schotter's *Captain Snap and the Children of Vinegar Lane. Problem:* How should children act and talk when they want to make friends with a lonely older man? How should the man respond to the children? Patricia C. McKissack's *The Honest-to-Goodness Truth. Problem:* What is the best way to tell the truth without hurting someone's feelings?

3. *Making difficult decisions.* Jeannie Baker's *Where the Forest Meets the Sea. Problem:* How can difficult ecological decisions be made so that the forest and seashore will be protected? How should the boy let his grandfather know that he understands the problem? Dayal Khalsa's *I Want a Dog. Problem:* How can you convince your family that you are responsible enough to own a pet? Theodore Taylor's *The Trouble with Tuck. Problem:* How should a family respond when the dog goes blind?

4. *Family disturbances.* Carol Lea Benjamin's *The Wicked Stepdog. Problem:* How should a girl, her father, and her new stepmother act when the father remarries? What can they each do to accept each other? Beverly Cleary's *Dear Mr. Henshaw. Problem:* How can a boy overcome his problems related to his parents' divorce? What should the mother, the father, and the boy say to each other? How can the parents help the boy understand what has happened to his family? Janet Taylor Lisle's *Afternoon of the Elves. Problem:* How should a family try to survive when a parent is mentally or physically incompetent? How can a friend help in this situation?

5. *Accepting others and overcoming prejudice.* Judy Blume's *Blubber. Problem:* How can students show sensitivity toward a student who is overweight? Betsy Byars's *The Summer of the Swans. Problem:* How should a sister and society respond to a child who is mentally retarded? Nicholasa Mohr's *Felita* and *Going Home. Problem:* In the first book, how can prejudice toward a Puerto Rican girl in New York be overcome? In the second book, how can the same girl overcome prejudice against a Puerto Rican American girl when she visits Puerto Rico?

Such stories allow children to empathize with characters who have problems that many children in elementary school experience. Through role playing, children may discover ways to handle problems and increase their sensitivity to the problems of others.

In addition to understandings gained through role playing, students gain understandings through discussions about books in which characters make moral choices. After reading Marion Dane Bauer's *On My Honor* with sixth- and seventh-grade students, Claudia Lepman-Logan (1989) states:

I was astonished at the response it provoked. I had thought that using a book with a moral choice as its theme might stimulate some interesting discussions, but I was quite unprepared for the intense and lively debates that engaged even the most passive students. . . . Throughout the reading of the book my students found themselves comparing and contrasting their own inclinations with Joel's motivations. The element of uncertainty is stretched out until the ending, which, interestingly enough, did not bring a close to either the events in the book or to our discussions. By following Joel's inner turmoil readers had to decide whether his final decision was indeed believable. (p. 108)

Lepman-Logan extended the initial discussion by asking her students to consider the choices that writers face when they resolve the problems that they create. Students who wanted more details to accompany *On My Honor* created additional dialogues among characters and explored further consequences that might result for the characters. Additional books that have moral choices and endings that lead to further consequences for the characters include Paula Fox's *One-Eyed Cat*, Walter Dean Myers's *Scorpions*, Gillian Cross's *On the Edge*, Cynthia Rylant's *A Fine White Dust*, Stephanie S. Tolan's *A Good Courage*, and Brock Cole's *The Goats*.

Using Survival Stories to Motivate Reading and Interaction with Literature

Many realistic fiction adventure stories portray physical survival and increased emotional maturity of the main characters. The plots and strong characterizations in this type of realistic fiction encourage children to live the adventures vicariously. Physical characteristics that cause major conflicts may help children understand the importance of setting.

Two very interesting instructional activities developed by university students and then shared with classrooms of children centered on the survival theme. One group developed an in-depth literature unit around physical and emotional survival on islands. Another group chose physical and emotional survival in mountains, on arctic tundra, and in Canadian wilderness. Each group used the webbing process to organize its unit.

Interdisciplinary Unit: Island Survival

The university students who chose the island survival theme identified the following books for ability to survive physically and grow in maturity because of the experiences:

Island of the Blue Dolphins, by Scott O'Dell
Call It Courage, by Armstrong Sperry
The Cay, by Theodore Taylor
The Swiss Family Robinson, by Johann David Wyss

The group read the books and identified the central themes and the main areas that challenged the physical survival: characteristics of the natural environment, including climatic conditions of the islands caused by their geographical locations, and survival needs related to other human needs. This central theme and six subtopics associated with survival were identified in the first phase of the island survival web (see Figure 9.1). During the next phase, the group identified subjects related to each subtopic on the web. The group developed the extended web shown in Figure 9.2.

After finishing the webs, the group planned activities to help children learn the importance of setting, realize that setting may cause major conflicts, and understand each identified physical survival topic. The university students also identified topics related to an upper-elementary science curriculum. They used interesting literature to increase children's understanding of scientific principles, and they developed activities to stimulate oral language, written language, and artistic interpretations of the plots and characters.

The examples in Chart 9.2 are taken from the physical survival activities developed around Scott O'Dell's *Island of the Blue Dolphins.* Several activities are included for each main subtopic in the web to allow you to visualize the types of physical survival activities that are possible in the classroom. Many of these activities are also appropriate for discussion in the library. The university students developed similar activities around each island survival book. Their discussions and activities stressed the importance of setting in developing the conflict and the effects upon the growth of the characters as they overcame problems connected with setting or loneliness. The students also compared the various characters, their settings, and the physical and emotional strategies that led to survival.

In a final activity, the university students set up an elementary-school classroom as an island. They divided the class into groups according to shelter, food, clothing, geography, medical care, and seasonal weather. For Island Day, the elementary-school children chose and developed activities that represented their areas of interest. The children constructed shelters in which they located

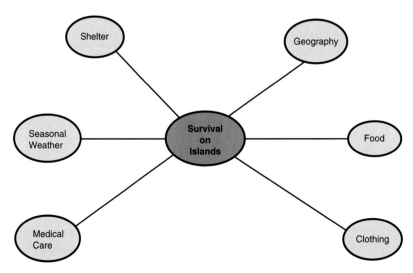

FIGURE 9.1   Island survival web, first phase

2. *Recall of sequence of events:* What sequence of events led Louise to believe that Caroline was the favored child in the family? What sequence of events caused Louise to move from an island to a mountain community?

3. *Recall of comparisons:* Compare the author's physical descriptions of Louise and Caroline. Compare the way in which Louise thought the family treated her with the way in which she thought they treated her twin sister, Caroline.

4. *Recall of character traits:* Describe Louise's response to the story about the birth of the twins, Louise and Caroline. How does Grandma respond to Caroline, to Louise, to Captain Wallace, to her son, and to her daughter-in-law?

Inference

When children infer an answer to a question, they go beyond the information that the author provides and hypothesize about such things as details, main ideas, and cause-and-effect relationships. Inference is usually considered a higher level thought process; the answers are not specifically stated within the text. Examples of inferential questions include the following:

1. *Inferring supporting details:* At the end of *Jacob Have I Loved,* Joseph Wojtkiewicz says, "God in heaven's been raising you for this valley from the day you were born." What do you believe he meant by this statement?

2. *Inferring main idea:* What do you believe is the theme of the book? What message do you think the author was trying to express? How does the author develop this theme?

3. *Inferring comparisons:* Think about Captain Wallace, who is such a part of Louise's story. Compare that character with the one who left the island when he was a young man. How do you believe they are alike and how do you believe they are different?

4. *Inferring cause-and-effect relationships:* If you identified any changes in Captain Wallace, what do you believe might have caused them? Why do you believe Louise dreamed about Caroline's death? Why do you believe that Louise felt wild exaltation and then terrible guilt after these dreams?

5. *Inferring character traits:* What do you believe caused Louise to change her mind about wanting Hiram Wallace to be an islander who escaped rather than a Nazi spy? What is Louise saying about herself when she emphasizes the word *escaped*? Why do you believe Louise became so upset whenever she was called "Wheeze"? Why do you think Louise was so upset when Call invited Caroline to join them during their visit to the captain? At the end of the book, after Louise has delivered twins to a mountain family,

she becomes very anxious over the healthier twin. Why do you think she gave this advice, "You should hold him. Hold him as much as you can. Or let his mother hold him" (p. 215)? What does this reaction say about Louise's own character and the changes in character that took place in her lifetime?

6. *Inferring outcomes:* There were several places in the book when the action and outcome of the story would have changed if characters had acted in different ways. Have students read or listen to the book up to a certain point. At various points, ask students to predict the outcomes. For example:

   a. At the end of Chapter Four, a mysterious man leaves the boat and walks alone toward an abandoned house. Who do you think he is? How do you think this man will influence the story?

   b. At the end of Chapter Twelve, Caroline finds and uses Louise's hidden hand lotion. What do you think will happen after Louise angrily breaks the bottle and runs out of the house?

   c. At the close of Chapter Fourteen, the captain has offered to send Caroline to Baltimore to continue her musical education. How do you think Caroline, her parents, and Louise will react to this suggestion?

   d. At the end of Chapter Seventeen, Louise and the captain are discussing what she plans to do with her life. Louise responds that she wants to become a doctor but cannot leave her family. Knowing Louise and her family, how do you think the story will end?

Evaluation

Evaluative questions require children to make judgments about the content of the literature by comparing it with external criteria, such as what authorities on a subject say, or internal criteria, such as experience or knowledge. The following are examples of evaluative questions:

1. *Judgment of adequacy or validity:* Do you agree that Louise in *Jacob Have I Loved* would not have been accepted as a student in a medical college? Why or why not? This story took place in the 1940s; would the author have been able to include the same scene between a woman and a university adviser if the story had taken place in the 1990s? Why or why not?

2. *Judgment of appropriateness:* What do you think the author meant by the reference to the quote, "Jacob have I loved, but Esau have I hated." How does this biblical line relate to the book? Do you think it is a good title for the book? Why or why not?

3. *Judgment of worth, desirability, or acceptability:* Was Louise right in her judgment that her parents always favored Caroline? What caused her to reach her final

decision? Do you believe that Louise made the right decision when she left the island? Why or why not?

Appreciation

Appreciation of literature requires a sensitivity to the techniques that authors use in order to have emotional impact on their readers. Questions can encourage children to respond emotionally to the plot, identify with the characters, react to an author's use of language, and react to an author's ability to create a visual image through word choices in the text. The following are examples of questions to stimulate appreciation:

1. *Emotional response to plot or theme:* How did you respond to the plot of *Jacob Have I Loved*? Did the author hold your interest? If so, how? Do you believe the theme of the story was worthwhile? Why or why not? Pretend that you are either recommending this book for someone else to read or recommending that this book not be read; what would you tell that person?

2. *Identification with characters and incidents:* Have you ever felt, or known anyone who felt, like thirteen-year-old Louise or her twin sister, Caroline? What caused you or the person to feel that way? How would you have reacted if you had been thirteen-year-old Louise? How would you have reacted if you had been Caroline? Pretend to be a grown-up Louise in Chapter Eighteen talking with your mother about leaving the island. What emotions do you think your mother would feel when you responded, "I'm not going to rot here like Grandma" (p. 200)? How would you feel when she told you, "I chose to leave my own people and build a life for myself somewhere else. I certainly wouldn't deny you that same choice. But . . . oh, Louise, we will miss you, your father and I" (p. 201)?

3. *Imagery:* How did the author encourage you to see the relationship between the island setting and changes in Louise's character over her lifetime?

4. *Appreciative comprehension and identification with characters and incidents:* Have you ever felt or known anyone who felt like thirteen-year-old Louise when she listened to the story about her birth and thought, "I felt cold all over, as though I was the newborn infant a second time, cast aside and forgotten" (p. 15)? How would you have reacted if you had been Louise and had heard this story repeatedly? What do you think could make you feel cold all over if you were Caroline and heard this story?

Suggested Activities

 For suggested activities for teaching children with contemporary realistic fiction, visit our Companion Website at www.prenhall.com/norton

Children's Literature

 For full descriptions, including plot summaries and award winner notations, of these and other titles for teaching children with contemporary realistic fiction, please visit the CD-ROM that accompanies this book.

Alcock, Vivien. *A Kind of Thief.* Delacorte, 1992 (I:10+ R:6).

Alcott, Louisa M. *Little Women* (first published in 1868). Crowell, 1995 (I:10+ R:7).

Anderson, Laurie Halse. *Speak.* Farrar, Straus & Giroux, 1999 (I:12+ R:5).

Anderson, Rachel. *The Bus People.* Holt, 1992 (I:10+ R:7).

Avi. *Nothing but the Truth: A Documentary Novel.* Orchard, 1991 (I:12+).

Baker, Jeannie. *Where the Forest Meets the Sea.* Greenwillow, 1988 (I:4–10).

Bartoletti, Susan Campbell. *Dancing with Dziadziu.* Illustrated by Annika Nelson. Harcourt Brace, 1997 (I:8–12 R:5).

Bauer, Joan. *Backwater.* Putnam, 1999 (I:10+ R:5).

_____. *Hope Was Here.* Putnam, 2000 (I:10+ R:5).

_____. *Rules of the Road.* Putnam, 1998 (I:12+ R:6).

_____. *Squashed.* Delacorte, 1992 (I:10+ R:5).

Bauer, Marion Dane. *On My Honor.* Clarion, 1986 (I:10+ R:4).

_____. *A Question of Trust.* Scholastic, 1994 (I:10+ R:5).

Bawden, Nina. *Humbug.* Clarion, 1992 (I:8+ R:5).

_____. *The Outside Child.* Lothrop, Lee & Shepard, 1989 (I:10+ R:6).

_____. *The Real Plato Jones.* Clarion, 1993 (I:12+ R:6).

Baylor, Byrd. *Hawk, I'm Your Brother.* Illustrated by Peter Parnall. Scribner, 1976 (I:all R:6).

Benjamin, Carol Lea. *The Wicked Stepdog.* Crowell, 1982 (I:9–12 R:4).

Berck, Judith. *No Place to Be: Voices of Homeless Children.* Houghton Mifflin, 1991 (I:12+).

Block, Francesca Lia. *Girl Goddess #9: Nine Stories.* HarperCollins, 1996 (I:14+ R:7).

Blume, Judy. *Are You There God? It's Me, Margaret.* Bradbury, 1970 (I:10+ R:6).

_____. *Blubber.* Bradbury, 1974 (I:10+ R:4).

_____. *Deenie.* Bradbury, 1973 (young adult).

_____. *Forever.* Bradbury, 1975 (young adult).

_____. *It's Not the End of the World.* Bradbury, 1972 (young adult).

_____. *The One in the Middle Is the Green Kangaroo.* Illustrated by Amy Aitken. Bradbury, 1981 (I:6–9 R:2).

_____. *Otherwise Known as Sheila the Great.* Dutton, 1972 (I:9–12 R:6).

_____. *Tales of a Fourth Grade Nothing.* Illustrated by Roy Doty. Dutton, 1972 (I:7–12 R:4).

_____. *Then Again, Maybe I Won't.* Bradbury, 1971 (young adult).

_____. *Tiger Eyes.* Bradbury, 1981. (I:12+ R:7).

I = Interest by age range.

R = Readability by grade level.

Bonham, Frank, *Durango Street*. Dutton, 1965 (I:12+ R:5).

Bridges, Ruby. *Through My Eyes*. Scholastic, 1999.

Brooks, Bruce. *Everywhere*. HarperCollins, 1990 (I:8+ R:4).

_____. *The Moves Make the Man*. Harper & Row, 1984 (I:10+ R:7).

_____. *What Hearts*. HarperCollins, 1992 (I:10+ R:5).

Burch, Robert. *Queenie Peavy*. Illustrated by Jerry Lazare. Viking, 1966 (I:10+ R:6).

Burnford, Sheila. *The Incredible Journey*. Illustrated by Carl Burger. Little, Brown, 1960, 1961 (I:8+ R:8).

Byars, Betsy. *After the Goat Man*. Illustrated by Ronald Himler. Viking, 1974 (I:9–12 R:7).

_____. *The Animal, the Vegetable, and John D. Jones*. Illustrated by Ruth Sanderson. Delacorte, 1982 (I:9–12 R:5).

_____. *Bingo Brown and the Language of Love*. Viking, 1989 (I:10+ R:5).

_____. *The Burning Questions of Bingo Brown*. Viking Kestrel, 1988 (I:10+ R:6).

_____. *Coast to Coast*. Delacorte, 1992 (I:10+ R:5).

_____. *Cracker Jackson*. Viking, 1985 (I:10+ R:6).

_____. *The Cybil War*. Illustrated by Gail Owens. Viking, 1981 (I:9–12 R:6).

_____. *The 18th Emergency*. Illustrated by Robert Grossman. Viking, 1973 (I:8–12 R:3).

_____. *The Night Swimmers*. Illustrated by Troy Howell. Delacorte, 1980 (I:8–12 R:5).

_____. *The Summer of the Swans*. Illustrated by Ted CoConis. Viking, 1970 (I:8–12 R:4).

Cadnum, Michael. *Zero to the Bone*. Viking, 1996 (I:12+ R:7).

Carrick, Carol. *The Accident*. Illustrated by Donald Carrick. Seabury, 1976 (I:5–8 R:4).

_____. *Stay Away from Simon*. Clarion, 1985 (I:7–10 R:3).

Carter, Alden R. *Between a Rock and a Hard Place*. Scholastic, 1995 (I:12+ R:7).

Christopher, Matt. *Dirt Bike Racer*. Illustrated by Barry Bomzer. Little, Brown, 1979 (I:10+ R:4).

_____. *Face-Off*. Illustrated by Harvey Kidder. Little, Brown, 1972 (I:8–12 R:4).

_____. *Football Fugitive*. Illustrated by Larry Johnson. Little, Brown, 1976 (I:9–12 R:6).

_____. *The Fox Steals Home*. Illustrated by Larry Johnson. Little, Brown, 1978 (I:8–12 R:6).

_____. *Skateboard Renegade*. Little, Brown, 2000 (I:8–12 R:4).

_____. *Soccer Duel*. Little, Brown, 2000 (I:8–12 R:4).

_____. *Tennis Ace*. Little, Brown, 2000 (I:8–12 R:4).

_____. *Wheel Wizards*. Little, Brown, 2000 (I:8–12 R:4).

Cleary, Beverly. *Dear Mr. Henshaw*. Illustrated by Paul O. Zelinsky. Morrow, 1983 (I:9–12 R:5).

_____. *Henry and Beezus*. Illustrated by Louis Darling. Morrow, 1952 (I:7–10 R:6).

_____. *Mitch and Amy*. Illustrated by George Porter. Morrow, 1967 (I:7–10 R:6).

_____. *Muggie Maggie*. Illustrated by Kay Life. Morrow, 1990 (I:7–10 R:5).

_____. *Ramona and Her Father*. Illustrated by Alan Tiegreen. Morrow, 1977 (I:7–10 R:6).

_____. *Ramona and Her Mother*. Illustrated by Alan Tiegreen. Morrow, 1979 (I:7–10 R:6).

_____. *Ramona the Brave*. Illustrated by Alan Tiegreen. Morrow, 1975 (I:7–10 R:6).

_____. *Ramona the Pest*. Illustrated by Louis Darling. Morrow, 1968 (I:7–10 R:4).

_____. *Ramona Quimby, Age 8*. Illustrated by Alan Tiegreen. Morrow, 1981 (I:7–10 R:6).

_____. *Strider*. Illustrated by Paul O. Zelinsky. Morrow, 1991 (I:10+ R:5).

Cleaver, Vera, and Bill Cleaver. *Trial Valley*. Lippincott, 1977 (I:11+ R:5).

_____. *Where the Lilies Bloom*. Illustrated by Jim Spanfeller. Lippincott, 1969 (I:11+ R:5).

Clements, Andrew. *The Janitor's Boy*. Simon & Schuster, 2000 (I:9+ R:5).

_____. *The Landry News*. Illustrated by Brian Selznick. Simon & Schuster, 1999 (I:8+ R:4).

Cole, Brock. *The Goats*. Farrar, Straus & Giroux, 1987 (I:10+ R:5).

Conly, Jane Leslie. *Crazy Lady!* HarperCollins, 1993 (I:10+ R:5).

Corcoran, Barbara. *The Potato Kit*. Atheneum, 1989 (I:10+ R:6).

Cormier, Robert. *The Bumblebee Flies Anyway*. Pantheon, 1983 (I:14+ R:6).

_____. *In the Middle of the Night*. Delacorte, 1995 (I:12+ R:6).

_____. *Tenderness*. Delacorte, 1997 (I:12+ R:6).

Couloumbis, Audrey. *Getting Near to Baby*. Putnam, 1999 (I:10+ R:4).

Creech, Sharon. *Chasing Redbird*. HarperCollins, 1997 (I:10+ R:6).

_____. *Walk Two Moons*. HarperCollins, 1994 (I:12+ R:6).

_____. *The Wanderer*. HarperCollins, 2000 (I:10+ R:6).

Cross, Gillian. *A Map to Nowhere*. Holiday House, 1989 (I:10+ R:5).

_____. *On the Edge*. Holiday House, 1985 (I:10+ R:5).

_____. *Roscoe's Leap*. Holiday House, 1987 (I:10+ R:6).

Crutcher, Chris. *Athletic Shorts*. Greenwillow, 1991 (I:10+ R:6).

Cunningham, Julia. *Burnish Me Bright*. Illustrated by Don Freeman. Pantheon, 1970 (I:8–12 R:8).

Curtis, Christopher Paul. *The Watsons Go to Birmingham—1963*. Delacorte, 1995 (I:10+ R:6).

Cutler, Jane. *No Dogs Allowed*. Farrar, Straus & Giroux, 1992 (I:8+ R:4).

_____. *Rats!* Illustrated by Tracey Campbell Pearson. HarperCollins, 1996 (I:8+ R:4).

Danziger, Paula. *Amber Brown Is Not a Crayon*. Illustrated by Tony Ross. Putnam, 1994 (I:6–9 R:4).

_____, and Ann M. Martin. *P. S. Longer Letter Later*. Scholastic, 1998 (I:10+ R:5).

Darling, Benjamin. *Valerie and the Silver Pear*. Illustrated by Dan Lane. Four Winds, 1992 (I:5–8 R:3).

Davis, Jenny. *Good-Bye and Keep Cold*. Orchard, 1987 (I:12+ R:6).

Delton, Judy. *Angel's Mother's Wedding*. Houghton Mifflin, 1987 (I:7–10 R:4).

DiCamillo, Kate. *Because of Winn-Dixie*. Candlewick, 2000 (I:8+ R:4).

Dickinson, Peter. *AK*. Delacorte, 1992 (I:12+ R:6).

Doherty, Berlie. *Dear Nobody*. Orchard, 1992 (I:12+ R:6).

Duncan, Lois. *Don't Look Behind You*. Delacorte, 1989 (I:12+ R:6).

Ellis, Sarah. *Next-Door Neighbors*. Macmillan, 1990 (I:10+ R:5).

_____. *Pick-up Sticks*. Macmillan, 1992 (I:10+ R:5).

Enright, Elizabeth. *Thimble Summer.* Holt, Rinehart & Winston, 1938, 1966 (I:7–12 R:5).

Estes, Eleanor. *The Hundred Dresses.* Harcourt, 1971.

_____. *The Moffats.* Illustrated by Louis Slobodkin. Harcourt Brace Jovanovich, 1941 (I:7–10 R:4).

Farley, Walter. *The Black Stallion.* Illustrated by Keith Ward. Random House, 1944 (I:8+ R:3).

_____. *The Black Stallion Returns.* Random House, 1945, 1973 (I:8+).

Fine, Anne. *Alias Madame Doubtfire.* Little, Brown, 1988 (I:9+ R:5).

_____. *Step by Wicked Step.* Little Brown, 1996 (I:10+ R:6).

_____. *The Tulip Touch.* Little, Brown, 1997 (I:10+ R:6).

Fitzhugh, Louise. *Harriet the Spy.* Harper & Row, 1964 (I:8–12 R:3).

_____. *The Long Secret.* Harper & Row, 1965 (I:8–12 R:3).

Fleischman, Paul. *Seedfolks.* Illustrated by Judy Pedersen. HarperCollins, 1997 (I:10+ R:6).

_____. *Whirligig.* Holt, 1998 (I:12+ R:6).

Foreman, Michael. *Seal Surfer.* Harcourt Brace, 1997 (I:5–9 R:4).

Fox, Paula. *Monkey Island.* Orchard, 1991 (I:10+ R:6).

_____. *The Moonlight Man.* Bradbury, 1986 (I:12+ R:5).

_____. *One-Eyed Cat.* Bradbury, 1984 (I:10+ R:5).

_____. *The Village by the Sea.* Watts, 1988 (I:10+ R:6).

_____. *Western Wind.* Orchard, 1993 (I:9+ R:5).

Franklin, Kristine L. *Lone Wolf.* Candlewick, 1997 (I:9+ R:5).

Freeman, Suzanne. *The Cucoo's Child.* Greenwillow, 1996 (I:10+ R:6).

Gantos, Jack. *Joey Pigza Loses Control.* Farrar, Straus & Giroux, 2000 (I:9+ R:4).

Garland, Sherry. *The Silent Storm.* Harcourt, 1993 (I:10+ R:6).

Gauch, Patricia. *Christina Katerina and the Time She Quit the Family.* Illustrated by Elise Primavera. Putnam, 1987 (I:4–8).

George, Jean Craighead. *The Cry of the Crow.* Harper & Row, 1980 (I:10+ R:5).

_____. *Julie of the Wolves.* Illustrated by John Schoenherr. Harper & Row, 1972 (I:10+ R:7).

_____. *My Side of the Mountain.* Dutton, 1959 (I:10+ R:6).

Gifaldi, David. *Toby Scudder, Ultimate Warrior.* Clarion, 1993 (I:9+ R:5).

Gipson, Fred. *Old Yeller.* Illustrated by Carl Burger. Harper & Row, 1956 (I:10+ R:6).

Godden, Rumer. *Listen to the Nightingale.* Viking, 1992 (I:10+ R:5).

Greenberg, Jan. *The Iceberg and Its Shadow.* Farrar, Straus & Giroux, 1980 (I:9–14 R:6).

Greene, Constance. *Beat the Turtle Drum.* Illustrated by Donna Diamond. Viking, 1976 (I:10+ R:7).

Greene, Stephanie. *Owen Foote, Frontiersman.* Illustrated by Martha Weston. Clarion, 1999 (I:6–9 R:4).

Grove, Vicki. *Reaching Dustin.* Putnam, 1998 (I:10+ R:5).

Haas, Jessie. *Keeping Barney.* Greenwillow, 1982 (I:9–12 R:5).

Hall, Lynn. *In Trouble Again, Zelda Hammersmith?* Harcourt Brace Jovanovich, 1987 (I:8–12 R:3).

Hamilton, Virginia. *The House of Dies Drear.* Macmillan, 1968 (I:11+ R:4).

_____. *Plain City.* Scholastic, 1993 (I:10+ R:5).

_____. *The Planet of Junior Brown.* Macmillan, 1971 (I:12+ R:6).

Hanel, Wolfram. *Abby.* Illustrated by Alan Marks. North-South, 1996 (I:7–9 R:4).

Harris, Rosemary. *Zed.* Farber & Farber, 1982 (I:12+ R:7).

Hartling, Peter. *Old John.* Translated by Elizabeth D. Crawford. Lothrop, Lee & Shepard, 1990 (I:8+ R:5).

Hathorn, Libby. *Thunderwith.* Little, Brown, 1991 (I:10+ R:5).

Haugen, Tormod. *The Night Birds.* Translated from the Norwegian by Sheila La Farge. Delacorte, 1982 (I:10+ R:3).

Hayes, Daniel. *Flyers.* Simon & Schuster, 1996 (I:12+ R:7).

Henkes, Kevin. *Words of Stone.* Greenwillow, 1992 (I:10+ R:5).

Henry, Marguerite. *Black Gold.* Illustrated by Wesley Dennis. Rand McNally, 1957 (I:8–12 R:6).

_____. *Justin Morgan Had a Horse.* Illustrated by Wesley Dennis. Rand McNally, 1954 (I:8–12 R:6).

_____. *King of the Wind.* Illustrated by Wesley Dennis. Rand McNally, 1948, 1976 (I:8–12 R:6).

_____. *Misty of Chincoteague.* Illustrated by Wesley Dennis. Rand McNally, 1947, 1963 (I:8–12 R:6).

_____. *San Domingo: The Medicine Hat Stallion.* Illustrated by Robert Lougheed. Rand McNally, 1972 (I:9–14 R:4).

Hermes, Patricia. *Mama, Let's Dance.* Little, Brown, 1991 (I:10+ R:5).

Hicyilmaz, Gaye. *Against the Storm.* Little, Brown, 1992 (I:10+ R:6).

Hoberman, Mary Ann. *And to Think That We Thought That We'd Never Be Friends.* Crown, 1999.

Holt, Kimberly Willis. *When Zachary Beaver Came to Town.* Holt, 1999 (I:10+ R:6).

Holtwijk, Ineke. *Asphalt Angels.* Translated by Wanda Boeke. Front Street, 1999 (I:12+ R:6).

Honeycutt, Natalie. *Twilight in Grace Falls.* Orchard, 1997 (I:10+ R:6).

Hopkins, Lee Bennett. *Mama.* Knopf, 1977 (I:7–10 R:6).

Horvath, Polly. *When the Circus Came to Town.* Farrar, Straus & Giroux, 1996 (I:9+ R:6).

Howard, Ellen. *Edith Herself.* Atheneum, 1987 (I:7–10 R:4).

Hughes, Dean. *Family Pose.* Atheneum, 1989 (I:10+ R:6).

_____. *Team Picture.* Simon & Schuster, 1996 (I:10+ R:6).

Hunt, Irene. *Up a Road Slowly.* Follett, 1966 (I:11+ R:7).

Hurwitz, Johanna. *Russell and Elisa.* Illustrated by Lillian Hoban. Morrow, 1989 (I:3–8 R:3).

Irwin, Hadley. *The Original Freddie Ackerman.* Macmillan, 1992 (I:10+ R:5).

Johnson, Angela. *Toning the Sweep.* Orchard, 1993 (I:12+ R:4).

Johnson, Scott. *Safe at Second.* Philomel, 1999 (I:10+ R:6).

Jorgensen, Gail. *Gotcha.* Scholastic, 1997.

Jukes, Mavis. *Like Jake and Me.* Illustrated by Lloyd Bloom. Knopf, 1984 (I:6–8).

Kaplan, Howard. *Waiting to Sing.* Illustrated by Hervé Blondon. DK, 2000 (I:5–8 R:4).

Kerr, M. E. *"Hello," I Lied.* HarperCollins, 1997 (I:14+ R:7).

Khalsa, Dayal. *I Want a Dog.* Clarkson, 1987 (I:4–7).

Kjelgaard, Jim. *Big Red.* Illustrated by Bob Kuhn. Holiday House, 1945, 1956 (I:10+ R:7).

Klein, Norma. *Mom, the Wolf Man and Me.* Pantheon, 1972 (I:12+ R:6).

Kline, Suzy. *Herbie Jones and the Monster Ball.* Illustrated by Richard Williams. Putnam, 1988 (I:8+ R:4).

Konigsburg, E. L. *About the B'nai Bagels.* Atheneum, 1969 (I:8–12 R:7).

_____. *From the Mixed-up Files of Mrs. Basil E. Frankweiler.* Atheneum, 1967 (I:9–12 R:7).

_____. *Jennifer, Hecate, Macbeth, William McKinley, and Me, Elizabeth.* Atheneum, 1967, 1976 (I:8–12 R:4).

_____. *Journey to an 800 Number.* Atheneum, 1982 (I:10+ R:7).

_____. *T-Backs, T-Shirts, Coat, and Suit.* Atheneum, 1993 (I:10+ R:5).

_____. *Throwing Shadows.* Atheneum, 1979 (I:11+ R:7).

_____. *The View from Saturday.* Atheneum, 1996 (I:9–12 R:5).

L'Engle, Madeleine. *Meet the Austins.* Vanguard, 1960 (I:10+ R:6).

Lisle, Janet Taylor. *Afternoon of the Elves.* Watts, 1989 (I:10+ R:5).

Little, Jean. *Different Dragons.* Illustrated by Laura Fernandez. Viking, 1986 (I:8–10 R:4).

_____. *From Anna.* Illustrated by Joan Sandin. Harper & Row, 1972 (I:8–12 R:5).

London, Jack. *Call of the Wild.* Photographs by Seymour Linden. Harmony, 1903, 1977 (I:10+ R:5).

Lorbiecki, Marybeth. *Sister Anne's Hands.* Dial, 1998.

Lowry, Lois. *All About Sam.* Illustrated by Diane deGroat. Houghton Mifflin, 1988 (I:8–12 R:5).

_____. *Anastasia Again!* Illustrated by Diane deGroat. Houghton Mifflin, 1981. (I:8–12 R:6).

_____. *Anastasia at Your Service.* Illustrated by Diane deGroat. Houghton Mifflin, 1982 (I:8–12 R:6).

_____. *Anastasia Krupnik.* Houghton Mifflin, 1979 (I:8–12 R:6).

_____. *Anastasia on Her Own.* Houghton Mifflin, 1985 (I:8–12 R:4).

_____. *Anastasia's Chosen Career.* Houghton Mifflin, 1987 (I:10+ R:6).

_____. *Attaboy, Sam!* Illustrated by Diane deGroat. Houghton, 1992 (I:8+ R:5).

_____. *The One Hundredth Thing About Caroline.* Houghton Mifflin, 1983 (I:8–12 R:3).

_____. *Rabble Starkey.* Houghton Mifflin, 1987 (I:10+ R:6).

_____. *See You Around, Sam!* Illustrated by Diane deGroat. Houghton Mifflin, 1996 (I:8+ R:5).

_____. *Your Move, J. P.!* Houghton Mifflin, 1990 (I:10+ R:6).

Lynch, Chris. *Shadow Boxer.* HarperCollins, 1993 (I:12+ R:6).

McDonald, Joyce. *Comfort Creek.* Delacorte, 1996 (I:10+ R:5).

McKay, Hilary. *The Exiles.* Macmillan, 1992 (I:9+ R:5).

McKissack, C. Patricia. *The Honest-to-Goodness Truth.* Illustrated by Giselle Potter. Atheneum, 2000 (I:5–9 R:4).

MacGregor, Rob. *Hawk Moon.* Simon & Schuster, 1996 (I:12+ R:6).

MacLachlan, Patricia. *The Facts and Fictions of Minna Pratt.* Harper & Row, 1988 (I:7–12 R:4).

_____. *Journey.* Delacorte, 1991 (I:8+ R:4).

_____. *Mama One, Mama Two.* Illustrated by Ruth Lercher Bornstein. Harper & Row, 1982 (I:4–8 R:3).

Marino, Jan. *For the Love of Pete.* Little, Brown, 1993 (I:10+ R:5).

Mathis, Sharon Bell. *The Hundred Penny Box.* Puffin, 1986 (I:6–9 R:3).

Mazer, Norma Fox. *After the Rain.* Morrow, 1987 (I:12+ R:5).

Mohr, Nicholasa. *Felita.* Illustrated by Ray Cruz. Dial, 1979 (I:9–12).

_____. *Going Home.* Dial, 1986 (I:10+).

Mooney, Bel. *The Voices of Silence.* Delacorte, 1997 (I:10+ R:6).

Mowry, Jess. *Babylon Boyz.* Simon & Schuster, 1997 (I:12+ R:7).

Myers, Walter Dean. *Mop, Moondance, and the Nagasaki Knights.* Delacorte, 1992 (I:9+ R:5).

_____. *Scorpions.* Harper & Row, 1988 (I:10+ R:5).

_____. *Somewhere in the Darkness.* Scholastic, 1992 (I:12+ R:5).

Naidoo, Beverly. *Journey to Jo'burg.* Harper, 1986 (I:10+ R:6).

Naylor, Phyllis Reynolds. *Alice in Rapture, Sort Of.* Atheneum, 1989 (I:10+ R:5).

_____. *All but Alice.* Atheneum, 1992 (I:10+ R:5).

_____. *Josie's Troubles.* Illustrated by Shelley Matheis. Atheneum, 1992 (I:8+ R:4).

_____. *Keeping a Christmas Secret.* Illustrated by Lena Schiffman. Atheneum, 1989 (I:5–8).

_____. *Reluctantly Alice.* Atheneum, 1991 (I:10+ R:5).

_____. *Shiloh.* Atheneum, 1991 (I:10+ R:5).

_____. *Shiloh Season.* Atheneum, 1996 (I:8+ R:5).

Nelson, Theresa. *The Beggars' Ride.* Orchard, 1992 (I:10+ R:5).

Neville, Emily. *It's Like This, Cat.* Illustrated by Emil Weiss. Harper & Row, 1963 (I:8–12 R:6).

Newman, Robert. *The Case of the Baker Street Irregular.* Atheneum, 1978 (I:10+ R:6).

_____. *The Case of the Vanishing Corpse.* Atheneum, 1980 (I:10+ R:6).

O'Connor, Barbara. *Beethoven In Paradise.* Farrar, Straus & Giroux, 1997 (I:10+ R:6).

O'Dell, Scott. *Island of the Blue Dolphins.* Houghton Mifflin, 1960 (I:10+ R:6).

Park, Barbara. *Don't Make Me Smile.* Knopf, 1981 (I:9–12 R:5).

_____. *The Kid in the Red Jacket.* Knopf, 1987 (I:7–11 R:3).

_____. *Maxie, Rosie, and Earl—Partners in Crime.* Knopf, 1990 (I:8–12 R:5).

Paterson, Katherine. *Bridge to Terabithia.* Illustrated by Donna Diamond. Crowell, 1977 (I:10–14 R:6).

_____. *Come Sing, Jimmy Jo.* Dutton, 1985 (I:10+ R:4).

_____. *Flip-Flop Girl.* Lodestar, 1994 (I:10+ R:5).

_____. *The Great Gilly Hopkins.* Crowell, 1978 (I:10+ R:6).

_____. *Jacob Have I Loved.* Crowell, 1980 (I:10+ R:7).

_____. *Park's Quest.* Lodestar Books, 1988 (I:10+ R:5+).

Patron, Susan. *Maybe Yes, Maybe No, Maybe Maybe.* Illustrated by Dorothy Donahue. Orchard, 1993 (I:7–10 R:4).

Paulsen, Gary. *Brian's Return.* Delacorte, 1999 (I:10+ R:6).

_____. *The Car.* Harcourt Brace Jovanovich, 1994 (I:10+ R:6).

_____. *Dancing Carl.* Bradbury, 1983 (I:10+ R:4).

_____. *Hatchet.* Bradbury, 1987 (I:10+ R:6).

_____. *The Schernoff Discoveries.* Delacorte, 1997 (I:10+ R:6).

Pearson, Gayle. *The Secret Box.* Atheneum, 1997 (I:8–12 R:5).

Peck, Richard. *Bel-Air Bambi and the Mall Rats.* Delacorte, 1993 (I:10+ R:5).

_____. *Remembering the Good Times.* Delacorte, 1985 (I:12+ R:4).

Perkins, Lynne Rae. *All Alone in the Universe.* Greenwillow, 1999 (I:10+ R:5).

_____. *Home Lovely.* Greenwillow, 1995 (I:6–9 R:3).

Petersen, P. J. *The Sub.* Illustrated by Meredith Johnson. Dutton, 1993 (I:8–10 R:4).

Powell, Randy. *My Underrated Year.* Farrar, Straus & Giroux, 1988 (I:10+ R:5).

Provost, Gary, and Gail Levine-Provost. *David and Max.* Jewish Publication Society, 1988 (I:10+ R:6).

Rapp, Adam. *The Buffalo Tree.* Front Street, 1997 (I:12+ R:6).

Raskin, Ellen. *Figgs & Phantoms.* Dutton, 1974 (I:10+ R:5).

_____. *The Mysterious Disappearance of Leon (I Mean Noel).* Dutton, 1971 (I:10+ R:5).

_____. *The Westing Game.* Dutton, 1978 (I:10+ R:5).

Riskind, Mary. *Apple Is My Sign.* Houghton Mifflin, 1981 (I:9–12 R:5).

Rocklin, Joanne. *For Your Eyes Only!* Illustrated by Mark Todd. Scholastic, 1997 (I:9–12 R:5).

Rodowsky, Colby. *Remembering Mog.* Farrar, Straus & Giroux, 1996 (I:12+ R:6).

_____. *Sydney, Herself.* Farrar, Straus & Giroux, 1989 (I:12+ R:6).

Rylant, Cynthia. *A Fine White Dust.* Bradbury, 1986 (I:11+ R:6).

_____. *A Kindness.* Orchard, 1988 (I:12+ R:6).

_____. *Missing May.* Orchard, 1992 (I:10+ R:6).

Sachar, Louis. *Holes.* Farrar, Straus & Giroux, 1998 (I:10+ R:5).

Sachs, Marilyn. *The Bears' House.* Illustrated by Louis Glanzman. Doubleday, 1971 (I:8–11 R:6).

Savage, Deborah. *Under a Different Sky.* Houghton Mifflin, 1997 (I:12+ R:6).

Schami, Rafik. *A Hand Full of Stars.* Translated by Rika Lesser. Dutton, 1990 (I:12+ R:6).

Schotter, Roni. *Captain Snap and the Children of Vinegar Lane.* Illustrated by Marcia Sewell. Orchard, 1989 (I:5–8).

Sheldon, Dyan. *Confessions of a Teenage Drama Queen.* Candlewick, 1999 (I:12+ R:6).

Shreve, Susan. *The Gift of the Girl Who Couldn't Hear.* Tambourine, 1991 (I:9+ R:5).

Shusterman, Neal. *Speeding Bullet.* Scholastic, 1992 (I:10+ R:6).

Slepian, Jan. *The Broccoli Tapes.* Philomel, 1989 (I:10+ R:6).

Slote, Alfred. *Hang Tough, Paul Mather.* Lippincott, 1973 (I:9–12 R:3).

_____. *The Trading Game.* Lippincott, 1990 (I:10+ R:4).

Smith, Janice Lee. *The Show-and-Tell War.* Illustrated by Dick Gackenbach. Harper & Row, 1988 (I:7–9 R:4).

Snyder, Zilpha Keatley. *The Egypt Game.* Illustrated by Alton Raible. Atheneum, 1967 (I:10+ R:6).

_____. *The Famous Stanley Kidnapping Case.* Atheneum, 1979 (I:10+ R:7).

Sobol, Donald J. *Encyclopedia Brown Sets the Pace.* Illustrated by Ib Ohlsson. Scholastic/Four Winds, 1982 (I:7–10 R:5).

_____. *Encyclopedia Brown Tracks Them Down.* Illustrated by Leonard Shortall. Crowell, 1971 (I:7–10 R:3).

Sperry, Armstrong. *Call It Courage.* Macmillan, 1940 (I:9–13 R:6).

Spinelli, Jerry. *Maniac Magee.* Little, Brown, 1996 (I:8+ R:5).

_____. *Wringer.* HarperCollins, 1997 (I:9+ R:4).

Staples, Suzanne Fisher. *Dangerous Skies.* Farrar, Straus & Giroux, 1996 (I:12+ R:6).

_____. *Shabanu: Daughter of the Wind.* Knopf, 1989 (I:12+ R:6).

Steig, William. *Spinky Sulks.* New York: Farrar, Straus & Giroux, 1988 (I:3–8 R:5).

Stolz, Mary. *Stealing Home.* HarperCollins, 1992 (I:8–12 R:4).

Strachan, Ian. *Flawed Glass.* Little, Brown, 1990 (I:10+ R:6).

Sykes, Shelley. *For Mike.* Delacorte, 1998 (I:12+ R:6).

Taylor, Clark. *The House That Crack Built.* Illustrated by Jan Thompson Dicks. Chronicle Books, 1992 (I:10+).

Taylor, Mildred. *Roll of Thunder, Hear My Cry.* Dial, 1976 (I:10+ R:6).

Taylor, Sydney. *All-of-a-Kind Family.* Illustrated by Helen John. Follett, 1951 (I:7–10 R:4).

Taylor, Theodore. *The Cay.* Doubleday, 1969 (I:10+ R:6).

_____. *The Trouble with Tuck.* Doubleday, 1981 (I:6–9 R:5).

Taylor, William. *Agnes the Sheep.* Scholastic, 1991 (I:8+ R:5).

Tolan, Stephanie S. *A Good Courage.* Morrow, 1988 (I:12+ R:6).

Voigt, Cynthia. *Bad Girls.* Scholastic, 1996 (I:9+ R:7).

_____. *Dicey's Song.* Atheneum, 1982 (I:10+ R:5).

_____. *Homecoming.* Atheneum, 1981 (I:10+ R:5).

_____. *A Solitary Blue.* Atheneum, 1983 (I:10+ R:6).

_____. *Sons from Afar.* Atheneum, 1987 (I:10+ R:6).

Walter, Virginia. *Making Up Megaboy.* Illustrated by Katrina Roeckelein. DK, 1998 (I:10+ R:6).

Watson, James. *Talking in Whispers.* Victor Gollancz, 1983 (I:12+ R:7).

White, Ruth. *Belle Prater's Boy.* Farrar, Straus & Giroux, 1996 (I:10+ R:6).

Williams, Carol Lynch. *The True Colors of Caitlynne Jackson.* Delacorte, 1997 (I:10+ R:5).

Wojciechowska, Maia. *Shadow of a Bull.* Illustrated by Alvin Smith. Atheneum, 1964 (I:10+ R:5).

Wolff, Virginia Euwer. *Probably Still Nick Swansen.* Holt, Rinehart & Winston, 1988 (I:10+ R:6).

Woodson, Jacqueline. *Maizon at Blue Hill.* Delacorte, 1992 (I:10+ R:5).

Wyeth, Sharon. *Something Beautiful.* Bantam, 1998 (I:4–8).

Wynne-Jones, Tim. *The Maestro.* Orchard, 1996 (I:11+ R:6).

Wyss, Johann David. *The Swiss Family Robinson.* Illustrated by Lynd Ward. Grosset & Dunlap, 1949 (I:10+ R:6).

Historical Fiction

Illustration from *A Boy Named Giotto* by Pablo Guarnieri, translated by Jonathan Galassi. Copyright © 1998 by Edizioni Arka Milano. Translation copyright © 1999 by Jonathan Galassi.

The thread of people's lives weaves through the past, through the present, and into the future. Many Americans have a deep desire to trace their roots—here in this hemisphere or back to Europe, Asia, or Africa. What did their ancestors experience? Why did their ancestors travel to North America? What were their ancestors' personal feelings and beliefs? What was life like for the settlers who pioneered the American frontier and for the native North Americans who greeted them? Did people of the past have the same concerns as people of the present do? Can their experiences suggest solutions for today's problems?

Through the pages of historical fiction, the past comes alive. It is not just dates, accomplishments, and battles; it is people, famous and unknown. This chapter discusses the values of historical fiction for children, gives criteria for evaluating historical fiction, looks at the need for historical authenticity, and provides examples of historical fiction. Books of historical fiction are linked to a short discussion of events in the time period that they reflect in the hope that this chronological framework will give you a better understanding of the sweep of history as portrayed in these books. One way to evaluate the importance of historical fiction is to analyze the genre of books awarded the Batchelder Award presented to the best book translated into English. More than one-half of the awards presented since 1968 are for historical fiction.

Values of Historical Fiction for Children

Children cannot actually cross the ocean on the *Mayflower* and see a new world for the first time, or experience the arrival of the first Europeans on their native shores, or feel the consequences of persecution during World War II. They can imagine these experiences, however, through the pages of historical fiction. With Patricia Clapp's *Constance: A Story of Early Plymouth,* they can imagine that they are standing on the swaying deck of the *Mayflower* and seeing their new home. With Scott O'Dell's *The Feathered Serpent,* they can imagine that they are witnessing Montezuma's tragic encounter with the Spanish conquistador Hernando Cortés. With Paul Fleischman's *Bull Run,* they can understand the various viewpoints associated with the Civil War. With Ida Vos's *Hide and Seek,* they can imagine that they are given sanctuary by Dutch gentiles during World War II.

As children read for enjoyment, they relive the past vicariously. Tales based on authentic historical settings or episodes are alive with adventures that appeal to many children. They may follow the adventures of a young girl living on the Wisconsin frontier in Carol Ryrie Brink's *Caddie Woodlawn.* They may follow the adventures of a girl in Victorian London, interacting with people in the sinister opium trade and conducting a quest for a missing ruby in Philip Pullman's *The Ruby in the Smoke*. They may discover that courage is required to take a stand during colonial times as they interact with the heroine in Ann Rinaldi's *The Fifth of March: A Story of the Boston Massacre*. They may follow the adventures of Jeff Bussey in Harold Keith's *Rifles for Watie* as Jeff tries to find information behind enemy lines during the Civil War. They may follow a family as the family prepares for an 1890s Christmas celebration in Virginia Hamilton's *The Bells of Christmas*. They may follow Patrick and his sister Keely as Keely tries to interest her polio-stricken brother in a challenge that sparks his interest in Julie Johnston's *Hero of Lesser Causes*. They may follow the rescue effort during the evacuation of Dunkirk in May 1940 in Louise Borden's *The Little Ships: The Heroic Rescue at Dunkirk in World War II*.

Children who read historical fiction gain an understanding of their own heritage. The research that precedes the writing of authentic historical stories enables authors to incorporate information about the period naturally. Children gain knowledge about the people, values, beliefs, hardships, and physical surroundings common to various periods. They discover the events that preceded their own time and made the present possible. Through historical fiction, children can begin to visualize the sweep of history. As characters in historical fiction from many different time periods face and overcome their problems, children may discover universal truths, identify feelings and behaviors that encourage them to consider alternative ways to handle their own problems, empathize with viewpoints that are different from their own, and realize that history consists of many people who have learned to work together.

Through historical fiction, children can discover that in all times, people have depended upon one another and that they have had similar needs. Children can learn that when human relationships deteriorate, tragedy usually results. Historical fiction allows children to judge relationships and realize that their present and future are linked to the actions in the past.

One of the strongest values of historical fiction is written by a character who is corresponding with a WW II survivor in Gregory Maguire's *The Good Liar*: "It makes me think that history really happens to ordinary people. That history is even happening to me, right now, even if I don't know it. I like that feeling" (p. 129).

Literary Criticism: Using Literary Elements to Evaluate Historical Fiction

When evaluating historical fiction for children, adults must be certain that a story adheres to the criteria for excellent literature discussed in Chapter 3. Historical fiction must also satisfy special requirements in terms of plot, characterization, setting, and theme. The questions in the

Evaluation Criteria box on this page summarize the criteria that you should consider (in addition to considerations of literary quality raised in Chapter 3) when evaluating historical fiction for children.

Plot

Credible plots in historical fiction emerge from authentically developed time periods. The experiences, conflicts, and resolutions of conflicts must reflect the times—whether the antagonist is another person, society, nature, or internal dilemmas faced by the protagonist. Conflict in historical fiction often develops when characters leave their environments and move into alien ones. Authors may highlight the problems, cultures, or diverse values of time periods by exploring the conflicts developed because of characters' inner turmoil or because of societal pressures. Author Russell Freedman (1992) presents interesting insights into the search for truth about the interactions between pioneers and Native Americans. He describes his own search for truth about the wagon-train journeys along the Oregon Trail. Freedman states:

Now, the movies and television have taught us that this journey was fraught with peril, since the hostile Indians were likely to attack at any moment. And yet, as I pursued my research, I found that Indian attacks were few and far between. Attacks were infrequent. I began to wonder, how menacing were the Indians. (p. 2)

In his search for the truth, Freedman describes differences in the impressions gained from diaries written by men and by women. Whereas men always emphasized the

---

EVALUATION CRITERIA

Literary Criticism: Historical Fiction

1. Do the characters' experiences, conflicts, and resolutions of conflicts reflect what is known about the time period?
2. Do the characters' actions express values and beliefs that are realistic for the time period?
3. Is the language authentic for the period without relying on so many colorful terms or dialects that the story is difficult to understand?
4. Is the setting authentic in every detail?
5. Are details integrated into the story so that they do not overwhelm readers or detract from the story?
6. If the setting is the antagonist, are the relationships between characters and setting clearly developed?
7. Is the theme worthwhile?
8. Does the style enhance the mood and clarify the conflicts, characterizations, settings, and themes?

dangers from Indians and described their battles with Indian war parties, women's diaries frequently showed initial fear of the Indians but usually described the Indians as friendly and helpful. Freedman speculates about the accuracy of the depiction of history for this period.

In Avi's *The True Confessions of Charlotte Doyle,* the conflicts develop after Charlotte leaves England to sail on the *Seahawk,* a merchant sailing ship crossing the Atlantic in 1832. Person-against-self conflicts develop when Charlotte faces her changing attitudes toward the captain and the crew and about her own family.

Scott O'Dell develops credible person-against-self conflict in *The Captive.* In this book, a young Jesuit seminarian faces moral dilemmas when he leaves his Spanish homeland in the early 1500s and accompanies an expedition to the Americas. O'Dell describes the Jesuit's faith and his desire to bring Christianity to the native Maya of New Spain, his turmoil when he discovers the real motives behind the Spaniards' actions, his refusal to betray the native people, his pondering over his inability to change them, and his justification for his own grasping for power by impersonating a Mayan god. The various characterizations help readers understand both good and bad human motives.

Circle of Fire, by William H. Hooks, explores the moral dilemmas created by prejudice. Hooks's story takes place in North Carolina in the 1930s. In this story, a white boy and his two black friends try to prevent a Ku Klux Klan attack on Irish gypsies. Hooks develops additional believable personal conflict when the eleven-year-old boy discovers that his father, whom he loves and respects, is probably involved in the Klan.

Historical fiction stories also develop plausible person-against-society conflicts. In Karen Cushman's *Catherine, Called Birdy* and *The Midwife's Apprentice,* both person-against-society and person-against-self conflicts develop as the heroines face conflicts caused by society in medieval England and their needs to overcome inner turmoils. The conflicts in *The True Confessions of Charlotte Doyle* are credible because Avi convincingly develops Victorian attitudes about people in various social classes. The conflict in *The Captive* develops because of greed and the Spaniards' socially supported prejudice against non-Europeans, which O'Dell compellingly portrays. Likewise, conflict develops in *Circle of Fire* because of social prejudice.

Authors who develop credible person-against-society conflicts must describe the values and beliefs of the time period or the attitudes of a segment of the population so that readers understand the nature of the antagonist. In Kathryn Lasky's *The Night Journey,* deadly anti-Semitism is the antagonist that forces a Jewish family to plan and execute a dangerous flight from czarist Russia. The story seems more credible because a modern-day family in this book believes that these memories would be so painful that the great-grandmother should not be encouraged to remember the experiences. In Carolyn Reeder's *Shades of Gray,* a boy who is orphaned by the Civil War learns to live with his uncle who has pacifist convictions. To make a believable story, Reeder develops the values and beliefs that cause societal conflicts.

Well-developed person-against-self and person-against-society conflicts such as those faced by the fourteen-year-old hero in Susan Campbell Bartoletti's *No Man's Land: A Young Soldier's Story* help readers understand the values expressed during a time period and the problems, moral dilemmas, and social issues faced by the people. Authors often use these conflicts and their resolutions to develop themes in historical fiction.

Characterization

The actions, beliefs, and values of characters in historical fiction must be realistic for the time period. Authors of historical novels admit that it is sometimes difficult not to give their historical characters contemporary actions and values. Historical fiction author Erik Haugaard (1988) emphasizes the need to accurately depict the beliefs and values of the time period. Haugaard differentiates between technical faults and spiritual errors in historical fiction. He contends that technical faults such as advancing the petroleum lamp by half a century do not bother him as much as do spiritual ones. He states:

The errors which I have dubbed spiritual I dislike much more, and I would be much harder on them than mere mistake of a date. By spiritual mistakes I mean giving people in one century the ideas and opinions of another. A citizen of Rome at the time of Christ might have considered slavery vile. But if he did, he was unique. There is no doubt that the vast majority did not even question the institution. If the author lets the character in his novel have extremely unorthodox views, he must explain why and how he came to hold those opinions. If the characters in a historical novel are merely twentieth century men and women dressed up to perform a masquerade, I see little point in applauding just because their dresses are described accurately. (p. 7)

Choosing the main and supporting characters can cause additional problems. For example, authors of historical fiction rarely use famous people as pivotal characters unless they can document evidence about specific dialogue or sentiments. Authors frequently place historical figures in the role of secondary characters. In Esther Forbes's *Johnny Tremain,* for example, a fictional silversmith's apprentice is the pivotal character, while Paul Revere and Samuel Adams are background characters.

Authors develop characters through dialogue, thoughts, actions, and descriptions. While all of these elements must appear authentic, the speech of the characters and the language of a period can cause problems for writers of historical fiction. In addition, authors of children's historical fiction must be careful not to use so many colorful terms from a period that the story is difficult for young readers to comprehend. Zena Sutherland (1997) agrees that creating natural conversations is one of the most difficult tasks for writers of historical fiction.

Technology Resources

Readers must believe that the characters in historical fiction are human beings like themselves. Belief in individual characters was one of the goals cited by Michael Dorris (1992) in his writing of *Morning Girl,* a story about the Taino people, who lived on the Bahama islands at the time of Columbus's arrival in 1492. Dorris states:

In the characters of Morning Girl and Star Boy, I allowed myself to speculate freely, to invite onto the page two fully invested children—curious, independent, self-analytical, strong, moving toward independence, whose flaws were the flaws of youth: redeemable with wisdom and maturity. (p. 3)

The resulting novel encourages readers to understand and believe in these characters who lived in a different time.

In *Bud, Not Buddy,* Christopher Paul Curtis uses an interesting technique to increase understanding of his character's motives and behaviors. Throughout the book he presents rules that Bud expresses when he has problems. For example, Rules and Things Number 328: "When You Make Up Your Mind to Do Something, Hurry Up and Do It, If You Wait You Might Talk Yourself Out of What You Wanted in the First Place" (p. 27).

In *Shadow Spinner,* Susan Fletcher introduces each chapter with "Lessons for Life and Storytelling." Through this technique, the author develops understanding of the characters and the conflicts in a story with an ancient Persian setting. In Linda Sue Park's *A Single Shard,* a story set in twelfth-century Korea, the main character fulfills his dream of making pottery. As in many historical fiction stories, the protagonist overcomes many obstacles to make his dream come true.

Setting

Because historical fiction must be authentic in every respect, the careful development of setting for a certain time period is essential. Historical fiction author Leon Garfield states that "historical fiction more than any other kind of fiction must be rooted in a particular place and time" (1988, p. 736). A setting this important to a story is called an integral setting.

An integral setting must be described in details so clear that readers understand how the story is related to a time and place. This is of particular concern in historical fiction written for children, because children cannot draw on memory for historical periods. Writers must provide images through vivid descriptions that do not overpower plot and characterization. John Stewig (1989) also emphasizes the need for integral settings when he concludes, "One mark of a skilled writer in any genre is the ability to

weave in details so they aren't noticed consciously, yet are available when needed later" (p. 135).

When writing lengthy books for older children, authors have more time to develop settings in which the actions and characters are influenced by both time and place. The setting in historical fiction may guide readers into the plot, create visual images that encourage them to accept a character's experiences, and encourage them to feel the excitement of a time period.

Setting plays the role of antagonist in many stories about exploration and pioneering. For example, in Honoré Morrow's *On to Oregon!,* sleet storms, rugged mountains, swift streams, and natural predators act as antagonists. Morrow's descriptions leave little doubt that the children are confronting a beautiful but awesome adversary.

Setting may also be the antagonist in a story set in a city. In *Anna, Grandpa, and the Big Storm,* Carla Stevens develops the 1888 blizzard in New York City into an antagonist.

Authors of historical fiction sometimes contrast settings in order to develop conflict. Both Ann Petry (*Tituba of Salem Village*) and Elizabeth George Speare (*The Witch of Blackbird Pond*) use this technique. Both authors have taken protagonists from the warm, colorful Caribbean and placed them in the bleak, somber surroundings of a Puritan village. Time and place then influence how other characters react to these protagonists and how these characters respond to their new environments.

Some settings in historical fiction create happy, nostalgic moods. In Cynthia Rylant's picture storybook *When I Was Young in the Mountains,* the illustrations and the text allow readers to glimpse a girl's happy years of growing up in the Appalachian mountains of Virginia. This peaceful setting includes swimming holes, country stores, and family evenings on the porch. The illustrations help integrate the details of the time period into the story. In contrast, the illustrations in Jo Hoestlandt's *Star of Fear, Star of Hope* reinforce a poignantly sad tale of separation in Nazi-occupied France in 1942.

Esther Forbes integrates many details of colonial life into the setting of her story for older readers, *Johnny Tremain.* The sights, sounds, and smells of revolutionary Boston are woven into the characters' daily routines. Readers know that Johnny sleeps in a loft, wears leather breeches and a coarse shirt, likes the bustling wharf, and is proud of his work in the silversmith's shop.

Smells, sounds, and light create believable settings in Gary Paulsen's *The Winter Room,* a story of farm life in an earlier American setting. Paulsen introduces *The Winter Room* by telling readers that if books could have smells, this book "would have the smell of new-mown hay as it falls off the oiled sickle blade when the horses pull the mower through the field, and the sour smell of manure steaming in a winter barn" (p. 1). If it could have sounds, it "would have the high, keening sound of the six-foot bucksaws as the men pull them back and forth through the

Through the Eyes of an AUTHOR

Mary E. Lyons

Visit the CD-ROM that accompanies this text to generate a complete list of Mary E. Lyons titles.

Selected Titles by Mary E. Lyons:

Sorrow's Kitchen: The Life and Folklore of Zora Neale Hurston

Raw Head, Bloody Bones: African-American Tales of the Supernatural

Letters from a Slave Girl: The Story of Harriet Jacobs

Catching the Fire: Philip Simmons, Blacksmith

Knockabeg: A Famine Tale

I was a teacher at the middle-school level for seventeen years and school librarian at the elementary, middle- and high-school levels for six years. One day I realized that half of my students were girls and half of my students were African Americans. And I thought, you know, I may just start putting some things in the curriculum that are especially for these two groups of students that I'm teaching. And I became very interested in African-American history and in women's history and did a lot throughout the whole year to celebrate that history.

Many of my books are about women, including my first book, *Sorrow's Kitchen: The Life and Folklore of Zora Neale Hurston.* As I delved into women's history, I found a lot of women writers whose work had been forgotten, and Zora Neale Hurston was one of them. So I collected some of her writings and shared them with my students, and I really liked to tell them the story of her life. She was quite a successful writer and an anthropologist. Sadly, she died alone and poor in a charity home in 1960.

The story of how Zora Neale Hurston educated herself, became a writer, a folklorist, and an anthropologist was so interesting to my students that I told it, and told it, and told it so many times that I finally decided to write it down—that is a short version of how I wrote my first book, *Sorrow's Kitchen.*

My second book, *Raw Head, Bloody Bones: African-American Tales of the Supernatural,* is a book that I edited. I did not write the stories, but I collected stories told by enslaved African Americans all over the world. Some of them are scary, some of them are funny/scary, and some are simply about the supernatural. There are a lot of wonderful supernatural elements in folklore from all over the world.

Another woman writer in whom I was interested was Harriet Jacobs. Harriet Jacobs was a real person. She was enslaved in North Carolina and for seven years she hid from the slaveholder in the eaves under her grandmother's roof. She finally escaped in 1845, but only when she knew that she could safely have her children join her in the North. She wrote of her experiences in a book called *Incidents of the Life of a Slave Girl.* That's a wonderful book to read when you're ready for it. For my readers, my students, I wanted to retell her story in a childhood voice, in a girlhood voice, so I wrote this historical novel. Writers of historical fiction start with what is true and then we add voice, and dialogue, and thought, and imagination, and, for want of a better word, heart. I really felt that Harriet's heart touched mine while I was writing this book.

Video Profiles: The accompanying video contains more of this conversation with Mary E. Lyons, as well as conversations with other writers of historical fiction, including Joseph Bruchac, Eve Bunting, and Leonard Everett Fisher.

The illustrations reflect a happy setting in an Appalachian mountain community. (From When I Was Young in the Mountains, *by Cynthia Rylant, illustrated by Diane Goode. Illustrations © 1982 by Diane Goode. E. P. Dutton, Inc. Reprinted by permission of E. P. Dutton, Inc.)*

trees to cut pine for paper pulp; the grunting-gassy sounds of the work teams snorting and slapping as they hit the harness to jerk the stumps out of the ground" (p. 2). And if the book could have light, it would have "the soft gold light—gold with bits of hay dust floating in it— that slips through the crack in the barn wall; the light of the Coleman lantern hissing flat-white in the kitchen; the silver-gray light of a middle winter day, the splattered, white-night light of a full moon on snow, the new light of dawn at the eastern edge of the pasture behind the cows coming in to be milked on a summer morning" (p. 2). But, Paulsen tells readers that because books cannot have smells, sounds, and light, the book needs readers who bring these sensations to the reading. Throughout his book, Paulsen's descriptions help readers visualize and vicariously experience details.

Theme

Themes in historical fiction, as in any literature, should be worthwhile and as relevant in today's society as they were in the historical periods represented. Many books of historical fiction have themes that have been relevant throughout history. The search for freedom is a theme in literature about all time periods. For example, Rosemary Sutcliff's *The Shining Company* is based on the develop-

Through the Eyes of a CHILD

Lindsay

Pam Wilson's Fourth Grade
Western Row Elementary
Mason, Ohio

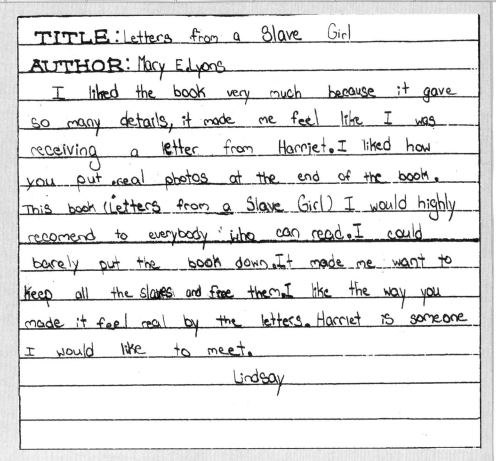

TITLE: Letters from a Slave Girl

AUTHOR: Mary E. Lyons

I liked the book very much because it gave so many details, it made me feel like I was receiving a letter from Harriet. I liked how you put real photos at the end of the book. This book (Letters from a Slave Girl) I would highly recomend to everybody who can read. I could barely put the book down. It made me want to keep all the slaves and free them. I like the way you made it feel real by the letters. Harriet is someone I would like to meet.

Lindsay

---

ment of a fighting brotherhood formed to battle the invading Saxons. Sutcliff's books develop stories in which searching for and defending freedom are primary goals. Sutcliff's books are memorable according to Sutherland (1997) because they are built around great themes. "Her characters live and die for principles they value and that people today still value" (p. 395). Freedom is one of the great themes in historical fiction. Elizabeth Yates's *Amos Fortune, Free Man* tells about an African slave searching for freedom in colonial Boston. The importance of justice is developed in many historical fiction books, such as Eve Ibbotson's *Journey to the River Sea.*

Love of the land and the independence that it provides are themes in books about the westward expansion of European settlers in North America and about the Native Americans that they displaced. Europeans leave relatives and established communities to face unknown dangers and acquire homesteads. Native Americans first attempt to share their beloved natural environment with the new arrivals. Then, they find themselves being pushed out of their homes. Love of land and the consequences caused by loss of land are developed by Scott O'Dell and

Elizabeth Hall in *Thunder Rolling in the Mountains.* This book, told through the viewpoint of Chief Joseph's daughter, develops the conflict and pain associated with being forced to leave the Wallowa Valley. Children in both the westward expansion literature and the Native American literature inherit their parents' dreams and fight to retain the land.

Loyalty and honor are also common themes in stories about all time periods. People are loyal to friends and family members, following them on difficult quests and avenging their deaths or dishonor. They are loyal to their principles and defend them. Many books of historical fiction for children stress the cruelty and futility of war, even when adherence to loyalty and honor have helped cause the conflict. Novels about war in various historical periods often develop the themes of overcoming injustice. They also show ways in which people on both sides of a conflict have much in common. For example, Susan Campbell Bartoletti's protagonist in *No Man's Land: A Young Soldier's Story* concludes as he prepares for battle: "It hit Thrasher, all of a sudden, how odd it was. The Yankees and Rebels spoke the same language, knew the same prayers, prayed to the same God" (p. 84). The beliefs of nonviolent people such as the

Quakers are the bases of themes in some historical novels. Many themes are relevant to understanding, whether the stories in which they are developed take place in ancient Rome or contemporary America.

Style

An author's style influences the mood in historical fiction. For example, the repetition of the line "When I was young in the mountains" in Cynthia Rylant's text helps create a warm, nostalgic mood, in which harmful occurrences seem improbable. Brett Harvey introduces her mostly happy pioneer adventure *Cassie's Journey: Going West in the 1860s* with a description that suggests anticipation and security: "We're on our way to California! I'm riding up high with Papa, and the wind is rocking the wagon. When I look back I can see a long line of wagons curling behind us like a snake in the dust" (unnumbered).

In contrast, Patricia MacLachlan's introduction to *Sarah, Plain and Tall* suggests that the story will be about a family but that some unhappiness may have entered the family's life:

"Did Mama sing every day?" asked Caleb. "Every-single-day?" He sat close to the fire, his chin in his hand. It was dusk, and the dogs lay beside him on the warm hearthstones. "Every-single-day," I told him for the second time this week. For the twentieth time this month. The hundredth time this year? And the past few years? (p. 3)

If a historical fiction story has elements of suspense and adventure, the introduction frequently hints at the intrigue to follow. Philip Pullman's *The Ruby in the Smoke* develops mystery and adventure in Victorian England. Pullman introduces his novel about the sinister opium trade and the quest for a missing ruby:

On a cold, fretful afternoon in early October, 1872, a hansom cab drew up outside the offices of Lockhart and Selby, Shipping Agents, in the financial heart of London, and a young girl got out and paid the driver. She was a person of sixteen or so—alone, and uncommonly pretty. . . . Her name was Sally Lockhart; and within fifteen minutes she was going to kill a man. (p. 3)

Various forms of figurative language may clarify the conflicts, characters, settings, and themes in historical fiction. Figurative language is especially powerful when it provides insights into time, place, and conflict. For example, Rudolf Frank in *No Hero for the Kaiser* creates vivid images of World War I settings. In the following example, Frank makes readers understand both the physical and psychological settings and introduces the antiwar theme through his choice of words:

The distant thud of cannon came closer, like a thunderstorm brewing. And as if the storm had already broken, women, boys, girls, and soldiers began to rush around in confusion; trumpets sounded, and suddenly the Russians had swept out of the village like the wind. Now they were firing down from the low hills into the village. It sounded like the high-pitched whine of mosquitoes as they fly past your ear looking for a place to settle and bite: zzzzzz—a thin, sharp noise, full of sly malice. Jan knew that any

one of these invisible whining bullets could kill man or beast on the spot. A dreadful feeling! But there was worse to come. (p. 2)

Allusions in historical fiction frequently provide insights into plots and characters. These same allusions, however, may require interpretation for less knowledgeable readers. For example, Frank uses allusions to the biblical flood, Napoleon, the skull of an African sultan, and the Maid of Orleans. Some of these allusions are explained in the text, while others are not. Karen Cushman identifies many of her journal entries in *Catherine, Called Birdy* with religious holidays that correspond with the dates. These "Feasts of Saint . . ." imply the importance of religion in medieval England.

In *The True Story of Spit MacPhee*, set in Australia in the 1920s, James Aldridge uses an unexplained allusion when Old Fyfe, the Scottish grandfather, looks at his grandson's friend, Sadie, and says with a grim laugh, "How are ye dressed, Jean Armour, aye sae clean and neat" (p. 37). This allusion depicts character and hints at possible conflict when readers understand that the grandfather is referring to poet Robert Burns's first real love. It is interesting to identify such allusions in historical fiction.

Historical Authenticity

In a review of the attitudes expressed by authors of historical fiction, Lawrence R. Sipe (1997) states, "The issue that receives the most attention from authors of historical fiction is how to write authentically" (p. 246). This concern for authenticity emphasizes the use of language; the depiction of the details of everyday life; the faithfulness to the historical record; and the need for readers to perceive that the language, situations, and characters are "true."

The need for authentic historical detail places special demands on authors of historical fiction. Some authors actually lived through the experiences that they write about or knew someone who lived through them. Other authors write about historical periods far removed from their personal experiences. To gather their data, they must rely on sources of information far different from the people who remember vividly a historical period. Diane Stanley (1994) emphasizes that authors of historical fiction must set high standards in the hope of coming close to the truth.

Laura Ingalls Wilder, the author of the "Little House" books, lived in the big woods of Wisconsin, traveled by covered wagon through Kansas, lived in a sod house in Minnesota, and shared her life with Pa, Ma, Mary, and Carrie when they finally settled in South Dakota. Wilder's books sound as if they were written immediately after an incident occurred, but Wilder actually wrote the stories describing her life from 1870 through 1889 much later, between 1926 and 1943. Authors who write about their own past experiences need to have both keen powers of observation and excellent memories in order to share the details of their lives with others.

Predominantly happy experiences in the past may be easy to remember. For authors who write about painful experiences in their own lives, however, the doors of memory may be more difficult to open. Johanna Reiss found herself remembering things that she had preferred to forget when she began writing the story of her experiences as a Jewish child hidden by Dutch gentiles during the Holocaust and World War II. According to the publishers of *The Upstairs Room,* Reiss (1972) "did not set out to write a book about her experiences during the Second World War; she simply wanted to record them for her two daughters, who are now about the age she was when she went to stay with the Oastervelds" (p. 197). When Reiss started to write, she began remembering experiences that she had never talked about with anyone because they were too painful. To reinforce her memory, she took her children back to Usselo, Holland, where she visited the Dutch family who had protected her and looked again at the upstairs room and the closet in which she had hidden from the Nazis.

Authors such as Carol Ryrie Brink write about relatives' experiences. In *Caddie Woodlawn,* Brink re-creates the story of her grandmother and her grandmother's family. In her author's note to the book, Brink (1973) tells how she lived with her grandmother and loved to listen to her tell stories about her pioneer childhood:

It was many years later that I remembered those stories of Caddie's childhood, and I said to myself, "If I loved them so much perhaps other children would like them too." Caddie was still alive when I was writing, and I sent letters to her, asking about the details that I did not remember clearly. She was pleased when the book was done. "There is only one thing that I do not understand," she said. "You never knew my mother and father and my brothers—how could you write about them exactly as they were?" "But, Gram," I said, "You told me." (p. 283)

Uri Orlev based his World War II story *The Man from the Other Side* on the memories of a journalist who as a child had lived on the outskirts of the Warsaw Ghetto and had helped his father provide assistance for the Jewish people in the ghetto. Consequently, the setting and the conflict seem very believable.

Of course, modern authors have no firsthand experience of some earlier times and cannot even talk to someone who lived during certain historical periods, so they must use other resources in researching their chosen time periods. To acquire this much knowledge about a time period demands much research. Some authors have chosen to research and write about one period; others have written books covering many different time periods.

Kathryn Lasky reveals the influence of extensive research in her author's note for *Beyond the Divide.* Lasky says that she based the book in part on Theodora Kroeber's biography of the last Yahi Indian, *Ishi: The Last of His Tribe,* and in part on J. Goldsborough Bruff's journal that describes his own experiences during the gold rush. Lasky (1983) describes her own discoveries about the West:

Mrs. Kroeber's story was the first true western tale I had ever read. This was not the West of television, nor was the gold rush the one written about in my school books. The bad guys were worse than I had ever imagined, and the greed for gold was pernicious and deadly to the human spirit. People did not just rob, they killed, and on occasion massacred. The conditions of survival were the most arduous imaginable, but there was one emigrant whose spirit was left miraculously intact. (p. 253)

These discoveries, characterizations, settings, and themes are apparent in her historical novel.

Likewise, Karen Hesse's author's note for *Stowaway* reveals that she based her historical fiction about Captain James Cook's 1768–1771 around-the-world expedition on Cook's and Banks's journals and the "Endeavor" CD-ROM, produced by the National Maritime Museum of Australia and the National Library of Australia.

Lois Lowry based *Number the Stars* on the experiences of the Danish Resistance. Lowry reveals that she was determined to tell the story of the Danish people and the Danish Resistance after seeing a photograph of Kim Malthe-Bruun and reading about his helping Jewish residents of Denmark. The Nazis captured and executed this resistance leader when he was only twenty-one.

Reading about any of the well-known authors of historical fiction whose books are noted for authentic backgrounds reveals that the authors first spend hundreds of hours researching county courthouse records and old letters, newspapers, and history books; conducting personal interviews; and visiting museums and historical locations. Authors must then write stories that develop believable plots, characters, and settings without sounding like history textbooks. In doing so, they must carefully consider the many conflicting points of view that surround particular events. Writing excellent historical fiction is a very demanding task.

A Chronology of Historical Fiction

In sharing historical fiction with children, you must understand at least some of the history of a time period in order to evaluate stories reflecting that period. Following a three-year study, Norton (1980) found that the understanding, evaluation, and utilization of historical fiction of students in children's literature courses improved if the students discussed books of historical fiction in a chronological order, briefly identified the actual historical happenings in each time period, identified major themes in literature written about a specific period (although, of course, some books have more than one theme), discussed the implications of recurring themes, identified how authors develop believable plots for a time period, and discussed the modern significance of the literature. To assist in the study of historical fiction, this chapter discusses books of historical fiction in an order similar to the one used during

CHART 10.1 Eras and themes in historical fiction

Date	Period	Themes
3000 B.C.	Ancient times through the Middle Ages	Loyalty is one of the noblest human traits. Ignorance, prejudice, and hatred can have destructive consequences for all concerned. Hatred, not people, is the great enemy. Love is stronger than hatred and prevails through times of great trouble. People will always search for freedom and riches. Courage is more important than physical strength. A physical disability does not reduce a person's humanity. People can overcome their handicaps.
A.D. 1492	Changes in the Old World and discovery of the New World	Greed is a strong motivational force and can have destructive consequences. Moral dilemmas must be faced and resolved. People will face severe hardships to acquire the political and religious freedom that they desire. People must work together if they are to survive. Overcoming problems can strengthen character. War creates tragedy. Life is more than physical survival. Land is important: People will endure numerous hardships to acquire land for personal reasons or for the glory of their country.
1692	The Salem witch-hunts	Prejudiced persecution of others is a frightening and destructive social phenomenon. People seek freedom from persecution. Moral obligations require some people to defend the rights of others.
1776	The American Revolution	Freedom is worth fighting for. Strong beliefs require strong commitments.
1780	Early expansion of the United States and Canada	Friendship and faith are important. People long for their own land and the freedom that ownership implies. People will withstand great hardships to retain their dreams. Strong family bonds help physical and spiritual survival. Prejudice and hatred are destructive forces. The greatest strength comes from within. Moral obligations require personal commitment.

Norton's study. Ideally, this framework will assist you as you discuss the literature in children's literature classes and undertake individual studies of historical fiction for children. Chart 10.1 presents a simple chronology of Western and North American history and the main themes developed in books in each period.

Ancient Times Through the Middle Ages

In pre-Roman times, various Celtic peoples, including the Britons and Gaels, inhabited the British Isles. These people lived in tribes ruled by chiefs and often warred with one another over land and people. In 55 B.C., Julius Caesar failed in an attempt to add present-day England and Scotland to the Roman Empire. One hundred years later, Emperor Claudius succeeded in annexing Britain. Roman legions were left behind to subdue the people and to keep peace among the tribes.

The Roman dominance lasted throughout Europe until about A.D. 410, when fierce tribes of Teutonic peoples from northern Europe invaded and sacked Rome,

CHART 10.1   Continued

Date	Period	Themes
1861	The Civil War	War creates tragedy. Moral obligations must be met even if one's life or freedom is in jeopardy. Moral sense does not depend on skin color, but on what is inside a person. People should take pride in themselves and their accomplishments. Prejudice and hatred are destructive forces. People search for freedom. Personal conscience may not allow some people to kill others. Strong family ties help people persevere.
1860s	The western frontier	People have moral obligations. People have strong dreams of owning land. Families can survive if they work together. People need each other and may work together for their mutual good. Battles can be won through legal means rather than through unlawful actions. Hatred and prejudice are destructive forces. Without spiritual hope, people may lose their will to live.
1900	The early twentieth century	People will strive for survival of the physical body and the spirit. Prejudice and discrimination are destructive forces. There is a bond between people who experience injustice. Monetary wealth does not create a rich life.
1939	World War II	People will seek freedom from religious and political persecution. Prejudice and hatred are destructive forces. Moral obligation and personal conscience are strong forces. Freedom is worth fighting for. Family love and loyalty help people endure catastrophic experiences.

beginning the long medieval period in European history that has sometimes been called the Dark Ages. In their great ships, Vikings from Norway were led by people such as Eric the Red. The Vikings raided the coasts of Europe and demonstrated their remarkable seafaring skills by exploring Greenland and Iceland. In about A.D. 1000, Norse explorers under Leif Ericson's command crossed the Atlantic Ocean and stayed briefly in a place in North America they called "Vinland."

Teutonic Saxons and Angles from the continent invaded and settled Britain. The once-unified Roman empire dissolved into many small domains ruled by competing feudal lords and the warrior nobility that served them in ongoing battles. The lords lived in fortified castles surrounded by cottages and fields in which enslaved peasants produced food and wealth for them. Constant warfare and rampant disease, such as the plague (also known as the Black Death), ravaged the developing towns of England, France, and elsewhere. The strong Christian beliefs of the Middle Ages led to the construction of magnificent cathedrals and to crusades in which Christian warriors attempted to capture Jerusalem for the Roman Catholic Church, which still survived in splendor and power after the fall of Rome.

Authors who write historical fiction about the ancient world and medieval times in Europe often tell their stories from the viewpoint of slaves or other people subjugated by the powerful. Other authors represent the perspectives of the mighty, such as Romans and Vikings, and show the ways in which all people have certain desires and fears in common and confront similar problems. Through these various perspectives, authors of historical fiction for children encourage young readers to imagine and empathize with the personal and social conflicts of people in the distant past. Themes emerge as the characters fight for their beliefs and personal freedoms, follow their dreams, struggle with moral dilemmas, or overcome prejudices or self-doubts that could destroy them.

In *The Bronze Bow*, Elizabeth George Speare focuses upon Israel during Roman rule. She portrays the harshness of the Roman conquerors by telling the story through the eyes of a boy who longs to avenge the death of his parents. (His father was crucified by Roman soldiers, and his mother died from grief and exposure.) Daniel bar Jamin's bitterness intensifies when he joins a guerrilla band and nurtures his hatred of the Romans. His person-against-self conflict comes to a turning point when he almost sacrifices his sister because of his hatred. Speare encourages readers to understand Daniel's real enemy. When Daniel talks to Jesus, both Daniel and readers realize that hatred, not Romans, is the enemy. In fact, the only thing stronger than hatred is love. Speare shows the magnitude of Daniel's change when he invites a Roman soldier into his home at the close of the story.

While the Vikings were roaming the seas, knights in armor all across Europe were challenging one another over land and power, and humble people were working in the fields of nobles or serving the mighty in the great halls of castles. In *The Door in the Wall*, Marguerite DeAngeli uses an English castle and its surroundings as the settings for her story about ten-year-old Robin, who is expected to train for knighthood. The plot has an unusual twist when Robin is stricken with a mysterious ailment that paralyzes his legs. The door in the title of the story becomes symbolic. A monk gives unhappy Robin difficult advice: "Thou hast only to follow the wall far enough and there will be a door in it" (p. 16).

This symbol is very important in the story. DeAngeli traces Robin's search for his own door and the preparation necessary to find it. The monk helps Robin by guiding his learning, encouraging him to carve and to read, and expressing the belief that Robin's hands and mind, if not his legs, must be taught because they represent other doors in the wall. Robin worries that as a person who walks with crutches, he will be useless as a knight. His father's friend Sir Peter reassures him by saying that if a person cannot serve in one way, another means of serving will present itself. Sir Peter is proven correct when Welsh forces attack the castle. Robin proves his worth to himself and the castle by escaping the enemy sentry and obtaining help from the neighboring castle.

DeAngeli encourages readers to understand the importance of accepting people for what they are, rather than rejecting them because of physical disability, when Robin's father congratulates him: "The courage you have

shown, the craftsmanship proven by the harp, and the spirit in your singing all make so bright a light that I cannot see whether or not your legs are misshapen" (p. 120).

Many children enjoy this beautiful story about a child who finds a door in his wall. One girl said that it was her favorite book because she liked the way in which Robin overcame his problem and was happy with his life. The theme is especially appropriate for teaching positive attitudes about individuals with disabilities.

Elizabeth Alder's *The King's Shadow*, set in Saxon England prior to the Battle of Hastings in 1066, has two strong themes that are characteristic of literature set in the Middle Ages: Loyalty is one of the noblest human traits, and physical disability does not reduce a person's humanity. Both themes are developed as a Welsh boy named Evyn first experiences violence at the murder of his father and then has his tongue cut off by his father's murderers. Even though he is now speechless and sold into slavery, he eventually comes under the control and guidance of an honorable lady who begins to see his worth and sends him to an abbey where he eventually learns to read and write. Evyn discovers the importance of loyalty when he becomes squire to Harold Godwinson, England's last Saxon king. As Evyn rides at Harold's side, he learns the importance of both the loyalty to England expressed by Harold and his own growing loyalty to a man who Evyn believes is one of the most noble of men. During his experience, Evyn discovers that his physical disability does not reduce his own humanity or value. Alder brings additional authenticity to her retelling of the time period through the inclusion of excerpts from *The Anglo Saxon Chronicle* and legends such as "The Song of Roland" and "Beowulf."

Three books by Karen Cushman have settings in medieval England in the thirteenth and fourteenth centuries. Interesting comparisons may be made among characteristics of the social levels, characterizations of the three different heroines, conflicts developed, and themes portrayed in *Catherine, Called Birdy, The Midwife's Apprentice*, and *Matilda Bone*. For example, readers may compare the social structure associated with a medieval English manor and the knight's family in *Catherine, Called Birdy* with the lowest level of poverty described in *The Midwife's Apprentice*. In the latter book, Cushman leaves no doubt about this lowly social level when she introduces both the setting and the heroine, Brat: "When animal droppings and garbage and spoiled straw are piled up in a great heap, the rotting and molding give forth heat. Usually no one gets close enough to notice because of the stench. But the girl noticed and, on that frosty night, burrowed deep into the warm, rotting muck, heedless of the smell. In any event, the dung heap probably smelled little worse than everything else in her life—the food scraps scavenged from kitchen yards, the stables and sties she slept in when she could, and her own unwashed, unnourished, unloved, and unlovely body" (p. 1). Contrasts in social structure are found in *Matilda Bone* as the heroine's life changes from that of a well-educated girl living in a fourteenth-century manor house to an abandoned orphan who serves as an assistant to a bone setter.

Although the positions of Cushman's three heroines are very different, there are similarities between the three characters. Catherine, Brat, and Matilda are strong-willed females who must face conflicts caused by the social structure in order to succeed. There is Catherine's desire for independence and an adventurous life versus society's requirements for females and her father's desire to marry his daughter to a wealthy suitor. There is Brat's need to rise above the ignorance and superstition surrounding her and the antagonism of the village midwife in order to gain the skills and self-respect she needs to succeed. There is Matilda's need to overcome her self-righteous, snobbish attitude before she develops into a compassionate assistant to the bone setter.

There are also similarities in themes between Cushman's books. In each of the books, the heroines discover, through their own actions, that the world is full of possibilities. But in order to realize these possibilities, they must continue trying. Brat, now Alyce, states this very well when she declares, " 'Jane Sharp! It is I, Alyce, your apprentice. I have come back. And if you do not let me in, I will try again and again. I can do what you tell me and take what you give me, and I know how to try and risk and fail and try again and not give up. I will not go away.' The door opened. Alyce went in. And the cat went with her" (pp. 116–117). This symbol of going through the door could be compared with DeAngeli's *The Door in the Wall* in which, as discussed, she traces a crippled boy's life as he searches for his own door and the preparation necessary to find it.

Two important themes are developed in Tracy Barrett's *Anna of Byzantium,* which is set in the eleventh century during the Byzantine Empire: (1) Searching for and trying to retain power can be destructive and (2) there were knowledgeable and scholarly women living during the eleventh century who should not be forgotten. Barrett develops these two themes by telling a fictional story through the viewpoint of the real Anna Comnena, daughter of the emperor Alexius I. The first theme is developed through the use of tragic Greek myths that are told to Anna by her tutor. The theme is reinforced as Anna discovers the intrigue and treachery conducted by her younger brother and her grandmother as they try to replace her as her father's appointed heir. The second theme is developed as the author describes Anna's joy as she writes down her memories, discovers the poetry written by the nun Kassia who wrote about injustice, and her excitement when she receives a gift of Kassia's books and journals. Readers discover that Anna wants to write history because "I admired anyone who could unravel the complicated stories of the past and show them in clear form to a reader" (p. 108).

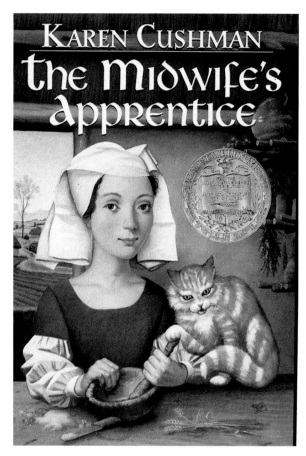

A book set in medieval England emphasizes the need to overcome person-versus-society and person-versus-self conflicts. (From **The Midwife's Apprentice,** *by Karen Cushman, text copyright © 1995, Clarion Books. Used by permission of E. P. Dutton, Inc.)*

Another book that develops the importance of writing and knowledge is Florence Parry Heide and Judith Heide Gilliland's picture storybook *The House of Wisdom.* The book is based on the Caliph al-Ma'mum's building in A.D. 830 of the House of Wisdom. This library and home of scholars is depicted as the center of civilization in Baghdad. Through the search for important manuscripts and the translations of books by scholars, the authors develop the theme that the creation and preservation of knowledge were some of the most important endeavors during this time period.

A different type of creation and preservation of knowledge is developed by Paolo Guarnieri is *A Boy Named Giotto.* The author creates the fictionalized boyhood of the artist who created frescoes in Assisi and Padua in late thirteenth- and early fourteenth-century Italy. The responses of viewers to his paintings suggest the importance of art in the preservation of a culture.

Books set in feudal Japan relate to the theme of overcoming racial and cultural conflict. Erik Christian Haugaard's *The Boy and the Samurai* is set in feudal Japan during the period of civil wars in the late 1400s and 1500s.

As do the authors of many other stories with wartime settings, Haugaard emphasizes the search for peace and the painful realities resulting from war. Haugaard's settings and characters allow readers to visualize the world of street orphans, warlords, samurais, and priests.

The following themes are expressed in historical fiction about ancient and medieval times. Consider how these themes relate to specific happenings in the time periods. Are any of these themes significant in our modern world?

1. Loyalty is one of the noblest human traits.
2. Ignorance, prejudice, and hatred can have destructive consequences for all concerned.
3. Hatred, not people, is the great enemy.
4. Love is stronger than hatred and prevails through times of great trouble.
5. People will always search for freedom and riches.
6. Courage is more important than physical strength.
7. A physical disability does not reduce a person's humanity.
8. People can overcome their handicaps.

Changes in the Old World and Encounters with the New World

By the fifteenth century, Europe had entered the Renaissance, a time of cultural rebirth and great social change. Large cities were bustling with trade, and middle-class merchants had attained more social prominence. Protestant Christianity was arising out of medieval Catholicism and challenging the religious and political power of the established church. In Germany, Johann Gutenberg was inventing the printing press, which William Caxton soon used to publish the first printed books in England. Great artists such as Michelangelo and William Shakespeare began to raise the visual arts and literature to new heights of creative glory, inspired by the rediscovery of ancient Greek and Roman culture. Ordinary people were expecting and demanding greater economic, political, and religious freedom. Explorers were sailing off to prove their belief that the world was round and then to acquire great riches in the New World, a land that was inhabited by native peoples in the Western Hemisphere.

The arrival of Christopher Columbus on a Caribbean island in 1492 was soon followed by conquest of ancient Mayan and Aztec cultures in Central America by Spanish explorers. By the late sixteenth and the early seventeenth centuries, colonies were springing up along the Atlantic coast of North America. People followed their lust for wealth and adventure or their desire for freedom from the religious persecution and political conflicts that were occurring in England and elsewhere.

Several books published in 1992, the five hundredth anniversary of Columbus's voyage, present the landing of Columbus from the viewpoint of the native peoples. Jane

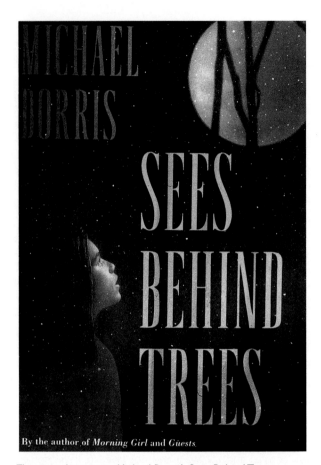

The main character in Michael Dorris's Sees Behind Trees encounters "strangers" for the first time. (From Sees Behind Trees by Michael Dorris, text copyright © 1996. Reprinted by permission of Hyperion Books for Children.)

Yolen's picture storybook *Encounter* develops a hypothetical interaction between a Taino Indian boy and Columbus and his men on the island of San Salvador in 1492. The text is developed on the premise that dreams forewarn the boy about the disastrous consequences of interacting with the explorers, whom the people believe have flown down from the sky. Yolen includes descriptions of the Taino Indians and their beliefs, details about the loss of culture and human life that resulted because of the exploration and colonization by the Spanish, and details describing trade between the explorers and the Taino people. Information provided in the author's notes indicates how disastrous this encounter was for the Taino people, who went from a population of 300,000 at the time of Columbus's landing to 500 only fifty years later. The book develops the theme that interaction with people who do not understand or respect your culture can have terrible consequences. As a result of this encounter, the Taino people lost their language, religion, and culture.

In *Morning Girl*, Michael Dorris writes from the perspective of Morning Girl and Star Boy, two Taino children who live on a Bahamian island at the time of Columbus's landing. By developing strong characters and detailing the settings, Dorris encourages readers to understand the nature of the Taino people and their culture. Unlike Yolen, Dorris concludes his book at the time of the first sighting of the Spanish sailors. Dorris includes an epilogue that quotes Columbus's journal on October 11, 1492, the day he first encounters the Taino people. Dorris's *Sees Behind Trees* is set in sixteenth-century America. The main character sees "strangers" for the first time and proves himself as he accompanies a village elder on a pilgrimage to find the land of the water.

Person-against-self conflicts, settings that depict Mayan and Aztec cultures, and themes that illustrate the consequences of greed are found in Scott O'Dell's historical novels based on the Spanish conquest of Mexico in the early 1500s. O'Dell's *The Captive, The Feathered Serpent,* and *The Amethyst Ring* focus not so much on the events of the time as on the moral dilemmas that a young priest faces in the New World.

A young, idealistic Jesuit seminarian, Julián Escobar, leaves his secure home in Spain and joins an expedition to Central America, inspired by the prospect of saving the souls of native peoples in New Spain. During the long voyage across the Atlantic, he begins to realize that the Spanish grandee leading the expedition actually intends to exploit and enslave the Maya and the Aztecs, rather than convert them to Christianity.

Later, Julián questions whether he has the spirit or the patience to spread the Christian faith within cultures so different from his own. O'Dell explores changes in Julián by stressing the changing conflicts in Julián's life: Should he take on the role of the mythical Kukulcán in order to save his life and make his views palatable to people with their own ancient beliefs? Should he advise attacking a neighboring city before his own Mayan city is attacked? How should he respond to the Mayan rites of sun worship? Why does God permit both good and evil? Julián's defense of his inability to change the Maya and of his own eventual grasping for power demonstrate changes in his character. In *The Feathered Serpent,* for example, Julián thinks back to Augustine's teachings and concludes that evil exists because God wills it. Therefore, idol worship and human sacrifice are beyond his control. Julián does admit, however, that this argument may be only a defense of his own actions.

O'Dell's descriptions of Mayan and Aztec cities and temples and other aspects of the cultures encourage readers to understand that an advanced civilization inhabited the Americas long before European exploration and settlement. Readers may also ponder the right of one culture to destroy another culture whose citizens worship different gods and possess riches desired by a foreign power.

In 1620, the *Mayflower* brought the first group of settlers to New England. The Pilgrims made no easy conquest of the wilderness. Their sponsors in England did not provide enough supplies, their first winter was filled with

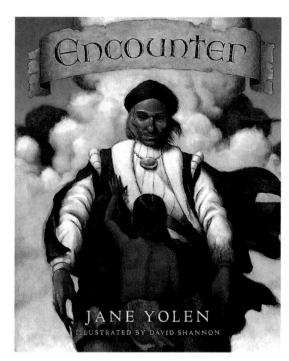

This text emphasizes the possible interaction between a Taino Indian boy and Columbus. (Illustration from Encounter *by Jane Yolen, copyright © 1992 by David Shannon. Reproduced by permission of Harcourt Brace & Company.)*

sickness and starvation, and the new settlers were apprehensive about the native peoples who lived beyond their settlement.

Authors who write about the settlement of Plymouth colony often look at the reasons for leaving England and the hardships faced by the Pilgrims. In *Constance: A Story of Early Plymouth,* for example, Patricia Clapp tells about the early settlement of New England from the viewpoint of a fourteen-year-old girl. Because Constance did not want to leave her cherished London, her first view of the new world from the deck of the *Mayflower* is an unpleasant one. Clapp encourages readers to understand the various viewpoints of the Pilgrims by contrasting Constance's view of a bleak and unfriendly land with the excitement and anticipation expressed by her father, William Bradford, John Alden, and Miles Standish.

While early colonists in North America were struggling to survive, ominous clouds were gathering over England. Conflict between Catholic King Charles I and the staunchly Protestant Parliament led to war in 1642. Authors who place their stories in England during this time frequently develop the theme that war is tragic and explore the influences that shape an awareness of the reality of war.

One of the strongest leaders to emerge during the English Civil War was Oliver Cromwell, an ordinary man but a great military organizer. In Erik Christian Haugaard's *Cromwell's Boy,* a thirteen-year-old boy discovers the tragic reality of war. The boy, also named Oliver, rides a horse well, does not divulge secrets, and looks inconspicuous. His ability to serve Cromwell extends beyond messages. Oliver goes into the dangerous stronghold of the king's army as a spy. Haugaard suggests the lessons that Oliver has learned, using a flashback in which Oliver remembers his youthful experiences:

In my youth there was little time for dreams. Life challenged me early. The leisure to reflect was not my lot; tomorrow was ever knocking on the door of today with new demands. It made me resourceful and sharpened my wit, but the purpose of life must be more than just to survive. You must be able—at least for short moments—to hold your precious soul in your hands and to contemplate that gift with love and understanding. (p. 1)

Consider the following themes developed in historical fiction about the age of cultural and social change in Europe and about early European settlement of the Western Hemisphere. Why and how are they related to specific happenings in the time periods? Do these themes have relevance in other periods of history? Do they have relevance for us today?

1. Greed is a strong motivational force and can have destructive consequences.

2. Moral dilemmas must be faced and resolved.

3. People will face severe hardships to acquire the political and religious freedom that they desire.

4. People must work together if they are to survive.

5. Overcoming problems can strengthen character.

6. War creates tragedy.

7. Life is more than physical survival.

8. Land is important: People will endure numerous hardships to acquire land for personal reasons or for the glory of their country.

The Salem Witch-Hunts

Belief in witchcraft was common in medieval Europe. Thousands of religious and political nonconformists, independent thinkers and artists, mentally ill persons, and other unusual people seemed to threaten the established social order. Such people were accused of witchcraft and were burned at the stake. Belief in witchcraft continued even in the relatively more enlightened sixteenth and seventeenth centuries and crossed the Atlantic with the first settlers of North America.

In the new England colonies of the late 1600s, strict Puritan religious beliefs governed every aspect of social life. Any kind of nonconformity was viewed as the work of the devil. The famous witch-hunts of 1692 in Salem, Massachusetts, began when a doctor stated that the hysterical behavior of several teenage girls was due to the "evil eye." Within six months, twenty persons had been sentenced to death and one hundred and fifty had been sent to prison.

Boston minister Cotton Mather was one of those who preached the power of the devil and the need to purge the world of witchcraft. People charged with witchcraft were pardoned in 1693 when Sir William Phipps, royal governor of the Massachusetts Bay Colony, said that the witch-hunt proceedings were too violent and not based upon fact. Belief in witchcraft faded in the 1700s as new scientific knowledge began to explain previously frightening phenomena.

The conflict in stories set in this short period of American history is usually person-against-society. Authors often place their characters in a hostile environment, where their usual behaviors create suspicion. For example, is a person a witch because he or she brews tea from herbs to give to the ill? Does spinning thread faster and better prove that a person is a witch? Does speaking to a cat indicate witchcraft? These are the charges that face the protagonist in Ann Petry's *Tituba of Salem Village*.

Contrasts in setting suggest the drama that follows. Petry describes two slaves who are living in comparative freedom by a sparkling sea on the coral-encrusted coastline of Barbados. Tituba and her husband lose their fairly permissive owner in Barbados and in his place acquire a solemn, dark-clothed minister from Boston. The setting changes rapidly from the tropical home to a dark ship that is taking the slaves to New England.

Petry completes the change in setting when she describes the minister's house in Salem. Rotten eggs on the doorstep of the gloomy, neglected building greet Reverend Parris, his family, and the two slaves to their new home. Soon, people in the town are muttering threats, teenage girls are becoming hysterical, and townspeople are testifying that Tituba can transform herself into a wolf or travel without her body. Tituba's crime is not witchcraft. Instead, she is not only a strange black person in a predominantly white community but also a more capable and intelligent person than many of the people around her.

This book develops insights into the consequences of inhumanity, regardless of time or place. Readers are encouraged to see and feel danger in mass accusations and a fear in people to defend what they know is right. Compare Petry's characterization and plot development with Patricia Clapp's in *Witches' Children: A Story of Salem*, which relates the Salem experience through the eyes of a bound girl.

The free white protagonist in Elizabeth George Speare's *The Witch of Blackbird Pond* comes from Barbados, but Kit's life is quite different from Tituba's. Contrasts between the people in Kit's early childhood environment and the people in New England encourage readers to anticipate the conflict. On Barbados, Kit was raised by a loving grandfather, who encouraged her to read history, poetry, and plays.

After the death of her grandfather, Kit travels to New England to live with her aunt. Several experiences on the ship suggest that her former lifestyle will not be appropriate for her new world. For example, when Kit tries to discuss Shakespeare with a fellow passenger, he is shocked because a girl should not read such things: "The proper use of reading is to improve our sinful nature, and to fill our minds with God's holy word" (p. 28). An even harsher response occurs after she jumps into a harbor and swims to rescue a child's doll. (The Puritans believe that only guilty people are able to stay afloat.)

When Kit's behavior in the Puritan village remains consistent with her earlier behavior, she raises the suspicions of the townspeople. When sickness breaks out in the town, the people believe that they are bewitched and blame Hannah, a Quaker believed to be a witch. Kit risks her life to warn her friend, and they escape before Hannah's cottage is burned by angry men.

Kit's action incurs the wrath of the settlement, and she is arrested for witchcraft. The charges brought against her are similar to those brought against Tituba. Unlike Tituba, however, Kit has friends and family who stand by her and assist in her acquittal. She learns that it is important to choose one's friends and then to stand by them.

The protagonists in Petry's and Speare's books have courage, high spirits, and honor in trying circumstances. Both remain true to their beliefs, even when faced with hostility and superstition. They cry out against injustices around them. Because of their actions, a few people realize the consequences of blind fear and hatred.

Various attitudes of the times and conflicts caused by the social and religious beliefs of Puritan Boston create person-against-society conflicts in Paul Fleischman's *Saturnalia*. Fleischman's characters strive to survive in a society that is suspicious of knowledge, education, and books; mistrustful of Native Americans; and filled with prejudice. Fleischman develops many of the same themes found in the stories about the Salem witch-hunts.

Consider the following themes developed in historical fiction about the Salem witch-hunts. What consequences of inhumanity and persecution are developed in other time periods? What historical events coincide with such persecution?

1. Prejudiced persecution of others is a frightening and destructive social phenomenon.

2. People seek freedom from persecution.

3. Moral obligations require some people to defend the rights of others.

The American Revolution

The inhabitants of the thirteen American colonies founded by the British came from different countries and had differing sympathies and practices. They did, however, have several strong antagonisms in common. They shared a fear of the native peoples of North America; they went through a period when they shared a dread of French conquest; and they came to conflict with their ruler, the British crown. Although British subjects, the colonists had

no elected representatives in the British Parliament that made decisions affecting their lives. For example, a series of demands made by the British government hastened the uniting of the colonies. In 1765, Britain tried to raise money by passing the Stamp Act, which placed a tax on all paper used in the colonies and declared all unstamped documents to be legally void. Then, the British demanded that British soldiers in the colonies be quartered by the colonists themselves. In 1773, when several British ships bearing tea arrived in Boston Harbor, the Bostonians would not accept the shipment. They refused to pay taxes without the right to vote for those who would represent them. Colonists disguised as Indians boarded the ships and dumped the tea into the harbor. The British Parliament responded by closing Boston Harbor, blocking it from trade. The sympathies of many colonists were in accord with the goal of independence from Great Britain.

Samuel Adams and others like him rallied the colonists in support of this cause. The Declaration of Independence and the long years of the Revolutionary War soon followed—an exciting time in American history. We are all familiar with the famous leaders of this period, but as Elizabeth Yates (1974) points out, many other Americans whose names we do not know played dynamic roles in creating a new nation:

Those who lived in small towns and villages and on distant farms, who thought and talked about events and made their feelings known: men who left their stock and crops and marched off to fight because they were convinced of the rightness of the stand that had been made, women who took over the work of the farms along with the care of their homes and families. Their names made no news. They did no particular acts of heroism, except as the living of each day was heroic in itself. Hard work they knew well, and hardship they could endure. Giving their lives or living their lives, they were as much the foundation of the new nation as were those whose names have long been known. (p. 6)

While famous people are found in the backgrounds of much historical fiction about the American Revolution that has been written for children, everyday people are the heroes of most of such books. In general, two types of stories are written about the revolutionary period: (1) tales about those who defend the home front while others go off to war and (2) tales about males and females who become actively involved in the war itself.

The best-known children's story about this period is Esther Forbes's *Johnny Tremain*. Forbes creates a superbly authentic setting. Paul Revere and Samuel Adams play important parts in the story, but a silversmith's apprentice named Johnny and other boys like him are the heroes. Through Johnny's observations, actions, and thoughts, Forbes emphasizes the issues of the times, the values of the people, and the feelings about freedom. Johnny discovers the political thinking of the time when he hears a minister preach sermons filled with anger against taxation without representation, delivers messages for the secret anti-British Boston Observers, and rides for the Boston Committee of Correspondence.

Forbes's writing style creates believable action and dialogue, as in this excerpt from a speech calling the rebels to action:

Friends! Brethren! Countrymen! That worst of Plagues, the detested tea shipped for this Port by the East Indian Company, is now arrived in the Harbour: the hour of destruction, of manly opposition to the machinations of Tyranny, stares you in the Face; Every Friend to his Country, to Himself, and to Posterity, is now called upon to meet. (p. 107)

Johnny is one of the "Indians" who throw the tea into Boston Harbor. He experiences the anger and resulting unity when British troops close the harbor. He is there when British troops and colonial rebels clash at Concord. Unhappily, he is also there when his best friend dies. He makes the discovery that a sixteen-year-old is considered a boy in times of peace but a man in times of war. As a man, he has the duty to risk his life for what he believes.

Consider the themes and the historical facts from this period. Why do you think the following themes are developed in the literature? How and why are these themes similar to or different from themes in stories about other wartime periods?

1. Freedom is worth fighting for.

2. Strong beliefs require strong commitments.

Early Expansion of the United States and Canada

Many Europeans who came to America during its early existence were escaping from poverty or the lack of freedom in their former lands. For example, the Irish potato famine of 1846–1851 devastated the people and resulted in approximately two million people emigrating to North America. Authors who write about this period focus on themes related to survival of the physical and emotional being, the importance of retaining family ties, and the need for friends in times of severe strife.

As more and more settlers came to America, a need for additional land became evident. Many settlers headed away from the Atlantic coastline into the rolling, tree-covered hills to the west, north, and south. These settlers had something in common: With courage, they sought freedom and land. Some settlers developed friendly relationships with the Native Americans,* and others experienced hostilities. It was not uncommon for settlers to be captured by Indians and taken into their tribes, sold as slaves, or held for ransom. Many abductions, however, were in retaliation for settlers' attacks.

---

*This book primarily uses the term *Native Americans* to denote the people historically referred to as *American Indians*. The term *Indian* is sometimes used interchangeably with *Native American* and in some contexts is used to name certain tribes of Native Americans.

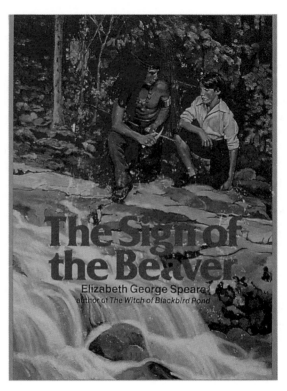

Survival and friendship are important in this story set in the 1700s. (From The Sign of the Beaver, *by Elizabeth George Speare. Copyright © 1983 by Elizabeth George Speare. Reprinted by permission of Dell Publishing Company.)*

Stories about early pioneer expansion are popular with children, who enjoy vivid characters and rapid action. The young characters may be popular with children because they often show extraordinary courage and prove that they can be equal to adults. Many of the stories depict strong family bonds. Vivid descriptions of the new land encourage readers to understand why a family is willing to give up a secure environment to live on a raw and dangerous frontier. Person-against-nature conflicts often appear in these stories. Person-against-self conflicts occur when characters face moral dilemmas, such as racial prejudice.

Themes of friendship, faith, moral obligation, working together, and love for land are found in Elizabeth George Speare's *The Sign of the Beaver*. The Maine wilderness in the 1700s can be either an antagonist or a friend. Matt, the thirteen-year-old main character, faces a life-and-death struggle when his father leaves him alone to guard their frontier cabin through the winter. Without food or a gun, Matt confronts a harsh natural environment, fear of the local Indians, and the possibility that he may never see his parents again. In spite of conflicts about the ways in which white settlers are changing their land, a Penobscot boy befriends Matt and teaches him how to survive.

The need to believe in oneself and the importance of retaining and respecting one's own beliefs are themes developed in Janet Lunn's person-against-society and person-against-self conflicts set in Hawthorn Bay, Ontario. Lunn's *Shadow in Hawthorn Bay,* winner of the Canadian children's literature award, follows fifteen-year-old Mary Urquhart as she leaves her Scottish highlands on the shores of Loch Ness to try to find and help her cousin in Canada. As Mary tends sheep in Scotland, she hears her cousin Duncan calling her to come to him. She does not consider this unusual, even though Duncan is over three thousand miles away. Her actions and the belief of her Scottish family make her ability to see into the future believable. This same ability, referred to as second sight, causes her conflict when she interacts with a society that not only does not believe in her special powers but also fears and distrusts them.

Lunn develops a related person-against-self conflict as Mary fights her powers and the consequences of her visions. As part of this inner conflict, Mary must overcome her fear of going into the forest, her fear of the black water, and her belief that something evil is trapped in the bay. Mary overcomes her fears and gains the insight that she needs to believe in herself and her powers. With this realization, Lunn develops the theme of the book: It is important to keep your beliefs and ways.

The importance of maintaining religious beliefs is a theme developed in Carolyn Otto's highly illustrated *Pioneer Church.* The fictional text and illustrations are based on the history of Old Zion, a landmark building in Brickerville, Pennsylvania.

The devastation caused by the potato famine in Ireland provides the background for Patricia Reilly Giff's *Nory Ryan's Song.* By writing the story through the viewpoint of twelve-year-old Nory, the author is able to develop themes associated with the importance of physical and emotional survival during times of stress and the need for family and friends.

Joan W. Blos's *A Gathering of Days: A New England Girl's Journal, 1830–32* is the fictional journal of a thirteen-year-old girl on a New Hampshire farm. Blos (1980) says that she tried to develop three types of truthfulness: "the social truthfulness of the situation, the psychological truthfulness of the characters, and the literary truthfulness of the manner of telling" (p. 371). Consequently, the characters are similar to those who stare from New England portraits. Likewise, the tone of the story is similar to that in *Leavitt's Almanac,* written for farmers, with the form and style found in journal writings of that period.

Both Elizabeth George Speare's *Calico Captive* and Lois Lenski's *Indian Captive: The Story of Mary Jemison* are stories about white girls captured by native tribespeople. Both girls face difficult conflicts and harsh circumstances, but their experiences eventually cause them to question their former prejudices. Speare's Miriam learns more about the Indians from Pierre, a *coureur des bois.* Mary Jemison, after much inner turmoil, finally decides that the Seneca are her people:

At that moment she saw Old Shagbark looking at her, his brown eyes overflowing with kindness and understanding. He knew how hard it was for her to decide. . . . She saw the Englishman, too. His lips were smiling, but his eyes of cold gray were hard. Even if she were able to put all her thoughts into words, she knew he would never, never understand. Better to live with those who understood her because they loved her so much, than with one who could never think with her, in sympathy, about anything. . . . Squirrel Woman's scowling face and even Gray Wolf's wicked one no longer held any terrors, because she understood them. (p. 268)

Books written from Native American viewpoints describe the harmful influences of an expanding white population. In *Sweetgrass,* a winner of the Canadian Library Association's Book of the Year Award, Jan Hudson focuses on the struggle for maturity of a young Blackfoot girl as she faces a life-and-death battle in 1837. Smallpox, the "white man's sickness," results in hunger and death. The themes in *Sweetgrass* are that it is important to honor moral obligation toward others and that it is important to retain one's dreams.

Hudson employs figurative language involving signs and omens that are meaningful to the characters and that reinforce themes related to retaining one's identity and meeting obligations toward family members. For example, the main character considers the importance of her name. She believes that it is appropriate because sweetgrass is "ordinary to look at but it's fragrant as the spring" (p. 12). Later, her grandmother tells her that sweetgrass has the power of memories. As Sweetgrass considers her future, readers discover that she is joyfully approaching womanhood. She says, "I felt mightier than a brave. . . . I felt I was holding the future like summer berries in my hands" (p. 26). Instead of allowing the signs and omens to control her life, Sweetgrass uses them to overcome taboos and to help her family in a time of great trouble. She decides, "I would make Father do what I wanted. I would find the signs, the power to control my own days. I would make my life be what I wanted" (p. 15).

The themes in books of historical fiction about the early expansion of the United States vary considerably. Consider the following themes. Why do you think that authors who write stories about this period chose them? How do these themes compare to themes found in different time periods? Are the themes significant today?

1. Friendship and faith are important.
2. People long for their own land and the freedom that ownership implies.
3. People will withstand great hardships to retain their dreams.
4. Strong family bonds help physical and spiritual survival.
5. Prejudice and hatred are destructive forces.
6. The greatest strength comes from within.
7. Moral obligations require personal commitment.

ISSUE Unbalanced Viewpoints in Historical Fiction

Reporting of history may change depending upon the viewpoint of an author. This is also true in the writing of historical fiction. Too many frontier books are told from the perspective of the white settlers rather than from the perspective of the Native Americans. In this context, some critics fear that children will not realize the hardships experienced by the Native Americans or the contributions that the Native Americans made. Stories from the perspective of the white settlers emphasize kidnappings of white children, attacks on wagon trains by warring tribes, the burning of white settlements, and rescues of settlers by soldiers. Many frontier heroes created their reputations as Indian fighters.

Some critics believe that historical fiction about the settlement of North America should include more stories told from the native perspective. These stories might include kidnappings of Native American children by white settlers or emphasize the reasons for the kidnappings of white children. The stories might portray the numerous peaceful tribes, who lived in harmony with settlers. They might emphasize the diversity of the Native American cultures. Students of children's literature should consider the viewpoints of authors and the consequences of unbalanced narratives of other time periods, including narratives about early explorers, the Roman invasion of Britain, religious freedom and the settlement of America, the Revolutionary War, the Civil War, and World War II.

Unbalanced viewpoints may be particularly harmful when presenting stories with a World War II Holocaust setting. Leslie Barban[1] emphasizes the importance of viewpoint in this literature when she states:

George Santayana once said, "Those who cannot remember the past are condemned to repeat it." This famous adage has proved itself to be true in many ways. Children's rooms in public libraries and school media centers across the nation house many important and memorable books not only about the Holocaust but about all types of racial prejudice. However, the Holocaust is often not discussed: many parents believe the subject will depress children, librarians often choose noncontroversial titles for booktalking, and teachers often feel that it's too disturbing or inappropriate to discuss in the classroom. Furthermore, some children are being told that the Holocaust is folklore and that the mass murder of 11 million people never happened. History textbooks mention it, but any true deliberation on the subject seems too much to ask of children. Is it? (p. 25)

In addition to evaluating the balance in historical fiction and in literary discussions, you should encourage students to evaluate and authenticate the historical accuracy in historical fiction. According to the findings of a study in *The Nation's Report Card*,[2] fourth-, eighth-, and twelfth-grade students "have a limited grasp of U.S. history." In addition, the study calls for assignments that encourage "thoughtful analytical essays" (p. 4). Evaluating and authenticating the historical accuracy in historical fiction and historical biography encourage thoughtful analytical essays.

As you consider the issue of unbalanced viewpoints and accuracy in historical fiction and the findings of *The Nation's Report Card*, what do you think is the role of historical fiction? What viewpoints should be expressed by the authors of historical fiction? How could you develop a balanced viewpoint of a historical time period through the use of historical fiction?

---

[1]Barban, Leslie. "Remember to Never Forget." *Book Links* 2 (March 1993): 25–29.

[2]Knight-Ridder News Service. "Most Students Have Limited Grasp of History, Study Finds." Bryan, College Station: *Eagle* (April 3, 1990): 1–4.

Slavery and the Civil War

In the early centuries of American history, white slave traders brought hundreds of thousands of black Africans to this continent in chains and sold them on auction blocks as field workers, house servants, and skilled craftspeople. Many people in both the North and the South believed that slavery was immoral; therefore, unable to pass laws against it, they assisted slaves in their flight toward Canada and freedom.

Helping runaway slaves was a dangerous undertaking, especially after the passage of the Fugitive Slave Act in 1850 made it a crime. Handbills offering rewards for the return of certain slaves added to the danger by urging slave catchers to hunt for suspected runaways. Because of the dangers and the need for secrecy, an illicit network of people dedicated to assisting fugitive slaves linked the North and South. Free people led the fugitives from one safe hiding place to another on each part of their journey along the Underground Railroad to Canada.

Conflicts between northern and southern interests that had emerged during the Constitutional Convention increased in the 1850s and led to the outbreak of the Civil War in 1861. The United States was torn apart. In some cases, relatives were on opposite sides of the conflict and faced one another on the battlefields of Bull Run and Gettysburg.

Some authors examine slavery and the experiences of slaves during captivity or as fugitives seeking freedom. Other authors examine the impact of the Civil War on young soldiers or on the people who remained at home. Person-against-society and person-against-self conflicts are common in historical fiction covering this period. Some characters confront prejudice and hatred and others wrestle with their consciences and discover the tragedy associated with slavery and war. Authors who create credible plots consider not only the historical events but also the conflicting social attitudes of the times. The themes developed in this literature reflect a need for personal freedom, ponder the right of one person to own another, consider the tragedies of war, and question the killing of one human by another.

The attitudes expressed toward blacks create special problems for authors who write about slavery. How accurately should historical fiction reflect the attitudes and circumstances of the times? Should authors use terms of the period that are considered insensitive and offensive today? For example, in their authors' note to *Jump Ship to Freedom*, James and Christopher Collier consider use of

The language and setting reflect the Blackfoot culture. (From
Sweetgrass by Jan Hudson. Illustration copyright © 1989 by Jan
Spivey Gilchrist. Reprinted by permission of Philomel Books, a
division of Putnam & Grosset Group.)

the word *nigger.* Although the word is considered offensive today, would avoiding it in a novel about slavery distort history? The Colliers chose to use the term in order
to illustrate their main character's change in attitude as he
develops self-respect and self-confidence and to highlight
the social attitudes of the other characters in the book.

In *Jump Ship to Freedom,* those who use the word *nigger* express racial bias toward blacks, and those who do
not are concerned with the rights and self-respect of all
humans. Consider, for example, how the slave Daniel uses
the word. At first, he refers to himself as a nigger. He considers himself unintelligent and inferior to whites and is
unable to think of himself as a person. He allows other
people's opinions to reinforce these beliefs. Self-realization
develops slowly. Daniel discovers that he can develop and
carry out a plan to recover his father's confiscated funds
and free himself, associate with people who consider him
capable and slavery immoral, meet his moral obligations
to his mother, and fight for his rights. After he makes these
personal discoveries, he refuses to call himself *nigger.*

A slave ship in which human cargo are chained
together in cramped quarters provides the setting for
Paula Fox's *The Slave Dancer.* The story is told from the
point of view of a thirteen-year-old white boy from New

Orleans who is kidnapped by slave traders to play his fife
on their ship. When the ship reaches Africa, Jessie learns
about the trade in human "Black Gold" and discovers that
in their greed for trade goods, African chiefs sell their own
people and people kidnapped from other tribes. For four
long nights, longboats bring their cargoes to the slave ship:
men and women who are half-conscious from the pressure of bodies and bruised by ankle shackles. The detailed
descriptions of the conditions on the ship are believable.
Jessie describes the holds as pits of misery, is horrified by
the low regard for human life, and is shocked when prisoners who die are thrown overboard. Jessie learns the
reason for having him aboard when slaves are dragged on
deck and forced to dance: A dead or weak slave cannot
be sold for profit, and the slave traders believe that dancing keeps their bodies strong.

This book has stirred much controversy. Some have
criticized the fact that the slaves in the book are not
treated like human beings or even given names. Many college students, however, say that while reading *The Slave
Dancer,* they realized for the first time the true inhumanity
of slavery. Fox reveals the impact of the experience on
Jessie by flashing ahead in time to Jessie's memories:

At the first note of a tune or a song, I would see once again as
though they'd never ceased their dancing in my mind, black men
and women and children lifting their tormented limbs in time to
a reedy martial air, the dust rising from their joyless thumping,
the sound of the fife finally drowned beneath the clanging of
their chains. (p. 176)

You may compare the descriptions in *The Slave Dancer*
with Tom Feelings's illustrations in *The Middle Passage:
White Ships/Black Cargo.*

A book written for young children explains the purposes of the Underground Railroad. F. N. Monjo's *The
Drinking Gourd* tells of a family that is part of the Underground Railroad and the role of that family in helping a
fugitive slave family escape. Even though this is an easy-to-
read book, it illustrates the importance of one family's
contributions. The dialogue between father and sons discloses the purpose of the railroad. Young readers also
experience excitement and danger as Tommy accompanies his father and an escaping black family on the next
part of their journey.

Kathryn Lasky's *True North* develops themes related
to moral obligations and the destructive forces of prejudice as a runaway slave dodges slave catchers as she travels the Underground Railroad on her way to Canada.
After a white girl discovers the runaway hiding in her
grandfather's house, the two girls join forces on this dangerous journey north. Lasky develops two strong heroines
who are committed to the abolitionist movement. In addition, the author emphasizes the restrictive roles of
women during the time period.

The impact of the Civil War on free whites in the
United States is the subject of several novels in which

Fugitive slaves follow the Underground Railroad to freedom. (From The Drinking Gourd, *by F. N. Monjo. Pictures by Fred Brenner. An I CAN READ History Book. Pictures copyright © 1970 by Fred Brenner. Reprinted by permission of Harper & Row Publishers.)*

idealistic young men come to realize that war is not simply a glamorous time of brass bands and heroic battles led by banner-carrying leaders. Stories about fighting soldiers often show men realizing the true horrors of war. Paul Fleischman's *Bull Run* is a series of short descriptive pieces that characterize the reactions of sixteen people who were involved in the first battle of the Civil War. Eight of these people express the Northern point of view and eight express the Southern point of view. Fleischman's characters allow readers to understand the many viewpoints associated with the war. The book is an excellent source for evaluating the importance of point of view when writing about historical time periods and controversial issues. Different points of view are also developed by Carolyn Reeder in *Across the Lines* as Edward and his slave and friend, Simon, struggle with issues of freedom and friendship.

One of the finest books to depict the wartime hardships and conflicts of family members who remain at home is Irene Hunt's *Across Five Aprils.* The beginning conflict is effectively introduced as members of a family in southern Illinois debate the issues related to the Civil War and choose their allegiances: Matt Creighton, the head of the family, argues that a strong union must be maintained; the majority of his sons agree with him, but one son argues that people in the South should be able to live without Northern interference.

Hunt develops a strong personal conflict. Jethro, the youngest son, is emotionally torn between two beloved brothers, one who joins the Union Army and another who fights for the Confederacy. The consequences of hatred are illustrated when young toughs burn the Creightons' barn and put oil into their well because of the family's divided allegiances. Readers also glimpse a different view of people when neighbors guard the farm, help put in the crops, and rebuild the barn.

This is the touching story of a heroic family overcoming problems at home and awaiting news of fighting sons. In spite of disagreement, the Creightons maintain strong family ties. When the son fighting for the South learns that

one of his brothers was killed at Pittsburgh Landing, he sends a message to his mother that he was not in that battle and did not fire the bullet that killed his brother. This story helps children understand the real tragedy of the Civil War: Brothers fought against brothers and neighbors against neighbors.

No Man's Land: A Young Soldier's Story by Susan Campbell Bartoletti is written from the viewpoint of a young Confederate soldier from the Twenty-Sixth Regiment Georgia Volunteer Infantry. The author develops themes related to the tragedy of war by describing the outcomes of the battles, the loss of friends, and the wounding of many young people. Through dialogue, the soldiers express their reasons for joining the army and their belief in the Confederate cause.

Consider the following themes developed around slavery and the Civil War. Why are so many of the themes related to overcoming great personal and social conflicts? How do these themes relate to the events and values of the times? Are they appropriate for the time period? What other time periods, if any, reflect similar themes, and what do they have in common with the Civil War period? Are any of these themes significant in contemporary life and literature?

1. War creates tragedy.
2. Moral obligations must be met even if one's life or freedom is in jeopardy.
3. Moral sense does not depend on skin color, but on what is inside a person.
4. People should take pride in themselves and their accomplishments.
5. Prejudice and hatred are destructive forces.
6. People search for freedom.
7. Personal conscience may not allow some people to kill others.
8. Strong family ties help people persevere.

The Western Frontier

The American frontier was extending farther and farther west in the 1800s. White Americans were giving up their settled towns and farms in the East to make their fortunes in unknown territories. Former slaves saw the frontier as a place to make a new start in freedom, and Asian immigrants to the West Coast moved inland to work on the railroads that were beginning to span the Great Plains. The Homestead Act of 1862 promised free land to settlers willing to stake their claims and develop the land. Stories of rich earth in fertile valleys caused families to travel thousands of miles over prairies and mountains to reach Oregon.

Sixteen different characters present their perspectives about the first battle of the Civil War. (From Bull Run, *text copyright © 1993 by Paul Fleischman. Jacket art copyright © 1993 by David Frampton/jacket copyright © 1993 by HarperCollins Publishers. Used by permission of HarperCollins Publishers.)*

Whether the pioneers stopped in the Midwest or went along the Oregon Trail, the journey was perilous. They fought nature, battling blizzards, dust storms, mountain crossings, and swollen rivers. They fought people as they met unfriendly Native Americans, outlaws, and cattle ranchers who did not want them to farm. Some demonstrated noble qualities as they helped each other search for new land and made friends with the Native Americans whom they encountered. Others demonstrated greed and prejudice in their interactions with other pioneers and Native Americans.

Native peoples themselves were experiencing a time of trauma. Outsiders invaded their ancient territories, staking claims to land that had once been without ownership or boundaries, and killing the buffalo and other wild animals on which the people relied for sustenance. The American government had begun its campaign to relocate Native Americans onto reservations that were minuscule in size and resources compared with the rich stretches of prairie and mountain that had long been the native people's domain.

This period of American history—with its high hopes, dangers, triumphs, and tragic conflicts—still cap-

tures the imagination of Americans. Stories about pioneer America are popular with children, as exemplified by the continuing interest in books such as Laura Ingalls Wilder's "Little House" series. Historical fiction for children includes three general types of stories about this period: (1) adventure stories in which the characters cross the prairies and mountains, (2) stories about family life on pioneer homesteads, and (3) stories about interactions between Native Americans and pioneers or Native Americans and military forces.

Authors who write about crossing the continent explore people's reasons for moving and their strong feelings for the land. Self-discovery may occur in young characters who begin to understand their parents' motivations and values. Detailed descriptions allow readers to understand the awesome continent as both inspiration and antagonist. Stories set on homesteads often develop relationships in which families seek to achieve their dreams. Like earlier stories about Native Americans and colonial settlers, these stories include tales of captive children and of the harsh treatment of Native Americans by white people who alter a traditional way of life.

Moving West. Barbara Brenner's *Wagon Wheels* is an enjoyable book for young readers. Based on fact, it tells about an African American pioneer family that leaves Kentucky after the Civil War and moves to Kansas to receive land under the Homestead Act. The family develops a friendly relationship with members of an Indian tribe, without whose help they would have starved. Young children enjoy the story because it shows that pioneer children were courageous: Three boys survive a prairie fire and travel over one hundred miles to join their father. This is one of the few books written about African Americans as a part of the frontier experience.

Two other books written for young readers follow pioneer families as they journey westward. Brett Harvey's *Cassie's Journey: Going West in the 1860s* develops the dangers and hardships as well as the close relationships of pioneers traveling from Illinois to California. The illustrations reinforce the need to work together if the families are to survive. Kerry Lydon's *A Birthday for Blue* tells about a pioneer boy who spends his seventh birthday traveling westward by covered wagon.

Honoré Morrow tells the story of earlier pioneers to the far West in *On to Oregon!,* a book for older children. Morrow's novel about pioneers from Missouri in the 1840s is more than an adventure story about crossing the continent; it is also a psychological story about the challenge of surviving in harsh circumstances. After his parents die on the trail, thirteen-year-old John Sager becomes head of the family and leads his brothers and sisters on to Oregon over a thousand miles of treacherous mountains, canyons, and rivers. The people in the wagon train do not want responsibility for the Sager children and plan to send them back East.

Morrow shows the strength of the father's dream by describing John's actions. John refuses to forfeit his father's dream; he works out a scheme so that the people think that he and his siblings will be traveling with Kit Carson. The children secretly pack their goods on oxen and head out on the lonely trail. The natural environment becomes the chief antagonist against which the children must struggle before reaching a warm, gentle valley in the Oregon of their dreams.

Morrow looks at the contributions of people who made westward expansion possible. Consider, for example, the possible impact of Morrow's closing statements:

You and I will never hear that magic call of the West, "Catch up! Catch up!" We never shall see the Rockies framed in the opening of our prairie schooner and tingle with the knowledge that if we and our fellow immigrants can reach the valleys in the blue beyond the mountains and there plow enough acreage, that acreage will belong forever to America. (p. 235)

Kathryn Lasky's *Beyond the Divide*, a story of survival set in the ruggedness of the far West just before the Civil War, develops themes related to the destructive nature of greed and prejudice and the constructive power of dreams, hope, and moral obligations. Louise Moeri effectively develops similar themes in *Save Queen of Sheba*, as twelve-year-old King David and his young sister Queen of Sheba (named after biblical characters) survive a Sioux raid and set out alone across the prairie in hope of finding the wagons that separated from their portion of the wagon train. Moeri effectively demonstrates the strength of King David's feeling of responsibility by developing his varied emotional responses during several emotionally and physically draining experiences.

The western frontier of the 1820s is the focus for Robert McClung's fictionalized biography of a legendary trapper in *Hugh Glass, Mountain Man*. Maps help readers follow the expedition and trace the route of Hugh Glass after he is attacked by a grizzly bear and then left for dead by his fellow trappers. The story follows a sequence of betrayal, survival, search for revenge, and ultimate forgiveness. McClung develops contrasts through the use of flashbacks. McClung also develops a wide variety of characters, including both friendly and hostile Native Americans and loyal and greedy trappers.

One of the more humorous western frontier stories is Kathleen Karr's *The Great Turkey Walk*. In 1860 a young man and several friends herd a flock of about a thousand turkeys from Missouri to Denver. The letter sent back to the person who loaned them money provides a summary of their adventures:

Well, I made it to Denver. . . . Along the way we also picked up Jabeth, met my long-lost pa and his no-good thieving gambler friend Cleave, and saved Lizzie from the godforsaken prairie. But what you're probably truly interested in hearing about is the turkeys. You'll never believe it, but they sold for six dollars the bird! The way I figure it, it comes out like this:

930 sold at $6, for $5,580
21 lost or stolen but paid back at $5, for $105
16 shot by U.S. Cavalry, eaten by coyotes, or given as a free-will gift to Pottawattomie (that's peaceful, hunting and farming Indians.)
33 saved for my new flock. (p. 196)

He then asks that any mail be sent to The Great Turkey Five Ranch, Denver, Kansas Territory.

Pioneer Family Life. Many stories about pioneer life depict the power of a family that is working to conquer outside dangers and build a home filled with love and decency. One author in particular has enabled children to vicariously experience family life on the frontier. Laura Ingalls Wilder, through her "Little House" books, re-created the world of her own frontier family from 1870 through 1889. The "Little House" books have sold in the millions and received literary acclaim. A popular television series introduced the Ingalls family to millions of new friends.

The first book, *Little House in the Big Woods*, takes place in a deep forest in Wisconsin. Unlike the settings in many other pioneer stories, this setting is not antagonistic. Although the woods are filled with bears and other wild animals, the danger never really enters the log cabin in the clearing. Any potential dangers are implied through Pa's stories about his adventures in the big woods, told in a close family environment inside the cabin. Other descriptions of family activities also suggest that the environment, while creating hard work for the pioneer family, is not dangerous. The family clears the land, plants and harvests the crops, gathers sap from the sugar bush, and hitches up the wagon and drives through the woods to Grandpa's house.

Wilder focuses upon the interactions of the family members. Pa's actions, for example, imply that he is a warm, loving father. After working all day, he has time to play the fiddle, play mad dog with the children, and tell stories. Likewise, Ma takes care of the physical needs of the children but also helps them create paper dolls. The impact of what it means to live in the relative isolation of the frontier, where a family must be self-sufficient, is also implied through the children's actions and thoughts: They feel secure when the attic is hung with smoked hams and filled with pumpkins, they are excited when they get new mittens and a cloth doll for Christmas, and they are astonished when they visit a town for the first time and see a store filled with marvelous treasures.

In other "Little House" books, Laura and her family leave the big woods of Wisconsin to live in the prairie states: Kansas, Minnesota, and South Dakota. The children go to a one-room school, build a fish trap, have a grasshopper invasion, worry when Pa must walk three hundred miles to find a job, and live through a blizzard. Wilder's description of the winter in *Little Town on the Prairie* encourages modern children to share the experience:

All winter long, they had been crowded in the little kitchen, cold and hungry and working hard in the dark and the cold to twist enough hay to keep the fire going and to grind wheat in the coffee mill for the day's bread. All that long, long winter, the only hope had been that sometime winter must end, sometime blizzards must stop, the sun would shine warm again. (p. 3)

When Laura gets her first job in the little town of De Smet, South Dakota, she earns twenty-five cents a day and her dinner for sewing shirts. Unselfishly, she saves this money to help send her sister Mary to a college for the blind in Vinton, Iowa. The series ends with stories about Laura's experiences as a schoolteacher, her marriage to Almanzo Wilder, and their early years together on a prairie homestead. One reason that children like these books so much is the feeling of closeness that they have with Laura.

Carol Ryrie Brink's *Caddie Woodlawn* presents another loving frontier family. The time and setting are similar to those of the first "Little House" book: the last half of the nineteenth century in Wisconsin. In fact, the real Caddie, Brink's grandmother, lived approximately thirty miles north of where Laura Ingalls Wilder was born. Caddie is a warm-hearted, brave, rambunctious girl who loves to play in the woods and along the river with her brothers. She is also a friend of Native Americans in the area.

In one dramatic situation, Caddie jumps on a horse and rides through the night woods to warn her friend Indian John about a plot by some settlers to attack John's people. Caddie's experiences differ from present-day ones, but her worries about growing up are similar to those of any girl, no matter when she lives. With Caddie, children know that everything will be all right:

When she awoke she knew that she need not be afraid of growing up. It was not just sewing and weaving and wearing stays. It was a responsibility, but, as Father spoke of it, it was a beautiful and precious one, and Caddie was ready to go and meet it. (p. 251)

Patricia MacLachlan's *Sarah, Plain and Tall* is a more recently published book about pioneer family life. In this book for younger readers, MacLachlan develops the strong need for a loving mother and a happy family life and introduces the children's need for singing in the home by contrasting the singing that took place before the mother's death with the quiet, sad atmosphere that dominates life after the mother's death. The father's needs are revealed through his actions: He places an advertisement for a wife in an eastern newspaper, in response to which "plain and tall" Sarah enters the family's life.

The children's need for a mother and a happy home is reflected in their desire for singing, in their rereading of Sarah's letters until the letters are worn out, their desire to be perfect for Sarah, their frightened reactions when Sarah misses the sea, their trying to bring characteristics of the sea into their prairie farm, and their complete happiness when they realize that Sarah will stay on the prairie. MacLachlan's Sarah is a strong, loving, independent pioneer

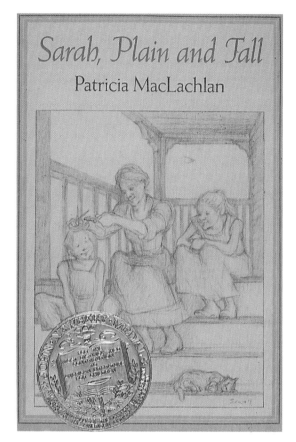

The need for warm family relationships provides the focus for this frontier story. (From Sarah, Plain and Tall, *by Patricia MacLachlan, Jacket art copyright © 1985 by Marcia Sewall. Reprinted by permission of HarperCollins.)*

woman who discovers that her love for her new family is stronger than her feelings of loneliness for the sea. Like Wilder's and Brink's, MacLachlan's characters may seem real because she drew them from her own family history.

Paul Fleischman's *The Borning Room* follows the happenings in a room on an Ohio farm. Family members experience both birth and death in a room set aside for such special occasions. Fleischman focuses on a baby born in 1851 and proceeds through her experiences on the Ohio frontier, through the life cycle of birth, marriage, and death. The time period between Georgina's birth and death allows Fleischman to include happenings that were influenced by changes in history, such as runaway slaves, the Civil War, and the introduction of chloroform. The book concludes as the now older lady, Georgina, awaits her own death in the borning room and thinks about the changes that have happened in the years between 1851 and 1918. In this conclusion, Fleischman encourages readers to understand the changes that have taken place in this one character's life and on the Ohio frontier:

I was born in this same month of January. The day might have looked precisely like this one. What a lot, though, has changed between that day and this. Automobiles, telephones, electric lights. And yet, nothing's changed. Here it is 1918 and a woman still can't vote. Over in Europe, we're fighting the Kaiser. A new set of buglers and battles. More dying. It's Shiloh and Vicksburg all over again. But you're too young to know that war. . . . I've got a grandson scuttling through the trenches and a daughter doctoring the wounded. And a son who teaches music at Princeton by day and writes pacifist pamphlets at night. That's Virgil you hear sawing wood. He alone of the four stayed here, as I did. (p. 100).

In *The Winter Room*, Gary Paulsen uses the stories told by family members through the long winter months on a northern farm. Paulsen encourages readers to see, hear, and feel the power of the stories and the memories revealed. He uses a sequence that follows the activities on a farm from spring through winter. The winter nights, however, bring out the stories. The family sits around the stove and watches the fire through the mica windows in the door and wait for the magic that begins, "It was when I was young . . . " (p. 69). Paulsen shows that stories provide a way to learn about others and to gain feelings of self-worth.

In a book that stresses self-realization, Jennifer L. Holm places her heroine in *Our Only May Amelia* within a Finnish American family on the Washington frontier in 1899. The author based her character on the life of her great-aunt, whose diary she found in an old suitcase. This actual source allows the author to develop settings, conflicts, and characters that are authentic for the time period. Readers will be enticed by adventures such as being trapped on a rope bridge with a growling cougar approaching from one end and a rushing river below.

Pioneers and Native Americans. The West Texas frontier of the 1860s provides the setting for Patricia Beatty's *Wait for Me, Watch for Me, Eula Bee.* The book tells of the capture of two farm children by Comanche and Kiowa Indians, the subsequent escape of the older boy, the changing loyalties of the very young girl who learns to love her Comanche foster parent, and her rescue by her brother. Beatty's descriptions of camp life, food, travel, and behavior create a vivid picture of the period. The author's notes list the sources for her information on Comanche and Kiowa tribes and their treatment of captives.

While Beatty depicts the Comanche as leading a harsh life built on raiding and warfare, she also depicts the value that the Comanche place on children. The little girl and her Comanche foster parent develop a warm, loving relationship. Sadness in this book stems from the tragic results of the lack of understanding of two cultures.

A tragic period in Navaho history, 1863–1865, is the setting for Scott O'Dell's *Sing Down the Moon.* The story of the three-hundred-mile forced march that culminates in holding Navahos prisoner at Fort Sumner, New Mexico, is told through the viewpoint of a Navaho girl, Bright Morning. O'Dell effectively uses both descriptions of physical settings and characterizations to depict tragedy. The Navahos are forced to leave their home, the beautiful

Canyon de Chelly, with its fruit trees, green grass, sheep, and cool water, for the harsh windswept landscape around Fort Sumner.

The greatest tragedy does not result from the loss of home, however, but from the loss of spiritual hope. Still, Bright Morning does not give up her dream of returning to her beautiful canyon, and O'Dell creates a thought-provoking, bittersweet ending. Bright Morning and her husband escape from the U.S. Army and return to her hidden valley. It is as she remembers it: The blossoms are on the trees, a sheep and a lamb are grazing on the green land, and the tools that she hid from the soldiers are waiting. However, a menacing shadow looms over their happiness. Readers cannot forget that the Navaho family is hiding from the soldiers whom they saw on the horizon.

In *Thunder Rolling in the Mountains*, Scott O'Dell and Elizabeth Hall write about another tragic Native American experience. The Nez Perce tribe and Chief Joseph are removed from their homeland in 1877. O'Dell and Hall develop the Nez Perce feelings for lost land and culture. The Nez Perce are moved from the Wallowa Valley in Oregon to Bear Paws in Montana and finally to reservation lands in Oklahoma. The story is told through the viewpoint of Chief Joseph's daughter.

In the foreword, Elizabeth Hall describes the immersion of Scott O'Dell in this story. O'Dell followed the trail taken by Chief Joseph in 1877 and researched the words, deeds, and recollections of the survivors who were part of this forced movement and the conflicts that occurred.

Many authors who write about the pioneer period stress the quest for and love of land and the conflicts between different cultures. Consider the following themes developed in historical fiction about pioneer America. How do the themes correspond with historical events? What other periods have similar themes? What are the similarities between times with similar themes?

1. People have moral obligations.

2. People have strong dreams of owning land.

3. Families can survive if they work together.

4. People need each other and may work together for their mutual good.

5. Battles can be won through legal means rather than through unlawful actions.

6. Hatred and prejudice are destructive forces.

7. Without spiritual hope, people may lose their will to live.

The Early Twentieth Century

Recent books of historical fiction with settings in the early 1900s often depict survival of immigrants who flee Europe or social conflicts and the Great Depression, which began in 1929. These stories stress both physical and spiritual survival as people strive to maintain pride and independence. Person-against-society and person-against-self conflicts develop when the characters experience or express racial prejudice and face financial hardships.

Even though Patricia Beatty's *Sarah and Me and the Lady from the Sea* takes place in 1894, shortly before the turn of the century, the father's bankruptcy caused by a flood is as devastating as the financial hardships caused by the Depression. Beatty shows the importance of family unity and a bond between people who are facing hardships. Beatty humorously contrasts the life of the family before and after the bankruptcy. For example, a family who has always had servants must learn to cook on a wood-burning stove, dress poultry, and wash clothes. At first, Beatty's family reflects prejudices against those who have less social standing than themselves. However, these characters show the family how to survive without servants and how to enjoy their new life.

In *No Hero for the Kaiser,* Rudolph Frank develops a strong antiwar theme through depictions of World War I and person-against-society conflict. For example, Frank suggests the destructive nature of war when he compares the peaceful Polish hamlet before and after the desolation caused by war. Person-against-society conflict is seen in the main character's conflict with the German officers and the foot soldiers' conflicts as they follow orders while dreaming of homes and families. Frank characterizes soldiers who are caught up in actions that are not of their doing. The final actions of the main character are especially effective in supporting the antiwar theme. When the supreme commander wants to honor Jan and make him a symbol for the war effort, Jan disappears, even though he is giving up personal glory. Frank develops the importance of this action through the words of one of Jan's friends:

Then Father Distelmann stood up, looked around the circle of his friends, and spoke slowly, "I knew him from the very beginning, isn't that right, Hottenrot, when we were advancing near Lodz. He always showed us the right way, always the right way. . . . I believe he's done the same thing this time." (p. 220)

The impact of the antiwar theme is strengthened when readers discover that this book was banned by Hitler.

In Karen Hesse's *Letters from Rifka,* a Jewish family flees Russia in 1919. The plot unfolds as Rifka writes letters to her cousin Tovah. The details show that degrading experiences and terror do not overcome the family's will to escape and survive. Rifka experiences additional conflict when she is prohibited from sailing to America because she has ringworm. Later, she is kept in detention at Ellis Island. Finally, after months of separation, she is reunited with her family. The story may be so believable because it is based on the true experiences of the author's great-aunt.

Anna Myers's *Fire in the Hills,* set in rural Oklahoma during World War I, develops themes related to prejudice and discrimination. For example, during the interactions with a conscientious objector and a German immigrant family, the author develops the themes that prejudice and

Historically accurate settings add to this World War I story. (From No Hero for the Kaiser *by Rudolf Frank, translated from the 1931 edition by Patricia Crampton, copyright © 1986. Illustrated by Klaus Steffens. Reprinted by permission of Lothrop, Lee & Shepard.)*

discrimination are destructive forces and that there is a bond between people who experience injustice. Through the actions of Hallie, the sixteen-year-old heroine, the author also develops themes related to the importance of dreams and working for a goal as Hallie discovers that her goal to become a teacher is possible, that women deserve to find a place for themselves in the world, and that women can work together to make their desires known.

Themes related to literature of the Depression suggest that people will strive for survival of the physical body and the spirit and that monetary wealth does not create a rich life. These themes are important in Mildred Ames's *Grandpa Jake and the Grand Christmas.* Through interactions with her grandfather, a girl, Lizzie, learns that life would have no meaning without dreams. The importance of a father and son working together to help the family survive hard times is the theme of David A. Adler's picture storybook, *The Babe & I.* The fictional story depicts a boy who meets Babe Ruth while he is selling newspapers at Yankee Stadium. *A Letter to Mrs. Roosevelt* by C. Coco DeYoung is based on the author's family stories. During the Depression a young girl's intervention through a letter saves the family home. The theme emphasizes the importance of being rich in happiness and health even though money is scarce.

Mildred D. Taylor's *Roll of Thunder, Hear My Cry* explores both the subtle and the explicit racial prejudice that many white Americans expressed toward African Americans in the early twentieth century. Consider, for example, the subtle discrimination developed by Taylor. Cassie and her brother, who live in rural Mississippi, excitedly await their new schoolbooks, only to receive badly worn, dirty castoffs from the white elementary school. When Cassie's brother looks at the inside cover of his book, he sees that on its twelfth date of issue—to him—it is described as being in very poor condition and the race of the student is listed as "nigra."

The warm family life of the children gives them the strength to confront such discrimination. First, they refuse the books. Then, they create a minor accident for the bus driver, who consistently and intentionally splashes the black children's clothes with dirty water as he drives the white children to their separate school. (There is no bus service for the black school.) After the children secretly deepen one of the puddles in the road, the bus breaks an axle and its riders must walk.

Other expressions of racism portrayed in this book are far less subtle, however, and they include the family's experiences with night riders and cross burnings. Understandably, the family feels fear as well as humiliation and indignation. In a sequel to this book, *Let the Circle Be Unbroken*, Taylor helps readers see how the estrangement of white and black people from each other results from ingrained social prejudices. The family in *Roll of Thunder, Hear My Cry* owns its own land, the mother has graduated from a teacher's college, and the children consistently attend school. The family experiences injustice, but a loving environment helps protect and strengthen the members.

The experiences in William H. Armstrong's *Sounder* are harsher and filled with tragedy. An early twentieth-century family of African American sharecroppers lives in one of numerous ramshackle cabins scattered across the vast fields of the white landlord. When the poverty-stricken father steals a ham to feed his hungry family, he is handcuffed, chained, and taken to jail. The futility of protest is suggested as Sounder, the family's faithful coon dog, tries to save the father and is wounded by the white sheriff's shotgun.

Comparisons between the two incidents are developed as both the father and Sounder are gone: the father to jail and then to a succession of chain gangs, and Sounder to the woods to heal his wounds. A strong bond between man and dog is implied when Sounder returns, a crippled remnant of his former self. He does not bark until the father returns home, himself crippled by a dynamite blast in the prison quarry. The two old friends are physically and emotionally tired and have only a short life together. The final vision of the two friends is one of remembered strength, as the son, grown to manhood, recalls his father and the faithful dog as they were before the tragic happenings:

The pine trees would look down forever on a lantern burning out of oil but not going out. A harvest moon would cast shadows forever of a man walking upright, his dog, bouncing after him. And the quiet of the night would fill and echo again with the deep voice of Sounder, the great coon dog. (p. 116)

Critics of *Sounder* believe that because the dog is the only character in the book with a name, the book implies that the characters need not be respected as human beings. Critics also object to the black family's being characterized as submissive and spiritless. Others argue that the family should be nameless because the tragedy depicted in the story was one shared by many poor black sharecroppers during that period. In the later view, tragedy is seen as a strong bond between all people who experience injustice. Readers may consider both viewpoints and form their own evaluations of *Sounder*.

In *Circle of Fire*, William H. Hooks also explores the consequences of hatred and prejudice. The setting is North Carolina in the 1930s. The conflict is between the Ku Klux Klan and a group of Irish gypsies. Hooks creates a believable person-against-society conflict, telling the story through the viewpoint of an eleven-year-old boy who befriends the gypsies. Readers may wish to consider an assertion that Hooks makes in his endnote:

The Ku Klux Klan grows and expands, reaching even into the alien territory of the North. *Circle of Fire,* set in the 1930s, is about the turbulent drama that occurred when someone dared step outside that "rightful place." These same events could happen today. (p. 147)

The themes developed in historical fiction set in the early twentieth century highlight both negative and positive attitudes and values. Consider the following themes found in the literature. How do the themes relate to the historical events? Are these themes found during any other time period in historical fiction?

1. People will strive for survival of the physical body and the spirit.
2. Prejudice and discrimination are destructive forces.
3. There is a bond between people who experience injustice.
4. Monetary wealth does not create a rich life.

World War II

In 1933, Adolf Hitler took power in Germany, and Germany resigned from the League of Nations. In 1935, Hitler reintroduced conscription of German soldiers and recommended rearmament, contrary to the Treaty of Versailles. Along with a rapid increase in military power came an obsessive hatred of the Jewish people. In March 1938, Hitler's war machine began moving across Europe. Austria

Teaching with Historical Fiction **445**

sure, to a pioneer family: quilts, tools (hammer, nails, spade, hoe, grindstone), tallow candles, lengths of cotton cloth, wooden buckets, iron pots, skillets, earthenware jugs, tin lanterns, dried herbs, food (a barrel of flour; yeast; dried beans, peas, and corn; salt; sugar; dried apples; a slab of bacon), seed corn, cornhusk dolls, a china-head doll, a yoke, a churn, a spinning wheel, a fiddle, a log cabin (made from Lincoln Logs), and pictures of pioneers. Accompany these objects by displays of historical fiction, books that pioneer children might have read, and books about pioneer art, music, and crafts.

One teacher introduced some third-grade students to the pioneer period by dressing in pioneer style, greeting the students at the classroom door, and taking them on a classroom tour. By enthusiastically presenting artifacts, the teacher excited the children and made them want to know more.

Values from the Past

Children can learn about the past and relate it to the present when they identify the values held and problems overcome by people living in pioneer America. Children can compare these values and problems and the solutions of problems, as depicted in historical fiction, with those of today. The pioneer period is filled with stories that stress love of the land and the need for positive relationships among family members, neighbors, pioneers, and Native Americans, including the struggle for survival and the need for bravery. The following experiences encourage children to clarify their own values as well as those of others.

Love of the Land. Pioneers were drawn to the West because of the opportunity to own rich farmland. Some people left their homes in the East when their land no longer produced good crops. Others traveled to the West because they wanted more room or fewer neighbors. Still others acquired the free land provided under the Homestead Act (see Figure 10.1). After children have read one of the books that place this emphasis on the land (such as Honoré Morrow's *On to Oregon!,* Barbara Brenner's *Wagon Wheels,* and Harold Keith's *The Obstinate Land*), ask them to identify the reasons of the pioneers for moving and conflicts that family members felt when they were deciding whether or not to move.

At this point, use role playing to help clarify the attitudes of pioneer family members. Ask the students to imagine that the year is 1866. The Civil War ended the year before. They are living on a small New England farm. They are sitting with their immediate family and their visiting aunt and uncle at the evening meal. Their aunt begins excitedly talking about an article in the paper telling how many people are going west to claim free land provided under the Homestead Act of 1862. The aunt and uncle are ready to sell their farm, pack a few belongings, and travel to the West in a covered wagon. The aunt wants

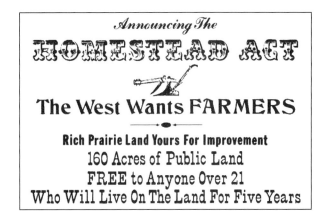

FIGURE 10.1 A poster for the Homestead Act

her brother's family to join them. Suggest that the students role-play the reactions of the different family characters and decide whether or not they should go. Based on characteristics found in historical fiction stories, the characters might express these concerns:

- *Mother:* She knows that her husband wants to own a better farm, but her family lives in the East and she doesn't want to leave it. In addition, she has lost one child, who is buried on the old farm. She is also concerned about living on the frontier away from a church, a school, and the protection of close neighbors.

- *Father:* He is unhappy with his rocky farm and the poor production it has provided. He has dreamed of a farm with rich soil to produce better crops and support his family.

- *Twelve-year-old daughter:* She is filled with the excitement of a new adventure. She wants to see new lands and Indians. In addition, she is not displeased with the prospect of leaving school for a while.

- *Seven-year-old son:* The farmhouse is the only home that he has ever known; his best friend and his relatives live in the surrounding countryside. He'd love to see some Indians and he wants to please his father but he doesn't know what to expect in a land that far from home.

Have the students consider each person's arguments and decide if they would have moved to a new land. Have the students continue by talking about what they would take with them if they decided to homestead.

Finally, draw the discussion into the present time. Do people still have a strong loyalty to the land? Do they want to own their own land? Encourage the students to provide reasons for their arguments. Place the desire for unspoiled land as well as adventure into a modern framework by having students pretend that their families are moving to a wilderness area in Alaska. Why would they want to move? Why would they not want to move? What problems do they think they would encounter before moving? How would they solve them? What problems would they encounter in the Alaskan wilderness? How would they solve them? Finally, do they believe that these problems and their solutions are similar to those experienced by pioneers?

Human Relations. Many stories about pioneer days present different ways of dealing with Native Americans and diverse attitudes toward them. The only solution that many books give is a battle between the Native Americans and whites. In contrast, Alice Dalgliesh's *The Courage of Sarah Noble* presents a family who settles on land for which the native people have been given a fair price, with the provision that they retain their right to fish in the river. Sarah's parents believe that all people must be treated fairly. Encourage children to discuss the reasons for various actions, the beliefs of the pioneers, and the consequences.

After children have read the "Massacre" and "Ambassador to the Enemy" chapters in Carol Ryrie Brink's *Caddie Woodlawn,* ask them to discuss the decision made by the settlers to attack the Indians because they thought the Indians were going to attack them. Why did the settlers reach their decision? Was it accurate? Why or why not?

Then, ask the students to place themselves in Caddie's role. If they were Caddie, would they have warned the Indians? Why or why not? What might have been the results if Caddie had not made her evening ride?

Finally, bring the discussion to contemporary times. Ask the students if there are times when people today might decide to act out of fright rather than out of knowledge. What events would they consider important enough to risk their own safety?

Books about pioneers also include many stories about need to help others. Neighbors and family members help each other and provide moral support during times of crisis. The "Little House" series, by Laura Ingalls Wilder, contains many incidents of family support and working with neighbors. *Sarah, Plain and Tall* by Patricia MacLachlan emphasizes the need for a mother and wife in pioneer times. Encourage children to discuss the values of positive relationships during both pioneer and contemporary times.

The Pioneer Environment

Pioneer stories are rich in descriptions of the homes, crafts, store goods, food, transportation, books, and pleasures of the pioneers.

Amusements of the Pioneer Family. Allowing children to take part in the same experiences that entertained pioneer children is a good way to help them feel closer to their counterparts in the past. For example, Laura Ingalls Wilder's *Little House in the Big Woods* describes happy moments that can be re-created with children:

1. For a special birthday treat, Pa played and sang "Pop Goes the Weasel" for Laura. Some of her happiest

memories were related to Pa's fiddle. Other songs mentioned in the book are "Rock of Ages" (the fiddle could not play weekday songs on Sunday) and "Yankee Doodle."

2. The family traveled through the woods to a square dance at Grandpa's house. At the dance, the fiddler played and the squaredance caller called the squares for "Buffalo Gals," "The Irish Washerwoman," and "The Arkansas Traveler."

3. After the day's work was finished, Ma sometimes cut paper dolls for the girls out of stiff white paper and made dresses, hats, ribbons, and laces out of colored paper.

4. In the winter evenings, Laura and Mary begged Pa to tell them stories. He told them about "Grandpa and the Panther," "Pa and the Bear in the Way," "Pa and the Voice in the Woods," and "Grandpa's Sled and the Pig." Enough details are included in these stories so that they can be retold to children.

A School Day with the Pioneer Family. A day in school for pioneer children (if a school was available) was quite different from a contemporary day in school. Historical fiction and other sources provide enough information about schools attended, books read, and parables memorized to interest children and re-create a school day that emphasizes spelling, reading, and arithmetic.

Modern children may be surprised that Ma in Laura Ingalls Wilder's *On the Banks of Plum Creek* considered three books on the subjects of spelling, reading, and arithmetic among her "best things" and gave them solemnly to the girls with the advice that they care for them and study faithfully.

A number of early textbooks and other stories have been reissued in their original form and can be shared with children. For example, children can read the rhyming alphabet; practice their letters; and learn to read words of one, two, three, four, and five syllables from *The New England Primer* (Ford, 1962).

Pioneer children also read and wrote maxims to practice their handwriting or as punishment for bad behavior. Joan W. Blos's *A Gathering of Days: A New England Girl's Journal, 1830–32* tells of this experience in the 1830s and lists some maxims that were written, such as:

> Speak the truth and lie not.
> To thine own self be true.
> Give to them that want.

Additional methods of instruction are described in other stories. Carol Ryrie Brink's *Caddie Woodlawn* describes an 1860 method for memorizing the multiplication tables: The children sang them to the tune of "Yankee Doodle." Re-creating a typical school day during which children read from the primer, recite and copy parables, have a spelling bee, and sing their multiplication tables would help them visualize the pioneer child's life and develop an understanding that education was considered important in earlier times.

A Day in the General Store. The country store was very different from the contemporary department store or large shopping mall. It fascinated children, however, just as malls create excitement in today's children. Laura Ingalls Wilder's first experience in a general store is described in *Little House in the Big Woods*. This store included bright materials, kegs of nails, kegs of shot, barrels of candy, cooking utensils, plowshares, knives, shoes, and dishes. In fact, it had just about everything.

A source of information about the kinds of materials that might be available to a pioneer family in the late 1800s is a reissue of an early Sears, Roebuck and Company catalogue (1997). Through these pages, children can acquire an understanding of the merchandise available and the fashions of the day. They can use the information found in such sources either to create a child-sized general store in one corner of the room or to create miniature stores in boxes.

While people may not keep the following kind of a work schedule today, the daily activities of the pioneer family associated with the house and other outside responsibilities are of interest to children.

Pioneer Chores

Wash on Monday
Iron on Tuesday
Mend on Wednesday
Churn on Thursday
Clean on Friday
Bake on Saturday
Rest on Sunday

Preparing food is mentioned in many stories. Because pioneer families could not go to the local store for supplies, they needed to prepare their own. Churning butter is one activity that children enjoy. A simple recipe for butter that children can make easily follows:

1/2 pint whipping cream
1/4 teaspoon salt
Pint jar with tight cover
Pour the 1/2 pint of whipping cream into the pint jar. Seal the cover tightly onto the jar. Shake the jar until the cream turns to butter. Remove the lid, pour off the liquid, and work out any excess liquid. Add salt and stir it into the butter. Remove the butter from jar and shape it.

According to Laura in *Little House in the Big Woods*, Ma was not always satisfied with white butter. Children may wish to experiment with the technique Ma used to add a yellow color to the butter. She rubbed a carrot over a pan that had nail holes punched across the bottom. She placed the soft, grated carrot into a pan of milk, then warmed the mixture and poured it into a cloth bag. When she squeezed the bag, bright yellow milk ran from the cloth and was added to the cream in the churn (p. 30).

Because pioneer families had no refrigerators or freezers, they had to find other ways to preserve their foods. If they lived in the North, they used nature's icebox in the winter. In Joan W. Blos's *A Gathering of Days: A New England Girl's Journal, 1830–32,* children read about chopping off a frozen wedge of soup and heating it in the kettle. Other stories describe the feeling of well-being when the pantry, shed, attic, and cellar were filled with food. In contrast, people experienced great concern when only seed corn remained between the family and starvation.

Children can learn about different ways that the pioneers preserved fruits and vegetables by reading Eliot Wigginton's *The Foxfire Book* (1972). Children enjoy drying their own apples and then having them for a special snack. Other books in this series provide details for many additional pioneer activities.

The people in pioneer fiction come alive for children who cannot actually live on a prairie homestead. Children can sing the same songs pioneer children sang, dance to the music of a pioneer fiddle, listen to the pioneer storyteller, imagine they attend a pioneer school, imagine they go to the general store, and do the chores of the homestead.

Trails in Westward Expansion

Deep ruts across a sea of prairie grass, markers along river crossings, and scars created by oxen hooves sliding down the rock sides of canyons were the pioneer equivalent of modern interstate highways. Like highways, these trails were important for moving people and commerce across the country; without them, the West could not have been opened for expansion. It is hard to imagine a thousand men, women, and children with two hundred covered wagons following such rough trails across prairies, deserts, and mountains to reach California or Oregon.

Have children discuss the purpose for the trails (such as cattle drives, wagon trails, fast movement of mail), the locations of the trails, the physical hardships found along the trails, forts built along the trails, and distances covered by the trails. Have them draw a large map of the United States, place on it the major westward trails, and then trace, using different colored pencils, the routes taken by pioneers in various books of historical fiction. The following books provide enough descriptions of locations to be of value in this activity:

1. Alice Dalgliesh, *The Courage of Sarah Noble.* Westfield, Massachusetts, to New Milford, Connecticut, by foot and horse backpack, 1707.

2. Brett Harvey, *Cassie's Journey: Going West in the 1860s.* Map shows the trail from Independence, Missouri, to Sacramento, California.

3. Honoré Morrow, *On to Oregon!* Missouri to Oregon by covered wagon, horse, and foot, 1844.

4. Laura Ingalls Wilder, "Little House" books: Pepin, Wisconsin, to Kansas, to Minnesota, and to Dakota Territory near De Smet by covered wagon, 1870s.

Research Skills

Many historical fiction books describe the sources used by the authors to develop the settings and authenticity of periods. Encouraging children to choose a specific time period and location and then to discover as much as possible about the people and their times will help the children develop respect for research skills and gain new insights.

In one class, children researched their own small city during the late 1800s. The group investigated documents at the historical society; searched old newspapers; found old family albums, journals, and letters; searched documents at the courthouse; interviewed people whose relatives had lived in the town during that time; read references to discover information about fashions, transportation, and food; and located buildings that would have existed during that time. After they had gathered this information, they pretended that they were living a hundred years earlier and wrote stories about themselves. The stories contained only authentic background information.

Additional Activities

Have children pretend that they are newspaper reporters sent from an eastern paper to discover what living on the frontier is really like. Encourage them to write news stories to send back to the newspaper. In addition, have them pretend that they can take tintype pictures to accompany their stories; have them draw pictures of the scenes that they would like to photograph.

Many pioneers moved to the West because they received encouraging letters from friends and relatives. Have children write letters to friends or relatives telling the Easterners why they should or should not sell all their property and move to _____.

Several books of historical fiction, such as Joan W. Blos's *A Gathering of Days: A New England Girl's Journal, 1830–32,* are written in journal format. Have children select a character from a historical fiction story and write several journal entries for a specific period in the story.

Many scenes from historical fiction about the pioneer period can be dramatized. The experiences of Alice Dalgliesh's Sarah Noble in playing and living with the Indian family when her father leaves her to return for his wife are interesting to dramatize.

You might try activities recommended by Frances F. Jacobson (2000) to bring a pioneer project into the twenty-first century. Jacobson describes how a group of elementary children combined an oral history project and research using primary sources to make history come alive. The teacher and librarian first provided background on family farming through class lectures and assigned reading. The students took a tour of the Farm Security Administration/Office of War Information collection of the Library of Congress American Memory website (http://lcweb2.loc.gov/ammem/fsahtml). The students searched the collection, chose a photograph, answered questions about it, and interpreted what they saw. Next they wrote stories about the people in the photographs and projected their stories into two succeeding imaginary generations. The students were asked to speculate about how the characters might have survived the Depression and about the role of farming in the lives of their descendants. Finally, they conducted oral history interviews with people involved with farming. Jacobson stated, "The project succeeded on a number of levels. First, the students had fun. They enjoyed searching the collection and debating the fate of their characters. Second, the fiction format was liberating, giving students a chance to use different literary techniques. . . . Finally, and the most important, the students got the point of the research. Even if their stories weren't always historically detailed and precise, they developed an understanding of the family farming tradition in this country, of its vibrant legacy and cyclical nature" (p. 35).

A Culminating Activity

Children enjoy sharing their knowledge about pioneer days with their parents or other children. Have a class plan a pioneer day in which the children display pioneer objects, food, arts, and crafts; demonstrate songs or dances learned; and share information gained, creative writing completed, and art projects made during their study of pioneer life and historical fiction.

Creating a Historical Fiction "Books on the Move" Source

Students in one class used Susan M. Knorr and Margaret Knorr's *Books on the Move: A Read-About-It Go-There Guide to America's Best Family Destinations* (1993) to create their own "Books on the Move" source. First, they looked at and discussed the authors' Chapter 8, "Stepping into the Past." In this chapter, the authors include children's books on such topics as history museums, dolls and toys, teddy bears, mummies, early American settlements, nineteenth-century New England, frontier living, the journey of Lewis and Clark, settling the West, gold rush days, cowhands and mountaineers, Native Americans, pueblo and cliff dwellers, striving for freedom, historic homes and sites, and various battles. In addition, the book includes destinations where people can go to see and discover more information about these time periods in history.

Next, the students conducted research on their own city and state. What historical sources did they have? What museums or other sites were found in their state? After selecting several of these sites, the students identified

Through the Eyes of a TEACHER

Robin Groce
Seventh/Eighth-Grade Teacher
Iola Junior High
Tyler, Texas

Literature Strategy Plan: Helping Children Become Knowledgeable About the Holocaust

The Holocaust is an aspect of world history well worth studying, although some people believe the horrifying nature of this historical event is too violent for children. Others agree with Eric Kimmell (1977) who says, "If the Holocaust remains incomprehensible, it will be forgotten. And if it is forgotten, it is certain to recur" (p. 84). To teach the Holocaust, Robin uses historical fiction, as discussed in this chapter, and biographies, as discussed in Chapter 12.

Robin Groce, seventh- and eighth-grade language arts teacher in Tyler, Texas, believes strongly that her students should know about this historical event—and she thinks historical fiction about the Holocaust is the best medium to make these events seem personal and real. Initially, she started by having them read Lois Lowry's *Number the Stars* (1989). However, she quickly realized that without any background on World War II and a fundamental knowledge of Judaism, they couldn't really understand the novel or the four additional ones she planned to use with the group.

Building Students' Background Knowledge

"I realized that for them to understand what was going on in these novels about the Holocaust, we needed some foundation in Judaism, the war itself, and then the events of the Holocaust, so I had the students write down everything they knew about that time period and was really surprised by their lack of knowledge. It was obvious that what they did know was very stereotyped," Robin commented.

Robin begins by using a series of picture books like Jane Yolen's *Milk and Honey* that describe some of the holidays and customs associated with the Jewish religion. The children also look at *The Jewish Kid's Catalogue* by Chaya Bernstein, which introduces specific information about their dietary system. The students also do research on the Internet. "I am always amazed at how much they learn," states Robin. "I was glad they were beginning to realize that Jewish people had very normal lives before the war. I just don't want to stereotype them as victims of the Holocaust."

Purposeful Reading and Writing

Robin next reads *Behind the Secret Window: A Memoir of a Hidden Childhood During World War II* by Nelly Toll, which is written in journal format. As she reads, she compares Toll's life to Anne Frank's. The children usually become fascinated by Frank's diary and discover there were several editions. To show them how cultural context influences a book, Robin has the group chart the additions and deletions made to the original 1952 edition regarding Anne's thoughts about other people in the Annex and her thoughts about the political situation. She wants them to think about *why* certain issues were restored or deleted. They discover, for example, that Anne's reflections on her relationship with her mother and her more graphic adolescent fantasies about Peter were not included until the 1991 edition. The group then evaluates three biographies: *Anne Frank—Beyond the Diary: A Photographic Remembrance* by Ruud van der Rol and Rian Verhoeven, *Anne Frank—Life in Hiding* by Johanna Hurwitz, and *Anne Frank* by Rachael Epstein, charting the following information as it pertains to each book:

- Author's notes (appendix, bibliography, suggested readings)
- Author's background
- Evidence of books, literature, or special interests that are associated with the main characters
- Fictional anecdotes, fake dialogue
- Evidence of an appeal to the emotional or affective domain
- Evidence of character bias/stereotypes (portrayals of victimized or sensationalized characters)
- Authenticity
- Historical context
- Personal documents (regarding self, family, friends, politics)
- Social/cultural inferences and references
- Questionable facts and opinions
- Political ideologies of advocacy and attack
- Chronology

"One biography said that the Franks were very Orthodox Jews; another stated they were Reformed. The process we use gets the students to look critically at the writing of the biographies and why the authors may have chosen one perspective over another."

Next Robin has her students experience *I Never Saw Another Butterfly*, edited by Hans Volavkov, which includes art created by children in the Terezin concentration camp in Czechoslovakia. "We first discuss how the Nazis tried to hold the camp up as a model for propaganda purposes. We compare that to propaganda we see in our own society. Then I have them write poetry and make art projects out of trash, just like the Terezin children did."

Emerging from Darkness, Half Circle
We don't really ever acknowledge the presence of evil on Earth.
We just know it's there like a black plague that hangs in the air and suffocates a
Child's laughter.
Sometimes it's worse than others, but usually evil is confined to one
Small area of a state or town where a serial killer is on the loose.

But in Germany in the years of 1939–1945 this was not the case.
Evil was airborne, and it didn't just confine itself to Germany.
It floated over Poland, Hungary, Czechoslovakia,
The U.S.S.R., the Netherlands, and France with its putrid, crazed,
Stench, that killed children's imaginations and hurt the pure of heart.
The Holocaust had begun.

Hitler's "Final Plan" murdered at least six million Jews.
Not only did Hitler want to kill all the Jewish people, but a whole rainbow of others.
Anyone who didn't fit his stone cold mold of "Master Race."
He conducted horrendous experiments on these human beings and broke their spirits.
All this as if he were no more than a child pulling the wings off a butterfly.
Hitler's nonchalant disregard for human life, and lack of humanity
Will haunt his survivors for the rest of their years.

Though the Holocaust was horrid, we must not forget it.
It is a part of all of us, not the hate, but the hope.
To know that even after such a blow people can, and did, overcome all odds,
And prosper.
It has been 50 years, and we have overcome oppression and risen out of the
Ashes like a phoenix rising from a smoldering pit of hate.

We are free.
We have emerged from the darkness and are stepping into the light of freedom.

By Christine Smith
Iola Junior High
Tyler, Texas

Reading Novels About the Holocaust

Following all this background work, Robin selects four novels for independent reading: Jane Yolen's *The Devil's Arithmetic, Friedrich* by Hans Richter, *The Man from the Other Side* by Uri Orlev, and Laura Williams's *Behind the Bedroom Wall*. Students decide which novel they want to read, then complete various response activities. For example, to document setting, they complete an activity on the five themes of geography, examining location, place (physical and human characteristics), interaction (cultural and physical), movement (of people, ideas and materials), and how regions form and change. They also collect pictures from travel brochures and other sources for a photo album of their story setting. For vocabulary development, they make vocabulary webs, choosing words they don't initially know the meaning of, putting them in their webs, and then finding synonyms for the web strands. Next the students do plot diagrams, in which they include the themes they might see emerging as the plot evolves. Robin also has them pull out some conflicts they see in the book, following the classic models of conflict: person versus self, person versus person, person versus society, and person versus nature.

"I also have them do weekly summaries about ideas they are pulling from their novels or things they might hear in their life about the Holocaust or World War II. One boy did a summary and cited a web site he found. And he had also come across an article in his Boy Scout magazine that related to the summary. I was really excited that he had collected all those sources."

Assessment

Every six weeks Robin has the children do an evaluation project in which they create a visual representation of something from their book. On the back of each project they have to include a note card with some response comments and some evidence of research. Some create movie posters, some do book jackets, and a few do videos where they interview different students. One student did computer animation with clay figures in which he responded to the plot of his novel.

"When I evaluate the projects, I look at whether they've depicted the major events that lead to the climax and they have a sense of some of the other story elements. I also look to see if they tried to further their knowledge of the time period. Most importantly, I want them to show their empathy for the people and the situations in which they found themselves. When we are finished, I have them compile another list of things they now know about World War II, Judaism, and the Holocaust. They are able to supply specifics about a much wider range of things."

Robin concludes, "It's really rewarding to see all these things they've learned . . . and it's all because of the literature. They get it all from all of these books that we studied."

 For ideas on adapting Robin Groce's lesson to meet the needs of older or younger readers, please visit Chapter 10 on our Companion Website at www.prenhall.com/norton

---

books that they could use to make connections with those sites and to learn more about the historical time period. They wrote to or visited various sites and wrote descriptions of the destinations that were similar to those developed by Knorr and Knorr. As a class, they read all of the material that they could find associated with a site near their school and then visited the site and wrote their impressions of the visit.

Finally, they published their own state source for historical sites and placed it in the school library. The activity and the book also provided motivation for family and group excursions.

Suggested Activities

 For suggested activities for teaching children with historical fiction, visit our Companion Website at www.prenhall.com/norton

Children's Literature

 For full descriptions, including plot summaries and award winner notations, of these and other titles for teaching children with historical fiction, visit the CD-ROM that accompanies this book.

Adler, David A. *The Babe & I.* Illustrated by Terry Widener. Harcourt Brace, 1999 (I:7+ R:4).

Alder, Elizabeth. *The King's Shadow.* Farrar, Straus & Giroux, 1995 (I:11+ R:7).

Aldridge, James. *The True Story of Spit MacPhee.* Viking Kestrel, 1986 (I:10+ R:6).

Ames, Mildred. *Grandpa Jake and the Grand Christmas.* Scribner, 1990 (I:8+ R:5).

Armstrong, Jennifer. *The Dreams of Mairhe Mehan: A Novel of the Civil War.* Knopf, 1996 (I:10+ R:6).

Armstrong, William H. *Sounder.* Illustrated by James Barkley. Harper & Row, 1969 (I:10+ R:6).

Auch, Mary Jane. *Frozen Summer.* Holt, 1998 (I:10+ R:5).

Avi. *The Fighting Ground.* Lippincott, 1984 (I:10+ R:6).

_____. *The True Confessions of Charlotte Doyle.* Orchard, 1990 (I:10+ R:6).

Barrett, Tracy. *Anna of Byzantium.* Delacorte, 1999 (I:10+ R:5).

Bartoletti, Susan Campbell. *No Man's Land: A Young Soldier's Story.* Blue Sky, 1999 (I:10+ R:5).

Bat-Ami, Miriam. *Two Suns in the Sky.* Front Street, 1999 (I:12+ R:6).

Beatty, Patricia. *Eight Mules from Monterey.* Morrow, 1982 (I:10+ R:6).

_____. *Sarah and Me and the Lady from the Sea.* Morrow, 1989 (I:10+ R:6).

_____. *Wait for Me, Watch for Me, Eula Bee.* Morrow, 1978 (I:12+ R:7).

Blackwood, Gary. *Shakespeare's Scribe.* Dutton, 2000 (I:10+ R:5).

Blos, Joan W. *A Gathering of Days: A New England Girl's Journal, 1830–32.* Scribner, 1979 (I:8–14 R:6).

Borden, Louise. *The Little Ships: The Heroic Rescue at Dunkirk in World War II.* Illustrated by Michael Foreman. Simon & Schuster, 1997 (I:8+ R:4).

Bradley, Kimberly Brubaker. *Ruthie's Gift.* Delacorte, 1998 (I:7–12 R:5).

Branford, Henrietta. *Fire, Bed, and Bone.* Candlewick, 1998 (I:10 + R:5).

Brenner, Barbara. *Wagon Wheels.* Illustrated by Don Bolognese. Harper & Row, 1978 (I:6–9 R:1).

Brink, Carol Ryrie. *Caddie Woodlawn.* Illustrated by Trina Schart Hyman. Macmillan, 1935, 1963, 1973 (I:8–12 R:6).

Bunting, Eve. *So Far from the Sea.* Clarion, 1998 (I:5–8).

Calvert, Patricia. *Bigger.* Scribner, 1994 (I:8+ R:5).

Carrick, Carol. *Stay Away from Simon!* Illustrated by Donald Carrick. Clarion, 1985 (I:7–10 R:3).

Clapp, Patricia. *Constance: A Story of Early Plymouth.* Lothrop, Lee & Shepard, 1968 (I:12+ R:7).

_____. *Witches' Children: A Story of Salem.* Lothrop, Lee & Shepard, 1982 (I:10+ R:7).

I = Interest by age range.
R = Readability by grade level.

Collier, James, and Christopher Collier. *Jump Ship to Freedom.* Delacorte, 1981 (I:10+ R:7).

Conrad, Pam. *My Daniel.* Harper & Row, 1989 (I:10+ R:5).

Cormier, Robert. *Other Bells for Us to Ring.* Illustrated by Deborah Kogan Ray. Delacorte, 1990 (I:8+ R:5).

Curtis, Christopher Paul. *Bud, Not Buddy.* Delacorte, 1999 (I:10+ R:5).

Cushman, Karen. *The Ballad of Lucy Whipple.* Clarion, 1996 (I:10+ R:8).

_____. *Catherine, Called Birdy.* Clarion, 1994 (I:12+ R:9).

_____. *Matilda Bone.* Clarion, 2000 (I:9+ R:8).

_____. *The Midwife's Apprentice.* Clarion, 1995 (I:12+ R:8).

Dalgliesh, Alice. *The Courage of Sarah Noble.* Illustrated by Leonard Weisgard. Scribner, 1954 (I:6–9 R:3).

DeAngeli, Marguerite. *The Door in the Wall.* Doubleday, 1949 (I:8–12 R:6).

DeYoung, C. Coco. *A Letter to Mrs. Roosevelt.* Delacorte, 1999 (I:8+ R:5).

Disher, Garry. *The Bamboo Flute.* Ticknor & Fields, 1993 (I:10+ R:5).

Dorris, Michael. *Morning Girl.* Hyperion, 1992 (I:8+ R:4).

_____. *Sees Behind Trees.* Hyperion, 1966 (I:9+ R:5).

Fleischman, Paul. *The Borning Room.* HarperCollins, 1991 (I:10+ R:5).

_____. *Bull Run.* HarperCollins, 1993 (I:10+ R:5).

_____. *Path of the Pale Horse.* Harper & Row, 1983 (I:10+ R:6).

_____. *Saturnalia.* HarperCollins, 1990 (I:12+ R:6).

Fletcher, Susan. *Shadow Spinner.* Atheneum, 1998 (I:10+ R:6).

Forbes, Esther. *Johnny Tremain.* Illustrated by Lynd Ward. Houghton Mifflin, 1943 (I:10–14 R:6).

Fox, Paula. *The Slave Dancer.* Illustrated by Eros Keith. Bradbury, 1973 (I:12+ R:7).

Frank, Rudolf. *No Hero for the Kaiser.* Translated by Patricia Crampton. Illustrated by Klaus Steffens. Lothrop, Lee & Shepard, 1986 (I:10+ R:7).

Giff, Patricia Reilly. *Lily's Crossing.* Delacorte, 1997 (I:10+ R:6).

_____. *Nory Ryan's Song.* Delacorte, 2000 (I:10+ R:5).

Graham, Harriet. *A Boy and His Bear.* Simon & Schuster, 1996 (I:9+ R:6).

Gray, Elizabeth Janet. *Adam of the Road.* Illustrated by Robert Lawson. Viking, 1942, 1970 (I:8–12 R:6).

Guarnieri, Paolo. *A Boy Named Giotto.* Translated by Jonathan Galassi. Illustrated by Bimba Landman. Farrar, Straus & Giroux, 1999 (I:5–8 R:4).

Haas, Jessie. *Westminster West.* Greenwillow, 1997 (I:11+ R:6).

Hahn, Mary Downing, *Following My Own Footsteps.* Clarion, 1996 (I:10+ R:6).

_____. *Stepping on the Cracks.* Clarion, 1991 (I:10+ R:6).

Hamilton, Virginia. *The Bells of Christmas.* Illustrated by Lambert Davis. Harcourt Brace Jovanovich, 1989 (I:8+ R:5).

Hartling, Peter. *Crutches.* Translated by Elizabeth D. Crawford. Lothrop, Lee & Shepard, 1988 (I:10+ R:6).

Harvey, Brett. *Cassie's Journey: Going West in the 1860s.* Illustrated by Deborah Kogan Ray. Holiday House, 1988 (I:7–9 R:3).

Haugaard, Erik Christian. *The Boy and the Samurai.* Houghton Mifflin, 1991 (I:11+ R:6).

_____. *Cromwell's Boy.* Houghton Mifflin, 1978 (I:11+ R:5).

Hautzig, Esther. *The Endless Steppe: A Girl in Exile.* Harper Junior Books, 1968 (I:12+ R:7).

Heide, Florence Parry, and Judith Heide Gilliland. *The House of Wisdom.* Illustrated by Mary Grandpré. DK, 1999 (I:8+ R:5).

Heneghan, James. *Wish Me Luck.* Farrar, Straus & Giroux, 1997 (I:12+ R:7).

Hesse, Karen. *Letters from Rifka.* Holt, 1992 (I:10 + R:6).

_____. *Out of the Dust.* Scholastic, 1997 (I:10 + R:6).

_____. *Stowaway.* Simon & Schuster, 2000 (I:10 + R:6).

Hill, Susan. *The Glass Angels.* Illustrated by Valerie Littlewood. Candlewick, 1992 (I:8+ R:5).

Hoestlandt, Jo. *Star of Fear, Star of Hope.* Translated from the French by Mark Polizzotti. Illustrated by Johanna Kang. Walker, 1995 (I:7–10 R:3).

Holm, Jennifer L. *Our Only May Amelia.* HarperCollins, 1999 (I:10+ R:5).

Holub, Josef. *The Robber and Me.* Translated by Elizabeth D. Crawford. Holt, 1997 (I:8+ R:6).

Hooks, William H. *Circle of Fire.* Atheneum, 1983 (I:10+ R:6).

Howard, Ellen. *Edith Herself.* Atheneum, 1987 (I:7–10 R:4).

Hudson, Jan. *Sweetgrass.* Tree Frog, 1984, Philomel, 1989 (I:10+ R:4).

Hunt, Irene. *Across Five Aprils.* Follett, 1964 (I:10+ R:7).

Ibbotson, Eva. *Journey to the River Sea.* Illustrated by Kevin Hawkes. Dutton, 2002 (I:9+ R:5).

Johnston, Julie. *Hero of Lesser Causes.* Little, Brown, 1993 (I:10+ R:5).

Karr, Kathleen. *The Great Turkey Walk.* Farrar, Straus & Giroux, 1998 (I:7+ R:5).

Keith, Harold. *Rifles for Watie.* Crowell, 1957 (I:12+ R:7).

Kerr, Judith. *When Hitler Stole Pink Rabbit.* Coward, McCann, 1972 (I:8–12 R:3).

Kinsey-Warnock, Natalie. *The Canada Geese Quilt.* Illustrated by Leslie W. Bowman. Dutton, 1989 (I:8+ R:5).

Kirkpatrick, Katherine. *Keeping the Good Light.* Delacorte, 1995 (I:12+ R:6).

Kodama, Tatsuharu. *Shin's Tricycle.* Illustrated by Noriyuki Ando. Walker, 1995 (I:all).

Lasky, Kathryn. *Beyond the Divide.* Macmillan, 1983 (I:9+ R:6).

_____. *The Night Journey.* Illustrated by Trina Schart Hyman. Warne, 1981 (I:10+ R:6).

_____. *True North.* Scholastic, 1996 (I:12+ R:7).

Lenski, Lois. *Indian Captive: The Story of Mary Jemison.* Stokes, 1941 (I:10+ R:7).

Levitin, Sonia. *Annie's Promise.* Atheneum, 1993 (I:12+ R:6).

_____. *Journey to America.* Illustrated by Charles Robinson. Atheneum, 1970 (I:12+ R:6).

_____. *Silver Days.* Atheneum, 1989 (I:12+ R:6).

Lisle, Janet Taylor. *The Art of Keeping Cool.* Simon & Schuster, 2000 (I:9+ R:5).

Longfellow, Henry Wadsworth. *Paul Revere's Ride.* Illustrated by Adrian J. Iorio and Frederick J. Alford. Houghton Mifflin (I:8+).

Lowry, Lois. *Number the Stars.* Houghton Mifflin, 1989 (I:10+ R:6).

Lunn, Janet. *Shadow in Hawthorn Bay.* Scribner, 1986 (I:10+ R:5).

Lydon, Kerry Raines. *A Birthday for Blue.* Illustrated by Michael Hayes Albert. Whitman, 1989 (I:5–8 R:4).

Lyon, George Ella. *Borrowed Children.* Watts, 1988 (I:10+ R:5).

MacLachlan, Patricia. *Sarah, Plain and Tall.* Harper & Row, 1985 (I:7–10 R:3).

Maguire, Gregory. *The Good Liar.* Clarion, 1999 (I:9+ R:5).

Mazer, Norma Fox. *Good Night, Maman.* Harcourt Brace, 1999 (I:12+ R:6).

McClung, Robert. *Hugh Glass, Mountain Man.* Morrow, 1990 (I:10+ R:6).

McGuigan, Mary Ann. *Where You Belong.* Simon & Schuster, 1997 (I:10+ R:6).

McSwigan, Marie. *Snow Treasure.* Illustrated by Mary Reardon. Dutton, 1942 (I:8–12 R:4).

Moeri, Louise. *Save Queen of Sheba.* Dutton, 1981 (I:10+ R:5).

Monjo, F. N. *The Drinking Gourd.* Illustrated by Fred Brenner. Harper & Row, 1970 (I:7–9 R:2).

Morrow, Honoré. *On to Oregon!* Illustrated by Edward Shenton. Morrow, 1926, 1948, 1954 (I:10+ R:6).

Myers, Anna. *Fire in the Hills.* Walker, 1996 (I:10+ R:8).

Namioka, Lensey. *The Coming of the Bear.* HarperCollins, 1992 (I:9+ R:6).

O'Dell, Scott. *The Amethyst Ring.* Houghton Mifflin, 1983 (I:10+ R:6).

_____. *The Captive.* Houghton Mifflin, 1979 (I:10+ R:6).

_____. *Carlota.* Houghton Mifflin, 1977 (I:9+ R:4).

_____. *The Feathered Serpent.* Houghton Mifflin, 1981 (I:10+ R:6).

_____. *Sing Down the Moon.* Houghton Mifflin, 1970 (I:10+ R:6).

_____, and Elizabeth Hall. *Thunder Rolling in the Mountains.* Houghton Mifflin, 1992 (I:10+ R:6).

Orlev, Uri. *The Island on Bird Street.* Translated by Hillel Halkin. Houghton Mifflin, 1984 (I:10+ R:6).

_____. *The Lady with the Hat.* Houghton Mifflin, 1995 (I:12+ R:5).

_____. *Lydia, Queen of Palestine.* Translated from the Hebrew by Hillel Halkin. Puffin, 1995 (I:10+ R:4).

_____. *The Man from the Other Side.* Houghton Mifflin, 1991 (I:10+ R:6).

Otto, Carolyn. *Pioneer Church.* Illustrated by Megan Lloyd. Henry Holt, 1999 (I:all).

Oughton, Jerrie. *The War in Georgia.* Houghton Mifflin, 1997 (I:12+ R:6).

Park, Linda Sue. *A Single Shard.* Clarion, 2001 (I:10+ R:5).

Paterson, Katherine. *Preacher's Boy.* Clarion, 1999 (I:10+ R:6).

Paulsen, Gary. *The Winter Room.* Orchard, 1989 (I:8+ R:5).

Pearson, Kit. *The Sky Is Falling.* Viking, 1989 (I:10+ R:6).

Petry, Ann. *Tituba of Salem Village.* Crowell, 1964 (I:11+ R:6).

Platt, Richard. *Castle Diary: The Journal of Tobias Burgess, Page.* Illustrated by Chris Riddell. Candlewick, 1999 (I:all).

Polacco, Patricia. *The Butterfly.* Philomel, 2000 (I:6–9 R:5).

Pullman, Philip. *The Ruby in the Smoke.* Knopf, 1985 (I:10+ R:6).

Reeder, Carolyn. *Across the Lines.* Simon & Schuster, 1997 (I:9+ R:6).

_____. *Shades of Gray.* Macmillan, 1989 (I:10+ R:6).

Reiss, Johanna. *The Upstairs Room.* Crowell, 1972 (I:11+ R:4).

Rinaldi, Ann. *The Fifth of March: A Story of the Boston Massacre.* Harcourt Brace Jovanovich, 1993 (I:10+ R:6).

Rylant, Cynthia. *When I Was Young in the Mountains.* Dutton, 1982 (I:4–9 R:3).

Salisbury, Graham. *Under the Blood Red Sun.* Delacorte, 1995 (I:8+ R:6).

Sandin, Joan. *The Long Way to a New Land.* Harper & Row, 1981 (I:7–9 R:3).

Siegal, Aranka. *Grace in the Wilderness: After the Liberation, 1945–1948.* Farrar, Straus & Giroux, 1985 (I:10+ R:7).

_____. *Upon the Head of the Goat: A Childhood in Hungary 1939–1944.* Farrar, Straus & Giroux, 1981 (I:10+ R:7).

Skolsky, Mindy Warshaw. *Love From Your Friend, Hannah.* DK, 1998 (I:8+ R:5).

Snyder, Zilpha Keatley. *Gib Rides Home.* Delacorte, 1998 (I:9+ R:5).

Speare, Elizabeth George. *The Bronze Bow.* Houghton Mifflin, 1961 (I:10+ R:6).

_____. *Calico Captive.* Illustrated by W. T. Mars. Houghton Mifflin, 1957 (I:10+ R:6).

_____. *The Sign of the Beaver.* Houghton Mifflin, 1983 (I:8–12 R:5).

_____. *The Witch of Blackbird Pond.* Houghton Mifflin, 1958 (I:9–14 R:4).

Stevens, Carla. *Anna, Grandpa, and the Big Storm.* Illustrated by Margot Tomes. Houghton Mifflin, 1982 (I:6–9 R:3).

Sutcliff, Rosemary. *Blood Feud.* Dutton, 1976 (I:11+ R:8)

_____. *The Eagle of the Ninth.* Illustrated by C. Walter Hodges. Walck, 1954 (I:11+ R:8).

_____. *The Lantern Bearers.* Illustrated by Charles Keeping. Walck, 1959 (I:11+ R:7).

_____. *The Shining Company.* Farrar, Straus & Giroux, 1990 (I:11+ R:8).

_____. *The Silver Branch.* Illustrated by Charles Keeping. Walck, 1958 (I:10+ R:8).

Taylor, Mildred D. *Let the Circle Be Unbroken.* Dial, 1981 (I:10 R:6).

_____. *Roll of Thunder, Hear My Cry.* Illustrated by Jerry Pinkney. Dial, 1976 (I:10+ R:6).

Uchida, Yoshiko. *Journey Home.* Illustrated by Charles Robinson. Atheneum, 1978 (I:10+ R:5).

_____. *Journey to Topaz.* Illustrated by Donald Carrick. Scribner, 1971 (I:10+ R:5).

Vos, Ida. *Hide and Seek.* Translated by Terese Edelstein and Inez Smidt. Houghton Mifflin, 1991 (I:8+ R:5).

Westall, Robert. *Time of Fire.* Scholastic, 1997 (I:10+ R:5).

Wilder, Laura Ingalls. *By the Shores of Silver Lake.* Illustrated by Garth Williams. Harper & Row, 1939, 1953 (I:8–12 R:6).

_____. *The First Four Years.* Illustrated by Garth Williams. Harper & Row, 1971 (I:8–12 R:6).

_____. *Little House in the Big Woods.* Illustrated by Garth Williams. Harper & Row, 1932, 1953 (I:8–12 R:6).

_____. *Little House on the Prairie.* Illustrated by Garth Williams. Harper & Row, 1935, 1953 (I:8–12 R:8).

_____. *Little Town on the Prairie.* Illustrated by Garth Williams. Harper & Row, 1941, 1953 (I:8–12 R:8).

_____. *The Long Winter.* Illustrated by Garth Williams. Harper & Row, 1940, 1953 (I:8–12 R:6).

_____. *On the Banks of Plum Creek.* Illustrated by Garth Williams. Harper & Row, 1937, 1953 (I:8–12 R:6).

_____. *These Happy Golden Years.* Illustrated by Garth Williams. Harper & Row, 1943, 1953 (I:8–12 R:6).

Williams, Laura. *Behind the Bedroom Wall.* Milkweed, 1996 (I:9+ R:5).

Yates, Elizabeth. *Amos Fortune, Free Man.* Illustrated by Nora S. Unwin. Dutton, 1950 (I:10+ R:6).

Yep, Laurence. *Hiroshima.* Scholastic, 1995 (I:9+ R:4).

Yolen, Jane. *The Devil's Arithmetic.* Viking/Kestrel, 1988 (I:8+ R:5).

_____. *Encounter.* Illustrated by David Shannon. Harcourt Brace Jovanovich, 1992 (I:6–10 R:5).

MULTICULTURAL LITERATURE

A heightened sensitivity to the needs of all people in American society has led to the realization that reading and literature programs for children should include literature by and about members of all cultural groups. Literature is appropriate for building respect across cultures, sharpening sensitivity toward the common features of all individuals, and improving the self-esteem of people who are members of racial and ethnic minority groups. The English Journal Forum (1990) states: "We believe that one of our country's strengths is its diversity. We deplore the attitude that bilingualism and multiculturalism are problems to be solved rather than boons to be celebrated" (p. 15).

The need for cross-cultural understanding is increasing as a result of the demographic shifts that are occurring in the United States. For example, William Booth (1998) stresses that the United States is experiencing its second great wave of immigration. The first wave occurred between 1890 and 1920, when the immigrants came mostly from European countries such as Germany, Poland, Ireland, Hungary, and Russia. According to Booth, this immigration pattern is now changing: "The overwhelming majority of immigrants come from Asia and Latin America—Mexico, the Central American countries, the Philippines, Korea and Southeast Asia" (p. 7). Educating the children of these immigrants requires cross-cultural understanding, just as it was needed in the past. According to James Hoffman and P. David Pearson (2000), "it is projected that between 2000 and 2020 there will be 47% more Hispanic children aged 5–13 in the United States than there are today" (p. 28). These educators conclude that teachers must have knowledge about the culture and linguistic diversity that is found in schools.

Educators and critics of children's literature maintain that children should be exposed to multicultural literature that heightens respect for the individuals, as well as the contributions and the values, of cultural minorities.

Many of the multicultural literature programs that have met these goals have accomplished them through preservice or in-service education of teachers and librarians. Such education stresses evaluating, selecting, and sharing multicultural literature (Norton, 1984–1987). The tasks related to developing such programs are enormous. Universities are beginning to require courses that include selecting and using multicultural literature. Until all educators have been trained in this way, school districts must provide in-service instruction so that teachers and librarians can select and use materials that create an atmosphere of respect for all children. One of the most formidable tasks is becoming familiar with the available literature and other teaching materials. Library selection committees, teachers, and administrators must all become involved in this process.

This chapter is not intended to isolate the literature and contributions of racial and ethnic minorities from other literature discussed in this book. Instead, it places multicultural literature in a context helpful to librarians, teachers, and parents who wish to select and share such materials with children or develop multicultural literature programs.

What Multicultural Literature Is

Multicultural literature is literature about racial or ethnic minority groups that are culturally and socially different from the white Anglo-Saxon majority in the United States, whose largely middle-class values and customs are most represented in American literature. Violet Harris (1992) defines multicultural literature as "literature that focuses on people of color, on religious minorities, on regional cultures, on the disabled, and on the aged."

Although, of course, ethnic diversity in the United States is extremely great, multicultural literature is usually viewed as literature about African Americans; Native Americans*; Latino Americans, including Mexican Americans, Puerto Ricans, Cuban Americans, and others of Spanish descent or cultural heritage; and Asian Americans, including Chinese Americans, Japanese Americans, Korean Americans, Vietnamese Americans, and others. This chapter focuses on the literature of these groups. Discussion of literature on religious minorities such as the Jewish people is found primarily in the traditional literature, historical fiction, and nonfiction chapters. Literature about individuals with disabilities and the elderly is found primarily in the contemporary realistic fiction chapter.

Values of Multicultural Literature

Many of the goals for multicultural education can be developed through multicultural literature. For example, Rena Lewis and Donald Doorlag (1987) state that multicultural education can restore cultural rights by emphasizing cultural equality and respect, enhance the self-concepts of students, and teach respect for various cultures while teaching basic skills. These goals for multicultural education are similar to the following goals of the UN Convention of the Rights of the Child and cited by Doni Kwolek Kobus (1992):

1. understanding and respect for each child's cultural group identities;
2. respect for and tolerance of cultural differences, including differences of gender, language, race, ethnicity, religion, region, and disabilities;

3. understanding of and respect for universal human rights and fundamental freedoms;
4. preparation of children for responsible life in a free society; and
5. knowledge of cross-cultural communication strategies, perspective taking, and conflict management skills to ensure understanding, peace, tolerance, and friendship among all peoples and groups. (p. 224)

Through multicultural literature, children who are members of racial or ethnic minority groups realize that they have a cultural heritage of which they can be proud, and that their culture has made important contributions to the United States and to the world. Pride in their heritage helps children who are members of minority groups improve their self-concepts and develop cultural identity. Learning about other cultures allows children to understand that people who belong to racial or ethnic groups other than theirs are individuals with feelings, emotions, and needs similar to their own—individual human beings, not stereotypes. Through multicultural literature, children discover that while not all people may share their personal beliefs and values, individuals can and must learn to live in harmony.

Through multicultural literature, children of the majority culture learn to respect the values and contributions of minority groups in the United States and the values and contributions of people in other parts of the world. In addition, children broaden their understanding of history, geography, and natural history when they read about cultural groups living in various regions of their country and the world. The wide range of multicultural themes also helps children develop an understanding of social change. Finally, reading about members of minority groups who have successfully solved their own problems and made notable achievements helps raise the aspirations of children who belong to a minority group.

Images of Racial and Ethnic Minorities in the Past

Only recently have Americans begun to realize that certain books—because of their illustrations, themes, characterizations, and language—can perpetuate stereotypes and result in psychological damage or discomfort for children. In the late 1940s, Americans began to express publicly their growing objections to the use of certain stereotypes in literature. In 1965, Nancy Larrick's article, "The All-White World of Children's Books," had much impact because her research showed both that there was a lack of books about minorities and that stereotypes were found in the few available books (*Saturday Review*, 1965). Many changes in American social life and literature have occurred since then, but further improvements are needed.

---

*This book primarily uses the term *Native Americans* to denote the people historically referred to as *American Indians*. The term *Indian* is sometimes used interchangeably with *Native American* and in some contexts is used to name certain tribes of Native Americans.

Eleven years later, in 1976, Bettye Latimer cautioned that through selection of books and instructional materials, some educators continue to communicate negative messages about minorities to children. Latimer states, "If your bulletin boards, your models, and your authority lines are White, and I am Black, Latino or Native American, then you have telegraphed me messages which I will reject" (p. 156). Latimer maintains that white children are taught a distorted image of American society and are not prepared to value American society's multiracial character because they are surrounded with literature and other instructional materials that either present minorities stereotypically or make minorities invisible by omitting them entirely. Latimer also stresses that because of the comparatively small number of books written about members of racial and ethnic minorities, well-meaning librarians, teachers, and other adults are likely to accept any book that describes or pictures members of minority groups, without carefully evaluating the stories and the stereotypes that they might be fostering. She believes that adults who work with children and literature should reeducate themselves to the social values that books pass on to children. To do this, adults must learn to assess books written about children from all ethnic backgrounds.

Nine years later, in 1985, author Eloise Greenfield is even harsher in her criticism of authors who perpetuate racism and stereotypes in literature. She states that books that express racism or negative attitudes toward any group "constrain rather than encourage human development. To perpetuate these attitudes through the use of the written word constitutes a gross and arrogant misuse of talent and skill" (p. 19).

The topic of images and stereotypes in multicultural literature became an important area of research, especially in the 1970s. As you read the following sections, remember the conclusions of these researchers and consider how their research may have influenced later multicultural literature.

African Americans

Several researchers have investigated images of African Americans in children's literature, focusing on stereotypes, attitudes that white characters express toward black characters, and the importance of black characters in the literature. Dorothy May Broderick (1971), for example, analyzed American children's literature published between 1827 and 1967. She reports that the personal characteristics of African American people portrayed in these books suggested that they (1) are not physically attractive, (2) are musical, (3) combine religious fervor with superstitious beliefs, (4) are required to select life goals that benefit black people, and (5) are dependent upon white people for whatever good things they could hope to acquire. Broderick concluded that in the 140-year period she studied, African American children would find little in literature to enhance pride in their heritage and that if these

books were white children's only contacts with black people, white children would develop a sense of superiority.

Beryle Banfield (1985) reviewed stereotypes found in pre–Civil War literature and found that stories set in the plantation South of the 1800s depicted slavery as idyllic, pastoral, and beneficial for the slave. In addition, these books frequently suggested that the slaves were so contented on the plantation that they were wretched when they tried to survive as free people.

In investigating whether or not changes in attitudes toward African Americans had occurred in more recent times, Julia Ann Carlson (1969) compared American children's literature of the 1930s with that of the 1960s. She discovered that many changes in the depiction of black characters occurred between the two time periods. Although 15 percent of the books from the earlier period mentioned African American characters, these characters tended to be stereotyped. Only 10 percent of the books in the later period mentioned African American characters at all, but when they did, they tended to present black people as individuals with either a racial problem or a universal problem. Betty M. Morgan (1973) reported that the number of books with African American people as the main characters has increased markedly. This chapter discusses numerous selections of excellent African American literature that do not perpetuate stereotypes from the past. In fact, there are more new African American selections than there are for any of the other peoples discussed in this chapter. In addition, fewer of the books go out of print.

Native Americans

Native Americans fared no better than African Americans in the literature of the past. According to Mary Gloyne Byler (1977):

There are too many books featuring painted, whooping, befeathered Indians closing in on too many forts, maliciously attacking "peaceful" settlers or simply leering menacingly from the background; too many books in which white benevolence is the only thing that saves the day for the incompetent childlike Indian; too many stories setting forth what is "best" for American Indians. (p. 28)

Researchers analyzing the images of Native Americans in children's literature written in the past have identified many negative stereotypes in a large percentage of the literature. According to Laura Herbst (1977), three of the most common stereotypes characterized Native Americans as (1) savage, depraved, and cruel; (2) noble, proud, silent, and close to nature; or (3) inferior, childlike, and helpless. Terms and comparisons suggesting negative and derogatory images often reinforced such stereotypes. A white family, for example, may be said to consist of a husband, a wife, and a child; members of Native American families, in contrast, may have been called bucks, squaws, and papooses. White authors often dehumanized Native Americans by comparing them to animals. Even Native American language is often described as "snarling," "grunting," or "yelping." *The Matchlock Gun,* by Walter Edmonds, compares the nameless Indians to trotting dogs, sniffing the scent of food. Often, Native American characters are depersonalized by not being given names, which implies that they are not individuals, or even full-fledged human beings.

In addition to stereotypes about Native American people, Laura Herbst identifies three stereotypical ways in which Native American culture has been portrayed in children's literature. First, the culture may be depicted as inferior to the white culture, treating the abandonment of the Native American way of life as an improvement. Native American characters are often depicted as gaining by going to white schools or taking on the values of the white culture, leaving their culture and even their people behind. A common theme in such literature is that white people must be responsible for remaking Native Americans.

Second, the culture may be depicted as valueless, and thus not worthy of respect. Depicting the rich diversity of spiritual beliefs and ceremonies, moral values, artistic skills, and the lifestyles in Native American cultures may be ignored in favor of depicting violence as the chief Native American value. Authors may be ignorant of the fact that Native American peoples have many different cultures.

Third, the culture may be depicted as quaint or superficial, without depth or warmth. White characters in children's literature of the past commonly ridicule or scorn customs that have spiritual significance to Native Americans. They disparage sacred ceremonies, medicine men, ancient artifacts, and traditional legends as belonging to "heathen savages." Any of these three stereotypical portrayals of a culture is offensive. More current books, however, especially those written by Native American authors or other authorities on Native American culture, are sensitive to the heritage and individuality of the native peoples of North America.

Latino Americans

Betty M. Morgan (1973) concluded that the number of children's books with members of minority groups as main characters has increased since World War II, but she also found that this is true only for books about either African Americans or Native Americans. Far fewer children's books have Latinos or Asian Americans as the main characters. Authors such as Gary Soto also lament the lack of Latino writers being published in the United States (Lodge, 1997).

Both the lack of children's literature about people of Latino descent and heritage and the negative stereotypes found in some of the literature have been criticized. At one children's literature conference, Mauricio Charpenel (1980), consultant to the Mexican Ministry of Education, reported that very few stories are written for or about Mexican or Mexican American children. He was especially concerned about poetry. While Latin American writers

publish beautiful poetry, the poems are not shared with Mexican American children in the United States. Both teachers and librarians at the conference expressed concern for literature that would appeal to Latino children and create positive images of their heritage.

The Council on Interracial Books for Children (1977a) has been critical of the depictions of Mexican Americans in children's literature of the past. After analyzing two hundred books, the council concluded that little in the stories would enable children to recognize a culture, a history, or a set of life circumstances. The council criticized the theme of poverty that recurs as if it is a "natural facet of the Chicano condition" (p. 57) and the tendency for Mexican American problems to be solved by the intervention of Anglo Americans. The council also felt that Mexican Americans' problems had been treated superficially in the books it studied. For example, many books suggest that if children learn English, all of their problems will be solved.

Even fewer books are being written about Puerto Rican Americans, Cuban Americans, and the many new Americans from Central American countries. The majority of books about Puerto Ricans, for example, lack literary merit and overuse a New York City ghetto setting. In addition to fewer books about Hispanic Americans, the available books tend to go out of print.

Asian Americans

Since few books about Asian Americans have been published for children, researchers who have tried to evaluate books about Asian Americans have had little to study. In 1976, the Asian American Children's Book Project (Council on Interracial Books for Children, 1977b) identified sixty-six books with Asian American central characters, and most of these books were about Chinese Americans. The members of the project concluded that with only a few exceptions, the books were grossly misleading. They presented stereotypes suggesting that all Asian Americans look alike, choose to live in "quaint" communities in the midst of large cities, and cling to "outworn, alien" customs. The project also criticized the books because they tended to measure success by the extent to which Asian Americans have assimilated white middle-class values and because they implied that hard work, learning to speak English, and keeping a low profile would enable them to overcome adversity and be successful.

Stereotypes of Asian characters change slowly. Bu Kunyu (1988) identifies past stereotypes of Chinese people and contrasts these stereotypes with current attitudes:

For hundreds of years, Chinese people have been described as diligent, conservative, obedient. In the wake of modernization, the three traditional words seem inappropriate. Today's students' slogan is: "Be a pioneer of reform, not a lamb of the traditional education system." Thus, three new words are used to describe the demands of modern society: *practical, efficient,* and *adventurous.* (p. 378)

Literary Criticism: Evaluating Multicultural Literature

To develop positive attitudes about and respect for individuals in all cultures, children need many opportunities to read and listen to literature that presents accurate and respectful images of everyone. Because fewer children's books in the United States are written from the perspective of racial or cultural minorities and because many stories perpetuate negative stereotypes, you should carefully evaluate books containing nonwhite characters. Outstanding multicultural literature meets the literary criteria applied to any fine book, but other criteria apply to the treatment of cultural and racial minorities. The following criteria related to literature that represents African Americans, Native Americans, Latino Americans, and Asian Americans reflect the recommendations of the earlier cited research studies and evaluations compiled by Donna Norton (1997):

Are African, Native, Latino, and Asian Americans portrayed as unique individuals, with their own thoughts, emotions, and philosophies, instead of as representatives of particular racial or cultural groups?

Does a book transcend stereotypes in the appearance, behavior, and character traits of its nonwhite characters? Does the depiction of nonwhite characters and lifestyles imply any stigma? Does a book suggest that all members of an ethnic or racial group live in poverty? Are the characters from a variety of socioeconomic backgrounds, educational levels, and occupations? Does the author avoid depicting Asian Americans as workers in restaurants and laundries, Latinos as illegal alien unskilled laborers, Native Americans as bloodthirsty warriors, African Americans as menial service employees, and so forth? Does the author avoid the "model minority" and "bad minority" syndrome? Are nonwhite characters respected for themselves, or must they display outstanding abilities to gain approval from white characters?

Is the physical diversity within a particular racial or cultural minority group authentically portrayed in the text and the illustrations? Do nonwhite characters have stereotypically exaggerated facial features or physiques that make them all look alike?

Will children be able to recognize the characters in the text and the illustrations as African Americans, Latinos, Asian Americans, or Native Americans and not mistake them for white? Are people of color shown as gray—that is, as simply darker versions of Caucasian-featured people?

Is the culture of a racial or ethnic minority group accurately portrayed? Is it treated with respect, or is it depicted as inferior to the majority white culture? Does the author believe the culture worthy of preservation? Is the cultural diversity within African American, Asian American, Latino, and Native American life clearly demonstrated? Are the customs and values of those diverse

EVALUATION CRITERIA

Literary Criticism: Multicultural Literature

1. Are the characters portrayed as individuals instead of as representatives of a group?
2. Does the book transcend stereotypes?
3. Does the book portray physical diversity?
4. Will children be able to recognize the characters in the text and illustrations?
5. Is the culture accurately portrayed?
6. Are social issues and problems depicted frankly, accurately, and without oversimplification?
7. Do nonwhite characters solve their problems without intervention by whites?
8. Are nonwhite characters shown as equals of white characters?
9. Does the author avoid glamorizing or glorifying nonwhite characters?
10. Is the setting authentic?
11. Are the factual and historical details accurate?
12. Does the author accurately describe contemporary settings?
13. Does the book rectify historical distortions or omissions?
14. Does dialect have a legitimate purpose and does it ring true?
15. Does the author avoid offensive or degrading vocabulary?
16. Are the illustrations authentic and nonstereotypical?
17. Does the book reflect an awareness of the changing status of females?

groups accurately portrayed? Must nonwhite characters fit into a cultural image acceptable to white characters? Is a nonwhite culture shown in an overly exotic or romanticized way instead of being placed within the context of everyday activities familiar to all people?

Are social issues and problems related to minority group status depicted frankly and accurately, without oversimplification? Must characters who are members of racial and cultural minority groups exercise all of the understanding and forgiveness?

Do nonwhite characters handle their problems individually, through their own efforts or with the assistance of close family and friends, or are problems solved through the intervention of whites? Are nonwhite characters shown as the equals of white characters? Are some characters placed in submissive or inferior positions? Are white people always the benefactors?

Are nonwhite characters glamorized or glorified, especially in biography? (Both excessive praise and excessive deprecation of nonwhite characters result in unreal and unbalanced characterizations.) If the book is a biography, are both the personality and the accomplishments of the main character shown in accurate detail and not oversimplified?

Is the setting of a story authentic, whether past, present, or future? Will children be able to recognize the setting as urban, rural, or fantasy? If a story deals with factual information or historical events, are the details accurate? If the setting is contemporary, does the author accurately describe the situations of nonwhite people in the United States and elsewhere today? Does a book rectify historical distortions and omissions?

If dialect is used, does it have a legitimate purpose? Does it ring true and blend in naturally with the story in a nonstereotypical way, or is it simply used as an example of substandard English? If non–English words are used, are they spelled and used correctly? Is offensive or degrading vocabulary used to describe the characters, their actions, their customs, or their lifestyles?

Are the illustrations authentic and nonstereotypical in every detail?

Does a book reflect an awareness of the changing status of females in all racial and cultural groups today? Does the author provide role models for girls other than subservient females?

See the Evaluation Criteria list on page 460.

African American Literature

Many fine books of traditional literature, contemporary realistic fiction, and nonfiction reflect the heritage and modern-day experiences of African Americans. Reading these enjoyable and well-written books will help children from all racial and cultural backgrounds identify with and appreciate the dreams, problems, and cultural contributions of black people on this continent. According to Hazel Rochman (1993):

African American literature is flourishing. In the last year, perhaps because African American history is now a required part of the curriculum in many states, there have been many new books about slavery and resistance, as well as several fine books about the civil rights movement. The focus has shifted from the role of the great leaders to the experience of ordinary people, including women and children. (p. 1052)

Traditional Literature

Traditional folk literature, the tales originally handed down through centuries of oral storytelling, includes many of the stories that children most enjoy. Through reading African and African American traditional tales, children discover a rich literary heritage, gain a respect for the creativity of the people who originated the stories, develop an understanding of the values of the originators, and share enjoyable experiences that have entertained others in centuries past. Modern writers of contemporary realistic fiction about African Americans often have their characters tell African tales in order to develop closer relationships to and understanding of the African heritage. Other authors write original modern fantasies based on African elements. The beliefs and values found in African and African American folklore are found in both poetry and contemporary stories; therefore, it is important to introduce a study of African American literature with traditional literature.

Traditional African and African American literature includes folktales that are indigenous to various countries on the African continent, African folk literature that was transported to one of the Caribbean islands and then altered in the new setting, and folk literature that originated in the American South. This final category includes many tales based on African themes and motifs or altered to meet the needs of southern African American storytellers.

African Tales. Africa has a long and rich history of oral literature. In 1828, the first known collection of African tales was published for European audiences. This collection, *Fables Sénégalaises Recueillies de l'Oulof*, was translated into French by le Bon Roger, the French Commandant of Senegal. More collections appeared as administrators, traders, and missionaries collected traditional African stories for various purposes. A brief review of these purposes shows how important an understanding of folklore is for understanding people. Daniel Crowley (1979) states:

Linguists collected tales as samples of language usage, teachers as a means of inculcating local languages, missionaries to study local values and beliefs, African elites in pursuit of vindication against colonialism, diffusionists in the search of distribution patterns on which to base migration theories, litterateurs and journalists looking for "authentic" themes.... (p. 11)

The collection of authentic folklore and artistic representations by ancient peoples is considered so important that Leo Frobenius and Douglas Fox (1983) state in the introduction to *African Genesis:*

Every fact, object, and belief which can help us to understand the growth of human culture should be recorded and indexed for use.... We will find that there are peoples of whom we do not know enough, and so it will be necessary to send out expeditions to find and gather the material we lack. (p. 16)

This is also a worthy attitude for students of children's literature, who can analyze the folklore to make discoveries about the types of stories represented, as well as the cultural patterns, values, and beliefs reflected in the ancient tales. Like other traditional lore, African folklore reveals ancient beliefs in the origins of the natural and tribal worlds, as well as certain physical and spiritual traits.

The beautifully expressed and illustrated traditional African tales discussed in this section represent some of the most noble values attributed to humanity: love of beauty, humor, work, courage, imagination, and perseverance. Children discover pride and hope in being black, as well as pleasure in the richness of cultural heritage.

Some tales explore societal problems and provide possible solutions. In the introduction to *The Dancing Palm Tree and Other Nigerian Folktales*, Barbara Walker (1990) describes this important role in Yoruba tales,

Many of the stories begin, "Far away and long ago in a small village," for this is a tradition in Yoruba storytelling. And somewhere in each story there is likely to be a "moral," a human truth which is taught through what happens in the story. For one of the main purposes of storytelling in Nigeria has always been to teach, to instruct, a very important function in a land where until just recently there were few schools and where many of the important lessons of life were learned at the knee of the storyteller. But you will find that the truths taught in these stories prevail not only in Nigeria but all around the world, truths that people must learn to live by no matter what country they call home. (p. 3)

As you read the stories in this section on African folklore, try to identify the truths, values, and beliefs that are important to the African people and to those from around the world.

For example, Verna Aardema's *Bringing the Rain to Kapiti Plain: A Nandi Tale* shows that individuals have obligations for the betterment of the people, the environment, and the animals that provide their welfare. Ashley Bryan's "The Husband Who Counted the Spoonfuls," found in *Beat the Story-Drum, Pum-Pum*, develops a need for stability in marital relationships. Solving family relationships is the theme found in Nancy Raines Day's *The Lion's Whiskers: An Ethiopian Folktale*. In this tale a caring stepmother discovers how to make her elusive stepson respond to her. In a variation of the "Lazy Jack" theme, *Gift of the Sun: A Tale from South Africa*, a man finds an occupation.

Ann Grifalconi's *The Village of Round and Square Houses* reveals how a social custom began. In this case, a volcanic eruption in the distant past leaves only two houses within the village: one round and one square. To meet the needs of the village, the women and children move into the round house while the men stay in the square house. According to the tale, the custom continues today because people "live together peacefully here— Because each one has a place to be apart, and a time to be together.... And that is how our way came about and will continue—Til Naka speaks again!" (unnumbered). The illustrations in *The Village of Round and Square Houses* add to the feeling of place. Likewise, the detailed drawings in many of the tales such as Trina Schart Hyman's illustra-

tions in Lloyd Alexander's *The Fortune-Tellers* provide readers with an understanding of the locations where the various values and beliefs are located.

As you read collections of African folktales for children, notice the values and beliefs such as the importance of maintaining friendship, a need for family loyalty, the desirability of genuine hospitality, the use of wit and trickery in unequal relationships, a strict code for ownership and borrowing, gratitude for help rendered, high risk in excessive pride, care for the feelings of those in authority, respect for individuality, and appropriate awe of the supernatural.

Notice that individuals who adhere to the values and beliefs are frequently rewarded, while individuals who reject the values and beliefs are usually punished. For example, traditional values reflected in the folklore of several African cultures are found in Harold Courlander's *The Crest and the Hide: And Other African Stories of Heroes, Chiefs, Bards, Hunters, Sorcerers, and Common People*. This collection of twenty tales from such cultures as the Ashanti, the Yoruba, the Swahili, and the Zulu emphasizes the values of wisdom, friendship, love, and heroism, as well as some behaviors that are not respected, such as foolishness and disloyalty.

Barbara K. Walker's *The Dancing Palm Tree and Other Nigerian Folktales* is a collection of eleven folktales told to Walker by Olawale Idewu, a Nigerian student. In addition to being an excellent source of tales that reflect the traditional values, this book includes a glossary of information to help readers interpret the stories. For example, the entry for NO-KING-IS-AS-GREAT-AS-GOD states: "Names such as this one are quite common in Yoruba life. In fact, the whole process of naming is an extremely interesting and complicated one. Each name which is used has a definite meaning and purpose, and it tells a great deal about its owner" (p. 95). The authors then explain that names may specify family positions, christening names, totem names, and pet names.

Wit and trickery are also appropriate actions found in Verna Aardema's *Anansi Does the Impossible!: An Ashanti Tale*. Now the little spider must outwit a python, a fairy, and forty-seven hornets in order to bring them to the Sky God in exchange for the Sky God's stories. With the help of his wife, Aso, Anansi succeeds in accomplishing the three impossible tasks and consequently brings the stories back to the people.

Additional folktales that develop the values of the people include John Steptoe's *Mufaro's Beautiful Daughters: An African Tale* which shows the importance of kindness and generosity toward others and the harmful results of greed and selfishness. The folktales in Brent Ashabranner and Russell Davis's *The Lion's Whiskers: And Other Ethiopian Tales* reveal important values such as courage and wisdom. *East African Folktales*, retold by Vincent Muli Wa Kituku, is a collection of eighteen tales retold in both English and the Kamba language from

Kenya. Each of the tales concludes with a moral that helps listeners interpret the tales and understand the values and messages developed in the tales.

David Wisniewski's *Sundiata: Lion King of Mali,* a legend, is the tale of a ruler who lived in the late 1200s. The tale begins in this fashion: "Listen to me, children of the Bright Country, and hear the great deeds of ages past. The words I speak are those of my father and his father before him, pure and full of truth ..." (p. 1, unnumbered). Sundiata's courage and leadership are especially valued in this tale. In addition, when he is returned to the throne, he tells his people that from that time on, no one shall interfere with another's destiny.

In endnotes, Wisniewski (1992) provides information about the source of this tale. For example, Wisniewski states:

Detailed drawings place the setting for this tale in central Africa. (From The Fortune-Tellers *by Lloyd Alexander, illustrated by Trina Schart Hyman. Copyright © 1992 by Trina Schart Hyman, illustrations. Used by permission of Dutton Children's Books, a division of Penguin Books USA Inc.)*

The story of Sundiata has reached modern ears through the unbroken oral tradition provided by griots. Many African ethnic groups rely on the prodigious memories of these people, rather than written accounts, to preserve the history and wisdom of the past. This version of the Sundiata epic is distilled from the words of Djeli Mamoudou Kouyate, a griot of the Keita clan, in *Sundiata: An Epic of Old Mali,* a compilation written by Djibril Tamsir Niane and translated from the original Malinke by G. D. Pickett (London, 1965). (endnote)

This information is valuable because it allows you to compare Wisniewski's retelling and interpretation with the earlier version.

Several myths from Virginia Hamilton's *In the Beginning: Creation Stories from Around the World* explore the origins of the natural world. For example, in "Spider Ananse Finds Something: Wulbarie the Creator," a myth from West Africa, Ananse brings the sun, moon, and darkness to earth. Unfortunately, he also causes blindness to come upon some of the people. The theme that weakness can overcome strength is developed as trickster Ananse outwits the more powerful sky god. In "Man Copies God: Nyambi the Creator," a myth from Zambia, Nyambi creates animals and man but is unhappy when man tries to copy god or disobeys his instructions. Consequently, Nyambi climbs into the sky and vanishes from earth. The only sign that god is still in the sky is the sun that rises every morning. The theme in this tale is that humans are at odds with the will of god.

Ruby Dee's *Tower to Heaven,* a tale from Ghana in West Africa, reveals why the great god of the sky, Onyankopon, no longer lives on the earth and why people tried to build a tower to communicate with him after he disappeared into the sky. Mary-Joan Gerson's *Why the Sky Is Far Away: A Nigerian Folktale* explains not only why the sky is far away but also why people have to plow the fields and hunt the forests rather than take food from the sky. The story contains the theme that people will be punished if they waste resources and take more than they need to satisfy hunger. The theme of the tale is very important in today's world, as it was in earlier times.

The ways in which animals and people acquired certain physical and spiritual traits are popular subjects in African tales. Barbara Knutson's *How the Guinea Fowl Got Her Spots: A Swahili Tale of Friendship,* the retelling of a Swahili tale, explains one such characteristic. In addition, the tale develops the relationships between cows and guinea fowl and shows the value of maintaining friendships and being loyal to friends. The tale reveals that wit and trickery are condoned when the unequal relationships are between the small guinea fowl and the much larger lion. Knutson's *Why the Crab Has No Head,* a tale from Zaire, explains two characteristics. First, Crab has no head because his pride offended the creator. Second, Crab walks sideways because he is filled with embarrassment instead of pride. A need to humble individuals who express excessive pride is a common theme in African folklore.

Two tales in Ashley Bryan's *Beat the Story-Drum, Pum-Pum* are also characteristic of explanation stories.

Through the Eyes of a STORYTELLER

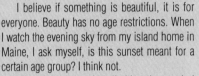

Ashley Bryan

Visit the CD-ROM that accompanies this text to generate a complete list of Ashley Bryan titles.

Selected Titles by Ashley Bryan:

Beat the Story-Drum, Pum-Pum

All Night, All Day: A Child's First Book of African-American Spirituals

Ashley Bryan's ABC of African-American Poetry

The Cat's Purr

Lion and the Ostrich Chicks, and Other African Folktales

The Oral Tradition: People to People, Voice to Voice

The oral tradition in literature is not exotic or something found only in pre-literate societies. Just listening to people is listening to their stories. While many tales are presented in circumstances where the wise elders answer the questions of children, the oral tradition is not limited to that. All life experience is rich, whether it is children talking to other children on the playground or families talking around the dinner table. The oral tradition will never die, even in this age of television and videocassettes, because each family has its own oral tradition.

Poetry always reminds me that language is man's greatest invention. The poet is more aware than most people of the wonder and mystery of language. Poetry deals with emotions, an area we are most ashamed of as human beings. But it is the emotion of poetry that allows it to reach out and touch the minds and hearts of the listeners in a way that no other medium can.

For this reason, I always begin each storytelling session by reciting a variety of poems written by black poets. I give most of my talks to adults. It is the adults who ask me to come and speak to the children. I try to prepare a range of material that cuts across all ages.

I believe if something is beautiful, it is for everyone. Beauty has no age restrictions. When I watch the evening sky from my island home in Maine, I ask myself, is this sunset meant for a certain age group? I think not.

Also, I never consider limiting the words I choose to tell my stories because children may not understand them. Children are always interested in what the voice is doing and children want to stretch. Whether or not they understand a poem completely, even young children will attend to it.

I choose the words of poetry for my stories, too, using the tools of close rhyme, rhythm, repetition, and alliteration. I spend months and years preparing stories and poems. I need that time to make the story or the poem truly mine. I always encourage teachers to allow their students three to four weeks to prepare to recite a poem. No poem should ever be read aloud "cold."

By allowing students time to investigate and play with the language of the poem, one automatically sets up a spirit of cooperation in the classroom. By the time children are asked to recite the poem, they can do so with confidence because now they know all the words and can read with expression.

I like my school visits to be a reminder that reading aloud should be an integral part of the entire school year, no matter what the age of the students. No one is "too old" to be read to, or to be told a story. No one is too young to tell a story that he or she has practiced.

Children always ask me how old I am. I tell them I am four. I tell them I am six. I tell them I am ten. I am forty-six, and I am sixty-four. I ask them to choose the age they want me to be. Invariably, young children will decide and be satisfied that I am four or six, close to their own age.

When I visit schools, I am often treated to wonderful performances of my stories, acted out by the children. It is important that the performance that I see not be the *only* performance. If students have taken time to prepare,

they should be allowed to perform again and again. Why not repeat the story to another group a week later? Why not perform again in a month? That way the story will always be truly theirs to own, and there will not be that "emotional letdown" that often occurs after a single performance. Children will also learn each performance can be special. Each time one can embellish a story, and it will grow richer through the retelling.

It is so important to be rooted in who you are, and then all flows naturally from this source. I have always been a teacher. And, I have always earned money to meet my responsibilities from areas other than my art. I write for myself. Since I don't sign contracts before I begin working on a project, I can be patient with a project and release it only when I feel it is ready. That way, my publisher can *choose* to accept my work. I am always prepared to take the work back.

The stories I write often evolve from very spare motifs, sometimes only four or five lines from an ancient journal. I sometimes play with a story for up to ten years before I will focus on it and make it a book.

My challenge is to open up the story from the printed word and try to match the expressive style of illustration to the story itself. That is why I don't use just a single artistic medium or style. When I wanted to concentrate on the movement in the illustrations in *The Dancing Granny,* I used the brushstroke style of painting from the Japanese and Chinese traditions. The characters needed to tumble around the pages. Bright, fresh watercolors captured the mood I wanted to create in *Turtle Knows Your Name.*

I hope that you will help the art of storytelling flourish in your own way—people to people, voice to voice.

Video Profiles: The accompanying video contains conversations with Joseph Bruchac, Gary Soto, Lynne Cherry, and other storytellers.

Drawn from an interview, March 30, 1990, by Linda James Scharp.

"How Animals Got Their Tails" reveals not only how animals received their individual tails but also why there is animosity between rabbits and foxes. "Why Bush Cow and Elephant Are Bad Friends" reveals why animals fight in the bush.

Verna Aardema's *Why Mosquitoes Buzz in People's Ears* explains why mosquitoes are noisy. Written as a cumulative tale, it is excellent for sharing orally with children. It suggests a rich language heritage and a respect for

storytelling. Ashley Bryan's retelling of Nigerian tales in *The Story of Lightning & Thunder* also reflects this rich language tradition. The oral language tradition is revealed in this introduction to the tale "Ma Sheep Thunder and Son Ram Lightning": "A long time ago, I mean a long, long, time ago, if you wanted to pat Lightning or chat with Thunder, you could do it. Uh-huh, you could . . ."

Aaron Shepard's retelling of *Master Man: A Tall Tale of Nigeria* reveals both why there is thunder in the sky and

The consequences of bragging are presented through Master Man: A Tall Tale of Nigeria, told by Aaron Shepard. (Cover art from Master Man: A Tall Tale of Nigeria, told by Aaron Shepard. Jacket illustrations © 2001 by David Wisniewski. Jacket © 2001 by HarperCollins Publishers. Used by permission of HarperCollins Publishers.)

the foolish consequences resulting from bragging: "Two fools fighting forever to see which one is Master Man." David Wisniewski's collage illustrations add power to this tall tale. In addition, a useful Author's Note adds information about the Hausa people and identifies the sources used for this retelling.

Several beautifully illustrated books contain single African folktales or legends retold for children of all ages. Aardema's *Who's in Rabbit's House?* is an unusual and humorous Masai tale about tricky animals. This tale is written in the form of a play performed by villagers for their townsfolk. In this tale, Caterpillar, who is smaller, slower, and weaker than any of the other animals (including Rabbit, Jackal, Leopard, Elephant, and Rhinoceros), must use wit and trickery to correct the imbalance. In addition, repetition of words adds to the vivid descriptions, and the dialogue suggests the richness of African language. The jackal trots off "kpata, kpata," the leopard jumps "pa, pa, pa," and the frog laughs "dgung, dgung, dgung." This is an excellent tale to stimulate creative dramatizations by children, who enjoy repeating the sound effects and dialogues out loud and creating masks of the various animals.

Another folktale rich in the language of the African storyteller is Gail E. Haley's *A Story, a Story.* This tale about Ananse, the spider man, repeats key words to make them

stronger, as Ananse's wit helps him overcome serious difficulties. Ananse seeks stories from the powerful sky god, and the god laughs: "How can a weak old man like you, so small, so small, so small, pay my price?" (p. 6, unnumbered). Ananse fools the god and is able to capture the leopard-of-the-terrible-teeth; Mmboro, the hornet who stings like fire; and Mmoatia, the fairy whom people never see. As a reward for these gifts, the sky god gives Ananse the stories that previously belonged only to the god. From this tale, children can understand the importance of storytelling on the African continent as well as recognize the occurrences in which wit and trickery may be legitimately used in African folklore.

American Tales. New folktales developed when Africans became slaves in North America, as Virginia Hamilton (1985) points out in her introduction to *The People Could Fly: American Black Folktales:*

Out of the contacts the plantation slaves made in their new world, combined with memories and habits from the old world of Africa, came a body of folk expression about the slaves and their experiences. The slaves created tales in which various animals . . . took on characteristics of the people found in the new environment of the plantation. (p. x)

For example, the favorite Brer Rabbit, who was small and apparently helpless when compared with the more powerful bear and fox, was smart, tricky, and clever, and usually won out over larger and stronger animals. The slaves, who identified with the rabbit, told many tales about his exploits.

Hamilton's collection of tales is divided into four parts: (1) animal tales, (2) extravagant and fanciful experiences, (3) supernatural tales, and (4) slave tales of freedom. The collection provides sources for listening, discussing, and comparing. For example, readers can compare the folklore elements, plot, and themes in Hamilton's "The Beautiful Girl of the Moon Tower," a folktale from the Cape Verde Islands, and Elizabeth Isele's retelling of the Russian tale "The Frog Princess."

The most famous collection of African American folktales originating in the southern United States are the stories originally collected and retold by Joel Chandler Harris's "Uncle Remus" in the late nineteenth century. Again, that "monstrous clever beast," Brer Rabbit, always survives by using his cunning against stronger enemies. William J. Faulkner's *The Days When the Animals Talked* (1977) presents background information on African American folktales about animals. Faulkner tells how the tales were created and what their significance is in American history.

Two authors, Van Dyke Parks and Julius Lester, have adapted highly acclaimed versions of the Uncle Remus stories originally written down by Joel Chandler Harris. The combination of Parks's text and Barry Moser's illustrations for *Jump! The Adventures of Brer Rabbit* and *Jump Again! More Adventures of Brer Rabbit* forms highly readable and visually satisfying experiences. It is interesting to analyze the animal characters, to consider the social

Through the Eyes of a CHILD

Danielle

Pam Wilson's Fourth Grade
Western Row Elementary
Mason, Ohio

TITLE: Jump Back, Honey   Illustrations: Ashley Bryan

AUTHOR: Paul Laurence Dunbar

I think the Illustrations are very beauitful and have very many details in them. Some are dark and gloomy and some are light and pretty. The book I read was Jump Back Honey it was a poem and song book. I liked it, but it was a long book but I enjoyed reading it. If there was no words on the page I could tell you what was happening because it has so many details and Illustrations in the picture. The thing that I like about the book was that all of the pictures would fill up the page and all the words would be either in the sky or on the grass so that there would be no white on the page.

Danielle

impact of slavery as depicted in the stories, to identify values that are similar to those found in African tales, to compare similar tales found in other cultures or in other versions of the Uncle Remus stories, and to consider the impact of the authors' styles.

For example, Brer Rabbit is considered a character who can use his head, outdo and outwit all other creatures, and rely on trickery if necessary. In this role, Brer Rabbit uses trickery if he is in conflict with bigger and more powerful characters, but Brer Rabbit also represents what happens when folks are full of conceit and proudness. They "are going to get it taken out of them. Brer Rabbit did get caught up with once, and it cooled him right off" (*Jump!*, p. 19). Notice that both of these values are also found in African folklore. In addition, the tales reflect changes caused by the new environment, where the storytellers are influenced by slavery and European colonization and the need to protect their families and develop friendships that are tempered with distrust.

Symbolism, onomatopoeia, and personification add to Parks's storytelling style. For example, Parks uses symbolic meaning to contrast the length of night and day in *Jump!:* "When the nights were long and the days were short, with plenty of wood on the fire and sweet potatoes in the embers, Brer Rabbit could outdo all the other creatures" (p. 3). Onomatopoeia is used to imitate actions. Brer Rabbit relies on his "lippity-clip and his blickety-blick" (p. 3). Personification is found in descriptions of nature: "Way back yonder when the moon was lots bigger than he is now . . ." (p. 3).

Make comparisons within and across cultures. For example, compare the stories retold in Parks's version, stories retold in Lester's *The Tales of Uncle Remus: The Adventures of Brer Rabbit,* and stories in earlier versions retold by Joel Chandler Harris. Make cross-cultural comparisons by analyzing "Brer Rabbit Finds His Match" (*Jump!*) and the Aesop fable, "The Tortoise and the Hare."

Stories such as these Brer Rabbit tales are filled with symbolism and alternate meanings. For example, in *The Adventures of High John the Conqueror*, Steve Sanfield states:

The slaves often told stories about Brer Rabbit, about how, through his cunning and his tricks, he would overcome all the might and power and meanness of Brer Fox and Brer Bear and Brer Wolf. Whites would hear those stories and think, "Oh, isn't that cute, little Brer Rabbit fooling big Brer Bear." But when the slaves told and heard them, they heard them differently. They saw themselves as Brer Rabbit and the slaveholders as Brer Wolf and Brer Fox, and the only way to defeat all that power and brute force was to be just a little bit more clever. (p. 5)

Symbolic meanings in many of the African American folktales are interpreted by Rex M. Ellis in his introductions to tales in *Beneath the Blazing Sun* (1997). For example, he states in "The Wolf and the Dog": "The following story addresses this phenomenon [symbolism and alternate meaning] using the character of a wolf, who, like many blacks of the period, chose to live a life of freedom, a life of running away and hiding out—with little comfort—and the dog who embraced a life of comfort—albeit accompanied by humiliation, degradation, and contempt" (p. 51).

There are distinct oral storytelling styles in African American folktales. Current retellers of these tales frequently mention the influence of storytellers in their own youth. For example, Patricia McKissack introduces *Flossie & the Fox* by telling readers:

Here is a story from my youth, retold in the same rich and colorful language that was my grandfather's. He began all his yarns with questions. "Did I ever tell you 'bout the time lil' Flossie Finley come out the Piney Woods heeling a fox?" I'd snuggle up beside him in the big porch swing, then he'd begin his tale. . . . (author's note, unnumbered)

Interestingly, Julius Lester also introduces *The Tales of Uncle Remus: The Adventures of Brer Rabbit* with the information that his most "lasting memories of my grandmother are of her telling me stories. . . . My favorites, and I'm sure they were hers as well, were the Brer Rabbit stories" (p. vii). Look for, compare, and analyze the influence of the storyteller's style in these selections.

Robert D. San Souci's *The Talking Eggs* is adapted from a Creole folktale collected in Louisiana. The tale shows that kindness is a respected value, while greed is not rewarded. William H. Hooks's *The Ballad of Belle*

Folklore elements and important themes are developed in this southern tale. (From The Talking Eggs: A Folktale from the American South *retold by Robert D. San Souci, pictures by Jerry Pinkney. Pictures copyright © 1989 by Jerry Pinkney. Reprinted by permission of Dial Books for Young Readers.)*

Dorcas is a tale set in the tidewater section of the Carolinas during the time of slavery. The protagonists are a free issue woman and a slave who fall in love, but they are threatened with separation when the master wishes to sell the slave. In addition to revealing the consequences of social injustice, the tale reveals the power of love and belief in the magical ability of the spells created by conjurers. Robert D. San Souci's *Sukey and the Mermaid*, collected from the Sea Islands off South Carolina's coast, is a melding of story elements from West Africa and the Caribbean. Virginia Hamilton's *Her Stories: African American Folktales, Fairy Tales, and True Tales* includes "Mary Belle and the Mermaid," collected in South Carolina.

John Henry, a real person and the great black hero of American folklore, is characterized as a "steel-driving" man. Ezra Jack Keats has written and illustrated an attractive edition of John Henry's story, *John Henry: An American Legend.* "Born with a hammer in his hand," the John Henry of folklore accomplishes seemingly impossible tasks, such as turning a huge broken paddle wheel and saving a ship from sinking, laying more railroad track than many men combined, hammering out a dangerous dynamite fuse and saving the men from a cave-in, and challenging and beating a steam drill in a race until he finally dies "with his hammer in his hand." The large, colorful illustrations in Keats's book suggest the power and heroism of this American legend.

Stories of another folk hero are retold, as we have discussed, by Steve Sanfield in *The Adventures of High John the Conqueror*. High John is similar to Brer Rabbit because he uses cleverness to outwit his more powerful adversary, the Old Master. The themes in these stories show that the spirit cannot be taken away even if people are living in the worst conditions. Sanfield's text includes factual information to help readers understand and interpret the tales.

Spirituals provide another source for understanding the values in the African American folktales. Spirituals provide the text to accompany Ashley Bryan's colorful illustrations in John Langstaff's *What a Morning! The Christmas Story in Black Spirituals*. The format of the book includes a colorful illustration and appropriate biblical text followed by the words and music for the accompanying spiritual. Another source for spirituals is Bryan's *All Night, All Day: A Child's First Book of African-American Spirituals*.

Fiction

There is currently an abundance of fiction written about the African American experience. Writing in *Publishers Weekly*, Bella Stander (1992) states, "Children's publishers are putting African American-themed books front and center in their catalogues these days, attesting to their growing importance" (p. 28). In a historical review of African American literature, Jean St. Clair (1989) comments on the increasing quality found in African American literature. St. Clair emphasizes that this is especially true, beginning in the 1970s, with the books written by African American authors.

Fiction written about African American characters differs, depending on the age of the intended audience. Books for younger readers emphasize the universal needs of children. Books for children in the middle-elementary grades emphasize searching for the past and understanding one's ancestry. Books for older children often have the characters face severe personal and social conflicts.

Books for Young Children. Fictional stories about African Americans written for young children mainly depict black children facing situations and problems common to all young children: overcoming jealousy, adjusting to a new baby, expressing a need for attention, experiencing rivalry with siblings, developing personal relationships, and overcoming family problems. Children from all ethnic backgrounds can realize from these books that African American children have the same needs, desires, and problems that other children have and solve their problems in similar ways.

Books for younger children frequently depict warm relationships between children and their parents or grandparents. Irene Smalls-Hector's *Jonathan and His Mommy* depicts a mother and her son walking in the neighborhood. On this walk, they try various movements, such as zigzag walking, making giant steps, and itsy-bitsy baby steps. Michael Hays's illustrations show the city neighborhood and the people who live there. The actions and the illustrations suggest warm relationships.

A different type of neighborhood walk is developed by Clifton L. Taulbert in *Little Cliff and the Porch People*. In this warm neighborhood story set in the Mississippi Delta of the 1950s, a young boy who lives with his great-grandparents is helped by the neighbors when he is sent on a task by his great-grandmother. The book develops the values of respecting one's elders, saying prayers, and helping one another. Jacqueline Woodson's *We Had a Picnic This Sunday Past* is another book that develops the universal qualities of families and keeping family traditions.

Sharon Bell Mathis depicts warm relationships between young children and elderly people in *The Hundred Penny Box*. In this book, Michael makes friends with his Great-great-aunt Dew and learns about the box in which she keeps a penny for every year of her life. "It's my old cracked-up, wacky-dacky box with the top broken," says Michael's Aunt Dew. "Them's my years in that box ....That's me in that box" (p. 19).

Imagination and desire to win a cakewalk combine to make a girl try to capture the wind as her dancing partner in Patricia McKissack's *Mirandy and Brother Wind*. The story may be so believable because the author was influenced by a picture of her grandparents after they won a cakewalk. Imagination also plays a role in Faith Ringgold's *Tar Beach*. The illustrations show a girl lying on the rooftop of her apartment building and flying over Harlem in the late 1930s.

Pride in a family member, persistence, and working for a dream are the themes developed in Deborah Hopkinson's *A Band of Angels*. The book is a fictional story based on real events associated with a group of former slaves who form a gospel singing group, the Jubilee Singers, in order to save Fisk University. The story is told through the viewpoint of a relative whose retelling expresses great pride in the accomplishments of the group. An author's note reveals the truth behind the story.

Retaining one's dreams and winning a father's admiration are important character traits in Gavin Curtis's *The Bat Boy & His Violin*. In this story, set during a time when African Americans had their own baseball league, a boy proves to his father that his own dreams of playing Mozart and Beethoven are as important to him as his father's dreams of coaching a winning baseball team.

Happy childhood memories also form the background for Donald Crews's *Bigmama's*, a story about warm family relationships that increase as the children visit Bigmama's house in Florida. Crews uses the same Florida setting for *Shortcut*. In this story, the children have a frightening experience. On the railroad track that they choose for a shortcut home, they encounter an oncoming train that sounds "WHOO WHOO" and "KLAKITY KLAKITY KLAKITY KLAK" in the night. The story has a happy ending: The children reach the warmth of Big-mama's house and decide that they will not take the shortcut again.

In *Working Cotton,* Sherley Anne Williams drew on her own childhood experiences in the cotton fields of Fresno, California. The text and the illustrations depict the hardworking life of a migrant family.

Several contemporary realistic picture books for younger children are set in Africa and focus on warm relationships between families and friends. Karen Lynn Williams's *When Africa Was Home* describes relationships between a white boy and his African neighbors. The strength of these relationships is shown when, after the family returns to America, they decide that their home is really in Africa. Consequently, they return to Africa and to their friends.

Virginia Kroll's *Masai and I* is an imaginative story in which a girl is learning about East Africa in her American school. The text describes and the illustrations show the girl thinking about what it would be like if she were Masai and were doing the same activities. For example, the text and illustrations contrast going home, eating dinner, getting dessert, playing at night, making the bed, looking at animals, running in the neighborhood, and attending a family dinner. Kroll's text stimulates readers to make other comparisons between their lives and those of people living in other countries.

Books with African settings may also show the consequences of segregated townships. Rachel Isadora's *At the Crossroads* follows South African children waiting to welcome their fathers, who are returning from working in the mines after being separated from their families for ten months. The text describes and illustrations show both the loving relationships between fathers and children, and the shanties in which they live.

In *The Day Gogo Went to Vote: South Africa, April 1994,* Elinor Batezal Sisulu creates a picture storybook with a strong character who voices her needs to vote. Gogo, Thembi's one-hundred-year-old great-great-grandmother, has not left her home in many years and now she explains why she is going out to vote: " 'Thembi, black people in South Africa have fought for many years for the right to vote. This is the first time we have a chance to vote for our own leaders, and it might be my last. This is why I must vote, no matter how many miles I have to stand in line!' " (unnumbered). The remainder of the book follows the process as the oldest woman in the township goes to vote and the township celebrates the election of Nelson Mandela.

Chapters 4 and 5 discuss additional picture storybooks written from the African American perspective.

Books for Children in the Middle-Elementary Grades. Many African American stories written for children in the middle-elementary grades are written by authors—black and white—who are sensitive to the black experience. Some themes—such as the discovery of oneself, the need to give and receive love, the problems experienced when children realize that the parents whom they love are getting a divorce, and the fears associated with nonachievement in school—are universal and suggest that all children have similar needs, fears, and problems. Other themes, such as searching for one's roots in the African past, speak of a special need by black children to know about their ancestry.

Virginia Hamilton's *Zeely* is a warm, sensitive story about an imaginative girl who makes an important discovery about herself and others when she and her brother spend the summer on their Uncle Ross's farm. Elizabeth is not satisfied with the status quo; she calls herself Geeder, renames her younger brother Toeboy, renames her uncle's town Crystal, and calls the asphalt highway Leadback. When the imaginative Geeder sees her uncle's neighbor, Miss Zeely Tayber, Hamilton describes Zeely's appearance in detail: Zeely is a thin and stately woman over six feet tall, with a calm and proud expression, skin the color of rich Ceylon ebony, and the most beautiful face that Geeder has ever seen. When Geeder discovers a photograph of a Watusi queen who looks exactly like Zeely, she decides that Zeely must have royal blood.

Geeder is swept up in this fantasy and shares her beliefs with the village children. Then, Zeely helps Geeder make her greatest discovery. As they talk, Geeder realizes that dreaming is fine, but being yourself is even better. This realization causes Geeder to see everything in a new way. She realizes that Zeely is indeed a queen, but not like the ones in books, with their servants, kingdoms, and wealth. Zeely is queen because she is a self-loving person who always does her work better than anybody else. Geeder realizes that what a person is inside is more important than how a person looks or what a person owns. When Hamilton shares Geeder's final thoughts about her wonderful summer and her discovery that even stars resemble people, readers understand just how much wisdom Elizabeth has gained:

Some stars were no more than bright arcs in the sky as they burned out. But others lived on and on. There was a blue star in the sky south of Hesperus, the evening star. She thought of naming it Miss Zeely Tayber. There it would be in Uncle Ross' sky forever. (p. 121)

Another book that explores a character's personal discovery and strength of character is *Sister,* by Eloise Greenfield. Sister, whose real name is Doretha, keeps a journal in which she records the hard times—and the good times that "rainbowed" their way through those harder times. Doretha's memory book helps her realize

"I'm me." The words of the school song sung in *Sister* are characteristic of the themes found in this and other books by Greenfield:

> We strong black brothers and sisters
> Working in unity,
> We strong black brothers and sisters,
> Building our community,
> We all work together, learn together
> Live in harmony
> We strong black brothers and sisters
> Building for you and for me. (p. 69)

Another book with strong characters is John Steptoe's *Creativity*, a story of friendship.

Mildred Taylor's *The Gold Cadillac* is a fictionalized story based on Taylor's painful memories, a story about family unity and the consequences of racial prejudice. The prejudice occurs in 1950, when a northern black family buys a gold Cadillac and tries to drive to Mississippi. For the first time, the children experience segregation and racial hostility. As in other books by Taylor, the theme is that family love and unity help them overcome such terrible experiences. The characters in Vaunda Micheaux Nelson's *Mayfield Crossing* also overcome prejudice after they move from their old school to their new school.

Books for Older Children. Outstanding realistic fiction written for older children is characterized by both strong characters and strong themes. The themes in these stories include searching for freedom and dignity, learning to live together, tackling problems personally rather than waiting for someone else to do so, survival of the body and the spirit, and the more humorous problems involved in living through a first crush.

Virginia Hamilton has written several fine novels that older children find engrossing. In her suspenseful contemporary story *The House of Dies Drear*, she skillfully presents historical information about slavery and the Underground Railroad through the conversations of a black history professor and his son who are interested in the history of the pre–Civil War mansion that they are about to rent. (Compare Hamilton's presentation of information about slavery with Belinda Hurmence's presentation of information in her time travel fantasy about slavery in *A Girl Called Boy*.) Hamilton provides details for a setting that seems perfect for the mysterious occurrences that begin soon after the family arrives:

The house of Dies Drear loomed out of mist and murky sky, not only gray and formless, but huge and unnatural. It seemed to crouch on the side of a high hill above the highway. And it had a dark, isolated look about it that set it at odds with all that was living. (p. 26)

Thomas learns that Dies Drear and two escaped slaves were murdered and that rumors say the abolitionist and the slaves haunt the old house and the hidden

The author sets the novel during the Depression. (Cover from Bud, Not Buddy *by Christopher Paul Curtis. Cover illustration © 1999 by Ernie Norcia. Published by Delacorte Press. Used by permission.)*

tunnels below. Mystery fans will enjoy this fast-paced book. In a sequel, *The Mystery of Drear House*, Hamilton answers questions that students may have after reading *The House of Dies Drear*. In this sequel, the characters protect the treasure accumulated by Dies Drear from nature and from the thieving Darrows.

In an interview conducted by Hazel Rochman (1992c), Virginia Hamilton discusses her interest in the Underground Railroad and mentions that her grandfather was a fugitive slave who came to Ohio from Virginia. She describes the houses in Ohio that are similar to the one in *The House of Dies Drear*. She states:

There are houses here with secret rooms and tunnels that were stations on the Underground going north into Oberlin and up to Shawnee territory. There's an octagonal house in Yellow Springs that was specifically designed to hide runaways. It had all these corners that could be cut off into little cubbyholes. (p. 1020)

Hamilton writes about the black experience with a universal appeal that speaks to readers of any heritage. Another of Hamilton's characters learns that choice and action lie within his power in *M. C. Higgins, the Great*. In this story, the enemy is the spoil heap remaining from strip mining of the mountains, an oozing pile that threatens to swallow a boy's home and even his mother's beloved sunflower. In *Cousins*, Hamilton explores interrelationships within an extended family.

For *Bud, Not Buddy*, Christopher Paul Curtis won both the 2000 Newbery award and the Coretta Scott King Award. Curtis places his ten-year-old protagonist in the setting of the Great Depression of the 1930s. By developing his main character as a mistreated orphan boy, Curtis describes a very dark side of the Depression as Bud experiences waiting in line for food at missions and living with other people in shanty towns. There is also a very positive side of the story as Bud, clutching the few possessions left to him by his mother, searches for the man he believes is his father. This search takes Bud into the world of a famous jazz band. Throughout the book, Curtis uses Bud's "Rules and Things for Having a Funnier Life" to explore Bud's character and to add humor to the story. It is interesting to learn in the author's afterword that Curtis modeled two of his characters after his own grandfathers: one a redcap for the railroad and the other a bandleader for several musical groups including "Herman E. Curtis and the Dusky Devastators of the Depression."

An In-Depth Analysis of African American Literature

Two in-depth discussions of African American stories are found in Chapter 3: plot and conflict in Christopher Paul Curtis's *The Watsons Go to Birmingham—1963* and characterization in Carol Fenner's *Yolonda's Genius*.

In *Scorpions*, Walter Dean Myers's characters face person-against-society conflicts created by the contemporary world of drug dealers and gangs. They also face person-against-self conflicts created by inner fears and consequences related to owning a gun. The characters of Mama and her younger son Jamal are especially strong. Myers develops Mama's character through numerous contrasts. For example, when Mama thinks about her older son, who is in jail for robbery, she remembers looking at him as a baby and feeling great expectations because "You got a baby and you hope so much for it. . . ." (p. 54). Later, Mama is torn between her need to help this older son and to protect her younger children. Myers develops Mama's inner conflict as she discusses her problems with her minister:

"And I know they convicted him of taking somebody's life, but that don't mean he ain't my flesh and blood." The minister replies: "Sometimes the herbs we take are bitter, sister, but we got to take them anyway. . . . You got to hold your family here together too. We can't let the bad mess up the good." (p. 153)

In a tragic ending, Jamal discovers the consequences of having the gun and makes an even greater personal discovery. There was "the part of him, a part that was small and afraid, that still wanted that gun" (p. 214). This poignant story reveals the complex problems facing two generations of people who are fighting for personal and family survival in a dangerous world. In *Slam!*, Myers also uses contemporary urban locations. Now basketball helps the main character learn truths about himself.

In another book that is also lighter in tone, *The Mouse Rap*, Walter Dean Myers uses a style that many readers enjoy. Students of children's literature can analyze the impact of the language as the main character, fourteen-year-old Mouse, presents many of his views in rap. For example, Myers introduces his character in this way:

Ka-phoomp! Ka-Phoomp! Da Doom Da Dooom!
Ka-phoomp! Ka-phoomp! Da Doom Da Dooom!
You can call me Mouse, 'cause that's my tag
I'm into it all, everything's my bag
You know I can run, you know I can hoop
I can do it alone, or in a group
My ace is Styx, he'll always do
Add Bev and Sheri, and you got my crew
My tag is Mouse, and it'll never fail
And just like a mouse I got me a tale
Ka-phoomp! Ka-phoomp! Da Doom Da Dooom!
Ka-phoomp! Ka-phoomp! Da Doom Da Dooom! (p. 3)

Read portions of the book aloud to gain the greatest response to the text. Another book that gains from being read aloud is Nikki Grimes's *Jazmin's Notebook*. The author includes considerable poetry within the pages of a book written in the form of a diary.

Chapter 10 discusses other stories about African Americans for older children, including Mildred D. Taylor's *Roll of Thunder, Hear My Cry*, James and Christopher Collier's *Jump Ship to Freedom*, and Kathryn Lasky's *True North*. Books such as Joyce Hansen's *Which Way Freedom* and *I Thought My Soul Would Rise and Fly: The Diary of Patsy, a Freed Girl*, and Colin A. Palmer's *The First Passage: Blacks in the Americas, 1502–1617* are based on historical information about African Americans during the Civil War and reconstruction. The characters in all of these stories meet the criteria for outstanding characterization in literature: They are memorable individuals who face the best and the worst that life offers. They are portrayed with dignity and without stereotype.

Characters such as the slave in Gary Paulsen's *Nightjohn* show both the ordeals experienced by the slaves and the hope and perseverance that kept them alive. Even though he is cruelly treated, Nightjohn brings his gifts of teaching reading and writing to the young slave children. Twelve-year-old Sarny reveals both his suffering and his personal value very well when she thinks:

In the night he come walking. Late in the night and when he walks he leaves the tracks that we find in the soft dirt down where the drive meets the road, in the soft warm dirt in the sun we see his tracks with the middle toe missing on the left foot and the middle toe missing on the right and we know.

We know.

It be Nightjohn.

Late he come walking and nobody else knows, nobody from the big house or the other big houses know but we do.

We know.

Late he come walking and it be Nightjohn and he bringing us the way to know. (p. 92)

As in the literature for young readers, the stories for older readers reflect varied settings and socioeconomic levels. The main character may be the child of a highly educated college professor or the child of a destitute sharecropper. The realistic stories for older readers do, however, reflect a harsh realism in the African American experience, whether in the past or in contemporary life. Some of these stories—such as Virginia Hamilton's *The Planet of Junior Brown* and Walter Dean Myers's *Scorpions*—portray an economically disadvantaged inner-city existence and problems of survival very different from those of the middle-class experience. However, children in the stories reflect pride in their individuality and in their decisions to be themselves. The courage and determination of the characters are inspirational to all.

Authors of contemporary realistic fiction that emphasizes the black experience may focus on characters who try to survive in modern repressive environments. For example, Frances Temple (1992) describes her reasons for writing *Taste of Salt: A Story of Modern Haiti.* She says:

I read about the firebombing of the boys' shelter, Lafanmi Selavi, in Haiti, heard some of Jean-Bertrand Aristide's speeches, saw pictures of children and teenagers working, demonstrating. I wondered what it would be like to be one of them, called to be a mover and shaker in a country trying to make a new start, pitted against the giants of political terrorism and our global economy. (endcover)

Temple's novel for older readers is based on the lives of a fictional street urchin and a young woman who writes the story about their experiences. It is a dramatic story of survival, in which the characters conclude, "'Is hope they want to kill, Jeremie.' 'Is hope we need to keep alive, then, Djo.' 'And we will, Jeri, don't you think?' " (p. 172). As in many of the African American stories, this book also concludes on a note of courage and determination.

The Batchelder Award winner, Anton Quintana's *The Baboon King,* translated by John Nieuwenhuizen, also develops a survival story that concludes on a note of

The importance of becoming literate is developed in this story set in the time of slavery. (Jacket cover from Nightjohn by Gary Paulsen. Copyright © 1993 by Lynn Brasswell. Used by permission of Delacorte Press, a division of Bantam Doubleday Dell Publishing Group, Inc.)

courage and determination. This time the survival setting is the African wilderness after Morengáru, a young man who is half Kikuya and half Masai, is banished. The author uses the first chapters of the book to develop the contrasting belief systems and settings for the Kikuya tribe and the Masai. For example, when discussing hunting and tracking, the author compares the trained farmers' sons of the Kikuya with the Masai who "left their parents when they turned twelve, and were only allowed back when they were thirty. All those years they wandered through the wilderness with the herds" (p. 21). When banishment from the Kikuya finally occurs, readers understand that the elders have used Morengáru's Masai pride against him.

The final portion of the book follows Morengáru as he is first challenged by the old leader of a baboon troop, and then is seen as the new leader after he is victorious. Through the months of observing and learning from the baboons, Morengáru discovers that he needs companionship and a sense of belonging even if his companions are not human. After he avenges the death of several baboons by capturing the black leopard responsible for these deaths, he realizes that he can now go back to the world of humans and reclaim his place among his own people.

Nonfiction

Because two of the strongest purposes for sharing literature by and about African Americans with children are to raise the aspirations of black children and to encourage understanding of the African American experience by nonblack children, biographies should be important in a multicultural literature program. Biographies of African American leaders and artists tell children about contributions to American society and the problems overcome. David A. Adler's highly illustrated biography *A Picture Book of George Washington Carver* presents not only a brief introduction to Carver's life and accomplishments, but also insights into Carver's beliefs and values such as "science shall set you free, because science is truth" (unnumbered).

Several biographies for children portray the life of nineteenth-century freedom fighter Frederick Douglass. For example, Lillie Patterson's *Frederick Douglass: Freedom Fighter* is a dramatic account of Douglass's life in slavery, protest against slavery, escape from the slave owners and then slave hunters, work on the Underground Railroad, and championing of the rights of not only black people but also the Chinese, the Irish, and females. Douglas Miller's *Frederick Douglass and the Fight for Freedom* covers similar events and is interesting for comparative study. Miller, a professor of American history, includes a valuable list of additional readings and discusses some of the problems in previous biographies. Michael McCurdy's *Escape from Slavery: The Boyhood of Frederick Douglass in His Own Words* preserves Douglass's original writings. Milton Meltzer's *Frederick Douglass: In His Own Words* is a collection of Douglass's speeches and writings. Through his writings, students will discover attitudes toward slavery.

Gwen Everett's *John Brown: One Man Against Slavery* presents the story of the abolitionist through the viewpoint of Brown's sixteen-year-old daughter. The book is illustrated with a series of paintings drawn in 1941 by a prominent African American artist, Jacob Lawrence. The reproductions of the paintings in Mike Venezia's biography *Jacob Lawrence* is another source in which the artist provides a view of historical events through his paintings.

Kathryn Lasky's *Vision of Beauty: The Story of Sarah Breedlove Walker* is the biography of an African American woman (1867–1919) who made two strong contributions: She developed a successful cosmetics business during a time when neither African Americans nor women had such opportunities and she worked for racial equality.

James T. DeKay's *Meet Martin Luther King, Jr.* stresses the magnitude of King's work and his reasons for fighting against injustice. Lillie Patterson's *Martin Luther King, Jr. and the Freedom Movement* begins with an account of the

1955–1956 Montgomery, Alabama, bus boycott and Martin Luther King, Jr.'s involvement in the boycott. Patterson then explores King's earlier background and discovers some of the influences that caused King to become a leader in the boycott and the civil rights movement. James Haskins's *The Life and Death of Martin Luther King, Jr.* presents a stirring account of both King's triumphs and tragedies. Haskins's *I Have a Dream: The Life and Words of Martin Luther King, Jr.* focuses on King's involvement with the civil rights movement. Compare these biographies of Martin Luther King, Jr., with the revised edition of *My Life with Martin Luther King, Jr.* by Coretta Scott King.

Interesting comparisons may be made between two highly illustrated biographies of Martin Luther King, Jr. Faith Ringgold's *My Dream of Martin Luther King* develops the biography through a dream sequence. The text begins appropriately, "I've always been a dreamer. But the only dreams I can remember are the ones I dream with my eyes wide open. Once I go to sleep, I rarely remember my dreams. However, one day while watching a television program about Martin Luther King, Jr., I slept and had a dream that I will never forget" (unnumbered). From that point on, the text and illustrations present various stages in developing King's vision for a better world such as joining demonstrations, listening to his father's sermons, being influenced by the teachings of Mahatma Gandhi, becoming an adult minister, and finally dying from an assassin's bullet. The text and dream sequence end as people in a crowd scene trade bags filled with prejudice, hate, ignorance, violence, and fear for Martin Luther King's dream for the promised land.

Rosemary L. Bray's biography, *Martin Luther King,* is illustrated with folk-art paintings. Bray's biography includes more details about King's life. Neither book includes source notes. Students of children's literature can compare the impact of the illustrations and the depiction of King's life in these two highly illustrated biographies written to appeal to younger audiences.

Eloise Greenfield's *Rosa Parks* focuses on the life of the seamstress in Montgomery who refused to give up her seat on the bus. Ruby Bridges's *Through My Eyes* focuses on the experiences of a six-year-old girl during the integration of her school in New Orleans in 1960. The book is illustrated with photographs taken during the time period.

Arnold Adoff's *Malcolm X* stresses how and why Malcolm X urged African Americans to be proud of their heritage and themselves. In books written for older readers, *Malcolm X: By Any Means Necessary,* by Walter Dean Myers, and Kevin Brown's *Malcolm X: His Life and Legacy* set their biographical character against the history of segregation and the civil rights movement. Compare the three books about Malcolm X. Patricia McKissack's *Jesse Jackson* focuses on the accomplishments of the first black man to run for president of the United States. Anne Schraff's *Ralph Bunche: Winner of the Nobel Peace Prize* focuses on the life of the diplomat, adviser to the U.S. delegation for drafting the United Nations charter, and mediator in Palestine during negotiations between Israel and Egypt.

Several books reflect the contributions of African Americans to the fine arts. James Weldon Johnson's *Lift Every Voice and Sing* is often referred to as the African American national anthem. This book combines the song with linocut prints that were originally created in the 1940s by Elizabeth Catlett. *Sweet Words So Brave: The Story of African American Literature* by Barbara K. Curry and James Michael Brodie provides an introduction to authors and literature.

Mary E. Lyons's *Sorrow's Kitchen: The Life and Folklore of Zora Neale Hurston* describes the life of a black author who was part of the Harlem Renaissance and recorded and published folklore collected from the southern United States and the West Indies. Hurston's writings enrich the biography, which is supported with notes, suggested readings, and a bibliography. Many contributions of African Americans in the area of poetry are included in Chapter 8, "Poetry."

Patricia and Fredrick McKissack focus attention on the contributions of African Americans in the labor movement. Their *A Long Hard Journey: The Story of the Pullman Porter* chronicles the struggle for African Americans to form a union for railroad porters. Walter Dean Myers's *Now Is Your Time! The African-American Struggle for Freedom* includes shorter episodes that explore the African American experience from slavery through the civil rights movement and into contemporary times. This book includes sources, a bibliography, and an index. Patricia and Fredrick McKissack have written a second edition of *The Civil Rights Movement in America from 1865 to the Present.* This large book is supported with numerous photographs and descriptions of people who influenced the civil rights movement.

Andrea Davis Pinkney's *Let It Shine: Stories of Black Women Freedom Fighters* develops short biographies written in chronological order beginning with Sojourner Truth and concluding with Shirley Chisholm. Milton Meltzer's *There Comes a Time: The Struggle for Civil Rights* uses biographical examples such as a college freshman who in 1960 staged a lunch counter sit-in. Meltzer concludes his book with a look to the future and a call for action.

The books discussed in this chapter have broad appeal for children and a wide range of content. The emergence of outstanding authors who write about the African American experience with sensitivity and honesty has provided more excellent books about African Americans than are available about other minorities in the United States. When shared with children, such books contribute toward positive self-images and respect for individuals across cultures. They also do much to lessen the negative stereotypes of African American people in American literature of the past.

Native American Literature

The copyright dates listed in the bibliography at the end of this chapter show that the majority of recommended books about Native Americans have been published relatively recently. Few copyright dates precede the 1970s, which indicates a recent increase in the number of books written from a Native American perspective. Many of these books are beautifully illustrated traditional tales, and several have won the Caldecott Medal. Some are written by Native Americans themselves; others have been written by non–Native American writers, such as anthropologist Joyce Rockwood, who have used their knowledge of native cultures to authentically portray the Native American past.

The lovely poetry written by Byrd Baylor and the tales that she has collected increase understanding of Native American values and heritage, but there are still too few stories with contemporary settings and Native American main characters. Consequently, most children have few opportunities to read about Native American children facing the problems of today.

Jon C. Stott (1992) focuses on another problem faced by people seeking authentic Native American literature. He states, "Works by native authors generally appear on the lists of smaller, regional publishers, and, unfortunately, seldom reach a wide audience" (p. 374). Consequently, some Native American literature is not easily available.

In a bulletin published by the National Council for the Social Studies, Karen D. Harvey, Lisa D. Harjo, and Jane K. Jackson (1990) identify the following facts that you should consider when choosing and evaluating materials about Native Americans. First, Native American cultures span twenty or more millennia, from before written history to today. Second, most of the Native American history is tentative, speculative, and written by European or Anglo-American explorers or scholars, and much of the oral history of the Native peoples was lost. Third, widely diverse physical environments influenced the development of ancient and contemporary native American cultures, including Arctic tundra, woodlands, deserts, Mesoamerican jungles, prairies, plateaus, plains, swamps, and mountains. Fourth, linguists believe that at least two hundred languages were spoken in North America before European contact, and scholars estimate that seventy-three language families existed in North America at the time of European contact. Fifth, currently, there are about five hundred federally recognized tribes and about three hundred federal Indian reservations. Sixth, no one federal or tribal definition establishes a person's identity as an Indian. Consequently, Harvey, Harjo, and Jackson conclude, "the subject is vast, complicated, diverse, and difficult" (p. 2).

Traditional Tales

Native American tales show that the North American continent had traditional tales centuries old before the European settlers arrived. Traditional Native American tales make up a heritage that all North Americans should take pride in and pass on to future generations. Clifford E. Trafzer (1992), Director of Native American Studies at the University of California, Riverside, stresses the importance of these traditional tales. He says:

The words of the old stories are not myths and fairy tales. They are a communion with the ancient dead—the Animal, Plant, and Earth Surface Peoples who once inhabited the world and whose spirits continue to influence the course of Native American history. (p. 381)

Trafzer also emphasizes the importance of these stories for children, saying, "There is something sacred in the old texts, the ancient literature of America. . . . The accounts provide children with a better understanding of this land and its first people" (p. 393).

Critics and reviewers of multicultural literature emphasize the need for authenticity in texts and in illustrations. For example, Betsy Hearne (1993a, 1993b) emphasizes that not only should the reteller provide information about the original source for the tale but also a text adapted from folklore should be judged for its balance of two traditions: the one from which it is drawn and the one that it is entering. Texts and illustrations, then, should ring true for the culture from which they are adapted and be meaningful to the culture that is reading them. When evaluating the works of John Bierhorst, Barbara Bader (1997) also emphasizes the importance of authenticity. Notice what elements of Bierhorst's writing she stresses: "Authentic, accessible, and uncommonly attractive; also, fully documented, with historical introductions, source notes, and explanatory page notes. At a time when freeform, embellished retellings were the norm, with perhaps a nod to an eminent anthropologist or native informant, Bierhorst's work stood out for integrity and intrinsic quality" (p. 270).

In an evaluation of children's literature about Native Americans, Trafzer (1992) emphasizes the need for citing tribal sources and creating works that are culturally authentic for the tribe. Stott (1992) adds that critics of Native American literature must employ a complex set of guidelines, including:

If it is based on oral materials, how well is its orality transferred to the page? For whom is the book intended, and are the needs of audience met? If the writer is non-native, how well is the process of translation carried out? If it is by a native writer, is the book subject to different evaluative guidelines? Does the reviewer take into account the distance between a native author and a young, non-native reader? (p. 374)

In his collection of traditional Native American tales, *Anpao: An American Indian Odyssey,* Jamake Highwater compares tellers of Native American folktales to weavers whose designs are the threads of their personal sagas as well as the history of their people. Stories of the Native American oral tradition have been passed down and often mingled with tales from other tribes. Says Highwater:

They exist as the river of memory of a people, surging with their images and their rich meanings from one place to another, from one generation to the next—the tellers and the told so intermingled in time and space that no one can separate them. (p. 239)

Highwater recounts the task of preserving and transmitting traditional stories described by the Santee Dakota Charles Eastman. Writing of his own boyhood, Eastman said that very early in life, Indian boys assumed the task of preserving and transmitting their legends. In the evening, a boy would listen as one of his parents or grandparents told a tale. Often, the boy would be required to repeat the story the following evening. The household became his audience and either criticized or applauded his endeavors.

Highwater has combined a number of traditional Indian tales in *Anpao: An American Indian Odyssey.* The story begins "In the days before the people fled into the water . . . [when] there was no war and the people were at peace" (p. 15). During this time, Anpao travels across the great prairies, through deep canyons, and along wooded ridges in search of his destiny. Along the way, he observes the cultures and customs of many different tribes. His odyssey illustrates the diversity of the land, lifestyles, and history found within the Indian cultures of North America.

Native American traditional literature is an excellent source for identifying and understanding tribal traditional values and beliefs. Stephen Dow Beckham (1997), in the introduction to *Echoes of the Elders: The Stories and Paintings of Chief Lelooska,* states:

The stories were the primary means of passing on the tribal memory. They recounted how the world had come to be, why things were named as they were, and how humans should act. They speak through time to listeners and readers today. (p. 5)

Several sources provide documentation for traditional Native American values and beliefs. For example, *Human Behavior and American Indians,* by Hanson and Eisenbise (1983), documents tribal traditional values and compares them to urban industrial values. *The Journal of American Indian Education* (Spang, 1965) identifies North American Indian cultural values and compares them to the values of the dominant non-Indian culture. The Coalition of Indian Controlled School Boards (Ross and Brave Eagle, 1975) identifies traditional Lakota values and compares them to non-Lakota values.

Technology Resources

Oyate is an excellent Internet site providing a Native American perspective and resources for children. Visit our Companion Website at www.prenhall.com/norton to link to this valuable site.

A review of these sources indicates that many of the traditional values, such as living in harmony with nature, viewing religion as a natural phenomenon closely related to nature, showing respect for wisdom gained through age and experience, acquiring patience, and emphasizing group and extended family needs rather than individual needs, are also dominant themes in the traditional tales from various tribal regions. As you read Native American tales, see if you can identify these values.

For example, living in harmony with nature is a dominant theme in Tomie dePaola's retelling of the Comanche tale, *The Legend of the Bluebonnet.* The theme is developed when selfishly taking from the land is punished by drought, while unselfishly giving of a prized possession is rewarded with bluebonnets and rain. The name change in the main character as she goes from She-Who-Is-Alone to One-Who-Dearly-Loved-Her-People supports the emphasis on extended family rather than the individual. Having reverence for animals is an important theme in Barbara Diamond Goldin's retelling of *The Girl Who Lived with the Bears,* a tale from the Pacific Northwest.

The interactions between buffalo and Great Plains Indians are developed in both Olaf Baker's *Where the Buffaloes Begin* and Paul Goble's *Buffalo Woman.* In *Where the Buffaloes Begin,* Stephen Gammell's marvelous black-and-white drawings capture the buffaloes surging out of a mythical lake after their birth, rampaging across the prairie, and eventually saving Little Wolf's people from their enemies. In traditional tales from the Great Plains, the buffalo people frequently save those who understand and respect them. Goble's tale ends with why the relationship between the Great Plains Indians and the buffaloes is so important:

The relationship was made between the People and the Buffalo Nation; it will last until the end of time. It will be remembered that a brave young man became a buffalo because he loved his wife and little child. In return the Buffalo People have given their flesh so that little children, and babies still unborn, will always have meat to eat. It is the Creator's wish. (unnumbered)

Showing respect for animals, keeping one's word, and listening to elders are interrelated themes in Frank Cushing's "The Poor Turkey Girl," found in *Zuni Folk Tales.* In this Cinderella-type tale, a Zuni maiden who cares for the turkeys is helped to go to a festival by old Gobble and the other turkeys. When the girl does not heed old Gobble's admonition and return on time to feed the turkeys, she loses everything because:

After all, the gods dispose of men according as men are fitted; and if the poor be poor in heart and spirit as well as in appearance, how will they be aught but poor to the end of their days? Thus shortens my story. (p. 64)

You may compare "Poor Turkey Girl" with Penny Pollock's retelling of the same tale, *The Turkey Girl: A Zuni Cinderella Story.* Pollock identifies her original source as Cushing's *Zuni Folk Tales.*

Traditional tales of legendary heroes reflect important values and beliefs of the people. These heroes have many of the same characteristics found in heroic tales from other cultures. Like Beowulf in the Norse legend, an Inuit hero shows bravery, honor, and a willingness to avenge wrongs. In the introduction to one of the tales included in *Stories from the Canadian North,* Muriel Whitaker states:

In order to understand fully the ending of "The Blind Boy and the Loon," one must realize that the Eskimo hero was predominantly an avenger. Just as the spirits of weather, thunder, lightning, and the sea took vengeance on those who mistreated them, so too was the mortal hero expected to have the will and the power to exact retribution for evil. (p. 20)

According to Robin McGrath (1988), the traditional tales in Inuit folklore can be divided into six classifications: creation myths or stories, which embody religious belief; stories of fabulous beings such as trolls, giants, or ghosts; tales of epic heroes; stories of murder and revenge; beast fables; and personal memoirs. Stories in these classifications can be found in the adult resource *The Eskimo Storyteller: Folktales from Noatak, Alaska* by Edwin S. Hall, Jr. (1976). Additional Inuit tales include John Bierhorst's *The Dancing Fox: Arctic Folktales,* Lydia Dabcovich's *The Polar Bear Son: An Inuit Tale,* and Howard Norman's *The Girl Who Dreamed Only Geese and Other Tales of the Far North.* Bierhorst and Norman include an introduction and notes that enhance understanding of the tales. Dabcovich discusses the background of the tale and her research into the subject.

Legends from the northwestern United States and Canada emphasize heroes who venture onto the unpredictable sea and overcome perils of the ocean wilderness. Tales from British Columbia are found in *Kwakiutl Legends,* retold by Chief James Wallas, and in *Echoes of the Elders: The Stories and Paintings Chief Lelooska,* edited by Christine Normandin.

Native North Americans, like people everywhere, evolved mythology that explained the origins of the universe and natural phenomena. Ron Querry (1995) defines traditional Native American literature as "that which was composed in an Indian language for an Indian audience at a time when tribal cultures were intact and contact with whites was minimal. It was literature made up of sacred stories, myths, legends, and songs" (p. 2).

Native Americans, Native Canadians, and the Inuit peoples developed a rich heritage of traditional myths and legends. John Bierhorst (1976) identifies the following four categories found in Native American mythology: (1) myths that emphasize "setting the world in order," in which the world is created out of or fashioned from the chaos of nature; (2) myths that emphasize "family drama" by centering on conflicts and affinities rising out of the kinship unit; (3) myths that emphasize "fair and foul," such as the trickster cycle tales, in which the hero progresses from a character of utter worthlessness to one that displays a gradual understanding of social virtue; and (4) myths that emphasize "crossing the threshold" by depicting the passage from unconsciousness to consciousness, the ordeal of puberty, the passage into and out of the animal world, the passage into and out of death, and the transition from nature to culture. In a book for adults, *The Red Swan: Myths and Tales of the American Indians,* Bierhorst presents and discusses examples of these various categories of myths. Bierhorst's categories are also found in single stories and anthologies that include several tales passed down in tribes across the North American continent.

Setting-the-World-in-Order Tales. Traditional tales that emphasize setting the world in order tell about creating the earth and various animal and plant life. Earth-diver type myths are found in the literature of numerous North American Indians. For example, Virginia Hamilton includes two earth-diver myths in *In the Beginning: Creation Stories from Around the World:* (1) "Turtle Dives to the Bottom of the Sea: Earth Starter the Creator," a Maidu tale from California, and (2) "The Woman Who Fell from the Sky: Divine Woman the Creator," a Huron myth from the northeastern United States. Hamilton's collection also includes a Blackfoot myth in which Na'pi, or Old Man the Creator, travels around the world creating people and animals and an Eskimo myth in which Raven, a trickster god, travels around the world instructing people how to live. Amy L. Cohn's *From Sea to Shining Sea: A Treasury of American Folklore and Folk Songs* includes a creation story told by the Iroquois people, as well as tales from other Native American peoples.

Creation stories from several tribes are found in *Keepers of the Earth: Native American Stories and Environmental Activities for Children,* by Michael J. Caduto and Joseph Bruchac. An Onondaga tale from the northeastern woodlands, "The Earth on Turtle's Back," tells about how Great Turtle gives his shell to hold Earth and the seeds brought to Earth by the Great Chief's wife. In a Navajo tale, "Four Worlds: The Dine Story of Creation," the Holy People move from the first world to the fourth world by way of a female reed. This tale shows the disastrous consequences of not taking care of Earth. The tale concludes with a warning: "So the Fourth World came to be. However, just as the worlds before it were destroyed when wrong was done, so too this Fourth World was destined to be destroyed when the people do not live the right way. That is what the Dine say to this day" (p. 34).

From Keepers of the Earth: Native American Stories and Environmental Activities for Children *by Michael J. Caduto and Joseph Bruchac; illustrations by John Kahionhes Fadden and Carol Wood. Cover illustration copyright © 1989 John Kahionhes Fadden. Published by Fulcrum, Inc., 1989. Reprinted by permission.*

"The Great Flood" is one of the creation stories found in *The Serpent's Tongue: Prose, Poetry, and Art of the New Mexico Pueblos,* edited by Nancy Wood. In this Zia tale, the people and animals leave their underworld via a reed that Spider Sussistinnako places on the top of the mesa. The people pass through the reed until they reach Earth. The creation stories in this volume develop the strong connection between people and the spirit world.

Carole G. Vogel's *Legends of Landforms: Native American Lore and the Geology of the Land* is a collection of fourteen tales about the creation of different landforms from "The Grand Canyon," an Aute legend, to "Martha's Vineyard and Nantucket Island," a Wampanoag legend. Each of the tales is first presented as told from a Native American source (sources of the original tales are included) and then each tale is followed by geological information about the landform. A map identifies the locations of each of the landforms.

Native American tales, such as Barbara Esbensen's *The Star Maiden,* account for the creation of plant life. In this lyrical rendition of an Ojibway tale, Star Maiden and her sisters leave their home in the sky and become the beautiful star-shaped water lilies. The Eskimo tale, "The Doll," found in Dale DeArmond's *The Boy Who Found the Light* is about a magical boy carved out of a tree, who comes to life and eventually locates and opens the covers over the sky wall. From these openings in the sky come the plants and animals that provide for the Eskimo people. Through the eastern hole emerge trees, bushes, and caribou. The second hole provides grasses, flowers, geese, and ptarmigan. Through the southern hole flow sea spray, seals, and whales. From the next hole, the western wind brings a rainstorm, sleet, and great walruses. From the final hole, the north wind brings blasts of ice and snow and two great white bears. When the boy returns to his village, he warns the people:

they must never kill for sport, but only for the meat they needed, and that meat must never be wasted. He taught the people that animals are just like people, and must be treated with respect. And he taught them that they should make masks and pay honor to the inuas, spirits of the animals with songs and dances. (p. 58)

This tale provides both a creation story and a lesson about how to care for the animals.

Many of the Native American traditional tales explain the creation of something in nature. Nina Jaffe's *The Golden Flower* is adapted from a Taino myth. Both the text and the illustrations develop a creation story in which an arid desert is turned into a lush forest. When a child finds seeds, he plants them on a mountaintop until a forest grows. A beautiful flower grows with a golden ball (a pumpkin) in the center. This ball becomes a coveted object. When two men fight over its possession, the pumpkin bursts open and the ocean comes forth. In addition to an explanatory tale, the story develops the importance of life and fertility even in once-harsh environments. John Bierhorst's *The People with Five Fingers: A Native Californian Creation Tale* tells how Coyote and the other animals created plants and people who live on the Earth.

The creation of horses and the four sacred directions are very important in many Native American tales. For example, in *Turquoise Boy: A Navajo Legend*, Terri Cohlene reveals how the son of Changing Woman visits the four sacred mountains and gains gifts from the Talking Gods who live on the sacred White Shell Mountain of the East, the sacred Turquoise Mountain of the South, the sacred Abalone Shell Mountain of the West, and the sacred Black Jet Mountain of the North. These gifts are eventually used by Changing Woman to create horses, which are very important to the Navajo people. In addition to the tale, this book provides information about the Navajo homeland, the Navajo people, and the Navajo beliefs.

Lois Duncan's *The Magic of Spider Woman* is a creation tale, an explanatory tale, and a cautionary tale. It is a tale about how Wandering Girl came to be known as Weaving Woman and also about the consequences when she disobeys Spider Woman. The story begins "before the beginning of time" when there were only animal beings and insects in the Third World. One of these insects is Spider Woman, who knows the secret of how to spin and weave. As in other traditional Navajo tales, the Third World floods and the beings escape to the Fourth World through a hollow reed. It is in this world that Spirit Being creates the first people, the Navajo. Now the Great Spirit teaches the people all they need to know to survive including the songs and chants called the Blessing Way that keep the people healthy and in harmony with nature. Unfortunately, Wandering Girl does not receive the instructions. During the cold winter, Spider Woman takes pity on Wandering Girl and teaches her to weave blankets. Spider Woman also gives a warning that is a moral lesson or theme for the story: "But there is one danger that you always must be aware of. The Navajo People must walk the Middle Way, which means that they must respect the boundaries and try to keep their lives in balance. They should not do too much of anything. You must promise not to weave for too long, or a terrible thing will happen to you" (unnumbered).

From that time she becomes known as Weaving Woman. Unfortunately, she does not take Spider Woman's warning and becomes completely engrossed in weaving a beautiful blanket and her spirit becomes trapped in the blanket. To free the spirit, a spirit trail is created in the blanket by pulling a yarn from the finished weaving and pulling the strand through so that it is now less perfect. After Weaving Woman is freed, her words reinforce the moral she should have heeded earlier: " 'Oh, Spirit Being! I have learned my lesson!" she cried. 'Never again will I weave for too long at a sitting and never again will I doubt the wisdom of my creators!' " (unnumbered). The tale concludes with a why explanation. Now every Navajo blanket includes a pathway so that the spirit of the weaver will not be imprisoned by the beauty of the blanket.

Family Drama Tales. Family drama tales focus on various family needs and conflicts, such as learning from elders, providing protection, obtaining food, and overcoming problems, including rivalry and aggression. The family in these stories may be the smaller tribal unit or the greater cosmos. If the tale deals with the greater world family, the storyteller may refer to Earth as mother, Sky as father, and humanity as children. Many of these stories reveal tribal standards.

The importance of tribal stories for providing instructions for life is emphasized in *The Serpent's Tongue*, edited by Nancy Wood: "Now people call our instructions legends because they were given as stories. But to the Indian people, that was like a reality at some point in history. . . . The instructions during that time, at the beginning, were to love and respect one another even with all the differences—different cultures, different languages. . . . We were told if the instructions were lost, then harm would come to the people" (p. 55).

Several tales in Jean Monroe and Ray Williamson's *They Dance in the Sky: Native American Star Myths* illustrate universal family concerns and appropriate behaviors. For example, "Bright Shining Old Man," an Onondaga tale from New York, shows that children will be punished if they ignore the warnings of their elders. In "The Little Girl Who Scatters the Stars," a tale from the Cochita Pueblo in New Mexico, a girl cannot overcome her curiosity. It is a universal family tale. In it, "Our Mother" tells the people that they are all brothers and sisters and instructs them to live as one large family.

Why there is chaos in the sky, society, and family life is revealed in Jerrie Oughton's *How the Stars Fell into the Sky: A Navajo Legend.* In this tale, First Woman wants to write the laws for the people to see. First Man makes several suggestions for places to write them, such as in the sand or on the water, but First Woman argues that they will be blown away or disappear into the water. Finally, First Man suggests that she take her jewels and write the laws in the sky. First Woman begins her mission by designing a pattern of stars so that all can read the laws. Coyote offers to help her complete her task, but he is unhappy when she tells him that writing the laws with the stars could take many moons. First Woman tries to convince Coyote that it is important to have the laws, so that the people will see them before they enter their hogans, mothers will sing of them to their children, and lonely warriors will warm themselves by them. However, Coyote impatiently gathers the corners of First Woman's blanket and flings the remaining stars out into the night, spilling them in disarray. The tale concludes: "As the pulse of the second day brought it into being, the people rose and went about their lives, never knowing in what foolish haste Coyote had tumbled the stars . . . never knowing the reason for the confusion that would always dwell among them" (p. 30). According to Oughton, this is a retelling of a traditional tale told to the Navajo Indians by Hosteen Klah, their great medicine man, at the turn of the century.

Trickster Tales. Trickster tales reveal both good and bad conduct. John Bierhorst (1976) states, "The trickster tale affords the narrator an opportunity to flirt with immoral or antisocial temptations" (p. 6) in humorous ways. Trickster characters are found throughout North America. On the northwestern coast of the Pacific Ocean, the trickster is called Raven. When evaluating the role of Raven, Bierhorst (1993) states:

Raven is tough. Whatever is ascribed to him, he can survive it. And when we look back on what has been said of him, we may find that there is more wisdom to these tales than we had realized. As for Raven himself, he is always off on a new adventure. One of the old Tsimshian narrators used to say that after each scrape Raven doggedly "journeys on." Or as another of the old texts once phrased it, the trickster simply "put on his raven garment and flew away."

Raven the trickster is the central character in Gerald McDermott's *Raven: A Trickster Tale from the Pacific Northwest.* In this tale, to bring light from Sky Chief, Raven changes himself into a pine needle that is in a drinking cup

of Sky Chief's daughter. After swallowing the needle, she eventually gives birth to a child that is really Raven in human form. Thus, Raven is able to acquire the sun that is in a set of nested boxes found in the sky lodge and bring light to the earth.

Iktomi is the Sioux name for trickster. In *Iktomi and the Boulder: A Plains Indian Story,* Paul Goble describes the fair and foul side of Iktomi, who is

beyond the realm of moral values. He lacks all sincerity. Tales about Iktomi remind us that unsociable and chaotic behavior is never far below the surface. We can see ourselves in him. Iktomi is also credited with greater things: in many of the older stories, the Creator entrusts him with much of Creation. People say that what seem to be the "mistakes" and "irrational" aspects of Creation, such as earthquakes, floods, disease, flies, and mosquitos, were surely made by Iktomi. (introduction)

In Goble's version of the Sioux tale, conceited Iktomi first gives his blanket to a boulder and then deceitfully takes the blanket back when he needs it for protection. Iktomi uses trickery to save himself from the angry boulder. Even though he eventually wins the confrontation, he is frightened and momentarily humbled by his experience. Goble's *Iktomi and the Berries* provides another humbling experience for the trickster character.

Another trickster character is Coyote, who may be a creator or a trickster in folklore from the Great Plains. In Barbara Diamond Goldin's *Coyote and the Fire Stick: A Pacific Northwest Indian Tale,* the crafty character teaches the People to start a fire by rubbing sticks together.

Coyote also may be a changer. William Morgan's *Navajo Coyote Tales* includes six tales about Coyote as both a trickster and a changer. The stories include such additional characters as Crow, Horned Toad, and Rabbit.

Threshold Tales. Numerous Native American tales depict crossing various thresholds. Transformations that allow characters to go into and out of the animal world are especially popular in stories retold for children. Paul Goble's *Buffalo Woman* uses transformations to show the bond between Native Americans and animals. Goble's retelling of a tale from the Great Plains reflects a bond between the humans and the buffalo herds, essential if both the people and the buffaloes were to prosper.

In *Beyond the Ridge,* Goble's main character goes from the land of the living to the spirit world. An elderly Plains Indian experiences the afterlife as believed by her people. On her way, she discovers Owl Maker. The spirits of individuals who have led good lives pass Owl Maker to the right, toward Wanagiyata, Land of Many Tipis. However, Owl Maker pushes the spirits of those who have led bad lives to the left, along a short path where they fall off, landing back on earth to wander for a time as ghosts.

Combination Tales. Many traditional tales have elements that include several of the folklore types. For example, John Bierhorst's *The Ring in the Prairie: A Shawnee Legend* has elements related to fair and foul tricksters, to crossing thresholds, and to family drama. First, the Shawnee hunter plays the trickster, turning himself into a mouse and creeping close to a beautiful young woman who descends from the sky. Then, he returns to his human form and captures his heart's desire. The tale contains several crossing-the-threshold experiences. The hunter passes into and out of the animal world before he and his family are permanently transformed into animals. His captured bride crosses from the world of the star people to the world of humans and back to the world of the star people before she is permanently transformed into a white hawk. The story also reflects strong family ties. The hunter mourns the loss of his wife and son and then goes on a difficult quest so that he can be reunited with his family.

"The Boy Who Found the Light," adapted by Dale DeArmond in a book by that name, exemplifies an Eskimo story that has elements of setting the world in order, trickster tales, and threshold tales. First, the orphan boy, Tulugac, sets out on a quest to return light to the Eskimo people. On this quest, Tulugac is helped by his old aunt, who is considered a witch because she has special powers. On his travels, Tulugac is assisted by a rabbit, a bear, and an owl. As the tale continues, Tulugac finds the sun and the moon and tricks an old man so that he (Tulugac) may retrieve the sun and the moon and return the light to the people. Finally, Tulugac is assisted by a small birdskin that he has been carrying with him. In his time of need, the birdskin surrounds him and he is transformed into a raven flying swiftly and smoothly through the air.

On Tulugac's return journey to his village, the story takes on setting-the-world-in-order elements. Tulugac, now the raven boy, breaks off pieces of the light and throws them away so that there is daylight everywhere. According to the tale, the intervals of darkness and light change throughout the year because, "Sometimes he waited a long time before he threw out another piece of light, and that is why we have the long nights of winter. Sometimes he threw out more light very soon, making the short nights and long days of summer" (p. 30).

In *Keepers of the Animals: Native American Stories and Wildlife Activities for Children*, Michael J. Caduto and Joseph Bruchac discuss the various circles found in "Salmon Boy," a Haida tale from the Pacific Northwest. They state:

"Salmon Boy" is an allegory of great importance, revealing a series of interlocking circles which, as the story proceeds, run progressively deeper into the life ways of the Haida. . . . There is an important, interdependent relationship here: The salmon give people food and the people show their appreciation through prayer and reverence. (p. 97)

Caduto and Bruchac identify the first circle as the great circle of life and death and as the reality of the spirit world. Another circle is transformation, depicted when Salmon Boy returns to his people as a healer and a teacher to instruct them in the ways of the Salmon People and to help them when they are sick. This circle shows the sense of interconnectedness between this world and the spirit world, and between animals and people. Finally, Salmon Boy's body is placed in the river, where it circles four times, a sacred number, and returns to the Salmon People.

In *Storm Boy*, Paul Owen Lewis also includes a combination of these characteristics in his original tale based on the mythology of the Northwest Coast of North America. For example, the author focuses on the motifs of separation, initiation, and return. Under separation are the motifs that wandering too far from the village invites supernatural encounters and there is a mysterious entrance into the Spirit World. Under initiation are the motifs that animals are encountered in human form and potlatching or exchanging of gifts and culture are important. Under return are the motifs that objects are given to assist in the return, a mysterious return is possible by wishing continually, there is a time disparity between two realms, and there is a claiming of a crest. As you read the Native American folklore, you will discover many of these combination tales.

Songs and Poetry

Songs, chants, and poems are very important in the various Native American cultures. Many poems express reverence for creation, nature, and beauty. Native Americans created poetry for a purpose; they believed that there was power in the word. Songs were often part of ceremonial rituals, with their symbolism portrayed through dance.

Native American author Joseph Bruchac stresses the importance of poetry to him when he says, "I believe that poetry is as much a part of human beings as is breath—and, like breath, poetry links us to all living things and is meant to be shared" (quoted in Whitson, 1999, p. 39).

The beauty of both ancient Native American poetry and contemporary poetry about Native American experiences can be shared with children. An interesting resource book that shares the music of Native Americans with children of many cultures is John Bierhorst's *A Cry from the Earth: Music of the North American Indians*. According to Bierhorst, native peoples throughout North America shared a belief in the supernatural power of music to cure disease, bring rain, win a lover, or defeat an enemy.

Many Native Americans today sing the songs for pleasure and to express pride in their heritage. Bierhorst's book contains words and music for many songs, including songs of prayer, magic, and dreams, songs to control the weather, and music to accompany various dances. There are greeting songs, love songs, a Hopi flute song, a Hopi sleep song, a Cherokee lullaby, and a Kwakiutl cradlesong. Music, words, and dance steps are included so that children can re-create, experience, and respect this musical heritage.

The wide range of subjects around which songs were created suggests a Native American heritage that is richly various. Bierhorst's anthology *The Sacred Path: Spells, Prayers, and Power Songs of the American Indians* is organized according to themes. An introduction, a glossary, and a list of notes and sources add authenticity and additional information.

Byrd Baylor has expressed her love and concern for the Native American peoples and the land of the Southwest in a series of books written in poetic form. One of them ponders the secrets of prehistoric people as seen through their drawings on pottery. In *When Clay Sings,* the designs on ancient shards of pottery created by the Anasazi, Mogollon, Hohokam, and Mimbres cultures of the Southwest are the models for Bahti's illustrations and suggest the inspiration for Baylor's poetry. According to Baylor:

Indians who find this pottery today say that everything has its own spirit—even a broken pot. . . . They say that every piece of clay is a piece of someone's life. They even say it has its own small voice and sings in its own way. (cover summary)

Poetry selections by Byrd Baylor and Jamake Highwater reflect foundations in traditional beliefs and mythological references. For example, Baylor's *The Other Way to Listen* and *The Desert Is Theirs* communicate to young readers the Native American closeness to nature. Peter Parnall's illustrations suggest the majesty of the desert and the respect of the Papago Indians for it. In *Moon Song,* Baylor presents a "why" tale in poetic form. She develops the closeness in nature between Moon and coyotes. Highwater's *Moonsong Lullaby* has foundations in traditional beliefs. The poem develops respect for nature, close relationships with animals, respect for older people, and belief in ancient knowledge.

Virginia Driving Hawk Sneve's collection, *Dancing Teepees: Poems of American Indian Youth,* includes poems from various tribes, such as the Hopi, the Zuni, and the Lakota Sioux. The poems vary from the words of heroes, such as Black Elk, to the prayers of ancient peoples to the writings of contemporary tribal poets. *When the Rain Sings: Poems by Young Native Americans,* published by the Smithsonian Institution, is another collection of poems from various tribes. Many of these poems such as "Ration Day," "The Fight," and "I Always Begin with I Remember," reflect historical conflict.

Susan Jeffers has adapted the words of Chief Seattle into a poetic text in *Brother Eagle, Sister Sky: A Message from Chief Seattle.* The text is based on the message that Chief Seattle supposedly presented in a speech describing his people's respect for the earth and his concern for the way the land will be treated in the future. (There is some disagreement about the actual rendition of Chief Seattle's message, however.) Compare the text for Jeffers's book with the version provided by Joseph Campbell in *Transformations of Myth Through Time* (1990). As you read both versions, analyze the variances, and consider any reasons for the variations.

Shonto Begay's *Navajo: Visions and Voices Across the Mesa* includes poems that reflect both an ancient past and a contemporary culture. Poems such as "Echoes" and "Creation" provide visions of the ancient culture of the

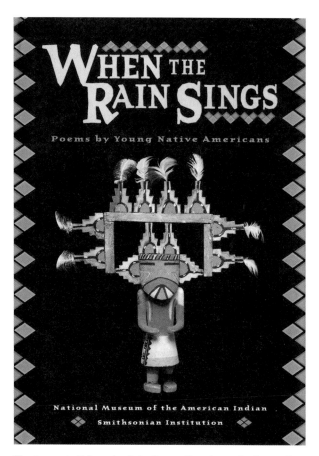

The poems in When the Rain Sings *reflect the work of poets from various tribes. (Reprinted with the permission of Simon & Schuster Books for Young Readers, an imprint of Simon & Schuster Children's Publishing Division, from* When the Rain Sings: Poems by Young Native Americans. *Jacket design by Anahid Hamparian. Copyright © 1999.)*

Navajo. Poems such as "Into the New World" reflect contemporary concerns related to damages done to the earth and the environment.

Inuit traditional beliefs are reflected in the poetry in Edward Field's *Magic Words.* Poems such as "The Earth and the People" and "Magic Words" reflect traditional stories told in poetic form.

Poetic texts reinforce the desirable understanding that Native American peoples have diverse cultures and great artistic traditions.

Historical Fiction

Themes and conflicts in historical fiction about Native Americans often emphasize the survival of the body or the spirit. Some authors emphasize periods in history in which contact with white settlers or cavalry resulted in catastrophic changes. Others emphasize growing interpersonal relationships between Native American and white characters. Four award-winning books provide examples for these two types of historical fiction.

Scott O'Dell's Newbery Honor book, *Sing Down the Moon,* focuses on the mid-1860s, when the U.S. Cavalry forced the Navaho to make the three-hundred-mile Long Walk from their beautiful and productive home in Canyon de Chelly to stark Fort Sumner. O'Dell effectively develops the resulting conflict through descriptions of the contrasting settings. He provides detailed descriptions of Canyon de Chelly, a place of miracles. This idealistic setting does not last. It is followed by horror when Colonel Kit Carson's soldiers first destroy the crops and livestock in the canyon and then force the Navaho to walk through desolate country to a setting that is unconducive to physical or spiritual survival. Fifteen hundred Navaho die, and many others lose their will to live.

O'Dell's protagonist, a Navaho woman named Bright Morning, retains an inner strength based on hope for the future. While she is a captive, she hoards food and plans for the day when she and her husband will return to their canyon. Susan Naramore Maher (1992) states that

O'Dell's female narrators are significant agents because as "strong, resistant purveyors of connection, they stand in opposition to the hermetic, invulnerable, unresponsive heroes of formulary westerns—the Orlovs and the Long Knives" (p. 226).

Jan Hudson's *Sweetgrass* is a story of a Blackfoot girl who survives a smallpox epidemic in the 1830s. Even though the girl does not interact with white characters, she battles the disease brought to her people. Hudson, the author of this Canadian Library Association Book of the Year Award winner, writes about native peoples with sensitivity. (See Chapter 10 for a discussion of *Sweetgrass*.)

Farley Mowat's Canadian Library Association Book of the Year, *Lost in the Barrens*, takes place in the twentieth century in a remote arctic wilderness, hundreds of miles from the nearest town. The two main characters are Awasin, a Woodland Cree, and Jamie, a white Canadian

An In-Depth Analysis of One Example of Multicultural Literature— Native American

The Birchbark House by Louise Erdrich was a National Book Award finalist. The book is set on an island in Lake Superior in 1847 and describes an Ojibwa girl's life as she experiences four seasons of the year. Consequently, our in-depth analysis must consider both the author's development of Native American values, specifically Ojibwa, and the ability of the author to create credible historical fiction for the time period.

First, the author creates credibility for the story by identifying herself as a member of the Turtle Mountain Band of Ojibwa and stating that she became interested in writing the book while researching her own family history. In her acknowledgments Erdrich states: "My mother, Rita Gourneau Erdrich, and my sister, Lise Erdrich, researched our family life and found ancestors on both sides who lived on Madeline Island during the time in which this book is set. One of them was Gatay Manomin, or Old Wild Rice. I'd like to thank him and all of his descendants, my extended family. . . . This book and those that will follow are an attempt to retrace my own family's history" (unpaged acknowledgments).

Two of the evaluative criteria for Native American literature are that the Native American characters belong to a specific identified tribe and not be grouped together under one category referred to as "Indian" and that the customs, values, and beliefs for the specific tribe should be authentic and respected.

In this book, the development of Ojibwa values is especially meaningful. For example, the author conveys the value of nature as the girl is taught by her grandmother to listen to and learn from nature. The importance of her lessons is reinforced as she nurses her family during a smallpox epidemic. The author reinforces Ojibwa values and beliefs through traditional stories

told by the girl's father and grandmother. One of the stories told by the grandmother is "Nanabozho and Muskrat Make an Earth." Grandmother uses the stories to teach lessons to her granddaughter. When you read the folklore from various Native American tribes, you will discover that the oral stories were told to pass on various beliefs and to educate the members of the tribe. In addition, the "Earth Diver" story as told by grandmother is one of the oldest and most common creation stories told among various North American Indian tribes. It is commonly told among the tribes living around the Great Lakes.

Another authentic Native American value and belief is developed as the author explores the importance of messages revealed in dreams and voices heard in nature. Notice in this quote how the grandmother reveals the importance of the fact that her granddaughter, Omakayas, can hear the voices: "Nokomis understood the meaning of what had happened, understood why the voices had spoken, understood what it meant for Omakayas's future and was proud and glad to have a granddaughter who was chosen to be a healer" (p. 206). When you read many of the autobiographies of early Native American leaders you will discover that showing respect for and relying on messages revealed in dreams and listening to voices found in nature are of considerable value. Consequently, only people of great stature within the tribe are given this special ability.

When analyzing the book for historical accuracy for settings and conflicts, you will discover that the author provides detailed descriptions of the island during each of the four seasons. A map of the general region of the island and Lake Superior and a detailed map of the Ojibwa village are included in the book. The major conflict that the village must overcome is the smallpox epidemic of 1847 during which time eighteen Ojibwa died from the disease. This is the kind of information that can easily be evaluated as you consider the authenticity of both the settings for the island and the major health conflicts of this period.

orphan who moves north to live with his uncle. The setting becomes an antagonist for both boys when they accompany the Crees on a hunting expedition and then become separated from the hunters. Mowat vividly describes searching for food and preparing for the rapidly approaching winter. Through long periods of isolation, the boys develop a close relationship and an understanding of each other. Elizabeth George Speare's Newbery Honor book, *The Sign of the Beaver,* focuses on the friendship between a Native American boy and a white boy in the Maine wilderness of the 1700s. (See Chapter 10 for a discussion of *The Sign of the Beaver.*)

In his latest book, *Thunder Rolling in the Mountains,* Scott O'Dell, with the assistance of his wife, Elizabeth Hall, again develops a story based on the removal of Indian peoples from their land. This time, the narrator is Chief Joseph's daughter, who tells from her point of view the story of the forced removal of the Nez Perce tribe from their homeland in 1877. In the foreword to the book, Hall describes O'Dell's fascination with this subject:

> At the time of his death, Scott O'Dell was immersed in the story of Chief Joseph and his people. Their courage and determination in the face of cruelty, betrayal, and bureaucratic ignorance moved him deeply. So deeply that he continued to work on the manuscript in the hospital until two days before he died. (p. ix)

Readers will also experience O'Dell's fascination with this time period and the plight of these brave people.

Two historical fiction books about Native Americans are set in 1492 at the time of Columbus's first contact with the native peoples. Jane Yolen's *Encounter* is a picture book written for younger audiences. Michael Dorris's *Morning Girl* is a book for older readers. (See Chapter 10 for a further discussion of these books.) Both books are written from the point of view of native children and both provide information about the beliefs and values of the Taino culture. Both authors also provide insights into their reasons for writing the stories and the research necessary for depicting the Taino culture, which was eliminated by the contact with Europeans. Yolen (1992) says:

> In order to create and recreate the characters in *Encounter,* I did the kind of research one might ordinarily do for a non-fiction book. And once I had the outlines of the Taino culture down (or at least what we know from the shards left), I could write the story as if I were a child of that culture. (p. 238)

The resulting text and illustrations provide insights into how the Taino people may have reacted to Columbus and his men. The final illustration in the text is symbolic: An old Taino Indian is sitting on a stump, but, like his people and his culture, his legs are disappearing. You may also find it interesting to compare *Encounter* and *Morning Girl.* In *Sees Behind Trees* Dorris places his characters in sixteenth-century America. Now a partially sighted boy discovers the importance of his other senses.

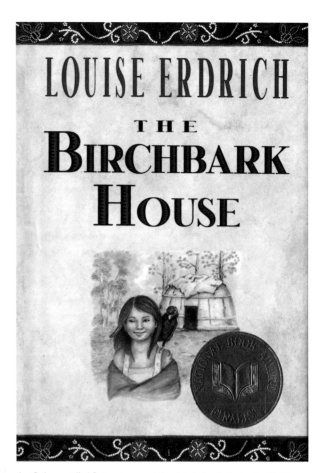

An Ojibwa girl's life is set on an island in Lake Superior in 1847. (From **The Birchbark House** by Louise Erdrich. Text and jacket illustration copyright © 1999 by Louise Erdrich. Reprinted by permission of Hyperion Books for Children.)

Through all of these stories, children can experience Native American characters who have personal thoughts and emotions and who live within a family as well as within a tribe. In addition, children will begin to understand the impact of white people on the Native American way of life. (Additional historical stories are discussed in Chapter 10.)

Contemporary Realistic Fiction

Little contemporary realistic fiction for children focuses on Native Americans. In the books that are available, Native Americans often express conflict between the old ways and the new ones. Characters must decide whether to preserve their heritage or to abandon it. Many of the stories allow Native Americans to honor the old ways but to live with the new ones. Some stories show life on modern reservations; others depict families who have left the reservation to live in cities. The needs of all individuals are shown: Characters search for their identities or express a desire for love. The Native American characters often express hostility toward white characters who have been unfair to them, but some stories develop strong friendships between people from different backgrounds.

Like other contemporary realistic fiction for younger children, stories about Native Americans for young audiences frequently develop themes related to love and family relationships. Barbara Joosse's *Mama, Do You Love Me?* and Nancy Luenn's *Nessa's Fish* are picture books set in the Arctic regions. In *Mama, Do You Love Me?* a young child tests her mother's love. Through satisfactory responses, the girl discovers that her mama loves her "more than the raven loves his treasure, more than the dog loves his tail, more than the whale loves his spout" (pp. 4–5). Each of the questions and responses relates to the culture. In *Nessa's Fish,* a young girl not only protects her ailing grandmother but also saves the fish that they caught from hungry arctic animals. Margaret Nicolai's *Kitaq Goes Ice Fishing* is a fictional account based on stories the author's husband told her about growing up in Kwethluk, Alaska, with the Yup'ik people. An excellent author's note provides an additional source of background information.

A loving relationship between a Navaho girl and her grandmother provides the foundation in Miska Miles's *Annie and the Old One.* The conflict in the story develops because Annie does not want to accept the natural order of aging and death. In an effort to hold back time, Annie tries to prevent her grandmother from completing the rug that she is weaving because her grandmother has said, "My children, when the new rug is taken from the loom, I will go to Mother Earth" (p. 15). The author emphasizes the way that Annie's inner conflict ends, and the theme that we are all part of nature emerges when Annie finally realizes:

The cactus did not bloom forever. Petals dried and fell to earth. She knew that she was a part of the earth and the things on it. She would always be a part of the earth, just as her grandmother had always been, just as her grandmother would always be, always and forever. And Annie was breathless with the wonder of it. (p. 41)

Annie's actions show that she has accepted nature's inevitable role. Annie picks up the weaving stick and begins to help her grandmother complete the rug.

Symbolism, ancient traditions, and person-against-self conflicts are important elements in Jean Craighead George's *The Talking Earth,* a book for middle-elementary readers in which a Seminole girl who lives on the Big Cypress Reservation questions the traditions of her people and searches for her heritage as she travels alone through the swamp.

Authors of contemporary stories about Native Americans frequently develop understandings about the past to help their characters respect their heritage. For example, in *High Elk's Treasure,* Virginia Driving Hawk Sneve ties the past to the present with a flashback to the year 1876, when the Sioux were taken to the reservation

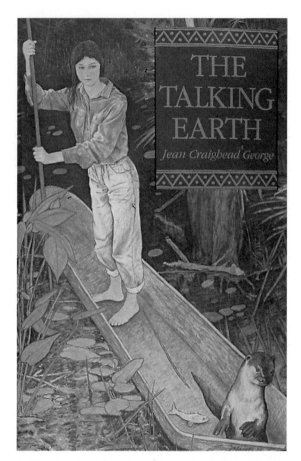

A contemporary Seminole girl searches for her heritage. (From **The Talking Earth** by Jean Craighead George. Jacket art copyright © 1983 by Bob Marstall. Reprinted by permission of HarperCollins Publishers.)

following the defeat of General Custer at the Battle of the Little Big Horn. One hundred years later, High Elk's descendants excitedly discover a pictograph of the Battle of the Little Big Horn. This pictograph is later authenticated by an expert from the university. Sneve develops a feeling for the past and pride in Native American heritage throughout this book. In *Bearstone,* Will Hobbs uses an ancient turquoise bear to help a Ute Indian boy clarify his beliefs and overcome his personal problems.

Three stories with Eskimo protagonists show the range of subjects and conflicts that are covered in contemporary literature. In Jean Craighead George's *Water Sky,* Lincoln, a boy from Massachusetts, journeys to Barrow, Alaska, in search of his uncle. The conflict between cultures is reinforced by the boy's mother, who does not want Lincoln to make this journey. During his quest, Lincoln lives at a whaling camp, where he learns to understand and respect his Eskimo heritage. Throughout this story, George combines vivid settings and information about Eskimo values and beliefs.

In Gary Paulsen's *Dogsong,* Russel, a contemporary Eskimo boy, leaves the mechanized world in which his people hunt seal and caribou by snowmobiles to discover the ways and beliefs that were there in the days of dogsleds. Russel's mentor is an elderly Eskimo who believes that the Eskimo people have lost the songs that made the whales and other animals come to the people in times of need. Russel's search for his own song takes him on a 1,400-mile dogsled trek across the isolated ice and tundra. In a traditional manner, dreams and visions become part of the learning experience. In a dream, Russel goes back in time, faces his fear, kills a mammoth, and sings a song in exultation. Through his ordeal with nature, Russel discovers the power of the old Eskimo ways.

In Scott O'Dell's *Black Star, Bright Dawn,* an Eskimo girl drives a dogsled team in the Iditarod Trail Sled Dog Race from Anchorage to Nome. Through her experiences, the girl learns to depend on her dogs and herself. In addition, she discovers the strength in her Eskimo heritage, values, and beliefs. Realistic fictional stories portray some conflicts in contemporary Native American children's lives, as well as some resolutions that reflect self-esteem and respect for an ancient heritage.

Nonfiction

Authors of informational books about Native Americans for young children often use illustrated texts to encourage identification with traditional ways of life and cultural contributions made by Native Americans. Authors of informational books for older readers often stress history, the struggle for survival, and various contemporary conflicts.

Artworks of Native American children in Bruce Hucko's *A Rainbow at Night: The World in Words and Pictures by Navajo Children* present a view of the children's life and culture through their drawings and paintings. George Littlechild's *This Land Is My Land* presents an illustrated history of Littlechild's ancestors. The illustrations by this well-known Cree artist provide an interesting subject for discussion and enjoyment.

Sandra DeCoteau Orie's *Did You Hear Wind Sing Your Name?: An Oneida Song of Spring* presents the Oneida Indians' view of nature. The author's note explains the symbolism of the pine tree as it represents the unity of the six nations of the Iroquois Confederacy; hawk, as the bringer of good news; the three sisters of corn, beans, and squash as sustaining staples; the flowers that give beauty; and the celebration of the circle of life.

In *People of the Breaking Day,* Marcia Sewall takes readers back to the Wampanoag nation of southeastern Massachusetts before the English settlers arrive. The text, which is divided into sections, presents information about the tribe, the belief in the Great Spirit, the celebrations, the role of warriors and other members of the tribe, and the family.

Paul Goble's *Death of the Iron Horse* and Russell Freedman's *Buffalo Hunt* and *An Indian Winter* also provide historical perspectives. Goble uses an actual incident in 1867, when a Union Pacific train was derailed by the Cheyenne. In this fictionalized story, Goble shows that the Cheyenne fought the encroaching white culture by attacking the railroad. In *Buffalo Hunt,* Freedman shows the importance of the buffaloes to the Indians living on the Great Plains. His text includes descriptions of the hunts, attitudes of the Indians toward the buffaloes, and the consequences to the Indians when the white culture all but eliminated the buffaloes. The text is illustrated with reproductions of paintings by such artists as George Catlin and Karl Bodmer, who actually saw the buffalo hunts. The titled and dated illustrations add interest to the text. Freedman uses a similar approach in *An Indian Winter,* accompanying his description of traditional Mandan life in the 1800s with paintings and drawings created by Karl Bodmer in 1832.

Diane Swanson's *Buffalo Sunrise: The Story of a North American Giant* includes a section on how the buffalo (bison) provided for the Blackfoot families living on the Alberta–Montana plains in the 1870s. According to the text, the buffalo provided a variety of activities and materials including laughter of children caused by antics of the young calves and the uses for the buffalo including hides for tipis and clothing, rattles from the hooves, and food. A chart shows examples of the more than one hundred uses for various parts of the buffalo including hides, horns, hooves, sinew, tails, bones, organs, fat, and hair. The author uses boxed materials that add to readers' understanding. For example, a boxed section tells about the importance of the birth of a white buffalo in 1994 and the belief in the miracles possible. Swanson quotes one of the Aani people who said, "Everything is reborn: thought, hope, life, all of these things" (p. 16). The text is illustrated with both early drawings and paintings and with contemporary photographs.

Caroline Arnold's *The Ancient Cliff Dwellers of Mesa Verde* describes the lives of the Anasazi, or ancient ones, through color photographs and text describing the cliff dwellings found in Mesa Verde National Park. Topics covered by Arnold include the discovery of Mesa Verde, uncovering the past, the history of the Anasazi, the daily life of the Anasazi, and speculations about why the Anasazi left Mesa Verde.

Michael Cooper's *Indian School: Teaching the White Man's Way* presents a sad time in the lives of many Native American youth. The author traces the importance of boarding schools in changing the lifestyles of young people who were separated from their families and land and sometimes moved thousands of miles away. The author begins the text by describing the experiences of eighty-four Lakota Sioux as they journey from the Great Plains to a boarding school in Carlisle, Pennsylvania. The author provides anecdotes that reveal the conflicts suffered by the youth as they are exposed to and expected to adapt to the ways of the white people. The author also presents the debates about the schooling that were held by the government during this time.

Nonfictional books also provide information about the Arctic regions and the native peoples who live there.

Illustration, "Mih-Tutta-Hang-Kusch, Mandan Village" by Karl Bodmer. (From An Indian Winter by Russell Freedman, illustration of "Mih-Tutta-Hang-Kusch, Mandan Village" by Karl Bodmer. Copyright © 1992. Reprinted by permission of Joslyn Art Museum, Omaha, Nebraska; gift of Enron Art Foundation.)

Normee Ekoomiak's *Arctic Memories* is written in both English and Inuktitut, the Inuit language. The illustrations by the Inuk artist also provide information about the culture, including the iglu, ice fishing, Okpik, traveling, games, and ancestral hunters. Carol Finley's *Art of the Far North: Inuit Sculpture, Drawing, and Printmaking* shows the art of contemporary Inuit people and discusses how the art is related to the environment and the culture. Tricia Brown's *Children of the Midnight Sun: Young Native Voices of Alaska* also provides a contemporary viewpoint.

Contemporary books about Native Americans frequently discuss both the advantages and problems related to growing up in two cultures. Books for younger readers usually present a positive view of these interactions. In *Pueblo Boy: Growing Up in Two Worlds*, Marcia Keegan depicts the life of a Pueblo Indian boy living in New Mexico. The text, in the form of a photographic essay, follows the boy as he learns to live in two cultures.

Biographies

Biographies are important reading for children because they encourage high aspirations and respect for the social contributions of outstanding people. However, there are fewer biographies about Native Americans than there are about African Americans.

Several biographies look at famous Native Americans who interacted with white settlers of this continent. For example, *Sacajawea, Wilderness Guide*, by Kate Jassem, is the biography of the Shoshone woman who guided the Lewis and Clark expedition across the Rocky Mountains to the Pacific Ocean. This book is appropriate for young readers.

Dennis Brindell Fradin's *Hiawatha: Messenger of Peace* is also appropriate for younger children. Fradin uses information that is known about the Iroquois who lived about five hundred years ago to re-create the role of Hiawatha as one of the founders of the Iroquois Confederacy. Fradin clearly separates what is actually known from the legend of Hiawatha. For example, Fradin states:

It is also said that around this time the Peacemaker chose the pine tree as a symbol of peace between the five Iroquois tribes and that Hiawatha invented a way to record important events. Hiawatha took large numbers of purple and white wampum beads and used them to make pictures that told a story. The Iroquois then began to record their major events on wampum belts in picture form. Some of these belts are now in museums, but they are not our main sources of information about Hiawatha. Our primary sources are the stories that the Iroquois elders have handed down to their young people for generations. (p. 30)

The title of Judith St. George's *To See With the Heart: The Life of Sitting Bull* is based on the Sioux Chief's ability to see "with the eyes in his heart rather than the eyes in his head." The biography covers his life on the Great Plains as he first leads raids against his people's enemies and later leads the fight against the European advancement that culminated in the Battle of Little Bighorn. St. George uses interviews found in archives to reconstruct Sitting Bull's life. You may compare St. George's biography with Albert Marrin's *Sitting Bull and His World*. Marrin places Sitting Bull into the context of the world he inhabited and the customs, culture, and spiritual beliefs that shaped his character. The author adds to the biography by including maps, drawings, and photographs.

Laurie Lawlor's *Shadow Catcher: The Life and Work of Edward S. Curtis* is a biography of the man who documented North American Indian culture beginning in 1898 and continuing for thirty years. The biography is illustrated with reproductions of Curtis's photographs that provide readers with a vivid view of Native American culture. The text includes a listing of Curtis's twenty volumes of the North American Indian, a bibliography of books for children, a bibliography of books by or about Edward Curtis, and an index.

Conflicts between worlds provide numerous opportunities for character and plot development in Jean Fritz's *The Double Life of Pocahontas*. Fritz effectively develops a character who is torn between loyalty to her father's tribe and to her new friends in the Jamestown colony. As in her other biographies, Fritz documents her historical interpretations. Notes, a bibliography, an index, and a map add to the authenticity.

Russell Freedman's *Indian Chiefs* includes short biographies about Red Cloud, Satanta, Quanah Parker, Washakie, Joseph, and Sitting Bull. The text is supported with photographs, a bibliography, and an index. Biographies of the various Native American leaders include Albert Marrin's *Plains Warrior: Chief Quanah Parker and the Comanches* and Russell Freedman's *The Life and Death of Crazy Horse*. Dorothy Morrison's *Chief Sarah: Sarah Winnemucca's Fight for Indian Rights* is one of the strongest biographies of this period. Morrison develops conflicts through contrasts when she describes Sarah's confusion:

The whites killed—but they had made her well. They took the Indians' meadows—but gave them horses and presents. They burned stores of food—but they gave food, too. Would she ever understand these strange people who were overrunning the land? (p. 31)

Morrison shows Sarah's battle for retention of Paiute culture when she describes Sarah's dream:

All this time Sarah had been lecturing and saving every penny, for she had another dream—of a school for Indian children, taught by Indians themselves, a school that would train its students as teachers for their own people. Up to then, Indian schools, both private and under the Bureau, had been taught and managed by white people who tried to "civilize" the students by wiping out native language and culture. Sarah, however, was sure her people's culture was worth preserving. (p. 149)

Additional Native American biographies are discussed in Chapter 12.

Latino Literature

As we discuss Latino literature, we discover that there is no clear preference for names to be applied to the literature. Terms such as *Hispanic, Latino,* and *Chicano* are frequently used. The U.S. Census Bureau uses the term *Hispanic*. Authors such as Sandra Cisneros prefer *Latino* because it is a term that shows more respect. The National Association of Hispanic and Latino Studies uses both terms. In this chapter we will, whenever possible, identify the literature with the specific area of the setting and the people.

Surprisingly, there are far fewer books about Latinos than there are books about either African Americans or Native Americans. In addition, the books about Latinos tend to go out of print faster than do the books about the other cultures. This phenomenon is readily seen between the third edition of this textbook (Norton, 1991) and the fourth edition published in 1995. A search of *Books in Print* disclosed that the following percentage of books from the 1991 text were no longer in print: 14 percent of African American, 25 percent of Asian American, 35 percent of Native American, and over 50 percent of Latino books. This trend continues into the fifth edition, published in 1999. More than 50 percent of the books are again out of print. Numerous new books about African Americans and Native Americans replaced most of the books that were out of print, but new books did not always replace the books about Latinos. Consequently, some out-of-print books about Latinos appear in the bibliography for this edition.

Most children's books about Latinos depict people of Mexican or Puerto Rican heritage, although the United States population contains numerous other Latino groups. People of Latino descent are the largest minority group in the United States, but relatively few children's books have been written about them. There is also an imbalance in the types of stories available. Award-winning picture storybooks about Latinos tend to examine Christmas celebrations. Award-winning novels are about a small segment of the Latino population, the sheepherders of Spanish Basque heritage, whose ancestors emigrated to parts of North America before those parts came under United States control. Although folktales and poetry are available for adults, a shortage of children's literature exists.

Many books for children about Latinos develop connections between the people and their religious faith. Celebrations, such as La Posada, suggest this cultural heritage. The respect for freedom is stressed through the celebration of Cinco de Mayo. Spanish vocabulary is also interspersed throughout many stories, allowing children to associate with a rich language heritage. (Misspelled and incorrectly used Spanish words have appeared all too often in this type of book, however. These errors have, understandably, caused criticism.) Several books are more factual, presenting the Spanish heritage that existed on the North American continent long before the United States became a nation. These stories suggest that Americans with Spanish ancestry have a heritage worthy of respect and of sharing with others.

Folklore

The wide cultural areas for Latino folklore include Mexico, South and Central America, Cuba, and the American Southwest. The folklore incorporates pre-Spanish tales of the Aztecs, Maya, and Incas. The Spaniards colonized the earlier populations, and different groups, such as the Apache and Pueblo Indians, interacted. As in other cultures, there are myths that explain (*ejemplo*), as well as folktales and fairy tales (collectively called *cuento*).

Many of the early Aztec and Mayan tales were recorded for European audiences by Spaniards in the sixteenth century. Others were written down by Aztecs who learned to read and write in the Texcoco Seminary. These tales were illustrated in pictographic forms on codices and provide many of the sources used by current folklorists and retellers of the tales.

Tales in John Bierhorst's *The Monkey's Haircut and Other Stories Told by the Maya,* collected from the Maya in Guatemala and southeastern Mexico, indicate many of the traditional Mayan values and cultural characteristics. For example, the extensive use of riddles in the folklore shows that the people value cleverness. In "Rabbit and Coyote," double meanings allow Rabbit to dupe Coyote and to escape from his cage. The plot of "Tup and the Ants" hinges on a pun. Cultural characteristics are shown in other tales, such as "The Mole Catcher," in which a husband must pay a price for his wife through a bride service. In *Song of Chirimia—A Guatemalan Folktale,* Jane Anne Volkmer retells the story of a young man who goes on a quest to win a Mayan princess. The illustrations, based on ancient stone carvings, provide a feeling for the Mayan civilization. The text is also printed in both English and Spanish.

The author's note in Gerald McDermott's *Musicians of the Sun* states that the tale is a fragment from the mythological tradition of the Aztecs. The tale reveals how Tezcatlipoca, Lord of the Night, commands Wind to fly to the house of the Sun and free the four musicians who are held prisoner: Red, Yellow, Blue, and Green. This becomes a creation myth as Wind overcomes Sun's power, frees

The reward of carob beans is presented to the Quechua Indians of Argentina. (Cover from The Magic Bean Tree: A Legend from Argentina *by Nancy Van Laan. Jacket illustration copyright © 1998 by Beatriz Vidal. Reprinted by permission of Houghton Mifflin Company. All rights reserved.)*

the musicians, and brings color and music to earth. The importance of the four directions is emphasized because each color faces a different direction.

Two highly illustrated books written by Nancy Van Laan and Pleasant DeSpain present Brazilian folktales for younger readers. Van Laan's *So Say the Little Monkeys* uses a rhyming text that incorporates the sounds of the mischievous and active monkeys with the sounds of the jungle. DeSpain's *The Dancing Turtle: A Folktale from Brazil* develops the theme that survival requires courage and wit.

Van Laan also uses South American sources for her retelling of *The Magic Bean Tree: A Legend from Argentina.* This tale from the Quechua Indians presents the reward of carob beans to a boy who brings rain back to his parched homeland.

Legends, myths, and riddles from South America are found in collections by John Bierhorst and Pleasant DeSpain. Bierhorst's *The Mythology of South America* provides scholarly background and selections that reflect the creation of the world and the origins of civilization as well as the conflicts between people. Bierhorst divides the sto-

Technology Resources

The Center for the Study of Children's Books in Spanish maintains an Internet site that provides recommendations for books in Spanish, as well as books about Latinos. Visit our Companion Website at www.prenhall.com/norton to link to this valuable resource.

ries and the discussions according to Greater Brazil, Guiana, Brazilian Highlands, Gran Chaco, Far South, Northwest, and Central Andes. Extensive notes on sources and references add to the text. Bierhorst's *Lightning Inside You and Other Native American Riddles* includes 150 riddles from several North and South American cultural regions, including southern Mexico and western South America. An annotated list of sources is helpful for students of children's literature. Pleasant DeSpain's *The Emerald Lizard: Fifteen Latin American Tales to Tell* is a collection of tales written in both English and Spanish. The author includes notes that discuss the tales, the sources, and the motifs.

Lois Ehlert's *Moon Rope* is adapted from a Peruvian tale called "The Fox and the Mole," in which Fox convinces Mole that they should try to climb to the moon on a rope woven of grass. The story ends as *a pourquoi* tale because after falling off the rope, Mole prefers to stay in the earth and come out only at night, avoiding other animals and never having to listen to Fox. Fox, however, may have made it to the moon because "The birds say that on a clear night they can see him in the full moon, looking down on earth. Mole says he hasn't seen him. Have you?" (unnumbered). The text, written in both English and Spanish, is illustrated with pictures that were inspired by ancient Peruvian textiles, jewelry, ceramics, sculpture, and architectural detail. Ehlert's *Cuckoo: A Mexican Folktale* is another *pourquoi* tale written in both English and Spanish.

Many of the folktales from Mexico, South and Central America, and Latino cultures in the United States reflect a blending of cultures as stated in the introduction to José Griego y Maestas and Rudolfo A. Anaya's *Cuentos: Tales from the Hispanic Southwest:*

> The stories also reflect a history of thirteen centuries of cultural infusing and blending in the Hispan mestizaje, from the Moors and Jews in Spain, to the Orientals in the Philippines, Africans in the Caribbean, and the Indians in America—be they Aztec, Apache or Pueblo. (p. 4)

For example, "The Man Who Knew the Language of the Animals," a folktale in *Cuentos: Tales from the Hispanic Southwest,* is based on a Moorish tale from "A Thousand and One Nights." The tale is also similar to Verna Aardema's African tale, *What's So Funny, Ketu?* Differences between the African and Latino tales reflect cultural values. The main character in the Latino tale portrays a stronger masculine role.

An In-Depth Analysis of a Folklore Collection

Tales from the Rain Forest is a collection of stories from the Amazonian Indians of Brazil as retold by Mercedes Dorson and Jeanne Wilmot. The collection begins with a detailed introduction of the cultural source of the stories: "The Brazilian Indians of Amazonia are the descendants of the Amerindian population that created and passed along the tales told in this book" (p. xv). The authors then provide historical background about the Brazilian Indians.

The introduction also focuses on the importance of the theme that emphasizes the need to respect the jungle:

> The message common in so many of the tales retold in these pages is the importance of respecting the needs of the formidable jungle. . . . The tales of the Brazilian Indians are dominated by animals, humans of animal ancestry, and even humans transformed into plants. Time is not linear. It is marked by the cycles of nature such as the ripening of fruit or the season of flood waters. Anything can be transformed or metamorphosized into anything else. A star can turn into a woman, a boy into a plant, a serpent can have a human daughter and a jaguar can be more civilized than a man. The animate and inanimate are interchangeable in a way that resists logical comprehension. (p. xix)

The authors also tell readers to be prepared to read stories that tell how various animals were created, how night was born, how fire was acquired, and how various aspects of the natural world originated. To further prepare readers or listeners, they tell readers that in the original stories the storytellers used pantomime, repetition, and mimicry.

The collection includes ten stories about motifs associated with creation. Each of the tales concludes with a comment that discusses the source of the tale and provides clarifying background information. Some of the comments such as the one associated with the tale "The Creation of Night" encourage understanding by defining the Water Serpent as the father of the sorceress and a symbol for the mobility between human and animal form and the feelings of equality with animals. Other comments such as those accompanying "The Young Man and the Star Maiden" clarify beliefs associated with cultivation, plant and animal management, and conservation.

The authors include a glossary, sources for each of the tales, a list of sources for illustrations, and a bibliography. The author information states that one of the authors was born in Brazil, has traveled in the Amazon region, and spent time among the Brazilian Indians. All of these sources add authenticity to the tales and could be used to further evaluate the stories and the illustrations.

John Bierhorst's *Doctor Coyote: A Native American Aesop's Fables,* a retelling, also indicates cultural infusion. Bierhorst identifies the text as Mexican in origin and

When they returned, the birds said,
"Your rope is ready." Fox started
climbing, paw over paw, eager
to be first on the moon.
Mole followed,
claw over claw.

Cuando regresaron los pájaros,
dijeron: — Ya está listo el lazo. —
El Zorro empezó a subir,
pata por pata, pues quería ser
el primero en llegar a la luna.
El Topo le siguió, garra por garra.

This pourquoi *tale explains the actions of Mole and Fox. (Illustration from* Moon Rope: A Peruvian Folktale, *copyright © 1992 by Lois Ehlert. Reproduced by permission of Harcourt Brace & Company.)*

shows the strong Spanish–Aztec connection. It is interesting to compare these fables with Aesop's fables and with coyote trickster tales.

Bierhorst's *Spirit Child: A Story of the Nativity* shows the fusion of Christian and Aztec beliefs. The text describes and Barbara Cooney's illustrations depict an Aztec setting for the birth of the Christ child. Extensive Aztec beliefs are infused. Likewise, various versions of "The Virgin of Guadalupe" represent the merger of Spanish–Catholic and Aztec Indian heritages.

Tomie dePaola's *The Lady of Guadalupe,* a retelling of a Mexican tale, develops the connection between the people and their religious faith. According to legend, the Lady of Guadalupe, now the patron saint of Mexico, appeared to a poor Mexican Indian on a December morning in 1531. Juan Diego, "He-who-speaks-like-an-eagle," was walking toward the Church of Santiago when he saw a hill covered with a brilliant white cloud. Out of the cloud came a gentle voice calling Juan's name and telling him that a church should be built on that site so that the Virgin Mary could show her love for Juan's people, the Indians of Mexico. On Juan's third visit to the bishop, he was believed because he brought with him a visual sign from the Lady of Guadalupe: His rough cape had been changed into a painting of the lady. The church was built on the location, and the cape with its miraculous change was placed inside the structure. DePaola says that he has had a lifelong interest in the legend of the Lady of Guadalupe. His drawings, based on careful research, depict the dress and architecture of sixteenth-century Mexico.

Two traditional tales adapted by Harriet Rohmer originate with the Miskito Indians of Nicaragua. *The Invisible Hunters* reflects the impact of European cultures on the Miskito people. The three hunters are punished when they break their promise and forsake their people. European traders influence the hunters' actions and create and expand their greed. *Mother Scorpion Country* is a tale of love. In this tale, a husband tries to accompany his wife into the land of the dead. According to the author's notes, "the compassionate figure of Mother Scorpion reflects a pre–Christian matriarchal past" (p. 32).

Both of Rohmer's texts include information about the author's research. For example, Rohmer began her research for *The Invisible Hunters* in anthropological archives, visited the Miskito communities in the company of an Afro-Indian Catholic priest, learned more details of the story from an elder Miskito Catholic deacon, and finally met a Miskito bishop of the Moravian Church, who provided many additional details. During this final contact, Rohmer was told, "According to the stories I heard as a child the Dar has a voice. I can take you to people who say they have heard that voice" (p. 31). In *Mother Scorpion Country,* Rohmer traces the story to the endeavors of a young Moravian minister who recorded the stories and customs of the Miskito Indians in the early 1900s. Early Inca life is reflected in Jane Kurtz's *Miro in the Kingdom of the Sun.*

Two retellers of Latino folklore have chosen to retell various versions of "La Llorona," the woman who killed her children and now wanders crying through the night. It is believed that because of loneliness she kidnaps children. *Prietita and the Ghost Woman,* by Gloria Anzaldua, is a story about a girl who goes in search of herbs to cure her mother and becomes lost in the woods. She has always heard about the ghost woman who steals children. Now she may be meeting the ghost woman. Rudolfo Anaya's *Maya's Children: The Story of La Llorona* tells about a Mayan woman who is immortal. When the god is angered by her immortality, he threatens to destroy her children. When she tries to trick the god, her children perish. Readers can compare the retellings and the illustrations in these two books.

Picture Storybooks

Listening to and saying rhymes from various cultures encourage children to interact with language as well as to discover the joy in language and in word play. Margot Griego's *Tortillitas Para Mama and Other Spanish Nursery Rhymes* and José-Luis Orozco's *Diez Deditos: Ten Little Fingers & Other Play Rhymes and Action Songs from Latin America* are written in both English and Spanish. These texts provide sources for sharing literature in either language.

My First Book of Proverbs by Ralfka Gonzalez and Ana Ruiz includes simple proverbs such as "A good listener needs few words." Each of the proverbs is illustrated in colorful illustrations that have the flavor of folk art. Jeanette Winter's *Josefina* is a counting story in which the illustrations also have the flavor of folk art. The illustrations include numerous Mexican motifs.

Deborah Lattimore's *The Flame of Peace: A Tale of the Aztecs* is a literary fairy tale based on the Aztec nine evil lords of darkness and the god of peace. Lattimore uses information from Aztec myth and hypothesizes about what might have caused the Alliance of Cities during the time of Itzcoatl. In the resulting story, a young boy uses his wits against the evil lords and brings peace to the cities. The illustrations reflect Aztec settings and characters.

Richard Garcia's *My Aunt Otilia's Spirits,* a fictional story set in contemporary San Francisco, includes elements of the supernatural. Garcia bases the story on a visit from a Puerto Rican relative. Consider the interrelationships between reality and fantasy as Garcia describes the story in the endnotes:

Like all stories, this one is based on a kernel of fact—that is that my Aunt Otilia was accompanied by bed shakings and wall knockings wherever she went. However, this was not regarded as unusual in my family, or a cause for much concern. The supernatural had a natural place in our life. Most of the time we ignored it—sometimes it meant something—as in the case of an omen or a dream. We had a large and well-worn copy of an old

dream book—and this was often consulted in the morning if a dream seemed significant. . . . And those who had died were never thought of as being very far away—and were often spoken to as if they were in the room. (p. 24)

Leo Politi has written and illustrated a number of award-winning picture storybooks about Mexican American children living in southern California. His *Song of the Swallows* tells the story of a young boy whose dear friend is the gardener and bell ringer at the mission of San Juan Capistrano. Politi shares Mexican American history with readers as the gardener tells Juan the story of the mission and of *las golondrinas,* the swallows who always return to the mission in the spring, on Saint Joseph's Day, and remain there until late summer. Politi's illustrations re-create the Spanish architecture of the mission and demonstrate a young boy's love for plants and birds.

Marie Hall Ets and Aurora Labastida's *Nine Days to Christmas: A Story of Mexico* tells of a kindergarten child who is excited because she is going to have her own special Christmas party, complete with a piñata. In the midst of numerous other everyday activities, Ceci chooses her piñata at the market, fills it with toys and candy, and joins the La Posada procession. After Ceci sees her beautiful piñata being broken at the party, she is unhappy until she sees a star in the sky that resembles her piñata. Children relate to the girl's feelings and learn about the Mexican celebration of Christmas when they read this book. This story depicts a middle-class family that lives in an attractive city home. Children can see that poverty is not the condition of all people with a Spanish heritage.

The themes of the importance of generosity and forgiveness are developed in Edith Hope Fine's *Under the Lemon Moon.* This is a contemporary story based on the belief that La Anciana, the Old One, walks the countryside during the full moon and helps things grow. A young girl discovers the importance of the Old One when someone steals the lemons from her cherished tree and the tree begins to wither. In an ending that highlights the importance of generosity and forgiveness, the young girl gives away all of the large lemons that grow on the tree after she follows the Old One's advice. She gives the last one to the poor thief whose family was in great need.

Mexican motifs are also important in Gerardo Suzan's illustrations for Virginia Kroll's *Butterfly Boy.* Suzan uses bright colors to develop the mood and setting for this tender story of a boy and his invalid grandfather as the boy tries to ensure that the red admiral butterflies will return.

Historical and Contemporary Realistic Fiction

Only a few books of historical and contemporary realistic fiction for children portray Latinos in suitably positive ways or as the main characters. Marian L. Martinello and Samuel P. Nesmith's *With Domingo Leal in San Antonio 1734* takes a documentary approach to Latino history and life in the United States. Published by the University of Texas Institute of Texas Cultures at San Antonio, this carefully researched book describes a day in the life of a young Spanish boy who travels with his family from the Canary Islands through Mexico to the Villa de San Fernando on the banks of the Rio San Antonio de Padua in present-day Texas. This historical novel can strengthen children's understanding of a lengthy Latino heritage in the southwestern United States. It also demonstrates that people of Spanish ancestry were living on the North American frontier before English-speaking settlers claimed it.

Another book of historical fiction depicting the early Spanish presence in western North America is Scott O'Dell's *Carlota.* In this story set in Spanish California in the mid-1800s, O'Dell explores the conflicts that occur between people who expect females to play a traditionally feminine role and others who encourage a different type of behavior. Carlota is the strong and independent daughter of Don Saturnino, a native Californian whose ancestors came from Spain. Her father supports her brave and adventurous inclinations. Discussions of O'Dell's *The Captive, The Feathered Serpent,* and *The Amethyst Ring* are found in Chapter 10.

Joseph Krumgold's *. . . And Now Miguel,* based on a full-length documentary film feature, is the story of the Chavez family, which has been raising sheep in New Mexico since before their region became part of the United States. Their ancestors raised sheep in Spain. Krumgold tells the story from the viewpoint of the middle child, Miguel, who unlike his older brother is too young to get everything he wants and, unlike his younger brother, is too old to be happy with everything he has. Miguel has a secret wish to accompany the older family members when they herd the sheep to the summer grazing land in the Sangre de Cristo Mountains. With the help of San Ysidro, the patron saint of farmers, Miguel strives to make everyone see that he is ready for this responsibility. When he is allowed to accompany his elders on the drive and reaches the summer camp, he feels pride in his family's traditions and in his own accomplishments:

In this place many men named Chavez had come. Those I could remember, and then my grandfather as well. And my father, Blas, and my uncles, Eli and Bonifacio. And my brothers, Blasito and Gabriel. And now, watching the shining world as I knew it would look when I came to this place, I stood, Miguel. (p. 244)

Krumgold visited the real Miguel and his family when the film was produced. Krumgold celebrated Saints' Day with them and observed all of the important functions of a sheep ranch. He grew to know a closely knit family with a heritage going back to ancient Spain.

The eight-year-old in Nicholasa Mohr's *Felita* has lived in her Puerto Rican neighborhood of New York City for as long as she can remember. Mohr depicts the reasons for Felita's great love of her neighborhood. When Felita walks down the street, she can greet everyone by name. Her dearest friends live in the apartments on the block, and her grandmother, Abuelita, lives nearby. Conflict results when Felita's father decides that the family must move to a neighborhood where the schools are better and the threats of gang violence are fewer. In the new neighborhood, Anglo children call Felita names, tear her clothes, and tell her to move away. Felita's mother is shocked by the attitudes of the children and tells Felita that she must not hate, because that could make her as mean inside as the people who are attacking her:

Instead you must learn to love yourself. This is more important. To love yourself and feel worthy, despite anything they might say against you and your family! That is the real victory. It will make you strong inside. (p. 39)

When violence against the family continues and no neighbors offer help, Felita's family moves back to the old neighborhood. Felita experiences anger, sorrow, and humiliation, but she finally regains her feeling of self-worth. With her grandmother's help, Felita returns to her happy, lively self, secure in the surroundings of her warm, loving family and friends. Perhaps the neighborhood and the people in *Felita* seem so real because Mohr herself was born and grew up in a similar neighborhood in New York City.

Mohr's *Going Home* provides additional adventures for Felita. Twelve-year-old Felita finds that she must face and overcome new person-against-self and person-against-society conflicts. During a trip to visit relatives in Puerto Rico, Felita finds that she is the object of attack because she is the gringa and not accepted by some of the Puerto Rican girls.

Latino author Gary Soto has several texts that appeal to readers. *Taking Sides* is a realistic fiction story about a Latino boy who moves from the barrio to the suburbs. The protagonist, who is a basketball player, must decide how he will respond when his new team plays his old team in a league game. Soto develops themes related to loyalty and friendship. In *Pacific Crossing,* the boys from the barrio participate in an exchange program in Japan. *Too Many Tamales* is the story of a girl who faces a dilemma on Christmas Eve when she misplaces her mother's diamond ring. *Neighborhood Odes* is a collection of twenty-one poems about a Latino neighborhood and the people who live in the neighborhood. *Snapshots from the Wedding* tells the story of a wedding through the point of view of the young flower girl.

Ben Mikaelsen and Frances Temple develop faster and more dangerous plots in books for older readers. Mikaelsen's *Sparrow Hawk Red* is a story of survival in the streets and drug traffic of Mexico. Thirteen-year-old Ricky Diaz discovers that his mother was murdered by drug smugglers because of his father's work for the Drug Enforcement Agency. In an effort to avenge his mother, Ricky disguises himself as a Mexican street urchin. With the help of Soledad, another street urchin, he enters the smugglers' compound, steals a plane containing the missing radar that allows smugglers to escape detection, and narrowly escapes. Through his adventures, Ricky discovers the importance of his heritage. Temple's *Grab Hands and Run* is set in El Salvador. The plot follows a family who tries to leave El Salvador after the father disappears.

Several books published by Pinata Books, a division of Arte Publico Press, provide interesting reading sources for older students. For example, *Hispanic, Female and Young: An Anthology* edited by Phyllis Tashlik is an example of a writing and literature project completed by young Latino students in New York City's El Barrio. The anthology includes interviews with both parents of the students and with Latino authors. In addition, the text includes poetry and other selections written by Latino female authors. Students of children's literature may be especially interested in an interview with Nicholasa Mohr in which she tells readers to "Hold Fast to Your Dreams." In this interview she discusses career choices for Latino women. This book could be used to motivate students to write similar texts.

Two additional books by the same publisher, Anilu Bernardo's *Jumping Off to Freedom* and Victor Villasenor's *Walking Stars: Stories of Magic and Power*, are stories in which young people overcome odds and succeed. *Jumping Off to Freedom* is the story of a fifteen-year-old boy and his father who seek freedom from Cuba's government by heading for Miami on a raft. This story includes both person-against-society and person-against-nature conflicts as the protagonists must escape the repressive Communist government and the dangerous ocean. *Walking Stars: Stories of Magic and Power* is a selection of stories about the author's family. Some of these stories are about escaping from persecution, while others are about more common occurrences. In the preface, the author explains that he wrote the book in order to tell children "that there's a way to live life, la viva, with power and magic, a way of triumphing over all odds and living life like a superhuman being" (p. 7).

Nonfiction

High-quality informational books about Latinos include books on history, geography, culture, and people. For example, several books look at the discoveries about and the accomplishments of the ancient native cultures of the Western Hemisphere. Carolyn Meyer and Charles Gallenkamp's *The Mystery of the Ancient Maya* provides a thoroughly documented presentation of Mayan history and accomplishments. The authors' writing style creates interest in the subject, and early photographs and drawings add to the authenticity. Jean Fritz et al. present the history of various parts of the world at the time of Columbus in *The World in 1492*. The section titled "The Americas in 1492" is written by Jamake Highwater. This chapter includes information on the Aztecs, the Incas, and other native peoples. Maps show

Information about the Aztecs and Incas focuses on the accomplishments of the native peoples. (From The World in 1492. *Copyright © 1992 by Henry Holt and Company, Inc. Illustrations copyright © 1992 by Stefano Vitale. Reprinted by permission of Henry Holt and Company, Inc.)*

the Aztec and Inca empires, and illustrations show art from the time period.

Elizabeth Mann's *Machu Picchu* provides an excellent introduction to the Incan empire. The author begins with the discovery in 1911 of the city, which was considered sacred by the Incas. The author then goes back in time to when the Incas and Machu Picchu represented a viable, living culture. The author's style is one that both captures interest and formulates the book. She asks the question "How can we ever really understand a culture so widely different from our own, where people celebrated rocks as sacred, thought strips of finely woven cloth were more precious than gold, administered a vast empire without knowledge of money or writing, and sacrificed children on mountain peaks?" The author then provides answers to her questions.

While the majority of books about Spanish American celebrations for young children concentrate on the Christmas holidays, Cinco de Mayo, the commemoration of the Mexican army's defeat of the French army on May 5, 1862, is also a major holiday for Mexican Americans. June Behrens's *Fiesta!* is an informational book describing the modern-day celebration of this holiday. Photographs show a Mexican American festival in which music is played by a mariachi band, costumed dancers perform traditional Mexican dances, and young and old enjoy the

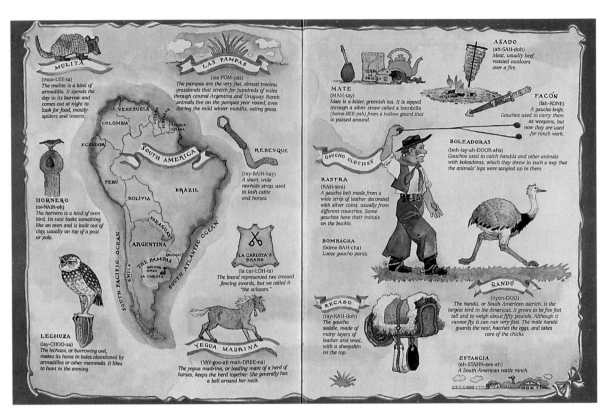

A map and an illustrated glossary add to understanding. (From On the Pampas *by Maria Cristina Brusca. Copyright © 1991 by Maria Cristina Brusca. Reprinted by permission of Henry Holt and Company.)*

celebration. Photographs also show children at school as they learn about and participate in the Cinco de Mayo activities. The book closes with a message from the author, who suggests that Americans of all heritages have become good amigos.

Information on the history of the Spanish involvement in the Americas is discussed in Albert Marrin's *Empires Lost and Won: The Spanish Heritage in the Southwest.* The history begins in 711 A.D. when the Moors told stories about the cities of gold. The text continues through the Middle Ages, into Coronado's expedition, and the westward expansion. The author includes maps and drawings.

Several nonfiction books provide information about Latino children and families. Tricia Brown's *Hello, Amigos!* is a photo essay for younger children. It chronicles a special day in the life of six-year-old Frankie Valdez, a Mexican American boy whose family lives in San Francisco's Mission District. Fran Ortiz's photographs show the boy as he goes to school, attends classes, plays with friends, reacts to a classroom birthday cake, goes to the boys' club, and shares his birthday celebration with his family. In *Calling the Doves,* Juan Felipe Herrera tells a story about his childhood as a migrant farmworker. The story portrays a strong relationship between the family and the land and depicts the grueling nature of farm labor. Maria Cristina Brusca's *On the Pampas* is a highly illustrated book that describes a girl's

experiences during a summer spent with her grandparents on their ranch in Argentina. The watercolor paintings provide visual images of the settings.

Two books for older children, Larry Dane Brimner's *A Migrant Family* and S. Beth Atkin's *Voices from the Fields: Children of Migrant Farmworkers Tell Their Stories,* tell about the lives of children of migrant laborers. Both books are illustrated with photographs. Atkin uses introductions and interviews to develop the stories of the children, who tell about their dreams and the joys of family relationships, as well as their hardships.

Asian American Literature

Few highly recommended books for children represent an Asian American perspective. Folktales from several Asian countries can help Asian American children and children from other ethnic backgrounds appreciate the traditional values and creative imagination of Asian peoples (see Chapter 6). Folktales, such as those found in *The Rainbow People,* retold by Laurence Yep, are especially good because they were collected from Chinese Americans living in California.

The widest range of Asian American experiences in current children's literature is found in the works of Laurence Yep, who writes with sensitivity about Chinese Americans who, like himself, have lived in San Francisco,

ISSUE   Who Should Write Multicultural Literature?

At a multicultural roundtable attended by various leaders in multicultural literature and education,[1] one of the debated questions was, "Who should write multicultural literature?" Many of the participants felt strongly that only members of an ethnic group should have ownership of the literature and be encouraged to write the literature and critique the literature written by others. According to this viewpoint, only African Americans, for example, have the experience and the perception to write authentically about the black experience. Others argued the viewpoint that anyone who writes with sensitivity and does the required research into the subject and the culture should be able to write about the culture.

Jane Yolen[2] maintains that demanding that only a person from a culture may write about that culture is "creating a kind of literature apartheid. Think of it: if I, a careful artist, am only allowed to write about the culture I grew up in—Jewish, Manhattan, Virginia, and Westport, Connecticut, 1940s–1960s—I could have written *The Devil's Arithmetic*, but not *Passager*; I could have created *All Those Secrets of the World*, but not *Piggins*. I could have made *And*

Twelve Chinese Acrobats, but not *The Emperor and the Kite*" (p. 289).

Betsy Hearne provides interesting thoughts about this issue in an article in *School Library Journal*.[3] Hearne states:

What defines an authority in creating or evaluating picture-book folklore? A well-read expert? Someone raised in the culture represented by the story? Can only members of an ethnic group truly represent the lore of that group? How can we tell? By the name? The skin color? Does the absence of an author or artist's photograph mean an African-American folktale has been adapted by a WASP? If so, does that mean a majority is ripping off a minority, or honoring it? Graciela Italiano has addressed this controversy in a paper delivered at the 1992 Allerton Institute.[4]

She underscores the importance of knowing a cultural tradition, from the standpoint of both experience and study, over the formal qualification of being a card-carrying member of the culture. At the same conference Hazel Rochman[5] argued eloquently against the misconception that "only Indians can really judge books about Indians, Jews about Jews . . . locking us into smaller and tighter boxes" (p. 34).

As you read Hearne's questions and concerns, ask yourself the same questions. What is your viewpoint on this important issue? What should be the qualifications of a person writing about a culture or evaluating the books written about that culture? Who should write and evaluate the books? What criteria should you use when selecting and evaluating the books about a culture that is different from your own?

---

[1]Roundtable on Multicultural Education, New York City, May 1993.
[2]Yolen, Jane. "Taking Time: Or How Things Have Changed in the Last Thirty-Five Years of Children's Publishing." *The New Advocate* 10 (Fall 1997): 285–291.
[3]Hearne, Betsy. "Respect the Source: Reducing Cultural Chaos in Picture Books, Part Two." *School Library Journal* 39 (August 1993): 33–37.
[4]Italiano, Graciela. "Reading Latin America: Issues in the Evaluation of Latino Children's Books in Spanish and English." In *Evaluating Children's Books: A Critical Look*, edited by Betsy Hearne and Roger Sutton. Champaign: University of Illinois Graduate School of Library and Information Science, 1993.
[5]Rochman, Hazel. "And Yet . . . Beyond Political Correctness." In *Evaluating Children's Books: A Critical Look*, edited by Betsy Hearne and Roger Sutton. Champaign: University of Illinois Graduate School of Library and Information Science, 1993.

California. His characters overcome the stereotypes associated with literature about Asian Americans, and his stories integrate information about Chinese cultural heritage into the everyday lives of the people involved. Yep has received the International Reading Association's 1976 Children's Book Award and a Newbery Honor Book award.

Mingshui Cai (1992) discusses examples of acculturation found within three of Yep's novels: *Dragonwings, Child of the Owl,* and *Star Fisher.* Cai states:

Although set in different times, these three novels have something in common: They cover themes like poverty, racial discrimination, marginalization, and loss of identity, which are typical of multicultural literature; and most significantly, they represent Chinese Americans' process of acculturation as a way out of the dilemma of being caught between two worlds. (p. 108)

Cai argues that Yep's novels contain two aspects of acculturation, "assimilating to the mainstream culture while maintaining Chinese identity" (p. 109).

Yep's *Dragonwings*, set in 1903 San Francisco, is based on a true incident in which a Chinese American built and flew an airplane. The characters are people who retain their values and respect for their heritage while adjusting to a new country. The "town of the Tang people" is eight-year-old Moon Shadow's destination when he leaves his

 Technology Resources

You can streamline your search by adding specifications in the Topic, Award, Genre, and Grade Level fields.

mother in the Middle Kingdom (China). He is filled with conflicting emotions when he first meets his father in the country that some call the "Land of the Demons" and others call the "Land of the Golden Mountain."

The Tang men in San Francisco give Moon Shadow clothing and things for the body, but his father gives him a marvelous, shimmering kite shaped like a butterfly, a gift designed to stir the soul. Moon Shadow joins his father in his dream to build a flying machine. Motivated by the work of Orville and Wilbur Wright, Moon Shadow's father builds an airplane, names it *Dragonwings*, and soars off the cliffs overlooking San Francisco Bay. Having achieved his dream, he decides to return to work so that his wife can join him in America.

In the process of the story, Moon Shadow learns that his stereotype of the white demons is not always accurate. When he and his father move away from the Tang men's protection, Moon Shadow meets and talks to his first demon. Instead of being ten feet tall, with blue skin and a face covered with warts, she is a petite woman who is very friendly and considerate. As Moon Shadow and his father get to know this Anglo-Saxon woman and her family, they all gain respect for one another. When they share knowledge, the father concludes: "We see the same thing and yet find different truths."

Readers also discover that many stereotypes about Chinese Americans are incorrect. This book is especially strong in its coverage of Chinese traditions and beliefs. For example, readers learn about the great respect that Chinese Americans feel for the aged and the dead. Family obligations do not end when a family member has retired or died. As Moon Shadow seeks to educate his white friend about the nature of dragons, readers discover traditional Chinese tales about a benevolent and wise dragon who is king among reptiles and emperor of animals. Readers realize the value of honor as the doubting Tang men pull *Dragonwings* up the hill for its maiden voyage. If the Tang men laugh at Moon Shadow's father, they laugh at a body of people who stand beside each other through times of adversity and honor. Children who read this story learn about the contributions and struggles of the Chinese Americans and the prejudice that they still experience.

The Serpent's Children is set in a time when China was battling both Manchu and British domination. In *Child of the Owl*, young Casey discovers that she knows more about racehorses than about her own Chinese heritage. *Star Fisher* is a story about a Chinese family overcoming prejudice in West Virginia during the late 1920s. The protagonists in all of these books by Yep are distinct and believable individuals, far from the conventional stereotypes of Asian people.

Two novels by Laurence Yep provide insights into Chinese American and white attitudes. In *Thief of Hearts*, a sequel to *Child of the Owl*, Yep writes another novel in which the main character develops cross-cultural understanding. Yep's *Later, Gater* develops themes related to sibling rivalry.

Stories about early immigration experiences in the New World are popular subjects in children's books. Allen Say's *Grandfather's Journey* is an immigration story that includes two journeys: one to California and then, many years later, one back to visit the Japan of his youth. The story also covers the time of World War II, when Grandfather cannot return to California again, but he tells his grandson, Allen Say, stories about America. *Grandfather's Journey* is an excellent companion for Say's *Tree of Cranes*, which is set in Japan. The story shows the melding of two cultures. The boy's mother, who was born in America, prepares a Christmas celebration that combines the Japanese and American cultures. In *Tea with Milk*, Say tells the story of a Japanese American girl who feels lonely and homesick for America when her parents return to Japan. After she meets a young man, they discover that they can make a home together.

The Japanese and American cultures combine in this book about the Christmas celebration. (Illustration from **Tree of Cranes** by Allen Say. Copyright © 1991 by Allen Say. Reprinted by permission of Houghton Mifflin Company. All rights reserved.)

Two picture books focus on the experiences of nineteenth-century Chinese immigrants. Elizabeth Partridge's *Oranges on Golden Mountain* explores a boy's life as he leaves his widowed mother in China, learns to fish in San Francisco Bay, saves money for his family's passage to America, and plants and tends cuttings from his mother's orange trees. Yin's *Coolies* is another picture book that focuses on the immigrant experience. This time the author develops the story of the immigrant workers who toiled to build the transcontinental railroad.

Bette Bao Lord, the author of *In the Year of the Boar and Jackie Robinson*, created a story that reflects her own experiences and beliefs. Like her protagonist Shirley Temple Wong, Lord was a Chinese immigrant to America. Lord says:

Many feel that loss of one's native culture is the price one must pay for becoming an American. I do not feel this way. I think we hyphenated Americans are doubly blessed. We can choose the best of both. (endcover)

In 1947, Shirley discovers that she can adore baseball, the Brooklyn Dodgers, and Jackie Robinson and still maintain the bond of family and the bond of culture.

Numerous experiences in the life of a Vietnamese American are shown through a photographic essay in Diane Hoyt-Goldsmith's *Hoang Anh: A Vietnamese-American Boy*. Lawrence Migdale's photographs show the daily activities of Hoang Anh and his family in San Rafael, California, as they work on their fishing boat, live and play at home, prepare for the New Year, and experience the Tet Festival. Patricia McMahon's *Chi-Hoon: A Korean Girl* is a photographic essay that presents one week in the life of a Korean girl.

Although Takaaki Nomura's picture storybook *Grandpa's Town* is set in Japan rather than North America, the themes of the story relate to the universality of loving relationships between grandfathers and grandsons, possible loneliness after the death of a loved one, and preferences for staying with old friends. This story, written in both Japanese and English, includes much cultural information. A young boy accompanies his grandfather around town, meets his grandfather's friends, and discovers that his grandfather is not willing to leave these friends to move in with the boy and his mother.

Eleanor Coerr's *Mieko and the Fifth Treasure,* a book for older children, is also set in Japan. Mieko's talent for painting, called "the fifth treasure," brings her great joy until her hand is damaged by a piece of glass when the bomb drops on Nagasaki. Mieko experiences a great sense of loss until she overcomes her unhappiness and discovers that she can still paint. Coerr develops the themes of the importance of friendship and the need for self-confidence. The setting allows Coerr to provide much information about the Japanese people, their customs, and their beliefs. You may compare Coerr's experiences with the atomic bomb with those developed in Tatsuharu Kodama's *Shin's Tricycle* and Laurence Yep's *Hiroshima.*

The setting for Sook Nyul Choi's *Year of Impossible Goodbyes* is Japanese-occupied Korea at the close of World War II. The author develops the person-against-society conflict experienced by Sookan, a ten-year-old Korean girl, and her family, who experience the oppressive treatment of both the Japanese and Russian occupation of North Korea. The author uses many small details and incidents to symbolize the oppression experienced by the family and the family's longing for freedom. For example, they are forbidden to grow flowers. In one incident, when the family manages to have a tiny patch of flowers, the Japanese police captain and his men trample the flowers. After that, the mother puts her packets of seeds carefully away. Each time she looks at them, she wonders if they will ever be able to plant the seeds. After another incident, the police punish the grandfather by chopping down his favorite pine tree. Shortly after the loss of the tree, the grandfather dies. After many dangerous experiences, the children and the mother escape to South Korea. In her endnotes, the author states her reasons for writing this book:

Having lived through this turbulent period of Korean history, I wanted to share my experiences. So little is known about my homeland, its rich culture and its sad history. My love for my

This photographic essay captures many experiences in the life of a Vietnamese American. (From Hoang Anh: A Vietnamese-American Boy *by Diane Hoyt-Goldsmith. Photographs copyright © 1992 by Lawrence Migdale. Reprinted by permission of Holiday House.)*

native country and for my adopted country prompted me to write this book to share some of my experiences and foster greater understanding. (unnumbered)

Seeds and memories and the future they represent are important in *Year of Impossible Goodbyes,* as they are in Sherry Garland's *The Lotus Seed,* written for younger children. In this story, a Vietnamese family resettles in America. During happier days in Vietnam, the grandmother picks a seed from a lotus plant in the emperor's garden to remember the special occasion. Throughout her life, she looks at this seed during important moments in her life or when she feels sad. The seed is so important that she brings it to America when her family escapes the war. Years later, a grandson carelessly throws out the seed, which saddens his grandmother tremendously. Luckily, the seed is thrown where it eventually grows into a lotus plant. When the blossom fades, the grandmother gives a seed to each of her grandchildren. Garland develops a universal theme: Small things and the memories that they evoke are important in our lives.

Huynh Quang Nhuong's *The Land I Lost: Adventures of a Boy in Vietnam* is also a story set in Vietnam. In this story, Huynh takes readers back to a time of family and village experiences. Traditions and beliefs are important elements in the stories of both Huynh and Garland.

Adjusting to a new culture and developing understanding of oneself and others are problems faced by many new Americans. Lensey Namioka's *Yang the Youngest and His Terrible Ear* is a humorous contemporary realistic fiction story that speaks to the needs of many readers. The author develops a protagonist, nine-year-old Yingtao,

An In-Depth Analysis of One Example of Multicultural Literature—Asian

Homeless Bird by Gloria Whelan is a 2000 National Book Award winner. The book is about a thirteen-year-old girl who must overcome difficulties associated with an arranged marriage. The book, set in modern India, is worthy of an in-depth analysis of both the author's development of cultural authenticity and literary style.

Let us first consider how the author develops the Hindu culture and the treatment of women within the culture. Koly, the female protagonist, is the young girl involved in an arranged marriage. Whelan's descriptions of this custom and the treatment of women are very similar to the traditional treatment of women described by Nandita Gurjar (1995) in her scholarly research about the position of women in Indian culture. Gurjar found that women were dependent on fathers until marriage, after which they were dependent on husbands and later on sons. Women are considered inferior in educational status, separated from men during many activities, strongly disciplined, and expected to become part of an arranged marriage. The dowry was an important part of these marriages: The better the dowry, the greater the prospects for a favorable marriage. Widows, especially those without sons, led very humble lives.

In *Homeless Bird*, Whelan develops a heroine who must adhere to these cultural standards for women. Koly is forbidden to attend school and is criticized by her mother when her father decides to teach her to read. Instead, Koly's mother teaches her to embroider, a skill that is considered by her mother to be more appropriate for females. When Koly is thirteen her family begins searching for a husband. Readers discover that the dowry is extremely important because the prospective bridegroom's family is very demanding. Notice in the following quote how Whelan uses similes to help readers understand Koly's reaction to the demands for a dowry: " 'You have brought the dowry, sir?' Until that moment I had believed it was me the Mehta family wanted; now it seemed that what they cared for most was the dowry. Was my marriage to be like the buying of a sack of yams in the marketplace?" (p. 13).

The fate of widows is developed as Koly discovers that the man she marries is actually a very sick boy whose family arranged the marriage to obtain the dowry. They hope to use the dowry money to take the boy to bathe in the Ganges River, this procedure is believed to be a cure for critically ill people.

Now the author uses additional figurative language to describe Koly's feelings: "It was not I who was wanted at all. It was the money. I felt as if I were tangled like a small fly in the web of a cunning spider. If Hari died, what would become of me? I would be a widow whom no one would want" (p. 33). The author uses descriptions detailing the journey to the Ganges, the visit to the Golden Temple of Vishvanath, the crowds making their pilgrimages, and the attitudes of the people who believe in this cure to develop the cultural setting and values of the people.

Throughout the book Whelan emphasizes various cultural beliefs and values. For example, she describes Holi, the feast that celebrates the god Krishna's love for Radha; she stresses the importance of the poetry written by Rabindranath Tagore, one of India's greatest poets; and she describes the fate of many widows when they are deserted in Vrindavan, a city with many widows who beg for food. Notice how the author uses a simile to describe Koly's emotions when she discovers that she has been deserted by her mother-in-law: "I suppose part of me had known all along. The thought had been waiting like a scorpion at the edge of my mind. Now it stung me, and I nearly cried out with the pain" (p. 121).

It is this desertion in the city that brings out Koly's strong character and sense of survival: Survival is possible when she is taken into a home for widows and discovers that her skills at embroidery make it possible for her to earn a living.

The author uses the theme of the homeless bird throughout the book. Her changing attitudes about the homeless bird also reflect her own development. Early in the book, Koly describes writing as caged birds that are caught forever; thinks of herself as a caged animal when contemplating her marriage; and discovers that her favorite poem is about a homeless bird that is always flying to somewhere else. Finally, when Koly meets a young man who she knows will make her happy, she feels like a homeless bird, but one that is flying at last to its home. Readers know that she has resolved her person-against-self conflicts when she embroiders a quilt that includes all of the items that make her happy. She knows immediately that the border will include the homeless bird and items from Tagore's poems.

As students of children's literature, you will find it interesting to analyze and appreciate how Whelan uses figurative language and various symbols to develop the cultural values, the themes, the settings, the conflicts, and the characterizations in her book. In addition, there are enough cultural details that the book lends itself to authentication.

who is out of place in his musical family. Although he has a great eye, he has a terrible ear. Students of children's literature can analyze Yingtao's reactions to both learning about English and trying to make his family understand that he is not, and will never be, a talented musician. The author helps readers visualize the problems by relating them to Yingtao's Chinese background. When Yingtao tries to work out inconsistencies in English, he states: "Talking to Americans is like walking along a country footpath in China. You think the path is nice and firm, but your foot suddenly slips on a muddy stretch and you land with a big splash in a wet rice paddy" (p. 60). In a satisfying ending, both the family of his American friend and Ying-tao's own family realize the importance of honoring one's gifts. Michele Surat's *Angel Child, Dragon Child* is a realistic story about a young Vietnamese girl's difficulties developing associations with her classmates after her family moves to the United States. The plots, characters, and themes in these books may encourage discussion and promote understanding.

The importance of even small cultural artifacts, such as eating utensils, stimulates a humorous plot in Ina R. Friedman's *How My Parents Learned to Eat*. Friedman suggests the solution to a problem on the first page of this picture storybook: "In our house, some days we eat with chopsticks and some days we eat with knives and forks. For me, it's natural" (p. 1, unnumbered). The rest of the story tells how an American sailor courts a Japanese girl, and each secretly tries to learn the other's way of eating. The couple reaches a satisfactory compromise because each person still respects the other's culture.

Yoshiko Uchida, the author of several historical fiction novels about the Japanese American experience during World War II (see Chapter 10), tells her personal experiences in *The Invisible Thread*. Students of children's literature may compare experiences described by Uchida in her autobiography with her historical fiction.

If children are to learn about the cultural heritage and the contributions of Asian American people, as well as discover the similarities between Asian and non–Asian Americans, more high-quality literature about Asian Americans is needed. Because biographies and autobiographies are especially good for raising children's aspirations and increasing understanding of the contributions and problems of individuals, multicultural literature programs need biographies about Asian Americans.

Suggested Activities

 For more suggested activities for understanding multicultural literature, visit our Companion Website at www.prenhall.com/norton

- Bettye I. Latimer (1976) surveyed trade books published in the mid-1960s and the 1970s and concluded that about 1 percent of the books involved African American characters. Choose a recent publication date, and select books that have been chosen as the best books of the year by the School Library Journal Book Review Editors or some other group that selects outstanding books. Tabulate the number of books that are about African Americans, Native Americans, Latinos, and Asian Americans. What percentage of the books selected as outstanding literature include characters who are members of minority groups?

- Choose one of the cultural groups discussed in the chapter. Read a number of myths, legends, and folktales from that culture. Summarize the traditional beliefs and values. Provide quotations from the tales to show the beliefs and values. Try to identify those same beliefs and values in other genres of literature depicting the same culture. What conclusions can you reach about the importance of traditional literature?

- Choose an outstanding author, such as Virginia Hamilton, Gary Soto, John Bierhorst, or Laurence Yep, and read several books by that author. What makes the plot and the characters memorable? What are the themes in the writer's work? Is there a common theme throughout the writing?

- With a group of your peers, choose an area of literature discussed in this chapter. Select five books that develop the values of multicultural literature discussed in this chapter. Also select five books that do not develop the values. Share the books and your rationales for selecting them with the rest of the class.

Teaching with Multicultural Literature

Educators are concerned about the quality and the quantity of multicultural materials available for sharing with children. They are also concerned about the teaching strategies used in developing understanding of and positive attitudes toward various cultural groups. Across the decades, educators have called for more involvement with multicultural concepts. For example, Kathryn H. Au (1993) argued for the inclusion of multicultural literature in the classroom when she stated:

Multiethnic literature can be used in the classroom to affirm the cultural identity of students of diverse backgrounds, and to develop all students' understanding and appreciation of other cultures. This view of literature is one of the new patterns of instruction that can help to support the school literacy development of students of diverse backgrounds. (p. 176)

Recent statistics indicate a greater need for multicultural education because there is a discrepancy among college graduation rates for different groups. For example, Alberta Gloria (2001) reports that 5 percent of Latinos complete four or more years of college. This is compared with 22 percent of whites. She states, "What's needed is a multidimensional approach. We need to welcome students at a psychological level, at a social level, at an environmental and cultural level. We need to step up to the challenge of inclusion" (p. 14).

This section considers many types of activities that can heighten the value of excellent multicultural literature and step up to the challenge of inclusion. Many of the teaching models and instructional ideas evolved from Donna Norton's (1984–1987; Norton and McNamara, 1988; Norton and Norton, 1999) research, including different approaches with undergraduate and graduate classes, research in elementary and middle school classes, multicultural literature evaluations, and development of multicultural literature curriculum and inservice activities.

Portions of the sequence of study that are recommended in this chapter were published in Norton's "Teaching Multicultural Literature in the Reading Curriculum" (1990). The journal article received the 1992 Virginia Hamilton Essay Award, which is presented by the Virginia Hamilton Conference Advisory Board at Kent State University. This annual award recognizes an article that "makes a significant contribution to the professional literature concerning multicultural literary

experiences for youth." I was very honored to be the recipient of this award, and I hope the sequence of study will help you as you prepare to use multicultural literature. The total sequence is developed with several cultural groups in Norton's *Multicultural Children's Literature: Through the Eyes of Many Children* (2001).

Research and experience as well as a search through the scholarly literature support a sequence of study in multicultural literature that proceeds from the ancient literature of a culture to the contemporary literature. For example, both Franchot Ballinger (1984) and Michael Dorris (1979) recommend a sequence of study of Native American literature that begins with a study of broad oral traditions, narrows to specific tribal experiences as expressed in mythology, continues with biographical and autobiographical study of specific cultural areas, and concludes with a study of contemporary Native American literature. Dorris supports this sequence because:

To investigate any Native American literature one must examine its evolution and development through time; one must know something of the language—its rules, its implied world view—of its creation; one must know something of the culture's history of contacts with other peoples, both Native American and Euro-American; and one must know something of the modern social setting of the culture. (p. 157)

The sequence of study used in Chart 11.1 modifies the Ballinger and Dorris models and emphasizes literature written for children. This study is a five-phase approach. It begins with a broad awareness of myths, legends, and folktales from one cultural group (for example, Native American). Then, it narrows to the myths, legends, and folktales of one or two tribal or cultural areas (for example, Native American myths and legends from the Plains Indians or Indians of the northwestern coast). It proceeds to autobiographies, biographies, and other informational literature about an earlier time in history, continues with historical fiction, and concludes with literature written for children by authors whose work represents that cultural group and contemporary time.

Follow the total sequence with one cultural group before proceeding to another cultural group. As you work through each phase, you are developing understandings that build upon each other. For example, after students can identify the traditional values and beliefs of the people as represented in their folktales, myths, and legends, they find it easier to identify values and beliefs in historical nonfiction. Students can use the knowledge gained from analyzing historical nonfiction, including autobiographies and biographies, to evaluate the appropriateness and authenticity of historical fiction and contemporary literature. As you proceed through the study, make cross-cultural comparisons. This series of activities can easily take the form of a unit.

CHART 11.1   Sequence for multicultural literature study

Phase I: Traditional Literature (Generalizations and Broad Views)
A. Identify distinctions among folktales, myths, and legends.
B. Identify ancient stories that have common features and that are found in many regions.
C. Identify types of stories that dominate a subject.
D. Summarize the nature of oral language, the role of traditional literature, the role of an audience, and the literary style.

Phase II: Traditional Tales from One Area (Narrower View)
A. Analyze traditional myths and other story types and compare findings with those in Phase I.
B. Analyze and identify values, beliefs, and themes in the traditional tales of one region.

Phase III: Historical Nonfiction
A. Analyze nonfiction for the values, beliefs, and themes identified in traditional literature.
B. Compare adult autobiographies and children's biographies (if possible).
C. Compare information in historical documents with autobiographies and biographies.

Phase IV: Historical Fiction
A. Evaluate historical fiction according to the authenticity of the conflicts, characterizations, settings, themes, language, and traditional beliefs and values.
B. Search for the role of traditional literature in historical fiction.
C. Compare historical fiction with autobiographies, biographies, and historical information.

Phase V: Contemporary Literature
A. Analyze the inclusion of any beliefs and values identified in traditional literature and nonfictional literature.
B. Analyze contemporary characterizations and conflicts.
C. Analyze the themes and look for threads that cross the literature.

Developing an Appreciation for African American Culture

To help students develop an appreciation of the culture of African Americans, encourage the students to read a number of literature selections in various genres. Use the following activities to develop higher comprehension abilities in literature-based reading programs and to add understanding to other areas of the curriculum, such as social studies.

Phase One: Traditional Literature

Before beginning a study of the folktales, myths, and legends from Africa, discuss the importance of the oral tradition in transmitting the beliefs and values of all people. Make sure that students know the background of the oral tradition and that tales were handed down for many generations before they were transcribed into written form. Share with the students that many contemporary storytellers prefer the stories that were part of the oral tradition. For example, Jack Maguire (1988) emphasizes that many storytellers and story listeners "prefer tales that developed within a predominately oral culture, such as the 'Ananasi the Spider' stories of Central America, the myths and legends of ancient Greece and Scandinavia, or the 'Jack Tales' of pioneer Appalachia" (p. 7). Also show and discuss a map of the African continent so that students understand the diversity of locations for folklore.

To help students understand the importance of oral language in transmitting cultural information, begin with a study of African folklore. Emphasize the power of oral storytellers and the impact of the language. Share with students that ancient Africans depended on oral storytellers to keep alive the cultural past. Storytellers chanted and sang, interacted with the audience, and acted out story elements. The art of storytelling was so highly valued that storytelling competitions were held to encourage the most vivid and entertaining stories. Tell the students that they will be listening to oral storytellers, identifying oral storytelling styles, and creating their own storytelling experiences.

Storytelling. Begin this enjoyable study by investigating how authentic storytellers selected their stories, what story openings were found in African folklore, what styles were common in storytelling, and how storytellers ended their stories. Relate to the students information about how contemporary storytellers such as Gail E. Haley (1986) find and retell their folktales. For example, Haley researches as far back as she can, to the earliest known version, and attempts to immerse herself in the culture that created the story. Haley states:

In the case of *A Story, a Story,* I took a course in African dance. I learned to prepare African food. I haunted museums and private collections of African artifacts. I even befriended a stranded African magic woman who shared our New York apartment for almost a year, imbuing me with her country and culture. But the

CHART 11.2 Introducing traditional tales with objects

Object	Association	Traditional Tales
1. A rabbit	The importance of sense	Gerald McDermott, *Zomo the Rabbit*
2. A cardboard python, a fairy, and a hornet	Anansi tricks the Sky God into returning stories	Verna Aardema, *Anansi Does the Impossible!*
3. A rabbit and a hut	Someone has taken possession of rabbit's house.	Verna Aardema, *Who's in Rabbit's House?*
4. A mosquito	The mosquito was not always noisy.	Verna Aardema, *Why Mosquitoes Buzz in People's Ears*
5. A crab	Pride causes Crab to be left without a head.	Barbara Knutson, *Why the Crab Has No Head*
6. A box containing stories	How did stories come to earth?	Gail Haley, *A Story, a Story*
7. Round and square houses	Why do men live in square houses and women live in round houses?	Ann Grifalconi, *The Village of Round and Square Houses*

basis remains the search for the primal roots of the story, the original tale. (p. 120)

Story Selections. Descriptions of storytellers from West Africa provide ideas for selecting a story from a number of possibilities. During her travels through Africa in the nineteenth century, Mary Kingsley (1964) discovered story minstrels who carried nets resembling fishing nets that contained such objects as bones, feathers, and china bits. When a listener chose an object, the storyteller would tell a story about it. Another interesting technique required storytellers to wear hats with articles suspended from the brims. A listener again would select an intriguing item, and the story would begin.

Teachers and librarians can easily use these techniques to help children select the story or stories to hear and to stimulate their interest. Cardboard cutouts, miniature objects, or real things that suggest a character or animal in a story can be chosen. Chart 11.2 gives examples of objects and the stories that they represent.

Story Openings. Storytellers from several African countries introduce stories by calling out sentences that elicit responses by the audiences. For example, Philip Noss (1972) relates that the following is a common story starter from Cameroon:

> Storyteller: Listen to a tale! Listen to a tale!
> Audience: A tale for fun, for fun. Your throat is a gong, your body a locust; bring it here for me to roast!
> Storyteller: Children, listen to a tale, a tale for fun, for fun.

If you prefer to use an opening statement and response in an African language, use the following Hausa opening from Nigeria, identified by A. J. Tremearne (1970):

> Storyteller: Ga ta, ga ta nan. (See it, see it here.)
> Audience: Ta zo, muii. (Let it come, for us to hear.)

If the stories are from the West Indies, one of the introductions identified by Elsie Clews Parsons (1918) would be appropriate:

> 1. Once upon a time, a very good time
>   Not my time, nor your time, old people's time
>
> 2. Once upon a time, a very good time
>   Monkey chew tobacco and spit white lime

Use these openings with any of the traditional African tales previously described, or use them to introduce a series of folktales. For example, Verna Aardema's humorous *Who's in Rabbit's House?* seems particularly appropriate for an introduction stressing a tale for fun. An enjoyable series of folktales might include "why" tales such as Aardema's *Why Mosquitoes Buzz in People's Ears* and Ashley Bryan's *The Cat's Purr* and "Why Frog and Snake Never Play Together" in *Beat the Story-Drum, Pum-Pum.* Another series might include hero or trickster tales.

Storytelling Styles. Listening to Ashley Bryan's tape, *The Dancing Granny and Other African Stories* (1985), is an excellent way to introduce storytelling styles. Have students listen to the tape and then describe this very vivid style. Have them search other sources for descriptions of storytelling styles. They will discover that the style of the traditional African storyteller, still found in many African countries today, can be characterized as a lively mixture of mimicking dialogue, body action, audience participation, and rhythm. Storytellers mimic the sounds of animals, change their voices to characterize both animal and human characters, develop dialogue, and encourage their listeners to interact with the story. Usually, they also add musical accompaniment with drums or other rhythm and string instruments such as thumb pianos. Anne Pellowski (1977) says that music and rhythm are important additions to African storytellers:

Taken as a whole, all storytelling in Africa, whether folk, religious, or bardic, whether in prose or poetry, seems to be strongly influenced by music and rhythm. It is rare to find stories that do not have some rhythmical or musical interlude or accompaniment, using either the voice, body parts, or special instruments. (p. 116)

Because children enjoy interacting with storytellers and interpreting tempos with drums or other musical instruments, such additions to storytelling can increase appreciation and understanding of traditional African tales. Stories such as Aardema's *Why Mosquitoes Buzz in People's Ears* and *Who's in Rabbit's House?*, with their strong oral language patterns and varied animal characterizations, can effectively introduce traditional African style.

Story Endings. Just as African storytellers use interesting story beginnings, they also often use certain types of story endings. A dramatic story could end with the Hausa *Suka zona* (they remained) or the Angolan *Mahezu* (finished). For an obvious exaggeration from the West Indies, the storyteller might choose this ending:

> Chase the rooster and catch the hen
> I'll never tell a lie like that again.

Storytellers from the West Indies also provide an appropriate ending for humorous folktales:

> They lived in peace, they died in peace
> And they were buried in a pot of candle grease.

A folktale from the West Indies, such as Ashley Bryan's retelling of *Turtle Knows Your Name,* is appropriate. Bryan's rhythmic language makes this tale an enjoyable choice for an oral experience.

Children enjoy re-creating the atmosphere of traditional African tales. African American children take special pride in the stories and the exciting ways in which the stories can be presented to an audience. Both adults and children can tell stories and then discuss the traditional African approaches to storytelling and the ways in which these approaches enhanced the enjoyment for both storyteller and listeners. After the stories are told, students may read them constantly. Conclude by asking students to identify and summarize the oral language styles that are found in traditional African folklore.

Values and Beliefs. After students consider the impact of the language on the folklore of Africa, ask them to read numerous examples of folklore from Africa to identify values and beliefs found in the tales. You may use several approaches to help students identify values and beliefs. Because themes are closely related to values and beliefs, have students search for themes in the folklore. Asking students to provide support for the themes helps them develop higher comprehension and cognitive skills.

In the following example, the themes in John Steptoe's *Mufaro's Beautiful Daughters: An African Tale* also illuminate values and beliefs. First, help students search for themes by asking them to listen to or to read the story and ask themselves: What is the author trying to tell me that would make a difference in my life? How do I know that the author is telling me _____? Remind the students that proof of theme may include many elements in the story, such as the characters' actions, the characters'

thoughts, the interaction of characters as shown through dialogue, the rewards and punishments that end the story, a statement of theme by the author, and illustrations.

Next, read *Mufaro's Beautiful Daughters* as students listen to answer the first question: What is the author trying to tell me that would make a difference in my life? After you complete the story, ask the students to provide at least two important themes in this book. They may say, for example, greed and selfishness are harmful, or bad, personal characteristics and that kindness and generosity are beneficial, or good, personal characteristics. The wording of these themes will differ depending on the age of the students.

Reread *Mufaro's Beautiful Daughters,* asking the students to identify support for each theme within the tale. Remind them of the different ways in which authors develop and support a theme. As support for "greed and selfishness are harmful personal characteristics," students may identify some of the following examples:

1. Illustrations show a bad-tempered girl (illustrations).

2. Manyara tries to trick her sister so that only Manyara will visit the king (actions).

3. Greed causes Manyara to leave the village secretly (actions).

4. Manyara refuses to give a hungry boy food and responds, "I have brought only enough for myself" (actions and dialogue).

5. Manyara shows anger when she says, "Out of my way, boy!" (actions and dialogue).

6. Manyara refuses to take advice from an older woman (actions that show disrespect for older people).

7. Manyara sees a monster snake with five heads (punishment as part of the ending).

8. Manyara becomes a servant to her sister, the queen (punishment as part of the ending).

9. Greed is punished (represented by the ending).

As support for "kindness and generosity are beneficial personal characteristics," students may identify some of the following examples:

1. Nyasha sings while she works, causing people to think that her singing makes the plants bountiful (actions).

2. Nyasha is kind to a garden snake (actions).

3. Nyasha does not complain because she is considerate of her father's feelings (actions and the author tells us).

4. Illustrations show Nyasha as a happy, thoughtful girl (illustrations).

5. Nyasha gives food to a hungry boy; she says, "You must be hungry," . . . and handed him a yam that she had brought for her lunch (actions and dialogue).

6. Nyasha takes advice from the older woman (actions show respect for older people).

7. Nyasha bravely approaches the chamber in which she is to meet the king (actions).

8. Nyasha sees a little snake and then the king (reward as part of the ending).

9. Nyasha proves herself to be both most worthy and most beautiful (ending).

10. Kindness and generosity are rewarded as Nyasha becomes queen (reward as ending).

After completing this activity, ask the students to identify any additional values and beliefs that they discovered. For example, in addition to admiring generosity and kindness and despising greed and selfishness, the African people represented in this tale value the advice of older people and consider worthiness to be more important than beauty. Again, students should support these values and beliefs with evidence from the tale.

Charting answers to questions related to folk characteristics is another technique that helps students identify values in folklore. First, discuss various ways in which students can identify traditional values found in folklore. For example, they can read the folklore to discover answers to each of the following questions:

1. What reward or rewards are desired?

2. What actions are rewarded or admired?

3. What actions are punished or despised?

4. What rewards are given to the heroes, the heroines, or the great people in the stories?

5. What are the personal characteristics of the heroes, the heroines, or the great people in the stories?

Next, print each of these questions on a chart. Allow room to include several African tales. When students read various African tales, have them use the chart to identify and discuss traditional values and beliefs.

Introduce the first book on the chart, Gail Haley's *A Story, a Story.* It is advisable to complete the first example together. Ask the students to listen carefully so that they will be able to answer the questions and identify the values on the chart. After reading *A Story, a Story* aloud, ask the students to identify the answers to the questions and to place them in the proper location on the chart. Chart 11.3 shows the results of this activity using *A Story, a Story* and Gerald McDermott's *Zomo the Rabbit: A Trickster Tale from West Africa.* For additional books, use a similar listening, listing, and discussing procedure, or have the students read these books independently and then discuss their results.

After each reading activity, discuss the values and beliefs that are developed in the story. Ask the students to notice ways that some of the values and beliefs express the importance of oral language discussed earlier. Read as many African tales as possible to find additional values and beliefs and to discover common values and beliefs in various folklore selections.

Notice that within these tales are many trickster tales. Tricksters may win or lose. Explain to students that in folklore, trickery is often considered necessary to create a balance. Consequently, students should consider what forces are out of balance.

Before leaving Phase One, review discoveries about oral storytelling and summarize the values and beliefs that the students discovered in reading African folklore.

Phase Two: Folklore of the American South

African American folktales and legends include many of the values and characteristics of the African tales. The resulting tales combine a past culture, a new environment, and new experiences. Many of the traditional values, including love for language, respect for wit, hospitality, generosity, gratitude, and reverence for elderly people, are also found in African American folklore. During Phase Two, identify the philosophy, values, and beliefs of the people as reflected in African American folklore. Have students identify similarities between the African folklore and the American folklore. Also, help students identify any differences that reflect the new environment and experiences.

CHART 11.3 Values identified in African folklore

Questions for Values	A Story, a Story	Zomo the Rabbit
What reward is desired?	Stories from the powerful sky god	Wisdom
What actions are rewarded or admired?	Outwitting the leopard, the hornet, and the fairy	Using wit, trickery, and courage
What actions are punished or despised?	—	Lacking caution
What rewards are given to heroes, heroines, or great people?	Oral stories to delight the people	Advice (the three things that are worth having are courage, good sense, and caution)
What are the personal characteristics of heroes, heroines, or great people?	Intelligence and verbal ability (in the small old man)	Courage and cleverness

Begin the study by sharing and discussing the stories found in Virginia Hamilton's *The People Could Fly: American Black Folktales.* Identify the types of tales, such as animal tales, supernatural tales, and slave tales of freedom. As you continue your study, encourage your students to identify values, beliefs, and language styles. Use the same techniques that encouraged students to search for values, beliefs, and themes in African folklore. For example, trace themes in several African American folktales and compare those themes with the themes found in African folklore. Develop charts that are similar to Chart 11.3. Analyze numerous African American folktales and compare the values. Read African American folktales aloud. Are there any similarities in language style? Identify stories that have similar story structures and discuss the similarities but also consider why there might be differences. In addition to Hamilton's book, the following books are excellent sources of tales: Julius Lester's adaptations of Joel Chandler Harris's tales in *The Tales of Uncle Remus: The Adventures of Brer Rabbit* and *More Tales of Uncle Remus: Further Adventures of Brer Rabbit, His Friends, Enemies, and Others;* Lester's *The Knee-High Man and Other Tales;* Van Dyke Parks's adaptation of Joel Chandler Harris's tales in *Jump! The Adventures of Brer Rabbit* and *Jump Again! More Adventures of Brer Rabbit;* Patricia McKissack's *Flossie & the Fox;* William H. Hooks's *The Ballad of Belle Dorcus;* Steve Sanfield's *The Adventures of High John the Conqueror;* and Robert D. San Souci's *Sukey and the Mermaid.*

Activities developed around John Henry, the tall tale hero, provide opportunities for creative dramatizations, discussions about values, learning about history, and writing. As a poem, a song, or a longer narrative, the tale can stimulate many creative activities. Because there are several versions of the John Henry tale, compare the books, poem, and song. Is the story the same in each version? Are the illustrations alike or different? Which version is the most effective? Why?

Teachers have used the tale in its various forms with children in all of the elementary grades. In the lower grades, children can listen to the story and discuss the large illustrations in the picture book *John Henry,* by Ezra Jack Keats, or in *John Henry,* by Julius Lester. The language of the books makes pleasant listening while children discover that American folk heroes are from different ethnic backgrounds. Through the story and pictures, children can gain an understanding of tall tales and the actions that heroes are supposed to perform. Discuss other folk heroes, such as Davy Crockett and Paul Bunyan. Have the children compare the remarkable feats of each hero and decide how much of each hero's story is exaggerated.

In poetic form, John Henry makes a good choral presentation. Classes have tried the poem as a refrain in which a leader reads the opening lines of each verse and the class enters in on each of the repetitive lines, such as "He laid down his hammer and he died." Alternatively, have students read each verse in a cumulative arrangement, in which one group begins the first verse, the second joins the second verse, and a third joins the third verse. This arrangement continues until the poem is complete.

Encourage creative writing by asking children to write their own work chants and tall tales. One class pretended that John Henry was a contemporary hero and wrote about the heroic deeds that he could do if he lived in their lifetime. Stories described him saving the nuclear reactor at Three Mile Island, rescuing people from the upper floors during a hotel fire, and completing work on a superhighway or a skyscraper. Illustrations accompanying the stories showed John Henry as a strong man who was also concerned with the lives of the people around him. Other classes have used tales about John Henry to stimulate creative drama.

As a conclusion to Phase Two, summarize the likenesses and differences between African and African American folklore. Identify stories that have close similarities, and consider any reasons for the similarities. Also consider reasons for the differences within the tales.

Phase Three: Historical Nonfiction

By this time, students should have gained understanding that they can use as they read, analyze, and evaluate both nonfictional and fictional literature. During Phase Three, have students read, discuss, and evaluate nonfictional literature that reflects a historical perspective. For example, as students read biographies and autobiographies, have them analyze the inclusion of values, beliefs, and philosophies found in the traditional literature. Have the students read a number of sources, evaluate the accuracy of the information, and identify historical happenings that influenced the culture. Include other types of nonfictional informational texts so that students may critically evaluate the accuracy of settings, happenings, and sources of conflict.

Use Chart 11.4 to help students as they proceed with this evaluation. Note, however, that the material included in Chart 11.4 is only a partial listing of the information that may be included. Notice a continuity within the literature of the language style, theme, and values found in earlier traditional literature. Also notice that the sources of conflict are authentic for this time period. The students who evaluated *Amos Fortune,* however, concluded after reading other nonfictional sources that many of the horrors of the period were not included in this biography.

Additional biographies that are excellent for analyzing during Phase Three include Lillie Patterson's *Frederick Douglass: Freedom Fighter,* Douglas Miller's *Frederick Douglass and the Fight for Freedom,* and Virginia Hamilton's *Anthony Burns: The Defeat and Triumph of a Fugitive Slave.* Milton Meltzer's *The Black Americans: A History in Their Own Words, 1619–1983* is an excellent source for shorter autobiographical sketches and information. Virginia Hamilton's *Many Thousand Gone: African Americans from Slavery to Freedom* also provides shorter sketches of people.

CHART 11.4   Analyzing historical biography and autobiography

Literature	Evidence of Philosophy, Values, Beliefs, and Language from Phases One and Two	Sources of Conflict	Historical Happenings and Evaluations
Yates's *Amos Fortune, Free Man*	African story told by Amos is in the style of African storytellers, using repetition, chants, and audience participation. *Theme:* Freedom is important. *Values:* Work, family, retribution, generosity, love of nature.	Person against society, as Amos fights mistreatment, injustice, and separation. Person against self, as Amos considers consequences of his actions.	New Hampshire, 1725–1801. Blacks are taken from Africa and sold as slaves. The horrors of the slave block are avoided in the text, so acceptance of the situations may be too easy.
Ferris's *Go Free or Die: A Story of Harriet Tubman*	*Themes:* Freedom is worth risking one's life. We must help others obtain their freedom. *Values:* Obligations to family and people, wit, trickery when needed for balance, responsibility, and gratitude.	Person against society, as Harriet fights to free blacks and to combat injustice.	America, mid-1800s to the end of the Civil War. This story is based on facts related to slavery, the Underground Railroad, the 1850 Fugitive Slave Act, and the 1863 Emancipation Proclamation. Tubman freed more than three hundred slaves in ten years.

Another type of activity using historical nonfiction is recommended by Wynell Burroughs Schamel and Jean West (1992). These educational specialists at the Education Branch, National Archives and Records Administration in Washington, D.C., recommend teaching about the Civil War and the fight for equal rights by analyzing documents from the time period, such as a recruiting poster for black soldiers in the Civil War. They provide a copy of a poster and recommend questions to analyze the poster, such as

Who do you believe is the intended audience for the poster? What does the government hope the audience will do? What references to pay do you find in this document? What references to treatment of prisoners of war do you find in this document? What evidence of government efforts to improve conditions for black soldiers do you find in this document? What purpose(s) of government is/are served by this poster? How is the design of this poster different from contemporary military recruitment posters? (p. 120)

Schamel and West also provide suggestions for creative writing, oral reports, and further research.

Phase Four: Historical Fiction

During Phase Four, have students read, analyze, and evaluate historical fiction and fiction with historical backgrounds

according to credibility of conflict, believability of characterization, authenticity of setting, authenticity of traditional beliefs expressed by the characters, appropriateness of themes, and appropriateness of the author's style. Understandings gained from the previously studied biographies, autobiographies, and informational books are especially important during Phase Four. For example, if students have read a number of biographies and other nonfictional texts about the time of slavery, then they can analyze a fictional book, such as Belinda Hurmence's *A Girl Called Boy*. Even though there is a time-warp experience in this story, the major portion of the story is set in North Carolina in the 1850s.

Have students evaluate the authenticity of the 1850s North Carolina plantation setting. Also, have them use the knowledge that they gained while reading biographies of this time period to analyze the credibility of the conflict. Have students provide evidence for answers to the following questions: Is the setting authentic for a plantation that included numerous slaves? If the setting is authentic, what makes it authentic? What proof do you have that this setting is or is not authentic? Does the plot parallel stories of actual slaves? How? Is the person-against-society conflict as believable as are the conflicts in biographies and autobiographies? What are the comparisons? Why is the conflict believable? How does the author develop believable characters?

Relate instances of characterization with examples from biographies and autobiographies. Are any of the traditional beliefs, themes, and language styles that were found during Phases One and Two also found in this book? Which ones? How are these beliefs developed in the story? Are any of the themes identified in biographies also found in this book? If so, how does the author develop these themes? Do you believe that the themes are appropriate for this story? Why or why not? Is the author's style appropriate for the story? Why or why not? Find examples of author's style that you think are either very good or inappropriate. What, if any, is the relationship of this book to the findings from Phases One, Two, and Three of this study? Defend your answer.

You may use numerous books for Phase Four. Additional books with historical settings about slavery include F. N. Monjo's *The Drinking Gourd,* Paula Fox's *Slave Dancer,* James and Christopher Collier's *Jump Ship to Freedom,* James Berry's *Ajeemah and His Son,* Gary Paulsen's *Nightjohn,* and Mary Stolz's *Cezanne Pinto: A Memoir.* Mildred Taylor's family survival stories set in the 1950s, *The Gold Cadillac, Roll of Thunder, Hear My Cry,* and *Let the Circle Be Unbroken,* are excellent sources for analysis and comparison. The themes related to family, physical, and spiritual survival have threads that may be traced to the earlier studies.

Molly Bannaky by Alice McGill is a picture storybook that allows readers to authenticate both the role of indentured servants and freed slaves. The book is set in the late seventeenth century when many immigrants from England exchanged the price of sea passage for seven years of work, after which they were declared free. In this story set in Maryland, the protagonist, after gaining her freedom, moves into the wilderness and settles her own farm. She buys a slave, frees him after the land is cleared, and they eventually marry. Students can use information found in the author's note to further research the lives of indentured servants and freed slaves. They can compare the lives of indentured servants and slaves. According to the author's note, the fictional story is based on the life of a former slave, Benjamin Banneker, 1731–1806, and Molly Bannaky.

Phase Five: Contemporary Literature

During the final phase, have students read, analyze, and evaluate contemporary literature, including poetry, fiction, and biography. Have the students search for continuity within the literature as reflected in the images, themes, values, and sources of conflict. Also, have them reflect on changes that have taken place. For example, ask the students to read the poetry of Langston Hughes, Gwendolyn Brooks, and Tom Feelings. Poetry selections such as Hughes's "Dreams" and "Merry-Go-Round" should have

special significance because the students should understand both the pain of prejudice and the joy of life experienced by people earlier in American history. Students also should gain respect for the poets who created such vivid images within their poems.

Some books are especially good for relating the past and the present. For example, ask students to read such contemporary realistic fiction selections as Sharon Bell Mathis's *The Hundred Penny Box* and Virginia Hamilton's *The House of Dies Drear.* The students should understand Mathis's characterization when Aunt Dew excitedly says, "18 and 74. Year I was born. Slavery over! Black men in Congress running things. They was in charge. It was the Reconstruction" (p. 26). In Hamilton's book, they should understand the pride in the African American family as it tries to unravel a mystery related to a home on the Underground Railroad.

Strong family relationships and respect for elders are found in books that span all five phases of this study. Ask students to search for support for these themes in such books as Lucille Clifton's *Everett Anderson's Goodbye,* Mildred Pitts Walter's *Justin and the Best Biscuits in the World,* and Mary Stolz's *Storm in the Night.* Pride in heritage and strength in character are also frequent themes and values. Ask the students to trace these themes and values in books such as Eloise Greenfield's *Sister* and Virginia Hamilton's *Zeely* and *Junius Over Far.*

Finally, ask the students to read biographies of contemporary African American people, such as Martin Luther King, Jr., Barbara Jordan, Malcolm X, Langston Hughes, and Arthur Mitchell. Ask them to search for conflicts, characterizations, values, and themes. Is there any evidence of continuity within the literature? If so, what aspects are also found in the other phases?

Comparisons between the more historical biographies and the contemporary biographies are especially interesting. Biographies lend themselves to numerous activities in the curriculum. The following activities include a study of biographies in history, science, literature, reading, art, music, and sports:

1. Have the children search the literature and develop a time line illustrating the contributions of famous African Americans in history. Develop the time line on a bulletin board and display literature selections that tell about the people.

2. Ask the children to share their reactions after reading a biography about Martin Luther King, Jr. Have them interview parents and other adults about the goals of the late civil rights leader.

3. After reading a biography, perform "A Day in the Life of _____ ."

4. Share literature written by African American authors. Discuss the contributions and styles of such authors as John Steptoe, Sharon Mathis, Eloise Greenfield, and Virginia Hamilton.

5. After reading biographies or stories about African American musicians, share and discuss their music.

6. Read biographies of African American athletes and discuss records set or other contributions.

7. After reading literature about the contributions and lives of African Americans, create a "What's My Line" game in which a panel of children asks questions while another group answers.

8. Using a "Meet the Press" format, ask children to take roles of famous African Americans or reporters who interview them. Prepare for the session by reading literature.

You can use similar activities to highlight the contributions of Native Americans, Latinos, and Asian Americans. However, before proceeding to the literature of another cultural group, review what the students have learned from this five-phase study. Review the evidence of both continuity and change. What do the students know about the literature of the African American culture that will make a difference in their lives?

Developing an Appreciation for Native American Culture

To study Native American cultures, use many of the same techniques that you used for African American culture. Begin with Native American folklore, in general. Then, narrow the study to the folklore of specific peoples. Proceed to historical nonfiction. Follow historical nonfiction with historical fiction, and end with contemporary literature.

Phase One: Native American Folklore

Before beginning a study of Native American culture, show and discuss a map of the North American continent to reveal to students the diversity of locations for Native American peoples. John Bierhorst's *The Mythology of North America* (1985) includes a useful map of North American mythological regions. A map is also located in Michael J. Caduto and Joseph Bruchac's *Keepers of the Animals: Native American Stories and Wildlife Activities for Children* (1991). According to the authors, this map indicates the cultural areas and tribal locations of Native North Americans as they appeared around 1600. Have students begin their study of Native American folklore with an investigation of the oral language.

Storytelling. Native American storytellers, like African storytellers, developed definite styles in their storytelling over centuries of oral tradition. Storytelling was an important part of early Indian life, and stories were carefully passed down from one generation to the next. It was quite common for Indians to gather around a fire or sit around their homes while listening to stories. The storytelling sessions often continued for long periods of time, with each person telling a story. Children have opportuni-

ties to empathize with members of Native American culture when they take part in storytelling activities that closely resemble the original experience. According to Michael J. Caduto and Joseph Bruchac (1989), "Stories form a link between our imagination and our surroundings. They are a way of reaching deep into a child's inner world, to the places where dreams and fantasies are constantly sculpting an ever-growing world view" (p. 7).

Caduto and Bruchac also emphasize the importance of the setting for the storytelling. They state:

In the American Indian culture, everyone was allowed to have their say and people listened with patience. People would sit in a circle during the time of storytelling because in a circle no person is at the head. All are "the same height." Remembering this may help you and it is good to remind your listeners—who are not just an audience but part of the story—of that. (p. 8)

Story Openings. Several collectors of Native American tales and observers of Native American storytellers have identified characteristic opening sentences that you may use when presenting Native American stories to children. Franc Newcomb (1967), for example, found that many Navaho storytellers opened their stories with one of the following tributes to the past:

In the beginning, when the world was new

At the time when men and animals were all the same and spoke the same language

A popular beginning with the White Mountain Apache was "long, long ago, they say." According to Caduto and Bruchac (1989), the Abenaki people begin a story with, "Here my story camps." The Iroquois often begin by saying, "Would you like to hear a story?"

Have the children search through stories from many Native American tribes and discover how interpreters and translators of traditional Indian folktales introduced their stories. Have the children investigate further and find the exact story openers a certain tribe would be likely to use so that they can use those openings when telling stories from that tribe.

Storytelling Styles. The storytelling styles used by various Indians of North America were quite different from the styles for African storytellers. Melville Jacobs (1959) describes the storytelling style of Northwest Indians as being terse, staccato, and rapid. It was usually compact, with little description, although storytellers might use pantomime and gestures to develop the story. Gladys Reichard (1974) found that the Coeur d'Alene Indians used dramatic movements to increase the drama of their tales.

The listening styles of the Native American audiences were also quite different. Native American children were expected to be very attentive and not to interrupt the storyteller. Their only response might be the Hopi's repetition of the last word in a sentence, or the Crow's responsive "E!" (yes) following every few sentences. According to Byrd Baylor (1976), this response was a sign that the audience was attentive and appreciative. Children in classroom and library story times may also enjoy using these signs to show that they are listening.

Morris Opler (1938) discovered an interesting detail about Jicarilla Apache storytellers that can be used to add authenticity and cultural understanding to Native American storytelling. Storytellers gave kernels of corn to children during story time. Because corn was very important, it was believed that if children ate the corn during the storytelling they would remember the content and the importance of the stories.

Story Endings. Melville Jacobs (1959) says that Clackama Indians ended many stories by telling an epilogue about an Indian's metamorphosis into an animal, bird, or fish. Most of the stories also had a final ending that meant "myth, myth" or "story, story." Jicarilla Apache storytellers sometimes ended their stories by giving gifts to the listeners because they had stolen a night from their audience. Caduto and Bruchac (1989) say that the Abenaki people closed their stories with phrases such as "That is the end" or "Then I left." The Iroquois often ended their stories with "Da neho!" which means, "That is all."

Teachers and librarians have found that adding authentic storytelling techniques increases understanding and respect for a cultural heritage and stimulates discussions about traditional values. Before leaving this portion of Phase One, ask students to summarize what they have learned about Native American folklore styles.

Types of Tales. Collect as many examples of North American Indian folklore as possible. Have the students use these tales to categorize stories that meet Bierhorst's story types found in Native American folklore: (1) setting-the-world-in-order tales, (2) family drama tales, (3) trickster tales, and (4) threshold tales. Chart 11.5 includes examples of literature that you may use for this purpose. Before leaving Phase One, summarize your generalizations about Native American folklore and review your discoveries about oral storytelling.

Phase Two: Folklore from Specific Peoples

During Phase Two, narrow the emphasis to the folklore of one or two Native American peoples. If the students work well in groups, you may choose several tribal regions and allow each group to do an in-depth study of the folklore of that region. For example, there are many stories from the Plains Indians, from the Southwest Pueblo peoples, and from Indians of the Pacific Northwest. Have students search for similarities in story types found in Phase One and analyze the literature for values and beliefs of the specific people. Have them consider the importance of variants in the story types and search for cultural and geographical reasons for these variants.

CHART 11.5 Literature for a study of Native American folklore

> **Setting the World in Order**
> Duncan's *The Magic of Spider Woman*
> Esbensen's *The Star Maiden*
> Hamilton's "Turtle Dives to the Bottom of the Sea"
>   in *In the Beginning: Creation Stories from Around the World*
> Monroe and Williamson's *They Dance in the Sky: Native American Star Myths*
> **Family Drama**
> Metayer's *Tales from the Igloo*
> Monroe and Williamson's *They Dance in the Sky: Native American Star Myths*
> Spencer's *Who Speaks for Wolf*
> **Tricksters**
> Goble's *Iktomi and the Boulder: A Plains Indian Story*
> Lame Deer's "Iktoml and the Ducks" in Cohn's *From Sea to Shining Sea: A Treasury of American Folklore and Folk Songs*
> McDermott's *Raven: A Trickster Tale from the Pacific Northwest*
> **Thresholds**
> Bierhorst's *The Ring in the Prairie: A Shawnee Legend*
> Goble's *Buffalo Woman*

Locate as many folktales, myths, and legends as possible from the specific regions to be studied. Several documented sources of Native American traditional values will help students as they search for evidence of those values. For example, Hanson and Eisenbise's *Human Behavior and American Indians* (1983) documents traditional values and compares them to urban industrial values. Ross and Brave Eagle (1975) identify traditional Lakota values. These Lakota values are especially important if the students are reading and analyzing literature from various Great Plains peoples.

Numerous collections of folklore contain selections from various tribal areas. These sources include Michael J. Caduto and Joseph Bruchac's *Keepers of the Earth: Native American Stories and Environmental Activities for Children* and *Keepers of the Animals: Native American Stories and Wildlife Activities for Children,* and Virginia Hamilton's *In the Beginning: Creation Stories from Around the World.* Chart 11.6 presents a few additional sources of folklore from the Great Plains, the Southwest, and the Northwest. Have students summarize the values, beliefs, and themes found in the traditional literature of a specific people and compare the types of stories found in Phase One and Phase Two. (Use similar techniques to help students discover themes and values like those developed under Phases One and Two of African American literature.)

At the conclusion of Phase Two, have older students analyze Jamake Highwater's *Anpao: An American Indian*

CHART 11.6 Folklore sources for a study of literature from the Great Plains, the Southwest, and the Northwest

Great Plains	Southwest	Northwest
Baker's *Where the Buffalos Begin* Bierhorst's *The Ring in the Prairie* dePaola's *The Legend of the Bluebonnet* Goble's *Buffalo Woman*	Baylor's *Moon Song* Cohlene's *Turquoise Boy: A Navajo Legend* Cushing's *Zuni Folk Tales*	Bierhorst's *The Girl Who Married a Ghost* McDermott's *Raven: A Trickster Tale from the Pacific Northwest* Normandin's *Echoes of the Elders: The Stories and Paintings of Chief Lelooska* Wallas's *Kwakiutl Legends*

Odyssey. This story combines a number of traditional Native American tales.

Many additional activities that you may develop with Native American folklore are found in Caduto and Bruchac's *Keepers of the Earth: Native American Stories and Environmental Activities for Children* and *Keepers of the Animals: Native American Stories and Wildlife Activities for Children*. The activities in these books encourage children to integrate science, geography, and environmental studies into the reading of Native American folklore.

Phase Three: Historical Nonfiction

As in the study of African American literature, students' previous knowledge should help them evaluate the inclusion of accurate values, beliefs, and philosophies in historical nonfiction. Have students read a number of sources to evaluate the authenticity of historical information and to identify the historical happenings that influenced the culture. Have the students develop a chart similar to Chart 11.4. This time, the sources should be Native American biographies and autobiographies from the particular region that the students are studying.

Comparison encourages students to consider the credibility of biographies from different regions. Nonfictional sources, such as Russell Freedman's *Buffalo Hunt, The Life and Death of Crazy Horse*, and *An Indian Winter* and Rayna Green's *Women in American Indian Society*, provide historical perspectives. Byrd Baylor's *When Clay Sings* is a poetic telling of the ancient way of life of Native Americans living in the Southwest desert.

Native American nonfiction is also an excellent source of material for integrating literature and geography. Books such as Marcia Sewall's *People of the Breaking Day* and Jane Yolen's *Encounter* present stories about the native peoples before or just at the time of Columbus. Use these books to help students analyze literature according to the five themes of geography (see next column), to integrate the study of literature and geography, to increase understanding of Native American peoples before and at the time of Columbus, and to motivate discussions related to geography and nonfiction literature (Norton and Norton, 1999).

Before reading either of these books to the students, provide some historical background about the time period and the locations. For *People of the Breaking Day*, explain that this story takes place before the English settlers arrive and change the lives of the people. Using a map or a globe, show and discuss the location of the story. For *Encounter*, explain that this is a story about what might have happened when the Taino Indians of the West Indies met Christopher Columbus and his Spanish explorers for the first time. Also show and discuss the location of San Salvador in the West Indies.

Introduce the five themes of geography that students will use to analyze and discuss the information in these books. Tell the students that geographers have developed this procedure to allow students to inquire about places on the earth and to analyze the relationships of these places to the people who live there. The following five fundamental themes in geography were developed by the Committee on Geographic Education (1983) and are also discussed in *GEO News Handbook* (1990):

1. *Location, including where and why:* Where does the story take place as far as city, country, continent, longitude, latitude, and so forth? Why does the story take place in this location?

2. *Place, including physical and human characteristics:* What are the physical features and characteristics? What are the characteristics of the people, including distinctive cultural traditions?

3. *Relationships within places, including cultural and physical interactions and how relationships develop:* How do human–environmental relationships develop and what are the consequences? What is the primary use of land? How have the people altered the environment? Where do most people live?

4. *Movement, including people, ideas, and materials:* How are the movements of people, ideas, and materials influenced and accomplished? What are the consequences of such movements?

5. *Regions, including how they form and change:* What are the major languages? What are the vegetation

CHART 11.7 Book title: *People of the Breaking Day*

Location	Place	Relationships	Movement	Regions
East Coast. Small settlement. "Where the sun rises." Close to the sea. Away from Mohawks, Penacooks, and Abanakis.	Climate has four seasons. Plentiful food. Cold winters. Wampanoag tribe. Hunt, fish, plant. Father is teacher. Ceremonies for war and death. Animals: fox, bear, deer, hawk.	Great Sachem or leader knows fields, forests, and water. He decides just punishments. Council decides issues of war. Men make arrows, build fences and canoes. Women garden, tend fields, care for needs. Relationships with Mother Earth.	Paths bind villages. Trade with Narragansetts for soapstone, pipes, bowls, and beads. Trade pipes, bowls, beads, and corn with Abanakis for birchbark. Make [birchbark] into canoes. Play games with other nations. Move for survival.	Vegetation: woods, fields, and forests. Regions divided according to hunting grounds. May fight over fishing and hunting grounds.

From Donna E. Norton and Saundra E. Norton, Language Arts Activities for Children, *4th ed. Upper Saddle River, N.J.: Merrill/Prentice Hall, 1999.*

regions? What are the country's political divisions? How do the regions change?

Discuss these themes using language that is appropriate for student understanding. Develop a chart for each of the books. On this chart, place the five themes of geography. As the students read or listen to each book, ask them to identify and discuss the information appropriate for each of the categories. See Chart 11.7 for an example of this analysis using *People of the Breaking Day*. You may use many additional books for this activity, including George DeLucenay Leon's *Explorers of the Americas Before Columbus*.

Phase Four: Historical Fiction

If students are examining literature from the Great Plains, Jan Hudson's *Sweetgrass* is excellent for analyzing historical fiction according to authenticity of setting, credibility of conflict, believability of characterization, authenticity of traditional beliefs, appropriateness of themes, and the author's style. The setting is among the Blackfoot people in southern Canada. The conflict presents a person-against-society problem. European expansion and smallpox cause the Native American characters to face disruption of their lives. The person-against-self conflicts result when characters must overcome differences in belief systems or taboos to survive within their cultures. Without an understanding of Blackfoot values and beliefs, these conflicts would not seem believable. *Sweetgrass* is especially effective for showing students that language should reflect the people, the setting, and the time period. Have students consider the effectiveness of the figurative language and prairie symbolism to describe characters, setting, and conflict.

In Paul Goble's *Beyond the Ridge,* students should discover a belief in the afterlife as experienced by an elderly Indian woman from the Great Plains. This belief is also found in traditional literature.

The following example shows how to present a historical fiction text from the Southwest. Scott O'Dell's *Sing Down the Moon* is based on a tragic time in Navaho history, spanning 1863 to 1865. The story begins during a beautiful spring in Canyon de Chelly. Life seems promising. Then, the United States government sends Colonel Kit Carson to the canyon to bring the Navahos to Fort Sumner, New Mexico. In order to force the Indians' surrender, the troops destroy the crops and livestock. Then, they drive the Navahos to the fort. This three-hundred-mile journey is known as The Long Walk. While at Fort Sumner, more than fifteen hundred Indians died, and many others lost their will to live.

The creation stories of the Navahos refer to creating the mountains as "singing up the mountains." Ask students: What is the significance of Scott O'Dell's title *Sing Down the Moon?* What happened to the Navaho way of life during the years depicted in the story? Why did the government force the Indians to leave their home? If people today were Navahos living at that time, how might they feel? How might a soldier feel?

When it was time for Bright Morning to become a woman, the tribe prepared for the Womanhood Ceremony. Have students investigate the ceremonies celebrated by Navaho Indians. In groups, have students demonstrate one ceremony to the rest of the class and explain its purpose.

Tall Boy made a lance to use against the Long Knives. The only materials with which he had to work were those available in nature. Have students investigate other weapons and tools that Native Americans used, review how the people made the weapons and tools, and draw a picture of each.

In *Sing Down the Moon,* Bright Morning steps on a spear and breaks it when her son reaches out toward a young lamb. Discuss the symbolic meaning of this action.

Many clues in *Sing Down the Moon* suggest the environment in which Bright Morning and her tribe live. For example, O'Dell develops a visual image, describing the canyons: "The stone walls of the canyons stand so close together that you can touch them with your outstretched hand" (p. 1). He describes the rain through Bright Morning's thoughts: "At first it was a whisper, like a wind among the dry corn stalks of our cornfield" (p. 2). O'Dell suggests that even the streams have a voice of their own: "The stream sounded like men's voices speaking" (p. 53). These descriptions also suggest characteristics of the Navahos' environment, as well as their respect for nature, and whether they were a hunting or a farming tribe.

Discuss the significance of the descriptions in O'Dell's language. How does O'Dell feel about the Navahos? Have students search for other visual language that describes the various environments experienced by the Navahos as they leave their canyon and go to Fort Sumner. Compare the canyon environment with that at Fort Sumner and draw pictures of both locations.

For creative writing, have the students describe two environments, one that is lovely and enjoyable to live in and one that is not. Have the students draw a picture illustrating each and describe the pictures using language that will allow someone else to visualize them. Before completing Phase Four, ask the students to summarize their findings and to trace any threads that continue through Phases One through Four.

Phase Five: Contemporary Literature

Contemporary Native American poetry is especially rich in symbolism and mythological references. Allow students to discover the close relationships between the folklore read in Phases One and Two and contemporary texts. For example, ask students to read or listen to the introduction to the Smithsonian Institution's *When the Rain Sings: Poems by Young Native Americans* before they read the poetry: "The strongest voices in contemporary Native poetry are those rooted in community. Neither the difficult landscape of the reservation nor the impact of urban relocation has diluted the strength of oral literature, which endures through new forms. Many contemporary poets speak from the power of oral tradition when they return to the primary sources of knowledge—their villages and tribes" (p. xiv). Before they read the poems, ask the students to also look carefully at the illustrations, which are pictures of people and Native art from an earlier time period. The introductory comments go on to reveal that "stories and objects are ways to understand one's place within the earth's benevolence, of learning about past hardships, of tracking the place of self and family in the

infinite cosmos. Master artists were not supreme beings but fluid connectors to the life force around them. Objects carry stories and bring information from their makers" (p. xvi).

After reading this introduction ask students to consider what subjects they might find in these poems written by Native Americans from eight different tribes. Ask students to locate examples of poems that reflect mythological references, historical information, geographical settings, and historical and contemporary conflicts.

Other excellent sources for this type of activity include Shonto Begay's *Navajo: Visions and Voices Across the Mesa* and Nancy Wood's *The Serpent's Tongue: Prose, Poetry, and Art of the New Mexico Pueblos.* The poetry of contemporary Native Americans provides an interesting means to relate past and present within the culture.

Several contemporary fiction books are interesting for analysis and comparison. For example, younger students may search for any evidence of continuity in the writings of Virginia Driving Hawk Sneve while older students analyze Robert Lipsyte's *The Brave.* White Deer of Autumn's contemporary story *Ceremony—In the Circle of Life* is an excellent book for comparing the values in realistic fiction and folklore. For example, ask the students to compare *Ceremony* and *The Legend of the Bluebonnet.* (Chart 11.8 compares these books.) Have the students discuss the results of the comparison and consider the reasons for the similarities between the values in the traditional tale and the contemporary story.

Byrd Baylor's contemporary story from the Southwest, *Hawk, I'm Your Brother,* is another excellent choice for comparative studies. Through this book, students can visualize the close relationships between a Native American boy and a hawk. There are also frequent references to dreams of flying and ancient knowledge. In addition to identifying relationships between traditional folklore and contemporary stories, you may use *Hawk, I'm Your Brother* to help children recognize differences in point of view and to motivate the writing of a story from another point of view. Such activities help students analyze the characterizations within the book. Use the following instructional sequence for developing understanding of point of view:

1. Introduce the story and tell the students that they will be listening to a story in which the author describes and develops the hero's aspirations. Ask the students to consider how they would feel as Rudy Soto. Also, ask them to consider the feelings and desires of the hawk.

2. After reading *Hawk, I'm Your Brother* aloud, lead a discussion in which the students characterize Rudy and the hawk, and identify the major sequence of events leading up to Rudy's decision to release the hawk.

3. Ask the students to consider the significance of the title of the book. Why did Baylor choose *Hawk, I'm*

CHART 11.8 A comparison of values in traditional and contemporary Native American literature

Comparisons	Traditional Folklore *The Legend of the Bluebonnet*	Contemporary Fiction *Ceremony—In the Circle of Life*
What is the problem?	Drought and famine that are killing the Comanche	Destruction of the land by humans
What reward is desired?	To end the drought and famine To save the land and people	To comfort and honor Mother Earth To teach humans about Mother Earth
What actions (or values) are rewarded or admired?	Sacrifice to save the land and tribe Belief in the Great Spirit	Honor and care for Mother Earth Living in harmony with nature Knowledge, truth, and belief
What actions are punished or despised?	Selfishness Taking from Earth without giving back	Pollution and destruction of Mother Earth
What rewards are given?	Bluebonnets, as a sign of forgiveness Rain to end the drought A name change	A living pipe to symbolize the vision of Mother Earth New strength, knowledge, and understanding
What are the personal characteristics of heroes, heroines, or great people?	Unselfish love of the people and land Respect for the Great Spirit Willingness to sacrifice to benefit others	Love of animals and the land Respect for the Star Spirit and the ways of the people Desire for knowledge and truth

Your Brother? Is it an accurate description of Rudy Soto's relationship to the hawk? How are Rudy and the hawk alike? How are they different? Why did Rudy release the hawk? How do you think Rudy felt after releasing the hawk? How do you think the hawk felt after being released? What would you do if you were Rudy Soto? How would you react if you were the hawk?

4. Tell the students that an incident may be described in different ways by several people who have the same experience. The details that characters describe, the feelings that they experience, and their beliefs in the right or wrong of an incident may vary. Consequently, the same story could change drastically, depending on the point of view of the storyteller. Ask the students to tell you whose point of view Baylor develops in *Hawk, I'm Your Brother.* How did they know that the story was told from Rudy Soto's point of view? Then, ask the students to consider how the story might be written if the author chose the hawk's point of view.

5. Ask the students to imagine that they are the hawk that Rudy captured. Have them write a story about what happened to them, beginning from the time of the capture from the nest high on Santos Mountain.

As a conclusion to Phase Five, summarize the findings and the threads discovered across the ages of literature.

Review examples of continuity and evidences of change. What do the students know about the literature of Native Americans that will make a difference in their lives?

Developing an Appreciation for Latino Culture

Latino literature and culture are very complex. This complexity results from the infusion of numerous influences. José Griego y Maestas and Rudolfo A. Anaya (1980) reinforce the importance of the traditional literature in understanding the culture and show the complexity of such a study. They say that the tales

are a great part of the soul of our culture, and they reflect the values of our forefathers. . . .

The stories reflect a history of thirteen centuries of infusing and blending from the Moors and Jews in Spain, to the orientals in the Philippines, Africans in the Caribbean, and the Indians in America—be they Aztec, Apache or Pueblo. (p. 4)

This chapter includes the ancient literature of the Aztecs and Maya, proceeds to the more recent folklore of Mexico and America, and then concludes with contemporary Latino poetry and fiction.

Phase One: Ancient Aztec and Mayan Folklore

Ancient folklore was first recorded for European audiences by the Spaniards in the sixteenth century. Introduce the folklore by showing students a map of Mexico and Central America that indicates locations of Aztec and Mayan peoples, such as those found in various adult sources, including *Atlas of Ancient America,* by Michael Coe, Dean Snow, and Elizabeth Benson (1986); *The Maya,* by Michael Coe (1992); and *The King Danced in the Marketplace,* by Frances Gillmor (1977). These books are also excellent sources for additional information about these ancient cultures.

Read and discuss several selections of Aztec folklore such as those found in C. Shana Greger's *The Fifth and Final Sun: An Ancient Aztec Myth of the Sun's Origin* and Gerald McDermott's *Musicians of the Sun.* Discuss the values and beliefs reflected in the stories.

After students read or listen to some of the Aztec tales and look at Aztec art in such sources as the *Atlas of Ancient America,* have them analyze the inclusion of Aztec tales and art in Deborah Nourse Lattimore's *The Flame of Peace: A Tale of the Aztecs.* Lattimore states that she combined "the known elements and the lively, authentic art with some educated guesses based on my research and knowledge of the period—to create a story with pictures that I hope will satisfy those two most critical audiences: scholars and children" (endcover). Students should use their own research abilities to decide if she reached her goal. What evidence do they have that Lattimore based her story on research and knowledge?

John Bierhorst's *The Monkey's Haircut and Other Stories Told by the Maya* provides a source for students to identify characteristics of and values in Mayan folklore. For example, have students search for stories that have the following values and characteristics identified by Bierhorst: (1) cleverness, as shown by stories that include riddles, puns, double meanings, and tricksters; (2) culture, such as paying a bride service and being godparents; (3) corn and farming practices.

Have students search for characteristics and values in other tales from before interaction with the Spanish culture. They will discover many of the values previously discussed. In addition, they will find stories that reflect such values as need to sacrifice for the betterment of the group and the worthiness of bravery and honor. Good choices for this activity include Harriet Rohmer and Dorminster Wilson's *Mother Scorpion Country,* Geraldine McGaughrean's "The Monster With Emerald Teeth" in *The Bronze Cauldron: Myths and Legends of the World,* and selections in Pleasant DeSpain's *The Emerald Lizard: Fifteen Latin American Tales to Tell.* Before leaving Phase One have the students summarize their findings.

Phase Two: Stories That Reflect Interaction with Other Cultures

Many of the values, beliefs, and characteristics of ancient literature are found in more recent traditional literature. The most dramatic difference coincides with the arrival of Cortés and the Spanish. A large body of folklore reflects the interactions between the ancient peoples and Christianity. Some tales show the clash of cultural values while others reflect stories that changed because of the settings. Teachers should choose tales according to the appropriateness for the ages of their students. For example, tales that reflect interactions between the people and Christianity include Tomie dePaola's *The Lady of Guadalupe* and John Bierhorst's *Spirit Child: A Story of the Nativity,* a translation. *The Invisible Hunters,* by Harriet Rohmer, Octavio Chow, and Morris Vidaure, may help students understand what happens when cultures clash.

Changes due to place are easy to identify in *Doctor Coyote: A Native American Aesop's Fables,* Bierhorst's retelling from an Aztec manuscript. Have students identify the relationships with the earlier Aesop and the trickster characters of Indian lore.

José Griego y Maestas and Rudolfo A. Anaya's *Cuentos: Tales from the Hispanic Southwest* includes numerous tales that are valuable for Phase Two. For example, students enjoy comparing one of the tales, "The Man Who Knew the Language of the Animals," with Verna Aardema's *What's So Funny, Ketu?,* which is based on an African tale. Have the students identify the similarities and differences and note ways in which the differences reflect cultural differences.

Older students may compare the "Hansel and Gretel" variants from Spain and Mexico found in James Taggart's article, " 'Hansel and Gretel' in Spain and Mexico" (1986). Have them compare these versions with the Grimms's tales. These variants are more complex and include changes in the tales due to male or female storytellers.

Before leaving Phase Two, have the students summarize similarities and differences between Phases One and Two and consider reasons for the stories to be either alike or different.

Phase Three: Historical Nonfiction

Several books can help students understand the Aztecs and Maya. For example, Albert Marrin's *Aztecs and Spaniards: Cortés and the Conquest of Mexico* describes the culture and the conquest. *The Mystery of the Ancient Maya,* by Carolyn Meyer and Charles Gallenkamp, explores the ancient culture. Albert Marrin's *Empires Lost and Won: The Spanish Heritage in the Southwest* traces the history of Spanish involvement.

Phase Four: Historical Fiction

An understanding of history is important for students to analyze historical fiction about the Spanish conquest. Older students may read and analyze the historical accuracy and trace the traditional beliefs in such books as Scott O'Dell's *The Captive, The Feathered Serpent,* and *The Amethyst Ring.* In *The King's Fifth,* O'Dell accompanies Coronado's army as it searches for the golden cities of the Southwest.

Siegelson, Kim L. *In the Time of the Drums.* Illustrated by Brian Pinkney. Hyperion, 1999 (I:7+ R:4).

Sisulu, Elinor Batezat. *The Day Gogo Went to Vote: South Africa, April 1994.* Little, Brown, 1996 (I:4–8 R:6).

Smalls-Hector, Irene. *Jonathan and His Mommy.* Illustrated by Michael Hays. Little, Brown, 1992 (I:3–8).

Stanley, Diane, and Peter Vennema. *Shaka: King of the Zulus.* Illustrated by Diane Stanley. Morrow, 1988 (I:6–10 R:6).

Steptoe, Javaka, ed. and illustrated by. *In Daddy's Arms I Am Tall: African Americans Celebrating Fathers.* Lee & Low, 1997 (I:all).

Steptoe, John. *Creativity.* Illustrated by E. B. Lewis. Clarion, 1997 (I:6+).

_____ . *Daddy Is a Monster . . . Sometimes.* Lippincott, 1980 (I:4–7 R:3).

_____ . *Mufaro's Beautiful Daughters: An African Tale.* Lothrop, Lee & Shepard, 1987 (I:all R:4).

_____ . *Stevie.* Harper & Row, 1969 (I:3–7 R:3).

Stewart, Dianne. *Gift of the Sun: A Tale from South Africa.* Illustrated by Jude Daly. Farrar, Straus & Giroux, 1996 (I:6–9 R:5).

Stolz, Mary. *Cezanne Pinto: A Memoir.* Knopf, 1994 (I:12+ R:6).

_____ . *Storm in the Night.* Illustrated by Pat Cummings. Harper & Row, 1988 (I:4–9 R:4).

Sullivan, Charles, ed. *Children of Promise: African-American Literature and Art for Young People.* Abrams, 1991 (I:10+ R:5).

Taulbert, Clifton L. *Little Cliff and the Porch People.* Illustrated by E. B. Lewis, Dial, 1999 (I:5–8 R:4).

Taylor, Mildred. *The Gold Cadillac.* Illustrated by Michael Hays. Dial, 1987 (I:8–10 R:3).

_____ . *Let the Circle Be Unbroken.* Dial, 1981 (I:10+ R:6).

_____ . *Roll of Thunder, Hear My Cry.* Dial, 1976 (I:10+ R:6).

Temple, Frances. *Taste of Salt: A Story of Modern Haiti.* Orchard, 1992 (I:12+ R:6).

Thomas, Jane Resh. *Celebration!* Illustrated by Raúl Colón. Hyperion, 1997 (I:5–8 R:4).

Towle, Wendy. *The Real McCoy: The Life of an African-American Inventor.* Scholastic, 1993 (I:8+ R:5).

Van Laan, Nancy. *With a Whoop and a Holler: A Bushel of Lore from Way Down South.* Illustrated by Scott Cook. Simon & Schuster, 1998 (I:all).

Venezia, Mike. *Jacob Lawrence.* Children's Press, 1999 (I:all).

Walker, Barbara K., retold by. *The Dancing Palm Tree and Other Nigerian Folktales.* Illustrated by Helen Siegl. Texas Tech University Press, 1990 (I:all).

Walter, Mildred Pitts. *Brother to the Wind.* Illustrated by Diane and Leo Dillon. Lothrop, Lee & Shepard, 1985 (I:all R:3).

_____ . *Justin and the Best Biscuits in the World.* Illustrated by Catherine Stock. Lothrop, Lee & Shepard, 1986 (I:7–10 R:5).

Ward, Leila. *I Am Eyes, Ni Macho.* Illustrated by Nonny Hogrogian. Greenwillow, 1978 (I:3–7 R:1).

Whitmore, Arvella. *Trapped Between the Lash and the Gun.* Dial, 1999 (I:10+ R:5).

Williams, Karen Lynn. *When Africa Was Home.* Illustrated by Floyd Cooper. Orchard, 1991 (I:4–8 R:4).

Williams, Sherley Anne. *Working Cotton.* Illustrated by Carole Byard. Harcourt Brace Jovanovich, 1992 (I:all).

Williams, Vera B. *Cherries and Cherry Pits.* Greenwillow, 1986 (I:3–8 R:3).

Wisniewski, David. *Sundiata: Lion King of Mali.* Clarion, 1992 (I:all).

Woodson, Jacqueline. *We Had a Picnic This Sunday Past.* Illustrated by Diane Greenseid. Hyperion, 1998 (I:5–8 R:3).

Yates, Elizabeth. *Amos Fortune, Free Man.* Illustrated by Nora S. Unwin. Dutton, 1950 (I:10+ R:6).

ASIAN AMERICAN LITERATURE

Allen, Judy. *Tiger.* Illustrated by Tudor Humphries. Candlewick, 1992 (I:5–8 R:4).

Asian Culture Centre for UNESCO. *Folktales from Asia for Children Everywhere.* 3 vols. Weatherhill, 1976, 1977 (I:8–12 R:6).

Choi, Sook Nyul. *Year of Impossible Goodbyes.* Houghton Mifflin, 1991 (I:10 R:5).

Coerr, Eleanor. *Mieko and the Fifth Treasure.* Putnam, 1993 (I:8+ R:5).

Czernecki, Stefan, retold by. *The Cricket's Cage: A Chinese Folktale.* Hyperion, 1997 (I:5–8 R:4).

Fang, Linda. *The ChiLin Purse: A Collection of Ancient Chinese Stories.* Farrar, Straus & Giroux, 1995.

Friedman, Ina R. *How My Parents Learned to Eat.* Illustrated by Allen Say. Houghton Mifflin, 1984 (I:6–8 R:3).

Fritz, Jean. *China Homecoming.* Putnam, 1985.

_____ . *Homesick: My Own Story.* Putnam, 1987.

Garland, Sherry. *The Lotus Seed.* Illustrated by Tatsuro Kivchi. Harcourt Brace Jovanovich, 1993 (I:5–8 R:4).

Ho, Minfong. *Hush! A Thai Lullaby.* Illustrated by Holly Meade. Orchard, 1996 (I:all).

Hoyt-Goldsmith, Diane. *Hoang Anh: A Vietnamese-American Boy.* Photographs by Lawrence Migdale. Holiday, 1992 (I:5–9 R:4).

Huynh, Quang Nhuong. *Water Buffalo Days: Growing Up in Vietnam.* Illustrated by Jean and Mou-sien Tseng. HarperCollins, 1997 (I:8+ R:4).

_____ . *The Land I Lost: Adventures of a Boy in Vietnam.* Illustrated by Vo-Dinh Mai. Harper & Row, 1982 (I:8–12 R:6).

Hyun, Peter, ed. *Korea's Favorite Tales and Lyrics.* Illustrated by Dong-il Park. Tuttle/Seoul International, 1986 (I:5–10 R:6).

Jiang, Ji-Li. *Red Scarf Girl: A Memoir of the Cultural Revolution.* Turtleback, 1998.

Kim, Helen. *The Long Season of Rain.* Holt, 1996 (I:12+ R:6).

Kodama, Tatsuharu. *Shin's Tricycle.* Illustrated by Noriyuki Ando. Walker, 1995 (I:all).

Lee, Millie. *Nim and the War Effort.* Farrar, Straus & Giroux, 1997.

Levine, Arthur. *The Boy Who Drew Cats: A Japanese Folktale.* Illustrated by Frédéric Clément. Dial, 1993 (I:8+ R:5).

Lobel, Arnold. *Ming Lo Moves the Mountain.* Turtleback, 1993.

Look, Lenore. *Henry's First-Moon Birthday.* Illustrated by Yumi Heo. Simon & Schuster, 2001 (I:4–8 R:4).

Lord, Bette Bao. *In the Year of the Boar and Jackie Robinson.* Illustrated by Marc Simont. Harper & Row, 1984 (I:8–12 R:4).

_____ . *Legacies: A Chinese Mosaic.* Diane, 1997.

McCully, Emily Arnold. *Beautiful Warrior: The Legend of the Nun's Kung Fu.* Scholastic, 1998 (I:6–10 R:5).

McMahon, Patricia. *Chi-Hoon: A Korean Girl.* Photographs by Michael O'Brien. Caroline House, 1993 (I:8+ R:4).

Melmed, Laura Krauss. *The First Song Ever Sung.* Illustrated by Ed Young. Lothrop Lee & Shepard, 1993 (I:4–8).

Mosel, Arlene. *The Funny Little Woman.* Illustrated by Blair Lent. Dutton, 1972 (I:6–8 R:6).

Namioka, Lensey. *Yang the Third and Her Impossible Family.* Turtleback, 1996.

_____ . *Yang the Youngest and His Terrible Ear.* Illustrated by Kees de Kiefe. Little, Brown, 1992 (I:8+ R:4).

Nomura, Takaaki. *Grandpa's Town.* Translated by Amanda Mayer Stinchecum. Kane-Miller, 1991 (I:3–7 R:4).

Partridge, Elizabeth. *Oranges on Golden Mountain.* Illustrated by Aki Sogabe. Dutton, 2001 (I:5–9 R:5).

Salisbury, Graham. *Under the Blood Red Sun.* Delacorte, 1995 (I:8+ R:6).

Say, Allen. *Grandfather's Journey.* Houghton Mifflin, 1993 (I:all).

_____ . *Tea with Milk.* Houghton Mifflin, 1999 (I:7+ R:4).

_____ . *Tree of Cranes.* Houghton Mifflin, 1991 (I:5–8 R:4).

Spivak, Dawnine. *Grass Sandals: The Travels of Basho.* Illustrated by Demi. Simon & Schuster, 1997 (I:8+).

Surat, Michele Maria. *Angel Child, Dragon Child.* Illustrated by Vo-Dinh Mai. Carnival/Raintree, 1983 (I:6–8 R:4).

Tompert, Ann. *Grandfather Tang's Story.* Random, 1990.

Uchida, Yoshiko. *Invisible Thread.* Messner, 1992 (I:10+ R:6).

Waters, Kate, and Madeline Slovenz-Low. *Lion Dancer: Ernie Wan's Chinese New Year.* Photographs by Martha Cooper. Scholastic, 1990 (I:5–8 R:3).

Whelan, Gloria. *Homeless Bird.* HarperCollins, 2000 (I:10+ R:5).

Yep, Laurence. *The Case of the Goblin Pearls.* HarperCollins, 1997 (I:8+ R:4).

_____ . *Child of the Owl.* Harper & Row, 1977 (I:10+ R:7).

_____ . *The City of Dragons.* Scholastic, 1995.

_____ . *Dragonwings.* Harper & Row, 1975 (I:10+ R:6).

_____ . *Hiroshima.* Scholastic, 1995 (I:9+ R:4).

_____ . *Later, Gater.* Hyperion, 1995 (I:9+ R:4).

_____ . *The Man Who Tricked a Ghost.* Illustrated by Isadore Seltzer. Troll, 1993 (I:5–8 R:4).

_____ . *The Rainbow People.* Illustrated by David Wiesner. Harper & Row, 1989 (I:8+ R:5).

_____ . *The Serpent's Children.* Harper & Row, 1984 (I:10+ R:6).

_____ . *Star Fisher.* Morrow, 1991 (I:10+ R:6).

_____ . *Thief of Hearts.* HarperCollins, 1995 (I:10+ R:6).

Yin. *Coolies.* Illustrated by Chris Soentpiet. Philomel, 2001 (I:5–9 R:5).

LATINO LITERATURE

Anaya, Rudolfo. *Farolitos for Akuelo.* Illustrated by Edward Gonzales. Hyperion, 1998 (I:5–9 R:4).

_____ . *Maya's Children: The Story of La Llorona.* Illustrated by Maria Baca. Hyperion, 1997 (I:5–9 R:4).

Anzaldua, Gloria. *Prietita and the Ghost Woman.* Children's, 1996 (I:5–8 R:5).

Atkin, S. Beth, ed. *Voices from the Fields: Children of Migrant Farmworkers Tell Their Stories.* Little, Brown, 1993 (I:10).

Behrens, June. *Fiesta!* Photographs by Scott Taylor. Children's Press, 1978 (I:5–8 R:4).

Belting, Natalia M. *Moon Was Tired of Walking on Air.* Illustrated by Will Hillenbrand. Houghton Mifflin, 1992 (I:all).

Bernardo, Anilu. *Jumping Off to Freedom.* Pinata, 1996 (I:12+ R:6).

Bertrand, Diane Gonzales. *Sip, Slurp, Soup, Soup/Caldo, Caldo, Caldo.* Illustrated by Alex Pardo DeLanga. Pinata, 1997 (I:4–7).

Bierhorst, John. *Doctor Coyote: A Native American Aesop's Fables.* Illustrated by Wendy Watson. Macmillan, 1987 (I:all).

_____ , ed. *Lightning Inside You and Other Native American Riddles.* Illustrated by Louise Brierley. Morrow, 1992 (I:8+).

_____ , ed. *The Monkey's Haircut and Other Stories Told by the Maya.* Illustrated by Robert Andrew Parker. Morrow, 1986 (I:8+ R:6).

_____ , *The Mythology of South America.* Morrow, 1988 (I:12+ R:7).

_____ , translated by. *Spirit Child: A Story of the Nativity.* Illustrated by Barbara Cooney. Morrow, 1984 (I:8–12 R:6).

Brimner, Larry Dane. *A Migrant Family.* Lerner, 1992 (I:all).

Brown, Tricia. *Hello, Amigos!* Photographs by Fran Ortiz. Holt, Rinehart & Winston, 1986 (I:3–8 R:3).

Brusca, Maria Cristina. *On the Pampas.* Henry Holt, 1991 (I:6–9 R:5).

Cherry, Lynne, and Mark J. Plotkin. *The Shaman's Apprentice: A Tale of the Amazon Rain Forest.* Harcourt Brace, 1998 (I:6–8 R:4).

Cisneros, Sandra. *The House on Mango Street.* Arte Publico, 1983 (I:12+ R:7).

Clark, Ann Nolan. *Secret of the Andes.* Illustrated by Jean Charlot. Viking, 1952, 1980 (I:8+ R:5).

dePaola, Tomie. *The Lady of Guadalupe.* Holiday House, 1980 (I:8+ R:6).

DeSpain, Pleasant. *The Dancing Turtle: A Folktale from Brazil.* Illustrated by David Boston. August House, 1998 (I:5–8 R:4).

_____ . *The Emerald Lizard: Fifteen Latin American Tales to Tell.* Illustrated by Don Bell. August House, 1999 (I:10+).

Dorros, Arthur. *Radio Man: A Story in English and Spanish.* HarperCollins, 1993 (I:6–10).

Dorson, Mercedes, and Jeanne Wilmot. *Tales from the Rain Forest: Myths and Legends from the Amazonian Indians of Brazil.* Ecco, 1997 (I:8+ R:7).

Ehlert, Lois. *Cuckoo: A Mexican Folktale.* Translated into Spanish by Gloria de Aragon Andujar. Harcourt Brace, 1997 (I:4–8).

_____ . *Moon Rope.* Harcourt Brace Jovanovich, 1992 (I:all).

Ets, Marie Hall, and Aurora Labastida. *Nine Days to Christmas: A Story of Mexico.* Illustrated by Marie Hall Ets. Viking, 1959 (I:5–8 R:3).

Fine, Edith Hope. *Under the Lemon Moon.* Illustrated by René King Moreno. Lee & Low, 1999 (I:5–8).

Fritz, Jean, Katherine Paterson, Patricia McKissack, Fredrick McKissack, Margaret Mahy, and Jamake Highwater. *The World in 1492.* Illustrated by Stefano Vitale. Holt, 1992 (I:8+).

Galvin, Irene Flum. *The Ancient Maya.* Benchmark, 1996 (I:10+ R:5).

Garcia, Richard. *My Aunt Otilia's Spirits.* Illustrated by Robin Cherin and Roger Reyes. Children's Press, 1987 (I:5–8 R:2).

Gonzalez, Ralfka, and Ana Ruiz. *My First Book of Proverbs.* Children's, 1995 (I:all).

Greger, C. Shana, retold by, *The Fifth and Final Sun: An Ancient Aztec Myth of the Sun's Origin.* Houghton Mifflin, 1994 (I:8+ R:5).

Griego, Margot C. *Tortillitas Para Mama and Other Spanish Nursery Rhymes.* Illustrated by Barbara Cooney. Holt, Rinehart & Winston, 1981 (I:3–7).

Griego y Maestas, José, and Rudolfo A. Anaya. *Cuentos: Tales from the Hispanic Southwest.* Illustrated by Jaime Valdez. Museum of New Mexico, 1980 (I:9+ R:5).

Herrera, Juan Felipe. *Calling the Doves.* Illustrated by Elly Simmons. Children's, 1995 (I:all).

Kroll, Virginia. *Butterfly Boy.* Illustrated by Gerardo Suzan. Boyds Mills, 1997 (I:5–8 R:4).

Krumgold, Joseph. *. . . And Now Miguel.* Illustrated by Jean Charlot. Crowell, 1953 (I:10+ R:3).

Kurtz, Jane. *Miro in the Kingdom of the Sun.* Illustrated by David Frampton. Houghton Mifflin, 1996 (I:4–7 R:4).

Lattimore, Deborah. *The Flame of Peace: A Tale of the Aztecs.* Harper & Row, 1987 (I:all R:6).

Mann, Elizabeth. *Machu Picchu.* Mikaya/Firefly, 2000 (I:9+ R:5).

Marrin, Albert. *Aztecs and Spaniards: Cortés and the Conquest of Mexico.* Atheneum, 1986 (I:12+ R:7).

_____ . *Empires Lost and Won: The Spanish Heritage in the Southwest.* Simon & Schuster, 1997 (I:12+ R:7).

Martinello, Marian L., and Samuel P. Nesmith. *With Domingo Leal in San Antonio 1734.* The University of Texas, Institute of Texas Cultures at San Antonio, 1979 (I:8+ R:4).

Martinez, Victor. *Parrot in the Oven: Mi Vida.* HarperCollins, 1996 (I:12+ R:6).

McCaughrean, Gerald. *The Bronze Cauldron: Myths and Legends of the World.* Illustrated by Bee Willey. Simon & Schuster, 1997 (I:9+ R:5).

McDermott, Gerald. *Musicians of the Sun.* Simon & Schuster, 1997 (I:all).

Meyer, Carolyn, and Charles Gallenkamp. *The Mystery of the Ancient Maya.* Atheneum, 1985 (I:10 R:8).

Mikaelsen, Ben. *Sparrow Hawk Red.* Hyperion/Little, Brown, 1993 (I:10+ R:6).

Mohr, Nicholasa. *El Bronx Remembered: A Novella and Stories.* Harper & Row, 1975 (I:10+ R:6).

_____ . *Felita.* Illustrated by Ray Cruz. Dial, 1979 (I:9–12 R:2).

_____ . *Going Home.* Dial, 1986 (I:10+ R:6).

O'Dell, Scott. *The Amethyst Ring.* Houghton Mifflin, 1983 (I:10+ R:6).

_____ . *The Captive.* Houghton Mifflin, 1979 (I:10+ R:6).

_____ . *Carlota.* Houghton Mifflin, 1981 (I:10+ R:6).

_____ . *The Feathered Serpent.* Houghton Mifflin, 1981 (I:10+ R:6).

_____ . *The King's Fifth.* Houghton Mifflin, 1966 (I:10+ R:6).

Orozco, José-Luis. *Diez Deditos: Ten Little Fingers & Other Play Rhymes and Action Songs from Latin America.* Illustrated by Elisa Kleven. Dutton, 1997 (I:4+).

Politi, Leo. *Song of the Swallows.* Scribner, 1949 (I:5–8 R:4).

Rohmer, Harriet, Octavio Chow, and Morris Viduare. *The Invisible Hunters.* Illustrated by Joe Sam. Children's Press, 1987 (I:all R:5).

_____ , and Dornminster Wilson. *Mother Scorpion Country.* Illustrated by Virginia Steams. Children's Press, 1987 (I:all R:4).

Soto, Gary. *Baseball in April and Other Stories.* Harcourt Brace Jovanovich, 1990 (I:11+ R:6).

_____ . *Neighborhood Odes.* Harcourt Brace Jovanovich, 1992 (I:all).

_____ . *Pacific Crossing.* Harcourt Brace Jovanovich, 1992 (I:10+ R:6).

_____ . *The Skirt.* Illustrated by Eric Velasquez. Delacorte, 1992 (I:6–8 R:4).

_____ . *Snapshots from the Wedding.* Illustrated by Stephanie Garcia. Putnam, 1997 (I:5–8 R:4).

_____ . *Taking Sides.* Harcourt Brace Jovanovich, 1991 (I:10+ R:6).

_____ . *Too Many Tamales.* Illustrated by Ed Martinez. Putnam, 1993 (I:6–8 R:4).

Stewig, John Warren, retold by. *Princess Florecita and the Iron Shoes: A Spanish Fairy Tale.* Knopf, 1995 (I:9+ R:5).

Tashlik, Phyllis, ed. *Hispanic, Female and Young: An Anthology.* Pinata, 1994 (I:12+ R:6).

Temple, Frances. *Grab Hands and Run.* Orchard, 1993 (I:10+ R:6).

VanLaan, Nancy. *The Magic Bean Tree: A Legend from Argentina.* Illustrated by Beatriz Vidal. Houghton Mifflin, 1998 (I:all).

_____ . *So Say the Little Monkeys.* Illustrated by Yumi Heo. Atheneum, 1998 (I:all).

Villasenor, Victor. *Walking Stars: Stories of Magic and Power.* Arte Publico Press, 1994 (I:10+ R:6).

Volkmer, Jane Anne, retold by. *Song of Chirimia—A Guatemalan Folktale.* Carolrhoda, 1990 (I:6–10 R:5).

Winter, Jeanette. *Josefina.* Harcourt Brace, 1996 (I:4–8 R:4).

NATIVE AMERICAN LITERATURE

Aliki. *Corn Is Maize: The Gift of the Indians.* Crowell, 1976 (I:6–8 R:2).

Ancona, George. *Powwow.* Harcourt Brace Jovanovich, 1993 (I:all).

Arnold, Caroline. *The Ancient Cliff Dwellers of Mesa Verde.* Photographs by Richard Hewett. Clarion, 1992 (I:8+ R:6).

Baker, Olaf. *Where the Buffaloes Begin.* Illustrated by Stephen Gammell. Warne, 1981 (I:all R:6).

Batherman, Muriel. *Before Columbus.* Houghton Mifflin, 1981 (I:6–9 R:5).

Baylor, Byrd. *The Desert Is Theirs.* Illustrated by Peter Parnall. Scribner, 1975 (I:all).

_____ . *Hawk, I'm Your Brother.* Illustrated by Peter Parnall. Scribner, 1976 (I:all).

_____ . *Moon Song.* Illustrated by Ronald Himler. Scribner, 1982 (I:all).

_____ . *The Other Way to Listen.* Illustrated by Peter Parnall. Scribner, 1978 (I:all).

_____ . *When Clay Sings.* Illustrated by Tom Bahti. Scribner, 1972 (I:all).

Begay, Shonto. *Ma'ii and Cousin Horned Toad: A Traditional Navajo Story.* Scholastic, 1992 (I:5–8 R:5).

_____ . *Navajo: Visions and Voices Across the Mesa.* Scholastic, 1995 (I:10+).

Bierhorst, John. *A Cry from the Earth: Music of the North American Indians.* Four Winds, 1979 (I:all).

_____ , ed. *The Dancing Fox: Arctic Folktales.* Illustrated by Mary K. Okheena. Morrow, 1997 (I:8+).

_____ , ed. *The Girl Who Married a Ghost.* Four Winds, 1978 (I:10+ R:6).

_____ , retold by. *The People with Five Fingers: A Native Californian Creation Tale.* Illustrated by Robert Andrew Parker. Cavendish, 2000 (I:all).

_____ . *The Ring in the Prairie, A Shawnee Legend.* Illustrated by Leo and Diane Dillon. Dial, 1970 (I:all R:6).

_____ , ed. *The Sacred Path: Spells, Prayers, and Power Songs of the American Indians*. Morrow, 1983 (I:8+).

Brown, Tricia. *Children of the Midnight Sun: Young Native Voices of Alaska*. Photographs by Roy Corral. Alaska Northwest, 1998 (I:8+ R:6).

Bruchac, Joseph. *The Boy Who Lived with the Bears and Other Iroquois Stories*. Illustrated by Murv Jacob. HarperCollins, 1995 (I:8+ R:5).

_____ . *Eagle Song*. Illustrated by Dan Andreasen. Dial, 1997 (I:7–10 R:4).

Caduto, Michael J., and Joseph Bruchac. *Keepers of the Animals: Native American Stories and Wildlife Activities for Children*. Illustrated by John Kahionhes Fadden. Fulcrum, 1991 (I:all).

_____ . *Keepers of the Earth: Native American Stories and Environmental Activities for Children*. Illustrated by John Kahionhes Fadden and Carol Wood. Fulcrum, 1989 (I:all).

Cohlene, Terri. *Turquoise Boy: A Navajo Legend*. Illustrated by Charles Reasoner. Watermill, 1990 (I:5–9 R:4).

Cohn, Amy L., compiled by. *From Sea to Shining Sea: A Treasury of American Folklore and Folk Songs*. Scholastic, 1993 (I:all).

Cooper, Michael L. *Indian School: Teaching the White Man's Way*. Clarion, 1999 (I:9+ R:5).

Cushing, Frank Hamilton. *Zuni Folk Tales*. University of Arizona Press, 1901, 1986.

Dabcovich, Lydia, retold by. *The Polar Bear Son: An Inuit Tale*. Clarion, 1997 (I:5–8 R:4).

DeArmond, Dale, retold by. *The Boy Who Found the Light*. Sierra Club/Little, Brown, 1990 (I:all).

DeCoteau Orie, Sandra. *Did You Hear Wind Sing Your Name?: An Oneida Song of Spring*. Illustrated by Christopher Canyon. Walker, 1995 (I:4–8).

dePaola, Tomie. *The Legend of the Bluebonnet*. Putnam, 1983 (I:all R:6).

Dorris, Michael. *Morning Girl*. Hyperion, 1992 (I:8+ R:5).

_____ . *Sees Behind Trees*. Hyperion, 1996 (I:8+ R:5).

Duncan, Lois. *The Magic of Spider Woman*. Illustrated by Shonto Begay. Scholastic, 1996 (I:all R:7).

Ekoomiak, Normee. *Arctic Memories*. Henry Holt, 1990 (I:all).

Erdrich, Louise. *The Birchbark House*. Hyperion, 1999 (I:8+ R:6).

Esbensen, Barbara Juster, ed. *The Star Maiden*. Illustrated by Helen K. Davie. Little, Brown, 1988 (I:all).

Field, Edward. *Magic Words*. Illustrated by Stefano Vitale. Harcourt Brace, 1998 (I:all).

Finley, Carol. *Art of the Far North: Inuit Sculpture, Drawing, and Printmaking*. Lerner, 1998 (I:8+ R:5).

Fradin, Dennis Brindell. *Hiawatha: Messenger of Peace*. Macmillan, 1992 (I:10+ R:5).

Freedman, Russell. *Buffalo Hunt*. Holiday House, 1988 (I:8+ R:6).

_____ . *Indian Chiefs*. Holiday House, 1987 (I:10+ R:6).

_____ . *An Indian Winter*. Illustrated by Karl Bodmer. Holiday, 1992 (I:8+ R:6).

_____ . *The Life and Death of Crazy Horse*. Photographs by Amos Bad Heart Bull. Holiday, 1996 (I:10+ R:5).

Fritz, Jean. *The Double Life of Pocahontas*. Illustrated by Ed Young. Putnam, 1983 (I:8–10 R:7).

_____ , et al. *The World in 1492*. Illustrated by Stefano Vitale. Holt, 1992 (I:8+).

George, Jean Craighead. *The Talking Earth*. Harper & Row, 1983 (I:10+ R:6).

_____ . *Water Sky*. Harper & Row, 1987 (I:10+ R:6).

Gleason, Katherine. *Native American Literature*. Chelsea, 1996 (I:10+ R:5).

Goble, Paul. *Beyond the Ridge*. Bradbury, 1989 (I:all R:5).

_____ . *Buffalo Woman*. Bradbury, 1984 (I:all R:6).

_____ . *Death of the Iron Horse*. Bradbury, 1987 (I:8+ R:5).

_____ . *The Dream Wolf*. Bradbury, 1990 (I:all R:6).

_____ . *The Gift of the Sacred Dog*. Bradbury, 1980 (I:all R:6).

_____ . *The Girl Who Loved Wild Horses*. Bradbury, 1978 (I:6–10 R:5).

_____ . *Iktomi and the Berries*. Watts, 1989 (I:4–10 R:4).

_____ . *Iktomi and the Boulder: A Plains Indian Story*. Orchard, 1988 (I:4–10 R:4).

Goldin, Barbara Diamond, retold by. *Coyote and the Fire Stick: A Pacific Northwest Indian Tale*. Illustrated by Will Hillenbrand. Harcourt Brace, 1996 (I:8+).

_____ , retold by. *The Girl Who Lived with the Bears*. Illustrated by Andrew Plewes. Harcourt Brace, 1997 (I:8+).

Green, Rayna. *Women in American Indian Society*. Chelsea, 1992 (I:12+ R:7).

Hamilton, Virginia. *In the Beginning: Creation Stories from Around the World*. Illustrated by Barry Moser. Harcourt Brace Jovanovich, 1988 (I:all R:5).

Highwater, Jamake. *Anpao: An American Indian Odyssey*. Illustrated by Fritz Scholder. Lippincott, 1977 (I:12+ R:5).

Hobbs, Will. *Bearstone*. Atheneum, 1989 (I:10+ R:6).

Hoyt-Goldsmith, Diane. *Arctic Hunter*. Photographs by Lawrence Migdale. Holiday, 1992 (I:8+ R:5).

_____ . *Buffalo Days*. Photographs by Lawrence Migdale. Holiday, 1997 (I:8+ R:5).

Hucko, Bruce. *A Rainbow at Night: The World in Words and Pictures by Navajo Children*. Chronicle, 1997 (I:all).

Hudson, Jan. *Sweetgrass*. Philomel, 1989; Tree Frog, 1984 (I:10+ R:4).

Hunter, Sally M. *Four Seasons of Corn: A Winnebago Tradition*. Photographs by Joe Allen. Lerner, 1997 (I:8+ R:4).

Jaffe, Nina. *The Golden Flower*. Illustrated by Enrique O. Sanchez. Simon & Schuster, 1966 (I:all R:5).

Jassem, Kate. *Sacajawea, Wilderness Guide*. Illustrated by Jan Palmer. Troll Associates, 1979 (I:6–9 R:2).

Jeffers, Susan. *Brother Eagle, Sister Sky: A Message from Chief Seattle*. Dial, 1991 (I:all).

Jones, Jennifer Berry. *Heetunka's Harvest: A Tale of the Plains Indians*. Illustrated by Shannon Keegan. Rinehart, 1994 (I:5–9 R:6).

Joosse, Barbara M. *Mama, Do You Love Me?* Illustrated by Barbara Lavalle. Chronicle, 1991 (I:3–7).

Keegan, Marcia. *Pueblo Boy: Growing Up in Two Worlds*. Cobblehill, 1991 (I:6–10 R:5).

Lawlor, Laurie. *Shadow Catcher: The Life and Work of Edward S. Curtis*. Walker, 1994 (I:10+ R:7).

Left Hand Bull, Jacqueline, and Suzanne Haldane. *Lakota Hoop Dance*. Dutton, 1999 (I:all).

Leon, George DeLucenay. *Explorers of the Americas Before Columbus*. Diane, 1989.

Lewis, Paul Owen. *Storm Boy*. Beyond Words, 1995 (I:7+ R:5).

Lipsyte, Robert. *The Brave.* HarperCollins, 1991 (I:12+ R:6).

Littlechild, George. *This Land Is My Land.* Children's, 1993 (I:7+ R:4).

Luenn, Nancy. *Nessa's Fish.* Atheneum, 1990 (I:4–8 R:4).

Lyon, George Ella. *Dreamplace.* Orchard, 1993 (I:5–9 R:4).

McDermott, Gerald. *Raven: A Trickster Tale from the Pacific Northwest.* Harcourt Brace & Jovanovich, 1993 (I:all).

Marrin, Albert. *Plains Warrior: Chief Quanah Parker and the Comanches.* Simon & Schuster, 1996 (I:10+ R:6).

_____ . *Sitting Bull and His World.* Dutton, 2000 (I:10+ R:7).

Martin, Bill, and John Archambault. *Knots on a Counting Rope.* Holt, Rinehart & Winston, 1987 (I:all).

Martin, Rafe. *The Boy Who Lived with the Seals.* Putnam, 1993 (I:10+ R:5).

Metayer, Maurice, ed. *Tales from the Igloo.* Illustrated by Agnes Nanogak. Hurtig, 1972 (I:all R:5).

Miles, Miska. *Annie and the Old One.* Illustrated by Peter Parnall. Little, Brown, 1971 (I:6–8 R:3).

Monroe, Jean Guard, and Ray A. Williamson. *They Dance in the Sky: Native American Star Myths.* Illustrated by Edgar Stewart. Houghton Mifflin, 1987 (I:10+ R:7).

Morgan, William. *Navajo Coyote Tales.* Ancient City Press, 1988 (I:6+).

Morrison, Dorothy Nafus. *Chief Sarah: Sarah Winnemucca's Fight for Indian Rights.* Atheneum, 1980 (I:10+ R:6).

Mowat, Farley. *Lost in the Barrens.* Illustrated by Charles Geer. McClelland & Stewart, 1966, 1984 (I:9+ R:6).

Nashone. *Grandmother Stories of the Northwest.* Sierra Oaks, 1988 (I:all).

Nicolai, Margaret. *Kitaq Goes Ice Fishing.* Illustrated by David Rubin. Alaska Northwest, 1998 (I:4–9 R:4).

Norman, Howard, retold by. *The Girl Who Dreamed Only Geese and Other Tales of the Far North.* Illustrated by Leo and Diane Dillon. Harcourt Brace, 1997 (I:9+ R:6).

Normandin, Christine, ed. *Echoes of the Elders: The Stories and Paintings of Chief Lelooska.* DK, 1997 (I:all).

O'Dell, Scott. *Black Star, Bright Dawn.* Houghton Mifflin, 1988 (I:8+ R:6).

_____ . *Sing Down the Moon.* Houghton Mifflin, 1970 (I:10+ R:6).

_____ , and Elizabeth Hall. *Thunder Rolling in the Mountains.* Houghton Mifflin, 1992 (I:10+ R:6).

Oughton, Jerrie. *How the Stars Fell into the Sky: A Navajo Legend.* Illustrated by Lisa Desimini. Houghton Mifflin, 1992 (I:4–8 R:5).

Paulsen, Gary. *Dogsong.* Bradbury, 1988 (I:10+ R:6).

Pollock, Penny, retold by. *The Turkey Girl: A Zuni Cinderella Story.* Illustrated by Ed Young. Little, Brown, 1996 (I:5–9 R:6).

Prusski, Jeffrey. *Bring Back the Deer.* Illustrated by Neil Waldman. Harcourt Brace Jovanovich, 1988 (I:6+ R:5).

St. George, Judith. *To See with the Heart: The Life of Sitting Bull.* Putnam, 1996 (I:10+ R:6).

Sewall, Marcia. *People of the Breaking Day.* Atheneum, 1990 (I:8+ R:5).

Sís, Peter. *A Small Tall Tale from the Far Far North.* Knopf, 1993 (I:6+ R:5).

Smithsonian Institution. *When the Rain Sings: Poems by Young Native Americans.* Simon & Schuster, 1999 (I:all).

Sneve, Virginia Driving Hawk, selected by. *Dancing Teepees: Poems of American Indian Youth.* Illustrated by Stephen Gammell. Holiday House, 1989 (I:all).

_____ . *High Elk's Treasure.* Illustrated by Oren Lyons. Holiday House, 1972 (I:8–12 R:6).

Speare, Elizabeth George. *The Sign of the Beaver.* Houghton Mifflin, 1983 (I:8–12 R:5).

Spencer, Paula Underwood. *Who Speaks for Wolf.* Illustrated by Frank Howell. Tribe of Two Press, 1983 (I:all R:5).

Steptoe, John. *The Story of Jumping Mouse.* Lothrop, Lee & Shepard, 1984 (I:all R:4).

Swanson, Diane. *Buffalo Sunrise: The Story of a North American Giant.* Little, Brown, 1996 (I:10+ R:9).

Tompert, Ann. *How Rabbit Lost His Tail.* Illustrated by Jacqueline Chwast. Houghton Mifflin, 1997 (I:7+ R:4).

Valgardson, W. D. *Sarah and the People of Sand River.* Illustrated by Ian Wallace. Douglas & McIntyre, 1996 (I:8+ R:4).

Van Laan, Nancy, retold by. *Shingebiss: An Ojibwe Legend.* Illustrated by Betsy Bowen. Houghton Mifflin, 1997 (I:7+ R:4).

Vogel, Carole G. *Legends of Landforms: Native American Lore and the Geology of the Land.* Millbrook, 1999 (I:10+ R:6).

Wallas, James. *Kwakiutl Legends.* Recorded by Pamela Whitaker. Hancock House, 1981 (I:all R:4).

Whitaker, Muriel, ed. *Stories from the Canadian North.* Illustrated by Vlasta van Kampen. Hurtig, 1980 (I:12+ R:7).

White Deer of Autumn. *Ceremony—In the Circle of Life.* Illustrated by Daniel San Souci. Raintree, 1983 (I:all R:5).

Wood, Nancy, ed. *The Serpent's Tongue: Prose, Poetry, and Art of the New Mexico Pueblos.* Dutton, 1997 (I:8+).

Yolen, Jane. *Encounter.* Illustrated by David Shannon. Harcourt Brace Jovanovich, 1992 (I:6–10 R:5).

12 Nonfiction: Biographies and Informational Books

Illustration by the National Park Service from Volcanoes by Semour Simon, 1988. William Morrow and Company, Inc.

Curiosity and the desire to make discoveries about the world strongly motivate children to read. Books of nonfiction encourage children to look at the world in new ways, to discover laws of nature and society, and to identify with people different from themselves. Biographer Russell Freedman (1992) develops the importance of and the purposes for nonfiction when he states:

Certainly the basic purpose of nonfiction is to inform, to instruct, hopefully to enlighten. But that's not enough. An effective nonfiction book must animate its subject, infuse it with life. It must create a vivid and believable world that the reader will enter willingly and leave only with reluctance. A good nonfiction book should be a pleasure to read. It should be just as compelling as a good story. After all, there's a story to everything. The task of the nonfiction writer is to find the story—the narrative line—that exists in nearly every subject. (p. 3)

Biographies

Many children who read well-written biographies feel as if the biographical subjects become personal friends. Often, these children carry with them into adulthood a love of nonfiction that portrays the lives of interesting people with whom they can identify and from whom they can learn. Biography offers children the high adventure and engrossing drama that fiction also supplies, but it also offers the special satisfaction of knowing that the people and events described are "really real."

Writers of biographies have a vast pool of real people from which to choose. There are brave men and women who conquer seas, encounter new continents, and explore space. There are equally brave and intelligent women and men who fight discrimination, change lives through their ministering or inventions, and overcome disabilities in their efforts to achieve. The ways in which writers of children's literature choose to portray these figures, however, change with historical time periods.

Changing Ideas About Biographies for Children

A brief review of biographies for children shows that the authors of biographies have been influenced by social attitudes toward children and attitudes about appropriate content. Children's biographies written in the seventeenth through the nineteenth centuries in Europe and North America were affected by the didactic themes of the Puritan era, the Victorian emphasis on duty to God and parents, the values associated with the American frontier, and the belief that children should be educated in a highly structured environment. In addition, early biographers believed that children's biographies should be tools for religious, political, or social education. Emulation of biographical heroes was considered desirable (Norton,

1984). Consequently, many pre-twentieth-century biographies reflected the belief that literature should save children's souls. Jon Stott (1979) concludes that this time produced numerous "biographies of good little children who died early and went to Heaven and of bad little children who died early and went to Hell" (p. 177). For example, in 1671, leading Puritan writer James Janeway published a series of stories about children who died at an early age after leading saintly lives.

In the mid-1800s, the religious zeal of many early Americans was replaced by concern for the nation and the acquisition of the "American dream." Salvation was no longer the primary goal. The supreme achievements were acquisition of power, fame, and wealth. Consequently, biography changed from a religious tool to a political tool.

Alan Wolfe (2001) describes changes between the nineteenth and twentieth centuries when he states:

In the 19th century, principles of economic liberty were instrumental in creating a society in which the right to own property, to hire workers, and to manufacture and dispose of goods was accepted as the most productive way for a society to create and distribute its wealth. This was followed, in the 20th century, by the spread of political freedom. By the century's end, the idea that people had a right to vote and to run for office—and that such a right could not be denied them on the basis of ownership of property, race or gender—had become so widely accepted that no society could be considered good unless its political system was organized along democratic lines. (p. 48)

These changing attitudes are also apparent in biographies written during different time periods.

The early twentieth century also brought new insights into child development. The developing science of psychology emphasized the vulnerability of youth and a need for protective legislation. Religious training placed less emphasis on sinfulness and more emphasis on moral development and responsibility toward others. In keeping with these ideas, biographers also protected children from the indiscretions of biographical subjects. Because idealized heroes were still believed to be desirable and necessary, biographers avoided areas concerning sensitive political beliefs and private lives. Taboos imposed by society included infamous people, unsavory or undistinguishing actions, and controversial subjects.

Furthermore, in the early 1900s, as in earlier periods of American history, the contributions of female and non-white Americans were either not highly regarded or were considered too controversial. Traditional social patterns kept most women and members of minority groups out of the positions of power and the fame that produced what American society considered the most appropriate subjects of biography. Consequently, few biographies dealt with women, African Americans, Native Americans, and members of other ethnic and racial minorities.

Biographies of most political leaders published through the 1960s continued to present role models for political and social instruction. Omissions and distortions allowed biographers to stress important contributions and to highlight dates of accomplishment. Biographers still did not explore motives. Literary critic Margery Fisher (1976) maintains that biographies for children were controlled by an establishment that exercised a powerful invisible influence. William Epstein (1987) argues, "State-supported American education is more or less a product of middle-class values and aspirations, and biography has almost always been an ally of the dominant structures of authority" (p. 179).

In an effort to increase the ability of children to empathize with political heroes, biographers writing for young readers often focused on the boyhood years of their characters. Still, these biographers tended to glorify the individuals. For example, the titles of several biographies published by Bobbs-Merrill before 1980 indicated the accomplishments that the subjects would achieve: *Thomas Paine: Common Sense Boy* and *John D. Rockefeller: Boy Financier.*

During the late 1960s and the 1970s, traditional social, family, and personal values were changing. The new openness was reflected in fiction for children. In addition, the previous instructional uses of, and role models in, children's biography were challenged. Some literary critics, educators, and authors of children's biographies maintained that idealizing subjects distorted not only history but also development. According to this argument, if prominent men and women were shown in favorable light only, children would assume that because they themselves make errors, they could never be great. In an effort to overcome past shortcomings in biographies for children, Marilyn Jurich (1972) advocated a greater variety in the choice of subjects—including great people who were not famous, ordinary people, and antiheroes—as well as a fuller and more honest treatment of all subjects. Biographer Russell Freedman (1988) summarizes the changes when he concludes:

The hero worship of the past has given way to a more realistic approach, which recognizes the warts and weaknesses that humanize the great. And fictionalization has become a naughty word. Many current biographies for children adhere as closely to documented evidence as any scholarly work. And the best of them manage to do so without becoming tedious or abstract or any less exciting than the most imaginative fictionalization. (p. 447)

As with realistic fiction, educators, authors, publishers, and parents today have different opinions about what the content of children's biographies should be. Jean Fritz (1976), a well-known author of historical biographies for young children, says:

Biographies have for the most part lagged behind other types of children's literature, bogged down, for one thing, by didacticism. Famous men and women must be shown in their best colors so children can emulate them. The idea of emulation has been a

Through the Eyes of an AUTHOR

Jean Fritz

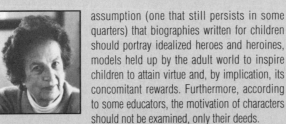

Visit the CD-ROM that accompanies this text to generate a complete list of Jean Fritz titles.

Selected Titles by Jean Fritz:

And Then What Happened, Paul Revere?

Bully for You, Teddy Roosevelt!

The Double Life of Pocahontas

The Great Little Madison

Make Way for Sam Houston

On Writing Biography

The reason for writing biography for children is the same as for writing biography for adults: to explore human behavior; to come to grips with specific characters interrelating with their specific times. This is not as obvious as it sounds. It was once a commonly held assumption (one that still persists in some quarters) that biographies written for children should portray idealized heroes and heroines, models held up by the adult world to inspire children to attain virtue and, by implication, its concomitant rewards. Furthermore, according to some educators, the motivation of characters should not be examined, only their deeds.

Such an approach, it seems to me, is dull, unrealistic, and unfair. Children look for clues to life. They want the truth, they need the truth, and they deserve it. So I try to present characters honestly with their paradoxes and their complexities, their strengths and their weaknesses. To do this, I involve myself in as much research as I would if I were writing a biography for adults. Contrary to what I call "old-fashioned" biography for children, I do not invent dialogue. I use dialogue only when I can document it. If the text is meaty enough, I do not think that children need facts dressed up in fictional trim-mings. Indeed, children welcome hard, specific facts that bring characters to life—not only the important facts but those small vivid details that have a way of lighting up an event or a person-ality. Had I been present, for instance, to hear Patrick Henry give his famous "liberty or death" speech, I would certainly have been impressed by his dramatic oratory, but I would also have remembered the man in the balcony who became so excited, he spit a wad of tobacco into the audience below. The trivial and the sig-nificant generally travel hand in hand and indeed I suspect that most people find that memory of trivial off-the-record detail serves to nail down memory itself. I think of history and biography as *story* and am convinced that the best stories are the true ones.

Video Profiles: The accompanying video contains conversations with Mary E. Lyons, Roland Smith, and other writers of nonfiction for children.

---

powerful factor in determining the nature of biography for chil-dren; you see the word over and over again in textbooks and courses of study. And I think it has done great harm in distorting history and breeding cynicism; the great men are all gone, the implication is. Because history is old, educators are often guilty of simply repeating it instead of taking a fresh look at it. Because it is complicated, they tend to simplify by watering down mater-ial for children, whereas children need more meat rather than less, but selected for their own interests. This, of course, involves original research, a great deal of it, which twenty years ago, I think was rather rare in children's biographies. (p. 125)

This rarity in children's biographies and Jean Fritz's role in changing biographies were recognized by Breen, Fader, Odean, and Sutherland (2000) when they identified Fritz's *And Then What Happened, Paul Revere?* as one of the "One Hundred Books That Shaped the Century." The authors of the article define Fritz's role when they conclude: "Starting with this book, Fritz enlivened the field of biography with short illustrated books that use well-chosen details and humor to attract young people to the genre" (p. 54).

Biographies now develop many sides of a person's character—as well as people who are female and non-white, like many young readers themselves. Readers may discover, through the work of such authors as Jean Fritz, that the heroes of biography were real people who, like other humans, often demonstrated negative qualities. In fact, a biographical subject who is a believable human being may be easier for children to emulate than a subject who is not.

Gertrude B. Herman (1977) relates changing understanding of biography to children's stages of per-sonal development. She maintains that until children are about eight years old, they have difficulty stepping out of their own time and space to explore the lives of real people whom they most likely can never meet. Herman believes that children in the fourth through sixth grades read biographies with increasing understanding and self-identification, as long as the books are about people they are interested in and the authors have written to hold the children's interest. In adolescence, says Herman, children are:

finally ready for causes . . . and for all those fascinating persons who are not necessarily models of perfection, but who are human beings through whose doubts and triumphs, courage or villainy, victories or defeats, young people may try on personali-ties, life styles, and modes of thought and commitment. It is in investigating, in sifting and winnowing facts and ideas, in empathizing with the deeds and sufferings of others that growth is helped along—intellectual, emotional, and spiritual growth. It is through this integrative function that biography and autobiog-raphy, honestly presented with literary and artistic merit, can make important contributions to self-integration and social real-ization. The testimony of many individuals over many years sup-ports a conviction that young people have much to gain from reading about real human beings in all their complexity, with all their sometimes troubled lives. (p. 88)

As we evaluate current biographies and other nonfiction materials, we should also consider Roger Sutton's (1996) concerns. He maintains that with the awarding of the Newbery Medal to Russell Freedman's *Lincoln: A Photobi-ography* "we were supposed to get a renaissance" because the award affirmed a groundswell of attention to juvenile nonfiction. However, he is not sure that this has happened. Sutton maintains that "real money has been in series books that are efficient, often eye-catching, and intellectually barren, merely rearranging and/or padding the facts that can be found in any reputable encyclopedia" (p. 665). He is concerned that books of literary quality and books that foster "passion and imagination" are in short supply. As you read biographies and other nonfictional works, try to separate the books that you consider of high-quality content from the books that Sutton classifies as merely "Great for Reports!"

Literary Criticism: Evaluating Biographies

Like other literature, biographies should be evaluated according to the criteria for good literature. They should carefully avoid negative stereotypes based on gender, race, ethnicity, and physical ability. With regard to literary elements, characterization is of primary concern, and authors of biography must place special emphasis on accuracy of detail and use sound research methods. (See the Evaluation Criteria box on this page for additional criteria.)

Characterization. Margaret Fleming and Jo McGinnis (1985) compare the artistry required in the writing of a good biography to the artistry required in the painting of a portrait: The "style and setting only enhance the portrayal of the subject. The development of character is the primary focus" (p. xi). Like other authors, biographers have a responsibility to portray their subjects three-dimensionally. Unlike authors of fiction, biographers are restricted from inventing characters and indicating unsupported thoughts and actions.

Elizabeth Robertson and Jo McGinnis (1985) provide the following guideline for evaluating characterization:

In biography, the writer can only infer from the actions of the subject and other characters what might be going on in the person's head. Look for evidence that the biographer is overstepping the bounds of scholarly writing in this respect. (p. 19)

Robertson and McGinnis recommend that readers analyze the supporting characters in a biography and the influence of these characters on the main character by answering the following questions:

Who are the people who most influenced the life of the subject? How important were these people in the development of the subject's character? Were they positive or negative influences? How are they developed as characters? What differences are there between a fictional development of character and this non-fictional work? How would life for the subject have been different if these influences had not been present? (p. 19)

Another way to analyze the characterization in a biography, according to Robertson and McGinnis, is to examine the biographical subject by analyzing the subject's thoughts about himself or herself as reflected in autobiographies, journals, essays, speeches, and letters. Does the subject perceive himself or herself in a way different from that developed by the biographer? What might account for differences in characterization?

Author Virginia Hamilton (1992) believes that characterization in biography must go beyond the known facts of a life. After the research:

then one proceeds in the same way as with a question. How did this person really move in time and space? Who was he inside, where no one is the wiser about him but himself? Is there any light in there, any way to see? The researcher-novelist must find an opening within the real person of the biography so that the life is in the spotlight in full view, and exists again. (p. 678)

Factual Accuracy. Comparisons between biographies for children and biographies for adults and between biographies and reference books often reveal differences in basic facts. Ann W. Moore (1985) reports:

Errors in contemporary children's biographies fall into one of the following three categories: (1) inaccuracies in numbers, dates, and names, items easily checked in reference books or authorized and/or reputable adult titles; (2) incomplete, unclear, or misleading statements caused by attempts at simplification; and (3) patently false, incorrect information. (p. 34)

Moore emphasizes the need for writers and publishers to improve the accuracy of biographies for children and for reviewers to check the facts against reputable sources. Biographies have a special responsibility to be accurate and authentic in characters and settings. The task is so important and demanding that

---

EVALUATION CRITERIA

Literary Criticism: Biography

1. Does the biography meet the criteria for good literature?

2. Is the subject of the biography worth reading about?

3. Is the biography factually accurate in relation to characters, plots, and settings?

4. Does the biographer distinguish between fact and judgment and fact and fiction?

5. Does the biographer use primary sources when conducting research for the text? Are these sources included in the bibliographies or other notes to the readers?

6. Does the biographer include photographs and other documents that increase the credibility of the text?

7. If the biographer uses illustrations other than photographs, are the illustrations accurate according to the life and time of the person?

8. Does the writing style appeal to readers?

Through the Eyes of a CHILD

Katie

Pam Wilson's Fourth Grade
Western Row Elementary
Mason, Ohio

TITLE: You want Women to Vote Lizze Stanto

AUTHOR: Jean Fritz

    I really like this book because, I am always trying to be a leader just like Elizabeth Cady-Stanton in this book.

    At one point in the book I thought I would actully go back in time and go to one of the Meetings with Elizabeth and Susan B. Anthony. Now that I am done with this book I think about how important women are, and how much they do for this country! I have a new hero, Elizabeth Cady - Stanton, she is my hero because, she stood up for herself and fought for freedom from the men. Sometims she put her lif on hold for the women of America. That is why she is my hero.

Katie.

May Hill Arbuthnot and Dorothy M. Broderick (1969) say that biographers "should be prepared to spend months, and probably longer, in study and research before touching the typewriter" (p. 225). Extensive research should use recent scholarly works and historical materials that indicate what the subjects and others of the time actually said and wrote.

Changes in the perception of a historical character are emphasized by Alessandra Stanley (2001) who argues that as cultural mores change, so does the writing of biographies. Consequently, historical viewpoints can influence biographical writing.

In a critical review of two biographies written about Roald Dahl and Dr. Seuss, Mark I. West (1996) concludes

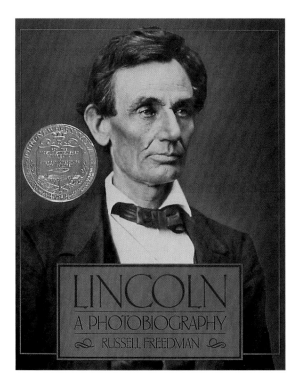

Russell Freedman develops a carefully documented biography in his book. (From Lincoln: A Photobiography *by Russell Freedman, copyright © 1987. Reprinted by permission of Clarion Books, a Houghton Mifflin Company.)*

that "most biographies do not simply record the events in the lives of their subjects; they also interpret these events" (p. 244). When selecting and evaluating biographies, this is a point to be considered. How accurate or biased is the interpretation of events in a person's life?

Any search for accuracy should include a wide range of sources. For example, Russell Freedman (1988), author of the 1988 Newbery Medal winner *Lincoln: A Photobiography,* stresses the importance of visiting original sites and studying original materials. Freedman states:

There's something magic about being able to lay your eyes on the real thing—something you can't get from your reading alone. As I sat at my desk in New York City and described Lincoln's arrival in New Salem at the age of twenty-two, I could picture the scene in my mind's eye, because I had walked down those same dusty lanes, where cattle still graze behind split-rail fences and geese flap about underfoot. When I wrote about Lincoln's morning walk from his house to his law office in downtown Springfield, I knew the route because I had walked it myself. (p. 449)

Frank J. Dempsey (1988) verifies Freedman's research in Springfield, Illinois, when he describes Freedman's fervor for on-site research. Other authors often mention research in historical societies, newspaper records, diaries, and letters. Often, they visit actual locations. Even simple biographies for young children must be accurate in the illustrations, as well as in the text, because young children

acquire much of their knowledge about a time or a setting from the illustrations rather than from detailed descriptions.

It is helpful if a biographer includes a bibliography. Freedman includes "A Lincoln Sampler" (a listing of quotes from Lincoln's speeches), "In Lincoln's Footsteps" (a listing of historical sites), and "Books About Lincoln" (a listing of additional sources). Virginia Hamilton's *Anthony Burns: The Defeat and Triumph of a Fugitive Slave* also includes extensive listings of the primary sources used by the authors.

According to biographer Olivia Coolidge (1974), authors of biographical literature must also distinguish fact from judgment. Coolidge says:

A good biography is also concerned with the effect its hero has on other people, with environment and background, with the nature of . . . achievements, and their value. I find that I examine facts in all these and many other spheres before I form judgments and that it needs great care to do what sounds quite easy, namely to distinguish a fact from a judgment. (p. 146)

Coolidge concludes her concern over fact and judgment by saying:

It simply seems that I need to know everything possible—because knowledge may affect judgment or because I am not yet really certain what I shall use or omit. In other words, I find it necessary to have a habit of worrying about facts, small or large, because my buildings are made up of these bricks, stones, or even pebbles. (p. 148)

In addition to separating fact and judgment, biographers also must contend with separating fact and legend. In her biography, *Calamity Jane: Her Life and Her Legend,* Doris Faber introduces her character by asking "Who Was She?" Then she states:

But was she a real person or just a made-up character in adventure stories? The answer to this question is a little complicated. Yes, there was a real woman nicknamed Calamity Jane, who loved to talk about having lived through many exciting adventures—but much of what she said could not really have happened the way she told it. There also was a writer who somehow got the idea of calling the imaginary heroine of some of his most popular tales Calamity Jane. Then, around a hundred years ago, the actual person and the fictional heroine began merging in the public mind, creating the same kind of legendary figure as Johnny Appleseed, for instance. (p. 1)

Throughout her biography, Faber separates fact from legend.

Worthiness of Subject. The subject of a biography should be worth reading about, just as she or he should be worthy of the meticulous research and time that the author spends in writing. Has the subject made a significant impact on the world—for good or for ill—that children should be aware of? Will children have a better understanding of the complexities of human nature after they have read the biography? Will they discover that history is made up of real people when they read the book? Will they appreciate the contributions of their ancestors or their heritage through the life of the person in the biography?

Tobie Brandriss (1999) stresses the importance of choosing biographies about scientists who could be models for students as they shape their own goals and values. In addition, Brandriss chooses biographies that help students "gaze into the lives of scientists whose discoveries we study" (p. 108).

The subjects of biography and autobiography need not be famous, infamous, or outstanding in a worldly sense in order for their lives to communicate important lessons about people and society. The subjects should be portrayed in believable ways, however. Whether a notable personage or an unsung hero of everyday life, the person upon whom a biographer focuses should have a many-faceted character, just like the people children know. Jean Fritz, for example, has written a series of historical biographies suggesting that leaders of the American Revolution were very human. Fritz portrays Patrick Henry as a practical joker who did not appreciate school in his youth, and Samuel Adams as a man who was not afraid to speak out against the British but who refused to ride a horse.

Balance Between Fact and Story Line. Writers of biographies for children must balance the requirement for accuracy with the requirement for a narrative that appeals to children. For example, authors may emphasize humorous facts as they develop plots and characters that present information in story formats. A poor balance between fact and story line may cause problems for young readers. Children have difficulty evaluating differences between fiction and nonfiction. Jean Fritz's (1982) foreword to her own fictionalized autobiography, *Homesick: My Own Story*, clarifies differences between fiction and biography:

Since my childhood feels like a story, I decided to tell it that way, letting the events fall as they would into the shape of a story, lacing them together with fictional bits, adding a piece here and there when memory didn't give me all I needed. I would use conversation freely, for I cannot think of my childhood without hearing voices. So although this book takes place within two years from October 1925 to September 1927, the events are drawn from the entire period of my childhood, but they are all, except in minor details, basically true. The people are real people; the places are dear to me. But most important, the form I have used has given me the freedom to recreate the emotions that I remember so vividly. Strictly speaking, I have to call this book fiction, but it does not feel like fiction to me. It is my story, told as truly as I can tell it. (foreword)

Writers of biographies for older children usually include extensive factual detail. Biographers such as John B. Severance in his biography *Einstein: Visionary Scientist* presents the theory of relativity in a way that can be understood by readers. This is extremely important when writing scientific biographies.

Biographies in Picture-Book Format. There are currently numerous biographies written as picture books in which much of the information about the character, the setting, and the times is reflected in the illustrations. The illustrations in many biographies written for younger children are especially important, according to Katheleen Odean (1996), because the illustrations supplement the spare texts by providing details about the historical era. John Malam's *Beatrix Potter*, for example, includes photographs of the author and her family, illustrations from her most famous work, *Peter Rabbit*, and paintings showing Hill Top Farm in the Lake District.

The dangers associated with being the country's first female steamboat captain are captured in Holly Meade's illustrations for Judith Heide Gilliland's *Steamboat! The Story of Captain Blanche Leathers*. By illustrating the often-hidden dangers of the river, the biography develops the strong courage associated with Captain Leathers. Sheila Moxley's illustrations for Laurence Anholt's *Stone Girl, Bone Girl: The Story of Mary Anning* develop the Dorset Coast in England during the early 1800s. The illustrations reinforce the character of a young girl who is fascinated by the hunt for fossils and shows her excitement when at the age of twelve she discovers the skeleton of an ichthyosaur and later expands her interest in paleontology.

Don Brown's *Uncommon Traveler: Mary Kingsley in Africa* is another illustrated biography that highlights the courage of nineteenth-century women. The text and illustrations develop the life of the British traveler who twice journeyed to West Africa, a journey which at the time was filled with many dangers. As you read this book notice how the illustrations develop the changing excitement in her life—contrast the drab colors in the early illustrations with the brightness of the African landscape.

When the illustrations provide this type of detail for a person's life, it is very important to critically evaluate the illustrations. Joanna Rudge Long (1997) provides several guidelines that should be considered when evaluating illustrated biographies. For example, the style and visual references should be appropriate for the intended audience. The pictorial motifs should be appropriate for the text. The author and illustrator should provide sources. The attitudes and points of view conveyed by the illustrations should be in harmony with the subject's true spirit. Long believes that illustrated biographies can enhance understandings of a person's life. She states, "An artist's eloquently expressed vision can transform a subject; at best, it can enhance understanding by heightening perceptions, or by presenting a familiar realm in an unexpected light" (p. 48). Long believes that Diane Stanley's *Leonardo da Vinci* and Peter Sís's *Starry Messenger* meet these guidelines for illustrated biographies.

Biographical Subjects

The subjects of biographies and autobiographies for children range from early European explorers and rulers to

American space travelers and ordinary people of today. Political leaders rise to eminence in times of need, and social activists speak out against oppression. Great achievers make contributions in science, art, literature, and sports. Common people express uncommon courage in their daily struggle for survival.

Explorers of Earth and Space. People who question existing boundaries and explore the unknown fascinate children and adults alike, and they are the subjects of numerous biographies. The consequences of the quest of Columbus are familiar to every schoolchild and are portrayed in many biographies. These biographies differ in literary style, focus, amount of detail, and development of character. Consequently, they are good for evaluation and comparison.

Before beginning a discussion of the biographies about early explorers, it is wise to consider some of the concerns generated about these materials in 1992, as numerous biographies and other information literature emerged about the Columbus experience. The National Council for the Social Studies (1992) lists some basic knowledge that critics and educators should consider when they evaluate the sources. First, neither Columbus nor any other of the early explorers discovered a new world. It was a world of people with rich and complex histories. Second, the real America that Columbus encountered in 1492 was different from the pre-contact America often portrayed in texts. It was a world of highly developed and complex civilizations. Third, in 1492, Africa was a part of the social, economic, and political system of the Eastern Hemisphere. Fourth, the encounters of Native Americans, Africans, and Europeans following 1492 are not stories of vigorous white actors confronting passive red and black spectators. All parties borrowed from and influenced the others and were influenced by them. Fifth, as a result of Columbus's arrival in 1492, Native Americans suffered catastrophic mortality rates. Sixth, Columbus's voyages were not just a European phenomenon. They were a facet of Europe's history of interaction with Asia and Africa. Seventh, Spain and Portugal, as well as northwestern Europe, had significant effects on the Americas. As you read various biographies and other informational literature about this time period, also consider how the biographies meet the concerns of the National Council for the Social Studies as well as the criteria for literary standards.

One of the earliest biographical subjects for explorers of earth and space is found in Kathryn Lasky's *The Librarian Who Measured the Earth.* Lasky develops the wonder associated with the Greek geographer Eratosthenes, who determined the circumference of the earth using techniques such as trying to calculate how long it took camels to get from one city to another, dropping plumb lines, and measuring the angles of shadows. Surprisingly, his measurements accomplished over two thousand years ago are within two hundred miles of those measured with the latest technology. Kevin Hawkes's illustrations develop the ancient setting, the importance of the Alexandria Museum, and Eratosthenes's quest to answer questions about the earth.

Biographies of Christopher Columbus are found in both highly illustrated versions for young children and carefully documented texts for older readers. Peter Sís's *Follow the Dream* is primarily a picture book that briefly describes the life of Columbus. The strength of the book is the art rather than the text. Compare the text and illustrations in Sís's book with the text and illustrations in David Adler's *Christopher Columbus: Great Explorer,* a book also written for young readers.

Ingri and Edgar Parin D'Aulaire's *Columbus,* written for slightly older children, includes details that develop a Columbus quite different from the Columbus in many highly illustrated versions. Additional information enables children to visualize an explorer who did not recognize the magnitude of his discovery and who considered himself a failure because he had not reached the Far East. The D'Aulaires say: "Old and tired, Columbus returned to Spain from his fourth and last voyage. While he was searching in vain, the Portuguese had found the seaway to the East by sailing south around Africa. Now Columbus stood in the shadow" (p. 54).

Jean Fritz's *Where Do You Think You're Going, Christopher Columbus?* is written in a light style that appeals to many children. Through use of detailed background information, Fritz creates a lively history inhabited by realistic people. For example, Columbus's sponsor, Queen Isabella of Spain, "was so religious that if she even found Christians who were not sincere Christians, she had them burned at the stake. (Choir boys sang during the burning so Isabella wouldn't have to hear the screams.)" (p. 17). Fritz ends her book with additional historical notes and an index of people and locations discussed in the book.

Biographies of Columbus written for older readers are interesting sources for analysis and comparison. You might choose for this comparison Milton Meltzer's *Columbus and the World Around Him.*

A Long and Uncertain Journey: The 27,000-Mile Voyage of Vasco da Gama by Joan Elizabeth Goodman details da Gama's 1497 voyage around Africa to the Orient. The author shows the importance of primary sources by including sidebars that are excerpts taken from a journal written by one of the members of the crew.

In the fifteenth and sixteenth centuries, astronomers, such as Nicolaus Copernicus and Galileo Galilei, shared and proved the belief of Christopher Columbus that the world is round. Through their explorations of the stars—by means of mathematical equations, naked-eye observations, and the earliest telescopes—such early explorers of space further shook the foundations of European world views. The astronomers discovered that the earth is not only round but also one of numerous planets rotating around the sun and that the sun itself is only one of many astral bodies moving through the universe. In a time when the church insisted that the earth was the stationary center of the one solar system created by God, these discoveries were radical.

In *Starry Messenger: Galileo Galilei,* Peter Sís presents a highly illustrated version of the scientist's life. By reading this biography, students discover Galileo's search for truth in a world in which the church considered his findings to be dangerous. Sís adds authenticity to the biography by including Galileo's own writings within the text. The highly detailed illustrations provide the major strength of the biography. As you read the text and view the illustrations, search for the techniques that Sís uses to develop the time period and to add important information about Galileo and the time period.

The inventions of the Wright Brothers encouraged explorers to open the next great frontier. In *The Wright Brothers: How They Invented the Airplane,* Russell Freedman places readers into the historical context of the time period, provides information about the history of flight, places the inventions of the Wright Brothers into the context of this historical development, supports his text with numerous photographs, and documents his sources.

Amelia Earhart, by Carol Ann Pearce, is the biography of the first woman to fly across the Atlantic Ocean. In showing the early life of Earhart and Earhart's experiences as an aviator, Pearce shows the role of women during early aviation. *Fly High! The Story of Bessie Coleman,* by Louise Borden and Mary Kay Kroeger, is a highly illustrated biography of the first African American aviator to earn a pilot's license. The rhythmic text describes her struggles to get an education in the early twentieth century and then go to France to earn her pilot's license because no American pilot would give her lessons.

Tomboy of the Air: Daredevil Pilot Blanche Stuart Scott by Julie Cummins is a biography of another trailblazer who was the first woman to fly in the United States and the first woman test pilot. Later in her career she became a writer and a talk show host on radio.

Political Leaders and Social Activists. Men and women who have achieved noteworthy political power or who have attempted to bring about social change are common subjects of biography. Often, these public figures are controversial—adored by some, deplored by others. As a result, biographers sometimes create unbalanced portraits of their subjects. Because biographers usually, but not always, choose to write about people they admire, hagiography (literally, "the biography of saints"), rather than objective biography, may result. Even authors who create well-rounded portrayals of political leaders and social activists inevitably express their own perspectives. For example, after reading three books about a certain political leader, one student of children's literature commented that she could have been reading about three dif-

ferent people. Because each author had a specific purpose in writing a biography, characterization of the person, choice of events to discuss, style, and tone created a different bias. If possible, read several biographies about the same person and draw your own conclusions.

Several biographies develop the lives of people who lived in early time periods. Biographies of Cleopatra, born in 69 B.C., are among the most common biographies of people living in the Middle East during this early time. Two biographies may be used for discussions and comparisons. *Cleopatra* by Diane Stanley and Peter Vennema is a highly illustrated biography about the Queen of Egypt. The authors provide an interesting note on ancient sources that might influence how readers approach these biographies: "Everything we know about Cleopatra was written by her enemies. It is not surprising, then, that she was portrayed as a conniving, immoral woman" (unnumbered note). The authors develop a queen who was strong willed, ambitious, and brilliant with a fine education and who also longed to return her country to the glory of its earlier years. The characterization suggests that her strength was her intelligence, courage, and charm. The text includes her relationships first with Caesar and then with Mark Antony. The illustrations, which depict the grandeur of Egypt, look like mosaics. The biography includes a historical atlas of Egypt and Roman Provinces during the accession of Cleopatra, a bibliography, and a pronunciation guide.

Ten Queens: Portraits of Women of Power by Milton Meltzer includes a biographical sketch of "Cleopatra—69 B.C.–30 B.C." Meltzer begins with historical perspectives about her time period, describes her intelligence (mastery of at least six languages), love for music, and her use of political power and intrigue. Meltzer chose his queens "not because they were heroines or saints. No, but because they were women who held power in their own hands and used it. Most had qualities to be wished for in any person, male or female: intellect, courage, independence" (preface, x). Meltzer also includes short biographies of Esther, Boudicca, Zenobia, Eleanor of Aquitaine, Isabel of Spain, Elizabeth I, Christina of Sweden, Martha Theresa, and Catherine the Great. The text includes a bibliography and an index.

Two biographies provide brief glimpses into the lives of important women in history and of children who were influenced by the political environment of both famous parents and the government. *HerStory: Women Who Changed the World,* edited by Ruth Ashby and Deborah Gore Ohrn, includes brief biographical histories of important women from prehistory through contemporary times. An introductory discussion compares the roles of women in various cultures such as ancient Egypt, China, and the Middle Ages. Katherine Leiner's *First Children: Growing Up in the White House* provides insights into the lives of the children or grandchildren who were raised in the executive mansion. The author uses a chronological order beginning with the

In Ten Queens: Portraits of Women of Power, *short biographies of portraits such as this one of Eleanor of Acquitaine provide a glimpse of some of the most powerful women in history. (From* Ten Queens: Portraits of Women of Power *by Milton Meltzer, illustrated by Bethanne Andersen. Copyright © 1998 by Bethanne Andersen, illustrations. Used by permission of Dutton Children's Books, an imprint of Penguin Putnam Books for Young Readers, a division of Penguin Putnam, Inc.*

grandchildren of George Washington, who lived with their grandfather in the executive mansion in Philadelphia, 1789–1797, and proceeds to Chelsea Clinton, 1993–2000. Leiner focuses on incidents in their lives that would be of interest to juvenile readers. For example, the author includes letters written to Chelsea from children around the country. The book includes an "Afterword" in which the author provides information about the children's lives after they reached adulthood. There is also a chart showing the various presidents' children and the dates of their lives, a bibliography of books categorized by each president, and a list of photographic credits.

The biographer of the following book uses many techniques to make the book an excellent example of biography. Polly Schoyer Brooks develops the characters and settings to capture the people and the times in *Queen Eleanor: Independent Spirit of the Medieval World*. Brooks portrays Eleanor of Aquitaine as she develops from a frivolous, immature girl who acts to satisfy her whims to a mature queen who has a shrewd talent for politics. Brooks uses a variety of techniques to develop colorful characters. Consider, for example, the picture that Brooks paints of Eleanor and her husband, Henry II, through the following comparisons:

Eleanor gradually restored some measure of peace and order to her duchy, using persuasion where Henry had used force. (p. 100)

While Eleanor had become serene, Henry had become more irascible. (p. 126)

From a queen of the troubadours, who had inspired romance and poetry, she became a queen with as much authority as a king. . . . Henry had been admired and feared; Eleanor was admired and loved. (p. 132)

Brooks includes verses composed about Eleanor to describe the attitudes expressed toward the queen and reinforce the mood of medieval chivalry. The following lyrics were written by troubadour Bernard de Ventadour and were included as an integral part of the text:

> Lady, I'm yours and yours shall be
> Vowed to your service constantly
> This is the oath of fealty
> I pledged to you this long time past,
> As my first joy was all in you,
> So shall my last be found there too,
> So long as life in me shall last. (p. 107)

Several highly illustrated biographies by Diane Stanley appeal to students in the lower-elementary grades. *Peter the Great* is supported by numerous full-page and half-page illustrations of Russian life in the late 1600s and early 1700s. *Shaka: King of the Zulus* is enhanced by illustrations that provide valuable details about the setting, Zululand in the early 1800s. The illustrations for Diane Stanley and Peter Vennema's *Good Queen Bess: The Story of Elizabeth I of England* encourage readers to visualize the world of the 1500s and the importance of the Elizabethan Age.

Founding Fathers and Mothers of America. Jean Fritz's stories about Patrick Henry, Samuel Adams, John Hancock, Benjamin Franklin, James Madison, and Sam Houston seem to come alive through Fritz's inclusion of little-known information. Through these books, children discover that heroes, like themselves, have fears, display good and bad characteristics, and are liked by some and disliked by others. For example, Fritz adds humor to *Where Was Patrick Henry on the 29th of May?* by developing the theory that unusual things always seemed to happen to Henry on the date of his birth. She characterizes Henry as not only a great patriot but also a practical joker and a person filled with "passion for fiddling, dancing, and pleasantry."

Similar insights enliven Fritz's biographies of other beloved figures from the Revolutionary War period. Fritz doesn't limit her writing to supporters of American

 Technology Resources

The accompanying CD-ROM is ideal for generating a list of titles to support a unit on explorers, a discussion of inventors, a career week focus, or a study of a specific historical figure.

independence from Great Britain, however. In *Traitor: The Case of Benedict Arnold,* Fritz describes a man who wanted to be a success and a hero. Fritz attracts interest in Arnold and prepares the readers for the apparently dramatic changes in a man who chose to support the British by suggesting early in the book the complete reversal of Arnold's popularity. In 1777, following Arnold's successes in the assault on Quebec and in the Saratoga Campaign, George Washington called him "the bravest of the brave." But by 1780, after his plot with John André to betray the American post at West Point, he was regarded as "the veriest villain of centuries past." The incidents that Fritz chooses to include develop many sides of Arnold's character and encourage readers to understand why Arnold joined forces with the British.

In *The Great Little Madison,* Fritz uses jokes that James Madison told on himself and humorous anecdotes to show how Madison overcame his small stature and his weak voice. The early experiences cited by Fritz show why Madison believed in logic, freedom of religion, and the written word.

In *Make Way for Sam Houston,* Fritz uses Houston's belief in destiny to emphasize Houston's interactions with other characters. For example, Houston accepted Andrew Jackson's vision of America because "now he had a picture and words for what he'd call Destiny" (p. 20). Fritz reinforces Houston's belief in destiny by describing Houston's responses each time he saw an eagle, the medicine bird that influenced major decisions in his life.

In *Benjamin Franklin: The New American,* Milton Meltzer carefully introduces readers to the historical background of Franklin. In the following quotation, Meltzer encourages readers to understand the time and place:

It is almost three hundred years since Benjamin Franklin was born in Boston. (The date was January 17, 1706.) It is hard to put yourself back in that time and grasp what it was like. About 12,000 people lived in Boston, and in all the English colonies of North America there were only 250,000. (That's about the same as the population of Rochester, New York, today.) Most of the people were clustered around Boston, the Connecticut and Hudson river valleys. . . . They had little connection with one another. Roads were really paths, and bad weather made them almost impassable. (p. 15)

Meltzer develops a many-sided person by revealing both strengths and weaknesses in Franklin. Meltzer adds credibility to the characterization through numerous quotations drawn from Franklin's writings and speeches.

Meltzer's *Thomas Jefferson: The Revolutionary Aristocrat* is an in-depth look at the author of the Declaration of Independence and the third president of the United States. The authenticity of the text is increased by Meltzer's use of historical photographs, list of sources, and maps showing locations discussed in the text. Another viewpoint of the Revolutionary War is found in Jim Murphy's *A Young Patriot: The American Revolution as Experi-*

enced by One Boy, the biography of a fifteen-year-old who enlisted in the army in 1776. *George Washington and the Founding of a Nation* by Albert Marrin includes quotes from Washington's writings, historical drawings, and maps. Marrin carefully develops a biographical character who is both someone to be admired and a personality with flaws. The biography also depicts the harshness of war.

Fiery words and bold actions are not the only forms of patriotism and leadership. Elizabeth Yates's *Amos Fortune, Free Man* depicts a man who advanced freedom. Fortune was an African who was brought to slavery in Boston, learned a trade, and eventually acquired freedom. He represents thousands of unsung heroes of the American Revolution—black and white, male and female. The words on his tombstone, erected in 1801, suggest the fundamental American values that Fortune exemplified: ". . . born free in Africa, a slave in America, he purchased liberty, professed Christianity, lived reputably, and died hopefully" (p. 181).

Leaders of a Growing America. As the United States became more confident in itself as a nation, it began to expand its interests overseas. Rhoda Blumberg's *Commodore Perry in the Land of the Shogun* depicts the attempts of the American naval officer Matthew Perry to open Japanese harbors to American trade in 1853. This book, an excellent choice for multicultural studies, strongly emphasizes the dramatic interactions between Perry and the Japanese. Reproductions of the original drawings that recorded the expedition, Japanese scrolls and handbills, and photographs provide documentation and enhance children's understanding of the setting and Japanese culture.

The best-known biographer of Abraham Lincoln is probably Carl Sandburg. His *Abraham Lincoln: The Prairie Years* was the basis for his biography for children, *Abe Lincoln Grows Up.* Children vicariously share the youth of a great American leader. They discover an impoverished young man of the backwoods who is starved for books, hungry for knowledge, eager to have fun, and ambitious to test himself and his principles in a wider world. Sandburg says:

It seemed that Abe made the books tell him more than they told other people. . . . Abe picked out questions . . . such as "Who has the most right to complain, the Indian or the Negro?" and Abe would talk about it, up one way and down the other, while they were in the cornfield pulling fodder for the winter. (p. 135)

Cheryl Harness's *Abe Lincoln Goes to Washington: 1837–1867* is a highly illustrated biography of Abraham Lincoln written for younger readers. The text presents interesting details including maps, portraits, and banners. Ann Turner's *Abe Lincoln Remembers* is another biography written for younger readers. Turner uses a chronological organization that depicts Lincoln's life through vignettes of some of the most memorable incidents.

Biographies of Charles Eastman and Theodore Roosevelt depict people who had great impact on the growth

In-Depth Analysis
of a Biographical Book

In 2000 Russell Freedman's biography *Lincoln: A Photobiography* was chosen unanimously as one of the "One Hundred Books That Shaped the Century" (Breen et al., 2000). In this 1988 Newbery Medal winner, Russell Freedman uses numerous techniques that students of children's literature should consider. First, Freedman introduces each of the seven chapters with quotations from Lincoln's own writing. For example, Freedman introduces chapter two, "A Backwoods Boy," with this quotation:

> It is a great piece of folly to attempt to make anything out of my early life. It can all be condensed into a simple sentence, and that sentence you will find in Gray's Elegy—"the short and simple annals of the poor." That's my life, and that's all you or anyone else can make out of it. (p. 7)

Second, Freedman clearly separates legend from fact. For example, in chapter three, "Law and Politics," Freedman states:

> He also fell in love—apparently for the first time in his life. Legend tells us that Lincoln once had a tragic love affair with Ann Rutledge . . . who died at the age of twenty-two. While this story has become part of American folklore, there isn't a shred of evidence that Lincoln ever had a romantic attachment with Ann. Historians believe that they were just good friends. (p. 28)

Third, Freedman supports his text with photographs of various documents of Lincoln's own writing. For example, the text includes a page of Lincoln's autobiographical sketch written in 1859 (p. 6), a page from Lincoln's homemade copybook (p. 13), and a copy of the handwritten Gettysburg Address (p. 103).

Fourth, Freedman includes historical photographs that support the settings and people. There are photographs of battlefields and of Lincoln and his family.

Fifth, the text includes photographs of authentic posters, newspaper ads, and documents. For example, there is a photograph of the marriage license of Abraham Lincoln and Mary Todd (p. 33), a wanted poster for a runaway slave (p. 44), a victory poster from 1860 (p. 62), and a newspaper cartoon from a Baltimore paper (p. 71).

Sixth, Freedman supports the text with references to sources for quotations and major speeches, lists of historical sites, sources for additional books about Lincoln, and lists of acknowledgments and picture credits. You may compare Freedman's biography with Albert Marrin's *Commander in Chief: Abraham Lincoln in the Civil War.*

of America. Charles Eastman, the most famous Native American of his time, was a Sioux of the Great Plains, born in 1858. Eastman overcame poverty and racial prejudice to become a physician and a crusader for Native American rights. Peter Anderson's *Charles Eastman: Physician, Reformer, and Native American Leader* looks at the influences that combined to make Eastman a spokesperson for his people, including the forced migration of the Sioux from Minnesota, Eastman's medical education, and Eastman's efforts to provide medical treatment and better living conditions for the Sioux. Eastman worked to restore broken treaties and to encourage Indians and whites to respect Native American culture. Anderson describes Eastman's motives for publishing his first book:

> It was Charles's intention to present an accurate picture of the Indian people and their way of life. Too often white people looked upon the Indian people as ignorant and backward. In his writing and lecturing, Charles was quick to correct them, pointing out the many strengths and contributions of America's native people. In addition to their deep respect for nature, Charles wrote about the beauty of their arts and crafts. Indian people, he said, also had developed their own herbal medicines and farming techniques. They knew, as well as anyone, how to live off the land. (p. 90)

Bully for You, Teddy Roosevelt!, by Jean Fritz, is a biography of the twenty-sixth president, who worked especially hard for conservation issues. Fritz's biography includes notes, a bibliography, and an index. It is interesting to compare this biography and the preceding one and to examine the time period through the viewpoints of a Native American man and a president of the United States.

Numerous biographies of escaped slaves develop the importance of freedom and the inhumanity of slavery. Virginia Hamilton's *Anthony Burns: The Defeat and Triumph of a Fugitive Slave* is a narrative history of events surrounding the life of Burns as well as a biography. In the research material, however, there existed no day-to-day calendar of the activities and movements of Burns as an ordinary slave child and youth. The life of Burns became well documented only after Burns's twentieth year, when Burns was hired out to Richmond, Virginia, and carefully began to plan his escape. Because of the lack of documentation, Hamilton draws from supporting materials to re-create the early life of Burns.

Hamilton uses an interesting technique to allow readers to understand the early life of Burns. After Burns is captured as a fugitive slave, he goes within himself and remembers his happier childhood days. In the following quotation, Hamilton transfers her character from his unhappy days of imprisonment to his memories: "Anthony was not aware Suttle had gone anywhere, for he had left first and gone deep inside himself, to his childhood. These days seemed endless, perfect. There mornings and waking up were the times he could hardly wait for, he loved them so" (p. 7).

Another interesting book about a nineteenth-century American with a strong social conscience is Leonard Everett Fisher's *Alexander Graham Bell.* Fisher focuses on Bell's achievements, first working with speech in Scotland and then emigrating to Canada after which he opens the

Boston school for teachers of the deaf. His work finally leads to the invention of the telephone. Fisher includes diagrams for the telephone patent in 1876.

Twentieth-Century Leaders in America and Abroad. Biographies written for young children and for older children differ in tone, focus, choice of content, amount of detail, and development of character. Because of the range in intended audiences, biographies about political leaders and social activists in the twentieth century provide opportunities to compare the techniques used by the authors and the content that they include.

First, consider several biographies written for young children: Barbara Cooney's *Eleanor* and Ruth Franchere's *Cesar Chavez.* The books share several features. The readability levels are for the fourth grade, indicating that the books are meant for independent reading. The books contain numerous illustrations, and they emphasize very positive characteristics and situations.

Barbara Cooney's *Eleanor* focuses on Roosevelt as a young girl. Both Cooney's text and illustrations develop characterization that shows her as a lonely and insecure child, especially after her father's death. The biography has a happy ending as the child realizes that she has special talents. Cooney's illustrations depict the time period and re-create the era of mansions and a wealthy social life.

Next, consider several biographies that have been written for older children. Longer format allows authors to include more details and to develop more information about the historical periods.

Appropriately for an older audience, Russell Freedman's *Franklin Delano Roosevelt* includes many photographs, lists books about Roosevelt, and provides acknowledgments for picture credits. Many of these photographs are from the Franklin D. Roosevelt Library, the Library of Congress, the Bettmann Archive, and the National Archives. The biography includes an in-depth look at Roosevelt's activities during World War II. Consequently, it is a valuable source for authenticating historical fiction about World War II. In *Eleanor Roosevelt: A Life of Discovery,* Freedman realistically portrays Eleanor Roosevelt by drawing heavily on her memoirs. Unlike biographies written for younger readers, Freedman's *Eleanor Roosevelt* includes her reactions when she discovers her husband's love affair. As in Freedman's other biographies, numerous photographs add to the depiction of this political leader's life.

Two biographies written by James Haskins about civil rights leaders encourage readers to understand the historical, political, and social perspectives of the time periods. For example, Haskins's *I Have a Dream: The Life and Words of Martin Luther King, Jr.* not only examines King's life and his achievements but also provides excerpts from his speeches and other communications that shed light on his beliefs and struggles. Haskins's *Thurgood Marshall: A Life for Justice* presents the fight against racism and segregation

waged by the first African American Supreme Court justice. The texts include bibliographies of books, articles, other sources, and indexes that encourage older readers to conduct specific research.

John B. Severance's *Gandhi, Great Soul* begins with a chapter that develops the impact of Gandhi's beliefs on other world leaders such as Martin Luther King, Jr. and Nelson Mandela. Severance's biography includes interesting details about his personal life as well as historical events and struggles with the British and various religious groups.

Elizabeth Ferber's *Yasir Arafat: A Life of War and Peace* is the biography of the Palestinian leader. The biographer combines the story of his life with information about the Arab and Israeli conflict. Ferber presents both points of view about the man: a popular leader among displaced Palestinians and a reviled figure in the occupied territories after the Hebron massacre in 1994. Labeled black-and-white photographs accompany the text. There is also a chronology of important dates, source notes for each chapter, a bibliography, and an index.

The importance of memories and friendship is developed in Vedat Dalokay's *Sister Shako and Kolo the Goat: Memories of My Childhood in Turkey.* This book, the winner of the 1995 Mildred Batchelder Honor Award, is a personal remembrance of the former mayor of Ankara, Turkey, in which he lovingly recalls his childhood in rural Turkey and his special friendship with a widow and her remarkable goat, Kolo. The author develops many of the values and beliefs identified in Turkish folklore. For example, the importance of hospitality is shown when the new goat comes into the family unexpectedly and is considered a "Guest of God" because, "If a traveler needs shelter or food, he knocks at the door of any house along the way. The host offers him whatever he needs, because the traveler is considered a guest sent by God. This is a very old Turkish tradition that is still practiced today" (p. 14).

Dalokay develops many of these Turkish values as he remembers Sister Shako's thoughts and advice about subjects such as holy places and death. For example, Sister Shako states her beliefs about death: "Now I am here in this hut, but after death, I shall be in the caterpillar on the black earth, I shall be in the rain seeping into the earth. Blowing winds and rapid rivers will carry me around this world. May death come nicely, smoothly, without pain, without suffering" (p. 58). To clarify understanding, the author includes footnotes that describe various customs and beliefs developed in the story. The cultural atmos-

Technology Resources

NCTE "has established an annual award for promoting and recognizing excellence in the writing of nonfiction for children"—the Orbis Pictus Award. Visit our Companion Website at www.prenhall.com/norton to link to the NCTE site.

phere is reinforced by the use of regional words, idioms, sayings, and traditions of eastern Turkey.

Achievers and American heroes are always popular subjects for children's biographies. In *The American Hero: The True Story of Charles A. Lindbergh,* Barry Denenberg uses several techniques that stimulate interest in the controversial aviator's life and add a feeling of authenticity. For example, he introduces each of the chapters with quotes from Charles or Anne Lindbergh's own writings. The introduction to the second chapter includes insights into the motivation to learn to fly an airplane: "When I was a child on our Minnesota farm, I spent hours lying on my back . . . hidden from passersby, watching white cumulus clouds drift overhead, staring into the sky. It was a different world up there. You had to be flat on your back, screened in by the grass stalks, to live in it. Those clouds, how far away were they? Nearer than the neighbor's house, untouchable as the moon—unless you had an airplane. How wonderful it would be, I'd thought, if I had an airplane—wings with which I could fly up to the clouds and explore their caves and canyons—wings like the hawk circling above me. Then, I would ride on the wind and be part of the sky . . .—Charles Lindbergh" (p. 19). In addition, photographs showing Lindbergh's experiences, charts, and maps illustrate the biography. The text includes source notes, a bibliography, and an index.

In *America's Champion Swimmer: Gertrude Ederle,* David A. Adler presents a biography of the first woman to swim the English channel. Adler uses newspaper comments that describe her as courageous, determined, modest, and poised to help define the character of the woman who also won three medals in the 1924 Olympics and set twenty-nine U.S. and world records.

When children do library research, they discover some of the techniques that biographers use. Such investigations may also lead children to outstanding, recently published biographies of other social leaders. (See Chapter 11 for a discussion of additional biographies.)

Artists and Authors. One of the most interesting new biographies develops both the biography of a world-famous photographer and a chronological view of history as shown through her photographs. In *Margaret Bourke-White: Her Pictures Were Her Life,* Susan Goldman Rubin uses a photobiography approach to blend the personal and professional life of this renowned photographer who was able to make a reputation in a profession that at the time was dominated by men. The biographer introduces her subject in a way that suggests to readers that they will be reading about a courageous and dedicated photographer. The biography begins as Bourke-White is ordered to abandon ship while she is on a troop carrier in World War II headed for North Africa and she takes pictures of the sinking ship while she is in a lifeboat. The major portion of the biography chronicles her development as one of the world's best known photojournalists. Her importance is reinforced through the reproductions of such photographs as the one of Churchill and Stalin that was on the cover of *Life* magazine. You may compare the biography and life of Margaret Bourke-White with the biography of another well-known photographer by reading Elizabeth Partridge's *Restless Spirit: The Life and Work of Dorothea Lang.* Lang was another photographer whose works chronicle the Depression and World War II.

Color reproductions of artworks add interest to Leslie Sills's *Inspirations: Stories About Women Artists.* This book includes four biographical sketches of contemporary women artists and artworks for which they are known. Sills's *Visions: Stories About Women Artists* includes additional biographical sketches of women artists and their works.

The series of books "Portraits of Women Artists for Children" includes both brief biographical sketches of the artists and color reproductions of their works. Several of the titles in this series include Robyn Montana Turner's *Frida Kahlo, Mary Cassatt, Georgia O'Keeffe,* and *Rosa Bonheur.* These books also provide much information about art.

In *Leonardo da Vinci,* Diane Stanley introduces readers to the art of the Renaissance artist. Through this biography, Stanley presents da Vinci's accomplishments both as a painter and as a scientist. Stanley incorporates miniature reproductions of da Vinci's paintings into her illustrations. Stanley uses a similar approach in *Michelangelo.* In this biography, Stanley also presents a historical perspective that allows readers to better understand how artists who worked during the Italian Renaissance were controlled by the desires of religious leaders and the wishes of wealthy patrons.

John Duggleby's *Artist in Overalls: The Life of Grant Wood,* the artist of the famous "American Gothic," traces the artist's life from his experiences as a farm boy who uses charcoal to sketch animals on an old cardboard to the emergence of an artist who developed his own style. Duggleby emphasizes the artist's development of self-esteem when he begins to express his feelings about art: " 'I want to reach everyday people, not just the artists and art critics of the world,' he explained. He talked about his years of trying to paint subjects from foreign lands, in other artists' styles, and about how he finally began painting the things he knew best, in the way he felt most comfortable" (p. 49). The biography is illustrated with reproductions of Grant Wood's paintings. Duggleby uses a similar approach in *Story Painter: The Life of Jacob Lawrence.* Full-color reproductions of Lawrence's paintings illustrate the life of an African American painter who was part of the Harlem Renaissance.

Several additional texts provide both biographical information about artists and introductions to their art. Gary Schwartz's *Rembrandt* and Richard Meryman's *Andrew Wyeth* include information that helps readers understand and interpret their works. Both texts are heavily illustrated with color reproductions of each artist's paintings. Both Schwartz and Meryman are considered leading authorities in art interpretations. Jan Greenberg and Sandra Jordan use numerous reproductions of the visionist artist's work in *Chuck Close, Up Close*. The authors list museums that show Close's art as well as a bibliography. In *My Name Is Georgia*, Jeanette Winter provides a highly illustrated introduction to artist Georgia O'Keeffe.

Other current biographies and autobiographies provide insights into the authors and illustrators of children's books. Read about the lives of the authors of *Little Women, The Secret Garden,* and *Charlotte's Web* and then compare the lives of the authors with those of their fictional heroines and heroes.

In *Louisa May: The World and Works of Louisa May Alcott*, Norma Johnston chronicles the life of Louisa May Alcott. Readers will be interested in Johnston's motivation for writing this biography and her point of view. As you read this biography, search for evidence that reflects Johnston's motivation and point of view. For example, Johnston states:

Like generations of readers, I grew up envying the March family everything but their poverty—their closeness, the way they never stayed angry, the way they always, always loved each other. As a young teen, I wept bitterly because I couldn't make my family as picture-perfect as the Marches, and resolved to be, like Louisa, a writer of books for girls. (author's note)

In *Frances Hodgson Burnett: Beyond the Secret Garden*, Angelica Shirley Carpenter and Jean Shirley explore the life of the author of *The Secret Garden* and *Little Lord Fauntleroy*. It is interesting to compare Burnett and Alcott, two successful women authors who wrote during approximately the same time period.

Beverly Gherman's *E. B. White: Some Writer!* chronicles the life of the popular author of *Charlotte's Web, Stuart Little,* and *The Trumpet of the Swan* as well as numerous articles in such journals as *The New Yorker*. Throughout her biography, Gherman relates White's character to scenes from and characters developed in his children's stories. For example, Gherman introduces the book in such a way that readers can visualize a many-sided person:

Whenever E. B. White was asked to accept an award for one of his books, he found an excuse for not attending the ceremony. In 1970, when *Charlotte's Web* won the Claremont Center's Award, he sent them a speech describing how Wilbur fainted with excitement after he won his special prize at the fair. It took a bite from Templeton the rat to revive him. White said he would faint just as Wilbur had if he were forced to stand up before the audience and read his own speech. But he thanked them for liking *Charlotte* and said he felt "very lucky to have gained the ear of children...." (p. 1)

Milton Meltzer's *Carl Sandburg: A Biography* presents the life of the poet and biographer who became known for his ability to speak for the common man. Meltzer presents early work that shows Sandburg as a journalist for the *International Socialist Review* as well as his extensive poetry focusing on working conditions in Chicago. Meltzer

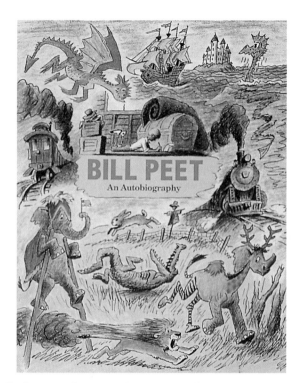

The humorous illustrations show the work of the author. (From Bill Peet: An Autobiography by Bill Peet, copyright © 1989 by Bill Peet. Reprinted by permission of Houghton Mifflin Company.)

presents a clear vision of the author by presenting and discussing Sandburg's poems and his reasons for writing the poems. A considerable portion of the biography focuses on Sandburg's role as a biographer of Lincoln and the success and recognition that came to Sandburg as a consequence of the Lincoln biographies.

Autobiographies give children insights into the illustrators and authors of children's books. *Bill Peet: An Autobiography* provides information about the artist's experiences as a Disney cartoonist. Peet worked on such films as *Dumbo* and *Fantasia*. This text is heavily illustrated with Peet's drawings. Beverly Cleary's *A Girl from Yamhill: A Memoir* is a chronicle of the early life of the popular realistic fiction author. Numerous photographs should intrigue readers of the "Ramona" series and *Dear Mr. Henshaw*.

Author Sid Fleischman, winner of the Newbery Medal, writes an autobiography of his life in *The Abracadabra Kid: A Writer's Life*. In addition to interesting information about his life, Fleischman introduces each chapter with quotes from his fan letters. The autobiography includes family photographs and illustrations that depict other experiences in his life.

Readers will discover the author's experiences when he was a young boy by reading Tomie dePaola's *26 Fairmount Avenue*. The autobiography begins with a hurricane in 1938 and includes such exciting memories as watching his house being built, spending time with his grandmothers, and attending kindergarten. The author reveals emotions that seem very real to many young children as he discovers that he will not learn to read until next year and he is infuriated when Walt Disney changes "Snow White and the Seven Dwarfs" from the "true" story in his folktale book.

In *War Boy: A Country Childhood,* British author and illustrator Michael Foreman describes his life growing up in England during the 1940s. This is not the normal life of a young boy; it is complicated by bombs, gas masks, and guns. It is also filled, however, with excitement, working together, and new friends. Foreman's detailed illustrations provide background for stories set in World War II. In *After the War Was Over,* Foreman continues illustrating and describing his experiences into his teenage years. Foreman's text and watercolor illustrations present a warm personal account of his post–World War II years in England.

Ellen Levine's *Anna Pavlova: Genius of the Dance* is a biography of the ballerina who became one of the most acclaimed dancers in Russia. The author uses excerpts from Pavlova's diary in addition to quotes from her contemporaries to develop a woman who had both a dream and determination. Through her story, readers discover some of the history of dance and the training required to be successful. Labeled black-and-white photographs provide background for Pavlova's career both in Russia and across the world. A feeling of her worldwide acclaim is found through the inclusion of illustrations such as a sketch of Pavlova used for a poster announcing the Russian Ballet's 1909 season in Paris. The author includes a glossary of ballet terms, an annotated bibliography, and an index.

The life of Louis Armstrong is developed in picture-book format in Roxane Orgill's *If I Only Had a Horn: Young Louis Armstrong.* The text and Leonard Jenkins's illustrations are set in New Orleans in the early 1900s. As you read the text and analyze the illustrations, notice how both author and illustrator re-create the emotions of jazz.

Spellbinder: The Life of Harry Houdini by Tom Lalicki presents the life of one of the most famous magicians and escape artists. Photographs of posters, experiences when handcuffed and chained, and life on Broadway add to the sensational nature of Houdini's life. The biography includes a chronology, a bibliography, and an index. The author also relates Houdini's life to the massive immigration movement of European Jews to America between 1880 and 1925.

People Who Have Persevered. Biographies are not always written about famous people or people of great material success. Some excellent biographies and autobiographies portray the courage and perseverance of ordinary people.

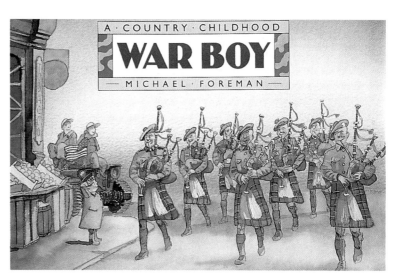

The author describes and illustrates his life growing up in England. (From War Boy: A Country Childhood *by Michael Foreman. Copyright © 1989 by Michael Foreman. Reprinted by permission of Little, Brown and Company.)*

Lisa Ketchum's *Into a New Country: Eight Remarkable Women of the West* focuses on women such as Mary McGladery Tape, who came to America as a Chinese immigrant and sought equal rights for Chinese, and Katherine Ryan, a nurse who joined the Gold Rush in the Klondike.

Biographies of immigrants to the United States frequently depict the harsh circumstances that forced them to leave their home countries. Rosemary Wells's *Streets of Gold* is based on Mary Austin's memoir written in the early twentieth century. The biography begins with her early life in Russia during which she experienced anti-Semitism, continues with her travels to America after her father earns enough money for his family's passage, and concludes with her life in Boston where she is finally able to attend school. The biography concludes with her joy on graduation day when she reads her poem written about George Washington in front of the school, and then sees her poem printed by *The Boston Herald.*

Another extraordinary woman is the subject of Rosemary Wells's *Mary on Horseback: Three Mountain Stories.* This biography chronicles many of the experiences of Mary Breckinridge, the first nurse to go to the Appalachian Mountains and provide medical services to families living in isolated locations. The influence of her work is developed through her formation of the Frontier Nursing Service, which began in 1925 with three nurses and grew to a service that visited about thirty-five thousand mountain homes each year. Joan Dash's *The World at Her Fingertips: The Story of Helen Keller* emphasizes how Keller influenced opinions about and treatment of the blind.

Peter Golenbock's biography *Hank Aaron: Brave in Every Way* develops the life of a major league baseball star who was born during the Depression during a time when the major leagues excluded black players. His father, however,

ISSUE How Should Authors Write About the Holocaust?

Selecting, researching, writing, and critically evaluating Holocaust biographies and other literature becomes especially important when we realize that fifty thousand books have been written about the Holocaust in the last fifty years.[1] One of the most important issues discussed in journals, conference presentations, and informational books written about the writing and critical analysis of Holocaust biographies is, How should authors write about the Holocaust?

Hazel Rochman[2] discusses how authors should and should not write about the Holocaust. In a review of Ruth Minsky Sender's *The Holocaust Lady,*[3] Rochman maintains that even though the book is much discussed, it is an example of how authors should not write about the Holocaust. Rochman states, "Sender's suffering as a Holocaust survivor is undeniable. What she has to tell us is of the utmost importance. . . . But, the writing is sentimental and self-centered, full of cliché about horror, pain, and degradation. On almost every page, at least once, her tears glide, glisten, or roll gently down her cheeks, and/or her heart skips a beat; people read her work with quivering hands, their faces distorted with pain" (p. 416).

In contrast, Rochman maintains that the writing in books such as Ida Vos's *Hide and Seek*[4] and Maus Spiegelman's *Maus: A Survivor's Tale*[5] is preferable because the writing represents a controlled style that has greater power.

The style of presentation in *The Diary of a Young Girl: The Definitive Edition*[6] is frequently presented as a role model for Holocaust biographies and autobiographies. In a review of the book, Patricia Hampl[7] states, "The 'Diary,' now 50 years old, remains astonishing and excruciating. It is a work almost sick with terror and tension, even as it performs its miracle of lucidity. . . . All that remains is this diary, evidence of her ferocious appetite for life. It gnaws at us still" (p. 21).

Geoffrey Short[8] is critical of both biographical writings and historical fiction about the Holocaust. He finds that books fail to emphasize the treatment of ethnic groups other than Jews and the Jewish resistance to Nazi oppression. Short concludes:

Teachers cannot rely on apparently germane literature either to plug gaps in their pupil's knowledge or to challenge their false beliefs. On the contrary, there is a real danger that some of this literature will either ignore or reinforce a range of misconceptions. Novels and autobiographies are not textbooks and it is understandable, though regrettable, if their literary merit is sometimes marred by historical inaccuracy and oversight. None of this would matter, of course, if history teachers were well informed about the Holocaust and had the time to raise all pertinent issues. To the extent that students are given a solid grounding in the history of the Holocaust they become that much less vulnerable to the factual errors and omissions in what is otherwise good literature. (p. 189)

As you read the various biographies set during the Holocaust, try to evaluate the impact of the writing style. For example, Anne Frank's style has been described as positive while Sender's has been described as a tear-stained style. As you read the biographies, consider the following questions: Should the writing style make a difference in Holocaust biographies? What is your viewpoint on the writing style of Holocaust literature? Which of the books are the most effective in their depictions of the time period and of your understanding of the issues surrounding the Holocaust? How would you write a book so that the conflict, the setting, and the characters are understood by your readers?

---

[1]Lustig, Arnost. "What We Will Never Understand About the Holocaust." Unexpected Encounters with the Holocaust Conference: Texas A&M University, College Station, Texas. April 2, 1997.
[2]Rochman, Hazel. "How Not to Write About the Holocaust." *Booklist* 89 (October 15, 1992): 416.
[3]Sender, Ruth Minsky. *The Holocaust Lady.* New York: Macmillan, 1992.
[4]Vos, Ida. *Hide and Seek.* Boston: Houghton Mifflin, 1991.
[5]Spiegelman, Maus. *Maus: A Survivor's Tale.* New York: Macmillan, 1992.
[6]Frank, Anne. *The Diary of a Young Girl: The Definitive Edition.* New York: Doubleday, 1995.
[7]Hampl, Patricia. "Anne Frank: Diary of a Young Girl: The Definitive Edition." *The New York Times Book Review* (March 5, 1995): 21.
[8]Short, Geoffrey. "Learning Through Literature: Historical Fiction, Autobiography, and the Holocaust." *Children's Literature in Education* 28 (1997): 179–189.

---

taught him to play baseball and his mother taught him determination. Through the biography, the author shows that determination can overcome obstacles.

Persevering may require the survival of body and soul through such terrible experiences as the Holocaust. When children of the Holocaust write their autobiographical experiences as adults, they frequently emphasize both the tragedies of their experiences and the hopes for the future that kept them alive during their hiding or internment.

Ana Novac writes about her own experiences in *The Beautiful Days of My Youth: My Six Months in Auschwitz and Plaszow.* She tells about finding a pencil stub and recording her experiences in a diary. In *I Have Lived a Thousand Years: Growing Up in the Holocaust,* Livia Bitton-Jackson also describes her experiences when her family is forced into a Jewish ghetto and later sent to Auschwitz. Both of these books are strengthened by the authors' use of personal observations.

Anne Frank's *The Diary of a Young Girl: The Definitive Edition* should be added to the original published version. This latest edition contains about 30 percent more material than was included in the earlier edition. Students of children's literature may compare the two editions as well as other biographies about Anne Frank.

Biographies of children who have persevered are popular subjects in the "Children of Conflict" series. For example, in *Children of Israel, Children of Palestine: Our Own True Stories,* Laurel Holliday includes memoirs from more than thirty Jewish and Arab subjects who tell about the struggle between Israeli Jews and Palestinians. Additional biographies and Jewish experiences are found in Edward T. Sullivan's *The Holocaust in Literature for Youth* (1999).

Authors who write biographies about people who have overcome physical disabilities frequently focus on the biographical character's ability to achieve success against considerable odds. In *Out of Darkness: The Story of Louis Braille,* Russell Freedman focuses on Braille's struggle to communicate after he loses his own sight and his additional difficulties in having his system accepted. In *Wilma Unlimited: How Wilma Rudolph Became the World's Fastest Woman,* Kathleen Krull stresses how Rudolph overcame her childhood polio to become at age twenty the first woman to win three gold medals in a single Olympics.

Eloise Greenfield and Lessie Jones Little's *Childtimes: A Three-Generation Memoir* traces a family's experiences. In three parts, an African American grandmother, mother, and daughter tell about growing up in time periods ranging from the late 1800s through the 1940s. Both Greenfield and Little are well-known authors of children's books. This book concludes poignantly:

It's been good, stopping for a while to catch up to the past. It has filled me with both great sadness and great joy. Sadness to look back at suffering, joy to feel the unbreakable threads of strength. Now, it's time for us to look forward again, to see where it is that we're going. Maybe years from now, our descendants will want to stop and tell the story of their time and their place in this procession of children. A childtime is a mighty thing. (p. 175)

The words provide a fitting conclusion to this discussion of biographies written for children. What better purposes are there for sharing biographies with children than allowing them to feel good, to catch up to the past, and to experience the sadness and great joy of other people's lives?

Informational Books

Informational books are available on almost any subject. They are valued by children, teachers, parents, and librarians. This nonfiction, however, requires careful evaluation of the contents.

Values of Informational Books

"I am curious." "It is easier to find the answer from reading than it is to ask my teacher." "I want to learn to take better pictures." "I want to learn about a career I might enjoy." "I like reading the books." These reasons were given to this author by children who were asked why they read informational books. The range of answers also reflects the many values of informational books for children. Nonfiction books provide information about hobbies, experiments, the ways in which things work, the characteristics of plants and animals, and many other phenomena.

Gaining knowledge is a good reason for reading informational books. Many recently published books contain information on timely subjects that children hear about on television or radio or read about in newspapers. For example, children excited by NASA's space explorations can consult Seymour Simon's *Jupiter* and *Saturn* for color photographs and information obtained during NASA's *Pioneer* and *Voyager* space explorations. Nic Bishop's *Digging for Bird-Dinosaurs: An Expedition to Madagascar* and Don Lessem's *Dinosaur Worlds* encourage children to expand their knowledge about dinosaurs and fossils and to learn about the current work and dis-

Color photographs taken during actual space explorations clarify the content of an informational book. (From Jupiter *by Seymour Simon. Published by William Morrow & Company, Inc., 1985. Photograph courtesy of NASA.)*

coveries of paleontologists. Joy Cowley's text and Nic Bishop's photographs help young children imagine the precarious life of the *Red-Eyed Tree Frog* in the rain forests of Costa Rica.

Informational books also provide opportunities for children to experience the excitement of new discoveries. For example, step-by-step directions also lead to creative problem solving in Joan Irvine's *How to Make Super Pop-Ups.* They can discover characteristics of the ocean when they follow Simon's directions in *How to Be an Ocean Scientist in Your Own Home.*

Another value of informational books is introduction to the scientific method. Through firsthand experience and reading about the work of scientists, children discover how scientists observe, compare, formulate and test hypotheses, and draw conclusions or withhold them until they uncover more evidence. Children also become familiar with the instruments used by scientists. As children learn about the scientific method, they gain appreciation for the attitudes of the people who use this method. Children discover the importance of careful observation over long periods of time, the need for gathering data from many sources, and the requirement that scientists, whatever their field, make no conclusions before all the data have been collected. For example, in Kathryn Lasky's *Dinosaur Dig,* students follow several families as they are guided by paleontologist Keith Rigby on a dig in eastern Montana. Books such as Susan E. Goodman's *Stones, Bones, and Petroglyphs: Digging Into Southwest Archaeology* not only introduce the scientific method, but motivate students to take part in field trips. Goodman's text and

Michael J. Doolittle's photographs accompany a group of eighth graders as they go on a field trip to the Mesa Verde region in Colorado.

Informational books also encourage self-reliance. One enjoyable discovery can motivate children to make further investigations. Parents and educators need to provide books such as David Macaulay's *The Way Things Work* to pique children's interest and then help children explore their environment. A high school student who likes to read informational books emphasizes the satisfaction in following his curiosity into broader and deeper exploration:

I enjoy reading to answer my own curiosity. Fictional books don't have the information that I want. I am more interested in real things. When I was in first grade, astronomy was the first science that interested me; the more I read, the more I learned I didn't know. As I became older I read a lot of books about the stars, space exploration, and theories about the black hole. I discovered that reality is stranger and more exciting than any fiction could be. I could not take fiction and transfer it into the real world; factual books help me learn about the real world.

Informational books can encourage children to develop critical reading and thinking skills. While reading books written on one subject by different authors, children can compare the books to evaluate the objectivity of the authors and determine their qualifications to write about the subject. They can check the copyright dates to see if the information is current. Texts about dinosaurs provide opportunities for developing critical reading and thinking skills. Readers can compare the information presented in Funston's *The Dinosaur Question and Answer Book*, J. Lynett Gillette's *Dinosaur Ghosts: The Mysteries of Coelophysis*, Patricia Lauber's *Living with Dinosaurs*, Don Lessem's *Dinosaur Worlds*, Margery Facklam's *Tracking Dinosaurs in the Gobi* and Pat Relf's *A Dinosaur Named Sue: The Story of the Colossal Fossil: The World's Most Complete T. Rex.*

Of course, informational books encourage children to stretch their minds. Chet Raymo (1992), a professor of physics and a science author, stresses:

Creative science depends crucially upon habits of mind that are most readily acquired by children: curiosity; voracious observation; sensitivity to rules and variations within the rules; and fantasy. Children's books that instill these habits of mind sustain science. (p. 561)

When children read Robert McClung's *Lost Wild America: The Story of Our Extinct and Vanishing Wildlife*, Dorothy Hinshaw Patent's *The Whooping Crane: A Comeback Story*, or Michelle Koch's *World Water Watch*, they may discover the perilous balance between animals, the environment, and humans and begin to think of ways in which their generation can conserve animals, plants, and other natural resources. Informational books also inform children about values, beliefs, lifestyles, and behaviors different from their own.

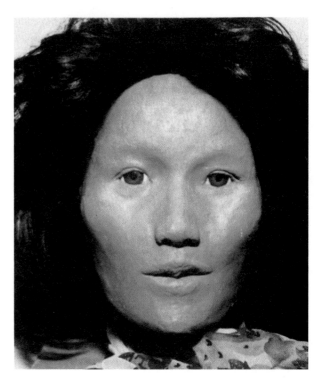

Children discover the importance of careful observation and research in Donna M. Jackson's The Bone Detectives: How Forensic Anthropologists Solve Crimes and Uncover Mysteries of the Dead. *(From* The Bone Detectives: How Forensic Anthropologists Solve Crimes and Uncover Mysteries of the Dead *by Donna M. Jackson, photographs by Charlie Fellenbaum, copyright © 1996. Photo courtesy of the Missouri State Highway Patrol.)*

Many well-written informational books expand children's vocabularies by introducing new words, including technical terms. Meanings of technical terms are often enriched through photographs or detailed illustrations. For example, in *The Life and Times of the Apple*, Charles Micucci develops the concept of grafting by presenting a series of illustrations that show how a cleft graft joins a scion to a rootstock. Detailed, labeled illustrations show each step in the grafting process.

Remember that one of the greatest values in informational books is *enjoyment*. Children who make new discoveries, become involved in the scientific process, or read because of curiosity are also reading for enjoyment. Enjoyment is often the primary reason children read informational literature. In addition, books such as Sue Macy's *Winning Ways: A Photohistory of American Women in Sports* or Steve Jenkins's *The Top of the World: Climbing Mount Everest* may inspire the next generation of climbers and adventurers.

Evaluating Informational Books

Several science associations concerned with the education of elementary-school children provide valuable guidelines for selecting informational books for children.

Books about climbing may inspire readers to prepare themselves for a challenge. (Illustration from The Top of the World: Climbing Mount Everest *by Steve Jenkins. Copyright © 1999 by Steve Jenkins. Reprinted by permission of Houghton Mifflin Company. All rights reserved.)*

These guidelines are specifically tailored to science books but are equally valid for all types of informational books. The guidelines in the Evaluation Criteria Box on this page are taken from recommendations made by the National Science Teachers Association (1997) and the American Association for the Advancement of Science (Johnston, 1991).

In addition to these criteria, Raymo (1992) emphasizes that good science books should develop "an attitude toward the world—curious, skeptical, undogmatic, forward-looking" (p. 562). Raymo recommends books that convey an "extraordinary adventure story of how the information was obtained, why we understand it to be true, or how it might embellish the landscape of the mind" (p. 561).

Accuracy. *Does the author have the scientific qualifications to write a book on the particular subject?* Franklyn M. Branley, author of *Saturn: The Spectacular Planet* and over one hundred other scientific books, has a doctorate, is an astronomer emeritus, and is the former chairman of the American Museum-Hayden Planetarium. Sylvia A. Earle, the author of *Hello, Fish!: Visiting the Coral Reef,* is a marine biologist and was the National Geographic Society's explorer-in-residence for 1998 and 1999. Mark A. Norell and Lowell Dingus, authors of *A Nest of Dinosaurs: The Story of Oviraptor,* are both scientists with the American Museum of Natural History and have led expeditions in the Gobi Desert in search of dinosaur fossils. Many books, however, provide little or no helpful information by which to evaluate the qualifications of the author.

Are facts and theory clearly distinguished? Children should know if something is a fact or if it is a theory that has not been substantiated. For example, in *Changes in the Wind: Earth's Shifting Climate,* Margery and Howard Facklam examine the changing climate. The Facklams begin their exploration of the subject by discussing several theories, such as the possibility of another ice age or global warming. The Facklams carefully separate fact from theory and opinion. As you read the following excerpt, consider why the authors use such terms as *might, if, could,* and *guess:*

Green plants might even be tapped for energy someday through bioengineering. If a super species of high hydrogen-producing plant could be genetically engineered, it might add to our energy supplies. The EPA closes its report by admitting we can only guess at the results of global warming. (p. 40)

Are significant facts omitted? Authors should present enough significant facts to make the text accurate. Specialized books that give complete histories of certain animals are valuable because they help children understand the evolution of a species, as well as its characteristics and its needs, if any, for protection. To acquire a balanced viewpoint on some topics, readers may require a book with a different focus for comparison. For example, Sneed B. Collard's *Animal Dads* could be used to show that it is not only the mother who protects, feeds, and teaches the young. Texts that provide historical information should also provide enough facts for readers to understand the concepts. For example, in *Smoke and Ashes: The Story of the Holocaust,* Barbara Rogasky traces the roots of anti-Semitism before presenting the World War II experiences.

Are differing views on controversial subjects presented? Subjects such as ecology and nuclear energy are controversial. A biased author should identify that his or her personal point of view is not necessarily a universally held position. Even the classifications of animals may present differing views. In her book about the history of various animals, *Who Harnessed the Horse? The Story of Animal Domestication,* Margery Facklam identifies various viewpoints when she states: "Scientists are still arguing over the vicuna, which is the smallest of the llamoids and has the softest, most lustrous hair. Some say it is a wild animal. Others say it, too, was domesticated from the guanaco but was allowed to roam wild on purpose" (p. 102).

History texts should present both sides of controversial issues. For example, as you read books such as Leonard A. Stevens's *The Case of Roe v. Wade,* try to decide if or how the author provides both sides of a controversial issue. In this book, the author not only presents history, he also discusses current and possible future ramifications of the decision. Natalie Bober uses an interesting technique in *Countdown to Independence: A Revolution of Ideas in England and Her American Colonies: 1760–1776.* She provides alternating viewpoints and actions. Reproductions of documents and portraits add to the depiction of differing views.

Is the information presented without relying on anthropomorphism? While it is perfectly acceptable for authors of fantasy to write about animals that think, talk, act, and dress like people, authors of informational books should not ascribe human thoughts, motives, or emotions to animals or to plants and other inanimate things (a practice called *anthropomorphism*). Writers of animal information books should describe the animals in terms that can be substantiated through careful observation. For example, in *The Snake Scientist,* Sy Montgomery describes information discovered about snakes at the Narcisse Wildlife Area in Manitoba, Canada. Notice in the following quote how the author relies on observations to answer questions about snakes:

Bob felt sure the males were searching for some clue to tell them which snake was the female. Bob checked off the information the snake could glean from its senses. Could the male snakes see which one was female? No—from the top and sides, males and females look similar (though the females are usually bigger). Could they tell by their sense of touch? That was unlikely, too. Males and females feel alike when you touch them: smoother than satin, softer than silk. How about hearing? Snakes can't talk to one another, and if they could, they couldn't hear what the others were saying—they don't have ears. Most researchers believe that snakes don't have the sense of taste as we know it, either. So that left only the sense of smell—a sense that is highly developed in snakes. (pp. 26–27)

Is the information as up to date as possible? Because knowledge in some areas is changing rapidly, copyright dates are very important for certain types of informational books. For example, the copyright date is very important in books about technology, such as Gloria Skurzynski's *Almost the Real Thing: Simulation in Your High-Tech World* and *Get the Message: Telecommunications in Your High-Tech World.* What was considered high technology in the 1970s, 1980s, and the 1990s may not be high technology in the 2000s. Likewise, books such as Bernard Wolf's *HIV Positive* require the latest information.

Attitudes and values also change. Comparing older factual books with more recent ones is one way to illustrate how attitudes and biases change. No educator or publisher today would condone the untrue and highly offensive descriptions of Native Americans presented in *Carpenter's Geographical Reader, North America* published by Frank G. Carpenter in 1898. For example, the following is Carpenter's depiction of the historical background of Native Americans:

The savage Indians were in former times dangerous and cruel foes. They took delight in killing women and children. They hid behind rocks and bushes to fight. . . . They used tomahawks to brain their victims, and delighted in torturing their captives and in burning them at the stake. (p. 293)

Information about Australian native people is just as biased in Charles Redway Dryer's *Geography, Physical, Economic, and Regional,* published in 1911, while V. M. Hillyer's 1929 text, *A Child's Geography of the World,* says that the most curious animals in Africa are the people. Students of children's literature may not realize how outdated, misinformed, and biased informational books can be until they discover books such as these that influenced the thinking of school children early in the twentieth century.

Stereotypes. *Does the book violate basic principles against racism and sexism?* As the above examples make clear, informational books, like all books, should be without demeaning racist or sexist stereotypes.

Some contemporary books reflect stereotypes through inclusion or exclusion of certain types of people in certain professions. For example, are people of both sexes and various racial and ethnic groups shown in illustrations of science or science professions? The illustrations in Joanna Cole's *The Magic School Bus: On the Ocean Floor* show that both boys and girls are interested in scientific subjects. The illustrations in Jackson's *The Bone Detectives: How Forensic Anthropologists Solve Crimes and Uncover Mysteries of the Dead* show that both boys and girls are interested in the subject. In addition, the text includes photographs of both male and female scientists. Informational books such as Nancy Loewen and Ann Bancroft's *Four to the Pole!: The American Women's Expedition to Antarctica, 1992–93* shows that women can succeed in very dangerous endeavors and environments.

Illustrations. *Are the illustrations accurate?* Illustrations should be as accurate as the text and should add to its clarity. Photographs and drawings should be accompanied by explanatory legends keyed directly to the text to allow children to expand their understanding of the principles or terminology presented. Literary critic Barbara Elleman (1992) emphasizes the importance of illustrations when evaluating trends in nonfiction. She states, "When done well, today's visuals are directly connected to the text, are made up of either meticulous, accurately produced drawings or clear, full-color photographs, and have captions that extend the information" (p. 30). David Macaulay's detailed illustrations in *The Way Things Work* are labeled to clarify concepts. *The Incredible Journey of Lewis and Clark,* by Rhoda Blumberg, includes maps showing both the journey west and the return journey east. Key locations are numbered and keyed to dates and pages of discussion within the text. *Money, Money, Money: The Meaning of the Art and Symbols on United States Paper Currency* by Nancy Winslow Parker includes detailed, labeled illustrations showing the symbols on the front and back of United States currency from $1 to $100,000. Detailed illustrations also strengthen the reader's understanding in David Weitzman's *Old Ironsides: Americans Build a Fighting Ship.*

Analytical Thinking. *Do children have an opportunity to become involved in solving problems logically?* Many informational books, particularly scientific ones, should encourage children to observe, gather data, experiment, compare, and formulate hypotheses. Informational books should encourage children to withhold judgment until enough data have been gathered or enough facts have been explored. Books that demonstrate scientific facts and principles should encourage children to do more experiments on their own and should stress the value of additional background reading. For example, in *How to Be an Ocean Scientist in Your Own Home,* Seymour Simon develops a series of experiments that proceed from "Let's Find Out" to "Here's What You Will Need" to "Here's What to Do." In addition, Simon includes a bibliography of books about the topics.

Good science writing should also encourage children to become involved with their world. Science writer Patricia Lauber (1992) states that the best science books, like any other literature, "have a point of view. They involve readers by making them care—care about the people, the animals, a town, an idea, and most of all, care how it all comes out. In short, they inspire feeling" (p. 13). This point of view is important when Lauber describes her own aims in writing science books: "Overall, my aims are to help children understand how the earth (or its parts) works and to try to imbue them with some of my own sense of wonderment, in the hope that they will grow up to be good stewards, who will take care of the earth, not just use (or abuse) it" (p. 14). As children read some of Lauber's books, such as *Volcano: The Eruption and Healing of Mount St. Helens, Flood: Wrestling with the Mississippi,* and *Hurricanes: Earth's Mightiest Storms,* decide if Lauber is able to involve her readers by making them care about the earth.

Organization. *Is the organization logical?* Ideas in informational books should be broken down into easily understood component parts. Authors often use an organization that progresses from the simple to the more complex, or from the familiar to the unfamiliar, or from early to later development. In Stephen R. Swinburne's *Once a Wolf: How Wildlife Biologists Fought to Bring Back the Gray Wolf,* the organization progresses from early attitudes to more contemporary ones. The author begins with a history of hatred toward wolves and their depiction as an enemy and a symbol of savagery that goes back as early as 5000 B.C. Swinburne brings the conflict to America by describing how ranchers massacred the animals. He then progresses to changing attitudes expressed by early conservationists and finally to the conservation movement that is bringing the gray wolf back to areas such as Yellowstone National Park.

Are organizational aids included? Reference aids such as a table of contents, an index, a glossary, a bibliography, and a list of suggested readings can encourage children to use organized reference skills. While very young children do not need all of these aids, older children find them helpful. For example, in *Commodore Perry in the Land of the Shogun,* Rhoda Blumberg includes a table of contents, notes, information about the illustrations, a bibliography, an index, and five appendices of additional information about the time period. Blumberg uses a similar approach in *What's the Deal? Jefferson, Napoleon, and the Louisiana Purchase.*

Style. *Is the writing style lively and not too difficult for children of a certain age to understand?* Kathryn Lasky's *Sugaring Time* is an excellent example of both stimulating literary style and careful documentation. For example, Lasky describes corn snow, large and granular snow crystals, as follows: "When Jonathan skis it sounds as if he is skimming across the thick frosting of a wedding cake" (p. 7). The maple sap "runs like streams of Christmas tinsel" (p. 19). The environment in the sugarhouse is "like sitting in a maple cloud surrounded by the muffled roar of the fire and the bubbling tumble of boiling sap" (p. 34). The photographs reinforce the language, following the family during all aspects of collecting and processing maple syrup.

Comparisons can help clarify complex ideas or startling facts. For example, in *Shadows of the Night: The Hidden World of the Little Brown Bat,* Barbara Bash compares the weight of a young bat with the weight of a pencil and provides diagrams that compare the structures of human hands and the wings of a bat.

Children's publisher and author of nonfiction James Cross Giblin (1992) emphasizes the importance of style when writing nonfiction and also presents some of the similarities and differences between writing nonfiction and fiction:

A nonfiction author is telling a story the same as any other author. The only difference is that it's a true story. So there's nothing wrong with using fictional techniques of scene setting and atmosphere building to make factual materials more interesting and involving for the reader. . . . A cautionary note: fictional techniques should never be confused by authors, editors, or

An In-Depth Analysis of an Informational Book

Life: Our Century in Pictures for Young People, edited by Richard B. Stolley, has been identified by *Publishers Weekly* as one of the best books published in 2000. Let us consider why the book might be so designated and how the book meets the evaluation criteria for informational books.

First, the book is a large glossy text that uses labeled photographs that have appeared in *Life* magazine. This format is one that is very appealing to readers of all ages.

Second, the book follows a format that aids understanding and helps readers clarify the major occurrences that happened in each of nine important time periods of the last century. The text uses a chronological order beginning in 1900 and progressing to 1999. Within each time period the text follows a similar format: An introduction by a children's author, numerous labeled photographs, a turning point incident, and a requiem. For example, the "1900–1913: Across the Threshold" section begins with an essay by Katherine Paterson titled "The Dawn of the American Century"; includes 13 pages of descriptive text with labeled photographs such as Teddy Roosevelt and his family, the receiving of the first Morse code message by Marconi, and the first flight of Orville Wright; features the turning point incident of the sinking of the *Titanic;* and concludes with a requiem section that includes labeled photographs and descriptions of Harriet Tubman, Geronimo, Florence Nightingale, Susan B. Anthony, and Mark Twain.

Third, the text continues in chronological order with the same inner format through the following historical periods: "1914–1919: The War to End All Wars," "1920–1929: All That Glitters," "1930–1939: Empty Pockets," "1940–1945: World on Fire," "1946–1963: Spreading the Wealth," "1976–1992: A Global Burst of Freedom," and "1993–1999: Our Future.Com."

Fourth, the writing styles of the various children's authors provide a lively introduction to the period and also challenge and stimulate readers' interests. For example, notice how Gary Paulsen stimulates interest and even debate in his essay "Liberty for All" that introduces the 1976–1992 time period. "It can of course be argued that there have been many outbursts of liberty in our history. Certainly America's declaration in 1776 that it would be independent from England. . . . And yet . . . there was something about the period between 1976 and 1992 that sets it apart, or perhaps more accurately, several things that make it a unique time in history. When viewed from a whole world perspective, this was the most volatile period since World War II" (p. 186). Paulsen then presents his reasons for his belief. These various essays lend themselves to discussions and additional research.

Fifth, the author of an informational book should have the expertise to write about the subject. Richard B. Stolley, the editor of the book, is also senior editorial adviser of Time Inc. Previously, he was a staff member for *Life* magazine for nineteen years. His expertise is visible in the editing of the book. In addition, the text includes helpful aids such as an index and a listing of photographic and illustration credits.

Finally, the text should be a useful companion to historical fiction units, biographical studies, and historical investigations. The text is extremely useful for authenticating literature that is written from one of the historical perspectives developed in the book.

book selectors with a distortion of the facts. Anthropomorphizing animals in natural history should be avoided at all costs, and invented dialogue should never be put into the mouths of the figures in biographies; anachronisms and inaccuracies of any type do not belong in nonfiction books. (p. 20)

Authors of credible informational books meet many of these guidelines. Consider in the following sections how authors develop credible books that may stimulate and inform readers.

History and Culture

Informational books about history and culture include books about ancient civilizations as well as more recent ones. The illustrations and photographs in many of the books help children visualize the past.

The Ancient World. Books on archaeology help readers understand the magnitude of history and develop an awareness of how archaeologists help uncover the past. In Kate Duke's *Archaeologists Dig for Clues,* a highly illustrated book for younger readers, an archaeologist explains the science of archaeology to three children who accompany her on a dig. Lively dialogue, realistic questions, and descriptions of the Archaic Era of six thousand years ago are discussed through such findings as stone knives. Sidebars add information about the content. In *Stone Age Farmers Beside the Sea: Scotland's Prehistoric Village of Skara Brae,* Caroline Arnold focuses on the work of archaeologists to uncover and preserve a prehistoric village inhabited from 3100 to 2500 B.C. Colored photographs, maps, and diagrams add to an understanding of the time period.

The discovery of an ancient world even older than described in these previous books is explored in Patricia Lauber's *Painters of the Caves.* Lauber begins with the discovery of Chauvet in southeastern France, a cave that holds paintings of Stone Age animals that lived about thirty-two thousand years ago. Lauber accompanies her descriptions of the Ice Age and Stone Age artists with labeled photographs showing the paintings discovered in the caves. The author includes a map of Europe that shows the locations of the caves, a discussion about how

Photographs from Life magazine provide a vivid history. (Cover from Our Century in Pictures for Young People, edited by Richard B. Stolley. Copyright © 2000 by Little, Brown and Company. Reprinted by permission of the publisher.)

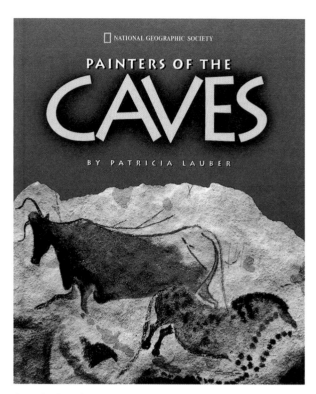

Animals of the Stone Age are brought to life through photographs of cave paintings. (From Painters of the Caves by Patricia Lauber. Copyright © 1998 by Patricia Lauber. Published by National Geographic Society. Reprinted by permission.)

scientists date ancient artifacts, a bibliography of related reading, and an index.

John S. Major's *The Silk Route: 7,000 Miles of History* follows the silk route from Chang'an, China, to Byzantium during the Tang Dynasty (A.D. 618–906). A map introduces the text. The remainder of the text and the illustrations focus on the major cities, geography, and obstacles along the route. Stephen Fieser's large, colored illustrations show people, culture, and settings. The book concludes with a section called "A Closer Look" in which the author provides additional background information on topics such as caravan life, invasion routes of inner Asia, and the religions of Central Asia.

Authors who write about the ancient world may develop credible books by citing the latest information gained from their own research or from that of others and by describing details so that readers can visualize an ancient world. Because readers cannot verify facts about the ancient world through their own experiences, authors may include drawings that clarify information or may use photographs of museum objects or archaeological sites.

Ancient Mayan and Aztec civilizations in Central America are the subjects of several books. Carolyn Meyer and Charles Gallenkamp create a hint of mystery and excitement in their introduction to *The Mystery of the Ancient Maya.* Consider the vivid setting, the motivation of

the two explorers, and the sense of discovery and anticipation in the following:

Two travelers—one American, one English—struggled through the jungle, hacking away the tangled vines with their machetes. New York City, which they had left that fall of 1839, seemed impossibly far away. Since their arrival in Central America the trip had been grueling. In the past few weeks they had endured hunger and had been thrown into a makeshift prison. They had hung on as their mules picked their way along the edges of cliffs. But now, standing on a river bank in Honduras, they felt hopeful again. On the opposite shore they could make out a stone wall, perhaps a hundred feet high but nearly hidden by the thick growth of trees. Maybe this was what they had been searching for—the lost city of Copan. (p. 3)

The book proceeds from a history of the early explorers, to revelations about the Mayan civilization, to disclosures about the Mayan people, and to the unanswered questions that are under investigation. Drawings, photographs, and excerpts from early journals add to the sense of time and place.

Archaeological investigations in Europe provide the sources for information in Susan Woodford's *The Parthenon.* Woodford's book, part of the Cambridge History Library, presents a detailed account of the building of the Greek Parthenon. This book follows a chronological order beginning in 490 B.C. and extending through current problems caused by air pollution. Use the labeled drawings, captioned photographs, and detailed descriptions of ancient Greek life and religious practices to expand a study of Greek culture and Greek mythology.

Shelley Tanaka's *Secrets of the Mummies* covers subjects related to creation of the mummies and building of elaborate tombs. In a section titled "Treasures of the Afterlife," Tanaka focuses on the work of Howard Carter and his discovery of Tutankhamen's tomb in the Valley of the Kings. Photographs and illustrations add understanding to both the historical times and the process of creating mummies.

One of the most baffling secrets associated with early Egypt was the hieroglyphics, a form of sacred writing that was used by ancient Egyptians. Carol Donoughue's *The Mystery of the Hieroglyphs: The Story of the Rosetta Stone and the Race to Decipher Egyptian Hieroglyphs* details the scholarship that went into breaking the early sacred secrets. The author creates both a sense of the importance of the discovery and the excitement associated with the finding. The author concludes the text with a list of twenty-five hieroglyphs and encourages readers to use them to write their names.

Readers who enjoy traditional literature and historical fiction set in medieval times and adults who would like to help children re-create medieval festivals should find several books rewarding. David Macaulay's *Castle* and *Cathedral: The Story of Its Construction* include detailed drawings to clarify how castles and cathedrals are constructed. Macaulay provides details about how he wrote and illustrated his book in *Building the Book Cathedral*. Leonard Everett Fisher's *The Tower of London* uses gray illustrations to add a feeling of ominousness to the surroundings. These books should be helpful to librarians, teachers, and other adults who are interested in giving children a feeling for earlier times and cultures.

In a highly illustrated book for younger readers, Ruth Freeman Swain traces the history of sleeping customs, including mattresses. *Bedtime!* explores how different ages and cultures used mattresses, various types of beds, and hammocks. The text proceeds from early peoples through sleeping facilities in space.

Informational books may trace the history of important developments that have changed the world such as the printing of books or the changes in medicine. In *Breaking into Print: Before and After the Invention of the Printing Press*, Stephen Krensky uses several techniques that increase understanding and interest. For example, the text follows a chronological order from the days of early parchment and monks creating hand-lettered texts with knife-sharpened quills through the printing press and computerized typesetting. Sidebars provide additional information about the time period; wood engravings add the feeling of historical accuracy; and a time line of the history of printing proceeds from 3500 B.C. through the 1980s. In *Just What the Doctor Ordered: The History of American Medicine*, Brandon Marie Miller

begins with descriptions of early Native American ceremonies and herbal remedies and continues through more modern times such as the impact on medical developments that resulted from the Revolutionary War and Civil War.

The Story of Clocks and Calendars: Making a Millennium by Betsy Maestro traces the history of calendars and clocks from early cave dwellers through modern atomic clocks. Giulio Maestro's illustrations are especially effective for depicting important milestones in the development of ways to mark the passing of time.

A history of people reputed to possess unusual abilities is the focus of Kathleen Krull's *They Saw the Future: Oracles, Psychics, Scientists, Great Thinkers, and Pretty Good Guessers*. The author presents in chronological order the stories of twelve visionaries who predicted the future. The text begins with "The Oracle of Delphi" in ancient Greece beginning about 700 B.C., and concludes with "Jeane Dixon," an American psychic who lived from 1918 to 1997. Each presentation includes information about how they may have made their predictions as well as predictions that have proven to be true and those that have not.

History also includes religious traditions. Betsy Maestro develops an introduction to various beliefs in *The Story of Religion*. The author begins with a discussion of early polytheistic beliefs and continues into a discussion of other religions such as Taoism, Hinduism, Christianity, and Islam. Giulio Maestro's illustrations relate to the culture of the religion. In *The Passover Journey: A Seder Companion*, Barbara Goldin explains the traditions associated with Passover. Gail Gibbons's *Santa Who?* includes both a religious and a secular history of Santa Claus. This history proceeds from the Wise Men bringing gifts to the Christ child to Saint Nicholas to the Dutch Sinter Cleas, and finally to many of the customs associated with contemporary practices.

Archaeologist and anthropologist Brian M. Fagan's *The Great Journey: The Peopling of Ancient America* explores in text and photographs the early people who lived in North America. The text is divided into five parts: (1) ideas, (2) ancestry, (3) the crossing, (4) the first Americans, and (5) the great diversity. In addition to photographs, Fagan uses drawings and maps to clarify concepts.

Just as there are numerous biographies resulting from the circa 1492 studies, there are also many informational books that either trace the early explorations of the New World or depict the period. Books such as George DeLucenay Leon's *Explorers of the Americas Before Columbus* focus on early settlers and explorers. In addition to Native Americans, Leon examines the voyages of Eric the Red and Leif Ericsson and explores the discovery of Norse settlements. In a book written for older students, *The Discoverers of America*, Harold Faber includes not only information on the earliest explorers but also information on European politics that influenced the explorations. The book includes important dates related to the discoveries of America, notes on sources, a bibliography, and an index.

In *If You Were There in 1492,* Barbara Brenner presents facts about everyday life during the fifteenth century. Chapters include information about such subjects as food and clothing, education, arts and entertainment, and crime and punishment. John Dyson's *Westward with Columbus* presents a re-enactment of the 1492 expedition. The photographs are taken from the 1990 voyage in a replica of the *Nina.* Charlotte and David Yue's *Christopher Columbus: How He Did It* focuses on the knowledge and technology that enabled Columbus to complete his voyage.

Norman Finkelstein's *The Other Fourteen Ninety-Two: Jewish Settlement in the New World* details the history of the Jewish people who were expelled from Spain in 1492. There is information about the Spanish Inquisition, anti-Semitism during the period, and the movement of people and ideas as the Jewish people searched for a location in which to live. The final chapter chronicles the positive Jewish experience in the American colonies. The text includes a bibliography of books and articles and an index.

The World in 1492 by Jean Fritz et al. is an interesting history for readers who are searching for a broader view of the world in 1492. The book includes five chapters, each written by a well-known author (or authors) of children's literature. For example, Jean Fritz writes "Europe in 1492." Additional authors and chapters include Katherine Paterson's "Asia in 1492," Patricia and Fredrick McKissack's "Africa in 1492," Margaret Mahy's "Australia and Oceania in 1492," and Jamake Highwater's "The Americas in 1492." Each author includes information about the history, customs, beliefs, and accomplishments of the people. Reproductions of various artworks help readers gain a deeper understanding of the world.

The Modern World. The factual data in informational books about the modern world may be made credible by citing research, quoting authorities, quoting original sources, and providing detailed descriptions of the setting, circumstances, or situations. Photographs also often add authenticity.

You may discover the impact of photographs and illustrations by analyzing books on historical places written for younger students and comparing them with books written for older students. For example, Karla Kuskin's *Jerusalem, Shining Still* is a highly illustrated book that tells the history of Jerusalem as a storyteller might reveal the battles, the people, and the rebuilding. Illustrations, rather than photographs and drawings, and emphasis on sequence of actions and plot, rather than exact historical dates, present the impression of a story rather than a history. In *The Golden City: Jerusalem's 3,000 Years,* a book for older readers, Neil Waldman focuses on the history of this sacred city

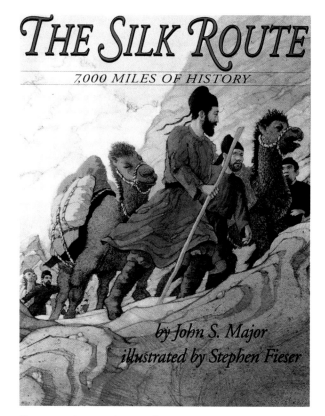

Illustrations focus on the route from Chang'an, China to Byzantium. (*From* The Silk Route: 7,000 Miles of History. *Text copyright © 1995 by John S. Major. Illustrations copyright © 1995 by Stephen Fieser. Used by permission of HarperCollins Publishers.*)

and includes information about the early conflicts. To add an additional feeling of historical change, Waldman's watercolor illustrations are labeled with both time and place. The author also includes Biblical text. Even though he includes the historic conflicts, he concludes his book on a positive note: "Just as in centuries past, thousands of people from faraway places come to visit Jerusalem each year. They are drawn by the splendor of the place, the magnificent domed mosques and the narrow alleyways, the delicate carvings and the massive ramparts, the ancient shrines and modern museums. But hidden beneath all these visible things is the mysterious feeling that, as you pass through the city gates, you are actually drifting back past the days of fabled knights and prophets, to the time when a young boy slew a giant with a slingshot" (unnumbered). In *Talking Walls,* a book for readers in the middle-elementary grades, Margy Burns Knight presents a history of some of the most famous walls in the world, including the Great Wall of China, the Vietnam Veterans Memorial, and the Berlin Wall.

The photographs included in Ruth Ashby's *Elizabethan England* provide an interesting introduction to sixteenth-century England. The author includes a cultural history that encourages readers to understand and to value the Golden

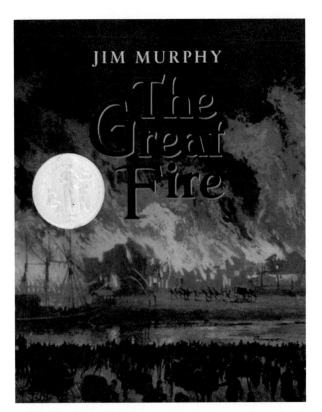

The Great Fire, by Jim Murphy, tells in story and pictures about the Chicago fire of 1871. (Dust jacket from THE GREAT FIRE by Jim Murphy. Copyright © 1995 by Jim Murphy. Reprinted by permission of Scholastic, Inc.)

Age of the Renaissance through poetry, Shakespearean theater, art, architecture, and music.

Jim Murphy's The Great Fire presents details associated with the Chicago fire of 1871. In addition to being selected a 1996 Newbery Honor award winner, the book received starred reviews in Booklist, Horn Book, and School Library Journal. Consequently, this book provides an excellent source for applying the evaluation criteria for information literature. For example, under accuracy of facts, students of children's literature will discover that Murphy provides a bibliography and sources for accounts that are presented in the book, and he uses carefully selected documents and personal accounts to provide the details associated with the fire. The author frequently distinguishes between fact and theory, or in this case facts and rumors. For example, when Murphy reports the common belief that the fire department had given up because they could do nothing, Murphy states, "That wasn't exactly accurate. Much of the fire department was still at work, even though they knew the fire was completely out of control. Engines and men had scattered as the fire advanced and were now operating on their own, essentially trying to save individual buildings here and there. Chief Marshall Williams, for instance, had jumped aboard a passing engine and was now at one of the remaining bridge crossings, hosing it down" (p. 67).

The author also separates facts from rumors in the concluding chapter, "Myth and Reality," in which he discusses questions such as "Did Mrs. O'Leary's cow cause the fire?" and "Was the drunken fire department to blame for the spread of the fire?"

The book is illustrated with reproductions of drawings that originated at the time of the event. Each drawing is labeled and includes its source and date of origin. For example, the drawing on page 44 shows fire ravaging the Crosby Opera House and identifies the source as Harper's Weekly, October 28, 1871.

In Blizzard! Murphy uses a similar approach to document the storm that paralyzed Northeastern United States.

The history of the early postal service is developed in Steven Kroll's Pony Express!. Kroll attracts the readers' attention by beginning the book with a help wanted ad:

Wanted.
YOUNG SKINNY WIRY FELLOWS
not over eighteen. Must be expert riders willing
to risk death daily. Orphans preferred. WAGES $25
perweek. Apply, Central Overland Express,
Alta Bldg., Montgomery St. (unnumbered)

Kroll then places the need for the pony express in its historical context by discussing the Gold Rush in California and the need to get mail from New York to California in less than the six months required for a ship to travel around Cape Horn. Kroll highlights the development of the overland routes including stagecoach travel and the impact of additional gold discoveries in Colorado and Nevada. The major part of the text then describes the pony express beginning with the first ride on April 3–April 13, 1860. Dan Andreasen's illustrations place the text into its historical context. The book concludes with an author's note that discusses the mail service through modern time. The text includes a map of the Pony Express Route, a Mini Photo Museum that traces the mail service from clipper ships to bar code sorters in a modern post office, a bibliography, and an index.

The influences of the Gold Rush on developing transportation and on human lives are found in Charlotte Foltz Jones's Yukon Gold: The Story of the Klondike Gold Rush in the late 1890s. The text includes maps, photographs, posters, a glossary, and a bibliography. Authors of various books about gold rushes may not agree about the human potential gained from the experience. Do you agree or disagree with Jones's conclusion about the Gold Rush?:

The men and women who rushed to the Klondike for gold were changed forever. They had achieved a goal they might never have attempted had they not been victims of gold fever. Almost everyone who survived was a better person for the experience. As the hardships faded in their memories, they realized they had endured conditions and accomplished a feat they would never have believed possible. Each man and woman had a new sense of his or her own incredible potential. (p. 88)

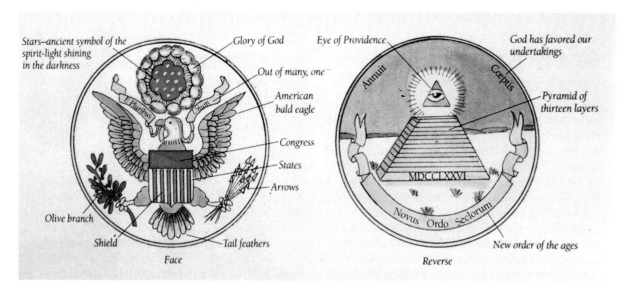

Detailed, labeled illustrations enhance understanding of currency. (From MONEY, MONEY, MONEY: The Meaning of the Art and Symbols on United States Paper Currency, *copyright © 1995 by Nancy Winslow Parker. HarperCollins Children's Books, a division of HarperCollins Publishers. Used by permission of HarperCollins Publishers.)*

You may compare Jones's text with Claire Rudolf Murphy and Jane G. Haigh's *Children of the Gold Rush.*

In Roxie Munro's almost wordless *The Inside-Outside Book of Washington, D.C.,* large, detailed illustrations provide a great deal of factual information. The only text provided in the book introduces each series of illustrations. Detailed illustrations include the Library of Congress, the Supreme Court of the United States, the National Air and Space Museum, the East Room of the White House, and the Senate Wing of the United States Capitol.

Nancy Winslow Parker's *Money, Money, Money: The Meaning of the Art and Symbols on United States Paper Currency* is both an informative text about the meaning of each of the figures or symbols on various paper currencies and a history that provides historical information about the people or symbols pictured on the bills. Parker introduces the subject with an enlarged fifty-dollar bill in which she identifies each of the symbols on the portrait. In the remainder of the book she provides information about the Secretary of the Treasury, the people whose portraits are on the bills, the seal of the United States, the White House, Independence Hall, engraving and printing, counterfeiters, the Federal Reserve System, and architectural capitals. To add clarity to the text, each of the illustrations are labeled.

The presidency and the White House provide interesting subjects for authors of informational books. Alice Provensen's *The Buck Stops Here: The Presidents of the United States* is a pictorial representation of the presidents and the major happenings during each time period. This heavily illustrated book contains excellent information for readers at all levels. The book also contains interesting background information for children reading stories set in various time periods. Younger children will enjoy Verla

Kay's *Iron Horses,* the race to construct the transcontinental railroad. Michael McCurdy's illustrations add a strong sense of history.

Many informational books about the modern world help children understand the varied peoples on the earth, including their struggles and achievements and their impact on history. Students may make interesting comparisons between books related to the writing of the Constitution and the people of that time. Jean Fritz's *Shh! We're Writing the Constitution* is for younger children. Fritz writes about the constitutional leaders in the lighter, often humorous style found in her biographies.

Milton Meltzer's *The American Revolutionaries: A History in Their Own Words, 1750–1800* is an excellent source for the original writings of the people who fought in the Revolutionary War or designed the Constitution. The text includes actual letters, diaries, journals, and speeches. In *Who Were the Founding Fathers? Two Hundred Years of Reinventing American History,* Steven H. Jaffe considers how various groups have interpreted the words of the founding fathers.

Peter W. and Cheryl Shaw Barnes use a lighter personified text to present details about the electoral process. In *Woodrow for President: A Tail of Voting, Campaigns and Elections,* they follow the life of a mouse as he grows up, registers to vote, runs for town council and later governor, and finally president.

Several current books explore the history of the United States at war. In *A Nation Torn: The Story of How the Civil War Began,* Delia Ray explores the causes of the Civil War. This book includes a map of the United States that designates free states and slave states, a glossary, a bibliography, and an index. In *The Long Road to Gettysburg,* Jim Murphy describes the events of the 1863 battle through the perspectives of two soldiers who took part in the battle. One is a nineteen-year-old Confederate soldier and the other is a seventeen-year-old Union soldier. You may compare the coverage of the events in Murphy's text with Mary Ann Fraser's *Vicksburg: The Battle That Won the Civil War.* Catherine Clinton's *Scholastic Encyclopedia of the Civil War* proceeds in chronological order from incidents that caused tensions before the war through 1865 and the consequences of the war.

Rhoda Blumberg presents three excellent histories of explorations in more modern times. *Commodore Perry in the Land of the Shogun* follows Commodore Perry as he opens Japan to world trade in the 1850s. The illustrations, which are reproductions of works of William Heine or Eliphalet Brown, Jr. (the official artists on Perry's expedition), add authenticity. *The Incredible Journey of Lewis and Clark* chronicles the 1803–1806 explorations of the Lewis and Clark expedition. Labeled maps and illustrations follow the quest for a water passage to the Pacific Ocean. Extensive notes, sources of illustrations, a bibliography, and an index add to the usefulness and scholarly feeling of the text. Blumberg's *What's the Deal? Jefferson, Napolean, and the Louisiana Purchase* presents the history behind the Louisiana Purchase of 1803. Maps, a time line, notes, and numerous illustrations add to the sense of history.

In 1845, Sir John Franklin, two ships, and the crews sailed the Arctic waters in search of the Northwest Passage. The ships and crews disappeared. In *Buried in Ice: The Mystery of a Lost Arctic Expedition,* Owen Beattie and John Geiger document the search for the missing ships. Photographs and drawings heighten the interest in the book.

Robert D. Ballard describes an even more recent exploration in *Exploring the Titanic.* Photographs from the 1912 *Titanic* are used extensively to show what the boat and interior rooms looked like before the "unsinkable" boat sank. Color photographs and text then document the finding of the *Titanic* in 1985 and subsequent exploration of the ship. A glossary of terms and a time line add to the text.

Highly emotional periods in history are difficult to present objectively. Seymour Rossel, however, approaches *The Holocaust* with a historian's detachment. He traces Adolf Hitler's rise to power; describes the harassment, internment, and extermination of many Jewish people; and discusses the Nuremberg trials of the Nazis. Rossel effectively quotes from original sources, such as diaries and letters, to allow readers to draw their own conclusions.

Barbara Rogasky's *Smoke and Ashes: The Story of the Holocaust* begins with the history of anti-Semitism and proceeds to the 1933–1945 experience. This text shows life in the camps and explores such questions as these: Why and how did it happen? Didn't anyone try to stop the Holocaust? Photographs add to the feeling of tragedy. Milton Meltzer's *Rescue: The Story of How Gentiles Saved Jews in the Holocaust* develops another side of the Holocaust and shows that many people risked their lives to help the Jewish people. Michael Leapman uses the experiences of eight children to depict the reality and cruelty of the Holocaust in *Witnesses to War: Eight True-Life Stories of Nazi Persecution.* In the introduction, Leapman provides information about the children as well as his purposes for writing the book. The text concludes with a listing of sources from which Leapman gained his information.

Ellen Levine's *Darkness over Denmark: The Danish Resistance and the Rescue of the Jews* is a comprehensive text that progresses from the invasion of Denmark in April 1940 through the liberation of Denmark in May 1945. The text includes source notes, a "Who's Who," a chronology, a bibliography, and an index.

Another interesting perspective on the history of Nazi Germany is developed in Susan D. Bachrach's *The Nazi Olympics: Berlin 1936.* The text based on an exhibit at the United States Holocaust Memorial includes numerous photographs taken during the time period. Readers will discover how a government can use a sporting event as a propaganda tool. This book could lead to interesting research and debates about political considerations that are identified in current Olympic games.

Through a photojournalism format, Stephen Ambrose surveys important incidents in *The Good Fight: How World War II Was Won.* Photographs and textual information cover topics from the D-Day invasion through the bombing of Hiroshima and Nagasaki. Ambrose uses quotes to reinforce experiences shown in the photographs.

Books that describe or depict nuclear war also vary depending on the intended audiences and the messages to be related. Compare the highly visual and personalized descriptions in Toshi Maruki's *Hiroshima No Pika (The Flash of Hiroshima)* with Carl B. Feldbaum and Ronald J. Bee's historical and scientific descriptions in *Looking the Tiger in the Eye: Confronting the Nuclear Threat.* Using a picture-storybook format, Maruki relates the experiences of seven-year-old Mii on August 6, 1945, as the child and her mother pass by fire, death, and destruction. Maruki, who actively campaigns for nuclear disarmament and world peace, concludes her book on a hopeful note: "It can't happen again if no one drops the bomb" (p. 43, unnumbered). Feldbaum and Bee's text includes the history of nuclear weapons and discusses decisions made by political, scientific, and military officials.

History is made up of people who immigrate to a new country, as developed in Dorothy and Thomas Hoobler's *The Jewish American Family Album.* According to the authors, about 2.5 million Jewish immigrants arrived in the United States between 1880 and 1924. This nonfictional book provides descriptions of families as they leave Europe, arrive in America, begin new lives, and become part of American life. Photographs and firsthand descriptions add to the authenticity of the book. It is interesting to compare these experiences with those described in historical fiction. Many of the

ISSUE Is There a Shortage of History Books for Children? Should Authors of History Books for Children Include Controversial Subjects?

Two writers of history informational books, Dorothy and Thomas Hoobler,[1] explore some of the issues associated with history books for children. They begin their article with the following concern:

> Studies show that children in the United States have little knowledge of history. . . . Certainly one of the most important reasons is that the subject is just not taught in the lower grades. This lack of knowledge has its effect on the reading students choose outside the classroom. Children who have no background in this area are unlikely to read it for recreation. . . . A look at the children's section of a bookstore will show little more than a few biographies, and many of these are about current sports figures and celebrities. (p. 37)

The Hooblers then suggest several additional reasons why few history books are written for children. For example, they argue that publishers are not interested in publishing children's books about periods before World War II. In addition, discussion of issues associated with conflicts in history may make the books controversial.

The Hooblers summarize their own experiences with the mixed reviews of *Vietnam: Why We Fought: An Illustrated History*. They state: "Unfortunately, we found that after almost 20 years, the controversy over the conflict is still very much alive. Our approach offended some people, although many publications praised our book" (p. 38).

After reading this article, discuss some of the following issues:

1. How pervasive is the lack of historical understanding in children in the elementary and middle grades? If there is a lack of understanding, how does this lack influence the history books read by children?
2. What should the publisher's role be in publishing and promoting books about history before World War II?
3. Should authors write controversial history books for children? Why or why not?

[1]Hoobler, Dorothy, and Thomas Hoobler. "Writing History for Children." *School Library Journal* 38 (January 1992): 37–38.

Jewish immigrants express desires for education and freedom. These desires mirror the conflicts, settings, and themes found in many historical fiction books written about this same time period. There are many excerpts from this book that may be used for comparisons and for authentication of historical fiction.

Detailed illustrations provide a strong sense of history in Andrew Langley's *Shakespeare's Theatre*. June Everett's paintings provide both historical views of Shakespeare's time and the modern reconstruction of the Globe Theatre. The illustrations for the book were selected from more than one hundred and fifty pictures drawn by Everett, who was the "Artist of Record" for the project.

Two books on history use both photographs of the times and writings by children's authors to present a history of the previous century. *Life: Our Century in Pictures for Young People*, edited by Richard B. Stolley, is a large glossy text that includes labeled photographs that have appeared in *Life* magazine. (See In-Depth Analysis on page 552.) *The Century That Was: Reflections on the Last One Hundred Years*, edited by James Cross Giblin, is a collection of essays written by authors of juvenile literature in which they reflect on various aspects of life in the twentieth century. For example, Russell Freedman discusses "Looking Back at Looking Forward: Predicting the Twentieth Century" in an essay that begins with predictions made by Jules Verne more than one hundred years ago. Eve Bunting writes about immigration, Albert Marrin explores World War I, and Milton Meltzer discusses politics from William McKinley through William Clinton. The text includes eleven essays, an introduction, a section of additional readings, and an index.

Nature

Effective informational books about nature encourage children to understand their own bodies, observe nature, explore the life cycles of animals, consider the impact of endangered species, experiment with plants, understand the balance of the smallest ecosystem, and explore the earth's geology. In order to create effective and credible books, authors must blend fact into narrative. The authors must gain these facts about animals from observation and research. Close-up photography is especially effective in clarifying information and stimulating interest. For example, photographs may illustrate what happens inside an egg or a nest or follow the life cycle of an animal or a plant. Labeled diagrams may clarify text descriptions. Maps may show natural habitats of animals, migration patterns of birds, or locations of earthquakes. If authors present new vocabulary or concepts, they should define the terms, illustrate them with diagrams or photographs, and proceed from known to unknown information. Clearly developed activities that encourage children to observe and experiment can make a book even more useful. A bibliography, an index, and a list of additional readings are helpful, too.

The Human Body. Informational books about the human body are especially interesting to readers who are curious about their own bodies and how they function. Books for children about the human body range from overviews to detailed discussions of one aspect of the body, such as the brain or the eyes. Some books also discuss body-related issues, such as the right to live or to die, genetic engineering, and human origins.

Three books on the human body illustrate the importance of labeled diagrams when studying anatomy.

Ruth and Bertel Bruun clarify their text, *The Human Body*, with diagrams and drawings that show the interiors of various body regions and the relationships of these regions to each other. Robie H. Harris's *It's So Amazing!: A Book About Eggs, Sperm, Birth, Babies, and Families* includes numerous labeled drawings. For example, Michael Emberley's drawings include detailed illustrations of the unborn child from a ball of cells through a nine-month fetus drawn in actual size. Joanna Cole's *How You Were Born* is a revision of her earlier book. Through text and illustrations, the author describes the process of conception and birth.

A series of books provides a history of various drugs and discusses their effects on the brain and the body, treatments for addicts, and ways to resist peer pressure. David Friedman's *Focus on Drugs and the Brain* discusses the brain and how drugs influence it. Friedman distinguishes differences between drugs used for medicine and drugs used for harmful purposes. These books emphasize specific drugs and provide clear warnings about their harmful influences: Catherine O'Neill's *Focus on Alcohol*, Robert Perry's *Focus on Nicotine and Caffeine*, Laurence Pringle's *Drinking: A Risky Business*, Jeffrey Shulman's *Focus on Cocaine and Crack*, and Paula Klevan Zeller's *Focus on Marijuana*.

Texts on the AIDS virus are available for both younger and older readers. Bernard Wolf's *HIV Positive* is a photoessay written for readers in the middle grades. He focuses on a mother with AIDS and her two young children. The author emphasizes the emotional and social impact of the illness. In another book written for older readers, *100 Questions and Answers About AIDS: A Guide for Young People*, Michael Thomas Ford uses a question-and-answer format to answer common questions about topics such as methods of transmission, diagnosis, treatment, and prevention. The text includes detailed diagrams on subjects related to the prevention of AIDS as well as interviews with AIDS patients and listings of support groups.

The world of forensics is explored in Donna M. Jackson's *The Bone Detectives: How Forensic Anthropologists Solve Crimes and Uncover Mysteries of the Dead*. The text discusses several cases in which forensic anthropology was used to solve crimes. The text includes labeled photographs. Several of the photographs clarify size by a measurement device. For example, one photograph is labeled, "Back at the police station, detectives organize and photograph evidence collected at the scene. A yardstick or ruler is usually included in such photographs to indicate scale" (p. 13). The text includes information on how sex, race, and age can be determined; how markings on bones can establish cause of death; and how a clay reconstructed face can help solve crimes.

Animals. Authors who write effectively about prehistoric animals or about modern-day reptiles and amphibians, birds, land invertebrates (earthworms), insects, and mammals must present their facts clearly, and they must not give their animals human qualities and emotions. Because books about animals are popular with many different age groups, authors must consider the readers' backgrounds when they develop new concepts.

Dinosaurs. With scientists as detectives and fossils as clues, twentieth-first-century children can experience the thrill of investigating the earth's prehuman past. Children who learn about dinosaurs in books, study about them in museums, search for fossilized footprints or bones, and make dinosaur models often become enthusiastic amateur paleontologists. Books depicting excavation sites, such as Caroline Arnold's *Dinosaur Mountain: Graveyard of the Past*, Margery Facklam's *Tracking Dinosaurs in the Gobi*, and Kathryn Lasky's *Dinosaur Dig*, present the work of paleontologists and show the careful work that has provided answers about dinosaurs. Books on dinosaurs range from highly illustrated texts for younger children, such as Russell Freedman's *Dinosaurs and Their Young* and Gail Gibbons's *Dinosaurs*, to texts for older children that provide extensive scientific details. Freedman's book explores the significance of a 1978 discovery that raised questions about how these animals raised their young. Drawings of both dinosaurs and excavation sites clarify the text. Nic Bishop's *Digging for Bird-Dinosaurs: An Expedition to Madagascar* follows the work of paleontologist Cathy Foster as she works in her laboratory and out on the dig. The author uses several techniques to create interest in the subject. For example, he introduces Foster's interest in the relationship between dinosaurs and birds by stating: "It's natural to wonder how they evolved. What did their ancestors look like? What events led to the evolution of flight?" (p. 4). Some of the greatest excitement occurs when the scientists begin to examine the bones brought back from Madagascar. The author details the scientific process used, the excitement when a sickle claw is found, and the evidence revealed through computer analysis. By reading this book, young scientists will discover the dedication and perseverance required to be a professional scientist.

The authors of books about ancient dinosaurs may develop their content through a question-and-answer approach. In *New Questions and Answers About Dinosaurs*, Seymour Simon asks and answers twenty-two questions about dinosaurs. These questions range from "What are dinosaurs?" to "Why did the dinosaurs become extinct?" and "What are some new discoveries about dinosaurs?" A helpful index includes a pronunciation guide.

The large illustrations and text in Patricia Lauber's *Living with Dinosaurs* take readers back into a time seventy-five million years ago when dinosaurs lived in prehistoric Montana. The book concludes with information about how fossils are formed and discovered. This book also includes an index and pronunciation guide. Lauber's *How Dinosaurs Came to Be* provides a highly interesting and factual account of the emergence of dinosaurs, explains how they evolved from the amphibians and reptiles, and discusses the appearance of mammals. Douglas Henderson's illustrations depict what dinosaurs might have looked like in their natural habitats.

J. Lynett Gillette focuses on one type of dinosaur in *Dinosaur Ghosts: The Mystery of Coelophysis*. The author attracts readers' attention by introducing the subject by showing the remains of three hundred dinosaurs who died very rapidly. The author explores various theories about their extinction.

William Mannetti's *Dinosaurs in Your Backyard* challenges some previous theories about dinosaurs and provides new interpretations suggesting that birds are feathered dinosaurs, dinosaurs may have been warm blooded, and some dinosaurs previously believed to be water inhabitants spent most of the time on land. Mannetti, however, implies that the theories he presents are accepted by all authorities, and he does not refer to opposing viewpoints or discuss how others have interpreted the same evidence.

Patricia Lauber makes comparisons and uses contrasts to clarify points in her *Dinosaurs Walked Here and Other Stories Fossils Tell*. For example, Lauber compares photographs of a 315-million-year-old amphibian and a bullfrog to highlight similarities. She also compares photographs of fossils of the oldest known bird and the skeleton of a barn owl. To illustrate contrasts among animals, Lauber compares photographs showing the teeth of a duckbill, which are meant to grind plants, and the teeth of a tyrannosaurus rex, which are suited for tearing flesh. In *The News About Dinosaurs*, Lauber presents past beliefs as well as newer information, which often refutes earlier beliefs.

Two books on dinosaurs cover expeditions in Mongolia. Brian Floca's *Dinosaurs at the Ends of the Earth: The Story of the Central Asian Expeditions* presents the story of the 1920s expeditions led by Dr. Roy Chapman Andrews that found the first fossilized eggs. This finding proved "that dinosaurs were not born, but hatched" (unnumbered). The author effectively develops both the excitement of and the requirements associated with being a paleontologist. In *A Nest of Dinosaurs; The Story of Oviraptor* authors Mark A. Norell and Lowell Dingus begin by describing the 1920 expeditions in Mongolia and then proceed to more recent expeditions such as one in 1993. The authors are respected scientists in their field. Norell is chairman of the American Museum of Natural History's Department of Paleontology and has led expeditions into the Gobi Desert. Dingus directed the American Museum of Natural History's fossil hall renovation and was head geologist for the Gobi Desert expeditions.

Pat Relf's *A Dinosaur Named Sue: The Story of the Colossal Fossil: The World's Most Complete T. Rex* traces the discovery and extraction of the fossil as well as the task of

Illustrations and text present old and new information about dinosaurs. (From The News About Dinosaurs *by Patricia Lauber, copyright © 1989 by Patricia Lauber. Reprinted by permission of Bradbury Press.)*

preparing and mounting it for display. The dinosaur fossil is now on display at the Field Museum in Chicago.

Insects, Spiders, Snakes, and Turtles. Books for younger children frequently present nature in familiar environments. Margery Facklam's *Creepy, Crawly Caterpillars* presents details about thirteen different types of caterpillars. There is a close-up of each of the caterpillars that provides information about its habitat. A band on the lower part of each double-page spread pictures the life cycle from eggs to caterpillar to cocoon to moth. The text includes a glossary of terms. Sandra Markle's *Creepy, Crawly Baby Bugs* provides color close-up photographs of various insects. Molly McLaughlin's *Dragonflies* follows the life cycle of these insects. Photographs of dragonflies resting on hands indicate sizes. Other photographs are magnified to reveal physical characteristics. Bianca Lavies's text and illustrations in *Backyard Hunter: The Praying Mantis* follow the life cycle of this interesting insect.

Books about butterflies provide both basic facts about and beautiful illustrations of butterflies. Kathryn Lasky's *Monarchs* takes readers through the life cycle of the monarch, discusses sites related to the monarch, and tells about people who are interested in the welfare of the monarch. Laurence Pringle's *An Extraordinary Life: The Story of a Monarch Butterfly* follows the often perilous route of the butterfly as it migrates from New England to Mexico. The illustrations and captions provide details about various aspects of the life cycle of the monarch. The text includes maps and diagrams that clarify information. There is also a list of further reading and an index. In *Butterfly House,* Eve Bunting develops a warm relationship between a girl and her grandfather as they build a house for a larva and then watch it turn into a butterfly. Bunting provides details about raising a butterfly including finding a larva, preparing the jar, building the butterfly house, feeding the butterfly, and releasing it back into nature.

Authors of informational books may entice children by presenting challenges or comparisons. Kathryn Lasky's *Interrupted Journey: Saving Endangered Sea Turtles* begins when a boy finds a nearly dead sea turtle and continues with the attempts by veterinarians to save the life of the endangered turtle. Christopher Knight's photographs and Lasky's text document various activities in different parts of the world designed to help save sea turtles.

Frank Staub's *Sea Turtles* stimulates reader involvement by asking readers to be word detectives as they search for words in the text and try to identify meaning. A glossary is included to help readers verify the meanings. Labeled, color photographs also clarify the meanings. Another way that the author clarifies meaning is by comparing characteristics of the turtles with known objects. For example, "Leatherbacks are the biggest reptiles alive today. They can grow as big as a bathtub" (p. 13). Brenda Z. Guiberson's *Into the Sea* follows the life cycle of a sea turtle. The author concludes the book with a discussion on ways people are trying to protect sea turtles.

Photographs and text in Sy Montgomery's *The Snake Scientist* describe the habitat of the red-sided garter snakes in Manitoba, Canada, as well as the work of scientists who study the snakes. Nic Bishop's photographs show the annual gathering of thousands of the snakes in the Narcisse National Management Area. Photographs show that people of all ages and both sexes are involved in the experiments.

Vivian French encourages reader involvement in *Growing Frogs* by providing directions for collecting frog eggs, placing them in a fish tank, watching the eggs hatch into tadpoles, and observing various stages as the tadpoles grow into frogs. Alison Bartlett's illustrations show each of these stages of growth. The book concludes with the need to return the frogs to the pond from which the eggs were collected.

Mammals. Sierra Club Book of Great Mammals is an introduction to the world of mammals. The heavily illustrated text begins with a general discussion about mammals and explores such topics as "What is a mammal?," "Three groups of mammals," "Mammal beginnings," "Where mammals live," and "Mammals in danger." The book then focuses on specific mammals, such as kangaroos, orangutans, bears, and whales. This book includes a glossary, a listing of classifications of mammals, and an index. *The Sierra Club Book of Small Mammals* is a companion book. This book provides an introduction to the world of such small mammals as monkeys, rabbits, and hyraxes.

Several books on animals are especially appropriate for young readers because the subjects are familiar. In *My Puppy Is Born,* Joanna Cole presents the birth of miniature dachshund puppies. Jerome Wexler's photographs show the pregnant dog going into her box, the emergence of the first puppy, born inside a sac, and the mother tearing the sac and licking the puppy. The book follows the growth of the puppies during their first eight weeks, as they are unable to see or hear, as they nurse, and then as they open their eyes and take their first steps.

Illustrated books about familiar animals help younger children develop their observational and descriptive abilities. Such books include David McPhail's *Farm Morning,* which accompanies a young girl and her father as they take care of the barnyard animals; zoologist Dorothy Hinshaw Patent's *Appaloosa Horses;* and Tana Hoban's *A Children's Zoo.*

The life of an endangered species is developed in Stephen R. Swinburne's *Once a Wolf: How Wildlife Biologists Fought to Bring Back the Gray Wolf.* Notice how the author summarizes the various conflicts associated with the wolf: "The wolf had come almost full circle. From the centuries-long war against them to the early research by scientists such as Olson, Murie, and Leopold and finally to the twenty-five-year battle to bring them back, the wolves' destiny was once again to be shaped by humans. And yet this is a unique experiment. Would wolves adjust to a new environment? Would they turn north and walk back to their home in Canada? Would ranchers shoot them. No one knew" (p. 28).

Through text and acrylic illustrations, Jonathan London's *Baby Whale's Journey* presents the world of the sperm whales as the pods travel the seas. To increase reader interest for younger children, the author focuses on the experiences of a young whale. The author uses comparisons to help understanding. Notice in the following quote how the author compares the characteristics of a giant squid with known objects and also infers the dangerous battles between squids and sperm whales: "A giant squid has tentacles 60 feet long (18 meters) and can weigh 1 to 2 tons. It has eyes the size of basketballs and a huge parrot-like beak. The beak and suction cups of a giant squid leave scars on the sperm whales who battle them" (Afterword, unnumbered).

Wild mammals, their contributions, and their survival are topics common in informational books. Authors may describe the contributions of animals, argue for their protection by means of responsible population control, and use statistics to develop points on survival and to demonstrate their plight. In *Whales, Giants of the Deep,* Dorothy Hinshaw Patent concludes her discussion of whales with a history of whaling and the consequences of an unregulated industry. While Patent states the arguments against a moratorium on whaling presented by Japan, Norway, and the former USSR, she concludes with a strong statement in favor of the moratorium:

In Once a Wolf, *the author explores the relationship between man and wolf and describes the role scientists have played in preserving the species. (From* Once a Wolf: How Wildlife Biologists Fought to Bring Back the Gray Wolf *by Steven R. Swinburne. Photographs copyright © 1999 by Jim Brandenburg. Published by Houghton Mifflin Company. Reprinted by permission.)*

While the whaling nations argue that some whale species are not diminishing and will not become extinct even with continued whaling, conservationists believe that without a ban on commercial whaling, whales will disappear from the Earth. Unfortunately, all nations that kill whales do not belong to the IWC. So even if Norway, Japan, and the U.S.S.R. decide to abide by the IWC moratorium, some whaling may continue. We can only hope that it is not enough to further endanger these magnificent animals. (p. 82)

The history of the whaling industry is presented in Catherine Gourley's *Hunting Neptune's Giants: True Stories of American Whaling.* The materials in the book came from sources such as stories preserved in maritime libraries, letters, diaries, and ships' logs. Each chapter is introduced with quotes selected to entice the interest of the reader. For example, the chapter "The Loss of the Arctic Fleet" is introduced with these thoughts by Clara Wheldon: "Through all this month I have been very comfortable; though very cold, and the ship has been covered with ice; the fog congealed to the rigging, and every rope encased in an icy tube . . . The men have looked very solemn, having neither danced nor sung. They can have no fire, and it's a mystery to me how they keep from freezing" (p. 51). The book is illustrated with paintings, lithographs, and drawings from this early time period. There is a list of sources, further information, places to visit and call, and an index.

Other excellent books about wild animals and protection of species include Dorothy Hinshaw Patent's *Back to the Wild* and Nicholas and Theodore Nirgiotis's *No More Dodos: How Zoos Help Endangered Wildlife.* Bruce McMillan's *Going on a Whale Watch* is a highly illustrated text that uses both photographs of whales and illustrations to show the major physical features of several types

of whales. The book shows the happy experiences that are possible when children are allowed to observe whales in their natural environment.

Eric S. Grace's *Seals* is an excellent introduction to seals, sea lions, and walruses. The photographs and charts clarify the text. For example, one drawing illustrates the ancestry of the pinniped. Another two-page illustration shows the differences between true seals and eared seals. Maps show the range of the northern fur seals and the routes of harp seal migration. The color photographs add even more information.

Depending upon their purposes and points of view, authors approach monkeys, apes, and chimpanzees quite differently. For example, Jane Goodall's *The Chimpanzee Family Book* explores chimpanzees in their natural habitat in the Gombe Natural Park, Tanzania. In this text, the natural environment seems to be the only appropriate one. The settings for Paul Hermann Burgel and Manfred Hartwig's *Gorillas* vary from the freedom of the Virunga Park in central Africa to the confines of zoos. The full-color photographs allow readers to glimpse the habitat of this endangered species. The differences between the photographs taken in the natural environment and in a zoo should generate interesting discussions about the future of this mammal.

Another animal that is often hunted is described in Ted and Betsy Lewin's *Gorilla Walk.* The authors introduce the relationship between mountain gorillas and humans as being tragic for animals. The text then describes an expedition to the native habitat in southern Uganda. Maps, a gorilla fact sheet, and an index add to the text.

Birds. The topics of informational books about birds range from common barnyard fowl to exotic tropical birds. In these books, the authors use various techniques to create interest for young children and to present new concepts to older children. The introduction to *The Emperor's Egg* by Martin Jenkins begins with a male Emperor penguin taking care of the egg laid by his mate. Notice in the following quote how the style of writing interests the reader by providing questions and statements: "Can you imagine it? Standing around in the freezing cold with an egg on your feet for two whole months" (unnumbered).

In *My Seasons with Penguins: An Antarctic Journal,* Sophie Webb uses journal entries and illustrations to cover her two-month expedition to study Adélie penguins. The author includes a glossary of technical vocabulary and the questions studied by the scientists. This approach helps readers understand the scientific method that is essential for animal study.

In *A First Look at Bird Nests,* a book written for young readers, Millicent Selsam and Joyce Hunt describe the nests of common American birds and tell how the nests are built. Selsam and Hunt stimulate observation by asking questions and providing puzzles. The answers to the questions are

The photographs follow a day in the life of Jane Goodall, the British naturalist. (From The Chimpanzee Family Book by Jane Goodall, copyright © 1989 by the Jane Goodall Institute for Wildlife Research, Education and Conservation. Photos copyright © 1989 by Michael Neugebauer. Reprinted by permission of Picture Book Studio.)

located in the accompanying illustrations. In *About Birds: A Guide for Children,* Cathryn Sill uses large illustrations and minimal text to appeal to young children. The author's afterword provides additional information about each illustration. In *Spoonbill Swamp,* Brenda Z. Guiberson focuses on one day in the lives of two animals that live in the swamp: spoonbills and alligators. The text and illustrations proceed back and forth between the lives of the two swamp creatures. Young readers will understand that both creatures live in the swamp and are dependent upon the swamp for survival. An endnote by Guiberson provides information about dangers to the animals and their environment.

In a book for younger readers, Barbara Juster Esbensen focuses on specific birds and their habitats. In *Tiger with Wings: The Great Horned Owl,* Esbensen and Mary Barrett Brown present insights into the life and habitat of horned owls. A combination of illustration and text allows vivid comparisons. For example, Esbensen describes the horned owl as:

The great horned owl is such a fierce hunter that it is often compared to a tiger. Like the tiger, the great horned owl hunts in the dark, and it kills instantly. Its stripes let it blend with the forest patterns of dim light and shadow. Its two-inch feather tufts look like a tiger's ears, and it has a face like an angry cat. It is a tiger with wings—a tiger that can fly almost unseen through the darkness. (p. 2, unnumbered)

Brown's two-page illustration shows an owl flying through the woods as a transparent tiger follows behind.

Think Like an Eagle: At Work with a Wildlife Photographer, a book for older readers, depicts both animal behavior and the requirements to be a wildlife photographer. In this book, Kathryn Lasky uses many effective writing techniques to appeal to older readers. For example, Lasky introduces the book with a language style that encourages readers to visualize the setting and the life of the wildlife photographer:

He follows a silver thread of moonlight through the forest. The tangled shadows of bare-branched trees spread across the snowy ground. . . . Now Jack crosses a stream that feeds into the reservoir. The water slides like a black satin ribbon under snow bridges and curls around billowing white banks. . . . Jack is wrapped in the silence of the forest when suddenly from somewhere behind him, deep in the heart of the woods, comes the flat hooo hoooo of the great horned owl. Hooo hoooo. The call thrums through the forest. (p. 5)

Such vivid language is found throughout the text. Lasky also makes comparisons that readers understand, such as the following comparison of time spent watching animals with time spent watching television:

But the most important part of the blind is the rectangular window slot. This slot is Jack's window on the world. He has spent as much time peering through it as many people spend in front of a television. He can't switch the channel. He can't change the scene. He must wait for the real-life action to happen in front of this small rectangle. It does. (p. 8)

Later, Lasky contrasts hunting and photography. Finally, she encourages critical thinking by suggesting to readers that an animal photographer must become a student of animal behavior and think like the animal, whether the animal is an eagle, a great egret, a beaver, or a deer. This concept provides interesting discussions when readers consider, What would a photographer of _____ need to know about the animal's behavior?

Powerful flying birds and exotic water birds have interested a number of eminent researchers, writers, and photographers. Because the birds and their environments may be new to young readers, many books for young children present most of their information through photographs. For example, in Caroline Arnold's *Saving the Peregrine Falcon,* the large photographs alone are sufficient to show scientists raising the endangered birds in captivity, encouraging them to identify with falcons rather than with humans, and releasing them into the environment.

Authors of nonfiction informational books frequently focus on endangered species. Dorothy Hinshaw Patent's *The Whooping Crane: A Comeback Story* explores attempts to save this bird, which was almost extinct. Peter and Connie Roop's *Seasons of the Cranes* begins in the spring and follows whooping cranes as they mate in northern Canada, raise their young, and migrate to their winter home in Texas. The Roops provide a map to let young readers follow the flyway of the cranes. The Roops also use the familiar to help clarify the unfamiliar. For example, when they describe the crane eggs, they say, "The two eggs, twice as long as chicken eggs, lie side by side in the shallow bowl of bulrushes" (p. 6). In *Operation Siberian Crane: The Story Behind the International Effort to Save an Amazing Bird,* Judi Friedman examines efforts to save this endangered bird through the International Crane Foundation, established by two Americans in 1972.

Readers may observe and compare three quite different habitats for birds by reading books by Barbara Bash, Joanne Ryder, and Mary Barrett Brown. Bash's *Urban Roosts: Where Birds Nest in the City* uses illustrations and text to disclose how birds adjust in this harsh environment. The illustrations, which show birds nesting on street lights, in traffic lights, and on buildings, should encourage observation by children who live in cities. San Francisco gardens are the settings for Ryder's *Dancers in the Garden.* Ryder's lyrical text is accompanied by Judith Lopez's watercolors, which enhance the delicate nature of the hummingbird. Brown's *Wings Along the Waterway* provides a short descriptive chapter on each of twenty-one types of birds that live in the wetlands of America. Brown's numerous color illustrations detail the environments. These three books encourage readers to understand that birds live in many different locations. All of the locations and the birds that live in them, however, are influenced by people.

Plants. Informational books about plants should develop clear details in logical order, include diagrams and photographs that illustrate terminology, and encourage children to become involved in learning. In *Cotton,* by Millicent E. Selsam, a dime next to the first two leaves of a cotton seedling clarifies the size, close-up photographs effectively illustrate the stages in plant development, and labeled photographs and drawings clarify the terminology.

The natural world of plants and the environment are depicted by Thomas Locker. Locker's *Sky Tree: Seeing Science Through Art* follows the sequence of the seasons through paintings of the same tree. The book concludes with a section, "Connecting Art and Science in Sky Tree" in which the author asks questions such as, "This is the same tree in the same place. What makes this painting different?" (unnumbered). The author then discusses the painting.

Desert Giant: The World of the Saguaro Cactus, by Barbara Bash, is part of the "Tree Tales" series of Sierra Club Books. This book is written for young readers. It emphasizes that the cactus provides food and shelter for desert inhabitants. Large illustrations show the interior as well as the exterior of the cactus. Labeled drawings clarify flower fertilization and detail seed interiors.

Detailed, labeled photographs and illustrations enhance books on plants. In *Roses Red, Violets Blue: Why Flowers Have Colors,* Sylvia Johnson explores the reasons for the variety of colors of flowers. Labeled color photographs by Yuko Sato clarify the text. The text also describes how readers can conduct an experiment with anthocyanin pigments. Photographs show readers how to conduct each step in the experiment.

Katya Arnold and Sam Swope also relate history to plants in *Katya's Book of Mushrooms.* They discuss the history and origin of mushrooms as well as provide basic facts about the types of scientific labels. Although they promote the hunting of mushrooms, they also caution readers about the dangers of poisonous varieties.

Charles Micucci's *The Life and Times of the Apple* is another book that combines information about the plant and its history. Detailed, labeled drawings show a cross-section of an apple and illustrate such concepts as cross-fertilization of apples, grafting, parts of an apple flower, pollination, growth, and harvesting. The text then discusses uses for apples, leading apple-growing states and countries, and apple varieties. The author provides a time line to show the history of the apple from 2,500,000 B.C. through the 1600s. An illustrated map of the United States shows the impact of the apple on America, from the first grafting of domestic apples in Virginia in 1647, to the legend of Johnny Appleseed, to the Franciscan priests who planted orchards in New Mexico and other Spanish territories, and to pioneers who brought apples west in covered wagons. *The Life and Times of the Apple* provides lessons in geography and history as well as plant science. Micucci uses a similar approach in *The Life and Times of the Peanut.* Marjorie Priceman's *How to Make an Apple Pie and See the World* is another entertaining book that also presents information on food origins. Catherine Paladino's *One Good Apple: Growing Our Food for the Sake of the Earth* explores one of the issues related to growing food. Do pesticides and fertilizers have a destructive influence on the earth? The author focuses on the benefits of organic farming.

Geology and Geography. Geology and geography books encourage readers to develop insights into changes in the earth, to understand the consequences of natural and human-produced disasters, and to understand the importance of developing cultural awareness. Kathryn Lasky's *Surtsey: The Newest Place on Earth* provides glimpses of what earlier land creations might have been like. Christopher G. Knight's photographs depict the birth of this island in the North Atlantic south of Iceland. Lasky's text provides a literary connection, with quotations from Snorri Sturluson's *Prose Edda* to enrich the prose.

Changes in a region resulting from interactions with humans are the major focus for Steve Noon's illustrations in Anne Millard's *A Street Through Time: A 12,000-Year Walk Through History.* The text and illustrations highlight changing times as a riverside settlement first draws Stone Age hunters seeking water and then proceeds through modern times. The author suggests that readers "trace the

PATRICIA LAUBER

VOLCANO

The Eruption and Healing of Mount St. Helens

BRADBURY PRESS · NEW YORK

Color photographs show important sequences in the Mount St. Helens eruption. (From Volcano: The Eruption and Healing of Mount St. Helens *by Patricia Lauber, copyright © 1986. Reprinted by permission of Bradbury Press.)*

changing role of the river from age to age as the story of the street unfolds" (p. 3).

Because children often see the results of earthquakes and various other disasters on television, geology may be a subject that interests them, especially if they live in portions of the world that have earthquakes or have experienced other disasters. Seymour Simon's *Earthquakes* has vivid photographs that show the consequences of earthquakes in various parts of North America. Books about earthquakes provide interesting background information for children who also read Laurence Yep's novel *Dragonwings,* which describes the great San Francisco earthquake of 1906. The photographs in Terry Carr's *Spill! The Story of the Exxon Valdez* vividly illustrate the environmental consequences of the oil spill and show the possible magnitude of human-produced disasters.

Since the eruption of Mount St. Helens, several books emphasizing volcanic activity have appeared. Patricia Lauber's *Volcano: The Eruption and Healing of Mount St. Helens* is an excellent photographic essay of the eruption and of the changes since the eruption. Photographs showing minute changes in time are effective, as are photographs of specific settings taken before and after the eruption. Seymour Simon's *Volcanoes* is a source for studying volcanic eruptions in other parts of the world.

Storms and other natural disasters are popular subjects for informational books. In *Hurricanes: Earth's Mightiest Storms,* Patricia Lauber discusses the weather conditions that create the storms and technological developments that allow meteorologists to track the storms. Color photographs, maps, and lists of further readings help clarify the subject. In *Flood: Wrestling with the Mississippi,* Lauber presents the history of the river, highlights the 1927 and 1993 floods, and discusses ways that people have tried to control the river. Color photographs provide dramatic examples of various types of storms including hurricanes and tornadoes in Stephen Kramer's *Eye of the Storm: Chasing Storms with Warren Faidley.* In *Lightning,* Seymour Simon provides a vivid introduction to lightning through color photographs, statistics about lightning, and explanatory information. In *Storm on the Desert,* Carolyn Lesser focuses on storms in the Sonoran Desert in Arizona. Ted Rand's illustrations depict the drama of nature.

Weather reporters frequently discuss the influences of El Niño or La Niña on the weather patterns, especially excessive rain or drought. Patricia Seibert's *Discovering El Niño: How Fable and Fact Together Help Explain the Weather* traces the weather phenomenon from its influence on early fishermen in Peruvian villages to recent times. The text includes maps that illustrate weather patterns.

Humor provides strong interest in Joanna Cole's *The Magic School Bus: Inside the Earth* and *The Magic School Bus: On the Ocean Floor.* Dialogue between children is presented in cartoon-type bubbles, while information is presented in both conventional text and examples of reports written by a school class. Magic and learning occur when the teacher drives a bus full of children into the earth, where they learn about rocks and the structure of the earth. In the second book, the school bus and Miss Frizzle's class take a trip in which they make discoveries about the ocean and the animals and plants that live there. Librarians and teachers who work with children indicate that many children enjoy the various books in Cole's "The Magic School Bus" series and that after reading the books, the children are frequently stimulated to make additional discoveries about the subject matter.

Books on cultural geography frequently focus on such questions as, How did the people who live here get here? How did they decide where to settle and how to make a living? How have they influenced their environment (land and climate) and how has it affected them? A major focus of cultural geography is the fit between culture and environment. Two books by Jim Brandenburg present the natural history of various locations on the continent. In *Sand and Fog: Adventures in Southern Africa,* the text and photographs focus on the Namib desert in southwestern Africa. The author provides information on the desert, the contrasts, and the animal life. *An American Safari: Adventures on the North American Prairie* provides a photographic essay of the prairie lands that extend from Texas into Canada. Labeled photographs provide visual images of scenes such as prairie dogs, bison, and rattlesnakes. Brandenburg urges readers to pay attention to the fragile nature of the environment and to conserve the prairie ecology. He includes addresses for prairie preserves. Interactions among people and geography are developed in Rebecca L. Johnson's *Braving the Frozen Frontier: Women Working in Antarctica,* Will Steger and Jon Bowermaster's *Over the Top of the World: Explorer Will Steger's Trek Across the Arctic,* and Lawrie Raskin and Debora Pearson's *My Sahara Adventure: 52 Days by Camel.*

Large colored photographs present the geography and inhabitants of various types of wetlands in Molly Cone's *Squishy, Misty, Damp & Muddy: The In-Between World of Wetlands.* In addition to the characteristics of wetlands, Cone discusses the ecological purposes of wetlands as they purify dirty water by filtering pollutants. Cone concludes her book by pleading for the preservation of the wetlands.

The undersea world of the marine biologist is presented in Diane Swanson's *Safari Beneath the Sea: The Wonder World of the North Pacific Coast.* The large color photographs by the Royal British Columbia Museum present a beautiful world of creatures such as jellyfish, mud crabs, sea stars, and sea anemone. This book won the Orbis Pictus Award for Outstanding Nonfiction for Children. Consequently, students of children's literature might analyze the book to decide what features it has that make it an award-winning text.

Books on ecology and conservation frequently introduce the importance of and the beauty associated with the subject and then present a plea to readers to help solve the problem. In *Everglades,* Jean Craighead George introduces the subject through a Native American storyteller who is taking five children through the Everglades and telling them a story about the environment. George allows readers to ponder the changes in the Everglades as the children question the storyteller: "Where are the clouds of egrets?" and "Where are the quantities of alligators?" The storyteller now tells the children why the numbers have diminished. George ends the ecology tale on a hopeful note in which the children grow up, run the earth, and return the Everglades to its former glory. The children have learned their lesson as George concludes, " 'That's a much better story,' said the children. 'Now pole us home quickly so we can grow up' " (unnumbered).

Books on protecting the planet range from humorous approaches that use cartoonlike drawings, such as Laurie Krasny Brown and Marc Brown's *Dinosaurs to the Rescue! A Guide to Protecting Our Planet,* to environmental protection books for slightly older readers, such as Vicki McVey's *The Sierra Club Kid's Guide to Planet Care & Repair,* to in-depth analysis of the problems for older readers, such as Barry Commoner's *Making Peace with the Planet.* McVey, who has a Ph.D. in cultural geography, writes frequently on this topic. Her book includes games, projects, and practical ideas that her readers may use. Commoner, the director of the Center for the Biol-

ogy of Natural Systems, is a frequent writer on the science of survival.

Other books on the earth and the need for environmental changes highlight actual projects that have resulted in change. One example is Molly Cone's *Come Back, Salmon.* The text and photographs by Sidnee Wheelwright follow the actions of a group of students in Everett, Washington, who cleaned up a stream, stocked the stream with salmon, and watched carefully to see if their efforts to improve the fish habitat succeeded. When reading this book, many children become personally involved in the students' efforts and are ready to try a similar project in their own neighborhoods. Most children understand the underlying message of the book: We can and must make a difference if we want the planet to improve.

Discoveries and How Things Work

Some informational books answer children's questions about discoveries of the past and present or provide explanations of how machines work. Authors may clarify their texts through step-by-step directions, carefully labeled diagrams, photographs that illustrate concepts, and content that proceeds from the simple to the complex or from the known to the unknown.

Discoveries. Books about discoveries may describe the basic principles of past discoveries or the latest space or computer technology. Some books combine information about discoveries with experiments designed to help children understand and duplicate earlier experiments. One such book is Seymour Simon's *How to Be an Ocean Scientist in Your Own Home.* Simon first asks a question, such as How can you make fresh water from seawater? Next, he presents information in a "Let's Find Out" section. Then, he tells students "Here's What You Will Need" and provides detailed directions in "Here's What to Do."

Patrick Moore's series of beginning astronomy books designed for children in the lower elementary grades presents basic information about comets, planets, stars, and the moon. The text and illustrations are presented to clarify understandings for young readers or listeners. For example, in *Comets and Shooting Stars* the author introduces the subject "What makes a shooting star?" and the friction in meteors this way: "If you pump up a bicycle tire, you will find that the pump gets hot, because the air inside is being squashed; this sets up friction, and this causes heat. A meteor moving into the upper air sets up so much heat by friction against the air that it catches fire, and burns away" (p. 11). Photographs of a child pointing a flashlight at a ball held by another child show how the planets are illuminated by the sun in *The Planets.* In *The Stars,* illustrations compare the size of the sun with Vega and Spica and show diagrams of the Great Bear or Big Dipper. In *The Sun and Moon,* the illustrations show the various phases of an eclipse.

Informational books about space and space travel should reflect current knowledge. Copyright dates may, therefore, be a very important consideration when selecting these books. Franklyn M. Branley, former chairman of the Hayden Planetarium in New York City, emphasizes the expanding nature of knowledge about space in *Saturn: The Spectacular Planet* by pointing out that the *Pioneer* and *Voyager* space probes have provided more knowledge than had previously been gathered during the more than three hundred years since Galileo first saw the planet in a telescope.

Patricia Lauber's *Journey to the Planets* contains large black-and-white NASA photographs of Earth and the other planets. These photographs clarify an interesting discussion of the search for intelligent life on other planets and the constructions that may indicate intelligent life, even from millions of miles out in space. Seymour Simon has written several readable books that, through words and photographs, take young readers into the far reaches of space and explain comets and planets. Simon's *The Long View into Space, Saturn, Jupiter,* and *Galaxies* provide information in a simple and illuminating way. For example, in *The Long View into Space,* Simon explains why space distances between earth and the planets are not measured in miles by saying that to measure in miles would be like "trying to measure the distance between New York and London in inches" (p. 4, unnumbered).

Questions related to the universe are explored in Heather Couper and Nigel Henbest's *The Space Atlas: A Pictorial Atlas of Our Universe.* Compare the coverage of the planets in this text with that in Seymour Simon's *Jupiter* and *Saturn.* Couper and Henbest's book is a highly illustrated overview of the planets, moon, and other bodies of the solar system. The text also includes star maps. An index helps readers find information.

A humorous and very visual introduction to the solar system is provided in Joanna Cole's *The Magic School Bus: Lost in the Solar System.* The facts about the solar system are introduced when Ms. Frizzle and her class enter the magic school bus, find themselves in outer space, and explore the planets in the solar system. Information about the solar system also is provided in reports written by the students in the class. Many of these reports use a question-and-answer format, such as What is the solar system?, What makes night and day?, Why are spaceships launched with rockets?, What is gravity?, and Why is it so hot on Venus? This book includes a planet chart and a mobile of the solar system. As with the other books in "The Magic School Bus" series, you may use this book to suggest various projects.

How Things Work. Several informational books appeal to children's curiosity about how common home appliances and bigger machines actually work. These books usually contain detailed diagrams or photographs that accompany two or three pages of descriptive text about each item. While the readability and interest levels are usually considered upper-elementary and above, many younger children ask questions about how percolators, dishwashers, or Thermos bottles work. Therefore, parents may find these books helpful when answering the questions of young children. (One mother said that her six-year-old son's favorite book was one containing diagrams of machines at work.)

David Macaulay's *The Way Things Work* includes over three hundred pages of detailed diagrams of almost every conceivable instrument. The text is arranged in four sections, including "The Mechanics of Movement," "Harnessing the Elements," "Working with Waves," and "Electricity & Automation." The book includes a glossary of technical terms and an index. The humorous analogies used throughout the text appeal to many readers. Macaulay's *Building Big* is a highly illustrated book that includes drawings of bridges, domes, and skyscrapers. Ronnie Krauss's *Take a Look, It's in a Book: How Television Is Made at Reading Rainbow* follows the process of producing the children's television show.

What You Never Knew About Tubs, Toilets, and Showers by Patricia Lauber traces the history of these devices by beginning with the Stone Age and tracing development through various cultures. The book presents a fascinating way to look at history.

Chronological order is an important concept in many books that explain how things work. Byron Barton's *Airport,* an excellent picture book for young children, answers many questions about airports and airline travel, following passengers from arrival at the airport to boarding the plane. *Inside the Hindenburg: A Giant Cutaway Book,* written by Mireille Majoor and illustrated by Ken Marschall, includes both the history of and detailed drawings showing the interior of the famous zeppelin. The illustrations and the text follow a chronological order beginning with the maiden voyage on April 4, 1936, and concluding on May 6, 1937, with the tragic fire that killed thirty-five passengers and crew.

Hobbies, Crafts, and How-To Books

One of the main reasons that older elementary-school children give for reading is learning more about their hobbies and interests. Children told one educator who asked them how teachers could improve enjoyment of reading that teachers should ask them about their hobbies and help them find books about them. Informational books cover almost every hobby and craft. The more useful books contain clearly written directions, provide guidelines for choosing equipment or other materials, or give interesting background information.

Books on hobbies, crafts, and how-to-projects are important for expanding children's interests. Developing art appreciation is a goal found in several new information books. For example, a series of four books written by Colleen Carroll focuses on different subjects in art includ-

ISSUE   Who Should Write Science Information Books for Children?

This topic is debated in two journal articles in the *School Library Journal.* In May 1991, Marsha Broadway and Malia Howland[1] published results of their research in "Science Books for Young People: Who Writes Them?" These researchers analyzed the qualifications of authors of children's science books reviewed over a five-year period in the journal *Science Books and Films,* published by the American Association for the Advancement of Science. Broadway and Howland found that 43 percent of the authors had degrees in English, journalism, or the humanities, and 37 percent of the authors had degrees in science-related fields. Only 12 percent of the respondents had science-related primary occupations. In addition, 19 percent of the authors indicated that they selected topics on the basis of their own experience and expertise. After analyzing the results of the returned questionnaires, Broadway and Howland conclude:

The findings suggest an insufficient concern about the qualifications and authority of those who write science and technology books for children and adolescents. Perhaps too many publishers and authors may believe that writing ability and interest qualify authors to write science books for children, regardless of credentials in a particular subject. (p. 37)

These researchers then provide several guidelines that they believe should be used for the authors of science books:

1. Ideally, the authors of science books for children and adolescents would be experts in their fields.
2. Another useful step in increasing the quality of informational books is to help make those who work with young people—and the young people themselves—more aware of the authors writing informational books and their credentials.
3. Publishers should recruit authors who are knowledgeable about specific topics and who have appropriate credentials and experience. (p. 38)

In the October 1992 issue of *School Library Journal,*[2] nonfiction author Gloria Skurzynski, who is an experienced writer but not a scientist, challenges Broadway and Howland's conclusions. Skurzynski argues that experienced writers are better at creating science books than are scientists, because experienced writers, even though they are not experienced in that specific scientific field

know how to bring the subject to life. Whether they write fiction or nonfiction, they're storytellers. They've learned all the ways to hook young readers. In contrast, books written by experts tend to be bogged down in the very weight of their expertise. (p. 46)

Further, Skurzynski believes:

Since experienced writers are generally not sci-tech savants, they'll be curious about the same aspects of a subject as the audience. They'll want to know what readers want to know. Experts are so familiar with their own spheres of knowledge that they rarely have a clue as to what fascinates, or bewilders, general readers. (p. 46)

Skurzynski also defends a technique used by many writers of nonfictional works, blending fact and fiction within the book. She states:

I'm willing to sugarcoat hardcore information with every sweetener in the storyteller's bag of tricks, provided the coating doesn't obscure the facts. My job is twofold: to attract young readers to the book, and to make sure the information in it is absolutely correct. (p. 46)

After reading these two articles, debate the following issues:

1. Should there be any requirements about who writes children's informational books that have scientific content?
2. What should be the qualifications of writers of nonfictional books for children?
3. What role does fiction have in nonfictional books written for children?

---

[1]Broadway, Marsha D., and Malia Howland. "Science Books for Young People: Who Writes Them?" *School Library Journal* 37 (May 1991): 35–38.

[2]Skurzynski, Gloria. "Blended Books." *School Library Journal* 38 (October 1992): 46–47.

---

ing animals, people, elements, and weather. In each of the books, Carroll discusses the art in a way that stimulates the imagination and the senses. The books in this series include *How Artists See Animals: Mammal Fish Bird Reptile; How Artists See People: Boy Girl Man Woman; How Artists See the Elements: Earth Air Fire Water;* and *How Artists See the Weather: Sun Rain Wind Snow.* Joy Richardson's *Looking at Pictures: An Introduction to Art for Young People* uses art from the National Gallery in London to show children how they can observe and appreciate paintings. Lucy Micklethwait's *A Child's Book of Play in Art* encourages children not only to look at art but to create their own works of art. Peggy Thomson and Barbara Moore's *The Nine-Ton Cat: Behind the Scenes at an Art Museum* takes readers behind the scenes at the National Gallery in Washington, D.C. This book may increase interest in visiting a museum or even in exploring careers associated with art and museums.

Some how-to books provide directions and information to expand special interests. For example, Colleen Aagesen and Marcia Blumberg's *Shakespeare for Kids: His Life and Times* presents both an introduction to Shakespeare and Elizabethan England and detailed directions for constructing objects associated with the period such as pomander balls, a juggler's beanbag, and games. This book provides interesting background and activities that might accompany a study of historical fiction set during Shakespeare's time period.

Lisa Bany-Winters's *Show Time!: Music, Dance, and Drama Activities for Kids* includes ideas that could be adapted for various ages. The book is divided into eight chapters beginning with "The History of Musical Theater" and concluding with "Show Time." The text includes "Suggested Musicals for Young Actors" and "Summaries of Plays Mentioned in the Book."

Creative Arts. Clear, detailed drawings that illustrate the points made in the text are important in informational books. Jim Arnosky's *Drawing from Nature* not only provides directions for drawing water, landforms, plants, and animals but also stimulates interest in carefully observing nature and increases understanding of science concepts. The step-by-step pencil sketches illustrate techniques that let artists accurately interpret nature. A careful reading

Detailed verbal directions are found in The Elements of Pop-Up, *a how-to book. (Reprinted with the permission of Little Simon, an imprint of Simon & Schuster Children's Publishing Division from* The Elements of Pop-Up *by David A. Carter and James Diaz. Copyright © 1999 David A. Carter and James Diaz.)*

and viewing of this text may encourage children to answer Arnosky's invitation:

Drawing from nature is discovering the upside down scene through a water drop. It is noticing how much of a fox is tail. Drawing from nature is learning how a tree grows and a flower blooms. It is sketching in the mountains and breathing air bears breathe. . . . I invite you to sharpen your pencils, your eyesight, and your sense of wonder. Turn to a fresh leaf in your drawing pad and come outdoors. (foreword)

Detailed directions and illustrations are important in books that show how to make various objects. Joan Irvine's *How to Make Super Pop-Ups* includes explicit, step-by-step directions and drawings to help readers measure, fold, cut, draw, or connect various parts to each project. *The Elements of Pop-Up* by David A. Carter and James Diaz provides detailed verbal and visual directions for making three-dimensional pop-up books. Examples of each type of paper engineering encourage readers to try to create their own artwork.

Step-by-step instructions for eleven art projects designed to be completed by young children are found in Denis Roche's *Loo-Loo, Boo, and Art You Can Do.* In addition to directions for such art projects as making potato prints, the author provides helpful hints that make cleaning up easier.

How-to-books should have clear directions for projects that can be accomplished by readers. Diane Rhoades's *Garden Crafts for Kids: 50 Great Reasons to Get Your Hands Dirty* includes detailed step-by-step directions for various outdoor projects. For example, chapter four, "Starting Your Garden," includes a list of needed materials, instructions that are numbered in the appropriate sequence, photographs that show children completing the various tasks, lists of plants that are grown from seeds and those that are set from transplants, and tips to make the activity successful. The section concludes with an experiment in which readers can try planting according to a moon planting calendar.

Marion Dane Bauer, a Newbery Medal author, provides guidance for young writers in her *What's Your Story? A Young Person's Guide to Writing Fiction.* The content covers such important subjects as developing a story plan, choosing your best idea, developing strong characters, focusing your story, developing the plot, choosing a point of view, and polishing the story. Bauer relates many of the subjects to her own writing. This book also provides guidelines for readers to use when they are evaluating literature.

Rachel Isadora, a professional dancer, focuses on her daughter's training in *Lili at Ballet.* The illustrations and the text show various aspects of ballet classes. Captioned drawings clarify the text and provide practical information for readers who may themselves become future ballet professionals. For music lovers, Anne Gatti's *The Magic Flute* includes a CD of the opera that is coded to each page of the book.

Children who read frontier stories and survival stories may be interested in discovering more about the foods eaten by the characters. Barbara M. Walker's *The Little House Cookbook: Frontier Foods from Laura Ingalls Wilder's Classic Stories* presents frontier foods that Wilder wrote about in her "Little House" stories. Walker searched for authentic recipes by reading the writings of Wilder and her daughter Rose, pioneer diaries, and local recipe collections. Her hope in sharing this collection is that children will rediscover basic connections between the foods on the table and the grains in the field and the cows in the pasture, as well as between people in the past and today. Walker uses liberal excerpts from the "Little House" books and the original Garth Williams illustrations in discussing the foods and their preparation.

Many books encourage children to consider new hobbies or to learn more about existing ones.

Suggested Activities

 For more suggested activities for understanding nonfiction, visit our Companion Website at www.prenhall.com/norton.

- Select a well-known author who has written several biographies for older children, such as Milton Meltzer, and another biographer who has written several biographies for younger children, such as Jean Fritz. What techniques does each author use in order to write a biography that will appeal to a specific age group?

- Select a content area, such as science or social studies, that is taught in an elementary- or middle-school grade. From the curriculum, identify names of men and women who are discussed in that content area. Develop an annotated bibliography of literature on a subject, such as biology, to stimulate interest in the subject and provide additional information about the contributors.

- Select the work of an outstanding author of informational books for children, such as Millicent E. Selsam, Seymour Simon, or Laurence Pringle. Evaluate the books according to the criteria listed in this chapter. Share with the class the characteristics of the books that make them highly recommended.

- Following suggestions recommended by Bamford and Kristo (2000), locate examples of books that use on-site research, books that identify the author's research process, books that present the author's credentials, books that allow readers to detect author bias, and books in which authors speculate using limited information. With a peer group, evaluate the effectiveness of each category of book.

Teaching with Nonfictional Literature

Children often find biographies and other informational books more exciting than textbooks. The lively dialogues, the confrontations between people and ideas, and the joys and sorrows in many biographies are natural sources for creative dramatizations and discussions. Thus, you can use biographies to help children understand people of the past and present. With informational books, you also can help children acquire abilities related to the content areas, such as using the parts of a book, locating sources of information, understanding science vocabulary, reading for meaning, evaluating science literature, and applying learning to practical problems.

Unit Plan: Using Biographies in Creative Dramatizations

The biographies of significant people of the past and present are filled with lively dialogue, confrontations, and the joys connected with discovery. Consequently, biographies provide many opportunities for children to dramatize the momentous experiences in people's lives. Children can create "You Are There" dramas based on scenes of historical significance. They can also create imaginary conversations between two people from the past or present or from different time periods who had some common traits but were never able to communicate because of time or distance. The following ideas are only samples of the creative dramatizations that can result from using biographies in the classroom.

Jean Fritz's stories of Revolutionary War heroes, with their humorous and human portrayals, are excellent sources for dramatizations. For example, you can read *Where Was Patrick Henry on the 29th of May?* and ask children how Patrick Henry acted and how they would act if they were Patrick Henry. Then read the story a second time, letting the children dramatize it.

There is another way to approach this dramatization. After the children listen to or read the book, have them identify and discuss scenes that they would like to depict and then act out each one. Children have identified the following scenes as being of special interest in Patrick Henry's life:

1. Going fishing with a pole over his shoulder.
2. Going hunting for deer or opossum, with a rifle in his hands, accompanied by a dog at his heels.

3. Walking barefoot through the woods, and then lying down while listening to the rippling of a creek or the singing of birds and imitating their songs.
4. Listening to rain on the roof, his father's fox horn, and the music of flutes and fiddles.
5. Teaching himself to play the flute while he is recovering from a broken collarbone.
6. Listening to his Uncle Langloo Winston making speeches.
7. Waiting for the school day to end.
8. Playing practical jokes on his friends, including upsetting a canoe.
9. Trying to be a storekeeper without success.
10. Attempting to be a tobacco farmer.
11. Attending court and discovering that he likes to watch and listen to lawyers.
12. Beginning his law practice and not finding many clients.
13. Defending his first big case in court and winning.
14. Arguing against taxation without representation as a member of Virginia's House of Burgesses.
15. Delivering his "give me liberty or give me death" speech at St. John's Church.
16. Governing Virginia.
17. Hearing the news that the Continental army has defeated the English troops at Saratoga, New York.
18. Speaking against the enactment of the Constitution of the United States and for individual and states' rights after the war is over.
19. Retiring on his estate in western Virginia.

These scenes may also be developed into a sequence game that involves careful observation by all players, who must interpret what someone else is doing and, according to directions written on their cue cards, stand and perform the next action at the correct time. (Players must be able to read to do this activity.) Prepare cue cards for scenes from Patrick Henry's life. The first cue card would look approximately like this:

You begin the game.
Pretend that you are a young, barefoot Patrick Henry happily going fishing with a pole over your shoulder.
When you are finished, sit down in your seat.

The second card would read:

Cue: Someone pretends to be a young Patrick Henry going fishing with a pole over his shoulder.
You are a young Patrick Henry happily going hunting for deer or opossum, with a rifle in your hands and accompanied by a dog running at your heels.
When you are finished, sit down in your seat.

Place the rest of the scenes, written in a similar manner, on cards. It is helpful if the cue and the directions for the dramatization are written in different colors. Mix the cards and distribute them randomly. There should be at least one cue card for each player, but you may add more scenes if a whole class is taking part in the activity. If there are fewer players, you can reduce the number of scenes or give each player more than one cue card. Ask the children to pay close attention and wait for each player to complete the dramatization.

It is helpful if you have a master cue sheet with all of the cues in correct order so that you can help if someone misinterprets a scene, the children seem uncertain, or the group loses its direction. To involve as many children as possible, you may divide large groups into three small groups. Have each small group dramatize a set of identical cue cards independently. Let a child act as leader of each group and follow the master sheet.

Incidents in the lives of other Fritz heroes—described in *Why Don't You Get a Horse, Sam Adams?, The Great Little Madison, What's the Big Idea, Ben Franklin?,* and *Bully for You, Teddy Roosevelt!*—also make enjoyable dramas.

When appropriate, encourage children to pantomime scenes. Children can pantomime the actions of writers and storytellers as in *Jump at de Sun: The Story of Zora Neale Hurston,* by A. P. Porter, and the actions of singers as in *Beverly Sills,* by Bridget Paolucci.

Reader Response: Developing Hypothetical Interviews with Authors

One reader response activity that is recommended for biographies, autobiographies, and other nonfictional literature is to have students develop hypothetical question-and-answer interviews between students and authors (Reissman, 1996). Reissman describes how she encourages sixth and seventh graders to read published interviews; to critically read, write, and interact with the issues and questions in the interview; and to develop their own question-and-answer imagined interviews with authors. She also asks her students to research the autobiographies and biographies of their favorite authors and place quotations from the authors into the hypothetical question-and-answer interviews.

There are numerous sources for interviews that allow students to read, to discuss, and to respond to the format for published interviews. Students could begin with interviews with favorite authors of fictional or informational books that they are currently reading. For example, the following interviews use a question-and-answer format: Feldman's interview with J. K. Rowling, the author of the "Harry Potter" books (1999); Kathleen T. Isaacs's interview with Gloria Whelan, the National Book Award winner of *Homeless Bird* (2001); Leonard Marcus's interviews with Bruce Brooks,

Nicholasa Mohr, and Laurence Yep (2000); and Marc Aronson's interview with the Grolier Award winner, Michael Cart (2000). All of these interviews are published in *School Library Journal* and are readily available in most libraries.

Ask the students to read the interviews critically and to respond to the questions and answers found in the interviews. For example, they could respond to Gloria Whelan's answers about how she accomplished the research for *Homeless Bird* and her need to write daily. Quotes from Michael Cart (Aronson, 2000) such as "Nonfiction can educate the mind, fiction can educate the heart" (p. 56) foster numerous responses. After students have read and discussed these interviews, they should develop a list of effective questions that they would ask if they had the opportunity to conduct an interview.

Books such as *Popular Nonfiction Authors for Children: A Biographical and Thematic Guide* (Wyatt, Coggins, and Imber, 1998) provide numerous examples of authors of nonfictional literature as well as a two-page biographical sketch, a message from the biographical subject, and a selected bibliography of each author's works. These biographical sketches, messages to students, and lists of books could easily form the structure for the question-and-answer interviews. Another source for selecting potential interview characters is Sharron L. McElmeel's *100 Most Popular Children's Authors' Biographical Sketches and Bibliographies* (1999). A "Genre Index" identifies the authors with their type of writing. There is a listing for both biographies and nonfiction.

If desired, students can develop and conduct their interviews in pairs or in small groups. An interesting activity results if students prepare an interview that is similar to those found when political leaders or scientists come to college campuses. For example, the speaker usually makes a formal presentation that is followed by questions that are written on cards by the audience and asked by the moderator of the session. This type of activity involves many of the class members in researching to determine what the speaker might say, acting the part of the speaker, and interviewing the personage.

Imaginary Conversations Between People of Two Time Periods

Children enjoy contemplating what historic personalities might say to each other if they had the opportunity to meet. Because this is impossible except through imagination, children can be motivated to read biographies in order to enter into such conversations. For example, an exciting conversation could result if Theodore Roosevelt (Jean Fritz's *Bully for You, Teddy Roosevelt!*) met with a panel of loggers from the Northwest and with the administration in Washington, D.C., as the group tries to develop policies about logging and the endangering of the owl (use newspaper, journal, or television reports).

Other historical biographical characters might have stimulating conversations if they could meet with world figures of the 2000s. What views would emerge if Patrick Henry could share his opinions on states' rights and the rights of individuals with the current president of the United States? What would be Amelia Earhart's or the Wright Brothers' response to space travel and exploration? What questions would they ask of a contemporary astronaut? What role would they want if they could be involved in the space program? When children read in order to role-play a character's actions, express a character's feelings, or state dialogue that a character might express, they interact with the character on a human level and often read until they feel empathy with that character and the historic time period.

Comparing Attitudes and Checking Facts in Biographies

Elizabeth Robertson and Jo McGinnis (1985) recommend that students compare the tone and attitude of a biographer as reflected in a biography about a specific person with the tone and attitude expressed by the biographical subject in his or her own writing. Ann W. Moore (1985) recommends that reviewers check the accuracy of facts in juvenile biographies by referring to reputable adult titles and other reference books.

Biographies about Eleanor Roosevelt are excellent sources for comparisons in the classroom. There are numerous children's biographies, including one written by her son Elliott Roosevelt, reputable adult biographies, and autobiographies written by Eleanor Roosevelt herself. The following books are sources for such comparisons. Biographies for children include Russell Freedman's *Eleanor Roosevelt: A Life of Discovery,* Jane Goodsell's *Eleanor Roosevelt,* and Sharon Whitney's *Eleanor Roosevelt.* A biography for children written by Elliott Roosevelt is *Eleanor Roosevelt, with Love.* Barbara Cooney's *Eleanor* is an illustrated biography for younger readers. Biographies for adults include Joseph P. Lash's *Eleanor and Franklin* and *Eleanor: The Years Alone,* Elliott Roosevelt and James Brough's *An Untold Story: The Roosevelts of Hyde Park* and *Mother R: Eleanor Roosevelt's Untold Story,* and Lorena Hickok's *Eleanor Roosevelt: Reluctant First Lady.* Autobiographies include Eleanor Roosevelt's *The Autobiography of Eleanor Roosevelt, On My Own, This I Remember, This Is My Story, Tomorrow Is Now,* and *You Learn by Living.*

Other good subjects for comparisons include Christopher Columbus, Abraham Lincoln, Franklin D. Roosevelt, Martin Luther King, Jr., and Benjamin Franklin. All of these biographical subjects have been chosen by numerous authors.

Analyzing Literary Elements in Biographies

In addition to evaluating the accuracy of characterization in biographies by comparing the characterizations in

biographies written by different authors, have students analyze and evaluate plot, setting, and theme in biographies. For example, to analyze plot in biographies, have students identify the pattern of action, locate examples of specific types of conflict developed in a biography, analyze why the biographer emphasizes those types of conflict, consider why and how the conflicts relate to the biographer's purpose in writing, and locate examples of ways in which the biographer develops the readers' interest. To evaluate setting in biographies, have students identify the various settings, identify the ways in which the biographer informs readers about the important details related to the time period; analyze how much influence the setting has on the plot and characters; find specific locations mentioned in the biography and locate these places on a map, in geography texts, or in other nonfictional sources; evaluate the authenticity of settings by comparing the various nonfictional sources; check the accuracy of dates and happenings in other nonfictional sources; draw a setting as if it were a backdrop for a stage production; and evaluate whether or not there is enough information about setting to complete a drawing. To evaluate theme in biography, have the students find the primary, or main, theme in a biography and several secondary themes. Have the students consider how these themes are integrated into the biography, analyze whether or not the title of the biography reflects the theme, search for evidence of the biographical subject's ability to triumph over obstacles, identify and compare the themes developed in several biographies written about the same person, and compare the themes in biographies written for younger children and those written for young adults.

One of the activities used by Tobie Brandriss (1999) in a study of biographies is to search for common themes in the lives of the scientists. The following themes emerged: The scientists exhibited a total preoccupation with the problem; scientists were undaunted by lack of money because each found a way to obtain funds; they had confidence in their experimental abilities; they had conviction that there was a solution; they had an independence of mind; they believed in intuition; they understood the importance of observation; and women scientists emphasized the importance of their fathers in encouraging their studies. This activity would be equally interesting when investigating the lives of other biographical subjects such as artists or authors.

Incorporating Literature into the Science Curriculum

James Rutherford (1991), the chief education officer of the American Association for the Advancement of Science, argues that trade books rather than textbooks should be a primary source of science materials in the early grades. He states:

I would say that the elementary school classroom, in the earliest grades, should not have science textbooks. They are too ordered, too assertive by their nature, too given to explanations.... Furthermore, textbooks are rarely very relevant to the real neighborhoods where the children go to school.... Nevertheless, despite this ban on textbooks in the early grades, books should be an essential part of science learning. What that means is that once we rule out the conventional textbook, we have to think very carefully and more creatively about the role that books really should play. (p. 27)

When recommending the types of books that should be used in the early grades Rutherford states, "The kind I am recommending are those which are adventurous, in which the story is built around finding things out, and which emphasize the excitement of discovery" (p. 29). Rutherford concludes: "elementary classroom books should promote the legitimacy of imaginative thinking, just as much as they promote activity. It is just this combination of action, thought, and imagination that makes science so powerful" (p. 30).

Lazer Goldberg (1991) reinforces Rutherford's beliefs about the quality of trade books in the science curriculum. He believes that good science books should foster questions and critical thinking because "critical thinking is at the heart of science" (p. 34).

Science author Laurence Pringle (1991) also argues the benefits of trade books over textbooks in the science curriculum. He states:

It is the process of science, and how scientists think, that needs more attention in children's books. Textbooks do a lot of telling and defining; they're often curiosity-killers. They usually fail to convey a sense of excitement in scientific research. (p. 52)

Pringle also believes that good trade books should foster critical thinking and reasoning. Pringle warns, however, that science trade books must be chosen with the same scrutiny used in choosing textbooks. Poorly written trade books can also kill curiosity and restrict critical thinking and reasoning.

Several values of informational books relate to the science curriculum. Interesting books—such as those by Seymour Simon, Millicent Selsam, and Laurence Pringle—allow children to experience the excitement of discovery. Through books such as Simon's *How to Be an Ocean Scientist in Your Own Home,* children can observe, experiment, compare, formulate hypotheses, test hypotheses, draw conclusions, and evaluate their evidence. Children can become directly involved in the scientific method. Even fairly young children can become interested in the scientific method by reading Kathryn Lasky's humorous *Science Fair Bunnies* in which two first graders (bunny characters) first face the problem of a failed project and then solve the problem by developing a new project. Through the project, readers discover the importance of keeping careful records as well as relying on originality and independent work. Through the experiments and

information found in many informational books, children can learn about the world of nature. Because many informational books that deal with science subjects have greater depth of coverage than do science textbooks, such informational books are valuable for extending knowledge and understanding.

Communication abilities, such as graphing, illustrating, recording, and reporting, are especially important to science. Authors of science information books frequently use these communication abilities when writing. Consequently, children are introduced to reading and interpreting graphs and can present their own ideas and findings in graphic form. Children need many opportunities to interpret data and to make predictions from them. Such experiences help children become actively involved in reading and discovery.

However, the nature of science materials—with their heavy concentration of facts and details, new scientific principles, and new technical vocabulary—may cause reading problems for children who are accustomed to the narrative writing style.

Use excellent informational materials on science-related topics to encourage children to develop their abilities to read science-related materials and to understand science-related concepts. This text considers abilities that relate to both literature and the content areas: using the parts of the book, locating sources of information, using science vocabulary, reading for meaning, evaluating science materials, and applying data from reading to practical problems. The specific books mentioned are only examples of the numerous books that you can use in the classroom. You may wish to add other informational books.

Using the Parts of a Book

Science informational books reinforce the ability to use parts of a book because many books contain a table of contents, a glossary, a bibliography of further readings, and an index. Children can use the table of contents in conjunction with an index to locate specific content. For example:

1. Find the chapter describing "The Battle to Bring the Gray Wolf Home" in Stephen R. Swinburne's *Once a Wolf: How Wildlife Biologists Fought to Bring Back the Gray Wolf* (Chapter 3, p. 21 and 28).

2. Find the page that describes the migration of caterpillars in Sy Montgomery's *The Snake Scientist* (p. 33).

3. Find the chapter on "People and Whales" in Dorothy Hinshaw Patent's *Whales: Giants of the Deep* (chapter 5, p. 73).

4. Find the number of entries that are classified as fossils in Nic Bishop's *Digging for Bird-Dinosaurs: An Expedition to Madagascar* (eleven entries plus "See also dinosaurs").

5. Find the chapter describing damage caused by mudflows in Patricia Lauber's *Volcano: The Eruption and Healing of Mount St. Helens* (Chapter 2, pp. 15–17).

Laurence Pringle's books usually have a glossary of technical terms, an index, and a list of further readings that can provide additional information about a subject. Use these books to reinforce the importance of each part of the book, the kind of information that is available, and locational aids. Books that include lists of further reading and biographical sources, such as Rhoda Blumberg's *Commodore Perry in the Land of the Shogun* and Jim Murphy's *The Great Fire*, provide opportunities for students to locate additional subjects.

Locating Sources of Information

You can use the lists of references at the back of many informational books to show children how to use a library filing system for more information. For example, Carol Donoughue's *The Mystery of the Hieroglyphs* includes nine additional sources. Jim Murphy's *The Great Fire* includes seventeen additional books about the Chicago fire. Charlotte and David Yue's *Christopher Columbus: How He Did It* includes twenty-two additional books that provide further information. Helping children learn how to make their own additional discoveries about a subject fosters important scientific goals.

Using Science Vocabulary

The glossary in many informational books is also a source of information about the meaning of technical terminology found in the book. Authors such as Caroline Arnold in *Saving the Peregrine Falcon* and Sally Walker in *Glaciers: Ice on the Move* and *Rhinos* use boldface type to identify terms that are defined in the glossary. Authors of informational books for children often present the meaning of new words through their context in the text. You should specifically point out this technique to children to help them understand the meanings of words. In *Almost the Real Thing: Simulation in Your High-Tech World,* Gloria Skurzynski presents meaning in both the text and a glossary. For example, in the text, she states: "Simulations are imitations of things that exist in the real world. Almost anything can be simulated—in images, in solid models you can touch, in sound, in motion, or in elements that you can feel, like the wind" (p. 7). In the glossary, she provides additional information for *simulation:* "an imitation that represents a real object, like an airplane's cockpit; or represents a force, like the wind; or an abstract idea, such as nuclear winter" (p. 63).

Authors also clarify the meanings of technical terminology through photographs, diagrams, and charts. Even books written for young children often use labeled drawings to clarify meanings of technical terminology. Millicent Selsam and Joyce Hunt's books for young children, including *A First Look at Caterpillars, A First Look at Animals with Horns,* and *A First Look at Seals, Sea Lions, and Walruses,* discuss specific characteristics that are easy to observe in illustrations. Selsam and Hunt use technical terms frequently and ask children to use their knowledge to answer questions. In *Creepy, Crawly Caterpillars,* Margery Facklam's terms are reinforced by Paul Facklam's illustrations that include labeled details in the lower portion of the page. For example, on a page showing the monarch caterpillar, the lower illustrations show the changes from egg to butterfly.

Reading for Meaning

A major reason that many students give for reading informational science books is to acquire facts; therefore, comprehending the meaning is important. Unlike writings that stress make-believe, informational science books are based on accuracy. Children often need encouragement to note main ideas and supporting details and to see organization. Reading methods books usually include several chapters on these comprehension abilities, but a few approaches considered here allow content area teachers and parents to reinforce and encourage the abilities through informational books.

Noting Main Ideas. Because many informational books written for children have a main idea as a topic sentence at the beginning of a paragraph, many teachers have children read a paragraph and then visualize the author's organization of the material according to the main idea and important details. (This technique may also help children evaluate whether the author uses a logical organization and help them use similar structures in their own nonfiction writing.) A typical paragraph may follow this organization (Norton, 1997):

Main Idea
Supporting Detail
Supporting Detail
Supporting Detail
Supporting Detail

Seymour Simon's writing tends to follow this structure. Use this diagram with material from *New Questions and Answers About Dinosaurs* to help children identify the main idea and supporting details and to evaluate whether or not the organization is logical. On page 4 of Simon's book are two paragraphs that answer the question, "What are dinosaurs?" Arrange the paragraph in the following way:

Main idea: Answer the question, What are dinosaurs?

Supporting details:

A group of reptiles that appeared about 225 million years ago.

Dinosaurs lived during the Mesozoic era, sometimes called the Age of Reptiles.

Dinosaurs died about 65 million years ago, long before there were humans.

There were hundreds of different kinds and sizes of dinosaurs.

Some dinosaurs were meat-eaters and some were plant-eaters.

Dinosaurs were spread across the world.

Dinosaurs lived for 160 million years.

Have children discuss whether or not Simon developed his main idea and answered the question with sufficient supporting details. The remainder of Simon's book uses a similar approach. Each two-page spread answers a question using one or two short paragraphs. The text includes such questions as Were all ancient reptiles dinosaurs?, How else are new dinosaurs discovered?, How are dinosaurs named?, and Were dinosaurs cold-blooded or warm-blooded? If children do not receive sufficient answers to any of their questions, encourage them to expand their knowledge through further reading and investigations.

Noting Supporting Details. When noting main ideas, children should learn to identify supporting details in diagrams and questions. In informational science books, size, color, number, location, and texture are also supporting details. Have the children listen to or read a description from an informational science book and draw a picture that shows the important details. The following descriptions are examples of sources that you can use:

1. The description of the process associated with grafting found on pages 8–9 in Charles Micucci's *The Life and Times of the Apple*.

2. The description of lightning found in Stephen Kramer's *Lightning* (various sections of this book).

Seeing an Author's Organization. A logical organization of information is often critical in the science content areas. Use books that emphasize the life cycles of plants and animals, the correct steps to use in following an experiment, or a chain of events to help children increase their ability to note scientific organization and to evaluate an author's ability to organize logically. Also use books that organize content according to subject. For example, discuss why David Macaulay chose the following organizational plan for the relationships among the objects pictured in *The Way Things Work*: (1) the mechanics of movement, (2) harnessing the elements, (3) working with waves, and (4) electricity and automation.

To organize content according to geographic area, on a large world map mark in different colors the six areas identified in Joyce Pope's *Kenneth Lilly's Animals: A Portfolio of Paintings*. Have students list the characteristics of the areas, the animals in each area, and the characteristics of the animals. The areas are (1) hot forests, (2) cool forests, (3) seas and rivers, (4) grasslands,

(5) deserts, and (6) mountains. Have the students search through geography texts to identify additional characteristics of these areas. Ask the students to consider why Pope's organization seems logical. Have them compare the effectiveness of Pope's organization with the effectiveness of organization in other texts in the library that use maps to identify locations of animals. Another book that encourages students to analyze author's organization through a map is John S. Major's *The Silk Route: 7,000 Miles of History*. The text follows the ancient route from Chang'an to Byzantium.

Evaluating Science Materials

Evaluation requires critical thinking. Critical reading and thinking go beyond factual comprehension; they require weighing the validity of facts, identifying the problem, making judgments, interpreting implied ideas, distinguishing fact from opinion, drawing conclusions, determining the adequacy of a source of information, and suspending judgment until all of the facts have been accumulated. For example, have students develop questions to ask when evaluating science materials. For this activity, have them consider the evaluation criteria used by the book review journal *Appraisal: Science Books for Young People* and develop questions around the following guidelines recommended by Diane Holzheimer (1991) for that journal. First, accuracy is extremely important. Consequently, materials should be completely correct and as up to date as possible. Second, the organization should be logical for the book. Third, the writing should be clear and logical. Fourth, writers should use language with precision and grace and should encourage readers to participate in the subject. Fifth, the illustrations should aid understanding and be appealing. Sixth, if the book includes activities and experiments, the instructions should be clear. Seventh, the book should exemplify scientific attitudes, stimulate imagination, and encourage readers to examine firsthand the wonders of the world.

In addition to developing questions that allow the students to evaluate the text, develop questions that allow students to consider authors' qualifications. For example, help students develop the following list of questions about the authors:

1. *Why did the author write this book?* Was it to present information? Was it to promote a point of view? Was it to advertise? Was it to propagandize? Was it to entertain?

2. *How competent is the author to write an article on this topic for this purpose?* What is the author's background? What is the author's reputation? Does the author have any vested interests in this topic? What is the author's professional position?

To help children critically evaluate authors of informational books (this list and activity are excellent for all informational books, not just those related to science), provide access to many books by different authors and biographical information about the authors. One teacher of upper-elementary students divided a class into five research groups according to a category of interest that each group chose to investigate. The categories were botany, birds, earth and geology, land mammals, and insects. (You may use the list of authors and books in the Children's Literature at the end of this chapter to help you and your students identify books and topics.)

Next, the students found as many books as possible on these categories in the library, including each author's most recent publications on the subject. The students read the information about the author on the dust jacket or elsewhere in the book and searched for biographical data and magazine or journal articles written by the author. Then, the students evaluated the author's background and read and reread the books, searching for each author's point of view and purpose for writing the book.

After the students had carefully read the books, they evaluated the content of the materials according to the criteria developed earlier.

The children also read background information in science textbooks, encyclopedias, and magazines or journals. They checked the copyright dates of the materials; scrutinized the photographs, graphs, charts, and diagrams; and evaluated whether or not the author differentiated fact from opinion. If the students found more than one viewpoint on the subject, they tried to discover if the author presented both.

Finally, the groups presented their information on the authors and their books to the rest of the class. The students learned how to critically evaluate informational books and authors. They also learned much about the content area and the procedures that writers of informational books should use when they research their subjects.

Several authors of informational science books develop themes related to endangered species and ecology. Books with these themes can provide stimulating sources for topics of debate and independent research. Have students use the criteria for evaluating authors and content that were given earlier in this section. In addition, have students test the validity of an argument presented in written materials. For example, have them strip the argument of any excess words or sentences; identify all of the premises upon which an author's conclusion rests; determine whether the author is referring to all of a group, some of a group, or none of a group; and determine whether the conclusion logically follows from the premises.

Then, have students independently evaluate whether the author's conclusion is logical and supported by facts. Also, have them enter into debates, choosing different sides of an issue, researching outside sources, and developing contrasting viewpoints. For example, use Stephen R. Swinburne's *Once a Wolf: How Wildlife Biologists Fought to*

Bring Back the Gray Wolf to help students debate about the plight of the wolf and the role of humans in this plight.

Have the students choose sides in these issues, complete additional research, and present their positions in debate format. They may include the following points that show humans as friends of wolves:

1. Wildlife biologists are attempting to bring the gray wolf back to its natural habitat in Yellowstone National Park.
2. The 1960s and 1970s saw sweeping environmental changes influenced by Rachel Carson's publication *Silent Spring*.
3. The Endangered Species Act guaranteed protection of wolves by imposing a ten-thousand-dollar fine and a jail sentence on anyone killing a wolf.
4. Overpopulation of elk, moose, and deer resulted without the wolf as predator to control their numbers. Animals killed by wolves were often diseased or crippled.
5. A 1991 environmental impact statement favored releasing Canadian wolves in Yellowstone.
6. The Native Americans, especially the Lakota, Blackfoot, and Shoshone, believed that the wolf was their spiritual brother and respected the wolf's endurance and hunting ability.

The following points show humans as foes to wolves:

1. Wolves have been hated and feared by Europeans throughout history.
2. Europeans who settled America in the seventeenth century brought their hatred of wolves with them. They feared wolves would kill cattle, horses, and sheep.
3. The wolf was killed because it was seen as an obstacle to civilization and progress.
4. Ranchers set cattle loose on the western ranges and attacked wolves when the wolves killed livestock.
5. Ranchers believed that wolf recovery was forced on them by easterners and city residents.

Some animals are not endangered because people hunt or poison them. Instead, pollution or land development has endangered their survival. Books on this subject can spark debates whether the interests of people are in opposition to the interests of animals and whether the protective measures designed for animals also protect humans. You also may use Caroline Arnold's *Saving the Peregrine Falcon* and Nicholas and Theodore Nirgiotis's *No More Dodos: How Zoos Help Endangered Wildlife* for this purpose.

Other books about animals that have been endangered include Dorothy Hinshaw Patent's *Whales: Giants of the Deep*, Judi Friedman's *Operation Siberian Crane: The Story Behind the International Effort to Save an Amazing Bird*, Dorothy Hinshaw Patent's *Where the Bald Eagles Gather*, and Brenda Z. Guiberson's *Into the Sea*.

Through the Eyes of a TEACHER

Ruth Nathan

Third-Grade Teacher
Rancho Romero Elementary
Alomo, California

Literature Strategy Plan: Using Nonfiction Trade Books in the Science Curriculum

S tudying scientific phenomena can be an exciting journey into the unknown for children. Scientific inquiries help change our preconceived notions about the world, expand our awareness, and show us that knowledge is constantly changing. Using well-written, intriguing science books with children is an excellent way to stimulate their interest in exploring a topic. However, just because we surround them with a variety of science books doesn't mean they will necessarily pursue a focused, in-depth inquiry. They need guidance in learning how to gather and organize information from a variety of resources. They need support as they consider multiple possibilities for communicating what they've learned. Ruth Nathan is adept at providing this guidance and support.

Building Students' Background Knowledge

Ruth believes it is important to integrate learning across the curriculum. Thus, when she reads *Charlotte's Web* by E. B. White aloud to her students, she introduces the study of insects and spiders in science. To introduce them to nonfiction about spiders, she reads Sandra Markle's *Outside and Inside Spiders.* "I like this book for several reasons. First, she takes a very holistic look at spiders. The book is nicely divided into sections where Markle describes spider body structure, predators, habitat, and the like. This really helps my children understand that nonfiction books often have an organizational structure that helps the reader access information. I try to introduce my students to different nonfictional organizational structures. For example, during our insect unit we read Laurence Pringle's *An Extraordinary Life,* a book about butterfly migration that has a narrative structure. The Markle book shows them yet another way that nonfiction texts can be organized. I also think the photographs are magnificently done with clearly written, accurate captions. My students find them very compelling. It helps me show the children that if they're going to do their own reports, carefully captioned illustrations are an important part of the final product. I also use the photographs to show my students different ways to use context to understand the meaning of words." The class spends a day examining this book, learning what makes a spider through discussion, close examination of the pictures, and comparisons with the insects they had studied in their previous unit. They also compare the information about spiders with research

they've pursued in their insect unit, focusing particularly on questions like "What makes a spider a spider?" and "How are spiders different from bugs?" "This kind of questioning helps them integrate new understandings with information they already know," says Ruth.

Purposeful Reading and Writing

Next, Ruth has the students go to the school library and find all the spider books. They spend two days perusing them, sharing interesting facts, intriguing pictures, gross habits, and the like with each other. Following this time of free exploration, the class develops a KWL chart—stating what the students Know already about the topic, what they Want to find out, and finally, at the end of the lesson, what they have Learned about spiders. "I think it's important that they get to muck around a bit—reading, talking, sharing ideas—before they do a KWL chart. Otherwise they can't tell you what they want to learn. The KWL chart doesn't work if they don't know much. So I let them look at lots of spider books, and then together we generate a lot of questions that we think we ought to find out. It's very organic. They learn things they wouldn't have been able to form a question about . . . and this leads to new questions. Usually they do this first as a class, then different children try to find answers to the various questions that have been generated."

The children next independently research self-selected questions. Some study individual spiders, learning what makes that spider unique. Others study specific aspects of spiders, like the different kinds of webs or how they protect their babies. As students work on their projects, new questions arise that send them back to their reading or to their peers for debates as to the validity of what they've discovered. Thus, children adjust their understandings through interactions with books, peers, and their teacher.

Once the children have collected their information, they brainstorm ways to share what they've learned. One of the most popular choices is through an informational "Big Book" that is eventually shared with their kindergarten buddies. "I bring in lots of big books so the children can see the format and get a better feel for what kindergartners like. One year they decided to do poetry. And I thought, sure, why not? We'd studied limericks, ballads, and Mother Goose rhymes and I'd shared a lot of insect and spider poetry during our studies, so they just wrote like crazy!"

The final product, *Amazing Spiders: Questions Kids Really Ask,* includes both illustrations and text. Each page features a large drawing of the spider or spider fact being described with an accompanying poem. Evan, who loves blood and gore, wrote "Why Do Spiders Have Fangs?" His poem was illustrated with a beautiful scientific drawing

How big is a Wolf Spider?

Some Spiders are as tiny as a piece of dust,
But some are as large as a big pizza Crust.
At three inches long, the Wolf Spider's
In the middle,
Not real big and not real Little.

by Grant

Grant combined an interest in the wolf spider and poetry to add to a Big Book
for kindergartners.

including the spider's fang and poison duct. Eric did a piece on jumping spiders in which he worked hard to convey the concept that these spiders can jump forty times their body length. In addition to the poem, he created a pocket on the page with string that could be pulled out to the exact length of the spider's jump. "Eric did this because he thought the kindergartners would like to pull the string and it would help them understand how long that jump really is," said Ruth. After much practice, the class presents the book to the younger children. The poems and pictures are also published in the classroom newspaper and on the class website.

Assessment

"When it comes to grading, I look for earnest effort. They all should read several books and have notes on their spi-

ders. When they're working on the project, I observe to make sure they're working and that they're helping others if they have useful information. So it is really a combination of factors that I think is important. I do have to consider the science standards established by our district and state. For example, two standards are 'understands scientific concepts' and 'participates in activities and discussions.' These projects clearly demonstrate that my students are at or above the required standard. What's neat with this unit is that they get to demonstrate what they really know so they can be evaluated fairly."

 For ideas on adapting Ruth Nathan's lesson to meet the needs of older or younger readers, please visit Chapter 12 on our Companion Website at www.prenhall.com/norton

Suggested Activities

 For suggested activities for teaching children with nonfiction, visit our Companion Website at www.prenhall.com/norton.

Children's Literature

 For full descriptions, including plot summaries and award winner notations, of these and other titles for teaching children with nonfiction, visit the CD-ROM that accompanies this book.

BIOGRAPHIES

Adler, David A. *America's Champion Swimmer: Gertrude Ederle.* Illustrated by Terry Widener. Harcourt, 2000 (I:7–9 R:4).

———. *Christopher Columbus: Great Explorer.* Illustrated by Lyle Miller. Holiday House, 1991 (I:6–10 R:4).

Aliki. *The King's Day: Louis XIV of France.* Crowell, 1989 (I:8+ R:6).

Anderson, William. *Pioneer Girl.* Illustrated by Dan Andreasen. HarperCollins, 1998 (I:7+ R:4).

Anholt, Laurence. *Stone Girl, Bone Girl: The Story of Mary Anning.* Illustrated by Sheila Moxley. Orchard, 1999 (I:all).

Ashby, Ruth, and Deborah Gore Ohrn, eds. *HerStory: Women Who Changed the World.* Viking, 1995 (I:9+ R:6).

Bains, Rae. *Harriet Tubman: The Road to Freedom.* Illustrated by Larry Johnson. Troll, 1982 (I:8–12 R:4).

Bitton-Jackson, Livia. *I Have Lived a Thousand Years: Growing Up in the Holocaust.* Simon & Schuster, 1997 (I:12+ R:6).

Blumberg, Rhoda. *Commodore Perry in the Land of the Shogun.* Lothrop, Lee & Shepard, 1985 (I:10+ R:6).

Bode, Janet. *Beating the Odds.* Watts, 1991 (I:12+ R:6).

Borden, Louise, and Mary Kay Kroeger. *Fly High! The Story of Bessie Coleman.* Illustrated by Teresa Flavin. Simon & Schuster, 2001 (I:8+).

Brenner, Barbara. *The Boy Who Loved to Draw: Benjamin West.* Illustrated by Olivier Dunrea. Houghton Mifflin, 1999 (I:all).

Brewster, Hugh. *Anastasia's Album.* Hyperion, 1996 (I:10+ R:6).

Brighton, Catherine. *The Fossil Girl: Mary Anning's Dinosaur Discovery.* Millbrook, 1999 (I:7+).

Brooks, Polly Schoyer. *Queen Eleanor: Independent Spirit of the Medieval World.* Lippincott, 1983 (I:10+ R:8).

Brown, Don. *Uncommon Traveler: Mary Kingsley in Africa.* Houghton Mifflin, 2000 (I:4–8).

Carpenter, Angelica Shirley, and Jean Shirley. *Frances Hodgson Burnett: Beyond the Secret Garden.* Lerner, 1990 (I:8+ R:5).

Christopher, Matt. *In the Huddle with . . . Steve Young.* Little, Brown, 1996 (I:9+ R:5).

Cleary, Beverly. *A Girl from Yamhill: A Memoir.* Morrow, 1988 (I:8+ R:5).

Cooney, Barbara. *Eleanor.* Viking, 1996 (I:5–9 R:4).

Cummins, Julie. *Tomboy of the Air: Daredevil Pilot Blanche Stuart Scott.* HarperCollins, 2001 (I:8–12 R:5).

Dalokay, Vedat. *Sister Shako and Kolo the Goat: Memories of My Childhood in Turkey.* Translated by Guner Ener. Lothrop, Lee & Shepard, 1994 (I:10+ R:5).

Dash, Joan. *The World at Her Fingertips: The Story of Helen Keller.* Scholastic, 2001 (I:10+ R:5).

D'Aulaire, Ingri, and Edgar Parin D'Aulaire. *Abraham Lincoln.* Doubleday, 1939, 1957 (I:8–11 R:5).

———. *Benjamin Franklin.* Doubleday, 1950 (I:8–12 R:6).

———. *Columbus.* Doubleday, 1955 (I:7–10 R:5).

Denenberg, Barry. *An American Hero: The True Story of Charles A. Lindbergh.* Scholastic, 1996 (I:12+ R:8).

dePaola, Tomie. *26 Fairmount Avenue.* Putnam, 1999 (I:6+).

Duggleby, John. *Artist in Overalls: The Life of Grant Wood.* Chronicle, 1995 (I:8+ R:8).

I = Interest by Age Range.

R = Readability by Grade Level.

_____ . Story Painter: The Life of Jacob Lawrence. Chronicle, 1998 (I:6–12 R:6).

Faber, Doris. Calamity Jane: Her Life and Her Legend. Houghton Mifflin, 1992 (I:8+ R:4).

Ferber, Elizabeth. Yasir Arafat: A Life of War and Peace. Millbrook, 1995 (I:12+ R:12).

Fisher, Leonard Everett. Alexander Graham Bell. Atheneum, 1999 (I:7–10 R:5).

Fleischman, Sid. The Abracadabra Kid: A Writer's Life. Greenwillow, 1996 (I:10+ R:6).

Foreman, Michael. After the War Was Over. Arcade, 1996 (I:all).

_____ . War Boy: A Country Childhood. Arcade, 1990 (I:all).

Frank, Anne. The Diary of a Young Girl: The Definitive Edition. Edited by Otto H. Frank and Mirjam Pressler. Translated by Susan Massotty. Doubleday, 1995 (I:12+ R:8).

Freedman, Russell. Eleanor Roosevelt: A Life of Discovery. Clarion, 1993 (I:8+ R:5).

_____ . Franklin Delano Roosevelt. Clarion, 1990 (I:8+ R:5).

_____ . Lincoln: A Photobiography. Clarion, 1987 (I:8+ R:6).

_____ . Out of Darkness: The Story of Louis Braille. Illustrated by Kate Kiesler. Clarion, 1997 (I:8+ R:5).

_____ . The Wright Brothers: How They Invented the Airplane. Holiday House, 1991 (I:all).

Fritz, Jean. And Then What Happened, Paul Revere? Illustrated by Margot Tomes. Putnam, 1996 (I:8+ R:5).

_____ . Bully for You, Teddy Roosevelt! Illustrated by Mike Wimmer. Putnam, 1991 (I:8+ R:5).

_____ . The Great Little Madison. Putnam, 1989 (I:9+ R:6).

_____ . Make Way for Sam Houston. Illustrated by Elise Primavera. Putnam, 1986 (I:9 R:6).

_____ . Stonewall. Illustrated by Stephen Gammell. Putnam, 1979 (I:10+ R:6).

_____ . Traitor: The Case of Benedict Arnold. Putnam, 1981 (I:8+ R:5).

_____ . What's the Big Idea, Ben Franklin? Illustrated by Margot Tomes. Coward, McCann, 1978 (I:7–10 R:5).

_____ . Where Do You Think You're Going, Christopher Columbus? Illustrated by Margot Tomes. Putnam, 1980 (I:7–12 R:5).

_____ . Where Was Patrick Henry on the 29th of May? Illustrated by Margot Tomes. Coward, McCann, 1975 (I:7–10 R:5).

_____ . Why Don't You Get a Horse, Sam Adams? Illustrated by Trina Schart Hyman. Coward, McCann, 1974 (I:7–10 R:5).

Gherman, Beverly. E. B. White: Some Writer! Atheneum, 1992 (I:10+ R:5).

Gilliland, Judith Heide. Steamboat! The Story of Captain Blanche Leathers. Illustrated by Holly Meade. DK, 2000 (I:7+).

Glass, Andrew. Mountain Men: True Grit and Tall Tales. Doubleday, 2001 (I:8+ R:4).

Gold, Alison Leslie. Memories of Anne Frank: Reflections of a Childhood Friend. Scholastic, 1997 (I:8+ R:6).

Golenbock, Peter. Hank Aaron: Brave in Every Way. Illustrated by Paul Lee. Harcourt, 2001 (I:6–9 R:4).

Goodman, Joan Elizabeth. A Long and Uncertain Journey: The 27,000-Mile Voyage of Vasco da Gama. Illustrated by Tom McNeely. Mikaya, 2001 (I:10+ R:5).

Goodsell, Jane. Eleanor Roosevelt. Illustrated by Wendell Minor. Crowell, 1970 (I:7–10 R:2).

Greenberg, Jan, and Sandra Jordan. Chuck Close, Up Close. DK, 1998 (I:10+ R:5).

Greenfield, Eloise, and Lessie Jones Little. Childtimes: A Three-Generation Memoir. Crowell, 1979 (I:10+ R:5).

Gross, Ruth Belov. True Stories About Abraham Lincoln. Illustrated by Jill Kastner. Lothrop, Lee & Shepard, 1990 (I:7–10 R:4).

Hamilton, Virginia. Anthony Burns: The Defeat and Triumph of a Fugitive Slave. Knopf, 1988 (I:10+ R:6).

Harness, Cheryl. Abe Lincoln Goes to Washington: 1837–1865. National Geographic, 1997 (I:5–9 R:4).

Haskins, James. I Have a Dream: The Life and Words of Martin Luther King, Jr. Millbrook, 1993 (I:10+ R:6).

_____ . Spike Lee: By Any Means Necessary. Walker, 1997 (I:12+ R:6).

_____ . Thurgood Marshall: A Life for Justice. Holt, 1992 (I:10+ R:6).

Holliday, Laurel. Children of Israel, Children of Palestine: Our Own True Stories. Pocket Books, 1998 (I:12+).

Hyman, Trina Schart. Self-Portrait: Trina Schart Hyman. Addison-Wesley, 1981 (I:9–12 R:5).

Jakes, John. Susanna of the Alamo. Illustrated by Paul Bacon. Harcourt Brace Jovanovich, 1986 (I:7–12 R:6).

Johnson, Rebecca L. Braving the Frozen Frontier: Women Working in Antarctica. Lerner, 1997 (I:9+ R:6).

Johnston, Norma. Louisa May: The World and Works of Louisa May Alcott. Four Winds, 1991 (I:10+ R:6).

Josephson, Judith Pinkerton. Mother Jones: Fierce Fighter for Workers' Rights. Lerner, 1997 (I:10+ R:6).

Kent, Zachary. Andrew Carnegie: Steel King and Friend to Libraries. Enslow, 1999 (I:10+ R:6).

Ketchum, Lisa. Into a New Country: Eight Remarkable Women of the West. Little, Brown, 2000 (I:10+ R:6).

Kherdian, David. The Road from Home: The Story of an Armenian Girl. Greenwillow, 1979 (I:12+ R:6).

Krull, Kathleen. Lives of the Musicians: Good Times, Bad Times (And What the Neighbors Thought). Harcourt Brace Jovanovich, 1993 (I:9+ R:5).

Kunhardt, Edith. Honest Abe. Illustrated by Malcah Zeldis. Greenwillow, 1993 (I:5–8 R:4).

Lalicki, Tom. Spellbinder: The Life of Harry Houdini. Holiday, 2000 (I:9+ R:5).

Lasky, Kathryn. The Librarian Who Measured the Earth. Illustrated by Kevin Hawkes. Little, Brown, 1994 (I:8+ R:6).

_____ . Vision of Beauty: The Story of Sarah Breedlove Walker. Illustrated by Nneka Bennett. Candlewick, 2000 (I:8–10 R:6).

Leiner, Katherine. First Children: Growing Up in the White House. Illustrated by Katie Keller. Tambourine, 1996 (I:10+ R:9).

Lester, Helen. Author: A True Story. Houghton Mifflin, 1997 (I:all).

Levine, Ellen. Anna Pavlova: Genius of the Dance. Scholastic, 1995 (I:12+ R:9).

Lipman, Jean, and Margaret Aspinwall. Alexander Calder and His Magical Mobiles. Hudson Hills, 1981 (I:9+ R:6).

Macy, Sue. Winning Ways: A Photohistory of American Women in Sports. Holt, 1996 (I:12+ R:7).

Malam, John. Beatrix Potter. Carolrhoda, 1998 (I:all).

Marrin, Albert. Commander In Chief: Abraham Lincoln and the Civil War. Dutton, 1997 (I:10+ R:7).

_____ . George Washington and the Founding of a Nation. Dutton, 2001 (I:10+ R:7).

_____ . *Stalin: Russia's Man of Steel.* Viking, 1988 (I:10+ R:7).

Meltzer, Milton. *Andrew Jackson and His America.* Watts, 1993 (I:10+ R:6).

_____ . *Carl Sandburg: A Biography.* Millbrook, 1999 (I:10+ R:5).

_____ . *Columbus and the World Around Him.* Watts, 1990 (I:10+ R:6).

_____ . *Dorothea Lange, Life Through the Camera.* Viking, 1985 (I:10+ R:5).

_____ . *Ten Queens: Portraits of Women to Power.* Illustrated by Bethanne Andersen. Dutton, 1998 (I:9+ R:5).

_____ . *Thomas Jefferson: The Revolutionary Aristocrat.* Watts, 1991 (I:10+ R:6).

Meryman, Richard. *Andrew Wyeth.* Abrams, 1991 (I:10+ R:6).

Miller, Douglas. *Frederick Douglass and the Fight for Freedom.* Facts on File, 1988 (I:10+ R:6).

Murphy, Jim. *A Young Patriot: The American Revolution as Experienced by One Boy.* Clarion, 1996 (I:10+ R:6).

Myers, Elizabeth. *John D. Rockefeller: Boy Financier.* Bobbs-Merrill, 1973 (I:8+ R:5).

_____ . *Thomas Paine: Common Sense Boy.* Bobbs-Merrill, 1976 (I:8+ R:5).

Novac, Ana. *The Beautiful Days of My Youth: My Six Months in Auschwitz and Plaszow.* Translated by George L. Newman. Holt, 1997 (I:12+).

Orgill, Roxane. *If I Only Had a Horn: Young Louis Armstrong.* Illustrated by Leonard Jenkins. Houghton Mifflin, 1997 (I:4–8 R:4).

Paolucci, Bridget. *Beverly Sills.* Chelsea House, 1990 (I:12+ R:7).

Partridge, Elizabeth. *Restless Spirit: The Life and Work of Dorothea Lang.* Viking, 1998 (I:10+ R:5).

Pasachoff, Naomi. *Alexander Graham Bell: Making Connections.* Oxford University Press, 1996 (I:10+ R:6).

Patterson, Lillie. *Frederick Douglass: Freedom Fighter.* Garrard, 1965 (I:6–9 R:3).

_____ . *Martin Luther King, Jr. and the Freedom Movement.* Facts on File, 1989 (I:10+ R:6).

Paulsen, Gary. *Woodsong.* Bradbury, 1990 (I:10+ R:6).

Pearce, Carol Ann. *Amelia Earhart.* Facts on File, 1988 (I:8+ R:5).

Peet, Bill. *Bill Peet: An Autobiography.* Houghton Mifflin, 1989 (I:all R:5).

Porter, A. P. *Jump at de Sun: The Story of Zora Neale Hurston.* Carolrhoda, 1992 (I:8+ R:5).

Provensen, Alice, and Martin Provensen. *The Glorious Flight Across the Channel with Louis Bleriot, July 25, 1909.* Viking, 1983 (I:all R:4).

Reiss, Johanna. *The Upstairs Room.* Crowell, 1972 (I:11 R:4).

Roop, Peter, and Connie Roop, eds. *I, Columbus—My Journal 1492.* Illustrated by Peter Hanson. Walker, 1900 (I:all).

Roosevelt, Elliott. *Eleanor Roosevelt, with Love.* Dutton, 1984 (I:10+ R:7).

Rubin, Susan Goldman. *Margaret Bourke-White: Her Pictures Were Her Life.* Photographs by Margaret Bourke-White. Abrams, 1999 (I:10+ R:5).

Sandburg, Carl. *Abe Lincoln Grows Up.* Illustrated by James Daugherty. Harcourt Brace Jovanovich, 1926, 1928, 1954 (I:10+ R:6).

_____ . *Abraham Lincoln: The Prairie Years.* Harcourt Brace Jovanovich, 1926 (I:12+ R:7).

Schwartz, Gary. *Rembrandt.* Abrams, 1992 (I:10+ R:6).

Scott, John Anthony, and Robert Alan Scott. *John Brown of Harper's Ferry.* Facts on File, 1988 (I:10+ R:6).

Severance, John B. *Einstein: Visionary Scientist.* Clarion, 1999 (I:10+ R:6).

_____ . *Gandhi, Great Soul.* Clarion, 1997 (I:10+ R:6).

Sills, Leslie. *Inspirations: Stories About Women Artists.* Whitman, 1989 (I:8+ R:5).

_____ . *Visions: Stories About Women Artists.* Whitman, 1993 (I:8+ R:5).

Sim, Dorrith M. *In My Pocket.* Illustrated by Gerald Fitzgerald. Harcourt Brace, 1997 (I:5–8 R:4).

Sís, Peter. *Follow the Dream.* Knopf, 1991 (I:5–9 R:4).

_____ . *Starry Messenger: Galileo Galilei.* Farrar, Straus & Giroux, 1996 (I:all).

Smith, Barry. *The First Voyage of Christopher Columbus.* Viking, 1992 (I:6–8 R:4).

Sofer, Barbara. *Shalom, Haver: Goodbye, Friend.* Kar-Ben, 1996 (I:7–9 R:5).

Stanley, Diane. *Leonardo da Vinci.* Morrow, 1996 (I:all).

_____ . *Michelangelo.* HarperCollins, 2000 (I:all).

_____ . *Peter the Great.* Four Winds, 1986 (I:8+ R:7).

_____ , and Peter Vennema. *Cleopatra.* Illustrated by Diane Stanley. Morrow, 1994 (I:all).

_____ , and Peter Vennema. *Good Queen Bess: The Story of Elizabeth I of England.* Four Winds, 1990 (I:7–10 R:5).

_____ , and Peter Vennema. *Shaka: King of the Zulus.* Illustrated by Diane Stanley. Morrow, 1988 (I:8+ R:5).

Stanley, Fay. *The Last Princess: The Story of Princess Ka'iulani of Hawai'i.* Illustrated by Diane Stanley. Four Winds, 1991 (I:7–10 R:6).

Szabo, Corinne. *Sky Pioneer: A Photobiography of Amelia Earhart.* National Geographic, 1997 (I:8–12 R:5).

Turner, Ann. *Abe Lincoln Remembers.* Illustrated by Wendell Minor. HarperCollins, 2001 (I:6+ R:5).

Turner, Robyn Montana. *Portraits of Women Artists for Children: Frida Kahlo.* Little, Brown, 1993 (I:8+ R:5).

_____ . *Portraits of Women Artists for Children: Georgia O'Keeffe.* Little, Brown, 1991 (I:8+ R:5).

_____ . *Portraits of Women Artists for Children: Mary Cassatt.* Little, Brown, 1992 (I:8+ R:5).

_____ . *Portraits of Women Artists for Children: Rosa Bonheur.* Little, Brown, 1991 (I:8+ R:5).

Wells, Rosemary. *Mary on Horseback: Three Mountain Stories.* Dial, 1998 (I:6+ R:5).

_____ . *Streets of Gold.* Illustrated by Dan Andreasen. Dial Books, 1999.

Whitney, Sharon. *Eleanor Roosevelt.* Watts, 1982 (I:10+ R:5).

Winter, Jeanette. *My Name Is Georgia.* Harcourt Brace, 1998 (I:5–9).

Yates, Elizabeth. *Amos Fortune, Free Man.* Illustrated by Nora S. Unwin. Dutton, 1950 (I:10+ R:6).

INFORMATIONAL BOOKS

Aagesen, Colleen, and Marcia Blumberg. *Shakespeare for Kids: His Life and Times.* Chicago Review Press, 1999 (I:9+).

Alonso, Karen. *Schenck v. United States: Restrictions on Free Speech.* Enslow, 1999 (I:10+ R:6).

Altman, Linda Jacobs. *Slavery and Abolition in American History.* Enslow, 1999 (I:10+ R:6).

Ambrose, Stephen E. *The Good Fight: How World War II Was Won.* Simon & Schuster, 2001 (I:9+ R:5).

Ammon, Richard. *Conestoga Wagons.* Illustrated by Bill Farnsworth. Holiday, 2000 (I:7+ R:4).

Anderson, Joan. *Cowboys: Roundup on an American Ranch.* Photographs by George Ancona. Scholastic, 1996 (I:8+ R:8).

Appelbaum, Diana. *Giants in the Land.* Illustrated by Michael McCurdy. Houghton Mifflin, 1993 (I:6–9 R:4).

Arnold, Caroline. *Dinosaur Mountain: Graveyard of the Past.* Photographs by Richard Hewett. Clarion, 1989 (I:8–12 R:6).

_____ . *On the Brink of Extinction: The California Condor.* Photographs by Michael Wallace. Harcourt, 1993 (I:9+ R:5).

_____ . *Saving the Peregrine Falcon.* Photographs by Richard R. Hewett. Carolrhoda, 1985 (I:8–12 R:7).

_____ . *Stone Age Farmers Beside the Sea: Scotland's Prehistoric Village of Skara Brae.* Photographs by Arthur P. Arnold. Clarion, 1997 (I:8–12 R:6).

Arnold, Katya, and Sam Swope. *Katya's Book of Mushrooms.* Illustrated by Katya Arnold. Holt, 1997 (I:6–10 R:5).

Arnosky, Jim. *Drawing Life in Motion.* Lothrop, Lee & Shepard, 1984 (I:all R:6).

_____ . *Drawing from Nature.* Lothrop, Lee & Shepard, 1982 (I:all R:6).

_____ . *Freshwater Fish and Fishing.* Four Winds, 1982 (I:8–12 R:5).

Arthur, Alex. *Shell.* Knopf, 1989 (I:9+ R:6).

Ash, Russell. *Incredible Comparisons.* DK, 1996 (I:10+ R:5).

Ashabranner, Brent. *To Seek a Better World: The Haitian Minority in America.* Photographs by Paul Conklin. Cobblehill, 1997 (I:10+ R:6).

Ashby, Ruth. *Elizabethan England.* Cavendish, 1999 (I:10+ R:6).

Bachrach, Susan D. *The Nazi Olympics: Berlin 1936.* Little, Brown, 2000 (I:10+ R:6).

Ballard, Robert D. *Exploring the Titanic.* Scholastic, 1988 (I:8+ R:5).

Bany-Winters, Lisa. *Show Time!: Music, Dance, and Drama Activities for Kids.* Chicago Review Press, 2000 (I:7+ R:5).

Barnes, Peter W., and Cheryl Shaw Barnes. *Woodrow for President: A Tail of Voting, Campaigns and Elections.* VSP, 1999 (I:7+).

Bartoletti, Susan Campbell. *Growing Up in Coal Country.* Houghton Mifflin, 1996 (I:10+ R:5).

Barton, Byron. *Airport.* Crowell, 1982 (I:3–8).

Bash, Barbara. *Desert Giant: The World of the Saguaro Cactus.* Sierra Club/Little Brown, 1989 (I:5–9 R:4).

_____ . *Shadows of Night: The Hidden World of the Little Brown Bat.* Sierra Club, 1993 (I:5–9 R:4).

_____ . *Urban Roosts: Where Birds Nest in the City.* Little, Brown, 1990 (I:4–9 R:5).

Bauer, Marion Dane. *What's Your Story? A Young Person's Guide to Writing Fiction.* Clarion, 1992 (I:10+ R:5).

Beattie, Owen, and John Geiger. *Buried in Ice: The Mystery of a Lost Arctic Expedition.* Scholastic, 1992 (I:9+ R:4).

Bergman, Thomas. *Finding a Common Language: Children Living with Deafness.* Gareth Stevens, 1989 (I:7–12 R:5).

Birdseye, Debbie Holsclaw and Tom Birdseye. *What I Believe: Kids Talk about Faith.* Photographs by Robert Crum. Holiday, 1996 (I:8+ R:4).

Bishop, Nic. *Digging for Bird-Dinosaurs: An Expedition to Madagascar.* Houghton Mifflin, 2000 (I:8+ R:5).

_____ . *The Secrets of Animal Flight.* Illustrated by Amy Bartlett Wright. Houghton Mifflin, 1997 (I:8+ R:4).

Bitton-Jackson, Livia. *I Have Lived a Thousand Years: Growing Up in the Holocaust.* Simon & Schuster, 1997 (I:12+ R:6).

Blumberg, Rhoda. *Commodore Perry in the Land of the Shogun.* Lothrop, Lee & Shepard, 1985 (I:9+ R:6).

_____ . *Full Steam Ahead: The Race to Build a Transcontinental Railroad.* National Geographic, 1996 (I:9+ R:6).

_____ . *The Incredible Journey of Lewis and Clark.* Lothrop, Lee & Shepard, 1987 (I:9+ R:6).

_____ . *What's the Deal? Jefferson, Napoleon, and the Louisiana Purchase.* National Geographic, 1999 (I:9+ R:6).

Bober, Natalie. *Countdown to Independence: A Revolution of Ideas in England and Her American Colonies: 1760–1776.* Simon & Schuster, 2001 (I:12+ R:7).

Boitano, Brian, and Suzanne Harper. *Boitano's Edge: Inside the Real World of Figure Skating.* Simon & Schuster, 1997 (I:8+ R:4).

Booth, Jerry. *You Animal!* Illustrated by Nancy King. Harcourt Brace, 1996 (I:8+ R:4).

Brandenburg, Jim. *An American Safari: Adventures on the North American Prairie.* Walker, 1995 (I:8+ R:5).

_____ . *Sand and Fog: Adventures in Southern Africa.* Walker, 1994 (I:10+ R:5).

Branley, Franklyn M. *Saturn: The Spectacular Planet.* Illustrated by Leonard Kessler. Harper & Row, 1983 (I:9+ R:6).

Brenner, Barbara. *If You Were There in 1492.* Macmillan, 1991 (I:8+ R:5).

Brown, Laurie Krasny, and Marc Brown. *Dinosaurs to the Rescue! A Guide to Protecting Our Planet.* Little, Brown, 1992 (I:5–8 R:4).

Brown, Mary Barrett. *Wings Along the Waterway.* Orchard, 1992 (I:10+ R:6).

Bruun, Ruth Dowling, and Bertel Bruun. *The Human Body.* Illustrated by Patricia J. Wynne. Random, 1982 (I:9+ R:6).

Bunting, Eve. *Butterfly House.* Illustrated by Greg Shed. Scholastic, 1999 (I:all).

_____ . *I Am the Mummy Heb-Nefert.* Illustrated by David Christiana. Harcourt Brace, 1997 (I:all).

Burandt, Harriet and Shelly Dale. *Tales from the Homeplace: Adventures of a Texas Farm Girl.* Holt, 1997 (I:9+ R:5).

Burgel, Paul Hermann, and Manfred Hartwig. *Gorillas.* Carolrhoda, 1992 (I:8+ R:5).

Carr, Terry. *Spill! The Story of the Exxon Valdez.* Watts, 1991 (I:8+ R:6).

Carrick, Carol. *Whaling Days.* Illustrated by David Frampton. Clarion, 1993 (I:8+ R:4).

Carroll, Colleen. *How Artists See Animals: Mammal Fish Bird Reptile.* Abbeville, 1996 (I:all).

_____ . *How Artists See the Elements: Earth Air Fire Water.* Abbeville, 1996 (I:all).

_____ . *How Artists See People: Boy Girl Man Woman.* Abbeville, 1996 (I:all).

Carter, David A., and James Diaz. *The Elements of Pop-Up.* Simon & Schuster, 1999 (I:10+).

Cerullo, Mary M. *The Octopus: Phantom of the Sea.* Photographs by Jeffery L. Rotman. Cobblehill, 1997 (I:9+ R:5).

_____ . *Sharks: Challengers of the Deep.* Photographs by Jeffrey L. Rotman. Cobblehill, 1993 (I:9↑ R:5).

Christian, Peggy. *If You Find a Rock.* Photographs by Barbara Hirsch Lember. Harcourt, 2000 (I:6–9).

Clinton, Catherine. *Scholastic Encyclopedia of the Civil War.* Scholastic, 1999 (I:10+).

Cole, Joanna. *How You Were Born.* Photographs by Margaret Miller. Morrow, 1993 (I:4–8 R:4).

_____ . *The Magic School Bus: Inside the Earth.* Illustrated by Bruce Degen. Scholastic, 1987 (I:6–8 R:4).

_____ . *The Magic School Bus: Lost in the Solar System.* Illustrated by Bruce Degen. Scholastic, 1990 (I:6–8 R:4).

_____ . *The Magic School Bus: On the Ocean Floor.* Illustrated by Bruce Degen. Scholastic, 1992 (I:6–8 R:4).

_____ . *My Puppy Is Born.* Photographs by Jerome Wexler. Morrow, 1991 (I:7–9 R:2).

Collard, Sneed B. *Animal Dads.* Illustrated by Steve Jenkins. Houghton Mifflin, 1997 (I:5–8 R:4).

Colman, Penny. *Corpses, Coffins, and Crypts; A History of Burial.* Holt, 1997 (I:10+ R:6).

Commoner, Barry. *Making Peace with the Planet.* Pantheon, 1990 (I:12+ R:7).

Cone, Molly. *Come Back, Salmon.* Photographs by Sidnee Wheelwright. Sierra Club, 1992 (I:8+ R:5).

_____ . *Squishy, Misty, Damp & Muddy: The In-Between World of Wetlands.* Sierra Club, 1996 (I:all R:7).

Couper, Heather, and Nigel Henbest. *The Space Atlas: A Pictorial Atlas of Our Universe.* Harcourt Brace Jovanovich, 1992 (I:8+ R:5).

Cowan, Paul. *A Torah Is Written.* Photographs by Rachel Cowan. Jewish Publication Society, 1986 (I:all R:5).

Cowley, Joy. *Red-Eyed Tree Frog.* Photographs by Nic Bishop. Scholastic, 1999 (I:5+).

Cummins, Julie. *The Inside-Outside Book of Libraries.* Illustrated by Roxie Munroe. Dutton, 1996 (I:6–9 R:4).

Curlee, Lynn. *Liberty.* Atheneum, 2000 (I:9+).

_____ . *Rushmore.* Scholastic, 1999 (I:9+).

dePaola, Tomie. *The Popcorn Book.* Holiday House, 1978 (I:3–8 R:5).

Donoughue, Carol. *The Mystery of the Hieroglyphs: The Story of the Rosetta Stone and the Race to Decipher Egyptian Hieroglyphs.* Oxford, 1999 (I:8+ R:5).

Duke, Kate. *Archaeologists Dig for Clues.* HarperCollins, 1997 (I:6–9 R:5).

Dyson, John. *Westward with Columbus.* Photographs by Peter Christopher. Scholastic, 1991 (I:10+ R:5).

Earle, Sylvia A. *Hello, Fish!: Visiting the Coral Reef.* Photographs by Wolcott Henry. National Geographic, 1999 (I:all).

Englander, Roger. *Opera, What's All the Screaming About?* Walker, 1983 (I:10+ R:7).

Esbensen, Barbara Juster. *Echoes for the Eye: Poems to Celebrate Patterns in Nature.* Illustrated by Helen K. Davie. HarperCollins, 1996 (I:all).

_____ . *Tiger with Wings: The Great Horned Owl.* Illustrated by Mary Barrett Brown. Orchard, 1991 (I:5–9 R:4).

Eschle, Lou. *The Curse of Tutankhamen.* Lucent, 1994 (I:9+ R:7).

Faber, Doris, and Harold Faber. *The Birth of a Nation: The Early Years of the United States.* Scribner, 1989 (I:10+ R:7).

Faber, Harold. *The Discoverers of America.* Scribner, 1992 (I:10+ R:7).

Facklam, Margery. *Creepy, Crawly Caterpillars.* Little, Brown, 1996 (I:4–9 R:7).

_____ . *Tracking Dinosaurs in the Gobi.* 21st Century, 1997 (I:10+ R:6).

_____ . *Who Harnessed the Horse? The Story of Animal Domestication.* Illustrated by Steven Parton. Little, Brown, 1992 (I:10+ R:5).

_____ , and Howard Facklam. *Changes in the Wind: Earth's Shifting Climate.* Harcourt Brace Jovanovich, 1986 (I:10+ R:7).

Fagan, Brian M. *The Great Journey: The Peopling of Ancient America.* Thames & Hudson, 1987 (I:10+ R:7).

Falk, John H., et al. *Bubble Monster: And Other Science Fun.* Illustrated by Charles C. Somerville. Chicago Review, 1996 (I:4–8).

Feldbaum, Carl B., and Ronald J. Bee. *Looking the Tiger in the Eye: Confronting the Nuclear Threat.* Harper & Row, 1988 (I:12+ R:7).

Finkelstein, Norman. *The Other Fourteen Ninety-Two: Jewish Settlement in the New World.* Scribner, 1989 (I:10+ R:6).

Fischer-Nagel, Heiderose, and Andraes Fischer-Nagel. *Life of the Honey Bee.* Carolrhoda, 1986 (I:6–10 R:6).

Fisher, Leonard Everett. *The Tower of London.* Macmillan, 1987 (I:all R:6).

_____ . *The Wailing Wall.* Macmillan, 1989 (I:all R:6).

Fleisher, Paul. *Life Cycles of a Dozen Diverse Creatures.* Millbrook, 1996 (I:9+ R:6).

Floca, Brian. *Dinosaurs at the Ends of the Earth: The Story of the Central Asiatic Expeditions.* Dorling Kindersley, 2000 (I:8+ R:6).

Ford, Michael Thomas. *100 Questions and Answers About AIDS: A Guide for Young People.* New Discovery Books, 1992 (I:10+ R:7).

Fraser, Mary Ann. *Vicksburg: The Battle That Won the Civil War.* Henry Holt, 1999 (I:10+ R:5).

Freedman, Russell. *Dinosaurs and Their Young.* Illustrated by Leslie Morrill. Holiday House, 1983 (I:6–9 R:4).

French, Vivian. *Growing Frogs.* Illustrated by Alison Bartlett. Candlewick, 2000 (I:5+).

Friedman, David. *Focus on Drugs and the Brain.* Illustrated by David Neuhaus. 21st Century Books, 1990 (I:10+ R:6).

Friedman, Judi. *Operation Siberian Crane: The Story Behind the International Effort to Save an Amazing Bird.* Macmillan, 1992 (I:10+ R:5).

Fritz, Jean. *Shh! We're Writing the Constitution.* Illustrated by Tomie dePaola. Putnam, 1987 (I:7–10 R:5).

_____ , et al. *The World in 1492.* Illustrated by Stefano Vitale. Holt, 1992 (I:8+).

Gatti, Anne, retold by. *The Magic Flute.* Illustrated by Peter Malone. Chronicle, 1997 (I:8+).

George, Jean Craighead. *Everglades.* Illustrated by Wendell Minor. HarperCollins, 1995 (I:7+ R:5).

George, Lindsay Barrett. *Around the World: Who's Been Here?* Greenwillow, 1999 (I:8+).

George, William T. *Box Turtle at Long Pond.* Illustrated by Lindsay Barrett George. Greenwillow, 1989 (I:3–8 R:3).

Gibbons, Gail. *Beacons of Light: Lighthouses*. Morrow, 1990 (I:7–9 R:4).

_____ . *Dinosaurs*. Holiday House, 1987 (I:4–8 R:3).

_____ . *Santa Who?* Morrow, 1999 (I:all).

Giblin, James Cross, ed. *The Century That Was: Reflections on the Last One Hundred Years*. Atheneum, 2000 (I:10+).

_____ . *From Hand to Mouth: Or, How We Invented Knives, Forks, Spoons, and Chopsticks & the Table Manners to Go with Them*. Crowell, 1987 (I:8+ R:6).

Gillette, J. Lynett. *Dinosaur Ghosts: The Mystery of Coelophysis*. Illustrated by Douglas Henderson. Dial, 1997 (I:9+ R:6).

Goldin, Barbara. *The Passover Journey: A Seder Companion*. Illustrated by Neil Waldman. Viking, 1994 (I:all).

Goodall, Jane. *The Chimpanzee Family Book*. Photographs by Michael Neugebauer. Picture Book Studio, 1989 (I:8+ R:5).

_____ . *The Chimpanzees I Love: Saving Their World and Ours*. Scholastic, 2001 (I:10+ R:5).

Goodman, Susan E. *Stones, Bones, and Petroglyphs: Digging Into Southwest Archaeology*. Photographs by Michael J. Doolittle. Atheneum, 1998 (I:10+ R:6).

Gourley, Catherine. *Hunting Neptune's Giants: True Stories of American Whaling*. Millbrook, 1995 (I:10+ R:8).

Grace, Eric S. *Seals*. Photographs by Fred Bruemmer. Sierra Club/Little, Brown, 1991 (I:8+ R:6).

Graff, Nancy Price. *The Strength of the Hills: A Portrait of a Family Farm*. Photographs by Richard Howard. Little, Brown, 1989 (I:all R:5).

Granfield, Linda. *Circus: An Album*. DK, 1998 (I:8+ R:6).

_____ . *In Flanders Fields: The Story of the Poem by John McCrae*. Doubleday, 1996 (I:9+ R:6).

Greene, Carol. *Police Officers Protect People*. Child's World, 1996 (I:4–7 R:4).

Guiberson, Brenda Z. *Into the Sea*. Illustrated by Alix Berenzy. Holt, 1996 (I:5–8 R:4).

_____ . *Spoonbill Swamp*. Illustrated by Megan Lloyd. Holt, 1992 (I:4–7 R:4).

Harris, Robie H. *It's So Amazing!: A Book About Eggs, Sperm, Birth, Babies, and Families*. Illustrated by Michael Emberley. Candlewick, 1999 (I:7+).

Hearne, Betsy. *Seven Brave Women*. Illustrated by Bethanne Andersen. Greenwillow, 1997 (I:5–8 R:5).

Heiligman, Deborah. *From Caterpillar to Butterfly*. Illustrated by Bari Weissman. HarperCollins, 1996 (I:5–8 R:4).

High, Linda Oatman. *Barn Savers*. Illustrated by Ted Lewin. Boyds Mills, 1999 (I:8+).

Hirst, Robin, and Sally Hirst. *My Place in Space*. Illustrated by Roland Harvey and Joe Levine. Orchard, 1990 (I:5–8 R:5).

Hoban, Tana. *A Children's Zoo*. Greenwillow, 1985 (I:2–6).

Hoobler, Dorothy, and Thomas Hoobler. *The Jewish American Family Album*. Oxford, 1995 (I:all R:10).

Hoose, Phillip. *We Were There, Too!: Young People in U.S. History*. Farrar, Straus & Giroux, 2001 (I:10+ R:6).

Irvine, Joan. *How to Make Super Pop-Ups*. Illustrated by Linda Hendry. Morrow, 1992 (I:8+ R:4).

Isadora, Rachel. *Lili at Ballet*. Putnam, 1993 (I:4–8 R:5).

Jackson, Donna M. *The Bone Detectives: How Forensic Anthropologists Solve Crimes and Uncover Mysteries of the Dead*. Photographs by Charlie Fellenbaum. Little, Brown, 1996 (I:10+ R:9).

Jacobs, Francine. *Follow That Trash! All About Recycling*. Illustrated by Mavis Smith. Grosset & Dunlap, 1996 (I:5 R:4).

Jaffe, Steven H. *Who Were the Founding Fathers? Two Hundred Years of Reinventing American History*. Holt, 1996 (I:12+ R:7).

Jarrow, Gail, and Paul Sherman. *The Naked Mole-Rat Mystery: Scientific Sleuths at Work*. Lerner, 1996 (I:9+ R:6).

Jenkins, Martin. *The Emperor's Egg*. Illustrated by Jane Chapman. Candlewick, 1999 (I:3–8).

Jenkins, Steve. *The Top of the World: Climbing Mount Everest*. Houghton Mifflin, 1999 (I:7+).

Johnson, Neil. *All in a Day's Work: Twelve Americans Talk About Their Jobs*. Little, Brown, 1989 (I:10+ R:6).

Johnson, Rebecca L. *Braving the Frozen Frontier: Women Working in Antarctica*. Lerner, 1997 (I:9+ R:6).

Johnson, Sylvia. *Roses Red, Violets Blue: Why Flowers Have Colors*. Photographs by Yuko Sato. Lerner, 1991 (I:10+ R:5).

Jones, Charlotte Foltz. *Yukon Gold: The Story of the Klondike Gold Rush*. Holiday, 1999 (I:8+ R:5).

Kay, Verla. *Iron Horses*. Illustrated by Michael McCurdy. Putnam, 1999 (I:5+).

King, Casey, and Linda Barrett Osborne. *Kids Talk About the Civil Rights Movement with the People Who Made It Happen*. Knopf, 1997 (I:9+).

King-Smith, Dick. *I Love Guinea Pigs*. Illustrated by Anita Jeram. Candlewick, 1995 (I:4–8 R:4).

Knight, Margy Burns. *Talking Walls*. Illustrated by Anne Sibley O'Brien. Tilbury House, 1992 (I:8+ R:5).

Koch, Michelle. *World Water Watch*. Greenwillow, 1993 (I:4–8 R:4).

Koscielniak, Bruce. *The Story of the Incredible Orchestra*. Houghton Mifflin, 2000 (I:8+ R:5).

Kovack, Deborah, and Kate Madin. *Beneath Blue Waters: Meetings with Remarkable Deep-Sea Creatures*. Viking, 1996 (I:10+ R:6).

Kramer, Stephen. *Eye of the Storm: Chasing Storms with Warren Faidley*. Putnam, 1997 (I:9+ R:5).

_____ . *Lightning*. Photographs by Warren Faidley. Carolrhoda, 1992 (I:8+ R:6).

Krauss, Ronnie. *Take a Look, It's in a Book: How Television Is Made at Reading Rainbow*. Walker, 1997 (I:all R:5).

Krensky, Steven B. *Breaking into Print: Before and After Invention of the Printing Press*. Little, Brown, 1996 (I:8+ R:5).

Kroll, Steven. *Pony Express!* Illustrated by Dan Andreasen. Scholastic, 1996 (I:10+ R:9).

Krull, Kathleen. *They Saw the Future: Oracles, Psychics, Scientists, Great Thinkers, and Pretty Good Guessers*. Illustrated by Kyrsten Brooker. Atheneum, 1999 (I:10+ R:5).

Kuskin, Karla. *Jerusalem, Shining Still*. Illustrated by David Frampton. Harper & Row, 1987 (I:8+ R:5).

Langley, Andrew. *Shakespeare's Theatre*. Illustrated by June Everett. Oxford, 1999 (I:10+ R:6).

Lasky, Kathryn. *Dinosaur Dig*. Photographs by Christopher Knight. Morrow, 1990 (I:9+ R:5).

_____ . *Interrupted Journey: Saving Endangered Sea Turtles*. Photographs by Christopher Knight. Candlewick, 2001 (I:8+ R:5).

_____ . *Monarchs*. Photographs by Christopher Knight. Harcourt Brace Jovanovich, 1993 (I:all).

_____ . *The Most Beautiful Roof in the World: Exploring the Rainforest Canopy*. Photographs by Christopher G. Knight. Harcourt Brace, 1997 (I:9+ R:6).

_____ . *Science Fair Bunnies*. Illustrated by Marylin Hafner. Candlewick, 2000 (I:6+).

_____ . *Sugaring Time*. Photographs by Christopher Knight. Macmillan, 1983 (I:all R:6).

_____ . *Think Like an Eagle: At Work with a Wildlife Photographer*. Photographs by Christopher G. Knight and Jack Swedberg. Little, Brown, 1992 (I:8+ R:6).

Lauber, Patricia. *Dinosaurs Walked Here and Other Stories Fossils Tell*. Bradbury, 1987 (I:all R:6).

_____ . *Flood: Wrestling with the Mississippi*. National Geographic, 1996 (I:8+ R:6).

_____ . *How Dinosaurs Came to Be*. Illustrated by Douglas Henderson. Simon & Schuster, 1996 (I:6–10 R:4).

_____ . *Hurricanes: Earth's Mightiest Storms*. Scholastic, 1996 (I:9+ R:6).

_____ . *Journey to the Planets*. Crown, 1982 (I:8–12 R:4).

_____ . *Living with Dinosaurs*. Illustrated by Douglas Henderson. Bradbury, 1991 (I:8+ R:6).

_____ . *The News About Dinosaurs*. Bradbury, 1989 (I:8+ R:6).

_____ . *Painters of the Caves*. National Geographic, 1998 (I:all).

_____ . *Snakes Are Hunters*. Illustrated by Holly Keller. Crowell, 1988 (I:4–8 R:3).

_____ . *Volcano: The Eruption and Healing of Mount St. Helens*. Bradbury, 1986 (I:all).

_____ . *What You Never Knew About Tubs, Toilets, and Showers*. Illustrated by John Manders. Simon & Schuster, 2001 (I:all).

Lavies, Bianca. *Backyard Hunter: The Praying Mantis*. Dutton, 1990 (I:5–9 R:4).

Lawlor, Laurie. *Where Will This Shoe Take You?: A Walk Through the History of Footwear*. Walker, 1996 (I:10+ R:5).

Leapman, Michael. *Witnesses to War: Eight True-Life Stories of Nazi Persecution*. Viking, 1998 (I:10+ R:5).

Leon, George DeLucenay. *Explorers of the Americas Before Columbus*. Watts, 1990 (I:8+ R:6).

Lessem, Don. *Bigger Than T. Rex*. Illustrated by Robert F. Walters. Crown, 1997 (I:9+ R:5).

_____ . *Dinosaur Worlds*. Boyds Mills, 1996 (I:10+ R:6).

Lesser, Carolyn. *Storm on the Desert*. Illustrated by Ted Rand. Harcourt Brace, 1997 (I:all).

Levine, Ellen. *Darkness over Denmark: The Danish Resistance and the Rescue of the Jews*. Holiday, 2000 (I:10+ R:6).

_____ . *The Tree That Would Not Die*. Illustrated by Ted Rand. Scholastic, 1995 (I:6–9 R:4).

Lewin, Ted. *Tiger Trek*. Macmillan, 1990 (I:10+ R:6).

_____ , and Betsy Lewin. *Gorilla Walk*. Lothrop, Lee & Shepard, 1999 (I:10+ R:6).

Locker, Thomas. *Sky Tree: Seeing Science Through Art*. HarperCollins, 1995 (I:6–8 R:5).

Loewen, Nancy, and Ann Bancroft. *Four to the Pole!: The American Women's Expedition to Antarctica, 1992–93*. Linnet, 2001 (I:10+ R:6).

London, Jonathan. *Baby Whale's Journey*. Illustrated by Jon VanZyle. Chronicle, 1999 (I:6–9).

McClung, Robert. *Lost Wild America: The Story of Our Extinct and Vanishing Wildlife*. Illustrated by Bob Hines. Linnet, 1993 (I:12+ R:7).

McDonald, Megan. *Is This a House for Hermit Crab?* Illustrated by S. D. Schindler. Orchard, 1990 (I:3–6).

McLaughlin, Molly. *Dragonflies*. Walker, 1989 (I:7–12 R:5).

McMillan, Bruce. *Going on a Whale Watch*. Scholastic, 1992 (I:3–8).

McPhail, David. *Farm Morning*. Harcourt Brace Jovanovich, 1985 (I:2–5).

McVey, Vicki. *The Sierra Club Kid's Guide to Planet Care & Repair*. Illustrated by Martha Weston. Sierra Club, 1993 (I:8+ R:5).

Macaulay, David. *Building Big*. Houghton Mifflin, 2000 (I:all).

_____ . *Building the Book Cathedral*. Houghton Mifflin, 1999 (I:all).

_____ . *Cathedral: The Story of Its Construction*. Houghton Mifflin, 1973 (I:all R:5).

_____ . *Mill*. Houghton Mifflin, 1983 (I:9+ R:5).

_____ . *Ship*. Houghton Mifflin, 1993 (I:10+ R:5).

_____ . *The Way Things Work*. Houghton Mifflin, 1988 (I:all R:6).

Macy, Sue. *A Whole New Ball Game: The Story of the All-American Girls Professional Baseball League*. Holt, 1993 (I:10+ R:5).

_____ . *Winning Ways: A Photohistory of American Women in Sports*. Henry Holt, 1996 (I:10+ R:7).

Maestro, Betsy. *The Story of Clocks and Calendars: Marking a Millennium*. Illustrated by Giulio Maestro. Lothrop, Lee & Shepard, 1999 (I:9+ R:5).

_____ . *The Story of Money*. Illustrated by Giulio Maestro. Clarion, 1993 (I:8+ R:4).

_____ . *The Story of Religion*. Illustrated by Giulio Maestro. Clarion, 1996 (I:8+ R:6).

Majoor, Mireille. *Inside the Hindenburg: A Giant Cutaway Book*. Illustrated by Ken Marschall. Little, Brown, 2000 (I:all).

Major, John S. *The Silk Route: 7,000 Miles of History*. Illustrated by Stephen Fieser. HarperCollins, 1995 (I:8+ R:6).

Mann, Elizabeth. *The Brooklyn Bridge*. Illustrated by Alan Witschonke. Mikaya, 1996 (I:9+ R:5).

_____ . *The Great Pyramid*. Illustrated by Laura Lo Turco. Mikaya, 1996 (I:9+ R:5).

Mannetti, William. *Dinosaurs in Your Backyard*. Atheneum, 1982 (I:9+ R:6).

Markle, Sandra. *Creepy, Crawly Baby Bugs*. Walker, 1996 (I:7–9 R:4).

_____ . *Outside and Inside Spiders*. Atheneum, 1994 (I:7–9 R:4).

Marrin, Albert. *Aztecs and Spaniards: Cortez and the Conquest of Mexico*. Atheneum, 1986 (I:12+ R:7).

_____ . *Terror of the Spanish Main: Sir Henry Morgan and His Buccaneers*. Dutton, 1998 (I:10+ R:7).

Maruki, Toshi. *Hiroshima No Pika*. Lothrop, Lee & Shepard, 1982 (I:8–12 R:4).

Maynard, Caitlin, and Thane Maynard. *Rain Forests & Reefs: A Kid's-Eye View of the Tropics*. Photographs by Stan Rullman. Watts, 1996 (I:9+ R:5).

Meltzer, Milton, ed. *The American Revolutionaries: A History in Their Own Words, 1750–1800*. Crowell, 1987 (I:10+).

_____ . *Rescue: The Story of How Gentiles Saved Jews in the Holocaust*. Harper & Row, 1988 (I:10+ R:7).

_____ . *Voices from the Civil War.* Crowell, 1989 (I:10+).

Merriman, Nick. *Early Humans.* Knopf, 1989 (I:all R:5).

Meyer, Carolyn, and Charles Gallenkamp. *The Mystery of the Ancient Maya.* Atheneum, 1985 (I:10+ R:8).

Micklethwait, Lucy. *A Child's Book of Play in Art.* Dorling Kindersley, 1996 (I:4–9 R:5).

Micucci, Charles. *The Life and Times of the Apple.* Orchard, 1992 (I:all).

_____ . *The Life and Times of the Peanut.* Houghton Mifflin, 1997 (I:5–9 R:4).

Millard, Anne. *A Street Through Time: A 12,000-Year Walk Through History.* Illustrated by Steve Noon. DK, 1998 (I:all).

Miller, Brandon Marie. *Just What the Doctor Ordered: The History of American Medicine.* Lerner, 1997 (I:10+ R:6).

Miller, Debbie S. *Disappearing Lake: Nature's Magic in Denali National Park.* Illustrated by Jon Van Zyle. Walker, 1997 (I:all).

_____ . *Flight of the Golden Plover: The Amazing Migration Between Hawaii and Alaska.* Illustrated by Daniel Van Zyle. Alaska Northwest, 1996 (I:8+ R:5).

Miller, Margaret. *Who Uses This?* Greenwillow, 1990 (I:2–5).

Montgomery, Sy. *The Snake Scientist.* Photographs by Nic Bishop. Houghton Mifflin, 1999 (I:8+ R:5).

Moore, Patrick. *Comets and Shooting Stars.* Illustrated by Paul Doherty. Copper Beech, 1995 (I:6–9 R:6).

_____ . *The Planets.* Illustrated by Paul Doherty. Copper Beech, 1995 (I:6–9 R:6).

_____ . *The Stars.* Illustrated by Paul Doherty. Copper Beech, 1995 (I:6–9 R:6).

_____ . *The Sun and Moon.* Illustrated by Paul Doherty. Copper Beech, 1995 (I:6–9 R:5).

Moses, Amy. *Doctors Help People.* Child's World, 1996 (I:5–7).

Munro, Roxie. *The Inside-Outside Book of Washington, D.C.* Dutton, 1987 (I:all).

Murphy, Claire Rudolf, and Jane G. Haigh. *Children of the Gold Rush.* Rinehart, 1999 (I:10+ R:5).

Murphy, Jim. *Blizzard!* Scholastic, 2000 (I:10+ R:7).

_____ . *The Great Fire.* Scholastic, 1995 (I:10+ R:7).

_____ . *The Long Road to Gettysburg.* Clarion, 1992 (I:10+ R:5).

Nirgiotis, Nicholas, and Theodore Nirgiotis. *No More Dodos: How Zoos Help Endangered Wildlife.* Lerner, 1996 (I:10+ R:6).

Norell, Mark A., and Lowell Dingus. *A Nest of Dinosaurs: The Story of Oviraptor.* Doubleday, 1999 (I:7+ R:5).

O'Neill, Catherine. *Focus on Alcohol.* Illustrated by David Neuhaus. 21st Century Books, 1990 (I:10+ R:6).

Paladino, Catherine. *One Good Apple: Growing Our Food for the Sake of the Earth.* Houghton Mifflin, 1999 (I:8+).

Pandell, Karen. *Animal Action ABC.* Photographs by Art Wolfe and Nancy Sheehan. Dutton, 1996 (I:all).

Parker, Nancy Winslow. *Money, Money, Money: The Meaning of the Art and Symbols on United States Paper Currency.* HarperCollins, 1995 (I:9+ R:6).

Parker, Steve. *Mammal.* Knopf, 1989 (I:8–12 R:7).

Pascoe, Elaine. *The Right to Vote.* Millbrook, 1997 (I:8+ R:4).

Patent, Dorothy Hinshaw. *Back to the Wild.* Illustrated by William Muñoz. Harcourt Brace, 1997 (I:9+ R:6).

_____ . *Biodiversity.* Photographs by William Muñoz. Clarion, 1996 (I:9+ R:6).

_____ . *Prairies.* Photographs by William Muñoz. Holiday, 1996 (I:8+ R:6).

_____ . *The Whooping Crane: A Comeback Story.* Photographs by William Muñoz. Clarion, 1988 (I:8+ R:6).

Perry, Robert. *Focus on Nicotine and Caffeine.* Illustrated by David Neuhaus. 21st Century Books, 1990 (I:10+ R:5).

Peters, David. *Giants of Land, Sea & Air: Past & Present.* Knopf/Sierra Club, 1986 (I:10+ R:10).

Platt, Richard. *Castle Diary: The Journal of Tobias Burgess, Page.* Illustrated by Chris Riddell. Candlewick, 1999 (I:all).

Pope, Joyce. *Kenneth Lilly's Animals: A Portfolio of Paintings.* Illustrated by Kenneth Lilly. Lothrop, Lee & Shepard, 1988 (I:all R:7).

Priceman, Marjorie. *How to Make an Apple Pie and See the World.* Knopf, 1994 (I:5–8).

Pringle, Laurence. *Drinking: A Risky Business.* Morrow, 1997 (I:10+ R:6).

_____ . *An Extraordinary Life: The Story of a Monarch Butterfly.* Illustrated by Bob Marstall. Orchard, 1997 (I:8+ R:6).

_____ . *Saving Our Wildlife.* Enslow, 1990 (I:10+ R:6).

Provensen, Alice. *The Buck Stops Here: The Presidents of the United States.* HarperCollins, 1990 (I:all).

Raskin, Lawrie, and Debora Pearson. *My Sahara Adventure: 52 Days by Camel.* Annick, 1998 (I:9+ R:5).

Ray, Delia. *A Nation Torn: The Story of How the Civil War Began.* Lodestar, 1990 (I:10+ R:6).

Relf, Pat. *A Dinosaur Named Sue: The Story of the Colossal Fossil: The World's Most Complete T. Rex.* Scholastic, 2000 (I:10+ R:6).

Reynolds, Jan. *Sahara Vanishing Cultures.* Harcourt Brace Jovanovich, 1991 (I:8+ R:4).

Rhoades, Diane. *Garden Crafts for Kids: 50 Great Reasons to Get Your Hands Dirty.* Sterling, 1995 (I:9+ R:8).

Richardson, Joy. *Looking at Pictures: An Introduction to Art for Young People.* Illustrated by Charlotte Voake. Abrams, 1997 (I:10+).

Roche, Denis. *Loo-Loo, Boo, and Art You Can Do.* Houghton Mifflin, 1996 (I:4–9).

Rogasky, Barbara. *Smoke and Ashes: The Story of the Holocaust.* Holiday House, 1988 (I:10+ R:6).

Roop, Peter, and Connie Roop. *Seasons of the Cranes.* Walker, 1989 (I:8+ R:5).

Rossel, Seymour. *The Holocaust.* Watts, 1981 (I:9+ R:6).

Ryder, Joan. *Dancers in the Garden.* Illustrated by Judith Lopez. Sierra Club, 1992 (I:all).

Sattler, Helen Roney. *The Earliest Americans.* Illustrated by Jean Day Zallinger. Clarion, 1993 (I:10+ R:6).

_____ . *Stegosaurs: The Solar-Powered Dinosaurs.* Illustrated by Turi MacCombie. Lothrop, Lee & Shepard, 1992 (I:all R:6).

Sayre, April Pulley. *Put on Some Antlers and Walk Like a Moose: How Scientists Find, Follow, and Study Wild Animals.* 21st Century, 1997 (I:10+ R:5).

Schmandt-Besserat, Denise. *The History of Counting.* Illustrated by Michael Hays. Morrow, 1999 (I:all).

Schmitt, Lois. *Smart Spending: A Young Consumer's Guide.* Scribner, 1989 (I:12+ R:6).

Schories, Pat. *Over Under in the Garden: An Alphabet Book.* Farrar, 1996 (I:5–8).

Seibert, Patricia. *Discovering El Niño: How Fable and Fact Together Help Explain the Weather.* Illustrated by Jan Davey Ellis. Millbrook, 1999 (I:8+ R:5).

Selsam, Millicent E. *Cotton.* Photographs by Jerome Wexler. Morrow, 1982 (I:7–10 R:5).

_____. *How to Be a Nature Detective.* Illustrated by Ezra Jack Keats. Harper & Row, 1958, 1963 (I:5–8 R:4).

_____, and Joyce Hunt. *A First Look at Animals with Horns.* Illustrated by Harriet Springer. Walker, 1989 (I:5–8 R:3).

Shahan, Sherry. *Dashing Through the Snow: The Story of the Jr. Iditarod.* Millbrook, 1997 (I:8+ R:5).

Shemie, Bonnie. *Houses of Snow, Skin, and Bones.* Tundra, 1989 (I:7–12 R:5).

Shulman, Jeffrey. *Focus on Cocaine and Crack.* Illustrated by David Neuhaus. 21st Century Books, 1990 (I:10+ R:6).

Sierra Club. *Sierra Club Book of Great Mammals.* Sierra Club, 1992 (I:8+ R:5).

_____. *The Sierra Club Book of Small Mammals.* Sierra Club, 1993 (I:8+ R:5).

Sill, Cathryn. *About Birds: A Guide for Children.* Illustrated by John Sill. Peachtree, 1991 (I:3–8).

Simon, Seymour. *Earthquakes.* Morrow, 1991 (I:8+ R:6).

_____. *Galaxies.* Morrow, 1988 (I:5–8 R:5).

_____. *How to Be an Ocean Scientist in Your Own Home.* Illustrated by David A. Carter. Lippincott, 1988 (I:8+ R:5).

_____. *Jupiter.* Morrow, 1985 (I:5–8 R:5).

_____. *Lightning.* Morrow, 1997 (I:8+ R:6).

_____. *New Questions and Answers About Dinosaurs.* Illustrated by Jennifer Dewey. Morrow, 1990 (I:7+ R:5).

_____. *Poisonous Snakes.* Illustrated by William R. Downey. Four Winds, 1981 (I:7–10 R:5).

_____. *Saturn.* Morrow, 1985 (I:5–8 R:5).

_____. *Storms.* Morrow, 1989 (I:8–12 R:5).

_____. *Volcanoes.* Morrow, 1988 (I:8–12 R:5).

Skurzynski, Gloria. *Almost the Real Thing: Simulation in Your High-Tech World.* Bradbury, 1991 (I:10+ R:5).

_____. *Get the Message: Telecommunications in Your High-Tech World.* Bradbury, 1993 (I:10+ R:5).

_____. *Waves: The Electromagnetic Universe.* National Geographic, 1996 (I:8+ R:6).

Staub, Frank. *Sea Turtles.* Lerner, 1995 (I:7+ R:5).

Stefoff, Rebecca. *Finding the Lost Cities.* Oxford, 1997 (I:8+ R:5).

Steger, Will, and Jon Bowermaster. *Over the Top of the World: Explorer Will Steger's Trek Across the Arctic.* Scholastic, 1997 (I:9+ R:6).

Stevens, Leonard A. *The Case of Roe v. Wade.* Putnam, 1996 (I:12+ R:7).

Stolley, Richard B., ed. *Life: Our Century in Pictures for Young People.* Little, Brown, 2000 (I:10+).

Swain, Ruth Freeman. *Bedtime!* Illustrated by Cat Bowman Smith. Holiday, 1999 (I:6–9 R:4).

Swanson, Diane. *Buffalo Sunrise: The Story of a North American Giant.* Little, Brown, 1996 (I:10+ R:8).

_____. *Safari Beneath the Sea: The Wonder World of the North Pacific Coast.* Photographs by the Royal British Columbia Museum. Sierra Club, 1994 (I:all).

Swinburne, Stephen R. *Once a Wolf: How Wildlife Biologists Fought to Bring Back the Gray Wolf.* Photographs by Jim Brandenburg. Houghton Mifflin, 1999 (I:10+ R:6).

Tanaka, Shelley. *Secrets of the Mummies.* Illustrated by Greg Ruhl. Hyperion, 1999 (I:10+ R:6).

_____, and Hugh Brewster, eds. *Anastasia's Album.* Hyperion, 1996 (I:10+ R:6).

Thomson, Peggy, and Barbara Moore. *The Nine-Ton Cat: Behind the Scenes at an Art Museum.* Houghton Mifflin, 1997 (I:9+ R:6).

Van Loon, Hendrik Willem. *The Story of Mankind.* Liveright, 1921, 1984 (I:9+ R:5).

Vogt, Gregory L. *Disasters in Space Exploration.* Millbrook, 2001 (I:9+ R:5).

Waldman, Neil. *The Golden City: Jerusalem's 3,000 Years.* Atheneum, 1995 (I:8–12 R:10).

Walker, Barbara M. *The Little House Cookbook: Frontier Foods from Laura Ingalls Wilder's Classic Stories.* Illustrated by Garth Williams. Harper & Row, 1979 (I:8–12 R:7).

Walker, Sally. *Glaciers: Ice on the Move.* Carolrhoda, 1990 (I:9+ R:5).

_____. *Rhinos.* Photographs by Gerry Ellis. Carolrhoda, 1996 (I:8+ R:5).

Wallace, Karen. *Imagine You Are a Crocodile.* Holt, 1997 (I:3–6).

Warren, James A. *Cold War: The American Crusade Against World Communism, 1945–1991.* Lothrop, Lee & Shepard, 1996 (I:12+ R:7).

Webb, Sophie. *My Seasons with Penguins: An Antarctic Journal.* Houghton Mifflin, 2000 (I:9+ R:5).

Weitzman, David. *Old Ironsides: Americans Build a Fighting Ship.* Houghton, Mifflin, 1997 (I:9+ R:6).

Wilcox, Charlotte. *Mummies & Their Mysteries.* Carolrhoda, 1993 (I:8–12 R:5).

_____. *Trash!* Photographs by Jerry Bushey. Carolrhoda, 1988 (I:8–12 R:5).

Wolf, Bernard. *HIV Positive.* Dutton, 1997 (I:8+ R:6).

Woodford, Susan. *The Parthenon.* Cambridge/Lerner, 1983 (I:10+ R:7).

Yue, Charlotte. *Shoes: Their History in Words and Pictures.* Illustrated by David Yue. Houghton Mifflin, 1997 (I:8+ R:6).

_____, and David Yue. *Christopher Columbus: How He Did It.* Houghton Mifflin, 1992 (I:9+ R:5).

Zeller, Paula Klevan. *Focus on Marijuana.* Illustrated by David Neuhaus. 21st Century Books, 1990 (I:10+ R:6).

Adams, Dennis, and Mary Hamm. *Media and Literacy*, 2nd ed. Springfield, Ill.: Charles C. Thomas, 2000.

Adams, Karen I. "The 'Born Again' Phenomenon and Children's Books." *Children's Literature Association Quarterly* 14 (Spring 1989): 5–9.

Aiken, Joan. "Interpreting the Past." *Children's Literature in Education* 16 (Summer 1985): 67–83.

Alderson, Brian. "Children Who Live in Boxes." *The New York Times Book Review* (November 14, 1993a): 17.

_____ . "Compass, Knife and Spyglass." *The New York Times Book Review* (November 19, 2000): 22.

_____ . *Ezra Jack Keats: Artist and Picture-Book Maker.* Gretna, Louisiana: Pelican, 1994.

_____ . "Harry Potter, Dido Twite, and Mr. Beowulf." *The Horn Book Magazine* LXXVI (May/June 2000): 349–352.

_____ . "Maurice Before Max: The Yonder Side of the See-Saw." *The Horn Book* (May/June 1993b): 291–295.

_____ . *Sing a Song of Sixpence.* New York: Cambridge University Press, 1986.

_____ , ed. and trans. *Three Centuries of Children's Books in Europe.* Cleveland, Ohio: World, 1959.

Allen, Marjorie N. *What Are Little Girls Made Of? A Guide to Female Role Models in Children's Books.* New York: Facts On File, 1999.

"An Adventure with Books." *Reading Today* (June/July 2001): 15.

Aoki, M. Elaine. "Are You Chinese? Are You Japanese? Or Are You Just a Mixed-Up Kid?—Using Asian American Children's Literature." *The Reading Teacher* 34 (January 1981): 382–385.

Applebee, Arthur S. "Children and Stories: Learning the Rules of the Game." *Language Arts* 56 (September 1979).

Apseloff, Marilyn Fain. "Abandonment: The New Realism of the Eighties." *Children's Literature in Education* 23 (December 1992): 101–106.

_____ . "New Trends in Children's Books from Europe and Japan." *School Library Journal* 32 (November 1985): 30–32.

Arbuthnot, May Hill, and Dorothy M. Broderick. *Time for Biography.* Glenview, Ill.: Scott, Foresman, 1969.

Aronson, Marc. "The World According to Cart." *School Library Journal.* 46 (September 2000): 54–57.

Ashe, Rosalind, and Lisa Tuttle. *Children's Literary Houses: Famous Dwellings in Children's Fiction.* New York: Facts on File, 1984.

Ashton, John. *Chap-Books of the Eighteenth Century.* London: Chatto & Windus, 1882.

Association of Women Psychologists. "Statement of Resolutions and Motions." Miami, Fla.: American Psychological Association Convention, September 1970.

Atwood, Ann. *Haiku: The Mood of Earth.* New York: Scribner's Sons, 1971.

Au, Kathryn H. *Literacy Instruction in Multicultural Settings.* Orlando: Harcourt Brace Jovanovich, 1993.

Avery, Gillian. "Beginnings of Children's Reading to c. 1700." In *Children's Literature: An Illustrated History,* edited by Peter Hunt. Oxford: Oxford University Press, 1995, 1–25.

Avi. "The Child in Children's Literature." *The Horn Book* 69 (January/February 1993): 40–50.

Babbitt, Natalie. "Read This, It's Good For You." *The New York Times Book Review.* (May 18, 1997): 23–24.

Bader, Barbara. " 'They Shall Not Wither': John Biehorst's Quiet Crusade for Native American Literature." *The Horn Book* 73 (May/June 1997): 268–281.

Baghban, Marcia. "Too Serious Too Soon: Where Is the Childishness in Children's Fiction?" New York: National Council of Teachers of English, March 16–18, 2000.

Bagley, Ayers. *An Invitation to Wisdom and Schooling.* Society of Professors of Education Monograph Series, 1985.

Baker, Gwendolyn C. "The Role of the School in Transmitting the Culture of All Learners in a Free and Democratic Society." *Educational Leadership* 36 (November 1978): 134–138.

Ballinger, Franchot. "A Matter of Emphasis: Teaching the 'Literature' in Native American Literature Courses." *American Indian Culture and Research Journal* 8 (1984): 1–12.

Bamford, Rosemary, and Janice V. Kristo. *Checking Out Nonfiction K–8: Good Choices for Best Learning.* Norwood, Mass.: Christopher-Gordon, 2000.

Banfield, Beryle. "Racism in Children's Books: An Afro-American Perspective." In *The Black American in Books for Children: Readings in Racism,* edited by Donnarae MacCann and Gloria Woodard. Metuchen, N.J.: Scarecrow, 1985.

Barclay, Donald A. "Interpreted Well Enough: Two Illustrators' Visions of Adventures of Huckleberry Finn." *The Horn Book* 68 (May/June 1992): 311–319.

Barnes, B. "Using Children's Literature in the Early Anthropology Curriculum." *Social Education* (January 1991): 17–18.

Barr, Rebecca, and Marilyn W. Sadow. "Influence of Basal Programs on Fourth-Grade Reading Instruction." *Reading Research Quarterly* 24 (Winter 1989): 44–71.

Barrett, Thomas C. "Taxonomy of Reading Comprehension." In *Reading 360 Monograph.* Lexington, Mass.: Ginn, 1972.

Barsam, Richard. *A Peaceable Kingdom: The Shaker Abecedarius.* New York: Viking, 1978.

Bartel, Nettie. "Assessing and Remediating Problems in Language Development." In *Teaching Children with Learning and Behavior Problems,* edited by Donald Hammill and Nettie Bartel. Boston: Allyn & Bacon, 1990.

Bascom, William. "The Forms of Folklore: Prose Narratives." *Journal of American Folklore* 78 (January/March 1965): 3–20.

Bauermeister, Erica, and Holly Smith. *Let's Hear It for the Girls.* New York: Penguin, 1997.

Baylor, Byrd. *And It Is Still That Way.* New York: Scribner's Sons, 1976.

Bean, Thomas W., and Nicole Rigoni. "Exploring the Intergenerational Dialogue Journal Discussion of a Multicultural Young Adult Novel." *Reading Research Quarterly* 36 (July/August/September 2001): 232–248.

Beckham, Stephen Dow. In *Echoes of the Elders: The Stories and Paintings of Chief Lelooska* by Christine Normandin. New York: DK, 1977, 4–5.

Bedard, Michael. *Emily.* New York: Delacorte, 1992.

Behn, Harry. *Chrysalis, Concerning Children and Poetry.* New York: Harcourt Brace Jovanovich, 1968.

Behn, Robin, and Chase Twichell, eds. *The Practice of Poetry: Writing Exercises from Poets Who Teach.* New York: Harper-Collins, 1992.

Bernstein, Joanne E. "Bibliotherapy: How Books Can Help Young Children Cope." In *Children's Literature: Resource for the Classroom,* edited by Masha Kabakow Rudman. Norwood, Mass.: Christopher Gordon, 1989.

_____ . *Books to Help Children Cope with Separation and Loss,* 2nd ed. New York: Bowker, 1983.

Bettelheim, Bruno. *The Uses of Enchantment: The Meaning and Importance of Fairy Tales.* New York: Knopf, 1976.

Bierhorst, John. "Children's Books." *New York Times Book Review* (May 23, 1993).

_____ . *The Mythology of North America.* New York: Morrow, 1985.

_____ , ed. *The Red Swan: Myths and Tales of the American Indians.* New York: Farrar, Straus & Giroux, 1976.

Bingham, Jane, and Grayce Scholt. *Fifteen Centuries of Children's Literature: An Annotated Chronology of British and American Works in Historical Context.* Westport, Conn.: Greenwood, 1980.

_____ . "The Great Glass Slipper Search: Using Folk Tales with Older Children." *Elementary English* 51 (October 1974): 990–998.

Bitzer, Lucy. "The Art of Picture Books: Beautiful Treasures of Bookmaking." *Top-of-the-News* 38 (Spring 1992): 226–232.

Blatt, Gloria Toby. "Violence in Children's Literature: A Content Analysis of a Select Sampling of Children's Literature and a Study of Children's Responses to Literary Episodes Depicting Violence." East Lansing, Mich.: Michigan State University, 1972. University Microfilm No. 72-29,931.

Blenz-Clucas, Beth. "History's Forgotten Heroes: Women on the Frontier." *School Library Journal* 39 (March 1993): 118–123.

Bloom, Benjamin. *Taxonomy of Educational Objectives.* New York: Longman, 1956.

Blos, Joan W. "Newbery Medal Acceptance." *The Horn Book* 56 (August 1980): 369–377.

Blough, Glenn O. "The Author and the Science Book." *Library Trends* 22 (April 1974): 419–424.

Bond, Nancy. "Conflict in Children's Fiction." *The Horn Book* 60 (June 1984): 297–306.

Book Review Subcommittee of the National Council for the Social Studies— Children's Book Council Joint Committee. "Notable 1991 Children's Trade Books in the Field of Social Studies." *Social Education* 56 (April/May 1992): 253–264.

Booss, Claire. *Scandinavian Folk & Fairy Tales.* New York: Avenel Books, 1984.

Booth, David. "Imaginary Gardens with Real Toads: Reading and Drama in Education." *Theory into Practice* 24 (1985): 193–198.

Booth, William. "Diversity and Division: America's New Wave of Immigration Is Changing Its 'Melting Pot' Image." *The Washington Post National Weekly Edition* 15 (March 2, 1998): 6–8.

Borgman, Harry. *Art and Illustration Techniques.* New York: Watson-Guptill, 1979.

Borusch, Barbara. Personal correspondence with author, December 1, 1980.

Bossert, Jill. *Children's Book Illustration: Step by Step Techniques.* New York: Watson-Guptill, 1998.

Boulanger, Susan. "Language, Imagination, Vision: Art Books for Children." *The Horn Book* 72 (May/June 1996): 295–304.

Braga, Laurie, and Joseph Braga. *Learning and Growing: A Guide to Child Development.* Englewood Cliffs, N.J.: Prentice-Hall, 1975.

Braine, Martin. "The Ontogeny of English Phrase Structure: The First Phase." In *Readings in Language Development,* edited by Lois Bloom. New York: John Wiley, 1978.

Brandriss, Tobie. "Heroes for Our Students." *The American Biology Teacher* 61 (February 1999): 108–114.

Breen, Karen, Ellen Fader, Kathleen Odean, and Zena Sutherland. "One Hundred Books That Shaped the Century." *School Library Journal* 46 (January 2000): 50–58.

Bridge, Ethel Brooks. "Using Children's Choices of and Reactions to Poetry as Determinants in Enriching Literary Experience in the Middle Grades." Philadelphia: Temple University, 1966. University Microfilm No. 67-6246.

Briggs, Katharine. *Dictionary of British Folk-Tales.* 4 volumes. London: Routledge & Kegan Paul, 1970–1971.

Briggs, Nancy E., and Joseph A. Wagner. *Children's Literature Through Storytelling and Drama.* Dubuque, Iowa: Brown, 1979.

Brink, Carol Ryrie. *Caddie Woodlawn.* Illustrated by Trina Schart Hyman. New York: Macmillan, 1935, 1973.

Broderick, Dorothy May. *The Image of the Black in Popular and Recommended American Juvenile Fiction, 1827–1967.* New York: Columbia University, 1971. University Microfilm No. 71-4090.

Broudy, H. S. "Arts Education As Artistic Perception." In G. W. Hardiman and T. Zernich (Eds.), *Foundations for Curriculum Development and Evaluation in Art Education.* Champaign, Ill.: Stipes, 1981, 9–17.

_____ , "How Basic Is Aesthetic Education? or Is It the Fourth R?" *Language Arts* 54 (September 1977): 631–637.

Brown, Jennifer M. "Flying Starts: Ian Falconer." *Publishers Weekly* 247 (December 18, 2000): 26.

Brown, June. "Critical Questions." *The Reading Teacher* 52 (February 1999): 520–521.

Brown, Roger. *A First Language/The Early Stages.* Cambridge, Mass.: Harvard Univ. Press, 1973.

Browne, C. A. *The Story of Our National Ballads.* Edited by Willard Heaps. New York: Crowell, 1960.

Bruchac, Joseph. *Tell Me A Tale.* San Diego: Harcourt Brace, 1997.

Bryan, Ashley. *The Dancing Granny and Other African Stories.* New York: Caedmon, 1985.

Buckley, Marilyn Hanf. "Focus on Research: We Listen a Book a Day: We Speak a Book a Week: Learning from Walter Loban." *Language Arts* 69 (December 1992): 622–626.

Bulzone, Marisa. "Children's Book Illustration: Is This the New Golden Age?" *Communication Arts* 34 (January/February 1993): 94–106.

Burke, Eileen M. *Early Childhood Literature: For Love of Child and Book.* Boston: Allyn & Bacon, 1986.

Burton, Hester. "The Writing of Historical Novels." In *Children and Literature: Views and Reviews,* edited by Virginia Haviland. Glenview, Ill.: Scott, Foresman, 1973, 299–304.

Bushnaq, Inea, ed. *Arab Folk Tales.* New York: Pantheon, 1986.

Butler, Dorothy. "From Books to Buttons: Reflections from the Thirties to the Eighties." *The Arbuthnot Lectures: 1980–1989.* Chicago: American Library Association, 1990.

Byars, Betsy. Interview conducted by Ilene Cooper. "The Booklist Interview." *Booklist* 89 (January 15, 1993): 906–907.

Byler, Mary Gloyne. "American Indian Authors for Young Readers." In *Cultural Conformity in Books for Children,* edited by Donnarae MacCann and Gloria Woodard. Metuchen, N.J.: Scarecrow, 1977.

Cadogan, Mary, and Patricia Craig. *You're a Brick, Angela! A New Look at Girls' Fiction from 1839 to 1975.* London: Gollancz, 1976.

Caduto, Michael J., and Joseph Bruchac. *Keepers of the Animals: Native American Stories and Wildlife Activities for Children.* Golden, Colo.: Fulcrum, 1991.

_____ . *Keepers of the Earth: Native American Stories and Environmental Activities for Children.* Golden, Colo.: Fulcrum, 1989.

Cafakum, Leslie. "Alphabet Books Grow Up!" *Book Links* 2 (May 1993): 41–45.

Cai, Mingshui. "A Balanced View of Acculturation: Comments on Laurence Yep's Three Novels." *Children's Literature in Education* 23 (June 1992): 107–118.

_____ . "Folks, Friends and Foes: Relationships Between Humans and Animals in Some Eastern and Western Folktales." *Children's Literature in Education* 24 (1993): 73–83.

Campbell, Joseph. *The Hero with a Thousand Faces.* Princeton, N.J.: Princeton University Press, 1949, 1968.

_____ . *The Power of Myth.* New York: Doubleday, 1988.

_____ . *Transformations of Myth Through Time.* New York: Harper & Row, 1990.

Carlson, Julia Ann. *A Comparison of the Treatment of the Negro in Children's Literature in the Periods 1929–1938 and 1959–1968.* Storrs, Conn.: University of Connecticut, 1969. University Microfilm No. 70-1245.

Carlson, Ruth Kearney. "World Understanding Through the Folktale." In *Folklore and Folk Tales Around the World,* edited by Ruth Kearney Carlson. Newark, Del.: International Reading Association, 1972.

Carmichael, Carolyn Wilson. "A Study of Selected Social Values as Reflected in Contemporary Realistic Fiction for Children," East Lansing, Mich.: Michigan State University, 1971, University Microfilm No. 71-31.

Caroff, Susan, and Elizabeth Moje. "A Conversation with David Wiesner: 1992 Caldecott Medal Winner." *The Reading Teacher* 46 (December 1992/January 1993): 284–289.

Carpenter, Frank G. *Carpenter's Geographical Reader, North America.* New York: American Book, 1898.

Carter, Betty. "Hold the Applause! Do Accelerated Reader & Electronic Bookshelf Send the Right Message?" *School Library Journal* 42 (October 1996): 22–25.

Carter, James. *Talking Books.* New York: Routledge, 1999.

Carvajal, Doreen. "In Kids' Pop Culture, Fear Rules." *The New York Times* (Sunday, June 1, 1997): E. 5.

Cavendish, Richard, ed. *Legends of the World.* New York: Schocken Books, 1982.

Cecil, Nancy Lee, and Patricia L. Roberts. *Families in Children's Literature: A Resource Guide, Grades 4–8.* Englewood, Colo.: Teacher Ideas Press, 1998.

Chall, Jeanne S., and Emily W. Marston. "The Reluctant Reader: Suggestions from Research and Practice." *Catholic Library World* 47 (February 1976): 274–275.

Chance, Rosemary. "A Portrait of Popularity: An Analysis of Characteristics of Novels from Young Adults' Choices for 1997." *The Alan Review* 27 (Fall 1999): 65–67.

Chapman, Raymond. *The Victorian Debate: English Literature and Society 1832–1901.* New York: Basic Books, 1968.

Charpenel, Mauricio. "Literature About Mexican American Children." College Station, Tex.: Texas A&M University, Children's Literature Conference, 1980.

Cheatham, Bertha M. "News of '85: SLJ's Annual Roundup." *School Library Journal* 32 (December 1985): 19–27.

"Children's Choices for 1992." *The Reading Teacher* 46 (October 1992): 127–141.

"Children's Choices for 1993: A Project of the International Reading Association and the Children's Book Council." *The Reading Teacher* 47 (October 1993): 127–141.

Children's Literature Association. *Touchstones: A List of Distinguished Children's Books.* Lafayette, Ind.: Purdue University; Children's Literature Association, 1985.

"Children's Voices: A Response to Harry Potter." *The New Advocate* 14 (Winter 2001): 86–87.

Cianciolo, Patricia J. "A Look at the Illustrations in Children's Favorite Picture Books." In *Children's Choices: Teaching with Books Children Like,* edited by Nancy Roser and Margaret Frith. Newark, Del.: International Reading Association, 1983.

_____ . *Picture Books for Children,* 3rd ed. Chicago: American Library Association, 1990.

_____ . *Picture Books for Children,* 4th ed. Chicago: American Library Association, 1997.

_____ . "Reading Literature, and Writing from Writers' Perspectives." *English Journal* 74 (December 1985): 65–69.

Cirker, Blanche. *The Book of Kells: Selected Plates in Full Color.* New York: Dover, 1982.

Clark, Anne. "Books in the Classroom: Poetry." *The Horn Book* 68 (September/October 1992): 624–627.

Clark, Beverly Lyon, and Margaret R. Higonnet, eds. *Girls, Boys, Books, Toys: Gender in Children's Literature and Culture.* Baltimore, Md.: Johns Hopkins University Press, 1999.

Clark, Leonard. "Poetry for the Youngest." In *Horn Book Reflections,* edited by Elinor Whitney Field. Boston: Horn Book, 1969.

Clay, Marie M. "Child Development." In *Handbook of Research on Teaching the English Language Arts,* edited by James Flood, Julie M. Jensen, Diane Lapp, and James R. Squire. Upper Saddle River, N.J.: Merrill/Prentice Hall, 1991, 40–45.

Coe, Michael. *The Maya,* 4th ed. New York: Thames & Hudson, 1992.

_____ , Dean Snow, and Elizabeth Benson. *Atlas of Ancient America.* New York: Facts on File, 1986.

Cohen, Caron Lee. "The Quest in Children's Literature." *School Library Journal* 31 (August 1985): 28–29.

Commire, Anne. *Something About the Author: Facts and Pictures About Contemporary Authors and Illustrators of Books for Young People.* Detroit: Gale, 1971.

Committee on Geographic Education. *Guidelines for Geographic Education: Elementary and Secondary Schools.* Washington, D.C.: National Council for Geographic Education and the Association of American Geographers, 1983.

Connell, Christopher. "Middle-Class Housewife Writes High-Class Children's Tales." *Bryan-College Station Eagle* (March 28, 1984): 1F.

Cook, Elizabeth. *The Ordinary and the Fabulous: An Introduction to Myths, Legends, and Fairy Tales,* 2d ed. Cambridge: University Press, 1976.

Coolidge, Olivia E. *Legends of the North.* Boston: Houghton Mifflin, 1951.

_____ . "My Struggle with Facts." *Wilson Library Bulletin* 49 (October 1974): 146–151.

Cooper, Ilene. "The African American Experience in Picture Books." *Booklist* 88 (February 1, 1992): 1036–1037.

Cooper-Solomon, Debra. "A Look at Eric Carle." *School Arts* 98 (May/June 1999): 18–19.

Council on Interracial Books for Children. "Chicano Culture in Children's Literature: Stereotypes, Distortions and Omissions." In *Cultural Conformity in Books for Children,* edited by Donnarae MacCann and Gloria Woodard. Metuchen, N.J.: Scarecrow, 1977a.

———. "Criteria for Analyzing Books on Asian Americans." In *Cultural Conformity in Books for Children,* edited by Donnarae MacCann and Gloria Woodard. Metuchen, N.J.: Scarecrow, 1977b.

Courlander, Harold. *A Treasury of African Folklore.* New York: Crown, 1975.

Cowen, John E. "Conversations with Poet Jose Garcia Villa on Teaching Poetry to Children." In *Teaching Reading Through the Arts,* edited by John E. Cowen. Newark, Del.: International Reading Association, 1983, 78–87.

Crane, Walter. *The Decorative Illustration of Books Old and New.* London: Bracken, 1984.

Creeden, Sharon. *Fair Is Fair: World Folktales of Justice.* Little Rock, Ark.: August House, 1995.

Crosscurrents. Aspen, Colo.: Aspen Music Festival and School, 2001.

Crossley-Holland, Kevin. *The Faber Book of Northern Legends.* Boston: Faber & Faber, 1983.

Crowley, Daniel. Foreword to *"On Another Day . . ." Tales Told Among the Nkundo of Zaire,* collected by Mabel Ross and Barbara Walker. Hamden, Conn.: Archon, 1979.

Cullinan, Beatrice, Marilyn C. Scalo, and Virginia Schroeder. *Three Voices: An Invitation to Poetry Across the Curriculum.* York, Me.: Stenhouse, 1995.

Cullingford, Cedric. *Children's Literature and Its Effects: The Formative Years.* London: Cassell, 1998.

Cullum, Carolyn N. *The Storytime Sourcebook: A Compendium of Ideas and Resources for Storytellers,* 2nd ed. New York: Neal-Schuman, 1999.

Cummins, Julie. "Taste Trends: A Cookie Lover's Assortment of Picture Book Art." *School Library Journal* 42 (September 1996): 118–123.

"Curriculum Connectors: Family Secrets." *School Library Journal* 43 (March 1997): 112–113.

Cushing, Frank Hamilton. *Zuni Folktales.* Tucson: University of Arizona Press, 1986.

Danoff, Michael. Quoted in *The Art of Nancy Ekholm Burkert,* edited by David Larkin. New York: Harper & Row, 1977.

Darton, F. J. Harvey. *Children's Books in England: Five Centuries of Social Life.* New York: Cambridge University Press, 1932, 1966.

Davis, Anita P., and Thomas R. McDaniel. "You've Come a Long Way, Baby—Or Have You: Research Evaluating Gender Portrayal in Recent Caldecott-Winning Books." *The Reading Teacher* 52 (February 1999): 532–536.

Davis, Joann. "Trade News: Sendak on Sendak." As told to Jean F. Mercier. *Publishers Weekly* (April 10, 1981): 45–46.

Davis, J. Madison. *Creating Plot.* Cincinnati, Ohio: Writers Digest Books, 2000.

Davis, Joy B., and Laurie MacGillivray. "Books About Teen Parents: Messages and Omissions." *English Journal* 90 (January 2001): 90–96.

Day-Lewis, Cecil. *Poetry for You.* New York: Oxford, 1947.

deCaro, Frank, ed. *The Folktale Cat.* Little Rock, Ark.: August House, 1992.

DelFattore, Joan. *What Johnny Shouldn't Read: Textbook Censorship in America.* New Haven: Yale University Press, 1992.

Dempsey, Frank J. "Russell Freedman." *The Horn Book* (July/August 1988): 452–456.

De Wit, Dorothy. *Children's Faces Looking Up: Program Building for the Storyteller.* Chicago: American Library Association, 1979.

Diakiw, J. "Children's Literature and Global Education: Understanding the Developing World." *The Reading Teacher* 43 (1990): 296–300.

Dole, J., G. Duffy, L. Roehler, and P. D. Pearson. "Moving from the Old to the New: Research on Reading Comprehension Instruction." *Review of Educational Research* 61 (1991): 239–264.

Donelson, Ken. "Almost 13 Years of Book Protests—Now What?" *School Library Journal* 31 (March 1985): 93–98.

Dorris, Michael. "Native American Literature in an Ethnohistorical Context." *College English* 41 (October 1979): 147–162.

———. "On *Morning Girl.*" Press Release by Hyperion Books, 1992.

Dressel, Janice Hartwick. "Abstraction in Illustration: Is It Appropriate for Children?" *Children's Literature in Education* 15 (Summer 1984): 103–112.

Drury, John. *The Poetry Dictionary.* Cincinnati, Ohio: Story Press, 1995.

Dryer, Charles Redway. *Geography, Physical, Economic, and Regional.* New York: American Books, 1911.

Duffy, Gerald G. "Crucial Elements in the Teaching of Poetry Writing." In *The Language Arts in the Middle School,* edited by Martha L. King, Robert Emans, and Patricia J. Cianciolo. Urbana, Ill.: National Council of Teachers of English, 1973.

Dundes, Alan. "Interpreting Little Red Riding Hood Psychoanalytically." In *The Brothers Grimm and Folktale,* edited by James M. McGlathey. Urbana: University of Illinois Press, 1988, 16–51.

Dunning, Stephen, and William Stafford. *Getting the Knack: 20 Poetry Writing Exercises.* Urbana: National Council of Teachers of English, 1992.

Early, Margaret. "What Ever Happened To . . . ?" *The Reading Teacher* 46 (December 1992/January 1993): 302–308.

Eccleshare, Julie. "Children's Books: Letter From London." *Publishers Weekly* 244 (August 18, 1997): 25.

Egoff, Sheila. "The Problem Novel." In *Only Connect: Readings on Children's Literature,* edited by Sheila Egoff, G. T. Stubbs, and L. F. Ashley. Toronto: Oxford University Press, 1980.

———. *Worlds Within: Children's Fantasy from the Middle Ages to Today.* Chicago: American Library Association, 1988.

Eichenberg, Fritz. "Bell, Book and Candle." In *The Arbuthnot Lectures: 1980–1989.* Chicago: American Library Association, 1990, 51–66.

Elleman, Barbara. "The Nonfiction Scene: What's Happening." In *Using Nonfiction Trade Books in the Elementary Classroom,* edited by Evelyn Freedman and Diane Person. Urbana, Ill.: National Council of Teachers of English, 1992, 26–33.

Ellis, Rex M. *Beneath the Blazing Sun.* Little Rock, Ark.: August House, 1997.

Engelfried, Steven. "The ABCs of ABCs: A Look at 26 of the Most Innovative Alphabet Books Around." *School Library Journal* 47 (January 2001): 32–33.

English Journal Forum. "When Minority Becomes Majority." *English Journal* 79 (January 1990): 15.

Epstein, William H. "Introducing Biography." *Children's Literature Association Quarterly* 12 (Winter, 1987): 177–179.

Erisman, Fred Raymond. "There Was a Child Went Forth: A Study of St. Nicholas Magazine and Selected Children's Authors, 1890–1915," Minneapolis: University of Minnesota, 1966, University Microfilm No. 66–12.

Ernest, Edward. *The Kate Greenaway Treasury.* Cleveland, Oh.: World, 1967.

Esmonde, Margaret P. "Children's Science Fiction." In *The First Steps: Best of the Early ChLA Quarterly.* Compiled by

Patricia Dooley. Lafayette, Ind.: Purdue University; Children's Literature Association, 1984.

Evans, Dilys. "An Extraordinary Vision: Picture Books of the Nineties." *The Horn Book* 68 (November/December 1992): 759–763.

Evans, Janet, ed. *What's in the Pictures?* London: Paul Chapman, 1998.

Faulkner, William J. *The Days When the Animals Talked*. Illustrated by Troy Howell. Chicago: Follett, 1977.

Favat, F. André. *Child and Tale: The Origins of Interest*. Urbana, Ill.: National Council of Teachers of English, 1977.

"Federal Technology Funding for Schools Jumps 450 Percent." *School Library Journal* 42 (November 1996): 14.

Feitelson, D., B. Kita, and Z. Goldstein. "Effects of Listening to Series Stories on First Graders' Comprehension and Use of Language." *Research in the Teaching of English* 20 (1986): 339–355.

Feldman, Edmund Burke. *Varieties of Visual Experience*. New York: Abrams, 1992.

Feldman, Roxanne. "The Truth About Harry." *School Library Journal*. 45 (September 1999): 136–139.

Feldstein, Barbara. "Selection as a Means of Diffusing Censorship." In *Children's Literature: Resource for the Classroom*, edited by Masha Kabakow Rudman. Norwood, Mass.: Christopher Gordon, 1993, 147–167.

Fillmore, Lily Wong. "Educating Citizens for a Multicultural 21st Century." *Multicultural Education* 1 (Summer 1993): 10–12, 37.

Fisher, Carol, and Margaret Natarella. "Young Children's Preferences in Poetry: A National Survey of First, Second, and Third Graders." *Research in the Teaching of English* 16 (December 1982): 339–354.

Fisher, Leonard Everett. "The Artist at Work: Creating Nonfiction." *The Horn Book* (May/June 1988): 315–323.

Fisher, Margery. "Life Course or Screaming Farce?" *Children's Literature in Education* 7 (Autumn 1976): 108–115.

Flack, Jerry D. *From the Land of Enchantment: Creative Teaching With Fairy Tales*. Englewood, Colo.: Libraries Unlimited, 1997.

Fleming, Margaret, and Jo McGinnis, eds. *Portraits: Biography and Autobiography in the Secondary School*. Urbana, Ill.: National Council of Teachers of English, 1985.

Flender, Mary G. "Charting Book Discussions: A Method of Presenting Literature in the Elementary Grades." *Children's Literature in Education* 16 (Summer 1985): 84–92.

Fohr, Samuel Denis. *Cinderella's Gold Slipper: Spiritual Symbolism in the Grimms' Tales*. Wheaton, Ill.: Quest Books, 1991.

Ford, Paul Leicester. *The New-England Primer*. New York: Columbia University, Teachers College, 1962.

"Forecasts: Children's Books." *Publishers Weekly* 247 (August 14, 2000): 354–356.

Forman, Jack. "Young Adult Books: Politics—The Last Taboo." *The Horn Book* 61 (July/August 1985): 469–471.

Fowke, Edith, and Joe Glazer. *Songs of Work and Protest*. New York: Dover, 1973.

Fox, Dan. *Go In and Out the Window: An Illustrated Songbook for Young People*. New York: The Metropolitan Museum of Art and H. Holt, 1987.

Fraser, James H., ed. *Society and Children's Literature*. Boston: Godine, 1978.

Frasher, Ramona. "A Feminist Look at Literature for Children: Ten Years Later." In *Sex Stereotypes and Reading: Research and Strategies*, edited by E. Marcia Sheridan. Newark, N.J.: International Reading Association, 1982.

Freedman, Russell. "Fact or Fiction?" In *Using Nonfiction Trade Books in the Elementary Classroom*, edited by Evelyn Freeman and Diane Person. Urbana, Ill.: National Council of Teachers of English, 1992, 2–10.

———. "Newbery Medal Acceptance." *The Horn Book* (July/August 1988): 444–451.

Friedan, Betty. "My Quest for the Fountain of Age." *Time* 142 (September 6, 1993): 61–64.

Fritz, Jean. *Homesick: My Own Story*. New York: Putnam, 1982.

———. "Making It Real." *Children's Literature in Education* 22 (Autumn 1976): 125–127.

Frobenius, Leo, and Douglas Fox. *African Genesis*. Berkeley, Calif.: Turtle Island for the Netzahualcoyatl Historical Society, 1983.

Fry, Edward. "Fry's Readability Graph: Clarifications, Validity, and Extension." *Journal of Reading* 21 (December 1977): 249.

Frye, Northrop, Sheridan Baker, and George Perkins. *The Harper Handbook to Literature*. New York: Harper & Row, 1985.

Furnivall, Frederick J., ed. *Caxton's Book of Curtesye*. London: Oxford University Press, 1868.

Gage, N. L., and David C. Berliner. *Educational Psychology*. Chicago: Rand McNally, 1979.

Galda, Lee. "Accent on Art." *The Reading Teacher* 44 (February 1991): 406–414.

———. "Readers, Texts and Contexts: A Response-Based View of Literature in the Classroom." *The New Advocate* 1 (Spring, 1988): 92–102.

Garfield, Leon. "Historical Fiction for Our Global Times." *The Horn Book* (November/December 1988): 736–742.

Garrett, Jeffrey. "Far-Away Wisdom: Three Nominees for the 1992 Andersen Prize." *The Reading Teacher* 46 (December 1992/January 1993): 310–314.

Gay, Carol. "Children's Literature and the Bicentennial." *Language Arts* 53 (January 1976): 11–16.

Geller, Linda Gibson. *Wordplay and Language Learning for Children*. Urbana, Ill.: National Council of Teachers of English, 1985.

Gensler, Kinereth, and Nina Nyhart. *The Poetry Connection: An Anthology of Contemporary Poems with Ideas to Stimulate Children's Writing*. New York: Teachers & Writers, 1978.

GEO News Handbook. (November 11–17, 1990): 7.

George, Jean Craighead. "Science Is Stories." In *Vital Connections: Children, Science, and Books*, edited by Wendy Saul and Sybille A. Jagusch. Washington: Library of Congress, 1991, 67–70.

Gerke, Pamela. *Multicultural Plays for Children, Volume II, Grades 4–6*. New Hampshire: Smith & Kraus, 1996.

Gibbons, Euell. *Stalking the Wild Asparagus*. New York: McKay, 1962, 1970.

Giblin, James Cross. "The Rise and Fall and Rise of Juvenile Nonfiction, 1961–1988." In *Using Nonfiction Trade Books in the Elementary Classroom*, edited by Evelyn Freedman and Diane Person. Urbana, Ill.: National Council of Teachers of English, 1992, 17–25.

Gibson, Louis Rauch, and Laura M. Zaidman. "Death in Children's Literature: Taboo or Not Taboo?" *Children's Literature Association Quarterly* 16 (Winter 1992): 232–234.

Gillespie, Margaret C. *Literature for Children: History and Trends*. Dubuque, Iowa: Brown, 1970.

Gillin, Richard. "Romantic Echoes in the Willow." *Children's Literature* 16 (1988): 169–174.

Gillmor, Frances. *The King Danced in the Marketplace*. Salt Lake City: University of Utah Press, 1977.

Gish, Kimbra Wilder. "Hunting Down Harry Potter: An Exploration of Religious

Concerns About Children's Literature." *The Horn Book* LXXVI (May/June 2000): 262–271.

Glazer, Joan. *Literature for Young Children.* Upper Saddle River, N.J.: Merrill/Prentice Hall, 1991.

Glazer, Tom. *A New Treasury of Folk Songs.* New York: Bantam Books, 1961.

Gleason, Katherine. *Native American Literature.* New York: Chelsea, 1996.

Glenn, Wendy J. "Brock Cole: The Good, the Bad, and the Humorously Ironic." *The Alan Review* 26 (Winter 1999): 26–29.

Gloria, Alberta. "Battling Against Attrition." *The Newsletter of the University of Wisconsin (Madison)* (Spring 2001): 14, 16.

Goble, Paul. *Notes by Goble About the Illustrations for* The Girl Who Loved Wild Horses. New York: Bradbury Press, 1978.

Godden, Rumer. "Shining Popocatapetl: Poetry for Children." *The Horn Book* (May/June 1988): 305–314.

"Going Places." *Reading Today* 18 (February/March 2001): 3.

Goldberg, Lazer. "Gaps and Emphases." In *Vital Connections: Children, Science, and Books,* edited by Wendy Saul and Sybille A. Jagusch. Washington: Library of Congress, 1991, 31–41.

Golman, Daniel. *Emotional Intelligence.* New York: Bantam, 1995.

Good, Carter. *Dictionary of Education.* New York: McGraw-Hill, 1973.

Gordon, Christine J. "Modeling Inference Awareness Across the Curriculum." *Journal of Reading* 28 (February 1985): 444–447.

Gosa, Cheryl. "Moral Development in Current Fiction for Children and Young Adults." *Language Arts* 54 (May 1977): 529–536.

Gough, John. "Experiencing a Sequence of Poem: Ted Hughes's *Season Songs.*" *Children's Literature Association Quarterly* 13 (Winter 1988): 191–194.

———. "Poems in a Context: Breaking the Anthology Trap." *Children's Literature in Education* 15 (Winter 1984): 204–210.

Granstrom, Jane, and Anita Silvey. "A Call for Help: Exploring the Black Experience in Children's Books." In *Cultural Conformity in Books for Children,* edited by Donnarae MacCann and Gloria Woodard. Metuchen, N.J.: Scarecrow, 1977.

Graves, Donald. *Writing: Teachers and Children at Work.* Exeter, N.H.: Heinemann, 1988.

Greaney, Vincent. "Factors Related to Amount and Type of Leisure Time Reading." *Reading Research Quarterly* 15 (1980): 337–357.

Green, Roland J. "Modern Science Fiction and Fantasy: A Frame of Reference." *Illinois School Journal* 57 (Fall 1977): 45–53.

Green, Thomas A., ed. *Folklore: An Encyclopedia of Beliefs, Customs, Tales, Music and Art,* Vol. 11. Santa Barbara, Calif.: ABC-CLIO, 1997.

Greenfield, Eloise. "Writing for Children—A Joy and a Responsibility." In *The Black American in Books for Children: Readings in Racism,* edited by Donnarae MacCann and Gloria Woodard. Metuchen, N.J.: Scarecrow, 1985.

Greenway, William, and Betty Greenway. "Meeting the Muse: Teaching Contemporary Poetry by Teaching Poetry Writing." *Children's Literature Association Quarterly* 15 (1990): 138–142.

Griego y Maestas, Jose, and Rudolfo A. Anaya. *Cuentos: Tales from the Hispanic Southwest.* Santa Fe: Museum of New Mexico, 1980.

Griffiths, Antony, ed. *Landmarks in Print Collecting.* London: British Museum, 1996.

Groce, Robin, and Patricia Wiese. *A Mosaic of Stories: Celebrating Cultures Through Classroom Storytelling.* College Station, Tex.: Texas A & M University, 2000.

Groff, Patrick. "Where Are We Going with Poetry for Children?" In *Horn Book Reflections,* edited by Elinor Whitney Field. Boston: Horn Book, 1969.

Gross, John. "Pop-Up Books: The Magical Art of Making Movable Pictures over the Years." *The New York Times* (Sunday, January 17, 1988): 33H.

Gurjar, Nandita. "Position of Women in Indian Culture and Literature." Paper presented at Multicultural Conference. Texas A & M University, 1995.

Haight, Anne Lyon. *Banned Books: 387 B.C. to 1978 A.D.* New York: R. R. Bowker, 1978.

Haining, Peter. *Movable Books: An Illustrated History.* London: New English Library Limited, 1979.

Haley, Gail E. "From the Ananse Stories to the Jack Tales: My Work with Folktales." *Children's Literature Association Quarterly* 11 (Fall 1986): 118–121.

Hall, Ann E. "Contemporary Realism in American Children's Books." *Choice* (November 1977): 1171–1178.

Hall, Christine, and Martin Coles. *Children's Reading Choices.* New York: Routledge, 1999.

Hall, Edwin S., Jr. *The Eskimo Storyteller: Folktales from Noatak, Alaska.* Knoxville: The University of Tennessee Press, 1976.

Hamilton, Martha, and Mitch Weiss. "Children as Storytellers: Teaching the Basic Tools." *School Library Journal* 39 (April 1993): 30–33.

———. *Children Tell Stories: A Teaching Guide.* Katonah, N.Y.: Richard C. Owen, 1990.

———. *How & Why Stories: World Tales Kids Can Read & Tell.* Little Rock, Ark.: August House, 1999.

Hamilton, Virginia. *The People Could Fly: American Black Folktales.* New York: Knopf, 1985.

———. "Planting Seeds." *The Horn Book* 68 (November/December 1992): 674–680.

Hampl, Patricia. "A Review of *The Diary of a Young Girl: Anne Frank, the Definitive Edition.*" *The New York Times Book Review* (March 5, 1995): 21.

Hanson, W. D., and M. O. Eisenbise. *Human Behavior and American Indians.* Rockville, Md.: National Institute of Mental Health, 1983. ERIC Document Reproduction Service, ED 231–589.

Harms, Jeanne McLain, and Lucille J. Lettow. "Book Design Elements: Integrating the Whole." *Childhood Education* 75 (Fall 1998): 17–24.

Harris, Violet. "Multiethnic Children's Literature." In *Exploring Literature in the Classroom: Content and Methods,* edited by K. D. Wood and A. Moss. Norwood, Mass.: Christopher-Gordon, 1992, 169–201.

Harrison, Barbara. "Howl Like the Wolves." *Children's Literature* 15 (1987): 67–90.

Harvey, Karen D., Lisa D. Harjo, and Jane K. Jackson. *Teaching About Native Americans.* Washington, D.C.: National Council for the Social Studies, 1990.

Haugaard, Erik. "When Does the Past Become History?" In *The Child and the Family: Selected Papers from International Conference of the Children's Literature Association,* edited by Susan R. Gannon and Ruth Anne Thompson. New York: Pace University, 1988, 5–11.

Haven, Kendall. *Super Simple Storytelling: A Can-Do Guide for Every Classroom, Every Day.* Englewood, Colo.: Libraries Unlimited, 2000.

Haviland, Virginia. *Children and Literature: View and Reviews.* Glenview, Ill.: Scott, Foresman, 1973.

———. *North American Legends.* New York: Collins, 1979.

Hawley, John C. "The Water-Babies as Catechetical Paradigm." *Children's Literature*

Association Quarterly 14 (Spring 1989): 19–21.

Hayden, Carla D., ed. *Venture into Cultures: A Resource Book of Multicultural Materials and Programs.* Chicago: American Library Association, 1992.

Hayden, Gretchen Purtell. "A Descriptive Study of the Treatment of Personal Development in Selected Children's Fiction Books Awarded the Newbery Medal." Detroit: Wayne State University, 1969, University Microfilm No. 70-19,060.

Hearn, Michael Patrick. Preface to *Histories or Tales of Past Times,* by Charles Perrault. New York: Garland, 1977.

Hearne, Betsy. *Beauty and the Beast: Visions and Revisions of an Old Tale.* Chicago: University of Chicago Press, 1989.

———. "Booking the Brothers Grimm: Art, Adaptations, and Economics." In *The Brothers Grimm and Folktale,* edited by James M. McGlathery. Urbana, Ill.: University of Illinois Press, 1988, 220–233.

———. "Circling Tuck: An Interview with Natalie Babbitt." *The Horn Book* LXXVI (March/April 2000): 153–161.

———. "Cite the Source: Reducing Cultural Chaos in Picture Books, Part One." *School Library Journal* 39 (July 1993a): 22–27.

———. "Contemporary Issues—Child Abuse." *Booklist* 81 (May 1, 1985): 1261–1262.

———. "Patterns of Sound, Sight, and Story: From Literature to Literacy." *The Lion and the Unicorn* 16 (June 1992): 17–42.

———. "Picture Books: More Than a Story." *Booklist* 30 (December 1, 1983): 577–578.

———. "Respect the Source: Reducing Cultural Chaos in Picture Books, Part Two." *School Library Journal* 39 (August 1993b): 33–37.

Heins, Paul. "Coming to Terms with Criticism." In *Crosscurrents of Criticism: Horn Book Essays 1968–1977.* Boston: The Horn Book, 1978a, 82–87.

———. "Out on a Limb with the Critics: Some Random Thoughts on the Present State of the Criticism of Children's Literature." In *Crosscurrents of Criticism: Horn Book Essays 1968–1977.* Boston: The Horn Book, 1978b, 72–81.

———. "A Second Look: The Adventures of Pinocchio." *The Horn Book* (April 1982): 200–204.

Hendrick, Joanne. *The Whole Child,* 4th ed. Upper Saddle River, N.J.: Merrill/Prentice Hall, 1992.

Henke, James T. "Dicey, Odysseus, and Hansel and Gretel: The Lost Children of Voigt's *Homecoming.*" *Children's Literature in Education* 16 (Spring 1985): 45–52.

Hepler, Susan Ingrid. "Profile, Tomie de Paola: A Gift to Children." *Language Arts* 56 (March 1979): 269–301.

Herb, Steve. "Building Blocks for Literacy: What Current Research Shows." *School Library Journal* 43 (July 1997): 23.

Herbst, Laura. "That's One Good Indian: Unacceptable Images in Children's Novels." In *Cultural Conformity in Books for Children,* edited by Donnarae MacCann and Gloria Woodard. Metuchen, N.J.: Scarecrow, 1977.

Herman, Gertrude B. "'Footprints on the Sands of Time': Biography for Children." *Children's Literature in Education* 9 (Summer 1977): 85–94.

Herring, William A. "Creating Rhythm with Color and Line." *American Artist* 61 (March 1997): 40–43.

Hewett, Gloria J., and Jean C. Rush. "Finding Buried Treasures: Aesthetic Scanning with Children." *Art Education* 40 (January 1987): 41–43.

Hillocks, George. *Research on Written Composition: New Directions for Teaching.* Urbana, Ill.: National Conference on Research in English, 1986.

Hillyer, V. M. *A Child's Geography of the World.* Illustrated by Mary Sherwood Wright Jones. New York: Century, 1929.

Hilts, Paul. "The Road Ahead: Publishing Visionaries Look at the Change That Digital Technology Might Bring." *Publishers Weekly* 244 (July 1997): 125–128.

Hipple, Ted, and Amy B. Maupin. "What's Good About the Best?" *English Journal* 90 (January 2001): 40–42.

Hockwald, Lambeth. "Little Book, Big Controversy." *Publishers Weekly,* 243 (July 29, 1996): 32–33.

Hoffman, James, and P. David Pearson. "Reading Teacher Education in the Next Millennium: What Your Grandmother's Teacher Didn't Know That Your Granddaughter's Teacher Should." *Reading Research Quarterly* 35 (January/February/March 2000): 28–44.

Hoffman, Lynn. "Picture Books at the Museum." *Joys* 14 (Fall 2000): 16–17.

Holt, David, and Bill Mooney, eds. *Ready-to-Tell Tales.* Little Rock, Ark.: August House, 1994.

Holzheimer, Diane. "Appraisal: A Book Review Journal." In *Vital Connections: Children, Science, and Books,* edited by Wendy Saul and Sybille A. Jagusch. Washington: Library of Congress, 1991, 91–96.

Homze, Alma Cross. "Interpersonal Relationships in Children's Literature from 1920 to 1960." University Park, Pa.: Pennsylvania State University, 1963. University Microfilm No. 64-5366.

Hopkins, Dianne McAfee. "Put It in Writing: What You Should Know About Challenges to School Library Materials." *School Library Journal* 39 (January 1993): 26–30.

Hopkins, Lee Bennett. *Pass the Poetry, Please!* New York: Harper & Row, 1987.

"The Horn Book Guide to Children's and Young Adult Books." *The Horn Book* 4 (Spring 1993): 18–51.

Houghton Mifflin Company. *Eliminating Stereotypes, School Division Guidelines.* Boston: Houghton Mifflin, 1981.

Houston, James. "A Primitive View of the World." In *The Arbuthnot Lectures, 1980–1989.* Chicago: American Library Association, 1990, 99–111.

Hsu, Richard C., and William E. Mitchell. "Books Have Endured for a Reason . . ." *The New York Times* 3 (Sunday, May 25, 1997): 12.

Huck, Charlotte S., Susan Hepler, and Janet Hickman. *Children's Literature in the Elementary School.* Madison, Wis.: Brown & Benchmark, 1997.

Hunt, Peter. "Censorship and Children's Literature in Britain Now, or, The Return of Abigail." *Children's Literature in Education* 28 (1997): 95–103.

———, ed. *Children's Literature: An Illustrated History.* New York: Oxford University Press, 1995.

———. "Dialogue and Dialectic: Language and Class in *The Wind in the Willows.*" *Children's Literature* 16 (1988): 159–168.

Hürlimann, Bettina. "Fortunate Moments in Children's Books." In *The Arbuthnot Lectures, 1970–1979,* compiled by Zena Sutherland. Chicago: American Library Association, 1980, 61–80.

Huus, Helen. "Teaching Literature at the Elementary School Level." *The Reading Teacher* 26 (May 1973): 795–801.

Isaacs, Kathleen T. "Flying High." *School Library Journal* 47 (March 2001): 52–55.

Iskander, Sylvia Patterson. "'Goody Two-Shoes' and *The Vicar of Wakefield.*" *Children's Literature Association Quarterly* 13 (Winter 1988): 165–168.

Jacobs, Melville. *The Content and Style of an Oral Literature: Clackamas Chinook Myths and Tales.* Chicago: University of Chicago Press, 1959.

Jacobson, Frances F. "Remembrance of Things Past: Making History Come Alive With Primary Sources." *School Library Journal* 46 (December 2000): 35.

Jaffe, Nina. "Reflections on the Work of Harold Courlander." *School Library Journal* 42 (September 1996): 132–133.

James, Grace. *Green Willow and Other Japanese Fairy Tales.* New York: Avenel, 1987.

Janson, H. W., and Anthony F. Janson. *History of Art for Young People,* 6th ed. New York: Abrams, 1999.

Jerome, Judson. *Poetry: Premeditated Art.* Boston: Houghton Mifflin, 1968.

Johannessen, Larry R. *Teaching the Literature of the Vietnam War.* Urbana, Ill.: National Council of Teachers of English, 1992.

Johnston, Kathleen S. "Choosing Books." In *Vital Connections: Children, Science, and Books,* edited by Wendy Saul and Sybille A. Jagusch. Washington, D.C.: Library of Congress, 1991, 97–103.

Jones, Leigh Ann. "Better Libraries Through Censorship." *School Library Journal* 42 (October 1996): 54.

Jorgensen, Karin. "Making the Reading, Writing, Social Studies Connection." *Social Studies and the Young Learner* 2 (March/April 1990): 20–22.

Judson, Hallowell. "What Is in a Picture?" *Children's Literature in Education* 20 (March 1989): 59–68.

Jurich, Marilyn. "What's Left Out of Biography for Children?" *Children's Literature: The Great Excluded* 1 (1972): 143–151.

Kaminski, Winfred. "War and Peace in Recent German Children's Literature." *Children's Literature* 15 (1987): 55–66.

Karl, Jean E. *How to Write and Sell Children's Books.* Cincinnati, Ohio: Writers Digest Books, 1994.

———. "What Sells—What's Good?" *The Horn Book* 63 (July/August 1987): 505–508.

Kean, John M., and Carl Personke. *The Language Arts: Teaching and Learning in the Elementary School.* New York: St. Martin, 1976.

Kehret, Peg. "Encouraging Empathy." *School Library Journal* 47 (August 2001): 44–45.

Keith, Harold. *The Obstinate Land.* New York: Crowell, 1977.

Kelly, Robert Gordon. "Mother Was a Lady: Self and Society in Selected American Children's Periodicals, 1865–1890," Iowa City, Iowa: University of Iowa, 1970, University Microfilm No. 71-5770.

———. "Social Factors Shaping Some Nineteenth-Century Children's Periodical Fiction." In *Society and Children's Literature,* edited by James H. Fraser. Boston: Godine, 1978.

Kennemer, Phyllis K. "Reviews of Fiction Books: How They Differ." *Top of the News* 40 (Summer 1984): 419–421.

Kherdian, David. *Feathers and Tails: Animal Fables from Around the World.* New York: Philomel, 1992.

Killheffer, Robert K. J. "Fantasy Charts New Realms." *Publishers Weekly* 244 (June 16, 1997): 34–40.

Kimmel, Mary, and Elizabeth Segel. *For Reading Out Loud.* New York: Dell, 1983.

King, Stephen. "Wild About Harry." *The New York Times Book Review* (July 23, 2000): 13–14.

Kingsbury, Mary. "Perspectives on Criticism." *The Horn Book* 60 (February 1984): 17–23.

Kingsley, Mary. *West African Studies,* 3rd ed. New York: Barnes & Noble, 1964.

Kiska, Paula. "Slavic Wonder Tales: An Overview." *Children's Literature Association Quarterly* 11 (Fall 1986): 123–128.

Knorr, Susan M., and Margaret Knorr. *Books on the Move: A Read-About-It Go-There Guide to America's Best Family Destinations.* Minneapolis: Free Spirit, 1993.

Kobus, Doni Kwolek. "Multicultural/Global Education: An Educational Agenda for the Rights of the Child." *Social Education* 56 (April/May 1992): 224–227.

Koch, Kenneth. *Wishes, Lies, and Dreams.* New York: Vintage Books/Chelsea House, 1970.

Kohlberg, Lawrence. *Essays on Moral Development: The Philosophy of Moral Development.* New York: Harper & Row, 1981.

Kukla, Kaile. "David Booth: Drama as a Way of Knowing." *Language Arts* 64 (January 1987): 73–78.

Kun-yu, Bu. "Between Two Cultures." *Social Education* 52 (September 1988): 378–383.

Kuo, Louise, and Yuan-hsi Kuo. *Chinese Folk Tales.* Millbrae, Calif.: Celestial Arts, 1976.

Kutiper, Karen Sue. "A Survey of the Adolescent Poetry Preferences of Seventh, Eighth, and Ninth Graders." University of Houston: Ed.D. Dissertation, 1985. DAI 47:451–452A.

Lacy, Lyn Ellen. *Art and Design in Children's Picture Books: An Analysis of Caldecott Award-Winning Illustrations.* Chicago: American Library Association, 1986.

Laliberté, Norman, and Alex Mogelon. *The Reinhold Book of Art Ideas.* New York: Van Nostrand Reinhold, 1976.

Lamb, Charles, and Mary Lamb. *Tales from Shakespeare.* New York: Children's Classics, 1986.

Lamme, Linda Leonard. "Reading Aloud to Young Children." *Language Arts* 53 (November/December 1976): 886–888.

———, and Frances Kane. "Children, Books, and Collage." *Language Arts* 53 (November/December 1976): 902–905.

Lanes, Selma. *The Art of Maurice Sendak.* New York: Abradale Press, 1980.

Larrick, Nancy. *Let's Do a Poem.* New York: Delacorte Press, 1991.

Lasky, Kathryn. *Beyond the Divide.* New York: Macmillan, 1983.

Latimer, Bettye I. *Starting Out Right: Choosing Books About Black People for Young Children.* Madison, Wis.: Wisconsin Department of Public Instruction, 1972, Bulletin No. 2314.

———. "Telegraphing Messages to Children About Minorities." *The Reading Teacher* 30 (November 1976): 151–156.

Lauber, Patricia. "The Evolution of a Science Writer." In *Using Nonfiction Trade Books in the Elementary Classroom,* edited by Evelyn Freedman and Diane Person. Urbana, Ill.: National Council of Teachers of English, 1992, 11–16.

———. "The Heart of the Matter." In *Vital Connections: Children, Science, and Books,* edited by Wendy Saul and Sybille A. Jagusch. Washington, D.C.: Library of Congress, 1991, 45–50.

Laws, Frederick. "Randolph Caldecott." In *Only Connect: Readings on Children's Literature,* edited by Sheila Egoff, G. T. Stubbs, and L. F. Ashley. 2nd ed. Toronto: Oxford University Press, 1980.

Leeson, Robert. *Children's Books and Class Society.* London: Writers & Readers, 1977.

Leggo, Carl. *Teaching to Wonder: Responding to Poetry in the Secondary Classroom.* Vancouver: Pacific Educational Press, 1997.

Lehr, Susan, ed. *Battling Dragons: Issues and Controversy in Children's Literature.* Portsmouth, N.H.: Heinemann, 1995.

Lenaghan, R. T., ed. *Caxton's Aesop.* Cambridge, Mass.: Harvard University Press, 1967.

Lenz, Liza. "Crossroads of Literacy and Orality: Reading Poetry Aloud. *Lan-*

guage Arts 69 (December 1992): 597–603.

Le Pere, Jean. "For Every Occasion: Poetry in the Reading Program." Albuquerque, N.M.: Eighth Southwest Regional Conference, International Reading Association, 1980.

Lepman-Logan, Claudia. "Books in the Classroom: Moral Choices in Literature." *The Horn Book* (January/February 1989): 108–111.

Leroi-Gourhan, Andre. *Treasures of Prehistoric Art.* New York: Abrams.

Lewis, Naomi. "Introduction." In Peter Christen Asbjörnsen and Jorgen Moe's *East O' the Sun and West O' the Moon.* Cambridge, Mass.: Candlewick, 1991.

Lewis, Rena, and Donald Doorlag. *Teaching Special Students in the Mainstream.* 2nd ed. Upper Saddle River, N.J.: Merrill/Prentice Hall, 1987.

Lindauer, Shelley L. Knudsen. "Wordless Books: An Approach to Visual Literacy." *Children's Literature in Education* 19 (1988): 136–142.

Linder, Enid, and Leslie Linder. *The Art of Beatrix Potter.* London: Frederick Warne, 1980.

Lipkis, Rita. "Books in the Classroom: Young Hands on Old Books." *The Horn Book* 69 (January/February 1993): 115–118.

Lipman, Doug. *Improving Your Storytelling: Beyond the Basics for All Who Tell Stories in Work or Play.* Little Rock, Ark.: August House, 1999.

_____ . *The Storytelling Coach.* Little Rock, Ark.: August House, 1995.

Lipson, Eden Ross. "Summer and the Reading Can Be Easy." *The New York Times Book Review* (May 20, 2001): 26–27.

Livingston, Myra Cohn. "Not the Rose . . ." In *Horn Book Reflections,* edited by Elinor Whitney Field. Boston: Horn Book, 1969.

_____ . *Poems of Lewis Carroll.* New York: Crowell, 1973.

_____ . *Poetry-Making: Ways to Begin Writing Poetry.* New York: Harper-Collins, 1991.

Loban, Walter. *Language Development: Kindergarten Through Grade Twelve.* Urbana, Ill.: National Council of Teachers of English, 1976.

Lobsenz, Norman. "News from the Home Front." *Family Weekly* (August 2, 1981): 9.

Locke, John. "Some Thoughts Concerning Education." In *English Philosophers,* edited by Charles W. Eliot. New York: Villier, 1910.

Lodge, Sally, compiled by. "Children's Books for Fall." *Publishers Weekly* 243 (July 22, 1996): 158–205.

_____ . "Rolling Out the Green Carpet: Environmental Books for Kids." *Publishers Weekly* 239 (March 2, 1992): 22–25.

_____ . "Spanish-Language Publishing for Kids in the U.S. Picks Up Speed." *Publishers Weekly* Special Supplement (August 25, 1997): 548–549.

Lofaro, Michael A. *The Tall Tales of Davy Crockett: The Second Nashville Series of Crockett Almanacs, 1839–1841.* Knoxville: University of Tennessee Press, 1987.

Long, Joanna Rudge. "Eloquent Visions: Perspectives In Picture Book Biography." *School Library Journal* 43 (April 1997): 48–49.

Lonsdale, Bernard J., and Helen K. Macintosh. *Children Experience Literature.* New York: Random House, 1973.

Lottman, Herbert R. "In the Studio with Satomi Ichikawa." *Publishers Weekly* 240 (June 7, 1993): 19.

Lowell, Amy. *Poetry and Poets.* New York: Biblo, 1971.

Lukens, Rebecca J. *A Critical Handbook of Children's Literature,* 6th ed. Reading, Mass.: Addison-Wesley, 1999.

Lunstrum, John P., and Bob L. Taylor. *Teaching Reading in the Social Studies.* Newark, Del.: International Reading Association, 1978.

Lustig, Arnost. "What We Will Never Understand About the Holocaust." Unexpected Encounters With the Holocaust Conference: Texas A&M University, College Station, Texas, April 2, 1997.

Lystad, Mary. *From Dr. Mather to Dr. Seuss: Two Hundred Years of American Books for Children.* Boston: G. K. Hall, 1980.

McCall, Cecelia. "A Historical Quest for Literacy." *Interracial Books for Children Bulletin* 19 (1989): 3–5.

MacCann, Donnarae, and Olga Richard. *The Child's First Books: A Critical Study of Pictures and Texts.* New York: Wilson, 1973.

MacLeod, Anne Scott. *American Childhood.* Athens: University of Georgia Press, 1994.

_____ . "Children's Literature in America from the Puritan Beginnings to 1870." In *Children's Literature: An Illustrated History,* edited by Peter Hunt. Oxford: Oxford University Press, 1995, 102–129.

McClenathan, Day Ann K. "Realism in Books for Young People. Some Thoughts on Management of Controversy." In *Developing Active Readers: Ideas for Parents, Teachers, and Librarians,* edited by Dianne L. Monson and Day Ann K. McClenathan. Newark, Del.: International Reading Association, 1979.

McCord, David. *One at a Time: Collected Poems for the Young.* Boston: Little, Brown, 1977.

McCord, Sue. *The Storybook Journey: Pathways to Literacy Through Story and Play.* Upper Saddle River, N.J.: Merrill/Prentice Hall, 1995.

McCulloch, Lou J. *An Introduction to Children's Literature: Children's Books of the 19th Century.* Des Moines, Iowa: Wallace-Honestead, 1979.

McDermott, Beverly Brodsky. *The Golem.* Philadelphia: Lippincott, 1976.

MacDonald, Margaret Read. *The Story-Teller's Start-Up Book.* Little Rock, Ark.: August House, 1993.

MacDonald, Robert. "Signs from the Imperial Quarter: Illustrations in *Chums,* 1892–1914." *Children's Literature* 16 (1988): 31–55.

McElderry, Margaret. "The Best Times, the Worst Times, Children's Book Publishing 1917–1974." *The Horn Book* (October 1974): 85–94.

McElmeel, Sharron L. *100 Most Popular Children's Authors: Biographical Sketches and Bibliographies.* Englewood, Colo.: Libraries Unlimited, 1999.

McElveen, Susan, and Connie Dierking, *Literature Modes to Teach Expository Writing.* Gainesville, Fla.: Maupin House, 2001.

_____ . *Teaching Writing Skills with Children's Literature.* Gainesville, Fla.: Maupin House, 1999.

McGarvey, Jack. ". . . But Computers Are Clearly the Future." *The New York Times* (Sunday, May 25, 1997): 12.

McGavran, James Holt, ed. *Literature and the Child: Romantic Continuations, Postmodern Contestations.* Iowa City: University of Iowa Press, 1999.

McGrath, Robin. "Words Melt Away Like Hills in Fog: Putting Inuit Legends Into Print." *Children's Literature Association Quarterly* 13 (Spring 1988): 9–12.

McGuire, Sandra. "Promoting Positive Attitudes Toward Aging." *Childhood Education* 69 (Summer 1993): 204–210.

McIntyre, Barbara M. *Creative Drama in the Elementary School.* Itasca, Ill.: Peacock, 1974.

McKay, Gwendda. "Poetry and the Young Child." *English in Australia* (June 1986): 52–58.

Madsen, Jane M., and Elaine B. Wickersham. "A Look at Young Children's Realistic Fiction." *The Reading Teacher* 34 (December 1980): 273–279.

Maguire, Jack. "Sounds and Sensibilities: Storytelling as an Educational Process." *Children's Literature Association Quarterly* 13 (Spring, 1988): 6–9.

Maher, Susan Naramore. "Encountering Others: The Meeting of Cultures in Scott O'Dell's *Island of the Blue Dolphins* and *Sing Down the Moon*." *Children's Literature in Education* 23 (1992): 215–227.

———. "Recasting Crusoe: Frederick Marryat, R. M. Ballantyne and the Nineteenth-Century Robinsonade." *Children's Literature Association Quarterly* 13 (Winter 1988): 169–175.

Manguel, Alberto. *A History of Reading*. New York: Viking, 1996.

———, and Gianni Guadalupi. *The Dictionary of Imaginary Places*. Illustrated by Graham Greenfield and James Cook. New York: Macmillan, 1980.

Marantz, Sylvia S. *Picture Books for Looking and Learning: Awakening Visual Perceptions Through the Art of Children's Books*. Phoenix: Oryx Press, 1992.

Marcus, Leonard S. "Awakened by the Moon." *Publishers Weekly* 238 (July 26, 1991): 16–20.

———. "Song of Myself." *School Library Journal* 46 (September 2000): 50–53.

Marshall, Cynthia. "Allegory, Orthodoxy, Ambivalence: MacDonald's *The Day Boy and the Night Girl*." *Children's Literature* 16 (1988): 57–75.

Martin, Sue Anne Gillespi. "The Caldecott Medal Award Books, 1938–1968: Their Literary and Oral Characteristics as They Relate to Storytelling." Detroit, Mich.: Wayne State University, 1969. University Microfilm No. 72-16,219.

Martinez, Miriam, and Nancy Roser. "Children's Responses to Literature." In *Handbook of Research on Teaching the English Language Arts*, edited by James Flood, Julie M. Jensen, Diane Lapp, and James R. Squire. New York: Macmillan, 1991, 643–654.

Maryles, Daisy. "Behind the Bestsellers." *Publishers Weekly* 243 (July 22, 1996): 141.

Maughan, Shannon. "Dealing the Straight Dope." *Publishers Weekly* 239 (April 13, 1992): 23.

Maxim, George. *The Very Young: Guiding Children from Infancy Through the Early Years*. Upper Saddle River, N.J.: Merrill/Prentice Hall, 1993.

Mediavilla, Cindy. *Arthurian Fiction: An Annotated Bibliography*. Lanham, Md.: Scarecrow Press, 1999.

Meigs, Cornelia, Elizabeth Nesbitt, Anne Thaxter Eaton, and Ruth Hill. *A Critical History of Children's Literature: A Survey of Children's Books in English*. New York: Macmillan, 1969.

Mendelson, Michael. "*The Wind in the Willows* and the Plotting of Contrast." *Children's Literature* 16 (1988): 125–144.

Mendoza, Alicia. "Reading to Children: Their Preferences." *The Reading Teacher* 38 (February 1985): 522–527.

Merriam, Eve. *Rainbow Writing*. New York: Atheneum, 1976.

Merrick, Brian. "With a Straight Eye: An Interview with Charles Causley." *Children's Literature in Education* 19 (Winter 1988): 123–135.

Metcalf, Eva-Maria, and Michael J. Meyer. "Society, Child Abuse, and Children's Literature." *Children's Literature Association Quarterly* 17 (Fall 1992): 2–3.

Miller, Peggy J. "Peter Rabbit and Mr. McGregor Reconciled, Charlotte Lives: Preschoolers Recreate the Classics." *The Horn Book* 73 (May/June 1997): 282–283.

Miller, Winifred. "Dragons—Fact or Fantasy?" *Elementary English* 52 (April 1975): 582–585.

Milne, A. A. *The Christopher Robin Story Book*. New York: Dutton, 1966.

Mittelstadt, Michelle. "Texas High on Watchdog Group's Censorship List." Associated Press. Bryan, College Station, Tex.: *The Eagle* (Thursday, September 2, 1993): A9.

Monson, Dianne, and Sam Sebesta. "Reading Preferences." In *Handbook of Research on Teaching the English Language Arts*, edited by James Flood, Julie M. Jensen, Diane Lapp, and James R. Squire. New York: Macmillan, 1991, 664–673.

Moore, Ann W. "A Question of Accuracy: Errors in Children's Biographies." *School Library Journal* 31 (February 1985): 34–35.

Moore, Eva. *The Fairy Tale Life of Hans Christian Andersen*. Illustrated by Trina Schart Hyman. New York: Scholastic, 1969.

Moore, Lilian. "A Second Look: The Poetry of Lillian Morrison." *The Horn Book* 69 (May/June 1993): 303–306.

———. "A Second Look: Small Poems." *The Horn Book* (July/August 1988): 470–473.

Moore, Robin. *Creating a Family Storytelling Tradition: Awakening the Hidden Storyteller*. Little Rock, Ark.: August House, 1999.

Morache, Jette. "Use of Quotes in Teaching Literature." *English Journal* 76 (October 1987): 61–63.

Morgan, Betty M. *An Investigation of Children's Books Containing Characters from Selected Minority Groups Based on Specified Criteria*. Carbondale, Ill.: Southern Illinois University, 1973. University Microfilm No. 74-6232.

Moritz, Charles. *Current Biography Yearbook*. New York: Wilson, 1968.

Morrison, Lillian. *The Sidewalk Racer and Other Poems of Sport and Motion*. New York: Lothrop, Lee & Shepard, 1977.

Morrow, Lesley Mandel. "Promoting Voluntary Reading." In *Handbook of Research on Teaching the English Language Arts*, edited by James Flood, Julie M. Jensen, Diane Lapp, and James R. Squire. New York: Macmillan, 1991, 681–690.

Morse, Samuel French. "Speaking of the Imagination." In *Horn Book Reflections*, edited by Elinor Whitney Field. Boston: Horn Book, 1969.

Muir, Percy. *English Children's Books, 1600 to 1900*. New York: Praeger, 1954.

Musleah, Rahel. "Rediscovering the Jewish Folktale." *Publishers Weekly* 239 (September 21, 1992): 42–43.

Mussen, Paul Henry, John Janeway Conger, and Jerome Kagan. *Child Development and Personality*. New York: Harper & Row, 1989.

National Council for the Social Studies. "The Columbian Quincentenary: An Educational Opportunity." *Social Education* 56 (April/May 1992): 248–249.

National Science Teachers Association. "Criteria for Selection—Outstanding Science Trade Books for Children." *Science and Children* 34 (March 1997): 23.

Natov, Roni. "Internal and External Journeys: The Child Hero in *The Zabajaba Jungle* and *Linnea in Monet's Garden*." *Children's Literature In Education* 20 (June 1989): 91–101.

Nelson, Mary Ann. *A Comparative Anthology of Children's Literature*. New York: Holt, Rinehart & Winston, 1972.

Nesbit, E., retold by. *Beautiful Stories from Shakespeare*. New York: Weathervane. Facsimile of 1907 edition.

Neufeld, John. "Preaching to the Unconverted." *School Library Journal* 42 (July 1996): 36.

Newcomb, Franc J. *Navajo Folk Tales*. Santa Fe: Museum of Navajo Ceremonial Art, 1967, xvi.

Nikolajeva, Maria, ed. *Aspects and Issues in the History of Children's Literature.* Westport, Conn.: Greenwood, 1995.

Nikola-Lisa, W. "Scribbles, Scrawls, and Scratches: Graphic Play as Subtext in the Picture Books of Ezra Jack Keats." *Children's Literature in Education* 22 (December 1991): 247–255.

Nilsen, Aileen Pace. "Women in Children's Literature." *College English* 32 (May 1971): 918–926.

———, and Kenneth L. Donelson. *Literature for Today's Young Adults,* 4th ed. New York: HarperCollins, 1993.

———. *Literature for Today's Young Adults,* 6th ed. New York: Longman, 2001.

Nitschke, August. "The Importance of Fairy Tales in German Families Before the Grimms." In *The Brothers Grimm and Folktale,* edited by James M. McGlathery. Urbana, Ill.: University of Illinois Press, 1988, 164–177.

Noble, Judith Ann. "The Home, the Church, and the School as Portrayed in American Realistic Fiction for Children 1965–1969." East Lansing, Mich.: Michigan State University, 1971. University Microfilm No. 31-271.

Noble, William. *Bookbanning in America: Who Bans Books?—and Why.* Middlebury, Vt.: Eriksson, 1990.

Nodelman, Perry. "How Children Respond to Art." *School Library Journal* 31 (December 1984a): 40–41.

———. "Some Presumptuous Generalizations About Fantasy." In *The First Steps: Best of the Early ChLA Quarterly.* Compiled by Patricia Dooley. Purdue University; Children's Literature Association, 1984b, 15–16.

———. "Which Children? Some Audiences for Children's Books." *The Horn Book* 63 (January/February 1987): 35–40.

———. *Words About Pictures.* Athens: University of Georgia Press, 1988.

———. *Words About Pictures,* 2nd ed. Athens: University of Georgia Press, 1990.

Noel, Ruth S. *The Mythology of Middle Earth.* Boston: Houghton Mifflin, 1977.

Norton, Donna E. "Centuries of Biographies for Childhood." *Vitae Scholasticae* 3 (Spring 1984): 113–129.

———. *The Effective Teaching of Language Arts,* 5th ed. Upper Saddle River, N.J.: Merrill/Prentice Hall, 1997.

———. "The Expansion and Evaluation of a Multiethnic Reading/Language Arts Program Designed for 5th, 6th, 7th, and 8th Grade Children." Meadows Foundation Grant, No. 55614, A Three Year Longitudinal Study. Texas A&M University, 1984–1987.

———. "Folklore and the Language Arts." In *Language Arts Instruction and the Beginning Teacher,* edited by Dale Johnson and Carl Personke. Englewood Cliffs, N.J.: Prentice-Hall, 1987a.

———. "Genres in Children's Literature: Identifying, Analyzing, and Appreciating." In *Children's Literature: Resource for the Classroom,* edited by Masha Kabakow Rudman. Norwood, Mass.: Christopher-Gordon, 1993, 75–94.

———. *The Impact of Literature-Based Reading.* Upper Saddle River, N.J.: Merrill/Prentice Hall, 1992.

———. "The Intrusion of an Alien Culture: The Impact and Reactions as Seen Through Biographies and Autobiographies of Native Americans." *Vitae Scholasticae* 6 (Spring 1987): 59–75.

———. "Moral Stages of Children's Biographical Literature: 1800s–1900s." *Vitae Scholasticae* (Fall 1986).

———. *Multicultural Literature: Through the Eyes of Many Children.* Upper Saddle River, N.J.: Merrill/Prentice Hall, 2001.

———. "Teaching Multicultural Literature in the Reading Program." *The Reading Teacher* 44 (September 1990): 28–40.

———. "A Three-Year Study Developing and Evaluating Children's Literature Units in Children's Literature Courses." Paper presented at the College Reading Association, National Conference, Baltimore, Md., October, 1980.

———. *Through the Eyes of a Child: An Introduction to Children's Literature,* 3rd ed. Upper Saddle River, N.J.: Merrill/Prentice Hall, 1991.

———. "A Web of Interest." *Language Arts* 54 (November 1977): 928–932.

———, and James F. McNamara. *An Evaluation of the Multicultural Reading/Language Arts Program for Elementary and Junior High School Students.* College Station, Tex.: Texas A&M University, 1988.

———, and Saundra E. Norton. *Language Arts Activities for Children,* 4th ed. Upper Saddle River, N.J.: Merrill/Prentice Hall, 1999.

Noss, Philip A. "Description in Gbaya Literary Art." In *African Folklore,* edited by Richard Dorse. Bloomington, Ind.: Indiana University Press, 1972.

"Notable Children's Trade Books in the Field of Social Studies." *Social Education* (April/May 1992): 253–264.

Odean, Katheleen. "Adventures and Accomplishments: Picture-Book Biographies of Women." *School Library Journal* 42 (December 1996): 664–665.

———. "The Story Master." *School Library Journal* 46 (October 2000): 50–54.

Olson, Renee. "When It Comes To Technology . . . The Postman Always Thinks Twice." *School Library Journal* 42 (May 1996): 19–22.

Opler, Morris Edward. *Myths and Tales of the Jicarilla Apache Indians.* Memoirs 31. New York: American Folklore Society, 1938.

Parsons, Elsie Clews. *Folktales of Andros Island, Bahamas.* New York: American Folklore Society, 1918.

Paterson, Katherine. *A Sense of Wonder: On Reading and Writing Books for Children.* New York: Penguin, 1995.

Paul, Lissa. "A Second Look: The Return of the Iron Man." *The Horn Book Magazine* LXXVI (March/April 2000): 218–225.

Paulin, Mary Ann. *Creative Uses of Children's Literature.* Hamden, Conn.: Library Professional Pubs., 1985.

Peck, Richard. "The Great Library-Shelf Witch Hunt." *Booklist* 88 (January 1, 1992): 816–817.

Pellowski, Anne. *The Family Story-Telling Handbook.* New York: Macmillan, 1987.

———. *Hidden Stories in Plants.* New York: Macmillan, 1990.

———. *The World of Storytelling.* New York: Bowker, 1977.

Perfect, Kathy A. "Rhyme and Reason: Poetry for the Heart and Head." *The Reading Teacher* 52 (April 1999): 728–737.

Perrine, Laurence. *Literature: Structure, Sound, and Sense,* 4th ed. San Diego: Harcourt Brace Jovanovich, 1983.

Phelan, Carolyn. "Talking with Mem Fox." *Book Links* 2 (May 1993): 29–32.

Phelps, Ruth M. "A Comparison of Newbery Award Winners in the First and Last Decade of the Award (1922–31 and 1976–85). Miami University, 1985, DAI 47: 453A.

Piaget, Jean, and B. Inhelder. *The Psychology of the Child.* New York: Basic Books, 1969.

Piper, David. "Language Growth in the Multiethnic Classroom." *Language Arts* 63 (January 1986): 23–36.

Polking, Kirk, ed. *Writing A to Z.* Cincinnati, Oh.: Writer's Digest Books, 1990.

Poole, Roger. "The Books Teachers Use." *Children's Literature in Education* 17 (Fall 1986): 159–180.

Preble, Duane. *Art Forms.* New York: Harper & Row, 1978.

Prewitt, Jana Wright. "Poetry for the Fourth-Grade Classroom." Paper, Texas A&M University, 2001.

Pringle, Laurence. "The Thinking Gap." In *Vital Connections: Children, Science, and Books,* edited by Wendy Saul and Sybille A. Jagusch. Washington: Library of Congress, 1991, 51–56.

_____ . *Wild Foods: A Beginner's Guide to Identifying, Harvesting and Preparing Safe and Tasty Plants from the Outdoors.* Illustrated by Paul Breeden. New York: Four Winds, 1978.

Probst, Robert. "Response to Literature." In *Handbook of Research on Teaching the English Language Arts,* edited by James Flood, Julie M. Jensen, Diane Lapp, and James R. Squire. New York: Macmillan, 1991, 633–655.

_____ . "Teaching the Reading of Literature." In *Content Area Reading and Learning: Instructional Strategies,* edited by Diane Lapp, James Flood, and N. Farnan. Englewood Cliffs, N.J.: Prentice Hall, 1989, 179–186.

Proett, Jackie, and Kent Gill. *The Writing Process in Action: A Handbook for Teachers.* Urbana, Ill.: National Council of Teachers of English, 1986.

Propp, Vladimir. *Morphology of the Folktale.* Translated by Laurence Scott. Austin, Tex.: University of Texas, 1968.

"Publishers Weekly: Children's Bestsellers." *Publishers Weekly* 244 (July 21, 1997): 177.

Purves, Alan C. "The School Subject Literature." In *Handbook of Research on Teaching the English Language Arts,* edited by James Flood, Julie M. Jensen, Diane Lapp, and James R. Squire. New York: Macmillan, 1991, 674–680.

_____ , and Dianne L. Monson. *Experiencing Children's Literature.* Glenview, Ill.: Scott, Foresman, 1984.

Quammen, David. "The Look of the Wild: How Styles of Illustration Have Changed the Way We Look at Animals." *The New York Times Book Review* (November 7, 1993): 12.

Quayle, Eric. *The Collector's Book of Children's Books.* New York: Clarkson N. Potter, 1971.

Querry, Ron. "Discovery of America: Stories Told by Indian Voices." In *American Diversity, American Identity: The Lives and Works of 145 Writers Who Define the American Experience,* edited by John K. Roth. New York: Holt, 1995.

Rauch, Alan. "A World of Faith on a Foundation of Science: Science and Religion in British Children's Literature: 1761–1878."

Children's Literature Association Quarterly 14 (Spring 1989): 13–19.

Raugust, Karen. "Sports Leagues Target Young Fans With Books." *Publishers Weekly* 244 (August 18, 1997): 34–35.

Raymo, Chet. "Dr. Seuss and Dr. Einstein: Children's Books and Scientific Imagination." *The Horn Book* 68 (September/October 1992): 560–567.

Reed, Susan Nugent. "Career Idea: Meet the Poet at His Craft." In *Using Literature and Poetry Affectively,* edited by Jon E. Shapiro. Newark, Del.: International Reading Association, 1979.

Rees, David. "The Virtues of Improbability: Joan Aiken." *Children's Literature in Education* 19 (Spring 1988): 42–54.

Rees-Williams, Gladys, and Brian Rees-Williams, eds. *What I Cannot Tell My Mother Is Not Fit for Me to Know.* New York: Oxford University Press, 1981.

Reichard, Gladys A. *An Analysis of Coeur d'Alene Indian Myths.* Philadelphia: American Folklore Society, 1974.

Reiss, Johanna. *The Upstairs Room.* New York: Crowell, 1972.

Reissman, Rose. "Writer/Author Q & A—Technology Takes the Published Interview to the Next Generation of Reader Response." *English Journal* 85 (February 1996): 78–79.

Reynolds, Kimberley and Nicholas Tucker, eds. *Children's Book Publishing in Britain Since 1945.* Brookfield, Vt.: Ashgate, 1998.

Rice, Daniel. "Vision and Culture: The Role of Museums in Visual Literacy." *The Journal of Museum Education* 13 (1988): 13–17.

Riley, Gail Blasser. *Censorship.* New York: Facts On File, 1998.

Roback, Diane, and Cindi Di Marzo. "Children's Book Survey: Consumer Awareness." *Publishers Weekly* 244 (June 16, 1997): 28–31.

Roback, Diane, and Shannon Maughan, eds. "Fall 1996 Children's Books: The Road Ahead." *Publishers Weekly* 243 (July 22, 1996): 151–153.

Robertson, Elizabeth, and Jo McGinnis. "Biography as Art: A Formal Approach." In *Portraits: Biography and Autobiography in the Secondary School,* edited by Margaret Fleming and Jo McGinnis. Urbana, Ill.: National Council of Teachers of English, 1985.

Rochman, Hazel. "The African American Journey: From Slavery to Freedom." *Booklist* 89 (February 15, 1993): 1052–1053.

_____ . *Against Borders: Promoting Books for a Multicultural World.* Chicago: American Library Association, 1992a.

_____ . "The Booklist Interview: Maurice Sendak." *Booklist* 88 (June 15, 1992b): 1848–1849.

_____ . "The Booklist Interview: Virginia Hamilton." *Booklist* 88 (February 1, 1992c): 1020–1021.

_____ . "Booktalking: Going Global." *The Horn Book* (January-February 1989): 30–35.

_____ . "How Not to Write About the Holocaust." *Booklist* 89 (October 15, 1992): 416.

_____ . "Loose Canon." *Booklist* 92 (September 1, 1996): 114–115.

_____ . "Young Adult Books: Childhood Terror." *The Horn Book* 61 (September/October 1985): 598–602.

Roehler, Laura, and Gerald G. Duffy. "Direct Explanation of Comprehension Processes." In *Comprehension Instruction,* edited by Gerald G. Duffy, Laura R. Roehler, and Jana Mason. New York: Longman, 1984, 265–280.

Roller, Cathy. "Classroom Interaction Patterns: Reflections of a Stratified Society." *Language Arts* 66 (September 1989): 492–500.

Root, Shelton L. "The New Realism—Some Personal Reflections." *Language Arts* 54 (January 1977): 19–24.

Rosenberg, Liz. "Has Poetry for Kids Become a Child's Garden of Rubbish?" *The New York Times Book Review* (November 10, 1991): 55.

Rosenblatt, Louise. "Language, Literature, and Values." In *Language, Schooling, and Society,* edited by S. N. Tchudi. Upper Montclair, N.J.: Boyton/Cook, 1985, 64–80.

_____ . "Literary Theory." In *Handbook of Research on Teaching the English Language Arts,* edited by James Flood, Julie M. Jensen, Diane Lapp, and James R. Squire. Upper Saddle River, N.J.: Merrill/Prentice Hall, 1991, 57–62.

_____ . *The Reader, the Text, and the Literary Work.* Carbondale, Ill.: Southern Illinois Press, 1978.

Ross, A. C., and D. Brave Eagle. *Value Orientation—A Strategy for Removing Barriers.* Denver, Colo.: Coalition of Indian Controlled School Boards, 1975. ERIC Document Reproduction, ED 125–811.

Ross, Elinor P. "Comparison of Folk Tale Variants." *Language Arts* 56 (April 1979): 422–426.

Ross, Jan. "Small Is Tall—Children and Self-Esteem." *Book Links* 2 (January 1993): 53–59.

Ross, Mabel, and Barbara Walker. *"On Another Day . . ." Tales Told Among the Nkundo of Zaire.* Hamden, Conn.: Archon, 1979.

Ross, Ramon R. *Storyteller,* 2d ed. Upper Saddle River, N.J.: Merrill/Prentice Hall, 1980.

Routman, Regle. *Literacy At the Crossroads: Crucial Talk About Reading, Writing, and Other Teaching Dilemmas.* Portsmouth, N.H.: Heineman, 1996.

Rovenger, Judith. "Fostering Emotional Intelligence: A Librarian Looks at the Role of Literature in a Child's Development." *School Library Journal* 46 (December 2000): 40–41.

Ruddell, Robert. "A Whole Language and Literature Perspective: Creating a Meaning-Making Instructional Environment." *Language Arts* 69 (December 1992): 612–619.

Rudman, Masha Kabakow. "Children's Literature in the Reading Program." In *Children's Literature: Resource for the Classroom,* edited by Masha Kabakow Rudman. Norwood, Mass.: Christopher-Gordon, 1993a, 171–199.

_____ . *Children's Literature: An Issues Approach,* 2d ed. New York: Longman, 1984.

_____ ."People Behind the Books: Illustrators." In *Children's Literature: Resource for the Classroom,* edited by Masha Kabakow Rudman. Norwood, Mass.: Christopher-Gordon, 1993b, 19–41.

_____ , and Anna Markus Pearce. *For Love of Reading: A Parent's Guide to Encouraging Young Readers from Infancy Through Age 5.* Mount Vernon, N.Y.: Consumers Union, 1988.

Ruggieri, Colleen A. "What About Our Girls? Considering Gender Roles with *Shabanu.*" *English Journal* 90 (January 2001): 48–53.

Russell, David L. *Scott O'Dell.* New York: Twayne, 1999.

Rutherford, James. "Vital Connections: Children, Books, and Science." In *Vital Connections: Children, Books, and Science,* edited by Wendy Saul and Sybille A. Jagusch. Washington D.C.: Library of Congress, 1991, 21–30.

Sacks, David. "Breathing New Life Into Ancient Greece and Rome." *School Library Journal,* 42 (November 1996): 38–39.

Sagan, Carl. *Cosmos.* Public Broadcasting System, October 26, 1980.

Sage, Mary. "A Study of the Handicapped in Children's Literature." In *Children's Literature, Selected Essays and Bibliographies,* edited by Anne S. MacLeod. College Park, Md.: University of Maryland College of Library and Informational Services, 1977.

Sale, Roger. *Fairy Tales and After: From Snow White to E. B. White.* Cambridge, Mass.: Harvard University Press, 1978.

Sam Houston Area Reading Conference, Sam Houston State University, February 1981.

Sandburg, Carl. *The American Songbag.* New York: Harcourt Brace Jovanovich, 1927.

San Diego Museum of Art. *Dr. Seuss from Then to Now.* New York: Random House, 1986.

Sarafino, Edward P., and James W. Armstrong. *Child and Adolescent Development.* Glenview, Ill.: Scott, Foresman, 1986.

Saturday Review 48 (September 11, 1965), 63–65, 84–85.

Saul, Wendy. "Introduction." In *Vital Connections: Children, Science, and Books,* edited by Wendy Saul and Sybille A. Jagusch. Washington D.C.: Library of Congress, 1991, 3–18.

Saylor, David. "Look Again." *School Library Journal* 46 (January 2000): 37–38.

Schafer, Elizabeth D. *Exploring Harry Potter.* Osprey, Fla.: Beacham, 2000.

Schafer, Elizabeth D. *Beacham's Sourcebook for Teaching Young Adult Fiction: Exploring Harry Potter.* Osprey, FL: Beacham Publishing, 2000.

Schamel, Wynell Burroughs, and Jean West. "The Fight for Equal Rights: A Recruiting Poster for Black Soldiers in the Civil War." *Social Education* 56 (February 1992): 118–120.

Schoenherr, John. "Caldecott Medal Acceptance." *The Horn Book* 64 (July/August 1988): 457–459.

School Library Journal 46 (September 2000). Cover.

Schwarcz, Joseph. *Ways of the Illustrator: Visual Communication in Children's Literature.* Chicago: American Library Association, 1982.

Schwartz, Alvin. *And the Green Grass Grew All Around.* New York: HarperCollins, 1992.

Scott, A. O. "The End of Innocence." *The New York Times Magazine* (July 2, 2000): 11–12.

Sealey, D. Bruce. "Measuring the Multicultural Quotient of a School." *TESL Canada Journal/Revue TESL Du Canada* 1 (March 1984): 21–28.

Sears, Roebuck and Co., Consumers Guide: 1900. Reprint. Northfield, Ill.: DBI Books, 1970.

Sebesta, Sam. "Choosing Poetry." In *Children's Choices,* edited by Nancy Roser and Margaret Frith. Newark, Del.: International Reading Association, 1983.

_____ ."What Do Young People Think About the Literature They Read?" *Reading Newsletter,* no. 8. Rockleigh, N.J.: Allyn & Bacon, 1979.

Seeger, Ruth Crawford. *American Folksongs for Children—In Home, School, and Nursery School.* New York: Doubleday, 1948.

Seki, Keigo, ed. *Folktales of Japan.* Translated by Robert J. Adams. Chicago: University of Chicago, 1963, xv.

Sendak, Maurice. *Posters by Maurice Sendak.* New York: Harmony Books, 1986.

Sender, Ruth Minsky. *The Holocaust Lady.* New York: Macmillan, 1992.

Sewell, Helen. *A Book of Myths, Selections from Bulfinch's Age of Fable.* New York: Macmillan, 1942, 1962.

Shaffer, David R. *Developmental Psychology: Childhood and Adolescence,* 2nd ed. Pacific Grove, Calif.: Brooks/Cole, 1989.

Shannon, George. "Once and Forever a Platypus: Child Reader to Writing Adult." *Children's Literature Association Quarterly* 13 (Fall 1988): 122–124.

_____ ."Sharing Honey from the Hive." *Children's Literature Association Quarterly* 11 (Fall, 1986): 115–118.

Shapiro, Jon E., ed. *Using Literature and Poetry Affectively.* Newark, Del.: International Reading Association, 1979.

Shavit, Zohar. "The Historical Model of the Development of Children's Literature." In *Aspects and Issues in the History of Children's Literature,* edited by Maria Nikolajeva. Westport, Conn.: Greenwood, 1995, 27–38.

Shaw, Jean Duncan. "An Historical Survey of Themes Recurrent in Selected Children's Books Published in America Since 1850," Philadelphia: Temple University, 1966, University Microfilm No. 67-11, 437.

Short, Geoffrey. "Learning Through Literature: Historical Fiction, Autobiography and the Holocaust." *Children's Literature in Education* 28 (1997) 179–189.

Shulevitz, Uri. *Writing with Pictures: How to Write and Illustrate Children's Books.* New York: Watson-Guptill, 1985.

Sibley, Brian. *The Land of Narnia.* New York: Harper & Row, 1989.

Sidney, Sir Philip. *An Apologie for Poetrie.* London: 1595.

Sierra, Judy. *Multicultural Folktales for the Feltboard and Readers' Theater.* Phoenix: Oryx, 1996.

Siks, Geraldine. *Drama with Children.* New York: Harper & Row, 1983.

Silvey, Anita. "Evaluation and Criticism: The Quest for Quality in Children's Books." In *Children's Literature: Resources for the Classroom,* edited by Masha Kabakow Rudman. Norwood, Mass.: Christopher-Gordon, 1993.

_____ . "The Goats." *The Horn Book* (January/February 1988): 23.

Simmons, John S. *Censorship: A Threat to Reading, Learning, Thinking.* Newark, Del.: International Reading Association, 1994.

Sipe, Lawrence R. "In Their Own Words: Author's Views on Issues in Historical Fiction." *The New Advocate* 10 (Summer 1997): 243–258.

Sis, Peter. "The Artist At Work." *The Horn Book* 68 (November/December 1992): 681–687.

Smith, Amanda. "The Lively Art of Leo Lionni." *Publishers Weekly* 238 (April 5, 1991): 118–119.

Smith, Lane. "The Artist at Work." *The Horn Book* 69 (January/February 1993): 64–70.

Smith, Sally A. "Talking About 'Real Stuff': Explorations of Agency and Romance in an All-Girls' Book Club." *Language Arts* 78 (September 2000): 30–37.

Smuskiewicz, Ted. *Oil Painting: Step by Step.* Cincinnati, Ohio: North Light Books, 1992.

Spang, A. "Counseling the Indian." *Journal of American Indian Education* 5 (1965): 10–15.

Spiegel, Dixie Lee. "Reader Response Approaches and the Growth of Readers." *Language Arts* 76 (September 1998): 41–48.

Sprague, Marsha M., and Kara K. Keeling. "A Library for Ophelia." *Journal of Adolescent & Adult Literacy* 43 (April 2000): 640–647.

St. Clair, Jean. "Recreating Black Life in Children's Literature." *Interracial Books for Children Bulletin* 19 (1989): 7–11.

Stacks, John F. "Aftershocks of the 'Me' Decade." *Time* (August 3, 1981): 18.

Stander, Bella. "Spring Titles for Kids Highlight Heroes and Their Times." *Publishers Weekly* 239 (December 14, 1992): 28–29.

Stanley, Alessandra. "Cleopatra, Career Woman." *The New York Times* (Saturday, January 20, 2001): A21, A23.

Stanley, Diane. "Is That Book Politically Correct? Truth and Trends in Historical Literature For Young People. A Writer Speaks . . ." *Journal of Youth Services in Libraries* 7 (Winter 1994): 172–175.

Stark, Myra. *Florence Nightingale.* New York: Feminist Press, 1979.

Steele, Mary Q. "Realism, Truth, and Honesty." *The Horn Book* 46 (February 1971): 17–27.

Sterck, Kenneth. "Landscape and Figures in the Poetry of De la Mare." *Children's Literature in Education* 19 (Spring 1988): 17–31.

Stewig, John Warren. "The Emperor's New Clothes." *Book Links* 2 (May 1993): 35–38.

_____ . "A Literary and Linguistic Analysis of Scott O'Dell's *The Captive.*" *Children's Literature Association Quarterly* 14 (Fall, 1989): 135–138.

_____ . *Reading Pictures: Exploring Illustrations with Children.* New Berlin, Wis.: Jenson, 1988.

Stokstad, Marilyn. *Art History: Volume One.* New York: Abrams, 1995.

_____ . *Art History: Volume Two.* New York: Abrams, 1995.

Storey, Denise C. "Fifth Graders Meet Elderly Book Characters." *Language Arts* 56 (April 1979): 408–412.

Stott, Jon C. "Biographies of Sports Heroes and the American Dream." *Children's Literature in Education* 10 (Winter 1979): 174–185.

_____ . "Native Tales and Traditions in Books for Children." *The American Indian Quarterly* 16 (Summer 1992): 373–380.

Strehle, Elizabeth. "Social Issues: Connecting Children With Their World." *Children's Literature in Education* 30 (1999): 213–220.

Strickland, Dorothy S. "Prompting Language and Concept Development." In *Literature and Young Children,* edited by Bernice Cullinan. Urbana, Ill.: National Conference of Teachers of English, 1977.

Sutherland, Zena. *Children and Books,* 9th ed. New York: Longman, 1997.

_____ , and Betsy Hearne. "In Search of the Perfect Picture Book Definition." In *Jump over the Moon: Selected Professional Readings,* edited by Pamela Barron and Jennifer Burley. New York: Holt, Rinehart & Winston, 1984.

_____ , and Myra Cohn Livingston. *The Scott, Foresman Anthology of Children's Literature.* Glenview, Ill.: Scott, Foresman, 1984.

Sutton, Roger. "Where's That Renaissance?" *The Horn Book* 72 (November/December 1996): 664–665.

Swanton, Susan. "Minds Alive: What and Why Gifted Students Read for Pleasure." *School Library Journal* 30 (March 1984): 99–102.

Symons, Ann K. "Sizing Up Sites: How to Judge What You Find on the Web." *School Library Journal* 43 (April 1997): 22–25.

Taggart, James. " 'Hansel and Gretel' in Spain and Mexico." *Journal of American Folklore* 99 (1986): 435–460.

Tanner, Fran. *Creative Communication: Projects in Acting, Speaking, Oral Reading.* Pocatello, Idaho: Clark, 1979.

Tarbox, Gwen Athene, ed. *American Popular History and Culture: Collective Impulses in Progressive-Era Girl's Fiction, 1890–1940.* New York: Garland, 2000.

Temple, Frances. *Taste of Salt: A Story of Modern Haiti.* New York: Orchard, 1992.

Terry, Ann. *Children's Poetry Preferences: A National Survey of the Upper Elementary Grades.* Urbana, Ill.: National Council of Teachers of English, 1974.

Thomas, Joyce. "The Tales of the Brothers Grimm: In the Black Forest." In *Touchstones: Reflections on the Best in Children's Literature,* edited by Perry Nodelman. West Lafayette, Ind.: Children's Literature Association, 1987, 104–117.

Thompson, Stith. *The Folktale.* Berkeley: University of California Press, 1977.

Thurman, Judith. *Flashlight and Other Poems.* New York: Atheneum, 1976.

Tolkien, J. R. R. *Fellowship of the Ring.* Boston: Houghton Mifflin, 1965.

Totten, Herman L., Carolyn Garner, and Risa W. Brown. *Culturally Diverse Library Collections for Youth.* New York: Neal-Schuman, 1996.

Townsend, John Rowe. *Written for Children: An Outline of English-Language Children's Literature.* New York: Lippincott, 1975.

Trafzer, Clifford E. "The Word Is Sacred to the Child: American Indians and Children's Literature." *The American Indian Quarterly* 16 (Summer 1992): 381–396.

Travers, P. T. *About the Sleeping Beauty.* Illustrated by Charles Keeping. New York: McGraw-Hill, 1975.

Trease, Geoffrey. "The Historical Story: Is It Relevant Today?" *The Horn Book* (February 1977): 21–28.

Trelease, Jim. *The New Read-Aloud Handbook.* New York: Viking, 1989.

Tremearne, A. J. *Hausa Superstitions and Customs: An Introduction to the Folklore and the Folk.* London: Frank Cass, 1970.

Tuer, Andrew W. *Stories from Forgotten Children's Books.* London: Leadenhall Press, 1898; Bracken Books, 1986.

Tunnell, Michael O. "Alexander's Chronicles of Prydain: Twenty Years Later." *School Library Journal* 34 (April 1988): 27–31.

_____ . "Books in the Classroom." *The Horn Book* 63 (July/August 1987): 509–511.

_____ , and James S. Jacobs. "Using 'Real' Books: Research Findings on Literature Based Reading Instruction." *The Reading Teacher* 42 (March 1989): 470–477.

Tway, Eileen. "Dimensions of Multicultural Literature for Children." In *Children's Literature: Resource for the Classroom,* edited by Masha Kabakow Rudman. Needham Heights, Mass.: Christopher-Gordon, 1989, 109–138.

Unsworth, Robert. "Welcome Home . . . I Think." *School Library Journal* 35 (May 1988): 48–49.

Vallone, Lynne. "The Crisis of Education: Eighteenth-Century Adolescent Fiction for Girls." *Children's Literature Association Quarterly* 14 (Summer 1988): 63–67.

Vasilakis, Nancy. "Young Adult Books: An Eighties Perspective." *The Horn Book* 61 (November/December 1985): 768–769.

Vogler, Christopher. *Writer's Journey: Mythic Structure for Storytellers & Screenwriters.* Studio City, Calif.: Michael Wiese Productions, 1992.

Vrooman, Diana. "Characterization Techniques in *Sarah, Plain and Tall.*" College Station: Texas A&M University, 1989.

Walker, Barbara. *The Dancing Palm Tree and Other Nigerian Folktales.* Illustrated by Helen Siegl. Lubbock: Texas Tech University Press, 1990.

Walmsley, S. A., and T. P. Walp. *Teaching Literature in Elementary School: A Report on the Elementary School Antecedents of Secondary School Literature Instruction.* Report Series 1.3 Albany, N.Y.: Center for the Teaching and Learning of Literature. University at Albany, State University of New York (ERIC No. ED 315 754), 1989.

Ward, Nel, and Patrick Jones. "Homelessness in America." *Booklist* 89 (October 1, 1992): 340–341.

Weaver, Warren. *Alice in Many Tongues.* Madison, Wis.: University of Wisconsin, 1964.

Weinberg, Steve. "Biography: Telling the Untold Story." *The Writer* (February 1993): 23–25.

Werner, Craig, and Frank P. Riga. "The Persistence of Religion in Children's Literature." *Children's Literature Association Quarterly* 14 (Spring, 1989): 2–3.

West, Mark I. "Essay Review: The Contrasting Biographies of Roald Dahl and Dr. Seuss." *Children's Literature in Education* 27 (1996): 243–247.

_____ . *Trust Your Children: Voices Against Censorship in Children's Literature.* New York: Neal-Schuman, 1988.

Western, Linda. "A Comparative Study of Literature Through Folk Tale Variants." *Language Arts* 57 (April 1980): 395–402.

Weston, Annette H. "Robert Lawson: Author and Illustrator." *Elementary English* 47 (January 1970): 74–84.

Whalen-Levitt, Peggy. "Making Picture Books Real: Reflections on a Child's-Eye View." In *The First Steps: Best of the Early ChLA Quarterly,* compiled by Patricia Dooley. Lafayette, Ind.: Purdue University, Children's Literature Association, 1984.

Whitehead, Jane. "'This Is Not What I Wrote!': The Americanization of British Children's Books—Part I." *The Horn Book* (November/December 1996): 687–693.

_____ . "'This Is Not What I Wrote!': The Americanization of British Children's Books—Part II." *The Horn Book* (January/February 1997): 27–34.

Whitson, Kathy J. *Native American Literatures: An Encyclopedia of Works, Characters, Authors, and Themes.* Santa Barbara, Calif.: ABC-CLIO, 1999.

Wigginton, Eliot. *The Foxfire Book.* New York: Doubleday, 1972.

Wilkin, Binnie Tate. *Survival Themes in Fiction for Children and Young People.* Metuchen, N.J.: Scarecrow, 1978.

Williams, Mary E., ed. *The Family: Opposing Viewpoints.* San Diego: Greenhaven Press, 1998.

Winkler, Karen J. "Academe and Children's Literature: Will They Live Happily Ever After?" *Chronicle of Higher Education* (June 15, 1981).

Wintle, Justin, and Emma Fisher. *The Pied Pipers: Interviews with the Influential Creators of Children's Literature.* New York: Paddington, 1974.

Wisniewski, David. *Sundiata: Lion King of Mali.* New York: Clarion, 1992.

Wolfe, Alan. "The Final Freedom." *The New York Times Magazine* (March 18, 2001): 48–51.

Wolkomir, Joyce, and Richard Wolkomir. "When Bandogs Howl & Spirits Walk." *Smithsonian* 31 (January 2001): 38–44.

Wolkstein, Diane. "Twenty-Five Years of Storytelling: The Spirit of the Art." *The Horn Book* 68 (November/December 1992): 702–708.

Worth, Valerie. "Capturing Objects in Words." *The Horn Book* 68 (September/October 1992): 568–569.

Worthy, M. Jo, and Janet W. Bloodgood. "Enchancing Reading Instruction Through Cinderella Tales." *The Reading Teacher* 46 (December 1992/January 1993): 290–301.

Wright, Jone P., and Elizabeth G. Allen. "Sixth-Graders Ride with Paul Revere." *Language Arts* 53 (January 1976): 46–50.

Wrightson, Patricia. "Stones into Pools." In *The Arbuthnot Lectures: 1980–1989.* Chicago: American Library Association, 1990, 67–77.

Wyatt, Flora R., Margaret Coggins, and Jane Hunter Imber. *Popular Nonfiction Authors for Children.* Englewood, Colo.: Libraries Unlimited, 1998.

Wyndham, Robert. *Tales the People Tell in China.* New York: Messner, 1971.

Yates, Elizabeth. *We, the People.* Illustrated by Nora Unwin. Hanover, N.H.: Regional Center for Educational Training, 1974.

Yep, Laurence. *The Rainbow People.* New York: Harper & Row, 1989.

Yolen, Jane. "Magic Mirrors: Society Reflected in the Glass of Fantasy." *Children's Literature Association Quarterly* 11 (Summer 1986): 88–90.

_____ . "Past Time: The Writing of the Picture Book *Encounter.*" *The New Advocate* (September 1992): 234–239.

_____ . "Taking Time: On How Things Have Changed in the Last Thirty-Five Years of Children's Publishing." *The New Advocate* 10 (Fall 1997): 285–291.

Young, Beverly. "The Young Female Protagonist in Juvenile Fiction: Three Decades of Evolution." Washington State University, 1985, DAI 46: 3276A.

Author, Illustrator, Title Index

CREDITS

Text Excerpts and Poems

Page 80–81, text excerpt from *Hatchet* by Gary Paulsen. Text, Copyright © 1987 by Gary Paulsen. Reprinted by permission of Bradbury Press, an Affiliate of Macmillan, Inc.

Pages 92, 418, and 437, text excerpts from *No Hero for the Kaiser* by Rudolf Frank. Text © 1986 by Rudolf Frank. By permission of Lothrop, Lee & Shepard, a division of William Morrow & Co.

Page 104, text excerpt from *Tuck Everlasting* by Natalie Babbitt. Copyright © 1975 by Natalie Babbitt. Reprinted by permission of Farrar, Straus and Giroux, Inc.

Page 162, poems from *Chinese Mother Goose Rhymes* by Robert Wyndham, with the permission of Philomel Books. Copyright © 1968 by Robert Wyndham.

Page 174, text excerpt from *The Cat in the Hat* by Dr. Seuss. Copyright © 1957 by Random House. Used by permission.

Page 174, text excerpt from *Frog and Toad Are Friends*, written and illustrated by Arnold Lobel. Copyright © 1970 by Arnold Lobel. By permission of Harper & Row Publishers, Inc. and World's Work Ltd.

Page 179, text excerpt from *No Such Things* by Bill Peet (New York: Houghton Mifflin, 1983).

Page 182, text excerpt from *A Baby Sister for Frances* by Russell Hoban, Courtesy of Harper & Row, Publishers, Inc.

Page 186, text excerpt from *The 500 Hats of Bartholomew Cubbins* by Dr. Seuss. Copyright © 1938 by Vanguard Press. Used by permission.

Page 240, text excerpted from "Gratitude" in *Aesop's Fables* by Tom Paxton. Copyright © 1988 by Tom Paxton. Reprinted by permission of William Morrow & Co.

Page 240, text excerpt reprinted with permission of Macmillan Publishing Company from *Doctor Coyote: A Native American Aesop's Fables* retold by John Bierhorst, pictures by Wendy Watson. © 1987 by John Bierhorst. Illus. Copyright © 1987 by Wendy Watson.

Page 285, text excerpts from *Redwall* by Brian Jacques. © 1986 by Brian Jacques. Reprinted by permission of Philomel Books.

Page 298, text essay Copyright © 1991, 1987, 1983, by Macmillan Publishing Company. Reprinted by permission of Madeleine L'Engle.

Page 318, poem "Rainbow Writing" from Eve Merriam. *Rainbow Writing*. Copyright © 1976 by Eve Merriam (New York: Atheneum, 1976). Reprinted by permission of Marian Reiner.

Page 322–323, poem "The Pickety Fence" from *Far and Few* by David McCord. Copyright 1952 by David McCord. By permission of Little, Brown and Company.

Page 324, "Poem to Mud" from Zilpha Keatley Snyder, *Today is Saturday*. Text copyright © 1969 by Zilpha Keatley Snyder (New York: Atheneum, 1969). Reprinted with the permission of Atheneum Publishers.

Page 324, poem "Don't Ever Seize a Weasel by the Tail" reprinted with permission of Macmillan Publishing Company, Inc. from *A Gopher in the Garden* by Jack Prelutsky. Copyright © by Jack Prelutsky, 1966, 1967.

Page 326, "Spill" from Judith Thurman, *Flashlights and Other Poems*. Copyright © 1976 by Judith Thurman (New York: Atheneum, 1976). Reprinted by permission of Marian Reiner for the author.

Page 328, poem "The Path on the Sea" reprinted with the permission of Simon & Schuster Children's Publishing Division from *The Moon Is Like a Silver Sickle*, compiled by Miriam Morton, © 1972. Reprinted by permission.

Page 328, poem "The Wind" reprinted by permission of Marian Reiner. From *The Covered Bridge House and Other Poems* by Kaye Starbird. Copyright © 1979 by Kaye Starbird.

Page 328, text of "Mummy Slept Late and Daddy Fixed Breakfast" from *You Read to Me, I'll Read to You* by John Ciardi. Copyright © 1962 by John Ciardi. By permission of J. B. Lippincott, Publishers.

Page 332, from Ann Atwood. *Haiku: The Mood of Earth*. Copyright © 1971 by Ann Atwood (New York: Charles Scribner's Sons, 1971). Reprinted with the permission of Charles Scribner's Sons, an imprint of Macmillan Publishing Company.

Page 334, poem excerpt from "The Man in the Marmalade Hat Arrives" from *A Visit to William Blake's Inn*, text © 1981 by Nancy Willard, reprinted by permission of Harcourt Brace & Company.

Page 335, poem "Eletelephony" from *Tirra Lirra* by Laura Richards. Copyright © 1930, 1932 by Laura E. Richards; Copyright © renewed 1960 by Hamilton Richards. By permission of Little, Brown and Company, (Inc.)

Page 335, poem "Ickle Me, Pickle Me, Tickle Me Too" from *Where the Sidewalk Ends* by Shel Silverstein (New York: Harper & Row, 1974). Copyright © by Evil Eye Music, Inc. Selection reprinted by permission of HarperCollins Publishers.

Page 335, poem "The Land of Ho-Ho-Hum" excerpted from the book *Laughing Time* by William Jay Smith. Copyright © 1953, 1955, 1956, 1957, 1959, 1968, 1974, 1977, 1980 by William Jay Smith. Reprinted by permission of Delacorte Press/Seymour Lawrence.

Page 336, poem "Bickering" from N. M. Bodecker, *Hurry, Hurry Mary Dear and Other Nonsense Poems*. Copyright © 1976 by N. M. Bodecker. A Margaret K. McElderry Book. (New York: Atheneum Publishers, 1976). Reprinted with permission of McElderry Books, an imprint of Macmillan Publishing Company.

Page 336–337, text of "Change" from *River Winding: Poems by Charlotte Zolotow*. Copyright © 1970 by Charlotte Zolotow. By permission of Thomas Y. Crowell, Publishers.

Page 337, poem from *The Poetry of Robert Frost* edited by Edward Connery Lathem. Copyright 1951 by Robert Frost. Copyright 1923, © 1969 by Henry Holt and Company, Inc. Reprinted by permission of Henry Holt and Company, Inc.

Page 337–338, text of "Frosted-Window World" from *In One Door and Out the*

ABOUT THE AUTHORS

Donna Norton

Following the completion of her doctorate at the University of Wisconsin, Madison, Donna E. Norton joined the College of Education faculty at Texas A&M University where she now holds the rank of professor. She teaches courses in children's literature, language arts, and reading. Dr. Norton is the recipient of the Texas A&M Faculty Distinguished Achievement Award in Teaching. This award is given "in recognition and appreciation of ability, personality, and methods which have resulted in distinguished achievements in the teaching and the inspiration of students." She is also the recipient of the Virginia Hamilton Essay Award, presented by the Virginia Hamilton Conference Advisory Board at Kent State University. This annual award recognizes an article that "makes a significant contribution to the professional literature concerning multicultural literature experiences for youth." She is listed in *Who's Who of American Women, Who's Who in America,* and *Who's Who in the World.* Several of her articles and chapters from books have been translated into Chinese and are used in Chinese universities.

Dr. Norton is the author of four books in addition to this volume: *The Effective Teaching of Language Arts,* 6th edition, *Language Arts Activities for Children,* 5th edition, *Multicultural Children's Literature: Through the Eyes of Many Children,* and *The Impact of Literature-Based Reading.* Her publications include 20 textbooks and over 100 journal articles. At the international level, she has been on the International Reading Association's Lee Bennett Hopkins Promising Poet Committee, President of the International Society of Educational Biography, on numerous editorial boards for professional journals, and presenter at international conferences including the Conference on Children's Literature at Providence University in Taiwan. The focus of her current research is on the authentication of biographical literature, historical fiction, and multicultural literature. She is also researching the literature and writing connection. Funded research has supported institutes in children's literature and the literacy connection as well as graduate courses that enable students to study children's literature and reading instruction in England and Scotland. She is currently the Grant Writing Chair for the Bush Museum Storytellers Guild. Her work with the Texas A&M University Evans Library and the Bush Library has resulted in several Storytelling Festivals that highlight the work of distinguished storytellers and provide training for university students in the art of storytelling.

Prior to her college teaching experience, Dr. Norton was an elementary teacher in River Falls, Wisconsin and in Madison, Wisconsin. She was a Language Arts/Reading Consultant for federally funded kindergarten through adult basic education programs. In this capacity she developed, provided in-service instruction, and evaluated kindergarten programs, summer reading and library programs, remedial reading programs, learning disability programs for middle school children, elementary and secondary literature programs for the gifted, and diagnostic and intervention programs for reading-disabled adults. Dr. Norton's continuing concern for literature results in frequent consultations with educators from various disciplines, librarians, and school administrators and teachers.

Saundra Norton

Saundra Norton completed her master's degree at Texas A&M University where she majored in American literature with an emphasis in children's literature and textual bibliography. Under the sponsorship of a Jordan Fellowship she studied German language, culture, and folklore at the Goethe Institute in Germany. Her current academic concentration is in 19th century American literature and biographical studies. She is a frequent participant at national and international conferences. Her paper presented at the 15th International Ezra Pound Conference in Italy was presented the Bates Award for the best essay written by a graduate student while in the doctoral program at the University of South Carolina. Saundra has won numerous competitions for her writing including being selected for the Prague Summer Seminars, the Paris Writer's Workshop, Bread Loaf Writer's Conference at Middlebury College, in Middlebury, Vermont, and Sewanee Writer's Conference at the University of the South. Her poetry has been published in several scholarly journals and she has given poetry readings in Prague, Key West, Paris, and at Wesleyan College. She is listed in *Who's Who Among Students in American Universities and Colleges.* Saundra is the co-author of *Language Arts Activities for Children,* 5th edition.

Amy McClure

Dr. Amy McClure is Rodefer Professor of Education and Director of the Early Childhood program at Ohio Wesleyan University, where she teaches courses in children's literature and early literacy and supervises student teachers. She also coordinates the University's Honors Program. Dr. McClure is the author and editor of several books including *Sunrises and Songs: Reading and Writing Poetry in an Elementary Classroom*, *Booktalk: Books That Invite Talk, Wonder and Play with Literature, Inviting Children's Responses to Literature,* and *Adventuring with Books*. She is also the author of numerous book chapters and articles and has presented at conferences throughout the United States and the world. She is the Past-President of the Children's Literature Assembly of NCTE, IRA's Children's Literature SIG and the Ohio International Reading Association. Dr. McClure was selected NCTE's Promising Young Researcher and her dissertation won Kappa Delti Pi's Outstanding Dissertation of the Year Award. She also received Ohio Wesleyan's Herbert Welch Meritorious Teaching Award. She lives in Dublin, Ohio, with her husband and two teen-aged daughters.